PRINCIPLES OF INTERNATIONAL BUSINESS TRANSACTIONS

Fourth Edition

Ralph H. Folsom

Professor of Law
University of San Diego School of Law

Michael Wallace Gordon

John H. and Mary Lou Dasburg Professor of Law Emeritus
University of Florida

Michael P. Van Alstine

Piper & Marbury Professor of Law
University of Maryland Francis King Carey School of Law

Michael D. Ramsey

Hugh and Hazel Darling Foundation Professor of Law
Director of International and Comparative Law Programs
University of San Diego School of Law

CONCISE HORNBOOK SERIES™

WEST
ACADEMIC
PUBLISHING

The publisher is not engaged in rendering legal or other professional advice, and this publication is not a substitute for the advice of an attorney. If you require legal or other expert advice, you should seek the services of a competent attorney or other professional.

Printed in the United States of America

ISBN: 978-1-63459-939-9

Preface

The authors have collaborated on *International Business Transactions: A Problem-Oriented Coursebook*, and its spin-off editions, *IBT: Contracting Across Borders; IBT: Trade and Economic Relations;* and *IBT: Foreign Investment*. Many students studying with these popular coursebooks, and others interested in an introduction to the field, have enjoyed our easy-to-read *International Business Transactions* Nutshell and its companion, the *International Trade and Economic Relations* Nutshell.

Principles of International Business Transactions is part of the West Academic Publishing's Concise Hornbook series. Our coverage moves sequentially from structuring the international sales transaction to the law governing international sales and letters of credit to regulation of international trade to transfers of technology to foreign investment and to dispute settlement. The authors gratefully acknowledge the prior contributions of Professor John A. Spanogle (professor emeritus, George Washington University Law School) and Professor Michael Gordon (professor emeritus, University of Florida Law School). Neither actively participated in the new edition of this book.

Principles of International Business Transactions is intended to provide a deeper of analysis of the subject matter, a more comprehensive examination of the relevant law, and detailed citations to caselaw and other supporting authorities. Our hope is that courts and legal practitioners will find it a valuable resource for research and analysis, and both professors and students will find it useful in connection with any international business, sales, trade, investment or economic law course, or even as an independent coursebook. For more detailed coverage of trade law see Professor Folsom's *Principles of International Trade Law, including the World Trade Organization, NAFTA and the European Union*.

We welcome feedback.

RALPH H. FOLSOM
rfolsom@sandiego.edu

MICHAEL P. VAN ALSTINE
mvanalstine@law.umaryland.edu

MICHAEL W. GORDON
gordon@law.ufl.edu

MICHAEL D. RAMSEY
mramsey@sandiego.edu

January 2017

Summary of Contents

Table of Contents

PRINCIPLES OF INTERNATIONAL BUSINESS TRANSACTIONS

Fourth Edition

Chapter 1

STRUCTURING THE INTERNATIONAL SALES TRANSACTION

Table of Sections

§ 1.1   Introduction

In some respects, an international sale of goods (*e.g.*, from Pittsburgh to Paris) does not differ substantially from one that occurs entirely within one jurisdiction (*e.g.*, from Pittsburgh to Philadelphia). Even in the entirely domestic transaction, the buyer and the seller must agree on the essential aspects of the deal, such as the type and quantity of goods and the price. Most often, the

1

parties also will address quality issues, the place and time of delivery, and the modalities of payment. And as the transaction becomes more complex, they even may take up questions of liability, dispute settlement, and a myriad of other matters relevant to their specific line of trade.

Once a sale of goods transaction crosses national borders, however, most of these otherwise prosaic issues become more complicated and a variety of new ones arise. The first, and most important, difference is that by definition an international transaction will touch on the interests of more than one legal sovereign. This creates difficult choice of law problems. If, for example, our Pittsburgh-based seller contracts with a Paris-based buyer to sell goods manufactured in China for delivery to Mexico, the law of any of the four countries may govern should a dispute arise (or perhaps even bits of each). Questions of court jurisdiction also will abound. And even if one were able to determine which court system(s) potentially could assert jurisdiction, a U.S. lawyer likely will lack the training and tools to research the content of the choice of law rules—which often are in a foreign language and are steeped in foreign conceptual structures—the foreign court(s) may apply.[1]

Other challenges arise from the very nature of a sale of physical objects between traders in different countries. One critical complication is that an international sale usually involves a greater geographic distance between the seller and the buyer, and this most often necessitates transportation by a third-party carrier. In addition, the parties' respective home countries likely will have different currencies, different banking and payment practices, different trade customs, and different insurance requirements. Still other challenges arise from the simple fact that an international transaction likely will cross cultural, linguistic, socio-economic, and jurisprudential lines. Thus, for example, different native languages create risks of miscommunication; different cultural expectations and practices may lead to misunderstandings; and different governmental philosophies in the respective home countries— regulatory rules, taxes, licensing requirements, disclosure laws, etc.—may set limitations on, and create expectations about, the proper subjects for contractual negotiation.

As a more fundamental matter, it also is more likely that the buyer and the seller will not know each other, or at least not well. As a result, neither will wish to perform first and then trust that the other will timely and fully perform later. This makes

---

[1]   For a more detailed analysis of this difficult choice of law problem in international sales transactions *see* Chapter 2, § 2.1.

negotiations over the details of delivery and payment substantially more difficult.

Distilled to a single theme, the challenge in an international sales transaction is the absence of a certain and stable foundation for contractual agreement. Fortunately, the international trading community has developed three principal solutions for this fundamental problem: (a) uniform international law that displaces the diverse rules of the domestic legal systems; (b) uniform international customs and practices that permit the parties to define their agreements with ease and clarity; and (c) standard transaction structures that address the trust problem concerning delivery and payment.

The subject-specific Chapters in this book—especially Chapters 2 through 8 on the various aspects of international sales of goods—will cover in detail the first two of these solutions. A brief review thus will suffice here. But as a foundation for those detailed examinations of the relevant legal rules, the bulk of this first Chapter will focus on the standard transaction structures that have developed over time for international sales of goods. These structures are able simultaneously to assure the seller of timely payment and the buyer of timely receipt of the contract goods.

(a) Uniform International Law. As noted, the most basic problem in an international sales transaction arises from uncertainty about the governing law: Absent express agreement, the parties cannot know in advance which of two (or more) bodies of domestic law will apply in the event of a dispute. Moreover, each likely will know little about the home law of the other. This uncertainly creates substantial transaction costs, for without a clear and stable set of background rules the parties must negotiate over a greatly expanded field of issues beyond the essential terms of the deal (subject, price, and performance time). The solution for this uncertainty is an international treaty that creates a uniform set of legal rules for all transactions in a given field of law. At best, such a treaty would be multi-lateral and thus apply to transactions in as many countries as possible.

Thankfully, treaties of this sort exist for many areas of international business transactions, and especially for the sale of goods. Chapter 2 examines in detail the most successful of these treaties: The United Nations Convention on Contracts for the International Sale of Goods (CISG)[2] as well as a related treaty on the limitations period for asserting claims.[3] Subsequent Chapters

---

2   *See* Chapter 2, §§ 2.2–2.43.

3   *See* Chapter 2, § 2.44.

review other treaties relevant to international sales, such as on the international carriage of goods by sea,[4] on independent guarantees and standby letters of credit,[5] and on electronic commerce.[6]

International treaties designed to create legal uniformity across jurisdictions are by no means limited to sales of goods. For example, Chapters 9 through 13 examine the extensive web of treaties on international trade in the World Trade Organization (WTO) system; Chapter 15 analyzes the OECD Convention on Combating Bribery of Foreign Public Officials in International Business Transactions;[7] Chapter 17 reviews the North American Free Trade Agreement (NAFTA), a treaty that governs trade between and among the United States, Canada, and Mexico; Chapters 18 and 19 explore a variety of treaties that protect international intellectual property rights; Chapter 23 reviews treaties on foreign investment; and Chapters 26 and 28 analyze treaties that regulate certain aspects of international dispute resolution, including the important New York Convention on the Recognition and Enforcement of Foreign Arbitral Awards.[8]

(b) *Uniform Customs and Practices.* A second way in which the international trading community has addressed the special challenges of international sales transactions is through widely accepted terminology, customs, and practices. Examples of accepted terminology include commercial terms, negotiable and non-negotiable bills of lading, negotiable drafts, and confirmed and irrevocable letters of credit. More important, various international institutions have developed "off-the-rack" sets of terms that parties may incorporate into their contracts by simple reference. In this way, the international trading community has sought to empower the parties to define their respective rights and obligations as clearly as possible and by reference to internationally accepted contract terms and forms.

The most prominent institution in this endeavor has been the International Chamber of Commerce (ICC) in Paris, which for nearly a century has prepared sets of uniform contractual terms for specific contract types. And the most important of these sets of contract terms is the so-called Incoterms© (for "International Commercial Terms"). These reflect an assortment of international customs that define the seller's delivery obligations and the buyer's reciprocal obligations, as well as the allocation of risk while the

---

[4]   *See* Chapter 4, § 4.5.

[5]   *See* Chapter 7, § 7.10.

[6]   *See* Chapter 8, § 8.7.

[7]   *See* Chapter 15, §§ 15.28–15.29.

[8]   *See* Chapter 28, § 28.28–28.29.

goods are in transit. The special feature of Incoterms is that they permit the parties, by a simple three-letter reference (*e.g.*, FOB or CIF), to choose the structure that best suits their mutual interests in a given transaction. Chapter 3 examines in detail the Incoterms and their special role in facilitating international sales transactions.

Another widely accepted set of contract terms published by the ICC, the Uniform Rules for Collections (URC)©, addresses the role of banks in collection transactions. A collection transaction is one in which a bank agrees merely to act as a forwarding agent for documents and a collection agent for receipt of payment on behalf of a seller of goods to a geographically distant buyer. Sections 1.6 and 1.7 below explain how the URC facilitate a transaction structure— Documents Against Payment (D/P)—that addresses the fundamental trust problem in an international sale of goods transaction.

The ICC rules for letters of credit, the Uniform Customs and Practice for Documentary Credits (UCP)©,[9] also have been influential in international business transactions. A letter of credit is a financing device under which a bank undertakes an independent obligation to pay the amount due the seller upon shipment of the goods. The UCP then define in detail the rights and obligations of the banks that issue international letters of credit. Sections 1.10 through 1.18 below explain how a letter of credit can solve in a particularly secure way the fundamental trust problem in an international sale of goods transaction. Chapter 6 analyzes the UCP's rules in greater detail. Chapter 7 then explores ICC contract terms for another important financing device, the standby letter of credit.[10]

(c) *Standard Transaction Structures.* As noted above, the principal function of this Chapter is to examine the standard transaction structures that enable distant, unfamiliar sellers and buyers to engage in mutually beneficial sale of goods transactions. Again, the fundamental challenge for international deals is what might be called the trust problem: Unlike many domestic transactions, in a sale of goods across national borders the exporter-seller and importer-buyer may not have previously dealt with one another; or each may know little about the reliability of the other; or each may be unfamiliar with the other's national legal system.

---

9   Uniform Customs and Practices for Documentary Credits (UCP) (ICC Publ. 600, 2007).

10   *See* International Standby Practices (ISP)©, Chapter 7, § 7.10. Chapter 7 also notes another financing device in civil law countries, the demand guarantee (or independent guarantee). *See* § 7.2. The ICC has issued another set of standard contract terms for this device, the Uniform Rules for Demand Guarantees (URDG)© (ICC Publ. 758, 2010).

The seller's specific concerns include (1) whether the buyer is trustworthy and, even if so, creditworthy; (2) whether exchange controls will hinder payment by the buyer (especially if the buyer's country has a "soft" currency, but payment is in a "hard" currency); (3) how great the exchange risk is if payment is to be in the buyer's currency; and (4) what delays may be involved in receiving unencumbered funds from the buyer.

The buyer's specific concerns, on the other hand, include (1) whether the seller can be trusted to ship the goods if the buyer prepays; (2) whether the goods shipped will be of the quantity and quality defined in the contract; (3) whether the goods will be shipped by a reliable carrier and properly insured; (4) whether the seller will furnish sufficient ownership documentation for the goods to allow the buyer to claim them from the carrier; (5) whether the seller will provide the documentation necessary to satisfy customs and valuation regulations (*e.g.*, country of origin certificates, health and other inspection certificates, *etc.*); and (6) what delays may be involved in receiving unencumbered possession and use of the goods at the buyer's location.

Thus, if the parties have not engaged in repeated transactions in the past or otherwise do not know each other well, neither will wish to perform first and trust that the other will do so later. That is, the seller will not be willing to ship the goods first, only to hope that the buyer will pay later; and the buyer will not be willing to pay first, only to hope that the seller will ship conforming goods later.

The solution to this trust problem is an arrangement in which the seller has a right to payment of the contract price once it has obtained and presented certain essential *documents* proving shipment of the contract goods to the buyer. We examine below the two principal forms of this transaction structure: Sections 1.2 through 1.9 first review the basic version in which the *buyer* agrees to pay the seller upon presentation of the documents. Sections 1.10 through 1.18 then address a more formal version in which, by issuing an international letter of credit, a *bank* agrees to pay the seller upon presentation of the documents.

Finally, Sections 1.19 through 1.21 briefly review arrangements in which one party is willing (or compelled) to trust the other, whether based on long-standing or institutional relationships or otherwise. Thus, either the seller is willing to ship first or the buyer is willing to pay first.

§ 1.2   The Documents Against Payment (D/P) Transaction

How does the "documents against payment" (D/P, aka "payment against documents"[11]) transaction work? In specific, how does it solve the fundamental problem that geographically distant sellers and buyers cannot concurrently exchange the *goods* for the purchase price? It does so by instead requiring a concurrent exchange of essential *documents* for the purchase price.

To facilitate this exchange, the documents against payment arrangement relies on independent third parties: an international carriage company and one or more banks. And it uses a specialized document, the negotiable bill of lading, that represents legal title to the goods. The carriage company will issue this document upon receipt of the goods from the seller for shipment to the buyer. The seller then will use the banks to present that essential document (among others) to the buyer on the condition that the buyer first pay the purchase price. The seller thus can ship the contract goods based on an assurance of payment when it presents—through the banks—documents that confirm shipment of the contract goods; and the buyer can make payment based on a documentary assurance that it has legal title to the contract goods already in transit.

§ 1.3   D/P Transaction__Requirement of a Contractual Agreement

A documents against payment arrangement in an international sale must result from a contractual agreement between the parties. As described in detail in Chapter 2 below, the law governing international sale of goods contracts in modern commerce is commonly, and increasingly so, the United Nations Convention on Contracts for the International Sale of Goods (CISG). But the CISG generally defers to the parties' agreement, and this is true as well on the modalities of payment.[12]

When the parties are forming their contract for the sale of goods, the seller must insist that the buyer "pay against the documents," rather than after delivery and inspection of the goods

---

[11]   This transaction structure also is known by a variety of similar names: "cash against documents" (CAD); "documentary sale" and, if banks are engaged as described in §§ 1.6 and 1.7 below, "documentary collection" (D/C). A slightly more nuanced version of the cash against documents arrangement involves the buyer first depositing with its bank the amount due under the sales contract. The buyer's bank then is obligated to pay on behalf of the buyer when the seller presents the proper documents, typically through collecting banks (*see* § 1.6 below).

[12]   *See* CISG, arts. 6, 58. For more detail on the CISG's default rules on this issue *see* Chapter 2, § 2.24.

themselves. As discussed in Chapter 3, such an agreement also may arise from the nature of specific commercial terms (such as CIF and CFR).[13] But it otherwise generally will not be implied. This arrangement often is especially important to the seller, because most legal systems—including the CISG[14]—grant the buyer a general right to inspect the goods before payment.[15]

Thus, an international seller often will wish to secure a contractual agreement from its buyer on a documents against payment arrangement. Of course, this agreement may occur as part of a carefully negotiated single contract document. But more often, the buyer initiates the contracting process through a "purchase order" form that describes the essential terms of a proposed deal (type and quantify of goods, price, delivery time). The seller then typically responds with an "order acknowledgement" form that agrees with those essential terms but also proposes a documents against payment arrangement. Both parties may then think that they have closed a deal. The problem is that the buyer's purchase order also often includes its standard business terms and the seller's order acknowledgement likewise includes its standard business terms. The result is a "battle of the forms." As discussed in Chapter 2,[16] this may leave substantial uncertainty for both parties about the content of their (possible) contractual deal, including for the seller on the time and modalities of payment.

§ 1.4   D/P Transaction__Seller's Shipment Obligations

If the parties' contract includes a documents against payment agreement, it is the seller's obligation to manufacturer (or otherwise procure), package, and ship the contract goods. For the last duty, it typically engages the services of a specialized company known as a "freight forwarder" (or in fancier modern terms, a "logistics company") with expertise in international shipping. The freight forwarder will arrange for transportation by an international carriage company, attend to any customs formalities, and otherwise perform the services required for an international shipment of goods.[17] If the agreed commercial term requires it (*e.g.*, under a CIF

---

[13]   *See* Chapter 3, §§ 3.10, 3.11.

[14]   *See* CISG, art. 58(3) ("The buyer is not bound to pay the price until he has had an opportunity to examine the goods[.]").

[15]   *See, e.g.,* UCC § 2–513(1).

[16]   *See* Chapter 2, § 2.17.

[17]   The seller—again, typically through its freight forwarder—also must provide detailed shipment information to the U.S. government through the online "Automated Export System (AES)." *See* http://aesdirect.census.gov. Supplying false information in connection with the AES is a federal crime. *See* 13 U.S.C. § 305.

term as discussed in Chapter 3[18]), the seller also will procure an insurance certificate covering the goods in transit. It then delivers the goods—again, typically through the freight forwarder—to an international carrier for transportation to the buyer.

Upon receipt of goods for transport, the carrier will issue a "bill of lading" covering the goods. The bill of lading serves three separate functions: (1) a contract of carriage between carrier and the "shipper" (the seller); (2) a receipt from the carrier describing the goods received from the shipper; and (3) a document of title defining who has rights to the goods and thus to whom the carrier is obligated to deliver them upon arrival at the defined destination.

In short, the essential purpose of a bill of lading is to provide proof—for the seller and the buyer alike—that the carrier has received the goods and that they are destined for the buyer. The carrier also will describe on the bill of lading itself the goods it has received (almost always from information provided by the seller). And, most important, the carrier then will be obligated to deliver (to "turn out") goods in accordance with that description.

Chapter 4 analyzes in detail the law governing international bills of lading. For present purposes it will suffice to observe that they come in two principal forms: nonnegotiable and negotiable. With a nonnegotiable (aka "straight") bill of lading, the carrier agrees to deliver the goods only to the person named therein (the "consignee"). In a sale of goods transaction, this is the shipper/seller. Thus, the seller alone retains full control over the carrier's delivery obligation. With a negotiable (aka "order") bill of lading, in contrast, the carrier agrees to deliver the goods only to the person properly in possession of the bill (the "holder"). For such a bill of lading, therefore, physical possession is essential to determining the rights to the goods as well as the delivery obligations of the carrier. This core feature of a negotiable bill, as § 1.5 immediately below explains, makes it the only appropriate form for a documents against payment transaction.

§ 1.5   D/P Transaction__Traditional Role of a Negotiable Bill of Lading

Unless otherwise agreed, a documents against payment transaction traditionally requires use of a negotiable bill of lading. A bill is negotiable if it states that the goods are to be delivered "to the order" of the consignee.[19] With these magic words, the physical bill of lading becomes the embodiment of the legal rights to the

---

[18]   *See* Chapter 3, § 3.10.

[19]   *See* Chapter 4, § 4.8.

goods. At the same time, such a bill creates a power of transfer (of "negotiation") in favor of the named consignee—that is, a power to give an "order" to the carrier. The consignee then may transfer the rights to the goods by transferring physical possession of the bill. The consignee exercises its power to give an order to the carrier by making an "indorsement" on the bill along with an instruction to deliver the goods to the named transferee.

This core feature of a negotiable bill of lading is essential to the payment against document arrangement. From its nature, a negotiable bill of lading controls the right to obtain the goods from carrier, and in this way provides valuable assurances to both the seller and the buyer. To the seller, it provides assurance that the carrier will deliver the goods to the buyer only if the buyer has obtained possession of the bill. And of course, the seller—acting through its collecting banks, see below—will deliver the negotiable bill of lading to the buyer only after the buyer has paid the purchase price for the goods. To the buyer, a negotiable bill of lading provides assurance that the goods—as described therein—have been delivered to the carrier and that, upon obtaining possession, the buyer will be the only person with the legal right to demand delivery from the carrier.

A recent federal district court aptly described the essence of this arrangement as follows:

> Negotiable bills of lading are a way of protecting a distant seller from fraud or insolvency of a buyer. The seller tenders shipping documents, including a negotiable bill of lading, rather than goods to the buyer. By paying for the documents, the buyer gets possession of the original bill of lading. Possession of the bill entitles him to possession of the goods; it represents the goods and conveys title to them.[20]

In short, the buyer will be able to obtain delivery of the goods if, *but only if*, it obtains physical possession of the properly indorsed bill of lading. And it will be able to obtain possession of the bill *only if* it first pays the price owed to the seller under the sales contract.

A nonnegotiable bill of lading makes little sense in this context. Because the physical bill does not control delivery of the goods from the carrier,[21] possession of the bill is irrelevant. As noted above, a

---

[20] Quanzhou Joerga Fashion Co., Inc. v. Brooks Fitch Apparel Group, LLC, 2012 WL 4767180, at *5 (S.D.N.Y. 2012) (*quoting* Allied Chem. Int'l Corp. v. Companhia de Navegacao Lloyd Brasileiro, 775 F.2d 476, 481 (2d Cir. 1985)).

[21] As explained in Chapter 4, some foreign legal systems require presentation to the carrier of even a straight bill of lading if it contains a so-called "surrender clause." *See* § 4.9. In these systems, stronger arguments exist that such a straight

nonnegotiable bill of lading instead obligates the carrier to deliver only to the named consignee. If such a bill were used in a documents against payment transaction, the parties would lose the ability to satisfy both of their interests through the identification of the consignee: If the seller were named as consignee, the buyer would be obligated to pay against a document that would not control the delivery of the goods from the carrier; but if the buyer were named as consignee, it would immediately have the right to delivery of the goods from the carrier, irrespective of whether the buyer has paid or ever will pay the purchase price to the seller. A nonnegotiable bill thus would destroy the essential aspect of a documents against payment transaction—a concurrent exchange of the purchase price for a document that controls delivery of the goods.

§ 1.6   D/P Transaction__Role of Banks as Collection Agents

Once the seller has obtained a negotiable bill of lading made out to its order, how does the payment arrangement actually work? First, the seller prepares a "draft" (aka "bill of exchange") drawn against the buyer (the "drawee") and naming the seller itself as "payee."[22] Like a check drawn on a bank, the draft functions as the formal legal vehicle for withdrawing from the buyer the money owed to the seller under the sales contract. It likewise will be payable to the seller's order; it thus also is a negotiable instrument, for it represents the physical embodiment of the seller's monetary claim against the buyer.[23] Therefore, the seller may sell its right to this payment to another person—such as a bank—by transferring physical possession of the piece of paper (see below).

The seller then uses the banking system to obtain payment on the draft from the buyer. It does so by indorsing both the negotiable draft and the negotiable bill of lading and delivering them to its local bank, along with any other documents required by the sales

---

bill of lading could control the goods as required for a documents against payment transaction.

   22   In the United States, Article 3 of the Uniform Commercial Code provides the governing rules for such "negotiable instruments." *See* § 3–102(a). The United Nations Commission on International Trade Law (UNCITRAL) has proposed a formal treaty for the same subject matter. *See* United Nations Convention on International Bills of Exchange and International Promissory Notes (New York, 1988), available at http://www.uncitral.org/uncitral/en/uncitral_texts/payments.html. This treaty has been accepted by only five countries, however, and has not entered into force.

   23   *See* UCC § 3–104(a), (e). *See also* § 4–104(6) (defining "documentary draft").

contract.[24] Typically, these other documents include a commercial invoice (which is the formal document generated by the seller's accounting department confirming the goods shipped and the amount the buyer owes) and sometimes also a packing list (which is a document generated by the seller's shipping department describing the goods actually packed and prepared for shipment).

The banks then serve as collection agents for the seller.[25] (For this reason, this aspect of a documents against payment transaction is referred to as "documentary collection" (or D/C)). And here again the negotiable bill of lading plays the significant role. When it undertakes to collect funds from the buyer, the bank receives from the seller the negotiable bill of lading issued by the carrier. This document permits the seller, acting through the banks, to retain control over the carrier's delivery of the goods—because the buyer cannot obtain possession of the goods from the carrier without possession of the negotiable bill of lading. And because the banks receive this document of title from the seller only on a conditional basis, they are obligated to obtain payment from the buyer before they are allowed to release the document to the buyer (see § 1.7 below).

It is here, also, that we confront the first set of uniform "customs and practices"[26] that facilitate international business transactions. The International Chamber of Commerce has prepared a set of standardized contract terms, the Uniform Rules for Collections (URC),[27] that banks may incorporate into their contracts governing the collection process.[28] Thus, the URC are not "governing law" in a formal sense, but instead gain their force through a contractual agreement between the seller and the banks in each particular transaction. A federal court aptly described the legal status of the URC this way:

> The crucial point here is that the URCs are a set of principles created by a nongovernmental organization. . . .

---

[24] The seller instead may indorse the bill of lading directly over to the buyer along with strict instructions to the banks not to release it to the buyer unless and until the buyer has paid the full amount of the related draft. Such an arrangement, however, leaves a bit less flexibility in the event the buyer wrongfully refuses to pay upon presentation. In such a case, the banks—again, acting as agents for the seller—would not be able indorse the bill of lading over to any new buyer the seller may find at the foreign destination.

[25] *See* URC, art. 3a(1) (referring to the person who engages a bank for collection as the "principal"); UCC § 4–201(a) ("Unless a contrary intent clearly appears . . . the bank, with respect to an item, is an agent or subagent of the owner of the item[.]").

[26] *See* § 1.1, *supra.*

[27] ICC Publication No. 522 (1995).

[28] In the United States, the governing legal rules are found in UCC Article 4. *See* especially §§ 4–501 through 4–504.

The operative legal mechanism is contractual: the URCs become binding when two parties enter into a contract which incorporates them.[29]

The contractual agreement on the URC occurs through a "collection instructions" form that describes the conditions for release of the documents to the buyer.[30] Upon incorporation in this way, the URC become "binding on all parties . . . unless otherwise expressly agreed or contrary to the provisions of a national, state or local law and/or regulation which cannot be departed from."[31] The effect of this last clause regarding mandatory domestic law is quite limited in the United States. The reason is that the domestic UCC expressly authorizes the parties, by agreement, to displace most of its provisions.[32] As a result, "the effect of the parties' adoption of URC 522 is to supersede those provisions."[33] The only limitation is that the parties "cannot disclaim a bank's responsibility for its lack of good faith or failure to exercise ordinary care."[34]

Under the URC, the seller's bank (the "remitting bank"[35]) is required to send the documents, along with the collection instructions, through customary banking channels "without delay" for presentation to the buyer.[36] If the seller's bank does not have a direct relationship with a bank in the buyer's trading area, it will engage a larger national or international bank as an intermediary. The URC refers to these intermediary banks as "collecting banks."[37] Whether directly or through such intermediary banks, the seller's bank must send the documents to a bank at the buyer's location. This final bank (the "presenting bank"[38]) then must notify the buyer of the arrival of the documents and present them to the buyer for inspection. Most important, the bank must demand, on behalf of the

---

[29]   Inox Wares Pvt. Ltd. v. Interchange Bank, 2008 WL 4691906, at *5 (D.N.J. 2008).

[30]   URC, arts. 2, 4.

[31]   Novara v. Manufacturers and Traders Trust Co., 2011 WL 3841538, at *8 (D. Md. 2011) (quoting URC, art. 1a).

[32]   See UCC §§ 1–302 ("Except as otherwise provided . . . the effect of the provisions of [the Uniform Commercial Code] may be varied by agreement."), 4–103(a) (same).

[33]   Novara v. Manufacturers and Traders Trust Co., 2011 WL 3841538, at *8–9 (D. Md. 2011) (quoting URC, art. 1a, but also holding that the URC's rule on reasonable care is "essentially identical" to the corresponding rule in UCC Article 4). See also SCADIF, S.A. v. First Union Nat'l Bank, 208 F. Supp. 2d 1352, 1373 (S.D. Fla. 2002) (same).

[34]   UCC § 4–103(a).

[35]   URC, art. 2a(2).

[36]   URC, arts. 5, 6. See also UCC § 4–501.

[37]   URC, art. 2a(3).

[38]   URC, art. 2a(4).

seller, that the buyer pay the draft (which, again, serves as the legal vehicle for obtaining the payment due under the sales contract).[39]

Because the seller's local bank usually takes the documents only "for collection," it will not even provisionally credit the seller's bank account prior to receiving payment from the buyer. It and any other involved banks likewise have no obligation regarding the authenticity of the documents[40] or the conformity of the goods.[41] Their only obligations are to follow the collection instructions and to "act in good faith and exercise reasonable care."[42]

Discounting of the Draft. Alternatively, but rarely, the seller's bank may decide to "discount" the draft. This means that it will purchase the draft outright from the seller at less than face value. Because the draft is a negotiable instrument, it represents the legal right to payment as against the buyer under the sales contract. Thus, the seller can sell ("negotiate") this valuable piece of paper to a discounting bank (or any other party). The seller does so by indorsing and transferring the draft over to the discounting bank. As security, the bank likely also will require that the seller negotiate over to it the related negotiable bill of lading covering the goods. Through these combined acts, the discounting bank will become the owner both of the right to payment from the buyer and of the goods covered by the bill of lading. By purchasing the draft at less than full value, the goal of such a discounting bank, of course, is to make a profit if the buyer ultimately pays in full. Nonetheless, the far more common arrangement is for the banks to act merely as collection agents for the seller as described above.

§ 1.7   D/P Transaction__Buyer's Payment Obligation

Documents against Payment (D/P). The payment arrangement in the great run of transactions involves a "sight draft" (aka

---

[39] For an application of these URC principles *see* Novara v. Manufacturers and Traders Trust Co., 2011 WL 3841538 (D. Md. 2011); Inox Wares Pvt. Ltd. v. Interchange Bank, 2008 WL 4691906 (D.N.J. 2008); Fashion Shop LLC v. Virtual Sales Group Corp. 525 F. Supp. 2d 436 (S.D.N.Y. 2007); Bank One Dearborn, N.A. v. Wachovia Bank, N.A. 2005 WL 67073 (E.D. PA. 2005).

[40] URC art. 13 (stating that the banks are not responsible for the "form, sufficiency, accuracy, genuineness, falsification, or legal effect of any documents"). *See also* Thiagarajar Mills, Ltd. v. Thornton, 242 F.2d 710, 713 (6th Cir. 2001).

[41] URC, art. 13 (stating that banks do not "assume any liability or responsibility for the description, quantity, weight, quality, condition, packing, delivery, value or existence of the goods represented by any document(s)"). *See also* UCC § 4–403 (stating that the bank presenting the draft "is under no obligation with respect to the goods represented by [a bill of lading] except to follow any reasonable instructions seasonably received").

[42] URC, arts. 4a, 9.

"demand draft"). This means that the buyer must pay the purchase price upon receipt of the draft. Thus, in a bank collection transaction the banks must demand that the buyer pay the stated amount—that it "honor" the draft—promptly upon the presentation. Under domestic U.S. law, the buyer breaches its payment obligation—*i.e.*, it "dishonors" the draft—if it does not pay the full amount within three business days.[43] And, again, the banks may not release the documents, especially the negotiable bill of lading, until the buyer has done so.[44] This is the essence of a documents against payment (D/P) arrangement. A bank that nonetheless releases the documents to the buyer before receiving payment is liable to the seller for any resulting damages.[45]

Documents against Acceptance (D/A). Alternatively, the seller may agree to extend credit to the buyer in the form of a "time draft." Such a draft requires payment at a defined time after presentment (*e.g.*, "30 days after sight"), and in this sense the seller extends credit because the buyer may pay at a time after receiving the documents (and thus the goods). Nonetheless, upon presentment the buyer must "accept" the draft in writing on the draft itself, most often simply in the form of a signature.[46] This is known as a "documents against acceptance" (or D/A) arrangement. The legal effect of an acceptance is a binding obligation of the buyer to pay at the later defined time.[47] In such a case, the presenting bank will release the documents upon the buyer's acceptance of the draft.[48] Again, even with such an arrangement a bank will be liable to the seller if it nonetheless releases the documents to the buyer before such an acceptance.[49]

In either a D/P or D/A arrangement, the buyer may require the presenting bank to "exhibit" the documents to allow the buyer to determine whether they conform to the contract. The buyer never sees the goods themselves, only the documents—so it will inspect the documents rigorously to determine that they comply exactly with the requirements of the sales contract. Substantial

---

[43] UCC § 3–502(c).

[44] *See* URC, art. 7b (stating that in absence of a contrary statement in the collection instructions, "commercial documents will be released only against payment"). *See also* UCC § 4–503(1).

[45] *See* Gathercrest, Ltd. v. First American Bank & Trust, 649 F. Supp. 106, 117 (M.D. Fla. 1985).

[46] *See* UCC § 5–102(b) (expressly incorporating the definition of "acceptance" from § 3–409(a)).

[47] *See* UCC § 3–413(a).

[48] URC, art. 7b. *See also* UCC § 4–503(1).

[49] *See* Kookmin Bank v. Sexton Dia-Tools, Inc., 33 A.D.3d 535, 823 N.Y.S.2d 378 (2006); Proin S.A. v. Lasalle Bank, N.A., 223 F. Supp. 2d 960, 965 (N.D. Ill. 2002).

performance by the seller in the tender of documents will not suffice. The most important document at this point is—once again— the negotiable bill of lading, for the buyer will inspect the description of the goods on the bill to ensure that it conforms to the seller's obligations under the sales contract. In short, the buyer must "pay against the documents" (or "accept" against the documents) and cannot wait until delivery of the goods themselves.

Once the buyer has paid, the banks must send the funds back to the seller "without delay."[50] The presenting bank then will give possession of the (properly indorsed) negotiable bill of lading to the buyer, who in turn will present it to the carrier to obtain delivery of the goods.

§ 1.8   D/P Transaction__Transaction Diagram

An international sale of goods transaction based on the standard documents against payment arrangement—with banks acting merely as collection agents—is illustrated by the following diagram:

---

[50]   URC, art. 16a (declaring that "[a]mounts collected (less charges and/or disbursements and/or expenses where applicable) must be made available without delay to the party from whom the collection instruction was received").

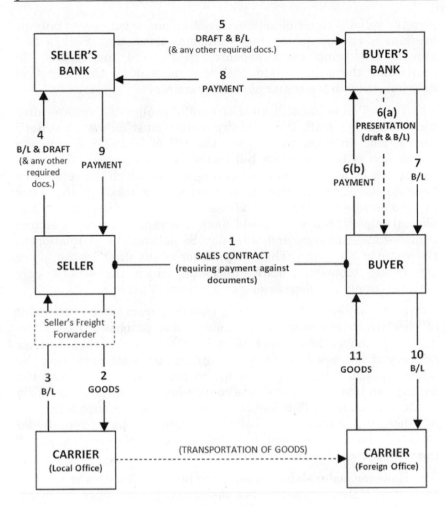

§ 1.9   D/P Transaction___Risk Allocation

Although the documents against payment transaction structure solves much of the trust problem noted in the Introduction, some risks remain for both the seller and the buyer.[51]

Risks for the Seller. What can go wrong from the seller's point of view? The principal risk is that it has shipped the goods to a foreign location prior to receiving payment from the buyer. The banks act merely as collection agents, and thus do not guarantee that the buyer will pay. To be sure, the buyer has a formal legal obligation to pay upon presentation of conforming documents. The problem is that the buyer simply may refuse to do so. This would

---

[51]   Chapter 4 addresses other special risks that relate directly to the use of bills of lading. *See* §§ 4.11 through 4.14.

give the seller a cause of action, but often one it can assert only by bringing a lawsuit in the buyer's home jurisdiction. Such a suit abroad will bring extra expense, delay, and uncertainty. In particular, the seller could feel that it will be the target of discrimination in the courts of another country.

The seller would still have control of the goods, because after dishonor of the draft, the collecting banks must follow the seller's instructions on what to do with the bill of lading.[52] A common instruction is to return the bill to the seller. However, the goods would now be at a foreign destination—one at which the seller may have no agent, and no particular prospects for resale. If the seller instead decides to bring the goods back to its base of operations (and normal sales territory), it would have to arrange and pay a second transportation charge, and this may be substantial in relation to the value of the goods. Thus, a dishonor of the draft by the buyer can create economic circumstances in which the seller's only rational option is a distress sale at a foreign location.[53]

Risks for the Buyer. What can go wrong from the buyer's point of view? In exchange for its payment of the purchase price of the goods, the buyer has a document from the carrier that controls delivery of the goods, likely an insurance certificate protecting the buyer against a loss of or damage to the goods in transit,[54] and perhaps an inspection certificate confirming that the goods conform to the sales contract (if it had the foresight to secure such a right in advance, see immediately below). Therefore, the buyer should receive what it bargained for—delivery of conforming goods or insurance proceeds sufficient to cover any loss.

However, as explained above, the buyer will have the right to inspect only the documents, not the actual goods, before payment. And the best information the buyer can obtain regarding the contract goods (description, quantity of packages, weight of the cargo, etc.) is provided in the bill of lading. But the buyer cannot be absolutely assured that the actual goods conform to the contract. The bill could contain a misstatement or misdescription of the goods; or the description could be accurate as a superficial matter,

---

[52]   *See* URC, art. 26c(3).

[53]   If the seller has indorsed the negotiable bill of lading to the banks (*See* § 1.16 above), such as sale would occur by the seller finding a second buyer and the last bank in the chain indorsing the bill over to that new buyer. With physical possession of such a bill properly indorsed over to it, the new buyer becomes the owner of the goods and obtains the right to delivery from the carrier.

[54]   For example, an agreement on a "CIF" commercial term (among others) obligates the seller to arrange and pay for insurance covering the goods after delivery to the carrier and until they reach the destination port. As Chapter 3 explains, the traditional view is that a CIF commercial term also implies an agreement on a documents against payment arrangement. *See* § 3.10

but the goods have latent defects; or the seller could ship the goods in sealed containers not subject to inspection by the carrier when it issued the bill. Thus, the goods could have a whole variety of actual nonconformities as compared to the requirements of the sales contract. Similarly, the buyer could find that the labeling on the packaging is deficient or incorrect in some way, such that customs agents prohibit or delay delivery of the goods.

Sophisticated buyers have responded to these risks with a separate protective device, the third-party inspection certificate. This involves the buyer contracting with an independent third party to inspect the goods *before* the seller delivers them to the carrier. The buyer then has the inspection certificate as a separate verification—beyond that of the seller in the invoice and of the carrier in the bill of lading—that the goods conform to the description in the sales contract. The buyer must separately secure a right for an inspection certificate in the negotiations over the sales contract. Like the documents against payment arrangement itself, such an agreement will not be implied. But even if the buyer secures this right, it must separately conclude a contract with the third-party inspection company—many multinational enterprises provide this service—and of course pay the required fee.

The buyer also may face risks relating to the conduct of the carrier. These include that the carrier will store or handle the goods inappropriately such that they are damaged in transit. Separately, the seller may have fabricated or forged the bill of lading (or even a required inspection certificate) in the first place, or a thief could have stolen and forged the bill later. Some of these risks are inherent in any transaction using a bill of lading, and Chapter 4 will examine them in detail.[55] But they assume special significance for the buyer in a documents against payment transaction under which it must pay before getting access to the goods themselves.

§ 1.10 The Documentary Sale Transaction with a Confirmed Letter of Credit

A second, and indeed more common, form of a documents against payment transaction in international sales is based on a "letter of credit" (aka "documentary letter of credit" transaction). Sellers greatly prefer this form—if they can secure a corresponding agreement from their buyers—for it involves a formal and independent payment obligation of a bank. A letter of credit in fact is just that: a letter from a bank that creates a credit at that bank in favor of the beneficiary (the seller in a sale of goods transaction).

---

[55]   *See* §§ 4.11–4.14.

The beneficiary then is entitled to payment of the credit when it presents to the bank the documents detailed in the letter.

Chapter 6 analyzes in detail the rights and obligations of the parties to an international letter of credit transaction. Our goal here is to examine how a letter of credit functions as a valuable payment vehicle to facilitate international sale of goods transactions.

A letter of credit is a particularly secure method—from a seller's perspective at least—of solving the fundamental trust problem that may exist between a distant seller and an unfamiliar buyer. It does so by distributing the potentially large risks reviewed in the Introduction above (see § 1.1) to third party intermediaries that have specialized knowledge and can more efficiently and effectively evaluate those risks.

In this form of a documentary sale, the third party intermediaries are banks (at least one in the buyer's home country and usually a second one in the seller's home country) and again at least one carrier. Thus, the parties involved are: (1) the buyer; (2) the bank at which the buyer does its banking (which for ease of reference we will term the "Buyer's Bank"); (3) the seller; (4) a bank with an office located near the seller; and (5) the carrier. These parties are able to take a large risk not subject to firm evaluation by any one of them, divide it into several small, calculable risks, and then allocate these smaller risks to the parties best able to evaluate them. This division and allocation of individual risks can reduce the uncertainties of the overall transaction to a point that it enables beneficial international sales transactions that otherwise might not take place.

The documentary letter of credit transaction involves a series of contracts—but not all of the parties to the transaction will be parties to each contract. The contracts include: the sale of goods contract between the buyer and the seller (see § 1.11); (b) the letter of credit transaction, which itself includes a contract between the buyer and its bank but also an independent promise by that bank to pay the seller, subject to defined documentary conditions (see § 1.12); and (c) the bill of lading issued by the carrier to the seller covering the goods in transit (see § 1.13).[56]

---

[56]   For a description of the overall transaction *see* Great Wall De Venezuela C.A. v. Interaudi Bank, 117 F. Supp. 3d 474, 485 (S.D.N.Y. 2015); Voest-Alpine Int'l Corp. v. Chase Manhattan Bank, N.A., 707 F.2d 680, 682 (2d Cir. 1983).

§ 1.11 L/C Transaction__Requirement of a Contractual Agreement

The contract underlying the entire series of transactions is the contract for the sale of goods. The buyer and the seller are parties to this contract, but not the banks or the carrier. This contract obligates the seller to deliver the agreed type, quantity, and quality of goods, and the buyer to take the goods and pay the agreed price. Again, for most international sale of goods contracts today the governing law is the United Nations Convention on Contracts for the International Sale of Goods (CISG) (see Chapter 2). But the CISG has no formal rules on letters of credit, and in any event generally defers to the parties' agreement regarding the modalities of payment.

The principal source for the rules governing international letters of credit is instead a second set of uniform customs and practices issued by the International Chamber of Commerce: the Uniform Customs and Practices for Documentary Credits (UCP). Indeed, although the Uniform Commercial Code in the United States has a separate Article (Article 5) for letters of credit, it expressly defers to the UCP rules if they are incorporated in a letter of credit.[57] Chapter 6 will examine these rules in detail, although we will to refer to some of the UCP's more basic notions as part the structural analysis here. Nonetheless, even the UCP generally defer to the agreements of the parties regarding the form and substance of a letter of credit.[58]

The process for arranging payment through an international letter of credit thus begins with the sale of goods contract. When the parties form their contract, the seller and the buyer of course must agree on a "price term." This is simply the amount of money the buyer must pay in exchange for the goods supplied by the seller.

But before it actually sends the goods to the buyer's foreign destination, the seller also will want assurance that the buyer will make the required payment in a timely fashion. As an expression of the fundamental trust problem sketched in the Introduction (see § 1.1), quite often a simple promise from the foreign buyer to pay in the future will not be enough. Experienced sellers thus will demand that the sales contract also include a "payment term." Such a term defines the time and the method by which the buyer must effect the payment of the purchase price.

---

[57]   *See* U.C.C § 5–116(c). For more detail on this point, see Chapter 6, § 6.3.

[58]   *See* Chapter 6, § 6.3.

Experienced or risk-averse sellers may be unwilling to assume even the limited risks associated with a basic documents against payment transaction reviewed above.[59] And the concerns of cautious sellers about shipment without a guarantee of return payment naturally increase for transactions that are especially large or involve especially unfamiliar (or financially unreliable) buyers.

In such cases, sellers may demand that the buyer arrange payment via an international letter of credit. A letter of credit is a particularly secure payment term, for it involves an independent obligation of a bank to pay the price stated in the sales contract, subject to defined conditions. Typically, that bank will be the buyer's own house bank. But the seller must bargain for and include in the sales contract a term that requires payment by a letter of credit. Such an agreement normally will not be implied.

A payment promise from an unfamiliar bank in the buyer's home country also may not provide enough security, however—for the seller may not fully trust a foreign bank either. Instead, the seller wants a firm, legally binding promise from a bank known to it, preferably one near its home. For maximum protection, therefore, the seller will seek payment by a "confirmed" letter of credit. This will require that the buyer arrange for a bank in the seller's home country and region to add its own independent promise to pay upon satisfaction of the defined conditions (see § 1.14 below). Again, however, the seller must separately secure an agreement on such a confirmation, for it too normally will not be implied from a simple requirement of a letter of credit.

Finally, experienced sellers will require that the letter of credit be "irrevocable." A revocable credit is of little value for a seller because the issuer may cancel its payment promise (most often, at the request of the buyer) at any time. Because of this, the UCP presumes that a credit is irrevocable unless it expressly states otherwise.[60]

§ 1.12 L/C Transaction___The Letter of Credit Contract

A letter of credit is a specialized contract involving a promise by a bank that it will pay to the seller the amount stated therein (typically, the amount due under the sales contract) subject to defined conditions. As described in § 1.14 below, the process begins with the buyer arranging for its bank to issue the credit in favor of the seller. In the distinctive language of letter of credit law, the

---

[59]   See § 1.9, *supra.*

[60]   UCP, art. 7b.

bank's formal promise will be to "honor drafts drawn" on the bank by the seller. A draft is the legal vehicle by which the seller withdraws from the bank the credit created by the bank's payment promise (see § 1.15 below). And if the seller also is able to secure a requirement of a confirmed letter of credit, it also will have a right to payment by the local confirming bank.

The essence of a standard letter of credit is that the seller's right to payment is conditioned on the presentation of the documents defined in the credit itself. For this reason, such a letter of credit often is known as a "documentary credit." To ensure that no problems arise later, the experienced seller will ensure that the sales contract contains clear specifications regarding the documents it must present to obtain payment. It then must ensure that the letter of credit issued by the banks in fact repeats those specifications precisely.

For a sale of goods transaction, the focus of the documentary conditions in the letter of credit of course will be the goods. Thus, the banks' payment promises will be conditioned upon the seller presenting documentary evidence that it has shipped the contract goods via a carrier for delivery at the buyer's location. What would furnish such evidence? The key document, again, is the bill of lading issued by the carrier, which will contain a description of the goods received from the seller for transportation to the buyer.

Further, most often the banks will require a negotiable bill of lading, because—as briefly described below[61] and as Chapter 4 will examine in detail—such a bill will control the right to obtain the goods from the carrier. Such a bill will assure the banks that they can control the ultimate delivery of the goods by retaining possession of the bill.

For maximum protection, the banks—based on information provided by the buyer regarding the sales contract—typically will require that the seller also present a variety of other documents as a condition to payment under the letter of credit. These documents provide either further evidence that the seller has shipped conforming goods or further protection for the banks and the buyer. In addition to the bill of lading (see § 1.13 below) and a draft (see § 1.15 below), the banks often require that the seller present the following additional documents in international transactions:

(1)   a commercial invoice, which is a form of an itemized bill prepared by the seller's accounting department that sets out the terms of the sale, grade and quantity of goods, amount owed, etc.;

---

[61]   *See* § 1.13, *infra.*

(2)   a packing list, which is a separate confirmation from the seller's shipping department of what goods actually were packed in any sealed cartons or containers;

(3)   a policy of marine insurance (if the goods are to be transported by sea);

(4)   a certificate of inspection, which is issued by a commercial inspecting firm and independently confirms that the required number and type of goods were shipped (although the buyer must separately contract for such an inspection, and then ensure that presentation of the certificate is included as a condition in the letter of credit); and

(5)   a certificate of origin, which documents the source of the goods sold and—depending on the trade agreements between the exporting and importing country—may be used by customs officials in the importing country to determine tariff assessments.

The parties' contract may require the presentation of other documents, depending on the nature of the goods or the specific line of trade.[62] In any event, the conditions to payment in a letter of credit must all be documentary in nature—for as Chapter 6 describes, the banks must disregard any conditions in a letter of credit (even if expressly stated) that do not require satisfaction through the presentation of a document.[63]

§ 1.13   L/C Transaction___The Bill of Lading Contract

As explained in the Introduction, a key challenge in international sales is that the geographic distance between the seller and the buyer most often requires the engagement of an international carrier of goods. Depending on the specific contractual agreements, either the seller or the buyer will make a contract with this carrier. At its most basic, this contract obligates the carrier, in return for payment of the freight charge, to transport the goods from the place of receipt to a defined foreign location (often, a port or terminal near the buyer's place of business).

Just as with the basic documents against payment transaction reviewed above,[64] this final contract in our letter of credit transaction is expressed in a bill of lading issued by the carrier.

---

[62]   Examples might include (depending on local law or custom), an export license, a food safety certificate, or a health inspection certificate.

[63]   *See* Chapter 6, § 6.9.

[64]   *See* § 1.5, *supra.*

Again, the bill may be either in a nonnegotiable ("straight") form or a negotiable ("order") form.[65] But for the same reasons examined in Section 1.5 above, the banks obligated to pay under a letter of credit most often will demand that the seller obtain and present a negotiable bill of lading covering the goods. The banks require this in order to ensure that the buyer is able to obtain delivery of the goods *only if* it has physical possession of the bill of lading properly indorsed over to it.[66] As a special form of a "document of title" covering the goods, such a bill of lading controls access to and delivery of the goods.

Thus, after paying the seller under the letter of credit and receiving the bill from the seller, the banks can preclude the buyer from obtaining the goods from the carrier until it has reimbursed the banks (or made a binding commitment to do so). In the worst case (such as if the buyer goes bankrupt), the negotiable bill of lading will give the banks control over the goods, which can be sold to cover the banks' losses.

Nonetheless, modern commercial and transportation practices are increasingly relying on various forms of nonnegotiable bills of lading.[67] This is especially true in transactions in which the goods may arrive as quickly as the physical bill of lading could, such as when the goods are sent by rapid means of transit (*e.g.*, airplane) or when the distance between the seller and buyer is small.

Because nonnegotiable bills of lading do not formally control access to the goods, banks that issue letters of credit in transactions that use such bills must look to other forms of security for their right to reimbursement by the buyer. For their regular, trusted customers, the banks may choose to rely on an existing financial relationship as well as a careful assessment of creditworthiness, and thus forego the default security of a negotiable bill of lading. For less reliable customers, the banks instead typically will require an upfront payment (*i.e.*, before the issuance of the letter of credit) of some or all of the credit amount, or the posting of sufficient collateral to guarantee payment later.

Nonetheless, the banks most often want the highest level of security that they can obtain, and thus, where possible, will require use of a negotiable bill of lading.

---

[65]   For more on these two different types of bills of lading *see* Chapter 4, §§ 4.8 and 4.9.

[66]   Again, Chapter 4 analyzes in detail the role of and rules governing international bills of lading.

[67]   For more details on this development *see* Chapter 4, §§ 4.9 and 4.10.

§ 1.14 L/C Transaction___Issuance Process for a Confirmed Letter of Credit

If the sale of goods contract includes a letter of credit payment term, the buyer—in the language of letter of credit law, the "applicant"[68]—will contract with a local bank (typically, its own house bank) to serve as the "issuing bank."[69] (Again, we will refer to this bank below as Buyer's Bank.) Today, the banks typically require that the applicant conclude a formal Reimbursement Agreement that sets forth the details on the contractual relationship concerning the issuance of the credit and the banks' right to reimbursement.[70] More advanced banks also may provide access to an electronic platform through which regular customers may apply for a letter of credit and enter the required substantive terms.

Buyer's Bank then will "issue" the letter of credit naming the seller as the "beneficiary."[71] Traditionally, the bank will not make a formal promise to pay money directly to the beneficiary; rather, it will promise "to honor a draft drawn" on the bank by the beneficiary in the amount of the credit, if and when the latter presents the documents specified therein. Again, Buyer's Bank will take care to assess the creditworthiness of the applicant/buyer, and will make appropriate arrangements to ensure easy reimbursement after it has paid the seller under the letter of credit. These arrangements will be made before the letter of credit is issued, for with an irrevocable[72] letter of credit, the bank is independently bound after issuance to pay according to the credit's terms.[73] And again, the bank is especially likely to require financial assurances from the applicant/buyer where the transaction will not involve the presentation of a negotiable bill of lading. Finally, for its services and risks the bank will charge a commission, although the amount is quite small (typically, about one percent of the amount of the credit).

If the sales contract requires a confirmed letter of credit, the buyer also must arrange for a payment promise by a local bank in

---

[68]   *See* UCP, art. 2; UCC § 5–102(a)(2).

[69]   *See* UCP, art. 2. *See also* UCC § 5–102(a)(9) (defining an "issuer").

[70]   UCC Article 5 generally permits such agreements, provided that they do not excuse liability or limit remedies for the issuer's failure to perform, or otherwise remove general obligations of good faith and reasonableness. *See* UCC § 5–103(c).

[71]   *See* UCP, art. 2; UCC § 5–102(a)(3).

[72]   Again, the UCP creates a presumption that a credit is irrevocable unless it expressly states otherwise. UCP, art. 7b.

[73]   UCP, art. 7b ("An issuing bank is irrevocably bound to honour as of the time it issues the credit.").

the seller's area. This occurs through the Buyer's Bank contacting, through correspondent relationships, a bank in the seller's location and requesting that it serve as a "confirming bank"[74]—that is, that the local bank *also* obligate itself to honor the draft presented by the seller. Most often, the Buyer's Bank does this by forwarding the terms of the original letter of credit to the local bank—through a dedicated electronic system for inter-bank communications known as SWIFT[75]—along with a request that the local bank add its confirmation. Thus, Buyer's Bank most often will not communicate directly with the foreign seller/beneficiary.

Instead, if the local bank agrees to confirm the credit, the common practice is for it to prepare and send to the seller a separate, formal letter (today, most often in an electronic form). This letter performs two distinct functions: (a) It informs the seller/beneficiary of the issuance of the letter of credit by Buyer's Bank; and (b) it declares the local bank's "confirmation" of that credit along with a restatement of the exact substantive terms in the original credit (required documents, etc.). Thus, most often the seller/beneficiary learns of both actions in the one confirmation letter from the local confirming bank. By confirming the original credit, the confirming bank makes a direct and independent promise that it will pay the stated amount to the seller/beneficiary, if the seller presents the required documents. In this respect, the confirming bank assumes the same basic obligations to the beneficiary as did the issuing bank.[76] But again, traditionally the formal promise of the confirming bank will not be simply to pay money upon demand; rather, it will be to "honor a draft" drawn on Buyer's Bank as the original issuer of the letter of credit (see § 1.14 below).

If the sales contract does not require a confirmed credit, Buyer's Bank nonetheless may choose to forward the letter of credit—again, through the SWIFT inter-bank communications system—to an "advising bank" located near the seller.[77] Such a bank does not make an independent payment promise to the seller; rather, it merely acts as the agent of the issuing bank and its only duty is to communicate the terms of the credit accurately.

---

[74]   *See* UCP, art. 2. *See also* UCC § 5–102(a)(4) (defining a "confirmer").

[75]   For a detailed examination of how the SWIFT system functions, see Chapter 6, § 6.16.

[76]   *See* UCP, art. 8b ("A confirming bank is irrevocably bound to honour or negotiate as of the time it adds its confirmation to the credit.").

[77]   UCP, art. 2. The UCC refers to such a bank as an "adviser." *See* § 5–102(a)(1).

Another role a bank in a letter of credit transaction may play is as a "nominated bank." This term broadly covers any bank "with which the credit is available,"[78] and thus would include a confirming bank as well. In its broadest sense, a nominated bank is one the issuer authorizes to accept documents presented under a credit and to pay the beneficiary.[79] A confirming bank is a nominated bank that also undertakes *in advance* to accept a presentation for payment under the credit; but a nominated bank that is *not also* a confirming bank is authorized, but not obligated, to do so.[80]

§ 1.15 L/C Transaction__Seller's Presentation of Documents to Obtain Payment

Once the letter of credit is issued and confirmed, the seller must produce and pack the goods, prepare a commercial invoice, and, where required, procure an insurance certificate (another form of contract) covering the goods in transit to the buyer. If an inspection certificate is required by the sales contract, the goods will be made available to the designated inspection firm (which is engaged according to another contract); this firm will issue a certificate stating whether the goods conform to the description in the sales contract. If so required by the sales contract, the seller also will prepare the necessary documents for the customs officials in its home country (*e.g.*, an export license) and those in the buyer's country (*e.g.*, a certificate of origin).[81]

The seller then will deliver the goods to the carrier. As discussed above,[82] often the seller will engage a specialized services firm (a "freight forwarder" or "logistics company") to attend to all of the necessary formalities. Once the goods are loaded on the ship (or train or airplane) for outbound transportation, the carrier will issue the bill of lading as a combination contract, receipt, and document of title. Again, the letter of credit commonly will require (at least for large transactions) a negotiable bill of lading, which obligates the carrier to deliver the goods only to the "order" of the shipper (*i.e.*, the seller). With such a negotiable bill of lading, the shipper/seller

---

[78] *See* UCP, art. 2; UCC §§ 5–102(a)(11), 5–107(b).

[79] The UCC terms such a bank a "nominated person." *See* UCC § 5–107(b).

[80] *See* UCP, art. 12(a) ("Unless a nominated bank is the confirming bank, an authorization to honour or negotiate does not impose any obligation on that nominated bank to honour or negotiate[.]")

[81] The details on the respective obligations of the seller and the buyer regarding transportation and delivery are typically defined by a "commercial term," such as FOB or CIF. Chapter 3 will examine the role and substance of the various commercial terms used in modern commerce.

[82] *See* § 1.4, *supra*.

has the power to transfer title to the goods by transferring the physical bill along with an appropriate indorsement.[83]

The seller also will take care to ensure that it obtains all of the documents required in the letter of credit, and that all of those documents conform precisely to the terms of the credit. As Chapter 6 explains in more detail,[84] "close" is not enough, for the banks' payment obligations are conditioned on the seller presenting documents that strictly conform to the requirements of the credit. The seller also must act promptly, because the letter of credit will have a variety of deadlines, including a date on which it "expires."[85] This concern is acute for documents issued by third parties (such as a carrier or an inspection firm). For such documents, it may be impractical or impossible to make corrections later. (It is quite unlikely that a carrier will re-issue a conforming bill of lading after the goods are securely stored on a ship that already has left the outbound port.)

Once the seller has the assembled a complete set of the required documents, it must "present" them to a bank obligated under on the letter of credit.[86] In the case of a confirmed letter of credit (as in our hypothetical), the whole point is to permit the seller to make the presentation to the local confirming bank.[87]

But as a formal matter, the letter of credit merely creates a credit available at the issuing bank. Thus, the seller must use a legal vehicle to withdraw that credit. And recall that in its confirmation letter, the confirming bank formally promised "to honor a draft" drawn on Buyer's Bank.[88] The legal vehicle the seller uses to withdraw the credit, therefore, is a "draft."[89] In a legal and practice sense, the draft functions like a personal check. With a standard check (which is one form of a draft[90]), the owner of the

---

[83]   Again, for more on these issues *see* Chapter 4.

[84]   *See* Chapter 6, § 6.6.

[85]   *See* UCP, art. 6.

[86]   *See* UCP, art. 2 (defining a "presentation"). *See also* UCC § 5–102(a)(12) (same).

[87]   For a letter of credit without a confirming bank, the seller/beneficiary must present the documents directly to the issuing bank. If the issuing bank is a distant foreign bank, the beneficiary nonetheless may request that a local bank serve as its collection agent for the presentation. Such "collecting bank" (*see* UCC § 4–105(5)) undertakes only the limited obligations examined in § 1.6 above. For international transactions, such a bank likely also will incorporate the URC in the collection instructions agreement. *See* again § 1.6, *supra*.

[88]   *See* § 1.14, *supra*.

[89]   *See* UCC §§ 3–104(e).

[90]   *See* UCC §§ 3–104(f) (stating that a check includes "a draft . . . payable on demand and drawn on a bank"). Because of the special role of a draft in documentary letter of credit transactions, the definition of a check excludes a draft that must be presented along with other documents to obtain payment. *See id.*, and § 4–104(6).

checking account (the Drawer) instructs its bank (the Drawee) to pay a designated person (the Payee) a defined amount of money from the credit in the account. The draft traditionally required under a letter of credit performs essentially the same function based on the credit created at Buyer's Bank (the issuing bank) in favor of the seller. Unlike the basic documents against payment transaction above—in which the obligated buyer is the drawee[91]—the draft under a letter of credit will be drawn on the issuing bank as drawee.

Thus, the seller/beneficiary will prepare a draft naming itself as payee that is drawn on Buyer's Bank in the amount of the credit created through that bank's issuance of the letter of credit. The draft (sometimes known by an earlier term, "bill of exchange") also is a negotiable document, *i.e.*, one that can be transferred from one holder to another. The seller then presents the draft to the confirming bank along with the other required documents.

As explained for the basic documents against payment transaction above,[92] a draft can be payable on demand or at a defined later time. If a demand draft (or "sight draft") is agreed, the confirming bank will pay the amount immediately, usually by crediting the seller's account at that same bank or by sending the funds to an account at another bank designated by the seller. If, in contrast, the sale of goods contract (and thus the letter of credit) specifies a "time draft" (*e.g.*, "30 days after sight"), actual payment is not due until the defined later time. In such a case, the confirming bank nonetheless must "accept" the time draft (*i.e.*, stamp its name on it).[93] This acceptance creates a binding obligation on the part of the bank to pay at the later time stated in the draft.[94] The obligation of an "acceptor" is directly enforceable by the original presenter of the draft or by any other holder[95] to whom that person sells ("negotiates") the draft after acceptance.[96] Thus, if a bank accepts a time draft and the buyer later becomes insolvent, the bank nonetheless must pay when the stated time expires. With the bank obligated on the time draft, the seller can immediately raise funds by selling the paper—or pledging it as collateral—on the strength of the bank's binding obligation to pay on maturity.

Upon the seller's presentation of the required documents (including the draft), the confirming bank must determine whether

---

[91]   *See* § 1.7, *supra*.

[92]   *See* § 1.7, *supra*.

[93]   *See* UCC § 5–102(b) (expressly incorporating the definition of "acceptance" from § 3–409(a)).

[94]   *See* UCC § 3–413.

[95]   *See* UCC §§ 1–201(b)(21), 3–301.

[96]   *See* UCC §§ 3–201, 3–301, 3–413.

they conform to the terms of the letter of credit.[97] If they do, the bank will "honor" the presentation and pay the seller the amount of the draft (or, as the case may be, accept the draft);[98] if not, it must "dishonor" and refuse to pay.[99] If it honors, the confirming bank also will require that the seller indorse over to it both the negotiable draft and the negotiable bill of lading. In this way, the bank will become the holder of both documents. As holder of the draft, the bank obtains the legal right to the payment from Buyer's Bank (the issuing bank under the letter of credit); and as holder of the negotiable bill of lading, the confirming bank obtains legal title to goods and—in the unlikely event that both the issuing bank and the buyer refuse to provide reimbursement—thus the right to demand delivery from the carrier.

The confirming bank, in turn, will present all of the documents to Buyer's Bank. And, in turn, Buyer's Bank will require that the confirming bank indorse the draft and the bill of lading over to it. As the issuing bank under the letter of credit, Buyer's Bank is obligated to honor the draft and thus to reimburse the confirming bank—if of course the presented documents conform to the requirements in the credit.[100] Indeed, because the two banks likely already have a correspondent relationship, the confirming bank typically will secure that reimbursement immediately—by simply debiting an account that Buyer's Bank holds at the confirming bank and notifying Buyer's Bank of this action.[101]

§ 1.16 L/C Transaction__Buyer's Reimbursement Obligation

Once it has paid the draft as required by the letter of credit, Buyer's Bank has a right of reimbursement from the buyer "in immediately available funds."[102] Because the parties usually have an established banking relationship, most often Buyer's Bank effects the reimbursement simply by taking the payment amount from the buyer's bank account. If the buyer has arranged for a loan, Buyer's Bank instead will add the payment to the loan amount. If

---

[97]   For more detail on the obligations of banks upon a presentation under a letter of credit *see* Chapter 6, §§ 6.8 through 6.10.

[98]   *See* UCP, art. 8. *See also* §§ 5–107(a), 5–108(a); § 5–102(a)(8) (defining "honor").

[99]   *See* § 5–102(a)(5). As explained in Chapter 6, the buyer/applicant may choose to waive any discrepancies found by the bank. *See* § 6.9.

[100]   *See* UCP, art. 7c.

[101]   The I.C.C. has issued a separate set of standard contract terms to cover such reimbursement obligations, The Uniform Rules for Bank-to-Bank Reimbursements under Documentary Credits (URR 725).

[102]   UCC § 5–108(i)(1). The UCP does not address the obligation of an applicant to reimburse the issuer of a letter of credit.

no preexisting relationship exists, Buyer's Bank likely already will have secured payment by the buyer at the time of issuance;[103] if not, the bank will demand that the buyer pay the full amount immediately or otherwise provide security (*i.e.*, collateral) of equal value.

The buyer, like the banks, must pay "against the documents" and not the goods themselves. This is why it is necessary to specify the terms of the documents in the original contract for the sale of goods, and then repeat those specifications precisely in the letter of credit. In any case, Buyer's Bank will not release the negotiable bill of lading covering the contract goods until reimbursement is made or secured. But upon obtaining such a reimbursement, Buyer's Bank will indorse the bill of lading over to the buyer. Because a negotiable bill of lading is a document of title that legally represents the goods, only then will the buyer have the power to obtain the goods from the carrier. This is so because, again, with a such a bill the carrier may release the goods only to the holder. This requires that the buyer both obtain possession of the bill and prove a proper chain of indorsements from the seller, to confirming bank, to Buyer's Bank (the issuing bank), and ultimately to the buyer.[104]

Note that, with large transactions involving ocean transport, the buyer effectively must pay for the goods while they are at sea, long before their arrival. If the goods fail to arrive or are damaged in transit, the buyer must look to its insurance certificate for protection and reimbursement. Alternatively, it may have a claim against the culpable carrier.[105] Further, from its nature a transaction involving a negotiable bill of lading will prohibit the buyer from even inspecting the goods—until it has obtained physical possession of the bill of lading and presented it to the carrier. Thus, until Buyer's Bank is satisfied that it will be reimbursed by the buyer, it can control the buyer's access to the goods by controlling the bill of lading.

§ 1.17 L/C Transaction__Transaction Diagram

With the separate payment obligation of one or more banks, the transaction structure for an international letter of credit is a bit more complicated than that for a basic documents against payment arrangement. Consult the following diagram as an illustration of how a documentary letter of credit functions:

---

[103] *See* § 1.14, *supra.*

[104] *See* Chapter 4, § 4.8 (describing in more detail these obligations of the carrier under a negotiable bill of lading).

[105] For a detailed examination of the liabilities of carriers under bills of lading *see* Chapter 4.

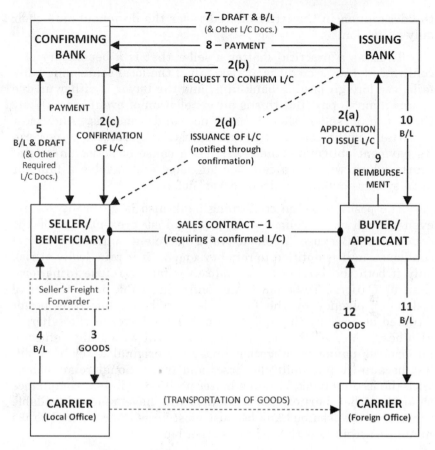

§ 1.18 L/C Transaction__Risk Allocation

The defining attribute of the irrevocable, confirmed letter of credit transaction is the allocation of risks to and among the various players. Without this financing vehicle, the seller merely has a promise of payment from the buyer. But with that vehicle, the seller also has a promise of payment from each of the two involved banks. Moreover, a fundamental principle of letter of credit law is that the banks' promises are independent of the underlying transaction.[106] Thus, the banks are obligated to pay despite assertions that the *goods* do not conform to the requirements of the sales contract, as long as the presented *documents* conform to the requirements of the letter of credit contract. For their part, the banks never see the goods, only the documents. Because of this, they inspect the documents rigorously to determine that they comply exactly with

---

[106] *See* Chapter 6, § 6.5.

the description in the letter of credit—for the documents are their only protection.

Thus, as a practical matter a seller that is a beneficiary of a confirmed letter of credit is at risk only if the local confirming bank fails, the foreign issuing bank fails, and the buyer is either unable or unwilling to pay. But this is a constellation of events so unlikely that such a seller should have no valid concerns. And most important, if the confirming bank unjustifiably refuses to perform its payment obligation, the seller has a cause of action in a local court—which will use a familiar language and involve a familiar legal system—against a "deep pocket" defendant.

The position of the confirming bank also is generally secure, even though it is obligated to pay against presentation of the documents. Because upon a valid payment pursuant to its confirmation it is entitled to reimbursement, it is practically at risk only if both the issuing bank and buyer fail or refuse to perform their obligations. To be sure, the confirming bank bears the small risk of insolvency by the foreign issuing bank; but it is better situated to evaluate this risk than either the buyer or the seller. It also bears the risk that the issuing bank will wrongfully refuse to perform its payment obligation under the original letter of credit; but because it has multiple direct and institutional relationships with the issuing bank, it is in a better position to induce compliance than the other parties. (And often it will have readily available funds from the issuing bank because most large international banks maintain accounts with numerous other banks.)

The issuing bank, in turn, is at risk only if the buyer fails or refuses to perform. This bank too has an independent obligation to pay if the documents conform to the requirements in the letter of credit, with the result that it bears the risk that the buyer cannot pay (becomes insolvent) or will not pay (refuses to reimburse). But these again are risks that the bank is best able to evaluate: It is in a particularly good position to investigate and evaluate the risk of insolvency by the buyer (its own customer), for it either has an established relationship with the buyer or can familiarize itself with the buyer's reputation and financial circumstances in the local market. It also is able either to obtain funds from the buyer as a condition to issuing the letter of credit or later sue the buyer for breach of contract (again, under the local legal system) if the buyer wrongfully refuses to pay. And the issuing bank has an opportunity to evaluate all of these risks before issuing the letter of credit, and thus can adjust its price (the fee or interest rate it charges) to compensate for any increased risk. Moreover, the issuing bank (and the confirming bank before it) often has the security of the negotiable bill of lading, which will enable it to control the goods until it obtains reimbursement. In the worst case, the banks can resell the goods into the market to limit their losses.

For the buyer's part, it may seem that the obligation to reimburse the issuing bank based only on an inspection of the documents leaves it in the most vulnerable position. But upon making the reimbursement, the buyer will obtain a document (the negotiable bill of lading) issued by a third-party carrier that describes goods conforming to the sales contract (as repeated in the letter of credit) and that entitles the buyer to delivery of those goods. The buyer also may secure an obligation from the seller to obtain an insurance certificate protecting it against casualty loss in transit, and perhaps a right to obtain an inspection certificate confirming that the goods conform to the sales contract. (If so, the buyer is well-advised to ensure that the letter of credit also lists an unconditional, positive certificate as one of the required documents.) In other words, the buyer should receive what it bargained for— delivery of conforming goods or insurance proceeds sufficient to cover any loss.

In short, with an irrevocable, confirmed letter of credit, one large risk in an international sales transaction is divided into several smaller ones. Each smaller risk then is allocated to the party best able to evaluate it. The lack of substantial remaining risk in the vast bulk of these transactions is evidenced by the usual bank charge for the issuance of a letter of credit: In developed countries, the usual fee is approximately one percent of the amount of the credit.

§ 1.19   Other Payment Structures__In General

Both the documents against payment transaction and the letter of credit transaction involve a certain amount of extra formality, principally to address the fundamental trust problem discussed repeatedly above. Both also require the payment of bank fees, and (although small) it is in the collective interest of the buyer and the seller to avoid such costs. The solution is for one party to perform first and then trust the other to perform later; but for the reasons sketched in the Introduction, it is particularly difficult in international transactions to convince a seller to assume the risks associated with shipping the goods without a secure payment arrangement, or the buyer to assume the risks associated with paying before shipment.

Nonetheless, as the next two sections explain, there are some circumstances in which one party may be convinced (or compelled) to perform first. Section 1.20 explores the Open Account arrangement, in which the seller ships the goods based merely on the buyer's promise that it will pay at a later defined time. Section 1.21 then analyzes the reverse situation (Cash in Advance), in which the buyer pays the purchase price even before the seller has shipped out the goods.

§ 1.20 Other Structures__Sale on Open Account (O/A)

An Open Account arrangement essentially involves the seller agreeing to extend credit to the buyer, and for this reason it is also known as a sale on "open credit." That is, the seller agrees to deliver the goods based solely on a promise by the buyer to pay at some defined later time, typically 30, 90, or 180 days after delivery. Thus, the buyer need not extend its own funds or borrow from a bank until this later time. Instead, it is the seller that often must arrange financing from a bank or other financial institution—for there will be a delay between when it expends the costs to produce the goods and when it receives payment to cover those costs.[107]

Most often, an O/A arrangement also dispenses with the formality of a negotiable bill of lading. Because the buyer will not pay until after delivery of the goods, there is no need for the seller to retain control after shipment. Instead, a nonnegotiable bill of lading will suffice; this bill commonly will name the buyer as consignee and thus immediately grant it the right to delivery of the goods from the carrier upon arrival.[108] Because, also, the seller need not engage the banks for collection, the standard practice is for it simply to send an invoice directly to the buyer confirming delivery of the goods and requesting payment at the agreed later time.[109]

Such an arrangement obviously involves substantial risks for an international seller. After shipment, the seller will lose control over the goods, and under nearly all legal systems the buyer also will become the owner of the goods.[110] Moreover, after delivery the

---

[107] A positive aspect is that the seller may pledge the future payment obligations of its buyers as collateral for a loan from a bank. This is known as accounts receivable financing (aka "factoring").

[108] As Chapter 4 describes in detail, with a nonnegotiable (aka "straight") bill of lading, the carrier agrees to deliver the goods only to the person named as consignee. *See* § 4.9.

[109] The buyer nonetheless may use the banking system for the payment process if it sends the purchase price to the seller via a bank transfer.

[110] Under the Uniform Commercial Code in the United States (which generally avoids title concepts), the buyer obtains title to the goods as soon as the seller completes its physical delivery of the goods, even if the latter retains a security interest or the goods are covered by a bill of lading. *See* § 2–401(2). *See also* § 1–201(b)(35) (providing that a seller's reservation of title merely has the effect of a security interest).

buyer will have ample time to inspect and assess the value of the goods (even against its later commercial needs and desires). In return, all that the seller has is a promise that the buyer will pay later. But of course the buyer may refuse to fulfill its promise, whether due to financial problems or dissatisfaction with the goods. The seller is then left with the unappealing options of suing the buyer (likely in the buyer's home jurisdiction) or accepting an unfavorable settlement. Moreover, the political, social, and economic circumstances in the buyer's home country may enhance the risk of nonpayment, as well as the desirability of filing suit against the buyer there.

Why then would a seller ever agree to such an arrangement? There are two general reasons. The first is that it already has high confidence that the buyer will pay on time. This confidence may come through institutional relationships, such as a sale to a related company in a large enterprise; or it may arise from a longstanding relationship built on numerous transactions in the past in which the buyer has faithfully fulfilled its payment obligations; or it may exist because the buyer is especially creditworthy and has a sterling reputation for principled conduct and timely payment.

The other reason that a seller may agree to an open account arrangement is simply competitive pressure. In some highly competitive markets, buyers have substantial leverage. Thus, even an established seller—let alone a new market entrant—may have no real choice but to sell on credit. Moreover, sales on open account are the established norm in some foreign markets. In such markets, sellers that are unwilling (or unable) to extend credit to their buyers will be at a competitive disadvantage as against other sellers of the same products.

Nonetheless, sellers on an open account basis must carefully monitor their repeat customers. Successive sales to the same buyer on credit may lead to a substantial cumulative balance. In such a case, the only real leverage a seller may have is to refuse future sales on that basis until the repeat buyer becomes current on overdue payment obligations.

§ 1.21 Other Structures__Cash in Advance (CIA)

An international sales transaction on a Cash in Advance (CIA) basis is at the opposite end of the risk spectrum as compared to an Open Account arrangement. With CIA, the buyer must pay the purchase price even before the seller ships the goods. From the seller's perspective, this is the most secure payment structure, for it displaces the default rule (in most legal systems) that the buyer has a right to inspect the actual goods before payment is due.[111] The most extreme form of such an arrangement is "Cash with Order" (CWO), under which the buyer must pay for the goods before the seller even will begin processing the buyer's order.

A CIA contract allocates nearly all of the risks in an international sales transaction to the buyer. With an advance payment, the buyer must trust that the seller later will fulfill its obligation to deliver the goods. But the seller of course may not do so; or it may ship goods that do not conform to the contract requirements; or it may fail to provide the documents necessary to clear the goods through customs in the buyer's home country. The buyer then is the one left with the unappealing options of filing a lawsuit (likely in the seller's home jurisdiction) or accepting an unfavorable settlement.

Why would a buyer agree to pay the purchase price before the seller ships the goods? Nearly always, the reason is that the buyer has no other choice. Typically, this is because it is experiencing severe financial problems, such that no seller would agree even to ship the goods on a payment against documents basis and no bank would agree to issue a letter of credit on the buyer's behalf. A less common reason is that the buyer has a specific or urgent need of goods from a particular seller. In either case, the buyer is in such a weak bargaining position that it must extend its own funds upfront—and then simply trust that the seller will ship conforming goods later.

---

[111] *See* CISG, art. 58(1) (noting also that the right to inspection before payment applies only if "the buyer is not bound to pay the price at any other specific time"); UCC § 2–513(1) (same).

Chapter 2

INTERNATIONAL SALES LAW

Table of Sections

---

§ 2.1   Background: Domestic Choice of Law Rules

The most common form of international business transactions is the sale of movable things (everything from pencils to pomegranates to petroleum). In the United States, the relevant law for sale of goods transactions is Article 2 of the Uniform Commercial Code (UCC), which the legislatures of all states (except Louisiana) have adopted as statutory law to ensure uniformity throughout the country. Specifically, § 2–102 provides that Article 2 governs "transactions in goods"; and § 2–105(1) defines the term "goods" to cover all things that are "movable at the time of identification to the contract for sale" (basically, when the seller designates the goods for the specific buyer at issue[1]). The remainder of UCC Article 2 then contains specialized rules for sale of goods transactions that apply in absence of a contrary agreement by the parties.[2]

The effect of the adoption of the UCC by effectively all of the individual states is to create uniform law for sales of goods transactions across the United States. Thus, if a seller in Seattle concludes a deal to sell gold (a moveable thing) to a buyer in Buffalo, it should matter little whether Washington or New York law governs in the event of a dispute. The law in the two states—subject to minor variations—should be the same.

The legal situation changes radically, however, if our seller in Seattle concludes a deal with a buyer in Beijing. Indeed, here we confront the most fundamental issue in international business (and

---

[1]   *See* § 2–501(1).

[2]   The UCC generally permits the parties to displace its statutory rules by contractual agreement. *See* § 1–302(a) (declaring that "except where otherwise provided . . . the effect of the provisions of [the UCC] may be varied by agreement").

other) transactions: Of its very nature, a transaction that touches the interests of two or more countries requires a choice of the governing law if any dispute arises—and for this choice, of course, we need a set of legal rules.[3] In U.S.-American legal terminology, these are "choice of law" (or "conflict of laws") rules. The parallel term in civil law countries is the "rules of private international law."

For a transaction involving a sale from Seattle to Beijing (unlike to Buffalo) this choice matters. The substantive law of China on the sale of goods—delivery and payment obligations, statutory warranties, extent of liability, etc.—may be strikingly different from the rules in the UCC. Indeed, in some cases the choice between Washington law and Chinese law may determine the very outcome of any legal disputes that arise between the parties.

The challenge is that each legal system also has its own choice of law rules, and often these, too, are quite different. This raises a kind of pre-question: Which jurisdiction's choice of law rules will govern the question of which jurisdiction's substantive laws will apply? Thankfully, broad agreement exists on the answer to this question: A court generally will apply its home choice of law rules (which also covers whether the parties may agree to displace the otherwise-applicable law, see immediately below).[4] Thus, where a lawsuit is filed determines which jurisdiction's choice of law rules will apply.

Choice of Law Under the UCC. If a lawsuit on a subject within the scope of the UCC—such as a sale of goods under Article 2—is filed in a U.S. court (whether state or federal[5]), the relevant choice of law rule is found in the UCC itself. Under § 1–301, a court must

---

3   *See* Restatement (Second) of Conflict of Laws, § 1 ("The world is composed of territorial states having separate and differing systems of law. Events and transactions occur, and issues arise, that may have a significant relationship to more than one state, making necessary a special body of rules and methods for their ordering and resolution.").

4   *See id.*, §§ 8(1) (directing a court to apply the law of a foreign state "[w]hen directed by its own choice-of-law rule"); 7(2) ("The classification and interpretation of Conflict of Laws concepts and terms are determined in accordance with the law of the forum[.]")

5   In the United States, federal law preempts state law. U.S. Const., art. VI (the so-called "Supremacy Clause"). In absence of controlling federal law, however, a court—even a federal court—will apply state choice of law rules. *See* Atlantic Marine Const. Co., Inc. v. U.S. Dist. Court for Western Dist. of Texas, ___ U.S. ___, 134 S.Ct. 568, 582 (2013) (citing Klaxon Co. v. Stentor Elec. Mfg. Co., 313 U.S. 487, 496 (1941)). *See also, e.g.,* Mazza v. Am. Honda Motor Co., 666 F.3d 581, 589 (9th Cir. 2012) ("A federal court sitting in diversity must look to the forum state's choice of law rules to determine the controlling substantive law.") (*quoting* Zinser v. Accufix Research Inst., Inc., 253 F.3d 1180, 1187 (9th Cir. 2001)); GlobalNet Financial.com, Inc. v. Frank Crystal & Co., Inc., 449 F.3d 377, 382 (2d Cir. 2006) (same).

apply the substantive rules of the UCC—for a sale of goods, Article 2—of the state where it is located if the transaction in dispute "bear[s] an appropriate relation" to that state.[6] Unfortunately, neither the text nor any official comment in the UCC contains a formal definition of "appropriate relation" and, as some courts have observed, the term otherwise provides little guidance for actual controversies.[7] The Official Comments to § 1–301 nonetheless clarify the concept in two important respects: First, although the natural inclination of a local court may be to apply its home law, "the mere fact that suit is brought in a state does not make it appropriate to apply the substantive law of that state."[8] Second, application of the home law is not appropriate where "the parties clearly have contracted on the basis of some other law," such as "where the law of the place of contracting and the law of the place of contemplated performance are the same."[9]

For most transjurisdictional disputes, however, the application of the "appropriate relation" test is not so clear. Failing more explicit guidance, U.S. courts generally have held that § 1–301 in effect adopts a "most significant relationship" test. In the words of one federal appellate court, "The majority of courts . . . has defined 'appropriate relation' in accord with the dominant trend in modern conflict of laws analysis, under which the law of the state with the 'most significant relationship' to the matter at issue is applied."[10] The modern trend referred to here derives from the Restatement (Second) of Conflicts of Law.[11]

As a foundational rule, the Second Restatement identifies seven "principles" that are relevant to a choice of law analysis on any substantive subject.[12] But it then adopts the "most significant

---

6   UCC § 1–301(b) (former § 1–105).

7   *See* In re Merritt Dredging Co., Inc., 839 F.2d 203, 206 (4th Cir. 1988) (noting the absence of any textual definition and that "[t]he UCC's Official Comments provide little guidance, stating only that 'the question what relation is 'appropriate' is left to judicial decision' "); Girard Bank v. Mount Holly State Bank, 474 F. Supp. 1225, 1238 n.12 (D.N.J. 1979) (observing that "the appropriate relation reference gives almost no guidance").

8   § 1–301, Official Comment 2.

9   *Id.*

10   In re Merritt Dredging Co., Inc., 839 F.2d 203, 206 (4th Cir. 1988). *See also* In re General Motors Corp. Dex-Cool Products Liability Litigation, 241 F.R.D. 305 (S.D. Ill. 2007) ("[T]he majority of courts treat the most significant relationship standard as being functionally identical to the 'appropriate relation' standard set out in the UCC."). For more recent affirmations, see Waters v. Electrolux Home Products, Inc., 2015 WL 9459949, at *3 (N.D. W.Va. 2015); Scheider v. Deutsche Bank Nat. Trust Co., 572 Fed. Appx. 185, 189 (4th Cir. 2014); Niagara Transformer Corp. v. Baldwin Technologies, Inc., 2013 WL 2919705, at *5 (D. Md. 2013).

11   Restatement (Second) of Conflicts of Laws (1971).

12   These seven principles are: "(a) the needs of the interstate and international systems, (b) the relevant policies of the forum, (c) the relevant policies of other

relationship" test specifically for issues of contract law.[13] For this test, the Second Restatement identifies five special "contacts" that a court should consider in choosing between the law of two or more interested jurisdictions: (a) the place of contracting; (b) the place of negotiation of the contract; (c) the place of performance; (d) the location of the subject matter of the contract; and (e) "the domicil, residence, nationality, place of incorporation and place of business of the parties."[14] A court then must evaluate these contacts "according to their relative importance with respect to the particular issue."[15] Of its nature, this multi-factor test leaves substantial discretion for a court, and thus substantial uncertainty for the contracting parties.[16] As one commentator observed about this approach long ago, "even a juggler, not to mention a trial judge, can only cope with a finite number of balls in the air."[17]

Choice of Law in Other Countries. Of course, other countries have their own choice of law rules, including for issues of contract law. One prominent example is the European Union's Regulation on the Law Applicable to Contractual Obligations (2009),[18] which applies in all twenty-eight EU member states. For sale of goods transactions, this so-called "Rome I" Regulation adopts as a bright line rule "the law of the country where the seller has his habitual residence."[19] This approach differs markedly from the intensely factual analysis required by the appropriate relation/most significant relationship test in the United States.

---

interested states and the relative interests of those states in the determination of the particular issue, (d) the protection of justified expectations, (e) the basic policies underlying the particular field of law, (f) certainty, predictability and uniformity of result, and (g) ease in the determination and application of the law to be applied." Restatement (Second) of Contracts, § 6.

[13]   *Id.*, § 188(1).

[14]   *Id.*, § 188(2).

[15]   *Id.* If the place of negotiation and the place of performance are in the same jurisdiction, the law of that jurisdiction "will usually be applied." *Id.*, § 188(3).

[16]   A closely related approach, followed by New York courts, seeks to identify the "center of gravity" of the contract. This approach considers essentially the same factors as the "most significant relationship" test. *See* Brink's Ltd. v. S. African Airways, 93 F.3d 1022, 1030–31 (2d Cir. 1996)). For a more recent application see Weihai Textile Grp. Imp. & Exp. Co. v. Level 8 Apparel, LLC, 2014 WL 1494327, at *7 (S.D.N.Y. 2014).

[17]   *See* Friedrich Juenger, *The E.E.C. Convention on the Law Applicable to Contractual Obligations: An American Assessment,* in CONTRACT CONFLICTS 295, 300 (P.M. North ed., 1982).

[18]   Regulation (EC) No. 593/2008 of the European Parliament and of the Council on the Law Applicable to Contractual Obligations of 17 June 2008, *available at* http://eur-lex.europa.eu/legal-content/EN/ALL/?uri=CELEX:32008R0593 (hereinafter, "Rome I Regulation").

[19]   *Id.*, art. 4(1).

A recent law in China specifically addresses choice of law for "foreign-related" matters.[20] For issues of contract law, this "Law of the Application of Law for Foreign-Related Civil Relations" (2011) instructs Chinese courts to apply—in absence of an effective choice by the parties, see below—"the laws at the habitual residence of the party whose fulfillment of obligations can best reflect the characteristics of this contract or other laws which have the closest relation with this contract."[21] The first part of this test has a substantial similarity to the Rome I Regulation's bright line test— for the seller performs the "characteristic" obligation of a sale of goods contract. The latter part of the test, however, introduces uncertainty, for it seems to permit a court instead to rely on a "closest relation" analysis similar to the most significant relationship test in the United States.

Choice of Law by Party Agreement. The choice of law rules of most countries nonetheless generally permit private parties to agree on the law that will govern their transaction (so-called "party autonomy"). The EU's Rome I Regulation places no limitation on such a choice,[22] except with regard to mandatory rules such as on the protection of consumers. Chinese law likewise grants the parties complete discretion to choose the governing law, as the Supreme People's Court recently declared in an "Interpretation" of the 2011 law noted above.[23] The UCC in the United States, in contrast, gives effect to such a party agreement on the application of a foreign country's laws only if the transaction "bears a reasonable relation" to that country.[24] Other countries may apply more or less stringent rules.

As should be readily apparent from this brief survey, significant differences exist in domestic choice of law rules. This leaves substantial uncertainty for parties engaged in international

---

[20]   Law of the Application of Law for Foreign-Related Civil Relations of the People's Republic of China (adopted October 28, 2010, effective April 1, 2011), *available at* http://www.wipo.int/wipolex/en/text.jsp?file_id=206611.

[21]   *Id.*, art. 41.

[22]   *See* Rome I Regulation, *supra* note 18, art. 3.

[23]   Interpretation (I) on Several Issues Concerning the Application of the "Law of the People's Republic of China on the Application of Laws to Foreign-Related Civil Relations", Article 7 (effective 7 January 2013) (affirming that a court should enforce a party choice of law even if "the law chosen by the parties in the agreement has no actual connection with the foreign-related civil relation in dispute").

[24]   UCC § 1–301(a) (former 1–105(1)). The drafters of the UCC proposed a change to this rule in the comprehensive overhaul of Article 1 in 2001. The new rule would have removed the "reasonable relation" limitation to a party choice of law. However, all states rejected this proposed change and instead readopted the substance of former § 1–105(1), but with the new section number 1–301. In 2008, the Uniform Law Commission acquiesced and formally re-endorsed the original rule of former § 1–105.

sale of goods transactions. Because they cannot know in advance where a lawsuit will be filed, they cannot know which country's choice of law rules will apply if any dispute arises. Of course, the parties to a particular transaction could agree on arbitration or on an exclusive state court forum for resolution of disputes.[25] But that would require that they have formed a contract or otherwise have concluded a corresponding, enforceable agreement in advance of their (possible) deal. Whether they have done so in a legally binding way is itself an issue of substantive law, and this, again, will turn on what law governs the agreement process in the first place.

To be sure, sellers and buyers also commonly include a choice of law clause in their standard business terms. But it is a common misconception that such a clause resolves the choice of law issue. Because the parties cannot know in advance what substantive legal rules will apply to their transaction, they cannot know whether they even have formed a contract; thus, they cannot know whether any such attempt to choose the governing law will have legal effect. Stated in more specific terms, where the parties to proposed deal exchange standard business terms, a "battle of the forms" arises. The outcome of that battle will turn on the substantive rules that govern the contract formation process. In absence of a carefully negotiated single contract document, neither party can know in advance which domestic contract formation rules will govern their (possible) deal. And it should not surprise that the battle of the forms rules in domestic legal systems diverge in significant respects. Neither party to a proposed deal can know in advance, therefore, whether it has formed a contract and, if so, whether its standard business terms—including the choice of law clause—is an effective part of such a contract.

The solution to this legal uncertainty is an international treaty that creates uniform rules across as many countries in the world as possible (and thus avoids the need for a choice of law analysis). For international sale of goods transactions, such a treaty in fact exists: The UN Convention on Contracts for the International Sale of Goods (1980). As explored below, the United States and over eighty other countries have ratified or otherwise accepted this treaty. The parties to a contract may "opt out" of the treaty,[26] but it must be the starting point for any analysis of international sales transactions.

---

[25]   *See* Chapter 28.
[26]   *See* § 2.5 *infra.*

§ 2.2   Introduction to the CISG

The United Nations Convention on Contracts for the International Sale of Goods (1980)[27]—which is commonly known, even internationally, by the acronym CISG—governs the sale of goods between parties in the United States and those in over eighty other countries. The Convention grew out of the failure of two earlier conventions—the so-called "ULIS" and "ULF"[28]—to address the diversity of cultures and legal traditions involved in international contracting. Following extensive, years-long negotiations, a UN-sponsored diplomatic conference held in Vienna in 1980 adopted the CISG as a formal international treaty. The Convention then entered into force on January 1, 1988, thirteen months after the ratifications of the United States, China, and Italy exceeded the prescribed acceptance threshold of ten member states (which the CISG somewhat confusingly refers to as "Contracting States").

As of the beginning of 2017, eighty-five countries are Contracting States to the CISG, representing well over three-quarters of the world's trade in goods. The list of Contracting States includes countries from all parts of the world and from all legal traditions, as well as nearly every major trading partner of the United States, from Canada and Mexico, to Japan and China, to Germany and France, and to South Korea and Singapore. Notable exceptions include the United Kingdom and India. As a result of this broad acceptance, courts and arbitral tribunals already have generated over ten thousand opinions applying the CISG.[29]

Each year, the roll of Contracting States of the CISG continues to grow, and more states are expected to ratify or otherwise accept the CISG in the near future. This will increase the impact and effectiveness of the CISG in unifying international sales law. A current list of Contracting States to the CISG is available at UNCITRAL's website, www.uncitral.org.

The CISG resulted from the work of a specialized body of the United Nations, the United Nations Commission on International Trade Law (UNCITRAL), whose mandate is the unification and harmonization of international trade law. The purpose of such

---

[27]   United Nations Convention on Contracts for the International Sale of Goods, Apr. 11, 1980, U.N. Doc. A/CONF. 97/18 (1980), *reprinted in* 19 I.L.M. 671 (1980).

[28]   The ULIS (Convention Relating to a Uniform Law on the International Sale of Goods (1964)) addressed substantive rights and obligations; the ULF (Convention Relating to a Uniform Law on the Formation of Contracts for the International Sale of Goods (1964)) addressed formation issues.

[29]   *See* CISG Database, http://www.cisg.law.pace.edu/cisg/text/digest-cases-toc. html.

unification is to reduce legal obstacles to international trade, decrease transaction costs, enhance predictability and certainty, and promote the orderly development of new legal concepts as international commerce evolves in the future.

Substantial English language resource materials are available for understanding and applying the CISG. These include prominent treatises,[30] hundreds of journal articles,[31] a comprehensive online compilation of materials[32] and court opinions,[33] and an authoritative collection of the drafting records for the Convention.[34] UNCITRAL also maintains a searchable database of abstracts of CISG cases from around the world[35] as well as a Digest with analytical summaries arranged by individual Articles of the Convention.[36] As explained below,[37] these materials are of particular importance for interpreting and applying the CISG because the Convention's interpretive rules require consideration of decisions by foreign courts.

§ 2.3   The Legal Status of the CISG

In the United States, the CISG has the constitutional status of preemptive federal law.[38] This is so because the Convention operates as a so-called "self-executing treaty,"[39] which means that it

---

[30]   *See* COMMENTARY ON THE UN CONVENTION ON THE INTERNATIONAL SALE OF GOODS (CISG) (P. Schlechtriem & I. Schwenzer, eds., 3rd ed., 2010); UN CONVENTION ON CONTRACTS FOR THE INTERNATIONAL SALE OF GOODS (CISG) (S. Kröll, L. Mistelis & M. Perales Viscasillas, eds., 2011); DRAFTING CONTRACTS UNDER THE CISG (H. Flechtner, R. Brand, and M. Walter, eds., 2008).

[31]   *See* CISG Database, http://www.cisg.law.pace.edu/cisg/biblio/bib2.html (listing over 1,600 journal articles on the CISG).

[32]   *See* the CISG Database of Pace University, www.cisg.law.pace.edu.

[33]   *See* http://www.unilex.info/dynasite.cfm?dssid=2376&dsmid=14315; http://www.cisg.law.pace.edu/cisg/text/caseschedule.html.

[34]   *See* John O. Honnold, DOCUMENTARY HISTORY FOR THE UNIFORM LAW ON INTERNATIONAL SALES (1989). These records are also *available at* http://www.cisg.law.pace.edu/cisg/conference.html.

[35]   *See* CASE LAW ON UNCITRAL TEXTS (CLOUT), *available at* http://www.uncitral.org/uncitral/en/case_law/abstracts.html.

[36]   UNCITRAL DIGEST OF CASE LAW ON THE CISG (2012 ed.), http://www.uncitral.org/uncitral/en/case_law/digests/cisg.html (hereinafter CISG DIGEST 2012).

[37]   *See* the analysis of CISG Article 7 in § 2.10 *infra*.

[38]   *See, e.g.,* Chicago Prime Packers, Inc. v. Northam Food Trading Co., 408 F.3d 894, 897 (7th Cir. 2005); Delchi Carrier v. Rotorex Corp., 71 F.3d 1024, 1027–28 (2d Cir. 1995); Honey Holdings I, Ltd. v. Alfred L. Wolff, Inc., 81 F. Supp. 3d 543, 551 (S.D. Tex. 2015); It's Intoxicating, Inc. v. Maritim Hotelgesellschaft mbH, 2013 WL 3973975, at *16 (M.D. Pa. 2013). *See also* Chateau des Charmes Wines Ltd. v. Sabata USA Inc., 328 F.3d 528, 530 (9th Cir. 2003) ("[T]here is no doubt that the [CISG] is valid and binding federal law.").

[39]   *See, e.g.,* VLM Food Trading Intern., Inc. v. Illinois Trading Co., 748 F.3d 780, 786 (7th Cir. 2014); Delchi Carrier v. Rotorex Corp., 71 F.3d 1024, 1027–28 (2d Cir. 1995).

functions as directly applicable federal law without the need for implementing legislation by Congress.[40] The CISG thus obtained domestic legal force by virtue of the Senate consent procedure defined in the treaty clause of Article II, Section 2, of the Constitution. And because ratified treaties function as supreme federal law under Article VI of the Constitution, the CISG preempts all state law within its scope, including Article 2 of the UCC.[41]

The CISG also creates a federal cause of action in favor of aggrieved buyers and sellers in ordinary commercial litigation in the courts of the United States.[42] Thus, for example, a sale of goods contract between a private party in the United States and one in Canada would be governed by the CISG, not by the UCC, and U.S. federal courts would have jurisdiction to hear disputes arising out of such a contract.[43] Moreover, as explored in more detail below,[44] the rules for interpreting the CISG and for filling gaps in its provisions impose severe restrictions on the ability of courts to resort to domestic law (such as the UCC) to resolve contested issues within the scope of the Convention.

§ 2.4   The CISG's Structure and Sphere of Application

The goal of the CISG is to promote legal certainty in international sales transactions by creating a uniform set of legal rules to operate in the place of the diverse domestic legal systems of the ratifying countries. The Convention does not even permit Contracting States to declare reservations to limit the effect of any of its substantive provisions[45] (but for a short list of expressly stated exceptions[46]). On the other hand, the CISG applies only to

---

[40]   *See* Medellín v. Texas, 552 U.S. 491, 505 (2008) (observing that a self-executing treaty "operates of itself" as domestic law "without the aid of any legislative provision"). President Reagan expressly declared that the CISG is self-executing upon submission to the Senate in 1983. *See Letter of Transmittal from the President of the United States to the Senate With Legal Analysis of the United Nations Convention on Contracts for the International Sale of Goods*, Sept. 21, 1983, Sen. Treaty Doc. No. 98–9, *reprinted in* 22 I.L.M. 1368, 1369 (1983).

[41]   *See, e.g.,* Beth Schiffer Fine Photographic Arts, Inc. v. Colex Imaging, Inc., 2012 WL 924380, at *7 (D.N.J. 2012); Usinor Industeel v. Leeco Steel Prods., Inc., 209 F. Supp. 2d 880, 884 (N.D. Ill. 2002).

[42]   *See* BP Oil Int'l, Ltd. v. Empresa Estatal Petróleos de Ecuador, 332 F.3d 333, 336 (5th Cir. 2003); Delchi Carrier v. Rotorex Corp., 71 F.3d 1024, 1027–28 (2d Cir. 1995). *See also* Honey Holdings I, Ltd. v. Alfred L. Wolff, Inc., 81 F. Supp. 3d 543, 551 (S.D. Tex. 2015).

[43]   This is so because 28 U.S.C. § 1331(a) confers on the district courts "original jurisdiction of all civil actions arising under . . . treaties of the United States."

[44]   *See* the discussion of CISG Article 7 in § 1.9 *infra*.

[45]   CISG, art. 98.

[46]   CISG, arts. 92–96.

international transactions as defined therein. It does not affect purely domestic sales transactions, and permits the parties (as explored below) to "opt out" of its application by a sufficiently clear contractual agreement.

In addition to rules governing its scope, the CISG contains provisions on contract formation; the respective rights and performance obligations of sellers and buyers; the rights and remedies upon breach; the passing of the risk of loss from the seller to the buyer; as well as most other significant subjects in international sales transactions. The Convention is structured in four principal parts:

Part I   Sphere of Application and General Principles (Articles 1–13);

Part II   Formation of the Contract (Articles 14–24);

Part III   Sale of Goods = the substantive rights and obligations of the buyer and the seller (Articles 25–88); and

Part IV   Final Provisions = the non-substantive "diplomatic" provisions relating to ratification, reservations, withdrawal, etc. (Articles 89–101).

As noted, in the United States the CISG operates as a "self-executing treaty," with the result that as of 1988 it has functioned as directly applicable, preemptive federal law without the need for separate implementing legislation.

To achieve its goal of certainty and predictability, it is important that the CISG's scope of application be clear, both as to the circumstances where it applies, and those where it does not. The first six articles of the CISG define its sphere of application, but the principal rules are found in Article 1. That Article provides that the CISG will apply if a transaction (1) involves a contract for the sale of goods; (2) is "international" (as defined therein); and (3) bears a stated relation to at least one country that has ratified or otherwise accepted the CISG (again, so-called "Contracting States").

(1) On the first requirement, the CISG unfortunately does not define "sale" or "goods." Nonetheless, pursuant to the basic rule for interpreting the CISG (see below[47]), these notions must be defined "autonomously," that is, by reference to the principles reflected in the Convention itself and not through a resort to domestic law. Thus, on the basis of the rules in Articles 30 and 53—which respectively require the seller to deliver "property in" the goods and

---

[47]   *See* the analysis of CISG Article 7 in § 2.10, *infra*.

the buyer to pay a "price"—it is broadly accepted that the subject matter of the transaction must involve the passing of title for a price (and thus not a bailment, gift, or lease). One court accordingly has observed that the essential nature of a contract governed by the CISG is that it involves the delivery of goods in exchange for money.[48]

An "autonomous" interpretation likewise permits a definition of the term "goods." A variety of CISG provisions make clear that the term refers to items that have a physical existence and are moveable at the time of agreed delivery.[49] Examples include provisions that refer to the "weight" of items, to the seller's "delivery" at a defined "place," and to the buyer taking "possession of" and the "preserv[ing]" the goods.[50] Courts accordingly have held that "goods" must be "moveable and tangible," irrespective of whether they are in solid form, are new or used, or are animate or inanimate.[51]

(2) The CISG clearly defines the requirement for an "international" sale of goods. This is determined not by the location or delivery of the goods (such as whether they cross a national border), but rather by the "places of business" of the persons involved in the transaction. Specifically, under Article 1(1) a contract for the sale of goods is international if, at the time of contract formation, the parties have their respective "places of business" in different states (with "states" being sovereign countries, not the states of the United States).

What is "a place of business"? The CISG does not define the term, but according to scholarly commentary and court opinions a "place of business" requires some level of both permanence and independence. Reference to the equally authoritative[52] French (*establissement*) and Spanish (*establecimiento*) language versions support this view. Judicial interpretations are in accord,[53] with one

---

[48] CLOUT Case No. 328, *Kantonsgericht* [Provincial Court] of Zug, Switzerland (21 October 1999).

[49] For an analysis of whether software may qualify as a "good" *see* § 2.4 *infra*.

[50] *See, e.g.,* CISG, art. 30 (referring to the seller's obligation to "deliver" goods); art. 31 (defining the "place" at which seller is obligated to deliver); art. 53 (stating buyer's obligation to "take delivery"); art. 56 (stating a rule for when the price is fixed according to the "weight of the goods"); and art. 86 (referring to the buyer's obligation to preserve the goods after taking possession of them).

[51] *See* CISG DIGEST 2012, *supra* note 36, art. 1, para. 28. *See also* Schwenzer/Hachem, art. 1, paras. 16–17, in Schlechtriem & Schwenzer, *supra* note 30.

[52] Like other UNCITRAL texts, the CISG has six official language texts: English, French, Spanish, Chinese, Russian, and Arabic.

[53] *See* CISG DIGEST 2012, *supra* note 36, art. 1, para. 5.

court observing that a place of business "requires a certain duration and stability as well as a certain amount of autonomy."[54]

On this basis, courts have found that none of the following constitutes a "place of business" under the CISG: a mere warehouse where the contract goods are located; a booth at an exhibition; the place where a party's representative happened to negotiate the contract; and a seller's "liaison office" that did not have autonomy in business decisions.[55] A branch office, on the other hand, may well suffice as long as it has some level of permanence and independent decision-making authority. If a party does not have a formal place of business, then the relevant location for purposes of CISG Article 1 is his "habitual residence."[56]

For emphasis, Article 1(3) declares that neither the nationality of the parties (*e.g.*, where a business is incorporated) nor their "civil or commercial character" (*e.g.*, whether or not domestic law would consider a party a "merchant") is relevant in determining whether the CISG applies. One Austrian appellate court thus held that the nationality of the parties is irrelevant to the application of the CISG in a transaction between an Austrian corporation and an Austrian-German joint venture because the relevant places of the business of the two sides were in different CISG member states.[57] However, under Article 1(2) the CISG will not apply even if the parties are from different states if this fact "does not appear" from information available to them upon the conclusion of the contract. Thus, if one party is represented by a local agent that does not disclose before contract formation the foreign place of business of its principal, the Convention should not govern the transaction. One should note, however, that the determination question of whether an intermediary is an agent or instead acts on its own account is a matter for domestic law, not the CISG.[58]

A special problem arises if a party has more than one location that qualifies as a "place of business" (which is quite common for large multi-national enterprises). If, for example, a seller has its place of business in the United States and the buyer has places of business in both Germany and the United States, the CISG may or may not apply depending on which place of business of the buyer is

---

[54]   *Oberlandesgericht* [Appellate Court] of Stuttgart, Germany, 28 February 2000, http://cisgw3.law.pace.edu/cases/000228g1.html.

[55]   *See* CISG DIGEST 2012, *supra* note 36, art. 1, para. 5.

[56]   CISG, art. 10(b).

[57]   CLOUT Case 746, *Oberlandesgericht* [Appellate Court] of Graz, Austria (29 July 2004).

[58]   *See* CISG DIGEST 2012, *supra* note 36, art. 1, para. 7; Caterpillar, Inc. v. Usinor Industeel, 393 F. Supp. 2d 659, 669–673 (N.D. Ill. 2005) (applying Illinois law of agency to a transaction otherwise governed by the CISG).

the relevant one. In such a case, CISG Article 10 provides that the relevant place of business is the one with the "closest relationship to the contract and its performance." Thus, the determinative place of business under the CISG is not a party's "main" or "principal" business location or even its "seat" under domestic law. Instead, the analysis will turn on which of a party's different business locations has the closest the relationship to the transaction. Applying this rule, one federal appellate court concluded that the CISG governed a transaction between an Illinois company and a company ("VLM") with offices in both Canada and New Jersey because "[m]ost of VLM's business is conducted from its headquarters near Montreal, including its performance of the contract" at issue.[59]

Nonetheless, the dual considerations of "the contract" and "its performance" may cause difficulties in application to specific facts. This is especially true where, for example, one office is more closely associated with the formation of the contract and a second office is more closely associated with a party's performance of its contractual obligations. When such circumstances arise, courts will need to weigh the relative significance of the two considerations to determine which predominates. Article 10(a)—in parallel to Article 1(2), see above—provides some assistance in this regard, for it limits the usable facts to those circumstances "known to or contemplated by *the parties*" (emphasis supplied) at or before the conclusion of the contract. The use of the plural here is important, for in choosing the relevant place of business a court may consider only those facts that were known to *both* parties at the time of contract formation. This should avoid a surprise application of the CISG where a domestic party deals principally with a local office and knows little about a possible foreign place of business. On the other hand, well-advised parties may ensure that the CISG, and not foreign domestic law, will apply by stating in the contract which office of each party they believe to have "the closest relationship" to the transaction. In short, because the Convention here focuses on the knowledge of "the parties," each party should ensure that the other is aware of its status.

A small number of courts have directly addressed the significance of Article 10(a) for the application of the CISG. Thus, for example, a U.S. District Court found that the CISG did not govern a transaction in which a U.S. company designed software for use in Germany by a German company, because the buyer's relevant place of business was its U.S. subsidiary to which the

---

[59]   VLM Food Trading Intern., Inc. v. Illinois Trading Co., 748 F.3d 780, 787 (7th Cir. 2014).

software was first sent and from which payment was made.[60] On the other hand, where a Canadian seller had a U.S. distributor, but the transaction was in part negotiated in Canada and the goods were manufactured there—all of which was known to the U.S.-based buyer—a court found that the transaction was between places of business in different states, and thus that the CISG applied.[61]

(3) Finally, the CISG governs only those contracts for the international sale of goods that have a sufficient relation to one or more Contracting States—that is, countries that have ratified, acceded to, or otherwise accepted the Convention before the relevant transaction (or, if contract formation is at issue, before the proposal to conclude a contract, see Article 100). The CISG defines two different ways to satisfy this requirement.

First, under Article 1(1)(a) the Convention will apply if the parties have their places of business in different states and *both* of these states are CISG Contracting States. Under this standard option, the CISG will govern a contract of sale where one party has its place of business in the United States and the other has its place of business in France, China, Mexico, or any other CISG Contracting State. This option thus does not depend upon the vagaries of conflicts of law doctrines, and provides certainty both to the parties in designing the transaction and to the courts in analyzing and deciding the issues that arise therein.

Second, under Article 1(1)(b) the Convention could apply if the applicable domestic conflict of law rules (known by the civil law term "the rules of private international law") lead to the application of the law of a Contracting State. Thus, the court in which a lawsuit is filed first will apply its domestic conflict of law rules; if those rules point to the application of the law of a country that has ratified the CISG, then the CISG will govern. As an illustration of this option, assume that a seller based in France (which has ratified the CISG) contracts to sell batteries to a buyer based in the U.K. (which has not). If one party files a lawsuit in France, the Rome I Regulation would require application of French law as it is the home state of the seller (see § 2.1 above). But because France is a CISG Contracting State, under Article 1(1)(b) the French court should apply the CISG (again, even though the U.K. has not accepted the CISG). This option is sometimes referred to as the "indirect application" of the CISG.

---

[60]   American Mint v. GO Software, Inc., 2006 WL 42090 (M.D. Pa. 2006). *See also* McDowell Valley Vineyards, Inc. v. Sabate USA Inc., 2005 WL 2893848 (N.D. Cal. 2005) (holding that the CISG did not apply because the relevant place of business of a French seller was its U.S.-based subsidiary).

[61]   Asante Technologies v. PMC-Sierra, Inc., 164 F. Supp. 2d 1142, 1147–1149 (N.D. Cal. 2001).

This possibility does not apply, however, for lawsuits filed in the courts in the United States. When it ratified the CISG, the United States declared an allowed reservation under Article 95 that it would not be bound by Article 1(1)(b). The effect of this reservation is that courts in the United States will apply the CISG only when the parties' respective places of business are in different states and *both* of those states are CISG Contracting States (*i.e.*, only if Article 1(1)(a) is satisfied). Thus, for example, the CISG will not apply to a sales contract between parties with respective places of business in the United States and the United Kingdom (again, a non-Contracting State), even if applicable choice of law rules would require that a U.S. court apply U.S. law. What law should the court apply in such a case? Instead of the CISG, the court would apply the otherwise-applicable choice of law rule for sales transactions (UCC § 1–301) in order to determine which domestic law will govern the transaction (see § 1.1 above).

The United States declared the Article 95 reservation upon ratification in 1986 based on a belief that the UCC is a superior approach to sales law as compared to the CISG.[62] At the time, the assumption was that the principal benefit of the uniform rules in the CISG was to avoid the uncertainty of the various choice of law regimes around the world and that resort to the alternative of Article 1(1)(b) would reintroduce that uncertainty. Certain U.S. interests also believed that if a court first had to resolve choice of law issues and then determined that domestic United States law applied, it might as well apply the "best" United States law—the UCC.

The U.S. reservation under Article 95 nonetheless has some unexpected consequences. Beyond the U.S., only six CISG states have declared a reservation to the application of Article 1(1)(b). Moreover, to ensure consistency of application the drafting history and scholarly commentary on the reservation indicate that even a foreign court should not consider the reserving states as CISG Contracting States for purposes of Article 1(1)(b).[63] (Germany in fact expressly declared this upon its ratification of the CISG.) Thus, assume that a dispute arises between a U.S.-based seller of goods and a U.K.-based buyer and that one party somehow is able to bring suit in France. Under the Rome I Regulation examined above,[64] the applicable law should be that of the U.S. (the home of the seller), which again is a CISG member state. But because of the U.S.'s

---

[62] *See* U.S. State Department, *Legal Analysis of the United Nations Convention on Contract for the Internal Sale of Goods* (1980), Appendix B, *reprinted in* 22 I.L.M. 1368, 1380 (1983).

[63] *See* CISG DIGEST 2012, *supra* note 36, art. 1, para. 19.

[64] *See* § 2.1 *supra*.

Article 95 reservation, the French court should apply the domestic UCC (not the CISG), because the U.S. would not be considered a CISG Contracting State *for purposes of Article 1(1)(b)*. Nonetheless, with the growing world-wide acceptance of the Convention (and thus the increasing application of Article 1(1)(a)), the Article 95 reservation of the United States is rapidly decreasing in significance.

§ 2.5   Party Autonomy and Choice of Law Clauses

One of the most important provisions for understanding the basic philosophy and scope of the CISG is Article 6. That provision states the core principle of party autonomy, that is, the power of the parties to "exclude application of th[e] Convention" and to "derogate from or vary the effect of any of its provisions." The agreements of the parties, in other words, take precedence over the provisions of the CISG. In its most fundamental sense, this includes the power of the parties to declare that the CISG will not govern their transaction at all (the power to "opt out" of the Convention).

Thus, even if the CISG otherwise is applicable under Article 1, the parties may choose to exclude it in favor of the application of the law of a specific domestic legal system. Special care is required, however, to exercise this power in an effective way. First, and most important, CISG Article 6 grants the power to the parties (in the plural). As a result, an international trader cannot be assured that a unilateral choice of law clause in its standard business terms will be effective. The recent case of *Hanwha Corp. v. Cedar Petrochemicals, Inc.* illustrates this point.[65] There, a South Korea-based buyer and a New York-based seller exchanged standard business forms that had conflicting choice of law clauses. Even though both parties tried to choose domestic law to govern the transaction, the absence of an agreement between them on one choice (in derogation of the CISG) meant that the court applied the CISG, and especially its contract formation rules.

Moreover, several courts have recognized that an effective exclusion of the CISG requires a clear, unequivocal, and affirmative agreement of the parties. To be sure, the documentary records of the CISG show that the drafters rejected a proposal to require an "express" exclusion, and on this basis some courts and arbitral tribunals have noted the possibility of an implied agreement to opt-out of the Convention. Nonetheless, the delegates at the 1980 Vienna Conference also rejected a proposal to include in Article 6 a textual recognition of "implicit" exclusions out of a fear that courts

---

[65]   760 F. Supp. 2d 426 (S.D.N.Y. 2011).

would reach such a result on insufficient evidence.[66] The result is that most courts have recognized high standards for an exclusion of the CISG, including an emphasis on the need for a real and unequivocal agreement between the parties.[67]

Finally, even an express choice of a specific domestic law will not suffice, for the parties also must affirmatively opt-out of the CISG by specific reference. Thus, a simple statement that, for example, a contract "shall be governed by New York law" will not effectively exclude the CISG. Indeed, courts addressing such clauses now commonly hold that a choice of the law of a CISG Contracting State means merely a choice of the CISG. As a U.S. federal Court of Appeals declared in a case where the parties' contract designated Ecuadorian law, "[g]iven that the CISG *is* Ecuadorian law, a choice of law provision designating Ecuadorian law merely confirms that the treaty governs the transaction."[68] The same rule applies, under preemption doctrines, if the parties choose the law of a state of the United States, and U.S. courts have consistently so held. As one recent federal court thus observed, "a choice of law provision, to be effective, must not only select the law that will apply but affirmatively state that the CISG will not apply to the contract."[69]

As a result, if the parties wish to exercise their Article 6 "opt out" power in favor of pure domestic law, they must do so through express language that both (a) affirmatively excludes the Convention by name, and (b) expressly identifies the agreed domestic law. (*E.g.*: "The law of the State of New York, including as applicable the New York Uniform Commercial Code, shall govern all disputes relating to this transaction. The parties hereby exclude application of the United Nations Convention on Contracts for the

---

[66] *See* Deliberations of the First Committee at the 1980 Vienna conference (A/CONF.97/C.I.SR.4), *reprinted in* Honnold, Documentary History, *supra* note 34, at 469–475.

[67] *See* CISG DIGEST 2012, *supra* note 36, art. 6, para. 2.

[68] BP Oil Int'l, Ltd. v. Empresa Estatal Petróleos de Ecuador, 332 F.3d 333, 337 (5th Cir. 2003) (emphasis in original). One U.S. court misleadingly indicated in dicta that a mere choice of domestic law may suffice to exclude the CISG, but the court's opinion only addressed the effectiveness of a forum selection clause. *See* American Biophysics v. Dubois Marine Specialties, 411 F. Supp. 2d 61 (D.R.I. 2006).

[69] It's Intoxicating, Inc. v. Maritim Hotelgesellschaft mbH, 2013 WL 3973975, at *16 (M.D. Pa. 2013). *See also, e.g.,* Microgem Corp. v. Homecast Co., 2012 WL 1608709, at *3 (S.D.N.Y. 2012) (holding that a contract's choice of "New York law" did not exclude the CISG because "[s]tating only that a contract will be governed by a particular jurisdiction's laws is generally insufficient to opt-out of the CISG when the CISG has been incorporated into that jurisdiction's laws"); Travelers Property Cas. Co. of America v. Saint-Gobain Technical Fabrics Canada Ltd., 474 F. Supp. 2d 1075, 1081–1082 (D. Minn. 2007); American Mint LLC v. GOSoftware, Inc., 2005 WL 2021248 (M.D. Pa. 2005).

International Sale of Goods (CISG)").[70] Even if the parties do not wish to exclude the CISG (or cannot reach a corresponding agreement), they are well advised to designate a default domestic law. This is so because the CISG, similar to other instruments, does not represent a complete legal regime for all issues that may arise between the parties.

Article 6 also permits partial derogation from the CISG, for it expressly empowers the parties to "derogate from or vary the effect of" any of its provisions. This more general implication of the principle of party autonomy means that the parties' agreement takes precedence even over the express rules in the CISG. Thus, for example, one court held that a contractual requirement of notice of breach "within five working days from the delivery" took precedence over Article 39(1)'s allowance of a "reasonable time."[71] In the same vein, courts and arbitral tribunals have held that the parties may, by agreement, derogate from CISG rules on the concept of "delivery," on the required place of delivery, and on liability upon breach.[72] The one exception to the principle of party autonomy relates to form requirements if one of the parties has its place of business in a Contracting State that has declared a reservation under CISG Article 96. Under that reservation, contracts must be evidenced by a writing if so required by the local law of the Contracting State.[73]

If the parties may "opt out" of the CISG, may they also "opt in"? Because the principle of party autonomy is widely accepted in domestic sale of goods law as well,[74] the answer here should be "yes." As a more specific matter, if the parties have their places of business in different states, CISG Article 1(1)(b) should permit them, by way of a choice of law clause, to use such rules of "private international law" to "opt in" to the Convention.[75] The choice of law clause used to accomplish this result can be relatively simple ("This contract shall be governed by the laws of France") because, as explained above, a choice of the laws of France (a CISG Contracting State) should yield an application of the CISG.[76] To avoid

---

[70]   Parties that have agreed so to exclude the CISG are also well advised to exclude application of the companion treaty on the Limitation Period in the International Sale of Goods. *See* Limitation Convention, § 2.44 *infra.*

[71]   *Rechtbank* [Local Court] of Arnhem, the Netherlands (11 February 2009), *available at* http://cisgw3.law.pace.edu/cases/090211n1.html.

[72]   *See* CISG DIGEST 2012, *supra* note 36, art. 6, para. 6 (with citations).

[73]   *See* discussion of CISG article 12 in § 2.12 *infra.*

[74]   *See, e.g.,* UCC § 1–301(a) (former § 1–105(1)); EU Rome I Regulation on the Law Applicable to Contractual Obligations, art. 3(1).

[75]   *See* § 2.4 *supra.*

[76]   *See* § 2.4 *supra.*

misunderstanding, however, parties are well advised to state their intent in this regard explicitly, *e.g.*: "This contract shall be governed by the laws of France, including the United Nations Convention on Contracts for the International Sale of Goods."

Unfortunately, many U.S. attorneys unthinkingly seek to opt out of the CISG for all contracts under all circumstances, simply because they do not understand it as well as they understand the UCC. Such an impulse, however, may work a disservice to their clients' interests. If an attorney represents the seller in an international transaction, for example, the UCC and its "perfect tender" and "implied warranty" rules may be less favorable than the corresponding rules under the CISG.[77] In such cases, automatic rejection of the CISG may prejudice the client's interests, unless the attorney can be assured that comparable seller-friendly rules will make it into the express terms of the contract. One respected author has observed in this vein that routinely opting out of the CISG, or even simply negotiating an international sales contract, without understanding how the treaty affects the client's interests, may constitute malpractice.[78]

§ 2.6   Software, "Hybrid," and Other Mixed Sales Transactions

Section 2.4 above noted that, by general consensus, the term "goods" means items with a physical existence that are moveable at the time of agreed delivery.[79] This straightforward definition nonetheless may mask a variety of subtle and important issues concerning the scope of the CISG.

Software Contracts. For modern commerce, the most prominent example of these difficult scope issues involves contracts for the transfer of intangible rights (such as intellectual property) contained or reflected in a tangible medium (*e.g.*, a computer disc). According to the general view, transactions that in their essence involve only the transfer of intangible rights are not within the scope of the Convention. Thus, a pure sale of know-how, information, or an ownership interest in a business enterprise is not

---

[77]   *See* §§ 2.19–2.21 *infra.*

[78]   *See* Ronald Brand, *Professional Responsibility in a Transnational Practice*, 17 J. LAW & COM. 301, 335–336 (1998). Unfortunately, knowledge of the CISG and its status as directly applicable and preemptive federal law is alarmingly limited. A 2008 survey across the spectrum of states (Florida, New York, California, Hawai'i, and Montana) revealed that only 30% of practitioners were "thoroughly" or "moderately" familiar with the CISG. The results for judges were even starker, with 82% reporting that they were "not at all familiar" with the CISG. *See* Peter Fitzgerald, *The International Contracting Practices Survey Project*, 27 J.L. & COM. 1 (2008).

[79]   *See supra* notes 50–51 and accompanying text.

subject to the CISG.[80] One court accordingly held that the CISG did not apply to a contract to conduct a marketing study, even though the contract required delivery in the form of a formal written report.[81] The court there emphasized that the concept of "goods" requires that the tangible thing delivered be the principal object of the contract. Similarly, contracts that solely involve a transfer of intellectual property rights (patents, copyrights, or trademarks) are licenses, and not a sale of goods (even if, again, the rights are delivered in a tangible medium). On the other hand, the mere fact that a sale of goods includes or is subject to intellectual property rights does not take the transaction out of the scope of the CISG.[82]

The applicability of the CISG to a sale of computer software, in contrast, has generated substantial controversy. One matter, however, is clear from the outset: The question of whether software transactions are within the scope of the CISG must be determined "autonomously," that is, on the basis of the CISG and without resort to rules or concepts of domestic law.[83] By general consensus, the CISG may indeed apply to a sale of software. A sale of physical electronic goods (*e.g.*, computers, electronic hardware, computer components), is certainly within the scope of the CISG.[84] And the mere fact that most modern products include embedded software also should not affect the nature of a transaction as a sale of goods.

The challenge comes with transactions whose essential nature is purely a sale of software. There seems to be general consensus that a sale of standard computer software through a tangible medium (such as a CD ROM) is within the scope of the CISG.[85] Some commentators go much further, however, and argue that the CISG should apply to any sale of software, irrespective of the mode of delivery (and even purely over the internet).[86]

---

[80]   *See* Schwenzer/Hachem, art. 1. paras. 19–22, in Schlechtriem & Schwenzer, *supra* note 30.

[81]   *See* CLOUT Case No. 122, *Oberlandesgericht* [Appellate Court] of Köln, Germany (26 August 1994).

[82]   Indeed, certain provisions of the CISG expressly cover the role of intellectual property rights in sales within its scope. *See, e.g.,* CISG, arts. 41 and 42 and § 2.2 *infra.*

[83]   *See* the analysis of CISG Article 7 in § 2.10 *infra.*

[84]   *See, e.g.,* CLOUT Case No. 281, *Oberlandesgericht* [Appellate Court] of Koblenz, Germany (17 September 1993); *Handelsgericht* [Commercial Court] of Zürich, Switzerland, February 17, 2000, *available at* http://cisgw3.law.pace.edu/cases/000217s1.html.

[85]   *See* CLOUT Case No. 749, *Oberster Gerichtshof* [Supreme Court] of Austria (21 June 2005); CLOUT Case No. 281, *Oberlandesgericht* [Appellate Court] of Koblenz, Germany (17 September 1993).

[86]   *See* Schwenzer/Hachem, art. 1. para. 18, in Schlechtriem & Schwenzer, *supra* note 30.

Courts and arbitral tribunals have delivered a mixed message. Some have seemed to follow the more liberal view that the CISG applies to all software sales;[87] at least one court has held, in contrast, that software developed and sold for an internet website did not involve goods.[88] Others have drawn a distinction between "standard" and specially designed software. Thus, two early German courts suggested that the CISG should apply only to sales of "standard software"—presumably, software generally available on a mass-market basis—as opposed to a program specially designed for the buyer and installed through the services of the seller.[89]

An analogy from the non-electronic world may be helpful in analyzing software sales. A contract calling for the submission of a manuscript for a book is not a contract for the sale of goods, even though the manuscript will be on paper or a disc. The essence of such a transaction is for the author's services. However, a contract for the sale of a commercial lot of printed books (or only one book) is for the sale of tangible items—the books, and not the printer's services. No such bright line may exist in software sales, because these may involve some adaptation to the user's precise situation. Nevertheless, a criterion based on the difference between "off the shelf" software and individually designed software may be helpful even when the software sold exhibits some characteristics of each, because one characteristic or the other may predominate.

In any event, most mass-market sales of software directly over the internet likely will be consumer sales (for "personal, family or household use") and thus will be excluded from the CISG under Article 2(a) (see § 2.7 below).

Hybrid Sales and Services Contracts. "Services" contracts are expressly excluded from the CISG.[90] Many contracts, however, involve obligations both to sell goods and to provide related services. CISG Article 3(2) provides a rule to address such situations. Under that rule, the CISG does not apply to a transaction in which the "preponderant part of the obligations of the party who furnishes the goods consists in the supply of labour or other services." The

---

[87]   Decision of District Court of Arnhem (Netherlands), 28 June 2006, *available at* http://cisgw3.law.pace.edu/cases/060628n1.html; CLOUT Case No. 281, *Oberlandesgericht* [Appellate Court] of Koblenz, Germany (17 September 1993).

[88]   *See Østre Landsret* [Appellate Court] of Denmark, March 7, 2002, *available at* http://cisgw3.law.pace.edu/cases/020307d1.html (with commentary by Joseph Lookofsky).

[89]   *See* CLOUT Case No. 122, *Oberlandesgericht* [Appellate Court] of Köln, Germany (26 August 1994): CLOUT Case No. 131, *Landgericht* [State Court] of München, Germany (8 February 1995).

[90]   CISG, art. 3(2).

authorities seem to be in agreement that the "preponderant part" test focuses on "the economic value of the obligations relating to the supply of labour and services and the economic value of the obligations regarding the goods."[91] One court thus held that the CISG applied to a transaction in which fifty percent or more of the purchase price was attributed to the sale of a water tank, even though the contract also required installation services for the tank.[92] This conclusion certainly obtains if the seller merely provides ancillary services such as onsite assembly, training of personnel, or continuing maintenance. If the CISG applies to a mixed sales and services contract, then it governs both aspects of the transaction (unless of course the parties actually conclude two separate contracts).[93]

Distribution Agreements. Distribution (or "framework") agreements in their usual form are not covered by the CISG.[94] The rationale is that such contracts address the "organization of the distribution" instead of the sale of specified goods.[95] Thus, distribution agreements, like franchising and marketing contracts, are service contracts and not contracts for sale of goods. The CISG will govern, however, the separate contracts under those distribution agreements that involve actual orders for goods.[96] As one U.S. court stated, a distribution contract would be within the CISG only if it contains definite terms for the delivery of specific goods.[97] That case involved a distribution contract that identified certain goods; the dispute between the parties involved, however, not those goods, but rather separate goods ordered under a later transaction. The same analysis applies to joint venture agreements.[98]

---

[91]   CISG DIGEST 2012, *supra* note 36, art. 3, para. 4 (citing cases).

[92]   CLOUT Case No. 196, *Handelsgericht* [Commercial Court] of Zürich, Switzerland (26 April 1995).

[93]   *See* Schwenzer/Hachem, art. 3, paras. 12, 16–17, in Schlechtriem & Schwenzer, *supra* note 30.

[94]   *See, e.g.,* Adonia Holding GmbH v. Adonia Organics LLC, 2014 WL 7178389, at *3 (D. Ariz. 2014); Multi-Juice, S.A. v. Snapple Beverage Corp., 2006 WL 1519981 (S.D.N.Y. 2006); Viva Vino Import Corp. v. Farnese Vini S.R.L., 2000 WL 1224903 (E.D. Pa. 2000). *See also* CISG DIGEST 2012, *supra* note 36, art. 1, para. 24 (citing numerous cases).

[95]   CLOUT Case No. 192, *Obergericht* [Appellate Court] of Luzern, Switzerland (8 January 1997).

[96]   *See, e.g.,* Foreign Trade Court of Arbitration Award No. T–8/08, Serbian Chamber of Commerce (28 January 2009); CLOUT Case No. 273, *Oberlandesgericht* [Appellate Court] of München, Germany (9 July 1997).

[97]   Helen Kaminski PTY Ltd. v. Marketing Australia Products Inc., 1997 WL 414137 (S.D.N.Y. 1997).

[98]   Amco Ukrservice v. American Meter Co., 2004 WL 816923 (E.D. Pa. 2004).

Hybrid Supply Contracts for Future Goods. CISG Article 3(1) also has a separate, though conceptually related, rule governing contracts "for the supply of goods to be manufactured or produced" in the future. This rule thus addresses what are known in the United States as "maquiladora" transactions, in which a domestic business ships component parts to a business in Mexico (or other low-wage country) for assembly and return shipment to the United States. (Mexico is a CISG Contracting State.) Article 3(1) states as a basic rule that such transactions "are to be considered sales." It then makes an exception, however, for those transactions in which the purported buyer ("the party who orders the goods") provides "a substantial part of the materials necessary for [the] manufacture or production" of the goods.

Note here the deliberate use of "a substantial part" in CISG Article 3(1), in contrast to "the preponderant part" rule in Article 3(2). This would seem to indicate that the purported buyer need not provide more than fifty percent of the necessary materials in order for this exclusion to apply. Substantial disagreement exists, however, over the precise contours of the term "a substantial part."[99] A reasonable resolution of this disagreement would rely principally on the relative value and volume of the buyer- and seller-supplied goods and, secondarily, on the importance of the buyer-supplied materials for the functionality or marketability of the final product.[100]

Hybrid Sales and Real Estate Transactions. The subject of contracts for the sale of goods attached to real estate has been a difficult one under domestic legal systems.[101] The CISG has no specific provision on the subject. Nonetheless, the consensus understanding on the definition of "goods" should resolve most of the difficult issues in practical application. Under that definition, goods must be moveable at the time of agreed delivery.[102] For sales of to-be-extracted minerals as well as of growing crops and timber, the CISG should apply if such goods are, or should be, moveable at the time of delivery according to the terms of the parties' contract.

Barter Transactions. Barter transactions (sometimes referred to internationally as "countertrade") represent a difficult conceptual issue for the application of the CISG. Is such a transaction, in which

---

[99] This dispute arises in part from a difference between the English ("a substantial part") and French language versions ("an essential part").

[100] *See* Schwenzer/Hachem, art. 3, para. 6, in Schlechtriem & Schwenzer, *supra* note 30. Contrary to the misguided view of one French court, purely knowledge-based specifications or instructions supplied by the buyer should not count as "materials" for purposes of Article 3(1).

[101] *See* UCC §§ 2–105(1), 2–107.

[102] *See* notes 50–51 and accompanying text *supra*.

goods are exchanged for other goods, a "sale"? A couple of Russian arbitral tribunals and some commentators have answered in the affirmative.[103] This view, however, runs contrary to the description in CISG Article 53 of the essential obligation of the buyer to "pay the price," words usually related to tender of money and not to a tender of goods. As a result, the "prevailing opinion" is that the CISG does not apply to purely barter transactions.[104]

Countertrade transactions sometime specify a price when structured to use three interrelated contracts—one for the sale of the primary goods, a second for the exchange sale of the countertrade goods, and a protocol to define the relationship between other two. In such a case, the two sales contracts could be governed by the CISG. However, many such sales contracts, especially structural arrangements on the exchange of the goods, are not sufficiently specific in identifying the quantities and types of goods to be purchased under the countertrade agreement. Thus, although the purported contract would be governed by the CISG, the Convention might well determine that no valid contract was formed.[105]

Other Mixed Transactions. As noted, the Convention does not define "sale," with the result that its application to some types of transactions is unclear. Nonetheless, a general consensus now exists on a variety of once-uncertain issues: Thus, the CISG does not apply to (a) franchise agreements (the essence of which is the temporary transfer of intellectual property rights); (b) "turn-key" contracts (the essence of which is that a contractor must complete a work, typically a building, for immediate operation); (c) financial leasing arrangements (which involve a transfer of only temporary rights); or (d) pure "consignments" (in which the consignee sells the goods solely for the account of the consignor, does not assume legal ownership of them, and may freely return them to the consignor/owner).[106] Nonetheless, by express terms the CISG applies to installment contracts as well as modification contracts for transactions already within its scope.[107]

---

[103]   *See, e.g.,* Tribunal of International Commercial Arbitration of the Russian Federation Chamber of Commerce and Industry (9 March 2004), *available at* http://cisgw3.law.pace.edu/cases/040309r1.html; Schwenzer/Hachem, art. 1, para. 11, in Schlechtriem & Schwenzer, *supra* note 30.

[104]   *See* Schwenzer/Hachem, art. 1, para. 11, in Schlechtriem & Schwenzer, *supra* note 30.

[105]   For further discussion of this issue, see § 2.14 *infra.*

[106]   *See* CISG DIGEST 2012, *supra* note 36, art. 1, paras. 25–26; Schwenzer/-Hachem, art. 3, paras. 21–22, in Schlechtriem & Schwenzer, *supra* note 30. On the specific issue of consignments, see Martini E Ricci Iamino S.P.A.–Consortile Societa Agricola v. Trinity Fruit Sales Co., Inc., 30 F. Supp. 3d 954, 971 (E.D. Cal. 2014).

[107]   *See* CISG, art. 73 and art. 29.

§ 2.7 Transactions Expressly Excluded from the CISG

CISG Article 2 expressly excludes from the scope of the Convention a number of specific types of transactions. The most prominent of these exclusions is a sale of goods to consumers. The drafters of the CISG excluded such transactions in order to avoid conflicts with special national legislation (usually mandatory law) designed to protect consumers. CISG Article 2(a) thus states that the Convention does not apply to goods "bought for personal, family or household use," a term that should be familiar to U.S. attorneys, since it is parallels language in the UCC[108] and the federal Truth in Lending Act.[109]

The specific linguistic formulation of Article 2(a) also has important implications for the application of its exclusion. Instead of the CISG's standard reference to a "sale" of goods, Article 2(a) uses the verb "bought" and the preposition "for". According to the widely prevailing view, the determinative fact thus is the buyer's intention regarding the use of the goods.[110] The relevant time for assessing this intention is the conclusion of the contract. Standard examples include automobiles, leisure boats, motorcycles, and recreational trailers.[111] An Austrian appellate court accordingly ruled in one case that the CISG did not apply to a purchase of Lamborghini automobile because the buyer's intent at the time of purchase was for personal use, even though he actually put it into use for other purposes.[112] On the other hand, a purchase of goods by an individual for commercial or professional purposes remains subject to the Convention. Moreover, the intended purchase must be *exclusively* for consumer use. As the drafters accordingly observed at the 1980 Vienna convention, the exclusion should not apply—and thus the CISG should apply—to the purchase of dual use items such as a camera partly used by a professional photographer, toiletries used by a business, and an automobile bought by a dealer for resale.[113]

Nonetheless, as protection for a surprise application of domestic law, CISG Article 2(a) states that the exclusion does not apply if, at the time of contract formation, the seller "neither knew nor ought to have known" of the buyer's intended use for personal

---

[108] UCC § 9–102(a)(23).

[109] 15 USC § 1602(i).

[110] *See* CISG DIGEST 2012, *supra* note 36, art. 2, para. 3.

[111] *Id.*

[112] *See* CLOUT Case No. 190, *Oberster Gerichtshof* [Supreme Court] of Austria (11 February 1997).

[113] *See* CISG DIGEST 2012, *supra* note 36, art. 2, para. 4.

purposes. Although the seller has the burden of proof on this score, this exception to the exclusion injects objective considerations into the analysis, such as the nature and quantity of the goods purchased, the extent to which the buyer's name indicates a business entity, and the delivery address. Thus, a German appellate court held that the CISG applied to the sale of a car from a salesman in Germany to a buyer in Finland, regardless of the buyer's subjective intent, because the seller reasonably assumed that the buyer also was an entrepreneur.[114] The allocation of the burden of proof nonetheless may explain the results in some cases. In the Lamborghini sale noted above, for example, the Austrian court observed that the seller had not presented sufficient evidence that it neither knew nor ought to have known of the buyer's personal use.[115]

Article 2(b) also excludes from the scope of the CISG sales by auction, whether public (*i.e.*, under authority of law) or private.[116] The rationale for this exclusion is that such transactions are held at a specific location and often under the assumption that the local law of that location governs. The necessary attributes of an auction—a pre-announced public sale in which the contract is awarded immediately to the highest bidder—place important limitations on the scope of this exclusion. Thus, the CISG should apply notwithstanding Article 2(b) to sales *to* an auction house, sales at commodity exchanges, and even public procurement transactions. For the same reason, online "auctions" (such as on eBay), where sales are drawn out over time and are open to international bidders, should not fall within the "auction" exclusion of Article 2(b)(subject of course to the separate consumer sale exception in Article 2(a)).[117]

Under Article 2(c) execution sales and sales made under governmental authority are also excluded from the CISG.[118] Such sales commonly are subject to mandatory special legislation or judicial rules. The word "otherwise" in Article 2(c) makes clear that the exclusion extends to sales by third parties as required or allowed under the authority of law. Thus, sales by creditors (such as in execution of a judgment), by judicial bodies, or in a bankruptcy proceeding all are excluded from the scope of the CISG.

---

[114] *See Oberlandesgericht* [Appellate Court] of Hamm, Germany, 2 April 2009, *available at* http://cisgw3.law.pace.edu/cases/090402g1.html.

[115] *See* CLOUT Case No. 190, *Oberster Gerichtshof* [Supreme Court] of Austria (11 February 1997).

[116] *Contrast* UCC § 2–328.

[117] *See* Schwenzer/Hachem, art. 2, para. 21, in Schlechtriem & Schwenzer, *supra* note 30.

[118] CISG, art. 2(c).

Sales of some intangible rights or claims—investment securities (stocks, shares), negotiable instruments, and money—are expressly excluded from the CISG, even though they may have a tangible "token."[119] Again, these exclusions were designed to avoid conflicts with mandatory rules of domestic law. Thus, a Swiss court held that a contract for the purchase of corporate shares is not covered by the CISG.[120] The "negotiable instruments" exclusion under Article 2(d) is, however, more limited than might appear at first glance. First, it only applies to documents that are formally negotiable (*i.e.*, those under which the transfer of the paper itself transfers a right to a monetary claim). Moreover, the exclusion does not extend to negotiable documents of title for goods (bills of lading, warehouse receipts), because the purchase of such a document (such as in documentary sale transactions, see Chapter 1) in legal substance involves a transfer of rights in the underlying goods. Finally, although Article 2(d) excludes sales of "money," one arbitral tribunal held that the CISG applied to a sale of souvenir coins.[121]

CISG Article 2(e) also states that the Convention does not apply to sales of "ships, vessels, hovercraft, or aircraft."[122] Under the two predecessor conventions to the CISG—the ULIS and ULF[123]—such sales were excluded only to the extent that the ships, etc., were subject to official registration (in the nature of real estate). This requirement does not appear in the text of the CISG, however. Moreover, sales of sailboats and other leisure watercraft should be excluded irrespective of the lack of knowledge exception for consumer sales discussed immediately above. Nonetheless, because such exclusions generally are interpreted narrowly, the prevailing view is that the CISG nonetheless applies to a sale of parts for such water- or aircraft, even if the parts may be subject to registration.[124] One must note, in any event, that Article 2(e) is quite specific, for it does not exclude contracts for other transportation vehicles such as locomotives, trains, and automobiles.

Finally, Article 2(f) excludes sales of electricity. Courts should interpret this exclusion, like the others in Article 2, narrowly. Thus,

---

[119]   CISG, art. 2(d).

[120]   *See* CLOUT Case No. 260, *Cour de Justice* [District Court] of Genève, Switzerland (9 October, 1998).

[121]   *See* CLOUT Case No. 988, China International Economic and Trade Arbitration Commission (2000).

[122]   CISG, art. 2(e).

[123]   *See supra* note 28.

[124]   *See* CISG DIGEST 2012, *supra* note 36, art. 2, para. 10. *See also, e.g.,* United Tech. Int'l v. Malev Hungarian Airlines (Metropolitan Court of Hungary (10 January 1992), *available at* http://cisgw3.law.pace.edu/cases/920110h1.html.

the exception does not apply—and thus the CISG should apply—to sales of other sources of energy such as gas, coal, or oil.

§ 2.8   Issues Expressly Excluded from the CISG

Sections 2.6 and 2.7 addressed entire *transactions* that are not within the CISG's sphere of application. But the Convention also has rules that address specific *issues* for transactions to which it otherwise applies: That is, it expressly *includes* in its coverage two sets of issues that arise under a sale contract, and expressly *excludes* three sets of issues. The issues expressly covered by the Convention—indeed, its sum and substance—are (a) the formation of the contract, and (b) the rights and obligations of the parties to the contract.[125] The expressly excluded issues are the (a) "validity" of the contract or its provisions,[126] (b) property (or title) to the goods,[127] and (c) liability for death or personal injury.[128] For these latter issues, a court must fall back on the domestic legal rules that otherwise would apply under choice of law doctrines.

The Substantive Scope of the CISG. CISG Article 4 defines the fundamental principle of the Convention's substantive scope: It governs "only the formation of the contract of sale and the rights and obligations of the seller and the buyer arising from such a contract." In the structure of the CISG, Article 4's basic inclusion of "formation" issues refers to Part II of the Convention[129] and its inclusion of the "rights and obligations" of the parties refers to Part III of the Convention.[130] Included within the concept of "obligations" is remedies for beach.[131]

CISG Article 4's reference to the rights and obligations "of the seller and the buyer" nonetheless leaves open an important issue over whether the CISG could also govern the rights and obligations of persons that were not immediate parties to the sales contract. Such persons would include both "remote sellers" (such as manufacturers of the product or its parts that had sold to an intermediate seller in the chain of distribution) and "remote buyers" (sub-buyers of the goods that purchased from an intermediate

---

[125]   CISG, art. 4.

[126]   CISG, art. 4(a).

[127]   CISG, art. 4(b).

[128]   CISG, art. 5.

[129]   CISG, arts. 14–24.

[130]   CISG, arts. 25–88.

[131]   The Convention includes within the general chapter on the "Obligations of the Seller" a section on the "Remedies for Breach of Contract by the Seller." *See* Part III, Ch. II, § III. It likewise includes within the general chapter on the "Obligations of the Buyer" a section on the "Remedies for Breach of Contract by the Buyer." *See* Part III, Ch. III, § III.

buyer). This issue has raised substantial challenges for courts and scholars, especially because the modern trend (under the UCC in the United States at least) has been to abolish such a "privity" bar for many "implied warranty" claims.[132]

The archetypical form of this issue involves a manufacturer that sells a product along with a standard form "warranty in a box" and a retailer that resells goods "as is" to a remote purchaser. The language of CISG Article 4 strongly suggests that the CISG provides no basis for a claim by the remote purchaser against the manufacturer, as the latter is not a *seller* in the "downstream" contract. And indeed, the strong trend of courts is to conclude that the CISG does not apply to such claims. As a U.S. federal court recently observed, "district courts have consistently found that, unless the buyer or the seller is acting through an agent that is selling the goods directly to a third party, a remote purchaser does not have a cause of action to sue an upstream seller under the CISG. Instead, the rights and obligations of remote purchasers are governed by the otherwise applicable state law."[133]

Note, however, that this conclusion may create substantial complexity in application to actual disputes. If all three parties—foreign manufacturer, U.S. reseller, and U.S. downstream purchaser—are brought into the same lawsuit, different bodies of law may apply to the different sides of the potential triangle: (a) As between the foreign manufacturer and the U.S. reseller, the CISG would govern (if the manufacturer is from a CISG member state); (b) as between the U.S. reseller and the U.S. purchaser, in contrast, the UCC likely would apply; but (c) although the CISG would not apply as between the foreign manufacturer and the U.S. remote purchaser because of the absence of a contractual relationship, the courts seem prepared to recognize a claim under the UCC (depending on the approach of the applicable state law to "privity" issues).

CISG Article 4 also impliedly excludes from its scope many non-sale issues. Of particular interest here is the law of principals and agents. This includes the liability of a purported "agent" that represented a non-existing principal; whether a person paid by a

---

[132]   This development is subject to important limitations. *See* Lee v. Mylan Inc., 806 F. Supp. 2d 1320, 1325–1326 (M.D. Ga. 2011) (observing that "[m]any states have eliminated the requirement of vertical privity" for certain implied warranty claims, but noting limitations); Pulte Home Corp. v. Parex, Inc., 579 S.E.2d 188, 192–193 (Va. 2003) (limiting remedies for such claims).

[133]   Beth Schiffer Fine Photographic Arts, Inc. v. Colex Imaging, Inc., 2012 WL 924380 (D.N.J. 2012). *See also* 2P Commercial Agency S.R.O. v. Familant, 2012 WL 6615889, at *3 (M.D. Fla. 2012) (same); Caterpillar Inc. v. Usinor Industeel, 393 F. Supp. 2d 659, 676 (N.D. Ill. 2005) (same).

buyer was an agent of the seller; and whether a right to payment could be assigned.[134] This issue—that is, who is an actual party to a potential contract—plays an important role in whether the CISG applies in the first place.[135]

Separately, some courts have held that the CISG does not displace "promissory estoppel" claims under domestic law,[136] but there are strong reasons to question this result. In its essence, promissory estoppel is a contract claim;[137] if, therefore, a party cannot satisfy the requirements for contractual liability under the CISG, it should not be permitted—under federal preemption—to circumvent that result by resort to an alternative version of contractual liability under state law. For similar reasons, the CISG should preempt state negligence and strict liability claims that in essence sound in contract. As federal district courts have thus held, "a tort that is in essence a contract claim and does not involve interests existing independently of contractual obligations . . . will fall within the scope of the CISG regardless of the label given to the claim."[138] The CISG clearly should not apply, in contrast, to free-standing, non-contractual unjust enrichment claims, unless in their essence they are merely an alternative label for a contract cause of action within the scope of the Convention.[139]

Expressly Excluded Issues. CISG Article 4(a) excludes issues of "validity" from the coverage of the Convention. Unfortunately, the CISG does not define "validity." Nonetheless, the exclusion of

---

[134]   *See, e.g.,* CLOUT Case No. 378, *Tribunale di Vigevano*, Italy (12 July 2000); CLOUT Case No. 189, *Oberster Gerichtshof* [Supreme Court] of Austria (20 March 1997). *See also generally* CISG DIGEST 2012, *supra* note 36, art. 1, para. 7 (citing cases).

[135]   *See supra* § 1.3. As one recent federal court noted, however, the mere allegation that a party is an agent does not preclude an analysis of whether that party is a co-seller under the CISG. *See* 2P Commercial Agency S.R.O. v. Familant, 2012 WL 6615889 (M.D. Fla. 2012).

[136]   Caterpillar, Inc. v. Usinor Industeel, 393 F. Supp. 2d 659, 675–676 (N.D. Ill. 2005); Geneva Pharmaceuticals Technology Corp. v. Barr Laboratories, Inc., 201 F. Supp. 2d 236 (S.D.N.Y. 2002), *rev. on other grounds*, 386 F.3d 485 (2d Cir. 2004).

[137]   The most authoritative recognition of promissory estoppel is § 90 of the Restatement (Second) of Contracts. Under the Restatement, the very definition of a "contract" is a "promise or set of promises for the breach of which the law gives a remedy" (*see id.*, § 1) and the result of an application of promissory estoppel is a binding promise. Thus, § 90 appears in a subpart of the Second Restatement entitled "Contracts without Consideration."

[138]   Electrocraft Arkansas, Inc. v. Super Electric Motors, Ltd. 2009 WL 5181854 at *5 (E.D. Ark. 2009). *See also* Weihai Textile Grp. Imp. & Exp. Co. v. Level 8 Apparel, LLC, 2014 WL 1494327, at *16 (S.D.N.Y. 2014) (same).

[139]   Weihai Textile Grp. Imp. & Exp. Co. v. Level 8 Apparel, LLC, 2014 WL 1494327, at *15 (S.D.N.Y. 2014). This conclusion is certainly correct regarding the remedies for breach of a contract within the scope of the Convention. CISG articles 81 through 84 provide specific rules for restitutionary remedies in the event of an avoidance of a contract.

validity issues clearly arose because the CISG was not designed to police sales contracts for fairness or otherwise address core defenses to contract enforcement. Thus, it is generally accepted that the concept of validity "refers to any issue by which the domestic law would render the contract void, voidable, or unenforceable."[140] As a result, domestic law will continue to apply even in CISG transactions for contract defenses based on fraud, negligent misrepresentation, duress, illegality, incapacity, and similar notions. Other domestic regulatory statutes, such as unfair competition laws, also are preserved under CISG Article 4(a).

The impact of the general contract doctrine of mistake, however, requires more careful analysis. Where the concept of mistake is based on facts existing at the time of contract formation and functions as a defense to enforcement, domestic law should apply.[141] But Article 4 permits such a resort to domestic law "except as otherwise expressly provided in this Convention," and the CISG has a number of provisions that might conflict with, and thus displace, some domestic law "mistake" doctrines. Thus, for example, if the "mistake" relates to a party's expression of intent, CISG Article 8(1) provides the governing rule.[142] Similarly, the CISG displaces domestic law claims based on post-formation events— which some legal systems categorize as a "subsequent mistake"— because CISG Article 79 exhaustively covers issues of impracticability, hardship, and the like.[143]

CISG Article 4(a) excludes from the Convention's scope not only issues of validity of a contract as a whole but also "of any of its provisions or of any usage." Thus, there has been a fair amount of litigation concerning the validity of individual clauses in standard business terms and concerning domestic statutes regulating the subject. There is now general agreement that such issues of validity are a matter of domestic law[144] (although not the basic question of whether such terms become part of the contract in the first

---

[140] *See* CISG DIGEST 2012, *supra* note 36, art. 4, para. 9 (quoting cases).

[141] *See, e.g.*, CLOUT Case No. 426, *Oberster Gerichtshof* [Supreme Court] of Austria (13 April 2000); *Bundesgerichtshof* [Federal Court of Justice] of Germany (27 November 2007), *available at* http://cisgw3.law.pace.edu/cases/071127g1.html.

[142] For more on CISG Article 8, see § 2.11 *infra*. Under U.S. law, such a mistaken expression of intent is known as a "misunderstanding." *See* Restatement (Second) of Contracts, §§ 20, 201.

[143] For more on CISG Article 79, see § 2.29 *infra*. Other examples of CISG rules that displace domestic law claims founded on a party's "mistake" include Article 27 (for errors in transmission); Articles 35–44 (for mistakes about the conformity or quality of the goods); and Article 71 (for mistakes about the solvency of the other party).

[144] *See* CISG DIGEST 2012, *supra* note 36, art. 4, para. 9; Schwenzer/Hachem, art. 4, para. 38, in Schlechtriem & Schwenzer, *supra* note 30.

place[145]). Thus, recent cases have held that the validity of clauses on the limitation of damages,[146] liquidated damages, non-competition, forum selection, and assignments of rights are a matter for domestic law.[147] Similarly, the validity of contracts or clauses on the settlement of disputes, assignment of receivables, set-offs, assumption or acknowledgement of debts, and the rights of third parties are not governed by the CISG.[148] The subject of the statute of limitations (the "limitation period") on claims in international sales transactions is covered by a companion treaty to the CISG.[149]

The validity exclusion in CISG Article 4 has triggered special issues with specific reference to United States law. The first is whether the restrictions in the UCC on disclaimers of warranty fall in this category. For example, UCC § 2–316 imposes special linguistic and form rules for a valid disclaimer of the warranty of merchantability, including the use of the term "merchantability" and a requirement that it be conspicuous.[150] Is this an issue of validity as contemplated by the CISG? A second issue concerns the UCC restrictions on clauses that exclude or limit the buyer's remedies to repair or replacement, and thereby exclude the remedies of avoidance of the contract (refusal to accept delivery of the goods) or an action for damages, especially consequential damages.[151] A third issue concerns clauses that provide for a significantly larger payment to the aggrieved party than any actual or reasonably expected damages. The relevant UCC provision makes such clauses "void as a penalty."[152]

On the first issue, one U.S. federal court has expressly concluded that the CISG does not displace the UCC's requirement for a valid warranty disclaimer.[153] This is in accord with the view originally expressed by Professor Helen Hartnell that, because the UCC warranty disclaimer provisions are designed to protect fairness, they qualify as rules of "validity" excluded from the scope of the CISG by Article 4(a).[154] Other scholars have disagreed with

---

[145]   Part II of the Convention exhaustively covers the issue of contract formation. *See* §§ 2.13—2.17 *infra.*

[146]   MSS, Inc. v. Maser Corp., 2011 WL 2938424, at *3 (M.D. Tenn. 2011).

[147]   *See* CISG DIGEST 2012, *supra* note 36, art. 4, paras. 9 and 14 (citing cases).

[148]   *See id.*, art. 4, para. 14 (citing cases).

[149]   *See* § 2.44 *infra.*

[150]   UCC § 2–316(2).

[151]   UCC § 2–719(2).

[152]   UCC § 2–718(1), last sentence.

[153]   Norfolk Southern Ry. Co. v. Power Source Supply, Inc., 2008 WL 2884102, at *5 (W.D. Pa. 2008).

[154]   *See* Helen Hartnell, *Rousing the Sleeping Dog: The Validity Exception to the Convention on Contracts for the International Sale of Goods*, 18 YALE INT'L L. 1 (1993).

this view.[155] As a general proposition, the CISG cases from other jurisdictions, especially those concerning pre-formulated standard business terms, have held that even agreements on warranty limitations are subject to a review for validity under domestic law.[156] But one might reasonably draw a distinction between (a) whether local public policy prohibits warranty or similar limitations completely and (b) whether it defines specific linguistic requirements for such a limitation. Under this approach, the courts would view general contract defenses (such as unconscionability) as issues of validity outside of the CISG; but, given that CISG Article 35 expressly permits the parties to "agree otherwise" regarding conformity of the goods, the courts could find that the specific linguistic formulations defined by the UCC for warranty disclaimers are displaced by the express provisions of the CISG.[157]

On the second issue, there seems to be general agreement that the validity of clauses limiting the amount of liability of the seller or the remedies of the buyer is a matter for domestic law.[158] Thus, one federal court has expressly concluded that the validity of a consequential damages limitation was governed by the UCC, not the CISG.[159] But the same result should obtain under the CISG in any event, for the core principle of "party autonomy" in Article 6 permits the parties to "vary the effect of any of its provisions."[160] However, such clauses may not leave a buyer with no remedy at all nor, as the Austrian Supreme Court has held, otherwise conflict with the core remedial values of the Convention (such as the right to declare a contract avoided).[161]

General agreement also exists on the third issue, the status of liquidated damages and penalty clauses: The validity of such clauses likewise is an issue for domestic law under CISG Article

---

[155] See John Honnold, UNIFORM LAW FOR INTERNATIONAL SALES UNDER THE 1980 UNITED NATIONS CONVENTION § 230 (H. Flechtner, ed., 4th ed. 2009) (declaring that "the particular verbal formulations or warranty requirements specified in the U.C.C. for disclaiming" implied warranties do not apply to CISG contracts); Bruno Zeller, CISG AND THE UNIFICATION OF INTERNATIONAL TRADE LAW 71 (2007) (same).

[156] See Oberster Gerichtshof [Supreme Court] of Austria (7 September 2000), available at http://cisgw3.law.pace.edu/cases/000907a3.html.

[157] See CISG, art. 35 and the discussion in § 2.21 infra.

[158] See Schwenzer/Hachem, art. 4, para. 43, in Schlechtriem & Schwenzer, supra note 30.

[159] See 2P Commercial Agency S.R.O. v. Familant, 2012 WL 6615889 (M.D. Fla. 2012).

[160] See § 2.5 supra.

[161] See Oberster Gerichtshof [Supreme Court] of Austria (7 September 2000), available at http://cisgw3.law.pace.edu/cases/000907a3.html. See also Schwenzer/ Hachem, art. 4, para. 43, in Schlechtriem & Schwenzer, supra note 30 and §§ 2.36, 2.41 infra.

4(a).[162] Common law courts hold such clauses to be invalid, even in contracts otherwise subject to the CISG. The wide acceptance of this conclusion may be due to the fact that the UCC makes such clauses substantively "void," rather than merely subject to special linguistic requirements. It also may be due to the foundations of the common law rule against "penalty" clauses in basic public policies against non-compensatory remedies and potential *in terrorem* use of such contract rights.[163]

Another set of issues excluded from CISG coverage concerns property rights to the goods, including title to the goods and the security rights and obligations of third parties to the contract.[164] It is clear that disputes over ownership of the goods are not covered by the CISG and must be determined under local law.[165] The primary issue raised in litigation over this provision has been the effect of "retention of title" clauses, by which the seller attempts to retain title in the goods after delivery and until the buyer pays for them. The legal status of such clauses is a property issue and is therefore outside the scope of the CISG.[166] Thus, any determination of the effect of such clauses depends upon applicable domestic law (in the U.S., UCC Article 9), even though the CISG applies to the analysis of the remainder of the contract.

Finally, CISG Article 5 provides that the Convention does not govern causes of action against the seller "for death or personal injury," even if they arise out of a sales transaction. The reason for this exclusion, again, was a desire not to have contract law rules conflict with core public policy values that underlie claims for personal injury under tort law.

§ 2.9   The General Provisions of the CISG

CISG Articles 7 through 13 contain the Convention's "general principles." These provisions deal with interpretation of the Convention and filling gaps in its provisions (Article 7), interpretation of party intent and usages of trade (Article 8 and 9), a definition relevant to the application of the Convention in the first place (Articles 10, see § 2.4 above), and a general removal of form

---

[162] *See* Schwenzer/Hachem, art. 4, para. 44, in Schlechtriem & Schwenzer, *supra* note 30, and, *e.g.*, decision of Appellate Court (*Oberlandesgericht*), Hamburg, Germany, 25 January 2008, *available at* http://cisgw3.law.pace.edu/cases/080125g1.html.

[163] For an historical perspective see Lloyd, *Penalties and Forfeitures*, 29 HARV. L. REV. 117 (1915).

[164] CISG, art. 4(b).

[165] *See, e.g.,* Usinor Industeel v. Leeco Steel Prods., 209 F. Supp. 2d 880 (N.D. Ill. 2002).

[166] *See* CISG DIGEST 2012, *supra* note 36, art. 4, para. 13 (citing cases).

requirements such as the Statute of Frauds (Articles 11–13). Article 7 is designed to assist in interpretation of the Convention itself, while Articles 8 and 9 provide rules on the interpretation of party intent, both pre-formation and as reflected in their contract terms. In specific, Article 8 concentrates on statements and conduct by the parties themselves as indications of their contractual agreement, while Article 9 concentrates on sources external to the parties, such as trade usages.

§ 2.10 General Provisions___Interpretation of the CISG

Beyond the "party autonomy" principle of Article 6 (see § 2.5 above), the most important provision for understanding the legal nature of the CISG is Article 7. At first glance, this Article seems merely to state standard rules of interpretation. But a more careful examination reveals that it declares the fundamental principles that define the Convention's relationship with domestic law.

Interpretation of the CISG. At its most fundamental, Article 7(1) is designed to prohibit local courts from applying local norms and rules, rather than the Convention, to international sales disputes within its scope. It first directs that interpretation of the Convention must heed its "international character." The purpose of this provision is to ensure that local courts respect the fact that the Convention reflects a broad international compromise among domestic legal systems. Courts thus must interpret the CISG on its own ("autonomously"), without resort to domestic interpretive norms or substantive rules. For example, in interpreting rules and concepts stated in the Convention, such as "reasonable time," the required regard for the "international character" of the Convention imposes on the courts an obligation to follow international practice developed within the CISG, rather than domestic precedents, norms, or customs.

The requirement of an international perspective is stressed further by a second directive in Article 7(1)—that interpretation of the CISG must "promote uniformity of its application." This directive serves both to highlight the persuasive authority of foreign decisions interpreting the CISG and to emphasize (again) that local decisions on domestic sales law should not be relevant. Even the doctrine of "good faith" under the CISG is muted. Although UCC § 1–304 imposes an obligation of good faith on the parties to sales (and other) transactions, CISG Article 7(1) only refers to good faith in the interpretation of the Convention, not of the parties' contract (although some courts have shown recent flexibility on this score via Article 7(2), see immediately below).

Unfortunately, some courts in the United States have missed the essential message of Article 7(1) when they have turned to the domestic UCC to assist in interpreting the CISG. The Second Circuit started U.S. courts on this false path in 1995 when it stated that, where the language of a CISG provision tracks that of an analogous UCC provision, UCC case law may inform the interpretation of the CISG.[167] Many subsequent courts have followed this statement without further analysis, even though they acknowledge that domestic law is not *"per se* applicable" to the CISG.[168] The Seventh Circuit, for example, has observed that the CISG is the "international analog" to Article 2 of the UCC, and that where provisions are "the same or similar" the UCC can be informative to the court.[169] These statements in principal part seem to serve as a means of easing the burden of the courts based on the equally misleading premise, often repeated, that there is "virtually no case law under the Convention."[170] Similarly, U.S. courts routinely fail to consider foreign interpretive decisions under the Convention.[171]

These observations fundamentally miss the core directives of Article 7(1) that interpretation of the Convention must heed its "international character" and "promote uniformity of its application."[172] Thus, unless the drafting history of the Convention reveals that a particular provision is based on a UCC rule (which is exceptionally rare), a coincidental linguistic parallel between the UCC and the CISG may be merely a "false friend" (just as a parallel with French or Chinese legal rules does not mean that the CISG

---

[167]   Delchi Carrier S.p.A. v. Rotorex, 71 F.3d 1024, 1028 (2d Cir. 1995).

[168]   *See, e.g.,* Eldesouky v. Aziz, 2015 WL 1573319, at *2 (S.D.N.Y. 2015) (*quoting* Delchi Carrier S.p.A. v. Rotorex Corp., 71 F.3d 1024, 1028 (2d Cir. 1995)).

[169]   Chicago Prime Packers, Inc. v. Northam Food Trading Co., 408 F.3d 894 (7th Cir. 2005).

[170]   *See, e.g.,* Hilaturas Miel, S.L. v. Republic of Iraq, 573 F. Supp. 2d 781, 799 (S.D.N.Y. 2008) (*quoting* Delchi Carrier S.p.A. v. Rotorex, 71 F.3d 1024, 1028 (2d Cir. 1995)).

[171]   For a positive counterexample see Forestal Guarani S.A. v. Daros Intern., Inc., 613 F.3d 395, 399–400 (3rd Cir. 2010) (examining the competing views of foreign courts on a disputed CISG issue).

[172]   A glaring example is the recent case of Eldesouky v. Aziz, 2015 WL 1573319 (S.D.N.Y. 2015). There, the court acknowledged that the CISG governed a sale of goods from a party in the United States to one in Egypt. The key issue was the calculation of damages. Although the CISG has comprehensive and highly detailed rules on this subject (*see* §§ 2.39 and 2.43 *infra*), the court held that "as a practical matter, whether the UCC or the CISG governs is likely immaterial." *Id.,* at *2. It thus simply applied the rules of the domestic UCC without reference to those in the CISG. *Id.* For a similarly misguided statement see Maxxsonics USA, Inc. v. Fengshun Peiying Electro Acoustic Co., 2012 WL 962698, at *4 (N.D. Ill. 2012) (observing that "in a breach of contract claim, relatively little turns on the choice between the CISG and the UCC [because] [t]he elements of a breach of contract claim are the same either way").

follows those domestic law approaches). As a matter of domestic law, a particular federal appellate decision may have a *stare decisis* effect on inferior courts. But within the scheme of an international treaty such as the CISG, decisions of foreign courts should have an equal persuasive value as domestic ones. Moreover, foreign interpretive decisions for the CISG are both abundant and easily accessible.[173] Indeed, one internet site alone lists 2,500 full text cases and 10,000 annotations.[174]

Filling Apparent Gaps in the CISG. Article 7(2) continues this internationalist approach with respect to apparent gaps in the express provisions of the Convention. Reflective of a civil code interpretive approach, this provision states as a primary rule that gaps in the CISG "are to be settled in conformity with the general principles on which it is based." This approach (unlike that of the domestic UCC) thus again mandates that courts first attempt to fill regulatory gaps on an "autonomous" basis—that is, with reference to the broader principles reflected in the *Convention itself.* On this basis, courts and scholars have distilled from common themes in the CISG's provisions certain fundamental principles (which might be viewed as "inductive general principles"), including: reasonableness (such as in the measurement of allowed time); a duty to communicate relevant information; full compensation in the event of breach; and a form of traditional estoppel ("*venire contra factum proprium*").[175] Based on this approach many courts also have found a general principle that the CISG includes an obligation of "good faith" *by the parties* in the formation and performance of international sales contracts.[176] In the same way, courts have found a general principle that a party relying on a CISG right or power has the burden to prove the factual prerequisites and a party claiming an exception to a CISG rule has the burden of proving the factual prerequisites of that exception, at least where the structure of the CISG implies such a result.[177]

It is only if a thorough search for relevant CISG general principles fails that Article 7(2) permits resort to domestic law

---

[173] For a comprehensive analysis of the CISG's interpretive scheme see Michael P. Van Alstine, *Dynamic Treaty Interpretation*, 146 U. PA. L. REV. 687 (1998).

[174] http://www.cisg.law.pace.edu/cisg/text/digest-cases-toc.html.

[175] *See* CISG DIGEST 2012, *supra* note 36, art. 16, para. 3 (citing CLOUT case No. 94, *Internationales Schiedsgericht der Bundeskammer der gewerblichen Wirtschaft-Wien*, Austria (15 June 1994)).

[176] *See* CISG DIGEST 2012, *supra* note 36, art. 7, paras. 10–32 (citing numerous cases). *See also* Van Alstine, *Dynamic Treaty Interpretation*, *supra* note 173, at 749–753.

[177] *See* CISG DIGEST 2012, *supra* note 36, art. 4, para. 4. *See also* Honnold/Flechtner, *supra* note 155, Article 4, § 70.1.

principles determined under applicable choice of law rules.[178] The danger to uniform application is that local courts will discover many "gaps" in the CISG and no usable internal "general principles", and then readily fall back on their own familiar domestic law rules. The fundamental philosophy of the CISG is that local courts must assiduously resist this impulse.

§ 2.11   General Provisions__Interpretation of Party Intent and Usages

Interpretation of Party Intent. Article 8 establishes rules for interpreting party expressions and conduct as well as any final contract between them. The Convention's approach to this issue reflects significant differences with prevailing norms under domestic U.S. law—a fact recent U.S. courts fortunately have recognized and applied in the CISG disputes before them.

Article 8 establishes a three-tier hierarchy of interpretation: (1) Although not expressly stated there, basic principles of party autonomy mean that if the parties in fact have a common understanding concerning their intent or the meaning of a provision, that common understanding will prevail. The difficulty with this obvious point, however, is that a supposed shared intent is very difficult to prove once a dispute arises between the parties.

(2)   The essence of the CISG's interpretive scheme instead is found in Article 8(1). That provision mandates as a primary principle that a party's actual (*i.e.*, subjective) intent governs where the other party "knew or could not have been unaware" of that intent. The idea here is that a party's *actual* intent should prevail where the other party knows—actually or constructively—of that *actual* intent. This is a blunt rejection of the strict objective standard of interpretation applied by many U.S. courts.

(3)   If this search for actual intent fails, Article 8(2) applies the traditional objective approach. Under that provision a party's statement or conduct is to be interpreted "according to the understanding that a reasonable person of the same kind as the other party would have had in the same circumstances."

Article 8(3) then further highlights the contrast of the CISG's interpretive rules with those of many U.S. courts. That provision declares that in interpreting party intent—including disputed provisions in written contracts—a court must consider "all relevant circumstances of the case." And this includes—in a clear rejection of

---

[178]   Again, to express this point Article 7(2) uses the civil law term "rules of private international law."

the American parol evidence rule—"the negotiations" of the parties as well as their prior practices, usages, and subsequent conduct.

As noted, U.S. courts fortunately have taken this hierarchy to heart. In an early significant case, *MCC-Marble Ceramic Center, Inc. v. Ceramica Nuova d'Agostino, S.p.A.*, for example, a federal Court of Appeals interpreted Article 8(1) to require consideration of a party's subjective intent in interpreting its statements and conduct in the formation of a contract.[179] As the court there correctly observed, "The plain language of the [CISG] . . . requires an inquiry into a party's subjective intent as long as the other party to the contract was aware of that intent."[180]

Article 8(3) also can direct a court to a very different approach to contract interpretation than is usual in domestic contract cases. Its requirement that a court give consideration to all relevant circumstances is a clear direction to consider parol evidence, even in interpreting a subsequent and final written agreement. As a more recent federal court has observed, "CISG allows all evidence of the parties' intent to be admitted to interpret the terms of the agreement" in direct rejection of domestic rules that favor final writings.[181] Other courts have recognized the point in even clearer terms: "[T]he CISG does not adopt the parol-evidence rule of American law, and instead 'allows all relevant information into evidence even if it contradicts the written documentation.' "[182] Some courts and scholars likewise have relied on the interpretive rules in Article 8 to promote the actual intent of the parties in "battle of the forms" situations and thus to avoid mechanical application of the traditional "last shot" doctrine.[183]

This does not mean, however, that fundamental principles of interpretation accepted throughout the world never can have relevance under CISG Article 8. Indeed, in a case governed by the CISG the German Federal Court of Justice (*Bundesgerichtshof*) recently applied the general notion that ambiguities should be interpreted against the drafter of a document. At issue there was an unclear provision in one party's standard business terms that had been incorporated into a contract. The court held that "in such a case, the internationally long established and broadly accepted rule

---

[179] 144 F.2d 1384 (11th Cir. 1998).

[180] *Id.*, at 1387. *See also* Orica Australia Pty Ltd v. Aston Evaporative Services, LLC, 2015 WL 4538534, at *6 (D. Colo. 2015) (*quoting* MCC-Marble with approval).

[181] ECEM European Chemical Marketing B.V. v. Purolite Co., 2010 WL 419444, at *13 (E.D. Pa. 2010).

[182] Korea Trade Ins. Corp. v. Oved Apparel Corp., 2015 WL 1345812, at *2 (S.D.N.Y. 2015) (*quoting* TeeVee Toons, Inc. v. Gerhard Schubert GmbH, 2006 WL 2463537, at *7 (S.D.N.Y. 2006)).

[183] *See* § 2.17 *infra*.

applies that unclear formulations are to be interpreted '*contra proferentem*,' that is, that ambiguities are to be interpreted against the drafter."[184]

Usages of Trade. CISG Article 9 addresses express and implied acceptance of usages of trade. Article 9(1) first provides that the parties are bound by "any usage" to which they have "agreed." Such agreements need not be in writing and, although the drafting history suggests a higher standard, the Austrian Supreme Court has held that even implicit agreements on usages are binding.[185] Further, "any" such usage may be so incorporated by agreement, including local ones. If so incorporated, a usage is considered to be part of the express contract items.[186] Indeed, because Article 6 allows the express terms of the contract to vary the provisions of the Convention (see § 2.5 above), agreed usages will prevail even over express CISG provisions.

Article 9(1) also binds the parties to "any practices which they have established between themselves." Where the parties have established such practices, they prevail over common industry usages. As the Eleventh Circuit observed in *Treibacher Industrie, A.G. v. Allegheny Technologies, Inc.*, "the parties' usage of a term in their course of dealings controls that term's meaning in the face of a conflicting customary usage of the term."[187]

Article 9(2) concerns the incorporation of usages by implication. In the drafting of the CISG, both less developed countries (LDCs) and nonmarket economies (NMEs) expressed strenuous concerns about the application of unfamiliar trade usages on this basis, and the careful language of Article 9(2) reflects those concerns. It states that "unless otherwise agreed," the parties are considered "impliedly" to have accepted a usage for their contract only if (a) they "knew or ought to have known" of it; (b) it is international (not merely local) in nature; and (c) it is both "widely known to" and "regularly observed by" others parties to "contracts of the type involved" in the "particular trade concerned." This seems to set a very high standard for a party seeking to rely on an implied trade usage, and in particular with regard to the identification of the specific *international* trade involved.

---

184   Decision of the *Bundesgerichtshof* [Federal Court of Justice] of Germany, VIII ZR 410/12, at 11–12 (28 May 2014) (translation by the authors).

185   *See* CLOUT Case No. 425, *Oberster Gerichtshof* [Supreme Court] of Austria (21 March 2000).

186   For numerous examples of such agreed usages see CISG DIGEST 2012, *supra* note 36, art. 9, para. 6.

187   464 F.3d 1235, 1239 (11th Cir. 2006).

§ 2.12 General Provisions___Form Requirements

CISG Article 11 rejects any writing or other form requirements for contract formation. It broadly states that a contract for the international sale of goods "need not be concluded in or evidenced by writing and is not subject to any requirement as to form." For emphasis—and fully consistent with the flexible interpretive rules of Article 8 discussed above—a second sentence of Article 11 declares that a contract "may be proved by any means, including witnesses." Thus, there is no equivalent in the Convention of the Anglo-American Statute of Frauds. This provision likewise makes clear that CISG contracts may be concluded or evidenced by electronic communications.[188]

Nonetheless, Articles 12 and 96 allow a Contracting State to declare a reservation that the local law of that Contracting State will govern the form requirements for a sales contract "where any party has his place of business in that State." Such a reservation extends not only to the contract of sale itself, but also to "its modification or termination by agreement" as well as to "any offer, acceptance or other indication of intention."[189] It applies, however, only to the extent that the domestic law of the declaring State itself "requires contracts of sale to be concluded in or evidence by writing."[190]

The United States has not made this declaration; as a result, the Statute of Frauds provisions in UCC § 2–201 do not apply to contracts under the CISG. In fact, only eight Contracting States have declared an Article 96 reservation; but prominently included among these are Russia, Chile, and Argentina, with the result that their domestic law on writing requirements would continue to apply for CISG contracts. (China and three other states initially declared, but subsequently withdrew, Article 96 reservations.[191])

The existence of an Article 96 reservation by one of these states may not, however, be the final word on transactions involving their residents. According to what appears to be the minority view, if one party has its relevant place of business in such a state, that state's writing requirements apply.[192] The apparent majority view, in

---

[188]   *See also* CISG Advisory Council Opinion No. 1, *Electronic Communications under CISG* (2003), *available at* http://www.cisgac.com/cisgac-opinion-no1/.

[189]   CISG, art. 12.

[190]   CISG, art. 96.

[191]   China withdrew its Article 96 reservation in 2013, as did Lithuania the same year, Latvia in 2012, and Estonia in 2004.

[192]   *See* CISG DIGEST 2012, *supra* note 36, art. 12, para. 4 (citing cases). *See also* Zhejiang Shaoxing Yongli Printing & Dyeing Co., Ltd. v. Microflock Textile Group Corp., 2008 WL 2098062, at *3 (S.D. Fla. 2008).

contrast, first requires application of the forum state's otherwise-applicable conflict of law rules. It is only if those rules lead to the application of a reserving state's law that its writing requirements will apply. In a carefully reasoned opinion, the Third Circuit endorsed this majority approach in 2010.[193]

If a state's Article 96 reservation applies to a transaction, however, the parties may not under CISG Article 6 agree otherwise.[194] This gives the local law the effect of "mandatory law" under the Convention. Nonetheless, Article 13 provides that a telex or a telegram may satisfy the "writing" requirement, and this should displace any contrary understanding of the term under local law. That is, Articles 12 and 96 only make unenforceable those contracts that are "other than in writing" (a Convention term), and Article 13 then defines "writing" to include a telex or telegram. Nonetheless, the telex and telegram of course long ago yielded to electronic communication, so the direct effect of Article 13 will be limited.

§ 2.13   Contract Formation＿In General

Part II of the CISG sets forth its contract formation provisions.[195] Under Article 92, a Contracting State may declare a reservation at the time of ratification that it will not be bound by Part II, even though it is bound by the rest of the CISG. Only the Scandinavian countries initially did so, however, and even these have since withdrawn their reservations.

Every first-year American law student learns about "offer, acceptance, and consideration," but all of these three elements of contract formation are not present in other legal systems. Civil law emphasizes the agreement process, and does not include a consideration requirement. Nonetheless, an examination of the domestic consideration cases will show that few such disputes arise in true commercial transactions. Rather, they tend to involve family members arguing over failed promises (uncles attempting to induce nephews not to smoke and the like). Thus, it should not be surprising to learn that the CISG has no requirement of consideration in its contract formation provisions.[196]

---

[193]   Forestal Guarani S.A. v. Daros Intern., Inc., 613 F.3d 395, 399–400 (3rd Cir. 2010). For an examination of the competing approaches see Weihai Textile Grp. Imp. & Exp. Co. v. Level 8 Apparel, LLC, 2014 WL 1494327, at *7 (S.D.N.Y. 2014).

[194]   CISG, art. 12.

[195]   CISG, arts. 14–24.

[196]   One U.S. court has concluded otherwise, but on the quite erroneous assumption that the common law requirement of consideration reflects an issue of "validity" as contemplated by CISG Article 4(a). Geneva Pharmaceuticals Technology

The essential building blocks of contract formation under Part II are the familiar notions of "offer"[197] and "acceptance."[198] In Convention terminology, a contract "is concluded at the moment when an acceptance of an offer becomes effective."[199] Again, there is no need for consideration, and no similar required formalities.

Nonetheless, it is clear that the parties can conclude a contract without a clearly identifiable offer and acceptance, and that such contracting arrangements fall within the scope of CISG rules.[200] Thus, the conduct of the parties can reflect an agreement on the existence of a contract between them, and the CISG would recognize such an agreement as a binding contract without a formal offer or acceptance. This results from the fundamental principle of "party autonomy" contained in CISG Article 6.[201] Whether this would allow recognition of a contract in the case of a "merchant's letter of confirmation," which in some countries will lead to contract formation in the absence of a timely objection, remains the subject of substantial dispute.[202]

§ 2.14 Formation___Offer: The Substantive Requirements

Article 14 defines three requirements for an "offer." First, it must be "a proposal for concluding a contract," which is a standard notion. Second, it must indicate "an intention to be bound in case of acceptance," which will distinguish an offer from a general sales catalogue, an advertisement, or a purchase inquiry. Article 14(2) elaborates on this concept by making proposals addressed to the general public presumptively not offers "unless the contrary is clearly indicated." Third, an offer must be "sufficiently definite." Article 14 expressly identifies in this regard only three essential elements: goods, quantity, and price; by implication, other terms can be left open, but not these three.[203]

Goods. A proposal satisfies Article 14's definiteness requirement if it merely "indicates" the goods. This term suggests substantial flexibility, for it does not seem to require that a proposal

---

Corp. v. Barr Laboratories, Inc., 201 F. Supp. 2d 236, 283–284 (S.D.N.Y. 2002), *rev. on other grounds*, 386 F.3d 485 (2004).

[197] CISG, arts. 14–17.

[198] CISG, arts. 18–22.

[199] CISG, art. 23.

[200] *See* CISG DIGEST 2012, *supra* note 36, *Formation of the Contract*, para. 5.

[201] *See* § 2.5 *supra.*

[202] *See* CISG DIGEST 2012, *supra* note 36, *Formation of the Contract*, para. 13 (citing cases).

[203] *See* CISG DIGEST 2012, *supra* note 36, art. 14, para. 7.

describe the goods with any particularity. Moreover, an indication of the goods may arise from the flexible interpretive rules in CISG Article 8 or from any practices established by the parties or usages common in the industry under Article 9. A proposal need not even describe the quality or grade of the goods, provided that a reasonable person in the position of the addressee would understand the goods indicated.[204]

Quantity. Likewise, Article 14 provides that a proposal is sufficiently definite if it "expressly or impliedly fixes or makes provision for determining the quantity[.]" Thus, flexible quantity provisions do not seem to prevent a proposal from qualifying as an offer. One court accordingly held that a proposal to sell a chemical "in commercial amounts" was "sufficiently definite."[205] In particular, open quantity contracts, such as those for requirements, output, or exclusive dealings, in most cases should cause little difficulty for the courts. In each such contract, a "provision for determining the quantity" likely will arise through party performance, even if the precise number cannot be fixed in advance. Thus, an order for an approximate quantity of natural gas met the requirements of Article 14 because it complied with usage regularly applied in the natural gas trade.[206] On the other hand, a mere distribution agreement without specific quantities was held not to make adequate provision for determining the quantity.[207] Thus, in view of the requirements of CISG Article 14 it is usually preferable to include either estimated quantity amounts or minimum quantity amounts, to assure that there is a fixed or determinable quantity.

Examples of sufficiently definite quantity terms include "an order of up to 250,000 pounds" of soy lecithin, "three truckloads" of eggs where the parties understood that this mean full truckloads, and "10,000 tons +/−5 per cent" of a particular good.[208]

Assortment arrangements, under which one party has discretion over the choice of goods from among an assortment, are a final problem concerning "definiteness" in both the description and quantity of the goods.[209] A clause that permits either the buyer or the seller to specify the assortment of goods during the performance of the contract would seem to "make[ ] provision for" determining

---

[204] *See* CISG DIGEST 2012, *supra* note 36, art. 14, para. 8.

[205] Geneva Pharmaceuticals Tech Corp. v. Barr Labs, Inc., 201 F. Supp. 2d 236, 281–282 (S.D.N.Y. 2002), *aff'd*, 386 F.3d 485 (2d Cir. 2004).

[206] CLOUT Case No. 176, *Oberster Gerichtshof* [Supreme Court] of Austria (6 February 1996), also *available at* http://cisgw3.law.pace.edu/cases/960206a3.html.

[207] Helen Kaminski PTY Ltd. v. Marketing Australia Products Inc. 1997 WL 414137 (S.D.N.Y. 1997).

[208] *See* CISG DIGEST 2012, *supra* note 36, art. 14, para. 93 (citing cases).

[209] Compare UCC § 2–311.

both quantity and type of goods. The major hurdle in such cases is the requirement that the offer "indicate[ ] the goods." But Article 14(1) does not require that the offer "specify" the goods, and so clauses that allow later selection of assortment should be effective, if the parties take care in describing the range or set from which the contract goods must be selected. Nonetheless, the alternatives also must satisfy the requirement of a definite price.[210]

Price. Article 14 seemingly also allows flexibility in the identification of the price. It states that a proposal is sufficiently definite if it "expressly or impliedly fixes or makes provision for determining . . . the price." Nonetheless, closer examination reveals that the requirement for a definite price is more restrictive than the comparable UCC provision on open, or flexible, price contracts,[211] and it was so intended. This is so because many civil law states do not recognize such open-price contracts. Some have argued that a true "open price" contract is possible under the CISG, provided that the parties have expressed a knowing intent to be bound.[212] This could be accomplished, however, only with a sufficiently clear party intent on a means to determine the price, and not, unlike the UCC, by a mere judicial resort to the market price (see § 2–305).

CISG Article 55 also may provide a foundation for flexible pricing arrangements. If a contract does not expressly or impliedly set the price, that provision permits reference to the price "generally charged at the time of the conclusion of the contract . . . under comparable circumstances in the trade concerned." But Article 55 only applies where a contract already has been "validly concluded," which assumes a valid offer (with an identification of the price). Most courts accordingly have held that Article 55 does not empower them to apply a market price if the proposal does not "fix[ ] or make[ ] provision for determining . . . the price" in the first place.[213]

Some courts have not been so doctrinaire. Most often these more accommodating courts have found that, by conduct or dealings, parties have "implicitly" agreed on a price under the interpretive rules of CISG Article 8.[214] These courts have utilized Article 55 as a subsidiary method for determining the price, especially where the parties have begun performance of the

---

[210]   *See* CLOUT Case No. 53, *Legfelsóbb Biróság* [Supreme Court] of Hungary (25 September 1992) (holding that proposals to an aircraft buyer did not satisfy the CISG's definiteness requirement because they did not provide the price for some elements of the various alternatives), also *available at* http://cisgw3.law.pace.edu/cases/920925h1.html.

[211]   *See* UCC § 2–305.

[212]   *See* Mohs, art. 55, para. 5, in Schlechtriem & Schwenzer, *supra* note 30.

[213]   *See* CISG DIGEST 2012, *supra* note 36, art. 14, para. 15.

[214]   *See* § 2.11 *supra*.

contemplated transaction. Thus, where the offer indicated a range of prices for goods with a range of quality, one court held that the offer was sufficiently definite, since it was possible to price each item according to its quality.[215] Likewise, in two cases where the seller and buyer agreed to a sale with no price term, but the seller then shipped and the buyer accepted the goods, the courts found that a binding contract existed.[216] Nonetheless, the cases are clear that CISG Article 55 is "not a means for judicial price-setting."[217] Thus, where the parties agreed to a sale without stating a price, but essentially "agreed to agree" later on the price for each shipment, the purported offer neither contained a price term nor made a provision for determining the price as required for a valid contract by Article 14(1).[218]

More generally, the Convention's language is flexible enough to authorize most forms of flexible pricing. A contract will sufficiently "make provision for determining the price" where the price is to follow a specified index, or is subject to an escalator clause, or is to be set by a third party. Arguably, the latter would include "lowest price to others" clauses. The only serious problem not resolved under this analysis may be an order for a replacement part in which no price is stated. It is here that Article 55 is certainly useful. The offeror may have "implicitly" agreed to pay the seller's current price for such goods, and Article 55 fixes the price as that generally charged at the time the contract was "concluded."

§ 2.15 Formation__Offer: Revocation and Related Process Issues

CISG Article 14 defines the requirements for an offer, but the three following articles address the process surrounding the making of an offer. That is, they concern when the offer becomes effective as well as how it may be withdrawn, revoked, or terminated. Many of these provisions resemble the civil law in substance, scope and style, more than comparable common law models.

When an Offer Becomes Effective. Article 15 first addresses when an offer becomes effective. In conformance with traditional notions, it requires that the offer be communicated to the offeree. But to describe this notion, Article 15(1) uses the civil law rule that

---

[215] CLOUT Case No. 106, *Oberster Gerichtshof* [Supreme Court] of Austria (10 November 1994).

[216] CLOUT Case No. 215, *Bezirksgericht* [District Court] of St. Gallen, Switzerland (3 July 1997); *Landgericht* [State Court] of Neubrandenburg, Germany (3 August 2005), also *available at* http://cisgw3.law.pace.edu/cases/050803g1.html.

[217] *See* CISG DIGEST 2012, *supra* note 36, art. 55, para. 3.

[218] CLOUT Case No. 139, Tribunal of International Commercial Arbitration of Russia (2 March 1995).

an offer becomes effective when it "reaches" the offeree. A separate article (Article 24) then defines when a communication—whether offer, acceptance, or "any other indication of intent"—reaches the addressee. This occurs when the communication "is made orally to him" or when it is "delivered" (a) personally, (b) to his place of business or mailing address or, (c) if no such place of business or mailing address exists, to his "habitual residence."

Withdrawal of an Offer. The right of the offeror to "withdraw" the offer under Article 15(1) is closely tied to the rule on effectiveness. Under the same article, an offer may be withdrawn freely—even if it is irrevocable—provided that the declaration of the withdrawal "reaches" the offeree "before or at the same time as the offer." If this occurs, the offer does not become effective, and thus could not have been accepted, in the first place. But after the offer reaches the offeree, the only recourse of the offeror is to attempt to "revoke" the offer.

Revocation of the Offer. One of the consequences of the abandonment of the CISG's rejection of any "consideration" requirement is that there is no foundation for the strict common law approach to the revocability of an unaccepted offer. Traditional common law doctrine makes an offer freely revocable until accepted, unless the parties had an agreement supported by consideration to keep it open (*i.e.*, had concluded a related "option contract").[219] In German law, in contrast, an offer is binding and irrevocable unless the offeror states that it is revocable.[220] These two approaches are in conflict, and the compromise adopted by the CISG uses neither.

CISG Article 16(1) first states the basic rule: An offer governed by the Convention[221] may be revoked "if the revocation reaches the offeree before he has dispatched an acceptance." Again, Article 24 defines when a communication reaches the addressee (see immediately above).[222] The remainder of Article 16, however, places important restrictions on the offeror's power of revocation.

Article 16(2) states two principal exceptions to the rule in Article 16(1). First, an offer is not revocable if it "indicates" that it is irrevocable.[223] Second, the offeror loses the power of revocation in the case of reasonable reliance by the offeree.[224] The first of these

---

[219]   *See* Restatement (Second) of Contracts, §§ 42, 25.

[220]   *See* German Civil Code art. 145.

[221]   Under CISG article 100, the Convention applies to a proposal made on or after the time when it has entered into force under CISG article 1. On this latter point see § 2.4 *supra*.

[222]   CISG, art. 16(1).

[223]   CISG, art. 16(2)(a).

[224]   CISG, art. 16(2)(b).

approaches incorporates civil law norms, while the second applies
common law norms. In adopting this position, the Convention
rejects both the common rule that an offer in principle always is
revocable and the German civil law rule that an offer is irrevocable
unless it is expressly states otherwise. This approach is similar in
concept—although decidedly not in particulars—to a merchant's
"firm offer" under the UCC,[225] but no "signed writing" is required.

An offer "indicates" that it is irrevocable "by stating a fixed
time for acceptance or otherwise."[226] The first reference seems
relatively clear, and would include a statement that an offer will be
held open for a specified period. But, what is included in "or
otherwise"? For example, does it include a statement that an offer
will *lapse* after a specified period? Such a statement, taken alone,
does not indicate a fixed intent that it will be held open prior to the
defined moment of lapse. This linguistic issue provoked substantial
controversy in the drafting of the Convention.[227] But carefully read,
the rule in Article 16(2) embraces the idea that the stating of any
such fixed time is "only one factor" indicating that the offer will not
be revoked.[228] In any event, the "or otherwise" language should
extend to any other indications of the offeror's intent not to revoke
as interpreted under Article 8, including the circumstances
surrounding the negotiation of the contract and the nature of the
parties' relationship.[229]

The possibility of irrevocability through reasonable and actual
offeree reliance is similar in concept to (but should not be influenced
by) the notion of an "option contract" created through reasonable
reliance by an offeree under Section 87(2) of the Second
Restatement of Contracts. For emphasis, however, the § 87(2)
requirements are idiosyncratic to U.S. domestic law and courts
should not consult them for guidance in developing the autonomous
law required by the CISG (for no gap exists as contemplated by
CISG Article 7(2)).[230] Finally, in either of the two means for

---

[225] UCC § 2–205.

[226] CISG, art. 16(2)(a).

[227] *See* Schroeter, art. 16, para. 9, in Schlechtriem & Schwenzer, *supra* note 30.
See also Gyula Eorsi, *Article 16*, in COMMENTARY ON THE INTERNATIONAL SALES LAW:
THE 1980 VIENNA CONVENTION (C.M. Bianca & M. Bonell, eds., 1987) (observing that
"[t]he common law delegations maintained that even if the offer states a fixed time
for acceptance, this, in itself, does not necessarily mean that the offer is
irrevocable. . . . Thus, the common law delegations were inclined to read the civil law
language in the common law way.").

[228] *See* Schroeter, art. 16, para. 9, in Schlechtriem & Schwenzer, *supra* note 30.

[229] *See* § 2.11 *supra*.

[230] *See* Geneva Pharmaceuticals Technology Corp. v. Barr Laboratories, Inc., 201
F. Supp. 2d 236, 286–287 (S.D.N.Y. 2002) (observing in dicta that domestic
promissory estoppel claims for reliance on an offer governed by the CISG would be
preempted).

irrevocability under Article 16, the offer of course must also meet the Article 14 requirements, including an indication of the goods and a fixed or determinable price and quantity.

Courts presented with these issues under CISG Article 16(2) may consult the principles of Article 8 on the interpretation of party intent. Under 8(1), the issue for the irrevocability of an offer would be whether the offeree knew or could not have been unaware that the offeror intended the offer to be revocable.[231] If both offeror and offeree are from common law states, there may be such an intention, although it is not conclusive since both parties' understandings arise from a common law background in which offers are revocable in the absence of consideration or a signed writing. If both parties are from civil law backgrounds the opposite construction of intention may be possible. One might argue that Article 8 is irrelevant to this determination, because CISG Article 16(2)(a) focuses on what the offer indicates, not on what the person making the offer intended to indicate. However, it is unlikely that the drafters of the CISG intended to set aside the general interpretive rules of Article 8 in the application of the Convention's substantive provisions, including the rules in Article 16. In any event, what is "reasonable" reliance for purposes of CISG Article 16(2)(b) must be determined on an international level and not based on domestic law practices or precedents.

§ 2.16 Formation__Acceptance: In General

Assent as Acceptance. The CISG's definition of an "acceptance" of an offer generally follows traditional notions. CISG Article 18(1) defines an acceptance as a statement or "other conduct" by an offeree "indicating assent to an offer." The same basic notion applies to proposals to modify or terminate a contract.[232] But in parallel with the rule for offers, an acceptance may be withdrawn provided the withdrawal declaration "reaches the offeror before or at the same time as the acceptance[.]"[233] Finally, an offer is "terminated" under Article 17—with the result that the offeree loses the power to accept it—when a rejection by the offeree "reaches the offeror."

Whether the particular words and conduct of an offeree indicate assent under Article 18(1) is, once again, determined by the interpretive rules in Article 8. Of particular importance in this regard is Article 8(3), which requires a court to consider all relevant circumstances, including the past relationship or practices of the parties, their contract negotiations, and any subsequent conduct, in

---

[231] *See* § 2.11 *supra.*

[232] *See* CISG DIGEST 2012, *supra* note 36, art. 18, para. 2.

[233] CISG, art. 22.

determining (as applicable) the subjective or objective intent of a party.[234] Also, a party that negotiates over or indicates acceptance of an offer in a foreign language bears the risk of the detailed meaning of that foreign language.[235]

Nonetheless, CISG Article 18(1) declares that "silence or inactivity" does not "in itself" amount to acceptance. This, too, is in accord with traditional notions. But again, the CISG's rules for interpreting party intent[236] make clear that negotiations and other prior conduct of the parties may establish an implicit understanding that lengthy silence followed by an absence of an affirmative objection indicates an acceptance. Thus, a U.S. District Court held in *Filanto, S.p.A. v. Chilewich Int'l Corp.* that a course of prior dealings, including exchanges of draft contracts, required an offeree to object promptly to an offer and that a lengthy failure to object to a proposed final draft, followed by the beginning of performance by the offeror, amounted to an acceptance.[237]

The *Filanto* decision creates some analytical challenges regarding the interaction between federal law on arbitration agreements and the contract formation rules of the CISG.[238] In part, the decision seems to indicate that there can be a contract to arbitrate formed separately from the sales contract. There is in principle no necessary conflict between federal arbitration law and the CISG in this regard, for the CISG elevates the agreement of the parties ("party autonomy") over even its express provisions.[239] But courts must take care to ensure that the parties' dealings in fact reflect a separate agreement to arbitrate. In any event, the true

---

[234]   *See* § 2.11 *supra.*

[235]   *See id.,* art. 18, para. 4.

[236]   *See* CISG, art. 8(3) and CISG, art. 9(1) (stating that the parties are bound by "any practices which they have established between themselves"). On both points see § 2.11 *supra.*

[237]   789 F. Supp. 1229, 1240 (S.D.N.Y. 1992) ("An offeree who, knowing that the offeror has commenced performance, fails to notify the offeror of its objection to the terms of the contract within a reasonable time will, under certain circumstances, be deemed to have assented to those terms."). Interestingly, this opinion analyzes whether, under the CISG's contract formation rules, the words and conduct of an offeree amounted to an agreement on arbitration under the 1958 New York Convention on the Recognition and Enforcement of Arbitral Awards and the federal legislation implementing that treaty. 9 U.S.C. §§ 201–209. The court found that the implicit acceptance by the offeree created an express "agreement in writing" for purposes of that treaty.

[238]   *See, e.g.,* Peter Winship, *The U.N. Convention and the Emerging Caselaw,* in EMPTIO-VENDITIO INTERNATIONES 227–237 (1997); Michael P. Van Alstine, *Consensus, Dissensus and Contractual Obligation Through the Prism of Uniform International Sales Law,* 37 VA. INT'L L. 1 (1996); Gary Nakata, *Filanto S.p.A. v. Chilewich Int'l Corp.: Sounds of Silence Bellow Forth Under the CISG's International Battle of the Forms,* 7 TRANSNAT'L LAW. 141 (1994).

[239]   *See* § 2.5 *supra.*

value of the *Filanto* decision lies in its recognition, on the foundation of the interpretive rules of the Convention, that a court "may consider previous relations between the parties in assessing whether a party's conduct constituted acceptance."[240] As discussed immediately below, the *Filanto* decisions—now reflected in later court decisions as well—also represents judicial hostility to a retreat to the dated "last shot" doctrine in a "battle of the forms" under the CISG.

When an Acceptance Becomes Effective. Article 18(2) defines when an acceptance "becomes effective." This is significant, for under Article 23 a contract is concluded under the Convention "when an acceptance of an offer becomes effective in accordance with the provisions of th[e] Convention." Thus, along with Articles 16(1) and 22, Article 18(2) forms the Convention's approach to "the mailbox rule"—except that the CISG rules are different. At common law, the mailbox rule (aka dispatched acceptance rule) passes the risk of loss or delay in the transmission of an acceptance to the offeror when the offeree dispatches the acceptance.[241] The common law also chooses that point in time to terminate the offeror's power to revoke an offer and to terminate the offeree's power to withdraw the acceptance.

Under CISG Article 18(2), in contrast, an acceptance is not effective until it "reaches" the offeror (as, again, defined in Article 24).[242] Thus, the risk of loss or delay in transmission of an acceptance is on the offeree, who now must ensure that its indication of acceptance actually reaches the offeror. Moreover, the acceptance must reach the offeror before the offer lapses[243]—*i.e.*, within any time fixed in the offer or, if the offer sets no such time, within a reasonable time under the circumstances.[244]

The arrival requirement in Article 18(2) is balanced by the rule, discussed above, for revocation of the offer in Article 16(1).

---

[240]   789 F. Supp. at 1240.

[241]   *See* Restatement (Second) of Contracts, § 63(a) ("[A]n acceptance made in a manner and by a medium invited by an offer is operative and completes the manifestation of mutual assent as soon as put out of the offeree's possession, without regard to whether it ever reaches the offeror"). The classic illustration of this rule is Adams v. Lindsell, 1 Barn. & Ald. 681, 106 Eng. Rep. 250 (K.B. 1818).

[242]   CISG, art. 18(2).

[243]   A late acceptance nonetheless is effective "if without delay" the offeror orally so informs the offeree or dispatches a notice to that effect. CISG, art. 21(1). On the other hand, if information in a late acceptance shows that it would have timely arrived under normal circumstances, it is effective to form a contract "unless, without delay" the offeror orally informs the offeree to the contrary or dispatches a notice to that effect. CISG, art. 21(2).

[244]   *Id.* The same provision states that an oral offer must be accepted "immediately, unless the circumstances indicate otherwise."

Under that rule, the offeror's power to revoke terminates upon dispatch of the acceptance. Thus, the offeree must ensure upon dispatch that its acceptance actually and timely reaches the offeror,[245] but is protected from a revocation in the interim.

This constellation nonetheless leaves a bit of room for manipulation by the offeree. Recall that the offeree's power to withdraw the acceptance terminates only when the acceptance reaches the offeror.[246] Thus, an acceptance sent by a slow transmission method (*e.g.*, the postal service) allows the offeree to speculate for a brief time while the offeror remains bound to its offer. An email message, for example, will release the offeree from the not-yet-received acceptance.

Notice and Acceptance by Conduct. Article 18(3) addresses the tricky issue of when an acceptance by conduct becomes effective (and thus forms a contract). It is a common misconception that this paragraph of Article 18 contains a substantive rule about acceptance by conduct. But such a rule would be superfluous because Article 18(1) already provides that acceptance can occur through "conduct of the offeree indicating asset to an offer." Careful review thus reveals that Article 18(3) only addresses the issue of *notice* to the offeror in such a case. If one parses the grammar, the key predicate words for the rule in Article 18(3) are the following: "if . . . the offeree may indicate assent by performing an act . . . *without notice to the offeror* . . . ". If this important predicate is satisfied, "the acceptance is effective at the moment the act is performed."

Article 18(3) provides, however, that such an acceptance by conduct without notice is possible only when that procedure is allowed by the offer, by usage, or by the parties' prior course of dealing. Therefore, not every expression of acceptance through conduct benefits from this rule; it instead sets as a premise an express or implied authorization for the offeree to conclude a contract without notice to the offeror. But if so allowed, the acceptance by conduct—such as shipment of the goods—is effective to form a contract immediately upon the performance of the act, rather than upon the offeror receiving notice of the acceptance under Article 18(2), such as through the actual arrival of the goods. (Even in such a case, the offeree must perform the relevant act within the time allowed for acceptance as described above.[247]) In the typical case, of course, the offeror also receives actual notification of

---

[245]   CISG Article 20 has detailed rules on the calculation of the period of time for acceptance of an offer.

[246]   CISG, art. 22.

[247]   CISG, art. 18(3), final sentence.

the acceptance indirectly such as through third-party banks or carriers.

Modification of a Contract. Separately, the CISG provides that a contract may be modified by the parties through a "mere agreement,"[248] a point emphasized by a U.S. Court of Appeals in a dispute over a settlement agreement.[249] If a contract writing permits modification only in writing, however, the contract cannot be otherwise modified, unless a party by its conduct induces the other party to act in reliance on an unwritten modification.[250]

§ 2.17 Formation___Acceptance: The Battle of the Forms

One of the most vexing of modern contract formation issues is the "battle of the forms." This "battle" arises when the respective lawyers of the buyer and the seller prepare carefully crafted forms, but the parties themselves pay little attention to the forms when they actually negotiate their contract. The parties focus instead on the business terms (price, specification and quantity of goods, performance time); it is only if and when a dispute arises that the parties pull out the forms (most often for the first time) and review them carefully. The CISG's approach to this vexing issue of the "battle of the forms" differs markedly from that of the UCC (the infamous § 2–207), as U.S. courts quite properly have recognized.[251]

To begin the battle, the CISG, although in a circuitous fashion, generally follows the traditional "mirror-image" analysis. Under CISG Article 19(1), if a reply to an offer contains "additions, limitations or other modifications" it functions not as an acceptance, but instead as a rejection and counteroffer. In the typical arrangement, this reply will be the seller's "order acknowledgement" form in response to the buyer's "purchase order" form. As a federal district court correctly has observed, in this fundamental respect the CISG is in "diametrical opposition" to the approach of UCC § 2–207.[252]

---

[248] CISG, art. 29.

[249] Valero Marketing & Supply Co. v. Greeni Oy, 242 Fed. Appx. 840, 844–845 (3rd Cir. 2007).

[250] CISG, art. 29(2). The same rules apply to a termination of a contract. *Id.*

[251] VLM Food Trading Intern., Inc. v. Illinois Trading Co., 748 F.3d 780, 786 (7th Cir. 2014) ("[T]he Convention's battle-of-the-forms provision, Article 19, is significantly different from § 2–207."); Miami Valley Paper, LLC v. Lebbing Engineering & Consulting GmbH, 2009 WL 818618, at *4 (S.D. Ohio 2009) ("There are several critical differences between the law governing contract formation under the CISG and the more familiar principles of the Uniform Commercial Code.")

[252] Roser Technologies, Inc. v. Carl Schreiber GmbH, 2013 WL 4852314, at *5 (W.D. Pa. 2013) (*quoting* Ronald A. Brand, I FUNDAMENTALS OF INTERNATIONAL BUSINESS TRANSACTIONS 75 (2013)). Under UCC § 2–207 a reply that agrees with the

Article 19(2) seems to inject some flexibility to this strict mirror image rule. It states that a reply may "constitute[ ] an acceptance"—and thus form a contract—even with additional or different terms if both (a) such terms do not "materially alter" the terms of the offer and (b) the offeror does not object "without undue delay." In such a case, the terms of the contract are those in the offer "with the modifications contained in the acceptance."[253]

What Article 19(2) gives, however, Article 19(3) takes away almost entirely. The latter defines as "material" nearly every term of noteworthy interest to the parties, including "among other things," those relating to "price, payment, quality and quantity of the goods, place and time of delivery, extent of one party's liability to the other or the settlement of disputes." In the great run of "battle of the forms" cases under the CISG, therefore, the seller's order acknowledgement form will not function as a legal acceptance of the buyer's offer. The simple reason is that this form document usually is the result of careful preparation by the seller's lawyers to protect its interests and thus will include many, and likely all, of the terms deemed material by Article 19(3). In short, in nearly all cases the seller's order acknowledgement—even if it states that it "accepts" the buyer's offer—will operate as a rejection of the offer and as a counteroffer. Pursuant to CISG Article 17, the rejection also terminates the original offer. Thus, the parties will not conclude a contract by exchanging forms, and if one party reneges on its promises before performance, no contract exists.

Nonetheless, in the vast majority of transactions involving exchanges of such forms, the parties fail to notice, or intentionally disregard, the technical conflicts between their forms and simply proceed to perform the contemplated transaction. Once the seller ships the goods and the buyer accepts and pays for them, there is little doubt—on the basis of the party autonomy principle of CISG Article 6—that the parties have formed a contract governing their transaction. But what are its terms? To put the same question in a different way, is the seller's shipment of the goods "conduct" by the seller under CISG Article 18(1) that accepts the terms in the buyer's purchase order? Or, is the buyer's acceptance of and payment for the goods "conduct" that accepts the terms in the seller's order acknowledgement form?

---

offer on the essential terms of the deal (subject, quantity, price, and delivery time) forms a contract "even if it states terms in additional to or different from those offered." For more on the approach of UCC § 2–207 *see* note 256 *infra*.

[253]   CISG, art. 19(2).

Traditional Anglo-American common law analysis would give effect to the terms of the last form sent by either party, with the reasoning that this last form (usually the seller's) would be a rejection and counteroffer and thereby terminate all prior unaccepted offers. The only offer left to accept through conduct, therefore, is this last counteroffer. This is the "last shot" principle, and, on the surface, CISG Article 19(1), together with Articles 17 and 18(3), seems to follow it. The drafting history of the CISG, however, is at best ambiguous; it shows instead that the drafters simply were unable to come to an agreement on this difficult issue and consciously left it unresolved.[254] By near universal consensus of courts and scholars, this does not, however, represent a gap in the CISG that would permit resort to domestic law.[255] Thus, the answer must be found within the structure and principles of the Convention itself.

It is worth noting that the United States and some civil law jurisdictions have developed more sophisticated methods of dealing with the "battle of the forms" than the "mirror-image" rule followed by the "last shot" principle—interestingly, in the United States by statute (UCC § 2–207) and in some civil code countries by judicial innovation. These approaches rely on different mechanisms, but commonly seek to rely on a deeper assessment of actual party intent in the place of the traditional inflexible rules.[256] Despite the superficial clarity of CISG Articles 18 and 19, it thus is not surprising that courts and scholars have shown great resistance to going back to 19th century contract principles.

---

[254] *See* Van Alstine, *Dynamic Treaty Interpretation, supra* note 173, at 771, note 348 (citing the relevant drafting history of the Convention).

[255] *See* Schroeter, art. 19, para. 33, in Schlechtriem & Schwenzer, *supra* note 30; Van Alstine, *Consensus, supra* note 238, at 84–92.

[256] Under UCC § 2–207 differences (even material ones) between the parties' forms do not preclude contract formation, unless the reply is "expressly" made conditional on the applicability of its terms. Without such a clause, the material additional terms in the reply (often the seller's acknowledgment form) drop out under UCC § 2–207(2). This in effect is a "first shot" rule, which rewards the initiator of the transaction (the first offeror) by giving it the terms of its offer. In the case of actual conflicts, however, the majority view holds that both offeror and offeree terms are "knocked out" of the contract. Where, in contrast, the reply is "expressly" conditional on the applicability of its terms, subsequent performance by the parties that recognizes the existence of a contract will form a contract, but only on the terms on which offer and acceptance forms agree (an "overlap" rule). *See* § 2–207(3).

The German Civil Code, as a formal matter, adopts a "mirror image" approach. *See* Art. 150(2). German courts nonetheless have focused on a fundamental norm of "good faith" (*"Treu und Glauben," see* Art. 242) to craft a more flexible solution. Under this view, the non-negotiated standard forms of the parties do not become part of the contract, especially if one or both has an express term that insists on the application of all of its own terms. For a review of this approach of German courts see Van Alstine, *Consensus, supra* note 238, at 97–100.

Nonetheless, the reflexive initial response under the CISG supported the traditional "last shot" approach. In this view, again, the ultimate performance by the parties was viewed as an expression of mutual assent to the *entirety* of whichever form happened to be sent last.[257] The more recent and growing trend of opinion among courts and scholars, however, has relied instead on the flexible interpretive rules of the Convention (*see* § 2.11 above) and the core principle of party autonomy (*see* § 2.5 above) to resolve this issue.[258]

The fundamental principle of party autonomy in CISG Article 6 makes clear that the parties may form a contract without regard to the formal offer–acceptance scheme. The more modern view on the battle of the forms under the CISG takes account of the fact that the parties rarely focus on, or even read, the standard business terms they commonly exchange as a matter of habit. Thus, the parties' performance of their transaction most often merely reflects an agreement on the existence of a contract—and decidedly not on the application of the form that happened to be last exchanged. In the words of CISG Article 8(1), each party "could not have been unaware" of the actual intent of the other to rely on its own standard terms. But if both nonetheless perform the essential aspects of their transaction, they obviously have agreed at least on the existence of a contract between them. As a result, their contract consists only of the terms on which their forms are in agreement (and of course any other agreed terms), together with the background rules of the Convention. All other proposed terms do not become part of the contract—a so-called "knock-out" rule (or better, "overlap" rule)—in absence of a clear agreement on those terms.[259] The German Federal Court of Justice (its highest civil court) in the so-called Powdered Milk case in fact described this modern approach as "most likely the prevailing view."[260]

United States courts, following on the *Filanto* case described in § 2.16 above, have agreed with this essential focus on the parties'

---

[257] *See, e.g.*, Allan E. Farnsworth, *Article 19*, at 179, in COMMENTARY ON THE INTERNATIONAL SALES LAW: THE 1980 VIENNA SALES CONVENTION (C. Bianca & M. Bonell, eds., 1987); Clark Kelso, *The United Nations Convention on Contracts for the International Sale of Goods: Contract Formation and the Battle of the Forms*, 21 COLUM. J. TRANSNAT'L L. 529, 554 (1983).

[258] To be sure, some residue of the traditional view remains in court decisions. *See* Larry A. Dimatteo, *et al.*, *The Interpretive Turn in International Sales Law: An Analysis of Fifteen Years of CISG Jurisprudence*, 24 NW. J. INT'L LAW & BUS. 299 (2004) (reviewing court decisions on the issue).

[259] For a comprehensive explanation of this approach see Van Alstine, *Consensus*, *supra* note 238, at 81–102.

[260] *See* Decision of the *Bundesgerichtshof* [Federal Court of Justice] of Germany (9 January 2002), *available at* http://cisgw3.law.pace.edu/cases/020109g1.html.

actual intent. In one prominent case, the Ninth Circuit Court of Appeals held that where the parties formed an oral contract their mere performance of the transaction did not indicate assent to the terms of a document sent by one of them.[261] And again, all that is required for a contract under the CISG is an agreement on the price, quantity and description.[262] In such cases, all of the additional terms in the parties' respective forms are proposals for modifications. Since a modification requires an agreement between the parties, none of the proposed additional terms become part of the contract.[263] The courts have held that a form sent out after such an oral agreement, followed by conduct of the other party, does not show agreement to the form's terms, thus rejecting a possible application of the "last shot" rule. In *Filanto* the court likewise used prior conduct of the parties to find the existence of a contract where exchange of forms was followed by one party's silence.

The approach of foreign courts tends to be in accord. Some French and several German court decisions have held that standard business terms become part of a contract only if the other party had notice of them and "easily" could have taken notice of their contents (about which more below). Where both parties send standard business terms without a formal agreement on either, these recent courts have applied what is in effect an "overlap" rule, under which the boilerplate provisions in the parties' respective standard business terms only become part of the contract to the extent they are in agreement. In the German Federal Court of Justice decision mentioned above, for example, a seller of dairy products received an oral order from a buyer. The seller responded with a written acceptance along with standard business terms that limited the buyer's warranty rights. The court found, however, that in battle of the forms cases under the CISG the parties respective standard business terms "become part of the contract only to the extent that they do not conflict."[264] Thus, although the buyer performed the transaction after receipt of the seller's reply, the seller's limitation on warranty claims did not become part of the contract.

All of these more recent authorities seem to agree that even though CISG Article 19(1) adopts the mirror-image rule, the last-shot doctrine should not be resurrected. A careful examination of the core principles of the CISG reveals that more sophisticated

---

[261] Chateau des Charmes Wines Ltd. v. Sabate USA Inc., 328 F.3d 528, 531 (9th Cir. 2003); Solae, LLC v. Hershey Can. Inc., 557 F. Supp. 2d 452, 457–458 (D. Del. 2008) (same).

[262] *See* §§ 2.14, 2.16.

[263] *See also* CISG, art. 29(1) (requiring an "agreement" to modify a contract).

[264] *See* Decision of *Bundesgerichtshof* [Federal Court of Justice] of Germany (January 9, 2002), *available at* http://cisgw3.law.pace.edu/cases/020109g1.html.

analytical tools are available to resolve the battle of the forms under the CISG, and that application of these tools yields results more faithful to the parties' actual shared intent as required by CISG Article 8.

Business enterprises nonetheless often believe they can "win" the battle of the forms by inserting a clause in their standard business terms to the effect that "our terms and conditions prevail over all others and we reject any terms proposed by [buyer/seller]." But if the other side does the same, and the parties nonetheless perform the transaction, they obviously have not insisted on their respective terms as a condition to contract formation. As the German Federal Court of Justice case demonstrates—where, incidentally, the seller's form included just such a clause—actual, express agreement is the only way to ensure application of one's desired contract terms.

Standard Business Terms. An issue closely related to, but conceptually distinct from, the battle of the forms is the effectiveness of the standard business terms that the parties routinely exchange but rarely discuss. These are the set of terms prepared by the parties' respective lawyers for repeat use without further negotiation. Following a trend precipitated again by the German Federal Court of Justice (see above), U.S. courts have recognized the propriety of treating such pre-formulated terms differently in the standard contract formation process.

In specific, a growing chorus of federal courts now holds that a party must have either actual knowledge of, or at least reasonable notice of the attempted inclusion of, standard business terms proposed by the other party.[265] Indeed, one federal district court—in an impressive recognition of the required persuasive authority of foreign decisions under CISG Article 7(1), see § 2.10 above)—quoted with approval the following observation of the German Federal Court of Justice regarding the effectiveness of standard business terms:

> [I]t is easily possible to attach to his offer the general terms and conditions, which generally favor him. It would, therefore, contradict the principle of good faith in international trade as well as the general obligations of cooperation and information of the parties to impose on the other party an obligation to inquire concerning the

---

[265] *See, e.g.,* Allied Dynamics Corp. v. Kennametal, Inc., 2014 WL 3845244, at *10 (E.D.N.Y. 2014); Roser Technologies, Inc. v. Carl Schreiber GmbH, 2013 WL 4852314, at *6 (W.D. Pa. 2013); CSS Antenna, Inc. v. Amphenol-Tuchel Elecs., GmbH, 764 F. Supp. 2d 745, 754 (D. Md. 2011); Tyco Valves & Controls Distribution GmbH v. Tippins, Inc., 2006 WL 2924814, at *5 (W.D. Pa. 2006).

clauses that have not been transmitted and to burden him with the risks and disadvantages of the unknown general terms and conditions of the other party.[266]

At a minimum, therefore, a party must have "reasonable notice" of the intent to include standard business terms in order for those terms to be an effective part of any offer or purported acceptance. Even an express reference will not suffice if the party has not actually received the terms.[267] This approach is fully consistent with CISG Article 8's primary reliance on the actual intent over inflexible notions of objective intent as well as "the principle of good faith in international trade."

In summary, and in comparison to the UCC, the CISG generally follows the traditional offer-acceptance scheme. But it may reduce the flexibility of the parties regarding some open price transactions, and it expands the protection of the offeree regarding revocation of an outstanding offer. On the battle of the forms, the courts have generally avoided the traditional "last shot" principle. Instead, based on a growing consensus among courts and scholars, the more modern approach has looked beyond the superficial wording of CISG Article 19 and focused on deeper principles in the Convention, especially the importance of the actual intent of the parties, to follow a "knock-out rule" that favors the standard terms of neither buyer nor seller.

§ 2.18 The Substantive Rights and Obligations of the Parties__In General

Part III of the CISG sets forth the basic performance obligations of the seller and the buyer. It is itself divided into four Chapters:

General Provisions (Chapter I);

Obligations of the Seller (Chapter II);

---

[266] Roser Technologies, Inc. v. Carl Schreiber GmbH, 2013 WL 4852314, at *6 (W.D. Pa. 2013) (*quoting* Decision of the German Federal Supreme Court, 2001 BGHZ No. 149 (Oct. 31, 2001)).

[267] Indeed, in Roser Technologies one party's declarations included an express reference to its standard business terms available at its own website. The court nonetheless held that the terms were not effective. Quoting the Austrian Supreme Court, the court held that "standard terms, in order to be applicable to a contract, must be included in the proposal of the party relying on them as intended to govern the contract in a way that the other party under the given circumstances knew or could not have been reasonably unaware of this intent." *Id.*, at *8 (*quoting Oberster Gerichtshof* of Austria (Dec. 17, 2003), *available at* http://cisgw3.law.pace.edu/cases/031217a3.html.).

Obligations of the Buyer (Chapter III); and

Passing of Risk (Chapter IV).

Sections 2.19 through 2.22 below examine the seller's performance obligations as set forth in Chapter II (Articles 30–50). The following three Sections (§§ 2.23 through and 2.26) examine the buyer's—substantially less complicated—performance obligations as set forth in Chapter III (Articles 53–65). Section 2.27 then analyzes the seller's rights to cure defects in its performance. Throughout, we will analyze the General Provisions as set forth in Chapter I that define fundamental principles relevant to the obligations of both parties. Finally, § 2.28 reviews the CISG's rules on the allocation of the risk of loss or damage to the goods as set forth in Chapter IV (Articles 66–70).

Notices and Other Communications. But one general matter is worthy of special emphasis in advance. A variety of provisions in Part III on substantive rights and obligations allow or require a notice, request, or other communication by one party to the other. Article 27 in the General Provisions of Part III addresses the corresponding requirements. That Article requires that, in addition to any expressly stated rules, any such communication be made "by means appropriate in the circumstances." But it then provides valuable protection for the sender: If the requirements are satisfied, any delay or error in the transmission or even a complete failure to arrive "does not deprive that party of the right to rely on the communication." Thus, a notice, request, or other communication may be effective even if the addressee never receives it.

§ 2.19 Seller's Performance Obligations

CISG Article 30 sets forth two fundamental obligations of the seller: First, "it must deliver the goods [and] hand over any documents related to them" (*see* § 2.20 below). But this obligation comes with the important qualifier that the seller must perform "as required by the contract and this Convention." Thus, subsequent provisions establish further obligations of the seller regarding the quantity, description, and quality of the goods (*see* § 2.22 below).[268] Second, Article 30 obligates the seller to "transfer the property in the goods" (the civil law term for title to the goods) (*see* § 2.22 below). Subsequent provisions then make clear that this includes an obligation to deliver goods free of all claims of third parties.[269]

Domestic law may influence the content of some of these obligations, because under Article 4(b) the Convention "is not

---

[268] CISG, arts. 35–40.
[269] CISG, arts. 41–42.

concerned with" the effect of the contract on "the property in the goods sold."[270] Domestic law, therefore, determines whether "the property" passes from the seller to the buyer at the "conclusion" (formation) of the contract, upon delivery, or at some other time;[271] whether a certificate of title is required;[272] and whether the seller may retain title as security for the purchase price or other debts.[273]

§ 2.20 Seller's Performance Obligations___ Delivery of the Goods

"Delivery" under the CISG is a limited concept, and relates only to transfer of possession of or control over the goods. The CISG's drafters did not attempt to consolidate all incidents of sale— physical delivery, passing of risk of loss, passing of title, liability for the price, and ability to obtain specific performance, etc.—into a single concept or make them turn on a single event, as has been done in some sales statutes.[274] Instead, they generally followed a format—in structure similar to, but in substance different from, that in the UCC—under which separate provisions address the different incidents of the delivery of the goods from the seller to the buyer.

Place of Delivery. As to the place of delivery, the CISG recognizes four distinct types of delivery terms: (1) delivery contracts, under which the seller must deliver the goods at a specified distant place; (2) shipment contracts, which "involve carriage of the goods," but do not require delivery at any particular distant place; (3) sales contracts where the goods are at a known location and are not expected to be transported; and (4) sales contracts without a specified place of delivery and where goods are not expected to be transported. Each of these options is examined below.

(1) In a delivery contract, the seller may be obligated to deliver the goods at the buyer's place, or at a sub-buyer's place, or at any other specified distant location. But, strangely, the CISG addresses this most common option only in the nature of a default in the event the parties have not agreed on one of the other three arrangements discussed below. In specific, CISG Article 31 provides express rules only for those contracts under which the seller "is not bound to deliver the goods at any other particular place." Thus, the

---

[270] *See* § 2.8 *supra.*

[271] For domestic law in the United States, see UCC §§ 2–401 to 2–403.

[272] For domestic law in the United States, see UCC §§ 2–319 to 2–323.

[273] For domestic law in the United States, see UCC §§ 2–507, 2–703 and 1–201(b)(35).

[274] *See* U.K. Sale of Goods Act 1979, §§ 17–20.

CISG has no specific rules describing the seller's duties in delivery contracts, and as a result the identification of the seller's specific delivery obligations is left to interpretation of the contract terms. A common practice in international sales transactions is to define such obligations through commercial terms such as "FOB," "DAP," or "DAT."[275] In any event, the goods must be conforming when delivered,[276] not merely when shipped.

(2) In a shipment contract, the seller has no obligation to deliver the goods at any particular place, but it is clear that transportation of the goods by an independent third party carrier is involved. Subject (as always) to the parties' contractual agreements, a shipment contract may require the seller to take more than one action to accomplish its obligation of "delivery." First, Article 31 requires that the seller transfer ("hand over") the goods to a carrier. But unlike some other legal systems, the seller's obligation here is merely to hand over the goods "to the first carrier," which may be only a local trucking company in a chain of carriers necessary for final delivery at a distant location.[277] To "hand over" the goods means that the seller must actually deliver possession to the carrier.[278] In contrast to the UCC,[279] in such a case the CISG does not obligate the seller to arrange for the carriage of the goods to the final foreign destination. Commercial terms may impose such a duty,[280] but the Convention does not. Second, Article 32 provides that if the goods are not "clearly identified to the contract" by the shipping documents or by their own markings, the seller must "give notice to the buyer of the consignment specifying the goods."[281] Third, if the seller *is* bound to arrange for carriage of the goods, it must make such carriage contracts as are "appropriate in the circumstances" and according to the "usual terms" for such transportation.[282] Finally, depending upon the contract's terms, the seller must either "effect insurance" coverage of the goods during transit or, at the buyer's request, give the buyer the information necessary to effect insurance.[283]

---

[275] For more detail on these commercial terms, see Chapter 3.

[276] *Cf.* CISG, arts. 36 (stating that the goods must be conforming when the risk of loss passes) and 69 (stating that the risk of loss passes when the buyer takes over the goods or wrongfully fails to do so). For more on risk of loss, see § 2.28 *infra*.

[277] CISG, art. 31(a).

[278] *See* CISG DIGEST 2012, *supra* note 36, art. 31, para. 7.

[279] *See* UCC § 2–504(a).

[280] For more detail see Chapter 3.

[281] CISG, art. 32(1).

[282] CISG, art. 32(2).

[283] CISG, art. 32(3).

(3) The CISG has different rules for transactions where carriage of the goods is not "involved." First, absent a contrary agreement, if the parties knew at the time of the conclusion of the contract where the goods were or were to be produced, the buyer is expected to pick them up at that location.[284] The seller's obligation then is merely to put the goods "at the buyer's disposal" at that location.[285] This means that "the seller has done that which is necessary for the buyer to be able to take possession."[286] The Convention is not clear on whether this requires notification to the buyer, but it would require notification to any third party bailees to allow the buyer to take possession.

(4) Second, in all other cases where transportation is not involved, delivery is required only at the seller's place of business.[287] Again, the seller's obligation in such a case is merely to put the goods "at the buyer's disposal" at that place.[288]

Where the delivery of the goods is to be accomplished by tender or delivery of documents (typically, a bill of lading), Article 34 requires only that the seller adhere to the terms of the contract. The second and third sentences of Article 34 also establish the principle that a seller that delivers defective documents early may cure the defects until the date due for delivery of the documents under the contract, provided that this does not cause the buyer "unreasonable inconvenience or unreasonable expense." Of course, in such a case the buyer nonetheless will retain a right to any damages caused by the original defective delivery and the cure.

Time of Delivery. CISG Article 33 defines the time requirements for the seller's performance. Not surprisingly, the primary focus is on the contract terms: the seller must deliver the goods or any documents covering them as follows: (a) if the date is fixed by or determinable from the contract, on that date; (b) if a period of time is fixed by or determinable from the contract, within that period, unless the circumstances indicate that the buyer has a power to choose a date; and (c) in all other cases, within a "reasonable time."[289] "Reasonable time" is not defined, and will depend on the surrounding circumstances and trade usage, but at least it should preclude a demand for immediate delivery.

---

[284]   CISG, art. 31(b).

[285]   CISG, art. 31(a), (b).

[286]   *See* CISG DIGEST 2012, *supra* note 36, art. 31, para. 9 (*quoting* the UNCITRAL Secretariat's commentary on the CISG).

[287]   CISG, art. 31(c).

[288]   CISG, art. 31(b), (c).

[289]   CISG, art. 33(a)–(c).

The Convention has no express provisions concerning the seller's duties regarding export and import licenses and taxes, and thus leaves the determination of these incidents of delivery to the contract terms, or usage. Where these issues are not covered by the contract terms or usage, the nature of the seller's delivery obligation often will provide the needed guidance. Thus, if the seller is not obligated to arrange transportation, these responsibilities should fall to the buyer; if, in contrast, the seller is obligated to deliver at a particular destination *inside* the buyer's country, the seller generally will have the responsibility to obtain export and import licenses. The issue becomes complicated where delivery is to be made only at a port in the buyer's country; in such a case, the *buyer's* separate obligation to perform all reasonable acts to "enable the seller to make delivery" generally will include the import (but not export) license.[290] In any event, it is quite common in international transactions for the parties to agree on an incorporation of an international "commercial term" ("FOB," "CIF," etc.), and in particular the so-called Incoterms©, which expressly address export and import licenses and related issues.[291]

§ 2.21 Seller's Performance Obligations__Quality of the Goods

Under the CISG, the seller's obligation is to deliver goods of the quantity, quality, description, and packaging required by the contract.[292] In determining whether the quality of the goods conforms to the contract, the Convention eschews such separate and independent doctrines as "warranty" and "strict product liability" from Anglo-American common law, as well as "fault" or "negligence" from the civil law. Instead, the CISG focuses on the simpler concept that the seller is obligated to deliver the goods as "required by" the contract.[293] It then defines certain default obligations of the seller and creates certain related presumptions.[294] This approach produces results that are comparable to the "warranty" structure of the UCC, but without the divisions between express and implied warranties.[295] This facial similarity should not, however, lead courts

---

[290]   *See* § 2.25 *infra* and in specific CISG, art. 60 (requiring buyer to "do[ ] all the acts which could reasonably be expected of him in order to enable the seller to make delivery"). *See also* CISG DIGEST 2012, *supra* note 36, art. 60, para. 2 (relating to import licenses).

[291]   For more detail on these commercial terms, see Chapter 3.

[292]   CISG, art. 35.

[293]   CISG, art. 35(1).

[294]   CISG, art. 35(2).

[295]   The UCC creates a series of "warranties" from seller to buyer. Some warranties are "express" (*see* UCC § 2–313), others are "implied" (*see* UCC §§ 2–314 and 2–315). The primary reason for the differentiation under the UCC is that

to apply idiosyncratic UCC notions, precedents, and practices to transactions governed by the CISG.[296] Thankfully, U.S. courts have recognized this important point. As one federal district court has observed, where the CISG governs a transaction all warranty claims under the UCC "are preempted and subsumed by the CISG."[297]

The basic obligation of the seller is that the goods must conform to the contract requirements regarding "quantity, quality and description" as well as in their packaging.[298] An early Federal Court of Appeals decision applying the CISG thus held that failure of the goods to comply with affirmative contractual performance standards (contractual specifications regarding cooling capacity and power consumption) constituted a breach.[299] Any trade usage recognized by the CISG also may add context for and content to the contractual description.[300]

To this, the CISG adds certain presumptions that will apply unless the seller secures a contractual limitation. First, the goods must be fit for "the purposes for which goods of the same description would ordinarily be used"[301] and be "contained or packaged in a manner usual for such goods."[302] The CISG imposes no conditions on this obligation of the seller relating to fitness for ordinary use. And because the CISG generally applies only to commercial contracts, there is no need for the UCC limitation to "merchant" sellers.[303]

Nonetheless, this leaves one important unresolved issue— whether the "ordinary use" is defined by the seller's location or the buyer's location, if the "ordinary use" in the two is different. Although some scholars support a contrary position, an early decision of the German Federal Court of Justice declared the now prevailing view that the seller generally is not obligated to deliver goods that conform to public laws and regulations enforced at the buyer's place of business, subject to three important exceptions: (1)

"implied" warranties can be "disclaimed" under UCC § 2–316(2), while "express" warranties generally cannot.

[296] *See* the discussion of the interpretive rules of the CISG, especially in Article 7(1), in § 2.10 *supra*.

[297] Electrocraft Arkansas, Inc. v. Super Electric Motors, Ltd. 2009 WL 5181854 at *4 (E.D. Ark. 2009).

[298] CISG, art. 35(1). Compare UCC § 2–313.

[299] Delchi Carrier S.p.A. v. Rotorex Corp., 71 F.3d 1024 (2d Cir. 1995).

[300] CISG, art. 9(2). *See also* § 2.11 *supra*.

[301] CISG, art. 35(2)(a). Compare UCC § 2–314(2)(c).

[302] CISG, art. 35(2)(d). Compare UCC § 2–314(2)(e).

[303] Compare UCC § 2–314(1).

if the public laws and regulations of the buyer's state are identical to those enforced in the seller's state; (2) if the buyer informed the seller about those regulations; or (3) if, due to "special circumstances," the seller knew or should have known about the regulations in the buyer's state.[304] The concept of "special circumstances" includes the seller having a branch office in the buyer's state. A U.S. federal court subsequently endorsed this approach,[305] as have courts of other jurisdictions.[306] Most notable, the Austrian Supreme Court came to the same conclusion after comprehensively analyzing foreign judicial opinions and scholarly commentary on this important aspect of Article 35(2).[307] One might also add that the seller likewise should be liable where a use is "ordinary" in the international trade of the goods involved. To secure a broader obligation, the buyer must conclude an express contractual agreement under Article 35(1) or satisfy the criteria for fitness for a "particular purpose" (see immediately below).

Second, the goods must be fit for any particular use made known to the seller at or before contract formation.[308] From its structure, this provision prescribes an interesting arrangement for the burden of proof. First, it will arise only if the buyer can prove that its "particular purpose" was "expressly or impliedly" made known to the seller at or before "the time of the conclusion of the contract." But if the buyer satisfies these factual predicates, the burden of proof switches to the seller.[309] That is, the seller will not be liable if it can prove either that the buyer in fact did not rely or that it was unreasonable for the buyer to rely on the seller's skill and judgment (which switches the burden of proof on this element as compared to the UCC[310]). The CISG states no express requirement that the buyer inform the seller of the buyer's reliance; the seller need only know of the buyer's particular purpose. More important, there is no requirement that the buyer inform the seller of any of the difficulties involved in designating or designing goods

---

[304]   *See* CLOUT Case No. 123, *Bundesgerichtshof* [Federal Court of Justice] of Germany (8 March 1995).

[305]   Medical Marketing Int'l, Inc. v. Internazionale Medico Scientifica, S.R.L., 1999 WL 311945 (E.D. La. 1999).

[306]   *See* CISG DIGEST 2012, *supra* note 36, art. 35, para. 9 (citing cases).

[307]   *See* Oberster Gerichtshof [Supreme Court] of Austria, No. 7 Ob 302/05w, (25 January 2006), *available at* http://cisgw3.law.pace.edu/cases/060125a3.html.

[308]   CISG, art. 35(2)(b). Compare UCC § 2–315.

[309]   Although courts have not agreed on the details, this allocation of the burden of proof arises from the structure of the rule in Article 35(2)(b): The obligation applies if the buyer proves the factual predicates, "except" if one of the latter two facts exists. If the seller wishes to rely on these latter exceptions, it must prove that one of them exists. *See* CISG DIGEST 2012, *supra* note 36, art. 35, para. 17 (citing cases).

[310]   *See* UCC § 2–315.

to accomplish the particular use. Courts may address abuse of this issue through a careful application of the "reasonable reliance" criterion.

Finally, the goods must conform to any goods the seller "has held out to the buyer as a sample or model."[311] This is in addition to any express contractual descriptions of the goods.[312]

Each of these obligations, however, arises out of the contract. As a result, the parties may "agree otherwise" and limit the seller's obligations concerning quality (a more flexible concept than "disclaimer of warranties" under the UCC[313]). And as a federal Court of Appeals correctly held in *Chicago Prime Packers, Inc. v. Northam Food Trading Co.*,[314] the buyer has the burden to prove any such a nonconformity (although some foreign courts unfortunately have left some ambiguity on the point[315]). In any event, the buyer need not prove the exact nature of the defect, only that the goods did not conform to contractual requirements.[316]

The obligations of the seller under Article 35(2) relating to non-conformities of quality do not apply where the buyer knew or "could not have been unaware" of a relevant nonconformity at the time the contract was "concluded."[317] Thus, knowledge gained at the time of delivery or inspection of the goods will not diminish the seller's general obligations. Moreover, courts have held that the seller may not rely on this exemption where, although the buyer has general knowledge of a defect or state of quality in the goods, the seller knows of specific facts not disclosed to the buyer.[318]

The relevant time for assessment of a nonconformity of the goods is "when the risk [of loss] passes to the buyer"[319]—a concept explored in more detail below.[320] This is true even if the fact of the nonconformity at the time the risk of loss passes is discovered

---

[311]   CISG, art. 35(2)(c). For the approach of the UCC, see § 2–313(1)(c) (which categorizes this obligation as an "express warranty").

[312]   *See* Schwenzer, art. 35, para. 26, in Schlechtriem & Schwenzer, *supra* note 30.

[313]   Compare UCC § 2–316(2).

[314]   408 F.3d 894 (7th Cir. 2005). *See also* CISG DIGEST 2012, *supra* note 36, art. 4, para. 7; Schwenzer, art. 35, para. 54, in Schlechtriem & Schwenzer, *supra* note 30.

[315]   *See* CISG DIGEST 2012, *supra* note 36, art. 35, para. 17.

[316]   Schmitz-Werke GmbH & Co. v. Rockland Indus., Inc., 37 Fed. Appx. 687 (4th Cir. 2002).

[317]   CISG, art. 35(3).

[318]   *See* CISG DIGEST 2012, *supra* note 36, art. 35, para. 16. *See also* Schwenzer, art. 35, para. 34, in Schlechtriem & Schwenzer, *supra* note 30.

[319]   CISG, art. 36(1).

[320]   *See* § 2.28 *infra*.

later.[321] The buyer must prove, however, that the defect actually was present at that point (typically, at delivery) and was not caused by third parties or the buyer's own use or lack of oversight of the goods. Nonetheless, the seller will be liable if defects arose later (such as in transit) due to inadequate packaging in violation of the seller's obligations under Article 35.[322] Pursuant to CISG Article 37, however, the seller may remedy any deficiencies in quantity, quality, and the like up to the agreed delivery date, provided this would not cause the buyer unreasonable inconvenience or expense (see § 2.27 below).

The seller's liability for nonconformities may extend beyond the passing of the risk of loss. Under CISG Article 36(2) the seller is liable for any nonconformity that occurs after that point and is "due to a breach of any of his obligations." This depends of course on the specific obligations undertaken by the seller in the contract (such as care for the goods, assembly, or installation) after the formal risk of loss has passed. The rule in Article 36(2) is of particular relevance for any "guarantcc of durability" assumed by the seller. Such a guarantee is one that, "for a period of time" after delivery, the goods either "will remain fit for their ordinary purpose, or for some particular purpose" or "will retain specified qualities or characteristics."[323] In such a case, the seller is liable for any nonconformity that occurs within the specified guarantee period.[324]

The CISG also imposes certain inspection and notice obligations on the buyer—explored in more detail below[325]—in order to preserve its rights relating to nonconforming goods. But, in turn, the seller loses the right to rely on the buyer's failure to fulfill these obligations if the seller knows of a specific nonconformity in advance. CISG Article 40 in effect imposes on the seller an obligation of disclosure regarding any facts relating to a nonconformity "of which he knew or could not have been unaware." If in such a case the seller does not disclose the relevant facts, then it may not rely on the buyer's failure to inspect the goods promptly or to notify the seller of any discovered defects (again, as discussed in more detail below).[326] Thus, even though the buyer may lose its right to rely on a nonconformity due its own failure to inspect or

---

[321]   CISG, art. 36(1).

[322]   See CISG DIGEST 2012, supra note 36, art. 36, para. 6 (citing cases).

[323]   CISG, art. 36(2).

[324]   Id. See also Schwenzer, art. 36, para. 7, in Schlechtriem & Schwenzer, supra note 30 (examining "guarantees of durability" as contemplated by Article 36(2)).

[325]   See § 2.26 infra.

[326]   See CISG, arts. 38 and 39. For more on these obligations of the buyer see § 2.26 infra.

notify, the right revives if the seller, in turn, knew of the nonconformity and did not notify the buyer of it.[327]

Exclusion of Quality Obligations. May the seller exclude the Article 35 obligations concerning the quality of the goods by terms in the parties' contract—and, if so, how? As a basic rule, CISG Article 6 states that the parties may, by agreement, derogate from *any* provision of the Convention. And Article 35 expressly affirms this point with the specific reference to the seller's obligations concerning the conformity of the goods with the statement that such obligations do not apply "where the parties have agreed otherwise."[328] Nonetheless, it is also clear that the standard formulation under the UCC—"disclaimer of implied warranties"[329]—will be inapposite, because the CISG describes the seller's obligations neither as "warranties" nor as "implied." Careful international sellers will need to employ different verbal formulations, ones that deal directly with the description of the goods and their expected use as defined in the CISG (not the UCC).

If a contract nonetheless is framed in the usual language for contracts subject to the UCC, but it is actually governed by the CISG, a court would have two possible analytical approaches. One would arise from the concept that the term "warranties" has little meaning in the CISG context, and the drafters deliberately avoided using it, because the term has many different meanings in different legal regimes. Thus, use of such language by a seller should not be allowed to destroy the obligations imposed by the express terms of the CISG. The other approach would allow a court to inquire into the intent of the parties (under the CISG's interpretive rules in Article 8) to determine what they meant with their contractual terms of "warranty," "express" and "implied"—*i.e.*, whether they were familiar with the United States domestic legal approach in this area. If so, CISG Article 8(1) would allow the court to interpret the language according to the parties' intentions.[330]

One continuing issue of controversy in this regard is the extent to which local law regulating disclaimers might apply for international contracts governed by the CISG. Such local law covers a spectrum, from prohibitions on "unconscionable" disclaimers (especially in printed standard terms) to the special linguistic and

---

[327]   CISG, art. 40.

[328]   CISG, art. 35(2).

[329]   *See* UCC § 2–316.

[330]   This would include, importantly, "all relevant circumstances" of the case, including the parties' prior dealings and negotiations. *See* § 2.11 *supra* and in particular MCC-Marble Ceramic Center, Inc. v. Ceramica Nuova d'Agostino, S.p.A., 144 F.3d 1384 (11th Cir. 1998).

similar requirements set out in the UCC.[331] Today, however, there seems to be agreement that the former raises a question of "validity", which CISG Article 4(a) excludes from the scope of the Convention, and leaves to applicable domestic law.[332] As argued above,[333] the latter, in contrast, should not raise questions of "validity" as contemplated by CISG Article 4(a). As a result, the UCC's specific statutory requirements for an exclusion of warranties should not apply for CISG contracts. The distinction should depend upon whether the local public policy prohibits conduct completely, as opposed to allowing the parties to limit the seller's obligations within certain specified conditions. Accordingly, the courts should draw a distinction between general contract defenses (such as unconscionability and fraud) and the specific UCC provisions that set requirements for exclusion of the express or implied warranties created by the UCC itself (*e.g.*, that the disclaimer be "conspicuous" or use particular words such "merchantability").

§ 2.22 Seller's Performance Obligations__ Property Issues

As noted above, CISG Article 4(b) states that the Convention "is not concerned with" the effect of the contract on "property in" (title to) the goods sold.[334] Nonetheless, the CISG imposes obligations on the seller that the goods be free of any claims concerning title and claims founded in infringement of intellectual property rights.[335] In specific, the seller generally is obligated to deliver goods "free from any right or claim of a third party."[336] Thus, the issue of who actually has valid title to particular goods is outside the scope of the Convention, but the seller's obligation to deliver what it has promised, including sufficiently clear title to the goods, is within the scope of the Convention. In other words, the CISG creates and defines the obligation, but otherwise-applicable domestic law determines whether the seller has fulfilled it.[337]

A subtler issue is whether the seller is required to convey only a valid title to the goods, or also title that will not be subject to

---

[331]   *See* UCC § 2–316.

[332]   *See* § 2.8 *supra.*

[333]   *See* text accompanying notes 155–157 in § 2.8 *supra.*

[334]   *See* § 2.8, *supra.*

[335]   CISG, arts. 41, 42.

[336]   CISG, art. 41. *Compare* UCC § 2–312.

[337]   *See* CISG DIGEST 2012, *supra* note 36, art. 30, para. 4 ("Whether the property in the goods has in fact been transferred to the buyer is not a question governed by the Convention; it must be determined by reference to the law designated by the rules of private international law of the forum.").

third-party claims at all. The UCC in the United States generally requires that the seller provide a warranty of "quiet possession."[338] The legal issue is whether the Convention language should be interpreted to require that the seller convey title that is free from all claims, or only title that is free from valid claims. The language in the English version is not clear, and the debates and drafting history suggest conflicting interpretations. Nonetheless, the language in the French and Spanish versions suggests that the goods are to be free from all claims. Some scholars have argued that the seller's obligation is not breached by third-party claims that are frivolous on their face (a notion that aligns somewhat with the general approach under the UCC).[339] The prevailing view, however, holds that the seller is obligated to protect the buyer even from spurious claims and if such arise, the seller must reimburse the buyer the costs of defense.[340] The parties may derogate from the terms of these provisions of the CISG by agreement, but the buyer's knowledge that the goods are subject to a bailee's lien does not necessarily imply such an agreement. Instead, buyer may expect the seller to discharge the lien before tender of delivery. This rule does not apply, however, if the buyer agreed to take the goods subject to the right or claim.[341]

In addition to good title, seller is obligated to deliver the goods free from patent, trademark, and copyright claims assertable under the law of the buyer's "place of business" or the place where both parties expect the goods to be used or resold.[342] This obligation is, however, subject to multiple qualifications. First, the seller's obligations arise only with respect to claims of which the seller "knew or could not have been unaware."[343] Second, the seller has no obligation with respect to intellectual property rights or claims of which the buyer "knew or could not have been unaware" when the contract was formed.[344] Third, the seller is not liable for claims that arise out of its use of technical drawings, designs or other specifications furnished by the buyer, if the seller's action is in "compliance with" the buyer's specifications.[345] It is clear that this provision applies when the seller is following specifications required

---

[338] See UCC § 2–312, and especially Comment 1.

[339] See, e.g., Pacific Sunwear of California, Inc. v. Olaes Enterprises, Inc., 84 Cal. Rptr. 3d 182 (2008) (holding that the seller's obligation in UCC § 2–312(3) does not extend to a "frivolous claim," one that is "totally and completely without merit").

[340] See Honnold/Flechtner, supra note 155, Article 41, § 266; Schwenzer, art. 41, para. 11, in Schlechtriem & Schwenzer, supra note 30.

[341] CISG, art. 41.

[342] CISG, art. 42.

[343] CISG, art. 42(1).

[344] CISG, art. 42(2)(a).

[345] CISG, art. 42(2)(b).

by the contract, but its application is not clear when the seller is merely following "suggestions" of the buyer as to how best to meet more general contract provisions. Fourth, the seller is excused from these obligations if the buyer does not give timely notice of breach[346]—unless the seller actually "knew" of the claim and "the nature of it" in the first place.[347]

With all these qualifications on the seller's obligation regarding intellectual property rights, does the mere assertion of an intellectual property infringement claim create a violation of the seller's title obligations? In order to have a violation, the buyer must show that "seller knew or could not have been unaware" of the third party claims. Moreover, there seems to be general agreement that the buyer bears the burden of proof that the seller had this level of knowledge.[348] And one survey of the legislative history concludes that it does not require the seller to research the trademark and copyright registries of the buyer's country, but to use due care.[349] That interpretation would preclude the absolutist view on frivolous third-party claims, because the buyer would have no strict liability claim, only a knowledge- or negligence-based claim.

A seller also might argue that mistake of law will provide an excuse, or at least that it has performed its obligations concerning intellectual property rights, if it has relied on trustworthy information from a lawyer. If it entered the transaction on the basis of such trustworthy information that the use or resale of the goods would not infringe on third-party intellectual property rights, the seller may be able to argue that it could not have "known" of the possible infringement claims.

The UCC approach to these problems is to allow the buyer, when sued by a third party claimant, to "vouch in" the seller, so as to allow the seller to defend itself directly.[350] Given the differences in local procedural rules, the CISG understandably contains no such provision. Thus, buyers that are confronted with third party claims are left to local procedural devices for protection.

§ 2.23 Buyer's Performance Obligations

In parallel with the structure for the seller, the CISG defines the buyer's principal obligations in a single provision (Article 53).

---

[346]   CISG, art. 43(1).

[347]   CISG, art. 43(2). Compare UCC § 2–312(3).

[348]   *See* CISG DIGEST 2012, *supra* note 36, art. 4, para. 7 (citing cases).

[349]   *See* Allen Shinn, *Liabilities Under Article 42 of the U.N. Convention on the International Sale of Goods*, 2 MINN. J. GLOBAL TRADE 115 (1993).

[350]   *See* UCC § 2–607(5).

That Article imposes two primary obligations on the buyer for a sales contract governed by the Convention: to pay the price, and to take delivery of the goods.[351] The following provisions then provide more detail on the payment obligation (Articles 54 through 59) and on the acceptance obligation (Article 60). Nonetheless, the CISG treats both these two principal obligations and all subsidiary ones defined in the subsequent provisions the same and applies the a single remedial scheme for all breaches of those obligations.[352]

§ 2.24 Buyer's Performance Obligations___ Payment of the Price

Of the two principal obligations of the buyer, the duty to pay the price is the more important. Of course, the buyer must pay the price "as required by the contract."[353] But on the modalities and time of payment, like nearly all other issues, the CISG also defers to the parties' agreement. Nonetheless, the Convention contains default provisions that impose on the buyer several derivative preliminary duties, which one might refer to as "enabling steps."[354] These include taking such actions as are required to enable payment[355] or enable delivery,[356] and providing specifications on "the form, measurement or other features of the goods."[357]

Time of Payment. Unless the sale contract expressly grants credit to the buyer, the sale is a cash sale, and the seller may make payment a condition of delivery of the goods or the handing over of documents controlling them.[358] Further, payment is due when the seller places the goods, or their documents of title, "at buyer's disposal" in accordance with the contract and the Convention.[359] If the sales contract involves carriage of the goods, the seller has the right to ship on terms under which the goods, or (more commonly) documents of title (*e.g.*, a negotiable bill of lading) controlling them,

---

[351] CISG, art. 53.

[352] *See* Mohs, art. 53, para. 1, in Schlechtriem & Schwenzer, *supra* note 30.

[353] CISG, art. 53. If the parties have validly concluded a contract by "fix[ing] or mak[ing] provision for determining . . . the price" (*see* § 2.14 *supra*), CISG Article 55 permits reference to "the price generally charged . . . for such goods under comparable circumstances in the trade concerned." This provision would have particular relevance when the parties actually perform a transaction without a prior price arrangement and for replacement parts. Separately, CISG Article 56 provides that an price fixed by weight of the goods "in cases of doubt" means the net weight.

[354] *See* Honnold/Flechtner, *supra* note 155, art. 54, § 323.

[355] CISG, art. 54.

[356] CISG, art. 60(a). *See also* § 2.25 below.

[357] CISG, art. 65. If the buyer fails to make such specifications, the seller may do so upon advance notice to the buyer. CISG, art. 65(1), (2).

[358] CISG, art. 58(1).

[359] *Id.*

are not released to the buyer except against payment of the purchase price—even if the parties have not agreed on any particular method of payment.[360]

Nonetheless, the buyer in general has a right to withhold payment until it has had an "opportunity to examine the goods."[361] This rule, however, creates a certain tension with the rights of a seller delivering to a geographically distant buyer. As noted immediately above, if a contract involves carriage of the goods the seller has a right to withhold delivery (whether of the goods or of documents controlling them) until the buyer pays the purchase price.[362] But as noted below, in such a case the buyer's right (and duty) to examine the goods "may be deferred until after the goods have arrived at their destination."[363] This constellation leaves the possibility of standoff between the seller's right to demand payment and the buyer's right to inspect the goods first.

CISG Article 58(3) attempts to temper the tension by providing that the buyer does not have a right to pre-payment examination of the goods if "the procedures for delivery or payment agreed by the parties are inconsistent with his having such an opportunity." But what this precisely means is subject to no small amount of ambiguity. To address the uncertainty, the parties are well-advised to address the issue in an express contractual agreement. Chapter 1 above examined the various modalities for such an agreement in modern commerce. At the ends of the spectrum, the seller may agree to deliver the goods on open credit,[364] or the buyer may agree to pay in advance.[365] A more common arrangement between remote and unfamiliar parties is a "documents against payment" (D/P) (aka "cash against documents") transaction.[366] In this arrangement, the buyer must pay against delivery of documents that control disposition of the goods, regardless of whether the goods have yet arrived, and without inspection of them.[367] This is a clear example of the exception to the buyer's general pre-payment right of inspection as contemplated by CISG Article 58(3). Traditionally, a

---

[360]   CISG, art. 58(2).

[361]   CISG, art. 58(3).

[362]   CISG, art. 58(2).

[363]   CISG, art. 38(2). *See also* § 2.26 *infra.*

[364]   *See* Chapter 1, § 1.20 (Sale on Open Account (O/A)).

[365]   *See* Chapter 1, § 1.21 (Cash in Advance (C/A)).

[366]   *See* Chapter 1, §§ 1.2–1.9.

[367]   For an examination of this issue, see CISG Advisory Council Opinion No. 11, *Issues Raised by Documents under the CISG Focusing on the Buyer's Payment Duty* (3 August 2012), *available at* http://www.cisgac.com/cisgac-opinion-no11/; Martin Davies, *Documents That Satisfy the Requirements of CISG Art. 58*, LIX Belgrade Law Review 39 (2011), *available at* http://www.cisg.law.pace.edu/cisg//biblio/davies.html.

documents against payment agreement also is implied with the use of the commercial terms CFR or CIF.[368] This traditional view should apply for CISG Article 58(3) as well,[369] although the matter is not entirely free of doubt.[370]

Place of Payment. If the buyer is to pay against "handing over" of the documents, or handing over the goods, the place of "handing over" is the place of payment. Otherwise, the seller's place of business is the place of payment, unless the contract provides otherwise.[371] Such a rule requires the buyer to "export" the funds to the seller, which is a critical issue when the buyer is from a country with a "soft" currency, or with other restrictions on the transfer of funds. The buyer's duty of payment also includes a cooperation obligation to the effect that it must take all necessary steps to enable payment to be made, including whatever formalities may be imposed by the buyer's country to obtain administrative authorization to make a payment abroad.[372] Like any other contractual obligation under the CISG, failure to take such steps may reflect a breach by the buyer even before payment is due.

§ 2.25 Buyer's Performance Obligations___ Acceptance of Delivery

Acceptance of Delivery. The buyer's second obligation is to take delivery, that is, to take physical possession of the goods from the seller at the time and place as defined by agreement or under the default rules of the CISG.[373] Article 60 refers to this as the duty to "tak[e] over the goods" (or, as applicable, the documents governing

---

[368] For a detailed examination of whether the CFR and CIF commercial terms imply a payment against documents transaction see Chapter 3, §§ 3.10 and 3.11.

[369] *See* BENJAMIN'S SALE OF GOODS, § 19–077 n.527 (M. Bridge, ed., 9th ed. 2014). The Secretariat Commentary on 1978 Draft of CISG expressly adopted this view as well. *See* Secretariat Commentary on Article 54 [draft counterpart to CISG art. 58] (providing with reference to the rule now in Article 58(3) that "the most common example is the agreement that payment of the price is due against the handing over of the documents controlling the disposition of the goods whether or not the goods have arrived. The quotation of the price on CIF terms contains such an agreement."), *available at* http://www.cisg.law.pace.edu/cisg/text/secomm/secomm-58.html.

[370] Thus, for example, one of the leading treatises on the CISG does not mention the CIF or CFR terms in its discussion of agreements that are inconsistent with the buyer's general right of pre-payment inspection under Article 58(3). *See* Mohs, art. 58, para. 35, in Schlechtriem & Schwenzer, *supra* note 30.

[371] CISG, art. 57(1). If the seller changes its place of business after contract formation, it must bear any resultant costs for the buyer. CISG, art. 57(2).

[372] CISG, art. 54.

[373] *See* CISG DIGEST 2012, *supra* note 36, art. 60, para. 6 (citing cases for the proposition that "taking over" the goods means accepting physical delivery). For the rules governing the time and place of delivery see § 2.20 *supra*.

the goods).[374] But the same provision goes much further. It also obligates the buyer "do[ ] all the acts which could reasonably be expected of him in order to enable the seller to make delivery."[375] In this respect, the buyer's obligation to take delivery is tied to the CISG provisions that define the seller's obligation to make delivery. Thus, the *place* where the buyer must cooperate to enable the seller's delivery will depend on the rules in Article 31; and the *time* at which the buyer must do so will depend on the rules in Article 33.[376] More generally, the broader obligation of cooperation includes a duty to make any necessary preparations to permit the seller to make delivery and may include such acts as providing for containers, arrangement of carriage (where this is not the seller's obligation), local transportation, unloading, and import licenses.[377]

This obligation also may have significance for the passing of the risk of loss when the contract contemplates shipment of the goods. In such a case, the risk of loss of or damage to the goods passes to the buyer when it fails to "take over" the goods in due time and the buyer thereby commits a breach by failing to take delivery.[378]

Taking delivery does not, however, imply acceptance of any defects; the buyer retains the right to inspect the goods, give notice of any lack of conformity, or resort to any remedies for late or improper delivery.[379] The buyer also may refuse to "tak[e] over" the goods if the seller delivers early or to the extent the seller delivers excess goods; and it is generally accepted that the buyer may reject in the event of a "fundamental breach" (*see* § 2.32 below).[380]

§ 2.26   Buyer's Performance Obligations___ Inspection and Notice of Defects

Duty of Timely Inspection. The buyer, as noted above, generally has a right to inspect the goods before payment.[381] But the CISG also imposes certain obligations on the buyer in order to preserve its rights relating to nonconformities that may exist in the goods. The first is a duty of timely inspection. Under CISG Article 38, the buyer loses the right to rely on a nonconformity if it does not inspect

---

[374]   CISG, art. 60(b).

[375]   CISG, art. 60(a).

[376]   On both issues, see § 2.20 *supra*.

[377]   *See* CISG DIGEST 2012, *supra* note 36, art. 60, para. 2.

[378]   CISG, art. 69(1). For more on the passing of the risk of loss see § 2.28 *infra*.

[379]   *See* CISG DIGEST 2012, *supra* note 36, art. 60, para. 8. *See also* § 2.36 *infra* (regarding these rights of the buyer).

[380]   *See* CISG DIGEST 2012, *supra* note 36, art. 60, para. 9.

[381]   CISG, art. 58(3).

the goods "within as short a time as is practicable in the circumstances."382 Timeliness of course will depend decisively upon the nature of the goods and similar circumstances. Thus, courts have held that a buyer fulfilled its duty by inspecting within a month, but other courts have reached the opposite conclusion where the buyer inspected two months, one month, one week, and even a few days after delivery.383 A U.S. court has found that a buyer lost its rights to rely on a nonconformity in frozen ribs when it failed to inspect them for over a month.384

Where the contract involves the carriage of goods, the buyer may defer the inspection until the goods have arrived at their destination.385 Likewise, if the seller knew or ought to have known at the conclusion of the contract that the buyer would redirect the goods in transit or redispatch them after arrival, the buyer's inspection obligation may be deferred until the ultimate arrival.386

The buyer nonetheless may have an incentive to inspect in the seller's home country (*i.e.*, at the point of the seller's shipment of the goods) because under the most commonly used commercial terms (FOB, FAS, CIF, CFR), the risk of loss in transit will pass to the buyer at the place or port of shipment.387 Numerous specialized inspection companies will, for a fee, inspect goods for a distant buyer.

Duty of Timely Notice. The buyer's second duty is to give timely notice to the seller of any nonconformities in the goods.388 This involves both timeliness and content. The buyer must notify the seller "within a reasonable time" after it "discovered or ought to have discovered" a nonconformity.389 The "ought to have discovered" option of course has direct relevance to the buyer's obligation to timely inspect the goods upon delivery as discussed immediately

---

382 CISG, art. 38(1). Compare UCC § 2–513, which gives the buyer a right to inspect the goods before it must either accept or pay for them. Even when shipment of the goods is involved, the buyer may inspect the goods after arrival and before acceptance or payment, unless otherwise agreed. UCC § 2–513(1). However, the buyer is not permitted to inspect before payment where the contract provides for payment against documents. UCC § 2–513(3).

383 *See* CISG DIGEST 2012, *supra* note 36, art. 38, paras. 16 and 17 (citing numerous cases).

384 Chicago Prime Packers, Inc. v. Northam Food Trading Co., 320 F. Supp. 2d 702, 711–14 (N.D. Ill. 2004).

385 CISG, art. 38(2).

386 CISG, art. 38(3).

387 *See* Chapter 3 and especially §§ 3.8–3.11.

388 CISG, art. 39(1).

389 As with all other notices respecting performance obligations, if a buyer chooses an appropriate means for sending a notice of a nonconformity to the seller, a delay or error in transmission does not deprive the buyer of the right to rely on the notice. *See* CISG, art. 27.

above. In contrast to the ambiguity on this point under the UCC,[390] the CISG also expressly addresses the required content of the buyer's notice: It must "specify[ ] the nature of the lack of conformity."[391]

If the buyer fails to fulfill this duty in a timely manner, it may not rely on any discovered or discoverable lack of conformity as a foundation for breach.[392] As a special protection for remote or unsophisticated parties, however, the buyer retains a right to reduce the contract price or to claim damages (but not lost profits),[393] if it has "a reasonable excuse" for the failure to give the required notice.[394] This latter provision was included in the CISG as a result of pressure from developing countries, which argued that it often is difficult for their businesses to inspect and notify promptly. In any event, the CISG contains an interesting rule requiring the buyer to give notice of a nonconformity "at the latest within a period of two years from the date on which the goods were actually handed over to the buyer."[395]

There has been more litigation over the effectiveness of notices of nonconformity than over almost any other single issue,[396] but the results usually are not surprising.[397] Several courts have attempted to set "presumptive periods" for notices of nonconformity. Unfortunately, the measuring points have differed: Some have set a presumptive period—from as short as eight days to as long as six weeks—measured as of the time of delivery (thus encompassing both the inspection period and the notice period). Others have set a presumptive period—from as little as a few days to as much as a month—measured only with reference to the duty of timely notice.

---

[390] Compare § 2–607(3)(a) (stating only that the buyer must "notify" the seller of any discovered breach).

[391] CISG, art. 39(1). For a comprehensive review of the cases examining the required content of such a notice see CISG DIGEST 2012, *supra* note 36, art. 39, paras. 16–17 (citing numerous cases).

[392] *Id.* (providing that if the buyer fails to notify the seller, it "loses the right" to rely on the lack of conformity in the goods).

[393] On these two remedies see §§ 2.37 and 2.39 *infra*.

[394] CISG, art. 44.

[395] CISG, art. 39(2).

[396] *See, e.g.*, Miami Valley Paper, LLC v. Lebbing Engineering & Consulting GmbH, 2009 WL 818618, at *7–8 (S.D. Ohio 2009); Chicago Prime Packers, Inc. v. Northam Food Trading Co., 320 F. Supp. 2d 702, 712 (N.D. Ill. 2004), *aff'd*, 2005 WL 1243344 (7th Cir. 2005); Shuttle Packaging Sys., L.L.C. v. Tsonakis, 2001 WL 34046276 (W.D. Mich. 2001).

[397] *See* CISG DIGEST 2012, *supra* note 36, art. 38, paras. 16 and 17 (citing numerous cases).

On the latter, many courts have argued for the "noble month" as a presumptive period of notice under normal circumstances.[398]

As with inspections, most often the issue of timeliness will turn on the specific facts of each case, but especially on the nature of the goods and the difficulty of discovering defects.[399] One U.S. court thus indicated that, for a complicated piece of machinery, notice "within a matter of weeks" was not practicable.[400] Another held, however, that a one-year delay in giving notice of a lack of conformity "plainly was unreasonable."[401] In any event, courts in the United States commonly have held that issues of the timeliness of notice under CISG Article 39 are so intensely factual as to preclude resolution by summary judgment.[402]

As noted above,[403] however, the seller may not rely on the failure of the buyer to give a timely notice if the relevant lack of conformity relates to facts already known to the seller or of which it "could not have been unaware" and did not disclose to the buyer.[404] Moreover, a seller may be deemed to have waived (as a "general principle" of the Convention[405]) its right to timely notice. The German Federal Court of Justice thus held in one case that the seller made such a waiver when it agreed to give credit to the buyer after the buyer raised potential concerns.[406]

§ 2.27 Seller's Rights to Cure

If the seller delivers nonconforming goods, it often will wish to cure the defects even after delivery. It is for this reason that the Convention requires early notice by the buyer to the seller of any defects in the goods. The primary issues arise from defects in quantity or quality of the goods and the timeliness of the delivery

---

[398]   On all of these points see CISG DIGEST 2012, *supra* note 36, art. 39, para. 24 (citing numerous cases).

[399]   For a comprehensive review of the relevant factors identified by the courts see CISG DIGEST 2012, *supra* note 36, art. 39, paras. 25–27 (citing numerous cases).

[400]   *See* Miami Valley Paper, LLC v. Lebbing Engineering & Consulting GmbH, 2009 WL 818618, *7 (S.D. Ohio 2009).

[401]   *See* Shantou Real Lingerie Manufacturing Co., Ltd. v. Native Group International, Ltd., 2016 WL 4532911, at *4 (S.D.N.Y. 2016).

[402]   *See, e.g.*, Electrocraft Arkansas, Inc. v. Super Elec. Motors, Ltd, 2010 WL 3307461 (E.D. Ark. 2010); Miami Valley Paper, LLC v. Lebbing Engineering & Consulting GmbH, 2009 WL 818618, *7 (S.D. Ohio 2009). *But see* Shantou Real Lingerie Manufacturing Co., Ltd. v. Native Group International, Ltd., 2016 WL 4532911, at *4 (S.D.N.Y. 2016) (granting summary judgment based on the conclusion that a one year delay "plainly was unreasonable").

[403]   *See* text accompanying notes 326–327 in § 2.21 *supra*.

[404]   CISG, art. 40.

[405]   *See* CISG, art. 7(2) and § 2.10 *supra*.

[406]   CLOUT case No. 235, *Bundesgerichtshof* [Federal Court of Justice] of Germany (25 June 1997).

(or tender of delivery). The Convention has different rules for cure depending upon whether the defects were discovered before or after the contract date for delivery.

Pre-Delivery-Date Cure. Where a non-conforming tender is made before the contract date for delivery, the seller has the right to remedy any lack of conformity, "provided that the exercise of this right does not cause the buyer unreasonable inconvenience or unreasonable expense."[407] If the seller cures the non-conformity, it is still liable to the buyer for any damages caused by the defects.[408] The same rules apply with respect to nonconformities in any documents covering the goods (such as a bill of lading).[409]

CISG Article 37 expressly identifies the cure options available to the seller: delivery of any missing part for or quantity of the goods; delivery of replacement goods; or "remedying any lack of conformity" in the goods delivered. Whether the seller has a "right" to rely on other forms of cure, such as offering a money allowance to the buyer,[410] is not clear. Given the objectives of Article 37, the list of specific forms of remedy should not be read as exclusive, and the buyer thus should be obligated to accept a tendered cure as long as it does not cause unreasonable inconvenience or unreasonable expense.

CISG Article 37 makes clear that the seller "may" cure the nonconformity of a tender before the date for delivery. Thus, if the buyer refuses to permit the seller to effect a cure, the buyer, at a minimum, will lose its right to rely on the nonconformity involved. Moreover, one could argue that such a refusal by the buyer may amount to a breach,[411] thus making the buyer liable for any damages suffered by the seller.[412]

Post-Delivery-Date Cure. Even after the date for delivery has passed, the CISG permits the seller to remedy a non-conformity; the right to do so, however, is subject to more exacting conditions. Similar to the pre-delivery-date option, the seller may resort to such a cure if it can do so "without causing the buyer unreasonable inconvenience or uncertainty of reimbursement by the seller of

---

[407] CISG, art. 37. Compare UCC § 2–508(1), which allows a seller that tenders delivery before the contract delivery date to cure any nonconformity, provided it gives timely notice of an intent to do so and accomplishes the cure before the contract delivery date.

[408] CISG, art. 37.

[409] CISG, art. 34.

[410] This would be the analog of the buyer's right to reduce the price corresponding to any nonconformity. *See* CISG, art. 50.

[411] CISG, art. 61(1).

[412] CISG, art. 74. For a general review of damages under the CISG see §§ 2.39 and 2.43 *infra*.

expenses advanced by the buyer."[413] But the seller also must cure "without unreasonable delay."[414] Unlike the specific references in CISG Article 37 to various ways a seller might remedy a nonconforming tender, CISG Article 48 states only that the seller "may remedy . . . any failure." Thus, the right to cure after delivery extends to every kind of breach of contract by the seller. And given that the basic objectives of Article 48 are the same as those of Article 37, the seller should not be limited in the form of cure as long as the conditions are satisfied. Even if the seller cures the non-conformity, it again will be liable to the buyer for any damages caused by the delay in providing conforming goods.[415]

The seller's right to post-delivery-date cure is expressly subject to the buyer's right to declare an "avoidance" of the contract, especially for a "fundamental" breach.[416] (On both notions, see § 2.32 below.) Nonetheless, the authorities are not in agreement on the details of this limitation, especially with respect to the influence of an offered cure on the existence of a fundamental breach in the first place (a point again explored in more detail in § 2.32 below).[417] In any event, if a buyer wishes to take such an action, it must comply with all of the requirements of CISG Article 49. For the standard case of a "fundamental breach," this would mean that the seller's breach must "substantially deprive" the buyer of its contractual rights. But in most cases it should be difficult for the buyer to meet this standard if the seller has made a timely offer of cure and can demonstrate an ability to effect that cure within a reasonable time.[418] Moreover, the entire thrust of the CISG provisions on the seller's right to cure (and more generally, the buyer's remedies) is to require cooperation between the parties in resolving disputes over timeliness of delivery and conformity of the goods.

If the conditions for post-delivery date cure are satisfied (*i.e.*, no unreasonable delay, expense, or inconvenience for the buyer), the

---

[413]   CISG, art. 48(1).

[414]   *Id.* Compare UCC § 2–508(2) which gives to the seller a more limited right to cure after the contract delivery date. It is available only if the seller had "reasonable grounds to believe" that, although defective, the nonconforming tender "would be acceptable" to the buyer. If so, the seller must notify the buyer of the intention to cure, and then may "substitute a conforming tender" within a reasonable time of the contract delivery date.

[415]   *Id.*

[416]   CISG, art. 48(1) (stating that the right to cure is "[s]ubject to article 49," which addresses the buyer's right to declare the contract avoided).

[417]   *See* Müller-Chen, art. 48, paras. 14–17, in Schlechtriem & Schwenzer, *supra* note 30.

[418]   For more on avoidance for a fundamental breach see § 2.32 *infra*.

buyer otherwise has no right to refuse a cure by the seller.[419] But given the factual uncertainty of the conditions, the CISG also has a special provision that permits the seller to force the buyer to take a position on any post-delivery cure: The seller may state a reasonable time within which it will effect the cure and then request that the buyer "make known" whether it will accept that performance.[420] If the buyer agrees or does not respond within a reasonable time, the seller has a right to perform within the stated period. And in the interim the buyer may not resort to any inconsistent remedy (including avoidance of the contract).[421]

§ 2.28   Risk of Loss

The identification of the moment at which the risk of loss of or damage to the goods passes from the seller to the buyer is especially important for transactions governed by the CISG. This is because significant geographical distances often separate the parties, and as a result most contracts governed by the CISG will involve transportation of the goods (although this is not required for the application of the CISG in the first place[422]).

The basic rule under the CISG is that the buyer bears the risk of loss to the goods during their transportation by a carrier, unless the contract provides otherwise.[423] Such a contractual agreement to allocate the risk of loss typically comes through the inclusion of a commercial term (such as FOB or CIF), and such agreements supersede the CISG provisions under CISG Articles 6 and 9.[424] More generally, the CISG makes clear that loss or damage to the goods after the risk of loss has passed to the buyer leaves it liable to pay the price (unless the loss or damage was due to an act or omission of the seller).[425]

---

[419]   CISG, art. 48(1).

[420]   CISG, art. 48(2).

[421]   *Id.*

[422]   *See* discussion of CISG Article 1 in § 2.4 *supra.*

[423]   CISG, art. 67(1). Compare UCC § 2–509(1).

[424]   For a full discussion of risk of loss under commercial terms, see Chapter 3. As noted there, the most widely accepted of these commercial terms are the Incoterms. Many courts have held that the Incoterms qualify under CISG Article 9(2) as a "usage . . . which in international trade is widely known to, and regularly observed by, parties to" international sales contracts. *See, e.g.,* BP Oil Int'l, Ltd. v. Empresa Estatal Petróleos de Ecuador, 332 F.3d 333, 336 (5th Cir. 2003) ("The CISG incorporates Incoterms through article 9(2)."); In re World Imports, Ltd., 549 B.R. 820, 824 (E.D. Pa. 2016) (same); Citgo Petroleum Corp. v. Odfjell Seachem, 2013 WL 2289951, at *5 (S.D. Tex. 2013) (same). Regarding CISG Article 9, see § 2.11 *supra.* As a result, the risk of loss rules of the Incoterms would supplant the default rules of the CISG.

[425]   CISG, art. 66.

In absence of a contrary contractual agreement, CISG Articles 67 through 70 set forth specific risk of loss rules which depend on the nature of the seller's delivery obligation.

A first set of rules relates to transactions that "involve[ ] carriage of the goods."

(a) If the contract does not obligate the seller to hand over the goods "at a particular place" (a "shipment contract"), the risk of loss will pass to the buyer when the goods are delivered "to the first carrier" for shipment to the buyer.[426] If instead the contract obligates the seller to hand over the goods to the *carrier* "at a particular place," then the risk of loss passes when the seller hands over goods to the carrier at that place.[427] In either situation, the goods need not be on board the means of transportation—any receipt by a carrier will do. Further, the seller need not "hand over" the goods to an ocean-going or international carrier—possession by the local trucker that will haul them to the port is sufficient. However, if the seller uses its own vehicle to transport the goods, the seller bears the risk until the goods are handed over to an independent carrier, or to the buyer.

(b) If, however, the contract requires the seller to deliver the goods to the *buyer* at the buyer's location or "at" some other distant location (a "destination contract"), the seller bears the risk of loss until it puts the goods at the buyer's disposal at that location at the delivery time and the buyer becomes aware of that fact.[428]

Thus, in a contract between Seattle-based seller and Beijing-based buyer governed by the CISG: (1) in a shipment contract, the seller would bear the risk only until the goods were delivered to the first carrier in Seattle; (2) in a destination contract (where the seller is obligated to deliver at Beijing), the seller would bear the risk during transit and until the goods were put at the buyer's disposal in Beijing. (Again, as discussed in Chapter 3, specific commercial terms—such as FOB, FAS, and CIF—have more detailed rules on risk of loss.)

A second set of risk of loss rules applies to transactions that do not involve carriage of the goods from the seller to the buyer.

(c) If the goods are not to be transported by a carrier (*e.g.*, when the buyer or an agent are close to the seller and will pick up the goods), the risk passes to the buyer when it "takes over" the goods or, if it is late in doing so, when the goods are "placed" at its

---

[426] CISG, art. 67(1), first sentence.
[427] *Id.*, second sentence.
[428] CISG, art. 69(2).

"disposal" and it commits a breach by not taking delivery.[429] The goods cannot, however, be at the buyer's "disposal" until they have first been identified to the contract.[430]

(d) If the goods are already in transit when sold, the risk passes when the contract is "concluded."[431] If, however, "the circumstances so indicate"—especially if the buyer has concluded insurance cover during transit—the risk of loss is assumed by the buyer from the time the goods were handed over to the carrier that issued documents governing the transit.[432] However, if in such a case the seller knew or ought to have known of a loss or damage to the goods at the conclusion of the contract and did not disclose this to the buyer, the risk of loss to that extent remains with the seller.[433]

The challenge for the buyer under this latter rule is that it may be practically impossible to determine whether damage to goods in a ship's cargo hold occurred before or after the parties concluded the sales contract.

In most situations, title and risk are treated separately. Thus, manipulation of title through the use of documents of title, such as negotiable bills of lading, is irrelevant and has no effect on the point of transfer of risk of loss.[434] Just as title and risk are treated separately, so also breach and risk generally are treated separately. The one exception to this approach (discussed immediately above) is where the buyer is obligated to pick up the goods and commits a breach by failing to do so in a timely manner.[435] In all other cases, including any breach by the seller, the basic risk of loss rules are not changed by claims of breach.[436] Thus, a breach by the seller, even if a "fundamental breach," is irrelevant to determining the point at which the risk of loss passes to the buyer. In specific, if the seller in fact already has committed a fundamental breach, the risk of loss rules in Articles 67, 68, and 69 will not impair the remedies available to the buyer on account of that breach (and especially the right to avoid the contract).[437] And an unrelated non-fundamental breach in a shipment contract will not create a right for the buyer to

---

[429]   CISG, art. 6(1).

[430]   CISG, art. 67(2).

[431]   CISG, art. 68, first sentence.

[432]   CISG, art. 68, second sentence. *See also* Hager/Schmidt-Kessel, art. 68, paras. 5–6, in Schlechtriem & Schwenzer, *supra* note 30.

[433]   CISG, art. 68, third sentence.

[434]   CISG, art. 67(1), third sentence.

[435]   CISG, art. 69(1).

[436]   This is different from the approach of the UCC. Compare UCC § 2–510.

[437]   CISG, art. 70.

avoid the contract simply because the goods are lost or damaged in transit (because the risk of loss already will have passed to the buyer upon delivery to the carrier).

§ 2.29 Exemption from Liability for Non-Performance

A common issue in the sometimes turbulent world of international trade is that events occur (wars, civil unrest, trade sanctions, etc.) that make one party's performance of a contract more difficult than anticipated, and maybe even impossible. To address such a situation, the CISG has a general provision, Article 79, that recognizes an "exemption" from liability for non-performance.

Unexpected Impediments. The CISG, like the domestic UCC,[438] has a general provision that relieves a party from liability in the event of unexpected impediments to performance. But CISG Article 79 is different in fundamental respects, and also comprehensively regulates the cognate subjects of impossibility, impracticability, frustration, and changed circumstances. Because of this, courts should not consult the rules and precedents developed under the UCC for guidance in applying CISG Article 79. As a fundamental matter, the CISG intentionally uses terms and concepts that do not correspond to domestic law approaches such as that in the UCC. Thus, Article 79 refers to an "exemption from liability" for non-performance (not, for example, an "excuse for non-performance"). Moreover, Article 79, unlike its UCC counterpart, provides relief for a non-performance by either the seller or the buyer, and extends to "any" obligations (not just the seller's delivery obligation).

A valid exemption under CISG Article 79 requires proof of three elements: First, the party asserting the exemption must prove that its failure to perform was "due to an impediment beyond [its] control."[439] The choice of the nontraditional notion of "impediment" here was a calculated one in order to avoid possible associations with any particular domestic legal regime.[440] The drafters of the CISG provisions thus deliberately rejected a proposal to use the word "circumstances," rather than "impediment."[441] Impediment was thought to reflect a requirement of a specific external force that prevents a party's performance, rather than a change in the general economic climate (even if unexpected). Thus, recessions or increases

---

[438]   *See* UCC § 2–615.

[439]   CISG, art. 79(1). Inherent in the phrase "due to" is a causation requirement, that is, that the impediment is the cause of the party's inability to perform.

[440]   *See* Honnold/Flechtner, *supra* note 155, Article 79, §§ 425–427.

[441]   *See id.,* § 427.

in inflation rates should not qualify as impediments. Nonetheless, and notwithstanding the reference to impediment, the standard for exemption is not strict impossibility. Rather, the prevailing view is that an extreme hardship will suffice, that is, such extreme difficulty in performance as constitutes impossibility as a practical matter under the circumstances.[442] The Court of Cassation (roughly, the Supreme Court) of Belgium has expressly so held.[443] Nonetheless, even this standard is an exacting one: Even a one hundred percent cost increase should not suffice, and "a party may have to accept even a tripled market price."[444]

Although Article 79 does not expressly address the point, in principle the exemption it describes should apply as well to a defective performance—such as delivery of nonconforming goods or a breach relating to third party property claims. This follows from the reference to an allowed exemption for a failure to perform "any" of a party's obligations. Nonetheless, as reflected in the drafting deliberations and in the concerns of some scholars, the circumstances in which such an exemption might be possible should be extremely narrow.[445]

Second, the affected party must show that it "could not reasonably be expected" to have taken the impediment into account at the time of the conclusion of the contract. This in effect is an unforeseeability test and it requires proof that a reasonable person in the claimant's position at the time of contract formation would not have anticipated that the impediment to performance would occur. This also is the element on which claims for exemption most often founder, for international buyers and sellers are expected to "take into account" the great variety of risks that attend the performance of international contracts.

Finally, the affected party must demonstrate that it could not reasonably have avoided or overcome the impediment or its consequences. The party thus must be expected to bear increased costs for overcoming even an unexpected impediment—such as from

---

[442] *See* Schwenzer, art. 79, para. 30, in Schlechtriem & Schwenzer, *supra* note 30; Honnold/Flechtner, *supra* note 155, Article 79, § 432.2.

[443] *Hof van Cassatie* [Court of Final Resort] of Belgium (19 June 2009), *available at* http://cisgw3.law.pace.edu/cases/090619b1.html.

[444] *See* Schwenzer, art. 79, para. 30, in Schlechtriem & Schwenzer, *supra* note 30.

[445] On the concerns about extending Article 79 to defective performances see Honnold/Flechtner, *supra* note 155, Article 79, § 427; Nicholas, *Impracticability and Impossibility in the U.N. Convention on Contracts for the International Sale of Goods*, in International Sales: The United Nations Convention on Contracts for the International Sale of Goods § 5–1 (N. Galston & H. Smit eds., 1984).

alternative modes or routes of transport, reallocation of supply, or the hiring of extra staff.[446]

While Article 79 may seem open-ended and subject to widely varying interpretations, the cases applying the provision have been remarkably consistent: With rare and narrow exceptions, the courts have ruled against the party seeking an exemption from liability. Thus, they have found that unexpected import regulations on radioactivity in food and increased costs for tomatoes from adverse weather conditions were not valid exemptions for sellers, and that significantly decreased market prices for purchased goods and a failure of a third party to transmit the buyer's payment to the seller were not valid exemptions for buyers.[447]

Many of the cases involve a default by the seller's suppliers. On the surface, CISG Article 79 seems to provide some protection for the seller in such cases. The Article's second paragraph states that a party has an exemption if its failure is "due to the failure by a third person whom [it] has engaged to perform the whole or part of the contract." But there is less here than appears at first read. First, and most important, Article 79(2) only applies when a party has "engaged" a third person "to perform . . . the contract." Based on this language, the strongly prevailing view among courts and scholars is that the exemption does not extend to mere upstream suppliers with which the seller has a separate contract, because the seller does not "engage" them to "perform" its formal contractual obligations to the buyer.[448]

Even in such a case, the standards for such an exemption are very stringent: A default of a third party (the supplier) provides an exemption from liability for the non-performing party (most often, the seller), only if it can show that *both* it and its supplier satisfy the requirements of CISG Article 79.[449] Thus, the seller also must prove that some unforeseeable and uncontrollable "impediment" prevented *the supplier* from performing. Financial difficulties of the supplier do not meet that standard, and the seller thus assumes the risk of the supplier's ability to continue to perform.

The exemption from liability under CISG Article 79 is available only for as long as the impediment continues.[450] In addition, the party seeking the exemption must notify the other party to the contract both of the "impediment" and of its effect on

---

[446]   See CISG DIGEST 2012, *supra* note 36, art. 79, para. 19 (citing cases).

[447]   See CISG DIGEST 2012, *supra* note 36, art. 79, para. 13 (citing cases).

[448]   See CISG DIGEST 2012, *supra* note 36, art. 79, para. 21; Schwenzer, art. 99, para. 37, in Schlechtriem & Schwenzer, *supra* note 30.

[449]   CISG, art. 79(2)(a) and (b).

[450]   CISG, art. 79(3).

performance.[451] Moreover, even if the party claiming the exemption proves all of the elements, it is protected only from damage claims. It is not protected from other remedial actions by the other party, such as avoidance of the contract or restitution of benefits received from the other party or derived from goods received.[452]

As a final note, some U.S. courts unfortunately have established a troubling pattern in the application of CISG Article 79. These courts, though small in number, have not looked to either the literature or the voluminous foreign case law under the CISG when applying Article 79. Instead, they have reflexively retreated to case law under the UCC merely because "no American court has specifically . . . interpreted Article 79."[453] Some arbitrators may be following the same misguided path.[454] These decisions fail to recognize that CISG Article 79 reflects a deliberately different approach and one that comprehensively regulates the subject—to the exclusion of domestic law regimes.[455]

Reliance on One's Own Acts or Omissions. CISG Article 80 separately declares that a party may not rely on a failure to perform "to the extent that such a failure was caused by" its own acts or omissions. Thus, where a party's own actions are the cause of a breach by the other party, the breach does not provide a ground to assert rights under the Convention. This is similar in concept to the notion of "good faith" under the UCC and the common law;[456] but like all other such facial similarities, the precedents and practices developed under U.S. law should not influence cases governed by the CISG. Nonetheless, in words that will be familiar to U.S. lawyers, the Supreme Court of Poland has declared that CISG Article 80 "imposes on the parties the duty of loyalty and abstention from any acts that would hinder the performance of the contract."[457] Courts thus have applied Article 80 to prevent a party from relying on a variety of remedies otherwise permitted for nonperformance,

---

[451] CISG, art. 79(4). On this point see Valero Marketing & Supply Company v. Greeni Oy, 2006 WL 891196, at *10 n.5 (D.N.J. 2006) (rejecting an Article 79 claim in part because the claimant failed to give the notice required by subparagraph 4).

[452] CISG, art. 79(5) (providing that the excuse does not prevent either party "from exercising any right other than a claim to damages").

[453] Raw Materials, Inc. v. Manfred Forberich GmbH & Co., 2004 WL 1535839 (N.D. Ill. 2004). *See also* Hilaturas Miel, S.L. v. Republic of Iraq, 573 F. Supp. 2d 781, 798–800 (S.D.N.Y. 2008).

[454] Macromex SRL v. Globex Int'l, Inc., 2008 WL 1752530 (S.D.N.Y. 2008) (affirming an arbitral award).

[455] *See, e.g.,* Carla Spivack, *Of Shrinking Sweatsuits and Poison Vine Wax: A Comparison of Basis for Excuse under UCC § 2–615 and CISG Article 79,* 27 U. PA. J. INT'L ECON. L. 757 (2006).

[456] *See* UCC § 1–304; Restatement (Second) of Contracts, § 205.

[457] Decision of Supreme Court of Poland (11 May 2007), *available at* http://cisgw3.law.pace.edu/cases/070511p1.html.

including a right to damages, to avoid the contract, and to use the non-performance as a contractual defense.[458]

§ 2.30 Breach and Remedies___In General

The CISG provides no formal definition for the traditional concept of breach of contract. Rather, it states simply that if the seller fails to perform "any" of its obligations, the buyer has a general right to damages as well as a right to certain more specific remedies.[459] Likewise, it states that if the buyer fails to perform "any" of its obligations, the seller has a general right to damages as well as a right to certain other more specific remedies.[460]

The CISG sets forth the rules for the buyer's and the seller's respective remedies upon breach in separate, though parallel, chapters. The buyer's remedies are in Part III, Chapter II (Articles 45 through 52). The seller's remedies are in Part III, Chapter III (Articles 61 through 65). The rules for determining damages for both parties, however, are combined in still another chapter, Part III, Chapter V (Articles 74 through 77).

The drafters of the remedy provisions of the CISG faced special challenges because of the divergent approaches of civil and common law legal systems. These challenges are illustrated by two facts: First, specific performance is the primary remedy at civil law, while an action for damages is preferred at common law. Second, at civil law a finding of "fault" is usually required for imposition of an obligation to pay damages, while under the common law an aggrieved party need show only breach of any nature. The CISG drafters attempted to bridge both gaps.

As described in more detail below, the buyer has four potential types of remedies under the CISG: "avoidance" of the contract;[461] a self-help right of price adjustment;[462] specific performance;[463] and an action for damages.[464] The first two of these remedies in many circumstances may be undertaken without judicial intervention, but the latter two will require proceedings in a court or before an arbitral tribunal. Separately, even in the event of a breach by the seller the buyer may have certain obligations to protect the goods after delivery.[465] The CISG also specifically provides that the buyer

---

[458] *See* CISG DIGEST 2012, *supra* note 36, art. 80, para. 7 (citing cases).
[459] CISG, art. 45(1)(a), (b).
[460] CISG, art. 61(1)(a), (b).
[461] *See* § 2.36 *infra* and CISG, art. 49.
[462] *See* § 2.37 *infra* and CISG, art. 50.
[463] *See* § 2.38 *infra* and CISG, art. 46.
[464] *See* § 2.39 *infra* and CISG, art. 45(1)(b), referring to arts. 74–77.
[465] *See* § 2.36 *infra* and CISG, arts. 86–88.

does not lose its right to damages by resorting to one of the other allowed remedies.[466]

If the buyer breaches, the seller has three potential types of remedies: "avoidance" of the contract (which may include a right to reclaim the goods);[467] an action for the price (which functions much in the nature of specific performance);[468] and an action for damages.[469] The first of these remedies may be undertaken without judicial intervention, but the last two involve proceedings in a court or before an arbitral tribunal. The seller likewise may have certain obligations to protect the goods upon non-payment by the buyer.[470] Like the buyer, the seller does not lose a right to damages by resorting to another allowed remedy.[471]

Like effectively all its provisions, the parties may agree to "derogate from or vary the effect of" the CISG's remedial rules (the principle of party autonomy).[472] Thus, the parties may agree to limit the amount of damages for breach or otherwise modify the available remedies.[473] Nonetheless, the widely accepted view of courts and scholars is that this power does not extend to a complete exclusion of all remedies in favor an aggrieved party.[474] The "validity" of such clauses, moreover, is an issue for otherwise-applicable domestic law.[475]

Separately, the buyer and the seller each may have a right to suspend performance in the event of well-grounded doubts about performance by the other.[476] Merchants commonly prefer such practical, informal rights because of their low cost; and merchants that have traded with each other in the past, and hope to do so in the future, are much more likely to use these rights than to go to

---

[466]   CISG, art. 45(2). A separate provision makes clear that no court may grant an additional grace period if the buyer resorts to one of its allowed remedies. CISG, art. 45(3).

[467]   See § 2.41 *infra* and CISG, art. 64.

[468]   See § 2.42 *infra* and CISG, art. 62.

[469]   See § 2.43 *infra* and CISG, art. 61(1)(b), referring to arts. 74–77.

[470]   See § 2.41 *infra* and CISG, arts. 85, 87–88.

[471]   CISG, art. 61(2). As with the buyer, no court may grant an additional grace period if the seller resorts to one of its allowed remedies. CISG, art. 61(3).

[472]   See CSIG, art. 6 and § 2.5 *supra*.

[473]   See CISG DIGEST 2012, *supra* note 36, Damages (articles 74–77), para. 6; Schwenzer/Hachem, art. 4, para. 43, in Schlechtriem & Schwenzer, *supra* note 30.

[474]   See Schwenzer/Hachem, art. 4, para. 43, in Schlechtriem & Schwenzer, *supra* note 30 (observing that the "the creditor must not be placed in a position where it is left with no remedies at all"); CISG Advisory Council Opinion 17, and Comment 1.16 (16 October 2015) (same), *available at* http://cisgac.com/opinion-17/.

[475]   See § 2.8 *supra* (examining CISG Article 4(a)) and CISG DIGEST 2012, *supra* note 36, Damages (articles 74–77), para. 6.

[476]   CISG, art. 71.

court. Similarly, when it is clear that the other party absolutely will not perform, merchants prefer to declare the entire transaction avoided without filing a lawsuit, and the CISG provides a mechanism for doing so.[477] Comparable rights exist with respect to installment contracts.[478] We thus will analyze these informal, practical, and non-judicial rights before turning to the more specific and formal remedies set forth in the CISG.[479]

§ 2.31 Breach and Remedies___Right to Suspend Performance

Under CISG Article 71, a party that has yet to perform may suspend its performance if it "becomes apparent" that the other party "will not perform a substantial part" of the required counter-performance.[480] A party that suspends performance must notify the other party of that suspension.[481] Although the CISG does not expressly identify the consequence of failing to do so, courts have uniformly held that in absence of timely notice the claimant may not rely on the right to suspend.[482] Even if substantive grounds exist, therefore, a suspension of performance without the requisite timely notice may trigger the other party's rights to a remedy for breach under the other provisions of the CISG, including a right to damages.[483]

CISG Article 71 is neutral between buyers and sellers. Thus, a buyer that has agreed to prepay for the goods may suspend that performance if it is apparent that the seller will not perform as a result of either (a) a "serious deficiency" in the seller's "ability to perform,"[484] or (b) the seller's conduct in preparing to perform or in actually performing.[485] Such obligations of the seller regarding preparation for performance may include making appropriate transportation arrangements,[486] assisting the buyer in concluding

---

[477] CISG, art. 72.

[478] CISG, art. 73.

[479] See §§ 2.31–2.33 infra.

[480] CISG, art. 71(1).

[481] CISG, art. 71(3). See also CISG, art. 27 (addressing the effect of delay or non-delivery of such a notice).

[482] See CISG DIGEST 2012, supra note 36, art. 71, para. 11 (citing cases).

[483] For the buyer's rights, see CISG, art. 45(1); for the seller's, see CISG, art. 61(1).

[484] CISG, art. 71(1)(a).

[485] CISG, art. 71(1)(b).

[486] CISG, art. 32(2).

insurance cover,[487] or obtaining and timely presenting proper documents covering the goods.[488]

In the same way, a seller that has not yet shipped the goods may suspend that performance if it learns that there is a "serious deficiency" in the creditworthiness of the buyer.[489] The seller also may suspend its performance if the buyer fails to perform necessary, agreed-upon preliminary steps, such setting up a required bank guarantee or a letter of credit[490] or providing specifications for the goods.[491]

Despite the facial neutrality of the provision between sellers and buyers, the right to suspend performance has the greatest significance for sellers. This is so because the sellers often must ship goods before payment, and thus assume the risk of later non-payment by the buyer. Unfortunately, the decisions under the CISG thus far have left some uncertainty for sellers wishing to rely on their right to suspend performance in such cases. The Austrian Supreme Court has held, for example, that a seller may not suspend performance merely because the buyer has failed to pay for prior installments of goods shipped under a contract.[492] It stated that, because there was insufficient proof of the buyer's *unwillingness* to pay, the seller was entitled to suspend its performance only if it could establish the buyer's *inability* to pay (such as due to financial difficulty or insolvency).

Two other decisions seem to send a less strict message. In one, a Belgian court held that a seven-month delay in the buyer's payment for an initial installment of goods allowed a seller to suspend performance in delivering the second installment.[493] The court reasoned that the seller could have a reasonable suspicion that the buyer would not pay for the second installment, but there is no indication that the buyer was in any financial difficulties or had any inability to pay. Thus, the unwillingness of the buyer to pay for prior deliveries was sufficient.

A case from the United States is in accord. In *Doolim Corp. v. R Doll, LLC*,[494] a U.S. district court held that a buyer's three-month

---

[487] CISG, art. 32(3).

[488] CISG, art. 34.

[489] CISG, art. 71(1)(a).

[490] CISG, art. 71(1)(b). *See* CISG DIGEST 2012, *supra* note 36, art. 71, para. 6 (citing cases).

[491] *See* CISG, art. 65.

[492] Clout Case No. 238, *Oberster Gerichtshof* [Supreme Court] of Austria (12 February 1998).

[493] *Rechtbank van Koophandel* [Commercial Court] of Hasselt, Belgium (1 March 1995), also *available at* UNILEX, Case D. 1995–7.0.

[494] 2009 WL 1514913 (S.D.N.Y. 2009).

delay in paying for two initial installments justified the seller in suspending future shipments. Along with a later failure to open a letter of credit, the court stated that the initial nonpayment made it apparent that the buyer "would be, at the very least, seriously deficient in its performance of its remaining contractual obligations."[495] But in a more recent case, *Weihai Textile Group Import & Export Co. v. Level 8 Apparel, LLC*, a U.S. district court refused to grant summary judgment on a similar claim even though the defendant had acknowledged that it was facing "imminent financial difficulties" and had been "several days late" in making two required payments.[496]

These seemingly inconsistent cases arise from a focus on different language in CISG Article 71: The Austrian court focused on Article 71(1)(a), which refers to a serious deficiency in an actual "ability" to pay; the other decisions focused on the basic rule in Article 71(1), which requires only that it become "apparent" that the other party will not perform. Certainly, the grounds stated in subparagraphs (a) and (b) to Article 71(1) reflect an exclusive list. But, as the court in *Doolim Corp.* correctly reasoned, the existence of objective, "well-grounded fears" of non-payment by the buyer should suffice to make it "apparent" that the buyer will not perform a substantial part of its overall payment obligation. This applies to both options, that is, as a result of (a) a "serious deficiency" in the buyer's ability to pay, or (b) the buyer's "conduct" in preparing or performing its already existing payment obligations. The *Weihai Textile Group* court, in contrast, emphasized the significance of the facts of each case, for it found that because of reasonable disputes about the words and conduct of the defendant there "a reasonable jury could find that Plaintiff . . . was not entitled to the protections of Articles 71 and 72."[497]

Separately, the CISG permits a seller to suspend performance after shipment but before delivery of the goods—a so-called right of stoppage in transit.[498] The CISG provision, however, only deals with rights and duties between the parties to the contract. Thus, it may give the seller the right, but not a practical ability, to prevent delivery by a carrier. The CISG does not require the carrier to comply with a seller's request; instead, it expressly leaves the carrier's obligations to other law.[499] If the seller has possession of a

---

[495]   *Id.*, at *6.

[496]   2014 WL 1494327, at *13 (S.D.N.Y. 2014).

[497]   *Id.*

[498]   CISG, art. 71(2). A related right to stop goods in transit may arise from an "avoidance" of the contract by the seller. *See infra* §§ 2.32 (on avoidance in general) and 2.41 (on the seller's specific rights upon avoidance).

[499]   CISG, art. 71(2), last sentence.

negotiable bill of lading to its order, then the carrier is obligated under the contract of carriage to follow the instructions of the seller. The CISG provision does not state any criteria for determining whether the stoppage is authorized; as a result, the buyer has no ground under the sales contract to object to the seller's stoppage or to challenge it.

However, if the buyer is already the holder of the negotiable bill of lading, then the carrier is obligated to follow the buyer's instructions.[500] Under the U.S. Federal Bills of Lading Act, moreover, if the buyer took the negotiation of the bill in good faith and for value, it has rights superior to any lien of the seller or right to stop the goods in transit.[501] And if the carrier follows the buyer's instructions and delivers the goods to the buyer in such a case, then the CISG provides no relief for the seller. If the carrier has not delivered the goods to the buyer, the seller may seek to obtain the bill of lading from the buyer and to enjoin the buyer from presenting the bill to the carrier. These remedies are not expressly provided for by the CISG; but the first sentence of CISG Article 71(2) expressly states that the seller is entitled to stop delivery even though the buyer "holds a document which entitles [it] to obtain [the goods]." The remedies discussed merely give effect to this right. This reasoning also applies to a transaction in which the buyer is the consignee of a non-negotiable bill of lading. But again, Article 71(2) expressly states that it covers only the rights as between the buyer and the seller, and thus does not preempt rules that protect a third-party carrier.

After the carrier has delivered the goods to the buyer, it is no longer possible to stop delivery under the CISG. All that the seller would have is an *in personam* claim against for the purchase price.[502] Although CISG Article 71 states the substantive grounds, the CISG is otherwise silent on whether the seller has an *in rem* right to recover the goods, and thus this is a matter for domestic law.[503]

Under CISG Article 71(3), the right to stop goods in transit— like the right to suspend in general—ceases if the other party "provides adequate assurance" that it will perform.[504] Although not expressly stated, the assurance must come within a reasonable

---

[500] For more on this point, see Chapter 4.

[501] 49 U.S.C. § 80105(b). *See also* UCC § 7–502(b) (same).

[502] CISG, arts. 61(1)(a), 62. *See also* § 2.42 *infra*.

[503] CISG, art. 4(b).

[504] CISG, art. 71(3).

time, as this is a "general principle" of the Convention.[505] In such a case, the original party must continue with its performance. As of 2016, no published cases have applied this provision.

§ 2.32 Breach and Remedies__Contract Avoidance and Fundamental Breach

Avoidance. Either a buyer or a seller may declare a contract "avoided" in the event of a nonperformance or defective performance by the other.[506] The CISG addresses the buyer's and the seller's respective rights to take such an action in separate sections of the Convention. The specific situations of buyers and sellers thus will be analyzed in separate sections below.[507]

Nonetheless, the concept of "avoidance of the contract" is central to the general breach and remedial scheme of the CISG and appears in a variety of provisions applicable to both buyer and seller.[508] In CISG terminology, "avoidance of the contract" is the rough equivalent of "cancellation of the contract" under the UCC.[509] But, importantly, this concept under the CISG is fundamentally different from the notion of "avoidance" under the UCC.[510]

In its essence, a justified declaration of avoidance brings a contract to an end and releases both parties from their obligations under it, but preserves the right to damages by the aggrieved party.[511] To be effective, a declaration of avoidance must be made by notice to the other party.[512]

For an aggrieved buyer, the legal result is a right to refuse to accept delivery of goods or to return defective goods, and in either case to refuse to pay for the goods. For an aggrieved seller, a justified avoidance means a right to stop goods in transit or to refuse to deliver them in the first place.

---

[505] *See* Fountoulakis, art. 71, para. 47, in Schlechtriem & Schwenzer, *supra* note 30. *See also* CISG, art. 7(2), and the discussion of the CISG's gap-filling "general principles" in § 2.10 *supra*.

[506] CISG, arts. 49(1), 64(1).

[507] *See* §§ 2.36 and 2.41.

[508] *See, e.g.,* §§ 2.36 and 2.41 *infra.* The concept of fundamental breach also may be relevant to the passage of risk. *See* CISG, art. 70 and § 2.28 *supra.*

[509] Compare UCC § 2–106(4). *See also* Dingxi Longhai Dairy, Ltd. v. Becwood Technology Group L.L.C., 635 F.3d 1106, 1108 n.2 (8th Cir. 2011) (recognizing this similarity). Under the UCC, where a party cancels a contract for breach, it nonetheless retains "any remedy for breach of the whole contract or any unperformed balance." *Id.*

[510] *See* UCC § 2–613 (stating that a contract is "avoided" if a "casualty to identified goods" causes a total loss).

[511] CISG, art. 81.

[512] CISG, art. 26. *But see* the final paragraph of § 2.30 *supra* (noting the special protections for the sender of such notices in Article 27).

Fundamental Breach. Again, the specific situations of the buyer and the seller regarding avoidance will be addressed below. But the principal ground for declaring a contract avoided under the CISG is in the event of a "fundamental breach."[513] What constitutes a "fundamental breach"? The Convention definition requires "such detriment to the other party as to substantially deprive him of what he is entitled to expect under the contract."[514] The drafting history of this provision seems to support a stricter standard than the "substantial impairment" test of the UCC;[515] and in any event courts should avoid any resort to UCC principles or precedents in analyzing a claimed "fundamental breach" under the CISG.[516]

A fundamental breach requires more than a failure of a party to perform a contractual obligation (whether from the terms of the contract itself or from the default rules of the CISG). The fundamental nature of such a breach also will arise not simply from the amount of damages it will cause but also, and especially, from "the importance of the interest which the contract and its individual obligations have created for the promisee."[517] The reference to expectation is defined with reference to the CISG's rules for interpreting contracts, and thus most often will involve an objective test that compares the claimed failure of performance to the reasonable expectation of the aggrieved party.[518] The consensus opinion is that the relevant point for assessing the justified expectations of the aggrieved party is the formation of the contract.[519] It follows, therefore, that the parties may define in their contract the standards for a fundamental breach.[520] The motivations or reasons for a party's breach, such as an economic desire to escape from a losing contract, are not relevant, however, to the analysis of a claimed fundamental breach.

A fundamental breach includes of course a complete failure to perform an essential contract duty (*e.g.*, final nondelivery or final nonpayment). Other possibilities of their nature will depend decisively on the facts of each case, but may include a failure to perform beyond a reasonable time where time is of the essence, defects in the goods such that they are unusable and cannot be resold, and an unjustified denial of contract rights. A cumulation of

---

[513]   *See* CISG, arts. 49(1)(a), 64(1)(a).

[514]   CISG, art. 25.

[515]   UCC §§ 2–608, 2–612.

[516]   *See* Schroeter, art. 25, para. 12, in Schlechtriem & Schwenzer, *supra* note 30.

[517]   *See id.*, para. 21.

[518]   *See* the discussion of CISG article 8 in § 2.11 *supra*.

[519]   *See* Schroeter, art. 25, para. 32, in Schlechtriem & Schwenzer, *supra* note 30.

[520]   *See* Björklund, art. 25, paras. 16–17, in Kröll, *et al.*, *supra* note 30; Schroeter, art. 25, paras. 21–22, in Schlechtriem & Schwenzer, *supra* note 30.

several violations also may suffice if as a result the aggrieved party loses the principal benefit of, or interest in, the expected contract performance.[521]

United States court decisions seem not to have required an overwhelmingly high standard for a "fundamental breach." In one early case, compressors for air conditioning units did not have either the cooling capacity or the power consumption contained in the contract specifications.[522] The court held that cooling capacity was an important factor in determining the value of air conditioner compressors, so that the buyer did not in fact receive the goods it was entitled to expect.[523] In another case, mammography units were seized for non-compliance with U.S. administrative regulations. When the court decided that the seller was obligated to furnish goods that conformed to the buyer's laws,[524] it held that a breach of that obligation was a fundamental breach.[525] A third U.S. court stated that a buyer's refusal to make "large" progress payments on schedule likely would be a fundamental breach.[526] In still another case, the court found that a buyer's refusal to accept substantially conforming substitute goods amounted to a fundamental breach.[527] And a more recent case held that a four-day delay in loading contract goods onto a ship did not constitute a fundamental breach.[528]

Foreign cases seem to have followed a similarly flexible approach. The German Federal Court of Justice thus found a fundamental breach where a buyer was unable to use, or otherwise reprocess, substandard steel wire delivered by the seller.[529] Similarly, a French court found a fundamental breach where a buyer of sugared wine was not able to use or resell it.[530] On the other hand, when a seller contracted to deliver in "July, August,

---

[521] See CISG DIGEST 2012, supra note 36, art. 25, paras. 6–12 (citing cases).

[522] Delchi Carrier S.p.A. v. Rotorex Corp., 71 F.3d 1024 (2d Cir. 1995).

[523] Id., at 1028.

[524] See analysis accompanying notes 304–305 in § 2.21 supra.

[525] Medical Marketing Int'l, Inc. v. Internazionale Medico Scientifica, S.R.L., 1999 WL 311945 (E.D. La. 1999).

[526] Shuttle Pkg. Syst. v. Tsonakis, 2001 WL 34046276 (W.D. Mich. 2001).

[527] Valero Marketing & Supply Company v. Greeni Oy, 2006 WL 891196 (D.N.J. 2006). On the other hand, one court held that a mere delay in delivery, absent special circumstances, would not amount to a fundamental breach. Macromex SRL v. Globex Int'l, Inc., 2008 WL 1752530 (S.D.N.Y. 2008).

[528] Citgo Petroleum Corp. v. Odfjell Seachem, 2013 WL 2289951, at *9 (S.D. Tex. 2013).

[529] CLOUT case No. 235, Bundesgerichtshof [Federal Court of Justice] of Germany (25 June 1997).

[530] CLOUT Case No. 150, Cour de Cassation [Court of Final Resort] of France (23 January 1996).

September" and thus the buyer expected monthly installment deliveries, it was not a fundamental breach to deliver the goods on September 26.[531] The court held that such tender of delivery was within the agreed delivery period, so any delay was not a fundamental defect.

A number of cases have related to resale of the goods. In one case, a court rejected a claim of a fundamental breach in an exclusive dealership arrangement merely because an agent of the seller sold to another retailer in the buyer's exclusive territory.[532] The court so held based on the reasoning that the seller had no knowledge of the agent's conduct and such knowledge also could not be imputed to the seller. On the other hand, where a seller stated at contract formation that a limitation on the resale location of the goods was critically important, and the buyer stated that it intended to resell in South America, a resale elsewhere was held to be a fundamental breach.[533] The court thus explicitly concluded that such a resale "substantially deprived" the seller of what it was entitled to expect under the contract.[534]

This last case also illustrates the final requirement for a fundamental breach: CISG Article 25 declares that a breach is not fundamental if "the party in breach did not foresee and a reasonable person of the same kind and in the same circumstances would not have foreseen such a result."[535] The relevant time for assessing this question of foreseeability is the conclusion of the contract.[536] Thus, in the last cited case, the court emphasized that the buyer knew, or could reasonably have foreseen, at the conclusion of the contract that an agreement precluding resale where other distributors of the seller sold the contract goods could cause a substantial detriment for the seller.[537]

---

[531] CLOUT Case No. 7, *Amtsgericht* [Local Court] of Oldenburg, Germany (24 April 1990).

[532] CLOUT Case No. 6, *Landgericht* [State Court] of Frankfurt a.M., Germany (16 September 1991).

[533] CLOUT Case No. 154, *Cour d'appel* [Court of Appeal] of Grenoble, France (22 February 1995).

[534] CISG, art. 25, first clause.

[535] CISG, art. 25, second clause.

[536] CLOUT Case No. 275, *Oberlandesgericht* [Appellate Court] of Düsseldorf, Germany (24 April 1997); CLOUT Case No. 681, China International Economic and Trade Arbitration Commission (18 August 1997).

[537] CLOUT Case No. 154, *Cour d'appel* [Court of Appeal] of Grenoble, France (22 February 1995).

§ 2.33 Breach and Remedies—Anticipatory Breach

Unlike the UCC,[538] the CISG describes no general right of an insecure party to request assurance when doubt exists about the other party's ability or willingness to perform. As described in § 2.31 above, CISG Article 71 sets forth certain grounds for a party to suspend its own performance, which the other party may cut off with an "adequate assurance" of performance on its part. But the CISG otherwise does not expressly empower an insecure party to initiate such a dialogue. Instead, CISG Article 72(1) states a general right to declare a contract entirely avoided if, prior to the date of performance, it "becomes clear" that the other party will commit a "fundamental breach" of contract.

This right is similar in premise, but more serious in consequence, than the right to suspend performance under CISG Article 71. Thus, "the preconditions for the more drastic remedy of avoidance [under Article 72] are more stringent than those for suspension, both as to the seriousness of the predicted breach and the probability that the breach will occur."[539] First, a declaring party must give reasonable notice to the other party, but only "if time allows." Second, and more important, the conduct of the other party must amount to a "fundamental breach" (as discussed in § 2.32 above). Third, the mere possibility of a breach in the future does not suffice: It must be "clear" under the circumstances that the other party will commit the required fundamental breach. Thus, for example, an Australian court held that the buyer's failure to open a letter of credit justified a declaration of avoidance by the seller.[540] Other examples include a buyer's failure to pay for prior deliveries; a seller's unfounded stoppage of the goods in transit; and one party's declaration that its own performance was contingent on conditions not defined by the contract.[541]

The combined requirement of a "clear" indication of a "fundamental breach," however, often will leave the other party in substantial doubt. This highlights a final requirement: that, after receipt of the notice, the other party does not give an "adequate assurance" that it in fact will perform.[542] One U.S. court in fact emphasized the absence of such an assurance in its determination

---

[538] *See* UCC § 2–609(4).

[539] *See* CISG DIGEST 2012, *supra* note 36, art. 72, para. 2.

[540] CLOUT Case No. 631, Supreme Court of Queensland, Australia (17 November 2000).

[541] *See* CISG DIGEST 2012, *supra* note 36, art. 72, paras. 6–7 (citing cases).

[542] CISG, art. 72(2).

that the seller had a right to declare the sales contract avoided due to an anticipatory fundamental breach by the buyer.[543]

Where the other party actually declares that it will not perform its obligations when due, the requirements for avoidance under Article 72 are less stringent. In such a case, CISG Article 72(3) provides that a party need not give notice of an intent to declare an avoidance. In addition, the other party does not have a right to cut off such an avoidance through a subsequent assurance of performance. Nonetheless, the twin requirements of a "clear" indication of a future "fundamental breach" remain. This often will leave an aggrieved party in substantial doubt about whether it has a right to declare an avoidance for anticipatory breach. It is in such circumstances that the right of a party to suspend its own performance, pending an adequate assurance from the other party, will be most valuable.[544]

§ 2.34 Breach and Remedies__Installment Contracts

The CISG has special rules for breach of an "instalment contract"—that is, where the contract involves at least two successive deliveries of the contract goods. For such a contract, the goods need not be of the same type; but the deliveries must be under the same contract (as opposed to under separate unrelated contracts). With respect to a breach of such contracts, CISG Article 73 defines different rules for an individual installment as opposed to a breach that affects the whole contract.

For an individual installment, if a party fails to perform in such a way as to constitute "a fundamental breach of contract with respect to that instalment," the other party may declare the contract avoided "with respect to that instalment."[545] If, however, such a breach also gives the aggrieved party "good grounds to conclude" that a fundamental breach will occur in the future installments, it may declare the contract avoided for the future as well (provided it does so within a reasonable time).[546] Thus, in one case a French court found that a buyer's breach of a resale limitation amounted to a fundamental breach with respect to the seller's delivery of a first installment of goods.[547] But the buyer also had stated unequivocally that "its resale actions are of no concern

---

[543]   Doolim Corp. v. R Doll, LLC, 2009 WL 1514913, at *6–7 (S.D.N.Y. 2009).

[544]   *See* CISG, art. 71 and § 2.31 *supra*.

[545]   CISG, art. 73(1).

[546]   CISG, art. 73(2).

[547]   CLOUT Case No. 154, *Cour d'appel* [Court of Appeal] of Grenoble, France (22 February 1995).

to" the seller. That statement gave the seller good grounds to conclude that the buyer would continue to breach the contract with regard to future installments as it had on the first installment. As a result, the court concluded that the seller was justified in declaring an avoidance of the entire contract.

Separately, the CISG grants a special right to an aggrieved buyer to declare an avoidance of the whole contract (or affected portions) if a breach on one delivery has a broader effect on the contract performances.[548] If the buyer can show that, "by reason of their interdependence," past or future deliveries "could not be used for the purpose contemplated by the parties at the time of the conclusion of the contract," it may declare an avoidance with respect to those past or future deliveries as well.[549] One court has held, however, that both parties must be aware of this interdependence in order to justify a buyer's resort to this special power of avoidance.[550]

§ 2.35 Buyer's Remedies for Breach by Seller

CISG Articles 45 through 52 define the remedies available to the buyer upon a breach by the seller. As described in detail below, if the seller breaches any of its obligations, the buyer has four basic types of remedies: (a) "avoidance" of the contract; (b) a special remedy that allows a "self-help" reduction in the price due; (c) specific performance; and in any event (d) an action for damages.

Before turning to those remedies, it is appropriate to recall that the CISG imposes certain conditions on the buyer's right to assert claims against the seller. As noted in § 2.26 above, to preserve any remedy for a delivery of nonconforming goods by the seller, the buyer must: inspect the goods in "as short a period as is practicable"; notify the seller of the nonconformity "within a reasonable time" of discovery; and permit the seller to attempt to cure any nonconformity, if the cure does not cause "unreasonable" delay, inconvenience, or expense. Similarly, the buyer loses the right to assert claims based on the existence of third-party property rights in the goods if it does not give notice to the seller of the claim "within a reasonable time" of discovery.[551]

---

[548] CISG, art. 73(3).

[549] This structure thus differs in important respects from the UCC provisions on installment contracts in § 2-612.

[550] CLOUT Case No. 880, Tribunal Cantonal of Vaud, Switzerland (11 April 2002).

[551] For more detail on all of these points see § 2.22 *supra*.

§ 2.36 Buyer's Remedies__Avoidance of the Contract

The CISG provides two separate grounds for the buyer to declare an "avoidance of the contract" upon a breach by the seller. First, CISG Article 49(1)(a) permits the buyer to use this remedy in the event of a "fundamental breach," regardless of the type of breach or when it occurs. Second, in the specific case of a non-delivery, CISG Article 49(1)(b) allows the buyer to declare an avoidance if the seller does not perform within an additional deadline set by the buyer. We will examine these two alternatives in turn.

As an essential background for both, recall first that an "avoidance of the contract" by the buyer is a method of refusing to accept or to keep defective goods, with a corresponding right not to pay for the goods.[552] In this respect, avoidance under the CISG is comparable to the rights of a buyer under the UCC to "reject" the goods actually delivered before "acceptance,"[553] or to "revoke the acceptance" of goods previously accepted.[554] However, the CISG does not adopt the UCC's distinctions between "rejection" of the goods, "acceptance" of the goods, and "revocation of acceptance."[555] Further, CISG does not attach special legal significance to the concept of acceptance of the goods; as a result, the buyer's taking delivery of the goods is not a crucial factual or legal step in the analysis of the buyer's position under the CISG.

Avoidance for Fundamental Breach. Instead, the core concept under the CISG is to limit use of the avoidance remedy to situations that involve a fundamental breach by the seller, regardless of when the breach occurs.[556] Section 2.32 above analyzed in detail the CISG's definition of a fundamental breach. In summary, a buyer has a right to declare an avoidance on this basis if a seller's failure to perform "any" of its obligations "substantially deprive[s]" the buyer of what it is "entitled to expect under the contract."[557] Such a declaration of avoidance must be made by notice to the seller.[558] But the right to declare an avoidance for a fundamental breach is lost if the buyer does not make the declaration (a) in respect of late delivery, within a reasonable time after the buyer has become

---

[552]   *See* the discussion in § 2.36 *supra.*

[553]   UCC §§ 2–601, 2–612.

[554]   UCC §§ 2–606, 2–608.

[555]   UCC §§ 2–601, 2–602, 2–608, 2–612.

[556]   CISG, art. 49(1)(a).

[557]   CISG, art. 25.

[558]   CISG, art. 26. But note again the special protections for the sender of such notices in Article 27. *See* the final paragraph of § 2.18.

aware of delivery, or (b) in respect of all other breaches, within a reasonable time after the buyer knew or ought to have known of the breach.[559] The purpose of this notice is to give the seller an opportunity to cure the defects.[560]

Even if the buyer seeks to avoid the contract after a "fundamental breach" by the seller, the latter has a right to "cure" any defect in its performance. As discussed in more detail in § 2.27 above, if the seller's nonconforming tender is early, the seller may cure by making a conforming tender up to the delivery date in the contract, whether the nonconformity would create a fundamental breach or not.[561] The seller's right to cure on this basis also survives the buyer's declaration of avoidance of the contract, because it will be very difficult to sustain a finding of fundamental breach where the seller has made a timely offer of cure before the delivery date has even arrived. If the seller's tender of a cure is made *after* the delivery date in the contract, it still has a right to cure through late performance, but only if it can do so "without unreasonable delay," and without causing the buyer unreasonable inconvenience or uncertainty of reimbursement of expenses.[562]

One controversy in this regard is whether the seller retains a post-delivery-date right to cure after a fundamental breach has already occurred. As noted above, the authorities seem to take conflicting views on the point.[563] One view holds that the buyer's right to declare a complete avoidance of the contract on such a basis takes priority over the seller's right to cure after the delivery date.[564] Nonetheless, one must be careful not to make too much of this argument, for the possibility of a timely cure will influence the existence of a fundamental breach in the first place. Thus, some courts have expressly held that the availability of timely repairs by the seller (or, presumably, third parties) precludes a finding of a fundamental breach. As UNCITRAL's Digest of Case Law on the CISG states, "[c]ourts are reluctant to consider a breach fundamental when the seller offers and effects speedy repair without any inconvenience to the buyer."[565] More generally, other courts have indicated that the assessment of a fundamental breach

---

[559] CISG, art. 49(2)(b)(i).

[560] *See* discussion of cure in § 2.27 *supra*.

[561] *See also* CISG, art. 37.

[562] CISG, art. 48(1). Again, for more detail on this point see § 2.27 *supra*.

[563] *See* § 2.27 and Müller-Chen, art. 48, paras. 14–17, in Schlechtriem & Schwenzer, *supra* note 30.

[564] *See* § 2.27 *supra*.

[565] *See* CISG DIGEST 2012, *supra* note 36, art. 25, para. 9 (citing cases).

is strongly influenced by the buyer's ability to procure suitable substitutes in a timely manner.[566]

In any event, the entire thrust of the CISG provisions on the buyer's remedies is to require cooperation between the parties in resolving disputes over timeliness of delivery and conformity of the goods. Moreover, as noted below, CISG Article 77 imposes an obligation on an aggrieved party to take reasonable steps to mitigate its damages.[567]

The CISG's rules on avoidance and cure may leave the seller of goods in a significantly better position as compared to the UCC, if the buyer claims a relatively minor fault in the goods. First, under the UCC the buyer may reject the goods merely because a tender is not "perfect;"[568] this definitely is not allowed under the CISG. In addition, although the seller has a right to cure defects under both regimes, the right under the UCC has either time limitations or knowledge requirements[569] that do not exist under the CISG. Finally, under either the UCC or the CISG the buyer will have a right to damages; but under the CISG, the buyer may return the goods only in the event of a "fundamental breach." Thus, the seller is less likely to find the goods rejected for an asserted minor nonconformity, and stranded an ocean or continent away.

Must performance offered as cure after delivery of defective goods meet a strict "nonconformity" test, or is it still subject to the fundamental breach test? The CISG has no express provision on this issue. Nonetheless, it would be paradoxical that if a seller effects a cure (*e.g.*, repair or replacement) that substantially gives the buyer what it entitled to expect under the contract,[570] the buyer nonetheless may declare an avoidance for fundamental breach. On the other hand, if the seller does not achieve this result on a first attempt at a cure, the likelihood of a subsequent cure "without unreasonable delay" and "without causing the buyer unreasonable inconvenience" decreases significantly.[571] Perhaps the seller, having breached once, should be considered to be on probation and must "get it right" during that probationary period (at least to clear up any existing fundamental breach).

---

[566]   *See id.*, art. 25, para. 8 (citing cases) and art. 49, para. 16 (citing cases).

[567]   *See* §§ 2.39 and 2.43 *infra*.

[568]   *See* UCC § 2–601.

[569]   *See* UCC § 2–508.

[570]   *See* CISG, art. 25 (defining the opposite of the statement in the text as a fundamental breach).

[571]   *See* CISG, art. 48(1).

In any event, even if the seller is able to effect a complete cure—whether before or after the delivery date—the buyer retains a right to damages caused by the defective goods.[572]

Recall, finally, that CISG Article 73(3) grants an aggrieved buyer with respect to a single installment a right to avoid the whole contract (or affected portions) if the interdependence of deliveries means that future deliveries cannot be used for the purpose contemplated at time of contracting.[573] Similarly, CISG Article 51 states that, even in the event of a partial delivery under a single delivery contract, the buyer may declare an avoidance of the entire contract if a seller's failure to make a complete delivery or a completely conforming delivery amounts to a fundamental breach of the entire contract.

Avoidance and "Nachfrist." Given the uncertainties of the fundamental breach test, it often will be difficult for the buyer, or its attorney, to know how to react to any particular breach—and whether avoidance of the contract is permissible or not. Incorrect analysis could put the buyer in the position of making a fundamental breach through its response. CISG Articles 47 and 49(1)(b) attempt to cure these uncertainties by offering the buyer an alternative method of formulating a supposedly strict standard for performance. Based on the German law notion of *Nachfrist* ("additional deadline"), if the seller fails to deliver the goods on the agreed delivery date, the buyer may notify the seller that performance is due by a stated new date.[574] If the seller fails to perform—or declares that it will not perform—by the new deadline, the buyer has a right to declare an avoidance of the contract even if no fundamental breach has yet occurred.[575] Such a declaration of avoidance again must be made by notice to the seller.[576] And if the seller has already delivered the goods, the buyer loses the right to declare an avoidance on this basis unless it does so within a reasonable time after the expiration of the *Nachfrist.*[577]

However, by its express terms, the CISG allows this alternative ground for avoidance by the buyer only for "non-delivery" by the seller. Thus, it is not clear whether the seller's delivery of nonconforming goods during the additional period permits

---

[572] CISG, arts. 37, 48(1).

[573] *See* § 2.34 *supra.*

[574] CISG, art. 47(1).

[575] CISG, art. 49(1)(b).

[576] CISG, art. 26. *But see* the final paragraph of § 2.18 *supra* (noting the special protections for the sender of such notices in Article 27).

[577] CISG, art. 49(2)(b)(ii). The same rule applies if the seller declared an intent to cure under CISG Article 48 and then (a) did not do so, or (b) the buyer rightfully refused to permit such a cure. CISG, art. 49(2)(b)(iii).

avoidance or not. In other words, must the quality of a late delivery by the seller meet a strict standard of "nonconformity," or only the standard of "fundamental breach"? The authorities are not in agreement. In any event, if the buyer sets such an additional deadline for performance, it may not resort in the interim to any remedy for breach of contract, unless the seller declares that it will not perform by the deadline.[578]

How long of an additional period must the buyer give the seller? Article 47 requires that it be "of reasonable length," but unless there is a custom on this issue the buyer will have no certainty that the period given in the *Nachfrist* notice is long enough, especially if long distances are involved. In one German decision, the court held that three to four weeks was a reasonable time for a car sale contract.[579] In another, however, the court indicated that an additional period of two weeks was too short, but nonetheless upheld the buyer's declaration of avoidance seven weeks later because the seller had offered only a partial delivery of conforming goods in the interim.[580] This latter holding conforms with a general practice of courts to substitute a reasonable period in the event the buyer fixes an unreasonably short period.[581]

The cases sometimes involve buyers that quickly complain about the goods, hoping that the seller will cure the defect, and then officially declare avoidance much later (often months). They usually are not permitted to avoid the contract—the courts holding that the buyers' original complaints about the goods do not amount either to the setting of a clear deadline as required for a *Nachfrist* or to a formal declaration of avoidance, and that their later declarations came too late.[582] The message of these cases is that buyers must make a clear choice either to set a deadline for final performance by the seller or make a timely declaration of avoidance for fundamental breach. As one U.S. Appellate Court observed, however, the CISG's flexible standard for a valid modification of a contract ("mere agreement") may mean that the parties' interactions after a defective or late delivery amount to a formal agreement to amend their contract.[583]

---

[578]   CISG, art. 47(2).

[579]   CLOUT Case No. 362, *Oberlandesgericht* [Appellate Court] of Naumburg, Germany (27 April 1999).

[580]   CLOUT Case No. 136, *Oberlandesgericht* [Appellate Court] of Celle, Germany (24 May 1995).

[581]   *See* CISG DIGEST 2012, *supra* note 36, art. 47, para. 5.

[582]   *Id.*, art. 49, para. 23 (citing cases).

[583]   Valero Marketing & Supply Co. v. Greeni Oy, 242 Fed. Appx. 840, 844–845 (3rd Cir. 2007) (citing CISG Article 29(1)).

Conditions on the Buyer's Avoidance Rights. The CISG imposes certain important conditions and obligations on a buyer that wishes to declare a contract avoided. First, the buyer loses the right to make such a declaration—or require delivery of substitute goods—if it cannot return the goods to the seller "substantially in the condition in which he received them."[584] This rule does not apply, however, if (a) the buyer was not at fault for the inability so to return the goods, (b) the harm to the goods was a result of a proper inspection upon delivery, or (c) the buyer sold or otherwise consumed the goods in the ordinary course of its business.[585] Even if one of these exceptions does not apply, the buyer retains all of the other remedies it has for seller's breach.[586]

Restitution and Obligation to Preserve Goods. As noted in § 2.32 above, avoidance of the contract releases both parties from their contractual obligations, but also preserves the right to damages for the aggrieved party.[587] A party that has already performed in such a case has a corresponding right of restitution against the other.[588] Thus, if the buyer properly avoids the contract, it is entitled to a return of any money already paid to the seller, but also must return to the seller any goods already delivered.

In addition, CISG Articles 85 through 88 impose certain obligations on the buyer to preserve the goods pending their return to the seller. A buyer that declares an avoidance after delivery of the goods must take "reasonable" steps to preserve them.[589] This may include depositing the goods in a warehouse at the seller's expense.[590] If the seller has no agent in the buyer's location, but the goods have been "placed at [the buyer's] disposal at their destination," the buyer must take possession of them "on behalf of the seller" if this can be done without payment of the price (*i.e.*, without paying for any negotiable bill of lading covering the goods) and without "unreasonable inconvenience or unreasonable expense."[591] After such a taking of possession on behalf of the seller, the buyer must again take "reasonable" steps to preserve them. If the goods are perishable, an aggrieved buyer in possession must take reasonable steps to sell them (and then apply to the proceeds to its expenses and damages, with any surplus presumably for the

---

[584] CISG, art. 82(1).
[585] CISG, art. 82(2).
[586] CISG, art. 83.
[587] CISG, art. 81(1).
[588] CISG, art. 81((2).
[589] CISG, art. 86(1).
[590] CISG, art. 87.
[591] CISG, art. 86(2).

seller).[592] The CISG does not, however, contain any provisions that would require an aggrieved buyer in possession to follow the seller's instructions, such as to resell on the seller's behalf, whether seemingly reasonable or not.[593]

Finally, the buyer must account to the seller for any benefits derived from temporary possession of the goods before return.[594]

§ 2.37 Buyer's Rememdies__Non-Judicial Reduction in Price

In addition to refusing to accept goods that do not conform to the contract based on a declaration of avoidance as discussed immediately above, an aggrieved buyer has a separate informal remedy that appears to give it a power of self-help. Under the CISG, a buyer that receives nonconforming goods "may reduce the price" it pays to the seller.[595] This remedy is available whether the buyer has already paid or not, but if the buyer has paid, the remedy is likely to require an action in court. The buyer may not resort to this remedy, however, if the seller has cured any defects in the goods[596] or the buyer wrongfully refuses to grant the seller an opportunity to make such a cure.[597]

The Convention spells out a formula for calculating the permissible amount of the price reduction: The buyer is entitled to reduce the price "in the same proportion as the value that the goods actually delivered bears to the value that conforming goods would have had at that time."[598] Thus, the buyer may reduce the price according to the difference between the actual value of the nonconforming goods and the contractually required value of those goods. If the market price has not changed between the time of contracting and the delivery date, this formula should give the same result as under the UCC.[599] In any event, one U.S. District Court has indicated that, if the buyer resells the defective goods, the

---

[592]   CISG, art. 88(2).

[593]   Compare UCC § 2–603.

[594]   CISG, art. 84(2).

[595]   CISG, art. 50.

[596]   *See* CISG, arts. 37 and 48 and § 2.27 *supra*.

[597]   CISG, art. 50.

[598]   *Id.*

[599]   *See* UCC § 2–714 (measuring damages for breach of warranty by the difference between the value of accepted goods and "the value they would have had if they had been as warranted"). The price reduction measure under the CISG may cause a different result as compared to the UCC if the market price of the goods has changed between formation and delivery. *See* Harry Flechtner, *More U.S. Decisions on the U.N. Sales Convention: Scope, Parol Evidence, "Validity," and Reduction of Price Under Article 50*, 14 J. LAW & COM. 153 (1995).

resale price is evidence of their value at the time of delivery and that the seller is entitled to discover that resale price.[600]

This type of a self-help remedy is familiar at civil law, as a method of compensating an aggrieved buyer when there is no civil law cause of action for damages (such as when the seller is not "at fault").[601] The UCC also allows an aggrieved buyer to exercise self-help in reducing the price of non-conforming goods, but this remedy does not appear to be widely used.[602] Unlike the UCC provision, CISG Article 50 states no requirement of prior notice to the seller by the buyer before exercising this option (although of course the buyer must give notice of the defect itself[603]). Proposals at the CISG Diplomatic Conference to require a "declaration of price reduction" by the buyer were not accepted.[604]

CISG Article 50 provides little guidance on how to determine the value of the goods at the time of delivery, or on what evidence of value should be presented to the seller. The provision, therefore, seems better suited to deliveries that are defective as to quantity, rather than as to quality. Nonetheless, the buyer's right to reduce the price clearly applies to defects in quality as well.[605] The general view among authorities is that the remedy is not available for defects in title or a breach founded on the existence of third-party property claims.[606]

As noted, a buyer intending to use this self-help remedy must allow the seller to attempt to cure, if the seller so requests.[607] But the buyer will retain the right to a price reduction under Article 50 even if the seller has a valid exemption due to an unexpected "impediment"[608] as provided in Article 79.[609] A buyer that has claimed a price reduction may not, however, simultaneously demand that a defect be remedied by repair or delivery of substitute

---

[600] Interag Co. Ltd. v. Stafford Phase Corp., 1990 WL 71478, at *4 (S.D.N.Y. 1990).

[601] On the civil law foundation of Article 50, see Eric Bergsten & Anthony Miller, *The Remedy of Reduction of Price*, 27 AM. J. COMP. L. 255 (1979).

[602] UCC § 2–717.

[603] *See* CISG, art. 39 and § 2.26 *supra*.

[604] *See* Bergsten & Miller, *supra* note 601.

[605] On the seller's obligations regarding the quality of goods see § 2.21 *supra*.

[606] *See* Müller-Chen, art. 50, para. 2, in Schlechtriem & Schwenzer, *supra* note 30.

[607] CISG, art. 50.

[608] *See* § 2.29 *supra*.

[609] Under CISG Article 79(5), a valid exemption from liability does not prevent either party from exercising "any right other than to damages."

goods,[610] although it may combine a price reduction with a claim for damages to obtain full compensation.[611]

§ 2.38   Buyer's Remedies__Specific Performance

The more formal remedies available to an aggrieved buyer through court or arbitral tribunal proceedings are an action for specific performance and an action for damages. (The seller has parallel judicial remedies in the form of an action for the price and an action for damages.[612])

The CISG gives to the buyer that has not received the agreed performance from the seller a specifically enforceable right to "require performance" by the seller.[613] This reflects the basic civil law theory that legal compulsion of performance is the best relief to an aggrieved buyer, and that the seller's actual performance is preferable to substitutional relief (such as a monetary award).[614] The reference to the seller's "obligations" is not limited, and so can include court compulsion to provide goods of the agreed description quantity, quality, and title (including intellectual property rights), as well as adhering to the agreed time, place, and manner of delivery.

The buyer's right to specific performance is subject to two important qualifications: First, the buyer must not have already resorted to an "inconsistent" remedy; and, second, a court (such as in a common law jurisdiction) need not grant such a remedy "unless the court would do so under its own law" for comparable contracts (see below).[615] Thus, the CISG gives the buyer the right to seek specific performance, rather than damages, but does not compel it to do so; and it permits a court to grant such a remedy, but does not compel it to do so.

Although the buyer may elect to seek specific performance, it often will prefer to purchase substitute goods and seek a recovery of damages, because of the expense and delays inherent in involving a court in ordering conforming performance by a recalcitrant seller.[616]

---

[610]   See CISG, art. 46 (although this remedy may not be available in the United States, see § 2.38 infra).

[611]   See Müller-Chen, art. 50, para. 18, in Schlechtriem & Schwenzer, supra note 30.

[612]   See §§ 2.42 and 2.43 infra.

[613]   CISG, art. 46.

[614]   For a background and comparison see Shael Herman, Specific Performance: A Comparative Analysis, 7 EDINBURGH L. REV. 5 [Part I] and 194 [Part II] (2003).

[615]   CISG, art. 28.

[616]   There is significant evidence that substitutional relief is often sought in civil law commercial disputes. See, e.g., Henrik Lando and Caspar Rose, On the Enforcement of Specific Performance in Civil Law Countries, 24 INT'L REV. L. &

Nonetheless, the first limitation noted above reflects the notion that a buyer cannot require *specific* performance of a contractual duty if it has already sought a *substitutional* remedy. The CISG in this respect imposes an election of remedies rule. Thus, the buyer is not entitled to specific performance if it has already declared an avoidance of the contract (whether for fundamental breach or failure of the seller to meet a *Nachfrist*);[617] effected a reduction in price;[618] or sought damages tied directly to the seller's failure to deliver the goods (as opposed to consequential damages).[619]

The second limitation on the remedy of specific performance is much more significant in the United States. Under CISG Article 28 a court "is not bound" to order specific performance "unless the court would do so under its own law" in respect of similar contracts of sale. This rule will have a negligible effect on civil law courts because they are authorized to order the seller's performance as a general rule.[620] Thus, if specific performance is sought in a civil law court, it usually will apply CISG Article 46 and order the seller to perform its obligations, and a buyer desiring this remedy should, if possible, bring its claim in such a court.

This would not, however, be the analytical approach of a common law court. Although the UCC empowers courts to order specific performance, the case law does not demonstrate widespread interest in doing so.[621] In any event, the result of the rule in Article 28, interestingly, is that a U.S. court will grant a remedy of specific performance in a case governed by the CISG only as allowed by UCC § 2–716. If the goods are "unique" and they exist, then it is more likely the court will order specific performance. If, however, substitute goods are readily available in the market it is less likely that the court would order specific performance. A U.S. court would be likely to issue a specific performance order for requirements or output contracts involving "particular or peculiarly available" goods.[622] With those exceptions, a U.S. court generally would not be required by CISG Article 46 to issue an order compelling the delivery of goods by the seller. And, in a noteworthy exception to the

---

ECON. 473, 478 (2004) (stating that damages are "by far the dominant form of relief" in civil law countries as well); Jacob Ziegel, *The Remedial Provisions of the Vienna Sales Convention: Common Law Perspectives*, Ch. 9, in INTERNATIONAL SALES (N. Galston and H. Smit, eds. 1984).

[617]   *See* § 2.32 *supra* and CISG, arts. 26, 49(1)(a), (b).

[618]   *See* § 2.36 *supra* and CISG, art. 50.

[619]   *See* § 2.39 *infra* and CISG, arts. 45(1)(b), 74–77.

[620]   *See* Tallon, *Remedies, The French Report*, in CONTRACT LAW TODAY 263–288 (D. Harris and D. Tallon, eds. 1989).

[621]   UCC § 2–716(1).

[622]   UCC § 2–716, comment 2.

general principle of "party autonomy" in CISG Article 6, the parties may not derogate from this limitation through contractual agreement.[623] Thus, a buyer desirous of a specific performance remedy should not bring its claim in a common law court.[624]

If the remedy of specific performance is available, the buyer may require performance by the seller of any of its breached obligations.[625] Where the goods have not been delivered, this would mean a requirement that the seller deliver the goods. If the seller has delivered, but the goods do not conform to the contract, the buyer may require delivery of conforming substitute goods if the nonconformity amounts to a fundamental breach, and the buyer has given the seller proper notice (either as part of the initial notice of nonconformity or separately within a reasonable time).[626] Likewise, the buyer may require the seller to repair nonconforming goods, unless this is "unreasonable having regard to all the circumstances."[627] In any event, the buyer, again, loses the right to demand specific performance in the form of repair or replacement if it has declared an "avoidance" of the contract, because this is an inconsistent remedy.

§ 2.39   Buyer's Remedies__Action for Damages

In accordance with traditional notions, the CISG also provides an aggrieved buyer (as well as an aggrieved seller, see below[628]) with an action for damages.[629] Like other remedies, the buyer's right to damages exists if the seller fails to perform any of its obligations under the contract.[630] The right to damages exists even when the buyer has avoided the contract and when the seller has successfully cured defects in its performance.[631] There is no requirement that the buyer prove that the seller was "at fault" as a prerequisite to a recovery of damages. Both direct and consequential damages are recoverable; and expectancy, reliance, and restitutionary interests are all protected depending on the specific context.

---

[623]   See CLOUT Case No. 651, *Tribunale di Padova*, Italy (11 January 2005).

[624]   Because the reference point in CISG Article 28 is "the court" in which an action is proceeding, the applicable law for granting specific performance is that of the forum, without regard to choice of law rules. *See* Müller-Chen, art. 28, para. 9, in Schlechtriem & Schwenzer, *supra* note 30.

[625]   CISG, art. 46(1).

[626]   CISG, art. 46(2).

[627]   CISG, art. 46(3).

[628]   See § 2.43 *infra*.

[629]   CISG, art. 45(1)(b).

[630]   *Id.*

[631]   CISG, art. 45(2).

CISG Articles 74 through 78 set forth the rules for the calculation of a claim for damages for both seller and buyer. Article 74 defines the basic principle that an aggrieved party is entitled to "a sum equal to the loss, including loss of profit, suffered as a consequence of the breach." As the Second Circuit correctly observed in *Delchi Carrier S.p.A. v. Rotorex Corp.*, this rule is "designed to place the aggrieved party in as good a position as if the other party had properly performed the contract,"[632] a formulation subsequent courts properly have adopted.[633] In a claim based on a seller's delivery of nonconforming goods, this court also concluded that the buyer may recover profits from any lost downstream sales, measured by the price less variable costs only (*i.e.*, not including fixed overhead costs).[634]

Recovery of damages under the CISG is subject to certain, in part familiar, limitations. First, CISG Article 74 expressly states that damages (especially consequential damages) may not exceed the loss that the party in breach "foresaw or ought to have foreseen at the time of the conclusion of the contract." Some U.S. courts have observed that this rule is "identical to the well-known rule of *Hadley v. Baxendale.*"[635] This, however, is an example of *faux amis* ("false friends"), in which courts wrongly assume that similar means "identical." First, unlike the common law foreseeability rule, CISG Article 74 states that recovery is available if the loss suffered is a "possible" (not "probable") consequence of the breach.[636] Second, the CISG rule has a more ambiguous reference to matters of which the party in breach "ought to have known" at the time of contract formation. Finally, the CISG rule refers explicitly to the two layers of foreseeability, that of the loss itself and, separately, that of the "facts and matters" of which the party in breach knew or ought to have known as a possible consequence of the breach.

---

[632]   71 F.3d 1024, 1029 (2d Cir. 1995) (*quoting* John Honnold, *Uniform Law for International Sales Under the 1980 United Nations Convention* 503 (2d ed. 1991)).

[633]   *See, e.g.,* Profi-Parkiet Sp. Zoo v. Seneca Hardwoods LLC, 2014 WL 2169769, at *7 (E.D.N.Y. 2014); Norfolk Southern Ry. Co. v. Power Source Supply, Inc., 2008 WL 2884102, at *7 (W.D. Pa. 2008).

[634]   *Id.* at 1029–1030. *See also* Al Hewar Environmental & Public Health Establishment v. Southeast Ranch, LLC, 2011 WL 7191744, at *2 (S.D. Fla. 2011) (awarding an aggrieved buyer damages from lost profits on downstream sales).

[635]   TeeVee Toons, Inc. v. Gerhard Schubert GmbH, 2006 WL 2463537, at *9 (S.D.N.Y. 2006) (citing Hadley v. Baxendale, 9 Ex. 341, 156 Eng. Rep. 145 (1854)). *See also* Delchi Carrier S.p.A. v. Rotorex Corp., 71 F.3d 1024, 1030 (2d Cir. 1995) (same).

[636]   *Compare* CISG, art. 74, last sentence, *with* RESTATEMENT (SECOND) OF CONTRACTS, § 351(1). For a thorough discussion of the differences between the Common Law and CISG, see Arthur Murphey, *Consequential Damages in CISG and the Legacy of Hadley*, 23 GEO. WASH. J. INT'L L. & ECON. 415 (1989).

Second, CISG Article 77 provides that an aggrieved party must take "reasonable measures" to mitigate its damages. If it fails to do so, the party in breach may claim a reduction in damages "in the amount by which the loss should have been mitigated."[637] With reference to a breach by the seller, this limitation commonly will require an aggrieved buyer to enter into a substitute purchase in order to prevent or mitigate its damages.[638]

Finally, it is generally understood that an aggrieved party must prove its damages to a reasonable degree of certainty.[639] This follows from the general principles of reasonableness and that a proponent has the burden of proof on a claim and of a claimant.[640]

Alternative Measures of Recovery. Where a buyer has declared an avoidance of the contract, the CISG provides alternative measures of recovery. If the buyer declares an avoidance of the contract (see § 2.36 above), Article 75 first grants it the right to buy replacement goods if it does so "in a reasonable manner and within a reasonable time after avoidance." The aggrieved buyer then is entitled to damages—in addition to consequential damages under Article 74—corresponding to the difference between the contract price and the "price in the substitute transaction," which in the case of an aggrieved buyer means the purchase price for the replacement goods.[641]

As an alternative, Article 76 grants the aggrieved buyer that has declared an avoidance of the contract the difference between the contract price and the "current price" (*i.e.*, the market price) for the goods. This, again, is in addition to consequential damages under Article 74. Where this current price differential is used, the price in the market is to be measured at the time of avoidance,[642] unless the buyer had already "taken over" the goods at the time of avoidance. In the latter case, the market price is measured at the time of "taking over."[643] The relevant market for determining the current price is the place where delivery of the goods should have been

---

[637]   CISG, art. 77.

[638]   *See* Schwenzer, art. 77, para. 10, in Schlechtriem & Schwenzer, *supra* note 30.

[639]   CISG Advisory Council Opinion No. 6, *Calculation of Damages under CISG Article 74*, § 2 (2006), *available at* http://www.cisgac.com/cisgac-opinion-no6/. *See also* Tee Vee Toons, Inc. v. Gerhard Schubert GmbH, 2006 WL 2463537, at *10 (S.D.N.Y. 2006) (referring to proof with "sufficient certainty") (citing Delchi Carrier S.p.A. v. Rotorex Corp., 71 F.3d 1024, 1029 (2d Cir. 1995)).

[640]   For a discussion of these "general principles" of the Convention see § 2.10 *supra*.

[641]   Compare UCC § 2–712 (providing for damages in the event of a "cover" purchase by the buyer).

[642]   CISG, art. 76(1), first sentence.

[643]   CISG, art. 76, second sentence.

made or, if no such price exists there, "at such other place as serves as a reasonable substitute."[644] The Article 76 measure may not be used at all, however, if no "current price" is available at any such place.

Although the Convention provides for recovery under either Article 75 or Article 76, if the buyer actually makes a replacement purchase, it may not use the latter.[645] The general requirement of "reasonable measures" to mitigate damages under Article 77 would seem to require this result. The Convention gives no guidance, however, on how to determine whether any particular purchase by the buyer is a replacement purchase, or is instead an ordinary buildup of inventory.

The CISG measures of the buyer's damages in many respects are similar to those in the UCC. The U.S. leading case applying the CISG's damages rules remains *Delchi Carrier S.p.A. v. Rotorex Corp.* There, the court correctly ruled that UCC case law could not be used to interpret CISG provisions unless the language of the UCC provision tracks that of the CISG provision.[646] But the court observed that the broad, general language of CISG Article 74 reflects a traditional and fundamental principle of full compensation[647] Nonetheless, U.S. courts should be very careful to ensure that the specific precedents developed under the specific rules of the domestic UCC do not frustrate the fundamental obligation to have "regard for [the Convention's] international character and the need to promote uniformity in its application."[648]

The case involved a buyer that had lost sales due to the seller's delivery of nonconforming goods, and that sought to recover the corresponding lost profits on the downstream sales until it was able to find suitable substitute goods. The court found that the standard contract price vs. market price differential would not fully compensate the buyer for the "loss, including lost profits, suffered by" the buyer as declared in CISG Article 74.[649] The lost profit damages were, however, recoverable only to the extent that they were reasonably foreseeable by the seller. In measuring the buyer's lost profits, the court found that the CISG had no specific provision

---

[644]   CISG, art. 76(2).

[645]   CISG, art. 76(1) (stating that the measure is available "if [the buyer] has not made a purchase . . . under article 75").

[646]   71 F.3d 1024, 1028 (2d Cir. 1995).

[647]   *Id.*, at 1029–1030 (emphasizing the language in CISG Article that "[d]amages . . . consist of a sum equal to the loss . . . suffered by the other party as a consequence of the breach").

[648]   CISG, art. 7(1). *See also* the discussion of the rules governing the interpretation of the Convention in § 2.10 above.

[649]   *Id.*

on the treatment of fixed and variable costs in determining the buyer's lost profits. It therefore followed the traditional principle that only the variable costs saved by the buyer are to be deducted from the lost sales revenues.

The courts also allowed the buyer to recover, as additional consequential and incidental damages: (1) the costs of the buyer's attempts to effect its own cure, including reinspection and testing; (2) the costs of expedited delivery of substitute conforming goods from another seller; (3) the costs of storing the non-conforming goods; (4) the shipping and customs costs for the non-conforming goods; (5) the costs of materials and tools usable only with the non-conforming goods; and (6) the labor costs related to the production line shutdown.[650]

Article 78 separately entitles an aggrieved party to recover interest on any "sum that is in arrears" (although a substantial dispute exists over how to calculate the interest rate).[651] Again, however, CISG Article 79 declares that damages are not recoverable in the event an unforeseeable impediment has prevented the other party's performance.[652]

Attorney's Fees. In most of the world, the losing party also must pay the winner's attorney's fees, typically according to a statutory formula. This—importantly—is regarded as part of the damages necessary to make the aggrieved party whole, not merely a local rule of procedure. One U.S. appellate court has held to the contrary, however, and, therefore, that the issue is not part of the substantive law of the Convention.[653] The problem with this decision is that it engaged neither with the interpretive rules in CISG Article 7 nor with the thoughtful analyses of foreign courts on the subject (which is required by Article 7(1)).[654] And essentially every court and arbitral tribunal outside of the United States has found that the basic principle of full compensation reflected in CISG Article 74

---

[650]   *Id.*, at 1029–031.

[651]   For a review of this controversy see Michael P. Van Alstine, *The UNCITRAL Digest, the Right to Interest, and the Interest Rate Controversy*, in DRAFTING CONTRACTS UNDER THE CISG (H. Flechtner, R. Brand & M. Walter, eds., 2008).

[652]   For more on this exemption for nonperformance see § 2.29 *supra*.

[653]   Zapata Hermanos Sucesores, S.A. v. Hearthside Baking Company, Inc., 313 F.3d 385, 389–390 (7th Cir. 2002). *See also* Profi-Parkiet Sp. Zoo v. Seneca Hardwoods LLC, 2014 WL 2169769, at *10 (E.D.N.Y. 2014); San Lucio, S.R.L. v. Import & Storage Services, LLC, 2009 WL 1010981 (D.N.J. 2009). *But see* Granjas Aquanova S.A. de C.V. v. House Mfg. Co. Inc., 2010 WL 4809342, at *2 (E.D. Ark. 2010) (noting the criticism of Zapata and observing the matter remains in doubt).

[654]   *See, e.g.,* CISG AC Opinion No. 6, *supra* note 639, Comment 5.2 (criticizing the procedural/substantive distinction in as reflected in Zapata as "outdated and unproductive"); Peter Schlechtriem, *Legal Costs as Damages in the Application of UN Sales Law,* 25 J.L. & COM. 71 (2007–08).

requires an award of reasonable attorney's fees as well.[655] The failure of these U.S. courts to recognize this world-wide consensus on the interpretation of the CISG thus fundamentally disregards the mandate in CISG Article 7(1) that they must "promote uniformity" in the application of the Convention.

§ 2.40   Seller's Remedies for Breach by Buyer

The CISG provisions on the seller's remedies for a breach by the buyer parallel the structure for the buyer's remedies upon breach discussed above. Under CISG Articles 61 through 65, if the buyer fails to perform "any" of its obligations,[656] the seller has three basic types of remedies: (a) a non-judicial "avoidance" of the contract; (b) an action for the price (a form of specific performance); and in any event (c) an action for damages.

§ 2.41   Seller's Remedies___Avoidance of the Contract

Again in parallel with the buyer's rights upon breach, the CISG provides two separate grounds for the seller to declare an "avoidance of the contract" upon a breach by the buyer. First, Article 64(1)(a) permits the seller to make such a declaration in the case of a "fundamental breach" by the buyer, regardless of the type of breach or when it occurs. Second, if the buyer does not pay the price or accept delivery of the goods, Articles 63 and 64(1)(b) give the seller a right to declare an avoidance if the buyer does not perform within an additional deadline set by the seller. We again will examine these two alternatives in turn.

Under either option, the effect of an "avoidance of the contract" by the seller is a right not to perform its contractual obligations, and especially to refuse to deliver the goods to the buyer.[657] Further, because the CISG does not attach special legal significance to the concept of "acceptance" of the goods, the seller's delivery of the goods to the buyer is not a crucial factual or legal step in the analysis of the seller's position under the CISG. Thus, as compared to the UCC, the CISG may put an aggrieved seller in a substantially better position regarding stopping the goods in transit or reclaiming them from the buyer (see immediately below).

To assert either option for avoidance, the seller must make a corresponding declaration by notice to the buyer.[658] In either case,

---

[655]   *See* CISG DIGEST 2012, *supra* note 36, art. 74, para. 27 (citing cases).

[656]   CISG, art. 61(1).

[657]   *See* the discussion in § 2.20 *supra*.

[658]   CISG, art. 26. *But see* the final paragraph of § 2.18 *supra* (noting the special protections for the sender of such notices in Article 27).

the seller also retains its right to any damages caused by the buyer's breach.[659]

Avoidance for Fundamental Breach. The seller's principal right to declare an avoidance of the contract arises upon a "fundamental breach" by the buyer.[660] Section 2.32 above analyzed in detail the CISG's definition of that core term. In summary, the seller has a right to declare an avoidance on this basis if the buyer's failure to perform "any" of its obligations[661] "substantially deprive[s]" the seller of what it is "entitled to expect under the contract."[662] The standard examples from the case law of such a fundamental breach by the buyer are a definitive failure to pay the price (or a significant portion thereof) and a final failure to take delivery of the goods (which is especially important in long-distance transactions).[663] But if the buyer already has paid the purchase price, the right to declare an avoidance for a fundamental breach is lost if the seller does not make the declaration (a) in respect of late performance, before the seller "has become aware that the performance has been rendered," or (b) in respect of any other breach, within a reasonable time after the seller knew or ought to have known of the breach.[664]

Avoidance and Nachfrist. The uncertainties over the precise application of the fundamental breach test in practice also affect a seller, for it too will have difficulty in knowing whether a particular breach by the buyer will justify a declaration of avoidance of the contract. Here as well, incorrect analysis could put the seller in the position of making a fundamental breach through its response. CISG Articles 63 and 64(1)(b) thus also give the seller an alternative method for ensuring that the buyer will perform its obligations—or at least making clear that the buyer will not do so. In the event the buyer fails to perform, the seller may set a *Nachfrist* ("additional deadline"), that is, "an additional period of time . . . for performance by the buyer."[665] Then, if the buyer fails to perform—or declares that it will not perform—by the new deadline, the seller has a right to declare an avoidance of the contract even if no fundamental breach has yet occurred.[666] This option only exists, however, with respect to the buyer's obligations to pay the price and take delivery of the goods.[667] Finally, the additional deadline for

---

[659] CISG, art. 61(2).

[660] CISG, art. 64(1)(a).

[661] CISG, arts. 61(1), 64(1)(a).

[662] CISG, art. 25.

[663] *See* CISG DIGEST 2012, *supra* note 36, art. 64, paras. 3–6 (citing cases).

[664] CISG, art. 64(2)(b)(i).

[665] CISG, art. 63(1).

[666] CISG, art. 64(1)(b).

[667] *Id.*

performance must be "of reasonable length"[668] in order to permit the buyer to perform at least to a level that will retain the integrity of the contract (especially, a right to delivery of the goods).

If the seller sets such an additional deadline for performance, it may not resort in the interim to any remedy for breach of contract, unless the buyer declares that it will not perform within the deadline. But even if the buyer so performs, the seller will retain its rights to any remaining damages from the delay in the buyer's performance.[669]

Again, such a declaration of avoidance must be made by notice to the buyer.[670] If the buyer has already paid the price, the seller loses the right to declare an avoidance on this basis unless it does so within a reasonable time after the expiration of the *Nachfrist* (or after the buyer has declared that it will not perform).[671]

The Seller's Right of Reclamation. A seller's justified declaration of avoidance also may trigger a right to reclaim the goods from the buyer after delivery. That is, if an unpaid seller is unable (for any reason) to obtain the price, it may through a declaration of avoidance seek to obtain the return of its goods from the defaulting buyer. The UCC places substantial limitations on such a right.[672] But the CISG's description of the rights upon avoidance may allow such a reclamation. First, the CISG's grant to the seller of a power of avoidance upon breach by the buyer does not distinguish between pre- and post-delivery situations.[673] In addition, if one party already has performed, an avoidance of the contract creates a right of "restitution from the other party of whatever the first party has supplied" under the contract.[674] In the case of the seller, this should mean a right of restitution of goods already delivered. This analysis is available only so long as third parties (*e.g.*, buyer's creditors and trustees in bankruptcy) are not involved, for the CISG excludes from its scope issues of title to the goods and third party rights.[675] Notwithstanding this rule, the CISG would seem to grant to the seller, as between it and the buyer, a right to *possession* of the goods upon a justified avoidance of the contract. This should create the legal ground for a right of

---

[668] CISG, art. 63(1). For a discussion of court decisions on what is a "reasonable" length of time in particular cases see § 2.26 *supra*.

[669] CISG, art. 63(2).

[670] CISG, art. 26. *But see* the final paragraph of § 2.18 *supra* (noting the special protections for the sender of such notices in Article 27).

[671] CISG, art. 64(2)(b)(ii).

[672] *See, e.g.*, UCC §§ 2–507 and 2–702, and their comments.

[673] CISG, art. 64.

[674] CISG, art. 81(2).

[675] CISG, art. 4(b). *See also* § 2.8 *supra*.

replevin under domestic law (and notwithstanding that the CISG generally does not require a court to order "specific performance" of a contract[676]).

Restitution and Obligation to Preserve Goods. Like the buyer's situation upon breach by the seller, avoidance of the contract releases both parties from their contractual obligations.[677] And as noted immediately above, if either party has already performed, it has a corresponding right of restitution against the other.[678]

If the buyer fails to take delivery of the goods or to pay the price when concurrent performance is required, the CISG imposes certain obligations on the seller regarding preservation of the goods. First, if the seller is in possession of or otherwise controls the goods, it must take reasonable steps to preserve them pending ultimate delivery to the buyer.[679] It may do so by depositing the goods in a public warehouse at the expense of the buyer.[680] The seller may then make payment of any such additional expenses a condition to delivery of the goods.[681] If, however, there is an "unreasonable delay" in the buyer taking delivery or paying the price, the seller may sell the goods to a third party "by any appropriate means"[682] and it must do so if the goods are subject to rapid deterioration.[683] It may then take out of the proceeds any related expenses, but must account to the buyer for any excess.[684]

§ 2.42 Seller's Remedies___Specific Performance: Action for the Price

The preferred remedy for an aggrieved seller, if the buyer should breach, is a cause of action for the price, which is the seller's functional equivalent of an action for specific performance. A cause of action for damages, but not the price, is distinctly secondary.

CISG Article 62 gives the seller an unqualified right to require the buyer to pay the price (although no other provision formally states that the seller has a cause of action for payment of the price). There are, however, important conditions on the exercise of such a right: First, the seller of course must itself have performed as

---

[676] *See* CISG, art. 28 and §§ 2.38 *supra* and 2.42 *infra*.

[677] CISG, art. 81(1).

[678] CISG, art. 81(2).

[679] CISG, art. 86(1).

[680] CISG, art. 87.

[681] CISG, art. 85.

[682] CISG, art. 88(1).

[683] CISG, art. 88(2). The same rule applies if the costs of preservation are excessive as compared to the value of the goods. *Id.*

[684] CISG, art. 88(3).

required by the contract.[685] Second, the payment of the price must actually be due.[686] Third, the seller must not have already resorted to an "inconsistent" remedy.[687] Prominent examples of this would be a declaration of an avoidance of the contract (for the seller may not "keep its contract and have it too") and a resale of the goods with an eye to recovering corresponding damages.

Finally, and perhaps most important, such an action for the price may reflect a claim "for specific performance." As noted for the buyer in § 2.38 above, CISG Article 28 declares that a court need only grant such a remedy if it would do so "in respect of similar contracts of sale not governed by the Convention."[688] For a time, some doubt existed on whether this rule was relevant to the seller's action for the price. The problem lay in the fact that the Convention and the UCC have different concepts of "specific performance." From the UCC perspective the only provision which specifically mentions an action for "specific performance" is UCC § 2–716, which is expressly limited to a cause of action by the buyer. The UCC gives the seller no comparable general cause of action to compel performance of the buyer's obligations, except for a limited right to seek payment of the price—a monetary award.[689] Thus, from the UCC perspective the action for the price under UCC § 2–709 is merely another action for a monetary judgment, not one to compel conduct. From the CISG perspective there is no separate action for the price as a monetary judgment, only CISG Article 62, which allows a court to compel three different types of conduct— payment of the price, taking delivery, or performance of other obligations. Payment of the price is within a list of specific performances which a court is authorized to compel.

Today, however, there is near universal agreement that an action for the price reflects a claim to specific performance.[690] As a result, an aggrieved seller seeking the full contract price must meet the requirements of UCC § 2–709, as well as those of CISG Article 62, before a U.S. court could order this remedy as opposed to calculating a general right to damages. This thus is one of the extremely rare circumstances in which a U.S. court may resort directly to the UCC even for a contract governed by the CISG.

---

[685]   See §§ 2.19–2.22 supra.

[686]   CISG, art. 58.

[687]   CISG, art. 62.

[688]   See again the discussion in § 2.38 supra (relating to a claim of specific performance by the buyer).

[689]   UCC § 2–709.

[690]   See CISG DIGEST 2012, supra note 36, art. 62, para. 6; Mohs, art. 62, para. 14, in Schlechtriem & Schwenzer, supra note 30; Bell, art. 62, paras. 11, in Kröll, et al., supra note 3.

Some of the buyer's obligations are not monetary, such as preparing to take delivery of the goods or opening a letter of credit. The CISG also authorizes a court to compel such conduct by the buyer,[691] if again the court would do so in a non-Convention case. In all such cases, therefore, a seller desirous of recovering the price should file its claim in a jurisdiction (such as a civil law court) that does not impose the more rigorous conditions of the UCC.

§ 2.43   Seller's Remedies___Action for Damages

The CISG also grants to the seller a right to damages if the buyer fails to perform "any" of its obligations.[692] This right exists even when the seller has avoided the contract.[693] Like the rights of the buyer, there is no requirement that the seller prove that the buyer was at fault in failing to perform as a prerequisite to a recovery of damages. And, again, both direct and consequential damages are recoverable and as appropriate expectancy, reliance, and restitutionary interests are all protected.

The general rules for the calculation of the seller's right to damages are the same as in the discussion of the buyer's remedies for a breach by the seller.[694] Again, CISG Article 74 defines the basic principle that an aggrieved party is entitled to "a sum equal to the loss, including loss of profit, suffered as a consequence of the breach." And as noted above, federal courts properly have observed that this rule is "designed to place the aggrieved party in as good a position as if the other party had properly performed the contract."[695] In parallel with the rules for recovery by the buyer,[696] however, certain familiar limitations apply: First, recoverable damages may not exceed the loss that the buyer "foresaw or ought to have foreseen at the time of the conclusion of the contract";[697] second, the seller may not recover damages that it could have

---

[691]   CISG, art. 62 (referring to requiring the buyer to "take delivery or perform [its] other obligations").

[692]   CISG, art. 61(1)(b).

[693]   CISG, art. 61(2).

[694]   CISG, arts. 74–77. *See also* § 2.39 *supra.*

[695]   Delchi Carrier S.p.A. v. Rotorex Corp., 71 F.3d 1024, 1029 (2d Cir. 1995) (*quoting* John Honnold, UNIFORM LAW FOR INTERNATIONAL SALES UNDER THE 1980 UNITED NATIONS CONVENTION 503 (2d ed. 1991)). *See also, e.g.,* Profi-Parkiet Sp. Zoo v. Seneca Hardwoods LLC, 2014 WL 2169769, at *7 (E.D.N.Y. 2014); Norfolk Southern Ry. Co. v. Power Source Supply, Inc., 2008 WL 2884102, at *7 (W.D. Pa. 2008).

[696]   *See* the discussion in § 2.39 *supra.*

[697]   CISG, art. 74.

avoided through "reasonable measures";[698] finally, the seller must prove its damages to a reasonable degree of certainty.[699]

Alternative Measures of Damages. The same two general alternatives also exist for the measurement of the seller's damages: (a) Under Article 75, the seller may recover the difference between the contract price and the price in a "substitute transaction," which in the case of an aggrieved seller is a resale of the goods;[700] and (b) under Article 76, the seller instead may recover the difference between the contract price and the "current price" (*i.e.*, the market price) for the goods at the time of avoidance of the contract.[701] The Convention provides for recovery according to either of these measures, but if the seller actually resells the goods, only the first is available.[702]

Again, the Article 76 recovery is based on the difference between the contract price and the "current price" for the goods. Where this current price differential is used, the price in the market is to be measured at the time of "avoidance,"[703] unless the goods had already been "taken over" at the time of avoidance. In the latter case, the current price is measured at the time of the "taking over."[704] The relevant place for determining the current price is where delivery of the goods should have been made or, if no such price exists there, "at such other place as serves as a reasonable substitute."[705] The Article 76 measure may not be used at all, however, if no "current price" is available at any such place.

The major practical issue concerning aggrieved sellers is that the "lost volume" seller is not adequately protected by these alternative measures of damages.[706] The idea here is that if an aggrieved seller resells the goods, the breaching buyer will argue that the seller has mitigated its damages. This argument overlooks the possibility that the seller would have concluded both sales. And properly understood, CISG Article 74 covers this situation as well. That fundamental provision for the definition of recoverable

---

[698]   CISG, art. 77.

[699]   CISG Advisory Council Opinion No. 6, *supra* note 639, § 2. *See also* Tee Vee Toons, Inc. v. Gerhard Schubert GmbH, 2006 WL 2463537, at *10 (S.D.N.Y. 2006) (referring to proof with "sufficient certainty") (citing Delchi Carrier S.p.A. v. Rotorex Corp., 71 F.3d 1024, 1029 (2d Cir. 1995)).

[700]   CISG, art. 75. Compare UCC § 2–706.

[701]   CISG, art. 76. Compare UCC § 2–708(1).

[702]   CISG, art. 76(1) (stating that this measure is available only if the seller "has not made a . . . resale").

[703]   CISG, art. 76, first sentence.

[704]   CISG, art. 76, second sentence.

[705]   CISG, art. 76(2).

[706]   Compare UCC § 2–708(2).

damages states that an aggrieved party is entitled to all damages "including loss of profit" suffered "as a consequence of the breach." On this basis, courts have granted full protection to aggrieved sellers by awarding "lost profits" damages, and by subtracting from those losses only the variable costs saved by the termination of the first sales contract.[707] Thus, for example, the Supreme Court of Austria held in one case that a seller could recover its lost volume profit, provided that it could have completed another sale at the market price.[708] As this case indicates, such a recovery requires, however, that the seller actually had the intent and capacity to conclude the second sale in addition to the breached first sales contract.

The seller likewise is entitled to incidental damages relating to interest on the unpaid purchase price as well as on any other "sum that is in arrears" (although, again, substantial dispute exists over how to calculate the interest rate).[709]

§ 2.44   The Limitation Convention

Following its acceptance of the CISG, the United States in 1994 also ratified a parallel treaty that addresses the limitation period for international sales contracts (which U.S. lawyers would know as the "statute of limitations"): The Convention on the Limitation Period in the International Sale of Goods.[710] Over two dozen other countries have ratified this Limitation Convention (as amended by a 1980 Protocol).

The provisions on the scope of the Limitation Convention in many respects parallel those of the CISG. The Limitation Convention applies to "claims . . . arising from a contract of international sale of goods or relating to its breach, termination, or invalidity."[711] Similar to the CISG, the Limitation Convention applies if, at the time of the conclusion of a contract, the parties have their "places of business" in different states and both such states are member states of the Convention.[712] But it also applies if the relevant conflict of law rules make the law of only one member

---

[707]   *See* CISG DIGEST 2012, *supra* note 36, art. 74, para. 32 (citing cases).

[708]   CLOUT case No. 427, *Oberster Gerichtshof* [Supreme Court] of Austria (28 April 2000).

[709]   CISG, art. 78. For a review of this controversy see Van Alstine, *supra* note 651.

[710]   Like the CISG, information about this Convention and the status of ratification is available on the website of UNCITRAL, http://www.uncitral.org/uncitral/en/uncitral_texts/sale_goods.html.

[711]   Limitation Convention art. 1(1).

[712]   Limitation Convention, arts. 2(a) (defining an "international" contract) and 3(1)(a) (stating the basic rule).

state applicable to the contract of sale.[713] Unlike the CISG, the United States has not declared a reservation to this latter option, with the result that the Limitation Convention may well apply to a transaction even if the CISG does not. If a party has more than one place of business, the relevant place is the one with the "closest relationship" to the contract and its performance.[714]

In parallel with CISG Article 6, Article 3(2) of the Limitation Convention permits the parties to exclude its application to their transaction.[715] The Limitation Convention also does not apply to sales to consumers, as well as a variety of other specific transaction types similarly excluded from the CISG.[716] The Limitation Convention likewise excludes a variety of specific types of claims, most notably those based on personal injuries, judgments, or negotiable instruments.[717] Finally, and again in parallel with the CISG, the Limitation Convention does not apply where the "preponderant part" of the seller's obligations consists of services or where the buyer supplies a "substantial part" of the component parts or materials the seller uses to sell the resultant goods to the buyer.[718]

The basic period of limitation under the Convention is four years,[719] a period that begins to run on the date on which the claim "accrues."[720] The Convention makes clear that the commencement of this period is not postponed by any notice requirement or by a provision in an arbitration agreement to the effect that no rights arise until the arbitration award is rendered.[721] Once the limitation period has expired, the Convention declares that the affected claim shall not "be recognized or enforced in any legal proceeding."[722] If, on the other hand, the obligated party (known as the "debtor"[723]) nonetheless performs his obligation thereafter, it does not have a claim to restitution.[724]

Article 10 of the Limitation Convention sets forth the important rules on when specific causes of action "accrue": (a) A

---

[713] Limitation Convention art. 2.

[714] Limitation Convention, art. 2(c). Compare CISG, art. 10.

[715] *Id.*, art. 3(2).

[716] *Id.*, art. 4. *See also* CISG art. 2 and § 2.4 *supra*.

[717] Limitation Convention, art. 5.

[718] *Id.*, art. 6. Compare CISG, art. 3.

[719] Limitation Convention, art. 8.

[720] *Id.*, art. 9(1).

[721] *Id.*, art. 9(2).

[722] *Id.*, art. 25(1).

[723] *Id.*, art. 1(3)(c).

[724] *Id.*, art. 26.

cause of action for a standard breach of contract accrues "on the date on which such breach occurs";[725] (b) a claim arising from "a defect or other lack of conformity" in the goods accrues on the date on which "the goods are actually handed over" to the buyer or the buyer refuses such delivery;[726] and (c) a claim based on fraud accrues on the date on which the fraud "was or reasonably could have been discovered."[727]

Articles 11 and 12 then state special accrual rules for two specific situations. Article 11 contains an analog to the UCC's "warranty of future performance" exception to when a cause of action for breach of warranty generally accrues.[728] Under that provision, if the seller has given an "express undertaking" relating to the goods "which is stated to have effect for a certain period of time," the limitation period for a breach of such undertaking will commence not on tender of delivery, but rather on the date on which the buyer "notifies the seller of the fact on which the claim is based."[729] Recall in this regard that under CISG Article 39 the buyer loses a right to rely on a nonconformity if it does not give sufficient notice to the seller within a reasonable time.[730] Putting the two rules together, if the buyer satisfies its notice obligation, a cause of action for breach of an express undertaking that extends to the future will accrue at the latest within a reasonable time after the buyer "discovered or ought to have discovered" the breach.[731]

Article 12 has a special rule for when one party has a right to declare a termination of a contract before the other party's performance is due.[732] If a party exercises such a right, the limitations period begins on the date on which the declaration is made to the other party. Otherwise, the period begins on the date on which the performance was due.

The Limitation Convention also has a number of—in part familiar—provisions on the "cessation and extension" of the defined limitations period. First, the period ceases when the aggrieved party undertakes an act that, under the law of the forum, "is recognized as commencing judicial proceedings" or as otherwise

---

[725]   *Id.*, art. 10(1).

[726]   *Id.*, art. 10(2).

[727]   *Id.*, art. 10(3).

[728]   Compare UCC § 2–725(2).

[729]   The same provision makes clear an issue left unresolved by UCC § 2–725(2), specifically that in such a case the limitation period will commence at the latest "on the date of the expiration of the period of the undertaking." Limitation Convention, art. 11.

[730]   *See* § 2.26 *supra*.

[731]   CISG, art. 39.

[732]   *See* CISG, art. 72.

raising a claim in an existing proceeding.[733] For arbitration proceedings, the period ceases when a claim is commenced according to the agreement or applicable law or, in absence of this, when the arbitration request is made.[734] Second, counterclaims are deemed raised at that same time as the claim against which they are directed.[735] Third, in the event a court dismisses a proceeding without prejudice, the applicable period of limitation "shall be deemed to have continued to run," but if less than one year remains at that time, a party will have one year to assert its claim.[736] Fourth, if a breaching party acknowledges its obligation either expressly in writing or implicitly by making a payment, a new four-year period of limitation applies. Finally, the Limitation Convention has a form of "impracticability" exception in the event of an uncontrollable and unavoidable circumstance that prevents a party from asserting a claim in a timely manner. In such a case, the limitation period is extended until one year after the circumstance ceases to exist.[737]

The Limitation Convention also has certain rules that differ from U.S. concepts in important particulars. First, Article 22 precludes the parties from modifying the Convention's limitation period in advance, even by an express contractual agreement. The party in breach may extend the period, but only after it has begun to run.[738] Second, the Convention also sets an absolute ten year limitation period from when any particular period has "commenced to run."[739] Finally, and unusually, the Limitation Convention includes a form of a procedural rule that precludes a party from relying on the expiration of a limitations period unless it has timely raised a corresponding defense in a relevant legal proceeding.[740]

§ 2.45   Other Efforts to Unify International Commercial Law

In addition to the CISG and the Limitations Convention, UNCITRAL is responsible for a series of further treaties in the field of international commercial law. The most influential of these

---

[733]   *Id.*, art. 13.

[734]   Limitation Convention, art. 14. *See also id.*, art. 15 (stating special rules for death or incapacity of the breaching party, bankruptcy, and dissolution or liquidation of a corporate entity).

[735]   *Id.*, art. 16.

[736]   *Id.*, art. 17. For claims against jointly and severally liable parties see *id.*, art. 18.

[737]   *Id.*, art. 21.

[738]   *Id.*, art. 22(b).

[739]   *Id.*, art. 23.

[740]   *Id.*, art. 24.

address international carriage of goods by sea (see Chapter 4),[741] and the enforcement of foreign arbitral awards (see Chapter 28).[742] A number of other UNCITRAL treaties in the field of commercial law, in contrast, have been substantially less successful in attracting ratifications. These include treaties on transparency in investor-state arbitration (2014)[743] and bills of exchange and promissory notes (1988).[744] Three other UNCITRAL treaties—on electronic communications (2005),[745] on assignment of receivables (2001),[746] and on letters of credit (1995)[747]—also have not yet found broad acceptance, although in February 2016 President Obama submitted them to the Senate for advice and consent to ratification. As of late 2016, however, the Senate has taken no action whatsoever on these treaties and the prospects for consent to ratification remain very uncertain.

Separately, UNCITRAL has prepared "model laws" for consideration by individual countries as domestic legislation.[748] Prominent among these are a Model Law on Public Procurement (2011); a Model Law on International Commercial Arbitration (1985, as amended in 2006), which has served as a model for legislation in over seventy countries as well as eight states of the United States and every province of Canada; a Model Law on International Commercial Conciliation (2002); a Model Law on Cross-Border Insolvency (1997), which the United States

---

[741] See Chapter 4, §§ 4.2, 4.5.

[742] Convention on the Recognition and Enforcement of Foreign Arbitral Awards (entered into force June 7, 1959), *available at* http://www.uncitral.org/uncitral/en/uncitral_texts/arbitration/NYConvention.html.

[743] UN Convention on Transparency in Treaty-based Investor-State Arbitration, *available at* http://www.uncitral.org/uncitral/en/uncitral_texts/arbitration.html.

[744] UN Convention on International Bills of Exchange and International Promissory Notes, *available at* http://www.uncitral.org/uncitral/en/uncitral_texts/payments.html.

[745] UN Convention on the Use of Electronic Communications in International Contracts, (entered into force March 1, 2013), *available at* http://www.uncitral.org/uncitral/en/uncitral_texts/electronic_commerce.html. President Obama submitted this treaty to the Senate on February 10, 2016. *See* Message of the President, Senate Treaty Doc. 114–5 (Feb. 10, 2016). Chapter 8 analyzes this treaty in more detail. *See* § 8.7.

[746] UN Convention on the Assignment of Receivables in International Trade *available at* http://www.uncitral.org/uncitral/uncitral_texts/security.html. President Obama submitted this treaty to the Senate on February 10, 2016. *See* Message of the President, Senate Treaty Doc. 114–7 (Feb. 10, 2016).

[747] UN Convention on Independent Guarantees and Standby Letters of Credit (entered into force January 1, 2000), *available at* http://www.uncitral.org/uncitral/en/uncitral_texts/payments.html. President Obama submitted this treaty to the Senate on February 10, 2016. *See* Message of the President, Senate Treaty Doc. 114–9 (Feb. 10, 2016). Chapter 7 analyzes this treaty in more detail. *See* §§ 7.10, 7.13.

[748] Information on these model laws along with a "Guide to Enactment" is available at http://www.uncitral.org/uncitral/en/uncitral_texts.html.

implemented through a new Chapter 15 of the Bankruptcy Code; and a Model Law on Electronic Commerce (1996), which has influenced nearly seventy national laws, uniform acts in nearly every state of the U.S. and in nearly every province of Canada, and various European Union directives. UNCITRAL is continuing its work on promoting international uniformity in other areas of commercial law, with present projects on the enforcement of international settlement agreements; on secured transactions; on the recognition of cross-border insolvency judgments; and on legal standards in respect of micro, small, and medium-sized enterprises.[749]

UNCITRAL is not the only international organization involved in proposing legal instruments for the unification and harmonization of international commercial law. Another prominent body, the International Institute for the Unification of Private Law (UNIDROIT), has prepared a variety of formal treaties in the field, including (a) a Convention on International Factoring (1988),[750] which entered into force in 1995 but has only nine ratifications; (b) a Convention on International Financial Leasing (1988),[751] which also entered into force in 1995 but has only ten ratifications; and (c) a Convention on International Interests in Mobile Equipment (2001),[752] which—with over 70 ratifications as of 2017—is already extremely successful.[753] The last instrument is designed to serve as a framework treaty to be supplemented by later "protocols" that focus on specific types of collateral. Thus far, UNIDROIT has concluded three such protocols (although only the first has entered into force as of 2017): on aircraft equipment,[754] on railroad rolling stock,[755] and on space assets.[756] The Organization of American

---

[749] Information on the UNCITRAL working groups for these projects is available at http://www.uncitral.org/uncitral/en/commission/working_groups.html.

[750] UNIDROIT Convention on International Factoring (entered into force January 5, 1995), *available at* http://www.unidroit.org/instruments/factoring.

[751] UNIDROIT Convention on International Financial Leasing (entered into force January 5, 1995), *available at* http://www.unidroit.org/instruments/leasing/convention-leasing.

[752] Convention on International Interests in Mobile Equipment (Capetown) (entered into force January 3, 2006), *available at* http://www.unidroit.org/instruments/security-interests/cape-town-convention.

[753] *See* http://www.unidroit.org/status-2001capetown.

[754] Protocol to the Convention on International Interests in Mobile Equipment on Matters Specific to Aircraft Equipment (Capetown) (entered into force January 3, 2006), *available at* http://www.unidroit.org/instruments/security-interests/aircraft-protocol.

[755] Protocol to the Convention on International Interests in Mobile Equipment on Matters Specific to Railway Rolling Stock (Luxembourg, 2007), *available at* http://www.unidroit.org/instruments/security-interests/rail-protocol.

States (OAS) also has been active in this field on a hemisphere-wide basis.[757]

In addition, UNIDROIT has prepared and issued the Principles of International Commercial Contracts (1994, as revised in 2004 and again in 2010). The Principles provide rules for all types of international commercial contracts, not just sales of goods, and their provisions are substantially more comprehensive. If the CISG is the international analog to UCC Article 2 in U.S. law, then the Principles are the international analog to the Restatement of Contracts in U.S. law. The Principles are not intended to be adopted as a convention or enacted as formal domestic law. Rather, they are designed for use principally by international commercial arbitrators, and even by judges where local law is ambiguous. Nonetheless, in contrast to the reception of the Restatements by common law courts, substantial institutional hurdles exist for judicial recognition of the Principles in civil law countries.

---

[756] Protocol to the Convention on International Interests in Mobile Equipment on Matters Specific to Space Assets (Berlin, 2012), *available at* http://www.unidroit. org/instruments/security-interests/space-protocol.

[757] A list of the multi-lateral treaties adopted by the Organization of American States is available here: http://www.oas.org/dil/treaties_subject.htm.

Chapter 3

COMMERCIAL TERMS

Table of Sections

§ 3.1   Introduction

Chapter 2 described how different rules may apply for domestic and international sales of goods—for the United States, the Uniform Commercial Code (UCC) and the UN Convention on Contracts for the International Sales of Goods (CISG), respectively.[1] It also explained how difficult choice of law issues arise for transactions that touch the interests of two (or more) countries.[2] And of course different countries may have different legal rules for sale of goods transactions.

---

[1]   United Nations Convention on Contracts for the International Sale of Goods, Apr. 11, 1980, U.N. Doc. A/CONF. 97/18 (1980), *reprinted in* 19 I.L.M. 671 (1980) (hereinafter CISG).

[2]   *See* Chapter 2, § 2.1.

Among the most important subjects for sellers and buyers in such transactions is the allocation of rights and responsibilities regarding the delivery of the goods. Given the complexity and detail of this subject, the parties often will wish to agree on a standard "commercial term," the very purpose of which—as Section 3.2 below explains—is to allocate the responsibilities for transportation of the goods, the passing of risk of loss, and numerous related matters. Such terms include, for example, FOB (Free on Board), FAS (Free Alongside Ship), and CIF (Cost, Insurance and Freight). The UCC provides definitions for such terms,[3] but other countries do as well[4]—and the differences can be substantial.

The CISG was designed to bridge such differences for international sales transactions. The drafters of the CISG decided, however, not to include formal definitions of commercial terms, and in general the Convention's provisions on the delivery and acceptance of the goods are quite sparse.[5] The drafters took this approach precisely because they were able to rely on a written formulation of industry norms on the meaning of individual commercial terms for international transactions. That written formulation is the "Incoterms"© published by the International Chamber of Commerce (ICC).[6] Indeed, as Section 3.3 below explains, the Incoterms are widely recognized as an international trade usage for contracts under the CISG, and therefore are available to fill in gaps in the CISG's provisions.

Incoterms is an acronym for "International Commercial Terms," a copyrighted set of rules the ICC first published in 1936. The ICC has updated the Incoterms periodically since that time. It published the current version in 2010 ("Incoterms 2010"). As explained in the review of the eleven different Incoterms "Rules" below (see §§ 3.7 through 3.19), these most recent revisions have made the Incoterms substantially different from the definitions in the domestic UCC.

§ 3.2   The Purpose of Commercial Terms

As Chapter 1 examined in detail, the parties to an international sale of goods transaction face a variety of more complicated, and in part entirely new, issues as compared to a

---

3   *See* UCC §§ 2–319 to 2–324.

4   *See, e.g.*, SCHMITTHOFF'S EXPORT TRADE, §§ 2–006, 2–007 (Murray, Holloway, Timson-Hunt, eds., 11th ed., 2007) (describing the different approach in the U.K. and other commonwealth countries to various commercial terms).

5   CISG, arts. 31–34. *See also* the more detailed discussion in Chapter 2, §§ 2.20, 2.25.

6   INCOTERMS 2010 (ICC Publ. No. 715, 2010) (hereinafter, INCOTERMS 2010).

purely domestic one.[7] Two of the most significant of these are (a) uncertainty over the application of potentially different domestic legal rules, and (b) the need to engage third-party carriers to transport the goods from the seller to a geographically distant buyer. In absence of uniform law to address these issues, the result is an increase in transaction costs, including the hassles and expense of negotiating in detail over the allocation of responsibility for transportation of the goods, the passing of risk of loss, and myriad related issues. Unfortunately, there is no specialized treaty on these matters, and as noted above the CISG addresses them only general terms.

But as Chapter 1 also explained, another method by which the international trading community has addressed such challenges is through widely accepted terminology, customs, and practices.[8] Most important in this regard is the development of sets of terms that parties may incorporate into their contracts by simple reference. The goal of these standard contract terms is to empower the parties to define their respective rights and obligations easily, clearly, and by reference to internationally accepted notions and norms.

The ICC in Paris is the most prominent institution in advancing this endeavor, and the Incoterms are its most successful product. The Incoterms provide the parties to a sales transaction a pallet of choices of specific commercial terms—referred to as "Rules"—to enable them to choose the structure that best suits their mutual interests. Another special feature of Incoterms is that they permit the parties to accomplish this result through a simple three-letter reference (*e.g.*, FOB or CIF) in their contract. Each Incoterm Rule then defines what acts the seller must do to deliver, what acts the buyer must do to accommodate delivery, what costs each party must bear, and at what point in the delivery process the risk of loss passes from the seller to the buyer. Each of these obligations may be different for different commercial terms. Thus, for example, the obligations and costs of the seller and the buyer are different under FOB than they are under CIF (although the rules governing the passing of risk are the same).

As noted in the Introduction, the domestic UCC also has provisions on some of these terms, but its definitions are seldom used in international trade. In fact, the UCC definitions are becoming obsolete in domestic trade as well, because they are premised primarily on water-borne traffic and do not address new

---

[7]   *See* Chapter 1, § 1.1.

[8]   *See id.*

business practices associated with air freight, containerization, or multi-modal transportation practices.[9]

§ 3.3 The Incoterms Rules as Trade Usages

Because the ICC is a non-governmental entity, Incoterms are neither national legislation nor an international treaty. Thus, they cannot be "the governing law" of any contract. Instead, they are a written form of custom and usage in the trade, which the parties can expressly incorporate in their contracts for the sale of goods. And all available evidence is that international traders very commonly do so.[10]

Even if the Incoterms are not expressly incorporated in a contract, they nonetheless may have effect as an implicit term in the form of an international trade usage. Courts in the United States have expressly so held,[11] as have courts in France, Germany, and elsewhere.[12] This description has allowed Incoterms to qualify under the CISG Article 9(2) as a "usage . . . which in international trade is widely known to, and regularly observed by, parties to" international sales contracts.[13]

Whether through express or implied incorporation, the legal nature of the Incoterms remains contractual. Thus, the Incoterms Rules themselves are subject to modification by the express terms of the parties' contract.

Although, as noted, the UCC has definitions for some commercial terms (*e.g.*, F.O.B., F.A.S., C.I.F.), these definitions are expressly subject to "agreement otherwise."[14] Thus, an express

---

[9] An effort at a comprehensive revision of UCC Article 2 would have deleted the commercial terms definitions entirely; but that effort failed because no state adopted the Revised Article 2 and the Uniform Law Commission subsequently withdrew its support as well.

[10] *See, e.g.*, Tian Long Fashion Co., Ltd. v. Fashion Avenue Sweater Knits, LLC, 2016 WL 4097801, at *4 (S.D.N.Y. 2016) (observing that "Incoterms are the most widely recognized non-statutory definitions of trade"); S.K.I Beer Corp. v. Baltika Brewery, 443 F. Supp. 2d 313, 315 n.4 (E.D.N.Y. 2006) (same).

[11] *See* BP Oil Int'l Ltd. v. Empresa Estatal Petróleos de Ecuador, 332 F.3d 333 (5th Cir. 2003); China North Chem. Indus. Corp. v. Beston Chem. Corp., 2006 WL 295395 (S.D. Tex. 2006); St. Paul Guardian Ins. Co. v. Neuromed Medical Systems & Support, GmbH, 2002 WL 465312 (S.D.N.Y. 2002); Texful Textile Ltd. v. Cotton Express Textile, Inc., 891 F. Supp. 1381 (C.D. Cal. 1995).

[12] *See* UNCITRAL DIGEST OF CASE LAW ON THE CISG (2012 ed.), art. 9, ¶ 19, available at http://www.uncitral.org/uncitral/en/case_law/digests/cisg.html.

[13] *See, e.g.*, BP Oil Int'l, Ltd. v. Empresa Estatal Petróleos de Ecuador, 332 F.3d 333, 336 (5th Cir. 2003) ("The CISG incorporates Incoterms through article 9(2)."); In re World Imports, Ltd. 549 B.R. 820, 824 (E.D. Pa. 2016) (same); Citgo Petroleum Corp. v. Odfjell Seachem, 2013 WL 2289951, at *5 (S.D. Tex. 2013) (same). Regarding CISG Article 9, see Chapter 2, § 2.11.

[14] UCC §§ 2–319(1), (2), 2–320(2).

reference to Incoterms will supersede the UCC provisions, and United States courts have so held.[15] Even if a contract does not include an express reference, and the UCC is the governing law rather than the CISG, Incoterms still can apply as a "usage of trade" under the UCC.[16] The UCC criteria for such a usage is "a practice or method of dealing having such regularity of observance . . . as to justify an expectation that it will be observed with respect to the transaction in question."[17] A usage need not be "universal" nor "ancient," just "currently observed by the great majority of decent dealers."[18] Thus, one federal court has held that a CFR term in a shipment from Ecuador to the United States implicitly incorporated the Incoterms as a usage.[19] Moreover, as noted in Section 3.4 immediately below, the Incoterms 2010 now expressly recognize that they may be used in "both domestic and international trade."

§ 3.4   The 2010 Revision of Incoterms

The ICC periodically updates the Incoterms, typically about every ten years. The last revision was in 2010 and is set forth in ICC Publication No. 715.

The 2010 revisions of the Incoterms, which formally entered into effect on January 1, 2011, were designed principally to respond to developments in international trade and transport practices and otherwise to simplify and clarify uncertain aspects of Incoterms 2000. The revisions had three principal purposes. First, they restructured and distilled the thirteen commercial terms (again, "Rules") defined in the 2000 revision into eleven Rules. Second, they then organized the eleven Rules into two general categories: those limited to sea and inland waterway transport, and those permitted for any mode of transport. The former category includes the most frequently used terms in large international transactions, CIF and FOB, as well as more specific versions CFR (Cost and Freight) and FAS (Free Alongside Ship). The latter category includes the seven

---

[15]   See, e.g., Phillips Puerto Rico Core, Inc. v. Tradax Petroleum Ltd., 782 F.2d 314 (2d Cir. 1985); Animal Science Products, Inc. v. China Nat. Metals & Minerals Import & Export Corp., 702 F. Supp. 2d 320, 371 n. 53 (D.N.J. 2010), rev'd on other grounds, 654 F.3d 462 (3rd Cir. 2011). See also Tian Long Fashion Co., Ltd. v. Fashion Avenue Sweater Knits, LLC, 2016 WL 4097801, at *4 (S.D.N.Y. 2016) (observing in a case the court considered as governed by the UCC that a court "may consider usage of trade to explain or supplement the terms in a [contract document], including Incoterms").

[16]   UCC § 1–303(c).

[17]   Id.

[18]   See UCC § 1–303, comment 4.

[19]   BP Oil Int'l Ltd. v. Empresa Estatal Petróleos de Ecuador, 332 F.3d 333, 337 (5th Cir. 2003).

other terms that are also occasionally used in water transport, but are more common for air, land, and rail transportation.

The final principal purpose of Incoterms 2010 was to address specific legal and factual developments relating to the transportation of goods. The most significant of these was electronic communication. Thus, the new Rules endorse the substitution of paper communications with an "equivalent electronic record or procedure." Moreover, they broadly embrace such electronic communications where either the parties so agree or such is "customary" in the trade.[20] This reference to trade custom is significant because it will increasingly authorize buyers and sellers to fulfill communication and documentation requirements with electronic equivalents. Moreover, the drafters of the new Incoterms intentionally adopted an open-ended definition of "electronic records" to permit the Rules to adapt to new technologies as they arise in the future.[21]

Incoterms 2010 also expressly recognize that they may be used in "both domestic and international trade."[22] The goal of this language was to facilitate the use of Incoterms in customs-free trade zones such as the European Union (where international borders are less significant) as well as in large domestic legal systems (such as in the place of the UCC in the United States).[23]

§ 3.5 The Format of Incoterms

The Incoterms obligations for each Rule are arranged in a mirror-image format that sets forth ten specific obligations in adjacent columns, with "the seller's obligations" in the left column and "the buyer's obligations" in the right. Each column has numbered paragraphs, and each numbered paragraph addresses a specific, corresponding obligation of each party. Thus, for example, for each Incoterm Rule, "A4" covers the seller's obligations regarding delivery and "B4" the buyer's obligations on the same subject. In summary, the ten paragraphs address the following subjects:

A1/B1. The first set of parallel paragraphs contains a statement of the basic obligations of the seller and the buyer: The seller must deliver the goods and a commercial

---

[20] In each of the eleven Incoterms Rules, A1 (for the seller) and B1 (for the buyer) state that a paper document may be replaced by "an equivalent electronic record or procedure" provided only that this is "agreed between the parties or customary."

[21] For more on electronic bills of lading see Chapter 4, § 4.15.

[22] *See* INCOTERMS 2010, *supra* note 6, at 8.

[23] *Id.*

invoice (or its electronic equivalent), and the buyer must pay the contract price.

A2/B2.   The second set of paragraphs allocates the responsibilities of the parties regarding export and import licenses, customs formalities, and (in a new reference) "security clearances."

A3/B3.   The third set of paragraphs allocates the responsibilities of the parties to arrange for carriage of the goods and for insurance covering them in transit.

A4/B4.   The fourth set of paragraphs specifies the extent of both the seller's delivery obligation and the buyer's obligation to take delivery.

A5/B5.   The fifth set of paragraphs specifies when the risk of loss is transferred from the seller to the buyer.

A6/B6.   The sixth set of paragraphs allocates the costs of transportation between the parties, including not only the freight and insurance costs already allocated in A3/B3, but also loading costs and the administrative costs of customs clearance, even when no import duties are charged.

A7/B7.   The seventh set of paragraphs defines what notices each party must give to the other, when such notices must be given, and what each notice must say.

A8/B8.   The eighth set of paragraphs specifies the type of transport document or other proof of delivery that the seller must provide to the buyer, and the buyer's obligation to accept such a document.

A9/B9.   The ninth set of paragraphs allocates responsibility for the costs of packaging the goods, marking the packages, "checking operations" (quality, measuring, weighing, counting), and any pre-shipment inspection. It does not, however, address whether the buyer has a right to post-shipment inspection before paying for the goods.

A10/B10. Finally, the tenth set of paragraphs sets forth miscellaneous obligations, such as duties of assistance and cooperation. New in Incoterms 2010 is a requirement of cooperation by both parties regarding any "security-related information" that either may need to provide to customs or other governmental authorities.

§ 3.6   The Categories of the Incoterms "Rules"

Incoterms 2010 give the parties a menu of eleven different Rules to describe the delivery obligations of the seller and the reciprocal obligations of the buyer to accommodate delivery. The eleven Rules, listed alphabetically, are as follows:

1.   CFR (Cost and Freight)

2.   CIF (Cost, Insurance and Freight)

3.   CIP (Carriage and Insurance Paid)

4.   CPT (Carriage Paid To)

5.   DAP (Delivered at Place)

6.   DAT (Delivered at Terminal)

7.   DDP (Delivered Duty Paid)

8.   EXW (Ex Works)

9.   FAS (Free Alongside Ship)

10.   FCA (Free Carrier)

11.   FOB (Free On Board).

One may organize these eleven different terms in a variety of ways. One is along a spectrum according to the respective responsibilities of the seller and the buyer. At one end would be EXW (Ex Works), under which the seller must merely make the goods available at its own place of business (or other named place);[24] at the other end would be DDP (Delivered Duty Paid), which obligates the seller to deliver the goods all the way to the buyer's foreign location and to assume the responsibility and cost of both export and import customs clearance.[25] The others would fall along the spectrum and thus permit the parties to choose the term that best fits their specific commercial transaction. Another division would be between the one term that does not assume that a carrier will be involved (EXW), and the ten other terms. A third division, suggested above, would be between those four terms that may only be used for water-borne transportation (FAS, FOB, CFR, CIF) and the seven other terms, which are applicable to any mode of transportation, including multi-modal transportation (CIP, CPT, DAP, DAT, DDP, EXW, and FCA). The UCC has none of the latter seven terms, even though the types of transactions they are

---

[24]   See id., at 15 (stating that "EXW represents the minimum obligation for the seller").

[25]   See id., at 69 (stating that "DDP represents the maximum obligation for the seller").

designed for arise routinely. The parties nonetheless may be able to achieve the same results—if, for some reason, they wished to assume the transaction costs of doing so—with careful adjustments to the UCC designations "F.O.B. place of shipment," "F.O.B. place of destination," "C. & F.", and "C.I.F."[26]

The ten terms requiring transportation also can be divided into "shipment contract" terms (FCA, FAS, FOB, CFR, CIF, CPT, and CIP) and "destination contract" terms (DAP, DAT, and DDP). The UCC and the CISG each distinguish in some form between "shipment" and "destination" contracts, although not with the same specific rules.[27] The underlying notion is that in shipment contracts the seller need merely put the goods in the hands of a carrier, but transportation is at the buyer's risk and expense.[28] In destination contracts, in contrast, the seller is responsible for putting the goods in the hands of the carrier, arranging their transportation, and bearing the cost and risk of transportation to the named location.[29] Unfortunately, many aspects of transportation usages have changed since the UCC was drafted in the 1950s, and the UCC concepts do not always fit the practices that the newly updated Incoterms now address.

§ 3.7   Rules for Sea and Inland Waterway Transport

The following sections examine each of the Incoterms Rules in turn. Following the structure of the Incoterms 2010, we address the Rules in two groups: the Rules for "sea and inland waterway transport" (§§ 3.8 through 3.11); and the Rules for "any mode or modes of transport" (§§ 3.12 through 3.19). Because FOB and CIF are by far the most commonly used terms in international trade, Sections 3.8 and 3.10, respectively, will provide more detail on the obligations of the parties under such terms.

§ 3.8   Water Transport__The Free on Board (FOB) Term

Under the Incoterms Free on Board (FOB) commercial term, the essential agreement between the parties is that the seller merely must deliver the goods on board a ship arranged by the buyer at a named port of (outbound) shipment. Thus, this term is appropriate only for water-borne transportation.

---

[26]   *See again* §§ 2–319 through 2–322.

[27]   Compare UCC §§ 2–503, 2–504, and CISG, art. 31. On the latter see also Chapter 2, § 2.20.

[28]   Compare UCC § 2–504.

[29]   Compare UCC § 2–503(1), (3).

Like the other Incoterm Rules, the basic obligation of the seller under an FOB term is to deliver the goods and a corresponding commercial invoice "in conformity with the contract of sale," as well as any other proof of conformity the parties specified in the sales contract.[30] For its part, the buyer is obligated to pay the price of the goods as specified in the sales contract.[31] And like the other Rules, any document (such as the commercial invoice) required under the FOB term may be in the form of an "equivalent electronic record or procedure if agreed between the parties" or such is "customary" in the trade.[32]

With respect to customs issues, the FOB term obligates the seller to obtain, "at its own risk and expense," any necessary *export* licenses and similar official authorizations and to "carry out all customs formalities necessary for the export of goods."[33] The buyer must procure "at its own risk and expense," any *import* licenses and similar authorizations, and also take care of any customs formalities "for the import of goods and their transport through any country."[34] The seller is responsible for the costs of packaging the goods, marking the packages, "checking operations" (quality, measuring, weighing, counting), and any pre-shipment inspection mandated by export authorities.[35] Each side also must provide assistance to the other regarding any documents or information, especially "security-related information," needed to fulfill their respective obligations to customs or other governmental authorities.[36]

The seller under an FOB term must bear the costs and risks of inland transportation to the named port of shipment (that is, the outbound port, typically in the seller's home country). But it has no obligation to arrange transportation or insurance for the goods in transit after delivery at that shipment port.[37] The FOB term instead expressly places on the buyer the obligation to arrange the contract for the carriage of goods.[38] The seller "may" arrange carriage "on usual terms at the buyer's risk and expense," if requested by the buyer, or if it is "commercial practice" for the seller

---

[30] INCOTERMS 2010, FOB A1.

[31] INCOTERMS 2010, FOB B1.

[32] *Id.*, second paragraph.

[33] INCOTERMS 2010, FOB A2.

[34] INCOTERMS 2010, FOB B2.

[35] INCOTERMS 2010, FOB A9, B9.

[36] INCOTERMS 2010, FOB A10, B10.

[37] INCOTERMS 2010, FOB A3.

[38] *See* INCOTERMS 2010, FOB B3(a) (stating that the buyer "must contract, at its own expense[,] for the carriage of goods from the named port of shipment," unless the seller has made the carriage contract on its behalf).

to do so and the buyer does not timely object.[39] But even under such circumstances, the seller may refuse to make such arrangements if it promptly so notifies the buyer.[40] Although the seller is not obligated to arrange for insurance, it must provide the buyer with any information necessary to obtain insurance.[41] The FOB term does not formally obligate the buyer to make a contract of insurance covering the goods in transit (but of course it is well-advised to do so).[42]

FOB A4 provides more detail on the seller's delivery obligation: The seller must deliver the goods "on board" the vessel nominated by the buyer within the time agreed and in the manner customary at the shipment port. Alternatively, the seller may "procure" rights to goods already loaded on a ship.[43] This option acknowledges the common practice of reselling goods, especially commodities, in "string sales," under which the seller obtains rights over the goods—such as by purchasing the corresponding negotiable bill of lading—when they are already in transit. In either case, the seller must notify the buyer of the delivery.[44] For its part, the FOB term obligates the buyer to notify the seller of the ship on which the goods are to be loaded[45] and to accept the delivery when made.[46]

The costs and risks for the buyer and seller under an FOB term track the seller's basic obligation regarding delivery of the goods. The risk of loss or damage to the goods will pass from the seller to the buyer once the goods are "on board the vessel" (or when the seller has otherwise "procured" the goods in transit).[47] But if the buyer fails to nominate the vessel in time or the vessel is delayed in arriving, the buyer will bear the risk of loss or damage from the contractually agreed delivery time for the goods.[48]

The cost point under an FOB term is the same (decidedly unlike the CIF term discussed below[49]): The seller bears the cost of transporting the goods only "until they have been delivered in accordance with A4" (i.e., until they are "on board" the vessel), and the buyer is responsible for the freight and other costs from that

---

[39] INCOTERMS 2010, FOB A3(a).

[40] Id.

[41] INCOTERMS 2010, FOB A3(b).

[42] INCOTERMS 2010, FOB B3(b).

[43] INCOTERMS 2010, FOB A4.

[44] INCOTERMS 2010, FOB A7. The seller must also notify the buyer if the nominated vessel is not timely available for loading. Id.

[45] INCOTERMS 2010, FOB B7.

[46] INCOTERMS 2010, FOB B4.

[47] INCOTERMS 2010, FOB A5, B5.

[48] INCOTERMS 2010, FOB B5.

[49] See § 3.10 infra.

point on.[50] As noted, the seller also is responsible for the "checking operations" that are necessary for delivering the goods "on board the vessel," as well as the costs of packaging the goods "in a manner appropriate for their transport."[51] However, the buyer must pay the cost of any pre-shipment inspection not required by the country of export (such as by a third-party firm engaged to inspect the goods prior to loading).[52] Moreover, the buyer is responsible for any additional costs that arise from its failure to nominate the vessel in time or from any delayed arrival of that ship.[53]

Because the seller has no obligations regarding the carriage of the goods after they are loaded on the outbound ship, its responsibility regarding the transport document are quite limited. It need merely provide to the buyer "usual proof that the goods have been delivered in accordance with A4."[54] Thus, the seller is not obligated to obtain a negotiable bill of lading covering the goods. As a result, the Incoterms FOB term is not appropriate for a "documents against payment" transaction (unless of course the parties otherwise so agree).[55]

The FOB term traditionally has been among the most common commercial terms in international carriage of goods, and it remains so today. But it is more problematic for the modern era of container transport in some lines of trade in which the goods are handed over to the carrier in a sealed, standardized container before loading on a vessel. As the ICC Commentary has observed. "[i]n such situations, the FCA rule should be used" (see § 3.14 below).[56]

The Incoterms FOB definition has no provisions on the time and place of payment[57] (and thus on any right of the buyer to pre-payment inspection of the goods). Such matters, therefore, must be resolved under otherwise-applicable law. In the United States, the UCC generally provides that payment is due at the time of delivery, but that the buyer has a right to inspect the goods themselves

---

[50]   INCOTERMS 2010, FOB A6, B6. The seller is responsible for the costs of any export licenses or formalities and the buyer for the costs of any import licenses or formalities. *Id.*, FOB A6(b), B6(c).

[51]   INCOTERMS 2010, FOB A9. The seller must assist the buyer with regard to obtaining any necessary documents or information required for security clearances or for the importation of the goods. *Id.*, FOB A10.

[52]   INCOTERMS 2010, FOB B9.

[53]   INCOTERMS 2010, FOB B6.

[54]   INCOTERMS 2010, FOB A8.

[55]   For more detail on the key role of a negotiable bill of lading in a documents against payment (D/P) transaction, see Chapter 1, § 1.5.

[56]   INCOTERMS 2010, FOB, Guidance Note, at 87.

[57]   INCOTERMS 2010, at 6 ("Incoterm Rules . . . say nothing about the price to be paid or the method of its payment.").

before such payment;[58] the CISG follows a similar approach.[59] The Incoterms likewise do not address the transfer of title from the seller to the buyer,[60] and thus otherwise-applicable domestic law governs this issue as well.[61] UCC Article 2 generally disdains title concepts regarding sale of goods transactions, but does provide that title passes when the seller completes its obligations regarding "physical delivery" of the goods.[62]

The UCC has a definition for "F.O.B.," but that definition is divided into "F.O.B. place of shipment," "F.O.B. place of destination," and "F.O.B. vessel" varieties.[63] Only the last—which also may be appended to either of the first two—relates directly to water-borne transportation. It is most closely aligned with the Incoterms FOB term in that it also obligates the seller to deliver the goods on board the ship and does not require the seller to arrange transportation to a final destination.[64] Under the UCC, however, the term "F.O.B. vessel" requires the buyer to pay against a tender of documents, such as a negotiable bill of lading, before the goods arrive at their destination and before the buyer has any post-shipment opportunity to inspect the goods.[65] This obligation does not align at all with the Incoterms FOB Rule.

§ 3.9 Water Transport__The Free Alongside Ship (FAS) Term

The Incoterms Free Alongside Ship (FAS) commercial term is similar to its FOB term except—as its title implies—with respect to the precise point of delivery. Under an FAS term, the seller is obligated to deliver the goods alongside a ship arranged by the buyer at a named port of shipment, whereas under the FOB term the seller is obligated to deliver the goods "on board" that ship.

---

[58] UCC §§ 2–511(1), 2–513(1).

[59] *See* Chapter 2, §§ 2.20, 2.24.

[60] INCOTERMS 2010, at 6 (declaring that the Incoterms do not address "transfer of ownership of the goods"). Courts in the United States have recognized this point as well. *See, e.g.,* Bristol-Myers Squibb Co. v. Matrix Laboratories Ltd., 2015 WL 4430614, *6 (S.D.N.Y. 2015); Nucor Corp. v. U.S., 612 F. Supp. 2d 1264, 1282 (U.S.C.I.T. 2009); Diesel Props S.R.L. v. Greystone Business Credit II LLC, 2009 WL 89115, at *10 (S.D.N.Y. 2009); Italverde Trading, Inc. v. Four Bills of Lading, 485 F. Supp. 2d 187, 200 (E.D.N.Y. 2007).

[61] The CISG also does not address issues of title. *See* art. 4(b) and Chapter 2, § 2.8.

[62] UCC § 2–401(2). This rule applies even if the seller has reserved title in the goods or has shipped them under a document of title. *Id.*

[63] UCC § 2–319(1)(a)–(c).

[64] UCC § 2–319(1)(c).

[65] UCC § 2–319(4).

Again, the seller instead may "procure" rights to goods already alongside that ship.[66]

The remainder of the FAS term parallels the FOB term. The seller must bear the costs of inland transportation to the named port of shipment.[67] The risk of loss of or damage to the goods also will transfer from the seller to the buyer at the time "they have been delivered in accordance with A4" (*i.e.*, for FAS when they are "alongside the ship").[68] The seller has no obligation to arrange transportation or insurance after that point,[69] but does have a duty to notify the buyer that the goods have been delivered alongside the ship.[70] The seller must provide a commercial invoice[71] and the "usual proof" that the goods have been so delivered[72] (or an equivalent electronic record for either[73]). The seller is obligated to obtain any licenses or other approvals for export clearance, and the buyer has the same obligation regarding import clearance.[74]

Again, the Incoterms FAS definition has no provisions on payment, pre-payment inspection, or title; as noted for the FOB term above, otherwise-applicable domestic law or the CISG must provide answers to these issues.[75] The UCC "F.A.S. vessel" term is similar in most respects to the Incoterms FAS term, including obligating the seller only to deliver the goods alongside a named vessel and not obligating the seller to arrange transportation to a final destination.[76] But the UCC's approach requires the buyer to pay against a tender of documents, such as a negotiable bill of lading, before the goods arrive at their destination and before it has any opportunity to inspect the goods after shipment.[77] The Incoterms FAS term does not require that the seller obtain a negotiable bill of lading covering the goods and does not address at all the timing of the buyer's obligation to pay for the goods or its right to inspect the goods before doing so (other than referring to the terms of the parties' contract[78]).

---

66   INCOTERMS 2010, FAS A4, B4.

67   INCOTERMS 2010, FAS A5, B5.

68   INCOTERMS 2010, FAS A6, B6.

69   INCOTERMS 2010, FAS A3, B3.

70   INCOTERMS 2010, FAS A7.

71   INCOTERMS 2010, FAS A1.

72   INCOTERMS 2010, FAS A8.

73   INCOTERMS 2010, FAS A1.

74   INCOTERMS 2010, FAS A2, B2.

75   *See* § 3.8 above.

76   UCC § 2–319(2).

77   UCC § 2–319(4).

78   INCOTERMS 2010, FAS B1 (providing merely that the buyer must pay "as provided in the contract of sale").

§ 3.10   Water Transport__The Cost, Insurance and Freight (CIF) Term

Under the Incoterms Cost, Insurance and Freight (CIF) commercial term, the seller is obligated to arrange for both transportation and insurance to a named destination port and to deliver the goods on board the vessel that it—not the buyer—must arrange. As the term "vessel" implies, the CIF commercial term also is appropriate only for water-borne transportation.

Many of the standard obligations of the seller and the buyer under a CIF term are similar to those under the FOB term. Under a CIF term as well, the seller is obligated to pay the cost of the goods and provide a commercial invoice "in conformity with the contract of sale,"[79] and the buyer is obligated to pay the price as provided in the contract.[80] Again, the parties may, by agreement or by custom, use an equivalent electronic record or procedure for any required document.[81] The seller is responsible for any license or other official authorization required for exporting the goods, and the buyer is responsible for the same issues regarding importing the goods.[82] The seller again is responsible for the costs of packaging the goods, marking the packages, "checking operations" (quality, measuring, weighing, counting), and any pre-shipment inspection mandated by export authorities.[83] And each side must provide assistance to the other regarding any documents or information, especially "security-related information," needed to fulfill their respective obligations to customs or other governmental authorities.[84]

Also similar to the FOB term, the seller under the CIF term must deliver the goods by "placing them on board the vessel" or by "procuring" goods already loaded on a ship.[85] In either case, the seller must perform its delivery obligation within the agreed time[86] and provide whatever notice is required "to enable the buyer to take the goods."[87]

The risk of loss point under a CIF term also is the same as that for an FOB term. Under CIF as well, the risk of loss or damage to the goods will pass from the seller to the buyer once the seller has

---

[79]   INCOTERMS 2010, CIF A1.

[80]   INCOTERMS 2010, CIF B1.

[81]   INCOTERMS 2010, CIF A1, B1.

[82]   INCOTERMS 2010, CIF A2, B2.

[83]   INCOTERMS 2010, CIF A9, B9.

[84]   INCOTERMS 2010, CIF A10, B10.

[85]   INCOTERMS 2010, CIF A4.

[86]   *Id.*

[87]   INCOTERMS 2010, CIF A7.

completed its delivery obligation, *i.e.*, when it has placed the goods "on board the vessel" at the shipment port (or "procured" the goods in transit).[88] But if the buyer fails to give any required notification to the seller, the buyer will bear the risk of loss or damage from the agreed date of shipment.[89]

The CIF term differs from the FOB term, however, in two fundamental respects:

(1) *Carriage and Insurance.* The first fundamental difference involves the seller's obligations regarding transport and insurance, and regarding the related costs. Under the CIF term, the seller is obligated to conclude a contract "for the carriage of the goods from . . . the place of delivery to the named port of destination."[90] (As noted immediately above, the place of delivery is the outbound shipment port.) The carriage contract must be on the "usual terms" and provide for carriage "by the usual route in a vessel of the type normally used" for the goods involved.[91] The seller also must bear the *costs* of such carriage to the destination port (as well as the transportation costs to and the loading costs at the shipment port).[92]

In addition, the seller is obligated to procure cargo insurance covering the goods from the point of delivery to the destination port.[93] The insurance must be from a company of "good repute," cover 110% of the contract price for the goods, and entitle the buyer to claim directly from the insurer.[94] Indeed, the 2010 Incoterms CIF Rule explicitly identifies the minimum allowed coverage with reference to the "Institute Cargo Clauses" prepared by maritime insurance carriers.[95] And, again, the seller is obligated to assume the *costs* of this insurance coverage to the destination port.[96]

---

[88] INCOTERMS 2010, CIF A5, B5.

[89] INCOTERMS 2010, CIF B5.

[90] INCOTERMS 2010, CIF A3(a).

[91] *Id.*

[92] INCOTERMS 2010, CIF A6(a), (b).

[93] INCOTERMS 2010, CIF A3(b).

[94] *Id.*

[95] CIF A3(b) states that the minimum allowed coverage is that "provided by Clauses (C) of the Institute Cargo Clauses (LMA/IUA) or any similar clauses." *Id.* The Institute Cargo Clauses (last updated in 2009) are the product of insurance industry working groups (including the International Underwriting Association and the Lloyds Market Association) and define levels of insurance according to the broadest coverage (Clauses A), an intermediate level of coverage (Clauses B), and the most limited coverage (Clauses C).

[96] INCOTERMS 2010, CIF A6(c). In addition, the seller must provide, at the buyer's "request, risk and expense," any information that the buyer needs to obtain additional insurance. CIF A3(b).

Thus, the CIF term establishes a system that separates the cost point from the delivery and risk of loss point. The seller must arrange and pay for the transportation to the *port of destination*, but has completed its delivery obligations when the goods are placed "on board the vessel" at the *port of shipment*. For its part, the buyer must "take delivery" of the goods at the *port of shipment*.[97] Similarly, the seller must arrange and pay for insurance during transportation to the *port of destination*, but the risk of loss transfers to the buyer at the time the goods are on board the vessel at the *port of shipment*. Thus, the buyer bears the risk of loss of or damage to the goods during transit, but should such an event occur it may resort to the insurance coverage arranged and paid for by the seller. And because the seller must pay for freight and insurance to the destination port, it must take those costs into account when it quotes a price to the buyer upon the formation of the sales contract.

(2) *Transport Document and Implied Agreement on Payment.* A second fundamental way in which the CIF term differs from the FOB term relates to the transport document the seller must obtain upon shipment of the goods. Indeed, this required transport document defines the essence of the CIF transaction as a "documents against payment" transaction. CIF A8 first states the basic obligation of the seller to provide the buyer "with the usual transport document for the agreed port of destination."[98] But the most important obligation of the seller lies in the description of the details for this transport document. In specific, the second paragraph of CIF A8 declares that the document must (a) "cover the contract goods," (b) "enable the buyer to claim the goods from the carrier at the port of destination," and (c) unless the parties agree otherwise, "enable the buyer to sell the goods in transit by the transfer of the document to a subsequent buyer or by notification to the carrier."[99]

The last requirement on this list the most important. As a practical matter, the most secure way for the seller to "enable the buyer to sell the goods in transit" is to obtain a *negotiable* bill of lading from the carrier and to tender that negotiable document to the buyer through a series of banks. As Chapter 4 will describe in greater detail,[100] traditionally only such a bill will "represent the

---

[97]   INCOTERMS 2010, CIF B4. The buyer also is obligated to "receive" the goods "from the carrier at the named port of destination." *Id.*

[98]   INCOTERMS 2010, CIF A8, first paragraph.

[99]   *Id.*, second paragraph.

[100] *See* in particular § 4.8.

goods" in a way that will permit the buyer to sell them "by the transfer of *the document* to a subsequent buyer."[101]

In modern transportation practice, a variety of intermediaries that fulfill the essential functions of formal carriers—known by the names "non-vessel-operating common carriers (NVOCCs)", full service freight forwarders, or "multimodal transport operators (MTOs)", among others—also may issue negotiable bills of lading. These intermediaries assume responsibility for arranging transportation of the goods through different modes of transport— road, rail, ocean, etc.—but perform little or none of the actual carriage themselves. Nonetheless, if negotiable in form and function, the bills issued by these intermediaries should satisfy the seller's obligation under a CIF term (or CFR, see below) for a valid and transferable transportation document. In contrast, as the ICC Guide to Incoterms 2010 declares, a nonnegotiable bill—aka an ocean waybill or sea waybill, among other names—"cannot be used . . . for transferring rights to the goods by the transfer of the document."[102]

Modern commercial practices nonetheless permit use of nonnegotiable waybills to fulfill the alternative noted in CIF A8 ("to sell the goods in transit . . . by notification to the carrier"). Unfortunately, however, most legal systems do not have rules to support this arrangement, and for this reason the ICC's Commentary for the CIF and CFR Rules expressly warns the parties about relying on nonnegotiable bills of lading for such terms.[103] It likewise warns buyers not to pay for the goods in advance and banks not to rely on any security in the goods merely because they are named as consignees in a nonnegotiable bill unless such a designation is *irrevocable*—for otherwise the seller may change the consignee simply by giving new instructions to the carrier.[104]

Nonetheless, the use of nonnegotiable waybills is increasingly common in modern commerce, especially for short transport distances or between parties with existing business relationships. Sellers subject to a CIF or CFR obligation that chose to rely on the "notification to the carrier" alternative should include in the contract of carriage a clear and irrevocable definition of the buyer's

---

[101] INCOTERMS 2010, CIF A8, second paragraph (emphasis supplied).

[102] *See* Jan Ramberg, ICC GUIDE TO INCOTERMS 2010, at 72 (ICC Publ. No. 720E, 2010). Regarding this nature of a nonnegotiable bill of lading see Chapter 4, § 4.9.

[103] *Id.* at 188–189 (observing that "international conventions and most national laws do not yet provide specific regulations for these non-negotiable transport documents").

[104] *Id.*, at 72–73. Again, for a more detailed analysis of the carrier's delivery obligation under a nonnegotiable bill of lading see Chapter 4, § 4.9.

corresponding rights *against the carrier* (such as through incorporation of the Comité Maritime International's "Uniform Rules for Sea Waybills").[105] But this arrangement also carries substantial risks for the seller, for upon giving the carrier an irrevocable direction to deliver the goods at the instruction of the buyer, the seller immediately loses all control over the goods (and thus the power to obtain payment against the document as explored immediately below).

A closely related issue is the identification of the point at which the buyer must pay the seller and whether the buyer has a right to inspect the goods prior to such payment. The Incoterms CIF Rule—like all of the others—has no express provisions on either subject.[106] Traditionally, however, a CIF term has been understood to reflect an agreement between the buyer and the seller on a "documents against payment" (aka "payment against documents") arrangement. Under such an arrangement, the buyer must pay when the seller presents the negotiable bill of lading (or similar document controlling disposition of the goods).[107] As noted above, the seller tenders those documents through the banking system. The banks allow the buyer to obtain possession of the negotiable bill of lading (and thus the right to the goods) only after it pays the price due the seller under the sale of goods contract. Thus, the buyer "pays against documents," most often while the goods are at sea, and before any inspection of the goods is possible.[108] The buyer's rights in this regard are limited to an inspection of the bill of lading to ensure that it describes the goods as provided in the parties' sale contract.[109]

The common law has long recognized the presumption that a CIF term implies an agreement by the buyer on such a payment against documents arrangement (although of course other terms in the parties' contract may indicate otherwise). In the United States, the UCC's C.I.F. definition *formally* requires the buyer to "make payment against tender of the required documents."[110] The

---

[105] *See* CMI Uniform Rules for Sea Waybills, Rule 6(i), (ii) (1990) (providing that upon receipt of the goods by the carrier the shipper may "transfer the right of control to the consignee" by a corresponding notation on the sea waybill, and in such a case the consignee shall have all rights "to give the carrier instructions in relation to the contract of carriage" and "the shipper shall cease to have such rights"), *available at* http://comitemaritime.org/Uniform-Rules-for-Sea-Waybills/0,2729,12932,00.html.

[106] *See* text accompanying notes 57 and 60 *supra*.

[107] *See* Chapter 1, §§ 1.2–1.7.

[108] *See id.*, § 1.7.

[109] INCOTERMS 2010, CIF B8 (stating that the buyer is obligated to accept the transport document as long as it is "in conformity with the contract").

[110] § 2–320(4).

overwhelming weight of authority among scholars[111] and courts[112]—at least in the English-speaking, common law world—continues to hold this view for any contractual agreement on a CIF or CFR term. However, the force of this interpretive presumption is unclear in civil law systems, and as noted the 2010 version of the Incoterms definition for CIF (and for CFR, see § 3.11 below) does not provide express guidance on the subject.

The Incoterms CIF Rule again does not address issues of the formal title to the goods themselves, as federal courts have expressly recognized.[113] Nonetheless, upon issuance of a negotiable bill of lading covering the goods, the person properly in possession of the bill (the "holder," see again Chapter 4[114]) will obtain title to the goods as well.[115] And again, because the nature of the CIF term contemplates a documents against payment transaction, the buyer as a practical matter will have to pay upon presentation of the negotiable bill of lading and without an opportunity to inspect the goods.

The UCC also has a definition of "C.I.F.," which as noted requires the buyer to "make payment against tender of the required documents."[116] The UCC C.I.F. term otherwise is similar to Incoterms CIF, in that it requires the seller to deliver the goods to the carrier at the port of shipment and bear the risk of loss only to

---

[111]　*See* BENJAMIN'S SALE OF GOODS, § 19–077 (9th ed., M. Bridge, ed., 2014) ("A c.i.f. buyer must pay against the documents: he is not entitled to refuse to pay until he has examined the goods."); SCHMITTHOFF'S EXPORT TRADE, § 2–031 (Murray, Holloway, Timson-Hunt, eds., 11th ed., 2007) ("In a c.i.f. contract, unless the parties have agreed otherwise, the payment of the price becomes due when documents conforming to the contract are tendered."); Alastair C.L. Mullis, *Termination for Breach of Contract in C.I.F. Contracts Under the Vienna Convention and English Law; Is There a Substantial Difference?* 137, 148–150, in CONTEMPORARY ISSUES IN COMMERCIAL LAW (1997) ("C.i.f. buyers are usually required to pay against the tender of documents before they have had an opportunity to inspect the goods.").

[112]　*See, e.g.*, P.T. Putrabali Adyamulia v. Socit Est Epices, 2 Lloyd's Rep. 700, 2003 WL 21353311, para. 24 (High Court of Justice of England and Wales, QB Commercial Court, 2003) (observing that under a CIF or C&F sale "[i]n general the buyer is bound to pay for documents if, on their face, they conform to the terms of the contract"); Attorney-General of Botswana v. Aussie Diamond Products Ltd. [No. 3] [2010] WASC 141, para. 219 (Supreme Court of Western Australia, 2010) (same); Phulchand Exports Ltd. vs. OOO Patriot, Civil Appeal 3343/2005, paras. 16–18 (Supreme Court of India, 2011) (citing with approval authorities to the effect that the "essential feature of a C.I.F. contract is that delivery is satisfied by delivery of documents and not by actual physical delivery of the goods" and that such delivery of the documents "entitl[es] the seller to payment of the[ ] price").

[113]　*See, e.g.*, Italverde Trading, Inc. v. Four Bills of Lading, 485 F. Supp. 2d 187, 200 (E.D.N.Y. 2007) ("CIF within the meaning of the Incoterms does not govern change in title."); St. Paul Guardian Ins. Co. v. Neuromed Medical Systems & Support, GmbH, 2002 WL 465312, at *4 (S.D.N.Y. 2002) (same).

[114]　*See* Chapter 4, § 4.8.

[115]　*See* Federal Bill of Lading Act, 49 U.S.C. § 80105(a), and UCC § 7–502(a)(2).

[116]　UCC § 2–320(4).

that port, but it also requires the seller to pay the freight and insurance costs to the port of destination.[117]

§ 3.11 Water Transport__The Cost and Freight (CFR) Term

The Incoterms Cost and Freight (CFR) commercial term is essentially identical to the CIF term, except that the seller has no obligations with respect to either arranging or paying for insurance coverage of the goods during transportation. Under the CFR term, the seller is obligated to arrange and pay for transportation to a named destination point and then to deliver the goods on board the ship that it must arrange (or to "procure" rights to the goods already in transit).[118] Thus, the term also is appropriate only for water-borne transportation.

Like the CIF term, the seller must arrange the transportation and pay the freight costs to the *destination port*,[119] but has completed its delivery obligations when the goods are placed "on board the vessel" at the *shipment port*.[120] But in contrast with CIF, the seller under a CFR term has no obligation to arrange or pay for insurance on the goods during transportation.[121] Nonetheless, the risk of loss also transfers to the buyer at the time the goods are on board the vessel at the *shipment port*.[122] The seller must give the buyer any notice needed to enable the buyer to take the goods and the buyer must notify the seller of any specific required location at the destination port.[123] The seller is responsible for any license or other official authorization required for the exportation of the goods, and the buyer is responsible for the same issues regarding the importation of the goods.[124] The seller must provide a commercial invoice and "the usual transport document" for the destination port (or an equivalent electronic record for either).[125] Finally, like the CIF term, the seller under a CFR term must procure a transport document that will "enable the buyer to sell the goods in transit by the transfer of the document to a subsequent buyer or by

---

[117] UCC § 2–320(1), (2).

[118] INCOTERMS 2010, CFR A1, A4.

[119] INCOTERMS 2010, CFR A3(a), A6.

[120] INCOTERMS 2010, CFR A4.

[121] INCOTERMS 2010, CFR A3(b).

[122] INCOTERMS 2010, CFR A5, B5.

[123] INCOTERMS 2010, CFR A7, B7.

[124] INCOTERMS 2010, CFR A2, B2.

[125] INCOTERMS 2010, CFR A1.

notification to the carrier."[126] The discussion above for the CIF term in this regard thus applies as well to the CFR term.

As with CIF, the Incoterms CFR Rule has no provisions on either payment or post-shipment inspection. However, like CIF, the practical requirement of a negotiable bill of lading will mean that a CFR term will involve a documents against payment transaction. Both the UCC[127] and prior versions of Incoterms regarded this term as requiring payment against documents while the goods were still at sea, thus restricting port-shipment inspection of the goods before payment. As explained for the CIF term above, the weight of authority is that the same norm should continue to apply under the 2010 version of Incoterms CFR.

§ 3.12   Rules for Any Mode or Modes of Transport

As noted in Sections 3.8 through 3.11 above, the Incoterms FOB, FAS, CIF, and CFR Rules are appropriate only for "sea and inland waterway transport." But the Incoterms also include Rules that are available for any mode of transport, including multi-modal transportation. The following Sections will describe the seven Rules that fall in this category (CIP, CPT, DAP, DAT, DDP, EXW, and FCA).

§ 3.13   Any Mode___The Ex Works (EXW) Term

Under the Incoterms Ex Works (EXW) term, the seller must only tender the goods by placing them "at the disposal of the buyer" at an agreed point. But if there is no agreed point, the seller "may select the point that best suits its purpose," and this most often will be its own premises. Thus, the seller has no obligation to deliver the goods to a carrier or to load the goods on any vehicle. Indeed, the seller is not even obligated to arrange for any licenses or authorizations necessary for export.[128] In short, the EXW term "represents the minimum obligation of the seller" and thus "should be used with care."[129] It is best suited for those sellers that are new to international export transactions or for buyers that have substantial experience and expertise. Foreign buyers, however, typically seek to avoid the EXW term because of the burden of

---

[126]   INCOTERMS 2010, CFR A8.

[127]   *See* UCC § 2–320(3) (referring to a "C&F" term that in most respects is functionally equivalent to the Incoterms CFR Rule).

[128]   INCOTERMS 2010, EXW, A2, B2.

[129]   INCOTERMS 2010, EXW, at 15.

navigating complex United States transportation and export regulations.[130]

The seller has no obligation to arrange for transportation or insurance,[131] but must give the buyer any notice necessary for it to take delivery of the goods.[132] The seller must provide a commercial invoice, or an equivalent electronic record, but has no obligation to obtain a document of title (or any other transport document).[133] The Incoterms definition of EXW does not address either payment modalities or inspection rights (although of course the buyer must assume any costs of pre-shipment inspection). The risk of loss transfers to the buyer at the time the goods are placed at the buyer's disposal.[134] This rule is contrary to the default rule for merchant sellers under the UCC and the CISG in general, which postpone passing of the risk in a non-delivery transaction until the buyer's actual receipt of the goods.[135] This approach of the UCC and the CISG is based on the assumption that a commercial seller is more likely both to have insurance and to be able to protect the goods pending actual delivery to the buyer.[136]

§ 3.14   Any Mode___The Free Carrier (FCA) Term

Under the Incoterms Free Carrier (FCA) commercial term the seller is obligated to deliver the goods, cleared for export, into the custody of a carrier nominated by the buyer, usually the first carrier in a multi-modal transportation scheme.[137] The FCA term is particularly appropriate for arrangements in which the seller delivers the goods in a sealed container—a dominant form of transport today—directly to a freight forwarder or other logistics company arranged by the buyer. It thus is the analog to the FOB term except that, instead of delivering the goods on board a ship at a defined outbound port, the seller delivers them to some other form of carrier at another defined place.

The seller has no obligation to pay for transportation costs or insurance.[138] However, the seller may arrange transportation at the buyer's expense if requested by the buyer, or if it is "commercial practice" for the seller to do so and the buyer does not timely

---

[130]   *See* Jacob Barron, *New Decade, New Upgrade: Incoterms 2010 Picks Up Where Incoterms 2000 Left Off*, 113 BUS. CREDIT 20, 21 (2011).

[131]   INCOTERMS 2010, EXW, A3.

[132]   INCOTERMS 2010, EXW, A7.

[133]   INCOTERMS 2010, EXW, A1, A8.

[134]   INCOTERMS 2010, EXW, A5, B5.

[135]   *See* UCC § 2–509(3) and CISG, *supra* note 1, art. 69(1).

[136]   *See* UCC § 2–509, Official Comment 3.

[137]   INCOTERMS 2010, FCA, A2, A4.

[138]   INCOTERMS 2010, FCA, A6.

object.[139] But even under these circumstances, the seller may refuse to make such arrangements as long as it so notifies the buyer. Even if the seller does arrange transportation, it has no obligation to arrange for insurance coverage during transportation.[140]

The seller's delivery obligation under an FCA term then consists of merely loading the goods on the transport arranged by the buyer (or delivering them into the custody of the carrier or other person nominated by the buyer).[141] The seller need only notify the buyer when the goods have been so delivered.[142] The risk of loss transfers to the buyer upon such delivery, although the buyer may not receive notice until after that time.[143] The seller must provide a commercial invoice or an equivalent electronic record, any necessary export license, and "the usual proof that the goods have been delivered."[144] The Incoterms definition for FCA has no provisions on either payment or post-shipment inspection.

This Incoterm FCA term is most comparable to the UCC's "F.O.B. place of shipment" term under § 2–319(1)(a). However, there are two sources of potential confusion in such a comparison. One is that Incoterms has its own FOB term, which is quite different (see § 3.8 above); this creates a risk of a *faux amis* ("false friends") as between the UCC's general F.O.B. term and the Incoterms FOB term. The other is that the obligations under Incoterms FCA and the UCC "F.O.B. place of shipment" term are, in fact, different. Under the UCC's F.O.B. place of shipment term, the seller must arrange transportation[145] while the seller need do so under Incoterms FCA only by special agreement. Further, under the UCC the seller must "obtain and promptly deliver . . . any document necessary to enable the buyer to obtain possession of the goods."[146] Under Incoterms FCA, the seller must merely provide, at the buyer's request, "assistance" in obtaining a transport document.[147]

§ 3.15 Any Mode___The Carriage and Insurance Paid to (CIP) Term

The Incoterms Carriage and Insurance To Paid (CIP) term and Carriage Paid To (CPT) term (see § 3.16 below) parallel its CIF and

---

[139]   INCOTERMS 2010, FCA, A3(a).

[140]   INCOTERMS 2010, FCA, A3(b).

[141]   INCOTERMS 2010, FCA, A4.

[142]   INCOTERMS 2010, FCA, A7.

[143]   INCOTERMS 2010, FCA, A5, B5.

[144]   INCOTERMS 2010, FCA, A1, A2, A8.

[145]   UCC §§ 3–319(1), 2–504.

[146]   UCC § 2–504(b).

[147]   INCOTERMS 2010, FCA, A8.

CFR terms, except that they may be used for any type of transportation (and thus not just for waterborne transportation). The CIP term is the analog to the CIF term (see § 3.10 above). Under the CIP term, the seller is obligated to arrange[148] and pay for[149] both transportation and insurance to a named *destination* place. However, the seller completes its delivery obligations by handing the goods over to the carrier at the place of *shipment* within the agreed time.[150] The risk of loss likewise passes to the buyer upon delivery to the first carrier at the place of *shipment*.[151] Thus, the CIP term—unlike CIF—is appropriate for multimodal transportation and for container transport.

Under CIP, the seller must notify the buyer that the goods have been delivered to the first carrier, and also give any other notice required to enable the buyer "to take the goods."[152] The seller must provide a commercial invoice, or an equivalent electronic record, any necessary export license, and "the usual transport document."[153] But—unlike CIF—the seller is obligated to obtain a document that would "enable the buyer to sell the goods in transit" (such as a negotiable bill of lading) *only if* this is "agreed or customary."[154] Thus, unless the parties expressly agree to a "documents against payment" arrangement or a special trade usage exists, the CIP commercial term does not require that the buyer pay upon presentation of a document controlling disposition of the goods or restrict its inspection rights before payment. The Incoterms definition of CIP contains no other payment or post-shipment inspection provisions.

As with all of the other seven Incoterms rules that apply for any mode of transport, the UCC does not recognize a CIP term.

§ 3.16 Any Mode__The Carriage Paid (CPT) Term

The Incoterms Carriage To Paid (CPT) term is the analog to the CFR term (see § 3.11 above), except that it may be used for any type of transportation, including multimodal transportation. Under the CPT term, the seller is obligated to arrange[155] and pay for[156] transportation to a named *destination* place. However, the seller

---

148   INCOTERMS 2010, CIP, A3.
149   INCOTERMS 2010, CIP, A6.
150   INCOTERMS 2010, CIP, A4.
151   INCOTERMS 2010, CIP, A5, B5.
152   INCOTERMS 2010, CIP, A7.
153   INCOTERMS 2010, CIP, A1, A2, A8.
154   INCOTERMS 2010, CIP, A8.
155   INCOTERMS 2010, CPT, A3(a).
156   INCOTERMS 2010, CPT, A6.

completes its delivery obligations by handing the goods over to the carrier at the place of *shipment* within the agreed time.[157] The risk of loss likewise passes to the buyer upon delivery to the first carrier at the place of *shipment*.[158] The seller completes its delivery obligations,[159] and the risk of loss passes to the buyer, upon delivery to the first carrier at the place of *shipment*.[160]

But unlike the CIP term, under a CPT term the seller has no obligation to arrange or pay for insurance covering the goods during transportation.[161] In other words, CPT has the same relationship to CIP that CFR has to CIF. The difference is that, because the seller under a CIP/CPT term completes its delivery obligation by "handing [the goods] over to the carrier" (and not by loading them on a waterborne vessel), these two terms—unlike CIF/CFR—are appropriate for multimodal transportation and for container transport.

The remaining rules for the CPT term are the same as those for CIP. Thus, the seller must provide a commercial invoice, or an equivalent electronic record, any necessary export license, and "the usual transport document," and then notify the buyer that the goods have been delivered.[162] Also, unlike CFR, the seller under a CPT term is obligated to obtain a document that would "enable the buyer to sell the goods in transit" *only if* such is "agreed or customary."[163] Thus, unless the parties expressly agree to a "documents against payment" term or a special trade usage exists, the CPT commercial term does not require that the buyer pay upon presentation of a document controlling disposition of the goods or restrict its inspection rights before payment. The Incoterms definition of CPT contains no other payment or post-shipment inspection provisions. And again, the UCC does not recognize a CPT term.

§ 3.17 Any Mode__The Delivered at Place (DAP) Term

The Incoterms 2010 have two new terms, DAP (Delivered at Place) and DAT (Delivered at Terminal), which replace four former terms (DES, DEQ, DAF, and DDU). Each can be used for any type of transportation, including multimodal transport. In both, the seller is required to arrange transportation to the defined distant

---

[157] INCOTERMS 2010, CPT, A4.

[158] INCOTERMS 2010, CPT, A5, B5.

[159] INCOTERMS 2010, CPT, A4.

[160] INCOTERMS 2010, CPT, A5, B5.

[161] INCOTERMS 2010, CPT A3(b).

[162] INCOTERMS 2010, CPT, A1, A2, A7, A8.

[163] INCOTERMS 2010, CPT, A8.

place, pay the freight costs, and bear the risk of loss to a named destination point. Although these definitions have no provisions on insurance during transportation, because the seller bears the risk of loss during transport, it is well-advised to arrange and pay for insurance, or it otherwise will assume the risks of a self-insurer.

Under the Incoterms DAP term, the seller bears the responsibility, costs, and risks of delivering the goods at the destination specified in the contract.[164] Because such destinations—cities, ports, or even terminals—can be extensive, the parties "are well advised to specify as clearly as possible the point within the agreed place of destination" to avoid disputes upon arrival.[165] The seller completes its delivery obligations under DAP when the goods reach the named place and are placed "at the disposal of the buyer on the arriving means of transport ready for unloading" by the buyer.[166] (In this respect, the DAP term is similar to the UCC's "Ex-Ship" term.[167]) Thus, the seller is obligated to arrange and pay for transportation to the named destination port and (although not obligated to do so) is again well advised to arrange and pay for insurance on the goods during transportation.[168] The risk of loss will transfer to the buyer when the seller completes its delivery obligation—that is, when the transportation vessel or vehicle arrives—at the named destination.[169] The seller must clear the goods for export and for transport "through any country prior to delivery," but is not responsible for import duties or other formalities for importation into the destination country.[170] The seller, finally, must provide to the buyer any document necessary to enable the buyer to take the goods.[171]

The DAP term has no provisions on payment or post-shipment inspection; but it does not require that the seller procure a negotiable bill of lading. Thus, there is no reason to imply a "documents against payment" requirement if the contract does not expressly include one. On the other hand, the parties (as always) are free to agree expressly on both a destination commercial term and a requirement that the buyer pay upon presentation of a document controlling disposition of the goods.

---

[164]   INCOTERMS 2010, DAP, A3, A4, A5, A6.

[165]   INCOTERMS 2010, DAP, Guidance Note, at 61.

[166]   INCOTERMS 2010, DAP, A4.

[167]   *See* UCC § 2–322.

[168]   INCOTERMS 2010, DAP, A3, A6.

[169]   INCOTERMS 2010, DAP, A5.

[170]   INCOTERMS 2010, DAP, A2.

[171]   INCOTERMS 2010, DAP, A8.

§ 3.18 Any Mode__The Delivered at Terminal (DAT) Term

The Incoterms DAT rule is similar to DAP, for the seller again bears the responsibility, costs, and risks of delivering the goods to the terminal at the location specified in the contract.[172] Unlike DAP, however, the seller also is responsible for *unloading* the goods from the arriving means of transport.[173] The seller completes its delivery obligations when the goods are unloaded from the arriving means of transport and are placed at the disposal of the buyer "at the named terminal" at the place of destination.[174] Terminal includes all forms of terminals (whether quay, container or rail yard, or road, rail, or air terminal). The risk of loss passes to the buyer upon unloading at that point.[175] Like DAP, the seller is responsible for export clearance and for clearance through any country along the way to the delivery terminal, but is not responsible for import duties or other import formalities.[176] Finally, the seller must again provide to the buyer any document necessary to enable the buyer to take the goods.[177]

The DAT term is especially valuable for sellers that wish to control their supply chain in order to signal reliability to customers, control costs, and maintain the quality of the goods. Sellers of this type also may wish to rely on established relationships with freight forwarders or carriers or to ship their goods to multiple customers under a single bill of lading or in a single container.

§ 3.19 Any Mode__The Delivered Duty Paid (DDP) Term

The final Incoterm rule, DDP (Delivered Duty Paid), places the highest level of responsibility on the seller (and thus the lowest responsibility on the buyer).[178] It thus sits at the opposite end of the responsibility spectrum from EXW, under which the seller must merely make the goods available at its own premises and all remaining responsibilities are on the buyer.[179]

---

[172] INCOTERMS 2010, DAT, A3, A4, A5, A6.

[173] INCOTERMS 2010, DAT, A4.

[174] *Id.*

[175] INCOTERMS 2010, DAT, A5.

[176] INCOTERMS 2010, DAT, A2.

[177] INCOTERMS 2010, DAT, A8.

[178] *See* INCOTERMS 2010, DDP, Guidance Note, at 69 (stating that "DDP represents the maximum obligation for the seller").

[179] *See* § 3.13 *supra.*

Under the DDP commercial term, delivery occurs and the risk of loss passes when the goods are placed at the buyer's disposal, "ready for unloading," at the named place in the country of destination.[180] The buyer's only noteworthy responsibility is to arrange and pay for the unloading of the goods from the arriving means of transport.[181]

But unlike all other Incoterms Rules, the seller under a DDP term not only is responsible for export clearance, but also must deliver the goods to the buyer cleared for importation into the destination country.[182] Thus, the seller must obtain the import license, pay all import duties and terminal charges, and complete all customs formalities for importation into the destination country at its risk and expense.[183] The seller again must provide to the buyer any document necessary to enable the buyer to take the goods at the named destination.[184] Because of the responsibility to clear the goods for importation into a foreign country, only the most sophisticated sellers (or those with established relationships with sophisticated international freight forwarders) are advised to use the DDP term. If the seller does not want to assume this obligation, "the DAP rule should be used."[185]

The UCC does not recognize a DDP term. The closest UCC commercial term is "F.O.B. destination,"[186] but it lacks substantial detail as compared to the Incoterms DDP term.

---

[180] INCOTERMS 2010, DDP, A4, A5.
[181] INCOTERMS 2010, DDP, B6.
[182] INCOTERMS 2010, DDP, A2.
[183] INCOTERMS 2010, DDP, A2, A3, A6.
[184] INCOTERMS 2010, DDP, A8.
[185] See INCOTERMS 2010, DDP, Guidance Note, at 69.
[186] UCC § 2–319(1)(b).

Chapter 4

BILLS OF LADING

Table of Sections

§ 4.1   Introduction to International Bills of Lading

Bills of lading play a significant, indeed essential, role in international sales transactions. A bill of lading is a document issued by a carrier upon receipt of goods from a shipper (commonly, the seller in a sales transaction). Such a document serves three independent, but related functions:

(1) It first serves as the shipper's contract of carriage with the carrier. This contract sets forth the terms under which the carrier undertakes to transport the goods to the named destination and either expressly includes the carrier's tariffs or incorporates them by reference;

(2) A contract of bailment, which serves as a receipt given by the carrier to the shipper describing the goods received from the shipper; and

(3)   A document of title covering the goods.[1]

Bills of lading are particularly important in the large international transactions that involve carriage (*i.e.*, transportation) of goods by sea—whether oil, foodstuffs, materials, or any other form of physical products. Indeed, the fundamental federal statute on this subject, the Carriage of Goods by Sea Act (see immediately below), requires that the carrier, on demand, "issue to the shipper a bill of lading" describing the goods received for international carriage.[2] And as Chapter 1 examined in detail, bills of lading form a critical building block in both the "documents against payment" transaction[3] and the documentary letter of credit transaction,[4] each of which plays an essential role in facilitating international business deals.

State, federal, and international law all have rules governing bills of lading. Uniform Commercial Code Article 7—which every state in the United States has adopted as statutory law—broadly regulates "Documents of Title," including bills of lading. But the regulation of bills of lading, and in particular the relationship of the carrier to its customers, also is the subject of four international conventions and three U.S. federal statutes. Until recently, only three conventions existed (the so-called Hague Rules, Hague–Visby Rules, and Hamburg Rules), each of which was progressively more customer-oriented. The multiplicity of treaties governing the terms and usage of bills of lading created, however, actual conflicts in the legal concepts that may apply to a single transaction. Concerns about these conflicts thus led to the negotiation and conclusion of an entirely new treaty, the so-called "Rotterdam Rules," and as of 2016 there are positive signs that the United States will adopt this treaty. Section 4.2 below will review the substance of these international conventions.

As of late 2016, however, the United States has accepted only the Hague Rules, which it has enacted into domestic law as the Carriage of Goods by Sea Act (COGSA).[5] The United States also has in force more limited pre-COGSA legislation, the Harter Act, which governs certain narrow aspects of purely domestic transport of

---

[1]   *See* Kawasaki Kisen Kaisha Ltd. v. Regal-Beloit Corp., 561 U.S. 89, 94 (2010) (stating that a bill of lading "records that a carrier has received goods from the party that wishes to ship them, states the terms of carriage, and serves as evidence of the contract for carriage") (*quoting* Norfolk Southern R. Co. v. Kirby, 543 U.S. 14, 18–19 (2004)).

[2]   *See* Carriage of Goods by Sea Act, § 3(3), 46 U.S.C. § 30701 (statutory note) [hereinafter, COGSA]. For more detail on COGSA, see § 4.5 *infra*.

[3]   *See* Chapter 1, § 1.5.

[4]   *See* Chapter 1, § 1.13.

[5]   *See* COGSA, *supra* note 2.

goods.[6] The most important federal law regulating bills of lading, however, is the Federal Bills of Lading Act (FBLA, also known by its earlier name, the Pomerene Act).[7] Sections 4.3 through 4.6 below will examine in detail these various U.S. laws governing bills of lading.

The fundamental function of a bill of lading lies in its status as a legal embodiment of the rights to the goods described therein. This status ensures that the carrier delivers ("turns out") the goods only according to the nature and terms of the bill of lading covering those goods. But this status also provides the material for the three most common disputes over bills of lading: (a) misdelivery of the goods by the carrier; (b) misdescription of the goods in the bill of lading; and (c) forgery of necessary signatures on the bill of lading. Sections 4.11 through 4.14 below will examine these disputes in detail.

§ 4.2   International Conventions

The regulation of the terms of a bill of lading, as well as the more general relationship between a carrier and its customers, is the subject of four international conventions. As noted in the Introduction to this Chapter, until recently only three conventions were in existence: The so-called Hague Rules;[8] the Hague–Visby Rules (which build on the Hague Rules, but amend them in noteworthy ways);[9] and the Hamburg Rules.[10] Each of these treaties governs contracts of carriage and related aspects of bills of lading, but they follow differing approaches.[11]

---

6   46 U.S.C. § 30701 *et seq.*

7   49 U.S.C. § 80101 *et seq.*

8   Convention for the Unification of Certain Rules of Law Relating to Bills of Lading, Aug. 25, 1924, 51 Stat. 233, T.S. No. 931, 120 L.N.T.S. 155. Nearly fifty countries are member states of only the Hague Rules. *See* the 2015 CMI YEARBOOK OF THE COMITÉ MARITIME INTERNATIONAL 449–450, *available at* http://comite maritime.org/Yearbooks/0,2714,11432,00.html.

9   Protocol to Amend the International Convention for the Unification of Certain Rules of Law Relating to Bills of Lading, Brussels, Feb. 23, 1968, 1412 U.N.T.S. 127 (entered into force June 23, 1977), *available at* http://www.admiraltylaw.com/statutes/hague.html. As of late 2016, twenty-six countries are member states of the Hague–Visby Rules. *See* the 2015 CMI YEARBOOK OF THE COMITÉ MARITIME INTERNATIONAL 455–456, *available at* http://comitemaritime.org/Yearbooks/0,2714,11432,00.html.

10   UN Convention on the Carriage of Goods by Sea, Mar. 31, 1978, U.N. Doc. A/RES/48/34 (entered into force Nov. 1, 1992), *available at* http://www.uncitral.org/uncitral/en/uncitral_texts/transport_goods.html. As of late 2016, thirty-four countries are member states of the Hamburg Rules. *See* http://www.uncitral.org/uncitral/en/uncitral_texts/transport_goods/Hamburg_status.html.

11   For discussions on the development of and change to these international conventions, see Francesco Berlingieri, I INTERNATIONAL MARITIME CONVENTIONS: THE CARRIAGE OF GOODS AND PASSENGERS BY SEA (2014); Hakan Karan, THE

The Hague Rules. The Hague Rules, adopted in 1924, set forth rules governing shipowner liability to shippers for cargo loss and damage. The Hague Rules define the basic "due diligence" obligations of the carrier,[12] provide seventeen defenses against carrier and shipowner liability,[13] preclude contractual exculpatory clauses in bills of lading,[14] and limit carrier liability to $500 per package or customary freight unit.[15] (Because the United States has enacted the Hague Rules into domestic law, Section 4.5 examines the content of these rules in more detail below.)

The Hague–Visby Rules. The Hague–Visby Rules of 1968 were based on, but made noteworthy amendments to, the Hague Rules. This "Visby Amendment" addressed certain issues that had arisen under the Hague Rules, such as the scope of carrier defenses and the inadequacy of the $500 per package liability provision in light of multimodal transportation and containerized packaging. The Hague–Visby Rules retain most of the long list of defenses for carriers[16] and define the term "package" to include containerized cargo.[17] These Rules also increase the liability limit of the carriers and made it adjustable with reference to the value of "special drawing rights (SDRs)," which is a unit of account based on a basket of currencies maintained by the International Monetary Fund.[18] The new liability amount is 666 SDRs per package (approximately US$926) or 2 SDRs per kilogram (approximately US$2.8), whichever is higher. But the Hague–Visby Rules also expressly remove that limitation for damage caused by the carrier's own intentional or reckless actions.[19]

The Hamburg Rules. The Hamburg Rules of 1978 were a major departure from the Hague and Hague–Visby Rules, for they substantially decreased the defenses of carriers and ship owners and increased their potential liability. The Hamburg Rules in fact leave only three of the seventeen defenses provided in the previous

---

CARRIER'S LIABILITY UNDER THE INTERNATIONAL MARITIME CONVENTIONS: THE HAGUE, HAGUE–VISBY, AND HAMBURG RULES (2004); and Samuel Mandelbaum, *Creating Uniform Worldwide Liability Standards for Sea Carriage of Goods Under the Hague, COGSA, Visby and Hamburg Conventions*, 23 TRANSP. L.J. 471, 477 (1996).

12   Hague Rules, art. 3.

13   *Id.*, art. 4(2).

14   *Id.*, art. 3(8).

15   *Id.*, art. 4(5) (as adjusted under COGSA, *supra* note 2, § 4(5)).

16   Hague–Visby Rules, art. IV(e).

17   *Id.*, art. IV(5)(c).

18   As of late 2016, an SDR was worth approximately 1.4 U.S. dollars.

19   *Id.*, art. IV(5)(e).

conventions;[20] they increase the liability per package to 835 SDRs (approximately US$1,169) per package (or customary shipping unit) or 2.35 SDRs (approximately US$3.7) per kilogram of cargo, whichever is higher;[21] and for the first time they include liability for on deck cargo and shipments without a bill of lading (such liability having been specifically excluded by the prior conventions).[22] A substantial majority of the thirty-four countries that have adopted the Hamburg Rules are developing or landlocked states, whose businesses are most likely to benefit from expansive liability rules for carriers.[23] The Hague Rules and the Hague–Visby Rules, in contrast, are more favorable to carriers and thus have been adopted mostly by the world's maritime states.[24]

Some countries have chosen one set of rules to apply as mandatory law for all transactions; others, such as those that have adopted the Hague–Visby Rules, apply different rules depending on whether a shipment is inbound or outbound (because those rules are not applicable of their own force for inbound shipments).[25]

The Rotterdam Rules. As noted in the Introduction, concerns about the conflicts between these three "international" treaty efforts led to comprehensive negotiations under the auspices of the United Nations Commission on International Trade Law (UNCITRAL) to bring about true international uniformity. The result of this new effort was a fourth treaty on the subject of the obligations of carriers in international trade, the United Nations Convention on Contracts for the International Carriage of Goods Wholly or Partly by Sea (2009).[26] These so-called Rotterdam Rules are the product of two decades of negotiation and drafting by interested parties from a broad range of perspectives and thus may be acceptable to a noteworthy majority of states, whether principally supportive of buyers, sellers, or carriers. As of late 2016, however, only three states (Congo, Spain, and Togo) have ratified the Rotterdam Rules, and it has not yet entered into force.[27] The United States has signed

---

[20]   Hamburg Rules, art. 5.

[21]   *Id.*, art. 6.

[22]   *Id.*, art. 9. For an in-depth review of the Hamburg Rules, see Robert Force, *A Comparison of the Hague, Hague–Visby, and Hamburg Rules: Much Ado About (?)*, 70 TUL. L. REV. 2051 (1996).

[23]   *See* Status of Convention, available at the website of UNCITRAL, http://www.uncitral.org/uncitral/en/uncitral_texts/transport_goods/Hamburg_status.html.

[24]   *See* 1 William Tetley, MARINE CARGO CLAIMS 11 (4th ed., 2008).

[25]   Hague–Visby Rules, *supra* note 9, art. X.

[26]   G.A. Res. 63/122, Annex, U.N. Doc. A/RES/63/122 (Feb. 2, 2009). The text of the Rotterdam Rules is available at http://www.uncitral.org/uncitral/en/uncitral_texts/transport_goods/2008rotterdam_rules.html.

[27]   The status of ratification of the Rotterdam Rules is available at http://www.uncitral.org/uncitral/en/uncitral_texts/transport_goods/rotterdam_status.html.

the treaty, and there are some positive indications that it may ratify in the near future.

If they were to enter into force, the Rotterdam Rules would comprehensively cover the relationship between the carrier and its customers, including with respect to the basic obligations of the carrier;[28] the carrier's liability for loss, damage, or delay,[29] as well as the limitations on that liability;[30] the rules for deck cargo and related issues;[31] the delivery of the goods;[32] the obligations of the shipper to the carrier;[33] the rules for "transport documents" (especially bills of lading);[34] the transfer of negotiable transport documents and the resultant rights of the party with control over the document;[35] and time limitations, jurisdiction, and arbitration.[36] These Rules also expressly contemplate, and create the legal framework for, the issuance and transfer of electronic bills of lading.[37]

As noted above and discussed in more detail below, as of late 2016 the United States has accepted only the original Hague Rules, which it has enacted into its domestic law as the Carriage of Goods by Sea Act (COGSA).

§ 4.3 Overview of United States Law

Under state law, UCC Article 7 governs the two principal forms of "documents of title"[38]: warehouse receipts[39] and, the subject of our interest here, bills of lading.[40] UCC Article 1 defines a bill of lading as a document of title "evidencing the receipt of goods for shipment issued by a person engaged in the business of directly or indirectly transporting or forwarding goods."[41] UCC Article 7 then

---

[28] Rotterdam Rules, *supra* note 26, arts. 11–16.

[29] *Id.*, arts. 17–23.

[30] *Id.*, arts. 59–61.

[31] *Id.*, arts. 24–26.

[32] *Id.*, arts. 43–49.

[33] *Id.*, arts. 27–34.

[34] *Id.*, arts. 35–42.

[35] *Id.*, arts. 50–58. For a comprehensive analysis of these Rotterdam Rules *see* Michael Sturley, Tomotaka Fujita & G.J. Van der Ziel, THE ROTTERDAM RULES: THE UN CONVENTION ON CONTRACTS FOR THE INTERNATIONAL CARRIAGE OF GOODS WHOLLY OR PARTLY BY SEA (2010).

[36] Rotterdam Rules, *supra* note 26, arts. 62–78.

[37] *Id.*, arts. 8–10, 35, 45–47, 57.

[38] *See* UCC § 1–201(b)(16) (defining the term "document of title" to include, *inter alia*, a bill of lading).

[39] UCC § 1–201(b)(42) (defining a warehouse receipt as a document of title "issued by a person engaged in the business of storing goods for hire").

[40] *See* UCC § 1–201(b)(6).

[41] *Id.*

has detailed rules on the rights and obligations arising out of the issuance[42] and transfer[43] of bills of lading.

These rules of the UCC have a curious relationship with federal law regarding international transactions. In large measure, the UCC is preempted by federal law.[44] As explained in more detail in § 4.6 below, the Federal Bills of Lading Act[45] governs bills of lading issued by any common carrier for the transportation of goods in either interstate commerce or international commerce from the United States to another country.[46] Because of this last clause, however, the rules of UCC Article 7 governing the issuance and transfer of bills of lading continue to apply to purely intrastate transactions, to *inbound* international shipments, and to international shipments not bound for a place in the United States (provided that a court somehow would find that U.S. law applies to such a shipment at all).[47]

As the next two Sections explore, both the Harter Act[48] and COGSA[49] have provisions that in some respects address the form and content of bills of lading. This multiplicity of statutes governing the terms and use of bill of ladings leaves considerable room for conflicts and confusion. Thus, for example, one federal court has observed that the Supreme Court has not "spoken directly to the question of whether COGSA completely preempts state law" and that "the courts that have reached the question have come to differing conclusions."[50] In many situations, therefore, lawyers will

---

[42]   *See* §§ 7–301 through 7–309, 7–401 through 7–404.

[43]   *See* §§ 7–501 through 7–509.

[44]   *See* National Union Fire Ins. Co. v. Allite, Inc., 430 Mass. 828, 724 N.E.2d 677, 679 (2000) (holding that the FBLA preempts Article 7 of the UCC for interstate and outbound international transportation of goods); BII Finance Co. v. U-States Forwarding Services Corp., 95 Cal. App. 4th 111, 115 Cal. Rptr. 2d 312, 319 (2002) (same).

[45]   49 U.S.C. §§ 80101 *et seq.*

[46]   49 U.S.C. § 80102.

[47]   *See* BII Finance Co. v. U-States Forwarding Services Corp., 95 Cal. App. 4th 111, 115 Cal. Rptr. 2d 312, 319 (2002) (holding that "[b]ecause the goods in this case did not travel through the United States, the Federal Bills of Lading Act does not supersede California law here"); Thypin Steel Co. v. Certain Bills of Lading, 1996 WL 223896 (S.D.N.Y. 1996); T.C. Ziraat Bankasi v. Standard Chartered Bank, 644 N.E.2d 272 (N.Y. 1994).

[48]   46 U.S.C. § 30701 *et seq.*

[49]   Again, COGSA now appears as a statutory note to 46 U.S.C. § 30701.

[50]   Continental Ins. Co. v. Kawasaki Kisen Kasha, Ltd., 542 F. Supp. 2d 1031, 1034 (N.D. Cal. 2008). *See also* UTI, U.S., Inc. v. Bernuth Agencies, Inc., 2012 WL 4511304 (S.D. Fla. 2012) (also examining the scope of COGSA preemption of state law).

need to consider the possible application of both state and federal law to a particular bill of lading transaction.[51]

§ 4.4   The Harter Act

The Harter Act, codified under the shipping title of the United States Code,[52] governs the liability of the vessel owner or carrier to the shipper for cargo transported solely in domestic trade. The Harter Act was a restatement of the common law as of 1893 governing the duties and liabilities in the relationship of a vessel to its cargo.[53]

The Harter Act nullifies language in a bill of lading that limits a carrier's liability for "negligence or fault in loading, stowage, custody, care, or proper delivery."[54] Distilled to its essence, the Act defines the carrier's basic obligation of "due diligence"[55] and limits the carrier's ability to contract away this liability in preparing the vessel for the carriage of the goods and in handling the goods while in its possession.[56]

In significant measure, COGSA (see immediately below) displaces the Harter Act for international shipments. The one area in which the Harter Act remains potentially relevant for international transactions is with respect to carrier liability for events that occur *after* the goods have been offloaded at a domestic port. This conclusion obtains, as the Supreme Court has emphasized, because COGSA governs bills of lading for the carriage of goods only "from the time when the goods are loaded on to the time when they are discharged from the ship."[57]

§ 4.5   The Carriage of Goods by Sea Act (COGSA)

The Carriage of Goods by Sea Act (COGSA) is the principal U.S. statute governing the international transport of goods. Together with the FBLA discussed in Section 4.6 below, COGSA defines the rights and obligations of a carrier in its relations with its customers (principally, the shipper and its transferees), including the rights and obligations that arise out of bills of lading issued for international transport.

---

[51]   For a more comprehensive discussion of the possible conflicts between state and federal law *see* Michael Crowley, *The Limited Scope of the Cargo Liability Regime Covering Carriage of Goods by Sea: The Multimodal Problem*, 79 TUL. L. REV. 1461, 1474–78 (2005).

[52]   46 U.S.C. § 30701 *et seq.*

[53]   *See* The Delaware, 161 U.S. 459, 471–72 (1896).

[54]   46 U.S.C § 30704.

[55]   *Id.*, § 30706.

[56]   *Id.*, § 30705.

[57]   Norfolk S. Ry. Co. v. Kirby, 543 U.S. 14, 29 (2004) (*quoting* COGSA § 1(e)).

COGSA resulted from the ratification by the United States of the Hague Rules.[58] Indeed, as one federal appellate court has observed, COGSA is "virtually identical" to the Hague Rules.[59] Prior to the Hague Rules, there was no international uniformity regarding the liability of carriers that accepted goods for international transport. For example, in the United States carriers could not limit their liability and were treated as insurers of the cargo, while in the United Kingdom they were permitted (under the principle of freedom of contract) to disclaim all liability. Because of this, a principal goal of the Hague Rules, and thus COGSA, was to establish uniform rules for goods transported under ocean bills of lading, and especially for the liability of the vessel owner or carrier to the shipper in international trade.[60]

COGSA applies to every bill of lading or document of title that evidences a contract for the carriage of goods by sea "to or from ports of the United States, in foreign trade."[61] Thus, it applies to bills of lading issued outside of the United States if the destination is a port in this country. But it does not *by its own terms* apply "to an ocean voyage between two foreign ports, even though the ultimate destination of a through bill of lading may be a city in the United States."[62] One appellate court nonetheless has held as a matter of federal common law that, in order to "advance the predictability and uniformity of maritime liability rules, which Congress sought to achieve in 1936 by passing COGSA," the Act applies to a multimodal bill of lading (see § 4.10 below) covering various stages in various countries as long as the "ultimate destination" of the goods is the United States.[63]

---

[58]   Upon a restructuring of the maritime laws in Title 46 of the U.S. Code in 2006, Congress moved COGSA to a "statutory note" in order not to interfere with the negotiations over the Rotterdam Rules. This change had no effect on the content or continued validity of COGSA.

[59]   Federal Ins. Co. v. Union Pacific R. Co., 651 F.3d 1175, 1179 (9th Cir. 2011).

[60]   *See* Robert C. Herd & Co., Inc. v. Krawill Mach. Corp., 359 U.S. 297, 301 (1959). The international counterpart in the United Kingdom in the early 1900s was the Carriage of Goods by Sea Act of 1924. More modern versions include the U.K.'s Carriage of Goods By Sea Act of 1971 (which implemented the Hague–Visby Rules) and the Carriage of Goods By Sea Act of 1992 (which provided more details for bills of lading).

[61]   COGSA, *supra* note 2, § 13. *See also id.* (defining the term "foreign trade" as "the transportation of goods between the ports of the United States and ports of foreign countries").

[62]   *See, e.g.,* Royal Ins. Co. of America v. Orient Overseas Container Line Ltd., 525 F.3d 409, 416 (6th Cir. 2008); Foster Wheeler Energy Corp. v. An Ning Jiang MV, 383 F.3d 349, 355 (5th Cir. 2004).

[63]   Royal Ins. Co. of America v. Orient Overseas Container Line Ltd., 525 F.3d 409, 414 (6th Cir. 2008). Regarding the notion of a "through" bill of lading, see § 4.10 *infra.*

The fundamental purpose of COGSA is to define the responsibilities and liabilities of the carrier and the ship in international carriage transactions. It thus addresses the seaworthiness of the vessel—which includes the proper manning, maintenance, equipment, supplies, and preparation of the vessel so that it is fit for the cargo[64]—and the proper care and loading of the cargo.[65] In addition, COGSA states that a carrier is liable for damaged cargo resulting from an unreasonable deviation from the terms of the contract of carriage—for example, discharging the cargo and reloading it on another vessel, stowage contrary to specific agreements with the shipper, or a delay in delivery resulting from a change in route in order to take on additional cargo.[66] Consistent with the Hague Rules, COGSA provides a carrier with seventeen defenses for uncontrollable causes of loss, including defective navigation or management of the ship; fires; dangers of the sea; acts of God or war or public enemies; seizure by foreign authorities; certain labor problems; inherent defects in the goods; insufficiency of packing or marks; and more generally any other cause "without the actual fault and privity of the carrier."[67] Unlike the Harter Act, COGSA does not require due diligence as a condition to reliance on these defenses,[68] except for liability under the seaworthiness requirement.[69]

One of the most well-known provisions of COGSA is the $500 per package limitation of liability for loss or damage to cargo.[70] This limitation was the regulatory trade-off for a prohibition limitation of liability clauses in the carriage contract itself.[71] The shipper may secure an increase in the $500 per package limit; indeed, some courts have found that the carrier must give the shipper a "fair opportunity" to do so.[72] But as one federal court has observed, "in the modern commercial context, it is rare for a shipper to declare the value of the goods [because] carriers typically demand a much

---

[64] COGSA, *supra* note 2, § 3(1).

[65] *Id.*, § 3(2).

[66] *Id.*, § 4(4).

[67] *Id.*, § 4(2).

[68] *Id.*

[69] *Id.*, § 4(1).

[70] *Id.*, § 4(5).

[71] *Id.*, § 3(8).

[72] *See e.g.*, Sompo Japan Ins. Co. of America v. Union Pacific R. Co., 456 F.3d 54, 58 (2d Cir. 2006); Kukje Hwajae Ins. Co. v. M/V Hyundai Liberty, 408 F.3d 1250, 1255 (9th Cir. 2005). *See also* Greenpack of Puerto Rico, Inc. v. American President Lines, 684 F.3d 20, 27 (1st Cir. 2012) (observing that "a carrier who does not provide adequate notice of this possibility does so at his own peril"). *But see* Ferrostaal, Inc. v. M/V Sea Phoenix, 447 F.3d 212, 228–229 (3rd Cir. 2006) (rejecting this doctrine as inconsistent with the express language of COGSA).

higher freight when a shipper declares the value of the cargo as compensation for shouldering increased potential liability."[73] Even if a higher amount is stated, neither the carrier nor the ship is liable for any increased liability if the shipper has "knowingly and fraudulently misstated the value of the goods on the bill of lading."[74] Regardless of the valuation or maximum amount of liability, a carrier or ship is not liable for more than the damage actually sustained.[75] An additional protection under COGSA is that claims must be filed within a year following delivery of the subject goods.[76]

COGSA contains some provisions that overlap with the Harter Act. But for international carriage "to or from ports of the United States" COGSA displaces the Harter Act regarding liability arising from negligence or a default in the navigation or management of a vessel used for carriage of goods by sea. That is, COGSA prevails during "the period from the time when the goods are loaded on to the time when they are discharged from the ship."[77] Courts refer to this as the "tackle-to-tackle" period.[78] As noted above, however, when damage to goods occurs on land (*i.e.*, after discharge from the ship), the Harter Act generally will prevail and prohibit any disclaimers against liability.[79] That is, the Harter Act by its terms still governs events prior to loading and after discharge of cargo until actual delivery as provided in the bill of lading.[80] Nonetheless, COGSA expressly allows the parties to enter into an agreement—typically through the carriage contract itself—that extends its scope to the time "prior to the loading on and subsequent to the discharge from the ship on which the goods are carried by sea."[81] The

---

[73]   Delphi-Delco Electronics Systems v. M/V Nedlloyd Europa, 324 F. Supp. 2d 403, 413 (S.D.N.Y. 2004).

[74]   COGSA, *supra* note 2, § 4(5).

[75]   *Id.*

[76]   *Id.*, § 6.

[77]   *Id.*, § 1(e).

[78]   For recent observations *see* M3 Midstream LLC v. South Jersey Port Corp., 1 F. Supp. 3d 289, 294–295 (D.N.J. 2014) ("COGSA applies from 'tackle to tackle' "); Crompton Greaves, Ltd. v. Shippers Stevedoring Co., 921 F. Supp. 2d 697, 722 (S.D. Tex. 2013) (observing that Courts refer to the phase of applicability of COGSA "as the 'tackle to tackle' period"). *See also* Pan Am. World Airways, Inc. v. Cal. Stevedore & Ballast Co., 559 F.2d 1173, 1177 n. 5 (9th Cir. 1977) (declaring that "COGSA has been continuously interpreted as being applicable from the time the ship's tackle is hooked onto the cargo at the port of loading until the time when cargo is released from the tackle at the port of discharge").

[79]   *See* § 4.4 *supra*. *Compare also* COGSA, *supra* note 2, § 4(2)(a), *with* Harter Act, 46 U.S.C. § 30704.

[80]   COGSA, *supra* note 2, § 11 (stating that COGSA does not supersede the Harter Act or other federal statutes insofar as they relate to duties, responsibilities, and liabilities of the ship or carrier prior to the time when the goods are loaded or after the time the goods are discharged from the ship).

[81]   *Id.*, § 7.

Supreme Court accordingly has held that COGSA "allows parties to extend its terms to an inland portion of a journey under a through bill of lading."[82]

COGSA also has important provisions relating to bills of lading. First, it expressly obligates the carrier, on the request of the shipper, to issue a bill of lading that describes "among other things" (a) the marks identifying the goods as provided by the shipper, (b) the number of packages or weight of the goods (as applicable), as furnished in writing by the shipper, and (c) "the apparent order and condition of the goods."[83] On the last issue, however, the carrier is not obligated to provide a description as to a fact that it "had no reasonable means of checking."[84] Once the carrier has provided such a description, COGSA declares that the bill of lading is "prima facie evidence of the receipt by the carrier of the goods as therein described."[85] As discussed in Section 4.13 below, this essential rule establishes the foundation for carrier liability for a "misdescription" of the goods in a bill of lading.

§ 4.6   The Federal Bills of Lading Act (FBLA)

The Federal Bills of Lading Act (FBLA), codified under the transportation title of the United States Code (Title 49), governs the creation, transferability, and transfer of bills of lading in defined international and interstate shipments. Congress originally enacted the Act (then known as the Pomerene Act) in 1916, and recodified it with slight clarifications as the FBLA in 1994. The recodification did not change the substance of the Act, but it did reword and consolidate the prior provisions and change all the section numbers.

The FBLA governs all interstate and outbound international shipments that use a bill of lading issued by a common carrier.[86] In specific, the statute governs a bill of lading if the goods are shipped between a place in one state and through to another state or from a place in the United States "to a place in a foreign country."[87] To that extent, the FBLA entirely preempts the UCC. But the UCC continues to cover *purely* intrastate shipments. Some courts have reasoned that the UCC also may apply by default to inbound

---

[82]   *See* Kawasaki Kisen Kaisha Ltd. v. Regal-Beloit Corp., 561 U.S. 89, 99 (2010) (*citing* Norfolk Southern R. Co. v. Kirby, 543 U.S. 14, 29 (2004)).

[83]   COGSA, *supra* note 2, § 3(3).

[84]   *Id.*, § 3(3)(c).

[85]   *Id.*, § 3(4).

[86]   49 U.S.C. § 80102.

[87]   *Id.*

international shipments[88] and international shipments that do not touch the United States, but are litigated in the United States.[89]

Unlike COGSA, the FBLA regulates only the rights and obligations arising out of bills of lading. It thus addresses the issuance of bills of lading;[90] the form and requirements for negotiation and the rights obtained upon transfer;[91] the rights of carriers upon nonpayment;[92] and the obligations of the carrier regarding descriptions and delivery of the goods.[93]

As Sections 4.7 through 4.9 below examine in detail, the most fundamental distinction in the FBLA is between negotiable (or "order") bills of lading and nonnegotiable (or "straight") bills of lading.[94] As those sections explain, this distinction is decisive in defining the carrier's obligations regarding delivery of the goods: For a nonnegotiable bill of lading, the carrier must deliver the goods only to the consignee named on the bill; for a negotiable bill of lading, in contrast, the carrier must deliver the goods only to the person in possession of the bill and only if the bill has been properly indorsed over to that person (the "holder").

§ 4.7   Forms and Types of Bills of Lading

In the United States, the common law and both state and federal statutory law recognize two fundamental types of bills of lading: a negotiable (or "order") bill of lading and a nonnegotiable bill of lading. Sections 4.8 and 4.9 examine these two fundamental types in detail. Section 4.10 then reviews the increasingly common practice in modern commerce in which intermediaries of various kinds issue "multimodal" (or "through" or "combined transport") bills of lading covering different modes of transport, but do not perform the actual carriage services. In such a case, a single bill of lading may govern many or even all of the links in the transportation chain.

Shippers and carriers use a variety of specialized terms to describe specific aspects of bills of lading. Thus, for example, they often refer to an "on board" bill of lading. An "on board" (aka

---

[88]   See Hual AS v. Expert Concrete, Inc., 45 UCC Rep. Serv. 2d 882 (N.Y. Sup. 2001).

[89]   See T.C. Ziraat Bankasi v. Standard Chartered Bank, 644 N.E.2d 272 (N.Y. 1994).

[90]   49 U.S.C. § 80103. See also 49 U.S.C. § 80114 (addressing lost, stolen, or destroyed bills of lading).

[91]   49 U.S.C. §§ 80104–80108.

[92]   49 U.S.C. § 80109.

[93]   49 U.S.C. §§ 80110–80113.

[94]   See especially 49 U.S.C. § 80103.

"loaded") bill of lading is issued once the goods have been loaded on board the vessel bound for the required destination. A "clean" bill of lading is one that has no clause or notation on its face indicating visible or possible defects in the packaging or condition of the goods. Simple comments regarding amount, weight, or other descriptions provided by the shipper will not, however, "foul" the bill of lading, provided that they do not incorporate other documents indicating defects in the cargo.

Finally, this area of law, like many others, is entering into the electronic age. Electronic substitutes for nonnegotiable bills of lading have been in use for about two decades and have proved to be successful. However, electronic substitutes for negotiable bills of lading have been less successful and are still in the developmental stage. Section 4.15 below will examine the progress toward the use of such electronic bills of lading.

§ 4.8   Negotiable ("Order") Bills of Lading

A negotiable, or "order," bill of lading serves as (1) a contract with the carrier, (2) a receipt for the goods, and, especially, (3) a document of title for the goods. For such a bill of lading, physical possession is essential to determining the rights to the goods and the delivery obligations of the carrier.

Under the FBLA, a bill of lading is negotiable if it states that the goods are to be delivered "to the order of a consignee,"[95] unless the bill states "on its face" that it is not negotiable.[96] With the words "to the order of," a bill of lading creates a power of transfer ("negotiation") in favor of the named consignee—that is, a power to give an order to the carrier. As a result, the consignee has the power to transfer rights over the goods by transferring the bill of lading along with a corresponding order to the carrier to deliver to the transferee.[97]

The consignee exercises its power of negotiation by delivering possession of the bill along with its "indorsement"[98] ("endorsement" in British English). The indorsement is made simply by stamping or

---

[95]   49 U.S.C. § 80103(a)(1)(a). *See also* UCC § 7–104(a). UCC Article 7 expressly recognizes a negotiable bill of lading in "bearer" form (*see* § 7–104(a)), but the FBLA does not refer to such a possibility. A bearer bill of lading is one made out simply to "bearer" and may be transferred by delivery alone. Thus, anyone in possession may demand delivery of the goods from the carrier. Because of the inherent risks of such a practice, negotiable bills of lading issued to "bearer" are substantially less common in international transactions.

[96]   49 U.S.C. § 80103(a)(1)(a).

[97]   *See* 49 U.S.C. § 80101(5) (defining an "order" as "an order by indorsement on a bill of lading").

[98]   49 U.S.C. § 80104(a)(1).

writing one's name on the back of the bill of lading. An indorsement may be made in two ways: (1) "in blank," that is, with the bare signature ("*Michael Van Alstine*"); or (2) by a "special indorsement," which identifies the next intended holder by name ("Deliver the goods to Ralph Folsom, or order. *Michael Van Alstine*").[99] In either case, such a proper negotiation of the bill of lading will make the transferee a "holder," that is, a person entitled to demand delivery from the carrier.[100]

The difference between a blank and a special indorsement is decisive in determining who can be the holder of the bill. With a blank indorsement, literally any person who obtains possession becomes the holder.[101] With a special indorsement, in contrast, only the named indorsee (if in possession) becomes the holder, and only that person can demand delivery from the carrier (or indorse the bill of lading to still another person so as to make the transferee the holder).[102] And only the original consignee/holder or, as applicable, a subsequent holder can make its own indorsement—a forgery of the holder's signature, however well made, is not effective as an indorsement.[103] Thus, the special indorsement protects the interests of the parties from thieves and forgers much better than does a blank indorsement.

By obtaining possession of the actual negotiable bill of lading, properly indorsed over to it, a person becomes the holder and acquires rights over the goods and against the carrier.[104] In turn, the carrier is liable to the holder of a negotiable bill of lading for misdelivery if it delivers the goods to anyone but the holder.[105] Thus, possession of the negotiable bill of lading becomes crucial. The carrier must see the actual bill of lading to confirm that the person demanding the goods has possession of the bill and that the bill has the proper chain of indorsements over to that person.[106] It is

---

[99]   *Id.*

[100]   49 U.S.C. § 80101(4) (defining a "holder" as "a person having possession of, and a property right in, a bill of lading").

[101]   49 U.S.C. § 80110(b)(3)(B).

[102]   *Id.*

[103]   *See* Adel Precision Products Corp. v. Grand Trunk Western R. Co., 332 Mich. 519, 51 N.W.2d 922 (1952). For a more detailed analysis of a forgery on a bill of lading *see* §§ 4.12 and 4.14 *infra*.

[104]   49 U.S.C. § 80110(a).

[105]   49 U.S.C. § 80113(a).

[106]   If the intended ultimate recipient of the goods cannot produce the negotiable bill of lading, but the circumstances otherwise indicate to the carrier that nothing is amiss, it may choose to release the goods in return for an "indemnity agreement" from the recipient. For examples of this *see, e.g.*, Evergreen Marine Corp. v. Six Consignments of Frozen Scallops, 4 F.3d 90, 92 (1st Cir. 1993); Orient Overseas Container Line v. Kids Int'l Corp., 1998 WL 531840, at *2 (S.D.N.Y. 1998); A/S Dampskibsselskabet Torm v. Beaumont Oil Ltd., 1990 WL 209637, at *1 n.2

in this sense that the negotiable bill of lading is an especially secure "document of title," because possession of it, properly indorsed to the possessor, controls title to the document, title to the goods, and the direct obligation of the carrier to deliver the goods only to the holder.[107]

A negotiable bill of lading retains its status as a transferrable document of title regardless of the number of transferees. Thus, a transferee by proper negotiation (*i.e.*, the new holder) from the original consignee/holder has the power to negotiate the bill of lading to a further transferee. With transfer of possession and a further proper indorsement, the downstream transferee then will become the new holder of the bill. Once again, this act of negotiation vests in the new holder the rights over the goods and against the carrier with regard to the delivery of those goods.

The holder of a negotiable bill of lading does not obtain absolute title to the goods in all cases, but nearly so. The FBLA provides that upon a proper negotiation the transferee acquires the title to the goods that the transferor "had the ability to convey to a purchaser in good faith for value."[108] Thus, if the consignee was not the owner of the goods in the first place—for example, if a thief originally stole the goods from the true owner at gunpoint—then no holder of the bill of lading will have title to the goods because the shipper's claim of title was "void" from the beginning. However, if the owner voluntarily parted with the goods but was defrauded by the shipper, then the shipper obtains "voidable" title and can pass good title to a holder of the document who purchases it in good faith, for value, and without notice.[109] The rights of such a good faith holder for value are also superior to any seller's lien or right to stop delivery of the goods in transit.[110]

Negotiable Bills and Documentary Sales. As Chapter 1 examined in detail, negotiable bills of lading play an essential role in "documents against payment" (D/P) transactions.[111] This form of bill solves the fundamental trust problem between distant and

---

(S.D.N.Y. 1990). If, then, a legitimate holder of the bill later appears, the carrier would be liable to that holder for misdelivery and must rely on its claim against the recipient under the indemnity agreement.

[107]   49 U.S.C. §§ 80105(a), 80110(b). For a more detailed examination of the delivery obligations of the carrier, and thus its liability for "misdelivery" *see* § 4.12 *infra.*

[108]   49 U.S.C. § 80105(a).

[109]   The FBLA does not define the "purchaser in good faith for value." The UCC, in contrast, provides more detailed guidance on the notion of a good faith purchaser of a bill of lading. *See* UCC § 7–503(a) (with reference to § 2–403).

[110]   49 U.S.C. § 80105(b).

[111]   *See* Chapter 1, §§ 1.1–1.9.

unfamiliar parties by permitting the buyer to pay the purchase price in exchange for a document that both describes and controls delivery of the goods.[112] This is typically accomplished through the issuance of the negotiable bill of lading by the carrier to the shipper/seller and the latter's use of banks as collection agents.[113] The banks will act on behalf of the seller and require that the buyer pay the price in full as a condition to delivery of physical possession of the negotiable bill of lading.[114] Because it serves as a special form of a document of title covering the goods, presentation of such a bill is a requirement for the carrier's delivery of the goods to the buyer.

Bills of lading commonly play an essential role in letter of credit transactions as well, as Chapter 1 again explained.[115] Typically, banks that issue letters of credit require as a condition of payment that the beneficiary (the seller) obtain and present a bill of lading covering the goods, and most often they demand a negotiable bill.[116] The banks require this in order to secure their right of reimbursement from the buyer after they have paid the seller under the letter of credit. With a negotiable bill of lading, the banks can ensure that the buyer is able to obtain delivery of the goods *only if* it has physical possession of the bill of lading properly indorsed over to it. They thus can preclude the buyer from obtaining the goods from the carrier until it has reimbursed the banks (or made a binding commitment to do so).[117]

For these and similar reasons the parties to international sales transactions traditionally have preferred the security of negotiable bills of lading. The traditional interpretation of Incoterms CIF and CFR contracts likewise has required that the seller obtain this form of transport document (although the most recent editions of Incoterms have introduced some flexibility on this score).[118] Modern commercial and transportation practices, however, increasingly rely on various forms of nonnegotiable bills. As the next Section explains, this is especially true in transactions in which the goods are sent by rapid means of transit (*e.g.*, airplane) or the distance between the seller and buyer is small—such that goods may arrive as quickly as the physical bill of lading could. Nonetheless, although less commonly used than in the past, negotiable bills of lading remain an essential feature of modern transportation practice,

---

[112] *See id.*, §§ 1.1–1.2.

[113] *See id.*, §§ 1.5–1.6.

[114] *See id.*, §§ 1.6–1.7.

[115] *See id.*, §§ 1.10–1.18.

[116] *See id.*, §§ 1.12–1.13.

[117] *See id.*, § 1.16.

[118] *See* Chapter 3, §§ 3.10 and 3.11.

especially for documents against payments and letter of credit transactions.

§ 4.9   Nonnegotiable Bills of Lading

A nonnegotiable (aka "straight") bill of lading differs in fundamental respects from a negotiable one. Such a bill likewise serves as a receipt for the goods and as a contract with the carrier stating the terms and conditions of carriage. But, significantly, it is issued only to a named person, the consignee.[119] Under the FBLA, a straight bill of lading is one stating that "the goods are to be delivered to a consignee." The FBLA also obligates a carrier issuing such a bill to state "nonnegotiable" or "not negotiable" on the bill of lading itself.[120]

Straight bills of lading are not negotiable documents, and thus are not transferable. As a result, an indorsement of such a bill "does not—(A) make the bill negotiable; or (B) give the transferee any additional right."[121] Instead, under the FBLA "the carrier must deliver goods covered by a bill of lading on demand of the consignee named in a nonnegotiable bill." Thus, the consignee retains all rights over the goods and against the carrier, and, even if actually transferred, possession of the actual bill does not confer such rights on the transferee. In fact, federal courts interpreting the FBLA have held that the consignee does not even need to be in possession of the bill of lading or produce the document in order to obtain the goods from the carrier.[122]

With a nonnegotiable bill of lading, therefore, the carrier is liable to the named consignee for misdelivery if it delivers the goods to any other person.[123] The shipper of the goods (often, the seller) even can change its mind at any time prior to the delivery of the

---

[119]   49 U.S.C. § 80101(1) (defining a consignee as "the person named in a bill of lading as the person to whom the goods are to be delivered").

[120]   49 U.S.C. § 80103(b)(2).

[121]   49 U.S.C. § 80103(b)(1).

[122]   *See, e.g.*, Dynamic Worldwide Logistics, Inc. v. Exclusive Expressions, LLC, 77 F. Supp. 3d 364, 374 n.13 (S.D.N.Y. 2015) ("Production of the original bill is not a pre-condition to delivery where a non-negotiable bill of lading is involved."); Quanzhou Joerga Fashion Co., Inc. v. Brooks Fitch Apparel Group, LLC, 2012 WL 4767180 (S.D.N.Y. 2012) (stating that for a nonnegotiable bill of lading "production of the original bill is not actually a precondition to the delivery of the goods"). *See also* Schoenbaum, 2 ADMIRALTY & MAR. LAW § 10–11 (5th ed. 2011) (observing that "[t]he carrier is not required to take up and cancel a straight bill of lading at the time of delivery of the goods"). The FBLA nonetheless has a curious provision that leaves some unnecessary ambiguity. *See* 49 U.S.C. § 80110(a) (stating that the carrier "must deliver goods covered by a bill of lading on demand of the consignee named in a nonnegotiable bill . . . when the consignee . . . (2) has possession of the bill").

[123]   49 U.S.C. § 80111(a)(1).

goods and stop delivery or reroute delivery to another party merely by so instructing the carrier.

Nonnegotiable bills of lading are commonly used between related parties or merchants with established business relationships, as it is the simplest method of conducting business. Similarly, such bills frequently are used in container transport, on short sea routes, and for air transport where the goods are likely to arrive as soon as the bill. Under U.S. practice, nonnegotiable bills of lading also are called "air waybills," "sea waybills" and "freight receipts," depending upon the intended method of main transportation for the goods. Such nonnegotiable receipts may be used under specific Incoterms (most notably, FOB and FAS) where no requirement of a transferrable document exists.[124] For the reasons discussed in detail in Chapter 1, however, nonnegotiable bills are not appropriate for documents against payment transactions, and are not preferred by banks under letter of credit transactions.[125]

Straight Bills in Other Legal Systems. In some other countries, the status of straight bills of lading does not conform with that under U.S. law and practice. For example, the House of Lords expressly held, after extensive analysis of foreign opinions and scholarly treatises, that a straight bill of lading also is a "document of title" within the contemplation of the Hague Rules—but it is one that runs only in favor of the named consignee and thus is not transferable. The court nonetheless held that, like the negotiable form, a straight bill of lading must be presented by the consignee as a condition to delivery of the goods from the carrier.[126] In this, the court drew a further distinction between both forms of bills of lading, on the one hand, and "waybills" on the other. The latter are not documents of title in any respect, the court reasoned, and thus need not be presented to the carrier. Courts from other jurisdictions and some commentators agree with this presentation requirement for a straight bill of lading.[127] The leading authority on English sale

---

[124] *See* INCOTERMS 2010, at 10 (ICC Publ. No. 715, 2010) (stating that "with EXW, FCA, FAS and FOB the delivery document may simply be a receipt"). *See also* Chapter 3, §§ 3.08, 3.09, and 3.13.

[125] *See* Chapter 1, §§ 1.5 and 1.13.

[126] J.I. MacWilliam v. Mediterranean Shipping Co., S.A. (*The Rafaela S.*), [2005] 2 A.C. 423 (H.L.).

[127] *See* APL Co. Pte Ltd v. Voss Peer, [2002] 2 Lloyd's Rep. 707 (Singapore Ct. App. 2002); Carewins Development (China) Ltd. v. Bright Fortune Shipping Ltd., 1 HKLRD 409 (Hong Kong Court of Final Appeal 2009); Beluga Shipping GmbH & Co v. Headway Shipping Ltd., [2008] FCA 1791 (Federal Court of Australia, 2008); Arrêt de la Cour de Cassation no. 891 (19 June 2007) [France]. On the basis of these holdings, the private Advisory Council for the CISG has expressed the view that a straight bill of lading also must be presented to the carrier. *See* CISG Advisory Council Opinion No. 11, *Issues Raised by Documents under the CISG Focusing on the*

of goods law has questioned this view, however, unless the presentation requirement arises from an express or implied agreement in the straight bill of lading itself.[128]

Effect of a "Surrender Clause." As discussed above, U.S. law as reflected in the FBLA does not impose a presentation requirement for delivery of goods covered by a nonnegotiable bill of lading. Nonetheless, some shippers even in the United States have sought to achieve the same result as described in the foreign cases noted immediately above by including a "surrender clause" in such a bill (*e.g.*, "Cargo to be released only against presentation of this bill of lading"). Absent such a clause, if the carrier delivered the goods to the consignee of a straight bill of lading without a surrender of the original bill, the shipper would not have a cause of action for misdelivery under the express terms of the FBLA.[129]

With such a clause, the carrier nonetheless may be liable to the shipper for *breach of contract* if it delivers the goods without requiring presentation of the original bill. The line of judicial authority on this point traces back to a famous 1921 case, *Pere Marquette Ry. Co. v. J.F. French and Co.*, in which the Supreme Court held that "such liability arises, not from the statute, but from the obligation which the carrier assumes under the bill of lading."[130] More recent federal courts have affirmed the vitality of this reasoning.[131] But the vagaries of contract interpretation—including continuing uncertainties over the proper standards for interpreting carriage contracts[132]—counsel against such a practice.

Buyer's Payment Duty (Art 58), available at http://www.cisgac.com/cisgac-opinion-no11/.

[128] BENJAMIN'S SALE OF GOODS, §§ 18–097, 18–098 (M. Bridge, ed., 9th ed. 2014).

[129] 49 U.S.C. § 80111(a)(1). For more on this point *see* § 4.12 *infra*.

[130] 254 U.S. 538, 546 (1921).

[131] *See* Lite-On Peripherals, Inc. v. Burlington Air Express, Inc., 255 F.3d 1189, 1192 (9th Cir. 2001) (holding that with a "surrender-upon-delivery" clause in a nonnegotiable bill of lading the carrier is liable for breach of contract if it delivers the goods without requiring a presentation of the bill); Allied Chemical Int'l Corp. v. Companhia de Navegacao Lloyd Brasileiro, 775 F.2d 476, 782 (2d Cir.1985) (same). *See also* Porky Products, Inc. v. Nippon Exp. U.S.A. (Illinois), Inc., 1 F. Supp. 2d 227, 232–233 (S.D.N.Y. 1997) (observing that "whether the bills [are] negotiable or nonnegotiable is relevant to a statutory claim for conversion under the Pomerene Act, but not relevant to a breach of contract claim").

[132] Some courts hold that "bills of lading are contracts of adhesion and, as such, are strictly construed against the carrier." Fernandez v. New England Motor Freight, Inc., 2015 WL 4002233, at * (S.D.N.Y 2015) (*quoting* Allied Chem. Int'l Corp. v. Companhia de Navegacao Lloyd Brasileiro, 775 F.2d 476, 482 (2d Cir. 1985)). *See also* Sompo Japan Ins. Co. of America v. Norfolk Southern Ry. Co., 966 F. Supp. 2d 270, 279 (S.D.N.Y. 2013) (same). Others have read the Supreme Court's opinion in Norfolk Southern R. Co. v. Kirby, 543 U.S. 14 (2004), to reject this rule of strict construction against the carrier. *See, e.g.*, Mazda Motors of America, Inc. v. M/V

§ 4.10   NVOCCs and Multimodal Bills of Lading

In modern international transportation practice, a variety of intermediaries increasingly assume responsibility for arranging the carriage of goods. These intermediaries are known by different names in different countries and circumstances—*e.g.*, non-vessel-operating common carriers, logistics companies, multimodal transport operators, or full-service freight forwarders.

Under U.S. law, the status of such an intermediary depends on the function it fulfills in a given transaction. A "freight forwarder" is merely a service company; that is, it merely agrees to arrange for the transportation of the goods as the agent of the seller. When, however, the intermediary issues a formal bill of lading and assumes the essential functions of carriage company, then it is subject to the obligations of a common carrier. Federal law formally defines such a party as "non-vessel operating common carrier (NVOCC)."[133]

One federal court appropriately described the distinction between a freight forwarder and a NVOCC in this way:

> A freight forwarder generally arranges for the movement of cargo at the request of a client. A non-vessel operating common carrier ("NVOCC"), in contrast, consolidates cargo from numerous shippers into larger groups for shipment by an ocean carrier. A NVOCC issues a bill of lading to each shipper and if anything happens to the goods during the voyage, then the NVOCC is liable to the shipper "because of the bill of lading that [the NVOCC] issued." But a freight forwarder, because it does not issue a bill of lading, is not liable to the shipper for anything that occurs to the goods as long as the freight forwarder limits its role to arranging for transportation.[134]

Overall, "[t]he most fundamental difference between a freight forwarder and an NVOCC is that an NVOCC issues a bill of

---

Cougar Ace, 565 F.3d 573, 579 (9th Cir. 2009) ("Now, absent any special rule of strict construction, we enforce the bills of lading as drafted[.]"); Diamond v. State Farm Mut. Auto. Ins. Co., 2010 WL 2904640, at *5 (E.D. Cal. 2010) (observing parenthetically that "following the decision in *Kirby*, bills of lading are not to be strictly construed but are to be enforced as drafted").

[133]   *See* 46 U.S.C. § 4102(16) (defining a non-vessel-operating common carrier as a common carrier that "(A) does not operate the vessels by which the ocean transportation is provided; and (B) is a shipper in its relationship with an ocean common carrier").

[134]   Talbots, Inc. v. Dynasty Intern., Inc., 808 F. Supp. 2d 351, 357 (D. Mass. 2011) (*quoting* Prima U.S., Inc. v. Panalpina, Inc., 223 F.3d 126, 129 (2d Cir. 2000)).

lading."[135] And when an intermediary does so and thus becomes an NVOCC, it is subject to the obligations under COGSA[136] as well as the FBLA[137] just like any other common carrier.

The essential value of NVOCCs in modern commerce is that they assume responsibility for end-to-end transportation of the goods, even though they may undertake none (or very little) of the actual carriage. That is, they neither own nor charter the transportation vehicles and vessels themselves. The end-to-end bills they issue are known by the various names "multimodal," "through," or "combined transport" bills of lading.[138] Such bills involve an agreement by the NVOCC to transport and deliver the goods to their final destination using any required connecting carriers. Thus, a single bill of lading covers all of the links in the transportation chain. As the Supreme Court has observed, "[a] through bill of lading covers both the ocean and inland portions of the transport in a single document."[139]

To fulfill their transportation obligations, NVOCCs sub-contract with individual carriers for each necessary link in the transportation chain (road, rail, ocean, and even air). The common practice is for the NVOCC to issue the multimodal bill of lading— often in negotiable form—to the shipper/seller when the goods are delivered to the first sub-contracting carrier. The NVOCC then obtains a bill of lading—often in nonnegotiable form—from that sub-contracting carrier, and thereafter from each other carrier responsible for a link in the transportation chain.[140] Because the overall multimodal bill issued by the NVOCC—commonly known as the "house bill"—is negotiable, the seller then is able to present that

---

[135]   Scholastic Inc. v. M/V KITANO, 362 F. Supp. 2d 449, 455 (S.D.N.Y. 2005).

[136]   *See, e.g.,* Strickland v. Evergreen Marine Corp. (Taiwan) Ltd., 2007 WL 539424, at *4 (D. Ore. 2007) ("Carriers, including NVOCCs, are subject to COGSA, while freight forwarders generally are not subject to COGSA."); Royal & Sun Alliance Ins., PLC v. Ocean World Lines, Inc., 612 F.3d 138, 141, 145 (2d Cir. 2010) (same).

[137]   *See, e.g.,* Jain Irr. System, Ltd. v. Chemcolit, Inc., 2000 WL 1802069 (S.D. Tex. 2000); Yang Ming Marine Transport Corp. v. Oceanbridge Shipping Intern., Inc. 48 F. Supp. 2d 1032, 1044 (C.D. Cal. 1999), *rev'd on other grounds,* 259 F.3d 1086 (9th Cir. 2001).

[138]   Slight differences of definition may arise between these terms depending on the specific functions of the intermediary. Under the common understanding of a "multimodal" bill, the intermediary is responsible for all links in the transportation chain; under some understandings of a "through" bill, in contrast, the intermediary is responsible only for its one link in the chain and then merely acts as the agent of the shipper in arranging the other links.

[139]   Kawasaki Kisen Kaisha Ltd. v. Regal-Beloit Corp., 561 U.S. 89, 94 (2010).

[140]   *See* Royal & Sun Alliance Ins., PLC v. Ocean World Lines, Inc., 612 F.3d 138, 141 (2d Cir. 2010) ("A NVOCC is a middleman that does not own and operate its own vessels. Instead, it enters into service contracts whereby it purchases large blocks of cargo space at a discount from vessel-operating common carriers (VOCCs). It then contracts with shippers to ship smaller amounts of cargo in that space.").

document to the buyer in "documents against payment" transaction.[141] (Many banks will not, however, accept house bills under letter of credit transactions.[142]) Upon negotiation of the house bill, the buyer becomes the holder and obtains the right to delivery of the goods as against the NVOCC (which, in turn, will fulfill its delivery obligation by enforcing its rights under the bill issued to it by the final individual carrier in the transportation chain).

§ 4.11   Liabilities and Risks Regarding Bills of Lading

The FBLA has several important liability rules that address certain risks uniquely related to transactions that use a bill of lading. The most prominent of these risks are the following: (1) where the carrier delivers the goods to the wrong person ("misdelivery"); (2) where the carrier delivers goods that do not conform to the description on the bill of lading ("misdescription"); and (3) where a bill of lading contains a forgery and thus creates potential warranty liability for transferors.

Sections 4.12 through 4.14 below will examine each of these subjects in detail. But to set the context, the FBLA establishes important obligations for a carrier regarding delivery of the goods and in this way it sets the foundation both for (a) analyzing whether the carrier is liable for misdelivery and (b) the available defenses to such a claim.[143] For example, the carrier (as noted above) must deliver the goods to the consignee under a nonnegotiable bill of lading or to the holder of a negotiable bill of lading.[144] For the latter, it also must obtain and cancel the bill as a condition to delivery of the goods.[145] As Section 4.12 explains in detail, these essential obligations will define whether the carrier has delivered the goods to the wrong person and thus is liable for misdelivery.

The FBLA's liability rules also set the foundation for an analysis of a misdescription claim. On the basis of COGSA's obligation that a bill of lading contain a description of the goods,[146] a carrier is liable under the FBLA for damages caused either by the fact that it never received all or any part of the described goods in the first place or "by failure of the goods to correspond with the

---

[141]   For an examination of the traditional role of negotiable bills of lading in such a transaction *see* Chapter 1, § 1.5.

[142]   For an examination of the traditional role of negotiable bills of lading in a letter of credit transaction *see* Chapter 1, § 1.13.

[143]   *See* 49 U.S.C. §§ 80110 and 80111, and § 4.12 *infra*.

[144]   49 U.S.C. § 80111(a). *See also* §§ 4.8 and 4.9 *supra*.

[145]   49 U.S.C. § 80111(c).

[146]   *See* COGSA, *supra* note 2, § 3(3), and § 4.5 *supra*.

description contained in the bill."[147] The FBLA provides, however, certain defenses for a carrier regarding nonreceipt and misdescription claims. As Section 4.13 explores in detail, the most prominent of these arises when all of the following are true: the goods are loaded by the shipper, the bill of lading indicates that the shipper provided the description for the goods, and the carrier is not aware of information contrary to that included on the bill.[148]

Finally, the FBLA provides for automatic representations and warranties by a person that negotiates or otherwise transfers a bill of lading for value. The statutory warranties set the foundation for analyzing which parties may be liable in the event of a forgery on a bill of lading.[149] Again, however, as Section 4.14 analyzes in detail, the FBLA recognizes an important defense to such liability.[150]

§ 4.12   Liability___Misdelivery

A claim against the carrier for delivering the goods to the wrong person depends decisively on whether it issued a nonnegotiable or a negotiable bill of lading covering the goods. Under a nonnegotiable bill of lading, the carrier (as described in § 4.9 above) obligates itself to deliver the goods at the stated destination point only to the consignee named in the bill.[151] As a result, the carrier is liable to the consignee of a straight bill of lading for misdelivery if it delivers the goods to anyone but the consignee.[152] Nonetheless, some courts have suggested the carrier may have a form of defense if it delivers according to the specific instructions of the consignee, even if not to the consignee itself.[153] In any event, straight bills of lading are not appropriate for a "documents against payment" transaction,[154] and the case reports are full of litigation where an attorney tried a short-cut using a straight bill of lading, and created unnecessary uncertainty for the client's interests in the process.

---

[147]   *See* 49 U.S.C. § 80113(a).

[148]   49 U.S.C. § 80113(b) and (c).

[149]   *See* 49 U.S.C. § 80107(a).

[150]   *See* 49 U.S.C. § 80107(a).

[151]   49 U.S.C. § 80110(b)(2). The carrier will have a defense, however, if it delivers to the person with the actual legal right to possession. 49 U.S.C. § 80110(b)(1).

[152]   49 U.S.C. § 80111(a)(1). For certain limited exceptions *see* 49 U.S.C. § 80111(d).

[153]   *See, e.g.,* PolyGram Group Distrib., Inc. v. Transus, Inc., 990 F. Supp. 1454, 1459 (N.D. Ga. 1997) (holding that delivery to a street address specified as consignee's place of business on a straight bill of lading along with the signature of a general contractor working at that address satisfied the delivery requirements imposed by the bill of lading).

[154]   *See also* § 4.9 *supra. See also* Chapter 1, § 1.5.

Under a negotiable bill of lading, in contrast, the FBLA obligates the carrier to deliver the goods at the destination point only to the "holder" of the bill of lading.[155] Thus, possession of the physical bill of lading becomes crucial. The carrier must see the bill of lading to determine both who has possession and to whom the indorsements run.

As a result, for goods covered by a negotiable bill of lading the carrier is liable for misdelivery if it delivers the goods to anyone but the holder.[156] As discussed above,[157] a negotiable bill of lading is a special form of a document of title. A person in possession of a negotiable bill of lading, if properly indorsed over to the person, is the holder and has title to the document, title to the goods, and the direct right against the carrier to delivery of the covered goods. For this reason, the negotiable bill of lading is appropriate for a "payment against documents" transaction. As the analysis in Chapter 1 illustrates, with "payment against documents" transactions, the collecting banks—acting on behalf of the seller—can use their possession of the required negotiable bill of lading to control title to and possession of the goods until the banks have collected the purchase price from the buyer.[158]

If, therefore, the carrier delivers goods covered by a negotiable bill of lading to someone other than the holder, the carrier is liable in damages to the person with ultimate rights over the goods (almost always the holder). As one federal court recently observed, "[a]bsent a valid agreement to the contrary, the carrier, the issuer of the bill of lading, is responsible for releasing the cargo only to the party who presents the original bill of lading . . . . If the carrier delivers the goods to one other than the authorized holder of the bill of lading, the carrier is liable for misdelivery."[159] However, some courts have observed, based on estoppel principles, that the carrier may deliver the goods to another person if it does so on the explicit instructions of the holder.[160]

---

[155]   49 U.S.C. § 80110(b)(3).

[156]   49 U.S.C. § 80111(a)(1).

[157]   See § 4.8 *supra* (analyzing negotiable bills of lading in more detail).

[158]   See Chapter 1, §§ 1.5 through 1.7.

[159]   OOCL (USA) Corp. v. Transco Shipping Corp., 2015 WL 1069339, at *4 (S.D.N.Y. 2015) (*quoting* Datas Indus. Ltd. v. OEC Freight (HK), Ltd., 2000 WL 1597843, at *3 (S.D.N.Y. 2000)). *See also* Ace Bag & Burlap Co., Inc. v. Sea-Land Service, Inc., 40 F. Supp. 2d 233, 239 (D.N.J. 1999) ("[W]here the carrier delivers goods to a person not entitled to their possession and without production of the bill of lading . . . , the carrier [is] liable for damages to anyone having title to or a right to possession of the goods.").

[160]   See, e.g., Chilewich Partners v. M.V. Alligator Fortune, 853 F. Supp. 744, 752–753 (S.D.N.Y. 1994) (holding that a carrier was not liable where it delivered

The difference between the carrier's delivery obligations for a nonnegotiable as compared to a negotiable bill of lading is illustrated by a recent federal court case that involved three separate bills of lading, all of which named a Russian buyer as consignee.[161] Two of the bills were nonnegotiable and one was negotiable, but the seller kept possession of all three pending payment by the buyer. The carrier nonetheless delivered all three shipments to the Russian buyer without requiring production of the physical bill of lading. The court held that the carrier properly delivered the goods to the consignee-buyer under the two nonnegotiable bills of lading; but it found that the carrier had misdelivered under the negotiable bill of lading because the carrier it did not require presentation of the physical bill as a condition to delivery of the goods to the buyer.[162]

The FBLA nonetheless recognizes a form of an excuse in the event of a technical misdelivery. If the carrier happens to deliver to the person with the actual legal right to possession of the goods, it will not be held liable to the holder of the bill of lading.[163] One federal court thus held that a carrier was not liable when goods were stolen while in the possession of Honduran customs authorities. Even though the bill of lading was not available upon delivery, the court found that under the applicable local law and circumstances the customs authorities were "persons entitled to possession" of the goods as contemplated by the FBLA.[164]

Nonetheless, a variety of other provisions in the FBLA highlight the significance of possession for a negotiable bill of lading. Thus, the FBLA sets forth a formal obligation of the carrier to take possession of the bill of lading and cancel it upon delivery of the goods. If the carrier does not do so, it will be liable in damages "to a person purchasing the bill for value in good faith whether the purchase was before or after delivery."[165] And this liability attaches

---

goods to a third-party at the specific direction of the holder of a negotiable bill of lading).

[161] Edelweiss (USA), Inc. v. Vengroff Williams & Assoc., Inc., 59 A.D.3d 588, 873 N.Y.S.2d 714 (2009). The case involved a malpractice claim against a lawyer for not timely filing the claim against the carrier, but the ultimate issue revolved around the delivery obligations of the carrier in the first place. Id., at 715.

[162] Id., at 717.

[163] 49 U.S.C. § 80110(b)(1). See also 49 U.S.C. § 8011(a)(1) (stating that basic liability rule for misdelivery applies if the carrier delivers the goods "to a person not entitled to their possession").

[164] Ace Bag & Burlap Co., Inc. v. Sea-Land Serv., Inc., 40 F. Supp. 2d 233, 239–40 (D.N.J. 1999). See also New Edge Intern., LLC v. Trans-Net, Inc., 2009 WL 5214414 (W.D. Wash. 2009) (same regarding delivery to Russian customs authorities).

[165] 49 U.S.C. § 80111(c).

even if the carrier had delivered the goods to "a person entitled to the goods" (such as an original holder),[166] unless the delivery was made by judicial process, to satisfy a lien for unpaid fees, or because the goods were unclaimed or perishable.[167] Even where a claimant obtains a court order for delivery because of a lost, stolen or destroyed bill of lading, the carrier will be liable to a good faith purchaser of a negotiable bill of lading without notice.[168] For this reason, the FBLA permits a court in such circumstances to require that the recipient of the delivery post a bond.[169]

Effect of Forgery. Under the FBLA, as under the UCC, any forgery of a necessary indorsement is not effective to create or transfer rights, regardless of the expertise of the forger. This is so because by definition a forgery is an unauthorized signature, and without the actual or authorized signature of a holder upon transfer (that is, a valid indorsement) the transferee cannot become the holder. Even a signature by a purported agent is treated as a forgery if the signature was made without actual, implied, or apparent authority. The force of this protection is illustrated by a situation in which a thief steals a negotiable bill of lading from the holder in possession under a special indorsement (that is, one made by naming that specific party only[170]). As such, the holder's indorsement is necessary to transfer rights to the document (and thus the goods) to any other party. Without that indorsement, the thief is not a holder and has no rights even if it is in possession.[171] If the thief transfers the document to another party, that party—even if it acted in good faith—also is not a holder and cannot obtain rights under the document without the true holder's signature. And the carrier is still obligated to deliver the goods only to the holder.[172] Thus, if a collecting bank or another party takes the document under a special indorsement, it is protected against theft of the paper and forgery, because the carrier does not discharge its obligation by delivering to the forger.

---

[166]　*Id.*

[167]　49 U.S.C. § 80111(d).

[168]　49 U.S.C. § 80114(b).

[169]　49 U.S.C. § 80114(a).

[170]　*See* 49 U.S.C. § 80104(a)(1) (stating that a negotiable bill of lading may be negotiated by an indorsement "to a specified person"). For an analysis of the distinction between a "special" and a "blank" indorsement see § 4.8 *supra.*

[171]　*See* 49 U.S.C. § 80104(a)(1) (declaring that "[i]f the goods are deliverable to the order of a specified person, then the bill must be indorsed by that person"). The situation is different if the prior holder indorsed "in blank." *See* 49 U.S.C. § 80104(a). In such a case, the bill becomes a "bearer" bill, and the carrier may deliver to anyone in possession. 49 U.S.C. § 80110(b)(3)(B).

[172]　49 U.S.C. § 80110(b)(3).

If, in short, the carrier delivers to a forger, or to someone who received the document from the forger, the carrier is liable for misdelivery.[173] The forger of course is also liable (in the unlikely event that he can be found).

Statutory Warranties upon Transfer. To protect innocent transferees of bills of lading (including in cases of forgery), the FBLA creates certain statutory warranties—a fancy term for statutorily imposed promises—by transferors. "Unless a contrary intention appears," every person who negotiates or otherwise transfers a bill of lading for value warrants that the bill is genuine; that the transferor has title to the goods and the right to transfer the bill; and that the transferor is not aware of any fact affecting the validity of the bill.[174] But the most important warranties are simply that the transferor had "a right to transfer the bill and title to the goods."[175]

A forged necessary indorsement will constitute a breach of this warranty. In the case of a forgery, each subsequent person in the chain is liable for breach of this statutory warranty because in fact it had no such right or title. The concept is that each person who takes the bill of lading should "know its transferor." If the carrier does not discover the forgery and misdelivers the goods, it will be liable to the person with legal rights to the goods.[176] In theory, the carrier may have a claim against the wrongful recipient of the goods, but that person may be difficult to find (and one federal court recently expressed doubt about the validity of such a claim in any event).[177] Under the structure of the system, the ultimately liability for misdelivery of the goods should lie with the carrier.

If, in contrast, the carrier discovers the forgery and refuses to deliver the goods, the person in possession of the forged bill of lading may assert a warranty claim against its transferor. That party of course is the one best situated to find its own transferor. Each such transferor, in turn, has a warranty action against its transferor—and so on back up the chain of transfers. This is not very efficient, but the purpose is to push liability back up the chain

---

[173] 49 U.S.C. § 80111(a)(1). *See also* Adel Precision Products Corp. v. Grand Trunk Western R. Co., 332 Mich. 519, 51 N.W.2d 922 (1952) (a famous case in which a buyer of goods obtained possession of a negotiable bill of lading and forged the indorsement of the seller/consignee).

[174] 49 U.S.C. § 80107(a)(1)–(4).

[175] 49 U.S.C. § 80107(a)(2). For more on the role of these statutory warranties *see* § 4.14 *infra.*

[176] An indorsement does not, however, by itself make the indorser a guarantor of the obligations of the carrier or previous indorsers. 49 U.S.C. § 80107(d).

[177] *See* Dynamic Worldwide Logistics, Inc. v. Exclusive Expressions, LLC, 2015 WL 5439217, at *8 (S.D.N.Y 2015).

of transfers to the person who took from the forger (and, if he can be found, to the forger himself).

This warranty liability also can extend to collecting banks that transfer the document for value. If the buyer pays, and the collecting banks transmit those funds to the forger, then an argument exists that the banks have received value. However, such banks have several potential escape valves. One is to disclaim the warranty liability when indorsing or transferring the bill of lading. As noted, the FBLA provides that its transfer warranties do not arise if "a contrary intention appears."[178] Thus, an indorsement, "XYZ Bank—no warranties, prior indorsements not guaranteed," would clearly disclaim liability for such a warranty. Banks may similarly argue that banking custom relieves them from any duty to examine documents, with the result that an implicit blanket "contrary intention" exists as a matter of custom. A second avenue arises in situations in which the bank takes a bill of lading "as security for a debt" and then transfers it only in that capacity. The FBLA exempts such a holder from warranty liability for the genuineness of the bill and the quantity or quality of the goods described therein.[179] This option should not be a viable one for a mere collecting bank, however, because it does not transmit funds to the original seller of the goods until after it receives payment, and thus never becomes a creditor, secured or otherwise. Finally, if a bank incorporates by reference the International Chamber of Commerce's (ICC) *Uniform Rules for Collections* (1995) when it forwards the documents, it may effectively avoid liability for problems not apparent on the face of the documents.[180]

Each of these approaches has analytical difficulties, but they may indicate a blanket intention to disclaim the statutory warranties by implication. In any event, any bank found to have warranty liability can pass this liability back to its transferor, as long as it can identify and find that transferor.

Liability of the Carrier. One party that clearly will be subject to liability in any case of a misdelivery, however, will be the carrier. The FBLA provides that upon a misdelivery the carrier is liable to

---

[178]   49 U.S.C. § 80107(a).

[179]   49 U.S.C. § 80107(b) ("A person holding a bill of lading as security for a debt and in good faith demanding or receiving payment of the debt from another person does not warrant by the demand or receipt (1) the genuineness of the bill; or (2) the quantity or quality of the goods described in the bill.").

[180]   Uniform Rules for Collections, art. 13 (ICC Publication No. 522, 1995) ("Banks assume no liability or responsibility for the form, sufficiency, accuracy, genuineness, falsification or legal effect of any document(s), or for the general and/or particular conditions stipulated in the document(s) or superimposed thereon[.]") For more on the URC *see* Chapter 1, § 1.6.

"a person having title to, or right to possession of," the goods.[181] For a negotiable bill of lading, this of course will be the holder. Indeed, FBLA § 80105(a) expressly states that a person to whom a bill of lading is negotiated "acquires title to the goods," as long as it is "a purchaser in good faith for value." This will be the standard case for misdelivery of goods covered by a negotiable bill of lading.

If, however, a thief forged the indorsement of the original consignee before the bill is transferred to the third party, no such negotiation will have occurred, and thus the transferee will not be a holder of the bill.[182] In such a case, the competing claimants will be the seller (the original consignee) and the buyer. If U.S. law applies, the proper claimant commonly will be the buyer because under the UCC title to the goods generally will pass from the seller to the buyer at the time of physical shipment of the goods (unless seller was obligated to deliver at the buyer's location).[183] But if the buyer has already wrongfully refused to pay, the seller may be able to rescind the sales contract and obtain superior rights against the liable carrier.[184] (This obviously will not be the case in a standard "documents against payment" transaction as discussed in Chapter 1, because the theft and forgery will mean that the bill of lading was not presented to the buyer at all and thus it will not yet have been obligated to pay the seller.[185])

For defects in transfer not based on a forgery, however, the FBLA is less forgiving for the original holder of a negotiable bill. If the owner of the bill is deprived of possession by "fraud, accident, mistake, duress, loss, theft, or conversion," the validity of the

---

[181]   49 U.S.C. § 80113(a).

[182]   49 U.S.C. § 80101(4) (defining a "holder" as "a person having possession of, and a property right in, a bill of lading").

[183]   UCC §§ 2–401(2) (providing that title passes to the buyer when the seller completes its obligations regarding the "physical delivery of the goods," even if a document of title is to be delivered at a different time).

[184]   The analysis of this point under the UCC is quite complicated. Under UCC § 2–505(1)(a), a seller who procures a negotiable bill of lading to its order is deemed to reserve a security interest in the goods. UCC Article 9 defines a seller with such a security interest under § 2–505 as a "secured party." See § 9–102(a)(73)(F). If in such a case the buyer defaults in its payment obligation, the seller—like any secured party—obtains a right to possession of the goods under UCC Article 9. See § 9–609(a)(1) (providing that "after default, a secured party . . . may take possession of the collateral"). See also § 9–102(a)(12) (defining "collateral" as the property subject to a security interest). Thus, if the buyer does not pay when obligated to do so, the seller should become the person with the "right to possession of the goods" as contemplated by FBLA § 80113(a). The same result should obtain if in the original sales contract the seller expressly reserves title to the goods until the buyer pays in full. See § 1–201(b)(35) (providing that a seller's reservation of title has the effect of a security interest).

[185]   For an analysis of this point concerning the timing of the buyer's payment obligation under a "documents against payment" transaction see Chapter 1, § 1.7.

owner's negotiation of the bill is not affected as against a transferee who has given value for the bill in good faith and without notice of the problem.[186] Such a transferee will become the holder as a result of a valid negotiation of the bill (assuming, again, that no forgery occurred).[187]

Finally, the UCC has rules on statutory warranties that are both clearer and more favorable to the banks. If the UCC governs a transaction, such as under an "inbound" international shipment,[188] statutory transfer warranties apply that are quite similar to those under the FBLA.[189] But the UCC has a special rule that generally releases collecting banks from these warranties. A collecting bank or "other intermediary known to be entrusted with documents of title on behalf of another" warrants "only its good faith and authority."[190] This protection of "mere intermediaries" applies even if they actually purchased the right to receive delivery of the goods (such as by purchasing the bill).[191]

§ 4.13 Liability__Misdescription

A carrier responsible for transporting goods under a contract with a shipper is not a party to the sales contract between (*i.e.*, is not in "privity" with) the seller and the buyer. Therefore, the carrier has no obligation to deliver goods that conform to the sales contract. However, when a shipper (most often the seller in the sales transaction) delivers goods to a carrier for transport in international trade, COGSA obligates the carrier on request to issue a bill of lading covering the goods.[192] As noted in Section 4.5 above, COGSA then obligates the carrier to provide in the bill of lading information on "[e]ither the number of packages or pieces, or the quantity, or weight, as the case may be, as furnished in writing by the shipper" as well as on "the apparent order and condition of the goods."[193] The carrier is not obligated to provide a description, however, with respect to facts it "had no reasonable means of checking."[194]

---

[186]   49 U.S.C. § 80104(b).

[187]   *Id.* The result under the UCC is similar. Under § 7–502(a)(2), if a bill of lading is "duly negotiated" to a holder, that person thereby obtains title to the underlying goods. Under § 7–501(a)(5), due negotiation requires that the transferee take in good faith, for value, and without notice of any defenses.

[188]   *See* 49 U.S.C. § 80102, and § 4.3 *supra.*

[189]   UCC § 7–507.

[190]   UCC § 7–508. *See also* T.C. Ziraat Bankasi v. Standard Chartered Bank, 644 N.E.2d 272 (N.Y. 1994).

[191]   UCC § 7–508.

[192]   COGSA, *supra* note 2, § 3(3).

[193]   *Id.*

[194]   *Id.*

Nonetheless, once the carrier has provided such a description of the goods on a bill of lading, COGSA declares that the bill is "prima facie evidence of the receipt by the carrier of the goods as therein described."[195] And under the FBLA, a carrier is liable for any failure to deliver goods that correspond to the description in the bill of lading.[196] This obligation is owed to the owner of the goods under a nonnegotiable bill of lading and to the holder of a negotiable bill of lading, provided that the owner or holder "gave value in good faith relying on the description of the goods in the bill."[197]

The problem with this obligation is that the carrier usually does not know what it is carrying, because (among other reasons) the goods often are in containers or other sealed packages. Thus, the carrier will know that it received a container labeled, for example, "1000 Apple iPads." But the carrier will not open, and is not expected to open, the container to check whether it in fact contains iPads or the stated number of them. Even if it opened the container, the carrier would not be expected to check whether each iPad is in working order. And even if it did so check, it is not likely to have the expertise to determine whether each iPad can perform as expected or is otherwise fit for the ordinary uses of such a device. Thus, the carrier is not expected to warrant the description and capability of packaged goods given to it for transport.

To solve this problem, the FBLA allows carriers to disclaim their obligations to deliver goods that conform to the description in the bill of lading. This is accomplished through what are generally known as "Shipper's weight, load, and count" or "SLC" clauses.[198] The FBLA defines three requirements for an effective SLC clause. First, the bill must have appropriately clear disclaimer language. The Act itself provides the following examples:

"contents or condition of contents of pack-ages unknown";

"said to contain"; and

"shipper's weight, load, and count."

These exact linguistic formulas are not required; rather, "words of the same meaning" will suffice.[199]

---

[195]   *Id.*, § 3(4). *See also* § 4.5 *supra.*

[196]   49 U.S.C. § 80113(a).

[197]   *Id.*

[198]   *See, e.g.,* Distribuidora Internacional Alimentos v. Amcar Forwarding, Inc., 2011 WL 902093, at *1 (S.D. Fla. 2011) (stating that " 'a bill of lading containing the recital 'shipper's load and count' places the burden of proof and correct loading on the shipper' who then accepts responsibility for the description and count of the goods") (*quoting* Dublin Co. v. Ryder Truck Lines, Inc., 417 F.2d 777 (5th Cir. 1969)).

[199]   49 U.S.C. § 80113(b).

Second, the goods must actually have been loaded on the vessel by the shipper (or the shipper's agent). If the carrier loads the goods, an SLC clause is not effective to disclaim liability for a description of the goods on the bill of lading.[200] When goods are loaded by the carrier, it has a direct ability to count the number of packages and at least note the condition of the packages. In such a case, it is obligated to "determine the kind and quantity" (although not the quality) of the goods.[201] Moreover, for bulk freight, even where it is loaded by the shipper the carrier must determine the kind and quantity of the freight if the shipper so requests and provides adequate facilities for the carrier to weigh the freight. In situations, disclaimers such as "shipper's weight, load, and count" will not be effective.[202]

The requirement that the shipper actually load the goods seems appropriate for disclaimers of the "shipper's weight, load, and count" variety; but it seems inapposite for disclaimers of the "said to contain" or "contents or condition of contents of packages unknown" variety. Nonetheless, the carrier will be liable for a misdescription even with an otherwise clear SLC disclaimer if it issues a bill of lading and the shipper in fact never loaded anything at all on board the carrier's vessels.

Third, a disclaimer is effective only to the extent that the carrier "does not know whether any part of the goods were received or conform to the description."[203] If the carrier has actual knowledge of a problem, it may not passively allow the shipper to provide a misdescription for the bill of lading. The protection of an SLC disclaimer, in other words, is available only to the uninformed carrier.

As noted, COGSA also permits the carrier to refuse to add to a bill of lading information that it has "no reasonable means of checking."[204] Nonetheless, the carrier must make at least a "reasonable inspection" of the goods under the circumstances.[205] If such an inspection reveals information that contradicts that provided by the shipper, the carrier must so note it on the bill of

---

[200] *Id.*, § 80113(b)(1).

[201] 49 U.S.C. § 80113(d)(2). *See also* Distribuidora Internacional Alimentos v. Amcar Forwarding, Inc., 2011 WL 902093, at *1 (S.D. Fla. 2011) ("When the goods are loaded by a common carrier, . . . the carrier is responsible for verifying that the quantity of the goods described on the bill of lading matches what is actually loaded for transit."); Elgie & Co. v. S.S. "S. A. Nederburg", 599 F.2d 1177, 1180–81 (2d Cir. 1979) (same).

[202] 49 U.S.C. § 80113(d)(1).

[203] *Id.*, § 80113(b)(3).

[204] COGSA, *supra* note 2, § 3(3)(c).

[205] *See* 1 William Tetley, MARINE CARGO CLAIMS 654 (4th ed., 2008).

lading. In such a case of readily apparent information about number, quantity, or weight, in other words, the carrier is not permitted to hide behind an SLC clause. However, the carrier is not required to check most quality terms, such as what goods are in a container and whether or not they are in operating condition.

The intersection of these rules arises when the carrier accepts a sealed container supposed to contain 2,000 tin ingots weighing 35 tons, and issues a bill of lading for a container "said to contain 2,000 tin ingots." If the container is empty or weighs less than a ton, and this information is readily apparent to the carrier, the carrier's disclaimer is not likely to provide protection.[206]

Indeed, some courts have connected a loss of SLC clause protection with a loss of the $500 per package limitation of liability set forth in COGSA.[207] Thus, a number of courts have found a carrier liable for the full value of misdescribed goods where a bill of lading contains false information that either is "readily apparent" to the carrier or relates to the carrier's own conduct in handling the goods.[208]

If, however, a carrier satisfies the three elements for a valid SLC clause, the bill of lading will no longer represent "*prima facie* evidence" (as stated in COGSA) of what the carrier received from the shipper.[209] In other words, the burden of proof will switch to the

---

[206]   *See, e.g.,* Berisford Metals Corp. v. S/S Salvador, 779 F.2d 841 (2d Cir. 1985); Delphi-Delco Elecs. Sys. v. M/V Nedlloyd Europa, 324 F. Supp. 2d 403, 10 (S.D.N.Y. 2004) (holding a carrier liable where a bill of lading "erroneously states that goods have been received on board when they have not been so loaded").

[207]   *See* text accompanying notes 70–76 *supra.*

[208]   *See, e.g.,* GIC Services, LLC v. Freightplus (USA), Inc., 120 F. Supp. 3d 572, 582 (E.D. La. 2015) (removing COGSA's limitation of liability based on intentionally false statements by the carrier on the bill of lading); Y-Tex Corp. v. Schenker, Inc., 2011 WL 2292352 (W.D. Wash. 2011) (removing the limitation because the carrier blindly accepted false information on two misidentified containers and did not "check[ ] the seal which was visible from the outside of the containers to verify the weight"); Mitsui Marine Fire & Ins. Co. v. Direct Container Line, Inc., 119 F. Supp. 2d 412, 416 (S.D.N.Y. 2000) (observing that "for a carrier to lose the package limitation, it is enough that a bill of lading be erroneous" with regard to the carrier's own conduct, "regardless of whether that carrier acted fraudulently"), *aff'd,* 21 Fed. Appx. 58 (2d Cir. 2001). The progenitor of this line of authority is Berisford Metals Corp. v. S/S Salvador, 779 F.2d 841, 846–848 (2d Cir. 1985). *But see* St. Paul Travelers Ins. Co. v. M/V Madame Butterfly, 700 F. Supp. 2d 496, 506 (S.D.N.Y. 2010) ("Courts have limited the false bill of lading exception to the COGSA package limitation 'to misrepresentations concerning the physical condition or location of the goods at the time the bill of lading was issued.' ") (*quoting* Delphi-Delco Electronics Systems v. M/V Nedlloyd Europa, 324 F. Supp. 2d 403, 411 (S.D.N.Y. 2004)), *aff'd,* 2011 WL 1901738 (2d Cir. 2011)).

[209]   COGSA expressly yields to the rules in the FBLA, including with reference to the effectiveness of SLC clauses. *See* COGSA, *supra* note 2, § 3(4) (stating with respect to the "*prima facie* evidence" rule for a bill of lading that "nothing in this chapter shall be construed as repealing or limiting the application of any part of" the FBLA).

shipper or other entitled party to prove that the carrier actually was the cause for the loss of or damage to the goods. As a federal court recently observed, in the case of a valid SLC clause "a shipper must prove that the goods were damaged or lost while in the carrier's custody."[210] In the typical case, the shipper will not have access to sufficient information to meet that burden.

Thus, what is established is a system in which the carrier is responsible for checking readily observable facts—quantity, the number of cartons, obvious information about the weight of a shipment, and the like. It is likely to check such matters in any event, at least to be certain that cartons are not inadvertently left behind and to determine the appropriate freight charge. For any information thus found that contradicts information provided by the shipper, the carrier must provide an appropriate notation on the bill of lading (although of course this likely will "foul" the bill from the shipper's perspective and thus trigger further discussions). However, the carrier is not required to check goods sealed in a container or otherwise investigate their quality or functionality. Thus, it can truthfully say that it has received 1,000 cartons "said to contain" Apple iPads, without opening the cartons or testing whether the tablets work. For such information, a valid SLC clause will protect the carrier from misdescriptions on the bill of lading. But it must note at least readily apparent information such as the number of cartons of claimed iPads or whether the cartons or containers are damaged.[211]

§ 4.14 Liability___Forged and Fraudulent Bills of Lading

Forgery upon Issuance. If the carrier issues a bill of lading for which there are no goods, the carrier is likely to be liable for misdescription as described above. However, suppose the carrier never issued a bill of lading in the first place. Instead, a person unrelated to the carrier created the bill of lading and then forged the carrier's signature or signature stamp (*i.e.*, without the authority of the carrier). A buyer who pays upon receipt of such a

---

[210] American Nat'l Fire Ins. v. M/V Seaboard Victory, 2009 WL 6465299 at *7 (S.D. Fla. 2009) (*citing* Plastique Tags, Inc. v. Asia Trans Line, Inc., 83 F.3d 1367, 1369–1370 (11th Cir. 1996)).

[211] *See, e.g.,* Jain Irrigation System, Ltd. v. Chemcolit, Inc., 2000 WL 1802069 (S.D. Tex. 2000) (holding that the carrier was not liable for goods misdescribed on a bill of lading because the bill contained a valid "said to contain" clause, the shipper loaded the goods, and the carrier knew of no contrary information); Dei Dogi Calzature S.P.A. v. Summa Trading Corp., 733 F. Supp. 773, 775–76 (S.D.N.Y. 1990) (holding that a carrier was not liable to a shipper for losses resulting from receipt of a container filled with water instead of leather items, where the bill of lading contained a "said to contain" clause and the shipper in fact loaded the freight).

forged bill of lading—such as in a "documents against payment" transaction as described in Chapter 1[212]—will have paid the purchase price for the goods, probably through a series of banks, but will find that the carrier has no goods to deliver. In such a case, the buyer will have no misdelivery or misdescription claim against the carrier, for no one ever delivered goods to the carrier that it could misdescribe or misdeliver. If the carrier did not issue the bill of lading and its signature is a forgery or is otherwise unauthorized, that signature is not "effective," and carrier will not be liable on the bill, absent collusion or (perhaps) some sort of actionable negligence. Indeed, by its own terms the FBLA—including of course its liability provisions—only applies in the case of a bill of lading "issued by" a common carrier.[213]

The forger is liable for the fraud, if he can be found. But unlike the forged indorsement situation discussed in Section 4.12 above, no carrier has misdelivered any goods, for there never were any goods to deliver. Nonetheless, like the forged indorsement situation each party that transferred the bill of lading for value makes warranties to later parties, and the first warranty is that "the bill is genuine."[214] If the bill of lading itself is forged, that warranty is breached. Thus, later transferees can assert breach of warranty actions against all parties who transferred the bill in return for payment. The concept again is that the last person to purchase the bill is bound to "know its transferor," and thus is best able to recover against that transferor. That transferor, in turn, can recover against its transferor, and so on up the chain of transfers, until the loss falls either on the forger or on the person that took the bill from the forger.

Again, collecting banks that have transferred the document for value can be subject to this warranty liability.[215] But such banks also will have the three potential escape valves discussed in Section 4.12 above regarding forged indorsements: (1) an express disclaimer of warranty that indicates "a contrary intention"; (2) a claim that the bank is holding the document only "as security for a debt"; and (3) the limitation in the ICC Uniform Rules on Collections that banks are not responsible for the authenticity of the documents they handle on behalf of their customers. Again, each of these approaches has analytical difficulties, but they may reflect a blanket, implicit indication to disclaim the statutory warranties. In any event, any bank found to have warranty liability can pass this

---

[212]   *See* Chapter 1, §§ 1.2–1.9

[213]   49 U.S.C. § 80102.

[214]   49 U.S.C. § 80107(a)(1).

[215]   *See* § 4.12 *supra*.

liability back to its transferor, as long as it can identify and find that transferor.

Finally, if UCC Article 7 applies, such as for an inbound shipment, it generally will exempt banks that are "mere intermediaries" (*e.g.*, collecting banks) from the transfer warranties regarding the genuineness of bills of lading.[216]

Other Forms of Fraud. Another (increasingly common) version of fraud in international bills of lading likewise involves criminal activity. In this version, fraudsters gain knowledge about a shipment of goods covered by an authentic bill of lading and then create an entirely fraudulent bill containing identical information. Upon arrival of the goods at the destination, the fraudsters present the fake bill to the carrier to obtain delivery of the goods before the holder of the authentic bill is able to do so. In such cases, the carrier—following the analysis above—ultimately is liable to the holder of the authentic bill for misdelivery.

One case in this vein involved "a series of international shipping frauds worthy of a bestselling adventure novel."[217] In this scam, criminals were able to defraud one of the world's largest carriage companies, Maersk Line, by forging bills of lading for goods destined for Kuwait. When Maersk released the goods against the fraudulent bills, the holders of the authentic bills (who were co-conspirators) obtained a judgment for misdelivery in Kuwait—and of course then disappeared.[218] Ultimately, Maersk sustained nearly $20 million of losses due to the scam.[219]

Another recent fraud of the same type prompted a worldwide warning by an insurance association for international carriers. The warning arose out of a case in which a carrier released six containers of goods valued at $270,000 against a fraudulent bill of lading. The fraud was revealed when the holder of the authentic bill demanded delivery of the goods at the destination.[220] Because of this and similar cases, the insurance association admonished international carriers that "it has never been easier for documents to be cleverly forged."[221]

---

[216] UCC §§ 7–507, 7–508.

[217] *See* Maersk, Inc. v. Neewra, Inc., 687 F. Supp. 2d 300, 308 (S.D.N.Y. 2009).

[218] *Id.*, at 313–317.

[219] *Id.*, at 309.

[220] *See* ITIC Press Release of October 29, 2013, *available at* http://www.itic-insure.com/knowledge-zone/article/press-release-october-2013-itic-issues-warning-on-forged-documents-129457/.

[221] *See id.*

§ 4.15 Electronic Bills of Lading

The FBLA does not define "bill of lading," but it also does not expressly require that a bill of lading be written on a piece of paper or signed in physical form. Thus, use of electronic bills of lading would seem to be a technical possibility. Nonetheless, all of the primary rules of the FBLA are founded on an implicit assumption that the bill of lading—at least a negotiable one—is a paper document. The references to indorsement (whether in blank or to a specified person), to transfer by "delivery," to "possession" of the bill, and to a "holder" all leave the impression that a paper document is required.

However, modern communications technology can provide electronic messages that perform the main functions of the bill of lading: as a receipt, a transport contract, and a document of title. Thus, several types of bill of lading equivalents are currently in use; but most of them are used only as receipts for the goods generated by the carrier. This is especially true for nonnegotiable bills of lading (a.k.a. waybills), which do not need to be presented to a carrier to obtain possession of the goods. Thus, as a federal court recently observed, "[s]ince the physical document is no longer necessary to the transaction, [a] waybill may be transmitted electronically or telexed between the parties."[222]

Efforts to Create Electronic Bills of Lading. With this foundation, several efforts have been made to facilitate and create electronic carrier-issued international receipts for goods. For example, the U.S. Interstate Commerce Commission (I.C.C.) authorizes the use of uniform electronic bills of lading, both negotiable and nonnegotiable, for motor carrier and rail carrier use.[223] More generally, as noted some federal courts have recognized the effectiveness of electronic bills of lading, at least in certain respects.[224] These developments, however, relate to the role of bills of lading merely in evidencing a carriage contract and in communicating information about the goods, the shipper, and the consignee. The recognition by the I.C.C. and the court cases does not, however, provide clear guidance on the formal legal rights and obligations of the parties to the electronic bill. Thus, the bills do not

---

[222] Delphi-Delco Elec. Sys. v. M/V Nedlloyd Europa, 324 F.Supp.2d 403, 425 n.12 (S.D.N.Y. 2004) (quoting Schoenbaum, 2 ADMIRALTY & MAR. LAW § 10–11 (5th ed. 2011)). *See also* Quanzhou Joerga Fashion Co., Inc. v. Brooks Fitch Apparel Group, LLC, 2012 WL 4767180 (S.D.N.Y. 2012) (same).

[223] *See* 49 C.F.R. Part 1035 and especially 49 CFR § 1035.1(b)(1).

[224] *See, e.g.,* Atlantic Container Line AB v. Volvo Car Corp., 2014 WL 4730152, at *1 n.1 (S.D.N.Y. 2014); Quanzhou Joerga Fashion Co., Inc. v. Brooks Fitch Apparel Group, LLC, 2012 WL 4767180 (S.D.N.Y. 2012); Delphi-Delco Electronics Systems v. M/V Nedlloyd Europa, 324 F. Supp. 2d 403, 413 (S.D.N.Y. 2004).

allow for further sale or rerouting of the goods in transit, or for using the bills of lading to finance the transaction. Under the I.C.C. regulations, for example, negotiable uniform electronic bills of lading must "provide for indorsement on the back portion,"[225] but there is no explanation of how an electronic message has a "back portion," or how "indorsement" is to be effected.

Carriers also have attempted to create programs that utilize electronic carrier-issued international receipts for goods. Most of these efforts relate to nonnegotiable electronic waybills under which shippers provide relevant information through the carrier's website and the shipper or consignee then prints out a waybill document at either the origin or destination. Atlantic Container Lines, for example, has used dedicated lines between terminals at its offices in different ports to send messages between those offices. It generates a Data Freight Receipt which is given to the consignee or notify party. Such a receipt is not negotiable, however, and gives buyers and banks little protection from further sale or rerouting of the goods by the shipper in transit. This program is an advance over the initial efforts because it includes a "no disposal" term in the shipper-carrier contract. Thus, this electronic message protects the buyer from further sale or rerouting by the seller in transit. But it still cannot be used to finance the transfer, because the electronic receipt, even if it named a bank as consignee, is not formally a negotiable document of title. The receipt is believed to give the bank only the right to prevent delivery to the buyer, not a positive right to take control of the goods for itself.

Chase Manhattan Bank also attempted to create the Seaborne Trade Documentation System (Seadocs), which involved a Registry for negotiable electronic bills of lading for oil shipments. The Registry acted as custodian for an actual paper negotiable bill of lading issued by a carrier, and maintained a registry of transfers of that bill from the original shipper to the ultimate "holder." The transfers were made by a series of electronic messages, each of which could be authenticated by "test keys", or identification numbers, generated by Seadocs. The Registry would then, as agent, indorse the paper bill of lading in its custody. At the end, Seadocs would electronically deliver a paper copy of the negotiable bill of lading to the last indorsee to enable it to obtain the goods from the carrier. While Seadocs was a legal success, showing that such a program was technically feasible, it was not a commercial success, and survived for less than a year.[226]

---

[225]   49 CFR §§ 1035.1(a)(3), (b)(1).

[226]   *See* Susan Beecher, *Can the Electronic Bill of Lading Go Paperless*, 40 INT. LAW. 627, 635–638 (2006).

The Comité Maritime International has adopted Rules for Electronic Bills of Lading (the "CMI Rules").[227] Under these rules, any carrier can issue an electronic bill of lading as long as it will act as a clearinghouse for subsequent transfers. Upon receiving goods, the carrier sends an electronic message to the shipper describing the goods, the contract terms, and a "private key."[228] The shipper then has the "right of control and transfer" over the goods, and is called a "holder."[229] Under CMI Rules 4 and 7, an electronic message from the shipper that includes the private key can be used to transfer the shipper's rights to a third party, who then becomes a new holder. The carrier then cancels the shipper's "private key" and issues a different private key to the new holder.[230] Upon arrival, the carrier delivers the goods to then-current holder or a consignee designated by the holder.

To take advantage of the CMI Rules, the original parties to the transaction must agree that the CMI Rules will govern the "communications" aspects of the transaction—the rules are voluntary and do not automatically have the force of law.[231] But such an agreement may come merely through a reference in the carriage contract. The CMI Rules are not intended to govern the substantive laws of bills of lading provisions, only the electronic transfers of the electronic bill of lading. The Rules thus reflect an attempt to create an electronic writing that functions as a negotiable document of title by contract and estoppel. However, this attempt by private parties to create a negotiable document cannot serve the essential function of binding third parties, a power usually reserved to legislatures. In addition, there is some concern that the CMI Rules do not address certain important issues, such as what happens when the system fails.

Separately, the Commission of the European Committees has sponsored the "Bolero" electronic bill of lading initiative (for "Bill of Lading Electronic Registry Organisation"). Bolero is based on a central electronic registry for bills of lading called the "title registry" that is independent of the shipper, the carrier, the ultimate buyer, and all intermediate parties. But it also requires all such parties to become bound to the system by agreeing to a master contract in the form of the "Bolero Rulebook."[232] This Rulebook defines the required communication system (through electronic

---

[227] Comité Maritime International Rules for Electronic Bills of Lading, available at http://comitemaritime.org/Rules-for-Electronic-Bills-of-Lading/0,2728,12832,00.html.

[228] *Id.*, art. 4.

[229] *Id.*, art. 7.

[230] *Id.*

[231] *Id.*, art. 1.

[232] Bolero Rulebook, available at http://www.bolero.net/integration/rulebook.

"Messages") and the rights and obligations of the parties. Conceptually, it is based on the traditional concept of paper bills of lading, but adapts the terminology and rules to an electronic environment.

The goal of Bolero's title registry is to permit the creation of electronic bills of lading and then enable the transfer of the rights that arise out of them. Upon receipt of the goods and shipping instructions from the shipper, the carrier creates a "Bolero Bill of Lading" (BBL) by digitally signing a corresponding electronic message and sending it to the title registry.[233] The registry then creates a record for the BBL along with a unique consignment number. The carrier's message must designate the shipper of the goods and indicate whether the bill is transferable or not transferable. It also must designate either a holder of the bill (whether by formal name or in bearer form) or a consignee (in which case the bill is not transferable).[234] In the case of a transferable BBL, the shipper becomes the first registered holder; it then can transfer the bill by sending to the title registry an electronic message that designates the new holder.[235] Upon receipt of such a message, the registry—acting as agent for the carrier[236]—issues a message confirming the rights of the new registered holder. The carrier then is obligated to acknowledge that "from that time on it holds the goods described in the Bolero Bill of Lading to the order of" the new designated holder.[237] All the electronic messages by the parties in the Bolero system are secured by digital signatures based on a private key. The ultimate goal of the system, according to Bolero, is to create "the legal framework allowing organisations to replicate the legal results currently achieved in a paper environment."[238]

The Bolero system has met with some success, especially for large enterprises with repeat business in a given line of trade. But this also is part of the problem, for Bolero is essentially a closed system. Infrequent shippers, small-scale carriage companies, and regional banks thus far have not participated. Any seller of goods covered by a Bolero Bill of Lading also will have challenges transferring the corresponding rights to a buyer that is not part of the Bolero system. And to attain anything near a comprehensive replacement of paper-based bills of lading will require substantially

---

[233]   *Id.*, Rule 3.1.

[234]   *Id.*, Rules 3.1(4), 3.3.

[235]   *Id.*, Rule 3.4.1(1).

[236]   *Id.*, Rule 3.4.2.

[237]   *Id.*, Rule 3.4.1(2).

[238]   *See* http://www.bolero.net/integration/rulebook.

broader acceptance than the approximately 500 enterprises that now participate in some form.

More recently, the Bolero system operators have teamed with the Society for Worldwide Interbank Financial Telecommunication (SWIFT) to create a "Core Messaging Platform" for the presentation of formal electronic documents such as bills of lading ("eBL"). (Indeed, in 2013 Bolero received a patent for this technology.) The system again involves all counterparties agreeing to a Rulebook, which provides for the dispatch and receipt of legally binding electronic bills of lading and, most important, a formal "fingerprinting" to ensure recognition of only one original bill. Thus far, however, this system also has not been able to establish a secure foundation for broad use of electronic bills of lading.

The largest challenge in all of these efforts has been in making an electronic bill of lading negotiable so that it remains authentic, unique, confidential, and transferrable in a way to bind third parties. Most bankers have been skeptical of the device created by the CMI Rules, including as expanded in the Bolero system. The registries maintained by each carrier do not have the same level of security associated with normal SWIFT procedures. (*See* "Electronic Letter of Credit Transactions" in Chapter 6.[239]) In addition to fraudulent transactions, there is a risk of misdirected messages. Thus, a bank could find itself relying on non-existent rights from a fraudulent actor impersonating the carrier. Although the new Bolero system seeks to minimize these risks, the banks are concerned about whether carriers will accept liability for losses due to such fraudulent practices. Thus, the CMI and Bolero Rules have not yet seemed to find wide acceptance, at least not in the United States, and bills of lading are still primarily paper-based in both the "documents against payment" and letter of credit transactions (although of course much internal communication is effected by electronic means[240]).

Other systems also have been tried. The "Global Trade System" employed a nonnegotiable waybill with a clause that tried to give it aspects of a negotiable bill of lading.[241] Another effort, the Trade Card System, was an Internet-based, paper-less system, which allowed electronic settlement of payments for purchases of goods and related services.[242] These systems were confined to registered

---

[239] *See* Chapter 6, § 6.14.

[240] *See id.*

[241] For further discussion of these systems, see Marek Dubovic, *The Problems and Possibilities for using Electronic Bills of Lading as Collateral*, 23 ARIZ. J. INT'L & COMP. L. 437 (2006).

[242] *Id.*

users, but both offered financing for commercial transactions." Both systems, however, had difficulties in providing bills of lading that could be used as collateral. The 2007 UNCITRAL Legislative Guide on Secured Transactions in fact is founded on the notion of paper documents of title.[243] Another effort that seems to be gaining some success with an electronic bill of lading system is "Cargodocs" offered by a private enterprise (Electronic Shipping Solutions).[244] This effort, like Bolero, is based on a central registry and a required, multilateral contract that binds all of the parties to the system.

Legal Developments. Two recent legal developments also may facilitate and promote the future development of secure and commercially viable electronic bills of lading. First, revisions to the UCC since the turn of the century expressly contemplate "electronic documents of title," including electronic bills of lading. The 2001 revisions to UCC Article 1 define an electronic document of title as one "evidenced by a record consisting of information stored in an electronic medium"[245] and then broadly defines a "record" to include information that is "stored in an electronic medium and is retrievable in perceivable form."[246] The 2003 revisions to UCC Article 7 then address the security of electronic bills of lading through the concept of "control."[247] At the core of this concept is a requirement that "a single authoritative copy of the document exists which is unique, identifiable, and . . . unalterable" (with certain defined exceptions).[248] Article 7 then has specifically tailored rules for the "negotiation" of an electronic document of title.[249]

Second, the "Rotterdam Rules" concluded in 2009[250] create an explicit legal framework for the creation, transfer, and enforcement of "negotiable electronic transport records."[251] Deliberately medium and technology neutral, these rules should both accommodate and foster future technological innovations.[252] Thus, the only

---

[243] Footnote 25 of the UNCITRAL Legislative Guide on Secured Transactions expressly notes that—although not designed to discourage use of electronic documents of title—it was "prepared against the background of negotiable instruments and negotiable documents in paper form." *See* http://www.uncitral.org/uncitral/uncitral_texts/security.html.

[244] *See* http://www.essdocs.com/solutions.

[245] UCC § 1–201(b)(16).

[246] UCC § 1–201(b)(31).

[247] UCC § 7–106(b).

[248] UCC § 7–106(b)(1).

[249] UCC § 7–501(b).

[250] *See* § 4.2 *supra*.

[251] Rotterdam Rules, *supra* note 26, arts. 1(10)(b), 1(19), 8–10.

[252] *Id.*, art. 1(21) (defining the "issuance" of a negotiable "electronic transport record" merely as requiring procedures "that ensure that the record is subject to

requirements for the use of a "negotiable electronic transport record" are functional: It must arise subject to procedures that provide for (a) a method for the issuance and the transfer of the record to an intended holder, (b) an assurance that the record "retains its integrity," (c) the manner by which the holder can "demonstrate that it is the holder," and (d) the manner of confirming the delivery to the holder or of terminating the record.[253] Although only three countries have ratified the Rotterdam Rules as of late 2016, as noted in § 4.2 above there are positive indications that many countries will do so (including the United States).

Separately, Customs and Border Protection (CPB) has established a system for paperless customs clearance through the use of an electronic interface on a dedicated agency website. Since September 2008, new Foreign Trade Regulations have mandated the electronic filing of export information via Electronic Export Information ("EEI") forms for any export over $2500 (other than to Canada). This new online Automated Export System ("AES") has replaced the filing of hard copy Shipper's Export Declaration (SED) forms. The purpose of the system was to assist U.S. Customs in enforcement goals and to spot potential terrorist threats.

---

exclusive control from its creation until it ceases to have any effect or validity"); and arts. 9, 51(4), and 57 (providing more detail).

[253]　*Id.*, art. 9.

Chapter 5

SALES AGENT AND DISTRIBUTORSHIP AGREEMENTS

Table of Sections

§ 5.1   Introduction___From Direct Sales to Agents or Distributors

The most straightforward means of engaging in international business is a direct sale of goods to a foreign buyer. Thus, for example, a manufacturer of goods in the United States may enter into a long-term deal to supply goods to a foreign wholesaler; or a U.S. wholesaler may conclude a large contract to sell goods to a foreign retailer; or a U.S. merchant may arrange a series of individual sales to foreign resellers identified through marketing efforts or established contacts; or a U.S. retailer may sell online to consumers in a foreign country. In the other direction, a U.S. manufacturer may buy raw materials from a foreign supplier; or a U.S. wholesaler may order finished goods from abroad; or (increasingly) a U.S. consumer may buy a product through an online site (perhaps not even knowing that the seller is located in a foreign country).

Chapters 1 and 2 examined the structure of and law governing international sale of goods transactions. Chapters 3 and 4 then analyzed, respectively, the important role of commercial terms and of bills of lading in such transactions. But as a particular U.S. enterprise finds greater success in a foreign market, the need arises for a more durable arrangement. Nonetheless, it may not be ready for a permanent presence in the foreign country, whether in the form of a branch office with formal employees (and attendant concerns over labor laws, licensing, etc.) or a formal corporate subsidiary (with attendant concerns over capital investments, local corporate and regulatory laws, etc.).[1]

Instead, the next stage in the expansion of a domestic enterprise into a foreign market commonly is the engagement of a local sales agent or distributor. That is the subject we take up in this Chapter. Taken in the aggregate, most sales of goods into foreign markets in fact involve the use of some such local person or entity that acts as an established intermediary. A small company may engage the services of a sale agent for the foreign market, although the agent also may handle other producers or products. A large company often has its own, exclusive foreign agent or distributor.

Unfortunately, unlike the UN Sales Convention (CISG) examined in Chapter 2, there is no widely accepted international treaty governing this subject. A proposed Convention on Agency in the International Sale of Goods (1983) has not garnered sufficient support to enter into force.[2] Another treaty limited to the choice of law for agency contracts[3] has been ratified only by four countries (Argentina, France, the Netherlands, and Portugal),[4] and as to the last three an EU Directive (see § 5.7 below) displaces many of its rules in any event. Likewise, there are no widely accepted international customs and practices for agents or distributors in the nature of the Incoterms discussed in Chapter 3 or the Uniform Customs and Practices for Documentary Credits (UCP) discussed in Chapters 6 and 7.[5]

Thus, the rights and obligations of the parties to a sales agent or distributorship relationship in nearly all respects is a matter for

---

[1]   Chapter 21 examines the issues that arise from these forms of investment in a foreign country.

[2]   UNIDROIT Convention on Agency in the International Sale of Goods, Geneva, 17 February 1983, *available at* http://www.unidroit.org/instruments/agency.

[3]   *See* Convention on the Law Applicable to Agency, The Hague, 14 March 1978, *available at* https://www.hcch.net/en/instruments/conventions/full-text/?cid=89.

[4]   *See* https://www.hcch.net/en/instruments/conventions/status-table/?cid=89.

[5]   The ICC recently published a "Model Contract on Distributorship." *See* ICC Product No. 776E (2016). The UNIDROIT Principles of International Commercial Contracts (2010) also contain some rules on the rights and powers of agents. *See* §§ 2.2.1–2.2.10, *available at* http://www.unidroit.org/instruments/commercial-contracts/unidroit-principles-2010.

the domestic law of each host country. Some important similarities exist across legal systems, especially regarding the protection of sales agents. But counsel for a U.S. enterprise desiring to engage a foreign sales agent or distributor must be aware that local law may have rules or norms that differ substantially from those in the United States.

The goal of this Chapter is to review the fundamental principles governing independent foreign sales agents and independent foreign distributors. Sections 5.2 and 5.3 first explore the important differences between these two most common forms of intermediaries in the distribution of goods in a foreign country. In broad strokes, a foreign agent is a small operation (most often simply a self-employed individual) that sells on behalf of a larger and more sophisticated principal; a foreign distributor, in contrast, often is a more substantial and established entity that buys goods for its own account and resells them through its own distribution network.

Sections 5.4 through 5.6 then examine the considerations relevant to choosing between, and defining the relationship with, a foreign agent or distributor. For ease of reference, we will analyze the choice between these two different types of foreign intermediaries from the perspective of a U.S. exporter.

Finally, Sections 5.7 through 5.13 analyze the mandatory rules many legal systems have adopted to protect local sales agents against mistreatment by their (typically more sophisticated) principals.

§ 5.2   The Basic Distinction Between a Sales Agent and a Distributor

The two forms of intermediaries most frequently engaged to distribute products abroad are (1) an independent foreign agent, and (2) an independent foreign distributor. Both are independent in the sense that they are not formal employees of the supplier (although, as noted below, the supplier must be careful not to exercise such a level of control that an agent is deemed to be an employee[6]).

Foreign Sales Agent. An independent foreign sales agent—also known as a "commercial agent," "sales representative," or "commission agent"—is a person or entity in the foreign country that does not buy the goods for its own account and thus does not take title to them. Instead, the agent markets the goods with the goal of finding customers for the U.S. exporter according to the

---

[6]   *See* § 5.4 *infra.*

responsibilities defined in the parties' contract. The agent's upfront financial outlays may be minimal, because it is not required to invest in facilities to store the goods, and it need not worry that any stored goods might decrease in value prior to resale (inventory risk). The U.S. exporter, not the foreign sales agent, also bears the risk that any customer/buyer might not pay (default risk). The form of compensation for the foreign sales agent instead is commissions tied to the number of deals closed by the U.S. exporter with local customers (and perhaps a base stipend).

The essential role of a sales agent is as a dedicated intermediary between the U.S. exporter and customers in the agent's defined local market. Because it works on commission, the agent's incentive is to secure as many orders for the U.S. exporter as possible. In this respect the standard notion of an "agent" as a person with the authority to bind its principal can be a bit misleading. Most often, the parties' contract includes an express agreement that the foreign sales agent does not have the authority to bind the U.S. exporter without prior written consent. In any event, the exact scope of the agent's authority is a subject for negotiation, and the U.S. exporter is well advised to address the issue in clear terms in the sales agent contract (see § 5.5 below).

The special challenge with foreign agents is that local (host country) law may define the status of "agent" in a completely different way from U.S. law. Local law also may impose different notions of implied or inherent authority, and limit the power of the principal to disclaim such authority. Thus, the formal rights and powers of an intended "agent" may vary depending on local law. Moreover, some aspects of local foreign law may, and likely will be, mandatory and thus not subject to modification by contract.[7]

All of this highlights the importance for a U.S. exporter of finding competent local legal counsel and then defining the exporter's contractual relationship with the foreign sales agent—within the permitted bounds—with clarity.

Foreign Distributor. An independent foreign distributor buys goods from the U.S. exporter and resells them through its own distribution network and on its own account. As a result, the distributor takes title to the goods and assumes the risk that it will not be able to resell them. It also has an independent payment obligation to the U.S. exporter, and thus bears the risk of non-payment by its downstream customers (default risk). The scope of its rights and responsibilities, including most often the terms of the

---

[7] Sections 5.7 through 5.13 below examine prominent examples of such mandatory local rules that protect sales agents.

future purchases of products, are a subject for contractual negotiations with the exporter (see § 5.6 below).

A distributor, in contrast to an agent, often must make significant financial investments in its own operations. Because it is buying the goods on its own account, typically in large volumes, it must arrange for storage prior to final sale. Sales from a permanent location will require investments in real estate, equipment, and fixtures. And because it sells through its own distribution network, success will depend on the extent of its commitment to developing that network. Closely related to this is the need to undertake active promotion and marketing efforts. For all of these reasons, a foreign distributor usually is a larger and more established entity than a foreign sales agent. A distributor makes money—like most other traders—on the difference between the price it pays the U.S. exporter and the price it charges its downstream customers ("buy low, sell high").

From its nature, an independent distributor—unlike the uncertainty with a sales agent—does not have the authority to bind the U.S. exporter. This arises from the simple fact that the distributor actually buys the goods for resale, rather than arranging sales for the account of an exporter/principal. The U.S. exporter and the distributor are fully separate entities. But this, too, is a matter for negotiation and definition in the parties' contract. Thus, for example, the U.S. exporter may find a value in granting the distributor the authority to act as its agent for defined purposes, such as arranging sales for the exporter outside of the distributor's otherwise-agreed territory or product lines.

§ 5.3   The Central Role of and Limits on Contract Law

Contract law obviously is the central focus for defining the rights and obligations of a sales agent or distributor. That certainly is the case in the United States, where the relationship between a supplier and the entities through which it distributes its products in nearly all respects is a subject for contractual negotiation. Some state and federal statutes provide limited protections, such as for franchises[8] or automobile dealers[9] or on the specific issue of the repurchase of inventory upon termination of a dealership.[10] In

---

[8]   *See, e.g.,* N.J. Stat. §§ 56:10 *et seq.*; Ind. Code §§ 23–2–2.7 *et seq.*; Del. Code Title 6, §§ 2552 *et seq.*

[9]   *See* The Automobile Dealers' Day in Court Act, 15 U.S.C. §§ 1221 *et seq.* For state law protections of motor vehicle dealers see, *e.g.,* N.H. Rev. Stat. §§ 357–C:1 *et seq.*; Mass. Gen. Laws ch. 93B *et seq.*; W. Va. Code §§ 17A–6A–1 *et seq.*

[10]   *See, e.g.,* Wis. Stat. §§ 135.01 *et seq.*; Miss. Stat. §§ 75–771 *et seq.*; Alaska Stat. §§ 45.45.700 *et seq.*

general, however, a U.S. seller/supplier is free to fashion its relationship with domestic agents or distributors through contractual agreements.

This is not so—at least not to the same extent—in many foreign countries. Even the choice between agent and distributor may not entirely be subject to party agreement. In order to protect local intermediaries, some foreign legal systems, especially in developing countries, require or allow only certain relationship structures. Thus, the choice of the form of distribution, or the specific attributes of that form, may not be the prerogative of the U.S. exporter.[11]

Moreover, some foreign countries, especially in the great majority that follow the civil law tradition, have detailed definitions for distributors and agents, and they apply different regulatory regimes for each. These laws likely are mandatory and thus not subject to displacement or modification by contract. This is especially true for self-employed sales agents (the definition of which itself may not conform to U.S. expectations[12]). As Sections 5.7 through 5.13 below examine in detail, a number of foreign legal systems have extensive rules that protect sales agents regarding disclosures, payment of commissions, notice periods for termination, and compensation upon termination.

Choice of Law. The limit on contractual autonomy may include the important issue of the applicable law in the first place.[13] Often, the U.S. exporter will have the bargaining edge by dint of size and legal resources; thus, it may demand a contractual agreement that the law of its home jurisdiction (*e.g.*, a state of the United States) will govern the entirety of the parties' contractual relationship.

As a general proposition, most countries allow the parties to a commercial contract to define the governing law.[14] The European Union's Regulation on the Law Applicable to Contractual Obligations (the "Rome I Regulation"),[15] for example, generally places no limitation on such a choice.[16] But, significantly for present

---

[11] For a comprehensive analysis of the law of forty-seven different countries governing sales agents and distributors see INTERNATIONAL AGENCY AND DISTRIBUTION LAW (Dennis Campbell, ed., 2009).

[12] *See* § 5.8 *infra.*

[13] The same applies for a franchise, a similar method for distributing products or services, but one that also involves an essential license of intellectual property rights.

[14] *See, e.g.*, Chapter 2, § 2.1.

[15] Regulation (EC) No. 593/2008 of the European Parliament and of the Council on the Law Applicable to Contractual Obligations of 17 June 2008, *available at* http://eur-lex.europa.eu/legal-content/EN/ALL/?uri=CELEX:32008R0593.

[16] *See id.*, art. 3.

purposes, the Regulation does not at all extend to the authority of an agent to bind a principal.[17]

In contrast, some legal systems, and not only in the developing world, refuse to give effect to choice of law clauses in agency and distributorship contracts and enforce local law only.[18] Moreover, even if this is not the case as a general proposition, as noted above many countries have mandatory legislation specifically for such contractual relationships. A prominent example is the EU Directive on Self-Employed Commercial Agents.[19] Indeed, local courts—including in industrialized Western countries—may not recognize choice of forum or even arbitration clauses if their effect is to avoid the protections of such mandatory law.[20] As explored in more detail Section 5.8 below, the European Court of Justice has expressly so concluded. As a more general matter, local protections of sales agents or distributors in EU member states may be viewed as "overriding mandatory provisions" under the Rome I Regulation and thus not subject to circumvention by a choice of law clause.[21]

Nonetheless, a U.S. exporter is well-advised to include a choice of law clause in a foreign agent or distributorship agreement. Where allowed, this will displace the general rule that such a contract is governed by the law of the location of the agent or distributor.[22] In addition, mandatory local law often is not comprehensive and thus does not define all aspects of the legal relationship; the choice of law clause then would apply for the gaps. To avoid local limitations, however, the clause should make clear that it applies only to the extent allowed by local law.

---

[17]   *See id.*, art. 1(2)(g) (excluding from its scope "the question whether an agent is able to bind a principal . . . in relation to a third party").

[18]   *See* Eberhard H. Rohm & Robert Koch, *Choice of Law in International Distribution Contracts: Obstacle or Opportunity*, 11 N.Y. INT'L L. REV. 1, 33 (1998) (observing that "many European and South American jurisdictions regard the sales agent, despite any contractual language to the contrary, as employees of the principal, and to that effect an evasion of national provisions regarding the termination and indemnification of agency agreements through choice of law and forum is impossible").

[19]   *See* Council Directive 86/653/EEC on the Coordination of the Laws of the Member States Relating to Self-Employed Commercial Agents (Dec. 18, 1986), *available at* http://eur-lex.europa.eu/legal-content/EN/TXT/?uri=CELEX:31986L0653. *See also* §§ 5.7–5.13 *infra* (analyzing this Directive in detail).

[20]   *See generally* Pilar Perales Viscasillasa, *The Good, the Bad, and the Ugly in Distribution Contracts: Limitation of Party Autonomy in Arbitration?*, 4 PENN ST. J. L. & INT'L AFF. 213 (2015).

[21]   *See* Rome I Regulation, *supra* note 15, art. 9.

[22]   *See, e.g., id.*, art. 4(1)(f) (providing that in absence of an effective choice "a distribution contract shall be governed by the law of the country where the distributor has his habitual residence").

The Need for a Writing. It should be obvious that the commercial relationship between a U.S. exporter and its foreign agent or distributor should be set forth in a formal writing. Because the agreement will involve two different legal systems, and probably two different languages and cultures, it should be reduced to a tangible form that addresses the differences in detail. Moreover, some foreign legal systems may require a writing for the effectiveness of a local agency or distributorship contract. The EU Directive on Commercial Agents, for example, expressly allows member states to impose such a requirement,[23] and provides in any event that upon demand the principal must produce a "signed written document setting out the terms of the agency contract."[24]

§ 5.4   Defining the Relationship—The Choice of Agent or Distributor

Independent Distributor. Perhaps the most important consideration in choosing between the foreign agent model and the foreign distributorship model is control. The choice of an independent distributor usually means that the U.S. exporter relinquishes control over important aspects of the distribution system, precisely because the distributor buys and then resells to its own customers on its own account. Thus, the U.S. exporter loses substantial control over the goods themselves (ensuring proper storage, preventing unauthorized modifications, etc.), over the customer base in the foreign market (establishing long-term good will, etc.), and over the quality of post-sale services. Monitoring the performance of a distributor also can be more difficult.

Perhaps most important, with the distributor model the U.S. exporter will lose the ability to control the price of its goods in the foreign market; as a result, it loses the chance to capture the full margin between its production costs and the price charged to the downstream customer in the foreign market. The reason for this is rooted in fundamental principles of antitrust/competition law: As independent entities, any agreement between the exporter and the foreign distributor on a resale price (aka "resale price maintenance") very likely will constitute a "contract, combination . . . or conspiracy, in restraint of trade" (in U.S. legal terminology).[25]

---

[23]   EU Commercial Agent Directive, *supra* note 19, art. 13(2) ("[A] Member State may provide that an agency contract shall not be valid unless evidenced in writing.").

[24]   *See id.,* art. 13 ("Each party shall be entitled to receive from the other on request a signed written document setting out the terms of the agency contract including any terms subsequently agreed. Waiver of this right shall not be permitted.").

[25]   *See* 15 U.S.C. § 1 (the "Sherman Act"). Indeed, prior to 2007, any agreement on resale price maintenance represented a "per se" violation of the Sherman Act. In

The choice of a distributor rather than an agent in fact is likely to raise a variety of concerns under antitrust/competition law. The simple reason again is that a distributorship involves a contract between two different and independent entities. Based on over a century of precedent under the Sherman Act, the law on this subject is well established in the United States. But for a U.S. exporter, the important point in this regard is that (of course) U.S. notions of antitrust law do not necessarily obtain in foreign countries. The European Union, for example, has adopted a detailed Regulation on such "vertical agreements" between suppliers and distributors that differs in material respects from U.S. antitrust law.[26] These include rules on (among others) exclusive territories, extra-territorial sales, resale price arrangements, and post-termination covenants not to compete.

The distributorship model nonetheless carries important advantages for a U.S. exporter. The return value from such an arrangement is that the U.S. exporter obtains a secure, established contract partner with expertise and business contacts in the foreign territory. The U.S. exporter thus does not need to invest in facilities or the development of its own distribution network (and may not have the capital to do so in any event). Instead, the distributor makes such investments and also assumes much of the inventory and default risks. The tradeoff, once again, is that the distributor will capture some of the margin between the U.S. exporter's production costs and the full price charged to the downstream buyer in the foreign market.

Independent Sales Agent. The loss of control over the foreign market, and especially over the price of its goods or services in the foreign market, may cause the U.S. exporter instead to choose independent agency model of distribution. Unlike a distributor, an agent does not buy for its own account; rather, it simply arranges a contract directly between the U.S. exporter and the foreign customer.[27] That is, the agent generally has authority only to find a buyer, not conclude the sale itself. Because title remains in the U.S. exporter/seller until the ultimate sale, the U.S. exporter should be able to control all aspects of the transaction in the foreign market

---

that year, the Supreme Court overruled prior precedent to that effect in favor of the "rule of reason." *See* Leegin Creative Leather Products, Inc. v. PSKS, Inc., 551 U.S. 877, 907 (2007).

[26] *See* Commission Regulation (EU) No 330/2010 on the Application of Article 101(3) of the Treaty on the Functioning of the European Union to Categories of Vertical Agreements and Concerted Practices (20 April 2010), *available at* http://eur-lex.europa.eu/legal-content/EN/ALL/?uri=CELEX:32010R0330.

[27] *See* § 5.2 *supra.*

(sale terms, customer development and relations, post-sale service, etc.). Indeed, the U.S. exporter even may control the price—for there is no "resale" at all—and thus capture for itself the full margin between its costs and the foreign sale price (less the commission for the agent).

The tradeoff is the inverse of that for the distributorship arrangement. What is lost through a sales agent arrangement is the opportunity for a more stable, established relationship with a distributor that likely has greater expertise and business contacts in the foreign market. Cultivating the customer base, providing secure post-sale servicing, and maintaining sufficient local inventory to meet short-term variations in local demand all require a local presence. This of course means investments of time, money, and human resources. Indeed, in industries in which close and intense support of customers is the norm, the sales agency model may not be feasible at all.

Risk of Employee Status. To address such demands of the local market, the temptation for the U.S. exporter will be to confer ever greater responsibilities on the sales agent. This raises the separate risk of exercising too much control, such that the agent is deemed a full employee under local law. Some foreign countries have quite expansive definitions of "employee"; and others do not have clear rules that distinguish between an agent who is an employee and one who is not. Through express agreement or actual practice, a U.S. exporter thus unwittingly may impose on the agent obligations or restrictions—such as on the time, place, or manner of the agent's activities—that stray into the definition of an employee under local law. Indeed, some developing countries may not recognize the status of "sales agent" at all, and thus default to an employer-employee relationship.

If this is the case, the U.S. exporter/employer must abide by local labor laws in its relationship with the "agent." Among other potential problems, this may remove the right to set term limits or to terminate the employee (nee "agent") at will, at least without making a substantial severance payment. Such a situation may not be limited to developing countries; some industrialized countries of Europe provide protections for employees that are far more extensive than in the United States.

The fact that some labor laws may not acknowledge the distinction between an agent-employee and an independent agent does not mean, however, that *all* local laws will overlook the distinction. For example, tax laws generally view income from sales by an employee as income to the U.S exporter, but some may not do so for income generated by a truly independent agent. In addition, the foreign host country may exert extraterritorial jurisdiction over a U.S. exporter that employs a local agent-employee, but not do so if the exporter uses a truly independent agent. In short, the laws of the host country may treat the same agent differently for different legal purposes.

For all of these reasons, the U.S. exporter is well advised to educate itself carefully about the status distinctions of local law and carefully define an agent as fully independent. This of course is something to be carefully addressed in writing in the agency contract; but the variability of host country laws also means that standard agreements developed for the U.S. market at best may fit awkwardly in a foreign environment and at worst may be entirely ineffective to accomplish the desired legal outcomes. Each agreement must be tailored to fit each host country. Adapting to local law also usually means engaging local counsel. No U.S. exporter intending to distribute products in many countries can be an expert in all the host-country laws; use of local counsel, therefore, is critical to avoiding the pitfalls reviewed above (and myriad others).

§ 5.5   Drafting the Independent Foreign Agent Contract

As Section 5.4 immediately above explained, a U.S. exporter generally will have much more latitude to control its relationship with a foreign sales agent than with a foreign distributor. The benefits to control are manifest. But with that arrangement may come responsibility for the actions of the agent on a broader range of issues. For this reason, the U.S. exporter must carefully define the rights and responsibilities of the agent, with a special emphasis on the limitations imposed by local law. The goal of this Section is to provide an overview of the issues typically addressed in a contract between a U.S. exporter/principal and its foreign sales agent.[28]

Some of the issues reviewed below are standard ones for any commercial relationship; others have a special significance for a contract between a U.S. exporter/principal and a sales agent. The international dimension plays a role as well: Some of the clauses below are customary for domestic sales agents, while others are necessary or appropriate specifically because the agent is in a foreign country.

---

[28]   For general treatments of this subject see *International Commercial Agency*, Ch. 7, IN MODEL CONTRACTS FOR SMALL FIRMS: LEGAL GUIDANCE FOR DOING INTERNATIONAL BUSINESS (Int'l Trade Centre, 2010); Campbell, *supra* note 11, Appendix APP/3.

- *Appointment.* Of course, the essential purpose of the contract is to appoint the sales agent as such. Thus, the contract should identify the U.S. exporter and appoint with particularity the person or entity with the authority to act as the sales agent.

- *Primary Duties of Agent.* The contract should define the basic duties of the sales agent. These typically include promoting the U.S. exporter's products, identifying interested purchasers, and conveying formal purchase orders to the U.S. exporter. A sales agent also may be expected to attend trade shows, assist the U.S. exporter in closing deals, and gather and relay information about local laws and market conditions.

- *U.S. Exporter Obligations.* In return, the contract should define the obligations of the U.S. exporter with regard to supplying promotional materials, training, marketing, advertising, etc. in the foreign market.

- *Scope of Authority.* A critical subject to address in a sales agent contract is the scope of the agent's authority. Curiously, this means a clear statement of *non*-agency. That is, the contract should contain unambiguous agreements that the agent is solely an independent contractor; is not an employee; is not the U.S. exporter's agent except with regard to the solicitation of orders; may not conclude sales without the express approval of the U.S. exporter; may not conclude other contracts or otherwise transact business on behalf or in the name of the U.S. exporter; and may not create binding obligations in any respect with third parties on behalf of the U.S. exporter.

  In the same vein, the contract should make clear that the U.S. exporter retains full control over the terms of the ultimate sale to customers, that the agent has no authority over such issues, and that the agent it will not make any representations to third parties to the contrary. This clear definition of an independent contractor status is important as well to ensure that the U.S. exporter is not deemed to have a presence in the foreign country such that it becomes subject to the jurisdiction of local courts or to local regulatory laws.

- *Product Range.* The contract should define the specific products or range of products within the agent's responsibility.

- *Territory.* In nearly all cases, the contract will define the geographic territory within which the agent may solicit business for the U.S. exporter. Worldwide sales agents are rare.

- *Market.* In addition or instead, the contract may define the scope of the agent's authority with reference to a specific market segment or identified group of potential customers. The purpose of such a limitation is to reserve to the U.S. exporter responsibility over defined customers or customer groups (whether for itself or for another representative in its distribution network).

- *Exclusivity.* The contract should define whether the agent has exclusive or non-exclusive rights within the defined product range, territory, and market. Most often, of course, the agent will prefer exclusive rights.

- *Competition.* On the other hand, the contract should define whether the agent may represent other companies or products that compete with those of the U.S. exporter.

- *Sub-agents and Assignment.* A key issue in choosing a foreign sales agent (as opposed to a distributor) is the ability to appoint sub-agents. This includes the more general right to assign the sales agent status to another party. Most often, a contract with a foreign sales agent reserves such powers to the U.S. exporter (subject to the agent's rights of exclusivity as noted above), because the agent cannot conclude deals without the approval of the U.S. exporter/principal in the first place.

- *Compensation.* Of course, the method and amount of compensation is a matter of great interest for both parties. Occasionally, the contract will set a basic retainer fee. But most often the compensation of a sales agent is based on a commission in the form of a defined percentage of the value of the sales closed through the efforts of the agent.

- *Goals.* The contract commonly also sets formal requirements or goals the agent must meet regarding the promotion of the exporter/principal's products in the local market. A failure to meet those expectations then becomes a ground for early termination of the contract.

- *Term and Termination.* The contract should define the duration of the contract, after which it automatically terminates. This may include rights of renewal for defined periods. It also should define the U.S. exporter's rights to terminate the contract for cause. Many foreign countries nonetheless have rules limiting the principal's right to terminate a sales agent contract and granting special rights to the agent upon termination.[29]

- *Compliance with Local Laws.* Many foreign legal systems impose citizenship, residency, and registration requirements for entities acting as representatives of foreign sellers. The contract thus should have a clause obligating the agent—on threat of termination for cause—to comply with these and all other local rules and regulations.

- *Foreign Corrupt Practices Act (FCPA).* An issue of increasing importance for U.S. multi-nationals—as Chapter 15 examines in detail—is compliance with the Foreign Corrupt Practices Act (and similar legal regimes of other countries). Among other things, that Act prohibits payments to an intermediary with actual or constructive knowledge that they will be used to influence a foreign public official for a corrupt purpose. The contract with the foreign sales agent thus must ensure that the agent complies with the FCPA's anti-bribery provisions. This also should include regular reporting obligations and periodic certifications of compliance with the requirements and prohibitions of the Act.

- *Intellectual Property Rights.* To the extent the U.S. exporter gives access to intellectual property rights, the contract must include an agreement by the agent to protect those rights and not to divulge trade secrets. More generally, such contracts commonly include a confidentiality agreement with regard to any non-public information acquired from the U.S. exporter.

---

[29]   *See* §§ 5.11 and 5.12 *infra.*

- *Choice of Law.* As noted in Section 5.3, a U.S. exporter is well-advised to include a choice of law clause in the sales agent contract. Where allowed, this will at a minimum serve to fill gaps in any mandatory local law governing the U.S. exporter–sales agent relationship.

Finally, a sales agent contract should contain the standard clauses of commercial contracts regarding, *e.g.*, notices, *force majeure*, severability, non-waiver, and integration (*i.e.*, that the writing supersedes all prior promises or representations). An agreement on mandatory private arbitration also is customary (although, as noted above, some doubt exists about whether local courts will recognize an arbitration agreement if it serves to circumvent mandatory local protections of sales agents[30]).

§ 5.6   Drafting the Independent Foreign Distributor Contract

If the U.S. exporter chooses the independent foreign distributor model, many of the contract issues will be the same as those for sales agents noted above. The core difference, once again, arises from the fundamental point that the distributor formally buys and resells the U.S. exporter's products through its own distribution network.[31]

The U.S. exporter instead could enter into a series of individual sales contracts with the foreign reseller; indeed, that often is where the relationship between the parties begins. As the sales become more frequent and regular, however, it increasingly is in the parties' mutual interest to conclude a formal distributorship arrangement. For the exporter, such an arrangement brings a stable relationship with a buyer that also will promote its products in the foreign market based on local knowledge and expertise; for the distributor, it brings a secure source of desired goods on fixed terms for a defined period of time into the future.

The principal function of a distributorship contract is to establish the terms for future sales and the framework for future cooperation. As with the sales agent, the contract between the U.S. exporter and the foreign distributor must cover basic issues such as scope of appointment, respective responsibilities of the parties, term

---

[30]   *See* § 5.3 *supra.*

[31]   For general treatments of this subject see Jeffrey R. Wahl, *International Distribution Contracts* 115–135, in UNDERSTANDING INTERNATIONAL COMMERCIAL CONTRACTS (2015); *International Distribution of Goods*, Ch. 6, in MODEL CONTRACTS FOR SMALL FIRMS: LEGAL GUIDANCE FOR DOING INTERNATIONAL BUSINESS (Int'l Trade Centre, 2010); ICC *Model Contract on Distributorship*, *supra* note 5.

and termination, etc. But because the distributorship contract will cover future purchases by the foreign distributor, it also must address the issues relevant to a sale of goods transaction. And because it separately serves as a framework for future cooperation, the contract must describe the distributor's responsibilities to promote and market the U.S. exporter's products in the foreign market, as well as the exporter's reciprocal obligations to support those efforts.

Of course, the allocation of rights and obligations will depend decisively on the parties' respective bargaining positions. A large U.S. company with an established brand may have a choice among many foreign distributors and thus considerable control over the outcome of negotiations. The distribution contract in such a case likely will contain a narrow definition of the distributor's authority and a broad definition of its obligations. A smaller U.S. enterprise seeking to break into a new foreign market, in contrast, may need to concede broad rights of exclusivity, a narrower description of the distributor's responsibilities, and favorable credit terms and return rights for future sales of goods.

The goal of this Section is to provide an overview of the issues typically addressed in a contract between a U.S. exporter and its independent foreign distributor. Again, some of the issues reviewed below are customary for domestic distribution contracts as well, while others have a special relevance for a distributor located in a foreign country:

- *Appointment.* The primary purpose of a distributorship contract is to establish the relationship between the exporter/supplier and its foreign distributor. Thus, one of the first clauses of the contract involves a formal appointment of the distributor. This clause will state in broad terms the scope of the appointment in terms of territory, product line, and market, all of which are defined in detail in the succeeding provisions.

- *Territory.* Foreign distribution contracts commonly describe a specific geographic territory (by region, country, province, etc.). The exporter will desire a limited geographic area in order to induce the distributor to concentrate its sales and marketing efforts. In return, the distributor likely will seek the exclusive right to conclude sales in the defined territory (see below) in order to reap all of the benefits from those efforts.

- *Market.* In addition or instead, the distribution contract may define a specific market in terms of defined customers or types of sales or service activities. Most often this is done to segment out the areas of expertise or strategic advantages of the distributor. Alternatively, a market definition may allow the exporter (or another distributor) to retain major "house" accounts or cultivate sales in areas of established expertise.

- *Product Line.* Because an essential purpose of a distributorship arrangement is to sell the exporter's products in the foreign market, the contract should specify the products or product lines within its scope. This is particularly important for exporters with a broad product pallet and numerous distribution channels. It also is important for distributors with expertise or strategic advantages in particular product areas. Most often, the contract addresses this specification through an appendix with a clear listing of the covered products or product lines.

- *Exclusivity.* The distributor's appointment may be either exclusive or nonexclusive. Most often, the distributor wants the sole right to resell the covered products in the defined territory and market; but most often, the exporter does not want to grant such a right, instead retaining the flexibility to open competing distribution channels. With a grant of exclusive rights, moreover, the exporter's fortunes in the defined territory and market are left in the hands of a single distributor. On the other hand, non-exclusivity may reduce the incentives for the distributor to devote its time and resources in promoting the exporter's products.

  If the exporter decides or is compelled to grant exclusive rights, the distribution contract should contain clear and rigorous performance standards for the distributor (see below). These standards may include required product purchases and promotional activities.

  However, exclusivity arrangements may raise issues under antitrust/competition law. Many foreign legal systems view such exclusive dealing agreements with suspicion, for they may represent an effort by the exporter to segment the market and thus limit competition. On the other hand, such arrangements may promote competition, such as by allowing a new exporter to enter the foreign market based on the corresponding incentives for the exclusive distributor. A common resolution of this tension, as reflected in the EU's Vertical Agreements Regulation, is to permit the supplier to restrict *active* sales by its distributors outside of their exclusive territories, as long as the restrictions do not limit *actual* sales to customers (*i.e.*, those that arise for reasons other than active sales efforts).[32]

- *Sub-Distributors.* Another common issue in distributorship contracts is the right to appoint sub-distributors. Such a right is more likely to be granted to a foreign distributor (as compared to a sales agent), for it may allow a better cultivation of the local market. If granted, however, most often the exporter retains some form of a review or approval right.

- *Sales Terms.* Because a distributorship arrangement contemplates formal sales by the exporter to the foreign distributor, the parties' contract must address the issues common to a sale of goods contract as well. In this sense, the distribution contract serves as a framework agreement for all future sales.[33] Thus, it commonly includes provisions on the price for the sale from the exporter to the distributor (including, especially, any volume or other discounts); shipment terms (*e.g.*, CIF or FOB[34]); transfer of title; passing of the risk of loss; time and terms of payment; specifications and required quality of the goods; disclaimer of "warranty" liability[35]; and limitations on consequential damages.

From its nature as a framework agreement, the distribution contract also commonly addresses the

---

[32]   *See* the EU Vertical Agreements Regulation, *supra* note 26, art. 4(b)(1).

[33]   Because the distributorship contract in this respect is only a framework arrangement and does not itself involve a sale of goods, the UN Sales Convention examined in Chapter 2 will not apply. But the Convention will govern the future transactions in which the exporter actually sells its goods to the distributor. *See* Chapter 2, § 2.6.

[34]   For a comprehensive examination of such commercial terms see Chapter 3.

[35]   The Uniform Commercial Code in the United States defines the seller's obligations regarding the quality of the goods in terms of "warranties." *See* UCC § 2–312 through 2–316. As explained in Chapter 2, the UN Sales Convention has not embraced this terminology. *See* § 2.21.

terms of any credit granted by the exporter as well as the distributor's rights to return inventory (something that is especially important for distant foreign distributors). Distributors will be very eager to secure generous credit terms. But the list is a long one of exporters that granted excessive lines of credit to foreign distributors and then were dragged into final distress when the distributors became insolvent.

- *Order Procedure.* A closely related issue is the order procedure. The distribution contract thus should address how the foreign distributor may or must place its orders and when and how the exporter must fill them. Often, this includes an agreement on a form purchase order. Another increasingly common arrangement is for the distributor to place orders on an electronic platform created and maintained by the exporter.

- *Distributor Performance Expectations.* From the exporter's perspective, the purpose of a distributorship contract, especially one that grants exclusive rights, is to initiate and/or increase the sales of its products in the foreign market. The contract thus commonly sets minimum purchase levels by the distributor as well as a general obligation to use "best efforts" to promote the exporter's products. Compliance with these obligations is subject to period review, and a failure to meet the defined expectations becomes a ground for early termination of the distributorship contract.

- *U.S. Exporter Obligations.* The distributorship contract should address the exporter's reciprocal obligations regarding sales promotions, marketing, advertising, etc. in the foreign market as well as regarding training, technical support, and service.

- *Term and Termination.* The distributorship contract should define its duration, as well as any rights of renewal by either or both parties. As indicated above, the contract separately should specify the exporter's rights to terminate the contract for cause, including based on a failure to meet minimum purchase or other performance obligations. Unlike sales agents,[36] foreign countries are less likely to have termination

---

[36]   *See* §§ 5.7 and 5.11 *infra.*

protections for fully independent distributors (although, again, the boundaries of these categories are subject to the vagaries of local law).

- *Compliance with Laws.* The distributorship contract should state a general obligation of the distributor to comply with local regulations, for the breach of which the exporter will have a right of early termination of the contract. The Foreign Corrupt Practices Act remains significant in this context as well—for again the FCPA (among other things) prohibits payments to any intermediary with actual or constructive knowledge that they will be used to influence a foreign public official for a corrupt purpose.[37] Although foreign distributors may resist, modern contracts increasingly require compliance with the exporter's anti-bribery, reporting, and accounting policies—as well as periodic certifications of compliance by the distributor.

- *Intellectual Property Rights.* Through a distributorship arrangement, especially an exclusive one, the exporter entrusts much of its reputation and goodwill in the foreign market to the distributor. The value of trademarks and trade names is very much tied to the value of such intangible assets. As a result, the distribution contract must clearly delineate the rights of the distributor to display and otherwise use the trademarks, trade names, logos, and related intellectual property of the exporter. More generally, the contract must include an obligation not to divulge trade secrets or any other confidential information.

- *Post-Termination Rights and Obligations.* A distributorship arrangement involves continuing investments of capital, time, and efforts by both parties. As a result, it is likely that at the time of a termination of the relationship both will be involved in activities that will have continuing effects. The contract thus commonly addresses the post-termination rights and obligations of the parties on issues such as outstanding orders, future warranty claims, use of trademarks and trade names, etc.

---

[37] *See* especially Chapter 15, § 15.7 (explaining that the FCPA prohibits corrupt payments to "any person . . . while knowing that" any portion will be offered or given, "directly or indirectly," to a foreign official, and that the definition of "knowing" includes "willful blindness").

- *Choice of Law.* As noted in Section 5.3, a U.S. exporter is well-advised to include a choice of law clause in a distributorship contract. These are more likely to be enforceable in foreign courts (though not certainly so), and in any event foreign law is less likely to impose mandatory protections in this context as compared with sales agents.

Like the sales agent contact, the foreign distributorship contract also should address a variety of standard subjects covered in domestic deals. This means that the contract should include clauses on notices, *force majeure*, severability, non-waiver, and the merger/integration of all prior promises or representations into the terms of the writing. Finally, an exporter likely will have more leeway in securing an enforceable agreement on mandatory private arbitration for all disputes, at least as compared to sales agent contracts.

§ 5.7   Laws Protecting Sales Agents

Section 5.2 above explored the basic distinction between an independent foreign sales agent and an independent foreign distributorship. As explained there, a sales agent is more likely to be a small operation, most often a self-employed individual; it also is more likely to be an agent for a single foreign supplier. In contrast, a foreign distributor commonly is a large and established enterprise that may sell products of a variety of different foreign suppliers.[38]

This difference in scale and sophistication—at least in the perception of lawmakers—has led to the adoption in many foreign countries of special laws designed to protect sales agents. The policy rationale is that the absence of effective bargaining power by sales agents justifies mandatory rules that override even express contractual agreements with the supplier. This is more likely to be true in developing countries; but many industrialized, advanced legal systems, especially those in the civil law tradition, have adopted statutes with wide-ranging protections of sales agents. To be sure, host countries may have distinctive rules for distributorship arrangements as well. But the protection of sales agents through comprehensive, non-disclaimable statutory regimes is a widespread phenomenon in foreign legal systems.

The following Sections will review the common elements of those statutory regimes. We use as a model the EU's Directive on

---

[38]   For a comprehensive analysis of the law of forty-seven different countries governing sales agents see Campbell, *supra* note 11.

the Coordination of the Laws of the Member States Relating to Self-Employed Commercial Agents (1986) (the "EU Directive" or simply "Directive").[39] This is a particularly good example because it has been implemented into the domestic law of all 28 member states of the European Union (including the impending departure state, the United Kingdom).[40] But as a point of emphasis, similar statutes are found in a number of other countries around the world.

§ 5.8 Laws Protecting Agents__Definitions and Scope

Laws protecting sales agents of course must begin with a definition of the core term, whether "sales agent" or "commercial agent." The EU Directive provides that it applies to "commercial agents"[41] engaged on behalf of a supplier of goods. The Directive defines this term as "a self-employed intermediary who has continuing authority" to do one of two things on behalf of another person ("the principal"): (a) "to negotiate the sale or the purchase of goods," or (b) "to negotiate and conclude such transactions on behalf of and in the name of that principal."[42] (The latter option of course involves a much more extensive grant of authority by the principal than the standard model discussed in Section 5.2 above.) Even a single transaction may suffice to convert an intermediary into a commercial agent if at the same time the supplier "conferred continuing authority on the intermediary."[43] The Directive does not apply, however, to unpaid commercial agents,[44] nor, as the European Court of Justice ruled in 2004, to commercial agents who act in their own name.[45]

Nearly all of the provisions of the EU Directive, like the similarly directed statutes of other countries, are mandatory. Thus, the Directive repeatedly states that "[t]he parties may not derogate from the[se] provisions."[46] Indeed, the European Court of Justice

---

[39] See EU Directive, *supra* note 19.

[40] In 2015 the EU Commission completed a comprehensive evaluation of this EU Directive. *See* European Commission Evaluation of the Council Directive on the Coordination of the Laws of the Member States Relating to Self-Employed Commercial Agents (Directive 86/653/EEC)/Refit Evaluation, SWD (2015) 146 final (July 16, 2015) (hereinafter, "Refit Evaluation").

[41] EU Directive, *supra* note 19, art. 1(1).

[42] *Id.*, art. 1(2). This definition does not include corporate officers, partners, or receivers or trustees in bankruptcy proceedings. *Id.*, art. 1(3).

[43] *See* Case C–3/04, Poseidon Chartering BV v. Marianne Zeeschip VOF, 2006 E.C.R. I–2518 (16 March 2006).

[44] EU Directive, *supra* note 19, art. 2(1).

[45] *See* Case C–85/03, Mavrona & Sia OE v. Delta Etaireia Symmetochon AE, 2004 E.C.R. I–01573 (10 February 2004).

[46] *See* EU Directive, *supra* note 19, arts. 5, 10, 11, 12, 19. *See also* Ellen Eftestøl-Wilhelmsson, *The EU Directive on Self-Employed Commercial Agents—*

(ECJ) concluded in the famous *Ingmar* case in 2000 that if an agent carries on activities in the territory of the EU, even an express choice of law clause—in that case in favor of California law by a principal located in California—cannot displace the mandatory protections of the Directive.[47] But the Directive sets a floor, not a ceiling: As the ECJ emphasized in another important decision in 2013, the EU Member States may adopt rules that are even more favorable for commercial agents.[48]

Moreover, the goal of the Directive is to establish only certain minimum protections on certain issues. As a 2015 Evaluation by the EU Commission explains, the Directive "does not regulate every aspect of the relationship between commercial agents and principals."[49] Thus, each EU Member State is free to regulate those other aspects of the relationship as it deems appropriate for the protection of local agents (or distributors for that matter).

The Directive begins with an identification of the basic obligations of the parties (see § 5.9 immediately below). Then, like other foreign statutes protecting sales agents, the Directive imposes three general groups of protections: (a) on "remuneration" (*i.e.*, payment of commissions and other forms of compensation); (b) on notice of termination; and (c) on compensation on termination. We will examine each of these subjects in turn. Finally, we review the EU Directive's rules on contractual limitations on the right of the agent to compete with the principal after the relationship has terminated.

§ 5.9   Laws Protecting Agents__Basic Obligations

The EU Directive first defines certain basic, non-derogatable[50] obligations of the principal and the agent. These are not particularly onerous or unusual, however.

The agent must "must look after his principal's interests and act dutifully and in good faith."[51] This basic obligation includes "proper efforts" to negotiate and conclude deals for his principal,

---

Applicability and Mandatory Scope, 39 TUL. MAR. L.J. 675 (2015) (analyzing recent case law from the European Court of Justice on this subject).

[47]   Case C–381/98, Ingmar GB Ltd v. Eaton Leonard Techs. Inc., 2000 E.C.R. I–9325, paras. 15–20 (9 November 2000).

[48]   Case C–184/12, United Antwerp Mar. Agencies (Unamar) NV v. Navigation Mar. Bulgare, EU:C:2013:663, at 50 (17 October 2013).

[49]   *See* Refit Evaluation, *supra* note 40, at 6.

[50]   EU Directive, *supra* note 19, art. 5 (declaring that the parties may not derogate from the provisions of Articles 3 and 4).

[51]   *Id.*, art. 3(1).

communicating "necessary information," and complying with "reasonable instructions" from the principal.[52]

In return, the principal likewise must "act dutifully and in good faith" in relations with the agent.[53] This basic obligation includes providing the agent with "necessary documentation" relating to the goods concerned, obtaining for the agent "information necessary for the performance of the agency contract,"[54] and informing the agent within a reasonable time if it has concluded or rejected any deals procured by the agent.[55]

Separately, the EU Directive grants either party the right to demand a signed and written description of the terms of the contract (although this typically will be more important to the agent).[56] This right cannot be waived and extends to any subsequent agreements.[57]

§ 5.10 Laws Protecting Agents__Compensation/ Commissions

The statutes that protect the position of sales agent not surprisingly address the agent's rights to timely and accurate compensation (which the EU Directive refers to as "remuneration"[58]). The EU Directive thus begins with a generic statement that, in absence of an agreement between the parties, the agent shall be entitled to remuneration that agents in the same area are "customarily allowed."[59]

Right to Commissions. The Directive then has special rules for situations in which an agent is compensated "wholly or in part by commission,"[60] a term it defines as remuneration that "varies with the number or value of business transactions."[61] The Directive first states that an agent is entitled to a commission in two circumstances. The first is obvious: where a transaction was

---

[52] *Id.*, art. 3(2).

[53] *Id.*, art. 4(1).

[54] *Id.*, art. 4(2)(b). This includes in particular a duty to notify the agent "within a reasonable period" that the volume of commercial transactions "will be significantly lower" than expected. *Id.*

[55] *Id.*, art. 4(3).

[56] *Id.*, art. 13.

[57] *Id.*

[58] *See id.*, Chapter III.

[59] *Id.*, art. 6(1). As an example of the principle that it sets a floor, not a ceiling, the Directive permits the individual EU Member States to adopt "compulsory provisions . . . concerning the level of remuneration." *Id.*

[60] *Id.*, arts. 7–12.

[61] *Id.*, art. 6(2).

concluded "as a result of his action."[62] But with the second we get a view into the special forms of protection imposed by laws such as the EU Directive: An agent also is entitled to a commission where the transaction is concluded "with a third party whom he has previously acquired as a customer for transactions of the same kind."[63] Thus, once the agent has secured a customer for the principal, the agent is entitled to a commission on all later transactions with that customer even if they do not result from any additional efforts by the agent.

The protections are even more extensive for an agent appointed for a defined territory or market. In such a case, the EU Directive grants a right to a commission for all transactions with customers in that area or market during the term of the contract[64] if the agent either (a) "is entrusted with a specific geographical area or group of customers" or (b) "has an exclusive right to a specific geographical area or group of customers."[65] (The Member States are entitled to choose either of the two models.[66]) The European Court of Justice has ruled that where an agent is entrusted with responsibility for a geographical area, he is entitled to commissions on all transactions concluded with customers in that area, even if the principal concluded them without any support of the agent.[67]

Post-Termination Rights to Commissions. The EU Directive even grants a commercial agent the right to a commission on certain transactions that occur after the agency contract has terminated. The right to such a commission arises in two situations: (a) if the post-termination transaction is "mainly attributable" to the agent's prior efforts and the transaction is closed "within a reasonable period" after the agency contract terminated;[68] and (b) if the order for the transaction "reached the principal or the commercial agent" before the termination (and the agent otherwise would have been entitled to the commission as described above).[69]

When Commissions Are Due. The EU Directive and similar protective statutes define in detail when commissions must be paid. Under the Directive, a commission becomes payable when (a) the

---

[62]   *Id.*, art. 7(1)(a).

[63]   *Id.*, art. 7(1)(b).

[64]   *Id.*, art. 7(2).

[65]   *Id.*

[66]   *Id.*, final paragraph.

[67]   Case No. 104/95, Kontogeorgas v. Kartonpak, 1996 E.C.R. I–6643 (12 December 1996).

[68]   *Id.*, art. 8(a).

[69]   *Id.*, art. 8(b). Article 11 provides that the right to a commission is extinguished if the corresponding contract with the customer is not executed, provided that this was not the fault of the principal.

principal has "executed the transaction"; (b) the principal "should have executed the transaction" under the contract with the third-party customer; or (c) "the third party has executed the transaction."[70] In a curiously worded provision, the principal must then actually pay the commission "not later than on the last day of the month following the quarter in which it became due."[71] The import of this provision is that the principal must pay accrued commissions at least on a quarterly basis, and then by the end of the month following each quarter.

Required Statements. The EU Directive requires the principal to account regularly to the commercial agent on the commissions due. It first declares that the principal must provide a statement on accrued commissions on the same quarterly basis as described immediately above.[72] The statement must contain "the main components used in calculating the amount of commission."[73] In addition, the agent has a right to demand further information from the principal, including "an extract from the books," as needed to "check the amount of the commission due to him."[74]

§ 5.11 Laws Protecting Agents___Notice of Termination

The most difficult issues involving sales agency contracts (and often for distributorship contracts as well) arise upon termination, especially when the foreign agent is terminated against its will.

Disputes over termination are difficult when both parties are in the United States. The difficulties often intensify and become more complicated when the supplier comes from one country, culture, and legal tradition—we have used the United States as an example in this Chapter—and the agent is located in another. The foreign agent, often an individual or other small business, may believe that it has been treated unfairly by the supplier, often a large multinational enterprise. This is especially true when the local agent has worked for a long time to develop clients and goodwill for the foreign supplier. Complaints by local agents on this basis led to the adoption of particularly detailed and extensive protections in the kind of laws, such as the EU Directive, we have been analyzing here.

---

[70]   *Id.*, art. 10(1). At the latest, the commission is payable "when the third party has executed his part of the transaction" (or would have done so but for a default by the principal). *Id.*, art. 10(2).

[71]   *Id.*, art. 10(3).

[72]   *Id.*, art. 12(1).

[73]   *Id.*

[74]   *Id.*, art. 12(2).

A first set of protections involves mandatory notice periods prior to termination. No notice is required if an agency contract has a fixed period, and the contract terminates at the end of that period. If, however, the parties in fact continue to perform after the end of that fixed period, then the EU Directive deems that the contract is "converted into an agency contract for an indefinite period."[75] At this point, or of course if the agency contract had no fixed period in the first place, the Directive imposes an obligation of advance notice of termination.

The length of the advance notice depends on the length of the relationship:

- For the first year of the contract, one month of advance notice is required.

- From the beginning of a second year of the contract, two months of advance notice is required.

- From the beginning of the third year and thereafter, three months of advance notice is required.[76]

The Directive allows the individual Member States to expand the notice periods for contractual relationships of a longer duration. Thus, the Member States may require advance notice of up to four months for the fourth year, five months for the fifth year, and six months for the sixth and subsequent years.[77]

In calculating all of these advance notice periods, the duration of any previously expired fixed term contract must be included.[78] As usual, the parties may not agree on shorter notice periods, but they may agree on longer periods (provided that the period is not longer for the principal than for the agent).[79] Unless the parties agree otherwise, any notice must take effect at the end of a calendar month.[80] The requirement of advance notice does not apply, however, if a Member State allows termination for cause[81] or in "exceptional circumstances."[82]

---

[75]   *Id.*, art. 14.

[76]   *Id.*, art. 15(2).

[77]   *Id.*, art. 15(4).

[78]   *Id.*, art. 15(6).

[79]   *Id.*, arts. 15(2), 15(5).

[80]   *Id.*, art. 15(3).

[81]   *Id.*, art. 16(a) (referring to a termination based on "the failure of one party to carry out all or part of his obligations").

[82]   *Id.*, art. 16(b).

§ 5.12 Laws Protecting Agents___Compensation upon Termination

From the perspective of a U.S. enterprise, perhaps the most surprising form of protection for a foreign sales agent is an automatic right to extra compensation upon termination. The policy behind such a protection is that the efforts of the agent to develop clients and create goodwill during the term of the contract continue to benefit the principal after the formal relationship has ended. Nonetheless, as explained below the EU Directive also recognizes an alternative form of compensation that is not based on this traditional rationale.

In specific, the Directive allows each Member State to choose between a "goodwill indemnity" (the German approach) and "termination compensation" (the French approach). As usual, the parties may not agree to derogate from these rights to the detriment of the agent,[83] but the Directive—contemplating settlements— allows such an agreement after the agency contract has expired.[84]

Indemnity. Most EU Member States have opted for the approach of German law, which grants an agent a right to an "indemnity" upon termination. Again, this approach proceeds from the premise that the agent's efforts during the term of the contract have secured longer-term benefits for the principal (*i.e.*, beyond the formal term of the agency contract). Thus, the right to indemnity does not depend on the reason the agency contract terminated. Instead, the right arises "if and to the extent that":

> (1) the agent has acquired new customers or "significantly increased the volume of business with existing customers" and the principal "continues to derive substantial benefits from the business with such customers,"

> *and*

> (2) the payment of this indemnity "is equitable having regard to all the circumstances." This particularly includes "the commission lost by the commercial agent on the business transacted with such customers."[85]

The key language from this rule is that the principal "continues to derive substantial benefits" from the customers acquired and cultivated by the agent during the term of the agency relationship.

---

[83]   *Id.*, art. 19.

[84]   *Id.*, art. 19.

[85]   *Id.*, art. 17(2)(a).

If this premise is satisfied, the agent is entitled to an indemnity of up to its average annual remuneration over the preceding five years (or over the full contract period if the contract has been in effect for less than that time).[86]

Compensation. The EU Directive allows each EU Member State instead to grant the agent a right to compensation for damages suffered "as a result of the termination of his relations with the principal."[87] No prerequisites exist for this right to compensation, and it does not require proof that the supplier was at fault in terminating the contract. In other words, the right to termination compensation in the Member States that have adopted this approach does not depend on a breach of contract or a tort by the principal; rather, the right arises simply out of a termination of the contractual relationship as such. The European Court of Justice affirmed this point in its significant *Quenon* decision in 2015.[88]

The EU Directive provides that the right to such compensation arises "particularly" when the termination deprives the agent of commissions he would have earned through "proper performance of the agency contract" in activities that would have provided "substantial benefits" to the principal.[89] The agent also is entitled to damages if a termination deprives the agent of the ability "to amortize the costs and expenses that he had incurred for the performance of the agency contract."[90] The idea here is that the agent separately should be able to recover the value of wasted investments made during the contract term at the request of the principal.

The indemnity and compensation models are not pure alternatives, however. The Directive expressly provides that the grant of an indemnity "shall not prevent the commercial agent from seeking damages."[91] In its 2015 *Quenon* opinion, the ECJ thus upheld a statutory scheme in Belgium that granted the right to indemnity but *also* allowed the agent to recover termination compensation. This is permitted, the Court reasoned, provided that the national legislation does not enable the agent to be compensated twice. For commercial agents located in EU Member States that follow this approach, therefore, the agent may recover up to one year's annual commission as an indemnity and, in addition,

---

[86]   *Id.*, art. 17(2)(b).

[87]   *Id.*, art. 17(3).

[88]   *See* Case C–338/14, Quenon K. SPRL v. Beobank SA, EU:C:2015:503 (3 December 2015).

[89]   *Id.*

[90]   *Id.*

[91]   *Id.*, art. 17(2)(c).

compensation for other commissions the agent would have earned over the expected duration of the contract as well as for any wasted expenditures.[92]

The agent nonetheless loses the right to the indemnity or the compensation under the EU Directive if (a) it does not give notice within one year of an intent to assert the rights;[93] (b) the principal terminated the contract "because of default attributable to the commercial agent which would justify immediate termination of the agency contract under national law"; or (c) the agent terminated the contract (unless the principal was at fault for inducing that termination).[94]

As a final point of emphasis, the EU Directive states only a floor, not a ceiling, of protection and only for the matters within its scope. Thus, for example, some EU Member States have extended the protections of the Directive to self-employed agents in the service sector.[95] Some have done so as well for distributorships (not merely self-employed agents). And other countries outside of the EU grant various forms of termination protection and compensation for agents and distributors alike (or do not recognize the distinction in the first place). This again highlights the importance of engaging competent local counsel.

§ 5.13 Law Protecting Agents__Post-Termination Rights of Competition

A final subject commonly addressed by the statutes that protect sales agents is post-termination agreements not to enter into competition with the principal. The EU Directive gives the sense of its general approach to this issue by referring to such an agreement as a "restraint of trade."[96]

The Directive states that such a restraint of trade is enforceable only under three conditions:

    (1) First, it must be concluded in writing.[97]

---

[92]   The right to indemnification or compensation also arises if the termination resulted from the agent's death. *Id.*, art. 17(4).

[93]   *Id.*, art. 17(5).

[94]   *Id.*, art. 18(b) (preserving the rights even though the agent terminated the contract if "such termination is justified by circumstances attributable to the principal"). The right to indemnification or compensation also exists if the agent terminated the contract "on grounds of age, infirmity or illness" such that it could not "reasonably be required to continue" its activities. *Id.* The agent nonetheless loses such rights if, with the agreement of the principal, it assigned all of its rights and obligations under the agency contract. *Id.*, art. 18(c).

[95]   *See* Refit Evaluation, *supra* note 40, at 7.

[96]   *Id.*, art. 20(1).

[97]   *Id.*, art. 20(2)(a).

(2) Second, it must be limited to the agent's defined territory and goods. Specifically, the restriction is only valid "to the extent that" it involves only (a) either "the geographical area" or "the group of customers and the geographical area" entrusted to the agent and (b) "the kind of goods" covered by the agent's contract with the principal.[98]

and

(3) Third, it may not extend for more than two years after the termination of the agent's contract.[99]

But this again is only a floor, not a ceiling. The Directive expressly authorizes the Member States to "impose other restrictions on the validity or enforceability of restraint of trade clauses" or to empower their courts to "reduce the obligations on the parties" under such restraints of trade.[100]

---

[98]   *Id.*, art. 20(2)(b).

[99]   *Id.*, art. 20(3).

[100]   *Id.*, art. 20(4).

Chapter 6

DOCUMENTARY LETTERS OF CREDIT

Table of Sections

§ 6.1   Introduction___The Essential Role of Letters of Credits

Letters of credit play an essential role in facilitating business transactions. As the word "credit" indicates, they are a financing vehicle that provide a guarantee of payment, in this case by a bank, on behalf of a distant, unfamiliar, or untrustworthy buyer. For this reason—as Chapter 1 explained in detail—letters of credit are especially important in international transactions.[1] A federal appellate court once explained their utility this way: "Originally devised to function in international trade, a letter of credit reduced

---

[1]   *See* Chapter 1, §§ 1.1, 1.10.

the risk of nonpayment in cases where credit was extended to strangers in distant places. Interposing a known and solvent institution's (usually a bank's) credit for that of a foreign buyer . . . accomplished this objective."[2]

Although they may support practically any payment obligation, international letters of credit play a particularly important role in international sales of good. In this context, a letter of credit transaction, as one federal court recently summarized, is founded on three separate contractual relationships:

(1) the underlying contract for the purchase and sale of goods between the buyer ("account party") and the seller ("beneficiary"), with payment to be made through a letter of credit to be issued by the buyer's bank in favor of the seller;

(2) the application agreement between the bank and the buyer, describing the terms the issuer must incorporate into the credit and establishing how the bank is to be reimbursed when it pays the seller under the letter of credit; and

(3) the actual letter of credit which is the bank's irrevocable promise to pay the seller-beneficiary when the latter presents certain documents (*e.g.*, documents of title, transport and insurance documents, and commercial invoices) that conform with the terms of the credit.[3]

Chapter 1 explained in detail the overall transaction structure,[4] and should be consulted for context in order to understand fully the examination of the law governing international letters of credit in this Chapter 6. At the center of the tripartite transaction is the bank that issues the credit. The purpose of this Chapter 6, therefore, is to analyze the rules governing the rights and obligations of banks that issue letters of credit in international business transactions.

---

[2] Voest-Alpine Int'l Corp. v. Chase Manhattan Bank, N.A., 707 F.2d 680, 682 (2d Cir. 1983). For more recent observations in the same vein see Great Wall De Venezuela C.A. v. Interaudi Bank, 117 F. Supp. 3d 474, 484 (S.D.N.Y. 2015); ACE American Ins. Co. v. Bank of the Ozarks, 2014 WL 4953566, at *7 (S.D.N.Y. 2014).

[3] Navana Logistics Limited v. TW Logistics, LLC, 2016 WL 796855, at *12 (S.D.N.Y. 2016) (paragraph breaks added for clarity). *See also* Great Wall De Venezuela C.A. v. Interaudi Bank, 117 F. Supp. 3d 474, 485 (S.D.N.Y. 2015); ACE American Ins. Co. v. Bank of the Ozarks, 2014 WL 4953566, at *6 (S.D.N.Y. 2014).

[4] *See* Chapter 1, §§ 1.10–1.18.

§ 6.2   The Law Governing Letters of Credit__ In General

The law relating to letters of credit developed before World War I principally in the courts of England, and thereafter in state and federal courts in the United States.[5] With the advent of the Uniform Commercial Code in the middle of the last century, however, letter of credit law became statutory law in the United States through the adoption of this uniform law by the individual states. In specific, Article 5 of the UCC (as revised in 1995) carefully regulates most rights and obligations arising out of letters of credit. It broadly defines its scope to cover any "definite undertaking . . . by an issuer to a beneficiary at the request or for the account of an applicant . . . to honor a documentary presentation by payment."[6] A letter of credit may be in any form that is authenticated (typically by signature) of the issuer or by agreement or practice.[7]

Nonetheless, as is true with the rest of the UCC, most of Article 5 is not mandatory law; rather, nearly all of its provisions defer to the agreement of the parties as expressed in the terms of their contract.[8]

Moreover, for international letters of credit, the practically more significant rules are found in the Uniform Customs and Practices for Documentary Credits (UCP). The UCP (like the Incoterms[9]) are a set of copyrighted contract terms prepared and published by the International Chamber of Commerce (ICC). The ICC published the original version of the UCP in 1933, and since then has updated approximately every ten years. The most recent version of the UCP is the 2007 Revision.[10]

The UCP applies, by its own terms, to any documentary credit (which it refers to merely as a "credit") "when the text of the credit expressly indicates that it is subject to these rules."[11] The overwhelming majority of international letters of credit in fact contain such an express reference to the UCP.[12] And as the next

---

[5]   *See* John F. Dolan, THE LAW OF LETTERS OF CREDIT §§ 3.01–3.04 (Rev. ed., 1999).

[6]   UCC § 5–102(10).

[7]   UCC § 5–104.

[8]   *See* UCC § 5–103(c).

[9]   For a detailed discussion of the Incoterms, see Chapter 3.

[10]   Uniform Customs and Practices for Documentary Credits (UCP) (ICC Publ. 600, 2007) (hereinafter, UCP 600).

[11]   UCP 600, art. 1.

[12]   *See* Great Wall De Venezuela C.A. v. Interaudi Bank, 117 F. Supp. 3d 474, 485 (S.D.N.Y. 2015) ("The UCP 'applies to most letters of credit . . . because issuers

Section describes in detail, UCC Article 5 explicitly validates an incorporation of the UCP rules into a letter of credit.

Finally, UNCITRAL—the UN institution responsible for the CISG[13]—has drafted a potentially relevant treaty, the United Nations Convention on Independent Guarantees and Stand-by Letters of Credit (1995).[14] Because this treaty principally addresses standby letters of credit, Chapter 7 will examine its provisions in more detail.[15] But if a standard documentary (aka "commercial") credit expressly so states, the treaty may apply in that context as well.[16] As of late 2016, however, only eight countries have ratified the treaty (and not the United States nor any other major trading country).[17]

§ 6.3 The Special Significance of the Uniform Customs and Practices for Documentary Credits (UCP)

The UCP constitutes a rather detailed set of rules that define the rights and obligations of the banks involved in a letter of credit transaction. But its legal status is as a statement of contract terms and banking trade usage, and not as generally applicable positive law. Thus, in an important sense there is no need for a "choice of law" analysis as between the UCC and the UCP. The former is legislation, and the latter merely reflects—through an incorporation by reference—agreed contractual terms. Nonetheless, because most of the provisions in UCC Article 5 are not mandatory law,[18] the UCP provisions would seem to prevail over the "gap-filler" provisions of UCC Article 5 without further analysis.

The unusual aspect of the UCP, however, is that it takes effect by a *unilateral* declaration of a bank in the letter of credit, and not by a contractual agreement with the beneficiary.[19] This would seem to require a more specialized authorization by law, but the UCC

generally incorporate it into their [letters of] credit[ ][.]") (*quoting* Alaska Textile Co. v. Chase Manhattan Bank, N.A., 982 F.2d 813, 816 (2d Cir. 1992)).

[13] *See* Chapter 2, § 2.2. *See also* Chapter 2, § 2.45 (describing other UNCITRAL efforts to unify the law governing international commercial transactions).

[14] Dec. 11, 1995, 2169 U.N.T.S. 190, available at UNCITRAL's website, http://www.uncitral.org/pdf/english/texts/payments/guarantees/guarantees.pdf.

[15] *See* Chapter 7, §§ 7.10, 7.13.

[16] *See* UN Standby Convention, *supra* note 14, art. 1(2).

[17] **As** Chapter 7 explains, in early 2016 President Obama submitted this treaty to the Senate for its advice and consent to ratification. As of late 2016, however, the Senate has taken no action on this treaty whatsoever. *See* Chapter 7, § 7.10.

[18] *See* text accompanying note 8 *supra*.

[19] *Compare* UCC § 1–301(a) (permitting "the parties" to agree that the law of another jurisdiction will govern their transaction).

expressly grants it. Section 5–116 declares that the liability of banks "is governed by any rules of custom or practice, such as the Uniform Customs and Practices for Documentary Credits, to which the letter of credit, confirmation, or other undertaking is expressly made subject."[20] This rule applies even in the case of a direct conflict between the UCC and the UCP, except with respect to the UCC's rare "nonvariable" provisions.[21] Thus, as one New York court recently observed, "[t]he UCP does not have the force of law, but is binding if the terms of a letter of credit explicitly incorporate its provisions."[22]

The rules set forth in the UCC and the UCP nonetheless generally are quite similar in scope and substance, and indeed one key purpose of the 1995 revision of UCC Article 5 was to align its provisions more closely with the UCP. However, some differences remain.[23] Moreover, the UCP does not purport to define a comprehensive regulatory system for letters of credit. UCC § 5–116(c) also makes clear that, even if incorporated in a specific letter of credit, the UCP controls only to the extent of a conflict with the UCC.

The most prominent example of this is that the UCP has no rules that address fraud or forgery or the enjoining of payment by a bank when such issues arise.[24] As a result, UCC Article 5, and not the UCP, will provide the legal rules to resolve issues related to allegations of fraud or forgery in letter of credit transactions. But the UCP provisions will govern the great variety of other letter of credit issues that do not involve fraud. Based on this relationship between the UCP and the UCC, this Chapter 6 will focus on the UCP rules for all non-fraud issues; Chapter 7 (on standby letters of credit) then will review the law governing fraud issues.[25] This division also aligns with the fact that litigation over allegations of fraud is comparatively rare for documentary credit transactions, but occurs with some frequency with standby letters of credit. For the latter cases, the UCC's fraud rules come into play with regularity.

Choice of Background Law. Finally, one provision noticeably absent from the UCP is a term that addresses the background law applicable to the transaction in absence of a party choice of one

---

[20]   UCC § 5–116(c).

[21]   UCC § 5–103(c) (listing the few provisions of Article 5 that the parties may not vary even by express agreement).

[22]   Fortis Bank (Nederland) N.V. v. Abu Dhabi Islamic Bank, 2010 WL 7326395, at *1 (N.Y. Sup. 2010).

[23]   For an important example of such a difference see note 124 *infra.*

[24]   *See* UCC § 5–109(a), (b).

[25]   *See* Chapter 7, §§ 7.11–7.13.

jurisdiction or another. For such choice of law issues, therefore, one must turn to otherwise applicable law. In the United States, the UCC allows the parties, or a bank through the letter of credit alone, to select the law of any jurisdiction as the applicable law.[26] Separately, it provides a default rule if such a choice is not made: The liability of a bank is governed by the law of the jurisdiction where it is "located."[27] In the case of multiple banks with different roles (issuing bank, confirming bank, etc.), this rule creates the very real possibility that no one body of law will govern an entire letter of credit transaction; instead, a series of different laws, each dependent on the location of the involved bank, may apply for each of the different parties' liabilities. Nonetheless, the UCC rule addresses only the liabilities of the issuing bank, a nominated person (including a confirming bank), and an adviser, and does not include the applicant. Apparently, the choice of law for the applicant is left to the contract between the applicant and the issuer, or to general choice of law doctrines.

Outside the United States, foreign courts will use their own choice of law doctrines. In absence of a choice of law clause, the traditional doctrine is that the applicable law is the law of the place of performance of the contract, or, in the letter of credit context, the place of payment of the credit against presentation of the documents. Thus, where only an issuer is involved, the law of the issuer's location is applicable. For a confirmed letter of credit, the law of the confirming bank applies, because that is the jurisdiction in which the beneficiary presents the documents and demands payment.

The traditional doctrine generally applies the same law to all segments of the credit transaction. Article 5 changes this approach, however, and permits the application of different rules to the obligations of the issuer and of the confirmer.[28] This, in turn, could lead, for example, to the use of different standards for determining strict compliance with the requirements of a letter of credit.[29] And the law governing the liability of a nominated bank most often cannot be determined until after the beneficiary has chosen to present the documents to such a bank for honor.

---

[26] UCC § 5–116(a). In contrast to the general choice of law provisions in UCC Article 1 (*see* § 1–301(a)), this provision in Article 5 expressly provides that the jurisdiction whose law is so chosen "need not bear any relation to that transaction."

[27] UCC § 5–116(b). If a bank has more than one, all branches are deemed to be "separate juridical entities." *Id.*

[28] *See* UCC § 5–116(b) and notes 26–27 *supra.*

[29] *See* the discussion of the "strict compliance" standard in § 6.6 *infra.*

Overview of the Different Statuses of Banks. As Section 6.7 below explains in more detail, the UCP recognizes four different types of banks in the letter of credit transaction: an issuing bank; an advising bank; a confirming bank, and a nominated bank.[30] In international transactions, these banks also commonly are in different jurisdictions: (a) An *issuing bank* is usually located in the buyer's jurisdiction; it promises to pay the seller (the beneficiary) according to the terms of the letter of credit.[31] (b) An *advising bank* is usually located in the seller's jurisdiction; it merely advises the seller of the issuance of the credit "at the request of the issuing bank."[32] (c) A *confirming bank* also is usually located in the seller's jurisdiction. Such a bank "adds its confirmation to a credit" and thus makes its own, independent promise to pay the beneficiary according to the terms of the letter of credit.[33] (d) A *nominated bank* is often located in the seller's jurisdiction as well, but may be in a third jurisdiction. The term "nominated bank" broadly covers any bank "with which the credit is available."[34] Thus, a nominated bank may or may not also be a confirming bank.[35]

§ 6.4   The Fundamental Legal Principles of Letter of Credit Law

Two fundamental principles underlie the UCP's regulatory scheme. The first is that the banks' obligations under the letter of credit are independent of the buyer's and seller's obligations under the sale of goods contract—the Independence Principle.[36] The second is that the banks deal only with documents, and not with the goods or any issues concerning performance of the sales contract.[37] Because they are obligated to pay the beneficiary on this basis alone (and thus never see the goods), the banks thus insist on strict compliance with all documentary conditions defined in the letter of credit—the Strict Compliance Principle.[38] Sections 6.5 and 6.6

---

[30]   *See* UCP 600, art. 2.

[31]   UCP 600, arts. 2 (tenth definition), 7. The UCC equivalent is an "issuer." *See* UCC §§ 5–102(a)(9), 5–108(a).

[32]   UCP 600, arts. 2 (first definition), 9. The UCC equivalent is an "adviser." *See* UCC §§ 5–102(a)(1), 5–107(c).

[33]   *See* UCP 600, arts. 2 (sixth definition), 8. The UCC equivalent is a "confirmer." *See* UCC §§ 5–102(a)(4), 5–107(a).

[34]   *See* UCP 600, art. 2 (twelfth definition). The UCC equivalent is a "nominated person." *See* UCC §§ 5–102(a)(11), 5–107(b).

[35]   Again, for more detail on these different statuses of banks in international letter of credit transactions see § 6.7 *infra.*

[36]   UCP 600, art. 4. *See also* In re Central Illinois Energy, L.L.C., 482 B.R. 772, 782 (C.D. Ill. 2012); Jaffe v. Bank of America, N.A. 395 Fed. Appx. 583 (11th Cir. 2010).

[37]   UCP 600, art. 5.

[38]   *See* UCP 600, art. 14(a), (d).

below will examine these two fundamental principles. The subsequent Sections then will analyze the more detailed obligations of the banks that issue, confirm, or otherwise are nominated to accept a presentation of documents under a letter of credit.

§ 6.5 Basic Principles__The Independence Principle

The most fundamental principle of letter of credit law is that the banks' obligations to pay upon the presentation of conforming *documents* is independent of the performance of the underlying transaction for the sale of the *goods*. As a U.S. District Court recently observed, the independence principle "means that a letter of credit 'takes on a life of its own,' endowing the transaction with the simplicity and certainty that are its hallmarks."[39] Indeed, the principle is essential to the very functioning of the system:

> Th[e] independence principle is predicated upon the fundamental policy that a letter of credit would lose its commercial vitality if before honoring drafts the issuer could look beyond the terms of the credit to the underlying contractual controversy or performance between its customer and the beneficiary.[40]

UCP Article 4 accordingly declares that a credit "by its nature is a separate transaction from the sale or other contract on which it may be based." Letters of credit often refer to the underlying contract between the buyer and the seller. But even with such a reference the UCP emphasizes that "[b]anks are in no way concerned with or bound by such contract."[41]

This basic principle carries with it two important corollaries. First, the obligations of an issuing bank or a confirming bank are not subject to claims or defenses by the applicant (the buyer) that the beneficiary (the seller) has not performed its obligations under the sales contract.[42] The banks have made their own, separate undertakings to the beneficiary that they will pay if the beneficiary performs its obligations under *the letter of credit contract,*

---

[39]   In re Central Illinois Energy, L.L.C., 482 B.R. 772, 782 (C.D. Ill. 2012).

[40]   Great Wall De Venezuela C.A. v. Interaudi Bank, 117 F. Supp. 3d 474, 485 (S.D.N.Y. 2015) (*quoting* Township of Burlington v. Apple Bank for Savings, 1995 WL 384442, at *5 (S.D.N.Y. 1995)). *See also* ACE American Ins. Co. v. Bank of the Ozarks, 2014 WL 4953566, at *7 (S.D.N.Y. 2014) ("Th[e] independence principle is universally viewed as essential to the proper functioning of letters of credit and to their particular value.") (*quoting* Semetex Corp. v. UBAF Arab Am. Bank, 853 F. Supp. 759, 770 (S.D.N.Y. 1994)); In re Central Illinois Energy, L.L.C., 482 B.R. 772, 782 (C.D. Ill. 2012) (same).

[41]   UCP 600, art. 4(a).

[42]   *Id.*

regardless of whether it performs its obligations under *the sales contract*. Indeed, this independence principle broadly relates to all events outside of the letter of credit transaction. A U.S. District Court recently summarized the breadth of this principle as follows:

> Because of the "independence principle," an issuing or confirming bank must honor a proper demand even though the beneficiary has breached the underlying contract; even though the insolvency of the account party renders reimbursement impossible; and notwithstanding supervening illegality, impossibility, war or insurrection.[43]

The second corollary of the independence principle runs in the opposite direction: In asserting its claim against a bank, the beneficiary may not rely on rights outside of the letter of credit transaction. UCP Article 4 thus states that the beneficiary "can in no case avail itself of the contractual relationships existing between banks or between the applicant and the issuing bank."

The one exception to the independence principle is for allegations of fraud or forgery. Although the banks' obligations under the letter of credit generally are independent of the sales contract, they may be subject to claims by the applicant (the buyer) that payment under a letter of credit will facilitate a material fraud by the beneficiary (the seller). As noted above,[44] the UCP has no provisions concerning fraud or forgery, and as a result UCC Article 5 (where U.S. law is applicable) will provide the governing rules.[45] Again, Chapter 7 will examine this law governing fraud and forgery in more detail.[46]

§ 6.6   Basic Principles__The Strict Compliance Principle

The second fundamental principle of letter of credit law— closely related to the first—begins with the premise that in fulfilling their obligations the banks deal only with the *documents* required by the letter of credit. UCP Article 5 thus declares, "Banks deal with documents and not with goods, services or performance to which the documents may relate." As Chapter 1 explained, the documents typically required by banks issuing international letters of credit include (1) a negotiable bill of lading (about which see § 6.11 below); (2) a commercial invoice; (3) a packing list; (4) an

---

[43]   ACE American Ins. Co. v. Bank of the Ozarks, 2012 WL 3240239, at *5 (S.D.N.Y. 2012) (*quoting* Alaska Textile Co., Inc. v. Chase Manhattan Bank, N.A., 982 F.2d 813, 815–816 (2d Cir. 1992)) (citations omitted).

[44]   *See* § 6.3 *supra*.

[45]   *See* UCC § 5–109.

[46]   *See* Chapter 7, §§ 7.11–7.13.

insurance policy covering the goods in transit; (5) a certificate of inspection (if required by the sales contract between the buyer and the seller); and, sometimes, (5) a certificate of origin (depending on the trade agreements between the involved countries).[47]

Because the documents are the only basis on which the banks may determine their payment obligations, the law imposes a standard of "strict compliance" with all documentary conditions. Under this longstanding approach of the UCP, "[e]ven slight discrepancies in compliance with the terms of a letter of credit justify refusal to pay."[48]

The modern versions of the UCP, including UCP 600, have embraced a slightly different linguistic formulation for the standard of conformity. As a general matter, the UCP now provides that a presentation of documents must be "in accordance with the terms and conditions of the credit."[49] UCP Article 14(a) then provides more detail. That article first states that the banks must examine a presentation to determine "on the basis of the documents alone" whether or not they appear, "on their face," to constitute a complying presentation. This provision thus makes clear that the banks must assess conformity by looking *only* at the "four corners" of the documents presented by the beneficiary as against the formal text of the letter of credit itself.

Unfortunately, the UCP 600 does not provide an explicit definition of a "complying presentation." Article 14(d) states only that data in a presented document "need not be identical to, but must not conflict with," the terms of other required documents and the letter of credit. The same provision defines the measurement standard as "the context of the credit" and "international standard banking practice."[50] This latter language has generated some judicial and scholarly debate, but, as described below, the prevailing view is that a "strict compliance" standard remains.[51]

The primary document for describing the goods in a documentary sale transaction is the commercial invoice. This is the formal document generated by the seller's accounting department confirming the goods shipped and the amount the buyer owes. The

---

[47]   See Chapter 1, § 1.12.

[48]   See, e.g., Creaciones Con Idea, S.A. de C.V. v. Mashreq Bank PSC, 51 F. Supp. 2d 423, 427 (S.D.N.Y. 1999) (*quoting* Hellenic Republic v. Standard Chartered Bank, 631 N.Y.S.2d 320, 321 (App. Div. 1995)).

[49]   UCP 600, art. 2.

[50]   UCP 600, art. 14(d).

[51]   To provide at least some guidance, the ICC publishes and periodically updates an "International Standard Banking Practice" (ISBP) manual. See ICC Publ. No. 745E (2013).

UCP states that the description in the commercial invoice "must correspond with that appearing in the credit."[52] Descriptions of the goods in all other documents "may be in general terms not conflicting with" the description in the credit.[53] And if a letter of credit requires, but does not provide specifics on, a document other than the commercial invoice, a transport document (usually, a bill of lading), or an insurance document, the UCP provides that the document need merely fulfill the general "function" of such a document.[54]

The archetypical case of the strict compliance doctrine is an English court's determination in the middle of the last century that "machine shelled groundnut kernels" was not the same description as "Coromandel groundnuts," even though merchants in the trade for such goods understood that the two terms meant the same thing.[55] The court there emphasized that the banks are not expected to know, or to find out, what specific terms mean outside of the banking world.

In recent years, the revisions to the linguistic formulation of the compliance standard in the UCP have generated debate about the status of the "strict compliance" test. The specific flash point for controversy has been the language that describes the touchstone of compliance as "international standard banking practice."[56] For guidance, the ICC periodically publishes a booklet entitled the "International Standard Banking Practice (ISBP)";[57] but this manual provides only guidelines and is not authoritative.

In any event, modern opinions (as well as UCC Article 5[58]) have rejected a nascent line in some American cases that seemed to permit payment upon substantial performance by the beneficiary.[59] Instead, the prevailing view among courts and scholars is that the "strict compliance" standard, properly calibrated, continues to apply

---

[52]   UCP 600, art. 18(c).

[53]   UCP 600, art. 14(e).

[54]   UCP 600, art. 14(f).

[55]   J.H. Rayner & Co. Ltd. v. Hambros Bank Ltd. [1943] 1 K.B. 37 (Court of Appeal).

[56]   UCP 600, arts. 2(a), 14(d).

[57]   See ISBP Manual, supra note 51.

[58]   See § 5–108(a) (providing that "an issuer shall honor a presentation that . . . appears on its face strictly to comply with the terms and conditions of the letter of credit" and that "an issuer shall dishonor a presentation that does not appear so to comply"). See also § 5–108, Official Comment 1 ("The standard of strict compliance governs the issuer's obligation to the beneficiary and to the applicant.").

[59]   See Flagship Cruises, Ltd. v. New England Merchants Nat. Bank, 569 F.2d 699 (1st Cir. 1978); Banco Español de Credito v. State Street Bank and Trust, 385 F.2d 230 (1st Cir. 1967), cert. denied, 390 U.S. 1013 (1968).

under the UCP as well.[60] As one recent federal court declared, "[t]he strict compliance standard means that the conditions of the letter of credit must be complied with precisely by all parties; documents that are 'nearly the same' will not suffice."[61]

Nonetheless, a clear typographical error seems to represent the edge of the strict compliance standard. The 2013 edition of the ICC's ISBP manual explains that "a misspelling or typing error that does not affect the meaning of a word or the sentence in which it occurs does not make a document discrepant." It cites as examples a description of goods as a "mashine" instead of "machine" or as a "fountan pen" instead of "fountain pen."[62] This seems to apply, however, only to a case of an obvious typographic or linguistic error. Thus, one court held that an issuer was justified in dishonoring where the letter of credit mistakenly identified the beneficiary as "Sung Jin Electronics," while the documents were correctly addressed to "Sung Jun Electronics."[63] The court found that it was not obvious in the context of the transaction that this reflected a mere linguistic error. More recently, an English court upheld a dishonor where a letter of credit identified the beneficiary as "Bulgrains Co. Ltd." but the presented documents referred to "Bulgrains & Co. Ltd."[64]

What is left, as the court in *Voest-Alpine Trading USA Corp. v. Bank of China* sensibly explained, is "a common sense, case-by-case approach [that] permit[s] minor deviations of a typographical nature because such a letter-for-letter correspondence between the letter of credit and the presentation documents is virtually impossible."[65] That case involved seven different discrepancies in the presented documents as compared to the requirements of the letter of credit. The discrepancies included failures to denote documents as originals, minor misstatements of the names of the parties, adding digits to the letter of credit number, and presenting a survey dated after the bill of lading was issued. Otherwise, however, the documents conformed, such that "the whole of the

---

[60]   *See, e.g.,* Continental Cas. Co. v. SouthTrust Bank, N.A., 933 So. 2d 337, 340 (Ala. 2006); Shin-Etsu Chemical Co., Ltd. v. 3033 ICICI Bank Ltd., 777 N.Y.S.2d 69, 74 (App. Div. 2004). *See also* J. White & R. Summers, UNIFORM COMMERCIAL CODE 1096 (6th ed., 2010) (observing that "although [UCP] Articles 2a and 14d refer to compliance with international banking standards, [this] arguably constitutes strict compliance in today's world").

[61]   ACE American Ins. Co. v. Bank of the Ozarks, 2014 WL 4953566, at *9 (S.D.N.Y 2014) (*quoting* Ocean Rig ASA v. Safra Nat. Bank of N.Y., 72 F. Supp. 2d 193, 199 (S.D.N.Y. 1999)) (internal quotations omitted).

[62]   *See* ISBP Manual, *supra* note 51, at 24.

[63]   Hanil Bank v. Pt. Bank Negara Indonesia, 148 F.3d 127 (2d Cir. 1998).

[64]   *See* Bulgrains & Co. Ltd. v. Shinhan Bank, [2013] EWHC 2498 (QB).

[65]   167 F. Supp. 2d 940, 947 (S.D. Tex. 2000).

documents relate[d] to the transaction."[66] The court thus held that the discrepancies were not sufficient, even under the strict compliance standard, to permit the issuing bank to reject the documents and dishonor.

§ 6.7   The Basic Obligations of Banks

The Issuing Bank. The issuing bank, as the originator of a letter of credit, has the primary obligation to pay the stated amount upon presentation of complying documents. UCP Article 7 thus states that if the presented documents "constitute a complying presentation," the issuing bank "must honour" and thus pay according to the terms of the letter of credit.[67] An issuing bank is "irrevocably" bound to do so "as of the time it issues the credit."[68] The obligation to honor arises either when the conforming documents are presented directly to the issuing bank or when a nominated bank (especially a confirming bank) refuses to take or pay for the documents.[69]

Where another bank is authorized to accept documents and pay under a letter of credit (*i.e.*, in the case of a "nominated bank"), the issuing bank also has an obligation to such a bank. In specific, UCP Article 7(c) provides that the issuing bank "undertakes to reimburse a nominated bank that has honoured or negotiated a complying presentation and forwarded the documents to the issuing bank."[70] The standard example of this is where a confirming bank has first honored a presentation by paying the beneficiary. (The concept of a "negotiation" covers the case where a confirming bank does not simply honor a presentation, but rather purchases the related drafts for its own account—*i.e.*, to make a profit beyond its small fee.[71]) The UCP also explicitly states that the issuing bank's obligation to reimburse a nominated bank "is independent of the issuing bank's undertaking to the beneficiary."[72]

Confirming Bank. Recall that a confirming bank is one that that "adds its confirmation" to a credit at the authorization or

---

[66]   *Id.*, at 947–949. For an analysis of this opinion see Lisa Pietrzak, *Sloping in the Right Direction: A First Look at UCP 600 and the New Standards as Applied to Voest-Alpine*, 7 ASPER REV. INT'L BUS. & TRADE L. 179 (2007).

[67]   The obligation to honor involves either immediate payment or, in the case of an agreed payment at a later date, an "acceptance" of the related draft or other documents. For the concept of acceptance, see Chapter 1, § 1.7.

[68]   UCP 600, art. 7(b).

[69]   UCP 600, art. 7(a)(i)–(v).

[70]   UCP 600, art. 7(c).

[71]   UCP 600, art. 2 (eleventh definition).

[72]   UCP 600, art. 7(c).

request of the issuing bank.[73] A "confirmation" represents an independent obligation, "in addition to that of the issuing bank," to honor a complying presentation under the letter of credit.[74] The confirming bank becomes "irrevocably" bound to do so as soon as it adds its confirmation.[75]

As against the beneficiary, the obligations of a confirming bank parallel those of the issuing bank. Under UCP Article 8, a confirming bank also "must honour" a presentation, provided as always that the documents comply with the requirements of the letter of credit.[76] Like the issuing bank, the confirming bank's obligation to honor arises either when the conforming documents are presented directly to it or when some other nominated bank refuses to take or pay for the documents.[77]

Nominated Bank. Under the UCP, a "nominated bank" is one that the issuer expressly or impliedly authorizes to accept documents presented under a credit. Indeed, the term includes any bank at all if the issuer makes the credit "available with any bank" (aka, a "freely negotiable credit").[78] Thus, a nominated bank may or may not also be a confirming bank. The distinguishing point is that a confirming bank also *obligates itself* in advance to accept a presentation, whereas other nominated banks are authorized, but not obligated, to do so.[79]

The legal position of the nominated bank flows directly from this description. Absent a confirmation or express agreement, the authorization to accept a presentation "does not impose any obligation on th[e] nominated bank to honour or negotiate."[80] Indeed, even the receipt and forwarding of documents by a nominated bank does not constitute an honor or negotiation of the documents.[81]

If, on the other hand, a nominated bank in fact chooses to honor or negotiate complying documents under a letter of credit, it

---

[73]   UCP 600, art. 2 (seventh definition). Again, for an examination of the role of a confirming bank in the standard international letter of credit transaction see Chapter 1, §§ 1.14–1.17.

[74]   UCP 600, art. 2 (sixth definition).

[75]   UCP 600, art. 8(b).

[76]   UCP 600, art. 8(a).

[77]   UCP 600, art. 8(a)(i)–(v). A confirming bank also owes an obligation to reimburse another nominated bank that has honored a complying presentation. This obligation is independent of that owed to the beneficiary. UCP 600, art. 8(c).

[78]   *See* UCP 600, art. 2 (twelfth definition).

[79]   *See* UCP 600, art. 12(a).

[80]   UCP 600, art. 12(a).

[81]   UCP 600, art. 12(c).

is entitled to reimbursement from the issuing bank or a confirming bank.[82]

Advising Bank. Another, though less important, status of a bank in an international letter of credit transaction is as an advising bank. Such a bank merely "advises" the seller-beneficiary of the issuance of the credit "at the request of the issuing bank." It thus makes no promise to pay the beneficiary against the documents.[83] The only obligations of an advising bank are to "satisf[y] itself as to the apparent authenticity of the credit" and to ensure that its advice to the beneficiary "accurately reflects the terms and conditions of the credit."[84]

§ 6.8   The Banks' Obligations upon Presentation of Documents

As noted above, under the UCP banks deal only in documents.[85] Indeed, the UCP's very definition of a "credit" is one that requires a "presentation," a term that relates only to "documents."[86] The UCP also provides a variety of more detailed requirements for letters of credit. These include that the credit must state: (1) either the specific bank(s) with which it is available (*i.e.*, to which bank(s) a presentation may be made) or that it is available with "any bank"; (2) when payment must be made upon presentation (*e.g.*, "on sight" or "30 days after presentation"); (3) an expiry date; and (4) the location of the bank(s) for presentation.[87]

When documents are presented to an issuing bank or to a confirming bank (or another nominated bank that has decided to act upon its nomination), the bank has two principal duties: One is to examine the documents to determine whether they conform to the terms of the letter of credit (see § 6.9 below); the second is to act upon any discrepancies found (see § 6.10 below).

§ 6.9   Obligation to Examine the Documents for Discrepancies

Unfortunately, discrepancies in documents presented under letters of credits are an everyday occurrence. Indeed, some estimates are that over two-thirds of all presentations contain at

---

[82]   UCP 600, art. 7(c), 8(c).

[83]   UCP 600, arts. 2 (first definition), 9.

[84]   *Id.*

[85]   *See* § 6.6 *infra* and UCP 600, art. 5.

[86]   UCP 600, art. 2 (thirteenth definition) (defining a "presentation" as "either the delivery of documents under a credit to the issuing bank or nominated bank or the documents so delivered").

[87]   UCP 600, art. 6(a)–(d).

least one discrepancy,[88] and that one-half of presentations are rejected on this basis. That rate of error should not be surprising if one understands that the presentation may consist of many pages of documents. Moreover, as described above, the prevailing view on the standard for identifying a discrepancy remains "strict compliance" with the terms of the letter of credit.[89]

The existence of a discrepancy in a presentation has direct consequences for the rights of the presenter, the obligations of the bank, and the right of the bank to seek reimbursement from another bank and the applicant (the buyer):

(1) If a presentation strictly complies with the terms of the letter of credit, the bank "must honour" and pay the beneficiary (or "accept" a time draft[90]).[91] In such a case, the bank is entitled to reimbursement from the buyer/applicant. But if the bank refuses to pay in such a case, it will be liable to the presenter ("wrongful dishonor");[92]

(2) If, in contrast, the documents do not comply, the bank "may refuse to honour."[93] In such a case, the presenter has no claim to payment under the letter of credit;[94]

(3) Finally, if the documents do not comply, but the bank nonetheless honors (or waives its right to dishonor), it generally is not entitled to reimbursement ("wrongful honor").[95]

Given the central importance of the assessment of a nonconformity, the UCP provides a variety of more detailed rules on the rights and performance obligations of the banks. The following paragraphs explore these rules.

Examination of Documents Alone. It is worth emphasizing that the first protection of banks is that they must determine the

---

[88]   *See* Ronald J. Mann, *The Role of Letters of Credit in Payment Transactions*, 98 MICH. L. REV. 2494, 2497 (2000) (finding that only twenty-seven percent of presentations conformed to the requirements of the letter of credit).

[89]   *See* § 6.6 *supra.*

[90]   For an examination of the concept of "acceptance" of a draft see Chapter 1, § 1.7.

[91]   UCP 600, art. 15(a), 15(b). Such a bank may also "negotiate," *i.e.*, purchase, the draft from the presenter. *Id.*

[92]   *See* § 6.12 *infra.*

[93]   UCP 600, art. 16(a).

[94]   For other obligations of the banks upon a dishonor (especially notice) *see* § 6.10 *infra.*

[95]   *See* § 6.13 *infra.*

existence of a discrepancy "on the basis of the documents alone."[96] The UCP stresses this point by stating that examination extends only to the "face" of the documents presented.[97] Thus, if an obligated bank finds that a document does not comply, it is under no obligation to investigate other circumstances that may or may not clarify the discrepancy.[98]

Irrelevance of Usages or Customs. The banks also are not responsible for knowing, and are not expected to investigate, the customs or usages that may apply in a particular trade outside of the banking trade. The famous case (noted above) of *J.H. Rayner & Co. Ltd. v. Hambros Bank, Ltd.* thus made clear that the bank there was not bound to know the general merchant's understanding of "Coromandel groundnuts."[99] The UCP has no explicit rule on this point, unlike the UCC.[100] It is nonetheless generally understood that for the UCP as well, as a U.S. District Court has declared, "[t]he bank is not expected or required to be familiar with or to consider the customs of, or the special meaning or effect given to particular terms in, the trade."[101]

Nondocumentary Conditions. As a corollary to the principle that the examination for conformity with the letter of credit involves "the documents alone," the banks may consider only those conditions that may be satisfied by documentary evidence. UCP Article 14 states this rule explicitly: "If a credit contains a condition without stipulating the document to indicate compliance with the condition," the banks must "deem such condition as not stated and . . . disregard it."[102] As a result, letters of credit must state precisely the documents, and the terms of those documents, against which payment is to be made. And if the issuing bank or the applicant (the buyer) wants to condition payment on a certain fact, it must ensure that the fact can be evidenced by a document. Upon a presentation, the banks are obligated to disregard any other form of a condition.

---

[96]   UCP 600, art. 14(a).

[97]   UCP 600, art. 14(a).

[98]   UCP 600 Article 14 also has some highly specific rules on information in a document. *See* UCP 600, art. 14(i) (stating that a required document may be dated before the issuance of the letter of credit, but not after the presentation); 14(j) (stating that the addresses of the beneficiary and the applicant need not be the same as stated in the credit, but must be within the stated country).

[99]   *See* text accompanying note 55 *supra*.

[100]   *See* UCC § 5–108(f)(3).

[101]   Thiagarajar Mills, Ltd. v. Thornton, 242 F.2d 710, 713 (6th Cir. 2001) (*quoting* Marino Indus. Corp. v. Chase Manhattan Bank, N.A., 686 F.2d 112, 115 (2d Cir. 1982)).

[102]   UCP 600, art. 14(h). *See also* In re Central Illinois Energy, L.L.C., 482 B.R. 772, 782 (C.D. Ill. 2012) ("If a letter of credit contains nondocumentary conditions, the issuer is authorized to disregard them and treat them as if they were not stated.").

Anomalous Documents. Another unfortunately common occurrence is that a beneficiary presents a document *not* required by the letter of credit. One might term these "anomalous documents." Derivative of the rule on nondocumentary conditions, the UCP requires that the banks ignore such documents: "A document presented but not required by the credit will be disregarded and may be returned to the presenter."[103]

Original Documents. The UCP 600 has a new provision designed specifically to address controversies over the subject of "original" documents engendered by ambiguities in earlier versions. The new version continues to require the presentation of "at least" one original of each document stipulated in the credit.[104] It also provides special detail on this requirement for the crucial commercial invoice: This document must (1) "appear to have been issued by the beneficiary," (2) "be made out in the name of the applicant," and (3) "be made out in the same currency as the credit."[105] But other provisions temper the seeming strictness of the "original document" requirement. First, one provision removes a requirement of a formal "signature" on the commercial invoice.[106] Two other provisions then require that a bank accept a presented document as an original, in absence of a contrary indication, if (a) it bears "an apparently original signature, mark, stamp, or label of the issuer," or (b) "states that it is original."[107]

Right to Seek a Waiver. In many situations, the discrepancies discovered by the banks are trivial, and the applicant/buyer may want the payment made despite the discrepancy. (Businesses most often are interested in "getting the deal done," not creating lawsuits.) To accommodate this, the UCP allows, but does not require, a bank, "in its sole judgement," to consult the applicant (its customer) for a waiver of discrepancies.[108] In the overwhelming majority of cases, applicants in fact waive the discrepancies discovered by the bank. Thus, the system has continued to work despite the frequency of discrepancies, because the non-bank parties (the buyer and the seller) typically want the transaction to

---

[103]   UCP 600, art. 14(g).

[104]   UCP 600, art. 17(a).

[105]   UCP 600, art. 18(a).

[106]   UCP 600, art. 18(a)(iv).

[107]   UCP 600, art. 17(b), 17(c).

[108]   UCP 600, art. 16(b). Some courts have held that an issuer may not consult in bad faith with the applicant for the sole purpose of discovering discrepancies. *See* E & H Partners v. Broadway Nat. Bank, 39 F. Supp. 2d 275, 284–285 (S.D.N.Y. 1998); Banker's Trust Co. v. State Bank of India, 1 Lloyd's Rept. 578 (1991), *aff'd*, 2 Lloyd's Rept. 443 (Ct. App. 1991).

be completed despite the technical protections offered by letter of credit law.

Errors in Transmission. The UCP has a general provision that protects banks against errors in the transmission of documents or similar technological problems.[109] In specific, Article 35 states that a bank "assumes no liability or responsibility for the consequences arising out of delay, loss in transit, mutilation or other errors arising in the transmission of" a letter of credit or associated communications. The same is true for errors in "translation or interpretation of technical terms."[110] Where the errors occur in the relationship with the beneficiary, these rules seem to provide complete protection to the banks. But as to transmissions *between* banks, the UCP has no specific rule.[111] And the UCC states only that the banks must observe "standard practice of financial institutions that regularly issue letters of credit" and are "not responsible for . . . an act or omission of others."[112]

§ 6.10 Obligation to Give Timely Notification of Discrepancies

The second principal obligation of a bank upon a presentation of documents is that it give timely notice of any discrepancies found. In this respect, UCP 600 provides a variety of important clarifications.

Duty of Notice. First, if a bank decides to dishonor a presentation (*i.e.*, not pay under the letter of credit), the UCP requires that it send a "notice to that effect" to the presenter.[113] This notice must state the following information: (a) that the bank is refusing to honor or negotiate (*i.e.*, purchase) the documents; (b) "each discrepancy in respect of which the bank refuses to honour or negotiate"; and (c) that the bank is either returning the documents to the presenter or holding them pending further instructions from the presenter or the applicant.[114] On this last issue, the UCP 600 has a new provision that allows the bank instead to follow *prior* instructions given by the beneficiary (the seller) or other presenter.[115] (This is separate from the right of the bank to consult

---

[109] As noted in § 6.16 below, most communications between banks occur via the SWIFT system.

[110] UCP 600, art. 35.

[111] The one exception is that a confirming or issuing bank must honor a presentation by a nominated bank even if the documents are lost in transit. *See* UCP 600, art. 35, second para.

[112] *See* UCC § 5–108(e), (f)(2).

[113] UCP 600, art. 16(c).

[114] *Id.*, art. 16(c)(i)–(iii).

[115] UCP 600, art. 16(c)(iii)(d).

the applicant for a waiver of discrepancies.[116]) This is an important provision, for it allows the seller/beneficiary to require direct consultations in order to correct any misunderstandings and to avoid any unnecessary delays occasioned by the bank's reflexive return of the documents.[117]

To ensure that the required notice of dishonor arrives in a timely fashion, the UCP specifies the means for communication. The notice must be sent "by telecommunication," and if this is not possible, "by other expeditious means."[118] As one court thus held, the use of a courier is not sufficiently expeditious to fulfill this obligation.[119]

Single Notice Requirement. UCP 600 also states that the bank has only one opportunity to give a notice of any discrepancy. In specific, Article 16(c) allows the bank to give only "a single notice," which, as noted above, must set forth all discrepancies on which the bank is relying for a dishonor decision. And, as noted below, the bank will be precluded from relying on any discrepancy not included in this single notice.[120]

Timing of Notice. The UCP 600 states a clear rule for the time within which a bank must make a decision on dishonoring a presentation. If it determines that a presentation does not comply, it must give a notice to that effect "no later than the close of the fifth banking day following the day of presentation."[121] This new rule—which replaced a flexible "reasonable time" standard under prior versions—extends to the issuing bank, any confirming bank, and any nominated bank that acts on its nomination.[122] A "banking day" means any day "on which a bank is regularly open" at the location of the presentation.[123] This strict five-day rule for letters of credit covered by the UCP differs from the traditional rule stated in UCC Article 5 ("a reasonable time . . . but not beyond the seventh business day" after presentation).[124] But when the UCP is

---

[116]   *See* the discussion of this right in § 6.9 *supra.*

[117]   For a comprehensive analysis of a bank's obligation regarding return of allegedly discrepant documents see Fortis Bank S.A./N.V. and Stemcor UK Ltd. v Indian Overseas Bank, [2011] EWHC 538 (Comm) (Ct. App.). *See also* Roberto Bergami, *What Can UCP 600 Do for You?*, 11 VINDONOBA J. INT'L L. & ARBITRATION 1, 9 (2007).

[118]   UCP 600, art. 16(d).

[119]   Hamilton Bank, N.A. v. Kookmin Bank, 245 F.3d 82, 89–90 (2d Cir. 2001).

[120]   *See* "Strict Preclusion Rule" immediately below.

[121]   UCP 600, art. 16(d). *See also id.*, art. 14(b) (stating that the banks shall have "a maximum of a five banking days . . . to determine if a presentation is complying").

[122]   UCP 600, art. 16(c), (d). This time period applies even if the letter of credit thereafter expires by its own terms. *See id.*, art. 14(b).

[123]   UCP 600, art. 2 (third definition).

[124]   UCC § 5–108(b).

incorporated in a particular letter of credit, its five-day deadline will prevail because (as discussed in § 6.3 above) the UCC defers to the UCP in the event of conflicts.

As noted above, the UCP allows, but does not require, the bank to consult with the applicant (the buyer) for a waiver of discrepancies. But the UCP makes clear that this does not extend the five-day notice period.[125] Thus, the "five banking days" deadline includes not only time to examine the documents, but also any time required to consult the buyer about waiving the discrepancies and to prepare and dispatch the notice of dishonor. The latter limitations had created difficulties in applying the earlier "reasonable time" standard (which, as noted, continues in the UCC).

Strict Preclusion Rule. UCP 600 also includes a strict rule on the failure of a bank to adhere to the timely notice requirement: If an issuing bank or a confirming bank fails to fulfill that obligation, "it shall be precluded from claiming that the documents do not constitute a complying presentation."[126] This preclusion thus covers both (a) a failure to give notice within the strict five-day period *and* (b) any discrepancies not stated in the allowed "single notice" of dishonor. Any such failure triggers an automatic preclusion for discrepancies not timely stated, and without requiring proof of a waiver or estoppel. Thus, banks that reject documents have only one chance to identify all the discrepancies on which they can ever rely. The rationale for this rule is that the presenter should have notice of all discrepancies at once, so that it can determine whether they are curable and whether the cure is cost-effective. But the rule also can lead the banks to delay notification as long as permitted to ensure that they discover all possible defects.

The strict rule of preclusion has two exceptions. First, because the formal language of the rule refers to "discrepancies," some courts properly have held that the preclusion does not apply if the letter of credit already had expired or been cancelled before the presentation.[127] However, the simple fact that the beneficiary sent documents that were clearly discrepant, or even that the beneficiary knew that they were discrepant, will not excuse an obligated bank from observing the notice requirements.[128] Indeed, one federal

---

125   UCP 600, art. 16(b).

126   UCP 600, art. 16(f).

127   *See, e.g.*, CVD Equipment Corp. v. Taiwan Glass Indus. Corp., 2011 WL 1210199, at *5 (S.D.N.Y. 2011); Todi Exports v. Amrav Sportswear, 1997 WL 61063, at *4 (S.D.N.Y. 1997).

128   *See, e.g.*, LaBarge Pipe & Steel Co. v. First Bank, 550 F.3d 442, 458–463 (5th Cir. 2008) (enforcing the notice requirement and preclusion rule even though the beneficiary knowingly presented discrepant documents); Voest-Alpine Trading USA Corp. v. Bank of China, 288 F.3d 262, 264 (5th Cir. 2002) (same); Hamilton Bank,

appellate court concluded that the preclusion rule for late or incomplete notices of dishonor applies even if the defects in the presented documents were incurable.[129]

Second, the notice requirement does not apply to fraud or forgery. As noted above, the UCP does not address such issues, with the result that otherwise applicable law will govern. Where UCC Article 5 applies, a failure to give a timely notice of dishonor "does not preclude the issuer from asserting as a basis for dishonor fraud or forgery."[130]

Rights of Confirming Banks. The requirement of timely notice of all grounds for dishonor applies as well to a presentation made by a confirming bank (or other nominated bank) to the issuing bank. The UCP does not explicitly address this point. But it states that the notice obligation applies in favor of a "presenter," and defines that term as a "beneficiary, *bank* or other party" that delivers documents to a bank seeking payment under a letter of credit.[131] Moreover, courts that have addressed a presentation by a confirming bank have applied the preclusion rule where the issuing bank failed to adhere to the notice obligations of UCP Article 16.[132] Thus, when, after paying the beneficiary, a confirming bank in turn presents the documents to the issuer, the latter has five banking days to give a "single notice" of all discrepancies on which it relies in refusing to reimburse the confirming bank.[133]

N.A. v. Kookmin Bank, 245 F.3d 82, 89–92 (2d Cir. 2001) (observing that the UCP's preclusion rule "is mandatory and admits of no exception"); Bombay Industries, Inc. v. Bank of New York, 1997 WL 860671, at *3–4 (N.Y. Sup. 1997).

[129] LaBarge Pipe & Steel Co. v. First Bank, 550 F.3d 442, 461–464 (5th Cir. 2008).

[130] UCC § 5–108(d).

[131] UCP 600, art. 2 (thirteenth definition) (emphasis supplied). *See also id.* (fourteenth definition) (defining a "presentation").

[132] *See* CVD Equipment Corp. v. Taiwan Glass Indus. Corp., 2011 WL 1210199, at *3 (S.D.N.Y. 2011) (holding in the case of a presentation by a confirming bank under the UCP that "[t]he rule could not be more clear" that the issuing bank must give notice within five banking days); Fortis Bank SA NV v. Stemcor UK Ltd., [2011] EWHC 538 (Comm) (2011) (applying the preclusion rule in UCP 16(f) to an issuing bank responding to a presentation by a confirming bank); Bank of Cochin, Ltd. v. Manufacturers Hanover Trust Co., 808 F.2d 209, 211–213 (2d Cir. 1986) (precluding an issuing bank from relying on discrepancies in documents presented by a confirming bank because of a failure to give the timely notice required by the UCP).

[133] The UCC addresses this point more clearly. The Official Comments to § 5–108 state that "confirmers [and] other nominated persons . . . can be presenters" and thus also "are entitled to the notice" required of an issuer upon discovery of a discrepancy in a presentation. § 5–108, cmt. 5.

§ 6.11   The Special Role of the Transport Document in Letter of Credit Transactions

As noted in the § 6.1 above (and as analyzed in detail in Chapter 1[134]), letters of credit play an especially significant role in facilitating international sale of goods transactions. But because they serve as an independent payment vehicle for such transactions, the description of the goods in the letter of credit, and therefore in the documents required as a condition to payment, is crucial. As a general matter, the UCP focuses in this regard on whether the seller's commercial invoice "strictly conforms" to the terms of the credit.[135] Nonetheless, the most important document in confirming the actual shipment of the contract goods commonly is the transportation document, precisely because it is issued by an independent third-party carrier. Prior versions of the UCP were premised on ocean bills of lading, evidencing an assumption that the goods would be carried by sea. Modern developments in the transport industry, however, have created new practices, vehicles, and methods. To accommodate these developments, UCP 600 now provides separate, detailed articles for multi-modal transport documents;[136] negotiable ocean bills of lading;[137] non-negotiable sea waybills;[138] charter party bills of lading;[139] air transport documents;[140] road, rail or inland waterway transport documents;[141] and courier receipts, post receipts, and certificates of posting.[142]

For letters of credit covering large international ocean shipments, however, banks traditionally require a negotiable bill of lading.[143] Under the UCP, an ocean bill of lading must name the port of loading, the port of discharge, and the carrier, and be signed by the carrier or its agent.[144] In addition, the document must be "clean," in the sense that banks may only accept such a document if it bears "no clause or notation expressly declaring a defective condition of the goods or their packaging."[145]

---

[134]   *See* Chapter 1, §§ 1.10–1.18.

[135]   *See* UCP 600, art. 18(c) and § 6.6 *supra*.

[136]   UCP 600, art. 19.

[137]   UCP 600, art. 20.

[138]   UCP 600, art. 21.

[139]   UCP 600, art. 22.

[140]   UCP 600, art. 23.

[141]   UCP 600, art. 24.

[142]   UCP 600, art. 25.

[143]   For more on this point see Chapter 1, § 1.13.

[144]   UCP 600, art. 20(a)(i). For more on negotiable bills of lading see Chapter 4, § 4.9.

[145]   UCP 600, art. 27.

Banks have no duty, however, to check the signature or initials accompanying an "on board" notation, absent a special arrangement.[146] The bill of lading also may merely identify an "intended vessel." In such a case, any "on board" notation must specify the vessel on which the goods have been loaded.[147] In any case, the bill of lading must "indicate shipment from the port of loading to the port of discharge stated in the credit."[148] The medieval custom of issuing "a set" of bills of lading (thereby increasing the chance that at least one of them would arrive and be honored) is now disapproved: The UCP requires as a norm only one original bill of lading.[149] In a curiously worded provision, the bill of lading also must contain the terms and conditions of carriage, but "the content" of those terms and conditions "will not be examined."[150]

Nonetheless, as Chapter 4 explained,[151] various forms of nonnegotiable transport documents have become increasingly common in international shipments, and the UCP accordingly contemplates their use in letter of credit transactions.[152] Under U.S. law and practice, the physical transfer of such bill (also known as "waybills") has no legal significance. Thus, banks are wary to allow presentation of nonnegotiable bills under letters of credit, except for transactions involving short distances or air transport where the goods are likely to arrive as soon as the bill of lading.[153] Other countries nonetheless draw a distinction between a "straight" bill of lading (which they consider a document of title, although a non-transferable one) and a waybill (which they consider not to be a document of title at all).[154] In such legal systems, therefore, banks may well be willing to accept the former but not the latter for letter of credit transactions.

Two other modern transportation practices are worthy of mention. A "charter party" bill of lading does not identify the carrier, and thus involves special risks. The UCP nonetheless now recognizes this as a permissible transport document for use with a letter of credit.[155] But it also relieves the banks from any duty to examine the terms of the charter party contract even if presentation

---

[146]   UCP 600, art. 20(a)(ii).

[147]   *Id.*

[148]   UCP 600, art. 20(a)(iii).

[149]   UCP 600, art. 20(a)(iv).

[150]   UCP 600, art. 20(a)(v).

[151]   *See* Chapter 4, § 4.9.

[152]   *See* UCP 600, art. 21.

[153]   For further analysis of this point see Chapter 1, § 1.13.

[154]   *See* Chapter 4, § 4.9.

[155]   UCP 600, art. 22.

is required under the credit,[156] under the assumption that only sophisticated parties with considerable knowledge of the trade will use them.

A second form of increasingly common transport document is a "multimodal" (or "combined transport") document. As Chapter 4 explained in detail,[157] in multimodal transportation arrangements the bill of lading—as its name implies—will cover the goods through "at least two different modes of transport."[158] An example is where the goods are first loaded on a truck and then transferred to a railroad, before being loaded on a ship for ocean transport. Such a bill of lading is likely to be issued by a freight forwarder and not by a single carrier (because many carriers may be involved). Under U.S. law, a freight forwarder that also fulfills the functions of a carrier by issuing a bill of lading is known as a "non-vessel operating common carrier (NVOCC)".[159] Thus, a multimodal bill does not formally name each carrier in the transportation chain and does not represent a receipt directly from such carriers. (The NVOCC instead will obtain a bill of lading from each carrier it engages for a link in the transportation chain.) However, the UCP allows its use if the letter of credit authorizes a signature by a named agent of the carrier and the freight forwarder issues it in that capacity as a multimodal transport document.[160]

§ 6.12   Wrongful Dishonor of a Credit

If the issuing bank or the confirming bank refuses to pay upon presentation of the documents, such a "dishonor" may be rightful or wrongful. If discrepancies in fact exist in the presented documents as against the specifications in the credit, the bank is entitled to dishonor, although to do so it must follow the notice procedures as described in § 6.10 above. If discrepancies in fact exist and the bank follows the procedures, it has no liability on the credit.[161] Most of the cases involving rightful dishonor involve litigation over the timeliness and effectiveness of the notice of dishonor required by the UCP rules.

If, in contrast, the bank refuses to pay when the presented documents in fact strictly comply with the letter of credit, it is in breach of one or more contracts. Most often this occurs at the behest

---

[156]   UCP 600, art. 22(b).

[157]   Chapter 4, § 4.10.

[158]   UCP 600, art. 19.

[159]   *See* again Chapter 4, § 4.10.

[160]   UCP 600, art. 19(a).

[161]   The buyer and the seller nonetheless may pursue their dispute under the sales contact. For this dispute, the CISG or (as applicable) the UCC will govern. *See* Chapter 2, §§ 2.1–2.4.

of its customer (the buyer) because of a dispute in the underlying sales transaction. But as one federal court recently observed, the rule in such a case "is simple: 'If the documents comply with the terms of the credit, the issuer's duty to pay is absolute, regardless of what occurs in the related transaction.' "[162] Thus, if the issuer does not pay in such a case it will be liable to the beneficiary for "wrongful dishonor."

The UCP has no provisions on the formal issue of causes of action, and as a result otherwise applicable law will provide the governing rules. UCC Article 5 expressly gives the beneficiary of a letter of credit whose presentation was wrongfully dishonored a cause of action against the issuer.[163] The elements of the cause of action are straightforward: To succeed on a claim of wrongful dishonor against a defendant bank, the beneficiary/plaintiff "must demonstrate that: (1) there exists a letter of credit issued by the defendant for the benefit of the plaintiff; (2) plaintiff timely presented strictly conforming documents to defendant as required by the letter of credit; and (3) defendant failed to pay plaintiff as provided by the letter of credit."[164]

The UCC provides in such a case that the aggrieved beneficiary may recover as damages "the amount of money that is the subject of the dishonor."[165] The beneficiary has no obligation to mitigate damages, but if it in fact avoids part of the loss, the recovery is reduced by the amount of the loss avoided. In addition, the aggrieved beneficiary can recover incidental damages and interest, but not consequential damages.[166] Thus, the damages allowed by the UCC for a wrongful dishonor may not provide compensation for all losses suffered by the beneficiary.

If the issuer wrongfully dishonors a presentation, the applicant (the buyer) also may be damaged. The most common harm is to the applicant's reputation in the trade, typically in the form of an unwillingness of suppliers to accept subsequent letters of credit from the buyer. Prior to the revision of UCC Article 5 in 1995, the consensus view was that, because it was not a formal party to the letter of credit, the applicant could not bring an action on the letter

---

[162]   Great Wall De Venezuela C.A. v. Interaudi Bank, 117 F. Supp. 3d 474, 485 (S.D.N.Y. 2015) (*quoting* ACE Am. Ins. Co. v. Bank of the Ozarks, 2014 WL 4953566, at *6 (S.D.N.Y. 2014)).

[163]   UCC § 5–111(a).

[164]   ACR Systems, Inc. v. Woori Bank, 2015 WL 1332337, at *5 (S.D.N.Y. 2015). *See also* Heritage Bank v. Redcom Labs., Inc., 250 F.3d 319, 325 (5th Cir. 2001) (same).

[165]   UCC § 5–111(a).

[166]   *Id.*

of credit itself for wrongful dishonor.[167] Instead, the applicant's right to sue the issuer for wrongful dishonor would arise out of (and follow the terms of) the credit application agreement, and would be analyzed under ordinary contract law. In fact, issuing banks commonly require the applicant to enter into "reimbursement agreements" that broadly cover their relationship.

The 1995 version of UCC Article 5 reverses this reasoning. UCC § 5–111(b) states that if the issuer wrongfully dishonors a presentation, the applicant also "may recover damages." The most important aspect of this rule is that the applicant may recover only incidental damages, and not consequential damages, even if foreseeable.[168] Thus, the applicant's recovery for the most common form of harm—damage to reputation—would seem to be foreclosed in the statutory right of action. However, the contract cause of action under the credit application agreement may survive the enactment of the statutory cause of action, because the Official Comments state that "this section does not bar recovery of consequential or even punitive damages for breach of statutory or common law duties outside of this article."[169] But because most rules of UCC Article 5 defer the agreement of the parties,[170] the contract between the issuer and the applicant may place noteworthy restrictions on the right of the applicant to seek damages for wrongful dishonor.

§ 6.13 Wrongful Honor of a Credit

If the issuing or confirming bank honors a presentation under a letter of credit and pays the beneficiary (or accepts a time draft[171]), its actions may be rightful or wrongful. If no discrepancies exist between the documents presented and the specifications in the credit, the banks are obligated to honor the presentation. They then are entitled to reimbursement from the applicant. In such a case, the beneficiary also has received payment or the acceptance of its time draft, so its claims should be satisfied and no litigation on the credit should ensue.

The bank then will seek reimbursement from the applicant under the credit application agreement or applicable law. If the documents conform to the credit, and thus the bank rightfully honored the beneficiary's presentation, the applicant has no defense

---

[167] *See, e.g.*, Interchemicals Co. v. Bank of Credit, 635 N.Y.S.2d 194 (App. Div. 1995).

[168] UCC § 5–111(b).

[169] *Id.*, Official Comment 4.

[170] § 5–103(c).

[171] *See* Chapter 1, § 1.15.

to the reimbursement claim. The issuer has performed its contractual obligation to the applicant and is entitled to the counter-performance (reimbursement). The UCC expressly recognizes this right.[172] Practical challenges nonetheless may exist for the issuer in asserting this right. If, for example, the issuer granted credit to the applicant, the issuer has consciously taken the risk that the applicant might be unable to pay. To avoid this risk, the issuer should insist on a pledge of collateral, obtain a third party's guarantee, or demand pre-payment.

On the other hand, if the documents have discrepancies and the issuer honors the beneficiary's presentation anyway, that is a wrongful honor. The issuer nonetheless may seek reimbursement from the applicant and may have the practical ability to debit the applicant's account with the bank. This would force the applicant to litigate in order to obtain a recrediting of its account.[173]

Curiously, the UCP has no provisions that directly address the subject of reimbursement of the issuing bank. It merely states that a "complying presentation" is one that does not "conflict with" the terms of the letter of credit under "international standard banking practice."[174] If this is the case, the UCP expressly recognizes that a confirming bank or other nominated bank that has honored a presentation is entitled to reimbursement from the issuing bank.[175] But it has no express rule on the right of the issuing bank to obtain reimbursement from the applicant.

UCC Article 5 also leaves at least some room for dispute on the issue. Its structure reflects a principle that the issuer is entitled to reimbursement only if it honored a complying presentation. Thus, it states that the issuer "shall dishonor a presentation that does not appear . . . to comply."[176] It then provides that the issuer is entitled to reimbursement only if it has honored a presentation "as permitted or required" in Article 5.[177] From this foundation, § 5–111(b) grants to the applicant a cause of action for damages in the event of a "wrongful honor." But this rule states that the right to

---

[172] *See* UCC § 5–108(i).

[173] For examples of wrongful honor claims see Steel v. ProTrade Steel Co., Ltd., 2016 WL 2944237 (N.D. Ohio 2016); Oei v. Citibank N.A., 957 F. Supp. 492 (S.D.N.Y 1997).

[174] UCP 600, art. 14(d).

[175] UCP 600, art. 7(c).

[176] UCC § 5–108(a).

[177] UCC § 5–108(i).

damages is founded on a "breach of [the issuer's] obligation to the applicant."[178]

The uncertainty comes from the fact that the UCC's statutory rights and obligations are subject to the parties' agreement. As a result, the terms of the credit application agreement (or "reimbursement agreement") may be more important than the provisions of either the UCC or the UCP. In specific, such agreements may include a disclaimer of, or limitation on, the liability of the issuer for wrongful honor, and thus may create a contractual right to reimbursement where no statutory right exists. Nonetheless, the UCC contains (unusually) a mandatory rule that limits bank's ability to exculpate itself through such agreements. In specific, § 5–103(c) denies effect to any term in an agreement "generally excusing liability or generally limiting liability for failure to perform obligations" set forth elsewhere in Article 5. This should disallow an agreement that grants a bank a blanket right to reimbursement notwithstanding its violation of the statutory obligation to dishonor a noncomplying presentation.

If the issuer has wrongfully honored the beneficiary's presentation, and cannot obtain reimbursement from the applicant, it nonetheless may seek to recover from the beneficiary. Such a right in favor of the issuer may exist directly against the beneficiary on a breach of warranty, or indirectly as an assignee or subrogee of the applicant's rights. The UCC provides that the beneficiary gives a warranty to the issuer that there is no fraud or forgery of the documents; but that warranty is not so broad as to cover all discrepancies in the documents, or even simple breach of contract.[179] The beneficiary also gives a warranty to the applicant, but the warranty is different in substance. The beneficiary warrants to the applicant only that the documents do not violate the sales contract or other agreement.[180] The difference between these warranties arises from a goal of promoting finality to the letter of credit transaction, so that litigation between parties to the letter of credit transaction is not infected with disputes over the sales transaction.[181]

---

[178]   UCC § 5–111(b). For examples, see Imptex Intern. Corp. v. HSBC Bank USA, N.A., 859 N.Y.S.2d 147 (App. Div. 2008); Oei v. Citibank, N.A., 957 F. Supp. 492 (S.D.N.Y. 1997).

[179]   UCC § 5–110(a)(1).

[180]   UCC § 5–110(a)(2).

[181]   UCC § 5–110, Official Comment 2.

§ 6.14   Other Letter of Credit Concepts and Terminology

A complete understanding of international letters of credit also requires familiarity with a range of specialized terminology. First, although the UCP presumes that letters of credit are irrevocable,[182] the parties instead may expressly agree that a letter of credit is revocable. The latter gives the beneficiary a right to payment, but only until it is cancelled by the issuer or applicant—something beneficiaries rarely are willing to accept.

Letters of credit may be payable by sight draft (on demand) or time draft (*e.g.*, one month after presentation of documents). In a time draft transaction, the issuing bank does not pay on presentation, but rather must "accept" the draft that accompanies the documents. This makes the bank liable to pay at the prescribed later time. The beneficiary then can negotiate (sell) the accepted draft to another financial institution to raise cash immediately. A "general" letter of credit is freely transferable by the beneficiary, while a "special" letter of credit limits permissible transferees, usually to one or more banks. A letter of credit "expires" when the time period stated therein for the presentation of drafts and other documents has passed.

A broker of goods may rely on a "back-to-back" letter of credit arrangement to finance an entire transaction without using (or even having) any of its own capital. By definition, a broker buys goods in one transaction and sells them in another. If a broker is able to structure the two deals such that it is, first, a beneficiary of a letter of credit in the downstream sales transaction (in which it is the seller), it can use this credit as collateral for a bank to issue a letter of credit to support the upstream transaction (in which the broker is the buyer). Both the terms and the timing, however, can be tricky. The broker must ensure that the bank credit in the downstream sale is set up *before* it is obligated to arrange for a bank credit to support the upstream purchase. In addition, it must ensure that the documents required by the two letters of credit are identical, such that it can use the exact documents from the upstream transaction to satisfy the requirements in the downstream letter of credit.

Back-to-back credits also can become unworkable if one of the credits is amended, and no similar amendment is made to the other credit. Thus, most banks prefer not to use the back-to-back letter of credit transaction. Instead, they recommend that sellers and

---

[182]   UCP 600, art. 7(b).

brokers obtain financing through a "transferable letter of credit" or an "assignment of proceeds" from a letter of credit.

A transferable letter of credit is one that expressly states that it can be transferred by the original beneficiary to a third party, who then becomes a new and substitute beneficiary.[183] Thus, a broker who is the beneficiary of a transferable letter of credit can use its rights under that credit to finance the purchase of the goods from suppliers by transferring all or part of its rights under the downstream credit to the upstream suppliers. Partial transfers are allowed, so the broker can use this device to finance purchases from several suppliers. However, although substitute commercial invoices and drafts may be used, all other necessary documents ultimately will be presented—through the issuing bank—to the original account party (applicant), which will reveal the identity of the substitute beneficiary. That may compromise commercially sensitive information, and so brokers tend to avoid use of such credits.

The beneficiary of a letter of credit instead may irrevocably assign a portion of the credit's proceeds to a third party. If the proceeds are assigned, an advising bank notifies the assignee of the assignment. Thus, a broker who is the beneficiary of a letter of credit that permits assignment of proceeds can use its rights under that credit to finance the purchase of the goods from a supplier by assigning a part of the broker's rights under the letter of credit to the upstream supplier. The assignment of proceeds does not change the parties to the letter of credit. Nonetheless, the issuer of the letter of credit is obligated to pay only if it receives documents that conform to the credit; thus, the assignee will not be paid unless it ships the goods using conforming documents. The assignee is not a party to the letter of credit and may not know what the terms of the credit are, so it must trust the broker (the beneficiary) to both accurately convey the content of and then later fulfill those terms. The assignment is not governed by the UCP, but by the applicable law of contract. Under the UCC, an issuer of a letter of credit need not recognize an assignment of proceeds until it consents to the assignment.[184]

Rapid expansion of turn-key construction contracts (*e.g.*, for building a complete steel mill or cement plant, such that a buyer need only to "turn a key" to begin plant operation) has expanded the use of "revolving" letters of credit. This form of a credit serves as a vehicle to enable contractors to receive progress payments promptly

---

[183]   UCP 600, art. 38. *See also* UCC § 5–112.
[184]   UCP 600, art. 39. *See also* UCC § 5–114.

as sequential construction phases are completed, and in turn to support further construction phases.

Revolving letters of credit are usually sight letters (*i.e.*, payable immediately upon a conforming presentation) that work in the same way and are subject to the same legal rules as fixed amount letters of credit. The principal difference relates to the amount of the credit and how much the beneficiary may draw at any given time. They commonly are used when an importer (often a developing country's government) imports services (*e.g.*, the building skills of a construction company) and raw materials rather than finished goods. The letter of credit is, however, funded in stages. Each time the construction company (the beneficiary) performs a defined set of services and then draws on the letter of credit for payment, the importer (the applicant under the letter of credit) is obligated to ensure that the issuing bank restores the amount of the letter to an agreed credit level in favor of the beneficiary. Revolving letters sometimes require presentation of specific documents such as certificates of construction phase completion (often prepared by a supervising architect). But a variety of administrative challenges of obtaining such interim certifications prompts many contractors to seek less formal arrangements, ones that may require the applicant to trust the contractor not to draw upon the letter before such action is appropriate. In such a case, the payment ceiling (amount of credit) under the revolving letter may be a substantially smaller amount than the total value of the construction contract.

§ 6.15   Letters of Credit and Electronic Commerce

Electronic communications have taken over some aspects of letter of credit practice, but not others. They dominate the issuance process in bank-to-bank communications, and are sometimes used by applicants to initiate the issuance process. However, for a variety of reasons banks and other interested parties have not yet been able to create an entirely paperless transaction. First, the beneficiary still commonly wants a piece of paper—or at least an electronic version of one, such as one in a pdf. form—committing the banks to pay upon specified conditions. Second, even with an electronic letter of credit, most industries have not accepted electronic forms in the place of the significant documents typically required by a letter of credit. The principal example is an electronic negotiable bill of lading, which, for the reasons discussed in Chapter 3, has not yet found broad or stable acceptance (although some promising platforms now exist).[185] Thus, in the presentation phase for letters

---

[185]   *See* Chapter 4, § 4.15.

of credit, the parties commonly still use physical documents, while funds settlement (payment) likely will be electronic.

Over three quarters of letter of credit communication between banks—including the issuance, advice, and confirmation of letters of credit—is paperless; and nearly all informal communication is electronic. While bank-to-bank communication is electronic, bank-to-beneficiary (seller) communication is still paper-based (or, again, electronic "paper-like-based" as noted immediately above). Letter of credit issuers now can communicate directly with beneficiaries' computers, however, and use of this practice is both widespread and increasing. The UCP rules also now expressly contemplate "teletransmission," which will continue to facilitate the use of electronic communications and documents.[186]

§ 6.16   The SWIFT Bank Communication System

Most bank-to-bank communications concerning letters of credit are routed through the dedicated lines of SWIFT (the Society for Worldwide Interbank Financial Telecommunication). SWIFT is a Belgian not-for-profit organization owned by banks as a cooperative venture for the transmission of financial transaction messages. It requires all such messages to be structured in a uniform format, and uses standardized elements for allocating message space and for message text. Each bank in the system has a unique SWIFT bank code (*e.g.*, Citibank in New York = CITIUS33), and each type of message has a unique number (*e.g.*, Issuance of Letter of Credit = MT700). Each message type has a set of uniform fields tailored to specific information relevant to that type (*e.g.*, in the standard letter of credit (MT700), 45A = Description of Goods and Services). In this way, banks may communicate their inter-bank messages on a computer-to-computer basis without human intervention.

A bank issuing a letter of credit communicates that message to the nearest SWIFT access point. The message is then routed on a dedicated data transmission line to a regional processor, where it is validated (see below). From the regional processor, it is routed over a dedicated line to one of three main data centers, one each in the United States, the Netherlands, and Switzerland. From there it is routed through a regional processor to a SWIFT access point and then to the receiving bank.

A bank that receives a SWIFT electronic letter of credit message need not send a reply stating that it accepts the request to confirm (or merely advise) or the authorization to negotiate or pay

---

[186]   UCP 600, art. 11.

the letter of credit.[187] It need only to perform by advising, confirming, negotiating, or paying. However, the SWIFT messages only transmit the letter of credit and their authorizations and requests. SWIFT messages do not effect the settlement of payments under letters of credit or other transfers of funds between issuing banks and other banks. SWIFT is not a clearing house for bank settlements like, for example, CHIPS (Clearing House for Interbank Payment Systems). Under the SWIFT letter of credit system, participating banks must use other arrangements (such as CHIPS) to settle their accounts and accomplish a transfer of funds.

SWIFT relies upon both encryption of messages and authentication to provide security to its users. The authentication of SWIFT messages is accomplished by the use of algorithms, which are mathematical formulas that calculate the contents of a message from header to trailer. If a SWIFT message requires authentication, and all letter of credit messages do, the issuing bank computes the contents and compiles a result based on the number of characters and data fields. At the regional processor, SWIFT checks the authentication trailer for the number of characters in the authentication. However, a more rigorous authentication will be performed by the receiving bank, using an algorithm contained in an authentication key provided by the issuing bank. The computations involving these authentication procedures will indicate a mismatch if the message is fraudulent or has been altered. There are also login procedures, application-selection procedures, message numbering and error-checking capabilities, and control of access to the system hardware. SWIFT also retains records of each transaction. In all, the security devices are numerous and complex.

Most SWIFT messages are delivered within minutes of their issuance by a bank, although longer delays are possible. Thus, delays in the system are slight, but present.

Under SWIFT rules, Belgian law governs all relations between SWIFT and its users. SWIFT is liable for negligence or fraud of its own employees and agents and for those parts of the communication system that it controls, such as regional processors, main switches, and the dedicated lines that connect them. But SWIFT disclaims liability for those parts of the communication system that it does not control, such as the bank computers that issue and receive messages and the dedicated lines from bank to a regional processor. Even where SWIFT is liable, its liability is limited to "direct"

---

[187] For an examination of these various statuses of banks under letters of credit see § 6.7 *supra*.

damages (loss of interest); the contracts with SWIFT thus expressly disclaim liability for indirect, special, or consequential damages.

It is now possible for an applicant (*e.g.*, the buyer in a sales transaction) to draft a proposed electronic letter of credit. The proposed electronic credit then can be transmitted to the issuing bank for issuance through the SWIFT system. This procedure is usually used where the applicant seeks multiple credits and there is a master agreement between the issuing bank and the applicant. The issuing bank will first check to see whether the proposed credit is authorized and contains the required security codes. Then, it will determine whether it is within the previously authorized credit limits and is stated in the standardized elements and uniform format for electronic messages. Both SWIFT and UCP requirements must be analyzed, and changes in the proposed message may be necessary.

On the other end of the electronic communications, the seller-beneficiary—which must be induced to part with value (*i.e.*, ship the goods) on the basis of the bank's promises—wants a "hard copy," a written letter of credit in the traditional form. The receiving bank (such as a confirming bank) will, therefore, convert the SWIFT electronic message into such a written, paper credit (although, once again, today this may be in an electronic pdf. Form). However, the SWIFT message has been designed for bank-to-bank use, and not necessarily for use by beneficiaries, which creates some problems. First, the message does not bear a signature in the traditional sense, even though it has been thoroughly authenticated within the computer-based transmission mechanisms. Thus, the beneficiary is entitled to doubt whether the sending bank is bound to the beneficiary to perform by the written credit derived from the SWIFT electronic message.

The fact that the SWIFT message is in electronic form should not be an issue. The UCP clearly contemplates electronic credits.[188] And UCC § 5–104 expressly provides that a letter of credit "may be issued in any form," including an electronic format. UCC § 5–106(a) in turn makes clear that such an electronic credit "is issued and becomes enforceable" when the issuer "transmits it," not when it is delivered to the receiving bank; and for their part, SWIFT rules do not require a reply. This UCC rule conforms to the understanding of bankers involved in the trade.

But from the perspective of the beneficiary the key question is this: Is the SWIFT message *the* operative credit instrument? This question is of importance to beneficiaries not only in the original

---

[188]   *See* UCP 600, art. 11.

issuance of the credit, but also in any amendments to the credit that may follow. Under SWIFT rules, SWIFT users treat the electronic message as a binding obligation, and treat the authentication by the issuer as the functional equivalent of a signature. However, the beneficiary is not a SWIFT user, and banking practice has been that a beneficiary can rely on an electronic message only after it has been issued in a paper-based format, properly signed or otherwise authenticated. The UCC rule that a letter of credit "may be issued in any form," including an electronic format, does not necessarily answer the question of whether a SWIFT message transmitted between banks is the operative credit instrument and binds the issuing bank.

Under the UCP, whether an electronic message is the operative credit instrument or not depends upon the terminology in the message itself. UCP Article 11(a) states a basic rule that an authenticated electronic message "will be deemed to be the operative credit," and that "any subsequent mail confirmation shall be disregarded."[189] It also provides, however, that if the electronic message states "full details to follow (or words of similar effect)," then the electronic message will not be the operative credit. In such a case, the issuing bank "must then issue the operative credit . . . without delay in terms not inconsistent" with the electronic message.[190]

However, there is some doubt as to whether SWIFT-generated transcriptions are subject to the UCP. SWIFT internal rules provide that credits issued through its system are subject to the UCP, but the transcription into a hard copy may bear no reference to the UCP. And UCP Article 1 states that the UCP provisions govern "where the text of the credit expressly indicates that it is subject to these rules."

§ 6.17 Efforts Toward an Electronic Letter of Credit

Chapter 4 discussed the attempts to create an electronic bill of lading.[191] If successful, an electronic bill of lading could facilitate the development of a totally electronic letter of credit transaction. However, while an electronic bill of lading can replace a nonnegotiable bill of lading, many market participants remain skeptical about its ability to replace a negotiable bill of lading (at least for large transactions). A number of institutions and business have tried, thus far without great success, to replicate the security

---

[189] UCP 600, art. 11(a).

[190] *Id.*

[191] *See* Chapter 4, § 4.15.

of paper-based negotiable bills of lading (although some are showing promise). In any event, some change may be on the horizon. As described in Chapter 4, the new provisions of UCC Articles 1 and 7 on "electronic documents of title" as well as the new "Rotterdam Rules" of 2009 may provide a stable legal foundation for a broader acceptance of electronic bills of lading in the future.[192] If these efforts gain traction, a fully electronic letter of credit transaction will not be far behind.

For its part, the ICC in 2002 and again in 2007 issued a Supplement to the UCP specifically tailored to electronic transactions—the Uniform Customs and Practice for Documentary Credits for Electronic Presentation. This "eUCP" is designed to "accommodate presentation of electronic records alone or in combination with paper documents." Thus, the eUCP permits a beneficiary to present equivalent "electronic records" for any required document. Its rules apply, however, only if a letter of credit specifically refers to it, not merely to the general UCP.

Separately, in July 2013, SWIFT and the ICC jointly issued a new electronic financing platform along with corresponding rules, the Uniform Rules on Bank Payment Obligations (URBPO).[193] This platform is designed to permit high-frequency corporate users—if agreed by both parties to the underlying transaction—to participate with banks in an entirely electronic financing transaction. In specific, it will allow sellers/exporters to present electronic documents or data and thus dispense with traditional hardcopy bills of lading and the like. It functions through the bank for the seller and the bank for the buyer each submitting data to the electronic platform (the transaction matching application, or TMA) on the underlying transaction. If the data match, the buyer's bank becomes irrevocably bound to the pay under the terms of the BPO. Upon shipment of the goods, the seller electronically communicates the relevant shipment data to its bank, which electronically uploads that data to the TMA. If the data match the original requirements, the TMA will send a notification to all of the parties, which triggers the formal payment obligation of the buyer's bank.

The ultimate goal of the BPO system is to replace the formal structure of international letters of credit with electronic (and increasingly automated) financing transactions. This system, however, differs from existing letters of credit in fundamental ways. First, and most important, the obligations under a BPO transaction exist solely between the involved banks. The seller in the underlying transaction has no direct claim against the buyer's bank

---

[192]   *See id.*
[193]   ICC Publication No. 750E (2103).

or, for that matter, its own bank. This contrasts sharply with the UCP and the UCC. Under both, the beneficiary of a letter of credit (the seller in a sales transaction) has a direct claim against the issuing bank.[194] And, in the common case of a confirmed credit in international transactions, the seller also has a direct claim against the confirming bank (which is located in its geographic area).[195]

Second, the ease of automation under the BPO in fact may be a liability. Because the data must match exactly, even the slightest errors can upset the payment transaction. In this way, it removes the necessary, although appropriately limited, flexibility of the presentation process under letters of credit. As noted above, even under the "strict compliance" standard obligated banks must honor a presentation notwithstanding a technical discrepancy if it is merely typographic or linguistic in nature.[196] This exercise of human judgment permits the letter of credit transaction to fulfill its essential role, without compromising its essential principles. For these reasons, the extent to which the new BPO system will find acceptance as an alternative to traditional letters of credit—except as between parties with established relationships—remains to be seen.

---

[194]   *See* §§ 6.7, 6.8, and 6.12 *supra.*
[195]   *See id.*
[196]   *See* § 6.6 *supra.*

Chapter 7

STANDBY LETTERS OF CREDIT

Table of Sections

§ 7.1   Introduction

Foreign governments, or other buyers or developers with sufficient bargaining power, often require a financial guarantee by multinational enterprises (MNEs) that they will supply goods, perform services, or construct a project competently and in accordance with the terms of the governing contract. Performance bonds can serve as an adequate assurance, but under prior U.S. federal law, banks were not allowed to issue guarantees, performance bonds, or insurance policies.[1] In response, however, banks developed an alternative: the "standby" (or stand-by) letter of credit. This form of a letter of credit is issued by the seller's (or other performer's) bank and runs in favor of the purchaser—truly a backwards arrangement as compared to the commercial letters of credit described in Chapter 6 above.

Like the traditional commercial (aka documentary) letters of credit examined in Chapter 6, standby letters of credit are

---

[1]   *See* 12 U.S.C. § 24 (Seventh).

mechanisms for allocating risks among parties in commercial transactions. By arranging for a payment by a neutral third party, if and when specified conditions are met, one party to a transaction is able to avoid the risk of nonpayment or nonperformance by the other.

A standby credit, however, is payable against a writing that certifies that the seller or other performer has not performed its obligations. Such a credit is not for the purpose of ensuring that *the buyer* performs its payment obligation to the seller upon shipment of goods; instead, it is used as a form of guarantee or insurance that *the seller* will perform its obligations to a foreign government or other buyer or developer. Thus, although once not allowed to issue guarantees, performance bonds, or insurance policies, banks came to achieve essentially the same end through standby letters of credit. The result was the creation of a new commercial device, which is now commercially accepted for its own value and has supplanted the performance bond in many fields of endeavor. In short, the standby letter of credit has become an indispensable tool for financing international commercial transactions.

§ 7.2   The Transaction Pattern of a Standby Letter of Credit

As noted in the Introduction, the financial assurance in a standby letter of credit runs in the opposite direction of a standard documentary letter of credit: Instead of assuring performance by the buyer (*i.e.*, payment), it backstops ("stands by") the performance by the seller (or other performing party). In international commerce, standbys often serve to back up a local "performance guarantee" issued by a foreign bank to support a construction or similar development project. As one U.S. court has observed, "such guarant[e]es, which are common in international construction contracts, provide a simple way for a buyer to obtain cash for substitute performance if a contractor defaults."[2]

These local financing devices under the civil law are known by a variety of names in different countries (guarantee on first demand, demand guarantee, independent guarantee, or performance guarantee); but they are the functional equivalent of standbys. Indeed, courts in the United States have held in light of this functional equivalence that demand guarantees are subject to letter of credit law (especially UCC Article 5, see § 7.5 below).[3] The

---

[2]   American Express Bank Ltd. v. Banco Español de Credito, S.A., 597 F. Supp. 2d 394, 401–402 (S.D.N.Y. 2009).

[3]   *See* Banque Paribas v. Hamilton Industries International, Inc., 767 F.2d 380, 384–386 (7th Cir. 1985); American Express Bank Ltd. v. Banco Espanõl de Credito, S.A., 597 F. Supp. 2d 394, 401–403 (S.D.N.Y. 2009).

ICC also has issued a set of standard customs and practices for such guarantees, the Uniform Rules for Demand Guarantees (URDG)©, which an issuer may incorporate by simple reference.[4]

The following diagram illustrates the standard transaction structure for a local performance guarantee backed by an international standby letter of credit—from the issuance stage through to demand and payment:

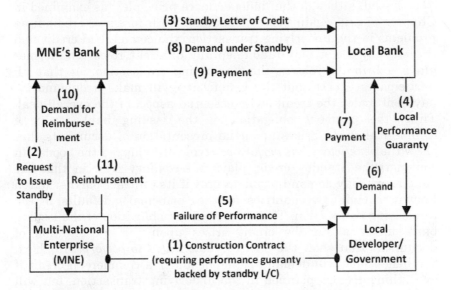

This transaction is almost the exact reverse structure of the letter of credit in the documentary sale as described in Chapters 1 and 6.[5] In the standby credit, the account party (applicant) is the seller or contractor, the beneficiary is the purchaser (not the seller), and—as described immediately below—the documents typically involved have no independent value of their own.

§ 7.3 Differences with a Commercial Letter of Credit

A standby letter of credit serves a quite different, though equally important, function in international business transactions as compared to a standard commercial (aka documentary) letter of credit. As illustrated in the transaction diagram above, a standby is a credit that is issued by the *seller's bank* and runs in favor of the *buyer*. It is payable against a writing certifying that the seller has not performed its contractual promises.

---

[4]   The most recent edition is "URDG 758." *See* ICC UNIFORM RULES FOR DEMAND GUARANTEES (ICC Publ. No. 758, 2010).

[5]   *See* Chapter 1, § 1.17; Chapter 6, § 6.1.

The standby credit—like its civil law cousin, the demand guarantee noted in § 7.2—differs from the commercial credit in three principal ways, even though the same basic rules apply to both: First, the commercial credit serves to fulfill a *payment* obligation (*e.g.*, a buyer's obligation to pay for goods), whereas the standby credit is used to guarantee *performance* of a non-monetary obligation (such as to construct a building or to deliver goods).[6]

Second, although the "independence principle" (as examined in Chapter 6[7] and again below[8]) insulates both forms of credit from problems in the underlying transaction, the commercial credit and the standby credit play fundamentally different roles. The former plays a *primary* role in the underlying transaction, in that all participants expect that the beneficiary will make a demand for payment under the credit as an essential aspect of the overall deal. Thus, the payment obligation of the issuing bank under a commercial credit arises upon the presentation of documents that show the *beneficiary has performed* (typically, shipped the goods). In contrast, the standby credit plays a *secondary* role, in that the beneficiary may demand payment only if its contract partner (often known in civil law countries as the "principal") defaults in the underlying transaction. Thus, the payment obligation of the issuing bank under a standby credit arises upon the presentation of documents that show the *principal has failed to perform*. In short, the beneficiary will demand payment under a commercial credit if everything goes as planned in the underlying transaction, but will do so under a standby credit only if something goes wrong.

In this respect, the standby letter of credit is primarily a risk-shifting device that protects the beneficiary in the event of default by its contractor. It thus provides the beneficiary with swift and easy access to funds upon default, much as if the contractor had left a cash deposit with the beneficiary. The standby letter of credit is often preferable to a cash deposit, however, because it does not require the contractor to part with any funds until after payment is demanded on the credit.

Finally, the required documents are quite different for the two forms of credit. The commercial credit requires that the beneficiary present numerous and detailed documents in order to obtain payment, typically including ones issued by disinterested third

---

[6]   It is possible, though unusual, for a buyer of goods to arrange for a standby letter of credit as default support for its primary payment obligation to the seller. *See, e.g.,* Mago International LLC v. LHB AG, 2015 WL 4653229, at *1–2 (S.D.N.Y. 2015).

[7]   *See* § 6.5.

[8]   *See* § 7.9 *infra*.

parties that have value in their own right (*e.g.*, a bill of lading). The issuing bank and the applicant can scrutinize those documents to confirm that the beneficiary is entitled to payment, and upon payment retain the valuable documents as security. With a standby, in contrast, the required documents often are skeletal at best.[9] Most often, all that is required is a statement by the beneficiary that its contract partner (the principal) has breached the underlying contract.

Due to their contingent nature, standby letters of credit are riskier for a bank than ordinary letters of credit. Similar to a commercial letter of credit, the bank does not and cannot "look behind" the documentary claim that its customer (the applicant) has failed to perform, nor may the bank delay payment in order to investigate the validity of the claim. The bank also cannot assert any defenses that the contractor may have against the beneficiary (except fraud or forgery, see below[10]). But with a standby letter of credit, the bank commonly will have few documents to examine in making its payment decision—often only an assertion by the beneficiary that the principal has breached. Standby letters of credit also typically are unfunded (that is, they are not supported by funds on deposit with the bank), because banks do not anticipate having to pay out on them; the customer simply promises to reimburse the bank if it is forced to pay out on the letter of credit.

Under "suicide" credits—*i.e.*, those payable upon a simple demand by the beneficiary—the exposure of the applicant may be enormous. This is so because the legal protections against arbitrary or unfounded demands are limited to cases of provable and material fraud or forgery.[11] Thus, standby credits tend, by their nature, to rely more heavily on the good faith of the parties than do commercial credit transactions. This necessary reliance on good faith—which carries with it an increased risk of fraud—exists because the payment decision by the issuing bank will be based solely on the unilateral decision of the beneficiary to demand payment. Again, this also is unlike a commercial credit, under which the beneficiary also must present documents prepared by third parties, such as carriers or inspection firms, to justify the demand for payment.

---

[9]   *See* American Express Bank Ltd. v. Banco Español de Credito, S.A., 597 F. Supp. 2d 394, 401–402 (S.D.N.Y. 2009) ("Unlike a commercial letter, a standby typically does not require the presentation of a negotiable bill of lading or other transport document; instead, the beneficiary may collect simply by certifying that the applicant failed to perform its underlying contractual obligations.").

[10]   *See* §§ 7.11–7.13 *infra.*

[11]   *See* §§ 7.12–7.13 *infra.*

§ 7.4 Overview of the Legal Landscape for Standby Letters of Credit

As with commercial letters of credit, the starting points for the legal rules applicable to standby letters of credit are Article 5 of the Uniform Commercial Code (UCC) and the Uniform Customs and Practices for Documentary Credits (UCP).[12] Both of these legal instruments make clear that they may apply to standby letters of credit as well.

Both UCC Article 5 and the UCP exist in revised versions. The Uniform Commissioners and the American Law Institute revised Article 5 in 1995, and all fifty-one U.S. jurisdictions have since enacted the revised version into law. The most recent version of the UCP is the 2007 Revision (UCP 600). The rules set forth in the UCC and the UCP generally are the same in substance, but some differences exist. The most prominent example of this is that the UCP rules do not address allegations of fraud or forgery, or the enjoining of payment by a bank in the event of such allegations. As a result, UCC Article 5, and not the UCP, will provide the legal rules to resolve issues related to such allegations in letter of credit transactions, including standby letters of credit.[13]

Nonetheless, from concept and content both the UCP and UCC Article 5 were designed to cover the documentary letter of credit transaction and not the standby transaction. Thus, they impose many unnecessary document-related conditions on the use of standbys.

In response to these difficulties, the United Nations Commission on International Trade Law (UNCITRAL) developed the UN Convention on Independent Guarantees and Stand-by Letters of Credit (1995).[14] For the same reason, the ICC developed a separate set of rules for standby credits, the International Standby Practices (ISP 98), which became effective in 1999.[15] The ISP 98 Rules were designed to replace the UCP as an equivalent set of international practices for standby letters of credit. (As noted in

---

[12] *See* ICC UNIFORM CUSTOMS AND PRACTICE FOR DOCUMENTARY CREDITS— UCP 600 (ICC Publ. No. 600, 2007) (hereinafter UCP).

[13] The application of UCC Article 5 itself of course will depend on the relevant choice of law rules. As explained in Chapter 6 (*see* § 6.2), for a lawsuit filed in a U.S. court Article 5 provides that the rights and obligations of a bank under a letter of credit are determined by the law of the jurisdiction where it is "located. *See* UCC § 5–116(b).

[14] United Nations Convention on Independent Guarantees and Standby Letters of Credit, December 11, 1995, 2169 U.N.T.S. 190, *available at* http://www.uncitral.org/uncitral/en/uncitral_texts/payments/1995Convention_guarantees_credit.html (hereinafter Convention on Standby Credits).

[15] INTERNATIONAL STANDBY PRACTICES 1998 (ISP 98) (ICC Publ. No. 590, 1998).

§ 7.2 above, the ICC has adopted a further set of ICC rules, The Uniform Rules for Demand Guarantees (URDG 758), for the civil law instrument of a demand guaranty.[16])

Sections 7.7 through 7.10 will analyze in turn the UCC, the UCP, the ISP 98, and the UN Convention on Standby Credits. But before turning to those detailed rules, the next section will examine the fundamental principles that underlie all four potential sources for legal rules governing standby letters of credit.

§ 7.5   The Fundamental Legal Principles Governing Standby Letters of Credit

The Independence Principle. The two fundamental principles of commercial letters of credit also apply to standby credits.[17] The first is that the banks' obligations under the letter of credit are independent of the buyer's and seller's obligations under the sale of goods or other underlying contract—the *independence principle*.[18] The UCC and UCP make no distinction in this regard for standby credits. Indeed, Even if a letter of credit refers to the underlying contract, the UCP emphasizes that "[b]anks are in no way concerned with or bound by such contract."[19] A bank's payment obligation thus is not subject to defenses arising out of the underlying transaction, with the result that, with exceptions noted below,[20] the disputes between the buyer and the seller in the underlying contract are irrelevant to the banks' payment decisions. This principle applies as well under the ISP 98[21] and the UN Convention on Standby Credits.[22]

The Strict Compliance Principle. The second fundamental principle of letter of credit law is that the banks deal only with documents required by and presented under the letter of credit.[23] Because of this limitation, the consensus view is that the UCP rules require that the presented documents strictly comply with the requirements of the letter of credit—the *strict compliance principle*. Thus, if the documents presented conform precisely to the terms of the letter of credit, the issuing bank and confirming bank (if any) are obligated to honor the presentation and either pay the beneficiary immediately or "accept" its time draft for later

---

16   *See* URDG, *supra* note 4.
17   *See* Chapter 6, §§ 6.6–6.8.
18   *See* UCP, art. 4 and Chapter 6, § 6.7.
19   UCP, art. 4(a).
20   *See* §§ 7.11–7.13 *infra* (addressing the subject of fraud and forgery).
21   ISP 98, *supra* note 15, Rule 1.06.
22   UN Standby Convention, art. 3.
23   *See* UCP, art. 5, and Chapter 6, § 6.6.

payment.[24] If, in contrast, the documents do not strictly comply, the banks may not pay out under the letter of credit. Again, the ISP 98 Rules[25] and the UN Convention on Standby Credits[26] embrace the same basic principle.

Some legal commentators question whether these traditional rules covering letters of credit should be applied to standby credits. The reasoning is that standby credits serve a different function: They do not provide a *primary* vehicle to assure payment to a seller/exporter, but rather a *secondary* assurance of performance for a foreign government or developer if a seller/contractor fails to deliver on its contract (to supply goods, services, or raw materials, or to construct a project). However, the text of both the UCP and UCC Article 5 make it clear that their respective drafters intended to cover standby letters of credit, and nothing in either of those sets of rules or in the ISP 98 or UN Convention suggests that the independence or the strict compliance principles should apply in any different way to standby credits.[27]

§ 7.6   The Rules Governing Standby Letters of Credit__In General

As noted above, four different legal regimes could govern the rights and obligations that arise out of a standby letter of credit.[28] Two are formal rules of positive law: (1) Uniform Commercial Code Article 5, and (2) the UN Convention on Standby Credits; two in contrast are uniform customs and practices proposed by the ICC: (3) the UCP, and (4) the ISP 98. The following sections explain the substance of these various bodies of law and how they may interact in relation to a given standby credit. We begin with UCC Article 5,

---

[24]   Regarding the concept of "acceptance" of a draft under a letter of credit see Chapter 1, § 1.15.

[25]   *See* ISP 98, *supra* note 15, Rules 4.01(a) ("Demands for honour of a standby must comply with the terms and conditions of the standby."); 4.01(b) (stating that "[w]hether a presentation appears to comply is determined by examining the presentation on its face against the terms and conditions stated in the standby as interpreted and supplemented by these Rules"). *Compare* UCP, arts. 2, 14. And as Chapter 6 explained, the consensus view is that this terminology means a strict compliance standard. *See* Chapter 6, § 6.6. For more on this issue *see* § 7.9 *infra*.

[26]   *See* Convention on Standby Credits, *supra* note 14, art. 14 (stating the basic principle that banks must adhere to "generally accepted standards of international practice" for standby letters of credit); art. 16 (providing that a bank must examine the presented documents whether they "are in facial conformity with the terms and conditions of the undertaking").

[27]   As noted in § 7.9 below, the ISP 98 Rules permit an issuer of a particular credit to define an even more exacting standard for a presentation. *See* ISP 98, Rule 4.09(c).

[28]   As noted in § 7.2, a further set of ICC rules, The Uniform Rules for Demand Guarantees (URDG 758), applies for the civil law instrument of a demand guaranty *See* URDG, *supra* note 4.

which had a substantial influence on the development of letter of credit law in general.

§ 7.7   Rules__Uniform Commercial Code Article 5

Article 5 of the UCC has had a considerable influence on the development of the law governing letters of credit. Until the formulation of the United Nations Convention on Independent Guarantees and Stand-by Letters of Credit in 1995, it was the only comprehensive statutory effort to regulate the subject. Although, like the rest of the UCC, Article 5 is merely an attempt at uniform law on a state level, every U.S. state (and the District of Columbia) adopted the original and has now adopted the revised version. The result is near complete statutory uniformity throughout the United States. Article 5's broad definition of a "letter of credit" also makes clear that it may apply to standby credits.[29]

Article 5 has provided a structure for the development of letter of credit law on an international basis as well. This is particularly true on issues of fraud: While the original version of UCC Article 5, released in 1952, reflected existing general principles of letter of credit law, it captured the fraud exception in a manner that has been highly influential. Reflective of the increasing relationship between state, national, and international law, the 1995 revision of Article 5 unfolded along with, and was influenced by, the formulation of the UN Convention and the revision of the UCP. The revised version of Article 5 also embraces new practices in letter of credit law, including by recognizing electronic communications and documents[30] and deferred payment arrangements.[31]

As is true with the rest of the UCC, most of Article 5 nonetheless is not mandatory law; rather, nearly all of its provisions defer to the agreement of the parties as expressed in the terms of their contract.[32] Indeed, in specific recognition of the great influence of uniform customs and practices for international letters of credit, the UCC—by express reference—permits a bank to displace its provisions in favor of the UCP: Section 5–116 declares that the liability of banks "is governed by any rules of custom or practice, such as the Uniform Customs and Practices for Documentary Credits, to which the letter of credit, confirmation, or other

---

[29]   UCC § 5–102(a)(10) (defining a letter of credit as any "definite undertaking . . . by an issuer to a beneficiary at the request or for the account of an applicant . . . to honor a documentary presentation by payment").

[30]   UCC §§ 5–102(a)(14) (defining a "record" as including "information . . . that is stored in an electronic form or other medium and is retrievable in perceivable form"); and 5–104 (providing that a letter of credit "may be issued in any form").

[31]   UCC §§ 5–102(a)(8)(iii), 5–108(a).

[32]   *See* UCC § 5–103(c).

undertaking is expressly made subject."[33] The reference to "any rules of customs or practice" obviously extends this displacement power to the ISP 98. Indeed, such rules or customs prevail even in the case of a direct conflict between the UCC and the UCP (except with respect to the UCC's rare "nonvariable" provisions).[34]

§ 7.8   Rules__The Uniform Customs and Practices for Documentary Credits (UCP)

Since 1933, the ICC has published and periodically updated the UCP to provide a uniform set of rules regarding the obligations of banks in letter of credit transactions. The legal status of the UCP is merely as a statement of contract terms and banking trade usage, and not as generally applicable positive law. Nonetheless, as Chapter 6 explained in detail, the UCP rules have broad international influence by virtue of an express incorporation of its terms in most letters of credit,[35] and the express validation of such incorporations by UCC Article 5.[36]

A standby letter of credit, like its commercial credit counterpart,[37] may incorporate the UCP. By its terms, the UCP rules apply to any documentary credit "when the text of the credit expressly indicates that it is subject to these rules."[38] And if a bank includes such an express reference in a credit, the UCP rules "are binding on all parties" to the credit except as otherwise expressly modified or excluded.[39] Since 1983, the UCP have included standby letters of credit within their scope as well. The present version (UCP 600) thus states that the UCP rules may apply "to the extent to which they may be applicable, [to] any standby letter of credit."[40] Standby letters of credit also may have confirming banks; but as explained in § 7.2 above it is quite common for a standby instead to serve as support for a local performance guarantee issued by a foreign bank.

---

[33]   UCC § 5–116(c).

[34]   UCC § 5–103(c) (listing the few provisions of Article 5 that the parties may not vary even by express agreement).

[35]   *See* Chapter 6, § 6.2. *See also* Great Wall De Venezuela C.A. v. Interaudi Bank, 117 F. Supp. 3d 474, 485 (S.D.N.Y. 2015) ("The UCP 'applies to most letters of credit . . . because issuers generally incorporate it into their [letters of] credit[ ][.]' ") (*quoting* Alaska Textile Co. v. Chase Manhattan Bank, N.A., 982 F.2d 813, 816 (2d Cir. 1992)).

[36]   *See* § 5–116(c) and Chapter 6, § 6.3.

[37]   *See* Chapter 6, § 6.5.

[38]   UCP, art. 1.

[39]   *Id.*

[40]   *Id.*

Chapter 6 examined in detail the UCP rules governing commercial letters of credit. Most important, these include the fundamental independence principle[41] and the strict compliance principle.[42] As examined there, the UCP also have detailed rules on the obligations of banks upon presentation of documents,[43] including on examination for discrepancies[44] and on timely notification of discrepancies.[45]

If incorporated in a particular credit, these rules apply to standbys as well. As noted, however, the UCP rules have an important disclaimer on this score—"to the extent to which they may be applicable."[46] This disclaimer was necessary because it is clear that the UCP rules were designed principally to cover the documentary letter of credit transaction and not the standby transaction. The UCP rules thus include numerous provisions that have little relevance to standbys.[47] In specific, the UCP's detail rules on transportation documents,[48] on insurance documents,[49] and on shipment of the goods[50] make little sense in the typical transaction supported by a standby credit.

As a more fundamental matter, the UCP rules are structured on the basis of extensive documentary presentations. Under a standby credit, the beneficiary is the party entitled to *receive* performance, and the credit serves as secondary support for that performance. The UCP rules, however, contemplate, in both concept and structure, that the beneficiary will create or procure a variety of documents in the course of its own performance, and then present those documents as a condition to payment under the credit.

The result is that most of the provisions of the UCP simply are not relevant to, or at least function oddly with, standby credits. It is for this reason that the ICC adopted the ISP 98, which as the next section explains reflect a set of rules specifically tailored to such credits.

---

41   *See* § 6.5.

42   *See* § 6.6.

43   *See* § 6.7.

44   *See* § 6.9.

45   *See* § 6.10.

46   *See* UCP, art. 1.

47   *See, e.g.,* Paul S. Turner, *New Rules for Standby Letters of Credit: The International Standby Practices,* 14 B.F.I.R. 457, 459 (1998–1999) (observing that "[m]any of the provisions of the UCP are either inapplicable or inappropriate in a standby credit context").

48   *See* UCP, arts. 19–25.

49   UCP, art. 28.

50   *See* UCP, arts. 26–27, 43.

§ 7.9   Rules__The International Standby Practices (ISP 98)

The ICC's International Standby Practices (ISP 98) define uniform rules with specific reference to standby letters of credit. The goal of the ISP 98 is to establish a set of widely accepted norms that will streamline and standardize the customs and practices for standby credits, and thus provide greater clarity on the issues unique to this special form of financial guarantee.

The ISP 98 provisions are structured in the form of ten general "Rules," each with sub-rules that generally are short and quite specific. The ISP Rules can dispense with the expansive provisions of the UCP on the permissible and required content of documents, especially transport documents, for the simple reason that most documentary conditions on standbys are quite skeletal (see §§ 7.1–7.3 above). The most important Rules of the ISP are the first five: (1) General Provisions; (2) Obligations; (3) Presentation; (4) Examination; and (5) Notice, Preclusion and Disposition of Documents. The analysis below thus will analyze these Rules in more detail. The latter five ISP Rules address more technical matters such as transfer and cancellation of credits.[51]

Applicability. The most basic rule of the ISP 98 of course is that they "are intended to apply to standby letters of credit";[52] but Rule 1.01 also states that the ISP 98 cover the various other forms of such credits, including "performance, financial, and direct pay standby letters of credit."[53] Like the UCP, the ISP 98 Rules apply simply through "an express reference to them" in the text of a particular credit.[54] The choice of which set of rules to select is, therefore, left to the parties (and as a practical matter to the issuing bank itself). And in this regard substance prevails over form and label. Thus, with such an express reference, the ISP 98 Rules may govern not only a standby credit but also any "similar undertaking, however named or described, whether for domestic or international use."[55]

If the ISP 98 Rules apply, then any such credit is deemed "an irrevocable, independent, documentary, and binding undertaking when issued," even if it does "not so state."[56] Nonetheless, the terms

---

[51]   In specific, Rules 6 through 10 cover the following topics: (6) Transfer and Assignment; (7) Cancellation; (8) Reimbursement Obligations; (9) Timing; and (10) Syndication/Participation.

[52]   ISP 98, *supra* note 15, Rule 1.01(a).

[53]   *Id.*

[54]   *Id.*, Rule 1.01(b).

[55]   *Id.*, Rule 1.01(b).

[56]   *Id.*, Rule 1.06(a).

of a credit may "expressly modify or exclude" the ISP Rules.[57] This confirms the legal status of the ISP Rules as contractual in nature, such that the agreement of the parties as expressed in a particular credit prevail over the customs and practices expressed in those Rules.

The ISP 98 Rules are designed to be compatible with the UN Convention on Stand-by Credits (see § 7.10 below) and also with local law, whether statutory or judicial. The ISP 98 Rules thus state that when incorporated in a particular credit they both "supplement the applicable law to the extent not prohibited by that law" and "supersede conflicting provisions in any other rules of practice to which a standby letter of credit is also made subject."[58]

The Basic Obligations of a Bank. The basic obligations of an issuing bank under the ISP 98 are quite similar to those under the UCP. The most basic one is to honor a complying presentation of documents. Thus, under Rule 2.01 "[a]n issuer undertakes to the beneficiary to honour a presentation that appears on its face to comply with the terms and conditions of the standby in accordance with these Rules supplemented by standard standby practice." Unless otherwise stated, the obligation is to pay "in immediately available funds."[59]

Presentation Rules. As compared to the UCP, the ISP 98 Rules have substantially more detailed provisions regarding the process for presentation of documents (although, again, not regarding the specific content). The Rules thus provide that a credit should indicate "the time, place . . . person to whom, and medium in which presentation should be made."[60] They also define when a presentation actually occurs;[61] the details on a presentation's identification of the relevant credit to which it applies;[62] where and to whom a presentation must be made;[63] the timeliness and medium of a presentation;[64] and the rights of various parties to waive these requirements.[65]

Regarding the medium, the ISP 98 Rules generally require presentation of paper documents,[66] unless the credit otherwise

---

[57] *Id.,* Rule 1.01(c).
[58] *Id.,* Rule 2.01(a).
[59] *Id.,* Rule 2.01(e).
[60] *Id.,* Rule 3.01.
[61] *Id.,* Rule 3.02.
[62] *Id.,* Rule 3.03.
[63] *Id.,* Rule 3.04.
[64] *Id.,* Rules 3.05, 3.06.
[65] *Id.,* Rule 3.11.
[66] *Id.,* Rules 3.06(b), 3.06(c).

provides or allows.[67] If, however, the only required document is a demand for payment, the Rules enable members of the SWIFT banking communication system to make an electronic presentation, whether or not the credit expressly permits it.[68] Where allowed by a credit, the ISP 98 Rules contained detailed definitions for the presentation of electronic documents.[69] (While electronic presentation is relatively easy for the skeletal documents typically required for standbys, it is much more difficult for commercial letters of credit that require presentation of documents of title.)

As noted in § 7.3 above, standbys sometimes are in the form of a "suicide" credit, under which the beneficiary need merely make a demand for payment. At the extreme end, a standby even may allow the beneficiary to do so without presenting any document. The ISP 98 nonetheless state that even where a standby "does not specify any required document, it will still be deemed to require a documentary demand for payment."[70] This is consistent with the rule that the issuer's obligation under a standby depends on the presentation of documents.

Examination and Compliance. Of necessity, the ISP Rules— given that they require a documentary presentation—also address the standards for compliance.[71] Like the UCP, the ISP 98 Rules do not expressly state a strict compliance standard. Nonetheless, they use terminology essentially identical to that of the UCP in describing a bank's obligation to examine presented documents. Rule 4.01(a) thus states that "[d]emands for honour of a standby must comply with the terms and conditions of the standby." Rule 4.01(b) then declares that "[w]hether a presentation appears to comply is determined by examining the presentation on its face against the terms and conditions stated in the standby" as interpreted and supplemented by the ISP 98 Rules. Like the UCP 600,[72] the ISP 98 Rules state that these standards "are to be read in the context of standard standby practice."[73] But as Chapter 6 explained, the parallel references in the UCP to "facial" conformity

---

[67]   *Id.*, Rule 3.06(a).

[68]   For more on the SWIFT system see Chapter 6, § 6.16. In any case, an issuer may, "in its sole discretion," allow an electronic presentation of documents. ISP 98, *supra* note 15, Rule 3.06(b)(2).

[69]   *Id.*, Rule 1.09(c).

[70]   *Id.*, Rule 4.08.

[71]   *Id.*, Rule 4.09.

[72]   *Compare* UCP, arts. 2, 14.

[73]   ISP 98, *supra* note 15, Rule 4.01(b).

and "standard practice" are generally understood to continue the traditional "strict compliance" standard.[74]

The limit of this strict compliance standard is obvious typographical, spelling, or similarly trivial errors.[75] The ISP 98 Rules capture this concept with a special provision that, unless the standby specifically requires "precise wording," the wording in a presentation need merely "appear to convey the same meaning as that required by the standby."[76] However, the practical relevance of a strict compliance standard for standby credits is quite limited. The simple reason is that—as noted repeatedly above—such credits often include only the most minimal documentary conditions. Commonly, all that is required is a simple statement by the beneficiary that the applicant/principal on the standby credit has not fulfilled its contractual obligations in the underlying transaction. There is, in short, very little with which a presentation must strictly comply.

Perhaps in recognition of this, the ISP Rules have a curious provision that permits an issuer to demand exact, mirror image conformity. Under Rule 4.09(c), if a standby describes the presentation requirements with quotation marks, blocked wording, or an attached form, "and also provides that the specified wording be 'exact' or 'identical'," then the presentation must "exactly reproduce[ ]" those requirements, "including typographical errors in spelling, punctuation, spacing and the like as well as blank lines."

Notice of Dishonor. Upon discovery of discrepancies in a presentation, a bank under the ISP 98 Rules must provide a notice of dishonor.[77] The notice need not be detailed, but it must state "all discrepancies upon which dishonor is based."[78] On the issue of the time frame for such a notice, the ISP 98 Rules follow the traditional standard of a "reasonable time" not to exceed seven banking days.[79] (As noted in Chapter 6, the UCP has replaced this traditional approach with a fixed five-day period.[80]). But to balance the uncertainty of the reasonable time standard, the ISP 98 Rules

---

[74]   *See* Chapter 6, § 6.6.

[75]   *See* again Chapter 6, § 6.6.

[76]   ISP 98, *supra* note 15, Rule 4.09(a). Indeed, the ISP 98 Rules have a specific provision on the reverse situation of an error in the credit: If a standby uses quotation marks, blocked wording, or an attached form, "typographical errors in spelling, punctuation, spacing, or the like that are apparent when read in context are not required to be duplicated in the presentation." Rule 4.09(b).

[77]   *Id.*, Rule 5.01. Upon dishonor the bank must return the documents to, or otherwise follow the instructions of, the presenter (typically, the beneficiary). *See id.*, Rule 5.07.

[78]   *Id.*, Rule 5.02.

[79]   *Id.*, Rule 5.01(a)(1).

[80]   *See* UCP, art. 16(c), (d) and Chapter 6, § 6.10.

establish a three-day safe harbor for examination of documents, within which notice of dishonor is deemed to be timely.[81] The issuer may, "in its sole discretion," seek a waiver of any discrepancy by the applicant, but doing so does not extend the time for giving the notice of dishonor.[82]

Finally, like the UCP a bank that issues a standby credit subject to the ISP 98 Rules is precluded from asserting any discrepancy in a particular presentation that it does not include in a timely notice of dishonor.[83] The one exception is a failure by the beneficiary to make the presentation before the credit expired.[84] But like the UCP, under the ISP 98 an issuer must disregard any documents presented that are not required by the credit as well as any non-documentary conditions in the credit.[85]

Reimbursement by the Applicant. Unlike the UCP, the ISP 98 Rules address the subject of reimbursement by the applicant. They state that where a bank has made payment "against a complying presentation in accordance with these Rules," the applicant must reimburse the issuer (and, where applicable, an issuer must reimburse a confirming or other nominated bank that has made such a payment).[86] They even create indemnification obligations on the part of the applicant against certain related costs of the issuer.[87] An issuer may waive certain provisions of a standby letter of credit, without affecting the applicant's reimbursement obligations.[88] But otherwise, and like the UCC and the UCP, the ISP 98 Rules do not address in any great detail the contractual rights as between the issuer and the applicant. Thus, the issuer's right to limit its liability to the applicant for wrongful honor or dishonor as well as the applicant's rights and defenses in that regard are beyond the scope of the ISP Rules.[89]

Fraud and Forgery. Neither the UCP nor the ISP 98 contain rules concerning when the issuer may or should refuse a complying presentation on the ground that the beneficiary's demand for payment is (allegedly) fraudulent. The UCP provisions contain no reference to the subject at all. The ISP 98 Rules are more explicit on

---

[81]   ISP 98, *supra* note 15, Rule 5.01(a)(1).

[82]   *Id.*, Rule 5.05. A separate rule makes clear that the beneficiary may not compel the issuer to seek a waiver from the applicant. *See id.*, Rule 5.06.

[83]   *Id.*, Rule 5.03.

[84]   *Id.*, Rule 5.04.

[85]   *Id.*, Rules 4.02 and 4.11.

[86]   *Id.*, Rule 8.01.

[87]   *Id.*, Rule 8.02.

[88]   *Id.*, Rule 3.11.

[89]   For more on the UCC and UCP approaches to these issues see Chapter 6, §§ 6.12 and 6.13.

the point, for Rule 1.05 states expressly that the ISP 98 Rules do not address "defenses to honor based on fraud, abuse or similar matters." For such issues, therefore, the parties must look to otherwise applicable law such as the UCC (or, where applicable, the UN Convention on Standby Credits). Sections 7.11 through 7.13 address this important subject matter for standby credits.

§ 7.10   Rules__The United Nations Convention on Stand-by Letters of Credit

The United Nations Convention on Independent Guarantees and Stand-by Letters of Credit, like the CISG, is a formal international treaty drafted under the auspices of UNCITRAL. The Convention was adopted and opened for signature by the UN General Assembly on December 11, 1995, and it entered into force by its own terms on January 1, 2000.[90] As of late 2016, however, the Convention has only eight Contracting States (Belarus, Ecuador, El Salvador, Gabon, Kuwait, Liberia, Panama and Tunisia), and no state has adopted the Convention in over ten years.

Nonetheless, one recent development may give the Convention impetus: In February, 2016, President Obama submitted the Convention to the Senate under Article II, Section 2, of the Constitution along with his recommendation that it grant consent to ratification.[91] A professed purpose of this act was "to encourage other countries to become parties to the Convention." Both the Uniform Law Commission and the American Law Institute have expressed support for U.S. ratification. As of late 2016, however, the Senate has taken no action whatsoever on this treaty.

Scope of Application. The Convention is designed to facilitate the use of independent guarantees and standby letters of credit. It applies to an "international undertaking" (see the following paragraphs) if either "the place of business of the guarantor/issuer . . . is in a Contracting State, or "the rules of private international law lead to the application of the law of a Contracting State."[92]

Because the Convention has entered into force, it also will govern any international credit that "expressly states that it is subject to th[e] Convention."[93] Indeed, even in countries that have

---

[90]   The status of the Convention is available on UNCITRAL's website http://www.uncitral.org/uncitral/en/uncitral_texts/payments/1995Convention_guarantees_status.html.

[91]   *See Letter of Transmittal from the President of the United States to the Senate With Legal Analysis of the United Nations Convention on Independent Guarantees and Standby Letters of Credit,* Feb. 10, 2016, Sen. Treaty Doc. No. 114–9.

[92]   Convention on Standby Credits, *supra* note 14, art. 1(1).

[93]   *Id.,* art. 1(2).

not adopted the Convention, standby letters of credit may be issued subject to it if so permitted by the choice of law rules of the issuer's state. Because most such rules emphasize party autonomy, the law of many different countries may permit an issuer to choose the Convention as the law governing a standby letter of credit. In other words, as allowed by applicable choice of law rules a particular standby credit may "opt into" the Convention by express reference.

The remaining requirements for application of the Convention are found in Articles 2 and 4, for they define the essential elements of the term "international undertaking." Starting with the first element, Article 4 states that a credit is "international" if the place of business of any two of the following typical actors are in different countries: the issuer, the beneficiary, the applicant, an "instructing party" (an entity that applies for the letter of credit on behalf of the applicant), and a confirmer.[94]

Article 2 defines the second element ("undertaking") as "an independent commitment . . . given by a bank or other institution or person . . . to pay to the beneficiary a certain or determinable amount upon simple demand or upon demand accompanied by other documents."[95] In simpler terms, it covers any independent promise by a financial institution to pay a beneficiary in accordance with defined conditions.

Article 3 then expressly addresses the "independence" of an undertaking as contemplated by the very definition of an undertaking in Article 2.[96] Under the basic rule, an undertaking is independent if the bank's obligation to the beneficiary is not dependent upon "the existence or validity of the underlying transaction, or upon any other undertaking."[97] Likewise, the undertaking must not be "subject to any term or condition not appearing in the undertaking."[98] Finally, the undertaking may not be subject to any "future, uncertain act or event" except for the presentation of documents.[99]

This of course is a standard notion in letter of credit law. As UNCITRAL's Explanatory Note for the Convention observes, a credit is not independent in this respect if the issuer is "called on to investigate the underlying transaction"; instead, the essential attribute of an independent credit is that the issuer "is merely to determine whether the documentary demand for payment conforms

---

[94]   *Id.*, art. 4(1).

[95]   *Id.*, art. 2(1).

[96]   *Id.*, art. 3.

[97]   *Id.*, art. 3(a).

[98]   *Id.*, art. 3(b).

[99]   *Id.*

on its face to the terms of the guarantee or stand-by letter of credit."[100] Implicit in Article 3's definition of "independent" is also the principle that any conditions on payment must have a "documentary" character. The effect of this rule is that an undertaking that is entirely subject to "non-documentary" conditions is outside the scope of the Convention.

The Convention nonetheless gives full freedom to the parties to exclude its application,[101] with the result that otherwise-applicable domestic law will apply. On the other hand, although it expressly applies only to independent guarantees and standby letters of credit, its flexible choice provisions should allow issuers of other forms of international credits—such as standard commercial credits—to "opt into" the Convention by express reference.[102]

The Convention provides choice of law rules, but allows the parties to choose the applicable background law. If the parties do not agree on a choice of law, the Convention provides a default rule that the law of the issuer's place of business governs the credit transaction.[103] More generally, the Convention's rules are not mandatory, and thus are subject to any contrary agreement of the parties. In this way, it allows the parties to choose rules more closely tailored to their specific transaction, such as the UCP, ISP, or URDG.

Like the UN Sale of Goods Convention (CISG) analyzed in Chapter 2, the Convention on Standbys contains a general rule that interpretation of its provisions must heed its "international character" and the need to promote uniformity in its application.[104] Likewise, interpretation of the Convention must have regard for the observance of good faith in the international practice associated with independent guarantees and standby credits.[105]

Issuance, Form, etc. The Convention addresses the elemental subjects of the issuance, form, and expiry of undertakings[106] as well as the amendment, transfer, or assignment of proceeds of undertakings.[107] Of special interest in this regard is a rule that expressly embraces electronic credits. Article 7(2) provides that "[a]n undertaking may be issued in any form which preserves a complete record of the text of the undertaking and provides

---

[100] *Id.*, UNCITRAL Explanatory Note, para. 9.

[101] *Id.*

[102] *Id.*, art. 1(2).

[103] *Id.*, arts. 21, 22.

[104] *Id.*, art. 5. *Compare* CISG, art. 7(1), and Chapter 2, § 2.10.

[105] Convention on Standby Credits, *supra* note 14, art. 5.

[106] *Id.*, arts. 7, 11, 12.

[107] *Id.*, arts. 8–10.

authentication of its source by generally accepted means." The reference to "any form" conforms with the similar rule on electronic letters of credit in UCC Article 5.[108]

The Core Provisions. The focus of the Convention is the relationship between the issuer and the beneficiary. Not surprisingly, the Convention states that the terms and conditions of the undertaking generally define the rights and obligations of the issuer and the beneficiary.[109] Beyond this, Article 14 of the Convention states the basic principle that an issuer must "act in good faith and exercise reasonable care" and must adhere to "generally accepted standards of international practice" for standby letters of credit.

The core provision of the Convention is found in Article 16 on "examination of [the] demand and accompanying documents." Under that provision, the issuer must examine any demand for payment in accordance with the Article 14 standard, and determine "whether documents are in facial conformity with the terms and conditions of the undertaking, and are consistent with one another." This "facial conformity" test comports with the strict compliance standard analyzed both above[110] and in Chapter 6.[111]

An issuer of an undertaking subject to the Convention has a "reasonable time, but not more than seven business days" following the demand to examine the documents and, if it decides not to honor, to give the beneficiary notice to that effect.[112] This conforms to the traditional rule in UCC Article 5,[113] but not the fixed five-day deadline in the UCP.[114] The required notice under the Convention must be by "expeditious means" and must "indicate the reason for the decision not to pay."[115]

The Convention also provides rules for allegations of fraud and the grounds for injunctive relief.[116] Section 7.13 below will analyze these provisions in more detail.

Finally, the relationship between the issuer and the applicant largely falls outside its scope. This includes the important subjects of the rights of an issuer to reimbursement and the defenses or

---

[108]   *See* UCC § 5–104.

[109]   Convention on Standby Credits, *supra* note 14, art. 13(1).

[110]   *See* § 7.5 *supra.*

[111]   *See* Chapter 6, § 6.6.

[112]   Convention on Standby Credits, *supra* note 14, art. 16(2).

[113]   *See* UCC § 5–108(b).

[114]   *See* UCP, art. 16(c), (d). *See also* Chapter 6, § 6.10.

[115]   Convention on Standby Credits, *supra* note 14, art. 16(2).

[116]   *Id.*, arts. 19, 20.

claims of the applicant against the issuer (such as for wrongful honor or dishonor[117]). For these matters, therefore, otherwise-applicable domestic law—such as UCC Article 5—will provide the governing legal rules.

§ 7.11   The Fraud Defense___In General

One important tension that arises from a strict application of the "independence principle" in letter of credit law is the effect of fraud. The independence principle promotes the utility of letter of credit transactions by offering certainty of payment to the beneficiary if it complies with the credit's requirements. Indeed, as noted in Chapter 6, U.S. courts repeatedly have emphasized that the independence principle "is predicated upon the fundamental policy that a letter of credit would lose its commercial vitality if before honoring drafts the issuer could look beyond the terms of the credit to the underlying contractual controversy or performance between its customer and the beneficiary."[118]

But when a required document is forged or fraudulent, or the beneficiary has engaged in material fraud beyond a "mere" breach of the underlying contract, a counter-principle comes into play. As one court observed in a famous case long ago, "[t]here is as much public interest in discouraging fraud as in encouraging the use of letters of credit."[119] That famous case is *Sztejn v. J. Henry Schroder Banking Corp.*[120] There, the court observed that the principle of "the independence of the bank's obligation" under a letter of credit "should not be extended to protect an unscrupulous seller" where its fraudulent actions become apparent before the bank decides to honor a presentation.[121]

Thus, the law is subject to two competing policies, and the courts have attempted to accommodate both when allegations arise that a payment will facilitate a material fraud or otherwise is tainted by forged or fraudulent documents. Nonetheless, the UCC and, in varying degrees, other legal systems recognize a "fraud exception" to the independence principle. As one federal court recently observed, "[f]raud is the 'well-established exception' to the

---

[117]   *See* Chapter 6, §§ 6.12 and 6.13.

[118]   Great Wall De Venezuela C.A. v. Interaudi Bank, 117 F. Supp. 3d 474, 485 (S.D.N.Y. 2015). *See also, e.g.,* ACE American Ins. Co. v. Bank of the Ozarks, 2012 WL 3240239, at *5 (S.D.N.Y. 2012); Alaska Textile Co., Inc. v. Chase Manhattan Bank, N.A., 982 F.2d 813, 815–816 (2d Cir. 1992). For a broader examination of the independence principle see Chapter 6, § 6.5.

[119]   Dynamics Corp. of America v. Citizens & Southern Nat. Bank, 356 F. Supp. 991 (N.D. Ga. 1973).

[120]   31 N.Y.S.2d 631 (N.Y. Sup. 1941).

[121]   *Id.*, at 634.

rule that an issuing bank must pay when a beneficiary submits documents that conform on their face to the terms of the letter of credit."[122] The policy underlying this exception is that the courts will not allow their process to be used by a dishonest person to carry out a fraud. However, an enduring debate exists about how broad this "fraud exception" should be.

§ 7.12   The Fraud Defense__Under the UCC

As noted in §§ 7.8 and 7.9 above, neither the UCP nor the ISP 98 Rules have provisions that address the subject of fraud. As a result, otherwise applicable law will step in to "fill the gap." Indeed, the UCC expressly provides that, even where a credit incorporates rules of custom or practice such as the UCP or ISP, the UCC will continue to apply in absence of a conflict.[123] With the UCP and ISP 98 silent, no such conflict exists on the issue of fraud.[124]

The courts generally have been skeptical of fraud claims in documentary letter of credit transactions.[125] Even there, however, some cases exist. An example is *Mid-America Tire, Inc. v. PTZ Trading Ltd.*[126] There, the Supreme Court of Ohio first observed that, given the UCP's silence on the subject, the UCC fraud rules apply even to a documentary credit that incorporates the UCP. Citing UCC § 5–109, the court then held that it had the authority to issue an injunction in the event of fraud in either the letter of credit transaction or in the underlying sales transaction. It further held that the relevant standard of "material fraud"[127] requires actions that "vitiate the transaction," and thereby deprive the applicant of the benefits of the underlying contract. It also observed that the courts must consider the fraudulent acts of agents of the beneficiary in deciding whether to enjoin payment under a letter of credit.

---

[122]   Great Wall De Venezuela C.A. v. Interaudi Bank, 117 F. Supp. 3d 474, 486 (S.D.N.Y. 2015) (*quoting* Semetex Corp. v. UBAF Arab Am. Bank, 853 F. Supp. 759, 773 (S.D.N.Y. 1994)).

[123]   UCC § 5–116(c). *See also, e.g.*, Northrop Grumman Overseas Serv. Corp. v. Banco Wiese Sudameris, 2004 WL 2199547, at *3 n.6 (S.D.N.Y. 2004); Amwest Sur. Ins. Co. v. Concord Bank, 248 F. Supp. 2d 867, 877 (E.D. Mo. 2003).

[124]   *See, e.g.*, Mid-America Tire, Inc. v. PTZ Trading Ltd., 768 N.E.2d 619, 636–67 (Ohio 2002); Brenntag International Chemicals, Inc. v. Norddeutsche Landesbank GZ, 970 F. Supp. 2d 399, 407 408 (S.D.N.Y. 1999).

[125]   *See, e.g.*, ACE Am. Ins. Co. v. Bank of the Ozarks, 2014 WL 4953566, at *11 (S.D.N.Y. 2014) ("Courts have observed . . . that 'because the smooth operation of international commerce requires that requests for payment under letters of credit not be routinely obstructed by prepayment litigation, the fraud exception to the independence principle 'is a narrow one' that is only available on a showing of 'intentional fraud.' ") (*quoting* BasicNet S.p.A. v. CFP Servs. Ltd., 120 A.D.3d 97, 111 (2014)).

[126]   768 N.E.2d 619 (Ohio 2002).

[127]   *See* UCC § 5–109(b).

In another case, a U.S. insurer sought to enjoin a draw by a Bermuda reinsurer on a letter of credit allegedly tainted by fraud.[128] The court granted injunctive relief, holding that the possibility of a later monetary award against a defendant already in receivership would be an inadequate legal remedy, and that a choice of forum clause in the underlying contract did not control the proper forum for actions involving the letter of credit.[129]

Such cases involving documentary credits, however, are comparatively rare. In contrast, claims of fraud are not at all uncommon in standby letter of credit transactions. A principal reason for the difference is that some of the limiting concepts for documentary credits, such as the extensive documentary requirements coupled with the "strict compliance" standard, become largely meaningless when the required document contains a mere allegation by the beneficiary that the other party failed to perform properly in the underlying contract. When the limitations that give structure to a transaction become meaningless, the transaction can become a breeding ground for fraud.

UCC § 5–109 imposes, however, a series of important limitations on the availability of the fraud exception.

Protection of Good Faith Intermediary Banks. The first is an absolute requirement that an issuer honor a presentation by certain intermediary banks that have already paid in good faith. Thus, § 5–109(a)(1) provides that "the issuer shall honor" a conforming presentation made by either (i) "a nominated person who has given value in good faith without notice of forgery or material fraud," or (ii) "a confirmer who has honored its confirmation in good faith."[130] Thus, a confirming bank that has paid against conforming documents in good faith is entitled to reimbursement even if strong evidence of fraud or forgery later surfaces. The same applies for other nominated banks (*i.e.*, those authorized, but not obligated, to honor a presentation) if they have paid in good faith and without notice. Under the UCC, therefore, if such a good faith intermediary bank has already paid the beneficiary, and the documents on their face appear to comply with the terms of the credit, the issuing bank *must* provide reimbursement, even if the documents are forged or fraudulent or the beneficiary has perpetrated a material fraud.

---

[128]   Hendricks v. Bank of America, N.A., 408 F.3d 1127 (9th Cir. 2005).

[129]   *Id.*, 1139–1141.

[130]   This protection also applies to certain other intermediaries in quite rare circumstances. *See* UCC § 5–109(a)(1) (requiring honor for a holder in due course of a draft taken after the issuer or a nominated bank has already accepted it); *id.* (requiring honor for certain good faith assignees of a deferred obligation already assumed by an issuer or nominated bank).

Authorization to Pay Even over Allegations of Fraud. A second protection for the banks applies to presentations by all other persons (*e.g.*, the beneficiary or any other intermediary party). In such cases, the issuing bank *may* choose to pay even if the applicant claims that the documents are forged or fraudulent, or that there was fraud in the underlying transaction.[131] Indeed, one essential rule that arises from the independence principle, as a federal district court recently observed, is that "when a beneficiary makes a presentation for payment under a letter of credit, the issuing bank is not required . . . to investigate any alleged underlying fraud."[132] The only requirement is that the issuer act "in good faith," and Article 5 defines this term with the very limited notion of "honesty in fact."[133] (This might be viewed as the "pure heart, empty head" test). Thus, an issuing bank or confirming bank may honor a presentation even in the face of allegations of fraud as long as it does not have *actual* (*i.e.*, subjective) knowledge of the fraud (which is extremely rare).[134]

Such a bank may accede to the applicant's desires and refuse to pay, but for a variety of reasons it is not very likely to do so. First, the banks have a limited ability to evaluate the available evidence of fraud, especially on their own, and have little desire to become involved in the buyer-seller dispute in any event. Second, the banks agree to take their small fee (typically, one to two percent of the credit amount) on the premise that they are mere administrative actors in the transaction, not the ultimate judge and jury of all disputes. Third, the banks likely will be reluctant to develop a reputation as an unreliable source of funds in letter of credit transactions. Fourth, a decision to dishonor almost certainly will cause a lawsuit by the beneficiary for wrongful dishonor,[135] with all of the attendant litigation costs and attorneys' fees for the bank. Finally, if the issuing bank honors a conforming presentation in good faith, even with no investigation whatsoever, Article 5 makes clear that it has an absolute right of reimbursement from the

---

[131]　UCC § 5–109(b).

[132]　CVD Equipment Corp. v. Taiwan Indus. Glass Corp., 2014 WL 641420, at *4 (S.D.N.Y. 2014). *See also* Cooperative Agricole Groupement De Producteurs Bovins De L'Ouest v. Banesto Banking Corp., 1989 WL 82454, at *21 (S.D.N.Y. 1989); Bank of Cochin Ltd. v. Mfrs. Hanover Trust Co., 612 F. Supp. 1533, 1537 (S.D.N.Y. 1985).

[133]　UCC § 5–102(a)(7).

[134]　*See* CVD Equipment Corp. v. Taiwan Indus. Glass Corp., 2014 WL 641420, at *5 (S.D.N.Y. 2014) ("To determine whether an issuing bank acted in bad faith, courts employ a subjective test which focuses on 'what [the issuer] itself actually knew,' rather than what a reasonable issuer in its position would know or might have inquired.") (*quoting* Chem. Bank of Rochester v. Haskell, 51 N.Y.2d 85, 92 (1980)).

[135]　*See* Chapter 6, § 6.12.

applicant.[136] Thus, all of the incentives point in the direction of the issuer honoring and allowing the applicant and the beneficiary to fight it out among themselves.

Direct Resort to Judicial Injunctions. The applicant (the seller/performer in a standby letter of credit transaction) may, however, seek to block payment on its own by requesting an injunction from a court. The UCC grants an applicant the right to seek such a court order based on fraud or forgery.[137] Indeed, it permits an injunction against payment if *either* (a) the beneficiary itself is involved in a "material fraud" in the underlying transaction, *or* (b) a document required by the letter of credit is "forged or materially fraudulent," even without the knowledge or involvement of the beneficiary.[138] In either case, if the applicant obtains an injunction from a court having proper jurisdiction, the issuing bank will be compelled to refuse to pay. But UCC Article 5 leaves only a very narrow avenue for this option, and for good reason. To beneficiaries, the possibility of an injunction creates great uncertainty about prompt payment, because they may know nothing about a foreign judicial system and may fear the worst. This undermines the basic utility of letters of credit as secure payment vehicles in international sales transactions.

UCC § 5–109(b) thus limits the right to an injunction based on the fraud exception in several important ways:

First, as indicated above, a court may not issue an injunction against payment to an intermediary bank that has already honored a conforming presentation in good faith.[139]

Second, the fraud must be "material," and this is a severe standard. The meaning of "material" of course will be decided on a case-by-case basis. Nonetheless, courts generally have imposed a very high burden, and have required proof of fraud that has "so vitiated the entire transaction that the legitimate purposes of the independence of the issuer's obligation would no longer be served."[140]

---

[136]   UCC § 5–108(i) (providing that an issuer that has honored a presentation "as permitted or required by this article: (1) is entitled to be reimbursed by the applicant in immediately available funds").

[137]   UCC § 5–109(b).

[138]   *Id.*

[139]   UCC § 5–109(b)(1).

[140]   For recent applications of this standard see ACE American Ins. Co. v. Bank of the Ozarks, 2014 WL 4953566, at *12 (S.D.N.Y. 2014); Hook Point, LLC v. Branch Banking and Trust Co., 725 S.E.2d 681, 684 (S.C. 2012); Smart & Associates LLC v. Independent Liquor (NZ) Ltd., 2012 WL 5463028, at *5–6 (W.D. Ky. 2012). *See also* § 5–109, Official Comment 1 (endorsing this standard).

Third, the applicant must present actual and sufficient evidence of fraud or forgery, not merely allegations of it.[141] This may be a difficult given the tight time frame for a decision by the bank (five banking days under the UCP) on honoring a presentation.[142]

Fourth, the applicant must satisfy all of the traditional equitable requirements for injunctive and similar relief. Thus, it must demonstrate that it would suffer irreparable harm without an injunction and that a later money judgment would not be an adequate remedy (that there is "no adequate remedy at law"). In most jurisdictions, the applicant also must show that the balance of harms does not weigh too heavily against the beneficiary and that an injunction would not be contrary to the public interest.[143]

Fifth, a court must require as a condition of an injunction that the beneficiary, the issuer, and any affected confirming or nominated banks are "adequately protected."[144] This typically means that the applicant must post a bond against any losses by affected third parties. The Comments to § 5–109 expand this concept to include even protection against incidental damages, such as legal fees.

Finally, UCC § 5–109(b) adds a noteworthy limitation regarding the "locus" of the fraud. A forgery or a fraud in a document required by the letter of credit may permit an injunction if perpetrated by anyone. But as to conduct in the underlying transaction, a court may issue an injunction only if payment would facilitate a material fraud "by the beneficiary," and not by some third party, such as a carrier.

The importance of this distinction is reflected in the approach of other common law courts. English and Canadian courts, for example, also have recognized the "fraud exception" based upon fundamental contract principles and the persuasive precedent of the American cases. These courts require, however, proof that the *beneficiary itself* was involved in the fraudulent activities; a fraud or forgery by any other party, including in the letter of credit transaction, will not suffice. Thus, the House of Lords in the famous case of *The American Accord*, while recognizing the basic fraud exception, refused to extend it to protect the buyer when the fraud

---

[141] UCC § 5–109(b)(4) (permitting an injunction "only . . . on the basis of information submitted to the court").

[142] *See* UCP, art. 16(d) and Chapter 6, § 6.10.

[143] UCC § 5–019(b)(3).

[144] UCC § 5–109(b)(2).

was committed by a third party (a loading broker) without the beneficiary's knowledge.[145]

This different approach is illustrated by comparing three different scenarios in which a credit requires an "on board" bill of lading dated May 15: (1) if the applicant can prove that the beneficiary fraudulently delivered worthless trash to the carrier (instead of the required goods) to meet the May 15 deadline, a court may issue an injunction against honor; (2) if the applicant can prove that the beneficiary fraudulently altered a May 16 bill of lading to state May 15, a court may issue an injunction against honor; but (3) if the carrier or another third party fraudulently put a May 15 date on a bill of lading actually issued on May 16, a court may *not* issue an injunction against honor. Indeed, the English Court of Appeals has refused to allow any flexibility in the requirement of beneficiary involvement, even if a document presented under the letter of credit is so fraudulent as to be a "nullity."[146]

Under § 5–109 of the UCC, in contrast, a court may issue an injunction in all three cases, including if a document required by the letter of credit is forged or materially fraudulent, and even if the beneficiary is not involved in any way (as in the third case). In such a case, the identity of the perpetrator is irrelevant.

The Meaning of Fraud. The traditional difference between fraud doctrines and breach of contract concepts was that the former considers the state of mind of a party, while the latter focuses only on whether a particular performance conformed to the contractually agreed standard. Fraud concepts have expanded enormously since the middle of the last century, however, and conduct that would not have been actionable then now may well amount to fraud. Modern fraud doctrines often do not require any evil intent; rather, the law now requires merely that a party state a fact with indifference about its truthfulness or make an innocent statement of fact under circumstances that leave the impression of complete knowledge, when that is not true.

In spite of all of this, in letter of credit law the courts have continued to place a high burden on applicants to demonstrate "material fraud" by the beneficiary. And with this high standard, courts commonly decline to enjoin payment because of insufficient evidence of fraud.

---

[145]   United City Merchants (Investments) Ltd. v. Royal Bank of Canada (The American Accord), [1983] 1.A.C.168.

[146]   *See* Montrod Ltd. v. Grundkötter Fleischvertriebs GmbH, [2002] 1 W.L.R. 1975.

Applicants thus have sought other means for protection. One option is a "notice injunction." Under this vehicle, an applicant with only limited evidence of fraud nonetheless may be able to convince a court to require that an issuer give notice to the applicant (usually a matter of days) before honoring a presentation by the beneficiary. This would permit the applicant to accelerate its efforts to obtain sufficient evidence to justify a preliminary or permanent injunction against payment by the issuer under the letter of credit.

As suggested above, injunctions against honor are rare in traditional commercial letters of credit, but occur with some frequency in standby letters of credit transactions. The principal reason for this is the extremely limited documentary presentations typically required with standbys. Often, the beneficiary need merely make a documentary demand that states an entitlement to payment, and this may create a special enticement to demand payment as soon as any problems arise. Substantial political and economic upheavals thus often trigger aggressive demands under standby letters of credit.

One prominent example is the political changes brought about by the revolution in Iran in the 1970s. After an initial period of strict adherence to the independence principle,[147] U.S. courts became increasingly skeptical of demands made by Iranian governmental institutions and began issuing injunctions against honor under standby letters of credit that supported pre-revolution projects.[148] One court found similarly convincing evidence of fraud in the chaos surrounding the recent events in Iraq, and thus entered an injunction against honoring a demand under a standby letter of credit.[149]

§ 7.13   The Fraud Defense___Under the UN Convention

One principal purpose of the UN Convention on Independent Guarantees and Stand-by Letters of Credit is to establish greater international uniformity regarding the proper response of issuers and courts to allegations of fraud or abuse under standby letters of credit. The Convention thus includes two important provisions that

---

[147]   *See, e.g.,* American Bell Int'l, Inc. v. Islamic Republic of Iran, 474 F. Supp. 420, 426 (S.D.N.Y. 1979) (observing regarding a party that had arranged for a standby letter of credit covering a project in Iran that a "party who undertakes by contract the risk of political uncertainty and governmental caprice must bear the consequences when the risk comes home to roost").

[148]   *See, e.g.,* Harris Corp. v. Nat'l Iranian Radio and Television, 691 F.2d 1344 (2d Cir. 1982).

[149]   *See* Archer Daniels Midland Co. v. JP Morgan Chase Bank, N.A., 2011 WL 855936 (S.D.N.Y. 2011).

address this subject: Article 19 covers the right of a bank to refuse payment, and Article 20 covers the authority of a court to grant a "provisional measure" against payment upon the request of an applicant.

Under Article 19, a bank, "acting in good faith," may refuse to pay if it is "manifest and clear" that: (1) a document is not genuine or has been falsified; (2) no payment is due on the basis asserted by the presenter; or (3) "the demand has no conceivable basis."[150] The same Article then describes five expansions on the third option. These include that (a) a covered risk "has undoubtedly not materialized"; (b) a court or arbitral tribunal has already declared the underlying obligation as "invalid"; (c) the underlying obligation "has undoubtedly been fulfilled to the satisfaction of the beneficiary"; (d) fulfillment of the underlying obligation "has clearly been prevented by wilful misconduct of the beneficiary"; or (e) a confirming or similar bank seeking reimbursement has made payment "in bad faith."[151]

As is apparent from these requirements, the Convention imposes a rigorous standard for dishonor based on allegations of fraud. Nonetheless, it seeks to strike a balance between the different interests involved in letter of credit transactions. By setting a high standard but granting discretion to the issuer, acting in good faith, the Convention permits dishonor in egregious cases of fraud, but also takes into account the concern of issuers over preserving the commercial reliability of undertakings as promises that are independent from underlying transactions.

At the same time, Article 20 provides that, if the issuer is nonetheless intent on honoring the presentation, the applicant may itself seek provisional court measures to prevent that action.[152] These measures may include blocking payment or freezing the proceeds of an undertaking.[153] But this right exists *only* for the grounds recognized in Article 19.[154]

Moreover, the Convention imposes other important limitations on the right to such "provisional relief" by a court. First, such relief must be based on "immediately available strong evidence."[155] Second, the evidence must show a "high probability" that one of the grounds recognized in Article 19 is present. Third, in deciding

---

[150]   Convention on Standby Credits, *supra* note 14, art. 19(1).

[151]   *Id.*, art. 19(2).

[152]   *Id.*, arts. 19(3), 20.

[153]   *Id.*, art. 20(1)(a), (b).

[154]   *Id.*, art. 20(3). Provisional court orders blocking payment or freezing proceeds are also authorized in the case of use of an undertaking for a criminal purpose. *Id.*

[155]   *Id.*, art. 20(1).

whether to block payment of the proceeds, the court must take into account whether failing to do so "likely" will cause the applicant "serious harm."[156] Finally, as a condition to issuing such an order, the court "may require the [applicant] to furnish such form of security as the court deems appropriate."[157] Like the UCC, therefore, the court may require that the applicant post a bond against any losses by affected third parties.

---

[156]   *Id.*, art. 20(1)(b).

[157]   *Id.*, art. 20(2).

Chapter 8

INTERNATIONAL ELECTRONIC COMMERCE

Table of Sections

§ 8.1   Introduction

The modern confluence of computerization, the Internet, dedicated intranets, cloud computing, and a variety of other communications technologies is having a profound effect on established business models and traditional contracting practices. This "eCommerce" (sometimes written E-Commerce) involves transactions in an intangible, digital world, one marked by an immediacy and rapidity of communication quite literally unthinkable only a few decades ago. This affects a whole variety of previously settled assumptions about transactional relationships, as well as the management, communication, and security of information.[1]

---

[1]   The phenomenon, of course, is not new. A concern about the impact of new technologies is a constant feature of commerce. Consider the following statement from the middle of the 1800s:

Initially, the rapid growth of eCommerce in the modern economy caught the legal regimes of the world unprepared. None was ready for the legal problems caused by the new means for concluding business deals, for effecting payment, and for exchanging communications and information. Although the courts at first did their best to bend or adapt traditional legal rules to accommodate the new transaction patterns, substantial uncertainties remained. Moreover, the rapidity of change has meant that modern communications and business technologies in significant respects represent a moving target for lawmakers and the courts. Even as lawmakers began to step in, the statutory rules were limited and uncoordinated. Thus, although some fundamental legal rules are the same across jurisdictions, even today noteworthy inconsistencies exist in the rules applicable to eCommerce transactions that cross national borders.

A lack of consistency across legal regimes of course is not new. But in one significant respect the problems that arise from such inconsistencies are especially challenging in the field of eCommerce transactions: Often, the parties often do not know when an eCommerce transaction involves dealings across national boundaries. A website with a ".com" address may be located anywhere in the world. Thus, the website addresses of the parties, which may be the only information each has about the other, may not reveal the transborder nature of their transaction.

As a more general matter, eCommerce raises a number of important challenges for the traditional rules of contract law. These include writing and signature requirements; the authentication of the parties' expressions of contractual assent; the security and integrity of communications; and express and implied terms for both commercial and consumer contracts. Transacting business through eCommerce also raises jurisdictional issues ranging from choice of law to sufficient contacts for the exercise of personal jurisdiction and to "presence" in a jurisdiction for purposes of regulation by public authorities. Public authorities may see a special need for such regulation in eCommerce transactions not only to prevent fraud, but also to address privacy concerns, intellectual property rights, and taxation, among other issues. In all of these areas, the traditional legal rules premised on paper transactions—

The businessman of the present day must be continually on the jump, the slow express train will not answer his purpose, and the poor merchant has no other way in which to work to secure a living for his family. He *must* use the telegraph.

Statement in 1868 by W.E. Dodge, *quoted in* Tom Standage, THE VICTORIAN INTERNET 166 (1999) (emphasis in the original).

whether statutory or common law—are inadequate to address the multiplicity of challenges that arise from electronic communications and contracting.

Thus, there was and is a need not only for statutory rules to facilitate eCommerce, but also for uniform solutions across jurisdictional borders. The most fundamental concern is over whether parties may form a contract by electronic means in the first place. This basic issue has led in recent years to a burst of legislative activity at the state, federal, and international levels:

International Efforts. At the international level, lawmakers could promote the adoption of similar rules across jurisdictions by either an international treaty or proposed model legislation. The initial, and still most influential, efforts in this direction came in the latter form. In 1996, UNCITRAL (the organization responsible for the CISG from Chapter 2) first proposed a Model Law on Electronic Commerce.[2] This Model Law reflects a minimalist approach to legislation, and merely seeks to facilitate eCommerce transactions, not regulate them. UNCITRAL followed this effort in 2001 with a Model Law on Electronic Signatures, the goal of which is merely to ensure that legal regimes do not deny legal effect to signatures made in an electronic form.[3] Both model laws are now available to domestic legal systems to provide a foundation for electronic contracting.

UNCITRAL subsequently proposed a formal treaty, the United Nations Convention on the Use of Electronic Communications in International Contracts (2005).[4] This treaty also is designed to ensure that a communication or contract is not "denied validity or enforceability on the sole ground that it is in the form of an electronic communication."[5] Unlike the Model Law, the goal of this treaty is to function as formal, positive law for ratifying countries. As Sections 8.4 and 8.7 explain, however, the Model Law has been substantially more influential, for it has influenced the law of nearly seventy countries, and very few countries have adopted the UN treaty.

Sections 8.4 through 8.7 below will examine in more detail these international efforts to facilitate electronic contracting.

---

[2] UN Doc. A/RES/51/162, 16 December, 1996, *available at* http://www.uncitral.org/uncitral/en/uncitral_texts/electronic_commerce/1996Model.html.

[3] UN Doc. A/CN.9/WG.IV/WP.88, 30 January 2001, *available at* http://www.uncitral.org/uncitral/en/uncitral_texts/electronic_commerce/2001Model_signatures.html.

[4] UN Doc. A/60/515, 22 November 2005, *available at* http://www.uncitral.org/uncitral/en/uncitral_texts/electronic_commerce/2005Convention.html.

[5] *Id.*, art. 8(1).

Domestic Legislation. In the United States, a federal statute from 2000, the Electronic Signatures in Global and National Commerce Act (E-SIGN),[6] has served as a significant impetus to the legal enforceability of eCommerce transactions. E-SIGN does not displace the substantive rules of contract law, but rather facilitates the use of electronic records and signatures in interstate and foreign commerce. At its core is the familiar principle that electronic signatures, records, and contracts may not be denied validity or effect solely because they are in an electronic form. E-SIGN permits the states to adopt their own conforming legislation in its place, but it has achieved its principal purpose because every State has done so.[7]

Indeed, even before E-SIGN, the National Conference of Commissioners on Uniform State Laws (now known as the Uniform Law Commission)—one of two institutions responsible for drafting the UCC—prepared two separate uniform acts to facilitate electronic commerce transactions. The first is the Uniform Electronic Transactions Act (UETA),[8] which is similar in scope and substance to the UNCITRAL Model Law. Forty-seven of the fifty states have adopted UETA (and in this way exercised their power to displace E-SIGN).[9] The second legal effort is the Uniform Computer Information Transactions Act (UCITA),[10] which applies specifically to transactions involving the transfer of computer information, such as software licensing transactions over the internet. Unlike UETA, however, UCITA has not been widely accepted, with only two state adoptions (Maryland and Virginia).

Sections 8.8 through 8.10 below will examine in more detail these various domestic legislative efforts to facilitate eCommerce transactions.

The European Union. The European Union also has been active in addressing electronic legal transactions on a regional level. In specific, it has adopted two "directives" on the subject: The Directive on Electronic Commerce[11] and the Directive on Electronic

---

[6]   15 U.S.C. §§ 7000 *et seq.* (hereinafter E-SIGN).

[7]   *See* §§ 8.9 and 8.10 *infra.*

[8]   *Available at* http://www.uniformlaws.org/shared/docs/electronic%20transactions/ueta_final_99.pdf (hereinafter UETA).

[9]   For more detail on this point see note 80, *infra.*

[10]   *Available   at*   http://www.uniformlaws.org/Act.aspx?title=Computer%20 Information%20Transactions%20Act (hereinafter, UCITA).

[11]   Directive 2000/31/EC of the European Parliament and of the Council of 8 June 2000 on Certain Legal Aspects of Information Society Services, in Particular Electronic Commerce, in the Internal Market ("Directive on Electronic Commerce"), *available at* http://eur-lex.europa.eu/LexUriServ/LexUriServ.do?uri=CELEX:32000 L0031:EN:HTML.

Signatures.[12] Separately, the European Union has recognized that the increased physical distance and increasingly impersonal interactions between sellers and buyers raise special legal challenges for consumer transactions, including an enhanced risk of deceptive practices and concerns about privacy and data protection. The European Union has adopted a variety of directives on these subjects as well.

Sections 8.11 through 8.14 below will examine these European Union initiatives in more detail.

Before turning to these more formal legal regimes, the next section will briefly address private efforts to take advantage of electronic means of communication and contracting. Against the backdrop of limited world-wide legal uniformity, private parties have attempted to regulate their dealings through traditional contractual arrangements. But as the legislative efforts to facilitate electronic commercial transactions at an international level take hold, the value of these private contractual arrangements will only increase.

§ 8.2   Private Contractual Measures Enabling Commerce

Trading Partner Agreements were among the first tools private parties developed to address the issues raised by eCommerce, but they continue to serve a valuable role in a number of different types of business relationships today. These agreements exist under a variety of different names and forms (including EDI or "electronic data interchange" agreements). They nonetheless share the central idea that a prearranged (or prescribed) contractual agreement regulates the transactions and communications between the parties through some form of electronic platform. The agreement may be between only two parties, such as where a supplier creates a platform for regular orders by a customer on a dedicated website on the supplier's server. But such an agreement also may regulate a whole network of interrelated business transactions, whether under a master contract covering all parties or under a series of standardized individual contracts based on an agreed model. Such trading partner arrangements function best—or perhaps only—in a "closed system," where every party is a member of the network pursuant to a single framework contractual arrangement.

---

[12]   Directive 1999/93/EC of the European Parliament and of the Council of 13 December 1999 on a Community Framework for Electronic Signatures, *available at* http://eur-lex.europa.eu/LexUriServ/LexUriServ.do?uri=CELEX:31999L0093:EN: HTML.

Modern cloud computing, under which electronic communications, documents, and information are saved on a single third-party server, is increasingly making such multi-party arrangements both feasible and practical. Whether provided by a telecommunications company, an internet service provider, or a more specialized business organization, cloud computing arrangements permit parties to create a platform for regularized interaction based on a master contract.

A quite promising modern form of this platform-based electronic contracting is known as "contract lifestyle management (CLM)," a product offered by various third-party software vendors. The concept involves an international seller of goods or services paying for a license that will enable it to create, negotiate, conclude, and monitor contracts with its customers through the vendor's electronic platform. The seller also may define standardized contract terms for its customers in ordering products and services. Unique keys serve to identify users and validate assent for each transaction. A variety of large software enterprises—Oracle, SAP, EMC, etc.—offer these platform services.

Another, more specific example is the effort by the organizers of the "Bolero" system to create the legal infrastructure for electronic bills of lading. As Chapter 4 analyzed in more detail,[13] the Bolero system requires all involved parties—shippers, carriers, banks, and consignees—to consent to a framework set of contractual rules (the "Bolero Rule Book").[14] The legal interactions between the parties are then conducted on a dedicated and secure cloud computing site under the control of the Bolero system.

§ 8.3 Legislative Measures Enabling eCommerce___In General

Given the speed with which electronic technology has been changing business practices, some lawmakers came to realize that a gradual adaptation of existing legal rules through case law was simply inadequate. Pressure by industry groups to create greater legal certainty also spurred national and state legislatures, as well as law reform bodies at the international level, to offer more comprehensive solutions tailored to the special characteristics of electronic transactions. The result has been a rapid increase in the number of statutes, codes, and model laws around the world designed to address eCommerce.

---

[13]   *See* Chapter 4, § 4.15.

[14]   *See* www.bolero.net.

The new statutory schemes nonetheless have different purposes. Some are enabling measures designed simply to clarify or confirm the ability to conclude contractual agreements in an electronic form. This is the most basic function for any statutory eCommerce measure. As legal systems become more comfortable with electronic communication and contracting, more modern statutory measures are turning to the special substantive issues that arise in cyberspace transactions.

Thus, for example, some new statutory schemes address the special challenges relating to standardized contracts in electronic transactions. This is a phenomenon as old as the printing press, but the ease of reproduction of contract terms in electronic form has raised with new urgency the traditional concerns about procedural and substantive fairness: Are the standard electronic terms unconscionable? Are they sufficiently clear and conspicuous so as to bind the user? Do electronic transactions raise special public policy issues, such as concerning rights to information and other forms of privacy? Do the customary legal remedies work with eCommerce transactions? And are there particular problems with choice of law and choice of forum in the global marketplaces that exist only in cyberspace? Since the advent of the internet age in particular, legislatures have grappled with these and similar questions and likely will need to do so with even greater urgency as electronic contracting grows in frequency and complexity around the world.

§ 8.4 The UNCITRAL Model Law on Electronic Commerce

The first significant international effort to address electronic commerce and contracting came in the form of a "model law" proposed by the United Nations Commission on International Trade Law (UNCITRAL), the organization that developed the CISG (see Chapter 2).[15] A model law is not designed to function as law by itself, but rather to serve as a coherent set of principles for adoption by individual domestic legal systems. In this respect, the Model Law on Electronic Commerce has been quite successful: As of late 2016, it already has influenced nearly seventy national laws,[16] various European Union Directives, and uniform acts in nearly every state

---

[15] For a detailed examination of the CISG see Chapter 2, §§ 2.2–2.43.

[16] Prominent examples of the countries that have adopted legislation based on the UNCITRAL Model Law on Electronic Commerce are China, Colombia, France, India, Iran, Ireland, Mexico, New Zealand, Pakistan, Panama, the Philippines, the Republic of Korea, Singapore, and South Africa. *See* http://www.uncitral.org/uncitral/en/uncitral_texts/electronic_commerce/1996Model_status.html.

or province in the United States, Canada, and Australia.[17] Further enactments are expected.

The Model Law follows a minimalist approach, for it seeks merely to validate and facilitate eCommerce transactions, not to regulate them comprehensively. Its fundamental principle is equality of treatment for paper documents and electronic "data messages" (see § 8.5 below).[18] With this foundation, Articles 5 to 10 of the Model Law address the legal recognition of data messages;[19] the admissibility and evidentiary weight of data messages;[20] the concepts of "writing," "signature," and "original document" in electronic commerce;[21] and the retention of data messages.[22] Articles 11 to 15 then furnish a set of rules that address the formation of electronic contracts and the communication of data messages.[23]

§ 8.5   UNCITRAL Model Law__Equality of Treatment

As noted above, the fundamental goal of the UNCITRAL Model Law on Electronic Commerce is to ensure that electronic messages enjoy the same legal status as paper documents. The Model Law thus provides that a "data message" is not to be denied legal effect, validity, or enforceability solely because it is in electronic form.[24] Similarly, if a rule of law requires that a party present or retain a document in its "original form," an electronic data message will suffice if: (a) "there exists a reliable assurance as to the integrity of the information from the time when it was first generated in its final form;" and (b) any such information "is capable of being displayed to the person to whom it is to be presented."[25] But like paper-based records, information contained in a data message of course is not necessarily valid simply because it is in an electronic form.[26]

The Model Law also addresses the admissibility and evidentiary weight of a data message in legal proceedings. Article 9

---

17   *See id.*

18   UNCITRAL Model Law on Electronic Commerce, *supra* note 2, art. 1(a) (defining a "data message" as "information generated, sent, received or stored by electronic, optical or similar means").

19   *Id.*, art. 5.

20   *Id.*, art. 9.

21   *Id.*, arts 6, 7, 8.

22   *Id.*, art. 10.

23   *Id.*, arts. 11–15.

24   *Id.*, art. 5.

25   *Id.*, art. 8(1).

26   *See id.*, Guide to Enactment, ¶ 46.

provides that information in a data message cannot be denied admissibility as evidence "on the sole ground that it is a data message" or, if the message is the best evidence that a party can obtain, "on the grounds that it is not in its original form."[27] Thus, the fact that evidence exists in electronic form is not a ground to deny the *admissibility* of a data message. But the evidentiary *weight* of the data message will depend on the extent to which it was generated, stored, and communicated in a reliable manner.[28]

Similarly, a data message may satisfy any applicable "writing" or record retention requirement under domestic law.[29] But to achieve a level of formality that parallels paper documents, the Model Law provides that the information in a data message satisfy three requirements: First, it must be "accessible so as to be usable for subsequent reference"; second, it must be "retained in the format in which it was generated, sent or received" or in a format that "can be demonstrated to represent accurately the information generated, sent or received"; and finally, it must be retained such that it permits "identification of the origin and destination of a data message and the date and time when it was sent or received."[30] The retention requirement thus implies that the information in an electronic data message must be accessible, retrievable, identifiable with the original, and accurate.

The legal requirements for a valid electronic "signature" are similar. The Model Law provides that a data message will satisfy the requirements for a signature under domestic law if a method exists that is "reasonable for the circumstances" to identify both the identity of the person sending the message and that person's approval of the message.[31] Thus, three requirements exist for an effective electronic signature: The method by which the electronic signature is made must be (1) reliable under the circumstances, (2) sufficient to identify the person, (3) sufficient to identify the person's approval of the data massage.

Because of the significance of signatures for a variety of legal rules (writing requirements, evidence of assent, etc.), UNCITRAL has prepared a Model Law on Electronic Signatures (2001) of similar content[32] that legal systems may adopt separately from the Model Law on Electronic Commerce. Intentionally medium-

---

[27]   *Id.*, art. 9(1).

[28]   *Id.*, art. 9(2).

[29]   *Id.*, art. 6.

[30]   *Id.*, art. 10(1).

[31]   *Id.*, art. 7(1)(b).

[32]   *See* UNCITRAL Model Law on Electronic Signatures, *supra* note 3.

neutral,[33] this Model Law likewise declares that an electronic signature is sufficient with respect to a "date message" if the signature "is as reliable as was appropriate for the purpose for which the data message was generated or communicated, in the light of all the circumstances."[34] As of late 2016, over thirty countries have adopted legislation based on the Model Law on Electronic Signatures.[35]

§ 8.6   UNCITRAL Model Law__Contract Formation

The UNCITRAL Model Law on Electronic Commerce also contains targeted provisions on the subjects of contract formation and the communication of data messages. In specific, it has rules on formation, the attribution of messages, and the acknowledgment and receipt of data messages. It provides, however, that these more specialized rules may be varied by agreement of the parties.[36]

Article 11 of the Model Law addresses the recognition of a contract formed through an exchange of data messages. Like its general principle on data messages, that provision declares that a contract may not be "denied validity or enforceability on the sole ground" that it was formed by exchange of data messages.[37] This rule extends to cases in which both the offer and the acceptance are communicated by electronic means as well as those in which only the offer or only the acceptance is so communicated.[38]

The Model Law also contains a set of rules on the "attribution" of data messages.[39] These rules address both sides of two-way electronic communications, that is, under what circumstances a data message is binding as a message of the originator, and under what circumstances the originator is bound by the addressee's response or action. First, a party is bound as an originator of a data message if it actually sent that message.[40] Second, a party is bound by a data message if the sender had the authority to act on the

---

[33]   *Id.*, art. 3.

[34]   *Id.*, art. 6(1).

[35]   For a list of the countries that have adopted such domestic legislation see http://www.uncitral.org/uncitral/en/uncitral_texts/electronic_commerce/2001Model_status.html.

[36]   UNCITRAL Model Law on Electronic Commerce, *supra* note 2, art. 11(1) (providing that the right to use electronic data messages in the formation of contracts applies "unless otherwise agreed by the parties").

[37]   *Id.*

[38]   *Id.*

[39]   *Id.*, art. 13.

[40]   *Id.*, art. 13(1).

party's behalf in respect of that data message.[41] On similar reasoning, a party is bound as an originator if the data message was sent automatically by an information system programmed by or on behalf of the party.[42] Third, the addressee is "entitled to regard" a data message as being that of the originator if either (a) the addressee properly applied an authentication procedure previously agreed to by the originator for that purpose,[43] or (b) the data message resulted from the action of a person whose relationship with the originator was such that it enabled that person to gain access to the method used by the originator to identify a message as its own.[44]

If a data message is deemed that of the originator, or the addressee is otherwise is entitled to rely it, then the addressee also is "entitled to act on th[e] assumption" that the data message was authorized.[45] This is not true, however, if the addressee "knew or ought to have known" that the data message in fact was not from or not authorized by the originator.[46]

A major problem with electronic data messages is that they get lost—or are caught in spam or similar computer filters—much more often than messages sent in paper form. Thus, acknowledgment of receipt of electronic messages is much more important to the parties than is acknowledgment of paper-based messages; as a result, parties engaging in electronic communications often agree that data messages must be acknowledged to be effective. If the parties so agree, the UNCITRAL Model Law provides that the required acknowledgment may be accomplished either by an agreed-upon method or, in absence of such a method, by any sufficiently clear communication or conduct.[47] Even where the parties have not agreed to require acknowledgment, the originator of a data message may unilaterally create such a requirement by stating in the body of the message that it is conditional on acknowledgment.[48] In such a case, the data message "is treated as though it has never been sent, until the acknowledgement is received."[49] Receipt of a message generally requires that the message enter an information system outside the control of the originator or its agents.[50] The UNCITRAL

---

[41]   *Id.*, art. 13(2)(a).

[42]   *Id.*, art. 13(2)(b).

[43]   *Id.*, art. 13(3)(a).

[44]   *Id.*, art. 13(3)(b).

[45]   *Id.*, art. 13(5).

[46]   *Id.*, art. 13(5), last sentence.

[47]   *Id.*, art. 14(2).

[48]   *Id.*, art. 14(3).

[49]   *Id.*

[50]   *Id.*, art. 15(1).

Model Law also contains detailed rules on when a data message is deemed sent and received.[51]

Other provisions in the Model Law are specific to the contracts for the carriage of goods and to transportation documents.[52] These provisions generally permit electronic data messages to replace bills of lading and waybills, even where local statutes require a paper document.[53] They also provide that legal requirements for the use of paper documents in carriage contracts are satisfied by such data messages.[54]

§ 8.7   United Nations Convention on Electronic Commerce

UNCITRAL also has prepared a formal treaty on the subject of electronic communications and contracting, the United Nations Convention on the Use of Electronic Communications in International Contracts (2005).[55] Like the Model Law on Electronic Commerce, the fundamental purpose of this treaty is to validate communications or contracts in electronic form. But unlike the Model Law, UNCITRAL has proposed this legal product as a treaty, which, like the CISG from Chapter 2, would take effect as formal, positive law in the ratifying countries.

By its terms, the Convention applies to electronic communications between parties whose "places of business" are in different states, provided at least one party has its place of business in a Contracting State.[56] The parties may "opt into" the Convention, but may also "opt out" or otherwise vary the effect of the Convention.[57] The Convention does not apply, however, to communications relating to contracts with consumers nor to those involving negotiable instruments, documents of title, wills or trusts, or certain types of financial matters.[58]

The core principles of the Convention parallel those of the Model Law on Electronic Commerce. First, the Convention declares that a communication or a contract may not be "denied validity or enforceability on the sole ground that it is in the form of an electronic communication."[59] Second, it emphasizes that nothing in

---

[51]   *Id.*, art. 15(2), (4).

[52]   *Id.*, arts. 16–17.

[53]   *Id.*, art. 16(1)–(5).

[54]   *Id.*, art. 16(6).

[55]   *See* UN Convention on Electronic Communications, *supra* note 4.

[56]   *Id.*, art. 1(1).

[57]   *Id.*, art. 3.

[58]   *Id.*, art. 2(1), (2).

[59]   *Id.*, art. 8(1).

its rules "requires that a communication or a contract be made or evidenced in any particular form."[60] Third, it expressly validates contracts concluded on an entirely automated basis,[61] but defines specific remedies for input errors by natural persons relating to automated message systems.[62] Finally, to further its general goal of ensuring functional equivalence between paper documents and electronic communications and contracts, it states that the electronic forms must be "accessible so as to be usable for subsequent reference"[63] and that electronic signatures must identify the person and indicate assent by sufficiently reliable methods.[64]

Although this Convention formally entered into force on March 1, 2013, thus far only seven countries have ratified it.[65] As a result, the extent of its future influence remains quite unclear. A principal reason for this is that many advanced countries, including the United States and the member states of the European Union, already have in place comprehensive legislative schemes that regulate the same subject as the Convention (as have the over seventy other countries that have adopted domestic legislation under UNCITRAL's Model Law as noted above).

Nonetheless, a recent development may enhance the Convention's prospects: In February, 2016, President Obama submitted the Convention to the Senate under Article II, Section 2, of the Constitution along with his recommendation that it grant consent to ratification.[66] Both the Uniform Law Commission and the American Bar Association have expressed support for U.S. ratification. The treaty would be implemented by separate federal legislation that would addresses its relationship with existing domestic legislation on the same subject (see §§ 8.8–8.10 below). As of late 2016, however, the Senate has taken no action whatsoever on this treaty.

---

[60]   *Id.*, art. 9(1).

[61]   *Id.*, art. 12.

[62]   *Id.*, art. 14.

[63]   *Id.*, art. 9(2).

[64]   *Id.*, art. 9(3).

[65]   The seven countries are the Congo, Dominican Republic, Honduras, Montenegro, the Russian Federation, Singapore, and Sri Lanka. *See* http://www. uncitral.org/uncitral/en/uncitral_texts/electronic_commerce/2005Convention_status. html.

[66]   *See Letter of Transmittal from the President of the United States to the Senate With Legal Analysis of the United Nations Convention on the Use of Electronic Communications in International Contracts*, Feb. 10, 2016, Sen. Treaty Doc. No. 114–5.

§ 8.8   eCommerce Legislation in the United States__In General

As noted in the Introduction to this Chapter, lawmakers in the United States have adopted legislation at both the national and state levels to validate and facilitate electronic commerce. The most important of these at the national level is the Electronic Signatures in Global and National Commerce Act (E-SIGN)[67] and at the state level the Uniform Electronic Transactions Act (UETA).[68] The following two Sections analyze these important statutes.

§ 8.9   Legislation__The Federal E-SIGN Act

As noted in the Introduction, the principal impetus for the recognition and validation of electronic commerce in the United States was the federal Electronic Signatures in Global and National Commerce Act (E-SIGN).[69] The provisions of E-SIGN broadly cover electronic signatures, electronic contracts, and electronic records in "any transaction in or affecting interstate or foreign commerce."[70] A "transaction" is similarly broadly defined in the Act as any "action or set of actions relating to the conduct of business, consumer, or commercial affairs between two or more persons."[71]

E-SIGN declares two fundamental principles, "notwithstanding any statute, regulation, or other rule of law": (1) "a signature, contract, or other record . . . may not be denied legal effect, validity, or enforceability solely because it is in electronic form"; and (2) "a contract . . . may not be denied legal effect, validity, or enforceability solely because an electronic signature or electronic record was used in its formation."[72] The Act also has more specific rules relating to the accuracy of and ability to retain contracts and other records,[73] to notarization of documents,[74] and to electronic agents.[75]

E-SIGN has special provisions for consumer contracts. It assumes that many consumers will want a paper (hardcopy) record of the transaction, while others prefer not to be bothered with

---

[67]   E-SIGN, *supra* note 6.

[68]   UETA, *supra* note 8.

[69]   *See* E-SIGN, *supra* note 6. For a case questioning, but not deciding on, the constitutionality of E-SIGN, see People v. McFarlan, 744 N.Y.S. 2d 287, 293 (Sup. Ct. 2002).

[70]   E-SIGN, *supra* note 6, 15 U.S.C. § 7001(a).

[71]   *Id.*, § 7006(13).

[72]   *Id.*, § 7001(a)(1), (2).

[73]   *Id.*, § 7001(d), (e).

[74]   *Id.*, § 7001(g).

[75]   *Id.*, § 7001(h).

paper. The Act thus provides that if a law requires that information be provided to a consumer in writing, the use of an electronic record satisfies the requirement if: (1) "the consumer has affirmatively consented to such use and had not withdrawn such consent," and (2) before such consent, the consumer is provided with a "clear and conspicuous statement" informing him or her of any right or option to have the record made available on paper and of the right to withdraw the consent.[76] The Act also requires that the consumer have some ability to access the electronic records to which the consent applies.[77] However, this requirement may be met if the consumer confirms electronically that he or she can access the electronic records in the specified formats, or acknowledges an ability to access the electronic record or responds affirmatively to an electronic query to that effect. If any changes occur to hardware or software requirements for such access, the consumer must be informed of this and that it may withdraw its consent to the use of electronic records.[78] Any consent by a consumer applies only to the particular transaction that gave rise to the obligation to provide the record.

The most important aspect of E-SIGN for present purposes, however, is that it may be superseded by a state statute. Indeed, the Act explicitly declares that a state may "modify, limit, or supersede" its provisions if the state either (a) enacts the Uniform Electronic Transactions Act (UETA) (see Section 8.10 below), or (b) otherwise specifies rules and procedures that are consistent with E-SIGN.[79] And in fact forty-seven states and the District of Colombia have taken advantage of this authorization by formally enacting UETA.[80] Thus, the most important practical statute for validating and facilitating electronic communications and contracting is not E-SIGN, but rather UETA.[81]

---

[76]   *Id.*, § 7001(c)(1)(A)–(B).

[77]   *Id.*, § 7001(c)(1)(C).

[78]   *Id.*, § 7001(c)(1)(D).

[79]   *Id.*, § 7002(a).

[80]   *See* http://www.uniformlaws.org/LegislativeFactSheet.aspx?title=Electronic%20Transactions%20Act. The three states that have not adopted UETA are New York, Illinois, and Washington. But the first two have adopted legislation that in nearly all significant respects parallels the rules in UETA. *See* Electronic Commerce Security Act, 1998 Ill. Laws 4191 (codified as amended at 5 ILL. COMP. STAT. ANN. § 175/1–101 *et seq.* (2016)); New York Electronic Signatures and Records Act, N.Y. STATE TECH. LAW §§ 301 *et seq.* (2016). Washington has adopted a more focused statute on electronic signatures. *See* Washington Electronic Authentication Act, 35 Wash. Rev. Code §§ 19.34.010 *et seq.* (1996) (as amended by the Act of May 13, 1999, ch. 287, 1999 Wash. Sess. Laws 1203).

[81]   One court has questioned whether the eCommerce statute adopted by New York conforms to E-SIGN in all respects. *See* People v. McFarlan, 744 N.Y.S. 2d 287, 294 (Sup. Ct. 2002). More recent courts have observed, however, that the New York legislation "appear[s] to have chosen to incorporate the substantive terms of E-SIGN

Moreover, even under E-SIGN, a party may give notice that it will not be bound by electronic messages, and thus negate E-SIGN's rules.[82] In addition, E-SIGN does not apply at all for transactions governed by the UCC, except for Article 2 (on sales of goods) and Article 2A (on leases of goods).[83] This elliptical phrasing means E-SIGN's rules on electronic signatures and records apply to transactions involving the sale and leasing of goods, but not to the other subjects within the scope of the UCC. More generally, E-SIGN makes clear that it does not alter the obligations of persons under any requirements imposed by another statute, regulation, or other rule of law except with respect to the validity and enforceability of electronic signatures, contracts or records.[84]

§ 8.10 Legislation__State Laws Enabling eCommerce, Especially UETA

UETA. As described in the preceding Section, the most important source for legal validation of electronic communications and contracts in the United States is uniform law adopted at the state level. In specific, the Uniform Law Commission (formerly known as the National Conference of Commissioners on Uniform State Laws) has produced two different uniform acts to facilitate electronic commerce. By far the more significant of the two is the Uniform Electronic Transactions Act (UETA).[85] As noted above, forty-seven states have enacted UETA into their domestic law to displace E-SIGN based on the express authorization in E-SIGN itself.[86]

Like E-SIGN, UETA is designed to validate and facilitate the use of electronic records at a very basic level. UETA also is similar in scope and substance to E-SIGN[87] as well as to the UNCITRAL Model Law on Electronic Commerce.[88] In fact, in nearly all significant respects, each of the principles discussed below regarding UETA conforms to the provisions in E-SIGN.

UETA applies to all types of electronic messages and contracts. It thus broadly defines its scope to cover any "action or set of actions occurring between two or more persons relating to the conduct of

---

into New York state law." Martin v. Portexit Corp. 948 N.Y.S.2d 21 (Ct. App. 2012) (*quoting* Naldi v. Grunberg, 80 A.D.3d 1,12, 908 N.Y.S.2d 639 (2010)).

[82]   E-SIGN, *supra* note 6, § 7001(b)(2).

[83]   *Id.*, § 7003.

[84]   *Id.*, § 7001(b)(1).

[85]   *See* UETA, *supra* note 8.

[86]   *See supra* note 80.

[87]   *See* § 8.9 *supra.*

[88]   *See* § 8.4 *supra.*

business, commercial, or governmental affairs."[89] Like E-SIGN, UETA does not apply to wills or to transactions governed by the UCC, with the exception of Articles 2 and Article 2A (to which UETA does apply).[90]

Nonetheless, UETA generally follows an "opt-in" approach; that is, it only applies to transactions "between parties each of which has agreed to conduct transactions by electronic means."[91] Several recent courts in fact have concluded that no such agreement existed between the parties to a disputed transaction.[92] And one emphasized that merely negotiating a potential deal via email does not, without more, equate to an agreement to conclude the final contract by electronic means.[93]

Nonetheless, such an agreement need not be express or explicit. As a general matter, UETA defines "agreement" to mean simply "the bargain of the parties in fact, as found in their language or inferred from other circumstances."[94] And on the specific issue, UETA provides that an agreement to conduct transactions by electronic means may arise "from the context and surrounding circumstances, including the parties' conduct."[95] Thus, one California federal court held that an employee agreed to binding arbitration by concluding an online application and then acknowledging that she had reviewed an arbitration program document available on the employer's website.[96]

---

[89]   UETA, *supra* note 8, §§ 2(16) (so defining the term "transaction"), and 3(a) (stating that the Act applies to electronic records and signatures "relating to a transaction").

[90]   *Id.*, § 3(b)(1), (2).

[91]   *Id.*, § 5(b).

[92]   *See, e.g.,* Celtic Marine Corp. v. James C. Justice Cos., 760 F.3d 477, 482–483 (5th Cir. 2014) (concluding that the parties had not agreed to amend a settlement agreement by electronic communications when in the past "the two settlement agreements and all contracts and guaranties between the parties had been typed and physically signed by authorized representatives of the parties"); WCT & D, LLC v. City of Kansas City, 476 S.W.3d 336, 341 (Mo. Ct. App. 2015) (holding with regard to a dispute over a liquor license that the applicant "offered no evidence that City had ever expressed a willingness to conduct these transactions electronically or that City had previously accepted electronic signatures" and thus that the City had not "agreed to conduct transactions by electronic means" as required by UETA).

[93]   SN4, LLC v. Anchor Bank, FSB, 848 N.W.2d 559, 567–569 (Minn. Ct. App. 2014) (declaring that "while contracting parties may agree to negotiate and form a contract by electronic means, doing so does not mean that they have also agreed to electronically subscribe to whatever agreement may result from their electronic negotiations").

[94]   UETA, *supra* note 8, § 2(1).

[95]   *Id.*, § 5(b).

[96]   Stover-Davis v. Aetna Life Ins. Co., 2016 WL 2756848, at *4 (E.D. Cal. 2016). *See also* Parks v. Seybold, 2015 WL 4481768, at *5 (Tex. Ct. App. 2015) (holding that by exchanging emails and other actions a party had agreed to conduct business electronically as contemplated by UETA).

The core principles of UETA are found in Section 7. At its most basic, that section mandates equal recognition of electronic contracts and communications with paper documents. In specific, it declares in four subparagraphs that:

(1) A record or signature "may not be denied legal effect or enforceability solely because it is in electronic form";

(2) A contract "may not be denied legal effect or enforceability solely because it is in electronic form";

(3) If a law requires a record to be in writing, "an electronic record satisfies the law"; and

(4) If a law requires a signature, "an electronic signature satisfies the law."[97]

Central to an understanding of these basic principles of UETA is its definition of "electronic records" and "electronic signatures." In both respects, UETA is technology-neutral, for it does not require that businesses and consumers use or accept any specific type or method of electronic interaction in order to conduct a transaction. The Act thus defines an "electronic record" very broadly as any record "created, generated, sent, communicated, received or stored by electronic means."[98] Following this broad conception, the Oklahoma Supreme Court recently held that a notice sent via Facebook satisfied the requirements of UETA.[99] As the court there observed, "[t]here is no support for an argument that Facebook is less dependable as an actual notice than a fax, a letter or some form of email other than Facebook."[100]

The definition of an "electronic signature" is similarly capacious. It includes any "electronic sound, symbol or process attached to or logically associated with a contract or other record and executed or adopted by a person with the intent to sign the record."[101] This definition is broad enough to include telephone keypad agreements (*e.g.*, "press 9 to agree") and internet "click wrap" agreements (*e.g.*, "click here if you agree").[102] The last phrase of the definition of an electronic signature—"with the intent to sign the record"—is significant, however. Although under UETA a

---

[97]   UETA, *supra* note 8, § 7(a)–(d).

[98]   *Id.*, § 2(7). UETA also has detailed rules on when and where electronic records are deemed sent and received. *See id.*, § 15.

[99]   Andrews v. McCall (In re K.P.M.A.), 341 P.3d 38, 56 (Okla. 2014).

[100]   *Id.*

[101]   UETA, *supra* note 8, § 2(8).

[102]   For a recent example see Harpham v. Big Moose Home Inspections, 2015 WL 5945842, at *3 (Mich. Ct. App. 2015) (holding in a dispute over an inspection contract that "[c]licking the button imposed on the inspection agreement evidences the intent to sign the contract").

recording may satisfy any writing requirement, a surreptitious recording cannot satisfy the signature requirement because the speaker did not intend the recording to be a signature.[103] Thus, the person or entity accepting an electronic "sound, symbol or process" as a signature must exercise care to ensure that the person supposedly bound in fact intended to connect itself with the electronic contract or record.

UETA also validates electronic retention of records. Thus, if a law requires that a record be retained, the requirement "is satisfied by retaining an electronic record of the information in the record." But this is subject to two requirements. First, the electronic record must "accurately reflect[ ] the information set forth in the record after it was first generated in its final form as an electronic record or otherwise."[104] Second, the electronic record must be "accessible for later reference."[105]

UETA (like E-SIGN) does not regulate the substantive rules of contract law as to the validity and enforceability of contracts.[106] Thus, although the Act has formal provisions on when an electronic record is deemed "sent"[107] and "received,"[108] these rules do not alter any substantive legal rules related to those concepts. For example, one recent court observed that UETA's rule on receipt does not control the issue under contract law of when an acceptance of an offer becomes effective (the so-called mailbox or dispatched acceptance rule).[109] Rather, UETA merely provides substitute methods to satisfy the basic formalities of contract (and other) law. For example, where a "Statute of Frauds" provision requires a contract to be in writing, UETA states that an electronic record will suffice. But as noted above regarding retention, to ensure a level of reliability comparable to paper documents, UETA requires that an electronic record be in a form that "accurately reflects the information" in the record and "remains accessible for later

---

[103]   See Sawyer v. Mills, 295 S.W.3d 79 (Ky. 2009).

[104]   UETA, supra note 8, § 12(a)(1).

[105]   Id., § 12(a)(2).

[106]   See, e.g., United States Life Ins. Co. v. Wilson, 18 A.3d 110, 127 n.5 (Md. Ct. Spec. App. 2011) ("[I]t must be borne in mind that neither UETA nor E-SIGN is intended to provide substantive rules of law; rather, each is essentially designed principally to validate electronic transactions, records and signatures.").

[107]   UETA, supra note 8, § 15(a).

[108]   Id., § 15(b).

[109]   See United States Life Ins. Co. v. Wilson, 18 A.3d 110, 127 n.5 (Md. Ct. Spec. App. 2011).

reference."[110] As a more general matter, the Act makes clear that all of its provisions "may be varied by agreement."[111]

UETA also has detailed "attribution" rules. Section 9 of the Act provides that an electronic signature or record is attributable to a person only if it is in fact produced by an act of that person.[112] This may poses challenges in some cases, but UETA is quite flexible on the point. The same provision thus states the act of a person "may be shown in any manner," including by security procedures designed to identify a person.[113] One interesting case in this regard involved a West Virginia statute governing public funding of campaigns that required candidates first to obtain a sufficient number of signed private contributions. When a dispute arose over electronic contribution records submitted by a candidate, the court held that under UETA "no evidentiary issues of intent or authenticity" existed because it was "undisputed in the record that the electronic contribution receipts submitted by [the candidate] contain unique transaction identifiers allowing the contributors to be identified."[114]

Finally, UETA expressly validates transactions concluded on an entirely automated basis (*i.e.*, by "electronic agents").[115] The Act likewise provides that a contract may be formed "by the interaction of an electronic agent and an individual."[116] Conceptually, this is essentially the extension of basic agency principles to the computer, with the computer acting on the instructions programmed by its "principal."[117]

UCITA. The second uniform law produced by the Uniform Law Commission (ULC) to address electronic commerce is the Uniform Computer Information Transactions Act (UCITA).[118] Unlike UETA, UCITA applies with specific reference to one category of transactions, *i.e.*, to those involving the sale or other distribution of, or access to, "computer information."[119] The term "computer

---

[110]   UETA, *supra* note 8, § 12.

[111]   *Id.*, § 5(d).

[112]   *Id.*, § 9(a).

[113]   *Id.*

[114]   Benjamin v. Walker, 786 S.E.2d 200, 212 (W. Va. 2016).

[115]   UETA, *supra* note 8, § 14(1).

[116]   *Id.*, § 14(2). *See also id.*, § 2(6) (defining an electronic agent as "a computer program or an electronic or other automated means used independently to initiate an action or respond to electronic records or performances in whole or in part, without review or action by an individual").

[117]   The Reporter for the Restatement of Agency does not fully agree with this analogy. *See* Restatement (Third) of Agency, § 1.04, Reporter's Note e (2006) (arguing that an agent must be a "person" and a computer cannot meet that definition).

[118]   *See* UCITA, *supra* note 10.

[119]   *Id.*, § 103.

information" is broadly defined as "information in electronic form which is obtained from or through the use of a computer."[120] Distilled to their essence, these rules mean that UCITA principally applies to software licensing transactions concluded or conducted via computer, and thus especially to transactions over the internet. UCITA then sets forth detailed provisions specifically tailored to such transactions. Thus, for example, UCITA has provisions on express and implied warranties that are customized for software transactions.[121]

The format of UCITA is similar to UCC Article 2 on sales of goods. Indeed, at an early stage in the process the drafters intended it to become UCC Article 2B; but this effort was rejected by the American Law Institute—the Uniform Law Commission's partner in UCC projects—as not sufficiently balanced. The Uniform Law Commission then took over the project on its own, and UCITA was the result. As of 2016, however, only two states have adopted UCITA (Maryland and Virginia).[122] Moreover, at least four states have enacted "bomb shelter" statutes to ensure that UCITA is not applied against their residents.[123] And in 2003, the Uniform Law Commission stated that it would not push for further enactments of UCITA, although it did not withdraw its original endorsement.

UCITA generally has provisions that parallel E-SIGN and UETA with regard to the validation of electronic records, contracts, and signatures.[124] But its rules on electronic signatures (which it refers to as "authentications"[125]) are even broader. Beyond executing or adopting "an electronic symbol, sound, message, or process," a party may be deemed to have authenticated (signed) a record under UCITA if it merely "made use of" or had "access to" computer information.[126] UCITA also has detailed substantive rules regarding offers and acceptances for electronic contracts,[127] including by electronic agents.[128]

The other controversial provisions of UCITA relate, first, to choice of law and choice of jurisdiction clauses. As to the former, it

---

[120]   *Id.*, § 102(10).

[121]   *Id.*, §§ 401–410. *See also* Baney Corp. v. Agilysis NV, L.L.C, 773 F. Supp. 2d 593 (D. Md. 2011) (holding a supplier liable for a breach of warranty under UCITA § 402(a) with regard to defects in a software program).

[122]   *See* http://www.uniformlaws.org/LegislativeFactSheet.aspx?title=Computer%20Information%20Transactions%20Act.

[123]   The four states are Iowa, North Carolina, Vermont and West Virginia.

[124]   UCITA, *supra* note 10, § 107.

[125]   *Id.*, § 102(6).

[126]   *Id.*, § 108.

[127]   *Id.*, §§ 201–207.

[128]   *Id.*, § 206.

broadly validates choice of law clauses (including, of course, a choice of UCITA), and then states that in absence of such a choice the licensor's home jurisdiction applies, "in all respects for purposes of contract law."[129] If a licensor has its place of business in a UCITA state (Maryland or Virginia), therefore, UCITA applies by default.[130]

As to choice of jurisdiction clauses, UCITA permits the parties to choose an exclusive forum for dispute resolution, unless the choice is "unreasonable and unjust."[131] Together with the broad rules choosing the governing law (and for proving "assent," see immediately below), the validation of choice of jurisdiction clauses gives substantial power to licensors—at least those in Maryland or Virginia—to ensure that UCITA governs their transactions.

Perhaps the most controversial aspects of UCITA relate to manifestations of assent. On this, UCITA first states the basic principle that both parties must indicate their assent to an electronic record (such as contractual terms prepared by a licensor) and that both must have had an opportunity to review the record or terms before manifesting assent.[132] The controversy comes with a rule that a person assents to contractual terms if, after an "opportunity to review,"[133] it engages in any conduct or makes any statement "with reason to know that the other party or its electronic agent may infer" such assent.[134] Moreover, under UCITA a licensor has the practical power to change a contract's terms unilaterally. This is so because it can demonstrate that a licensee has assented to a change merely by subsequently "obtain[ing] or us[ing]" the licensed product.[135] Thus, a licensee could become bound to contract modifications merely by using the product it has already purchased.[136]

---

[129]   *Id.*, § 109(a), (b). A choice of law clause will not, however, displace mandatory consumer protection laws. *Id.*, § 109(a).

[130]   *Id.*, § 109(d).

[131]   *Id.*, § 110.

[132]   *Id.*, § 112(a).

[133]   A person has such an "opportunity to review" a record if, *inter alia*, "it is made available in a manner that ought to call it to the attention of a reasonable person and permit review." *Id.*, § 112(e)(1). For a case holding that a person did not have such an opportunity to review with respect to terms not prominently displayed on an internet website see Cvent, Inc. v. Eventbrite, Inc., 739 F. Supp. 2d 927, 937 (E.D. Va. 2010).

[134]   UCITA, *supra* note 10, § 112(a)(2).

[135]   *Id.*, § 112(d).

[136]   Such a licensee may then have a "right to return" the related software, but that right is limited in noteworthy respects. *See id.*, § 112(e)(3).

§ 8.11   The European Union___Background to the eEurope Initiative

Like the United States, the European Union has made substantial efforts to develop regulatory solutions to the issues raised by electronic commerce. Beginning with an "eEurope Initiative" in the late 1990s,[137] as supplemented by "action plans" (eEurope 2002 and eEurope 2005[138]), these efforts attempted to address in a comprehensive way the impact of technology on European society.

From a legal perspective, the eEurope Initiative resulted in legislative products that in some ways are quite similar to the federal and state statutes in the United States noted above, but in other ways are quite different (especially regarding consumer protection). The principal measures designed as "enabling legislation" for eCommerce are the 1999 Electronic Signatures Directive,[139] and the 2000 Electronic Commerce Directive.[140] Section 8.12 below will review the substance of these Directives.

Separately, the European Union has adopted legislation designed to protect the legal and economic interests of consumers in the impersonal and distant transactions that electronic communications and commerce make possible. Section 8.13 will review the substance of these Directives.

Finally, the European Union's distinctive approach to data privacy is worthy of review. In 1995, the European Union adopted the Data Protection Directive[141] which required that member states adopt local legislation to limit in substantial respects the collection and sharing of information relating to natural persons. This was replaced in 2016 with a formal Regulation on the subject.[142]

This issue of course is of ever increasing significance as Facebook, Google, and myriad similar social media sites collect ever more detailed information on the lives of their users. Although

---

[137]   *eEurope 2002, available at* http://eur-lex.europa.eu/legal-content/EN/TXT/?uri=uriserv:l24226a.

[138]   *eEurope 2005 Action Plan: An Information Society for Everyone, available at* http://eur-lex.europa.eu/legal-content/EN/TXT/?uri=URISERV:l24226.

[139]   *See* Electronic Signatures Directive, *supra* note 12.

[140]   *See* Electronic Commerce Directive, *supra* note 11.

[141]   Directive 95/46/EC of 24 October 1995 on the Protection of Individuals with Regard to the Processing of Personal Data and on the Free Movement of Such Data, http://eur-lex.europa.eu/LexUriServ/LexUriServ.do?uri=CELEX:31995L0046:EN:HTML.

[142]   *See* Regulation (EU) 2016/679 of the European Parliament and of the Council On the Protection of Natural Persons with Regard to the Processing of Personal Data and on the Free Movement of Such Data (27 April 2016), *available at* http://eur-lex.europa.eu/legal-content/EN/TXT/HTML/?uri=CELEX:32016R0679&from=EN.

beyond the scope of "enabling legislation" as such, the significance of this issue justifies a brief review of the Data Protection Directive and the Data Protection Regulation (see Section 8.14 below).

§ 8.12   EU Directives Enabling eCommerce

The European Union's two principal legislative vehicles that recognize and facilitate electronic commerce are the Electronic Signatures Directive and the Electronic Commerce Directive.[143] Under the European Union's legal infrastructure, a "Directive" does not function as directly applicable law on its own, but rather requires that the twenty-eight member states adopt or adapt their own domestic legislation to conform to principles described therein.

Electronic Signatures Directive. The Electronic Signatures Directive, as the name implies, establishes the basic principle that the European Union member states must "ensure that an electronic signature is not denied legal effectiveness and admissibility solely on the grounds" that it is in electronic form.[144] More generally, the Directive requires that the member states ensure that electronic signatures are permitted "to circulate freely" within the European Union.[145] The definition of "electronic signature" is intentionally flexible and means merely "data in electronic form which are attached to or logically associated with other electronic data and which serve as a method of authentication."[146] In this respect, the Electronic Signatures Directive is technology-neutral, in that it seeks merely to associate an electronic record with a particular party.

The Directive also contemplates a more secure, high-tech system in the form of "advanced electronic signatures."[147] The idea here was that third party "Certification Services Providers" (CSPs) would issue unique and highly secure "qualified certificates" for specific transactions.[148] However, subsequent technological advances—as well as risks of liability for CSPs in the event of

---

[143]   *See* Electronic Signatures Directive, *supra* note 12, and Electronic Commerce Directive, *supra* note 11.

[144]   Electronic Signatures Directive, *supra* note 12, art. 5(2).

[145]   *Id.*, art. 4(2).

[146]   *Id.*, art. 2(1).

[147]   *See id.*, art. 2(2) (defining an "advanced electronic signature").

[148]   *See id.*, arts. 2(9) (defining a "certificate" to mean "an electronic attestation which links signature-verification data to a person and confirms the identity of that person"); and 2(10) (defining a "certification service provider" as an entity that, *inter alia*, "issues certificates"). *See also id.*, art. 5(1) (conferring special legal significance on "advanced electronic signatures" subject to certain other requirements).

errors[149]—have meant that this option has disappeared almost entirely in favor of the more flexible general electronic signature.

Electronic Commerce Directive. The second major piece of European Union legislation designed to facilitate electronic commerce is, appropriately, the Electronic Commerce Directive.[150] Issued in 2000, the broad goal of this Directive is to facilitate the provision of "information society services," including, among other things, the establishment of service providers and the use of electronic communications and contracts.[151] On the first point, the Directive thus precludes member states from requiring prior approval for online providers of commercial services ("information society service providers—ISSPs") or from imposing "any other requirement having equivalent effect."[152]

But a more specific goal of the Directive is a familiar one: to remove the legal obstacles to the enforceability of electronic contracts. Article 9 of the Directive thus states that European Union member states "shall ensure that their legal system allows contracts to be concluded by electronic means."[153] The same provision obligates member states to ensure that the legal requirements for contract formation "neither create obstacles for the use of electronic contracts nor result in such contracts being deprived of legal effectiveness and validity on account of their having been made by electronic means."[154]

The Directive provides, however, that any contract terms and general conditions for the transaction "must be made available in a way that allows [the recipient] to store and reproduce them."[155] It also requires that electronic communications from ISSPs "clearly identify" both their sender and their specific nature. Thus, "commercial communications," "promotional offers," and "promotional competitions or games," respectively, must be "clearly identifiable as such."[156]

The Directive establishes greater disclosure requirements for ISSPs in transactions with consumers. In specific, in such transactions ISSPs must provide the following information "clearly, comprehensibly and unambiguously and prior to the order being

---

[149]   *Id.*, art. 6.

[150]   Electronic Commerce Directive, *supra* note 11.

[151]   *Id.*, Preamble, ¶¶ 1, 2.

[152]   *Id.*, art. 4(1). The Directive separately has specific rules on required disclosures by ISSPs, see *id.*, art. 5, and on their liability. *See id.*, arts. 12–15.

[153]   *Id.*, art. 9(1).

[154]   *Id.*

[155]   *Id.*, art. 10(3).

[156]   *Id.*, art. 6(a)–(d).

placed by the recipient of the service": (a) the required technical actions to conclude the contract; (b) whether the contract will be filed and be accessible; (c) the technical means to correct "input errors" by the consumer prior to concluding the contract; and (d) the language(s) offered for contracting. Where a consumer places an order by electronic means, ISSPs must acknowledge receipt "without undue delay and by electronic means."[157]

Taken together, the EU's Electronic Signatures Directive and the Electronic Commerce Directive thus create the same basic legal framework for electronic contracting as UNCITRAL's Model Law and UETA.

§ 8.13   EU Directives on Distance Selling and Other Forms of Consumer Protection

For transactions with consumers, the European Union generally follows a much more protective policy than does the United States. The significance of this issue has only increased as electronic commerce has enabled transactions at much greater distances and on a much more impersonal basis. This has prompted the European Union to adopted a variety of directives aimed at protecting consumers from unfair and deceptive practices.

The most significant of these in practical terms is the 1997 Directive on the Protection of Consumers in respect of Distance Contracts (the Distance Selling Directive).[158] The Distance Selling Directive is intended to promote European consumer confidence in eCommerce by defining certain minimum protections for contracts concluded at a distance. The Directive thus imposes disclosure requirements on suppliers and grants a general right of withdrawal to consumers. In this way, it seeks to limit the effect of the aggressive marketing techniques and deceptive practices that may be particularly prevalent in online transactions. And to secure this goal, the Directive expressly provides that the consumer may not waive its protections[159] and may not lose them through choice of law clauses.[160]

The Directive applies to contracts concerning goods or services concluded by any means where the supplier is not in "the

---

[157]   *Id.*, art. 11.

[158]   Directive 1997/7/EC of the European Parliament and of the Council of 20 May 1997 on *the* Protection of Consumers in respect of Distance Contracts, *available at* http://eur-lex.europa.eu/legal-content/en/ALL/?uri=CELEX:31997L0007.

[159]   *Id.*, art. 12(1).

[160]   *Id.*, art. 12(2).

simultaneous physical presence" of the consumer.[161] Thus, it applies to contracts created, for example, by mail, telephone, videophone, fax, and email, as well as those concluded online.[162] In order to achieve its goal of an "approximate" level of consumer protection in such distance selling transactions throughout the European Union, the Directive required each member state to implement its provisions in their national law by the end of 2000.[163] All member states in fact have "transposed" the protections of the Directive into domestic law.[164]

The Distance Selling Directive imposes a number of obligations on suppliers and grants certain important rights to consumers in distance selling contracts. The most important of these is the right of consumers to "withdraw" from the contract. The Directive required member states to grant the consumer a right to withdraw from a distance selling contract "without penalty and without giving any reason" for at least seven days from the receipt of the goods or the provision of the services.[165] In fact, many member states have extended this right, some up to 15 days.[166] The only cost that may be imposed on the consumer is the cost of returning the goods.[167] Thereafter, the supplier must process the consumer's reimbursement as soon as possible and in any event within thirty days.[168] The supplier must inform the consumer of this right upon contract formation and again in writing in the course of contract performance,[169] and, if the supplier fails to do so, the time period for the consumer to exercise the right of withdrawal expands to three months.[170]

The Directive requires specific disclosures to consumers, in a "clear and comprehensible form," prior to concluding a distance selling contract. These include information on a variety of basic

---

[161]   *Id.*, arts. 2(1) (defining a "distance contract" as one involving the use of a "means of distance communication"); and 2(4) (defining "means of distance communication" as "any means which, without the simultaneous physical presence of the supplier and the consumer, may be used for the conclusion of a contract between those parties").

[162]   *See id.*, Annex 1.

[163]   *Id.*, art. 15.

[164]   *See* Press Release of the EU Commission, Questions and Answers on Distance Selling (21 September 2006), *available at* http://europa.eu/rapid/press-release_MEMO-06-339_en.htm.

[165]   Distance Selling Directive, *supra* note 158, art. 6(1).

[166]   *See* Commission Press Release, *supra* note 164.

[167]   Distance Selling Directive, *supra* note 158, art. 6(1). For limitations on the right of withdrawal see *id.*, art. 6(3).

[168]   *Id.*, art. 6(2).

[169]   *Id.*, arts. 4(1)(f), 5(1).

[170]   *Id.*, art. 6(1).

details about the supplier; the cost, terms, and conditions of the transaction; and, significantly, the consumer's right to withdraw or cancel the transaction.[171] In addition, the supplier must provide a confirmation of most of this information either in writing or in some other "durable" medium accessible to the consumer prior to delivery or completion of performance of the contract.[172] Orders placed through distance selling ordinarily must be filled within thirty days.[173] The Distance Selling Directive completely bans unsolicited marketing by certain types of technologies, including automated calling machines or faxes (and presumably, by extension, email spam), and allows others only if there is no clear objection by the consumer.[174]

The European Union also has adopted consumer protection directives of general application that are relevant to transactions conducted by electronic means. The first is the Directive on Unfair Contract Terms of 1993.[175] This rule-based Directive governs non-negotiated contracts with consumers and reflects a much more paternalistic approach than the general unconscionability doctrine of U.S. law. It contains a list of terms that are never effective in contracts with consumers and subjects all others to a substantive review for fairness.[176]

A second consumer protection directive of note is the Consumer Goods Directive of 1999.[177] This Directive might be seen as a complement to the Directive on Unfair Contract Terms, but with reference to contractual promises made regarding the quality of goods sold to consumers. In general, the seller must ensure that the goods conform to the contract, comply with any description given by the seller, are fit for any specific purpose made known to the seller, and are of a comparable quality to similar goods.[178] If the seller fails

---

[171]   *Id.*, art. 4.

[172]   *Id.*, art. 5. This confirmation obligation does not apply to services provided on a one-time basis. *Id.*, art. 5(2).

[173]   *Id.*, art. 7.

[174]   *Id.*, art. 10. A more specialized EU Directive addresses distance marketing of financial services. *See* Directive 2002/65/EC of the European Parliament and of the Council of 23 September 2002 Concerning the Distance Marketing of Consumer Financial Services, *available at* http://eur-lex.europa.eu/LexUriServ/LexUriServ.do? uri=CELEX:32002L0065:EN:HTML.

[175]   Council Directive 93/13/EEC of 5 April 1993 on Unfair Terms in Consumer Contracts, *available at* http://eur-lex.europa.eu/legal-content/EN/TXT/HTML/?uri= CELEX:31993L0013&from=EN.

[176]   *Id.*, art. 3, and Annex.

[177]   Directive 1999/44/EC of the European Parliament and of the Council of 25 May 1999 on Certain Aspects of the Sale of Consumer Goods and Associated Guarantees, *available at* http://eur-lex.europa.eu/LexUriServ/LexUriServ.do?uri= CELEX:31999L0044:EN:HTML.

[178]   *Id.*, art. 2.

to meet these obligations, it is liable to the consumer for any resultant damages.[179]

A final consumer protection directive relevant to electronic commerce is the Unfair Commercial Practices Directive of 2005.[180] This Directive broadly prohibits commercial practices that distort the economic decision-making of consumers. Included among such practices are advertising with misleading information,[181] misleading omissions,[182] and other aggressive commercial tactics.[183]

§ 8.14   EU Laws on Protection of Personal Data

The European Union has adopted a comprehensive legal regime for the protection of personal data that extends far beyond the market-based approach in the United States. The EU's first legal instrument on this subject was a Data Protection Directive, which required each European Union member state to regulate the processing of personal data in accordance with certain described principles.[184] In 2016, the EU then adopted a formal Regulation on the same subject, which (unlike a Directive) has direct effect as law throughout the European Union without implementing legislation by the member states.[185] Because this Regulation will not enter into effect until 2018, the following materials briefly review the Data Protection Directive. We then highlight some of the more significant changes to be introduced by the Data Protection Regulation.

The Data Protection Directive. The purpose of the Data Protection Directive is to protect "the fundamental rights and freedoms of natural persons, and in particular their right to privacy with respect to the processing of personal data."[186] It accomplishes this goal by declaring that the processing of any information relating to natural persons must be fair, current, legitimate, accurate, and proportional to the related purpose. "Personal data" is broadly defined as "any information relating to an identified or

---

[179]   *Id.*, art. 4.

[180]   Directive 2005/29/EC of the European Parliament and of the Council of 11 May 2005 Concerning Unfair Business-to-Consumer Commercial Practices, *available at* http://eur-lex.europa.eu/legal-content/EN/TXT/HTML/?uri=CELEX:32005L0029&qid=1470324464167&from=EN.

[181]   *Id.*, art. 6 (also defining a practice as misleading if it contains false information or otherwise deceives the consumer).

[182]   *Id.*, art. 7.

[183]   *Id.*, art. 8.

[184]   The Data Protection Directive, *supra* note 141. Switzerland—which is not an EU member state—also has adopted a "Federal Act on Data Protection" (1992, as amended 2008), *available at* http://www.admin.ch/ch/e/rs/2/235.1.en.pdf.

[185]   *See* Data Protection Regulation, *supra* note 142.

[186]   *Id.*, art. 1(1).

identifiable natural person."[187] The Directive then places severe restrictions on the "processing" of such personal data. This term is exceptionally broad and covers "any operation or set of operations which is performed upon personal data, whether or not by automatic means."[188]

The Data Protection Directive applies to any processing of personal data by entities ("controllers"[189]) that are established in, or use any equipment in, a member state of the European Union.[190] In most cases, it permits the processing of personal data only with the "unambiguous" consent of the individual involved or when the processing is "necessary" for contract performance (*e.g.*, billing), to serve "important public interests," or to protect the individual's "vital interests."[191] The processing of data revealing racial or ethnic origin, political opinions, religious beliefs, philosophical or ethical persuasion, or health or sexual life is rarely permitted without the individual's "explicit" consent.[192]

The Directive requires that controllers provide information to the affected individuals on a variety of subjects, including the purposes for both the collection and the processing of personal data.[193] Such disclosure obligations apply to virtually all websites that invite registration or otherwise collect data on users. Affected individuals have a right to obtain access to the personal data collected by controllers "without constraint at reasonable intervals and without excessive delay or expense."[194] The individuals then may object either to any processing of personal data for marketing purposes or, "on compelling legitimate grounds," to processing of any kind.[195] All processing also must also be confidential and secure.[196] The Directive requires that member states provide for private civil liability and public administrative remedies for violations of its requirements.[197]

---

[187]   *Id.*, art. 2(a).

[188]   *Id.*, art. 2(b). The term "processing" expressly includes the "collection, recording, organization, storage, adaptation or alteration, retrieval, consultation, use, disclosure by transmission, dissemination or otherwise making available, alignment or combination, blocking, erasure or destruction." *Id.*

[189]   *Id.*, art. 2(d).

[190]   *Id.*, art. 4.

[191]   *Id.*, art. 7.

[192]   *Id.*, art. 8.

[193]   *Id.*, arts. 10, 11.

[194]   *Id.*, art. 12.

[195]   *Id.*, art. 14.

[196]   *Id.*, arts. 16, 17.

[197]   *Id.*, arts. 22–24.

Data processors are required to make extensive disclosures to governments authorities as well. Each member state is obligated to designate or establish a "supervisory authority" to implement and oversee compliance with the Directive's requirements.[198] Data controllers then must provide extensive disclosures to these supervisory authorities regarding the processing of personal data.[199] The national authorities are empowered where appropriate to access, demand erasure, or block the processing of information held by data processors.[200]

For international commercial transactions, the most important provision in the Data Protection Directive is Article 25. That provision mandates that member states prohibit the transfer of personal data to persons in non-member states (such as the United States) unless those states offer an "adequate level of protection." This prohibition applies unless the Directive otherwise permits the processing of personal data, such as with the "unambiguous" consent of the affected individual or (within the narrow confines noted above) when "necessary" and for a "legitimate purpose."[201]

Practically speaking, the Data Protection Directive governs most global businesses, for the simple reason that is difficult to segregate European Union data from data collected elsewhere. Both online and offline data processors fall within its scope. The Directive's impact has been felt, for example, in restrictive orders denying U.S. direct marketing companies access to European customer, email, and mailing lists.

The Invalidated "Safe Harbor" Agreement. Early in 2000, the United States and the European Union reached a "safe harbor" agreement for U.S. firms based on seven privacy principles designed to satisfy the "adequacy" requirement in Article 25 of the Data Protection Directive. The twist in that safe harbor arrangement was that compliance took place in the United States in accordance with U.S. law and was carried out primarily by the private sector. Thousands of U.S. companies took advantage of this agreement by adopting procedures to verify compliance and to investigate and resolve individual complaints.

In its landmark *Schrems v. Data Protection Commissioner* case in October, 2015, however, the European Court of Justice (ECJ) declared that the Safe Harbor Agreement was "invalid" under the Data Protection Directive and contrary to fundamental personal

---

[198]   *Id.,* art. 28(1).

[199]   *Id.,* arts. 18, 19.

[200]   *Id.,* art. 28.

[201]   *Id.,* art. 7.

rights protected under EU law.[202] This immediately placed in jeopardy the business operations of the thousands of U.S. internet and telecommunications companies that collected personal data in Europe and transferred it to the U.S. under the protection of the Safe Harbor Agreement.

The EU-U.S. Privacy Shield Framework. To remedy this situation, the EU Commission and the U.S. Department of Commerce in July, 2016, announced a new "Privacy Shield Framework" to replace the Safe Harbor Agreement in conformity with the ECJ's *Schrems* judgment. This new form of a "safe harbor" arrangement allows organizations to self-certify annually their compliance with the Framework's requirements in a filing with the International Trade Administration (ITA) of the Commerce Department.[203]

In order to rely on the Privacy Shield to transfer personal data from the EU, an organization must provide to the ITA a variety of information about itself and its privacy policies, and self-certify its adherence to certain "Principles" (see below) that conform to the fundamental protections in the EU Data Protection Directive. In addition, the organization must (1) publicly disclose its privacy policies; (2) publicly declare its commitment to comply with the Principles; (3) fully implement and regularly verify its compliance with the Principles; and (4) be subject to the investigatory and enforcement powers of the Federal Trade Commission or the Department of Transportation (depending on the industry).

The Commerce Department then will regularly review self-certifying organizations to ensure continued compliance with the requirements of Privacy Shield. (Participating organizations pay a fee based on annual revenue to support the costs of the review program.[204]) If an organization fails to comply with its commitments, it will be subject to an enforcement action under Section 5 of the Federal Trade Commission Act (which prohibits unfair and deceptive acts and practices[205]) and other similarly directed federal laws and regulations.

The Privacy Shield Framework requires U.S. organizations that collect personal data in the EU to develop and enforce a

---

[202]   Case No. C–362/14, Schrems v. Data Protection Commissioner, ECLI:EU: C:2015:650 (6 October 2015).

[203]   Information on the Privacy Shield Framework is available at the Department of Commerce's dedicated webpages, https://www.privacyshield.gov/welcome.

[204]   *See* https://www.privacyshield.gov/Program-Overview.

[205]   *See* 15 U.S.C. § 45(a).

privacy policy consistent with seven fundamental Principles.[206] In summary, those Principles are:

(1) *Notice.* The organization's privacy policy must provide individuals "in clear and conspicuous language" information on a variety of subjects, including the purposes for collecting and using their personal information, their rights to access and limit use of their personal information, and options for resolution of disputes;

(2) *Choice.* The organization must offer individuals the opportunity to choose not to have their personal information disclosed to a third party or used for unauthorized purposes ("opt out"). Individuals must be provided with "clear, conspicuous, and readily available mechanisms" to exercise this choice. For sensitive information—on health, racial or ethnic origin, religious beliefs, or the individual's s sex life, etc.—the organization must obtain "affirmative express consent" to disclose collected information to a third party or to use it for an unauthorized purpose ("opt in");

(3) *Accountability for Onward Transfer.* The Privacy Shield Framework sets forth detailed requirements and limitations regarding transfer of personal information to third parties;

(4) *Security.* The organization must take "reasonable and appropriate measures" to protect against the loss, misuse, disclosure, etc. of personal information;

(5) *Data Integrity and Purpose Limitation.* Personal information collected by an organization must be limited to information that is relevant to processing and may be retained only for as long as is necessary for that purpose;

(6) *Access.* A "right of access" is an essential aspect of the protection of personal information. Thus, individuals must have access to the personal information collected about them and "be able to correct, amend, or delete that information where it is inaccurate, or has been processed in violation of the Principles"; and

(7) *Recourse, Enforcement and Liability.* The organization's privacy policy must include "robust mechanisms for assuring compliance with the Principles,"

---

[206] More information on these seven Principles of the EU-U.S. Privacy Shield Framework is available at https://www.privacyshield.gov/EU-US-Framework.

including recourse mechanisms, procedures for verifying compliance, dispute resolution processes to remedy problems, and internal sanctions that are "sufficiently rigorous to ensure compliance." This means in particular that the organization's privacy policy must include a right of an individual to pursue binding arbitration for claims that the organization has violated its obligations under the Principles or that any such past violations remain fully or partially unremedied (so-called "residual claims"). A separate Annex describes in more detail the requirements for this binding arbitration.[207]

In addition, the Privacy Shield Framework has sixteen "Supplemental Principles," which contain clarifications, limitations, exceptions, and procedural rules relating to self-certification, compliance, audits, and dispute resolution.[208] The last of these Supplemental Principles, which addresses "Access Requests by Public Authorities," is of particular note. A principal reason for the ECJ's invalidation of the Safe Harbor agreement in the *Schrems* case was the gathering of private data by the National Security Agency and other U.S. public authorities. To address these concerns, the Office of the Director of National Intelligence and the Department of Justice each submitted letters describing the safeguards and limitations governing their access to data covered by the EU Data Protection Directive. The sixteenth Supplemental Principle of the Privacy Shield Framework then addresses transparency regarding requests by public authorities. In specific, it authorizes organizations, on a voluntary basis, to "issue periodic transparency reports on the number of requests for personal information they receive by public authorities for law enforcement or national security reasons" (to the extent allowed by law).

As a practical matter, compliance with the new Privacy Shield Framework is mandatory for U.S. search companies, social media sites, and essentially any other entities that offer goods or services on the internet and wish to integrate their European data

---

[207]　More information on this Annex regarding binding arbitration is available at https://www.privacyshield.gov/article?id=ANNEX-I-introduction.

[208]　The sixteen Supplemental Principles address the following general subjects: (1) Sensitive Data; (2) Journalistic Exceptions; (3) Secondary Liability (actually the absence of such liability for internet service providers that "merely transmit, route, switch, or cache information"); (4) Performing Due Diligence and Conducting Audits; (5) The Role of the Data Protection Authorities; (6) Self-Certification; (7) Verification; (8) Access; (9) Human Resources Data; (10) Obligatory Contracts for Onward Transfers; (11) Dispute Resolution and Enforcement; (12) Choice–Timing of Opt-Out; (13) Travel Information; (14) Pharmaceutical and Medical Products; (15) Public Record and Publicly Available Information; and (16) Access Requests by Public Authorities. More information on these sixteen Supplemental Principles is available at https://www.privacyshield.gov/EU-US-Framework.

operations with those outside of the EU. If such organizations comply, they may transfer personal data from the European Union to the United States. If not, they have little choice but to maintain separate data centers in Europe for personal data collected there (which apparently is increasingly occurring in any event).

The New Data Protection Regulation. In April, 2016, the EU adopted a comprehensive Data Protection Regulation (the "Regulation")[209] designed to replace the Data Protection Directive. Under the EU legal system, a Regulation functions as directly applicable law (like a federal statute in the United States), without the need for implementing legislation by the individual EU member states. Under its terms, however, the Regulation will not take effect until two years later (May, 2018). A review of its fundamental principles nonetheless is appropriate here.

The essential purpose of the Regulation, like the Directive, is to protect "natural persons with regard to the processing of personal data." To advance the goal of a single European market the Regulation also seeks to ensure the free movement of personal data within the EU.[210] The Regulation broadly applies to the processing of "personal data"[211] of individuals (known as "data subjects"[212]) in the EU where the processing relates to (a) "the offering of goods or services" (even on an unpaid basis) in the EU, or (b) "the monitoring of their behaviour" in the EU.[213] If this is the case, the Regulation applies "regardless of whether the [data] processing takes place in the [European] Union or not."[214]

In basic principles, the Regulation (not surprisingly) is quite similar to the Directive on the protection of the personal data. In large measure, therefore, it has the same basic rules on the protection of personal data;[215] conditions for consent by individuals;[216] processing data;[217] transparency;[218] notification

---

[209] *See* Data Protection Regulation, *supra* note 142.

[210] *Id.*, art. 1.

[211] Article 4(1) defines personal data broadly to mean "any information relating to an identified or identifiable natural person ('data subject')." An individual may be so identifiable "by reference to an identifier such as a name, an identification number, location data, an online identifier or to one or more factors specific to the physical, physiological, genetic, mental, economic, cultural or social identity of that natural person." *Id.*

[212] *Id.*

[213] *Id.*, art. 3(2).

[214] *Id.*, art. 3(1).

[215] *Id.*, arts. 5–6.

[216] *Id.*, arts. 7–8.

[217] *Id.*, arts. 9–11.

[218] *Id.*, art. 12.

requirements on the collection of personal data;[219] and the rights of individuals to have access to,[220] correct errors in,[221] and restrict processing of their own personal data. The Regulation has extremely detailed provisions on the administrative, monitoring, and reporting obligations of data "controllers" (*i.e.*, entities that collect and use personal data)[222] and data "processors" (*i.e.*, entities that "process personal data on behalf of the controller").[223] Data controllers also have an obligation to inform individuals of their rights regarding the processing of their personal data.[224]

Again, in a fundamental sense the Regulation provides the same protections for personal data as the does the Directive. But when it enters into force in 2018, the Regulation will introduce some important new protections, concepts, and obligations:

Expanded Scope. First, the scope of the Regulation is broader, for as noted above its protections apply even to "monitoring of [individuals'] behaviour . . . within the Union,"[225] even if no actual processing of data occurs in the EU. The Regulation also applies to the activities of data processors[226] and imposes obligations on data controllers on the choice and oversight of their data processors.[227]

Consent. Article 7 of the Regulation imposes a heightened burden on data collectors and processers to obtain consent from a covered individual. In specific, they must demonstrate that the consent was "freely given" and ensure that it must be "as easy to withdraw consent as to give consent."[228] In addition, if a request for consent to collect and process personal data is given in connection with other matters on a form or website, it "shall be presented in a manner which is clearly distinguishable from the other matters, in an intelligible and easily accessible form, using clear and plain language."[229]

---

[219]   *Id.*, arts. 13–14.

[220]   *Id.*, art. 15.

[221]   *Id.*, art. 16.

[222]   *See id.*, art. 4(7) (defining a controller as "the natural or legal person, public authority, agency or other body which, alone or jointly with others, determines the purposes and means of the processing of personal data").

[223]   *See id.*, art. 4(8).

[224]   *Id.*, art. 19.

[225]   *Id.*, art. 3(2).

[226]   *Id.*, art. 28(4).

[227]   *Id.*, art. 28(1)–3. *See also* arts. 82, 83 (making processors liable for an infringement of the obligations in the Regulation).

[228]   *Id.*, art. 7(3).

[229]   *Id.*, art. 7(2).

Right to Erasure. The Regulation formally introduces a "right to be forgotten."[230] Article 17 grants individual "the right to obtain from the controller the erasure of personal data concerning him or her without undue delay" in a variety of circumstances.[231]

Right to Object to Profiling. Article 22 grants individuals a right "not to be subject to a decision based solely on automated processing, including profiling, which produces legal effects concerning him or her or similarly significantly affects him or her."[232] The concept of "profiling" is defined broadly to include "any form of automated processing of personal data consisting of the use of personal data to evaluate certain personal aspects relating to a natural person."[233] It thus embraces most common forms of online tracking for analytical purposes as well as behavioral and targeted advertising. This will impose significant burdens on the myriad businesses that engage in such activities to obtain corresponding consent from individuals.

Right to Data Portability. Article 20 grants to individuals both the right to receive their personal data from data controllers "in a structured, commonly used and machine-readable format" and the right to demand that the controllers "transmit those data to another controller."

Compliance Programs. The Regulation includes an obligation of data controllers to establish rigorous compliance programs. In particular, Article 24 obligates controllers to retain accurate records of processing activities and more generally to "implement appropriate technical and organisational measures" to ensure compliance with the Regulation.[234] These measures must be reviewed and updated "where necessary."[235] A controller may use only those data processors that "provide sufficient guarantees" that they, too, have in place "appropriate technical and organizational measures" to ensure compliance with the Regulation.[236]

As a separate but related matter, controllers must appoint a formal "data protection officer (DPO)" in a variety of common

---

[230] The European Court of Justice had inferred a similar right under the Data Control Directive in 2014. *See* Case No. C–131/12, Google Spain SL v. Agencia Española de Protección de Datos (AEPD), ECLI:EU:C:2013:424 (13 May 2014).

[231] *Id.*, art. 17(1).

[232] *Id.*, art. 22(1).

[233] *Id.*, art. 4(4) (also providing that profiling applies to the use of personal data "in particular to analyse or predict aspects concerning that natural person's performance at work, economic situation, health, personal preferences, interests, reliability, behaviour, location or movements").

[234] *Id.*, art. 24(1).

[235] *Id.*

[236] *Id.*, art. 28.

circumstances.[237] In some respects this position is similar to the Chief Privacy Officer (CPO) in many large U.S. companies; but the extensive and detailed requirements of the Regulation will heighten the significance of this role. A separate Article in the Regulation sets forth the minimum obligations of a DPO.[238]

Notification of Data Breaches. The Regulation imposes on data controllers strict notification obligations in the event of a personal data breach.[239] A notification (with defined minimum content requirements) first must be made to the relevant Supervisory Authority that each member state must establish under the Regulation.[240] The notification must be made "without undue delay and, where feasible, not later than 72 hours."[241] Separately, the controller must give such a notification to affected individuals "without undue delay" if the personal data breach "is likely to result in a high risk to the rights and freedoms of natural persons."[242]

Liability for Violations of the Regulation. The Regulation's tough new liability rules are likely the most important issue for businesses that collect personal data. Article 82 first makes data controllers and data processors directly liable "[t]o any person who has suffered material or non-material damage as a result of an infringement of this Regulation." Article 83 then imposes on the Supervisory Authorities of each member state both the right and the obligation to impose "effective, proportionate and dissuasive" administrative fines for violations of the Regulation.[243] Depending on the specific violation, the administrative fines may be up to (a) 10,000,000 Euros or 2% of the total worldwide annual turnover of the preceding financial year, "whichever is higher,"[244] or (b) 20,000,000 Euros or 4% of the total worldwide sales of an enterprise in the preceding year, again "whichever is higher."[245]

---

[237] *See id.*, arts. 37–38.

[238] *See id.*, art. 39.

[239] Such a data breach involves the "destruction, loss, alteration, unauthorised disclosure of, or access to, personal data." *See id.*, art. 4(12).

[240] *Id.*, art. 33. With regard to the competent domestic supervisory authority see *id.*, arts. 4(21) (defining the term); 51 (imposing the obligation to establish a supervisory authority); and 55 (defining which supervisory authority is competent for specific matters).

[241] *Id.*, art. 33.

[242] *Id.*, art. 34.

[243] *Id.*, art. 83(1).

[244] *Id.*, art. 83(4).

[245] *Id.*, art. 83(5).

Chapter 9

AN INTRODUCTION TO THE WTO AND U.S. TRADE AUTHORITIES

Table of Sections

The need to balance the protection of local industries from harm by foreign competitors and the encouragement of trade across national borders is a recurrent theme in the law of international business transactions. There has been a shift in recent years toward freer international trade because of diminished restrictions on imported goods. However, trade problems associated with the movement of goods across national borders still arise because of restrictive trade devices which impede or distort trade. Common devices include tariff barriers: For example, there are "normal" import and export duties, as well as additional antidumping and subsidy countervailing duties. The law of tariffs is heavily influenced by the World Trade Organization (WTO).

The General Agreement on Tariffs and Trade (GATT 1947), the predecessor to the WTO, was an international arrangement with over one hundred countries as Contracting States which regularly held multilateral trade negotiations (MTN) seeking ways of making international trade more open. These periodic negotiations cumulatively reduced tariff barriers by an average of up to eighty percent below those existing three decades before. After the most recent multilateral negotiations, the Uruguay Round, average tariff rates of developed countries on dutiable manufactured imports were cut from 6.3 percent to 3.9 percent. Tariff reductions are one of the success stories of GATT. But not all nations participated in the GATT or are members of its replacement, the WTO. For example, Iran is still seeking membership in the WTO. China did not join until 2001, Vietnam in 2007, and Russia in 2012.

There are also nontariff trade barriers (NTBs). The latter can take the form of import quotas, import licensing procedures, health, safety, environmental and other product standards, import testing requirements, complex customs procedures (including valuation), and government procurement policies. For example, the United States employs numerous import quotas on agricultural goods. The European Union (EU) places a variable tariff on imported agricultural goods designed to ensure that their cost is always higher than many EU farm products supported by its Common Agricultural Policy.

The WTO plays a significant role in the law of nontariff trade barriers. NTBs are addressed in the WTO Covered Agreements, which include agreements designed to lessen or to eliminate NTBs such as complex customs valuation procedures, import licensing systems, and product standards. Needless to say, developing world exporters are pushing within the WTO for a reduction in major-market nontariff trade barriers.

United States Trade Law. U.S. international trade law is primarily found in the frequently amended Tariff Act of 1930 and the Trade Act of 1974. Much of the content of these statutes is derived from World Trade Organization principles. Additional statutes of note include the NAFTA Implementation Act of 1993, the Uruguay Round Agreements Act of 1994, the Export Administration Act of 1979, the Foreign Corrupt Practices Act of 1977, and the Caribbean Basin Economic Recovery Act of 1983.

The international trade of the United States is regulated by a number of different governmental bodies. The International Trade Administration is part of the Commerce Department, which in turn is part of the Executive Branch of the federal government. The Commerce Department also contains the Office of Export Licensing and the Office of Anti-boycott Compliance. The International Trade Commission is an independent federal government agency, and the

Court of International Trade is part of the Judicial Branch of the United States government. Lastly, the Office of the United States Trade Representative works directly under the President.

§ 9.1   The General Agreement on Tariffs and Trade (1947)

Participants in the Bretton Woods meetings in 1944 recognized a post-War need to reduce trade obstacles in order to foster freer trade. They envisioned the creation of an International Trade Organization (ITO) to achieve the desired result. Fifty-three countries met in Havana in 1948 to complete drafting the Charter of an ITO that would be the international organizational umbrella underneath which negotiations could occur periodically to deal with tariff reductions. A framework for such negotiations had already been staked out in Geneva in 1947, in a document entitled the General Agreement on Tariffs and Trade (GATT). Twenty-three nations participated in that first GATT session, India, Chile, Cuba and Brazil representing the developing world. China participated; Japan and West Germany did not. Stringent trading rules were adopted only where there were no special interests of major participants to alter them. The developing nations objected to many of the strict rules, arguing for special treatment justified on development needs, but they achieved few successes in drafting GATT.

The ITO Charter was never ratified. The United States Congress in the late 1940s was unwilling to join more new international organizations, thus U.S. ratification of the ITO Charter could not be secured. Nonetheless, and moving by way of the President's power to make executive agreements, the United States did join twenty-one other countries, as Contracting Parties, in signing a Protocol of Provisional Application of the General Agreement on Tariffs and Trade (61 Stat.Pts. 5, 6) (popularly called the "GATT Agreement"). One notable feature of this protocol was the exemption of existing trade restraints of the Contracting States. The GATT 1947 Agreement evolved from its "provisional" status into the premier international trade body, GATT the organization based in Geneva. It was through this organization that tariffs were steadily reduced over decades by means of increased membership and GATT negotiating Rounds. Today, the GATT 1947 Agreement has been superseded by the substantially similar GATT 1994 Agreement, part of the World Trade Organization "package" of trade agreements that took effect in 1995.

Trade in Goods: Core GATT Principles. One of the central features of GATT 1947 and 1994 is Article I, which makes a general commitment to the long standing practice of "most favored nation treatment" (MFN) by requiring each Contracting Party to accord unconditional MFN status to goods from all other Contracting Parties. Thus, any privilege or tariff granted by a Contracting Party to products imported from any other country (not necessarily a WTO member) must also be "immediately and unconditionally" granted to any "like product" imported from any Contracting Parties. There are two major exceptions to the MFN obligation of Article I: Free trade areas and customs unions (see Chapter 17) and differential and more favorable treatment of goods from developing countries (see Chapter 10).

GATT Article III incorporates the practice of according "national treatment" to imported goods by providing, with enumerated exceptions, that they shall receive the same tax and regulatory treatment as domestic goods. In this context, national treatment requires that the products of the exporting GATT Contracting State be treated no less favorably than domestic products of the importing State under its laws and regulations concerning sale, internal resale, purchase, transportation and use. Two major exceptions apply to Article III: Government procurement policies (see Section 9.10) and some subsidization of domestic industries (see Chapter 13).

In addition to requiring MFN and national treatment, GATT prohibits use of certain kinds of quantitative restrictions. Subject to exceptions such as balance of payment crises, Article XI prohibits "prohibitions or restrictions" on imports and it specifically prohibits the use of "quotas, import or export licenses or other measures" to restrict imports from a Contracting Party. If utilized, Article XIII requires non-discrimination in quantitative trade restrictions, by barring an importing Contracting State from applying any prohibition or restriction to the products of another Contracting State, "unless the importation of the like product of all third countries . . . is similarly prohibited or restricted." (emphasis added).

The WTO has significantly reduced the number of trade quotas. The Agreement on Textiles eliminated quotas long maintained under the Multi-Fibre Arrangement. Voluntary export restraints (quotas) are severely limited by the Safeguards Agreement. In addition, the WTO removes trade quotas by advancing "tariffication," replacing quotas with tariffs—sometimes even at extraordinarily high tariff rates. Tariffication is the approach adopted in the WTO Agricultural Agreement. Import licensing schemes are also being phased out under WTO agreements.

There are four important exceptions to all GATT 1994 rules. These concern national security (Article XXI), balance of payments (Articles XII and XVII:B), and public health, morals or policy (such as product standards or conservation of exhaustible natural resources) (Article XX).

GATT Procedures. While GATT does permit nondiscriminatory "duties, taxes and other charges," the powers of a Contracting Party are limited even as to these devices. First, GATT Article X requires that notice be given of any new or changed national regulations which affect international trade, by requiring the prompt publication of those "laws, regulations, judicial decisions and administrative rulings of general application." Second, the Contracting Parties commit themselves "from time to time" to a continuing series of multilateral tariff negotiations (MTN) to seek further reductions in tariff levels and other barriers to international trade. Such negotiations are to be "on a reciprocal and mutually advantageous basis." GATT negotiated tariff rates (called "concessions" or "bindings"), which are listed in the "tariff Schedules", are deposited with GATT by each participating country. These concessions must be granted to imports from any Contracting Party, both because of the GATT requires MFN treatment, and also because Article II specifically requires use of the negotiated rates.

The 1947 GATT Agreement and its subsequent multinational negotiating rounds were quite successful in reducing tariff duty levels on trade in goods. See Section 9.2 below. This was its original purpose, and the mechanism was well-adapted to accomplishing that purpose. However, its effectiveness was also limited to trade in goods, and primarily to reduction of tariffs in such trade. It was not designed to affect trade in services, trade-related intellectual property rights or trade-related investment measures. As tariff duty rates declined, the trade-distorting effects of these other issues became relatively more important.

Even within "trade in goods," the 1947 GATT had limitations. It included a Protocol of Provisional Application which allowed numerous grandfathered exceptions to Members' obligations under the GATT Agreement. The Protocol exempted from GATT disciplines the national laws of Member States which were already enacted and in force at the time of adoption of the Protocol. Further, the 1947 GATT did not have an institutional charter, and was not intended to become an international organization on trade. It did later develop institutional structures and acquired quasi-organizational status, but there was always a lack of a recognized structure. This lack was most often perceived in the inability of GATT to resolve disputes which were brought to it. Dispute settlement procedures were dependent upon the acquiescence of all Member States, including the losing state, which understandably almost never acquiesced.

Framers of GATT 1947 were well aware that a commitment to freer trade could cause serious, adverse economic consequences from time to time within part or all of a country's domestic economy, particularly its labor sector. The GATT contains at least seven safety valves (in nine clauses of the Agreement) to permit a country, in appropriate circumstances, to respond to domestic pressures while remaining a participant in GATT. Two safety valves deal with antidumping duties and countervailing subsidies. See Chapters 12 and 13.

§ 9.2   The GATT Multinational Trade Negotiations (Rounds)

Under the auspices of GATT Article XXVIII, the Contracting Parties committed themselves to hold periodic multinational trade negotiations (MTN or "Rounds"). They have completed eight such Rounds to date, and the WTO Doha Round is marginally ongoing.

While the first five Rounds concentrated on item by item tariff reductions, the "Kennedy Round" (1964–1967) was noted for its achievement of across-the-board tariff reductions. In 1961, GATT began to consider how to approach the increasing trade disparity with the developing world. In 1964, GATT adopted Part IV, which introduced a principle of "diminished expectations of reciprocity". Reciprocity remained a goal, but developed nations would not expect concessions from developing nations which were inconsistent with developmental needs. For the developing nations, nonreciprocity meant freedom to protect domestic markets from import competition. Import substitution was a major focus of developmental theory in the 1960s, and developing nations saw keeping their markets closed as a way to save these domestic industries. Although they also sought preferential treatment of their exports, that was a demand which would remain unsatisfied for another decade and longer.

The "Tokyo Round" (1973–1979) engendered agreements about several areas of nontariff barrier (NTB) trade restraints. Nearly a dozen major agreements on nontariff barrier issues were produced in the Tokyo Round. In the early 1970s, national and regional generalized preference schemes (GSP) developed to favor the exports of developing nations. The foreign debt payment problems of the developing nations suggest that they need to generate revenue to pay these debts, and that developmental theory must shift from import substitution to export promotion.

In 1986, the "Uruguay Round" of multilateral trade negotiations began at a Special Session of the GATT Contracting States. This Uruguay Round included separate negotiations on trade in goods and on trade in services, with separate groups of negotiators dealing with each topic. Subtopics for negotiation by subgroups included nontariff barriers, agriculture, subsidies and countervailing duties, intellectual property rights and counterfeit goods, safeguards, tropical products, textiles, investment policies, and dispute resolution. The negotiating sessions were extraordinarily complex, but were able to achieve a successful conclusion at the end of 1993, giving birth to the World Trade organization in 1995.

In 1999 an attempt at launching a "Seattle Round" led by President Clinton failed with violence in the streets. Two years later, the "Doha Round" was successfully launched in Qatar covering all existing WTO fields as well as E-commerce, trade and the environment, debt and finance, and special and differential treatment and assistance for developing countries. Developed WTO countries have been pushing foreign investment, competition policy, transparency in procurement, and trade facilitation topics. At Cancun in 2003, the WTO developing nations rejected these topics, focusing on agricultural trade barriers to their exports. Scheduled for completion in 2005, in July 2008 the Doha Round of WTO negotiations collapsed after marathon sessions. India and China, in particular, insisted upon Special Safeguard Mechanisms against surges in agricultural imports, provisions the U.S. and EU did not accept. Apart from cotton, the members were in agreement on all other areas of the Doha Round negotiations. At this writing, the Doha Round remains on life support.

The GATT completed eight Rounds with the GATT membership steadily increasing:

Geneva (1947) with 19 countries

Annecy (1948) with 27 countries

Torquay (1950) with 33 countries

"Dillon Round" Geneva (1960–62) with 36 countries

"Kennedy Round" Geneva (1964–67) with 74 countries

"Tokyo Round" Geneva (1973–79) with 85 countries

"Uruguay Round" Geneva (1986–94) with 128 countries

The WTO Doha Round (2001–___) with 164 countries is marginally ongoing.

§ 9.3 The World Trade Organization (WTO) and GATT 1994

The WTO is the product of the Uruguay Round of GATT negotiations, which was successfully completed in 1994. The Uruguay Round produced a package of agreements, the Agreement Establishing the World Trade Organization and its Annexes, which include the General Agreement on Tariffs and Trade 1994 (GATT 1994) and a series of Multilateral Trade Agreements (the Covered Agreements), and a series of Plurilateral Trade Agreements.[1]

GATT 1947 and GATT 1994 are two distinct agreements. GATT 1994 incorporates the provisions of GATT 1947, except for the Protocol of Provisional Application, which is expressly excluded. Thus, the problems created by exempting the existing national laws at the time of the adoption of the Protocol will now be avoided by this exclusion in the Covered Agreements. Otherwise, in cases involving a conflict between GATT 1947 and GATT 1994, GATT 1947 controls. The WTO will be guided by the decisions, procedures and customary practices under GATT.

Annexed to the WTO Agreement are several Multilateral Trade Agreements. As to trade in goods, they include Agreements on Agriculture, Textiles, Antidumping, Subsidies and Countervailing Measures, Safeguards, Technical Barriers to Trade, Sanitary and Phytosanitary Measures, Pre-shipment Inspection, Rules of Origin, and Import License Procedures. In addition to trade in goods, they include a General Agreement on Trade in Services and Agreements on Trade-Related Aspects of Intellectual Property Rights and Trade-Related Investment Measures. Affecting all of these agreements is the Understanding on Rules and Procedures Governing the Settlement of Disputes. All of the Multilateral Trade Agreements are binding on all Members of the World Trade Organization.

In addition to the Multilateral Trade Agreements, there are also Plurilateral Trade Agreements which are annexed to the WTO Agreement. These agreements, however, are not binding on all WTO Members, and Members can choose to adhere to them or not. They include Agreements on Government Procurement, Trade in Civil Aircraft, International Dairy and an Arrangement Regarding Bovine Meat. States which do not join the plurilateral trade agreements do not receive reciprocal benefits under them.

---

[1]   See 33 I.L.M. 1130 (1994).

WORLD TRADE ORGANIZATION AGREEMENTS

AGREEMENT ESTABLISHING THE WORLD TRADE ORGANIZATION

AGREEMENTS ON TRADE IN GOODS

1   **General Agreement on Tariffs and Trade 1994 (GATT)**

   (a)   Understanding on the Interpretation of Article II:1(b)

   (b)   Understanding on the Interpretation of Article XVII

   (c)   Understanding on Balance-of-Payments Provisions

   (d)   Understanding on the Interpretation of Article XXIV

   (e)   Understanding on the Interpretation of Article XXV

   (f)   Understanding on the Interpretation of Article XXVIII

   (g)   Understanding on the Interpretation of Article XXXV

2   Uruguay Round Protocol GATT 1994

3   **Agreement on Agriculture**

4   **Agreement on Sanitary and Phytosanitary Measures (SPS)**

5   **Agreement on Textiles and Clothing**

6   **Agreement on Technical Barriers to Trade (TBT)**

7   **Agreement on Trade-Related Investment Measures (TRIMs)**

8   Agreement on Implementation of GATT Article VI

9   Agreement on Implementation of GATT Article VII

10 **Agreement on Preshipment Inspection**

11 **Agreement on Rules of Origin**

12 **Agreement on Import Licensing Procedures**

13 **Agreement on Subsidies and Countervailing Measures (SCM)**

14 **Agreement on Safeguards**

   General Agreement on Trade in Services (GATS)

   Agreement on Trade-Related Aspects of Intellectual Property Rights (TRIPs)

   Understanding on Rules and Procedures Governing the Settlement of Disputes (DSU)

   Trade Policy Review Mechanism

   Plurilateral Trade Agreements (optional)

      ANNEX 4(a) Agreement on Trade in Civil Aircraft

      ANNEX 4(b) Agreement on Government Procurement

      ANNEX 4(c) International Dairy Arrangement (rescinded)

      ANNEX 4(d) Arrangement Regarding Bovine Meat (rescinded)

The duties of the World Trade Organization are to facilitate the implementation, administer the operations and further the objectives of all these agreements. Its duties also include the resolution of disputes under the agreements, reviews of trade policy and cooperation with the International Monetary Fund (IMF) and the World Bank. To achieve these goals, the WTO Agreement provides a charter for the new organization, but for only minimalist institutional and procedural capabilities, and no substantive competence. Thus, there is a unified administration of pre-existing and new obligations under all agreements concerning trade in goods, including the Uruguay Round Agreements. In addition, the administration of the new obligations on trade in services and intellectual property were brought under the same roof.

The WTO as an institution has no power to bring actions on its own initiative. Under the provisions of the WTO Agreement, only the Members of WTO can initiate actions under the Dispute Settlement Understanding. Enforcement of WTO obligations is primarily through permitting Members to retaliate or cross retaliate against other members, rather than by execution of WTO institutional orders. See Section 9.6 below.

§ 9.4   WTO Decision-Making, Admission, and Withdrawal

The World Trade Organization is structured in three tiers. One tier is the Ministerial Conference, which meets biennially and is composed of representatives of all WTO Members. Each Member has an equal voting weight, which is unlike the representation in the IMF and World Bank where there is weighted voting, and financially powerful states have more power over the decision-making process. The Ministerial Conference is responsible for all WTO functions, and is able to make any decisions necessary. It has the power to authorize new multilateral negotiations and to adopt the results of such negotiations. The Ministerial Conference, by a three-fourths vote, is authorized to grant waivers of obligations to Members in exceptional circumstances. It also has the power to adopt interpretations of Covered Agreements. When the Ministerial Conference is in recess, its functions are performed by the General Council.

The second tier is the General Council which has executive authority over the day to day operations and functions of the WTO. It is composed of representatives of all WTO Members, and each member has an equal voting weight. It meets whenever it is appropriate. The General Council also has the power to adopt interpretations of Covered Agreements.

The third tier comprises the councils, bodies and committees which are accountable to the Ministerial Conference or General Council. Ministerial Conference committees include Committees on Trade and Development, Balance of Payment Restrictions, Budget, Finance and Administration. General Council bodies include the Dispute Settlement Body, the Trade Policy Review Body, and Councils for Trade in Goods, Trade in Services and Trade-Related Intellectual Property Rights. The Councils are all created by the WTO Agreement and are open to representatives of all Member States. The Councils also have the authority to create subordinate organizations. Other committees, such as the Committee on Subsidies and Countervailing Measures are created by specific individual agreements.

Of the General Council bodies, the most important are the Dispute Settlement Body (DSB) and the Trade Policy Review Body (TPRB). The DSB is a special meeting of the General Council, and therefore includes all WTO Members. It has responsibility for resolution of disputes under all the Covered Agreements, and will be discussed in more detail below under Dispute Resolution.

The purpose of the Trade Policy Review-Mechanism (TPRM) is to improve adherence to the WTO agreements and obligations, and to obtain greater transparency. Individual Members of WTO each prepare a "Country Report" on their trade policies and perceived adherence to the WTO Covered Agreements. The WTO Secretariat also prepares a report on each Member, but from the perspective of the Secretariat. The Trade Policy Review Body (TPRB) then reviews the trade policies of each Member based on these two reports. At the end of the review, the TPRB issues its own report concerning the adherence of the Member's trade policy to the WTO Covered Agreements. The TPRB has no enforcement capability, but the report is sent to the next meeting of the WTO Ministerial Conference. It is then up to the Ministerial Conference to evaluate the trade practices and policies of the Member.

Consensus Rules. The process of decision-making in the WTO Ministerial Conference and General Council relies upon "consensus" as the norm, just as it did for decision-making under GATT 1947. "Consensus", in this context means that no Member formally objects to a proposed decision. Thus, consensus is not obtained if any one Member formally objects, and has often been very difficult to obtain, which proved to be a weakness in the operation of GATT. However, there are many exceptions to the consensus formula under WTO, and some new concepts (such as "inverted consensus", discussed below) which are designed to ease the process of decision-making under WTO.

Article IX(1) of the WTO Agreement first provides that "the practice of decision-making by consensus" followed under GATT shall be continued. The next sentence of that provision, however, states that "where a decision cannot be arrived at by consensus, the matter at issue shall be decided by voting," except where otherwise provided. The ultimate resolution of the conflict between these two sentences is not completely clear.

There are a number of exceptions to the requirement for consensus that are expressly created under the WTO Agreement. One such exception is decisions by the Dispute Settlement Body, which has its own rules (see below). Another set of exceptions concerns decisions on waivers, interpretations and amendments of the Covered Agreements. Waivers of obligations may be granted and amendments adopted to Covered Agreements only by the Ministerial Conference. Amendments of Multilateral Trade Agreements usually require a consensus, but where a decision on a proposed amendment cannot obtain consensus, the decision on that amendment is to be made in certain circumstances by a two-thirds majority vote. In "exceptional circumstances", the Ministerial Conference is authorized to grant waivers of obligations under a Covered Agreement by a three-fourths vote. Another exception to the consensus requirement allows procedural rules in both the Ministerial Conference and the General Council to be decided by a majority vote of the Members, unless otherwise provided.

Admission to the WTO. Admission to the World Trade Organization is by "consensus." In theory, this gives each member a veto over applicant countries. In reality, no nation wishing to join has ever formally been vetoed, though many have been long delayed. Iran's desire to join has basically been frustrated by U.S. refusal to negotiate on WTO entry. It took, for example, well over a decade to negotiate acceptable terms of entry for the People's Republic of China and Russia. Such negotiations are handled individually by member states, not by the WTO as an organization. U.S. negotiations with China were particularly lengthy and difficult, one principal issue being whether China should be admitted as a developing or developed nation. (The issue was fudged, with China treated differently within the WTO package of agreements.)

Essentially, applicant counties make an offer of trade liberalization commitments to join the WTO. This offer is renegotiated with interested member nations, some 40 nations regarding China including the European Union which negotiates as a unit (NAFTA does not). Regarding China, the last member to reach agreement on WTO admission was Mexico, which extracted stiff promises against the dumping of Chinese goods. The various commitments made by the applicant in these negotiations are consolidated into a final accession protocol which is then approved by "consensus."

Withdrawal. As of 2017, there were over 164 member states of the World Trade Organization. Any member state may withdraw from the WTO upon six months' notice, something that has never happened but could conceivably become an issue under the administration of U.S. President Donald Trump.

§ 9.5   WTO Agreements and U.S. Law

The WTO Covered Agreements concern not only trade in goods, but also trade in services (GATS), and trade-related aspects of intellectual property (TRIPS). The basic concepts that GATT applied to trade in goods (described above) are now applied to these areas through GATS and TRIPS. In the WTO Covered Agreements, the basic concepts of GATT 1947 and its associated agreements are elaborated and clarified. In addition, there is an attempt to transform all protectionist measures relating to agriculture (such as import bans and quotas, etc.) into only tariff barriers, which can then be lowered in subsequent MTN Rounds (a process known as "tariffication"). WTO also contains some provisions on trade-related investment measures (TRIMs) (see Chapter 23 below). Some of the WTO provisions, particularly those concerning trade in goods, will be discussed in more detail below in relation to United States trade law.

The United States enacted legislation to implement WTO and the Covered Agreements on December 3, 1994. The implementing legislation was submitted to Congress under the "fast track" procedures of 19 U.S.C. § 2112, which required that the agreement and its implementing legislation be considered as a whole by Congress, and which also prohibits Congressional amendments to the implementing legislation. The Congressional authority for "fast track" procedures also required that the President give ninety days' notice of his intention to enter into such an agreement.

Neither GATT 1947 nor the WTO Agreement, GATT 1994 and the other Covered Agreements have been ratified as treaties, and therefore comprise domestic obligations of the United States only to the extent that they are incorporated in United States' implementing legislation. GATT 1947 was not considered controlling by the courts of the United States, and these courts have always held themselves bound to the U.S. legislation actually enacted.[2]

§ 9.6   WTO Dispute Settlement/U.S. Disputes/ China Disputes

The WTO provides a unified system for settling international trade disputes through the Dispute Settlement Understanding (DSU) and using the Dispute Settlement Body (DSB). The DSB is a special assembly of the WTO General Council, and includes all WTO Members. There are five stages in the resolution of disputes under WTO: 1) Consultation; 2) Panel establishment, investigation and report; 3) Appellate review of the panel report; 4) Adoption of the panel and appellate decision; and 5) Implementation of the decision adopted. There is also a parallel process for binding arbitration, if both parties agree to submit this dispute to arbitration, rather than to a DSB panel. In addition, during the implementation phase (5), the party subject to an adverse decision may seek arbitration as a matter of right on issues of compliance and authorized retaliation.

Although the DSU offers a unified dispute resolution system that is applicable across all sectors and all WTO Covered Agreements, there are many specialized rules for disputes which arise under them. Such specialized rules appear in the Agreements on Textiles, Antidumping, Subsidies and Countervailing Measures, Technical Barriers to Trade, Sanitary and Phytosanitary Measures, Customs Valuation, General Agreement on Trade in Services, Financial Services and Air Transport Services. The special provisions in these individual Covered Agreements govern, where applicable, and prevail in any conflict with the general provisions of the DSU.

Under the WTO, unlike under GATT 1947, the DSU practically assures that panels will be established upon request by a Member. Further, under the WTO, unlike under GATT 1947, the DSU virtually ensures the adoption of unmodified panel and appellate body decisions. It accomplishes this by requiring the DSB to adopt panel reports and appellate body decisions automatically and without amendment unless they are rejected by a consensus of all Members. This "inverted consensus" requires that all Members of the DSB, including the Member who prevailed in the dispute, decide to reject the dispute resolution decision, and that no Member formally favor that decision. Such an outcome seems unlikely. This inverted consensus requirement is imposed on both the adoption of

---

[2]   *See, e.g.*, Suramerica de Aleaciones Laminadas, C.A. v. United States, 966 F.2d 660 (Fed. Cir. 1992).

panel reports or appellate body decisions and also on the decision to establish a panel.

The potential resolutions of a dispute under the DSU range from a "mutually satisfactory solution" agreed to by the parties under the first, or consultation phase, to authorized retaliation under the last, or implementation, phase. The preferred solution is always any resolution that is mutually satisfactory to the parties. After a panel decision, there are three types of remedies available to the prevailing party, if a mutually satisfactory solution cannot be obtained. One is for the respondent to bring the measure found to violate a Covered Agreement into conformity with the Agreement. A second is for the prevailing Member to receive compensation from the respondent which both parties agree is sufficient to compensate for any injury caused by the measure found to violate a Covered Agreement.

Finally, if no such agreement can be reached, a prevailing party can be authorized to suspend some of its concessions under the Covered Agreements to the respondent. These suspended concessions, called "retaliation," can be authorized within the same trade sector and agreement; or, if that will not create sufficient compensation, can be authorized across trade sectors and agreements.

Consultation. Any WTO Member who believes that the Measures of another Member are not in conformity with the Covered Agreements may call for consultations on those measures. The respondent has ten days to reply to the call for consultations and must agree to enter into consultation within 30 days. If the respondent does not enter into consultations within the 30 day period, the party seeking consultations can immediately request the establishment of a panel under the DSU, which puts the dispute into Phase 2.

Once consultations begin, the parties have 60 days to achieve a settlement. The goal is to seek a positive solution to the dispute, and the preferred resolution is to reach whatever solution is mutually satisfactory to the parties. If such a settlement cannot be obtained after 60 days of consultations, the party seeking consultations may request the establishment of a panel under the DSU, which moves the dispute into Phase 2.

Third parties with an interest in the subject matter of the consultations may seek to be included in them. If such inclusion is rejected, they may seek their own consultations with the other Member. Alternatives to consultations may be provided through the use of conciliation, mediation or good offices, where all parties agree to use the alternative process. Any party can terminate the use of conciliation, mediation or good offices and then seek the establishment of a panel under the DSU, which will move the dispute into Phase 2.

Panel Establishment, Investigation and Report. If consultations between the parties fail, the party seeking the consultations (the complainant) may request the DSB to establish a panel to investigate, report and resolve the dispute. The DSB must establish such a panel upon request, unless the DSB expressly decides by consensus not to establish the panel. Since an "inverted consensus" is required to reject the establishment of the panel and the complainant Member must be part of that consensus, it is very likely that a panel will be established.

The WTO Secretariat is to maintain a list of well-qualified persons who are available to serve as panelists. The panels are usually composed of three individuals from that list who are not citizens of either party. If the parties agree, a panel can be composed of five such individuals. The parties can also agree to appoint citizens of a party to a panel. Panelists may be either nongovernmental individuals or governmental officials, but they are to be selected so as to ensure their independence. Thus, there is a bias towards independent individuals who are not citizens of any party. If a citizen of a party is appointed, his government may not instruct that citizen how to vote, for the panelist must be independent. By the same reasoning, a governmental official of a non-party Member who is subject to instructions from his government would not seem to fit the profile of an independent panelist.

The WTO Secretariat proposes nominations of the panelists. Parties may not normally oppose the nominations, except for "compelling reasons." The parties are given twenty days to agree on the panelists and the composition of the panel. If such agreement is not forthcoming, the WTO Director-General is authorized to appoint the panelists, in consultation with other persons in the Secretariat.

Complaints brought to DSB panels can involve either violations of Covered Agreements or nonviolation nullification and impairment of benefits under the Covered Agreements. A prima facie case of nullification or impairment arises when one Member infringes upon the "obligations assumed under a Covered Agreement." Such infringement creates a presumption against the infringing Member, but the presumption can be rebutted by a showing that the complaining Member has suffered no adverse effect from the infringement.

The panels receive pleadings and rebuttals and hear oral arguments. Panels can also engage in fact development from sources outside those presented by the parties. Thus, the procedure has aspects familiar to civil law courts. A panel can, on its own initiative, request information from any body, including experts selected by the panel. It can also obtain confidential information in some circumstances from an administrative body which is part of the government of a Member, without any prior consent from that Member. A panel can establish its own group of experts to provide reports to it on factual or scientific issues. In a series of rulings commencing with the *Shrimp-Turtles* decision in 1998, the WTO Appellate Body affirmed the right of panels and itself to elect to receive unsolicited informational and argumentative briefs or letters from non-governmental organizations (NGOs), business groups and law firms.

A panel is obligated to produce two written reports—an interim and a final report. A panel is supposed to submit a final written report to the DSB within six months of its establishment. The report will contain its findings of fact, findings of law, decision and the rationale for its decision. Before the final report is issued, the panel is supposed to provide an interim report to the parties. The purpose of this interim report is to apprize the parties of the panel's current analysis of the issues and to permit the parties to comment on that analysis. The final report of the panel need not change any of the findings or conclusions in its interim report unless it is persuaded to do so by a party's comments. However, if it is not so persuaded, it is obligated to explain in its final report why it is not so persuaded.

The decisions in panel reports are final as to issues of fact. The decisions in panel reports are not necessarily final as to issues of law. Panel decisions on issues of law are subject to review by the Appellate Body, which is Phase 3, and explained below. Any party can appeal a panel report, and as is explained below it is expected that appeals will usually be taken.

Appellate Review of the Panel Report. Appellate review of panel reports is available at the request of any party, unless the DSB rejects that request by an "inverted consensus." There is no threshold requirement for an appellant to present a substantial substantive legal issue. Thus, most panel decisions are appealed as a matter of course. However, the Appellate Body can only review the panel reports on questions of law or legal interpretation.

The Appellate Body was a new institution in the international trade organization and its process. GATT 1947 had nothing comparable to it. The Appellate Body is composed of seven members (or judges) who are appointed by the DSB to four year terms. Each judge may be reappointed, but only once, to a second four year term. Each judge is to be a recognized authority on international trade law and the Covered Agreements. To date, Appellate Body members have been drawn mostly from the academe and retired justices. They have come from Germany, Japan, Egypt, India, New Zealand, the Philippines, Argentina, the United States and other WTO member nations. The review of any panel decision is performed by three judges out of the seven. The parties do not, however, have any influence on which judges are selected to review a particular panel report. There is a schedule, created by the Appellate Body itself, for the rotation for sitting of each of the judges. Thus, a party might try to appear before a favored judge by timing the start of the dispute settlement process to arrive at the Appellate Body at the right moment on the rotation schedule, but even this limited approach has difficulties.

The Appellate Body receives written submissions from the parties and has 60, or in some cases 90, days in which to render its decision. The Appellate Body review is limited to issues of law and legal interpretation. The panel decision may be upheld, modified, or reversed by the Appellate Body decision. Appellate Body decisions will be anonymous, and ex parte communications are not permitted, which will make judge-shopping by parties more than usually difficult.

Adoption of the Panel or Appellate Body Decision. Appellate Body determinations are submitted to the DSB. Panel decisions which are not appealed are also submitted to the DSB. Once either type of decision is submitted to the DSB, the DSB must automatically adopt them without modification or amendment at its next meeting unless the decision is rejected by all Members of the DSB through the form of "inverted consensus" discussed previously.

An alternative to Phases 2 through 4 is arbitration, if both parties agree. The arbitration must be binding on the parties, and there is no appeal from the arbitral tribunal's decision to the DSB Appellate Body.

Implementation of the Decision Adopted. Once a panel or Appellate Body decision is adopted by the DSB, implementation is a three-step process. In the first step, the Member found to have a measure which violates its WTO obligations has "a reasonable time" (usually 15 months) to bring those measures into conformity with the WTO obligations. That remedy is the preferred one, and this form of implementation is the principal goal of the WTO implementation system. To date, most disputes have resulted in compliance in this manner. If the adequacy of compliance is disputed, such disputes typically return to the WTO panel that rendered decision on the merits which also determines, acting as an arbitrator, the amount (if any) of authorized retaliation. The retaliation process is discussed below.

Compensation. If the violating measures are not brought into conformity within a reasonable time, the parties proceed to the second step. In that second step, the parties negotiate to reach an agreement upon a form of compensation which will be granted by the party in violation to the injured party. Such compensation will usually comprise trade concessions by the violating party to the injured party, which are over and above those already available under the WTO and Covered Agreements. The nature, scope, amount and duration of these additional concessions is at the negotiating parties' discretion, but each side must agree that the final compensation package is fair and is properly related to the injury caused by the violating measures. Presumably, any such concessions need not be extended under MFN principles to all WTO members.

Few such compensation agreements have ever been achieved. though the United States compensated most of the membership after losing a dispute to Antigua about whether it had "reserved" (excepted) Internet gambling from coverage under the GATS. The United States also compensated the EU in a copyright dispute involving small business use of music, and Brazil after losing a subsidies dispute concerning cotton.

Authorized Retaliation. If the parties cannot agree on an appropriate amount of compensation within twenty days, the complainant may proceed to the third step. In the third step, the party injured by the violating measures seeks authority from the DSB to retaliate against the party whose measures violated its WTO obligations. Thus complainant seeks authority to suspend some of its WTO obligations in regard to the respondent. The retaliation must ordinarily be within the same sector and agreement as the violating measure. "Sector" is sometimes broadly defined, as all trade in goods, and sometimes narrowly defined, as in individual services in the Services Sectoral Classification List. "Agreement" is also broadly defined. All the agreements listed in Annex IA to the WTO Agreement are considered a single agreement. If retaliation within the sector and agreement of the violating measure is considered insufficient compensation, the complainant may seek suspension of its obligations across sectors and agreements.

The DSB must grant the complainant's request to retaliate within 30 days unless all WTO members reject it through an "inverted consensus." (Article 22.6, DSU) However, the respondent may object to the level or scope of the retaliation. The issues raised by the objection will be examined by either the Appellate Body or by an arbitrator. The respondent has a right, even if arbitration was not used in Phases 2 through 4, to have an arbitrator review in Phase 5 the appropriateness of the complainant's proposed level and scope of retaliation. The arbitrator will also examine whether the proper procedures and criteria to establish retaliation have been followed. The Phase 5 arbitration is final and binding and the arbitrator's decision is not subject to DSB review.

In addition to objecting to the level of authorized retaliation, the responding WTO member may simultaneously challenge the assertion of noncompliance (Article 21.5, DSU). This challenge will ordinarily be heard by the original panel and must be resolved within 90 days. Thus the request for authorized retaliation and objections thereto could conceivably be accomplished before noncompliance is formally determined. In practice, WTO dispute settlement has melded these conflicting procedures such that compliance and retaliation issues are decided together, typically by the original panel.

Retaliation in Action, Cross-Sector Retaliation. Retaliation has rarely been authorized and even less rarely imposed. The amount of a U.S. retaliation permitted against the EU after the WTO *Bananas* and *Beef Hormones* decisions were not implemented by the EU was contested. The arbitration tribunals for this issue were the original WTO panels, which did not allow the entire amount of the almost $700 million in retaliatory tariffs proposed by the United States. The United States was authorized and levied retaliatory tariffs amounting to about $300 million against European goods because of the EU failure to implement those WTO decisions. Since 2000, Congress has authorized rotating these tariffs in "carousel" fashion upon different European goods. The threat of carousel retaliation contributed to settlements of these disputes. The $300 million in authorized U.S. retaliation was dwarfed by a WTO decision allowing the EU to impose up to $4 billion in retaliatory tariffs on U.S. exports after twice finding U.S. extraterritorial export tax benefits (FSCs) to be illegal subsidies. The EU commenced imposing this retaliation gradually in 2004, which caused Congress to repeal the offending IRC provisions shortly thereafter.

In a landmark ruling, a WTO panel acting as an arbitrator authorized Ecuador to remove protection of intellectual property rights regarding geographical indicators, copyrights and industrial designs on European Union goods for sale in Ecuador. This authorization is part of Ecuador's $200 million compensation in the

Bananas dispute. The WTO panel acknowledged that Ecuador imports mostly capital goods and raw materials from the European Union and that imposing retaliatory tariffs on them would adversely harm its manufacturing industries. This risk supported "cross-retaliation" under Article 22.3 of the DSU outside the sector of the EU trade violation. Cross-sector intellectual property retaliation, a very powerful WTO remedy, was also authorized against the United States after it lost a GATS dispute to Antigua on Internet gambling restraints. The United States settled this services dispute with nearly all other WTO members via compensation. Antigua is still meditating on whether to engage in cross-sector retaliation.

Both "compensation" in the second step and "retaliation" in the third step of implementation provide only for indirect enforcement of DSB decisions. There is no mechanism for direct enforcement by the WTO of its decisions through WTO orders to suspend trade obligations. Some commentators believe that retaliation will be an effective implementation device; others believe that it will prove ineffective. The division represented by these conflicting views represents two different approaches to the nature of both international law and international trade law.

One approach seeks a rule-oriented use of the "rule of law"; the other seeks a power-oriented use of diplomacy. The United States and less developed countries have traditionally sought to develop a rule-oriented approach to international trade disputes. The European Union and Japan have traditionally sought to use the GATT/WTO primarily as a forum for diplomatic negotiations, although the EU now ranks second in number of WTO proceedings. These different views created part of the conflict at the December 1999 Seattle WTO meeting (which failed to launch the Millennium Round). If the DSB is a court, its proceedings should be open and "transparent." However, if it is just another form of government-to-government diplomacy, that has always been held in secret.

U.S. Involvement in WTO Dispute Resolution. The WTO dispute resolution process has been invoked more frequently than many expected. The United States has been a complainant or a respondent in dozens of disputes. It lost a dispute initiated by Venezuela and Brazil (WT/DS 2 and 4) concerning U.S. standards for reformulated and conventional gasoline. The offending U.S. law was amended to conform to the WTO ruling. It won on a complaint initiated jointly with Canada and the European Union (WT/DS 8, 10 and 11) regarding Japanese taxes on alcoholic beverages. Japan subsequently changed its law. When Costa Rica complained about U.S. restraints on imports of underwear (WT/DS 24), the U.S. let the restraints expire prior to any formal DSB ruling at the WTO. Similar results were reached when India complained of U.S. restraints on wool shirts and blouses (WT/DS 23). The United States won a major dispute with Canada concerning trade and subsidies for periodicals (WT/DS 31). This celebrated *Sports Illustrated* dispute proved that WTO remedies can be used to avoid Canada's cultural industries exclusion under NAFTA.

In the longstanding *Bananas* dispute (WT/DS 27) noted above, the United States joined Ecuador, Guatemala, Honduras and Mexico in successfully challenging EU import restraints against so-called "dollar bananas." The EU failed to comply with the Appellate Body's ruling, and retaliatory measures were authorized and imposed. In April 2001, the *Bananas* dispute was settled on terms that converted EU quotas to tariffs by 2006. A patent law complaint by the U.S. against India (WT/DS 50) prevailed in the DSB and ultimately brought changes in Indian law regarding pharmaceuticals and agricultural chemicals.

In *Beef Hormones* (WT/DS 26 and 48), also noted above, the European Union lost twice before the Appellate Body for want of proof of a "scientific basis" for its ban on hormone beef. It refused to alter its import restraints and absorbed $200 million in retaliatory tariffs on selected exports to Canada and the United States. In 2009, an arguably pro-European settlement was reached. The U.S. effectively got a higher quota to export hormone-free beef to the EU, in return for phasing out over four years its retaliatory tariffs on EU goods. The U.S. threat of carousel sanctions, i.e. rotating goods subject to retaliation, was instrumental to this settlement. Meanwhile, because the U.S. beef industry failed to timely ask for a continuation of the retaliatory tariffs, the Federal Circuit ruled in 2010 that they expired in 2007. Refunds were given to importers of EU products who paid those tariffs.

The United States prevailed against Argentina regarding tariffs and taxes on footwear, textiles and apparel (WT/DS 56). It lost a challenge (strongly supported by Kodak) to Japan's distribution rules regarding photo film and paper (WT/DS 44). In this dispute the U.S. elected *not* to appeal the adverse WTO panel ruling to the Appellate Body. In contrast, the European Union took an appeal which reversed an adverse panel ruling on its customs classification of computer equipment (WT/DS 62, 67 and 68). The U.S. had commenced this proceeding. Opponents in many disputes, Japan, the United States and the European Union united to complain in WT/DS 54, 55, 59 and 64 that Indonesia's National Car Programme was discriminatory and in breach of several WTO agreements. They prevailed and Indonesia altered its program.

India, Malaysia, Pakistan and Thailand teamed up to challenge U.S. shrimp import restraints enacted to protect endangered sea turtles (WT/DS 58). The WTO Appellate Body generally upheld their complaint and the U.S. has moved to comply. The adequacy of U.S. compliance is being challenged by Malaysia. The European Union and the United States jointly opposed Korea's discriminatory taxes on alcoholic beverages (WT/DS 75 and 84). This challenge was successful and Korea now imposes flat non-discriminatory taxes. The United States also complained of Japan's quarantine, testing and other agricultural import rules (WT/DS 76/1). The U.S. won at the WTO and Japan has changed its procedures.

In a semiconductor dumping dispute, Korea successfully argued that the U.S. was not in compliance with the WTO Antidumping Agreement (WT/DS 99/1). The United States amended its law, but Korea has instituted further proceedings alleging that these amendments are inadequate. The United States did likewise after Australia lost a subsidies dispute relating to auto leather exports (WT/DS 126/1). The reconvened WTO panel ruled that Australia had indeed failed to conform to the original adverse DSB decision. A U.S. challenge concerning India's quotas on imports of agricultural, textile and industrial products was upheld (WT/DS 90/1). India and the United States subsequently reached agreement on a timeline for removal of these restraints.

Closer to home, New Zealand and the United States complained of Canada's import/export rules regarding milk (WT/DS 103/1). Losing at the WTO, Canada agreed to a phased removal of the offending measures. The United States also won against Mexico in an antidumping dispute involving corn syrup (WT/DS 132/1), but lost a "big one" when the DSB determined that export tax preferences granted to "Foreign Sales Corporations" of U.S. companies were illegal (WT/DS 108/1). Another "big one" went in favor of the United States. The European Union challenged the validity under the DSU of unilateral retaliation under Section 301 of the Trade Act of 1974 (WT/DS 152/1). Section 301 has been something of a bete noire in U.S. trade law, but the WTO panel affirmed its legality in light of Presidential undertakings to administer it in accordance with U.S. obligations to adhere to multilateral WTO dispute settlement.

U.S. involvement in WTO dispute settlement continues to be extensive. The Appellate Body ruled that U.S. countervailing duties against British steel based upon pre-privatization subsidies were unlawful (WT/DS 138/1). The European Union prevailed before a WTO panel in its challenge of the U.S. Antidumping Act of 1916

(WT/DS 136), since repealed. U.S. complaints against Korean beef import restraints and procurement practices were upheld (WT/DS 161/1, 163/1). Canada's patent protection term was also invalidated by the WTO under a U.S. complaint (WT/DS 170/1). European Union complaints concerning U.S. wheat gluten quotas (WT/DS 166/1) and the royalty free small business provisions of the Fairness in Music Licensing Act of 1998 (WT/DS 160/1) have been sustained. The *Wheat Gluten* dispute questions the legality of U.S. "causation" rules in escape clause proceedings under Section 201 of the Trade Act of 1974.

A WTO Panel ruled in 2002 that the Byrd Amendment violates the WTO antidumping and subsidy codes. The Byrd Amendment (Continued Dumping and Subsidy Act of 2000) authorizes the Customs Service to forward AD and CVD duties to affected domestic producers for qualified expenses. Eleven WTO members including the EU, Canada and Mexico challenged the Amendment. This ruling was affirmed by the WTO Appellate Body and retaliation was authorized. Late in 2005, the U.S. repealed the Byrd Amendment, subject to a contested two-year phase out. The Appellate Body also ruled against Section 211 of the Omnibus Appropriations Act of 1998 denying trademark protection in connection with confiscated assets (the "HAVANA CLUB" dispute). U.S. compliance with these rulings has been slow in forthcoming. The United States and other complainants prevailed in a 2002 WTO proceeding against Indian local content and trade balancing requirements for foreign auto manufacturers. These requirements violated the TRIMs agreement.

In March of 2004, the European Union commenced raising tariffs against U.S. goods under the WTO retaliation authorized out of the FSC/export tax subsidy dispute. Monthly increments were planned until either the U.S. complied or the EU reached the maximum of roughly $4 billion annually it was authorized to retaliate. In the Fall of 2004, the United States repealed the extraterritorial income exclusion and the EU subsequently removed its retaliatory tariffs. In 2004, also, Antigua-Barbuda won a WTO panel ruling under the GATS against certain U.S. Internet gambling restraints. Retaliation was authorized, and the U.S. settled by offering compensation to all WTO members. The U.S. won a panel decision against Mexico's exorbitant telecom interconnection rates, but lost a 2004 cotton subsidy challenge by Brazil. Retaliation by Brazil was authorized.

The United States also lost a second dispute with the EU about pre-privatization countervailable subsidies, in particular the legality of the U.S. "same person" methodology. (WT/DS212/AB/R).

The U.S. won an SPS dispute against Japanese quarantine of U.S. apples (WT/DS245/AB/R), while losing an important softwood lumber "zeroing" methodology complaint brought by Canada. (WT/DS257/AB/R). In 2006, the Mexico-United States "sugar war" came to a head before the Appellate Body. Mexico's 20% soft drink tax on beverages not using cane sugar, its 20% distribution tax on those beverages, and related bookkeeping requirements were found to violate GATT Article III and not exempt under Article XX(d). Subsequently, the two countries settled their dispute by agreeing, effective in 2008, to free trade in sugar and high fructose corn syrup. Further in 2006, the U.S. failed to persuade the Appellate Body to require the European Union under GATT Article X (3) to undertake a major overhaul of its customs law system targeting inconsistencies therein among the 27 member states.

In 2010, the United States agreed to pay $147 million annually to provide technical assistance to Brazilian cotton farmers. In return, Brazil suspended retaliatory tariffs and cross-sector IP sanctions authorized by the WTO because of U.S. cotton subsidy violations. In 2009, a WTO panel ruled that Airbus had received $20 billion in illegal EU "launch" subsidies. By 2010, that same panel found Boeing the recipient of $5 billion in U.S. federal research contract subsidies that violated the WTO Subsidies Code.

The United States has also settled a number of disputes prior to WTO panel decisions, and remains in consultation on other disputes that may be decided by a WTO panel. For the latest summary of all WTO disputes, including many not involving the United States, see www.wto.org.

China and WTO Disputes. Canada, the European Union and the United States complained against Chinese duties on imported auto parts (10 percent) that rose to those on complete autos (25 percent) if the imported parts exceeded a fixed percentage of the final vehicle content or price, or if specific combinations of imported auto parts were used in the final vehicle. In addition, extensive record keeping, reporting and verification requirements were imposed when Chinese auto companies used imported parts. In 2008, a WTO panel ruled that these "internal charges" violated Articles III (2) and III (4) of the GATT. The core Panel ruling found China's auto parts measures discriminatory in favor of domestic producers, a violation of the national treatment standard for taxes and regulations. This ruling marked the first time since China's admission to the WTO in 2001 that China had been held in breach of its WTO commitments and obligations. See WT/DS 339, 340, 342/R (July 18, 2008) (Affirmed by the Appellate Body Oct. 16, 2008).

Less than one month after losing this dispute, China enacted a clever "green tax" on gas-guzzling autos, most of which just happen to be imported. The sales tax on cars with engine capacities over 4.1 litres doubled to 40%. Autos with engines between 3 and 4.1 litres are taxed at 25%, up from 15%. Most Chinese-made cars have engines with 2.5 litres or less. Autos with engines between 1 and 3 litres remain taxed at 8% and 10%. The smallest cars with engines below 1 litre have their sales tax reduced from 3 to 1 percent. This green tax could achieve protective results similar to China's Auto Parts tariff structure and could be challenged under GATT Article III.

Other disputes challenging China's compliance with WTO law are pending. They concern China's value-added tax on integrated circuits, discriminatory tax refunds, reductions and exemptions, protection and enforcement of intellectual property rights (2009 WTO panel ruled against China), trade and distribution of publications and audiovisual entertainment products (2009 WTO panel ruled against China), commodity export tariffs and restrictions (2012 WTO Appellate Body ruled against China), Chinese antidumping duties against U.S. steel exports (2012 Appellate Body ruled against China), discriminatory treatment of foreign financial information suppliers (2012 Appellate Body ruled against China), and rare earth export restraints (2014 WTO Panel ruled against China). The United States is a complaining party to all of these disputes.

China, in turn, has challenged U.S. safeguard measures applied to Chinese steel exports (2010 WTO Panel rejected challenge) and tires (2010 WTO Panel rejected challenge), and U.S. antidumping and countervailing duties on paper products from China (2011 WTO Panel ruled against U.S. dual assessment of AD and CVD duties). It has also applied AD duties to U.S. exports, *e.g.* chicken.

§ 9.7   Import Quotas and Licenses Under the WTO

Quantity restrictions, such as numerical quotas on the importation of an item or upon a type of item, continue to exist, despite GATT Article XI which calls for their elimination. Import quotas may be "global" limitations (applying to items originating from anywhere in the world), "bilateral" limitations (applying to items originating from a particular country) and "discretionary" limitations. Quantitative limitations may have arisen from a Treaty of Friendship, Commerce and Navigation or from a narrow international agreement, such as agreements on trade in textiles and textile products. Discretionary limitations, when coupled with a requirement that importation of items must be licensed in advance by local authorities, provide an effective vehicle for gathering statistical data and for raising local revenues. "Tariff-rate quotas" admit a specified quantity of goods at a preferential rate of duty. Once imports reach that quantity, tariffs are normally increased.

The WTO has significantly reduced the number of trade quotas. The Agreement on Textiles eliminates in 2005 the quotas long maintained under the Multi-Fibre Arrangement. The demise of MFA textile quotas in 2005, as widely expected, accelerated Chinese and other Asian textile exports to the United States. Responding to domestic pressures, President Bush set temporary quotas in the Fall of 2004 against surges of Chinese bras, bathrobes and knit fabrics. More such restraints are permitted until 2008. Voluntary export restraints (quotas) are severely limited by the Safeguards Agreement. In addition, the WTO removes trade quotas by pressuring for "tariffication," or replacing them with tariffs— sometimes even at extraordinarily high tariff rates. Tariffication is the approach adopted in the Agriculture Agreement. It is expected that such high tariff rates will be reduced in subsequent negotiating Rounds. Import licensing schemes are also being phased out under WTO agreements.

§ 9.8   GATT/WTO Nontariff Trade Barrier Codes

There are numerous nontariff trade barriers applicable to imports. Many of these barriers arise out of safety and health regulations. Others concern the environment, consumer protection, product standards and government procurement. Many of the relevant rules were created for legitimate consumer and public protection reasons. They were often created without extensive consideration of their international impact as potential nontariff trade barriers. Nevertheless, the practical impact of legislation of this type is to ban the importation of nonconforming products. Thus, unlike tariffs which can always be paid, and unlike quotas which permit a certain amount of goods to enter the market, nontariff trade barriers have the potential to totally exclude foreign exports.

Multilateral GATT negotiations since the end of World War II have led to a significant decline in world tariff levels, particularly on trade with developed nations. As steadily as tariff barriers have disappeared, nontariff trade barriers (NTBs) have emerged. Health and safety regulations, environmental laws, rules regulating products standards, procurement legislation and customs procedures are often said to present NTB problems. Negotiations over nontariff trade barriers dominated the Tokyo Round of the GATT negotiations during the late 1970s. A number of optional

NTB "codes" (sometimes called "side agreements") emerged from the Tokyo Round. These concerned subsidies, dumping, government procurement, technical barriers (products standards), customs valuation and import licensing. In addition, specific agreements regarding trade in bovine meats, dairy products and civil aircraft were also reached. The United States accepted all of these NTB codes and agreements except the one on dairy products. Most of the necessary implementation of these agreements was accomplished in the Trade Agreements Act of 1979.

Additional GATT codes were agreed upon under the Uruguay Round ending in late 1993. They revisit all of the NTB areas covered by the Tokyo Round Codes and create new codes for sanitary and phyto-sanitary measures (SPS), trade-related investment measures (TRIMs), preshipment inspection, rules of origin, escape clause safeguards and trade-related intellectual property rights (TRIPs). However, the WTO nontariff barrier codes (save a few plurilateral codes) are **mandatory** for all members. The United States Congress approved and implemented these Codes in December of 1994 under the Uruguay Round Agreements Act.

One problem with nontariff trade barriers is that they are so numerous. Intergovernmental negotiation intended to reduce their trade restricting impact is both tedious and difficult. There are continuing attempts through the World Trade Organization to come to grips with additional specific NTB problems. Furthermore, various trade agreements of the United States have been undertaken in this field. For example, the Canadian-United States Free Trade Area Agreement and NAFTA built upon the existing GATT agreements to further reduce NTB problems between the United States, Canada and Mexico.

Some of the difficulties of NTBs are illustrated in the *EU Beef Hormones* case. The EU, adhering to "precautionary principles," banned imports of growth-enhancing hormone-treated beef from the U.S. and Canada as a health hazard. The Appellate Body ruled that, since the ban was more strict than international standards, the EU needed scientific evidence to back it up. However, the EU had failed to undertake a scientific risk assessment, and the EU's scientific reports did not provide any rational basis to uphold the ban. In fact, the primary EU study had found no evidence of harm to humans from the growth-enhancing-hormones. The Appellate Body ruled that the ban violated the EU's SPS obligations and required the EU to produce scientific evidence to justify the ban within a reasonable time, or to revoke the ban. Arbitrators later determined that 15 months was a reasonable time, but the EU failed to produce such evidence and the U.S. retaliated. Late in

2004, the EU commenced new WTO proceedings asserting that more recent scientific studies and precaution justified its ban and require removal of U.S. retaliation. This WTO proceeding also went against the EU, again for want of adequate proof of scientific basis.

§ 9.9   The WTO Agreement on Agriculture

Agricultural issues played a central role in the Uruguay Round negotiations and are critical to the Doha Round as well. More than any other issue, they delayed completion of the Uruguay Round from 1990 to 1993. The agreement reached in December of 1993 is a trade liberalizing, market-oriented effort. Each country has made a number of commitments on market access, reduced domestic agricultural support levels and export subsidies. The United States Congress approved of these commitments in December of 1994 by adopting the Uruguay Round Agreements Act.

Broadly speaking nontariff barriers (NTBs) to international agricultural trade are replaced by tariffs that provide substantially the same level of protection. This is known as "tariffication." It applies to virtually all NTBs, including variable levies, import bans, voluntary export restraints and import quotas. Tariffication applies specifically to U.S. agricultural quotas adopted under Section 22 of the Agricultural Adjustment Act. All agricultural tariffs, including those converted from NTBs, are to be reduced by 36 and 24 percent by developed and developing countries, respectively, over 6 and 10 year periods. Certain minimum access tariff quotas apply when imports amount to less than 3 to 5 percent of domestic consumption. An escape clause exists for tariffed imports at low prices or upon a surge of importation depending upon the existing degree of import penetration.

Regarding domestic support for agriculture, some programs with minimal impact on trade are exempt from change. These programs are known as "green box policies." They include governmental support for agricultural research, disease control, infrastructure and food security. Green box policies were also exempt from GATT/WTO challenge or countervailing duties for 9 years. Direct payments to producers that are not linked to production are also generally exempt. This will include income support, adjustment assistance, and environmental and regional assistance payments. Furthermore, direct payments to support crop reductions and *de minimis* payments are exempted in most cases.

After removing all of the exempted domestic agricultural support programs, the agreement on agriculture arrives at a calculation known as the Total Aggregate Measurement of Support (Total AMS). This measure is the basis for agricultural support reductions under the agreement. Developed nations reduced their Total AMS by 20 percent over 6 years, developing nations by 13.3 percent over 10 years. United States reductions undertaken in 1985 and 1990 meant that little or no U.S. action was required to meet this obligation. Agricultural export subsidies of developed nations were reduced by 36 percent below 1986–1990 levels over 6 years and the quantity of subsidized agricultural exports by 21 percent. Developing nations had corresponding 24 and 14 percent reductions over 10 years.

All conforming tariffications, reductions in domestic support for agriculture and export subsidy alterations were essentially exempt from challenge for 9 years within the GATT/WTO on grounds such as serious prejudice in export markets or nullification and impairment of agreement benefits. However, countervailing duties could be levied against all unlawfully subsidized exports of agricultural goods except for subsidies derived from so-called national "green box policies" (discussed above).

§ 9.10   The Optional WTO Public Procurement Code

Where public procurement is involved, and the taxpayer's money is at issue, virtually every nation has some form of legislation or tradition that favors buying from domestic suppliers. The Tokyo Round GATT Procurement Code was not particularly successful at opening up government purchasing. Only Austria, Canada, the twelve European Union states, Finland, Hong Kong, Israel, Japan, Norway, Singapore, Sweden, Switzerland and the United States adhered to that Procurement Code. This was also partly the result of the 1979 Code's many exceptions. For example, the Code did not apply to contracts below its threshold amount of $150,000 SDR (about $171,000 since 1988), service contracts, and procurement by entities on each country's reserve list (including most national defense items). Because procurement in the European Union and Japan is often decentralized, many contracts fell below the SDR threshold and were therefore GATT exempt. By dividing up procurement into smaller contracts national preferences were retained. United States government procurement tends to be more centralized and thus more likely to be covered by the GATT Code. This pattern may help explain why Congress restrictively amended the Buy American Act in 1988.

Chapter 13 of the North American Free Trade Area Agreement opened government procurement to U.S., Canadian and Mexican suppliers on contracts as small as $25,000. However, the goods supplied must have at least 50 percent North American content.

These special procurement rules effectively created an exception to the GATT Procurement Code which otherwise applied. The thresholds are $50,000 for goods and services provided to federal agencies and $250,000 for government-owned enterprises (notably PEMEX and CFE). These regulations are particularly important because Mexico, unlike Canada, has not traditionally joined in GATT/WTO procurement codes. In December 2011 Canada-U.S. procurement provisions were incorporated in a long awaited agreement to expand the WTO Procurement Code. This expansion selectively brings more types of procurement contracts, notable service contracts, and more sub-central government entities within the Code's coverage. Contract value thresholds are also selectively lowered.

The Uruguay Round Procurement Code took effect in 1996 and replaced the 1979 Tokyo Round GATT Procurement Code. The Uruguay Round (WTO) Code expanded the coverage of the prior GATT Code to include procurement of services, construction, government-owned utilities, and some state and local (subcentral) contracts. The U.S. and the European Union applied the new Code's provisions on government-owned utilities and subcentral contracts as early as April 15, 1994. Most developing nations have opted out of the WTO Procurement Code.

Various improvements to the procedural rules surrounding procurement practices and dispute settlement under the WTO Code attempt to reduce tensions in this difficult area. For example, an elaborate system for bid protests is established. Bidders who believe the 1979 Code's procedural rules have been abused will be able to lodge, litigate and appeal their protests. The WTO Procurement Code became part of U.S. law in December of 1994 under the Uruguay Round Agreements Act. The United States has made, with few exceptions, all procurement by executive agencies subject to the Federal Acquisition Regulations under the Code's coverage (i.e., to suspend application of the normal Buy American preferences to such procurement). Thirteen U.S. states have not ratified the WTO Procurement Code. The economic stimulus and auto bail-out legislation of the Obama administration have raised questions of U.S. compliance with the Code.

§ 9.11   The General Agreement on Trade in Services (GATS)

Because protectionist barriers to international trade in services were stifling, the United States and several other countries insisted that there should be a General Agreement on Trade in Services (GATS). In the United States, services account for over two-thirds of the Nation's GNP and provide jobs for nearly two-thirds of the work force. Services account for almost one-third of U.S. exports.

Market access for services is a major focus of the General Agreement on Trade in Services (GATS), a product of the Uruguay Round of Negotiations. The GATS defines the supply of services broadly to include providing services across borders or inside member states with or without a commercial presence therein. The core commitment is to afford most-favored-nation treatment to service providers, subject to country-specific exemptions, such as audio-visual services in the EU.

The U.S. Congress approved and implemented the GATS agreement in December of 1994 under the Uruguay Round Agreements Act. Subsequently, early in 1995, the United States refused to extend most-favored-nation treatment to financial services. The European Union, Japan and other GATS nations then entered into an interim 2-year agreement which operated on MFN principles. Financial services was revisited in 1996–97 with further negotiations aimed at bringing the United States into the fold. These negotiations bore fruit late in 1997 with 70 nations (including the United States) joining in an agreement that covers 95 percent of trade in banking, insurance, securities and financial information. This agreement took effect March 1, 1999.

National laws that restrict the number of firms in a market, that are dependent upon local "needs tests" or that mandate local incorporation are regulated by the GATS. Various "transparency" rules require disclosure of all relevant laws and regulations, and these must be administered reasonably, objectively and impartially. Specific service market access and national treatment commitments are made by various governments in schedules attached to the agreement. These commitments may be modified or withdrawn after 3 years, subject to a right of compensation that can be arbitrated. Certain mutual recognition of education and training for service-sector licensing will occur. State monopolies or exclusive service providers may continue, but must not abuse their positions. Detailed rules are created in annexes to the GATS on financial, telecommunications and air transport services.

The GATS has reduced unilateral U.S. action under Section 301 to gain access to foreign markets for U.S. service providers. This reduction flows from U.S. adherence to the Dispute Settlement Understanding (DSU) that accompanies the Uruguay Round accords. The DSU obligates its signatories to follow streamlined dispute settlement procedures under which unilateral retaliation is restrained until the offending nation has failed to conform to a World Trade Organization ruling.

GATS, and the 1996 Protocol on Telecommunications and 1997 Protocol on Financial Services, have generated only a handful of WTO disputes. Here is a sampling of GATS disputes:

(1) EC—Regime for the Importation, Sale and Distribution of Bananas, WT/DS 27/AB/R (1997) (traders of goods may also be traders of services, such as wholesaling or retailing, GATS Articles II and XVII apply to de jure and de facto discrimination).

(2) Canada—Certain Measures Concerning Periodicals, WT/DS 31/AB/R (1997) (GATT and GATS co-exist, no override).

(3) Canada—Certain Measures Affecting The Automotive Industry, WT/DS 139, 142/ R (2000) (coverage under GATS must be determined before assessment of consistency with GATS obligations).

(4) Mexico—Measures Affecting Telecommunication Services WT/DS 204/R (2004) (Mexican cross-border interconnection rates not cost-oriented and unreasonable in breach of Telecoms Annex, failure to allow access to private leased-circuits also violated commitments) (settled with rate reductions and increased access).

(5) United States—Measures Affecting The Cross-Border Supply of Gambling and Betting Services, WT/DS 285/AB/R (2005) (gambling included in U.S. recreational services' commitments, U.S. import ban amounted to "zero quota" in breach of GATS Article XVI, necessary to protect public morals under Article XIV defense but discriminatory enforcement regarding Interstate Horseracing Act fails to meet "chapeau" requirements) (U.S. pays compensation to all GATS signatories except Antigua and Barbuda, the complaining party. . . . $21 million retaliation authorized in 2008).

§ 9.12   The WTO and Rules of Origin

The Uruguay Round accord on rules of origin is, in reality, an agreement to agree. A negotiations schedule was established along with a WTO Committee to work with the Customs Cooperation Council on harmonized rules of origin. Certain broad guiding principles for the negotiations are given and considered binding until agreement is reached. These principles are:

- rules of origin applied to foreign trade must not be more stringent than applied to domestic goods.

- rules of origin must be administered consistently, uniformly, impartially and reasonably.

- origin assessments must be issued within 150 days of a request and remain valid for three years.

- new or modified rules or origin may not be applied retroactively.

- strict confidentiality rules apply to information submitted confidentially for rule of origin determinations.

§ 9.13   The WTO TRIPs Agreement

The Uruguay Round accords of late 1993 include an Agreement on Trade-Related Aspects of Intellectual Property Rights (TRIPs). This agreement is binding upon the over 155 nations that are members of the World Trade Organization. There is a general requirement of national and most-favored-nation treatment among the parties.

The TRIPs Code covers the gamut of intellectual property. On copyrights, there is protection for computer programs and databases, rental authorization controls for owners of computer software and sound recordings, a 50-year motion picture and sound recording copyright term, and a general obligation to comply with the Berne Convention (except for its provisions on moral rights). On patents, the Paris Convention prevails, product and process patents are to be available for pharmaceuticals and agricultural chemicals, limits are placed on compulsory licensing, and a general 20-year patent term is created. For trademarks, service marks become registrable, internationally prominent marks receive enhanced protection, the linking of local marks with foreign trademarks is prohibited, and compulsory licensing is banned. In addition, trade secret protection is assisted by TRIPs rules enabling owners to prevent unauthorized use or disclosure. Integrated circuits are covered by rules intended to improve upon the Washington Treaty. Lastly, industrial designs and geographic indicators of alcoholic beverages (*e.g.*, Canadian Whiskey) are also part of the TRIPs regime.

Infringement and anticounterfeiting remedies are included in the TRIPs agreement, for both domestic and international trade protection. There are specific provisions governing injunctions, damages, customs seizures, and discovery of evidence.

Late in 2001, the Doha Round of WTO negotiations were launched. These negotiations have reconsidered the TRIPs agreement, particularly as it applies to developing nations. In addition, a Declaration on the TRIPs Agreement and Public Health was issued at the Qatar Ministerial Conference. This Declaration includes the following statement:

> We agree that the TRIPs Agreement does not prevent Members from taking measures to protect public health. Accordingly, while reiterating our commitment to the TRIPs Agreement, we affirm that the Agreement can and should be interpreted and implemented in a manner supportive of WTO Members' right to protect public health and, in particular, to promote access to medicines for all.

By mid-2003, a "Medicines Agreement" was finally reached on how to implement this Declaration. Compulsory licensing and/or importation of generic copies of patented medicines needed to address developing nation public health problems are authorized. Such activities may not pursue industrial or commercial policy objectives, and different packaging and labeling must be used in an effort at minimizing the risk of diversion of the generics to developed country markets. Under pressure from the United States, a number of more advanced developing nations (such as Mexico, Singapore and Qatar) agreed not to employ compulsory licensing except in situations of national emergency or extreme urgency. Canada, on the other hand has licensed production of drugs of Rwanda and other nations incapable of pharmaceutical production.

Dozens of TRIPs complaints have been initiated under WTO dispute settlement procedures. Most have been settled, but a few have resulted in WTO Panel and Appellate Body Reports. Here is a sampling of TRIPs disputes:

> (1) India—Patent Protection for Pharmaceutical and Agricultural Chemical Products, WT/DS 50/AB/R (1998) ("mailbox rule" patent applications for subjects not patentable in India until 2005 inadequate, denial of exclusive marketing rights in breach of TRIPs Article 70.9).

> (2) Canada—Term of Patent Protection, WT/DS 170/AB/R (2000) (pre-TRIPs Canadian patents must receive 20 year term).

> (3) U.S.—Section 110 (5) Copyright Act, WT/DS 160/R (2000) (copyright exemption for "homestyle" dramatic musical works consistent with Berne Convention, "business use" exemption inconsistent with Berne and therefore in breach of TRIPs) (settled by payment).

(4) Canada—Pharmaceutical Patents, WT/DS 114/R (2000) (Canadian generic pharmaceutical regulatory review and stockpiling patent rights' exceptions not sufficiently "limited").

(5) U.S.—Section 211 Appropriations Act, WT/DS 176/AB/R (2002) (prohibition against registering marks confiscated by Cuban government, *e.g.* HAVANA CLUB rum, without original owner's consent violates Paris Convention and TRIPs, trade names covered by TRIPs).

(6) EC—Trademarks and Geographical Indications WT/DS 174, 290/R (2005) (EC regulation violates national treatment and most-favored treatment obligations to non-EC nationals, procedural violations also found).

(7) China—Measures Affecting The Protection and Enforcement of Intellectual Property Rights, WT/DS 362R (Jan.26, 2009) (China's implementation of TRIPs upheld as to criminal law thresholds and disposal of confiscated, infringing goods by customs authorities, rejected as to denial of copyright protection for works not authorized for release in China).

(8) China—Measures Affecting Trading Rights and Distribution Services for Certain Publications and Audiovisuals Entertainment Products, WT/DS 363/AB/R (Dec. 31, 2009) (China's ADV restrictions limited to state-owned or approved channels violate WTO Accession Protocol, GATT 1994 and GATS; Restraints not necessary to protect public morals).

(9) European Communities—Information Technology Tariffs, WT/DS 375–377 (Aug.16, 2010) (EU tariffs on cable converter boxes with Net capacity, flat panel computer screens and printers that also scan, fax or copy violated 1996 Information Technology Agreement zero tariff rules).

§ 9.14 U.S. International Trade Administration (ITA)

The international trade of the United States is regulated by a number of different governmental bodies. The International Trade Administration is part of the Commerce Department, which in turn is part of the Executive Branch of the federal government. The Commerce Department also contains the Office of Export Licensing and the Office of Anti-boycott Compliance. The International Trade Commission is an independent federal government agency, and the

Court of International Trade is part of the Judicial Branch of the United States government. Lastly, the Office of the United States Trade Representative works directly under the President.

The International Trade Administration (ITA) is an administrative agency. In broadest terms, the ITA is to foster, promote and develop world trade, and to bring U.S. companies into the business of selling overseas. At a practical level, the ITA is designed to be helpful to the individual business by providing it with information concerning the "what, where, how and when" of imports and exports, such as information sources, requirements for a particular trade license, forms for an international license agreement or procedures to start a business in a foreign country. The ITA provides business data and educational programs to United States businesses. In addition to these duties, the ITA also decides whether there are subsidies in countervailing duty (CVD)[3] cases or sales at less than fair value in antidumping duty (AD) cases.[4] Prior to 1980, such decisions were made by the Treasury Department. The ITA is not, however, involved in decision-making in escape clause (Section 201), market disruption (Section 406) and unfair import practices (Section 337) proceedings.

§ 9.15 U.S. International Trade Commission (ITC)

The United States International Trade Commission (ITC) is an independent bipartisan agency created in 1916 by an act of Congress. The ITC is the successor to the United States Tariff Commission. In 1974, the name was changed and the ITC was given additional authority, powers and responsibilities. The Commission's present powers and duties include preparing reports pertaining to international economics and foreign trade for the Executive Branch, the Congress, other government agencies and the public. To carry out this responsibility, the ITC conducts investigations which entail extensive research, specialized studies and a high degree of expertise in all matters relating to the commercial and international trade policies of the United States. Statutory investigations conducted by the ITC include unfair import trade practice determinations (Section 337 proceedings),[5] domestic industry injury determinations in antidumping and countervailing duty cases,[6] and escape clause and market disruption import relief recommendations. The ITC also advises the President about probable economic effects on domestic industries and consumers of

---

3   See Chapter 13.
4   See Chapter 12.
5   See Chapter 20.
6   See Chapters 12 and 13.

modifications on duties and other trade barriers incident to proposed trade agreements with foreign countries.

The ITC is intended to be a quasi-judicial, bipartisan, independent agency providing trade expertise to both Congress and the Executive. Congress went to great lengths to create a bipartisan body to conduct international trade studies and provide reliable expert information. The six Commissioners of the ITC are appointed by the President and confirmed by the United States Senate for nine year terms, unless appointed to fill an unexpired term. The presence of entrenched points of view is inhibited because a Commissioner who has served for more than five years is not eligible for reappointment. Not more than three Commissioners may be members of the same political party. The Chairman and Vice-Chairman are designated by the President for two year terms. No Chairman may be of the same political party as the preceding Chairman, nor may the President designate two Commissioners of the same political party as Chairman and Vice-Chairman. Congress further guaranteed the independence of the ITC from the Executive Branch by having its budget submitted directly to the Congress. This means that its budget is not subject to review by the Office of Management and Budget.

§ 9.16 U.S. Court of International Trade (CIT)

The United States Court of International Trade (CIT) is an Article III court under the United States Constitution for judicial review of civil actions arising out of import transactions and certain federal statutes affecting international trade. It grew out of the Board of General Appraisers (a quasi-judicial administrative unit within the Treasury Department which reviewed decisions by United States Customs officials concerning the amount of duties to be paid on imports in actions arising under the tariff acts) and the United States Customs Court which had essentially the same jurisdiction and powers. The President, with the advice and consent of the Senate, appoints the nine judges who constitute the Court of International Trade. Not more than five of the nine judges may belong to any one political party.

The geographical jurisdiction of the Court of International Trade extends throughout the United States, and it is also authorized to hold hearings in foreign countries. The court has exclusive subject-matter jurisdiction to decide any civil action commenced against the United States, its agencies or its officers arising from any law pertaining to revenue from imports, tariffs, duties or embargoes or enforcement of these and other customs regulations. This includes disputes regarding trade embargoes, quotas, customs classification and valuation, country of origin determinations and denials of protests by the U.S. Customs Service.

The court's exclusive jurisdiction also includes any civil action commenced by the United States that arises out of an import transaction, and authority to review final agency decisions concerning antidumping and countervailing duty matters, the eligibility of workers, firms and communities who are economically harmed by foreign imports for trade adjustment assistance, disputes concerning the release of confidential business information, and decisions to deny, revoke or suspend the licenses of customs brokers. However, the CIT does *not* have jurisdiction over disputes involving restrictions on imported merchandise where public safety or health issues are raised. This limitation on CIT jurisdiction arises because such issues involving domestic goods would be determined by other regulatory bodies, and only referral to United States District Courts can ensure uniform treatment of both imports and domestically produced goods.

The standard for the judicial review exercised by the CIT varies from case to case. In some instances, such as confidentiality orders, a *de novo* trial is undertaken. In others, notably antidumping and countervailing duty cases, the standard is one of substantial evidence or arbitrary, capricious or unlawful action or an abuse of discretion. In trade adjustment assistance litigation, the administrative determinations are considered conclusive absent substantial evidentiary support in the record with the CIT empowered to order the taking of further evidence. Unless otherwise specified by statute, the Administrative Procedure Act governs the judicial review by the CIT of U.S. international trade law. The CIT possesses all the remedial powers, legal and equitable, of a United States District Court, including authority to enter money judgments for or against the United States, but with three limitations. First, in an action challenging a trade adjustment ruling, the court may not issue an injunction or writ of mandamus. Second, the CIT may order disclosure of confidential information only as specified in Section 777(c)(2) of the Tariff Act of 1930. Third, the CIT may order only declaratory relief for suits brought under the provision allowing the court accelerated review because of a showing of irreparable harm.

The CIT must give due deference to Customs Service regulations under *Chevron* rules[7] even when undertaking *de novo* review.[8] CIT decisions are first appealed to the Court of Appeals for

---

[7]   Chevron, U.S.A., Inc. v. Natural Resources Defense Council, Inc., 467 U.S. 837 (1984).

[8]   United States v. Haggar Apparel Co., 526 U.S. 380 (1999).

the Federal Circuit (formerly to the Court of Customs and Patent Appeals), and ultimately to the United States Supreme Court.

§ 9.17 The USTR and U.S. Trade Agreements

Removing trade barriers is usually done on a reciprocal basis, and requires lengthy bargaining and negotiations between the sovereigns. Congress is not adapted to carry on such negotiations, so it routinely delegates limited authority to the President to negotiate agreements reducing trade restrictions. Recent efforts to reduce trade restrictions have been multilateral, bilateral and trilateral. Congress has intermittently given quite broad authority to the President, or his representative, to reduce or eliminate United States tariffs on a reciprocal "fast track" basis. Fast track originated as a compromise after Congress refused to ratify two major components of the Kennedy Round of GATT negotiations. NAFTA and the Uruguay Round WTO agreements were negotiated and implemented under fast track procedures, discussed below.

In response to Section 1104 of the Trade Agreements Act of 1979,[9] the President reviewed the structure of the international trade functions of the Executive Branch. Although this did not lead to the establishment of a new Department of International Trade and Investment, it did lead to enhancement of the Office of the Special Representative for Trade Negotiations,[10] which has since been renamed the United States Trade Representative (USTR). The powers of the USTR were expanded and its authority given a legislative foundation. The USTR is appointed by the President, with the advice and consent of the Senate.[11] The Office of the USTR has been the principal vehicle through which trade negotiations have been conducted on behalf of the United States. Among other things, the USTR has had continuing responsibility in connection with implementation of the WTO Agreements and U.S. free trade agreements. The USTR is the contact point for persons who desire an investigation of instances of noncompliance with any trade agreement.

In 1988, the duties of the USTR were significantly expanded in conjunction with an overhaul of Section 301 of the Trade Act of 1974. Section 301 creates a controversial unilateral trade remedy which principally has been used to obtain foreign market access for U.S. exports. Prior to 1988, the President directly administered Section 301. Thereafter, as amended by the Omnibus Trade and Competitiveness Act, the USTR assumed this role along with new

---

[9] P.L. 96–39.

[10] The office had been established by an Executive Order in 1963.

[11] 19 U.S.C. § 2171.

duties governing the Super 301 and Special 301 procedures created in 1988. Moreover, since the 1988 Act expanded the coverage of Section 301 and introduced mandatory (not discretionary) remedies, the USTR has been in the spotlight of many domestic industry complaints about foreign governments. Such complaints can reach breaches of international agreements as well as unjustifiable, unreasonable or discriminatory foreign country practices.

Chapter 10

UNITED STATES TARIFFS AND DUTY FREE IMPORTS

Table of Sections

§ 10.1 U.S. Tariffs, Duty Free Entry

This chapter focuses on United States tariffs under the Harmonized Tariff Schedule (HTS). Column 1 tariffs, known as most-favored-nation (MFN) tariffs, are the lower and most likely to be applicable. Column 2 tariffs, originating in the Smoot-Hawley Tariff Act of 1930, are the higher and least likely to be applicable. United States tariffs generally take one of three forms. The most common is an ad valorem rate. Such tariffs are assessed in proportion to the value of the article. Tariffs may also be assessed at specific rates or compound rates. Specific rates may be measured by

425

the pound or other weight. A compound rate is a mixture of an ad valorem and specific rate tariff. Tariff rate quotas involve limitations on imports at a specific tariff up to a certain amount. Imports in excess of that amount are not prohibited, but are subject to a higher rate of tariff. Thus tariff rate quotas tend to restrict imports that are in excess of the specified quota for the lower tariff level.

Some goods may enter the United States at less than most-favored-nation tariff levels or duty free. This occurs because of special tariff preferences incorporated into United States law (outlined below). It is important to realize that these preferences create valuable trading opportunities for U.S. importers and exporters located in qualified nations. These people are the clients for whom lawyers work to secure duty free entry into the United States market. Duty free entry is, of course, the ultimate goal of all exporters and importers involved in United States trade. Various free trade and customs union agreements (including NAFTA and other FTAs of the United States) achieving duty free outcomes are discussed in Chapter 17.

Perhaps the widest of the duty free programs is known as the Generalized System of Preferences (GSP) adopted through the GATT. The GSP is a complex system of duty free tariff preferences benefiting selected goods originating in developing nations and intended to foster their economic improvement. A second program is the Caribbean Basin Economic Recovery Act of 1983 (also known as the Caribbean Basin Initiative), which permits certain goods to enter the United States market duty free. To a significant degree, the CBI duty free program was duplicated in the Andean Trade Preference Act of 1991 initially benefiting Colombian, Ecuadorian, Bolivian and Peruvian goods. Another important "duty free" category allows fabricated U.S.-made components shipped abroad for assembly to return to the U.S. without tariffs on the value of the components. Authorization for this importation is found in Section 9802.00.80 of the Harmonized Tariff Schedule. Goods of this type are subject to a United States Customs duty limited in amount to the value added by foreign assembly operations. This provision is perhaps best known in connection with maquiladora assembly plants.

- The least restrictive rules of origin for duty free entry of goods into the United States apply to its insular possessions. These include American Samoa, Guam, Johnson Island, Kingman Reef, Midway Islands, Puerto Rico, the U.S. Virgin Islands and Wake Island. Generally speaking, goods from such possessions may contain up to 70 percent foreign value and still be admitted duty free.

- Some of these duty free programs overlap and effectively compete with each other. It might be helpful to think of them in terms of concentric geographic circles. The widest circle is Section 9802.00.80 which applies to the entire globe. The next circle represents the GSP system and most developing nations. Inside that circle is the Caribbean Basin Initiative, the Andean Initiative, and U.S. insular possessions followed by the North American, and other U.S. Free Trade Agreements. A manufacturer based in the Caribbean may seek duty free entry into the United States market under Section 9802.00.80, the GSP program or the CBI, but not U.S. free trade agreements, save the Dominican Republic. To most developing   nations,   these   are   selectively discriminatory duty free programs that undermine their GSP benefits.

- Unusual trade opportunities can arise by linking U.S. duty free entry programs with those of the European Union (EU). For example, the Union has its own complicated   and   different   GSP   program,   its equivalent of Section 9802.00.80, and two selective duty free programs for developing nations. The latter are   known   as   its   Mediterranean   Policy   and Lomé/Cotonou Conventions.[1] A producer in Israel can quite possibly gain duty free access to the EU (under its Mediterranean Policy) and to the United States (under the Israeli-U.S. FTA). A producer in Jamaica might   achieve   similar   results   under   the Lomé/Cotonou Conventions, the CBI and/or the GSP programs of the EU and the United States.

§ 10.2   The Origins of United States Tariffs

Article I, Section 8, of the United States Constitution authorizes Congress to levy uniform tariffs on imports. Tariff legislation must originate in the House of Representatives. Although tariffs were primarily viewed as revenue-raising measures at the founding of the nation, it was not long before tariffs became used for openly protectionist purposes. The Tariff Act of 1816 initiated this change in outlook. During much of the Nineteenth

---

[1]   *See generally* Ralph Folsom, PRINCIPLES OF EUROPEAN UNION LAW Chapter 6 (4th ed. 2014).

Century, the United States legislated heavy protective tariffs. These were justified as necessary to protect the country's infant industries and to force the South to engage in more trade with the North (not with Europe). Exceptions were made to the high level of tariffs for selected United States imports under conditional most-favored-nation reciprocity treaties. The first of these treaties involved Canada (1854) and Hawaii (1875).

As the United States moved into the 20th Century, additional tariffs in excess of the already high level of protection were authorized. "Countervailing duty" tariffs were created in 1890 to combat export subsidies of European nations, particularly Germany. After 1916, additional duties could also be assessed if "dumping practices" were involved. Early American dumping legislation was largely a reaction to marketplace competition from foreign cartels. Throughout all of these years the constitutionality of protective tariffs was never clearly resolved. In 1928, however, the United States Supreme Court firmly ruled that the enactment of protective tariffs was constitutional.[2] This decision, followed by the crash of the stock market in 1929, led to the enactment of the Smoot-Hawley Tariff Act of 1930. This Act set some of the highest rates of tariff duties in the history of the United States. It represents the last piece of tariff legislation that Congress passed without international negotiations. These tariffs remain part of United States law and are generally referred to as "Column 2 tariffs" under the Harmonized Tariff Schedule (HTS).

Since 1930, changes in the levels of tariffs applicable to goods entering the United States have chiefly been achieved through international trade agreements negotiated by the President and affirmed by Congress. During the 1930s and 40s, the Smoot-Hawley tariffs generally applied unless altered through bilateral trade agreements. The Reciprocal Trade Agreements Act of 1934[3] gives the President the authority to enter into such agreements, and under various extensions this authority remains in effect today. An early agreement of this type was the Canadian Reciprocal Trade Agreement of 1935.

§ 10.3 Column 1 Tariffs and the GATT/WTO

The Trade Agreements Extension Act of 1945 authorized the President to conduct multilateral negotiations in the trade field. It was out of this authority that the General Agreement on Tariffs and Trade (GATT) was negotiated. The GATT became effective on January 1, 1948 and was implemented in the United States by

---

2   J.W. Hampton, Jr. & Co. v. United States, 276 U.S. 394 (1928).

3   48 Stat. 943 (1934).

executive order. Indeed, despite its wide-ranging impact on United States tariff levels since 1948, the GATT was never approved by the United States Congress. Nevertheless, it is the source of the principal tariffs assessed today on imports into the United States. These duties, known as most-favored-nation (MFN) tariffs or "Column 1 tariffs," have been dramatically reduced over the years through successive rounds of trade negotiations. They are unconditional MFN tariffs, meaning that reciprocity is not required in order for them to apply. Multilateral tariff agreements have predominated over bilateral negotiations since 1948.

The term "most-favored-nation" is misleading in its suggestion of special tariff arrangements. It is more appropriate and since 1998 officially correct to think of MFN tariffs as the "normal" level of U.S. tariffs, to which there are exceptions resulting in the application of higher or lower tariffs. After the Tokyo Round of GATT negotiations in 1978, the average MFN tariff applied to manufactured imports into the United States was approximately 5.6 percent. Reductions in this level to approximately 3.5 percent have been accomplished under the Uruguay Round of 1994.

Tariff cuts on a wide range of information technology products were agreed to late in 1996. By the year 2000, the United States, the European Union and most of East Asia had abolished tariffs on computers, electrical capacitors, calculators, ATM's, fax and answering machines, digital copiers and video cameras, computer diskettes, CD-ROM drives, computer software, fiber optical cables and hundreds of other items. This agreement covers more than 90 percent of all information technology trade.

In early 1997, agreement on liberalizing trade and reducing tariffs on basic telecommunications equipment was reached by 69 nations. This agreement took effect Feb. 5, 1998. Later that year, a WTO declaration imposed standstill obligations on all members to continue to refrain from applying customs duties to electronic commerce while negotiations are underway for more permanent rules in this area.

§ 10.4   Column 2 Tariffs

Between 1948 and 1951 the United States granted Column 1 most-favored-nation tariff treatment to goods originating from virtually every part of the world. Commencing in 1951, goods originating in nations controlled by communists were withdrawn from such tariff treatment. This had, and to some degree continues to have, the effect of treating the importation of goods from communist nations under Column 2 United States tariff headings.

As a practical matter, very few such imports can overcome the high Smoot-Hawley tariffs embodied in Column 2.

The designation of which nations are "communist" for these purposes has varied over time. Yugoslavia was generally not treated as a communist country and its goods therefore entered under Column 1 MFN tariffs. Goods from the Balkans presently do so as well. Central and Eastern European nations were sometimes treated as communist countries, particularly during the 1950s and 1960s. This is no longer the case, and at this point nearly every European and Baltic nation has been granted MFN status under United States tariff law. Belarus, Kazakhstan, Turkmenistan, Georgia, Azerbaijan, Tajikistan, Moldova, Kyrgyzstan, Armenia, Uzbekistan, the Russian Federation and Ukraine are also MFN beneficiaries. It is perhaps more useful, therefore, to indicate those nations that do not presently benefit from most-favored-nation tariff treatment. These include Cuba and North Korea. Goods from some of these nations are totally embargoed as a matter of national security; the law in this area is covered in Chapter 16. The most current listing of those nations whose products are subject to Column 2 tariffs can be found in General Headnote 3(b) to the HTS.

§ 10.5   The Jackson-Vanik Amendment

Section 402 of the 1974 Trade Act presently governs American grants of most-favored-nation tariff status.[4] This is commonly known as the "Jackson-Vanik Amendment." Under its terms, no products from a nonmarket economy nation may receive MFN treatment, nor may that country participate in U.S. financial credit or guaranty programs, whenever the President determines that it denies its citizens the right or opportunity to emigrate, imposes more than nominal taxes on visas or other emigration documents, or imposes more than nominal charges on its citizens as a result of their desire to leave. These statutory conditions are widely thought to have been the product of United States desires to have the Soviet Union permit greater exodus of its Jewish population during the early 1970s. However, the passage of the Jackson-Vanik Amendment was an important factor in the Soviet decision to withdraw from a broad trade agreement with the United States at that time, and led to sharply curtailed Jewish emigration from the Soviet Union.

The application of Jackson-Vanik by the President is subject to a waiver by executive order whenever the President determines that such a waiver will substantially promote the objectives of freedom of emigration and the President has received assurances

---

[4]   19 U.S.C. § 2432.

that the emigration practices of a particular nonmarket economy nation will lead substantially to the achievement of those objectives. If the President decides to exercise this waiver authority, the waiver must be renewed annually and reported to Congress. These reports and the exercise of presidential waivers have over the years been contentious. At one point Congress had the power to veto presidential waivers under the Jackson-Vanik Amendment. However, a 1983 decision of the United States Supreme Court strongly suggested that these veto powers were unconstitutional.[5] The Customs and Trade Act of 1990 amended the Trade Act of 1974 so as to permit Congress to jointly resolve against presidential Jackson-Vanik waivers. These resolutions can be vetoed by the President, and the President's veto can in turn by overridden by Congress. It is thought that these amendments resolved the constitutional problems associated with Congressional vetoes of presidential action.

Congress and the President disagreed significantly over the renewal of most-favored-nation treatment for Chinese goods. Questions surrounding China's emigration policies, and its general human rights record, were downplayed by U.S. authorities for many years prior to Tiananmen Square. As internal discord within China increased, especially in Tibet and more generally in connection with the Democracy Movement, the Jackson-Vanik amendment came to the forefront of Sino-American trade relations. President Bush's renewal of China's most favored nation status in 1990, 1991 and 1992 was heavily criticized.

Jackson-Vanik became the political fulcrum of Sino-American trade relations. Congress threatened but did not achieve a veto of the President's renewal of MFN tariffs for Chinese goods. Early in 1992, Congress adopted the United States-China Act of 1991. This law would have prohibited the President from recommending further extensions of MFN status to China unless he reported that the PRC has accounted for citizens detained or accused in connection with Tiananmen Square and had made significant progress in achieving specified objectives on human rights, trade and weapons proliferation. President Bush vetoed the Act and the Congress was unable to override that veto.

In 1993, President Clinton renewed China's MFN status subject to some general human-rights conditions, including "significant progress" in releasing political prisoners, allowing international groups access to prisons and respect for human rights in Tibet. This seemed to pacify Congress for the moment. But it

---

5   *See* Immigration and Naturalization Service v. Chadha, 462 U.S. 919 (1983).

engendered hostility and resistance in China. Less publicly, the United States business community opposed the linkage of human rights to MFN tariffs as its PRC trade and investment commitments and opportunities were endangered. China, meanwhile, had developed the world's fastest growing economy and it decided to force the issue. If anything, abuse of human rights in the PRC actually increased early in 1994, notably prior to a well-publicized visit of the U.S. Secretary of State. With Congress increasingly split on the issue, President Clinton made an historic reversal in policy. In June of 1994, he renewed China's MFN tariff status without human rights conditions, limiting its coverage only as regards Chinese-made ammunition and guns.

President Clinton renewed China's MFN tariff status each year after 1994. Congress did not seek to override these decisions. In 1998, for the first time, President Clinton waived the Jackson-Vanik requirements for Vietnam. President George W. Bush did likewise. This waiver survived Congressional scrutiny. It opened the door to EXIMBANK and OPIC programs, as well as Column 1 MFN tariffs on Vietnamese goods entering the United States.

WTO members like China since 2001, Vietnam since 2007 and Russia since 2012 receive MFN tariff status automatically and unconditionally. Hence the Jackson-Vanik amendment no longer has significant application.

§ 10.6 U.S. Generalized System of Tariff Preferences___Statutory Authorization

The Generalized System of Preferences (GSP) originated in United Nations dialogues between the developed and the developing world. The third world successfully argued that it needed special access to industrial markets in order to improve and advance their economies. One problem with this approach is that it is contrary to the unconditional most-favored-nation principle contained in the GATT. Nevertheless, in 1971 the GATT authorized its parties to establish generalized systems of tariff preferences for developing nations. The European Union, Japan and nearly all other developed nations adopted GSP systems before the United States. Although similar in purpose, each of these systems is governed by a unique body of law of the "donor" country.

It was not until the Trade Act of 1974 that a GSP system was incorporated into United States tariff law. The Trade Act authorized GSP tariff preferences for ten years. The program was renewed in the Trade Act of 1984 for an additional nine years ending in July 1993. Incremental extensions have since been made pending a program review. The Trade Promotion Authority-Trade

Adjustment Assistance Act of 2002 (TPA-TAA) renewed the GSP program through 2006 retroactive to its expiration on Sept. 30, 2001. Regular GSP renewals have followed, notably in 2015. At this point, tens of billions of dollars worth of goods enter the U.S. market duty free under the GSP program, but it is estimated that more imports could achieve this status if traders better understood the GSP.

Title V of the Trade Act of 1974 contains the provisions authorizing the United States GSP program.[6] The United States GSP system, as presently operated, designates certain nations as "beneficiary developing countries." Unless a country is so designated, none of its imports can enter duty free under the GSP program. In addition, only selected goods are designated "eligible articles" for purposes of the GSP program. Thus, for duty free entry under the GSP program to occur, the goods must originate from a beneficiary nation and qualify as eligible articles.

§ 10.7   U.S. Generalized System of Tariff Preferences___USTR Petition Procedures

Any United States producer of an article that competes with GSP imports can file a petition with the United States Trade Representative (USTR) to have a country or particular products withdrawn from the program. This petitioning procedure can also be used in the reverse by importers and exporters to obtain product or beneficiary country status under the United States GSP program. The President is given broad authority to withdraw, suspend or limit the application of duty free entry under the GSP system.[7] Specific products from specific countries may be excluded from GSP benefits. In one case, for example, the President's decision to withdraw GSP benefits for "buffalo leather and goat and kid leather (not fancy)" from India was affirmed.[8] In another decision, the President's discretionary authority to deny GSP benefits to cut flowers from Colombia was similarly upheld.[9]

The President is required to take into consideration the impact of duty free entry on U.S. producers of like or directly competitive products. There is a set of regulations, codified at 15 C.F.R. Part 2007, which details the petitioning procedures used in connection with the certification of GSP eligible products or countries. These regulations require the domestic competitor to cite injury caused by duty free GSP imports. Within 6 months after the petition is filed,

---

6   19 U.S.C. §§ 501–506.

7   *See* 19 U.S.C. § 2464(a).

8   Florsheim Shoe Co. v. United States, 744 F.2d 787 (Fed. Cir. 1984).

9   Sunburst Farms, Inc. v. United States, 797 F.2d 973 (Fed. Cir. 1986).

and a review by the United States Trade Representative (USTR) acting with the advice of the International Trade Commission (ITC) has been undertaken, a decision on the petition will be rendered by the USTR.

§ 10.8   U.S. Generalized System of Tariff Preferences___Competitive Need Limitations

There are two statutory limitations on the applicability of duty free GSP entry. These are known as the "competitive need" limitations. They are found in Section 504 of the Trade Act of 1974, codified at 19 U.S.C. § 2464(c). The first statutory limitation focuses upon dollar volumes. Duty free entry is not permitted to any eligible product from a beneficiary country if during the preceding year that country exported to the United States more than a designated dollar volume of the article in question. There is a statutory formula for establishing this dollar volume limitation. In recent years, the maximum dollar volume limitation has approximated $170 million dollars. The second statutory limitation on duty free GSP entry is framed in terms of percentages. Duty free entry is denied to products if during the preceding year the beneficiary country exported to the United States 50 percent or more of the total U.S. imports of that particular product.[10]

A complex system of waivers applies to the competitive need formulae. These are administered by the USTR and the President acting on advice of the International Trade Commission.[11] Basically, there are five possibilities for waivers of the competitive need limitations. The first can occur if the President decides that there is no like or directly competitive article produced in the United States and the imported product is exempt from the percentage but not the dollar value competitive need limitation. The second can occur under circumstances where the President determines that the imports in question are *de minimis*. The third possibility involves imports from the least developed developing nations, after notice to Congress. A list of these countries can be found in HTS General Note 3(c)(ii)(B). A fourth opportunity for a competitive need waiver exists when there has been an historical preferential trade relationship between the United States and the source country, and there is a trade agreement between that country and the United States, and the source country does not discriminate against or

---

[10]   *See* West Bend Co. v. United States, 10 C.I.T. 146 (1986) (competitive impact still must be proven).

[11]   *See* 19 U.S.C. § 2464(c).

otherwise impose unjustifiable or unreasonable barriers to United States commerce.

Lastly, the President is authorized to waive the competitive need requirements of the GSP program if the International Trade Commission decides that the imports in question are not likely to have an adverse effect on the United States industry with which they compete, and the President determines that such a waiver is in the national economic interest.[12] In making waiver determinations, the President must consider generally the extent to which the beneficiary country has assured the United States that it will provide equitable and reasonable access to its markets and basic commodity resources. The President must also consider the extent to which the country provides adequate and effective means for foreigners to secure and exercise intellectual property rights. Once a waiver of the competitive need limitations is granted, it remains in effect until circumstances change and the President decides that it is no longer justified. Attorneys can play a useful role in monitoring Department of Commerce trade statistics to determine how close imports are coming under the competitive need formulae to restriction. By shifting to purchases of similar goods from another country, importers can preserve duty free entry and avoid the effects of these statutory restraints.

§ 10.9   U.S. Generalized System of Tariff Preferences__Country Eligibility

At present, thousands of products from over one hundred countries benefit from duty free GSP entry into the United States.[13] A list of GSP qualified nations and territories is presented in HTS General Note 3(c)(ii). Goods from insular possessions of the United States (*e.g.*, American Samoa and the U.S. Virgin Islands) ordinarily receive duty free GSP entry "no less favorable" than allowed GSP beneficiary nations.[14] The President's power over the list of eligible countries and eligible products is wide and politically sensitive. For example, the President is required to evaluate, in determining whether a country is eligible under the U.S. GSP program, if it is upholding "internationally recognized workers' rights." Such rights include the right of association, the right to organize and bargain collectively, a prohibition against forced or compulsory labor, a minimum age for employment of children, and acceptable working conditions (minimum wages, hours of work, and

---

[12] *See* 19 U.S.C. § 2464(c)(3)(A).

[13] See Executive Order 11888 (Nov. 24, 1975, 40 F.R. 55276, extensively amended) for a detailed listing of eligible products and countries).

[14] 19 U.S.C. § 2462(d).

occupational safety and health.)[15] In 2002, the definition of "core worker rights" for GSP country eligibility purposes was updated to include the ILO prohibition on the worst forms of child labor. The President must report annually to the Congress on the status of internationally recognized workers' rights in every GSP beneficiary country, but the issue is not open to private challenge.[16]

The President must also consider whether the foreign country is adequately protecting United States owners of intellectual property, (compliance with TRIPs is not necessarily sufficient), and whether its investment laws adversely affect U.S. exports. In addition, when designating GSP beneficiary nations, the Trade Act requires the President to take into account various factors which amount to a U.S. agenda on international economic relations:

(1)   the desires of the country;

(2)   its level of economic development;

(3)   whether the EU, Japan or others extend GSP treatment to it;

(4)   the extent to which the country provides equitable and reasonable access to its markets and its basic commodity resources, and the extent to which it will refrain from unreasonable export practices;

(5)   the extent to which it provides adequate and effective intellectual property rights; and

(6)   the extent to which it has taken action to reduce trade distorting investment practices (including export performance requirements) and reduced barriers to trade in services.[17]

No communist nations and no oil restraining OPEC nations (Indonesia, Ecuador and Venezuela are excepted) may benefit from the GSP program. Furthermore, the President must not designate countries that grant trade preferences to other *developed* nations. The President must also consider, in making GSP decisions, whether beneficiary countries are cooperative on drug enforcement, whether they are expropriators of U.S. property interests, whether they offer assistance to terrorists, and whether they are willing to recognize international arbitration awards. The President may waive the expropriation requirement if it is determined that the country in question has paid prompt, adequate and effective

---

[15]   19 U.S.C. § 2462(a).

[16]   *See* International Labor Rights Education & Research Fund v. Bush, 752 F. Supp. 495 (D.D.C. 1990), *aff'd* 954 F.2d 745 (D.C. Cir. 1992).

[17]   19 U.S.C. § 2462(c).

compensation or entered into good faith negotiations or arbitration with the intent to do so.

The statutory bar against communist, oil restricting OPEC and preferentially trading countries as GSP beneficiaries is absolute. The bar against expropriating, drug dealing, arbitration award nonenforcement, terrorist aiding and workers' rights nonrecognition beneficiaries is discretionary with the President. The goods of such nations may still qualify if the President determines that GSP duty free entry would be in the national economic interest of the United States.[18] In applying these country eligibility criteria, past Presidents have disqualified a variety of nations from the U.S. GSP program. For example, Romania, Nicaragua, Paraguay, Chile, Burma, the Central African Republic and Liberia have all been disqualified in the past for failure to meet the workers' rights standards. Argentina and Honduras have lost GSP benefits for perceived failures to adequately protect U.S. pharmaceutical patents. Panama under General Noriega was rendered ineligible because of the failure to cooperate on narcotics. Intellectual property piracy led to the suspension of Ukraine's country eligibility in the GSP program.

The President's review of a country's eligibility under the GSP program is ongoing. This has led to the reinstatement of GSP beneficiary nations. Russia was made a GSP beneficiary by President Clinton in the Fall of 1993. Any country designated as a beneficiary nation under the GSP program that is subsequently disqualified by exercise of Presidential discretion, or graduated, must receive 60 days' notice from the President with an explanation of this decision.[19] This, in effect, presents the opportunity to reply and negotiate.

Since the GSP program originated within the GATT/WTO nearly all the beneficiary countries are members of that organization. It is not, however, mandatory for a developing nation to be a member of the WTO in order to receive GSP trade benefits from the United States. China is a WTO member, but for other reasons its goods do not qualify for GSP duty free entry. Other nations whose goods are not eligible are specifically listed in the Trade Act: Australia, Austria, Canada, European Union States, Finland, Iceland, Japan, Monaco, New Zealand, Norway, Republic of South Africa, Sweden, and Switzerland.[20] Lastly, there is a competitive need formula for automatic removal of country eligibility based upon per capita income (about $15,000 in 2016).

---

[18]   19 U.S.C. § 2462(b).

[19]   19 U.S.C. § 2462(a).

[20]   19 U.S.C. § 2462(b).

Bahrain, Brunei, Nauru, Bermuda, The Seychelles, Uruguay, Venezuela and other countries have been disqualified under this formula.

All developing nation U.S. free trade partners, for example Mexico, Jordan, Morocco, the CAFTA nations, Colombia and Peru, have been removed from the GSP list of eligible countries.

§ 10.10   U.S. Generalized System of Tariff Preferences___Product Eligibility

For each designated GSP beneficiary country, the President also issues a list of products from that country that qualify for duty free entry into the United States. The statutory authorization for the United States GSP program generally excludes leather products, textiles and apparel,[21] watches,[22] selected electronics and, certain steel, footwear and categories of glass from being designated as eligible articles.[23] All these goods are thought to involve particular "import sensitivity."

The UNCTAD Certificate of Origin Form A is ordinarily required of the foreign exporter when GSP eligible merchandise is involved. A complex body of "rules of origin" determine where goods are from for purposes of the United States GSP program. Basically, for goods to originate in a beneficiary country, at least 35 percent of the appraised value of those goods must be added in that nation.[24] The statutory rules of origin for GSP eligible goods are found in 19 U.S.C. § 2463(b).[25] A federal Circuit Court of Appeals ruled that a

---

[21]   *See* Luggage and Leather Goods Mfrs. of America, Inc. v. United States, 588 F. Supp. 1413 (C.I.T. 1984) (man-made fiber flat goods are textile and apparel articles).

[22]   *See* North American Foreign Trading Corp. v. United States, 600 F. Supp. 226 (C.I.T. 1984), *aff'd* 783 F.2d 1031 (Fed. Cir. 1986) (exemption for watches includes solid-state digital watches).

[23]   19 U.S.C. § 2463(c).

[24]   *See* Madison Galleries, Ltd. v. United States, 870 F.2d 627 (Fed. Cir. 1989).

[25]   19 U.S.C. § 2463(b). Eligible articles qualifying for duty-free treatment:

(b)(1) The duty-free treatment provided under section 501 shall apply to any eligible article which is the growth, product, or manufacture of a beneficiary developing country if—

   (A) that article is imported directly from a beneficiary developing country into the customs territory of the United States; and

   (B) the sum of (i) the cost or value of the materials produced in the beneficiary developing country or any 2 or more countries which are members of the same association of countries which is treated as one country under section 502(a)(3), plus (ii) the direct costs of processing operations performed in such beneficiary developing country or such member countries is not less than 35 percent of the appraised value of such article at the time of its entry into the customs territory of the United States.

"two-stage" substantial transformation process must also occur in order to qualify goods for GSP purposes.[26] Thus, the value of U.S.-grown corn did not count towards meeting the 35 percent requirement because the intermediate products into which it was turned did not qualify as Mexican in origin for lack of substantial transformation into a new and different article of commerce.[27] But the assembly of integrated circuits in Taiwan from slices containing many integrated circuit chips, gold wire, lead frame strips, molding compound and epoxy (all of which were U.S. in origin) did constitute a substantial transformation of such items into a new article of commerce. Thus the circuits could be deemed from Taiwan for purposes of the 35 percent value added GSP rule.[28]

One unusual feature of the rules of origin for the United States GSP program is that which favors selected regional economic groups. Goods made in the ANDEAN pact, ASEAN or CARICOM may be designated as "one country" for purposes of origin. So too may goods produced in the East African Community, the West African Economic and Monetary Union and the Southern African Development Community. This means that the value added requirement as applied in these regions is met if 35 percent of the value added has been created inside each group as opposed to inside any one nation of the group. It is notable that many other third world regional economic groups are not similarly treated, *e.g.* MERCOSUR, and the Gulf Council of the Middle East.

---

(2)   The Secretary of the Treasury, after consulting with the United States Trade Representative, shall prescribe such regulations as may be necessary to carry out this subsection, including, but not limited to, regulations providing that, in order to be eligible for duty-free treatment under this title, an article must be wholly the growth, product, or manufacture of a beneficiary developing country, or must be a new or different article of commerce which has been grown, produced, or manufactured in the beneficiary developing country; but no article or material of a beneficiary developing country shall be eligible for such treatment by virtue of having merely undergone—

    (A) simple combining or packaging operations, or

    (B) mere dilution with water or mere dilution with another substance that does not materially alter the characteristics of the article.

[26]   *See* Torrington Company v. United States, 764 F.2d 1563 (Fed. Cir. 1985). *See generally* Cutler, *United States Generalized System of Preferences: the Problem of Substantial Transformation*, 5 N.C. J. INT'L L. COM. REG. 393 (1980).

[27]   Azteca Mill. Co. v. United States, 890 F.2d 1150 (Fed. Cir. 1989).

[28]   Texas Instruments Inc. v. United States, 681 F.2d 778 (C.C.P.A. 1982). *See* Madison Galleries, Ltd. v. United States, 688 F. Supp. 1544 (C.I.T. 1988) (blank porcelain from Taiwan substantially transformed when painted and fired in Hong Kong).

§ 10.11   U.S. Generalized System of Tariff Preferences___Graduation

As nations develop, U.S. law either bars their participation in the GSP program absolutely or vests discretion in the President to remove nations or products from its scope. Since 1984, developing nations with a per capita gross national product in excess of $8,500 are totally ineligible for GSP duty free entry. The Bahamas, Bahrain, Brunei, Israel, Nauru and Bermuda have been disqualified under this rule. In addition, the President has a broad authority to "graduate" countries from the United States GSP program. The basic concept here is that certain nations are sufficiently developed so as to not need the benefits of duty free entry into the United States market. Discretionary graduation is based on an assessment of the economic development level of the beneficiary country, the competitive position of the imports and the overall national economic interests of the United States.[29]

In recent years, Presidents have been graduating more and more products from countries like India and Brazil. In January of 1989, President Reagan graduated all products from Hong Kong, Singapore, South Korea and Taiwan. At that time, these countries were the source of about 60 percent of all goods benefiting from the United States GSP program. Mexico then emerged as the chief beneficiary country under the program until late in 1993 when all of its products were removed from the GSP treatment in anticipation of the North American Free Trade Agreement. In 1997, President Clinton graduated Malaysia entirely from the GSP program. President Obama graduated Russia entirely in 2014.

§ 10.12   U.S. Generalized System of Tariff Preferences___Judicial and Administrative Remedies

Legal challenges to presidential revocations of duty free GSP treatment were originally filed with the U.S. Customs Court. This was the case despite contentions of inadequate legal remedies in that court and the fact that plaintiff could not pursue class action relief except in federal district court.[30] Litigation involving the GSP program is now commenced in the U.S. Court of International Trade.

The goods entering the United States duty free through the GSP program remain subject to the possibility of escape clause

---

[29]   *See* 47 Fed. Reg. 31,099, 31,000 (July 16, 1982).
[30]   Barclay Industries, Inc. v. Carter, 494 F. Supp. 912 (D.D.C. 1980).

relief under Section 201 of the Trade Act of 1974.[31] Moreover, such goods may also be restrained pursuant to Section 232 of the Trade Expansion Act of 1962 in the name of the national security of the United States.[32]

§ 10.13   Caribbean Basin Initiative (CBI)

The European Union has had for many years a policy which grants substantial duty free entry into its market for goods originating in Mediterranean Basin countries. The United States has duplicated this approach for the Caribbean Basin. This is accomplished through the Caribbean Basin Economic Recovery Act of 1983.[33] For these purposes, the Caribbean Basin is broadly defined to include nearly all of the islands in that Sea, and a significant number of Central and South American nations bordering the Caribbean. So defined, there are 28 nations which could qualify for purposes of the United States Caribbean Basin Initiative. As with the GSP program, the Caribbean Basin Initiative (CBI) involves presidential determinations to confer beneficiary status upon any of these eligible countries. However, unlike the GSP, there are no presidential determinations as to which specific products of these countries shall be allowed into the United States on a duty free basis. All Caribbean products except those excluded by statute are eligible. Moreover, there are no "competitive need" or annual per capita income limits under the CBI. Lastly, unlike the GSP program which must be renewed periodically, the Caribbean Basin Initiative is a permanent part of the U.S. tariff system.

The United States has maintained a steady trade surplus with Caribbean Basin countries. Leading export items under the CBI are typically beef, raw cane sugar, medical instruments, cigars, fruits and rum. The leading source countries have often been the Dominican Republic, Costa Rica and Guatemala, now all U.S. free trade partners. The value of all CBI duty free imports now exceeds $1 billion annually, but the CBI countries fear a diversion of trade and investment to Mexico and Central America as the North American Free Trade Agreement (NAFTA) and the Central American Free Trade Agreement (CAFTA) mature.

§ 10.14   CBI Country Eligibility

The President is forbidden from designating Caribbean Basin Initiative beneficiaries if they are communist, have engaged in expropriation activities, nullified contracts or intellectual property

---

[31]   See 19 U.S.C. § 2251.
[32]   See 19 U.S.C. § 2463(c)(2).
[33]   Public Law 98–67, 97 Stat. 384, codified at 19 U.S.C. § 2701 et seq.

rights of the U.S. citizens, failed to recognize and enforce arbitral awards, given preferential treatment to products of another developed nation, broadcast through a government-owned entity United States copyrighted material without consent, failed to sign a treaty or other agreement regarding extradition of United States citizens, failed to cooperate on narcotics enforcement, or failed to afford internationally recognized workers' rights. For these purposes, the definition of workers' rights enacted in connection with the GSP program applies.[34] Since 2000, CBI countries must also show a commitment to implementing WTO pledges.

These prohibitions notwithstanding, the President can still designate a Caribbean Basin country as a beneficiary if he or she determines that this will be in the national economic or security interest of the United States. However, this can be done only in connection with countries that are disqualified as being communist, expropriators, contract or intellectual property nullifiers, nonenforcers of arbitral awards, unauthorized broadcasters, or those who fail to provide for internationally recognized workers' rights. Thus, if a Caribbean nation is disqualified because it grants preferential trade treatment to products of another developed nation or refuses to sign an extradition treaty with the United States, there is no possibility of its designation as a beneficiary nation under the Caribbean Basin Initiative. As with the GSP statutory requirements, if the basis for the disqualification is expropriation or nullification of benefits, the President may override this disqualification if that nation is engaged in payment of prompt, adequate and effective compensation or good faith negotiations intended to lead to such compensation.

In addition, the President is required to take various factors into account in designating beneficiary countries under the Caribbean Basin Initiative. These include:

(1) the desire of that country to participate;

(2) the economic conditions and living standards of that nation;

(3) the extent to which the country has promised to provide equitable and reasonable access to its markets and basic commodity resources;

(4) the degree to which it follows accepted GATT rules on international trade;

---

[34]   *See* § 10.9, *supra.*

(5) the degree to which it uses export subsidies or imposes export performance requirements or local content requirements which distort international trade;

(6) the degree to which its trade policies help revitalize the region;

(7) the degree to which it is undertaking self-help measures to promote its own economic development;

(8) whether it has taken steps to provide internationally recognized workers' rights;

(9) the extent to which it provides adequate and effective means for foreigners to secure and enforce exclusive intellectual property rights;

(10) the extent to which the country prohibits unauthorized broadcasts of copyrighted material belonging to U.S. owners; and

(11) the extent to which it is prepared to cooperate with the United States in connection with the Caribbean Basin Initiative, particularly by signing a tax information exchange agreement.

Under these criteria, the President has designated a large number of the 28 eligible nations as beneficiary countries under the Caribbean Basin Initiative. These include Antigua and Barbuda, Aruba, the Bahamas, Barbados, Belize, the British Virgin Islands, Costa Rica, Dominica, the Dominican Republic, El Salvador, Grenada, Guatemala, Guyana, Haiti, Honduras, Jamaica, Monserrat, the Netherlands Antilles, Nicaragua, Panama, St. Christopher-Nevis, St. Lucia, St. Vincent and the Grenadines, and Trinidad and Tobago. Cuba is not even listed among the nations eligible for consideration in connection with the Caribbean Basin Initiative. Some of these countries are now U.S. free trade partners and therefore no longer CBI eligible.

U.S. Presidents have typically required of each potential beneficiary a concise written presentation of its policies and practices directly related to the issues raised by the country designation criteria listed in the Caribbean Basin Economic Recovery Act. Wherever measures were in effect which were inconsistent with the objectives of these criteria, U.S. presidents have sought assurances that such measures would be progressively eliminated or modified. For example, the Dominican Republic promised to take steps to reduce the degree of book piracy and the

Jamaican and Bahamian governments promised to stop the unauthorized broadcast of U.S. films and television programs.[35]

§ 10.15   CBI Product Eligibility

Unless specifically excluded, all products of Caribbean Basin nations are eligible for duty free entry into the United States market. Certain goods are absolutely excluded from such treatment.[36] These include footwear, canned tuna, petroleum and petroleum derivatives, watches, and certain leather products. It should be noted that this listing of "import sensitive" products is different from but overlaps with that used in connection with the United States GSP program. Since 2000, products ineligible for CBI benefits enter at reduced tariff levels corresponding to Mexican goods under NAFTA . . . so-called "NAFTA parity."

One of the most critical of the products that may enter the United States on a duty free basis is sugar. But the President is given the authority to suspend duty free treatment for both sugar and beef products originating in the Caribbean Basin or to impose quotas in order to protect United States domestic price support programs for these products.[37] Sugar exports have traditionally been critical to many Caribbean Basin economies. Nevertheless, sugar import quotas into the United States from the Caribbean have been steadily reduced in recent years. For example, by 1988 the sugar quota allocations for some CBI countries reached a low of 25 percent of their 1983 pre-Caribbean Basin Initiative allocations.[38] Many consider the few duty free import benefits obtained under the Initiative to be more than counterbalanced by the loss in sugar exports to the United States market.

The rules of origin for determining product eligibility in connection with the Caribbean Basin Initiative are virtually the same as discussed previously under the GSP.[39] As a general rule, a substantial transformation must occur and a 35 percent value added requirement is imposed (but 15 percent may come from the United States). This percentage is calculated by adding the sum of the cost or value of the materials produced in the beneficiary country or two or more beneficiary countries plus the direct cost of processing operations performed in those countries.[40] It should be

---

[35]   19 U.S.C. § 2702.

[36]   *See* 19 U.S.C. § 2703(b).

[37]   19 U.S.C. § 2073(c) and (d).

[38]   *See* Betty Ruth Fox, *Interaction of the Caribbean Basin Initiative and U.S. Domestic Sugar Price Support: A Political Contradiction*, 8 MISS. COL. L. REV. 197 (1988).

[39]   *See* HTS General Note 3(c)(v).

[40]   19 U.S.C. § 2703(a).

noted that this approach effectively treats all of the CBI-eligible nations as a regional beneficiary since the 35 percent required value can be cumulated among them.

As under the GSP program, the President is given broad powers to suspend duty free treatment with reference to any eligible product or any designated beneficiary country.[41] Import injury relief under Section 201 of the Trade Act of 1974 can be invoked in connection with Caribbean Basin imports. And the equivalent of that relief is authorized specifically for agricultural imports upon similar determinations by the Secretary of Agriculture.[42] The effects of these protective proceedings may be diminished in the context of Caribbean Basin imports. Whenever the International Trade Commission is studying whether increased imports are a substantial cause of serious injury to a domestic industry under Section 201 or its agricultural equivalent, the ITC is required to break out the Caribbean Basin beneficiary countries. The President is given the discretion if he or she decides to impose escape clause relief to suspend that relief relative to Caribbean Basin imports. A similar discretion is granted to the President in connection with national security import restraints under Section 232 of the Trade Expansion Act of 1962. However, these discretionary provisions relate only to those goods that are eligible for duty free entry under the Caribbean Basin Initiative.[43]

In 1986, President Reagan initiated a special program for textiles produced in the Caribbean. Essentially, this program increases the opportunity to sell Caribbean textile products when the fabric involved has been previously formed and cut in the United States. If this is the case, there are minimum guaranteed access levels. This program is run in conjunction with Section 9802.00.80 of the Harmonized Tariff Schedule of the United States.[44]

The U.S.-Caribbean Basin Trade Partnership Act of 2000 grants duty-free and quota-free access to the U.S. market for apparel made from U.S. fabric and yarn. Apparel made from CBI fabric is capped for duty free into the United States. CBI textiles and apparel are subject to market surge safeguards comparable to those under NAFTA. Late in 2006, duty free treatment of Haitian apparel products was expanded under the HOPE Act. In certain cases, Haiti may utilize third country fabrics and still ship apparel duty free into the United States.

---

[41]   19 U.S.C. § 2702(e).

[42]   19 U.S.C. § 2703(f).

[43]   *See* 29 U.S.C. § 2703(e).

[44]   *See* 51 Fed. Reg. 21,208 (June 11, 1986).

§ 10.16   Andean Trade Preferences

The Andean Trade Preference Act (ATPA) of 1991[45] authorizes the President to grant duty free treatment to imports of eligible articles from Colombia, Peru, Bolivia and Ecuador. Venezuela is not included as a beneficiary country under this Act. The Andean Trade Preference Act is patterned after the Caribbean Basin Economic Recovery Act of 1983. Goods that ordinarily enter duty free into the United States from Caribbean Basin nations will also enter duty free from these four Andean countries. The same exceptions and exclusions discussed above in connection with the Caribbean Basin Initiative generally apply. However, while the CBI is a permanent part of United States Customs law, the ATPA was only authorized initially for a period of ten years. Furthermore, the guaranteed access levels for Caribbean Basin textile products, separate cumulation for antidumping and countervailing duty investigations, and the waiver of the Buy American Act for procurement purposes are not authorized by the ATPA.

The Andean Trade Preference Act was renewed by the TPA-TAA through February 2006 retroactive to its expiry Dec. 4, 2001. Periodic renewals have followed. Textile and apparel products, and most other products previously excluded, are now included under the ATPA. Country eligibility for enhanced benefits includes consideration of steps taken to comply with WTO obligations, the protection of worker rights and combating corruption. Broadly speaking, the passage of the ATPA represents fulfillment of the elder President Bush's commitment to assist these nations economically in return for their help in containing narcotics. Peru and Colombia are now U.S. free partners, a status that removes ATPA benefits. Free trade negotiations with Ecuador and Bolivia have not succeeded, leaving their Andean benefits uncertain.

§ 10.17   African Trade Preferences

The Africa Growth and Opportunity Act of 2000[46] granted duty-free and quota-free access to the U.S. market for apparel made from U.S. fabric and yarn. Apparel made from African fabric is capped for duty free entry. The least developed sub-Saharan countries enjoy duty-free and quota-free apparel access regardless of the origin of the fabric. In 2008, the so-called "abundant supply" provision of AGOA was repealed, thus assuring least-developed country textile exports to the United States. U.S. imports of AGOA textiles using third country fabrics have also been liberalized.

---

[45]   Public Law 102–82, 19 U.S.C. § 3201 et seq.

[46]   Public Law No. 106–200, 114 Stat. 252.

The Act also altered U.S. GSP rules to admit certain previously excluded African products on a duty-free basis, including petroleum, watches and flat goods. Sub-Saharan countries can export almost all products duty-free to the United States. These countries are encouraged to create a free trade area with U.S. support. African exports are subject to import surge (escape clause) protection and stringent rules against transshipments between countries for purposes of taking advantage of U.S. trade benefits.

AGOA was renewed in 2015 subject to eligibility rules concerning market-based economies, poverty reduction, rule of law, and anti-corruption and human rights efforts, including internationally recognized workers' rights.

§ 10.18　Section 9802.00.80 of the HTS

Section 9802.00.80 of the Harmonized Tariff Schedule of the United States (formerly Section 807.00 of the Tariff Schedule of the United States) is an unusual "duty free" provision. This section allows for the duty free importation of United States fabricated components that were exported ready for assembly abroad. If qualified, goods assembled abroad containing U.S. components are subject only to a duty upon the value added through foreign assembly operations regardless of where assembled. In order for this to be the case, Section 9802.00.80 requires that the components be fabricated and a product of the United States, that they be exported in a condition ready for assembly without further fabrication, that they not lose their physical identity by change in form, shape or otherwise, and that they not be advanced in value or improved in condition abroad except by being assembled and except by operations incidental to the assembly process such as cleaning, lubricating and painting.

The regulations issued in connection with Section 9802.00.80 indicate that there are other incidental operations which will not disqualify components from duty free re-entry into the United States. These include removing rust, grease, paint or other preservative coatings, the application of similar preservative coatings, the trimming or other removal of small amounts of excess material, adjustments in the shape or form of a component required by the assembly that is being undertaken, the cutting to length of wire, thread, tape, foil or similar products, the separation by cutting of finished components (such as integrated circuits exported in strips), and the calibration, testing, marking, sorting, pressing and folding and assembly of the final product.[47] In contrast, the regulations also provide examples of operations that are not

---

[47]　19 C.F.R. § 10.16(b).

considered incidental to assembly for these purposes. These examples include the melting of ingots to produce cast metal parts, the cutting of garments according to patterns, painting which is intended to enhance the appearance or impart distinctive features to the product, chemical treatment so as to realize new characteristics (such as moisture-proofing), and the machining, polishing or other treatment of metals which create significant new characteristics or qualities.[48]

If all of the Section 9802.00.80 criteria are met, the tariff that will be assessed upon the imported assembled product will be limited to a duty upon the full value of that product less the cost or value of U.S. made components that have been incorporated into it.[49] Those who seek to take advantage of Section 9802.00.80 must provide the United States Customs Service with a Foreign Assembler's Declaration and Certification. This is known as Form 3317. The assembly plant operator certifies that the requirements of Section 9802.00.80 are met, and the importer declares that this certification is correct. Billions of dollars of ordinarily tariffed value have been excluded as a result of this Customs law provision. Motor vehicles, semiconductors, office machines, textiles and apparel, and furniture are good examples of the kinds of products assembled abroad with fabricated U.S. components so as to meet the requirements of Section 9802.00.80. Historically, many of these products have been assembled in Japan, Germany or Canada. In more recent times, the assembly operations to which Section 9802.00.80 frequently applies have more commonly been found in the developing world.

§ 10.19 Maquiladoras

Section 9802.00.80 is applicable to goods imported into the United States from anywhere in the world. However, it is most frequently associated with maquiladoras. Maquiladoras are "in-bond" assembly plants that often take advantage of the duty free potential of Section 9802.00.80. Maquiladoras enjoyed a phenomenal popularity after 1982 when the Mexican peso was dramatically devalued. This had the practical effect of rendering Mexican labor costs lower than those of Taiwan, Hong Kong, Singapore and South Korea. These Asian nations were traditionally low-cost assembly plant centers. Thousands of maquiladoras have been established in Tijuana, Ciudad Juarez, Nuevo Laredo and other border cities. They provide Mexico with hundreds of thousands of jobs and are a major source of foreign currency

---

[48]   19 C.F.R. § 10.16(c).

[49]   *See generally* 19 C.F.R. § 10.14 *et seq.*

earnings. Electronics, apparel, toys, medical supplies, transport equipment, furniture and sporting goods are examples of the types of industries that have been attracted south of the border.

United States components, when assembled in maquiladoras and qualifying under Section 9802.00.80, are exported and then reimported on a duty free basis. Maquiladoras have been developed throughout the Caribbean Basin and Central America. Much to the frustration of organized labor, such offshore assembly operations exemplify the internationalization of the United States manufacturing sector.

The maquiladora industry enjoyed explosive growth before and in the early years of NAFTA. Mexican law, like Section 9802.00.80, supports this growth. Various decrees permit goods to enter Mexico on a duty free basis *under bond* for purposes of assembly in maquiladoras. Mexican law permits duty free importation of equipment, technology and components for six months. At the end of that period the goods must be exported from Mexico, typically back to the United States. Except with special permission, which has been increasingly granted by the authorities, maquiladora-assembled goods may not enter the Mexican market. Investors may own maquiladoras, typically using 30-year land trusts (fideicomiso) and Mexican subsidiaries. Alternatively, they may lease assembly plant space from a Mexican company and operate a maquiladora from that space. The simplest way to enter into maquiladora assembly operations is to contract with a Mexican company to assemble the goods in question.

In 1998, Mexico's Ministry of Commerce and Industry Development (SECOFI) published an amended Maquiladora Decree. The revised Decree streamlines regulation of maquiladoras in Mexico, notably reducing SECOFI's discretion to deny, suspend or cancel maquila programs. A translation of the new Decree can be found at www.natlaw.com. Mexico was responding, in part, to increased assembly plant competition from Asia, especially China after its 2001 admission to the WTO.

The net result of the United States and Mexican law in this area is to create an interdependent legal framework mutually supportive of maquiladora operations. Many have characterized this legal framework as a "co-production" or "production sharing" arrangement between the two countries. However, utilization of maquiladoras is not limited to U.S. firms nor United States' components. Japanese and Korean companies have become major investors in maquiladora industries. To the extent that they utilize U.S. components, they may benefit from the duty free entry provisions of Section 9802.00.80. At this stage, however, some firms have moved their plants to Asia where lower labor costs prevail.

Until late in 1993, there was also a link between the United States System of Generalized Preferences (GSP) and Mexican maquiladoras. Under the rules of origin that govern the GSP program, if at least 35 percent of the value of a maquiladora product was of Mexican origin, it could qualify entirely for duty free entry into the United States. The possibility of this result caused many users of maquiladoras to seek out Mexican suppliers in order to try to meet the 35 percent rule of origin. This incentive was enhanced by the fact that South Korea, Singapore, Taiwan and Hong Kong were all graduated from the United States GSP program in 1989. Mexico was the largest source of GSP qualified goods entering the United States market prior to December 1993, when all of its products were removed from the GSP program as a result of NAFTA.

The North American Free Trade Area incorporating Mexico, Canada and the United States creates an incentive to invest in Mexico. Nearly all Mexican-made goods are able to enter the United States market on a duty free basis. NAFTA phased out over seven years the duty free entry Section 9802.00.80 benefits applied to Mexican maquiladoras, but not as regards goods assembled with United States components from outside North America.

There is an evolutionary cycle in assembly plants-from cheap raw labor to more skill-oriented operations to capital-intensive manufacturing. One of the most interesting comparative questions is whether there is also an evolutionary process in the applicable laws of these countries. In other words, what legal regimes do developing nations have to adopt in order to first attract assembly operations and do they evolve from extremely accommodating to more demanding as the cycle reaches completion? Or, does the manufacturer's ability to go elsewhere to even cheaper labor markets (*e.g.*, from Mexico to Guatemala to Haiti or from Hong Kong to the People's Republic of China to Vietnam) constantly temper the legal regimes regulating assembly plants? Some assembly plants withdrawn from Mexico have been based in China and Vietnam, with a few actually returning to North America due to rising costs.

§ 10.20   Section 9802.00.80 Case Law

There is a surprisingly large body of case law interpreting Section 9802.00.80. Much of it was developed when this provision was formally known as Section 807 of the Tariff Schedule of the United States. One issue is whether the United States components have been advanced in value or improved in condition abroad. If this is the case, duty free re-entry into the United States is prohibited. An early decision of the Court of Customs and Patent Appeals held that the export of U.S. fish hooks, which were assembled abroad into individually packaged assortments so as to meet the requirements of retail purchasers in the United States, were not advanced in value or improved in condition so as to be disqualified.[50] In another decision, U.S. revolvers were rechambered in Canada such that they no longer fired with accuracy .38 caliber bullets as originally designed. This change in condition caused the revolvers to be disqualified under Section 9802.00.80.[51] United States tomatoes shipped to Canada in bulk and sorted, graded as to color and size, and repackaged in smaller cartons were not changed, advanced in value or improved in condition so as to be disqualified from duty free re-entry.[52]

The buttonholing in Mexico of U.S. shirt components (cuffs and collar-bands) did not advance them in value nor improve their condition as a result of this incidental operation.[53] But polyester fabric exported from the United States to Canada where it was dyed and processed, and then exported back to the United States as finished fabric did involve an advancement in value and changing of the condition of the U.S. component so as to disqualify it from duty free entry.[54] Similarly, glass pieces produced in annealed form in the United States which were sent to Canada for heat treatment and returned for use as pieces of tempered glass were not capable of benefiting from duty free entry.[55] Terminal pins of U.S. origin were shipped to Mexico and incorporated into header assemblies and relays. This operation constituted an assembly which did not advance the value of the terminals nor improve their condition.[56]

Another requirement of Section 9802.00.80 is that the United States component be fabricated and ready for assembly without further fabrication. Circuit boards for computers made in the

---

[50]   United States v. John V. Carr & Son, Inc., 496 F.2d 1225 (C.C.P.A. 1974).

[51]   A D Deringer, Inc. v. United States, 386 F. Supp. 518, 73 Cust. Ct. 144 (1974).

[52]   Border Brokerage Co., Inc. v. United States, 314 F. Supp. 788, 65 Cust. Ct. 50 (1970).

[53]   United States v. Oxford Industries, Inc., 668 F.2d 507 (C.C.P.A. 1981). See United States v. Mast Industries, Inc., 668 F.2d 501 (C.C.P.A. 1981) (buttonholing and pocket slitting operations incidental to assembly process do not lead to duty free entry disqualification.)

[54]   Dolliff & Co., Inc. v. United States, 455 F. Supp. 618 (Cust. Ct. 1978), aff'd 599 F.2d 1015 (C.C.P.A. 1979).

[55]   Guardian Industries Corp. v. United States, 3 C.I.T. 9 (1982).

[56]   Sigma Instruments, Inc. v. United States, 565 F.Supp. 1036 (C.I.T.), aff'd 724 F.2d 930 (Fed.Cir.1983).

United States from foreign and U.S. parts qualify as fabricated components for these purposes.[57] In this case, the programmable read only memory (PROM) was programmed in the United States causing it to undergo a substantial transformation and become a United States product. Aluminum foil, tabs, tape, paper and mylar made in the United States and shipped to Taiwan in role form where they were used together with other articles of U.S. origin to produce aluminum electrolytic capacitors were not eligible for duty free entry because they were not "fabricated components" upon departure from the United States to Taiwan.[58] The fact that gold wire made in the United States was not cut until used for transistors assembled in Taiwan did not make it a U.S. component that was not ready for assembly abroad without further fabrication. The cutting of the gold wire was an incident of the assembly process.[59] But the assembly in Ecuador of flattened cylinders and ends into tunafish cans which were then packed with tuna and shipped back to the United States did not qualify under Section 9802.00.80.[60]

The failure to lock knitting loops to keep the knitting from unravelling in the United States meant that knitted glove shelves were not exported in a condition ready for assembly without further fabrication. The importer of those gloves was not entitled to duty free entry for the value of the shelves.[61] On the other hand, pantyhose tubes made in the United States were fully constructed and secured from unravelling by stitches. A closing operation did not create a new toe portion and the goods were permitted the benefits of Section 9802.00.80.[62] Likewise the joinder of molten plastic to the upper portion of a shoe abroad did not prevent the shoe vamp from duty free entry upon return to the United States. This operation did not constitute further fabrication of the vamp.[63]

The scoring and breaking of silicon slices along designated "streets" was an incidental operation to the assembly of transistors and therefore the slices were entitled to duty free entry into the United States.[64] Magnet and lead wire made in the U.S. and exported to Taiwan where it was wound into coils and cable harness put into television deflection yolks were entitled to duty free entry.[65]

---

[57]   Data General Corp. v. United States, 4 C.I.T. 182 (1982).

[58]   General Instrument Corp. v. United States, 67 Cust. Ct. 127 (1971).

[59]   General Instrument Corp. v. United States, 462 F.2d 1156 (C.C.P.A. 1972).

[60]   Van Camp Sea Food Co. v. United States, 73 Cust. Ct. 35 (1974).

[61]   Zwicker Knitting Mills v. United States, 613 F.2d 295 (C.C.P.A. 1980).

[62]   L'Eggs Products, Inc. v. United States, 704 F. Supp. 1127 (C.I.T. 1989).

[63]   Carter Footwear, Inc. v. United States, 669 F. Supp. 439 (C.I.T. 1987).

[64]   United States v. Texas Instruments, Inc., 545 F.2d 739 (C.C.P.A. 1976).

[65]   General Instrument Corp. v. United States, 499 F.2d 1318 (C.C.P.A. 1974).

The two-step assembly process in this case did not defeat the application of Section 9802.00.80. The burning of slots and holes in steel Z-beams in order to incorporate them into railroad cars was an operation incidental to the assembly process and therefore the beams were not dutiable.[66]

For Section 9802.00.80 to apply the components must be assembled abroad. It has been held that a needling operation causing fibers to be entwined with exported fabric in order to create papermaker's felts constituted an assembly abroad for these purposes.[67] Likewise the adhesion of Canadian chemicals to sheets of the United States polyester involved an assembly.[68] Another requirement of Section 9802.00.80 is that the components not lose their physical identity by change in form, shape or otherwise. Fabric components used to make papermaker's felts which were needled abroad and thus perforated with holes and changed in width did not lose their physical identity and therefore continued to qualify for duty free re-entry.[69] The absence of a loss of physical identity was apparently included as a requirement of Section 9802.00.80 in order to exclude U.S. components that are chemical products, food ingredients, liquids, gases, powders and the like. These products would presumably lose their physical identity when "assembled" abroad.[70]

---

[66]   Miles v. United States, 567 F.2d 979 (C.C.P.A. 1978).

[67]   E. Dillingham, Inc. v. United States, 470 F.2d 629 (C.C.P.A. 1972).

[68]   C.J. Tower & Sons of Buffalo, Inc. v. United States, 304 F. Supp. 1187 (Cust. Ct. 1969).

[69]   E. Dillingham, Inc. v. United States, 470 F.2d 629 (C.C.P.A. 1972).

[70]   See United States v. Baylis Bros. Co., 451 F.2d 643 (C.C.P.A. 1971).

Chapter 11

CUSTOMS CLASSIFICATION, VALUATION AND ORIGIN

Table of Sections

---

§ 11.1   Purpose of Classification, Valuation and Origin

To calculate import duties, you must first determine the classification, country of origin and the customs valuation of goods. In other words, what is it, where is it from, and what is its customs value? Customs officials classify, value and identify the origin of imported merchandise. In some cases, the importer (and the

455

exporter) may disagree with those conclusions reached by the official regarding the classification of the merchandise, its country of origin, and its valuation. This chapter concentrates on the customs process, those who play a role in the process, and some of the difficulties that may arise.

All foreign goods entering the United States must be identified in a process called classification. Classification takes two forms determining (1) the nature of the product, and (2) the product's country of origin. The first, looks to the nature of a product, such as whether an imported doll wig made from human hair should be classified as a wig of human hair, part of a doll, or as a toy. The second, looks at what country or countries a product was made. For example, if the doll wig was made in Argentina from human hair from Cuba, is the doll wig a product of Argentina or Cuba? This form of classification by country may involve formal rules of origin.

Knowing the nature of the product allows Customs to determine the proper tariff that applies, because tariffs differ from nation to nation. In other words, knowing the country of origin informs Customs which tariff column to use. For example, different tariffs apply to countries granted most favored nation (MFN) status, countries denied such status, or countries with special or duty free tariff levels such as Canada and Mexico under the North American Free Trade Agreement (NAFTA), Caribbean Basin beneficiaries under the Caribbean Basin Economic Recovery Act, or other such agreements. Additionally, identification of the country of origin informs Customs of products that cannot be imported for reasons such as an embargo by the United States, like Cuba.

But even when the product and its source of origin have been identified, Customs must know the value of the product before the tariff can be determined. Assigning a value to an import is called valuation. Customs officials must be able to determine a value in order to calculate the appropriate import tariff, usually calculated as a percentage of the value. The task is easier if the product is entitled to duty free entry. In such case the valuation is not needed for purposes of collecting a tariff. But valuation remains useful for gathering information regarding the value of various classes of imports for statistical purposes.

§ 11.2 The Actors Who Classify and Value___
The Customs Service

The United States Customs Service, as part of the Department of the Treasury, administers the entry of goods into the Customs Territory of the United States, which includes the fifty states, the

District of Columbia, and Puerto Rico.[1] This process allows Customs officials to detain and examine goods to determine compliance with all laws and regulations. Title 19 of the Code of Federal Regulations sets out extensive regulations governing such entry.[2]

An importable item must "pass customs". Usually, the passage through customs and physical entry into a country occur simultaneously. When goods arrive at the United States border, the consignee (or an agent, such as a customs broker) files both "entry" and "entry summary" forms which are used to determine the classification, valuation, origin and conformity to product standards of the imported goods. At the same time, a deposit of the amount of estimated customs duties is made with customs officials. A procedure for immediate release of imported goods is available, as is the use of consolidated periodic statements for all entries made during a billing period.

Because the entry process requires the importer to classify and value goods, a Customs Service official must determine the correctness of the documentation presented by the importer. If the Customs official rejects the importer's documentation, the decision may be appealed to the District Director (Regional Commissioner if for the port of New York), and to the Commissioner of Customs.[3]

Customs' decisions may be reviewed by the judiciary.[4] Specifically, the United States Court of International Trade (CIT)[5] has exclusive jurisdiction.[6] Appeals from the CIT may be made to the Court of Appeals for the Federal Circuit (CAFC).[7] From these specialized courts, appeals are ultimately made to the United States Supreme Court. In *United States v. Mead Corp.,* the U.S. Supreme Court held Customs Service classification rulings are not entitled to full administrative deference, but rather, such rulings are entitled to limited deference depending on their "thoroughness, logic and

---

[1]   19 U.S.C. § 1500, granting Customs authority to appraise, classify and liquidate merchandise entering the United States.

[2]   Title 19 of the C.F.R. is divided into three chapters. Chapter I includes parts 1–199 entitled United States Customs Service, Department of the Treasury. Chapter II and Chapter III include parts 200 to the end and are entitled United States International Trade Commission, and International Trade Administration, Department of Commerce, respectively.

[3]   19 C.F.R. §§ 173–174. There is a process for omitting the review by the district director in certain instances, by application for "further review." *See* 19 C.F.R. § 174.23–174.27.

[4]   *See* Dell Products LP v. United States, 642 F.3d 1055 (Fed. Cir. 2011) (affirming an appeal from importer regarding Customs and Border Protection decision under Harmonized Tariff Schedule of the United States);

[5]   19 C.F.R. § 176.

[6]   The CIT is the successor to the Customs Court.

[7]   The CAFC is the successor to the Court of Customs and Patent Appeals.

expertness, fit with prior interpretations, and any other sources of weight."[8]

As an additional precaution, on February 28, 2012, President Barack Obama, by way of an executive order, created the Interagency Trade Enforcement Center within the Office of the United States Trade Representative.[9] The primary purpose of the Center focuses on strengthening and coordinating the enforcement of U.S. trade rights under international law. The Order ensures compliance with domestic trade laws and international trade agreements through coordination between government agencies that have "trade related responsibilities."

On the international level, other actors involved in classification and valuation play an important role, including:

Secretariat of the World Customs Organization Council (WCO). This Brussels-based organization formed under the Convention on the Commodity Description and Coding System (the Convention) as an administrative entity. Since 1970, the WCO (formerly the CCC) has sought to develop an internationally accepted "Harmonized Commodity Coding and Description System." This system, initially called the Customs Cooperation Council Nomenclature (CCCN) gave nations a domestic law for classifying goods for all purposes, including the application of tariffs and gathering statistics. It was formerly known as the Brussels Tariff Nomenclature (BTN). The CCCN evolved into the Harmonized Tariff Schedule (HTS), which is the system in currently used by the United States.

The World Customs Organization(WCO) is composed of four committees. These committees have worked closely with the HTS, however, only one remains active today, the Harmonized System Committee.

§ 11.3 The Sources of Law for Classification, Valuation and Origin

The process of classification of the item and its country of origin and valuation requires us to turn to separate rules. Classification of products or materials requires use of the Harmonized Tariff Schedule, adopted by the enactment of the Omnibus Trade and Competitiveness Act of 1988. Classification of the country of origin tends to focus on theory developed in cases, whereas the process of valuation utilizes provisions in the Tariff Act of 1930, which generally follow the GATT Customs Valuation Code.

---

8   533 U.S. 218 (2001).
9   Exec. Order No. 13601, 77 Fed. Reg. 12981 (March 5, 2012).

The statutory development of classification of products and valuation follows.

Classification. Although most nations used the internationally accepted Brussels Tariff Nomenclature (BTN), the United States refused to participate in the system. Instead, the United States used its own system of classification, found within the Tariff Schedule of the United States (TSUS). These two systems created very different classifications for United States exports destined to a nation using the BTN, and those classifications of products entering the United States from other nations. What might be very narrowly defined in one system, might be very broadly defined in another. It made achieving fairness in lower tariffs for certain products quite difficult. What was called a widget in the foreign nation, might be a gadget in the United States.

As a result of using a separate system, the United States became increasingly isolated, and it became apparent that the United States TSUS would have to give way to the BTN. In 1982, after much urging from other major trading partners, the United States began converting to the HTS, the effective successor to the BTN. The HTS is administered by the World Customs Organization (WCO) in Brussels. This conversion was completed by adoption of the HTS for all imports in the Omnibus Trade and Competitiveness Act of 1988, effective January 1, 1989.[10] Most United States exports enter other nations under the HTS, and now the same is true for products of those other nations entering the United States.

The HTS "nomenclature" has twenty sections, the majority of which group articles from similar branches of industry or commerce. For example, Section I includes live animals and animal products, Section II includes vegetable products, Section III includes animal or vegetable fats, Section IV includes prepared foodstuffs, and Section V mineral products. The twenty sections are subdivided into 99 chapters, which in total list approximately 5,000 article descriptions in the heading and sub-heading format. These provisions apply to all goods entering the customs territory of the United States. Most problems arise when it is possible to classify imported goods under more than one heading.

Valuation. For many years the United States used the American Selling Price (ASP) system to determine the value of an imported good. This system valued an imported good at the level of

---

10   P.L. 100–418, title I, §§ 1202–1217, Aug. 23, 1988, 102 Stat. 1107. The HTS is not published in the U.S. Code. The United States International Trade Commission maintains the current version, which is available from the Superintendent of Documents, U.S. Government Printing Office, Washington, D.C., 20402.

the usual wholesale price that the same product was offered for sale, if manufactured and sold in the United States. Thus, the valuation had no relation to the cost of production in the foreign nation, which caused the system to be much criticized abroad.[11] Many other nations, especially in Europe, used a system based on the 1950 convention that established the Brussels Definition of Value. To many, the Brussels Definition was too general, and was not adopted by either the United States or Canada.

Harmonization of customs valuation became one of the most important topics at the 1979 GATT Tokyo Round, which produced the GATT Customs Valuation Code.[12] The United States abandoned the ASP when it adopted the GATT Customs Valuation Code in the Trade Agreements Act of 1979.[13] The GATT's approach to valuation differs significantly from the ASP because it values goods based on "positive" rather than "normative" economic principles. In other words, the Code values goods based on the transaction price (price paid or payable) and not what the value of the good should be. If the transaction price cannot be determined, several fallback methods in a descending order of applicability may be used.

Because the United States replaced the TSUS with the HTS for the classification of imports, and the ASP with the GATT Customs Valuation Code for valuation of imports, its classification and valuation systems obtained greater harmony with its major trading partners.

The Uruguay Round of negotiations ushered in the next stage of development of customs valuation. The World Trade Organization replaced the GATT, and incorporated customs valuation provisions rather than having them exist as a separate external code. The three principal amendments to the Customs Valuation Code are discussed below. The provisions, which allow pre-shipment inspection are of considerable importance to customs procedures.[14] These provisions attempt to balance the interests of some nations in contracting with outside companies to determine whether imports were fairly valued in the invoice, with the interest of exporting nations to reduce or remove impediments to trade, not to increase them.

---

[11]   Such criticism was quite expected since United States domestic producers could indirectly control the valuation applied to foreign competitors' imports

[12]   Its importance is reflected by its adoption by the European Union, Canada and the United States, plus such major trading nations as Australia, Japan, Spain (prior to joining the EU) and Sweden, and even important developing nations such as Argentina, Brazil, and India.

[13]   19 U.S.C. § 1401a.

[14]   *See* Creskoff, *Pre-Shipment Inspection Programs: The Myth of Inconsistency with GATT Customs Valuation Provisions*, 35 FED. BAR NEWS & J. 83 (1988).

§ 11.4   Classification__Sample Provisions of the Harmonized Tariff System

In any classification dispute, two issues must be resolved: (1) under what category or categories is it proper to classify the goods; and, (2) if there are several permissible classifications, which one takes priority over the others? Although the HTSUS updates every five years to account for new products, obsolete products, and provide more thorough classifications, multiple classifications can still result.[15]

As to the first question, no provisions in the HTSUS "General Rules of Interpretation" (GRI) purport to limit the categorization of a product to a single categorization. In other words, the General Rule of Interpretation 2 (GRI 2) is inclusive, not exclusory, and the GRI 3 assumes that multiple categorizations will occur.

To solve the issue of multiple classifications, the GRIs provide priorities among competing categories, and the GRI 3(c) provides a "last resort" provision for cases where all else fails. However, even within the GRI, interesting ambiguities exist. For example, even though an international treaty produced the HTS and attempts to avoid the now-repealed TSUS system, a U.S. court may consult prior U.S. cases under the TSUS to interpret GRI 3(a)'s preference for "the most specific description."[16]

In addition to the GRI, the U.S. has allowed "[a]dditional U.S. Rules of Interpretation" and "the General Notes" in the HTS. These allow any determined attorney to create additional interpretations, and have particular importance because it is unclear whether the General Notes prevail over the GRIs and the Additional U.S. Rules, or vice versa. The best example of these possible conflicts arises when one tries to determine the priority between competing classifications. Should one first attempt to use the provisions of GRI 3, including the "last resort" provision in GRI 3(c)? Or, should one first attempt to apply the General Notes, especially Note 3(f)? And, what is the role of the Additional U.S. Notes to the Chapter Headnotes?

---

[15]   For example, in 2012 Chapter 3, covering "Fish and crustaceans, mollusks, and other aquatic invertebrates," gained a new heading for aquatic invertebrates (i.e. sea urchin and jellyfish), which had previously been classified only under "Other" or "Not Elsewhere Included." *See* Harmonized Tariff Schedule of the U.S., Annotated for Statistical Reporting Purposes (USITC Publ. 4299).

[16]   *See* Mitsui Petrochemicals v. United States, 21 C.I.T. 882, 887 (1997) (citing United States v. Siemens America, Inc., 653 F.2d 471 (C.C.P.A. 1981) (applying the "relative specificity" test under the Tariff Schedules of the United States)).

Below is a small portion of the extensive classification schedule of the United States.[17] The provision illustrates two features of the HTS. First, the notes preceding the chart provide comments on what the chapter does or does not cover. And second, the illustration shows the schedule of tariffs in the various columns.

CHAPTER 67

PREPARED FEATHERS AND DOWN AND ARTICLES MADE OF FEATHERS OR OF DOWN; ARTIFICIAL FLOWERS; ARTICLES OF HUMAN HAIR

Notes

1.   This chapter does not cover:

(a)   Straining cloth of human hair (heading 5911);

(b)   Floral motifs of lace, of embroidery or other textile fabric (section XI);

(c)   Footwear (chapter 65);

(d)   Headgear or hair-nets (chapter 65);

(e)   Toys, sports equipment, or carnival articles (chapter 95); or

(f)   Feather dusters, powder-puffs or hair sieves (chapter 96).

---

[17]   *See* Harmonized Tariff Schedule of the U.S., Annotated for Statistical Reporting Purposes (USITC Publ. 4299).

Heading Subheading	Stat. Suf. & cd		Article Description	Units of Quantity	Rates of Duty		
					General	Special	
6703.00			Human hair, dressed, thinned, bleached or otherwise worked; wool or other animal hair or other textile materials, prepared for use in making wigs or the like:				
6703.00.30	00	1	Human hair	kg	Free		20%
6703.00.60	00	4	Other...........................	kg	Free		35%
6704			Wigs, false beards, eyebrows and eyelashes, switches and the like, of human or animal hair or of textile materials; articles of human hair not elsewhere specified or included:				
			Of synthetic textile materials:				
6704.11.00	00	3	Complete wigs	No..........	Free		35%
6704.19.00	00	5	Other	X............	Free		35%
6704.20.00	00	2	Of human hair	X............	Free		35%
6704.90.00	00	7	Of other materials.........	X............	Free		35%

§ 11.5   Classification___The Meaning of the Headings in the HTS

The heading in the above excerpt is used under the General Rules of Interpretation to determine classification of products. Customs must apply the rule of relative specificity in the classification process, which requires that goods be classified under the provision that most specifically describes it. Here, false eyelashes made of human hair, for human adult use appear to fall under Chapter 67 because it is an article of human hair. However, it seems that this commodity may fit under more than one heading. This potential problem will be discussed in the next section.

§ 11.6   Classification___The Meaning of the Notes in the HTS

The notes at the beginning of chapters in the HTS provide a useful tool in classification. They are to be used in addition to the terms of the headings, under the General Rules of Interpretation. For example, Note 1 in Chapter 67 states footwear cannot be classified under Chapter 67, but is the subject of Chapter 64. These "chapter notes" should not be confused with the Explanatory Notes to the Harmonized System,[18] nor the General Notes to the HTS.[19]

§ 11.7 Classification___The Meaning of the Columns in the HTS

After looking through the applicable chapter notes, the next step is to look at the columns. The United States HTS utilizes a combined number system, including the six digits used internationally, and adding further digits for more subdivisions and statistical use. As seen in the above excerpt the first column, titled "Heading/Subheading", has eight digits. The first six are the heart of the IITS, and must be adopted by all contracting nations. The first two (67 in the excerpt) repeat the chapter. The second two designate the heading (03 for Human hair, etc., 04 for Wigs, etc., in the excerpt). The next two are subheadings. The additional two numbers provide further sub-subheadings (.30 for Human hair and .60 for Other in the excerpt),[20] and the columns titled "Stat. Suf. & cd" help maintain records for statistical purposes.

The three-column section entitled "Rates of Duty" discloses the rate of duty for the particular article. The Column 1 rates apply to nations that receive most favored nation (MFN) status. MFN tariffs are set by GATT/WTO negotiations and are now referred to officially as "normal" tariffs. The "General" column applies to most MFN nations. The "Special" column applies to nations that have tariff preferences, making these nations even more favored than the most favored. The tariffs may be commodities, which enter duty free or with less than the general MFN rate. The capital letters denote different special preferential tariff programs. For example, A means nations qualifying under the Generalized System of Preferences (GSP),[21] B means commodities under the Automotive Products Trade Act, C means products under the Agreement on Trade in Civil Aircraft, CA means commodities under the Canada-United States Free Trade Agreement, E means commodities under the Caribbean Basin Economic Recovery Act,[22] IL means commodities

---

[18] The Explanatory Notes to the Harmonized System are part of the documents of the Customs Cooperation Council in Brussels which may have some influence on the classification. They are discussed in § 10.8, *infra*.

[19] These General Notes identify the customs territory of the United States, list nations to which Column 2 rates of duty apply, define symbols for special treatment such as the Caribbean Basin nations, give definitions, abbreviations, items exempted from coverage and rules on commingled goods. *See* ITC Pub. 2333 (1991).

[20] The use of an additional four digits is permitted by the Convention and other nations have adopted their own form of using these additional digits. Such use will lead to some lessening of the uniformity of the system.

[21] An A* appears if a country is specifically ineligible.

[22] The symbol E* appears if a country is ineligible.

under the United States-Israel Free Trade Area, and NA means commodities under the North American Free Trade Agreement.

Column 2 applies to all nations, which are not entitled to Column 1 rates of duty. These countries are listed in General Note 3(b). They include principally nations under communist or socialist rule. Essentially these counties are "least" favored nations, although that term perhaps ought to be saved for those nations that are excluded from trading with the United States altogether.

While it might seem the HTS offers a fairly easy resolution to classification, it does only when a commodity clearly fits into one chapter, one heading, and if present one sub-heading. Fortunately, that is often the case, but many commodities are not clearly allocated within the system, and multiple possibilities for their classification may exist. This is the subject of much of the remainder of this chapter.

§ 11.8   Classification__Applying the General Rules of Interpretation

While the Customs Service classifies goods, the importer (also the foreign exporter) has an obvious interest in the classification, because when the goods are classified at a high rate of duty applicable, the transaction may not go forward. Thus, the United States importer may consider the classification themselves. If the importer's conclusion is not the same as the Customs Service (meaning undoubtedly that the latter will be a classification at a higher rate of duty), the importer may (1) decide not to import the goods, (2) pay the higher duty, or (3) challenge the Customs' determination.

The process of determination, whether conducted by Customs or the importer, must use the rules of interpretation of the United States (*e.g.* the General Rules of Interpretation and the Additional U.S. Rules of Interpretation). A walk through those rules illustrates how difficult the classification process can be.

Headings and Relevant Section or Chapter Notes (Rule 1). The legal classification of a good is determined according to (1) the terms of the *headings*; (2) any relative *section*; and (3) *chapter notes*.[23] This means the section, chapter and sub-headings are subordinated to the headings in importance. If the headings and notes do not otherwise require, one turns to the additional provisions of the General Rules,[24] and also to the Additional U.S. Rules of

---

[23]   General Rules of Interpretation 1.

[24]   *Id.*

Interpretation.[25] The General Rules specifically note that the "table of contents, alphabetical index, and titles of sections, chapters and sub-chapters" are only for reference, not legal classification.[26]

Heading References to Articles (Rule 2(a)). When any reference in a heading is to an *article,* as opposed to a material or substance, the reference is to be understood to include that article in an incomplete or unfinished state as long as it "has the essential character" of the complete or finished article.[27] The reference also includes that article unassembled or disassembled.[28] This emphasis on the *material* as well as on the *function* of the good replaces emphasis on how the goods are used under the TSUS.

Heading References to a Material or Substance (Rule 2(b)). If the reference heading describes a *material* or *substance,* as opposed to an article, it should be understood to refer to mixtures or combinations of that material or substance with other materials or substances.[29] Also, any reference to goods of a given material or substance should include a reference to goods consisting wholly or partly of such material or substance. The obvious problem with this is that when the goods are only partly of a material or substance, the other party may have its own classification. This can also occur when there are mixtures or combinations. The Rules acknowledge this and require one to move on to Rule 3.

Classification under Two or More Headings—Most Specific Description (Rule 3(a)). When goods may be classified under two or more headings,[30] the most specific description is preferred over the *more general description.*[31] This rule parallels the long used "rule of relative specificity," and decisions under that rule may continue to be of some use.[32] However, if each possible heading refers only to a *part* of the material or substances in mixed or composite goods, or of the items in a set for retail sale,[33] the headings must be considered

---

[25]   The Additional U.S. Rules of Interpretation are found immediately following the General Rules in the HTS, as adopted in the United States. These additional rules often include methods of interpretation used under the prior classification system in the United States.

[26]   General Rules of Interpretation 1.

[27]   General Rules 2(a).

[28]   *Id.* Rule 2 generally follows the previous position under the TSUS.

[29]   General Rules 2(b).

[30]   This applies to Rule 2(b) discussed above and to any other situation where two or more headings seem possibly applicable.

[31]   General Rules 3(a).

[32]   That includes the doctrine that an *eo nomine* description prevails over headings having only general or functional descriptions.

[33]   In 2011, the Federal Circuit held that "goods put up in sets for retail sale" include goods that are packaged together in a certain manner at the time they enter the United States, and does not include secondary materials that the customer must

equally specific. This is so even if one heading provides a more complete or precise description of the goods.[34] If this occurs, one must move to Rule 3(b).

Classification under Two or More Headings—Essential Character (Rule 3(b)). If an item cannot be classified under the most specific description test in Rule 3(a), then it must be classified with regard the material or component that gives the items their *essential character.*[35] While no similar provision existed in the TSUS[36] and the HTS does not strictly define "essential character," it has some parallel under the TSUS definition of the term "almost wholly of." Even some United States cases hold "almost wholly of" may be used while defining "essential character." However, the determination is fact-intensive[37] and should still be made on a case-by-case basis.

Classification under Two or More Headings—Last in Numerical Order (Rule 3(c)). If classification is not possible using either the most specific description or essential character tests, the rules move from a substantive classification method to one based simply on location. More specifically, the proper classification is the one heading, which occurs last in numerical order among those which might be applicable.[38]

Goods Unclassifiable under Rules 1–3—Most Akin (Rule 4). When no headings appear directly applicable, the goods should be classified under the heading the goods are *most akin.* While this test has been used very infrequently, it is essentially a "do the best the headings allow" test, and may result in two or more headings being equally "most akin." In such case one should try to find which is "more" akin. However, if uncertainty still results, move on to Rule 5.

Specially Shaped or Fitted Cases for Goods—Classed with Their Contents (Rule 5(a)). Containers, such as camera cases, musical instrument cases, gun cases, drawing instrument cases, and necklace cases, which are "specially shaped or fitted" are classified with the goods they serve, if they enter with those goods and are suitable for long term.[39]

---

purchase separately. Dell Products LP v. United States, 642 F.3d 1055, 1060 (Fed. Cir. 2011).

[34] General Rules 3(a).

[35] General Rules 3(b).

[36] A "chief value" determination applied, no less capable of exact determination.

[37] CamelBak Prod. LLC v. United States, 649 F.3d 1361, 1369 (Fed. Cir. 2011).

[38] General Rules 3(c).

[39] General Rules 5(a).

However, the rule does not apply if the containers give the whole its essential character. For example, expensive carved tea caddies containing tea would not be classified as tea, because the container is not shaped to fit the tea (as is a musical instrument case) and the container gives the whole (tea plus caddy) the essential character.

Packing Materials and Containers—Classed with Their Contents (Rule 5(b)). Subject to the provisions of Rule 5(a), packing materials and containers that enter with goods are classified as the goods if they are the normal kind used in packaging or containers.[40] However, this is not true when the materials or containers are suitable for repetitive use.

Rules 5(a) and (b) are specific and apply only in limited situations. In fact, in most cases when a clear classification cannot be determined after using Rule 4, it will be necessary to go on to the final General Rule 6 for additional guidance.

Subheadings and Subheading Notes (Rule 6). The subheadings, found in the first "Heading/Subheading" column of each chapter in the tariff schedules define goods more specifically than the heading. When subheadings or subheading notes are used, and two or more subheadings on the same level seem applicable, the process follows the outline in the rules discussed above.[41]

§ 11.9 Classification___The Additional U.S. Rules of Interpretation

The six General Rules of Interpretation make up the classification system provided by the HTS. However, when the United States adopted this system, it added its own rules, called the "Additional U.S. Rules of Interpretation." In addition to applying the General Rules, these rules must also be examined to determine whether a use is (1) consistent with the General Rules; (2) helpful where the General Rules do not lead to a satisfactory conclusion; or (3) conflict with the conclusion reached under the General Rules.

Classification Controlled by Use Other Than Actual Use (U.S. Rule 1(a)). If a classification is controlled by use other than actual use, and there is no special language or context mandating otherwise, it must be the use in the United States. More specifically, the use in the United States at, or immediately prior to, the time of importation. Furthermore, the controlling use must be the *principal* use (which exceeds any other single use).[42] This

---

40   General Rule 5(b).
41   General Rules 6.
42   U.S. Rules 1(a).

requirement steps away from the Rule's past reference to chief use (which exceeds all other uses).

Classification Controlled by Actual Use (U.S. Rule 1(b)). The rule is similar to the above. However, to satisfy this provision, the imported goods must, (1) be the use intended at the time of importation, (2) the goods are so used, and (3) proof thereof is furnished within three years after the date the goods are entered.[43]

Parts and Accessories—General vs. Specific (U.S. Rule 1(c)). Where a provision specifically describes a part or accessory, it must be used over a general "parts and accessories" provision.[44] Thus, the import of bicycle chains would be classified as bicycle chains if described specifically, and not under a "catch-all" "other parts and accessories" category. This rule provides consistency with the General Rules' preference for specificity, even though the General Rules do not specifically contain a rule for parts.[45]

Textile Materials (U.S. Rule 1(d)). The principles of section XI, which govern mixtures of two or more *textile* materials, apply to any goods in any provision where textile material are named.[46] Textiles have their own mystique, and are subject to special trading rules throughout the world. These provisions assure the special rules of classification for textile materials are applied throughout the tariff schedules wherever textile material is mentioned.

Conflicts Between General Rules and Additional U.S. Rules. When a conflict arises between the application of the General Rules and the Additional U.S. Rules, no guidance exists within the rules to handle that situation. However, it seems likely that the Additional U.S. Rules would supplant as well as supplement the General Rules. But, the likelihood for such conflict is slim because the Additional U.S. Rules were not intended to set forth views where the United States differs with the HTS. Instead, the Rules provide a necessary supplement.

Fair and accurate application of the above rules is not an easy task, and certainly does not mean that all reasonable minds (including those found in the Customs Service) will reach the same conclusion. However, another important source should be considered while classifying products, the "United States Customs Service, Guidance for Interpretation of Harmonized System."

---

[43]   U.S. Rules 1(b).

[44]   U.S. Rules 1(c).

[45]   However, individual chapter and section notes sometimes include parts rules.

[46]   U.S. Rules 1(d).

§ 11.10 Classification___United States Customs Service, Guidance for Interpretation of Harmonized System

When the HTS was adopted in 1989, some questions existed as to how Customs would classify some of the materials developed over the years. Of specific concern was the use of the Explanatory Notes to the Harmonized System, and reports of the Nomenclature Committee, which administered the Customs Cooperation Council (CCC) Nomenclature. Additionally, how letters from the Secretariat of the CCC would be used was unclear, and rulings and regulations from the customs administrations of other nations. The United States Customs Service soon issued the *Guidance for Interpretation of Harmonized System*.[47] The guide makes several points quite clear.

United States Customs Service Does Not Seek Uniformity of Interpretation with Other Nations. While the Harmonized System Committee (HSC) under Article 7 of the Convention functions to provide uniformity, the United States Customs Service does not. To illustrate, the United States does not seek to alter "sections, chapters, headings or subheadings" of the HTS, and will consider background documents to avoid such alterations. However, the Customs Service will not purposely make its interpretations of the HTS consistent with the interpretations of other HTS member nations. If serious inconsistencies in interpretation result, the HTS will likely be modified to minimize the inconsistency, such as by further refining the classification.

Use of Explanatory Notes to the Harmonized System. These notes are the official interpretation of the Harmonized System created by the World Customs Organization. According to the Custom Service, Customs should use the notes as a useful tool, providing guidance, but should not treat them as dispositive.[48] Further, because the Explanatory Notes are amended from time to time and reflect changes in interpretation, they should be consulted periodically as changes are adopted. The only other document given this status by Congress are the "similar publications of the Council," which essentially refers to the Compendium of Classification Opinions because it is the only similar publication.

Use of the Compendium of Classification Opinions. The Harmonized System Committee (HSC) writes these opinions on the classification of different products. They are the result of requests

---

47   54 Fed. Reg. 35127 (1989).
48   *See* Conf. Rep. No. 100–576, 100th Cong., 2d Sess. 549 (1988).

presented to the HSC, and have the same weight as Explanatory Notes. Additionally, the Opinions are the official interpretation of the HSC on the particular issue decided.

Harmonized System Committee Reports. In addition to opinions, the HSC periodically issues reports on various subjects. While they do not have the same weight as the Explanatory Notes or Compendium of Classification Opinions, they may be helpful in determining the intention of the HSC. However, the reports of committees within the HSC, such as the Nomenclature Committee, carry virtually no weight, but may nevertheless be of some assistance in interpretation. Of even less use are the "working documents" of the Nomenclature and Classification Directorate of the WCO. They are the basis of discussions in HSC sessions, but they may not necessarily reflect the intent of the HSC.

Rulings of Other Countries. Because other nations that have adopted the HTS use the same General Rules of Interpretation, Section and Chapter Notes, and first six digits in the classification tables, their customs administration decisions are sometimes presented to the United States Customs Service. In general, U.S. Customs does not follow other nations' rulings because their decisions "may have been subject to political realities or domestic regulations which are different from our own." The meaning of this has not been further defined, but illustrates that there may be political pressure to classify goods so as to more readily admit them to, or more readily exclude them from, the United States. In any event, these foreign rulings are considered "merely instructive of how others" classify imports.

Position Papers. Before a session of the HSC, U.S. Customs, the International Trade Commission, and the Bureau of Census prepare position papers for the session. These papers do not reflect Customs' position in the interpretation of the HTS and are considered to have no value, although they are occasionally circulated and obtained by importers or their counsel.

These notes, opinions, reports, rulings and papers all add to the process of interpretation, a layer which did not exist before the adoption of the HTS by the United States. Awareness of their use by the Customs Service may be helpful to United States counsel, but should not expect to be given weight beyond that announced by the Customs Service and as described above.

§ 11.11   Classification__Decisions of United States Courts

While it may seem strange to suggest that decisions of United States courts may not be applicable in interpreting the HTS, that may be correct for decisions interpreting the prior TSUS.[49] Interpretations of the United States HTS must follow the procedure outlined above. Certainly decisions rendered subsequent to the adoption of the HTS in 1988, which interpret the HTS, will be useful. But in many cases decisions have little usefulness because they apply to a narrow set of issues affecting specific goods where two or more classification possibilities exist. Although the HTS has a different process, the approach used in the past may find use in the future. Thus, some earlier decisions may be useful to understand the analytical process used by the courts.[50]

For example, prior United States decisions applying the rule of relative specificity may be used in interpreting General Rule of Interpretation Rule 3(a), which uses a kind of "rule of relative specificity" under the wording "most specific description."[51]

§ 11.12   Rules of Origin__Substantial Transformation, Proposed Uniform Approach

The second form of classification determines the country of origin of the items to be imported. Unlike, the determination of the proper classification discussed above, the country of origin determination discloses whether Column 1 or Column 2 rates of duty apply. If Column 1 rates of duty apply, the goods may qualify for preferential or duty free treatment, if from a country of origin that qualifies under "Special" in Column 1.[52]

Additionally, knowing the country of origin uncovers more general prohibitions of trade with that country, because the United States nearly always has several nations with which it does not

---

[49]   *See* JVC Company of America v. United States, 234 F.3d 1348 (Fed. Cir. 2000).

[50]   For example, the decision in Mattel, Inc. v. United States, 287 F.Supp. 999 (Cust. Ct. 1968), might be used when the issue involves priority of one classification over another.

[51]   *See, e.g.*, Great Western Sugar Co. v. United States, 452 F.2d 1394 (C.C.P.A. 1972).

[52]   The Court of International Trade requires importers seeking preferential tariff treatment to verify the country of origin of their goods. "Reasonable care" must be exercised, not just simple reliance on the exporter's assertions of origin. Failures in this regard can result in collection of lost duties and penalties. United States v. Golden Ship Trading Co., 2001 WL 65751 (C.I.T. 2001) (T-shirts imported from Dominican Republic under Caribbean Basin Act were from China).

trade by legislative or presidential declaration.[53] The United States may also put limits on products entering from a specific foreign nation. This limitation may be the result of a formal quota,[54] or an informal voluntary restraint agreement (VRA). VRAs have in the past covered a wide range of products (*e.g.*, steel, vehicles, electronics), and have been a device adopted by the United States (and other areas such as the European Union) as executive policy in order to discourage legislative action to establish mandatory and involuntary quotas to reduce trade imbalances.[55] VRAs are now generally prohibited under the WTO Safeguards Agreement (1995).

Counsel representing an importer must know the framework for determining the country of origin of articles.[56] Eligibility of entry often depends on country of origin determination.[57] Country of origin law does not have as consolidated a framework as for classification of the goods discussed above. Although the classification is dealt with exclusively in the HTS, working within that system is not a simple matter. Determination of the country of origin requires using rules that may apply in a spectrum of different areas. While there are several references to various aspects of the rule of origin in different sources of law, the *substantial transformation* test (treated below) in its various costumes, has traditionally been *the* test.

In 2008, the Bureau of Customs and Border Protection proposed shifting to a single uniform approach to determine the origin of imported goods.[58] Although Customs and Border Protection withdrew the proposal, if adopted, it would have abandoned the historic test for the "substantial transformation" of foreign goods. The proposal elicited so many responses that the time for public comment on the proposal was extended twice. Most of the responses opposed the proposal because the rule could have substantially impacted the cost of entry into the United States, place undue burdens on those in the trading community, and cause the importation process to become more complex.[59] Eventually, in 2010

---

[53] These prohibitions may extend to both exports and imports, but may have certain exceptions, such as medical supplies.

[54] Quotas are regulated by the Customs Service. *See* 19 C.F.R. Part 132.

[55] *See, e.g.*, Note, *Voluntary Restraint Agreements: Effects and Implications of the Steel and Auto Cases*, 11 N.C. J. INT'L L. & COM. REG. 101 (1986).

[56] Counsel may wish to obtain a ruling from Customs in advance of importation. *See* 19 C.F.R. §§ 177.1–177.11.

[57] The United States must know whether the country of origin is one entitled to most favored nation treatment.

[58] *Uniform Rules of Origin for Imported Merchandise, Notice of Proposed Rulemaking*, 73 Fed. Reg. 43,385 (2008).

[59] Vivian C. Jones and Michael F. Martin, INTERNATIONAL TRADE: RULES OF ORIGIN, Cong. Res. Serv., RL 34524 at 2 (January 5, 2012).

the Bureau of Customs and Border Protection abandoned the proposal.

Under the proposed WTO Agreement on Rules of Origin, there will be an effort to harmonize the rules of origin on a world-wide basis. A committee of experts is charged with creating rules which are "objective, understandable, and predictable." They are likely to differ from the core U.S. rule. Special rules of origin apply to the various U.S. duty free entry programs, most notably NAFTA which relies principally on changes in tariff classifications and regional value content to determine which goods may freely be traded. See Chapter 17. It is expected that any WTO agreement on rules of origin will adopt similar approaches.

§ 11.13   Rules of Origin___Sources of Law

Tariff Act of 1930. Section 304 of the Tariff Act requires every article of foreign origin, or its container imported into the United States to be marked in a conspicuous place with the English name of the country of origin.[60]

Trade Agreements Act of 1979. Section 308 of the Act provides various definitions, including the rule of origin for eligible products.[61] The definition focuses on the concept of substantial transformation,[62] leaving the courts to interpret the meaning of substantial transformation.

Code of Federal Regulations, Country of Origin Marking. Part 134 of 19 C.F.R. provides rules governing the country of origin *marking*. These regulations implement or reflect the provisions noted above in both the Tariff Act of 1930 and the HTS. The regulations define articles subject to the marking, with special rules for articles repacked or manipulated, and ones usually combined with another article.[63] Rules also specify how containers or holders

---

[60]   19 U.S.C. § 1304. For example the product has to say "Made in Spain" rather than "Made in España." The HTS governs treatment of containers and holders for imported merchandise. *See* 19 C.F.R. § 1202. The purpose of the rule is essentially to inform the public. Also, the Trademark Act of 1946, 15 U.S.C. §§ 1051–1127, does not allow admission of goods of foreign origin if they have a mark or name intended to lead the United States public to believe the product was made in the United States, or any country other than its true country of origin.

[61]   19 U.S.C. § 2518.

[62]   "An article is a product of a country or instrumentality only if (i) it is wholly the growth, product, or manufacture of that country or instrumentality, or (ii) in the case of an article which consists in whole or in part of materials from another country or instrumentality, it has been substantially transformed into a new and different article of commerce with a name, character, or use distinct from that of the article or articles from which it was so transformed." 19 U.S.C. § 2518(4)(B).

[63]   19 C.F.R. §§ 134.13–134.14.

must be marked,[64] exceptions to the marking requirements,[65] method and location of marking,[66] and the consequences of finding articles not legally marked.[67] Essentially, the consequences for not properly marking a good are (1) properly mark the goods; (2) return the goods to the foreign nation; or (3) destroy the goods.[68]

Generally, a single country of origin must be determined for labeling purposes, even though the product may have been made in several countries. The country of origin, as determined by Customs, may not disclose other nations that may have participated in the process. While this may be important to the United States consumer, who may not wish to purchase products from a country substantially benefiting from the sale, but it is not important to the determination of the official country of origin. It may also be important to the United States government because it may not trade with the country that has substantially benefited from the importation, but was not the official country of origin.

Special Rules—The North American Free Trade Agreement (NAFTA). In drafting NAFTA, as with drafting the earlier Canada-United States Free Trade Agreement, there was considerable concern that products entering the United States, as products of Canada or Mexico, actually had little fabrication or processing in those countries. To prevent this, special NAFTA rules of origin (discussed in Chapter 17) were adopted, which include articles governing customs procedures for the certification of origin.

The procedures create a North American "Certificate of Origin" and require extensive verification provisions. The exporter provides the Certificate of Origin when the importer tries to claim the duty free tariff treatment offered by NAFTA.[69] However, a Certificate of Origin is not required for goods valuing $1,000 or less, or where a member state has waived their use.[70] A member state may conduct verification through written questionnaires, visits to the premises exporter/producer, or other procedures the member states agree.[71] Verification is of considerable concern to the United States because it does not want Mexico to be used as a base for transshipping products from outside the NAFTA area, especially from Asia. The Court of International Trade requires importers seeking

---

[64]   19 C.F.R. §§ 134.21–134.26.

[65]   19 C.F.R. §§ 134.31–134.36.

[66]   19 C.F.R. §§ 134.41–134.47.

[67]   19 C.F.R. §§ 134.41–134.55.

[68]   19 C.F.R. § 134.51(a).

[69]   NAFTA Art. 501.

[70]   NAFTA Art. 503.

[71]   NAFTA Art. 506.

preferential tariff treatment to verify the country of origin of their goods. "Reasonable care" must be exercised, which requires more than simple reliance on the exporter's assertions of origin. Failure to do so can result in collection of lost duties and penalties.[72]

Decisions of United States Courts. There are several areas where Customs is required to determine the country of origin. However, the determinations sometimes lead to problems. For example, products from countries with which the United States does not trade are sometimes transshipped through a country which with the United States does trade. For example, products from countries subject to high rates of duty in Column 2 could be transshipped through countries subject to lower rates of duty in Column 1. Products with most favored nation status, Column 1 rates of duty, could be transshipped through a country with special access, such as a Caribbean nation. Exporters from a nation that has agreed to a voluntary restraint agreement could try to exceed the agreed upon numbers by having the products transshipped through a nation without such a quota. As the United States enters into free trade agreements such as NAFTA, other nations could attempt to take advantage of that relationship by having goods transshipped through Canada or Mexico into the United States.

Fortunately, some case law has evolved, addressing the country of origin issue. Those cases, which involve one specific area, may be helpful in addressing another. For example, a case that has identified the country of origin, may be useful in determining whether the agreed amount under a voluntary restraint agreement has been exceeded.[73] Or such a case may be helpful where products are allegedly violating the rules of the generalized system of preferences. Thus, when dealing with a country of origin issue, cases outside the scope of the form of entry (i.e., GSP, VRA, NAFTA, etc.) must be consulted. However, overall the cases utilize the same substantial transformation test, whether the matter involves quota restrictions or trade preferences.[74]

---

[72]   United States v. Golden Ship Trading Co., 2001 WL 65751 (C.I.T. 2001) (T-shirts imported from Dominican Republic under Caribbean Basin Act were from China).

[73]   *See, e.g.*, Superior Wire, A Div. of Superior Products Co. v. United States, 669 F.Supp. 472 (C.I.T. 1987), *aff'd,* 867 F.2d 1409 (Fed. Cir. 1989).

[74]   *See* Ferrostaal Metals Corp. v. United States, 664 F.Supp. 535, 538 (C.I.T. 1987) (holding that case law does not suggest that the court should depart from "policy-neutral rules governing substantial transformation in order to achieve wider import restrictions in particular cases").

§ 11.14 Rules of Origin___Applicable Legal Theories

While some consistency in the identification of the country of origin exists, the process requires more than simply reading the label, which states the country of origin. Because a nation may do little more to an item than sew on the country of origin label, the product itself must be measured. The tests tend to be product specific, and because so many product variations exist, many variations in application may result.

Substantial Transformation Test. As stated above, the principal focus in a country of origin determination examines whether the product was substantially transformed in the country claiming the country of origin status.[75] One of the principal cases defining substantial transformation in the United States, an early United States Supreme Court decision, involves drawbacks.[76] The Court held substantial transformation occurs when a product is transformed into a new and different article "having a distinctive *name, character or use.*"[77] However, while this case provides a standard, it has been applied in many different ways.[78] For example, while a name change alone would not always be sufficient, such as from "wire" to "wire rod,"[79] a court held that changing heat-treated steel to galvanized steel was sufficient. More specifically, because the annealing process involved substantial manufacturing, which ultimate strengthened the steel and made it resistant to corrosion, it caused a substantial transformation to occur.[80]

Courts tend to concentrate on changes in *character* or *use* rather than in the name of the product. Also, they often develop subtests appropriate for a particular kind of article. For example, whether a *significant value* was added, or *additional costs* were incurred. But each test leads to some subjective evaluation, which provides a sort of sense of whether the product is really from the

---

[75]   This test is in the Trade Agreements Act of 1979. *See* 19 U.S.C. § 2518(4)(B).

[76]   Anheuser-Busch Brewing Ass'n v. United States, 207 U.S. 556 (1908).

[77]   *Id.* at 562.

[78]   But it is applied by the courts. *See, e.g.*, Texas Instruments Inc. v. United States, 681 F.2d 778, 782 (C.C.P.A. 1982).

[79]   *See* Superior Wire, A Div. of Superior Products Co. v. United States, 669 F.Supp. 472 (C.I.T. 1987) (the court noted that in recent years the focus was on a change in use or character).

[80]   Ferrostaal Metals Corp. v. United States, 664 F. Supp. 535 (C.I.T. 1987) (there was a "significant altering" of the "mechanical properties and chemical composition of the steel").

state country. While the substantial transformation test has been criticized,[81] it remains the applicable law.

Value-Added Test. This test provides a more exacting process. It looks at how much value has been added as a percent of the value of the original product. There may be situations where no substantial transformation has occurred, but where significant value has been added to the original product.[82] What if a completed shirt with K-Mart logo buttons has those buttons removed and buttons are added with the logo of the most prestigious (currently) designer? If the result is the retail price may be trebled would that satisfy the value added test? There has certainly been minimal processing. Was the added value any more than the cost of the new buttons and their application? Isn't the high price really added in the United States by the consumers' willingness to pay more for apparent prestige? It seems that there must be some real value, such as labor or capital equipment, added in the country claiming to be the country of origin.

Considerations. However a court reaches a decision in a country of origin question, it is likely to have considered most of the following changes:

(1) Change in name (and change in tariff classification);

(2) Change in physical appearance;

(3) Change in material substance (at each stage of manufacture);

(4) Change in apparent use;

(5) Change in value of item in the mind of the consumer;

(6) Additional capital vested in article;

(7) Additional labor vested in article;

(8) Type of processing;

(9) Effect of processing; and

(10) Change in method of distribution.

There is no secret formula for determining which factor, if any, plays the most significant role. The end result may seem much like a test parallel to Justice Stewart's obscenity test—"I'll know it when I see it."

---

[81] Michael P. Maxwell, *Formulating Rules of Origin for Imported Merchandise: Transforming the Substantial Transformation Test*, 23 GEO. WASH J. INT'L L. & ECON. 669 (1990).

[82] One may nevertheless claim this to be a substantial transformation of value, if not of substance.

§ 11.15   Valuation__United States Law

The law applicable to classification of products is limited by the United States adoption of the HTS. The case law tends to evolve through variations of the substantial transformation test. The law applicable to valuation can be found in the United States Tariff Act of 1930, as amended. However, the United States' commitment to the GATT Customs Valuation Code, and the successor World Trade Organization must be considered.

For the most part, the United States Tariff Act of 1930 incorporates the GATT Customs Valuation Code of 1979.[83] However, because the United States adopted that GATT Code in 1979 amendments to the Tariff Act of 1930, some of the prior methods of interpretation of valuation may continue to be considered by courts.[84]

§ 11.16   Valuation__The Law of the GATT/WTO

Of the several codes adopted by the GATT in the Tokyo Round and renewed in the Uruguay WTO Round, the Agreement on the Implementation of Article VII of the General Agreement on Tariffs and Trade (GATT Customs Valuation Code) is of considerable importance to the United States.[85] While Article VII of the GATT, titled "Valuation for Customs Purposes," established a form of transaction value before, it was not until the Customs Valuation Code was adopted that the form of valuation by a descending order of tests was introduced. This form of valuation was incorporated into the United States law in 1979, and is the source of law one must turn for valuation of imports.

§ 11.17   Valuation__Appraisal of Imported Merchandise

Imports of merchandise are valued according to a series of alternative methods,[86] but not alternative methods in the sense that Customs may use any method it chooses. Nor may Customs reject information provided if based on the use of generally accepted

---

[83]   19 U.S.C. § 1401a. *See* Saul L. Sherman, *Reflections on the New Customs Valuation Code*, 12 LAW & POL'Y INT'L BUS. 119 (1980).

[84]   The same is true of other areas with pre-Code established procedures. *See* William M. Snyder, *Customs Valuation in the European Economic Community*, 11 GA. J. INT'L & COMP. L. 79 (1981).

[85]   Geneve, 1979, GATT, 26th Supp. BISD 116 (1980). *See* Saul L. Sherman & Hinrich Glashoff, CUSTOMS VALUATION: COMMENTARY ON THE GATT CUSTOMS VALUATION CODE (1988).

[86]   Merchandise is defined as of the same class or kind as other merchandise if within a group or range which is produced by a particular industry or industrial sector. 19 U.S.C. § 1401a(e)(2).

accounting procedures.[87] The methods of valuation are set forth in the order of use. Most valuations never go beyond the first, the transaction value.

§ 11.18 Valuation__Transaction Value

All merchandise imported into the United States must be appraised. First, Customs considers the transaction value of the merchandise.[88] The transaction value is often referred to as the *invoice value* because in the absence of over or under invoicing, it would be the value of the transaction. The statute describes the transaction value as the *price actually paid or payable*.[89] In other words, it is the price when sold for exportation to the United States, also known as the wholesale price.[90] This may be confusing where there are several contracts, in addition to the actual contract between the buyer-seller. This situation can occur as between a party to the sale and the party's parent entity,[91] or between a foreign seller and United States company acquiring items purchased by the foreign seller from a foreign manufacturer.[92]

Also, the transaction value may include some elements that create doubt as to application of duties. For example, quota charges clearly separated on the invoice are nevertheless includable.[93] Rebates to the price actually paid or payable made after the merchandise has entered the United States are disregarded in determining the transaction value.[94] However, dividing the assembly (service) price from the consumer (sale of goods) price for made-to measure clothing does not relieve the importer from duty on the former portion, the full cost is subject to duty.[95]

---

[87]   19 U.S.C. § 1401a(g)(3).

[88]   19 U.S.C. § 1401a(a)(1)(A).

[89]   19 U.S.C. § 1401a(b)(1). Price actually paid or payable is defined in 19 U.S.C. § 1401a(b)(4). Disbursements by the buyer for the benefit of the seller are included, as when the buyer disburses some funds to the agent's seller who assists in bringing about the sale. Moss Mfg. Co., Inc. v. United States, 714 F.Supp. 1223 (C.I.T. 1989), *affirmed* 896 F.2d 535 (Fed.Cir.1990).

[90]   As of January 1, 2011, Customs and Border Protection.

[91]   Nissho Iwai American Corp. v. United States, 786 F.Supp. 1002 (C.I.T. 1992), *aff'd in part, rev'd in part* 982 F.2d 505 (Fed. Cir. 1992) (holding the master contract between the buyer and seller controls, rather than the contract price paid by the seller's Japanese company's parent to primary manufacturer).

[92]   *See* Brosterhous, Coleman & Co. v. United States, 737 F. Supp. 1197 (C.I.T. 1990)

[93]   Generra Sportswear Co. v. United States, 905 F.2d 377 (Fed. Cir. 1990).

[94]   19 U.S.C. § 1401a(b)(4)(B). *See* Allied Int'l v. United States, 795 F. Supp. 449 (C.I.T. 1992) (importer has the burden of showing that the rebate occurred on or before date of entry).

[95]   E.C. McAfee Co. v. United States, 842 F.2d 314 (Fed. Cir. 1988).

Five other categories of associated costs must be also added to the transaction value. Some are costs, which may be part of the price paid or payable, but some are costs, which, if not subject to tariffs, could be split off from the price of the goods and paid separately, thus avoiding or evading proper duty.[96] These additional costs subject to duty are:

(1)   Packing costs incurred by the buyer.[97] If incurred by the seller they would be part of the price paid for the merchandise, probably buried in the price of the goods.

(2)   All selling commission incurred by the buyer with respect to the imported merchandise.[98]

(3)   The value of any assist, apportioned as appropriate.[99] An assist includes a very broad range of benefits, and is the subject of an extensive definitional provision.[100]

(4)   Any royalty or license fee related to the goods, which the buyer pays directly or indirectly as a condition of the sale.[101] This can be a difficult provision to interpret. However, if a buyer pays a flat fee per year directly to the designer of the goods, no matter how many are sold, the buyer may escape duty. But, any payment related to the number sold seems subject to duty.

(5)   Any direct or indirect accrual to the seller from the subsequent resale, disposal, or use of the goods.[102] This prevents the sale at a low base price, with the buyer required to pass on a percentage to the seller after the goods are resold.

The price paid or payable shall be increased by any of the above five additions, if it can be shown that they have not already been included in the price paid or payable by "sufficient" information.[103] The statute defines sufficient information as that which

---

[96]   See All Channel Products v. United States, 787 F. Supp. 1457 (C.I.T. 1992), aff'd 982 F.2d 513 (Fed. Cir. 1992) (inland freight charges separately invoiced properly included in transaction value); United States v. Arnold Pickle & Olive Co., 659 F.2d 1049 (C.C.P.A. 1981) (inspection costs).

[97]   19 U.S.C. § 1401a(b)(1)(A).

[98]   19 U.S.C. § 1401a(b)(1)(B). See Jay-Arr Slimwear Inc. v. United States, 681 F. Supp. 875 (C.I.T. 1988).

[99]   19 U.S.C. § 1401a(b)(1)(C).

[100]   19 U.S.C. § 1401a(h)(1). See, e.g., Texas Apparel Co. v. United States, 883 F.2d 66 (Fed. Cir. 1989) (sewing machine costs constitute an assist in manufacturing jeans). See Thomas R. Collins, The Concept of Assist as Applied to Customs Valuation of Imported Merchandise, 1991 DETROIT COL. L.R. 239.

[101]   19 U.S.C. § 1401a(b)(1)(D).

[102]   19 U.S.C. § 1401a(b)(1)(E).

[103]   19 U.S.C. § 1401a(b)(1).

"establishes the accuracy of such amount, difference, or adjustment."[104] Where sufficient information is not available, and it seems like one or more of the five additional amounts exist, the transaction value is not determinable, and one must move to the next section in the chronology of applicable provisions.[105]

Where the transaction value is determinable, as discussed above, it will be considered the *appraised* value only if certain further conditions exist. The first of these conditions requires the buyer to dispose of or use the goods without restriction, except restrictions that (1) are required by law, (2) limit resale to a geographical area, or (3) do not substantially affect the value.[106]

The second condition requires that there may not be any condition or consideration affecting the sale of or the price paid or payable where the value of the condition or consideration cannot be determined.[107]

The third states that no part of the proceeds from the use or resale may accrue directly or indirectly to the seller, unless that amount is calculable under the provisions noted above.[108]

The fourth requires the buyer and seller to be either unrelated, or if related that the transaction is acceptable.[109] Because buyers and sellers are often related through a parent and subsidiary relationship, the statute sets forth special rules. Often the prices reflected in transfers within an organization do not truly reflect arm's length prices because they want to avoid taxes, avoid tariff duties, or for other purposes.[110] The transaction value in such a transaction will be the appraised value, as long as (1) the circumstances of the sale do not suggest the relationship influenced the price, and (2) the transaction value approximates either the transaction value in an unrelated parties transaction, the deductive value, or computed value for identical or similar merchandise.[111]

This exception introduces the concepts of *deductive* value and *computed* value, both alternative valuations methods discussed below. The exception also requires defining both *identical* merchandise and *similar* merchandise.[112] The comparison values

---

[104]   19 U.S.C. § 1401a(b)(5).

[105]   *Id.*

[106]   19 U.S.C. § 1401a(b)(2)(A)(i).

[107]   19 U.S.C. § 1401a(b)(2)(A)(ii).

[108]   19 U.S.C. § 1401a(b)(2)(A)(iii). The above provision is 19 U.S.C. § 1401a(b)(1)(E).

[109]   19 U.S.C. § 1401a(b)(2)(A)(iv).

[110]   Transfer pricing is discussed in Chapter 21.

[111]   19 U.S.C. § 1401a(b)(2)(B).

[112]   19 U.S.C. § 1401a(h)(2) & (4).

referred to above must be values for merchandise entering the United States on or around the same time as the merchandise in question.

The values used for comparison purposes usually consists of identical or similar goods,[113] however, varying method of sales may distort the comparison between the goods. Consequently, the values used must consider these differences, if based on sufficient information, in commercial levels, quantity levels and any costs, commissions, values, fees and proceeds in § 1401a(b)(1), discussed above.[114]

While the above identifies provisions designating the composition of the transaction value, specific items should not be included in the transaction value, including:

First, transaction value should not include any reasonable cost or charge for either (1) construction, erection, assembly, or maintenance of, or technical assistance to the merchandise after importation, or (2) transportation after importation.[115]

Second, transaction value should not include the customs duties or other federal taxes imposed upon importation, nor federal excise tax.[116]

Transaction Value of Identical and Similar Merchandise. This separate section largely draws from the above section applicable to transaction value. The identical merchandise value method is used when the transaction value cannot be determined or used. When the identical merchandise value cannot be used, the similar merchandise value should be used.[117] Where the transaction value has been determined above for identical merchandise or for similar merchandise, as defined in the statute,[118] it must be adjusted. This adjustment requires consideration of all different commercial level or quantity level of sales for identical or similar merchandise.[119] It must also be based on sufficient information. Where two or more comparison transactions exist, the appraisal of the imported

---

[113]   *See* Walter Holm & Co. v. United States, 3 C.I.T. 119 (1982) (use of value of exports of cantaloupes through Laredo, Texas, to determine value of same items through Nogales, Arizona).

[114]   19 U.S.C. § 1401a(b)(2)(C).

[115]   19 U.S.C. § 1401a(b)(3)(A). International transportation is separately excluded in 19 U.S.C. § 1401a(b)(4)(A).

[116]   19 U.S.C. § 1401a(b)(3)(B).

[117]   19 U.S.C. §§ 1401a(a)(1)(B) & (C).

[118]   19 U.S.C. § 1401a(h)(2) & (4).

[119]   19 U.S.C. § 1401a(c)(2).

merchandise will be based on the lower or lowest of the comparison values.[120]

§ 11.19 Valuation__Deductive Value

The most important question is when will the deductive method of valuation be used? Deductive value should be used when the above transaction value does not lead to an acceptable determination to Customs.[121] However, the importer may request that the computed value discussed below be used in place of the deductive value.[122] If computed value does not prove possible, the deductive value must be used next.[123]

Deductive value may be applied to the merchandise being appraised, or to either identical or similar merchandise.[124] The deductive value focuses on unit value,[125] and constitutes the most appropriate value as determined in one of three ways.

The first method applies when the merchandise imported is sold (1) in the condition as imported, and (2) at or about the date of importation. The deductive value is the unit price at which the merchandise is sold in the greatest quantity.[126]

The second method applies when the merchandise imported is sold in the condition as imported, but not at or about the date of importation. The deductive value in this case is the unit price at which the merchandise is sold in the greatest quantity, but within 90 days after importation.[127]

The third method is where the merchandise is neither sold in the condition imported nor within 90 days after importation. The deductive value is the unit price at which the merchandise, after further processing, is sold in the greatest quantity within 180 days of importation.[128] This third method only applies at the election of the importer and upon notification to the customs officer.[129]

---

[120]   *Id.*

[121]   19 U.S.C. § 1401a(a)(1)(D).

[122]   19 U.S.C. § 1401a(a)(2).

[123]   *Id.*

[124]   19 U.S.C. § 1401a(d)(1).

[125]   Unit value is the price the merchandise is sold (1) in the greatest aggregate quantity, (2) to unrelated persons, (3) at the first commercial level after importation (at level i and ii discussed below), or after further processing (at level iii discussed below), (4) in a total volume which is both greater than the total volume sold at any other unit price, and sufficient to establish the unit price. 19 U.S.C. § 1401a(d)(2)(B).

[126]   19 U.S.C. § 1401a(d)(2)(A)(i).

[127]   19 U.S.C. § 1401a(d)(2)(A)(ii).

[128]   19 U.S.C. § 1401a(d)(2)(A)(iii).

[129]   *Id.*

If the deductive method applies, some reductions from the unit price may result, including commissions, additions for profit and expenses, costs of domestic and international transportation, customs duties and other federal taxes on the merchandise. If the third method of deductive value is used, the costs of additional processing may reduce the unit price.[130] However, deductions for profits and expenses must be consistent with profits and expenses in the United States for similar merchandise, and any state or local taxes on the importer relating to the sale of the merchandise is considered an expense.[131]

There may also be an increase to the unit price, if such costs have not already been included, amounting to the packing costs incurred by the importer or buyer.[132]

A final provision requires one to disregard any sale to a person who supplies an assist for use in connection with the merchandise.[133]

Where deductive value is inapplicable, or where the importer has chosen to pass over deductive value, the next method is computed value.

§ 11.20 Valuation___Computed Value

Computed value should be used when transaction and deductive value methods do not provide an appropriate result. However, the importer may skip over the deductive value tests and go straight to the computed value test.[134] The computed value determination consists of the sum of four parts.[135]

First, computed value considers the cost or value of materials and fabrication or processing,[136] but it does not include any internal tax by the exporting country if the tax is remitted upon exportation.[137]

---

[130]   19 U.S.C. § 1401a(d)(3)(A).

[131]   19 U.S.C. § 1401a(d)(3)(B).

[132]   19 U.S.C. § 1401a(d)(3)(C).

[133]   19 U.S.C. § 1401a(d)(3)(D).

[134]   19 U.S.C. § 1401a(a).

[135]   19 U.S.C. § 1401a(e)(1). For cases which have used the constructed value approach, see Campbell Soup Co., Inc. v. United States, 107 F.3d 1556 (Fed. Cir. 1997) (calculating the computed value of transported tomato paste from Mexico to United States); New York Credit Men's Adjustment Bureau, Inc. v. United States, 314 F. Supp. 1246 (Cust. Ct. 1970), affirmed 342 F. Supp. 745 (Cust. Ct. 1972).

[136]   19 U.S.C. § 1401a(e)(1)(A). See Texas Apparel Co. v. United States, 698 F.Supp. 932 (C.I.T. 1988), affirmed 883 F.2d 66 (Fed. Cir. 1989).

[137]   19 U.S.C. § 1401a(e)(2)(A).

Second, computed value considers the profit and expenses of the amount usually associated with the same kind of merchandise.[138] They are based on producer's profits and expenses, unless inconsistent with those for sales of the same class or kind of merchandise by producers in the country exporting to the United States, in which case there is a calculation of such profits and expenses using the "sufficient information" procedure.[139] For example, freight costs incurred through the shipment of tomato paste from Mexico to the United States should be included in the computed value.[140] Also, the costs of a warranty for aircraft should be included as profit, less expenditures the manufacturer-seller establishes as incurred by the warranty obligations in curing defects.[141]

Third, computed value includes any assist if not already included in the amount above.[142] Computing the value of jeans would allow the addition of the cost or value of the sewing machines used to produce the jeans.[143] Finally, packing costs are included in the computed value.[144]

§ 11.21 Valuation___Value When Other Methods Are Not Effective

If the value cannot be determined under the above-discussed methods, there is a final method for calculating value. It is to derive a value using the methods set forth above, and then adjusting them to the extent necessary to achieve a reasonable result.[145] But in making such an appraisal, the statute prohibits using any of seven items:[146]

(1) United States selling price of United States produced merchandise,

(2) any system using the higher of two alternatives,

(3) domestic market price in country of exportation,

---

[138] 19 U.S.C. § 1401a(e)(1)(B). *See* Braniff Airways, Inc. v. United States, 2 C.I.T. 26 (1981).

[139] 19 U.S.C. § 1401a(e)(2)(B).

[140] Campbell Soup Co., Inc. v. United States, 107 F.3d 1556 (Fed. Cir. 1997)

[141] Braniff Airways, Inc. v. United States, 2 C.I.T. 26 (1981).

[142] 19 U.S.C. § 1401a(e)(1)(C).

[143] Texas Apparel Co. v. United States, 698 F. Supp. 932 (C.I.T. 1988), *aff'd* 883 F.2d 66 (Fed. Cir. 1989).

[144] 19 U.S.C. § 1401a(e)(1)(D).

[145] 19 U.S.C. § 1401a(f)(1).

[146] 19 U.S.C. § 1401a(f)(2).

(4)   cost of production for identical or similar merchandise which differs from such cost of production determined under the computed value method,

(5)   price for export to a country other than the United States,

(6)   minimum values, or

(7)   arbitrary or fictitious values.

As first noted, transaction value expressed in the invoice is used in the vast majority of cases. However, when challenges to transaction value appear, the procedure may become more complex. While any of the determinations of Customs may be challenged, the cost of such challenge for all but the largest importers will often result in paying the Customs determined value, or not importing the goods. Counsel should calculate the possible rates of duty under all the possible alternatives and should only import the products if the rate of duty is acceptable and does not cause the price for resale to be either excessive, or more than would result from using United States products which may cost more to produce, but do not have added duty.

Chapter 12

ANTIDUMPING DUTIES

Table of Sections

§ 12.1 Overview of Antidumping Duties (ADs) and Countervailing Duties (CVDs)

Chapters 9, 10, and 11 examined governmental regulation of international trade, and in particular the international and national rules for the imposition of tariffs. At the core of the international system defined by the various agreements in the World Trade Organization (WTO) system is a principle of binding tariffs applied equally to all WTO member states (the most-favored-nation principle). The WTO system allows, however, certain exceptions, the two most important of which are "antidumping duties" (ADs) and "countervailing duties" (CVDs). This Chapter will analyze antidumping duties; Chapter 13 will then examine the subject of governmental subsidies and the allowed response of countervailing duties.

Under both antidumping duties and countervailing duties, a country may impose duties on an imported item above that otherwise allowed by the generally applicable tariff schedule. Antidumping duties are an allowed trade response where an enterprise prices its goods for sale in the country of importation at a level that is less than that charged for comparable sales in the home country (*i.e.*, at "less than fair value" (LTFV)). Countervailing duties are allowed as a trade response to direct or indirect "subsidies" granted by another country in order to position its exports more competitively in the international marketplace.

The WTO system recognizes and permits both antidumping duties and countervailing duties, providing of course the respective requirements are satisfied. Each "trade remedy" also is governed by a separate WTO Covered Agreement that provides more detail on the circumstances under which member states may impose the exceptional duties. Because each is mandatory in the WTO system, the special WTO agreements provide the foundation for a reasonably uniform body of legal rules for trade remedies among the more than 160 WTO member states.

The substantive grounds for the imposition of trade remedies are different for each of the two exceptions, but the injury standard is essentially the same. Under the WTO Antidumping Agreement and the WTO Subsidies and Countervailing Measures Agreement, generally a country may impose a special duty on products of another WTO member state only if two requirements are met. First, the country must find sufficient evidence of an unfair trade practice, either dumping (sales at less than fair value) or prohibited or actionable subsidies. Second, the practice must cause a sufficiently significant injury to a domestic industry. In the case of dumping or subsidies, this requires proof that the practice has caused or threatens to cause a "material injury" to a domestic industry or that it has "materially retarded" the establishment of such an industry.

Neither of the two trade remedies in favor of domestic producers is based, however, on any notion of reciprocity. That is, neither arises because another country has restricted the importation of U.S. goods into its markets. Antidumping and countervailing duties instead address only unfair selling prices for the dutiable imported goods themselves.

§ 12.2   Dumping: What Is It and Why Is It Done?

Dumping involves an exporter selling goods abroad at a lower price than it charges for the same goods in the home market (the "normal" or *"fair"* value). This alone is not sufficient however. Antidumping duties are allowed as a trade response only if the practice causes or threatens to cause a material injury to an industry in the export market. Dumping is recognized by most of the trading world as an unfair practice (akin to price discrimination as an antitrust offense). As noted, dumping is the subject of a special WTO Agreement that defines when dumping occurs, what constitutes a material injury, and the rules on the calculation of an allowed antidumping duty response by the offended country.

The economics of dumping arise from a producer's opportunity to compartmentalize the overall market for its product, thus permitting it to offer the product for sale at different prices in different geographic areas. Only if trade barriers or other factors insulate each market sector from others is there opportunity to vary substantially the product's price in different sectors of the global market. For example, a producer can securely "dump" products in an overseas market at cheap prices and at high volume only if it can be sure that the product market in its home country is immune from return penetration by these products. The objectives of dumping include increasing marginal revenues, ruining a competitor's market position, and developing a new market on an expeditious basis.

On the other hand, a sale at less than the home price may not necessarily represent an unfair trade practice; it may instead merely result from a short-term need to introduce new products, sell off excess inventory, or conduct a distress sale in difficult financial circumstances. Indeed, "dumping" products in order to establish a foothold in a new foreign market or to raise brand awareness in an existing market may make sense as a marketing technique. Because the motivations for selling a product at low prices are numerous and varied, it often is very difficult to determine whether "actionable" dumping is occurring in any particular case. In any event, the ultimate economic rationality of dumping remains the subject of vigorous debate among economists.

§ 12.3 The WTO Antidumping Agreement (1994)

The law regarding dumping has been the repeated subject of discussion in the various rounds of negotiations under the General Agreement on Tariffs and Trade (GATT) and (later) the WTO. A technical area, antidumping remedies were for many years principally used by developed nations to protect against competition from developing country imports. Then, in a remarkable transfer of legal technology, the principles endorsed by various GATT antidumping agreements took hold in newly developing countries. Today, antidumping duties are as likely to be imposed on U.S. exports by Mexico, India or China, as vice-versa. Antidumping proceedings remain the preferred trade remedy of domestic producers. The European Union and India are the top users of antidumping remedies, with products from China by far the top target of antidumping duties.

Late in 1993, the Uruguay Round of GATT negotiations came to a successful conclusion and President Clinton notified Congress of his intent to sign the many "covered agreements" that resulted from those negotiations. One of those agreements was yet another attempt at a codification of antidumping law. As a basic matter, Article VI of the longstanding GATT grants WTO member states the right to impose antidumping duties. But the more detailed standards for such duties are set forth in a separate WTO Agreement, "The Agreement on Implementation of Article VI of GATT 1994."

The WTO Antidumping Agreement, adopted from the earlier Tokyo Round GATT "Antidumping Code," focuses on dumping determinations (particularly criteria for allocating costs) and material injury determinations (particularly causation). The Antidumping Agreement provides that dumping occurs with respect to a product if its export price is less than the "normal value." It defines the "normal value" of a good as the comparable price, in the ordinary course of trade, for the same or a similar product "when destined for consumption in the exporting country." Thus, in evaluating whether an export price constitutes dumping, the best baseline for comparison is the domestic sales price of comparable goods in the exporting country (*i.e.*, the home country).

However, such comparable sales may not be available, either because comparable products are not sold domestically or because the usual retail transaction there is not comparable (*e.g.*, leasing rather than a sale). In that situation, the Antidumping Agreement provides a hierarchy of alternative computation methods to achieve an approximate evaluation. Among these alternatives, the preferred one uses the *price* for the same or a similar product in the ordinary course of trade for export to a third country. The next preferred alternative is to calculate the *cost* of production of the exported goods in the country of origin, plus a reasonable amount for profits and for administrative, selling and any other general costs. In either case, the value thus determined is then compared against the price charged on the export price to the target country.

The Agreement then has detailed rules that permit a member state to impose an antidumping duty only if a sale at less than fair value has caused a sufficient injury to a domestic industry. The Agreement defines the required level of injury as a "material injury" or "threat of material injury" to a domestic industry or a "material retardation of the establishment of such an industry." And such an injury determination is permitted only on "positive evidence" and an "objective determination" of the volume of dumped imports and the effect on domestic prices as well as the consequent impact on domestic producers of the dumped product.

Because the United States has agreed to abide by the Antidumping Agreement, each of these requirements is reflected in conforming provisions of the U.S. Tariff Act of 1930. The remaining Sections of this Chapter will examine in detail these rules of antidumping law.

The WTO Antidumping Agreement also has a few special rules that are worthy of emphasis. First, it forbids duties for *de minimis* dumping, defined as less than two percent of the product's export price; in such cases member states must terminate any antidumping investigations immediately. Second, the Agreement permits "cumulation" of imports—*i.e.*, imports of the same goods from more than one country—if the dumping from each is more than *de minimis* and this is otherwise appropriate under the circumstances. Third, it recognizes, but does not expressly allow or disallow, antidumping petitions by employees and their union representatives. Fourth, the Agreement obligates member states to notify the WTO of any changes to their domestic antidumping laws as well as any related administrative actions. More generally, a special WTO "Committee on Anti-Dumping Practices" oversees implementation of the Agreement by member states.

Finally, when another member state challenges the imposition of antidumping duties before the WTO, the Dispute Settlement Body (DSB) panel may rely on the facts developed in the domestic administrative proceedings and must accept those facts if the domestic evaluation "was unbiased and objective, even if the panel might have reached a different conclusion." The Agreement also expressly allows for "competing, reasonable interpretations" of its obligations under the domestic law of its member states.

§ 12.4   The Evolution of U.S. Antidumping Law

The United States was an early advocate of the perspective that dumping constitutes an unfair trade practice. Indeed, complaints about dumping were recorded as the subject of a protest by Secretary of the Treasury Alexander Hamilton in 1791. In general, U.S. antidumping statutes compare the price at which articles are imported or sold within the United States with their price in the country of production at the time of their export to the United States. This approach was first established by the Antidumping Act of 1916, a rarely-invoked criminal statute prohibiting "predatorily low price levels."[1] This statute, which also created a private remedy for treble damages, required proof of an intent to seriously injure or destroy a U.S. industry. The European Union, Japan, and other states successfully challenged this 1916 Act in WTO dispute settlement proceedings as inconsistent with the Antidumping Agreement. The pressure of the adverse rulings by the WTO's DSB ultimately led the United States to repeal the Act in 2004.

The modern U.S. rules and procedures governing antidumping duties are set forth in a statute that is still known as the Tariff Act of 1930;[2] but Congress has enacted amendments to this statute numerous times. The most important of these for present purposes came through the Uruguay Round Agreements Act of 1994 (URAA),[3] by which (as the name suggests) Congress amended the Tariff Act to implement the numerous Uruguay Round WTO agreements, including the Antidumping Agreement. Finally, the Code of Federal Regulations contains more detailed rules on the requirements for, calculation of, and process for assessing antidumping duties.[4]

U.S. law places authority for administering antidumping law in two different governmental agencies.[5] Generally, the Secretary of Commerce (which in turn has delegated specific authority to its International Trade Administration (ITA)) is the "Administering

---

[1]   15 U.S.C. §§ 71–77.

[2]   Codified at 19 U.S.C. §§ 1671–1677g.

[3]   Public Law No. 103–465, 108 Stat. 4809.

[4]   The principal U.S. antidumping regulations are found in 19 C.F.R. Part 351.

[5]   For more on the administrative processes governing antidumping duties see Sections 12.22 through 12.25 *infra*.

Authority,"[6] which is responsible for all administration determinations except those relating to injury to a domestic industry. Injury determinations are the responsibility of the International Trade Commission (ITC).[7] To provide guidance on the application of the applicable statutory and regulatory rules, the International Trade Administration publishes an "Antidumping Manual," the most recent version of which is from 2009.[8]

Sections 12.5 through 12.19 below will examine in detail the substantive rules of U.S. law on antidumping determinations. In brief, and in conformity with the WTO Antidumping Agreement, the fundamental determination under U.S. law is whether a sale is at "less than fair value" (LTFV).[9] This requires a comparison of the U.S. price of imported goods with their "normal value." "Normal value" is usually determined by the price charged for the goods in the exporter's *domestic* market (the home market) in the ordinary course of business.[10] The ITA then compares this value with the price of the goods for export to the United States.[11] As noted, the ITC separately makes determinations on injury and causation in antidumping proceedings. In order to impose antidumping duties, the Tariff Act requires an affirmative determination by the ITC that a challenged practice presents an actual or threatened "material injury" to a domestic industry or that it has "materially retarded" the establishment of such an industry.[12]

If sales are both at LTFV and cause or threaten "material injury" to a domestic industry, then the Tariff Act declares that an antidumping duty "shall be imposed."[13] Thus, antidumping duties are a statutory remedy, one which the President cannot veto or affect (except by the extraordinary act of negotiating an international trade agreement).

---

[6]   19 U.S.C. § 1677(1). Prior to 1980, the Treasury Department was the "administering authority," but the Secretary of Commerce was so designated in 1980. *See President's Reorganization Plan No. 3 of 1979*, 44 Fed. Reg. 69,273 (1979), and Executive Order 12188, 45 Fed. Reg. 989 (1980).

[7]   19 U.S.C. §§ 1673(2) and 1677(2).

[8]   Import Administration Antidumping Manual (2009), http://ia.ita.doc.gov/admanual/index.html.

[9]   19 U.S.C. § 1673(1).

[10]   19 U.S.C. §§ 1673(1), 1677b. *See also* Sections 12.6–12.9 *infra*.

[11]   19 U.S.C. §§ 1673(1), 1677a. *See also* Section 12.10 *infra*.

[12]   19 U.S.C. § 1673(2). *See also* Sections 12.12–12.18 *infra*.

[13]   19 U.S.C. § 1673.

§ 12.5   The Basic Dumping Determination

The Basic Measure. The ITA determines whether foreign merchandise[14] is, or is likely to be, sold in the United States at less than fair value (LTFV) by comparing the foreign market value (the "normal value") of the goods to the price charged for export to the United States (the "United States price"). If the former exceeds the latter, dumping has occurred. Much turns, therefore, on the definitions of these two central concepts. Sections 12.6 through 12.9 below will examine the calculation of the foreign market value. Section 12.10 below will then analyze the appropriate comparison price regarding the export of the goods to the United States.

The Dumping Margin. As noted, if a sale both (a) is at LTFV and (b) meets the statutory material injury requirement, then the Tariff Act provides that an antidumping duty "shall be imposed."[15] The amount of the duty will correspond to the "dumping margin." The ITA normally compares the "weighted-average" foreign market value with the "weighted-average" U.S. price for the dumped product.[16] The term "weighted average dumping margin" is a percentage that is determined with reference to the "aggregate dumping margins" of the exporter or producer for the type of products at issue.[17] For large capital goods, however, the ITA will typically use the actual normal value and the U.S. price on a transaction-to-transaction basis.[18] Whichever calculation method is used, the "dumping margin"—and thus the amount of the antidumping duty—corresponds to the amount by which the foreign market "normal value" of the goods exceeds the price charged in the export to the United States.[19] The dumping margin may be different for similar merchandise from different foreign states, and may also be different for different manufacturers from the same foreign state.

§ 12.6   Foreign Market Value__"Normal Value"

The first step in the analysis is to determine the appropriate value of the allegedly dumped goods in a relevant foreign market. The Tariff Act refers to this value as the "normal value."[20] It recognizes three different measures for this normal value:

---

[14]   Antidumping law generally does not apply to services, but also is not limited to "cash-only sales." *See* United States v. Eurodif S. A., 555 U.S. 305 (2009).

[15]   19 U.S.C. § 1673.

[16]   19 U.S.C. § 1677(35)(B).

[17]   *Id.*

[18]   19 U.S.C. § 1677(35)(A).

[19]   *Id.*

[20]   19 U.S.C. § 1677b.

Home Market Price. The standard measure of the "normal value" is the price at which the foreign merchandise is first sold for consumption—in usual quantities, in the ordinary course of trade, and preferably at the same level of trade—in the exporting country ("home market price").[21]

Third Country Price. If, however, sales in the home market are nonexistent or too small to form an adequate basis for comparison (usually, less than five percent of the total sales of the goods to the United States), then export sales to other countries may be used for the normal value ("third country price").[22] Sales intended to establish fictitious markets in the source country, however, cannot be considered.[23]

Constructed Value. If comparable merchandise is not offered for sale either in the home market or for export to third countries, the ITA is authorized to calculate a "constructed" value.[24] In such a case, the ITA will build a figure based on the sum of three elements: (1) First, it will calculate the actual costs of production and processing of the goods. (2) To this basic cost figure it will add the exporter's actual "selling, general, and administrative expenses" as well as actual profits for the goods. If actual numbers are not available for this element, then the ITA will use one of three alternatives: (a) the specific exporter's costs and profits for goods of the "same general category," (b) the weighted average of costs and profits for like goods by other exporters subject to the investigation, or (c) the costs and profits determined by the ITA "based on any other reasonable method." (3) Finally, the ITA will add the costs of containers and other coverings for the goods as well as all other expenses incidental to shipping the goods to the United States.[25] If the foreign producer is in a non-market economy, then the ITA will construct an appropriate value based either on various "factors of production" or on "surrogate country prices" (see Section 12.8 below).[26]

The time and place for determining the normal value is often crucial. The Tariff Act requires that the relevant time for measuring the sales in the foreign country must "reasonably correspond[ ]" to the time used to calculate the comparison export price to the United States.[27] That is the time when the product is "first sold (or agreed

---

[21]   19 U.S.C. § 1677b(a)(1)(B)(i).

[22]   19 U.S.C. § 1677b(a)(1)(B)(ii).

[23]   19 U.S.C. § 1677b(a)(2).

[24]   19 U.S.C. § 1677b(a)(4), (e).

[25]   19 U.S.C. § 1677b(e).

[26]   19 U.S.C. § 1677b(c). For more detail on this issue see Section 12.9 *infra*.

[27]   19 U.S.C. § 1677b(a)(1)(A).

to be sold) before the date of importation by the producer or exporter of the subject merchandise outside of the United States to an unaffiliated purchaser in the United States."[28] That is also the date for determining the appropriate exchange rate for converting prices in foreign currency into U.S. dollars.[29]

In determining foreign market value, the ITA may use averaging and generally recognized sampling techniques whenever there is a significant volume of sales or number of adjustments.[30] The authority to select averages and statistical sampling "rests exclusively" with the Secretary of Commerce (and thus the ITA).[31]

When the goods are manufactured in one country and then shipped to another, from which they are exported to the United States, a question arises as to which foreign country is the relevant one. The Act provides a partial answer. Generally, the price in country of transshipment (the "intermediate country") is the correct one *unless*:

(1) the producer knew at the time of the sale that the subject merchandise was destined for exportation;

(2) the goods are merely transshipped through the intermediate country;

(3) sales of the goods in the intermediate country are too small to form an adequate basis for comparison; or

(4) the goods are not produced in the intermediate country.[32]

Other issues relating to the determination of foreign market value are discussed below. These problems include issues arising out of sales at less than the costs of production; constructed values; imports from nonmarket economy countries; special rules for multinational corporations; and adjustments necessary to ensure a proper comparison of value with price.

§ 12.7 Foreign Market Value__Sales Below Cost Disregarded

The central question in most antidumping proceedings is whether and to what degree the foreign producer or exporter is selling its goods in the home market below the cost of production. Sales are below cost if they do not recover total costs, both fixed and

---

[28]   19 U.S.C. § 1677a(a).

[29]   *See* 19 U.S.C. § 1677b–1.

[30]   19 U.S.C. § 1677f–1.

[31]   19 U.S.C. § 1677f–1(b).

[32]   19 U.S.C. § 1677(a)(3).

variable, over a commercially reasonable period. Thus, a significant volume of sales by a foreign producer at prices that cover only its variable costs can be disregarded by the ITA in its calculation of the foreign market value of the goods. The Tariff Act explicitly authorizes the ITA to disregard sales at less than the cost of production when it makes its "normal value" determinations.[33]

The ITA will investigate this issue whenever it "has reasonable grounds to believe or suspect" that sales of the goods under investigation "have been made at prices which represent less than the cost of production." If the ITA determines that such sales (a) have occurred "within an extended period of time in substantial quantities," and (b) "were not at prices which permit recovery of all costs within a reasonable period of time," then it "may" disregard the sales in determining the "normal value."[34] Thus, recovery of start-up costs may be prorated over commercially reasonable periods. A decision to disregard sales below cost from the normal value calculation naturally raises the average cost and thus increases the potential to find dumping. A decision to include such sales has the opposite effect.

If the ITA disregards sales as below the cost of production, it will make its "normal value" determination based on the remaining sales of the goods "in the ordinary course of trade."[35] And if no sales are made in the ordinary course of trade, the ITA must instead use the "constructed value" of the goods.[36]

§ 12.8 Foreign Market Value__Nonmarket Economy Constructed Values

The ITA will always use the "constructed value" to determine the foreign market value of imports from nonmarket economy countries.[37] The actual prices used in the exporter's (home) foreign market are deemed irrelevant because they are assumed to be determined bureaucratically and not by market forces. That is, they are not sufficiently subject to the forces of competition to form an accurate standard for comparison.

The Tariff Act delegates to the ITA the authority to determine when imports are from a "nonmarket economy country,"[38] and then insulates that administrative determination from judicial review.[39]

---

[33]   19 U.S.C. § 1677b(b).

[34]   *Id.*

[35]   *Id.*

[36]   *See* Section 12.9 *infra.*

[37]   19 U.S.C. § 1677b(c).

[38]   19 U.S.C. § 1677(18)(A), (C).

[39]   19 U.S.C. § 1677(18)(D).

The Act nonetheless gives the ITA a basic definition—whether the country's economy operates on "market principles" so that home market sales reflect "fair value." It then provides five factors to consider.[40] The factors include the convertibility of the foreign country's currency, the extent to which wages and prices are determined by government action or free bargaining, the extent of government ownership of the means of production, the receptivity to private foreign investment, and "such other factors as the [Commerce Department] considers appropriate."[41] Although the Act speaks in terms of a country by country decision, the ITA has more often analyzed the particular industrial segment involved.

If the imports are from a nonmarket economy (NME) country, the Act directs the ITA to "construct" a foreign market value by determining the factors of production (labor, materials, energy, capital, etc.) actually used by the NME to produce the imported goods.[42] The ITA then determines a value for each of those "factors of production" according to the prices or costs in a market economy that is appropriate under the circumstances. Surrogate countries are appropriate if they are "at a level of economic development comparable to that of the nonmarket economy country" and also are "significant producers of comparable merchandise."[43]

The Act then directs the ITA to add to the cost of production—again, as constructed based on the factors of production—appropriate amounts for general expenses, profits, and the packaging of the goods for shipment to the United States. The amounts for general expenses and profits are to be derived from sales of the same class or kind of merchandise in the "country of exportation,"[44] but this term simply means an "appropriate" market economy country.

In recognition of some of the difficulties with a "cost of production" approach, the Act provides an exception to the constructed value method outlined above, by allowing the use of a method of constructing a foreign market value for imports from a NME based on actual sale *prices*. The ITA may use this alternative method if it finds that the best available information on the factors of production is not adequate. In such a case, the ITA will find a "surrogate" market economy country (a) that produces goods that

---

[40] 19 U.S.C. § 1677(18)(B).

[41] *Id.*

[42] 19 U.S.C. § 1677b(c)(1).

[43] 19 U.S.C. § 1677b(c)(4). *See also, e.g.*, Ad Hoc Shrimp Trade Action Comm. v. United States, 618 F.3d. 1316 (Fed. Cir. 2010) (upholding the ITA's decisions in an antidumping order covering shrimp from Vietnam that calculated surrogate values based on survey data from comparable suppliers as "the best available information").

[44] 19 U.S.C. § 1677b(e)(1)(B).

are the same as or similar to the merchandise imported from the NME, and (b) that is "at a level of economic development comparable to that of the nonmarket economy country." Then, the ITA will construct a value based on the *price* at which such goods are "sold in other countries, including the United States."[45] Such a methodology does not require the ITA to construct a value based on the factors of production.

Several problems arise in the application of this scheme. First, "appropriate" market economy countries may be limited or unavailable. Second, the surrogate market economy countries selected may be obviously inappropriate, when compared to the level of economic development of the NME. Third, producers in such countries may not furnish the necessary information, even though the ITA is authorized to use the "best available information."[46] Fourth, there is no necessary relationship between the price so constructed by the ITA and any price that the NME producer may decide to charge. This leaves the NME producer or exporter always open to antidumping duties, and there is no pre-transaction analytical path for avoiding such duties.

§ 12.9   Foreign Market Value__Market Economy Constructed Values

The ITA may use constructed values not only for imports from NME countries, but in other circumstances as well. It is directed to construct a foreign market value whenever merchandise comparable to the imported merchandise is not offered for sale either in the home market of the foreign producer or exporter or for export from that home market to other countries.[47] A constructed foreign market value is also to be used when so many sales in the home market are below the cost of production, and therefore are disregarded, such that the remaining sales provide an inadequate basis for determining foreign market value.[48]

In such a case, the ITA will calculate the foreign market value based on one of three methodologies: (1) the producer's actual costs, plus sales, general, and administrative expenses, and plus a profit for the specific product under investigation; *or* (2) the producer's actual costs and profit for the products in the same category as those under investigation; *or* (3) a weighted average of other

---

45   19 U.S.C. § 1677b(c)(2).

46   19 U.S.C. § 1677b(c)(1).

47   19 U.S.C. § 1677b(a)(4).

48   19 U.S.C. § 1677b(b).

producers' actual costs and profit for the category of products under investigation.[49]

Special Rule for Multinational Corporations. The Act also has a special rule for determining the foreign market value of merchandise produced by a corporation with production facilities in two or more countries. This "special rule for certain multinational corporations" applies when there are insufficient sales by that producer in its home market on which to base a comparison of its export sales to the United States.[50] If the foreign market value of the goods produced in the country of exportation is less than the price of the goods produced in the corporation's facilities in another country, the ITA "shall" construct a foreign market value which reflects the price of the goods produced in the nonexporting country.

§ 12.10   United States Price

To determine whether dumping exists, the ITA will compare the foreign market value ("normal value") of the goods with the price charged for export to the United States. The Tariff Act recognizes two different methods for calculating this price:

Export Price. The ITA generally uses the "export price" for the price of the goods for exportation to the United States. This is the price at which the goods are first sold *outside* of the United States to an unaffiliated person before the goods are imported into the United States.[51] The standard example of this is when a foreign producer or exporter contacts an unaffiliated U.S. business in order to distribute a foreign product in the United States and the parties agree on the sale terms (price, quantity, delivery, etc.).

Constructed Export Price. If, however, the foreign exporter first sells the goods to an *affiliated* person outside the United States (such that this "export" price is not a reliable one), then the ITA may use the "constructed export price."[52] This is the price at which the goods are first sold to an unaffiliated person *in* the United States irrespective of whether it occurs before or after importation. This typically occurs when a foreign exporter or producer first sells to a U.S. subsidiary, and in that case the relevant price is that charged by the subsidiary to the first unaffiliated U.S. buyer.

---

[49]   19 U.S.C. § 1677b(e).

[50]   19 U.S.C. § 1677b(d).

[51]   19 U.S.C. § 1677a(a).

[52]   19 U.S.C. § 1677a(b).

§ 12.11 "Foreign Like Product" Determinations and Required Adjustments

The entire analysis above depends upon a comparison of the United States price against the price of a "foreign like product,"[53] a concept also relevant in injury determinations by the ITC.[54] Because merchandise sold in foreign markets is often different, due to cultural, technical or legal constraints, the determination of comparability of merchandise sold in the foreign market to the imported merchandise is often a crucial one. The Act provides a definition, with a hierarchy of criteria.[55] Under the basic definition, merchandise that is identical in physical characteristics, and produced in the same country by the same person as the imported merchandise, is to be categorized as a "foreign like product."[56]

If such identical merchandise is not available, the ITA next looks for merchandise that is (a) produced in the same country by the same person, (b) has similar component materials, and (c) is approximately equal in value to the imported merchandise.[57]

If neither of these reference points is available, the ITA is to look at merchandise that (a) is produced in the same country by the same person and is of "the same general class or kind as the subject merchandise," (b) is like that merchandise "in the purposes for which used," and (c) in the judgment of the ITA "may reasonably be compared with" the imported merchandise.[58] In practice, the ITA considers similarities in the physical characteristics, use and expectations of ultimate purchasers, including advertising of the product, and distribution channels.

A considerable number of adjustments are necessary to obtain comparable prices for goods sold in home markets and for export to the United States. To determine the United States price, packing costs and container costs are added to the purchase price or exporter's sales price, if they are not already included in that price.[59] If generally applicable taxes are either not collected or are rebated by the exporting government, these also may be included in the determining United States price.

Adjustments deducted from the purchase price or exporter's sales price include any expenses, such as freight or insurance costs,

---

[53] 19 U.S.C. § 1677b(a)(1)(A), (B).

[54] *See* Section 12.13 *infra.*

[55] 19 U.S.C. § 1677(16).

[56] 19 U.S.C. § 1677(16)(A).

[57] 19 U.S.C. § 1677(16)(B).

[58] 19 U.S.C. § 1677(16)(C).

[59] 19 U.S.C. § 1677a(c)(1)(A).

included in that price and attributable to the costs of bringing the goods from the country of export to the United States as well as most export taxes of the exporting country.[60] Deductions also are appropriate for any commissions and other expenses for making sales in the United States and for the costs of additional processing or assembly in the United States after importation and before sale.[61] However, the additional cost of U.S. product liability insurance is not a permitted adjustment.[62]

Adjustments and exchange rate conversions are also made to determine the foreign market value of the goods. Exchange rate conversions are required whenever the foreign market price or the United States price is not in U.S. dollars. The rates for the relevant sales period as determined quarterly by the Federal Reserve Bank of New York are ordinarily used except when those rates are fluctuating rapidly. In such cases, the ITA will test whether the dumping margin remains if the rates from the prior quarter are used. If the margin disappears, the dumping is attributed to exchange rate fluctuations and the ITA may determine that no dumping occurred.

To obtain an equivalent of the United States price, the ITA will add to the foreign market value an amount equal to the packing costs and container costs for shipment to the United States.[63] Allowances may be made for sales at different trade levels (wholesale versus retail), quantity or production cost discounts, differences in the circumstances of sale, and physical differences in the merchandise.[64] Differences in the circumstances of the sale include credit terms, warranties, servicing, technical assistance, and advertising allowances. Adjustments for cost differences in the circumstances of sale are allowed even if they do not give rise to comparable price increases in the foreign market. This is true even if they involve rebates or discounts not made available to all purchasers.[65] These decisions reflect the substantial deference the courts give to the ITA on the important issue of adjustments to its price and value calculations.

---

[60]   19 U.S.C. § 1677a(c)(1)(B)–(C).

[61]   19 U.S.C. § 1677a(d).

[62]   *See* Carlisle Tire & Rubber Co. v. United States, 622 F. Supp. 1071 (C.I.T. 1985).

[63]   19 U.S.C. § 1677b(a)(6).

[64]   *See* 19 U.S.C. § 1677b(a), (b).

[65]   *See* Zenith Radio Corp. v. United States, 783 F.2d 184 (Fed. Cir. 1986).

§ 12.12 The Injury Determination

As noted in the Overview in Section 12.1, antidumping proceedings in the United States are conducted in two stages. In the second stage, the International Trade Commission (ITC) must determine whether the dumping has caused material injury to concerned domestic industries.[66] The following sections review the material injury determination under U.S. law, including market definition, injury factors, and causation.

Thus, the injury determination by the ITC involves three separate inquiries:

(1) First, the ITC must define the relevant "domestic like product" and relevant domestic industry;

(2) Second, the ITC must determine whether that industry is suffering or threatened with a sufficiently serious injury; and

(3) Third, the ITC must determine whether a causal link exists between the injury and the sale at LTFV (*i.e.*, the dumping).

The most important of these steps is the determination of whether a domestic industry is suffering a sufficient injury due to a dumping practice. The Tariff Act provides that an affirmative injury determination is required when an industry in the United States is materially injured or is threatened with material injury by reason of dumped imports, or the establishment of an industry in the United States is materially retarded.[67] Both the "material injury"[68] and the "threat of material injury"[69] standards apply to established industries, and substantial overlap exists between the two. Nonetheless, the Act makes clear that they are independent grounds for a sufficient injury to justify antidumping duties.[70]

§ 12.13 Injury Determination___The "Like Product" and Relevant Domestic Industry Determinations

In order to assess "material injury," the ITC and the ITA must first identify the relevant products and relevant domestic industry affected by an alleged dumping practice. The ITA necessarily focuses on which foreign products are like those alleged to be

---

[66]   19 U.S.C. § 1673(2).

[67]   *Id.*

[68]   19 U.S.C. § 1677(7).

[69]   19 U.S.C. § 1677(7)(F).

[70]   19 U.S.C. § 1673(2).

dumped in the United States. For its part, the ITC also must define the relevant domestic industry that produces like products in order to make its injury determinations.

The term "domestic like product" is defined by the Tariff Act as one that is "like, or in the absence of like, most similar in characteristics and uses with" the foreign product under investigation.[71] The "like product" determination is a factual issue for which the ITC weighs six relevant factors: "(1) physical characteristics and uses; (2) common manufacturing facilities and production employees; (3) interchangeability; (4) customer perceptions; (5) channels of distribution; and, where appropriate, (6) price."[72]

Separately, the ITA and the ITC must define the relevant domestic industry potentially affected by dumped products. The Tariff Act defines the relevant domestic "industry" as those domestic producers, "as a whole," of a "domestic like product" or as those producers "whose collective output of a domestic like product constitutes a major proportion" of the total domestic production.[73] Although these definitions apply to both the ITA and the ITC, they do not always agree on the outcome. The ITA and ITC may assess injury on a geographically regional basis if local producers sell most of their production in the regional market, and the demand in the regional market is not supplied by other U.S. producers outside that region.[74]

The determination of domestic "like products" and the relevant domestic industry can be decisive for ITA dumping determinations, but especially for ITC injury determinations. Some early cases on the subject, which have paved the way for later determinations, illustrate the point. In one early case, for example, the ITC excluded large screen TVs from the U.S. domestic industry definition. This had the effect of giving Japanese TV exports a much larger market share in the United States, thus supporting an affirmative injury determination.[75] In another early decision, the ITC narrowly defined the relevant U.S. industry as the canned mushrooms industry, noting that fresh and canned mushrooms were not always interchangeable. This narrow market definition again supported a

---

[71]   19 U.S.C. § 1667(10).

[72]   Cleo Inc. v. United States, 501 F.3d 1291, 1295 (Fed. Cir. 2007). The ITA's identification of the category of goods sold at less than fair value is not binding on the ITC's "like product" determination for injury purposes. *See* Hosiden Corp. v. Advanced Display Mfrs. of Am., 85 F.3d 1561, 1568 (Fed. Cir. 1996).

[73]   19 U.S.C. § 1677(4)(A).

[74]   19 U.S.C. § 1677(4)(C).

[75]   *See Television Sets from Japan*, U.S.I.T.C. Publ. No. 367 (March 1971).

preliminary injury determination.[76] Variations on the theme of defining "domestic like products" can occur if the ITC decides it is appropriate to exclude domestic companies that also import the allegedly dumped goods or are related to the importer or foreign producer.[77] The ITC may also define the domestic industry regionally in situations where this reflects market realities.[78] Thus, which U.S. firms the ITC chooses to include or exclude in its "domestic like product" definition is an important threshold issue in material injury analysis.

§ 12.14   Injury Determination__Material Injury

There are two potential perspectives on the appropriate meaning of "material." The first is that the term means any economic harm that is more than trivial, inconsequential, or *de minimis*. The second is that it contemplates a higher threshold, something serious in the ordinary sense of that word. The consensus view is that the spirit of Article VI of the GATT embraces the higher standard.

The Tariff Act thus defines material injury as "harm which is not inconsequential, immaterial, or unimportant."[79] (The same standard applies in CVD proceedings[80] and much of the law in the area is therefore interchangeable.) In assessing this essential "material injury" standard, the Act *requires* the ITC to consider three factors:

(1)   The volume of imports of the merchandise subject to investigation;

(2)   The effect of these imports on prices in the United States for like products; and

(3)   The impact of these imports on domestic producers of like products, but only in the context of domestic U.S. production operations.[81]

The Act also *permits* the ITC to consider "such other economic factors as are relevant to the determination regarding whether there is material injury by reason of imports."[82]

---

[76]   Canned Mushrooms from the People's Republic of China, U.S.I.T.C. Publ. No. 1324 (Dec. 1982).

[77]   19 U.S.C. § 1677(4)(B).

[78]   19 U.S.C. § 1677(4)(C).

[79]   19 U.S.C. § 1677(7)(A).

[80]   *See* Chapter 13.

[81]   19 U.S.C. § 1677(7)(B)(i). *See also* Angus Chemical Co. v. United States, 140 F.3d 1478 (Fed. Cir. 1998) (holding that consideration of these three factors is mandatory).

The ITC is required to explain its analysis of each factor considered and the relevance of each to its determination.[83] The Tariff Act nonetheless provides that the "presence or absence" of any of the three mandatory factors should "not necessarily give decisive guidance" to the ITC in its material injury determination, and the ITC is not required to give any particular weight to any one factor.[84] The factors are examined through extensive statistical analyses. This analysis occurs on industry-wide basis and not on a company-by-company basis. The ITC may select whatever time period best represents the business cycle, best captures the competitive conditions in the industry, and most reasonably allows it to determine whether an injury exists.[85]

The Tariff Act also gives detailed guidance for the ITC's assessment of each of the three mandatory considerations for a material injury determination:

Volume of Imports. The Tariff Act requires the ITC to consider the absolute volume of imports or any increase in volume of imports in evaluating the volume of imports subject to investigation. This assessment may be made in relation to production or consumption in the United States. The standard in this evaluation is whether the volume of imports, viewed in any of the above ways, is significant.[86]

Data relating to the volume of imports are an important factor in the ITC's injury determinations. In particular, the ITC is more concerned with the dynamics of the market share, such as a significant increase in market penetration, than it is with the size of market share. It is also primarily concerned with the effects that market share changes might have on profits and lost sales. The ITC may also find a sufficient injury even where a specific producer has a small market share, but imports from its home country as a whole are increasing rapidly, such that the U.S. domestic industry must reduce its prices in response. On the other hand, a large market share for the importer, coupled with increases in production, domestic shipments, exports, employment and profits of the domestic industry, may indicate that no material injury is occurring.

Price Effects. While price issues are obviously crucial to any determination of dumping margins, they have no strict correlation to injury determinations. However, under the Tariff Act, the ITC

---

[82]   19 U.S.C. § 1677(7)(B)(ii).

[83]   19 U.S.C. § 1677(7)(B).

[84]   19 U.S.C. § 1677(7)(E)(ii).

[85]   19 U.S.C. § 1677(7)(C).

[86]   19 U.S.C. § 1677(7)(C)(i).

may consider the effect of the dumped imports upon prices for like products in the domestic market. This is done to the extent that such a consideration assists in evaluating whether (1) there is significant "price underselling" in the imported merchandise as compared with the price of like products of the United States;[87] and (2) the effect of the imported merchandise is otherwise to depress domestic prices to a significant degree or to prevent price increases that otherwise would occur.[88] If there is no price underselling, but instead the exporters cut their U.S. prices to effectively meet price competition from U.S. producers, this is traditionally considered only "technical dumping" and precludes a finding of material injury. The rationale for this approach focuses upon the purposes behind antidumping law, *i.e.*, to prevent unfair dumping not to protect against pro-competitive trade practices. Thus, technical dumping constitutes a defense to U.S. material injury determinations.

Price underselling is not a *per se* basis for a finding of injury. For example, if the demand for the product is not price sensitive, price underselling will not be a central consideration. Price underselling in fact may be irrelevant, even if domestic producers are losing sales in the United States, if their inability to sell goods is not attributable to dumped imports. For example, the industry's decline may have been caused by its failure to develop, produce, and market a competitive product. (The next Section will analyze causation issues in more detail.)

Substantial underselling, on the other hand, will lead to an affirmative injury finding where the market is price sensitive. The ITC looks for a pervasive pattern of underselling. If the ITC finds that demand for a specific product is price sensitive and importers are engaging in price underselling, it will then examine whether domestic producers are being forced into price suppression[89] or actual price cutting.[90] Because price suppression can be as severe a burden to domestic producers as can an actual price cutting, the ITC will find an injury if it determines that, in order to respond to dumping practices, domestic producers have lowered or have been unable to raise their prices to accommodate rising costs.

Domestic Industry Impact. The impact on a domestic industry of an allegedly dumped product commonly is the most important

---

[87]   19 U.S.C. § 1677(7)(C)(ii)(I).

[88]   19 U.S.C. § 1677(7)(C)(ii)(II).

[89]   Price suppression arises when the domestic industry can affect smaller price increases on those articles directly competitive with dumped imports than it can on those articles that directly compete with non-dumped imports.

[90]   Price cutting arises when the domestic industry is compelled to lower its prices to meet the prices of dumped imports in an attempt to protect its market share.

consideration in the ITC's injury analysis. Because of this, the Tariff Act provides supplemental factors for the ITC to consider. These include (1) actual and potential decline in "output, sales, market share, profits, productivity, return on investments, and utilization of capacity," (2) impact on domestic prices, (3) actual and potential "negative effects on cash flow, inventories, employment, wages, growth, ability to raise capital, and investment," (4) actual and potential negative effects "on the existing development and production efforts of the domestic industry," and (5) in specific cases, the magnitude of the margin of dumping.[91]

The ITC must evaluate all these relevant economic factors within the context of the business cycle and conditions of competition in the affected industry.[92] But the ITC traditionally relies primarily on two of the factors in making this determination. First, the industry must be in a distressed or a stagnant condition. Second, the low domestic price levels must be a factor in the industry's difficulties (*e.g.*, high unemployment or low capacity utilization rate), and these low prices must be having a serious negative effect on profits.

The ITC will often base an affirmative determination of material injury on severe downward trends in profitability among domestic producers. In one early case, the ITC found that a drop in the ratio of net profit to sales from 5.55 percent to 1.05 percent over a three year period, coupled with a seventy-five percent decline in the aggregate profit in the relevant industry in the same period, justified an affirmative determination of material injury.[93] Thus, it is not necessary that an industry suffer an actual loss as a prerequisite to a finding of material injury. On the other hand, simply because an industry is experiencing a decline in profitability does not require a finding of material injury due to dumping.[94] Other factors unrelated to dumping, such as general economic conditions and industry overexpansion, may be the cause.

The effect of dumped imports on employment in the relevant domestic industry often is a significant factor. Employment data are not dispositive, because decreases in the level or rate of employment may be due to a broad spectrum of economic factors unrelated to dumping. (The economic downturn since 2008 provides ample proof of this point.) Nonetheless, sudden changes in domestic employment

---

[91]   19 U.S.C. § 1677(7)(C)(iii).

[92]   19 U.S.C. § 1677(7)(C), last paragraph.

[93]   Sugars and Syrups from Canada, 46 Fed. Reg. 51,086–01 (1981).

[94]   *See* GEO Specialty Chems. Inc. v. United States, 2009 WL 424468 (C.I.T. 2009) (upholding an ITC determination that imports of glycine did not cause a material injury because the declining profits were the fault of the domestic industry).

during the period of dumping can be an important signal for the ITC that dumping is causing a material injury. For example, in one early case the ITC found that a thirty-five percent drop in employment during the period of dumping was a reasonable indication of material injury.[95] On the other hand, an increase in employment levels and hours worked can be a strong indication that dumping did not cause a material injury to the relevant industry.

Finally, the utilization of plant capacity can be a significant factor in material injury determinations. Again, however, such capacity utilization data commonly is affected by a variety of factors. For example, the ITC found a reasonable indication of material injury from the fact that capacity utilization in the affected industry fell from eighty-eight percent to seventy-seven percent in two years.[96] In contrast, the ITC found no material injury in a case where capacity utilization similarly dropped from eighty-five to seventy-seven percent, because in that instance frequent equipment breakdowns and quality control disruptions were the actual cause of the decline.[97]

§ 12.15   Injury Determination__Threat of Material Injury

The ITC may also make an affirmative determination of injury if it finds that dumped imports represent a "threat of material injury" to a domestic industry. The Tariff Act lists a variety of "economic factors" that the ITC "shall consider" in making such a determination in an antidumping proceeding:

(1) any "unused production capacity or imminent, substantial increase in production capacity in the exporting country . . . indicating the likelihood of substantially increased imports" into the United States;

(2) "a significant rate of increase of the volume or market penetration of imports . . . indicating the likelihood of substantially increased imports";

(3) whether imports are coming to the United States "at prices that are likely to have a significant depressing or suppressing effect on domestic prices, and are likely to increase demand for further imports";

(4) the existing inventories of the imported products;

---

95   Montan Wax from East Germany, 45 Fed. Reg. 73,821–02 (1980).

96   Carbon Steel Wire Rod from Brazil, Belgium, France, and Venezuela, 47 Fed. Reg. 13,927–01 (1982).

97   Crystal from Italy and Austria, 45 Fed. Reg. 31,830–03 (1980).

(5) the potential that the low prices for the imports will cause other production facilities in the foreign country to switch to the products at issue; and

(6) "the actual and potential negative effects on the existing development and production efforts" of the industry in the United States.[98]

Beyond these, the Tariff Act requires the ITC to consider "any other demonstrable adverse trends that indicate the probability" of a material injury to a domestic industry.[99]

The Tariff Act obligates the ITC to consider these factors "as a whole" in making a determination of a threat of material injury. Therefore, the presence or absence of any one factor is not determinative. In any event, the determination "may not be made on the basis of mere conjecture or supposition."[100]

The case of *Rhone Poulenc, S.A. v. United States* represents a good example of the analysis of the *threat* of material injury standard.[101] That case involved the shipment of package anhydrous sodium metasilicate from France to the United States. The U.S. industry comprised four companies, only one of which was demonstrably injured. *Rhone Poulenc* was an appeal to the U.S. Court of International Trade (CIT) from an ITC decision concerning the "threat of material injury" standard. The court first rejected the importers' argument that the extent of market penetration by imports is the crucial factor in determining whether such a threat exists. Instead, the court found that it is proper for the ITC to consider, in determining the likelihood of future injury, the developing trends in the indicators used to determine whether an actual injury has occurred. These indicators of actual injury include the volume of imports, the effect of imports on prices, and the impact of the imports on the domestic industry. The court also held that the ITC also may look at likely future conduct of the producers or exporters of the dumped products.

§ 12.16 Injury Determination__Material Retardation

The Tariff Act recognizes as an independent ground for an affirmative injury determination by the ITC that a dumped import product has "materially retarded" the establishment of an industry in the United States. The standard for "material retardation" is

---

[98] 19 U.S.C. § 1677(7)(F)(i).

[99] *Id.*

[100] 19 U.S.C. § 1677(7)(F)(ii).

[101] 592 F. Supp. 1318 (C.I.T. 1984).

applied to new industries, *i.e.*, those that have made a substantial commitment to begin production, or have recently begun production.[102] As the ITA notes in its Antidumping Manual, however, this ground "has rarely been asserted by a petitioner in an antidumping duty investigation. Nearly all antidumping investigations have been initiated on the basis of petitions by established manufacturers of the domestic like product."[103]

§ 12.17 Causation

Causation of material injury by dumping is a required element in addition to, and independent of, the finding of material injury, threat of material injury or the material retardation of the establishment of a domestic industry. As a practical matter, however, the two separate inquiries (injury and causation) are closely linked. As a result, when it has found a material injury from a dumping practice the ITC has tended to make an affirmative injury determination without a lengthy analysis of the causal link between them. In a negative injury determination, on the other hand, the ITC may engage in a rather detailed analysis of causation.

The Tariff Act requires a simple causation element: that the material injury to a domestic industry is "by reason of" the dumped imports.[104] (Again, the same standard applies in CVD proceedings and the law in this area is largely interchangeable.[105]) The causation requirement is not a high one. Imports need only be *a* cause of material injury, and need not be the most substantial or primary cause of injury suffered by domestic industry.[106] The "by reason of" standard nonetheless "mandates a showing of causal— not merely temporal—connection between the LTFV goods and the material injury."[107] The Tariff Act does not require that the ITC use any particular methodology in making such a determination, and it "need not isolate the injury caused by other factors from injury caused by unfair imports."[108] Nonetheless, the Federal Circuit has made clear that "causation is not shown if the subject imports

---

[102] For a rare analysis of this standard see BMT Commodity Corp. v. United States, 667 F. Supp. 880 (C.I.T. 1987), *affirmed* 852 F.2d 1285 (Fed. Cir. 1988).

[103] Antidumping Manual, *supra* footnote 8, Ch. 18, I, § III.D.

[104] 19 U.S.C. § 1673(2).

[105] *See* Chapter 13, Section 13.18.

[106] *See* Nippon Steel Corp. v. U.S. Int'l Trade Comm'n, 345 F.3d 1379, 1381 (Fed. Cir. 2003) (observing that " 'dumping' need not be the sole or principal cause of injury").

[107] Gerald Metals, Inc. v. United States, 132 F.3d 716, 720 (Fed. Cir. 1997).

[108] Bratsk Aluminium Smelter v. United States, 444 F.3d 1369, 1373 (Fed. Cir. 2006) (*quoting* Taiwan Semiconductors Industry Ass'n v. U.S. Int'l Trade Comm'n, 266 F.3d 1339, 1345 (Fed. Cir. 2001)).

contributed only 'minimally or tangentially to the material harm.' "[109]

In short, the causation element of an affirmative injury determination can be satisfied if the dumped products contribute in any noteworthy way to the conditions of the domestic injury.[110] Under this "contributing cause" standard, causation of injuries may be found despite the absence of correlation between dumped imports and the alleged injuries if there is substantial evidence that the volume of dumped imports was a contributing factor to the price depression experienced by the domestic injury.

In examining the causal link between the dumped imports and the material injury, the ITC must consider other causal factors that might be responsible for the alleged injury. The Federal Circuit has observed that, for example, "the increase in volume of subject imports priced below domestic products and the decline in the domestic market share are not in and of themselves sufficient to establish causation."[111] On this reasoning, the Federal Circuit has held that the ITC must consider "fairly traded imports" of non-dumped products as a relevant "other economic factor" for causation inquiries.[112] Thus, the ITC may uncover other major causes for the problems of the domestic industry. These may include huge unnecessary expenses, chronic excess capacity, inefficiency, poor quality, price sensitivity or increased domestic competition. Nonetheless, the presence of such major alternative causes of injury does not foreclose the possibility that imports have been *a* contributing cause of the industry's problems.[113]

The ITC may, but is not required to, consider the margin of dumping when evaluating causation. In practice the margin of dumping is an important factor in the ITC's causation analysis. If the dumping margin is slight or substantially lower than the margin of underselling, this may indicate that the injury was not caused by the dumped imports. The imports will still be able to

---

[109] *Id.*, 444 F.3d at 1373 (*quoting* Gerald Metals, Inc. v. United States, 132 F.3d 716, 722 (Fed. Cir. 1997)).

[110] Antidumping Manual, *supra* footnote 8, Ch. 18, I, § III.F (observing that: "[t]he courts have held that this causation standard is satisfied if the dumped imports contribute, more than minimally or tangentially, to the injured condition of the domestic industry").

[111] *See* Bratsk Aluminium Smelter v. United States., 444 F.3d 1369, 1374 (Fed. Cir. 2006).

[112] *See, e.g.,* Gerald Metals, Inc. v. United States, 132 F.3d 716, 723 (Fed. Cir. 1997).

[113] *See, e.g.,* Iwatsu Electric Co., Ltd. v. United States, 758 F. Supp. 1506 (C.I.T. 1991) (regarding small telephone systems); United Engineering & Forging v. United States, 779 F. Supp. 1375 (C.I.T. 1991), *opinion after remand* 14 ITRD 1748 (C.I.T. 1992) (regarding crankshafts).

undersell domestic producers, even if the prices of the imports are raised to their fair values. If, on the other hand, the dumping margin is higher than the margin of underselling, thereby enabling the foreign exporters to undersell domestic producers, the dumping can be the cause of the material injury because the foreign exporters may be able to undersell only because of the higher dumping margin.

§ 12.18 Cumulative Causation

Can "material injury" be caused by imports from exporters from more than one country through the cumulative effect of many small injuries? There are arguments against cumulating the sources of dumping to determine whether they collectively are a cause of material injury. For example, cumulation could penalize small suppliers who would not have caused injury if their dumping had been examined in isolation. Nevertheless, the WTO Antidumping Agreement expressly permits cumulation.[114]

In turn, the Tariff Act requires that the ITC cumulatively assess the impact of reasonably coincident dumped imports from two or more countries if the imports compete with like U.S. products. In specific, the Act requires the ITC to "cumulatively assess the volume and price effects of imports of the subject merchandise from all countries" with respect to which antidumping petitions were initiated on the same day, "if such imports compete with each other and with domestic like products in the United States market."[115] (An exception exists, however, for imports from beneficiary countries of the Caribbean Basin Initiative.[116]) The injury to a domestic industry is measured by the cumulated results of dumping on the ground that an injury caused by the collective effect of "many nibbles" is just as harmful as one caused by "one large bite." Cumulation also provides administrative ease, since the ITC is not required to allocate the amount of injury caused by each individual exporter.

The CIT has observed that to support a cumulation decision, the ITC "must find a reasonable overlap of competition between imports from the subject countries and the domestic like product."[117] In applying this "reasonable overlap" test, the ITC traditionally has applied a "four factor" test: "(1) fungibility; (2)

---

[114]   See Antidumping Agreement, art. 3.3.

[115]   19 U.S.C. § 1677(7)(G)(i). See also Hosiden Corp. v. Advanced Display Mfrs. of America, 85 F.3d 1561 (Fed. Cir. 1996).

[116]   19 U.S.C. § 1677(7)(G)(ii)(III).

[117]   Nucor Corp. v. United States, 594 F. Supp. 2d 1320, 1347 (C.I.T. 2008) (quoting Noviant OY v. United States, 451 F. Supp. 2d 1367, 1379 (C.I.T. 2006)), aff'd, 601 F.3d 1291 (Fed. Cir. 2010).

sales or offers in the same geographic markets; (3) common or similar channels of distribution; and (4) simultaneous presence."[118]

§ 12.19 Negligible Dumping

The Tariff Act requires that an investigation be terminated with a negative injury determination if imports of the subject merchandise are negligible. The Act defines imports as "negligible" if they "account for less than three percent of the volume of all such merchandise imported into the United States" during a defined twelve-month period."[119] In the case of cumulated imports from a number of countries,[120] however, the "negligible" threshold rises to seven percent.[121] In computing import volumes for these purposes, the ITC "may make reasonable estimates on the basis of available statistics."[122]

§ 12.20 Specific Issues in the U.S. Implementation of the WTO Antidumping Agreement

As noted above, Congress approved and implemented the Uruguay Round accords of 1994 under the Uruguay Round Agreements Act (URAA).[123] For present purposes, the most significant aspect of the URAA was the amendment of the Tariff Act to conform to the WTO Antidumping Agreement. In nearly all respects, therefore, the important rules on dumping determinations as described in the Sections above conform to the requirements of the Antidumping Agreement. Nonetheless, the URAA brought about a few more specific changes that are worthy of emphasis here.

De Minimis Dumping. First, the URAA amended the Tariff Act to address "*de minimis*" dumping.[124] In specific, the Tariff Act now requires that, in making its preliminary determination, the administrating authority (the Secretary of Commerce/ITA) disregard any weighted average dumping margin less than two percent ad valorem or the equivalent specific rate for the subject merchandise. Any weighted average dumping margin that is *de minimis* must also be disregarded by the administrating authority when making its final determinations.[125]

---

[118] Nucor Corp. v. United States, 594 F. Supp. 2d 1320, 1347 (C.I.T. 2008).

[119] 19 U.S.C. § 1677(24)(A)(i).

[120] *See* Section 12.18 *supra.*

[121] 19 U.S.C. § 1677(24)(A)(ii).

[122] 19 U.S.C. § 1677(24)(C).

[123] Public Law No. 103–465, 108 Stat. 4809.

[124] 19 U.S.C. § 1673b(b)(3).

[125] 19 U.S.C. § 1673d(a)(4).

Statutory Time Limits. A significant new effect from the adoption of the URAA is the imposition of strict new statutory timelines for dumping determinations by the ITA. In the case of an antidumping petition, the ITA must make an initial determination within twenty days after the date on which a petition is filed. This time limit may be extended to forty days if the ITA is required to poll or otherwise determine support for the petition by the industry and exceptional circumstances exist.[126] Time limits are also imposed on the ITC in its determination of whether there is a reasonable indication of injury.[127] Separately, the ITC must conduct a review no later than five years after an antidumping duty order is issued to determine whether revoking the order would likely lead to continuation or recurrence of dumping and material injury. Known as the "sunset provision," this new requirement has resulted in periodic reviews of antidumping orders.[128]

Notice and Comment. The URAA requires that the ITC provide all parties to a proceeding with an opportunity to comment, prior to a formal decision, on *all* information collected in the investigation.

Other Issues. The URAA requires the ITC to consider the magnitude of the dumping margin (although not the magnitude of the margin of subsidization) in making material injury determinations. It also authorizes an adjustment to sales-below-cost calculations to accommodate start-up costs,[129] a new rule thought to be particularly beneficial to high-tech products. It also adds a new "captive production" section intended to remove such internal sales from ITC injury determinations.[130]

§ 12.21 WTO Dispute Resolution and U.S. Antidumping Actions

The WTO Appellate Body (AB) has taken a restrictive view of what constitutes permissible antidumping duties and in fact has repeatedly ruled against the United States in disputes with other countries. In the *Thai-Steel from Poland* dispute, for example, the WTO rejected a cursory material injury determination by the ITC, stressing that all relevant economic factors must be considered. Similarly, in the *United States-Hot-Rolled Steel from Japan* dispute, the AB found bias in the determination of normal value when low-priced sales from a respondent to an exporter were automatically excluded. The AB also indicated that injury determinations must

---

126   19 U.S.C. § 1673a(c).

127   19 U.S.C. § 1673b(a).

128   19 U.S.C. § 1675(c).

129   19 U.S.C. § 1677b(f)(1)(c).

130   19 U.S.C. § 1677b(f)(1)(c)(iii).

include an analysis of captive production markets in addition to merchant markets. It thus observed that causation in such determinations must be rigorously scrutinized.

Separately, a WTO panel ruled that the Commerce Department's refusal to revoke an antidumping order against South Korean DRAMS was inconsistent with Article 11.2 of the Antidumping Agreement. Hence, U.S. regulations regarding the likelihood of continued dumping after a three-year hiatus are suspect under the Antidumping Agreement. The Court of International Trade, on the other hand, has found that the U.S. regulations in question are consistent with the WTO Antidumping Agreement. The Court took the position that the WTO panel ruling was not binding precedent, merely persuasive.

The Zeroing Controversy. In a series of decisions that ran through 2011, the WTO's Appellate Body also repeatedly ruled against "zeroing," a methodology used in dumping margin calculations by the United States and other countries. To understand this practice, first note that a foreign producer likely will have numerous sales in its home country. As a result, in order to calculate the "home market price," the ITA must use the *average* price from all such sales.[131] This average price is then compared to the "export price" to yield the dumping margin. Under zeroing, however, the ITA in effect considered only those home market sales that were *above* the export price; for sales *below* the export price, it simply assigned a "zero" (*i.e.*, not a negative number). Because on average this meant a higher home country comparison price, it also resulted in a higher average dumping margin.

In a series of decisions, WTO panels declared that this practice violates the United States' obligations under the Article 2.4 of the Antidumping Agreement.[132] Notwithstanding these decisions, the Federal Circuit repeatedly upheld the methodology as a reasonable interpretation of the actual language in the Tariff Act.[133] In response to the repeated adverse rulings by the WTO, however, the ITA has limited the practice of zeroing in antidumping investigations.[134]

---

[131]   *See* 19 U.S.C. § 1677(35).

[132]   *See, e.g.,* Appellate Body Report, *United States—Laws, Regulations and Methodology for Calculating Dumping Margins ("Zeroing"),* ¶ 222, WT/DS294/AB/R, adopted May 9, 2006.

[133]   *See, e.g.,* Corus Staal BV v. U.S. Dep't of Commerce, 395 F.3d 1343 (Fed. Cir. 2005).

[134]   *See* Antidumping Proceedings: Calculation of the Weighted Average Dumping Margin and Assessment Rate in Certain Antidumping Proceedings, 75 Fed. Reg. 81533 (Dep't Commerce Dec. 28, 2010).

The "Byrd Amendment" Controversy. The WTO Appellate Body also ruled against the United States with respect to the Continued Dumping and Subsidy Offset Act of 2000 (CDSOA, also known as the "Byrd Amendment"). The controversial aspect of that Act was a mechanism under which the U.S. government funneled the antidumping duties it collected back to the members of the affected domestic industry. As a result, CDSOA in effect subsidized domestic industries through antidumping procedures, because it made those industries the financial beneficiaries of any duties ultimately assessed.

Nine other member states of the WTO promptly challenged CDSOA pursuant to the procedures set forth in the WTO's Dispute Settlement Understanding (DSU). Following unsuccessful negotiations, a WTO panel concluded that CDSOA was inconsistent with Articles 5.4, 18.1, and 18.4 of the antidumping Agreement (as well as various provisions of other WTO Agreements). The United States then appealed to the WTO's AB. In its report, the AB first observed that CDSOA was subject to the obligations in the Antidumping Agreement because it was a "specific action against" dumping. It also found that the only permitted responses to dumping under the Antidumping Agreement are "definitive antidumping duties, provisional measures and price undertakings." The AB ultimately concluded that, because CDSOA did not fall into any of these allowed responses to dumping, it was inconsistent with the United States' obligations under the Antidumping Agreement.[135]

When the United State failed to comply with this decision, the WTO authorized the claimant countries to retaliate in their domestic trade laws as permitted under Article 22 of the DSU.[136] Congress then bowed to the pressure created by the WTO decisions and repealed CDSOA effective October 1, 2007.

§ 12.22   AD Procedures__Petition and Response

In an antidumping proceeding, the ITA determines whether the imports are being sold at less than fair value (LTFV), and the ITC makes a separate determination concerning injury to the domestic industry making like or similar products.

United States antidumping proceedings may be initiated by a petition of the Commerce Department itself or by a union or

---

[135]   *See* Appellate Body Report, *United States—Continued Dumping and Subsidy Offset Act of 2000*, WT/DS217/R, WT/DS234/R, Jan. 16, 2003.

[136]   *See, e.g.,* United States—Continued Dumping and Subsidy Offset Act of 2000, Original Complaint by Canada—Recourse to Arbitration by the United States under Article 22.6 of the DSU, WT/DS234/ARB/CAN, 31 August 2004.

aggrieved business (or by a group association of aggrieved workers or businesses).[137] The petition requirements are set forth by regulation.[138] In general, antidumping proceedings involve the ITA first making a determination that a petition adequately alleges the relevant statutory requirements. But before initiating an investigation, the ITA must find that a sufficient percentage of the affected domestic industry supports the petition—for the Tariff Act requires that a petition be filed "by or on behalf of" the entire domestic industry.[139] Generally, this requires that the industry or workers who support the petition account for (a) at least twenty-five percent of the total industry, and (b) more than fifty percent of those that have actually expressed an opinion for or against the petition.[140]

After an initial review, the ITA makes a determination—"on the basis of information readily available to it"—on whether the petition (a) alleges the elements necessary for the imposition of an antidumping duty and "contains information reasonably available to the petitioner supporting the allegations," and (b) has been filed "by or on behalf of the industry."[141] This inquiry cannot include any information furnished by respondents or a respondent's government. In other words, the ITA accepts or rejects the petition almost entirely on the basis of the information supplied by the petitioner.

Once the petition is accepted, the proceeding becomes genuinely adversarial if (as is commonly the case) the parties alleged to be dumping respond to the questionnaires on sales volumes and prices that the ITA creates and later verifies through on-site investigations. It is rare for the "defense" to have more than one month to respond. Any failure to respond or permit verification risks an ITA dumping decision on the "best information available" (see Section 12.23 immediately below), i.e. most likely the petitioner's or other respondent's submissions.[142] Because this obviously is an undesirable result, the best information available rule functions much like a subpoena. Most respondents answer the ITA's questionnaires. Protective orders preserve the confidentiality of the often strategically valuable information submitted to the ITA and ITC in dumping proceedings.[143] Such orders ordinarily preclude

---

[137]   19 U.S.C. § 1673a.

[138]   *See* 19 C.F.R. § 351.202.

[139]   19 U.S.C. § 1673a(b), (c)(4).

[140]   19 U.S.C. § 1673a(c)(4).

[141]   19 U.S.C. § 1673a(c).

[142]   *See* 19 U.S.C. § 1677e(b).

[143]   19 U.S.C. § 1677f.

release to corporate counsel engaged in competitive decision-making, but permit release to outside counsel and outside experts.

§ 12.23 AD Procedures__Administrative Determinations

Antidumping proceedings under U.S. law involve four stages. The ITC first makes a "preliminary determination," based on "the information available to it at that time," on whether there is "a reasonable indication" that the challenged practice presents a real or threatened material injury to the affected domestic industry.[144] If the ITC makes such a finding, the ITA then makes a preliminary determination, again based on the best "information available to it at that time," on whether there is "a reasonable basis to believe" that goods are being sold at LTFV.[145] If the ITA makes such a preliminary determination, it proceeds to make a "final determination" concerning sales at LTFV.[146] If the ITA finds sales at LTFV as a final determination, the ITC then must make a final determination concerning injury.[147] Thus the chain of decision-making in antidumping proceedings runs as follows:

ITC Preliminary Injury Determination

ITA Preliminary Dumping Determination

ITA Final Dumping Determination

ITC Final Injury Determination

Congress has repeatedly amended U.S. antidumping law so as to accelerate the rate at which these determinations are made. At this point, it is common for the proceeding to be completed within one year. U.S. antidumping duties are then and in the future assessed retrospectively for each importation such that the amount payable varies for each importer and transaction.

Any goods imported after an ITA preliminary determination of sales at LTFV (Stage Two) will be subject to any antidumping duties imposed later, after final determinations are made.[148] In customs law parlance, liquidation of the goods is suspended. In "critical circumstances," the antidumping duties will also be imposed on goods entered ninety days *before* suspension of liquidation.[149] Critical circumstances exist when there is a prior

---

144   19 U.S.C. § 1673b(a).

145   19 U.S.C. § 1673b(b).

146   19 U.S.C. § 1673d(a).

147   19 U.S.C. § 1673d(b).

148   19 U.S.C. § 1673b(d).

149   19 U.S.C. § 1673b(e).

history of dumping or the importer knew or should have known that the sales were below fair value, and there have been massive imports over a relatively short period of time.[150] Because the ITA has demonstrated a willingness to order retroactive antidumping duties and need not find injury as a result of the massive imports, the importer's risks in such a case may be substantial.

§ 12.24　AD Procedures__The Importance of the ITA Preliminary Dumping Determination

As a practical matter, the ITA's *preliminary* determination that dumping has occurred will place significant, often overwhelming, pressure on the importers of the covered goods. This is so because at that point any covered goods become subject to antidumping duties that are ultimately determined once the ITA and ITC complete their investigations and make any affirmative final determinations. The preliminary determination, therefore, tends to discourage or even cut off the imports, because at that point importers generally must post cash or bonds to cover any duties as determined by the ITA in its preliminary determination. At a minimum, they likely will have to raise their import prices—unless and until either the ITA or the ITC makes a contrary final determination once the agencies have completed their respective administrative proceedings.

Thus, once a petition is filed, importers will not know what their liabilities for duties will be and must post an expensive bond in the meantime to gain entry. Foreign exporters frequently raise their "United States prices" to the level of home market prices soon after such a preliminary determination. If they do, antidumping law will have accomplished its essential purpose. However, the WTO GATT Antidumping Agreement and the U.S. Tariff Act disfavor termination of the proceeding on the basis of voluntary undertakings of compliance.[151]

United States antidumping proceedings may be settled by the ITA if the respondents formally agree to cease exporting to the United States within six months or agree to revise their prices so as to eliminate the margin of the dumping.[152] Because price revision agreements are hard to monitor, they are disfavored by the ITA. But an agreement to cease exports also cancels any outstanding suspension of liquidation. The total time secured in this manner may allow foreigners a window of opportunity to establish market presence prior to shifting production to the United States. If requested, the ITA and ITC may proceed to their final

---

[150]　19 U.S.C. § 1673b(e)(1).

[151]　19 U.S.C. § 1673c.

[152]　19 U.S.C. § 1673c(b).

determinations after a settlement is agreed. If the respondents prevail, normal trading will resume; but if the petitioners prevail, the settlement agreement will remain in effect. The ITA monitors all settlement agreements and may assess civil penalties (in addition to antidumping duties) in the event of a breach.[153]

§ 12.25 Antidumping Duties and Reviews

The ITA's final determination of sales at LTFV establishes the amount of any antidumping duties. Because duties are not imposed to support any specific domestic price, they are set at the "margin of dumping" (the amount the "normal value" exceeds the United States price).[154] In the ordinary case, antidumping duties are retroactive to the date of the suspension of liquidation that occurred when the ITA made its preliminarily determination on dumping. However, if the ITC's final determination is one of threatened (not actual) domestic injury, the duties usually apply as from the ITC's final decision and not retroactively to the suspension date. The antidumping duty remains in force only as long as the dumping occurs. Upon request, annual ITA reviews are conducted.[155] The ITA also may review and revoke or modify any antidumping order if changed circumstances warrant such an action, but the burden of proof is on the proponent.[156] As noted above, in accordance with the WTO Antidumping Agreement the ITA must also conduct a review of final antidumping determinations every five years.[157]

Problems in assessing and collecting antidumping duties may arise because the antidumping duty order applies to goods that do not exactly correspond to normal U.S. Harmonized Tariff Schedule (HTS) classifications. While the ITA is given some leeway to modify an antidumping order to accommodate such problems, it may not use them as an excuse to exclude merchandise falling within the scope of the order. Where, on the other hand, merchandise is deliberately excluded from an original antidumping order, the ITA may not subsequently include that merchandise in an anticircumvention order (see Section 12.26 immediately below).[158]

---

[153] 19 U.S.C. § 1673c(i).

[154] 19 U.S.C. § 1677(35).

[155] 19 U.S.C. § 1675(a).

[156] 19 U.S.C. § 1675(b).

[157] 19 U.S.C. § 1675(c).

[158] *See, e.g.*, Wheatland Tube Co. v. United States, 161 F.3d 1365 (Fed. Cir. 1998).

§ 12.26   Anticircumvention

In 1988, Congress enacted important amendments to the Tariff Act to address the "circumvention" of antidumping duties. These "anticircumvention" rules entered into force while the subject was under discussion in the GATT Uruguay Round negotiations. Ultimately, the WTO Antidumping Agreement included no substantive rules on anticircumvention, but also did not forbid the practice.

The Tariff Act addresses circumvention in a variety of ways. First, it allows the ITA to ignore fictitious markets in the source country—a form of advance circumvention—when calculating the foreign market "normal value."[159] In addition, the ITA may include within the scope of an antidumping order merchandise "completed or assembled" in the United States if such merchandise includes "parts or components produced in the foreign country" that is the original subject of the order.[160] The principal requirements are that the process of completion or assembly in the United States is "minor or insignificant" and the value of the components themselves is a "significant portion of the total value of the merchandise."[161] Similarly, when the exporter ships the components to a third country for assembly and subsequent exportation to the United States, such circumvention efforts can be defeated by extending an antidumping order to those goods as well.[162] Again, such an action is appropriate if the assembly in the third country is "minor or insignificant" and the components themselves represent the principal value of the merchandise.[163]

§ 12.27   Appeals to United States Courts

The U.S. Court of International Trade. A party to an administrative antidumping proceeding may appeal an adverse final determination of the ITA or ITC to the U.S. Court of International Trade (CIT). The CIT was established in 1980 as the successor to the U.S. Court of Customs. The CIT is an Article III court, and its nine judges are appointed by the President with the advice and consent of the Senate. The CIT possesses all the powers in law and equity of a U.S. District Court, including the authority to enter money judgments against the United States, but with three general limitations. These limitations (a) prohibit its issuance of injunctions or writs of mandamus in challenges to trade adjustment

---

[159]   19 U.S.C. § 1677b(a)(2).

[160]   19 U.S.C. § 1677j(a).

[161]   19 U.S.C. § 1677j(a)(2).

[162]   19 U.S.C. § 1677j(b).

[163]   *Id.*

rulings, (b) allow it to issue only declaratory relief in suits for accelerated review of pre-importation administrative actions, and (c) limit its power to order disclosure of confidential information to a narrowly defined class of cases.

The CIT has "exclusive" subject matter jurisdiction over suits against the United States, its agencies, or its officers arising from any law pertaining to revenue from imports, tariffs, duties or embargoes, or the enforcement of such laws and certain related regulations. The court's exclusive jurisdiction also includes any civil action commenced by the United States that arises out of an import transaction, the authority to review final agency decisions concerning antidumping duties and countervailing duties, and a review of eligibility determinations for trade adjustment assistance.

Further Appeals. CIT decisions may be appealed first to the Court of Appeals for the Federal Circuit (formerly the Court of Customs and Patent Appeals), and ultimately to the U.S. Supreme Court.

§ 12.28 Appeals to International Tribunals (WTO and NAFTA)

International institutions also play an increasingly significant role in the resolution of trade disputes. The most important of these is the WTO's Dispute Settlement Body ("DSB"). Dissatisfied parties in domestic administrative proceedings may convince their government to challenge an adverse antidumping ruling before the DSB based on alleged violations of the WTO Antidumping Agreement. As Chapter 9 examines in detail, proceedings before the DSB are governed by a separate WTO Agreement, the Dispute Settlement Understanding (DSU). The DSU generally provides that the involved member states first must pursue consultations. If those consultations are not successful, either party may request that the DSB establish a panel to investigate the dispute and issue a written report. Panel decisions are appealable on issues of law to the WTO's Appellate Body.

Three points are worthy of emphasis concerning proceedings before the DSB. First, since the WTO came into being in 1994 dispute settlement before the DSB, once initiated, is compulsory and binding. Second, this dispute settlement option is not open to private litigants, for only WTO member state governments may file an action before the DSB. Finally, although formally binding, the WTO has no direct power to compel compliance with its decisions. Nonetheless, it may order compensation for the aggrieved state(s) or authorize retaliatory trade sanctions, and these may provide a significant incentive for an offending state to bring its domestic law into compliance.

Separately, a special international institution exists for trade disputes involving the three member states of the North American Free Trade Agreement (NAFTA)—the United States, Canada, and Mexico. NAFTA uniquely provides for resolution of antidumping disputes through "binational panels." Such panels apply the domestic law of the importing country, and provide a substitute for judicial review of the decisions of administrative agencies of the importing country. Indeed, the initiation of a review under NAFTA divests the CIT of jurisdiction over the same dispute. Although the decisions of such binational panels are not formally binding in U.S. law, the ITA or ITC may decide to review any administrative action to conform to an adverse panel decision, including through a revocation or reduction of antidumping duties.

Chapter 13

SUBSIDIES AND COUNTERVAILING DUTIES

Table of Sections

---

§ 13.1 Subsidies and International Trade

A member state of the World Trade Organization (WTO) may impose an increased tariff on an imported item beyond the regular tariff schedule as a "countervailing duty." Such duties are based not on a foreign exporter selling goods at less than fair value, but rather on a foreign government providing "subsidies" that support production for exportation and thus permit the exporter to sell at lower prices in other countries. Subsidies come in many forms, including, among others, tax reductions or rebates; tax credits; loan guarantees; subsidized financing; equity infusions; and outright grants. Rapidly developing countries also routinely offer to give some form of subsidy for initial foreign investments designed to produce exports. But subsidies are not only a phenomenon for developing countries. In the United States, for example the Export-Import Bank (EXIMBANK)—the financing for which Congress extended and expanded in 2012—offers low cost loans to overseas buyers of products exported from the United States. Other developed countries have similar programs.

In theory, a countervailing duty offsets exactly the unfair subsidy. Proponents of countervailing duties argue that they are necessary to keep imports from being unfairly competitive based on foreign government support. Opponents of countervailing duties argue that there is no coherent standard of "fairness" to justify a rational assessment of such duties. They point out that, absent a predatory motive by a foreign government, there is no more reason to justify government action to protect a domestic producer disadvantaged by foreign competition than one disadvantaged by domestic competition. The result in each case is that the domestic resources used by the disadvantaged producer are shifted to their next highest value use and, viewing the world market as a unit, production efficiency worldwide is increased thereby. Opponents of countervailing duties also point out that it is often difficult to identify precisely when a subsidy exists as compared with general governmental actions to support beneficial commercial activity.

Countervailing duties (CVDs) complement the antidumping duties (ADs) examined in Chapter 12 above. These alternatives recognize that unfair international trade practices can arise either through practices of producers or exporters, or through unfair practices of foreign governments. The former are subject to AD law; the latter are subject to CVD law. The two can be equally harmful to domestic industries, and such domestic interests thus often simultaneously pursue both trade remedies.

§ 13.2 The WTO Agreement on Subsidies and Countervailing Measures (1994)

International concern with unfair subsidies and countervailing duties is reflected in Articles VI, XVI, and XXIII of the General

Agreement on Tariffs and Trade (GATT) and in the more specific 1994 WTO "Agreement on Subsidies and Countervailing Measures" (SCM Agreement). Like the Antidumping Agreement, Congress approved and implemented the SCM Agreement through the Uruguay Round Agreements Act of 1994 (URAA).[1]

Under the SCM Agreement, government authorities in an importing member state may impose a CVD in the amount of the subsidy for as long as the subsidy continues. The SCM Agreement also provides substantive rules governing when, and under what circumstances, a member state may impose CVDs to offset a claimed subsidy. The CVD may only be imposed after an investigation, begun on the request of an affected industry, has "demonstrated" the existence of (1) a subsidy; (2) that has adverse trade effects, such as injury to a domestic industry; and (3) a causal link between the subsidy and the alleged injury.

The SCM Agreement attempts to shift the focus of subsidy rules from a national forum, as was the exclusive case under the GATT, to the multinational forum provided by the WTO. As a result, disputes over subsidies may occur either before national administrative authorities (according to prescribed procedures) or before the WTO's Dispute Settlement Body (or both).[2] In addition, a special WTO "Committee on Subsidies and Countervailing Measures" supervises the implementation of the SCM Agreement by the WTO member states.

The SCM Agreement generally defines a subsidy as a financial contribution provided by a government that confers a benefit on an exporter. The Agreement initially established three classes of subsidies: (1) prohibited subsidies (also known as "red light" subsidies); (2) actionable subsidies, *i.e.*, those that are permissible unless they cause adverse trade effects ("yellow light" subsidies); and (3) non-actionable and non-countervailable subsidies ("green light" subsidies). Under the terms of the SCM Agreement, however, the "green light" category expired in 2000. The SCM Agreement also granted special exemptions for developing countries that permitted them to phase out their export subsidies and local content rules on a gradual basis. These exemptions were to have expired by 2003, but as of 2017, eighteen countries—principally in the Caribbean and Central America—continue to operate under an extension of this deadline granted by the WTO's Committee on Subsidies and Countervailing Measures.

---

1   Public Law No. 103–465, 108 Stat. 4809.
2   *See* Sections 13.20 and 13.25 *infra*.

The SCM Agreement also prescribes procedural rules for the investigation and imposition of CVDs by domestic authorities. These rules address, among other things, the initiation of CVD proceedings, the conduct of investigations, the calculation of the amount of the subsidy, and the right of all interested parties to present information. The Agreement also has special rules relating to subsidies that cause a "serious prejudice" to the interests of another member state (although most of these rules have lapsed). Finally, the SCM Agreement has rules on the gathering of evidence in CVD proceedings, on the imposition and collection of CVDs, on provisional measures, and on the permitted length of any allowed CVDs (typically five years).

§ 13.3   Historical Introduction to U.S. CVD Law

United States law has long considered the grant of a subsidy by a foreign government to aid its exporters to be an unfair trade practice. Laws granting a right to impose countervailing duties to counter unfair subsidies have existed since 1897, long before the creation of the GATT. The origin of U.S. laws against export "bounties" or "grants" can be traced to Section 5 of the Tariff Act of 1897.[3] For many years, this law vested almost complete discretion in the Treasury Department to levy CVDs as it saw fit. Several early CVD tariffs targeted tax subsidies on sugar exports.[4] And the U.S. Supreme Court essentially gave the Treasury Department *carte blanche* to impose CVDs whenever foreign governments favored exports reaching the United States.[5]

Prior to the Trade Act of 1974, U.S. law on CVDs was largely administered as a branch of U.S. foreign policy, not as a private international trade remedy.[6] Indeed, it was not until 1974 that negative bounty or grant determinations by the Treasury Department became subject to judicial review. The Trade Act of 1974 also gave private parties a number of procedural rights, notably time limits for Treasury decisions on their petitions for CVD relief and mandatory publication of Treasury rulings. It is from this point, therefore, that a systematic body of case law interpreting and applying U.S. bounty, grant, and CVD provisions began to develop.

---

³   30 Stat. 205.

⁴   *See* Downs v. United States, 187 U.S. 496 (1903) (relating to Russia); United States v. Hills Bros., 107 Fed. 107 (2d Cir. 1901) (relating to the Netherlands).

⁵   *See* G.S. Nicholas & Co. v. United States, 249 U.S. 34 (1919).

⁶   *See* Energetic Worsted Corp. v. United States, 53 C.C.P.A. 36 (1966) (relating to wool from Uruguay); United States v. Hammond Lead Products, 440 F.2d 1024 (C.C.P.A. 1971) (Mexican lead).

The next major development in the U.S. statutes governing this field arrived in the Trade Agreements Act of 1979. This Act, *inter alia,* codified the rules on the use of CVDs to counteract unfair "export subsidies" as agreed in the Tokyo Round GATT Subsidies Code. In addition, the 1979 Act authorized limited use of CVDs against foreign *domestic* subsidies, a subject the GATT Subsidies Code did not address. The 1979 Act also adopted the GATT requirement of proof of an actual injury to a domestic industry.

The Uruguay Round Agreements Act of 1994 then implemented the numerous changes of the new WTO SCM Agreement into U.S. law. Most important, the URAA amended the Tariff Act of 1930 to reflect a rough arrangement similar to the "red light," "yellow light," and "green light" (now lapsed) categories of the SCM Agreement. The requirements of the earlier Tokyo Round Subsidies Code relating to material injury continued in substantially the same form.

§ 13.4   Two Statutory Tests

The United States currently has two statutory structures on countervailing duties. That is, Section 1671 of the Tariff Act of 1930 provides a different test for products imported from countries that participate in the WTO SCM Agreement (or its equivalent),[7] as compared to products imported from other countries.[8] The most important difference between the two is that for imports from a "Subsidies Agreement Country,"[9] CVDs may be imposed only upon an affirmative determination both that a countervailable subsidy exists *and* that a U.S. industry is "materially" injured, or threatened with such injury, or its development is materially retarded; for other countries, CVDs may be imposed *without* any finding of injury to a domestic industry. In most other significant respects, the two tests are the same.[10] Nonetheless, with the continuing growth in the membership of the WTO (over 160 member states as of 2017), the possibility of imposing CVDs without a showing of material injury is rapidly decreasing in significance.

---

[7]   19 U.S.C. § 1671(a)(2).

[8]   19 U.S.C. § 1671(a)(1).

[9]   19 U.S.C. § 1671(b) (defining a "Subsidies Agreement Country" as a WTO member state or a country the President has determined has laws that are "substantially equivalent" to the SCM Agreement).

[10]   *But see* 19 U.S.C. § 1671(c) (identifying certain other general provisions that do not apply for countries that are not "Subsidies Agreement Countries").

§ 13.5   U.S. Implementation of the WTO SCM Agreement

The U.S. statutory provisions on countervailing duties are set forth principally in Section 1671 of the Tariff Act of 1930.[11] As derived from the SCM Agreement, Section 1671 imposes two general conditions on the imposition of countervailing duties. First, the International Trade Administration (ITA) in the Department of Commerce (the "administering authority") must determine that a foreign state is providing a countervailable subsidy to its exporters. Second, the International Trade Commission (ITC) must determine that imports benefiting from the subsidy injure, threaten to injure, or retard the establishment of a domestic industry in "material" way.[12] This second condition embraces proof of causation, a difficult CVD issue. If these conditions are met, a duty equal to the net subsidy "shall be imposed" upon the imports.

Like antidumping duties, countervailing duties are a statutory remedy, one which the President cannot veto or (in general) otherwise affect. If an injured U.S. industry believes that a countervailable subsidy exists, it generally may pursue CVD proceedings to their conclusion over the President's objection simply by refusing to withdraw a petition once filed.[13] The President nonetheless may have substantial influence in bringing a CVD proceeding to a positive end. Section 1671 allows the suspension of a proceeding if the subsidizing foreign government or exporters accounting for substantially all of the exports agree to cease exporting to the United States or to eliminate the subsidy within six months.[14] The subsidy may be eliminated by imposition of either an export tax or a price increase amounting to the net subsidy. In "extraordinary circumstances" benefiting the domestic industry, the ITA may also suspend a proceeding in the case of a settlement agreement reducing the subsidy by at least eighty-five percent and preventing price cutting in the United States.[15] These approaches, which are increasingly common, may effectively give exporters a brief window of opportunity to enter the U.S. market at subsidized price levels prior to shifting production to the United States.

Although an exporter may receive the subsidy through public or private sources, all U.S. determinations to date have involved foreign governmental subsidies. Thus, these cases are usually

---

[11]   19 U.S.C. § 1671 *et seq.*

[12]   19 U.S.C. § 1671(a).

[13]   19 U.S.C. § 1671(a) (providing that in the event of a countervailable subsidy that causes a sufficient injury, a CVD "shall be imposed").

[14]   19 U.S.C. § 1671c(b).

[15]   19 U.S.C. § 1671c(c).

determined on a country-wide basis (for instance, steel from India[16]), and CVD orders usually apply to all imported goods of a particular tariff classification from a particular country—including indirect imports shipped via other countries. This is one of the few instances in which the GATT/WTO allows an importing country to engage in discriminatory conduct.

As noted, the United States amended its rules on countervailing duties in 1994 to conform to the SCM Agreement. The amendments changed many concepts under U.S. law and, although with a slightly different structure, the U.S. rules on CVDs in large measure are consistent with the substance of the SCM Agreement. In nearly all respects, therefore, the important rules on the imposition of CVDs under U.S. law as described in the Sections below conform to the substance of the WTO SCM Agreement.

In general, the U.S. rules state that "there shall be imposed . . . a countervailing duty" (CVD) if the ITA determines that an exporting country is providing, "directly or indirectly," a "countervailable subsidy," and the ITC makes an affirmative injury determination.[17] U.S. law defines three elements for the imposition of a CVD: (1) a "subsidy," (2) that is "specific," and (3) that causes or threatens to cause a material injury to a domestic industry.[18] If all three elements are satisfied, the ITA must impose a CVD "equal to the amount of the net countervailable subsidy."[19]

The following sections will analyze in detail each of the three required elements for the imposition of a CVD.

§ 13.6   The Subsidy Requirement

The first step in the analysis for the imposition of a CVD is a finding of a "subsidy." The Tariff Act defines this term as a "financial contribution" by a governmental entity that confers a "benefit" on the producer or exporter of the subsidized product.[20] It includes governmental grants, loans, equity infusions, and loan guarantees, as well as tax credits and the failure to collect taxes. It can also include a governmental purchase or sale of goods or services on advantageous terms.[21] Further, direct governmental

---

[16]   *See* United States Steel Corp. v. United States, 2009 WL 5125921 (CIT 2009), *aff'd*, 425 Fed. Appx. 900 (Fed. Cir. 2011).

[17]   19 U.S.C. § 1671(a).

[18]   *Id.*

[19]   *Id.*

[20]   19 U.S.C. § 1677(5).

[21]   19 U.S.C. § 1677(5)(D). *See also* United States Steel Corp. v. United States, 2009 WL 5125921 (CIT 2009) (upholding an imposition of CVDs on steel from India because the Indian government sold input goods to exporters "for less than adequate remuneration"), *aff'd*, 425 Fed. Appx. 900 (Fed. Cir. 2011).

action is not required: A subsidy may also arise if a government provides any of the above through a private body.

A financial contribution provides a "benefit" if it grants an exporter a better deal than would be available through normal market mechanisms. The Tariff Act states that this "normally" occurs: (1) in the case of an equity infusion, "if the investment decision is inconsistent with the usual investment practice of private investors"; (2) in the case of a loan, if the recipient gains an advantage as against a "comparable commercial loan"; (3) in the case of a loan guarantee, if there is a difference between the fee the recipient paid as compared to the fee for "a comparable commercial loan"; (4) in the case of governmental goods or services, if they "are provided for less than adequate remuneration"; and (5) in the case of goods purchased from the exporter, if the goods are purchased "for more than adequate remuneration."[22]

§ 13.7 The Specificity Requirement

In addition to a financial contribution that confers a benefit, the Tariff Act requires that the resulting subsidy be "specific" to a particular industry or enterprise. This is where U.S. law uses a slightly different structure as compared to the SCM Agreement (although, again, the substance is largely the same). U.S. law thus refers to "export subsidies" (see § 13.8 below) to correspond to the "prohibited" (red light) subsidies under the SCM Agreement. These are deemed to be specific as a matter of law. Similarly, U.S. law refers to "domestic subsidies" (see § 13.9 below) to correspond to "actionable" (yellow light) subsidies under the SCM Agreement. These may be subject to CVDs if they cause adverse effects to a domestic industry based on a variety of further factual considerations.

Two other categories originally recognized under the SCM Agreement, and incorporated into U.S. law, have lapsed.[23] A so-called "dark amber" subsidy was one that exceeded five percent of the cost basis of the product, or provided debt forgiveness, or covered the operating losses of a specific enterprise industry more than once. The dark amber provisions lapsed in 2000. As noted above, the "green light" category of allowed subsidies—for industrial research and development, regional development, and adaptation of existing facilities to new environmental standards—also lapsed after five years and was not renewed.[24]

---

[22]   19 U.S.C. § 1677(5)(E).

[23]   *See* 19 U.S.C. § 1677(5B)(A)–(E).

[24]   *See* Section 13.2, *supra*.

§ 13.8   The Specificity Requirement__Export Subsidies

The clearest example of a "specific" subsidy is a direct export incentive provided by a foreign government, such as an export credit on taxes or export loan guarantees at less than commercial rates. U.S. CVD law provides that a subsidy is an "export subsidy," and thus is specific as a matter of law, if "in law or in fact" it is "contingent upon export performance," even where the condition is only one of several.[25] The same applies for a subsidy that is "contingent upon the use of domestic goods over imported goods" ("import substitution subsidy").[26]

As noted, these rules correspond to the "prohibited" (red light) subsidies under the SCM Agreement. (Annex I to the SCM Agreement also provides an "Illustrative List of Export Subsidies.") A footnote to the SCM Agreement explains that a subsidy also is contingent on exports if it is "in fact tied to actual or anticipated exportation or export earnings."[27] A 2011 WTO Appellate Body decision in the long-running dispute between the European Union and the United States over aircraft subsidies explained that this concept applies, "[w]here the evidence shows, all other things being equal, that the granting of the subsidy provides an incentive to skew anticipated sales towards exports."[28] Although U.S. law does not expressly incorporate the language of the SCM Agreement footnote, a fair interpretation of the definition of an "export subsidy" would seem to capture it as well.

Other examples of an export subsidy might include governmental loans at below market interest rates or with uncompensated deferrals of payments of the principal. If these benefits are used to induce the building of a plant with a capacity too large for the local market, an export subsidy may exist. Outright cash payments to exporters, export tax credits, and accelerated depreciation benefits specifically for exporters provide additional examples of clearly countervailable export subsidies.

More difficulties arise in analyzing whether tax rebates confer the type of benefits that would equate with an export subsidy. Remission or deferral of, or exemption from, a direct tax on exports is a countervailable subsidy. But the remission of an indirect tax (sales tax, value added tax, etc.) is not a "specific" subsidy, as long

---

[25]   19 U.S.C. § 1677(5A)(B).

[26]   19 U.S.C. § 1677(5A)(C).

[27]   *See* SCM Agreement, art. 3.1(a), footnote 4.

[28]   *See* Report, *European Communities and Certain Member States—Measures Affecting Trade in Large Civil Aircraft*, ¶ 1047, WT/DS316/AB/ (May 18, 2011).

as it is not excessive. However, a foreign government that makes payments to exporters must show a clear link between the amount, eligibility, and purpose of the payments and the actual payment of indirect taxes, and then document the link.

At one time, the amount of a U.S. CVD would be reduced by the "nonexcessive" amount of the remission of an indirect tax. The Tariff Act now provides, however, a definition of "net subsidy" that allows certain subtractions. These include (1) application fees to qualify for the subsidy, (2) any reduction in the value of the subsidy due to a governmentally mandated deferral in payment, and (3) export taxes intended to offset the subsidy.[29]

§ 13.9   The Specificity Requirement__Domestic Subsidies

The Tariff Act as amended by the URAA in 1994 generally covers the SCM Agreement category of "actionable" (yellow light) subsidies under the concept of a "domestic subsidy." Under the SCM Agreement such subsidies are permissible (and thus may not be subject to CVDs), but only if they do not cause "adverse effects."[30]

Under the Tariff Act, a domestic subsidy exists if as a matter of law or fact it is provided to a specific enterprise or industry, even if not linked to export performance.[31] The Act lists four "guidelines" for determining whether a subsidy so qualifies as a domestic subsidy:

(1)   If the subsidizing country "expressly limits access" to the subsidy to an enterprise or industry, then it is "specific as a matter of law."

(2)   If the subsidy is in fact automatically granted to all enterprises or industries that meet written and objective criteria or conditions, it is "not specific as a matter of law."

(3)   But a subsidy may be "specific as a matter of fact" where the actual recipients are limited in number; one enterprise or industry is the predominant user or receives a "disproportionately large amount" of the subsidy; or the manner in which the granting authority exercises its discretion indicates that one enterprise or industry is favored over others.

(4)   Finally, a subsidy is specific if it is limited to an enterprise or industry in a "designated geographic region"

---

[29]   19 U.S.C. § 1677(6).

[30]   SCM Agreement, art. 5.

[31]   19 U.S.C. § 1677(5A)(D).

and is granted by the governmental authority of that region.[32]

For purposes of each of these guidelines, the Tariff Act makes clear that a reference to an enterprise or industry includes "a group of such enterprises or industries."[33]

§ 13.10   Upstream Subsidies

A foreign government may, as discussed in the preceding two Sections, subsidize the actual exportation of a product, whether in law or in fact. Alternatively, it may subsidize component parts or raw materials that are incorporated into the final exported product. The latter are called "upstream subsidies" and are subject to CVDs if they both bestow a competitive benefit on the product exported to the United States and have a significant effect on its cost of production.[34] A competitive benefit arises if the price of the subsidized "input product" (the component or raw material) to the producer of the final product is less than it would have been "in an arms-length transaction."[35] Upstream subsidies then become "countervailable subsidies" if this competitive benefit functions to create or support an import substitution subsidy or a domestic subsidy.[36]

The amount of the benefit from an upstream subsidy is determined by calculating the subsidy rate on the input and then determining what percentage of the cost of the final product is represented by the subsidized input. By regulation the ITA has stated that, if the subsidy so calculated represents more than five percent of the total cost, it will presume that there is a "significant effect;" if it is less than one percent. The ITA will presume no significant effect.[37] However, both presumptions are rebuttable, and the ITA also will consider whether "factors other than price, such as quality differences," are "important determinants" in the competitiveness of the final product.[38]

The Tariff Act has specialized rules for processed agricultural products. A subsidy provided to producers of a "raw agricultural product" is deemed to be provided to the producer of the processed

---

[32]   19 U.S.C. § 1677(5A)(D)(i)–(iv).

[33]   19 U.S.C. § 1677(5A)(D), last paragraph.

[34]   19 U.S.C. § 1677–1(a). *See also* 19 U.S.C. § 1671(e) (providing for the inclusion of upstream subsidies in CVDs).

[35]   19 U.S.C. § 1677–1(b).

[36]   19 U.S.C. § 1677–1(a) (stating that an upstream subsidy is one "other than an export subsidy"); 19 U.S.C. §§ 1677(5)(C) (referring to import substitution subsidies), and 1677(5)(D) (referring to domestic subsidies).

[37]   19 CFR § 351.523(d)(1) (2013).

[38]   19 CFR § 351.523(d)(2) (2013).

agricultural product if (1) the demand for the "raw" product is substantially dependent upon the demand for the processed product, and (2) the processing adds only limited value to the raw product.[39]

§ 13.11 *De Minimis* Subsidies

De minimis subsidies, defined in Tariff Act as subsidies of "less than 0.5 percent *ad valorem*," are disregarded, with the result that the Act does not permit the imposition of CVDs on the imported goods.[40] However, when the ITA calculates country-wide CVD rates, it uses a fair average of aggregate subsidy benefits to exports of all firms from that country. In making such calculations, the ITA must include not only sales by exporters who receive substantial subsidy benefits, but also sales by exporters who receive zero or *de minimis* subsidies, when calculating the weighted average benefit conferred.[41] Thus, in such circumstances, the CVD imposed may not exceed the weighted average benefit received by all exporters of the goods subject to the CVD proceeding. The *de minimis* 0.5 percent rule need not be utilized in sunset reviews of CVDs every five years.[42]

§ 13.12 CVDs and Nonmarket Economies

The subject of subsidies is particularly difficult with respect to non-market economies (NMEs). The longstanding view was that CVDs for products from NMEs are not appropriate because the NME government in effect is responsible for the entire economy. In accordance with this view, the Federal Circuit Court of Appeals ruled in 1986 that economic incentives given to encourage exportation by the government of an NME cannot create a countervailable "subsidy."[43] The court's rationale was that, even though an NME government provides export-oriented benefits, the NME can direct sales to be at any price, so the benefits themselves do not distort competition. The court also suggested that imports from NMEs with unreasonably low prices should be analyzed under the rules for antidumping duties.

For some time, one strong view was that Congress implicitly approved of this reasoning when it enacted important amendments

---

[39]   19 U.S.C. § 1677–2.

[40]   Although the Tariff Act generally refers to one percent, see 19 U.S.C. § 1671b(b)(4), the ITA has refined the standard to .05 percent. *See* 19 CFR § 351.106(c)(1) (2013).

[41]   *See* Ipsco, Inc. v. United States, 899 F.2d 1192 (Fed. Cir. 1990).

[42]   *See* Report of the Appellate Body, *U.S. CVD on Certain Corrosion—Resistant Steel Flat Products from Germany*, WT/DS213/AB/R (Dec. 19, 2002).

[43]   Georgetown Steel Corp. v. United States, 801 F.2d 1308 (Fed. Cir. 1986).

to the Tariff Act in 1988, and again in 1994. Those amendments addressed *dumping* from NMEs, but did not address *subsidies* for exports from NMEs.[44] Thus, for many years it was assumed that unfair trade practices by NMEs would only be subject to antidumping reviews and not CVD reviews. But in a major reversal, the Commerce Department in 2007 started pursuing CVD cases against China despite its NME status under U.S. trade law. In 2008, it then imposed substantial CVDs on steel pipe from China.[45] It did the same in 2010 for certain imports from Vietnam.[46]

In 2011, however, the Federal Circuit rejected this effort based on its reading of congressional intent in the substantial amendments of CVD law in 1994.[47] But in March, 2012, Congress then stepped in and annulled the Federal Circuit's decision by special legislation, with the result that countervailing duties also may be imposed on goods from non-market economies such as China and Vietnam.[48] Thus, the criteria used to determine whether a country has a nonmarket economy in antidumping proceedings[49] will apply for U.S. countervailing duty law as well. These criteria focus principally upon government involvement in setting prices or production levels, private versus collective ownership, and market pricing of inputs.[50]

§ 13.13 The Injury Determination

CVD proceedings in the United States for Subsidies Agreement Countries (and only such countries[51]), are conducted in two stages. The ITA is responsible for assessing the substantive grounds for the imposition of a CVD as discussed in Sections 13.5 through 13.11 above.[52] In the second stage, the International Trade Commission (ITC) must determine whether the subsidization of the imported merchandise has caused or threatens material injury to a domestic industry.[53] The following sections review the material injury

---

[44]   *See, e.g.,* 19 U.S.C. §§ 1677b(c) and 1677(18).

[45]   *See* 73 Fed. Reg. 40,480 (July 15, 2008).

[46]   *See* 75 Fed. Reg. 23,670 (May 4, 2010).

[47]   *See* GPX Int'l Tire Corp. v. United States, 666 F.3d 732, 745 (Fed. Cir. 2011).

[48]   *See* PL 112–99 (March 12, 2012), codified at 19 U.S.C. § 1671(f). In 2013, the Court of International Trade held that retroactive application of this statute to past CVDs on NMEs was not unconstitutional. Guangdong Wireking Housewares & Hardware Co., Ltd. v. United States, 2013 WL 951006 (C.I.T. 2013).

[49]   *See* Chapter 12, § 12.8.

[50]   *See id.*

[51]   *See* Section 13.2 *supra* (noting that an injury determination is required only for "Subsidies Agreement Countries").

[52]   *See generally* 19 U.S.C. § 1671(a)(1).

[53]   19 U.S.C. § 1671(a)(2).

determination under U.S. law, including market definition, injury factors, and causation.

The injury determination by the ITC involves three separate inquiries:

(1)   First, the ITC must define the relevant "domestic like product" and relevant domestic industry;

(2)   Second, the ITC must determine whether that industry is suffering or threatened with a sufficiently serious injury; and

(3)   Third, the ITC must determine whether a causal link exists between the injury and the "countervailable subsidy."

The most important of these steps is the determination of whether a countervailable subsidy causes a sufficient injury to a domestic industry. The Tariff Act provides that an affirmative injury determination is required when an industry in the United States is materially injured or is threatened with material injury by reason of dumped imports, or the establishment of an industry in the United States is materially retarded.[54] Both the "material injury"[55] and the "threat of material injury"[56] standards apply to established industries, and substantial overlap exists between the two. Nonetheless, the Act makes clear that they are independent grounds for a sufficient injury to justify a CVD.[57]

The law governing the injury determination for the imposition of CVDs in nearly all significant respects is the same as that for imposing antidumping duties. Indeed, the definitions of the relevant product market, the relevant industry, and the three alternatives for an affirmative injury determination are essentially identical for CVDs and ADs. Thus, the analysis of the injury determination for CVDs below will often be the same as, or will liberally refer to, the injury analysis for ADs in Chapter 12.

§ 13.14   The Injury Determination__The "Like Product" and Relevant Domestic Industry Determinations

In order to assess "material injury," the ITC must first identify the relevant products and relevant domestic industry affected by a countervailable subsidy.

---

[54]   *Id.*

[55]   19 U.S.C. § 1677(7).

[56]   19 U.S.C. § 1677(7)(F).

[57]   19 U.S.C. § 1671(a)(2).

With regard to the product market, the Tariff Act uses the term "domestic like product." This term is defined, for both CVDs and ADs, as one that is "like, or in the absence of like, most similar in characteristics and uses with" the foreign product under investigation.[58] The "like product" determination is a factual issue for which the ITC weighs six relevant factors: "(1) physical characteristics and uses; (2) common manufacturing facilities and production employees; (3) interchangeability; (4) customer perceptions; (5) channels of distribution; and, where appropriate, (6) price."[59] In a CVD proceeding, the ITC must define the relevant product and industry for an assessment of the harm caused by a subsidized product upon importation. The ITA undertakes a similar analysis in AD proceedings in order to determine the foreign market value ("normal value") for the imported merchandise.[60] Because the concept of "like product" is used for a different purpose, the ITA's definition and methodology in determining whether dumping has occurred is not binding on the ITC's analysis of "like product" for CVD cases.[61]

Separately, the ITC in a CVD proceeding must define the relevant domestic industry potentially affected by a proscribed subsidy practice. The Tariff Act defines the relevant domestic "industry" as those domestic producers, "as a whole," of a "domestic like product" or as those producers "whose collective output of a domestic like product constitutes a major proportion" of the total domestic production.[62] Again, although these definitions apply to both the ITA and the ITC, they do not always agree on the methodology or outcome.

In addition, the ITC may create regional geographic product markets if the local producers sell most of their production in the regional market, and the demand in the regional market is not supplied by other U.S. producers outside that region.[63] If the relevant domestic injury in such a region is harmed, then there is material injury to a domestic industry.

---

[58]   19 U.S.C. § 1667(10).

[59]   Cleo Inc. v. United States, 501 F.3d 1291, 11294–1295 (Fed. Cir. 2007).

[60]   *See* Chapter 12, § 12.6.

[61]   Cleo Inc. v. United States, 501 F.3d 1291, 1295 (Fed. Cir. 2007); Mitsubishi Elec. Corp. v. United States, 898 F.2d 1577 (Fed. Cir. 1990).

[62]   19 U.S.C. § 1677(4)(A).

[63]   19 U.S.C. § 1677(4)(C).

§ 13.15   The Injury Determination__Material Injury

The Tariff Act defines material injury as "harm which is not inconsequential, immaterial, or unimportant."[64] (The same standard applies in AD proceedings,[65] and again much of the law in the area is therefore interchangeable.) In assessing this essential "material injury" standard, the Act *requires* the ITC to consider three factors:

> (1)   The volume of imports of the merchandise subject to investigation;

> (2)   The effect of these imports on prices in the United States for like products; and

> (3)   The impact of these imports on domestic producers of like products, but only in the context of domestic United States production operations.[66]

The Act also *permits* the ITC to consider "such other economic factors as are relevant to the determination regarding whether there is material injury by reason of imports."[67]

The ITC is required to explain its analysis of each factor it considers and the relevance of each to its determination.[68] The Tariff Act nonetheless provides that the "presence or absence" of any of the three mandatory factors should "not necessarily give decisive guidance" to the ITC in its material injury determination, and the ITC is not required to assign any particular weight to any one factor.[69] The factors are examined through extensive statistical analyses. This analysis occurs on industry-wide basis and not on a company-by-company basis. The ITC may select whatever time period best represents the business cycle and competitive conditions in the industry and most reasonably allows it to determine whether an injury exists.[70]

The Tariff Act also gives detailed guidance for the ITC's assessment of each of the three mandatory considerations for a

---

[64]   19 U.S.C. § 1677(7)(A).

[65]   *See* Chapter 12, § 12.14.

[66]   19 U.S.C. § 1677(7)(B)(i). *See also* Angus Chemical Co. v. United States, 140 F.3d 1478 (Fed. Cir. 1998) (holding that consideration of these three factors is mandatory).

[67]   19 U.S.C. § 1677(7)(B)(ii).

[68]   19 U.S.C. § 1677(7)(B).

[69]   19 U.S.C. § 1677(7)(E)(ii).

[70]   19 U.S.C. § 1677(7)(C).

material injury determination. This guidance applies to both CVD and AD proceedings.

Volume of Imports. The Tariff Act requires the ITC to consider the absolute volume of imports or any increases in volume in evaluating the volume of imports subject to investigation. This assessment may be made in relation to production or consumption in the United States. The standard in this evaluation is whether the volume of imports, viewed in any of the above ways, is significant.[71]

Price Effects. Under the Tariff Act, the ITC must consider the effect of the subsidized imports on prices for like products in the domestic market. This is done to the extent that such a consideration assists in evaluating whether (1) there is significant price underselling by the imported merchandise as compared with the price of like products of the United States,[72] and (2) whether the effect of the imported merchandise is otherwise to depress domestic prices to a significant degree or to prevent price increases that otherwise would have occurred to a significant degree.[73]

Domestic Industry Impact. Similar to AD proceedings, the impact on a domestic industry of an allegedly subsidized product commonly is the most important consideration in the ITC's injury analysis. Because of this, the Tariff Act provides supplemental factors for the ITC to consider. These include: (1) actual and potential decline in "output, sales, market share, profits, productivity, return on investments, and utilization of capacity"; (2) impact on domestic prices; (3) actual and potential "negative effects on cash flow, inventories, employment, wages, growth, ability to raise capital, and investment"; and (4) actual and potential negative effects "on the existing development and production efforts of the domestic industry."[74]

The ITC must evaluate all these relevant economic factors within the context of the business cycle and conditions of competition in the affected industry.[75] But traditionally the ITC has relied primarily on two of the factors in making this determination. First, the industry must be in a distressed or a stagnant condition. Second, the low domestic price levels must be a factor in the industry's difficulties (*e.g.*, high unemployment or low capacity utilization rate), and these low prices must have a serious negative effect on profits.

---

[71]   19 U.S.C. § 1677(7)(C)(i).

[72]   19 U.S.C. § 1677(7)(C)(ii)(I).

[73]   19 U.S.C. § 1677(7)(C)(ii)(II). For more detail on the role of "price underselling" in the ITC's determination of injury see Chapter 12, § 12.14.

[74]   19 U.S.C. § 1677(7)(C)(iii).

[75]   19 U.S.C. § 1677(7)(C), last paragraph.

The ITC will often base an affirmative determination of material injury on severe downward trends in profitability among domestic producers. But even in a case of declining profitability, increasing production, shipments, capacity, and market share may demonstrate to the ITC that the affected industry is in a healthy state.[76] Thus, the ITC may make a negative determination concerning material injury even if the industry is experiencing decreases in profitability.

Like AD proceedings, the effect of subsidized imports on employment in the relevant domestic industry may also be significant. Again, employment data are not dispositive due to the broad spectrum of economic factors that may affect such data, many of which may not be attributable to foreign subsidization. However, a change in domestic employment during the period under investigation is one factor to be considered. A decrease in employment during the period of investigation may be an indication of injury, whereas increasing employment commonly is a fact that supports a negative injury determination.

Finally, and again like AD proceedings, plant capacity utilization can be an important factor. Falling capacity utilization may indicate material injury if no other explanation exists, but the ITC can make negative injury determinations despite falling capacity utilization, if the decline is caused by other factors, such as frequent equipment breakdowns and quality control disruptions.

§ 13.16   The Injury Determination__Threat of Material Injury

The ITC may also make an affirmative determination of injury if it finds that a proscribed subsidy practice represents a "threat of material injury" to a domestic industry. The Tariff Act lists a variety of "economic factors" that the ITC "shall consider" in making such a determination in an antidumping proceeding. Again, these factors apply for AD proceedings as well, and Chapter 12 analyzes them in detail.[77]

The Tariff Act nonetheless adds one "economic factor" that is relevant only for CVD proceedings. For such proceedings, the ITC must also consider "the nature of the subsidy . . . and whether imports of the subject merchandise are likely to increase."[78]

---

[76]   *See, e.g.,* Nucor Corp. v. United States, 675 F. Supp. 2d 1340 (C.I.T. 2010) (relating to a revocation of CVDs after a review); American Spring Wire Corp. v. United States, 590 F. Supp. 1273 (C.I.T. 1984), *affirmed sub nom.* Armco, Inc. v. United States, 760 F.2d 249 (Fed. Cir. 1985).

[77]   *See* Chapter 12, § 12.15.

[78]   19 U.S.C. § 1677(7)(F)(i)(I).

§ 13.17   The Injury Determination__Material Retardation

For a CVD proceeding as well, the Tariff Act recognizes as an independent ground for an affirmative injury determination by the ITC that a countervailable subsidy has "materially retarded" the establishment of an industry in the United States. This standard of its nature is relevant to new or nascent domestic industries. Like AD proceedings,[79] this ground for an affirmative injury determination has not been a significant one in CVD cases.

§ 13.18   Causation

In addition to a sufficient injury to a domestic industry as described in Sections 13.15 through 13.17 above, the ITC must also find causation. As with AD proceedings, however, when the subsidization and material injury already exist, there is a natural tendency to make an affirmative determination for a CVD without a lengthy analysis of the causal link between the two. In a negative injury determination, on the other hand, the ITC may engage in a rather detailed analysis of causation.

The Tariff Act sets out a simple causation standard: that material injury must occur "by reason of" the subsidization of the imports.[80] The same standard applies in AD proceedings, and once again the law in this area is largely interchangeable.[81] The Tariff Act does not require that the ITC use any particular methodology in making such a determination, and it "need not isolate the injury caused by other factors from injury caused by unfair imports."[82] Thus, the causation requirement is not a high one. Imports need only be a cause of material injury, and need not be the most substantial or even primary cause. Again, the causation standard may be satisfied if the subsidized imports simply contribute to the conditions of the domestic injury. Under this "contributing cause" standard, causation may exist despite the absence of a correlation between subsidized imports and the alleged injuries, if substantial evidence exists that the volume of subsidized imports was a contributing factor in the price depression experienced by the domestic injury. Nonetheless, as the Federal Circuit has made clear in an AD case, "causation is not shown if the subject imports

---

[79]   *See* Chapter 12, § 12.16.

[80]   19 U.S.C. § 1671(a)(2).

[81]   *See* Chapter 12, § 12.17.

[82]   Bratsk Aluminium Smelter v. United States, 444 F.3d 1369, 1373 (Fed. Cir. 2006) (*quoting* Taiwan Semiconductors Industry Ass'n v. U.S. Int'l Trade Comm'n, 266 F.3d 1339, 1345 (Fed. Cir. 2001)).

contributed only 'minimally or tangentially to the material harm.' "[83]

Like AD proceedings, the ITC must consider causal factors other than subsidies in CVD cases.[84] An industry that is prospering during times of greater import penetration will find it difficult to persuade the ITC that subsidized imports are the cause of any material injury to it. The existence of extraneous injury factors will not, however, necessarily preclude an affirmative finding of material injury for purposes of the Tariff Act, as long as the subsidies are a contributing cause to the material injury of the domestic industry. The ITC is not required to weigh the effects from the subsidized imports against the effects associated with other factors, if the subsidization is a contributing cause of the injury. Nonetheless, the ITC may uncover other major causes for the problems of the domestic industry. These may include huge unnecessary expenses, chronic excess capacity, inefficiency, poor quality, price sensitivity or increased domestic competition.

§ 13.19 Cumulative Causation

Similar to an AD proceeding,[85] the Tariff Act requires that the ITC cumulatively assess the impact of reasonably coincident subsidized imports from two or more countries if the imports compete with "like products" in the United States. In specific, the Act requires the ITC to "cumulatively assess the volume and price effects of imports of the subject merchandise from all countries" with respect to which CVD proceedings were initiated on the same day, "if such imports compete with each other and with domestic like products in the United States market."[86] The reasoning for this approach, again, is that the injury caused by the cumulative effect of "many nibbles" is just as harmful as that caused by "one large bite."

The Court of International Trade has observed that to support a cumulation decision, the ITC "must find a reasonable overlap of competition between imports from the subject countries and the domestic like product."[87] In applying this "reasonable overlap" test, the ITC traditionally has applied a four factor test: (1) the degree of

---

[83]   *Id.*, 444 F.3d at 1373 (*quoting* Gerald Metals, Inc. v. United States, 132 F.3d 716, 722 (Fed. Cir. 1997)).

[84]   Taiwan Semiconductors Industry Ass'n v. U.S. Int'l Trade Comm'n, 266 F.3d 1339, 1345 (Fed. Cir. 2001) (so holding with respect to an AD proceeding).

[85]   *See* Chapter 12, § 12.18.

[86]   19 U.S.C. § 1677(7)(G)(i).

[87]   Nucor Corp. v. United States, 594 F. Supp. 2d 1320, 1347 (C.I.T. 2008) (*quoting* Noviant OY v. United States, 451 F. Supp. 2d 1367, 1379 (C.I.T. 2006)), *aff'd*, Nucor Corp. v. United States, 601 F.3d 1291 (Fed. Cir. 2010).

fungibility; (2) the presence of sales or offers in the same geographic markets; (3) the existence of common or similar channels of distribution; and (4) whether there is a simultaneous presence in the relevant market.[88] However, neither the "reasonable overlap" test nor the four factors test is "singularly dispositive or the sole factors the ITC may consider."[89]

When cumulating, it is not necessary to find, for each country, a separate causal link between imports and U.S. material injury. Such multiple country cumulation should be distinguished from the "cross cumulation," which is also allowed by the Tariff Act. Cross cumulation involves consideration by the ITC of both dumped and subsidized imports into the United States. The net effect of U.S. rules on cumulation of import injury is to encourage petitioners to name as many countries as possible as the source of their problems and combine these in a single proceeding.

§ 13.20   Countervailing Duty Procedures

As noted in Section 13.4 above, the Tariff Act applies different rules for the imposition of CVDs depending on whether the source country is or is not a "Subsidies Agreement Country."[90] The major difference between the two is that for a "Subsidies Agreement Country" a determination of both a countervailable subsidy and an injury is required; for other countries, only a finding of a countervailable subsidy is necessary.[91] Thus, the administrative procedure for deciding whether to impose CVDs for a Subsidies Agreement Country is the same as that for antidumping duties[92] and involves the ITA and ITC (see below) making both preliminary and final determinations. But for subsidized products from other countries, a decision by the ITA on the existence of a countervailable subsidy is alone sufficient to impose CVDs.

§ 13.21   Administrative Determinations

Two different governmental agencies are involved in administering U.S. CVD law: The International Trade Administration (ITA), which is part of the Commerce Department and thus the Executive Branch, and the International Trade Commission (ITC), which is an independent agency created by Congress.

---

[88]   *Id.*, at 1347.

[89]   *Id.*

[90]   *See* Section 13.4 *supra*.

[91]   19 U.S.C. § 1671(a)(1), (2).

[92]   *See* Chapter 12, § 12.22.

The chain of decision-making in CVD proceedings depends, again, on whether a Subsidies Agreement Country is involved. If not, the proceeding is totally before the ITA. This will be a two-stage proceeding:

ITA Preliminary Countervailable Subsidy Determination.

ITA Final Countervailable Subsidy Determination.

If, in contrast, a Subsidies Agreement Country is the source of the challenged goods, then a four-stage proceeding will apply:

ITC Preliminary Injury Determination.

ITA Preliminary Countervailable Subsidy Determination.

ITA Final Countervailable Subsidy Determination.

ITC Final Injury Determination.

The CVD process may be initiated by either the Department of Commerce or by a union or business (or group or association of aggrieved workers or businesses).[93] The petition requirements are set forth by regulation.[94] Pre-filing contact with the ITA and (if necessary) the ITC can often resolve any problems regarding the contents of the petition. Petitioners may also access the ITA's library of information on foreign subsidy practices.

The ITA first examines, "on the basis of sources readily available" to it, the "accuracy and adequacy" of the evidence provided in the petition, and determines whether the petition (a) alleges the elements necessary for the imposition of a CVD and "contains information reasonably available to the petitioner supporting the allegations," and (b) has been filed "by or on behalf of the industry."[95] In other words, the ITA essentially accepts or rejects the petition based only on readily available information, which most often means only that provided by the petitioner.

Like AD proceedings, the ITA must find that a sufficient percentage of the affected domestic industry supports a CVD petition—for the Tariff Act requires that a petition be filed "by or on behalf of" the entire domestic industry.[96] Generally, this requires that the industry or workers who support the petition account for (a) at least twenty-five percent of the total industry, and (b) more

---

[93]   19 U.S.C. § 1671a(a), (b). *See also* 19 U.S.C. § 1677(9)(C)–(G) (defining such entities as a relevant "interested party" that may initiate a CVD petition).

[94]   *See* 19 C.F.R. § 351.202.

[95]   19 U.S.C. § 1671a(c).

[96]   19 U.S.C. § 1671a(c)(1)(A).

than fifty percent of those that have actually expressed an opinion for or against the petition.[97]

Once the petition is accepted, the ITC makes a preliminary determination as to a real or threatened material injury within sixty-five days of the filing of the petition based on the best information available to it at that time.[98] If the ITC makes such a finding, the ITA must then make a preliminary determination on whether there is "a reasonable basis to believe or suspect" based on the best information available that there is a countervailable subsidy with respect to the covered merchandise.[99] The time for making this decision may be extended if the petitioner so requests, or if the ITA determines both that the parties are cooperating and that the case is extraordinarily complicated.[100] The time period may also be extended for "upstream subsidy" investigations.[101]

If the ITA makes a preliminary determination that a countervailable subsidy exists, it must, within seventy-five days, both make a "final determination" on the existence of a countervailable subsidy and calculate the amount of the proposed CVD.[102] If the ITA makes a positive finding on a countervailable subsidy, the ITC then must make a final determination on material injury within 120 days after the ITA's preliminary determination or forty-five days after the ITA's final determination.[103] If both the ITA and ITC make affirmative final determinations in their respective areas of responsibility, then the ITA must enter a CVD order and assess the CVD on the covered goods "equal to the amount of the net countervailable subsidy."[104] If the ITA makes a negative preliminary determination, but then an affirmative final determination, the ITC must thereafter make its final determination within seventy-five days.[105]

In reaching their determinations, both the ITA and the ITC frequently circulate questionnaires to interested parties, including foreign governments and exporters. Since any failure to respond risks a determination on the "best information available," this results in the flow of significant and often strategically valuable business information to the government.

---

[97]   19 U.S.C. § 1671a(c)(4).
[98]   19 U.S.C. § 1671b(a).
[99]   19 U.S.C. § 1671b(b).
[100] 19 U.S.C. § 1671b(c).
[101] 19 U.S.C. § 1671b(g).
[102] 19 U.S.C. § 1671d(a).
[103] 19 U.S.C. § 1671d(b)(2).
[104] 19 U.S.C. §§ 1671(a), (c), 1671e.
[105] 19 U.S.C. § 1671d(b)(3).

§ 13.22   The Importance of the ITA Preliminary Subsidy Determination

An ITA preliminary determination that a countervailable subsidy exists places great pressure on the importers of the foreign goods. Liquidation (entry of the goods subject to a determined rate of tariff) of all such merchandise is suspended by order of customs. Goods imported after an ITA preliminary determination of a countervailable subsidy will be subject to any CVD imposed later, after final determinations are made.[106] Such a preliminary determination, although subject to final determinations by the ITA and the ITC and appealable to the CIT, will effectively cut off further importation of the disputed goods unless an expensive bond is posted pending completion of the process. The respondent importer thus will want a speedy resolution, as its total costs for the imports will have become uncertain. It is for this reason that the Tariff Act is replete with time provisions designed to protect the importer by requiring decisions within specified time limits (see § 13.21 above). As with antidumping proceedings, most CVD proceedings are completed within one year.

At one level, then, a useful intermediate goal in representing a petitioner is to obtain an ITA preliminary determination concerning a "subsidy" that meets the statutory requirements. The respondent's "defense" to such efforts must be organized quickly, usually within thirty days of the filing of a CVD petition. The importer's ability to present a defense is handicapped by the nature of CVD proceedings—the actual target of the petition is the subsidy practices of foreign governments. Unlike most foreign exporters whose pricing decisions are the focus in AD proceedings, many foreign governments are loath to provide information necessary for an adequate response to a CVD complaint. Because the ITA and ITC are authorized to make decisions on the basis of the "information available to it," any failure to adequately respond to a CVD complaint can contribute to adverse rulings. Moreover, responses by foreign governments and exporters to ITA questionnaires that cannot be verified by on-the-spot investigations are ignored and thus removed from the best information available for decision-making. This may leave only the petitioner's or other respondents' submissions for review—a one-sided proceeding almost sure to result in affirmative determinations.

The respondent-importer's uncertainties over the amount of duty owed after a preliminary ITA determination that a countervailable subsidy exists can increase for Subsidies Agreement

---

[106]   19 U.S.C. § 1671b(d).

Countries if the ITA decides that "critical circumstances" are present. In such cases, the suspension of liquidation of the goods applies not only prospectively from the date of such determination, but also retrospectively for ninety days.[107] For other countries, moreover, there is *no* time limit on retroactivity and no need for a "critical circumstances" determination.

§ 13.23 CVDs and Anticircumvention

The ITA final determination of the existence of a subsidy establishes the amount of any CVDs. Because duties are not imposed to support any specific domestic price, they are set only to equal the amount of the net subsidy.[108] The CVDs remain in force as long as the subsidization continues.

Like antidumping duties,[109] the Tariff Act also has rules that address the "circumvention" of CVDs. First, the ITA may include within the scope of a CVD order merchandise "completed or assembled" in the United States if such merchandise includes "parts or components produced in the foreign country" that are the original subject of the order.[110] The principal requirements are that the process of completion or assembly in the United States is "minor or insignificant" and the value of the components themselves is a "significant portion of the total value of the merchandise."[111] Second, when the exporter ships components to a third country for assembly and subsequent exportation to the United States, such circumvention efforts can be defeated by extending an antidumping order to those goods as well.[112] Again, such an action is appropriate if the assembly in the third country is "minor or insignificant" and the value of the components represents a "significant portion" of the total value.

Many petitioners in countervailing duty cases also seek antidumping duties[113] and other relief through "escape clause" or market disruption proceedings. Thus, domestic producers seeking relief from import competition will often use a "shotgun" approach to obtain protective relief.

---

[107] 19 U.S.C. § 1671b(e).

[108] 19 U.S.C. § 1671e.

[109] *See* Chapter 12, § 12.26.

[110] 19 U.S.C. § 1677j(a).

[111] 19 U.S.C. § 1677j(a)(2).

[112] 19 U.S.C. § 1677j(b).

[113] *See* Chapter 12.

§ 13.24 Appeals

Judicial review "on the record" of final (not preliminary) decisions by the ITA and the ITC in both CVD and AD proceedings may be sought before the Court of International Trade (CIT). In turn, CIT decisions may be appealed first to the Court of Appeals for the Federal Circuit and ultimately to the U.S. Supreme Court.

§ 13.25 Appeals__WTO and NAFTA Proceedings

As noted in Chapter 12, international institutions also play an increasingly significant role in the resolution of trade disputes. The most important of these is the WTO's Dispute Settlement Body (DSB). Dissatisfied parties in domestic administrative proceedings may convince their government to challenge an adverse countervailing duty determination before the DSB based on alleged violations of the WTO SCM Agreement. As Chapter 9 examines in detail, proceedings before the DSB are governed by a separate WTO Agreement, the Dispute Settlement Understanding (DSU).

The SCM Agreement also has special rules regarding the resolution of subsidy disputes. The multilateral procedure under the WTO first provides for consultations between the complaining state and the subsidizing state. If these do not resolve the dispute within thirty days for a "red light" subsidy, or sixty days for a "yellow light" subsidy, either party is entitled to request that the DSB establish a panel to investigate the dispute and issue a written decision and report. The DSB panel will have ninety days (red light) or 120 days (yellow light) to investigate and prepare its report. The panel report is appealable on issues of law to the Appellate Body. The Appellate Body has thirty days (red light) or sixty days (yellow light) to decide the appeal. Panel and Appellate Body decisions are adopted without modification by the DSB unless rejected by an "inverted consensus" (again, see Chapter 9).

If a prohibited or actionable subsidy is found to exist, the subsidizing state is obligated under the WTO to withdraw the subsidy. If the subsidy is not withdrawn within a six-month period, the AB may authorize the complaining state to take countermeasures. Such countermeasures need not be in the form of countervailing duties, but may instead comprise increased tariffs by the complaining state on exports from the subsidizing state.

Separately, a special international institution exists for trade remedy disputes involving the three member states of the North American Free Trade Agreement (NAFTA)—the United States, Canada, and Mexico. NAFTA uniquely provides for resolution of CVD disputes through "binational panels." Such panels apply the domestic law of the importing country, and provide a substitute for judicial review of the decisions of administrative agencies of the importing country. Indeed, the initiation of a review under NAFTA divests the CIT of jurisdiction over the same dispute. Although the decisions of such binational panels are not formally binding in U.S. law, the ITA or ITC may decide to review any administrative action to conform to an adverse panel decision, including through a revocation or reduction of CVD duties.

Chapter 14

UNITED STATES EXPORT CONTROLS

Table of Sections

---

§ 14.1 U.S. Governance of Exports

Why does a nation control exports? Exports earn revenue and create jobs. This suggests that export controls are imposed more for political or foreign policy reasons than for economic reasons. But sometimes the controls have a mixture of these goals. For example, exports may be limited to protect national security (military weapons and technology, regulated in the U.S. by the Arms Export

Control Act of 1976), to limit the spread of nuclear components (partly controlled by the Nuclear Nonproliferation Act), to preserve natural resources (endangered species, subject to an international convention—CITES), to reserve resources for domestic use (certain hardwoods for making furniture), or to hold resources for sale at expected higher prices in the future (oil).

Apart from the law of export subsidies and countervailing duties and to a degree the law of export quotas, the WTO package of agreements marginally touches upon export issues. See Chapter 9. Why does the World Trade Organization fail to have extensive legal disciplines regarding exports?

The answer is less than clear. National export controls have certainly been less numerous, and therefore less on the international trade radar screen. Restricting exports is often counterintuitive to trade policy. Exports represent local production, employment and earnings, whereas imports may disrupt domestic companies, jobs and economic growth. Governments are therefore inclined to promote exports, not inhibit them. In the developing world, there has been a major policy shift away from import substitution in favor of export enhancement.

In the absence of WTO rules on export controls, member states have pursued different policies. The United States, one of the world's top exporters, shipping trillions of dollars of exports each year, has nevertheless maintained an extensive system of export controls. This system is the focus of this Chapter.

United States export controls involve three primary laws and government agencies. The U.S. Department of Commerce, Bureau of Industry and Security (BIS), administers the Export Administration Act Regulations (EAR, 22 C.F.R. Parts 730–774), and the U.S. antiboycott laws. The U.S. Department of the Treasury, Office of Foreign Asset Controls (OFAC), administers U.S. boycott laws. Lastly, the U.S. Department of State administers the International Traffic in Arms Regulations (ITAR, 22 C.F.R. Parts 120–130).

Unlike the control of imports, the laws regulating exports are briefer and rely on the issuance of extensive administrative regulations. For example, the *statutes* prohibiting U.S. persons from assisting boycotts against friendly nations fill only a few pages. But the *regulations* and examples of prohibited and permissible conduct fill dozens of pages in the Code of Federal Regulations. The control of exports, meaning their limitation, quite expectantly creates some conflict by way of the diminished economic benefit to the United States that might otherwise be gained from export trade. Indeed, the statement of policy in the Export Administration Act indicates that it is only after consideration of the impact of restrictions on the economy that export restrictions are adopted, and only to the extent necessary.[1]

Exports are controlled for three reasons stated in the governing rules—(1) to protect against the drain of scarce materials and reduce inflation from foreign demand, (2) to further U.S. foreign policy, and (3) to assure national security.[2] These goals are expressed in the principal export enactment, the Export Administration Act (EAA), and are implemented by means of licensing requirements.[3] But the EAA does not contain many substantive provisions regulating exports. They are contained in the Export Administration Regulations (EAR). These regulations constitute an extensive set of provisions detailing the governance of exports.

Governance of exports is principally by The Department of Commerce's Bureau of Industry and Security (BIS). But other departments also have some regulatory authority, especially the Department of State where the goods are "dual-use" items, meaning that they have both commercial and military application. Application for a license may be done electronically under the Simplified Network Application Process Redesign (SNAP-R), but only if the exporter has a BIS granted Company Identification Number (CIN).

§ 14.2   The Meaning of an "Export License"

Prior to 1996 changes, exporters sent items abroad under either a "general" license or a "validated" license. The general license was used for most exports and did not require prior approval

---

[1]   50 U.S.C. App. § 2402.

[2]   15 C.F.R. § 730.6.

[3]   The EAA of 1979 has been amended several times. It expired in 1994 but has been kept in force ever since by the President declaring a state of emergency under the International Emergency Economic Powers Act (IEEPA). 50 U.S.C. §§ 1701–1706. The President is required to report to Congress every six months on the national emergency. The report is more an outline of changes in export rules and actions taken than a disclosure of any conditions which any "reasonable man" might conclude constitute a national emergency. The Congress and the President have allowed the EAA to expire because of the continuing conflict between the Congress and the President regarding control over export trade. Unhappy with what Congress presents as a new framework for regulating exports, usually granting little discretion to the President to curtail exports to countries for U.S. foreign policy reasons, the President threatens a veto, the act is not passed, and the provisions of the old act remain in force under the International Emergency Economic Powers Act. Waiting for a "better" new law from Congress which does not so severely limit discretionary power of the President, with legislators annually predicting that it will be passed "this year," the wait has reached twenty years without any reasonable expectation that a new law will be forthcoming "this year or next."

by the Department of Commerce. When most goods were shipped and a "Shipper's Export Declaration (SED)" was filled out, the SED constituted a general license. Validated licenses were issued only upon application to and approval by the Department of Commerce.

The current regulations eliminate the terms "general license" and "validated license." "License" refers to an authorization to export granted by the Department of Commerce. The change is to some degree a matter of semantics. General licenses, which were in a sense "self-granted," are abolished in favor of referring to such exports as exports permitted without any license. The new "license" replaces the old "validated license." But much more was accomplished in the rearrangement of the regulations. The myriad of "special" licenses has been redone. There are now ten general prohibitions making up Part 736 of the C.F.R., rather than the previous scattering of the prohibitions throughout the regulations. These prohibitions indicate the circumstances where a license must be obtained.

§ 14.3 Export Administration Regulations

The EAA does not contain many substantive provisions regulating exports. They are contained in the Export Administration Regulations (EAR). These regulations constitute an extensive set of provisions detailing the governance of U.S. exports, "deemed exports" (disclosure of controlled technology *in the United States* to a foreign national) and re-exports. Following the "nationality of the goods," the EAR are primarily focused on the "end-use" or "end-user" of U.S. exports, including technology. The EAR rely heavily on "know your customer" determinations by exporters.

Important questions to which the exporter must give thought include:

What is the item?

Where is it going?

Who will actually receive and use it?

What will the item be used for?

Answers to these questions will help the exporter determine whether the EAR are applicable. The BIS maintains a list of "Red Flags" to assist with compliance and signal the need for further inquiries by exporter.

The Export Administration Regulations[4] govern most export activity, including the issuance of licenses. The regulations are implemented and enforced by the Bureau of Industry and Security (BIS). The regulations include helpful provisions for the exporter that attempt to explain the regulations in simple terms. The regulations introduce the exporter to considerable new terminology.[5] The export of some commodities and technical data is absolutely prohibited, while other commodities are permitted to be exported under a range of lenient to severe restrictions. Special provisions of the EAA apply to further control the proliferation of missiles, and chemical and biological weapons.[6] The EAR has integrated the role of the former Coordinating Committee for Multilateral Export Controls (COCOM), a group of nations which sought to keep sensitive material from communist dominated nations. COCOM was abolished soon after the Soviet Union was dismantled.[7] The United States enacted the Enhanced Proliferation Control Initiative (EPCI), motivated by the Iraq conflict. This enactment seeks to establish greater control where commodities or technical data are destined for a prohibited nuclear, chemical or biological weapons or missile development use or end user. Considerable emphasis is placed on making the exporter aware of the nature of the buyer and where the items are going.

The Department of Commerce has considerable discretion to allow or block exports where they are subject to licensing. In addition, certain *items* may be subject to mandatory controls, just as certain *destinations* may be subject to mandatory controls (*e.g.*, a boycott that disallows most or all exports, such as with Cuba or North Korea). Actually, these mandatory controls allow some deviation, usually by the President rather than an agency exercising discretion. Some examples of mandatory controls include the Nuclear Non-Proliferation Act regulations governing exports that have nuclear explosive capability, unprocessed timber under the Forest Resources Conservation and Shortage Relief Act (FRCSRA 1990), oil for purposes of conservation or to establish reserves, and oil from certain locations such as the North Slope of Alaska. Exports are thus subject to a mix of regulations *by* different persons or agencies, *of* different products, *for* different purposes, and *to* different places.

---

4   15 C.F.R. §§ 730–774.

5   Terms are defined in 50 U.S.C. App. § 2415 and in 15 C.F.R. § 772.

6   50 U.S.C. App. §§ 2410b and c.

7   COCOM expired in 1994. It has been replaced by the Wassenaar Arrangement, discussed below in § 14.17.

§ 14.4 Steps for Using the Export Administration Regulations

Part 730 provides a general introduction to the EAR. It outlines the scope of the regulations, statutory authority, defines "dual use" exports (generally civil versus military), other agencies which participate in the regulation of exports, extraterritorial application of regulations, purposes of control, and limited situations requiring licenses. Part 732 includes the 29 steps for using the EAR. They include an overview, steps regarding the scope of the EAR, the ten general prohibitions, License Exceptions, Shipper's Export Declaration and other documents and records, and other requirements.

The overview notes some important questions to which the exporter must give thought, such as: What is the item? Where is it going? Who will actually receive and use it? What will it be used for?[8] This will help the exporter determine whether the EAR are applicable. The first six steps regarding the scope of the EAR cover (1) items subject to the exclusive jurisdiction of another federal agency; (2) publicly available technology and software; (3) reexport of U.S. origin items; (4) foreign made items incorporating less than a *de minimis* level of U.S. parts, components and materials; (5) foreign made items incorporating more than a *de minimis* level of U.S. parts, components and materials; and (6) foreign made items produced with certain U.S. technology for export to specified destinations.

§ 14.5 General Prohibitions[9]

If an export is subject to the EAR, the general prohibitions, as well as the License Exceptions, must be reviewed to determine if a license is necessary. This part informs the exporter of both the facts that make the proposed transaction subject to the general prohibitions, and the nature of the general prohibitions.

§ 14.6 Determination of the Applicability of the General Prohibitions

Five factors help determine the obligations of the exporter under the ten general prohibitions.[10] They are:

(1) Classification of the item using the Country Control List (CCL).

---

8   15 C.F.R. § 732.1.
9   15 C.F.R. Part 736.
10   15 C.F.R. § 736.2.

(2)   Destination of the item using the CCL and Country Chart.

(3)   End-user referring to a list of persons the exporter may not deal with.

(4)   End-use.

(5)   Conduct such as contracting, financing, and freight forwarding in support of a proliferation project.

The ten general prohibitions follow, with commentary under the following headings:

(1)   General Prohibition One—Export and reexport of controlled items to listed countries (Exports and Reexports).

(2)   General Prohibition Two—Reexport and export from abroad of foreign-made items incorporating more than a *de minimis* amount of controlled U.S. content (Parts and Components Reexports).

(3)   General Prohibition Three—Reexport and export from abroad of the foreign-produced direct product of U.S. technology and software (Foreign-Produced Direct Product Reexports).

(4)   General Prohibition Four—Engaging in actions prohibited by a denial order (Denial Orders).

(5)   General Prohibition Five—Export or reexport to prohibited end-uses or end-users (End-Use End-User).

(6)   General Prohibition Six—Export or reexport to embargoed destinations (Embargo).

(7)   General Prohibition Seven—Support of Proliferation Activities (U.S. Person Proliferation Activity).

(8)   General Prohibition Eight—In transit shipments and items to be unladen from vessels or aircraft (Intransit).

(9)   General Prohibition Nine—Violation of any order, terms, and conditions (Orders, Terms, and Conditions).

(10) General Prohibition Ten—Proceeding with transactions with knowledge that a violation has occurred or is about to occur (Knowledge Violation to Occur).

In preparing these prohibitions, the Commerce Department rejected a number of suggestions to liberalize existing reexport controls, such as to create a separate part for reexports. Reexports create a problem with the nation from which the item may be reexported, which nation may object to any extraterritorial application of the U.S. rules. Some comments noted that although the new regulations were intended to be easier to use and less complex than the old, the new regulations created a system just as complex.

§ 14.7   Overview of Export Controls

The Commerce Control List (CCL—Part 774) is maintained by the BIS. The CCL includes all items (i.e., commodities, software, and technology) subject to BIS controls. The CCL does not include items exclusively governed by other agencies. But where there is shared governance, the CCL will note other agency participation. Knowing the Harmonized Code (customs classification for tariff purposes) Schedule B number does not help to determine whether or not an export license is required. That number is used by the Census Bureau for trade statistics. It is only the ECCN that will indicate whether or not an export license is required. If no license is required it is considered to be NLR.

§ 14.8   The Commerce Control List (CCL)

The CCL is contained in Supplement No. 1 to Part 774. Supplement No. 2 to Part 774 contains the General Technology and Software Notes relevant to entries in the CCL. The CCL basic structure includes the following ten general categories:

(0)   Nuclear Materials, Facilities, and Equipment (and Miscellaneous Items)

(1)   Materials, Chemicals, "Microorganisms," and Toxins

(2)   Materials Processing

(3)   Electronics

(4)   Computers

(5)   Telecommunications and Information Security

(6)   Sensors and Lasers

(7)   Navigation and Avionics

(8)   Marine

(9)   Propulsion Systems, Space Vehicles, and Related Equipment

Within each of the above ten categories are five different groups of items, identified by the letters A through E, as follows:

A.   Systems, Equipment, and Components

B.   Test, Inspection, and Production Equipment

C.   Material

D.   Software

E.   Technology

To classify an item the exporter determines the general characteristics that will usually be expressed by one of the categories. Having the appropriate category, the next step is to match the characteristics and functions with one of the groups. For example, a common television would be in category 3 and group A. The first digit and letter of the ECCN would thus be 3A.

This is followed by another digit that differentiates individual entries by the types of controls associated with the second digit. The Reasons for Control are as follows:

0.   National Security reasons (including Dual Use and International Munitions List) and Items on the NSG Dual Use Annex and Trigger List

   (1) Missile Technology reasons

   (2) Nuclear Nonproliferation reasons

   (3) Chemical & Biological Weapons reasons. . .

   (9) Anti-terrorism, Crime Control, Regional Stability, Firearms Convention, etc.

There may be more than one reason for control of a particular item. If so the first digit in the above list would appear as the second digit in the ECCN. The third digit in the ECCN reflects the possible unilateral and multilateral controls.

§ 14.9 License Requirements, License Exceptions and List of Items Controlled Sections

Next to each ECCN is a brief description, followed by "License Requirements", "License Exceptions", and "List of Items Controlled" sections.

"License Requirements" identifies all possible Reasons for Control in order of precedence. Items within a particular ECCN number may be controlled for more than one reason. All the possible Reasons for Control are as follows:[11]

AT   Anti-Terrorism

CB   Chemical & Biological Weapons

---

[11]   15 C.F.R. § 738.2(d)(2)(i).

CC Crime Control

EI Encryption Items

MT Missile Technology

NS National Security

NP Nuclear Nonproliferation

RS Regional Stability

SS Short Supply

XP Computers

SI Significant Items

The applicable reasons appear in one of two columns in the License Requirements, entitled "Control(s)". The second column, entitled "Country Chart", identifies a column name and number for each applicable Reason for Control (*e.g.*, CB Column 1). Once the exporter has determined that the item is controlled by a specific ECCN, information contained in the "License Requirements" section of the ECCN in combination with the Country Chart will allow a decision regarding the need for a license.

"License Exceptions" is used after it is determined that a license is required. It provides a brief eligibility statement for each ECCN-driven License Exception that may be applicable to the transaction. This is intended to help the exporter decide which ECCN-driven License Exception should be considered before submitting an application.[12] License Exceptions, the subject of Part 740, includes numerous categories. In the regulations, several exceptions were "bundled" under the grouping symbol LST (limited value shipments (LVS), shipments to group B countries (GBS), civil end-users (CIV), technology and software under restriction (TSR) and computers (APP)).

But objections by exporters with automated processes, who complained that an additional step was created, resulted in 1996 changes which dropped the LST, "debundled" the process, putting each exception into its own section. This makes them similar to other separated exceptions (i.e., temporary imports and exports (TMP), servicing and parts replacement (RPL), governments and international organizations (GOV), gift parcels and humanitarian donations (GFT), some technology and software (TSU), baggage (BAG), aircraft and vessels (AVS) and additional permissive reexports (APR)). Part 740 is an extensive and important part of the EAR. It is followed by three supplements to Part 740, including (1)

---

[12]   15 C.F.R. § 738.2(d)(2)(ii).

Country Groups, (2) meeting basic human needs, and (3) favorable treatment countries (ENC).

§ 14.10   The Commerce Country Chart

Consulting the Country Chart is an essential step in determining the need for a license. It is useful in all cases except where short-supply reasons apply, or where there are unique entries.[13] The Country Chart is Supplement No. 1 to Part 738, and over several pages lists countries alphabetically. Territories, possessions, and departments are not listed, but are subject to the same rules as the governing country. On the right of the listed countries are the numerous columns identifying the various Reasons for Control. There may be one, two or three columns under a particular Reason for Control. They correlate to references in the License Requirements section of the applicable ECCN. There may be an "x" in one or more of the cells. Where it appears in more than one cell, there will be multiple reviews.

§ 14.11   Determining the Need for an Export License[14]

Having determined that the item to be exported is controlled by a specific ECCN number, the exporter uses information in the "License Requirements" section of the ECCN entry in combination with the Country Chart. The need for a license is thus determined. Using the CCL "Controls" the exporter learns the reasons for control. Turning to the Country Chart and finding the appropriate country and the heading(s) for the reason(s), and with the column identifiers from the ECCN, the exporter looks for an "x". If found in the cell on the Country Chart, the exporter knows a license is required. A license application must be submitted unless a License Exception applies. Turning to the License Exceptions in the ECCN entry list, if a "yes" appears a further search of Part 740 will disclose whether an exception is available. Where there is no "x" in the cell on the Country Chart, a license is not required for control and destination, but one or more of General Prohibitions Four through Ten may prohibit the export. One can thus go to Parts 758 and 762 for information on export clearance procedures and record keeping.

§ 14.12   Advisory Opinions

A party who wishes to know whether a license is required may obtain an Advisory Opinion from the BIS.[15] Receipt of an opinion

---

[13]   15 C.F.R. § 738.3.

[14]   15 C.F.R. § 738.4.

does not mean the subsequent application will be granted. Opinions are not binding. But the BIS is likely to help the applicant in the preparation of an application which will meet the Advisory Opinion's requirements. An applicant may wish to avoid asking for an Advisory Opinion for fear that the opinion will be unfavorable. But if an export is made without an opinion and is in violation of the law, the sanctions may be severe.[16] Certainly, obtaining an unfavorable opinion and then exporting without a license creates a rather clear case of intent to disregard the law. But the Advisory Opinion is a good route to follow. If an unfavorable opinion is received, the BIS may explain what is required to obtain permission, unless the case is a clear one where no exports are permitted.

Support documents may be required along with an application.[17] Numerous countries are exempt from the need of support documents, mostly (1) any exports or reexports in the Western Hemisphere, (2) sales to government purchasers, and licenses submitted under special procedures, such as by A.I.D., or under the Special Comprehensive License procedure. When support documentation is required, the required data is to gain information about the disposition of the items, and to answer questions about national security controls and certain destinations. The transaction may require an End-User Certificate, or a Statement of Ultimate Consignee and Purchaser.[18]

§ 14.13 Issuance and/or Denial of Applications[19]

Part 750 describes the BIS's process for reviewing a license application, including processing times, denials, revocations, issuance, duplicates, transfers, and shipping tolerances on approved licenses. The part also includes information on processing Advisory Opinion requests.

The BIS undertakes a complete review of the application, including an analysis of the license and support documentation, plus a consideration of the reliability of each party to the transaction, including any intelligence information. The Departments of Defense, Energy, State, and the Arms Control and Disarmament Agency may also have review authority.

---

[15]   15 C.F.R. § 748.3.

[16]   Persons convicted of a violation of any statute specified in § 11(h) of the EAA may not apply for any export license for ten years. 15 C.F.R. § 748.4(c).

[17]   15 C.F.R. § 748.9.

[18]   *See also* 15 C.F.R. § 748.10–13 and Supplements.

[19]   15 C.F.R. Part 750.

Furthermore, the BIS may request review by other departments or agencies, which may agree to review, or waive review.

There has been a continuing dispute between Commerce and State over control of technology that seems to fall within the jurisdiction of each department. While the Arms Export Control Act gives State exclusive authority to issue jurisdiction determinations, Commerce has attempted to obtain concurrent authority to issue commodity jurisdiction determinations. Hearings were held in 1995 by the Senate Armed Services Committee after complaints that Commerce had issued export licenses for stealth technology that was under the jurisdiction of State. State intervened to stop the shipments, determined that they had jurisdiction, and denied the license. This kind of dispute has made it difficult to reach agreement on a new Export Administration Act. With proposals to abolish Commerce and transfer much of its export jurisdiction to State, the issue could become moot. There is little likelihood that State will agree to the transfer of any authority to Commerce.

Delay has been used by the government, especially by the Department of Defense, as a means of discouraging exports which might be permissible, but to which the Department objects. The *Daedalus Enterprises, Inc. v. Baldrige* case is an example.[20] Twenty-nine months after the filing of an application, the Department of Commerce had not reached a decision. The company had to seek a court order that the Secretary comply with the statutory timetable. There is little a company can do. It may not export the goods when the time period has expired if no response has been made by the government. It must go to court at each stage when the government fails to comply with the statute. Fortunately, the *Daedalus* case is an exception, and this kind of delay has been much diminished. The filing process is considerably improved.

§ 14.14 Timetable for Application Review

The BIS is required to resolve all applications, or refer them to the President, within 90 calendar days from the date of registration by the BIS. That is the date the BIS enters the application into the electronic license processing system.[21] Where there are deficiencies, the BIS tries to contact the applicant to obtain needed information. If no contact is made, the license is returned with notations of the deficiencies. This may cause a suspension in the processing time. If another department or agency is involved, or if government-to-government assurances or consultations are involved, there are additional time requirements for making requests and analyzing

---

[20]   563 F. Supp. 1345 (D.D.C. 1983).

[21]   15 C.F.R. § 750.4.

their results. When certain countries are involved, such as Congressional designated terrorist supporting nations, Congress may have to be notified, delaying the application for another 60 days.

§ 14.15 Issuance of an Export License[22]

A license is issued for a transaction, or series of transactions. The application may be approved in whole or in part. A license number is issued along with and a validation date. The license number must be used when discussing the license with the Department of Commerce. Nonmaterial changes may be made without obtaining a "Replacement" license.

§ 14.16 Revocation or Suspension of a License[23]

All licenses may be revised, suspended, or revoked. This may occur without notice when the BIS learns that the EAR have been violated or are about to be violated. The exporter may have to stop a shipment about to be made, or if possible one that is already en route. When revocation or suspension occurs, the exporter is required to return the license to the BIS. Appeals from actions taken under the EAA or the EAR by the BIS are allowed for most actions.[24] There is an internal appeal process prior to appealing to the federal courts.

§ 14.17 Review of Export Applications by International Agencies

In 1995, 28 nations,[25] including the United States, agreed to establish a new export control regime that would assume some of the functions of the expired COCOM. The Wassenaar Arrangement on Export Controls for Conventional Arms and Dual-Use Goods and Technologies (the organizational meeting was in Wassenaar, the Netherlands; the secretariat was established in Vienna) fell short of U.S. expectations, not containing a requirement of prior notification of sales by one country to other countries in the group. A second concern is the lack of agreement on prohibiting dual-use goods and conventional weapons to civilian as well as military end-users in such nations as Iran, Iraq, Libya, and North Korea. An additional

---

22   15 C.F.R. § 750.7.

23   15 C.F.R. § 750.8.

24   15 C.F.R. § 756.1.

25   Australia, Austria, Belgium, Canada, the Czech Republic, Denmark, Finland, France, Germany, Greece, Hungary, Iceland, Italy, Japan, Luxembourg, the Netherlands, New Zealand, Norway, Poland, Portugal, the Russian Federation, the Slovak Republic, Spain, Sweden, Switzerland, Turkey, the United Kingdom, and the United States. Several other nations have since joined.

concern is the lack of transparency in exchanging information on exports of dual use goods and conventional arms.

There are other multilateral export regimes, including the Nuclear Suppliers group (NSG), the Australia Group (AG), the Missile Technology Control Regime (MTCR), and the Technical Advisory Committees (TACs). It is reasonably safe to assume that the goals of these groups govern products carefully controlled under U.S. law.

§ 14.18   Shipper's Export Declaration (SED) and Automated Export System (AES)

The exporter is responsible for following the regulations that govern carrying out the export.[26] This is so whether a license is issued or the exporter relies on a License Exception. The most important responsibility is the proper preparation of the Shipper's Export Declaration (SED), or Automated Export System (AES) record. They are primarily statements to the U.S. government used for gathering information to prepare trade statistics. There are numerous exemptions, such as gift parcels, aircraft and vessels, governments and international organizations, technology and software, and tools of trade.

As many as one-half the filings contain errors of omission or commission, according to the Bureau of Census and U.S. Customs Service. The two organizations have compared SEDs with outbound vessel manifests and discovered numerous inaccuracies in the vessel manifests as well as the SEDs. Cargo is often manifested not on the vessel actually carrying the goods, but on the manifest of a later departing vessel. The reason is the failure of exporters (and forwarders) to supply SEDs with complete and accurate information when the goods are shipped. This causes difficulties for Customs in detecting export law violations, and creates inaccurate trade statistics. Unless voluntary compliance improves, Customs may delay or detain an increasing number of shipments where filings are not presented with complete and accurate information.

§ 14.19   Fines, Suspensions and Revocation of Export Authority

Some means of enforcement is necessary to assure compliance with rules. The export laws and regulations are no exception. Violation of laws and regulations governing exports brings into play both the basic law and the regulations. The EAA contains

---

[26]   15 C.F.R. § 758.3.

provisions governing violations of both the EAA and EAR.[27] The Export Administrative Regulations contain supplementary provisions.[28] The general sanction for violations of the export laws, where the conduct was entered into *knowingly,* is a fine of the higher of $50,000 or five times the value of the exports.[29] This can obviously be *very* substantial.[30] *Willful* violations, with knowledge that the commodities or technology will be used to benefit, or are destined for, a controlled country, may result in a fine for business entities of the higher of $1 million or five times the value of the exports.[31] For individuals who engage in such willful violations the fine is $250,000 and/or 10 years imprisonment. This provision covers misuse of licenses. Cases involving violations of the licensing requirements tend to be quite complex.[32] If the party exported to a controlled country commodities or technology under a license with knowledge that the commodities or technology were being used for military or intelligence gathering purposes, and willfully fails to report this use, the business entity fine is the same as above, the higher of $1 million or five times the value of the exports, but for the individual the imprisonment drops to five years, with the fine remaining the same, $250,000.[33] Even possession of goods or technology either with the intent to export in violation of the law or knowing that the goods might be so exported, can result in a fine.

Perhaps the most severe statutory penalty in the EAA is in the civil penalty section. The Department of Commerce may impose a fine of $10,000 for violations (in certain cases up to $100,000), and they may *suspend or revoke the authority to export.*[34] This is a most severe sanction used only in extreme cases. It was used in the Toshiba dispute, where Toshiba (Japan) and Köngsberg (Norway) enterprises sold the Soviet Union technology allegedly useful for developing submarine propellers which would be sufficiently silent to avoid detection.[35] The result was enactment of the Multilateral

---

[27]   50 U.S.C. App. § 2410. See www.bis.doc.gov for considerable information concerning enforcement.

[28]   15 C.F.R. Part 764.

[29]   50 U.S.C. App. § 2410(a).

[30]   *See* United States v. Ortiz de Zevallos, 748 F. Supp. 1569, 1573 (S.D. Fla. 1990), *judgment reversed* in United States v. Macko, 994 F.2d 1526 (11th Cir. 1993). *See also* United States v. Brodie, 403 F.3d 123 (3d Cir. 2005).

[31]   50 U.S.C. App. § 2410(b)(1).

[32]   United States v. Pervez, 871 F.2d 310 (3d Cir. 1989).

[33]   50 U.S.C. App. § 2410(b)(2).

[34]   50 U.S.C. § 2410(c).

[35]   *See* Robert van den Hoven van Genderen, *Cooperation on Export Control Between the United States and Europe: A Cradle of Conflict in Technology Transfer?* 14 N.C. J. INT'L L. & COM. REG. 391 (1989).

Export Control Enhancements Act in 1988,[36] amending the EAA and providing trade prohibition sanctions for two to five years.[37] These sanctions are applied whether or not the other nations take action against their companies. The EAR repeat and expand upon these statutory sanctions. They further add provisions dealing with actions including "causing, aiding, or abetting" a violation,[38] and "solicitation and attempt", and "conspiracy."[39] Further details are provided addressing misrepresentation and concealment of facts, or evasion,[40] failing to comply with reporting and record keeping requirements',[41] alterations of documents,[42] and acting contrary to the terms of a denial order.[43]

The political nature of export controls is emphasized by judicial refusal to agree to a settlement negotiated between a company accused of violations of the export laws and the Justice Department. In one instance a bargained for $1 million fine was rejected by the court, which imposed a $3 million fine.[44]

§ 14.20 Administrative Proceedings and Denial Orders

Administrative procedures which supplement the Administrative Procedures Act are the subject of a separate Part of the EAA and EAR.[45] They provide the framework for proceedings dealing largely with denial of export privileges and civil penalties. Appeals are the subject of several parts of the regulations.[46] The denial of export rights occurs principally either as an administrative sanction for violation of the EAR, or as a temporary measure when there is evidence of an imminent violation of the EAR. A denial order prohibits the party from any exports, unless there are exceptions in the order. The denial order states the extent to which exports are restricted. Because all denial orders are not

---

[36] It was part of the 1988 Omnibus Trade and Competitiveness Act. *See* 50 U.S.C. App. § 2410a.

[37] 50 U.S.C. App. § 2410a.

[38] 15 C.F.R. § 764(2)(b).

[39] 15 C.F.R. § 764(2)(c) & (d).

[40] 15 C.F.R. § 764.2(g) & (h).

[41] 15 C.F.R. § 764.2(i).

[42] 15 C.F.R. § 764.2(j).

[43] 15 C.F.R. § 764.2(k).

[44] United States v. Datasaab Contracting A.B. (D.D.C. Criminal No. § 84–00130, 4–27–84).

[45] 50 U.S.C. App. § 2412; 15 C.F.R. Parts 756, 764, and 766. One court has held that attorneys' fees of a prevailing defendant are not allowable under § 2412, because Congress did not make the Equal Access to Justice Act part of the EAA. *See* Dart v. United States, 961 F.2d 284 (D.C. Cir. 1992).

[46] 15 C.F.R. Part 764. *See* Iran Air v. Kugelman, 996 F.2d 1253 (D.C. Cir. 1993).

the same, it is important to read carefully any specific denial order to determine the extent of the denial.

The denial order also affects persons dealing with the denied party.[47] The denied party may not be part of a transaction nor receive any benefit from a transaction. What are subject to regulation are essentially items of U.S. origin, or foreign items which require reexport permission. A person who deals with a denied party is not innocent if there is no knowledge of the denial status; everyone is responsible for knowing that any person with whom they engage in transactions is *not* on the denial list.

Licensed items to be shipped to a denied party may place the exporter at risk. The denial order must be checked to determine the extent of the loss of export privileges *if* the sale to the denied party is a product to be reexported, or it releases controlled technical data to a denied foreign national. A person may buy products from a denied party in the United States, however, unless the intention is to subsequently export the product, which would give a "benefit" to the denied party. A transaction within a foreign country may be prohibited, as the foreign recipient of U.S. origin items may not sell them to a denied party even if the sale occurs within the foreign nation.[48] This purportedly applies whether or not the foreign firm is a U.S. subsidiary.

§ 14.21 Enhanced Proliferation Control Initiative (EPCI)

The EPCI consists of Sections 744.1–744.6 of the C.F.R. The initiative addresses how technology and goods are *used* rather than by their *description*. They include essentially the "design, development, production, stockpiling, or use" of nuclear explosive devices, missiles, or chemical or biological weapons. The end result is that a license is required where otherwise it might not be. Exporters are thus given the responsibility to know more about their dual-use goods. The use of the EPCI in the control of weapons of mass destruction, especially after September 11, 2001, is clear.

§ 14.22 Designation as a Foreign National

Although it is part of sanctions, being designated a foreign national merits separate consideration because it is so potentially restrictive. The Office of Foreign Assets Control (OFAC) in the

---

[47] It could even limit employment of a denied party, to the extent that the party could not engage in transactions subject to the EAR.

[48] This is not likely to be acceptable to the foreign country, which is apt to consider the prohibition an unreasonable extension of U.S. laws into its territory. A foreign court might order the transaction to take place.

Department of the Treasury may designate individuals and companies owned or controlled by, or acting for or on behalf of, targeted companies. They become so-called "specially designated nationals" or "SDNs." Their assets are blocked and U.S. persons are for the most part prohibited in dealing with them. The list of such designated nationals exceeds 550 pages. It can be a devastating designation and effectively end trade with the United States.

Chapter 15

THE FOREIGN CORRUPT PRACTICES ACT AND THE OECD ANTI-BRIBERY CONVENTION

Table of Sections

§ 15.1   Background and Introduction

History of the FCPA. The Foreign Corrupt Practices Act (FCPA) resulted from disclosures made to the Special Prosecutor in the Watergate scandal in the 1970s that many U.S. corporations had made payments to foreign officials to influence formal governmental policies and decisions. The FCPA was a response to the real and perceived harm to U.S. foreign policy interests arising from corrupt payments made by private corporations to influence foreign public officials in the performance of their official duties.

Subsequent investigations by the Securities and Exchange Commission (SEC) and a special Congressional Subcommittee on Multinational Corporations (the so-called Church Committee) revealed that the problem was serious and widespread.[1] A focal point of the investigations was the large defense contractor Lockheed Corporation, and for good reason: An investigation revealed that from 1970 to 1975 Lockheed had paid millions of dollars in bribes to public figures in Germany, Italy, Japan, the Netherlands, and other countries.[2] The names of alleged recipients also became public, causing considerable embarrassment (*e.g.*, Prince Bernard of the Netherlands). The revelations even led to the formal arrest of some prominent foreign officials, including Prime Minister Kakuei Tanaka of Japan.[3]

Congress responded in 1977 with the enactment of the FCPA.[4] This Act is not a free-standing statute in the U.S. Code. Rather, as the remaining Sections of this Chapter explain in detail, the FCPA amended the Securities Exchange Act of 1934 in two important respects: First, in three substantive sections the Act establishes criminal liability for a broad range of entities with connections to the United States concerning corrupt payments to foreign officials (see Sections 15.2 through 15.14 below).[5] Second, it requires issuers of securities in the United States to maintain accurate financial records that would tend to disclose the existence of such payments (see Sections 15.15 through 15.18 below).[6] Violations of these criminal statutes carry substantial monetary penalties and even

---

[1]   *See* S. Comm. on Banking, Housing and Urban Affairs, 94th Cong., *Report of the Securities & Exchange Commission on Questionable and Illegal Corporate Payments and Practices* (May, 1976).

[2]   *See* Brent Fisse & John Braithwaite, THE IMPACT OF PUBLICITY ON CORPORATE OFFENDERS 144 (1984).

[3]   *Id.*, at 152.

[4]   The Foreign Corrupt Practices Act, Pub. L. 95–213, 91 Stat. 1494 (Dec. 19, 1977).

[5]   *See* 15 U.S.C. §§ 78dd–1, 78dd–2, 78dd–3.

[6]   *See* 15 U.S.C. § 78m(b)(2).

incarceration for individuals (see Sections 15.19 through 15.23 below). And although no formal private right of action exists under the FCPA, violations may create a basis for indirect enforcement by private parties (see Sections 15.24 through 15.27 below).

The 1988 Amendments of the FCPA. Upon its adoption in 1977, U.S. corporations recognized that the FCPA placed them at a significant competitive disadvantage. At the time, many other industrialized countries both permitted bribery of foreign officials and made the payments tax deductible.[7] As a special Task Force reported to Congress during the debates over the FCPA, the solution to this problem of an uneven playing field was an international treaty "to assure that all nations, and the competing firms of differing nations, are treated on the same basis."[8] To address these concerns, Congress amended the FCPA in 1988 to remove some of the strictness and thus perceived competitive disadvantages for U.S. corporations in international business.[9] Those amendments also added two affirmative defenses, one based on local law and the other permitting payments for "reasonable and bona fide" promotional expenses.[10] At the same time, Congress renewed its call for the President to negotiate an international treaty to ensure a level playing field for U.S. companies engaged in international business transactions.[11]

The OECD Convention and the 1998 Amendments to the FCPA. As noted above, even before the adoption of the FCPA the United States began efforts to secure an international treaty prohibiting bribery of foreign officials. The U.S. pursued this goal principally through the Organization for Economic Cooperation and Development (OECD), and the result in 1997 was the OECD Convention on Combating Bribery of Foreign Public Officials in International Business Transactions.[12] The U.S. promptly ratified this treaty and in 1998 Congress passed conforming legislation that amended the FCPA in significant respects. Section 15.28 below will

---

[7] *See* Convention on Combating Bribery of Foreign Public Officials in International Business Transaction, S. EXEC. REP. NO. 105–19, at 12 (1998).

[8] *See Foreign Payments Disclosure: Hearings Before the Subcomm. on Consumer Protection and Fin. of the Comm. on Interstate and Foreign Commerce*, 94 Cong. Rec. 1, 45–46 (1976).

[9] *See* Omnibus Trade and Competitiveness Act of 1988, Pub. L. No. 100–418, § 5003, 102 Stat. 1107, 1415–25 (1988).

[10] For more on these affirmative defenses see §§ 15.12 and 15.13 below.

[11] *See* Omnibus Trade and Competitiveness Act of 1988, *supra* note 9., § 5003(d).

[12] Convention on Combating Bribery of Foreign Public Officials in International Business Transactions, Dec. 17, 1997, S. Treaty Doc. No. 105–43, *available at* http:// www.oecd.org/daf/anti-bribery/oecdantibriberyconvention.htm [hereinafter "OECD Anti-Bribery Convention"].

examine in detail both this OECD Convention and these 1998 amendments to the FCPA.

§ 15.2 The FCPA's Anti-Bribery Provisions: Elements of the Substantive Offense

The principal way in which the FCPA combats corruption in international business transactions is through a direct prohibition on corrupt payments to foreign officials. The Act achieves this goal in three sections of the U.S. Code covering three different sets of entities connected to the United States. These three parallel provisions define the following elements of the criminal offense of bribery of a foreign official (although some commentators cut the pie somewhat differently): (1) a covered entity; (2) nexus with interstate commerce (with important exceptions); (3) corruption and intent; (4) prohibited act; (5) foreign official as intended recipient; (6) purpose to gain influence or secure an improper advantage; and (7) goal to obtain or retain business.[13] Sections 15.3 through 15.9 below examine these elements in turn. Sections 15.10 through 15.14 then review the recognized exceptions and defenses to FCPA liability.

One overarching comment nonetheless is appropriate to set the context. The principal difficulty with criminalizing payments in a foreign country and culture is defining the concept of "corrupt." In some cultures, gift-giving reflects an essential, deeply ingrained component in the development of business (and other) relationships (*e.g.*, *ttokkap* in South Korea, *guanxi* in China, *baksheesh* in India and the Middle East). To turn a common phrase, one person's bribe is another's courtesy. To be sure, no country is likely to endorse bribery of its public officials in formal, written laws; but the "operational code"—the unwritten norms of required conduct—in many countries makes that very practice commonplace, and indeed expected. The FCPA nonetheless criminalizes corrupt payments to foreign officials as defined in that Act. But the last clause is worthy of emphasis: The FCPA does not prohibit bribes qua bribes; it prohibits only payments that violate its statutory standard. The following sections analyze that standard.

§ 15.3 Elements__Covered Entities

The FCPA's prohibitions against corrupt payments cover three sets of "persons" with connections to the United States as set forth in three separate sections of the Securities Exchange Act: 15 U.S.C.

---

[13]   *See, e.g.*, Worldwide Directories, S.A. De C.V. v. Yahoo! Inc., 2016 WL 1298987, at *7 (S.D.N.Y. 2016) (although failing to list the final element of a business goal, see § 15.9 below); Chevron Corp. v. Donziger, 974 F. Supp. 2d 362 (S.D.N.Y. 2014), *aff'd*, 833 F.3d 74 (2d Cir. 2016) (same); Ariztegui v. Sikorsky Aircraft Corp., 2011 WL 1216089, at *11 (D. Conn. 2011) (same).

§§ 78dd–1 ("issuers"), 78dd–2 ("domestic concerns"), and 78dd–3 ("any person" who acts in the United States).

(1) *Issuers.* Section 78dd–1 includes within the scope of the FCPA any "issuer" of securities on a national exchange[14] as well as any entity whose securities are traded on the over-the-counter market in the United States and thus is required to file periodic reports with the SEC.[15] This latter category includes the over 900 foreign companies with American Depository Receipts (ADRs) listed on a U.S. exchange.[16] Section 78dd–1 also covers "any officer, director, employee, or agent of such issuer or any stockholder thereof acting on behalf of such issuer."[17] Separately, a U.S. issuer that is a parent of and exercises sufficient control over its foreign subsidiary may be liable for the acts of that subsidiary/agent based on *respondeat superior* principles.[18] In the same vein, Section 78dd–1 covers a foreign national that "aids and abets [or] conspires with" an issuer, "regardless of whether the foreign national or company itself takes any action in the United States."[19]

(2) *Domestic Concerns.* Section 78dd–2 includes within the scope of the FCPA any "domestic concern." This very broad term includes (i) an individual who is a "citizen, national, or resident" of the United States, (ii) "any corporation, partnership, association, joint-stock company, business trust, unincorporated organization or sole proprietorship" that is organized under the laws of a State of the United States or the United States,[20] and (iii) any corporation, etc. with a principal place of business in the United States.[21] Again, this provision also covers officers, directors, agents, etc. as well as foreign nationals that aid, abet, or conspire with such a domestic concern.[22]

(3) *Any Person.* Section 78dd–3 is even broader. It includes within the scope of the FCPA "any person" who does "any . . . act . . . while in the territory of the United States" in furtherance of a

---

14   *See* 15 U.S.C. § 78*l*.

15   *See* 15 U.S.C. § 78o(d).

16   *See* https://www.sec.gov/divisions/corpfin/internatl/foreignsummary2014.pdf.

17   15 U.S.C. § 78dd–1(a).

18   *See Resource Guide to the U.S. Foreign Corrupt Practices Act*, at 27–28 (Criminal Division of the U.S. DOJ and the Enforcement Division of the U.S. SEC, Nov. 14, 2012), *available at* http://www.justice.gov/criminal/fraud/fcpa/guidance (hereinafter, FCPA Resource Guide).

19   *Id.*, at 11.

20   15 U.S.C. § 78dd–2(a).

21   *See* 15 U.S.C. § 78dd–2(h)(1) (defining the term "domestic concern"). This includes entities organized under the law of a "territory, possession, or commonwealth of the United States." *Id.*

22   15 U.S.C. § 78dd–2(a).

foreign bribery scheme.[23] Thus, the FCPA extends even to a foreign person engaged in a foreign bribery scheme for a foreign company in a foreign transaction if she commits a relevant single act in the territory of the United States (such as sending an email while on vacation here). Indeed, the U.S. government has taken a very liberal view of the required territorial nexus. In a submission to the OECD, the United States declared that § 78dd–3 extends to any act beyond "merely conceiv[ing] the idea of paying a bribe without undertaking to do so."[24] Again, this provision covers officers, directors, agents, etc. of such a person.

The FCPA does not formally cover foreign *recipients* of a prohibited corrupt payment.[25] But they too may be subject to prosecution if, in connection with a foreign bribery scheme, they function as an agent of a covered issuer, domestic concern, or other person who commits a relevant act in the United States. Nonetheless, as a federal district court recently reiterated, no criminal liability attaches to a foreign national who does not act as an agent of a covered person, qualify as a domestic concern, or commit any relevant act in the territory of the United States.[26]

§ 15.4   Elements__Nexus to Interstate Commerce

Each of the three basic provisions of the FCPA (78dd–1, 78dd–2, and 78dd–3) states as an element that the prohibited actor must "make use of the mails or any means or instrumentality of interstate commerce in furtherance of" a prohibited payment to a foreign official.[27] The Act defines "interstate commerce" to mean "trade, commerce, transportation, or communication among the several States, or between any foreign country and any State or between any State and any place or ship outside thereof."[28] This of course is a common notion when Congress legislates on the basis of its constitutional authority under Commerce Clause of Article I.[29]

The significance of this element has diminished substantially, however, in light of the 1998 amendments to the FCPA. On the

---

[23]   15 U.S.C. § 78dd–3(a).

[24]   *See* United States: Review of the Implementation of the Convention and 1997 Recommendation ("Phase 1 Report"), at 3 (April, 1999), *available at* http://www. oecd.org/dataoecd/16/50/2390377.pdf.

[25]   United States v. Blondek, 741 F. Supp. 116, 117 (N.D. Tex. 1990) (observing that the FCPA "does not criminalize the receipt of a bribe by a foreign official"), *aff'd, sub nom* United States v. Castle, 925 F.2d 831 (5th Cir. 1991).

[26]   *See* United States v. Hoskins, 123 F. Supp. 3d 316, 319 (D. Conn. 2015).

[27]   15 U.S.C. §§ 78dd–1(a), 78dd–2(a), 78dd–3(a). As to the last provision (78dd–3) this language is largely irrelevant because, as noted in § 15.3 above, that provision also covers "any other act" while in the territory of the United States.

[28]   15 U.S.C. § 78dd–2(h)(5).

[29]   *See* U.S. CONST., art. I, § 8, cl. 3.

basis of a requirement in the OECD Anti-Bribery Convention that member states assert jurisdiction based on the "nationality" principle,[30] those amendments included a provision on "alternative jurisdiction" for a "United States person."[31] This broad term means any national of the United States and "any corporation, partnership, association, joint-stock company, business trust, unincorporated organization, or sole proprietorship" that is organized under the laws of the United States or any State, territory, etc. of the United States.[32] These "United States Persons" may be prosecuted for violating the FCPA irrespective of whether they use an instrumentality of interstate commerce.[33]

§ 15.5   Elements__"Corruptly" and Intent

Corruptly. A violation of the FCPA requires that a prohibited act be done "corruptly."[34] Unfortunately, the Act does not define this term, and its meaning cannot "be determined 'simply by reading it in context.'"[35] The legislative history of the FCPA nonetheless indicates that it "connotes an evil motive or purpose" or a "wrongful" intent to influence a prohibited recipient.[36]

Federal courts have interpreted the term much in the same sense. One court thus held that "corruptly" means "an act done with an evil motive or wrongful purpose of influencing a foreign official to misuse his position."[37] Another emphasized that a person meets this

---

[30]   *See* OECD Anti-Bribery Convention, *supra* note 12, art. 4.2. For more on this point see § 15.28 and text accompanying notes 189–190 *infra*.

[31]   15 U.S.C. §§ 78dd–1(g), 78dd–2(i).

[32]   15 U.S.C. §§ 78dd–1(g)(2), 78dd–2(i)(2).

[33]   15 U.S.C. §§ 78dd–1(g)(1), 78dd–2(i)(1).

[34]   15 U.S.C. §§ 78dd–1(a), 78dd–2(a), 78dd–3(a).

[35]   SEC v. Jackson, 908 F. Supp. 2d 834, 860 (S.D. Tex. 2012) (*quoting* Stichting Ter Behartiging Van de Belangen Van Oudaandeelhouders In Het Kapitaal Van Saybolt Int'l B.V. v. Schreiber, 327 F.3d 173, 181 (2d Cir. 2003)).

[36]   *See* S. Rep. No. 95–114, at 10 (1977). Because this Report has played prominently in analyses of the word "corruptly" under the FCPA, it is worthy of full quotation:

> The word "corruptly" is used in order to make clear that the offer, payment, promise, or gift, must be intended to induce the recipient to misuse his official position in order to wrongfully direct business to the payor or his client, or to obtain preferential legislation or a favorable regulation. The "corruptly" connotes an evil motive or purpose, an intent to wrongfully influence the recipient.

See also Stichting Ter Behartiging Van de Belangen Van Oudaandeelhouders In Het Kapitaal Van Saybolt Int'l B.V. v. Schreiber, 327 F.3d 173, 182 (2d Cir. 2003) (*quoting* this report); SEC v. Straub, 921 F. Supp. 2d 244, 263 (S.D.N.Y. 2013) (same). The House Report at the time described the term "corruptly" in much the same way. *See* H. Rep. 95–640, at 7–8 (1977).

[37]   SEC v. Jackson 908 F. Supp. 2d 834, 859 (S.D. Tex. 2012). *See also* SEC v. Straub, 921 F. Supp. 2d 244, 263 (S.D.N.Y. 2013) (observing that "the word 'corruptly' is used in order to make clear that the offer, payment, promise or gift

test if she merely knows that her actions are unlawful in some way; it thus held that the government is not required to prove that a defendant knew her actions would constitute a violation of the FCPA.[38] If a person has such a corrupt intent, it is irrelevant whether she knows the identity of the proposed recipient.[39] It likewise is irrelevant whether the bribe actually is made or whether the overall scheme is successful in achieving its goal.[40]

Willfulness. Individual *criminal* liability for violating the anti-bribery provisions of the FCPA also requires proof that the defendant act "willfully." This requirement is set forth directly for an individual who is or acts on behalf a "domestic concern" (§ 78dd–2) and for individuals acting in the territory of the United States (§ 78dd–3).[41] A separate provision states this requirement for officers, directors, etc. acting on behalf of an issuer covered by § 78dd–1.[42] The government is not required to prove willfulness for corporate criminal liability,[43] although of course the corruption element discussed immediately above remains.

The FCPA again does not define the term "willfully." In absence of textual guidance, courts have resorted to the common understanding from a variety of federal criminal statutes. Following these general notions, they have held that the defendant (of course) must have acted intentionally, that is, not by mistake or accident.[44] Beyond this, all that is required for a criminal violation of the FCPA is that the defendant knew that his actions "were in some way

---

must be intended to induce the recipient to misuse his official position in order to wrongfully direct business to the payor or his client, or to obtain preferential legislation or a favorable reputation").

[38] Stichting Ter Behartiging Van de Belangen Van Oudaandeelhouders In Het Kapitaal Van Saybolt Int'l B.V. v. Schreiber, 327 F.3d 173, 183 (2d Cir. 2003). *See also* SEC v. Jackson 908 F. Supp. 2d 834, 859–860 (S.D. Tex. 2012) (same).

[39] *See, e.g.,* United States v. Harder, 168 F. Supp. 3d 732, 739 (E.D. Pa. 2016); SEC v. Straub, 921 F. Supp. 2d 244, 265 (S.D.N.Y. 2013); SEC v. Jackson 908 F. Supp. 2d 834, 851–853 (S.D. Tex. 2012).

[40] *See* FCPA Resource Guide, *supra* note 18, at 14.

[41] *See* 15 U.S.C. §§ 78dd–2(g)(2)(A), 78dd–3(e)(2)(A).

[42] *See* 15 U.S.C. § 78ff(c)(2)(A).

[43] *Compare* 15 U.S.C. §§ 78ff(c)(2)(A) (stating a willfulness requirement for individuals acting on behalf of an issuer) with 78ff(c)(1)(A) (stating no such requirement for issuers); §§ 78dd–2(g)(2)(A) (stating a willfulness requirement for a natural person acting on behalf of a domestic concern) with 78dd–2(g)(1)(A) (stating no such requirement for a domestic concern that is not a natural person); and §§ 78dd–3(e)(2)(A) (stating a willfulness requirement for natural persons who violate 78dd–3) with § 78dd–3(e)(1)(A) (stating no such requirement for a juridical person that violates § 78dd–3).

[44] United States v. Kay, 513 F.3d 432, 447–448 (5th Cir. 2007); United States v. Kozeny, 667 F.3d 122, 135–136 (2d Cir. 2011) (endorsing the trial court's jury instruction on this point).

unlawful."[45] The courts thus have emphasized that the defendant "need not have known of the specific [criminal] statute[;] rather he must have acted with the knowledge that he was doing a 'bad' act under the general rules of law."[46]

In contrast, willfulness is not required for civil liability of an individual (*i.e.*, monetary penalties)[47] or for criminal or civil liability of a corporate entity.[48]

§ 15.6   Elements__Prohibited Acts

The fundamental goal of the FCPA is to prohibit bribery of foreign public officials. But the Act recognizes that such corruption can come in a variety of vehicles and types. Each of its three principal sections thus defines the prohibited acts in very broad terms to include "an offer, payment, promise to pay, or authorization of the payment of any money" as well as any "offer, gift, promise to give, or authorization of the giving of anything of value" to a foreign official.[49]

By its nature, the notion of "anything of value" is extremely broad. It includes of course direct gifts of valuable items, but also, for example, travel and entertainment, payment of medical and other expenses, lavish dinners, and beneficial services of myriad forms. In one early case, an official of an American company was convicted of violating the FCPA for giving a foreign official airplane tickets for his honeymoon.[50] The DOJ's and SEC's *Resource Guide to the U.S. Foreign Corrupt Practices Act* lists as further examples in the same vein "a $12,000 birthday trip for a government decisionmaker"; "$10,000 spent on dinners, drinks, and entertainment for a government official"; "a trip to Italy for eight . . . government officials that consisted primarily of sightseeing and included $1,000 in 'pocket money' for each official"; and "a trip to Paris for a government official and his wife that consisted primarily

---

[45]   United States v. Kay, 513 F.3d. 432, 447–448 (5th Cir. 2007) (citing the general discussion of criminal willfulness by the Supreme Court in Bryan v. United States, 524 U.S. 184, 191–92 (1998), and Ratzlaf v. United States, 510 U.S. 135, 137 (1994)).

[46]   *Id.* (punctuation mark added). *See also* Stichting Ter Behartiging Van de Belangen Van Oudaandeelhouders In Het Kapitaal Van Saybolt Int'l B.V. v. Schreiber, 327 F.3d 173, 181 (2d Cir. 2003); United States v. Kozeny, 667 F.3d 122, 135–136 (2d Cir. 2011).

[47]   *See* 15 U.S.C. §§ 78dd–2(g)(2)(B), 78dd–3(e)(2)(B), 78ff(c)(2)(B). For more on these penalties see § 15.20 *infra*.

[48]   *See* 15 U.S.C. §§ 78dd–2(g)(1), 78dd–3(e)(1), 78ff(c)(1). For more on these penalties see § 15.20 *infra*.

[49]   15 U.S.C. §§ 78dd–1(a), 78dd–2(a), 78dd–3(a).

[50]   United States v. Liebo, 923 F.2d 1308, 1311 (8th Cir. 1991).

of touring activities via a chauffeur driven vehicle."[51] Even gifts made to a charitable organization may suffice if it is affiliated with a foreign public official and the purpose is to secure a corrupt advantage from or through that official.[52]

There is no *de minimis* exemption for these prohibited acts. Nonetheless, as the government's *FCPA Resource Guide* emphasizes in this connection, the giving of "anything of value" must have a corrupt purpose. Thus, "it is difficult to envision any scenario in which the provision of cups of coffee, taxi fare, or company promotional items of nominal value would ever evidence corrupt intent."[53]

§ 15.7 Elements__Foreign Official

The FCPA does not prohibit all payments, only those made with the corrupt intent to influence foreign officials. Nonetheless, in parallel language in each of its three principal sections, the FCPA defines the prohibited recipients and the prohibited purposes of a corrupt payment in very broad terms. In this Section, we analyze the FCPA's definition of the prohibited recipients under the general heading "foreign official." The next Section examines the prohibited purposes of corrupt payments under the general heading "purpose to influence."

The FCPA prohibits corrupt payments to a whole range of actors related to a foreign government. First, it prohibits payments to "any foreign official."[54] This term includes not only "any officer or employee of a foreign government or any department, agency, or instrumentality thereof" but also "any person acting in an official capacity for or on behalf of any such government or department[.]"[55] Thus, the Act covers high- and low-ranking officials, employees, and government agents alike.

Second, the Act prohibits payments to "any foreign political party or official thereof or any candidate for foreign political office."[56] The latter category thus covers payments with a long-term goal to gain favor with a candidate who might become a formal "foreign official" in the future.

---

[51] *See* FCPA Resource Guide, *supra* note 18, at 15.

[52] *See id.*, at 16–19.

[53] *Id.*

[54] 15 U.S.C. §§ 78dd–1(a)(1), 78dd–2(a)(1), 78dd–3(a)(1).

[55] 15 U.S.C. §§ 78dd–(f)(1)(A), 78dd–2(h)(2)(A), and 78dd–3(f)(2)(A) (each defining the term "foreign official").

[56] 15 U.S.C. §§ 78dd–1(a)(2), 78dd–2(a)(2), 78dd–3(a)(2).

Third, the set of prohibited recipients includes "public international organizations" as designated by the President.[57] Dozens of organizations are on the list, from highly significant ones such as the World Bank, International Monetary Fund, and World Trade Organization to highly specialized ones such as the "International Cotton Advisory Committee" and the "International Fertilizer Development Center."[58]

Fourth, the term "instrumentality" in the definition of a "foreign official" opens the possibility of a prohibited bribery for a host of organizations affiliated with a foreign government. A particular flashpoint has been the status of state-owned and state-controlled companies, which clearly may qualify as an instrumentality of a foreign government.[59] As a result, a U.S. company doing business with a state-controlled enterprise—for example, in China, India, or Vietnam—must comply with the FCPA's anti-bribery provisions regarding all payments to such an enterprise.

Courts have considered a variety of non-exclusive factors in assessing whether an enterprise is an "instrumentality" of a foreign state. As summarized by one court, these include:

- The foreign state's characterization of the entity and its employees;

- The foreign state's degree of control over the entity;

- The purpose of the entity's activities;

- The entity's obligations and privileges under the foreign state's law, including whether the entity exercises exclusive or controlling power to administer its designated functions;

- The circumstances surrounding the entity's creation; and

---

[57]   15 U.S.C. §§ 78dd–(f)(1)(A), 78dd–2(h)(2)(A), and 78dd–3(f)(2)(A) (each defining the term "foreign official" to include an officer, employee, etc. of a "public international organization"); and §§ 78dd–(f)(1)(B), 78dd–2(h)(2)(B), and 78dd–3(f)(2)(B) (each defining "public international organization" to mean any organization so designated by the President under the International Organizations Immunities Act, 22 U.S.C. § 288, or otherwise).

[58]   See 22 U.S.C. § 288, Note.

[59]   See, e.g., United States v. Duperval, 777 F.3d 1324, 1333–1334 (11th Cir. 2015); Aluminum Bahrain B.S.C. v. Alcoa Inc., 2012 WL 2094029, at *3 (W.D. Pa. 2012); United States v. Carlson, 2011 WL 5101701, at *3–4 (C.D. Cal. 2011); United States v. Aguilar, 783 F. Supp. 2d 1108, 1113–1114 (C.D. Cal. 2011).

- The foreign state's extent of ownership of the entity, including the level of financial support by the state (*e.g.*, subsidies, special tax treatment, and loans).[60]

Separately, the Eleventh Circuit has emphasized—on the basis of the drafting history of the OECD Convention[61]—that the term instrumentality is not limited "to entities that perform traditional, core government functions."[62]

Finally, and perhaps most important, the FCPA prohibits corrupt offers, payments, etc. to "any person . . . while knowing that" any portion of the payment will be offered or given, "directly or indirectly," to a foreign official, political party, etc. as described above.[63] The definition of "knowing" extends far beyond actual knowledge. Each of the three parallel provisions of the FCPA defines the term to include an awareness that a result is "substantially certain to occur" as well as an awareness of "a high probability" of the existence of a relevant circumstance (unless the defendant "actually believes" that it does not exist).[64]

The courts in turn have interpreted this definition to embrace a "willful blindness" test. Thus, a covered person may commit a criminal act under the FCPA if he is aware of a "high probability" that a consultant, broker, or other intermediary will direct any part of a payment to a foreign official. "Conscious ignorance" or "conscious avoidance" also will suffice. As the Second Circuit observed in *U.S. v. Kozeny* in 2011, a trial court may give an instruction in FCPA cases that "permits a jury to find that a defendant had culpable knowledge of a fact when the evidence shows that the defendant intentionally avoided confirming the fact."[65]

According to the government's *FCPA Resource Guide*, the "common red flags" associated with willful blindness/conscious avoidance involving payments through intermediaries include the

---

[60]   United States v. Carlson, 2011 WL 5101701, at *3–4 (C.D. Cal. 2011). *See also, e.g.*, United States v. Duperval, 777 F.3d 1324, 1333–1334 (11th Cir. 2015) (providing more detail on (a) whether "the government controls the entity" and (b) whether "the entity performs a function that the government treats as its owns"); United States v. Aguilar, 783 F. Supp. 2d 1108, 1113–1114 (C.D. Cal. 2011). A 2012 DOJ Opinion Release under the FCPA also addressed this subject. *See* U.S. Department of Justice FCPA Op. Release 12–01 (September 18, 2012).

[61]   For more on this point see § 15.28 and text accompanying notes 194–195 *infra*.

[62]   United States v. Esquenazi, 752 F.3d 912, 924 (11th Cir. 2014).

[63]   15 U.S.C. §§ 78dd–1(a)(3), 78dd–2(a)(3), 78dd–3(a)(3).

[64]   15 U.S.C. §§ 78dd–1(f)(2), 78dd–2(h)(2), and 78dd–3(f)(2).

[65]   United States v. Kozeny, 667 F.3d 122, 132–133 (2d Cir. 2011) (*quoting* United States v. Ferrarini, 219 F.3d 145, 154 (2d Cir. 2000)).

following: excessive commissions; unreasonably large discounts; consulting agreements that include "only vaguely described services"; activities beyond the intermediary's traditional expertise; a close association between the intermediary and a foreign official; a foreign official's express request for a particular intermediary; engagement of an intermediary that is "merely a shell company incorporated in an offshore jurisdiction"; and requested payments to a third-country bank account.[66]

§ 15.8 Elements__Purpose to Influence or Secure Improper Advantage

The prohibited payment to a foreign official must be for a defined corrupt purpose. The three parallel FCPA provisions prohibit an offer, payment, etc. for the *direct* purpose of (a) influencing any act or decision of a foreign official, political party, etc. "in his official capacity," or (b) inducing such a foreign official to do or omit to do any act "in violation of the lawful duty of such official."[67] They also prohibit an offer, payment, etc. for the *indirect* purpose of "inducing" any a foreign official, political party, etc. "to use his influence" with a foreign government or official in order to "affect or influence" any act or decision.[68]

Finally, the 1998 FCPA amendments added—on the basis of the OECD Anti-Bribery Convention[69]—an even broader prohibited purpose of "securing any improper advantage."[70] Federal courts have interpreted this term broadly as well. The Fifth Circuit thus quoted with approval a commentary on the OECD Convention to the effect that " 'improper advantage' refers to something to which the company concerned was not clearly entitled," and it gave as an example "an operating permit for a factory which fails to meet the statutory requirements."[71]

§ 15.9 Elements__Business Goal

Finally, the corrupt payment to a foreign official, political party, etc. must have as its purpose to assist the covered party "in obtaining or retaining business for or with, or directing business to,

---

[66]   *See* FCPA Resource Guide, *supra* note 18, at 22–23.

[67]   15 U.S.C. §§ 78dd–1(a)(1)(A), (2)(A), 3(A); 78dd–2(a)(1)(A), (2)(A), 3(A); 78dd–3(a)(1)(A), (2)(A), 3(A).

[68]   15 U.S.C. §§ 78dd–1(a)(1)(B), (2)(B), (3)(B); 78dd–2(a)(1)(B), (2)(B), (3)(B); 78dd–3(a)(1)(B), (2)(B), (3)(B).

[69]   *See* § 15.28 *infra.*

[70]   15 U.S.C. §§ 78dd–1(a)(1)(A), (2)(A), (3)(A); 78dd–2(a)(1)(A), (2)(A), (3)(A); 78dd–3(a)(1)(A), (2)(A), (3)(A).

[71]   United States v. Kay, 359 F.3d 738, 754 (5th Cir. 2004).

any person."[72] It should not surprise that this element of the test has a quite expansive reach. The Fifth Circuit provided perhaps the definitive statement of this point in *United States v. Kay*.[73] After an extensive analysis of the drafting history of the FCPA as well as of the OECD Anti-Bribery Convention the court declared:

> [W]e cannot hold as a matter of law that Congress meant to limit the FCPA's applicability to cover only bribes that lead directly to the award or renewal of contracts. Instead, we hold that Congress intended for the FCPA to apply broadly to payments intended to assist the payor, either directly or indirectly, in obtaining or retaining business for some person[.] . . . The FCPA's legislative history instructs that Congress was concerned about both the kind of bribery that leads to discrete contractual arrangements and the kind that more generally helps a domestic payor obtain or retain business for some person in a foreign country[.][74]

As this quote indicates, virtually any direct or indirect benefit to a business interest may satisfy this final element of the test for a prohibited corrupt payment to a foreign official. The government's *FCPA Resource Guide* thus provides the following examples: "winning a contract; influencing the procurement process; circumventing the rules for importation of products; gaining access to non-public bid tender information; evading taxes or penalties; influencing the adjudication of lawsuits or enforcement actions; obtaining exceptions to regulations; [and] avoiding contract termination."[75]

§ 15.10 Exception and Affirmative Defenses

The FCPA expressly recognizes one exception and two defenses to liability under its anti-bribery provisions. A form of implied defense also arises in cases of true extortion. The following Sections examine these limitations on the FCPA's anti-bribery provisions.

§ 15.11 Exception__Facilitating or Expediting Payments

The principal exception under the FCPA commonly is known as the "grease payments" exception.[76] This covers any "facilitating or expediting payment" made to a foreign official when the purpose is

---

[72]   15 U.S.C. §§ 78dd–1(a)(1), (2), (3); 78dd–2(a)(1), (2), (3); 78dd–3(a)(1), (2), (3).

[73]   359 F.3d 738 (5th Cir. 2004).

[74]   *Id.*, at 755–756.

[75]   *See* FCPA Resource Guide, *supra* note 18, at 13.

[76]   *See* §§ 78dd–1(b), 78dd–2(b), 78dd–3(b).

"to expedite or to secure the performance" of a "routine governmental action."[77] The Act defines the latter term in four specific provisions and one general catch-all clause. Specifically, a covered party does not violate the FCPA in making a payment to secure an action that is "ordinarily and commonly performed" by a foreign official in:

(i) obtaining permits, licenses, or other official documents to qualify a person to do business in a foreign country;

(ii) processing governmental papers, such as visas and work orders;

(iii) providing police protection, mail pick-up and delivery, or scheduling inspections associated with contract performance or inspections related to transit of goods across country;

(iv) providing phone service, power and water supply, loading and unloading cargo, or protecting perishable products or commodities from deterioration.[78]

A general clause at the end of the list protects payment made to obtain "actions of a similar nature."[79]

Nonetheless, an immediately succeeding proviso makes clear that this is not an open-ended invitation to conceal bribes as an effort to facilitate a routine government action. Each of the FCPA's three substantive provisions specifically declares that this exception does not include any decision by a foreign official "to award new business to or to continue business with a particular party" or "to encourage a decision to award new business to or continue business with a particular party."[80]

§ 15.12   Defenses__Permitted Under Written Laws

The FCPA recognizes two affirmative defenses. The first is when the payment, gift, offer, or promise is lawful under the *written* laws and regulations of the foreign country.[81] The word "written" of course is significant. Few foreign countries have formal, written laws that specifically allow bribery of their governmental officials or candidates for public office. As a result, this affirmative defense will

---

[77]   *Id.*

[78]   15 U.S.C. §§ 78dd–1(f)(3)(A), 78dd–2(h)(4)(A), 78dd–3(f)(4)(A).

[79]   *Id.*

[80]   15 U.S.C. §§ 78dd–1(f)(3)(B), 78dd–2(h)(4)(B), 78dd–3(f)(4)(B).

[81]   15 U.S.C. §§ 78dd–1(c)(1) (providing an affirmative defense for payments that are "lawful under the written laws and regulations" of the foreign country); § 78dd–2(c)(1)(same); 78dd–3(c)(1) (same).

rarely be of relevance. When confronted with claims by a foreign official that a desired payment is legal under local law, U.S. firms and their lawyers are well advised to obtain an opinion in writing from foreign local counsel that identifies the specific written law or regulation that allows the payment.

§ 15.13   Defenses___Reasonable and Bona Fide Expenditures

The second affirmative defense recognized by the FCPA is for payments made to a foreign official as a "reasonable and bona fide expenditure, such as travel and lodging expenses."[82] Such an expenditure must be "directly related to" one of two specifically defined purposes: (a) "the promotion, demonstration, or explanation of products or services," or (b) "the execution or performance of a contract with a foreign government or agency thereof."[83]

Whether a particular promotional expense satisfies this defense of course will be highly dependent on the facts of each case. To provide guidance the Department of Justice has issued a number of "opinion releases"[84] in response to specific inquiries on this subject. As summarized by the government's *FCPA Resource Guide*, these opinions indicate that a covered party should observe the following "safeguards" to ensure that a particular payment qualifies as "reasonable and bona fide" expenditure under this defense: (a) It should not select specific foreign officials for trips or meetings; (b) it should make payments directly to travel and lodging vendors or otherwise provide reimbursement only against qualified receipts; (c) it should not advance funds for expenditures in cash; (d) it should ensure that any flat amount stipends are "reasonable approximations" of expected costs; (e) it should pay for expenditures in manner that is transparent both within the company and to the foreign government; (f) it should not condition payments on any action by the foreign official; (g) it should ensure that any payment is not contrary to local law; and (h) it should ensure that any such expenditure is accurately recorded in the company's books.[85]

---

[82]   15 U.S.C. §§ 78dd–1(c)(2), 78dd–2(c)(2), 78dd–3(c)(2).

[83]   *Id.*

[84]   The FCPA obligates the Department of Justice to provide such opinions for issuers and domestic concerns. For more on this point see § 15.22 *infra.*

[85]   *See* FCPA Resource Guide, *supra* note 18, at 24. The following DOJ Opinion Releases address the "reasonable and bona fide expenditures" defense: FCPA Op. Release 11–01 (June 30, 2011); FCPA Op. Release 08–03 (July 11, 2008); FCPA Op. Release 07–02 (September 11, 2007); FCPA Op. Release 07–01 (July 24, 2007); FCPA Op. Release 04–04 (September 3, 2004); FCPA Op. Release 04–03 (June 14, 2004); FCPA Op. Release 04–01 (January 6, 2004); FCPA Op. Release 96–01 (November 25, 1996).

§ 15.14   Defenses—True Extortion

Although no provision in the FCPA expressly recognizes this, a company may have a defense in the case of true extortion. The Senate Committee Report on the FCPA in 1977 thus contained this observation:

> That the payment may have been first proposed by the recipient rather than the U.S. company does not alter the corrupt purpose on the part of the person paying the bribe. On the other hand true extortion situations would not be covered by this provision since a payment to an official to keep an oil rig from being dynamited should not be held to be made with the requisite corrupt purpose.[86]

On this basis, both the government's *FCPA Resource Guide*[87] and one court[88] have recognized that a "extortion" defense exists for payments demanded by a foreign official. These authorities have made clear, however, that mere economic coercion—such as the loss of a contract or an inability to break into a foreign market—will not suffice.

§ 15.15   The FCPA's Accounting Provisions—In General

The second pillar of the FCPA is directed to accounting practices. In general terms, the Act requires issuers of securities in the United States to maintain accurate financial records and to put in place internal controls to ensure that those records remain accurate.[89] The simple idea is that these separate requirements directed to a firm's accounting and compliance departments will serve as checks on the activities of the sales and marketing departments.

The accounting requirements apply both to formal "issuers" of securities under the Securities Exchange Act[90] and to those other companies that are required to file periodic reports under that Act[91] (thus, those entities that are covered by the first substantive anti-bribery provision of the Act, 78dd–1[92]). In addition, such entities are required to ensure compliance with the accounting provisions by

---

[86]   Senate Report No. 114, 95th Cong. 10 (1977).

[87]   *See* FCPA Resource Guide, *supra* note 18, at 27.

[88]   United States v. Kozeny, 582 F. Supp. 2d 535, 540 (S.D.N.Y. 2008).

[89]   *See* 15 U.S.C. § 78m(b)(2).

[90]   *See* 15 U.S.C. § 78*l*.

[91]   *See* 15 U.S.C. § 78*o*(d).

[92]   *See* § 15.3 *supra*.

any foreign subsidiary in which they hold a majority interest (*i.e.*, more than 50%).[93]

§ 15.16   Accounting___The Books and Records Provision

The basic accounting requirement of the FCPA is to "make and keep books, records, and accounts, which, in reasonable detail, accurately and fairly reflect the transactions and dispositions of the assets of the issuer."[94] The Act defines "reasonable detail" to mean a "level of detail . . . that would satisfy prudent officials in the conduct of their own affairs."[95] Congress adopted the "reasonable" adjective specifically out of a concern that an unqualified standard "might connote a degree of exactitude and precision which is unrealistic."[96]

As noted above, the goal of this books and records provision to facilitate detection—by other company officials as well as the SEC— of corrupt practices including, of course, bribery of foreign officials. It advances this goal by subjecting accounting officials of a covered company—who often are not involved in, and thus do not personally benefit from, a bribery scheme—to criminal liability for knowingly failing to record the payments and other transactions of their company accurately.[97]

§ 15.17   Accounting___The Internal Controls Provision

As further support for the goal of combating corruption, the FCPA requires covered entities to "devise and maintain a system of internal accounting controls sufficient to provide reasonable assurances" of accurate books and records.[98] In more specific terms, such internal controls must ensure that:

(i)   transactions are executed in accordance with management's general or specific authorization;

(ii)   transactions are recorded as necessary (I) to permit preparation of financial statements in conformity with generally accepted accounting principles or any other

---

[93]   *See* 15 U.S.C. § 78m(b)(6). If a U.S. issuer holds less than 50% of the stock of a foreign subsidiary it nonetheless must "proceed in good faith to use its influence, to the extent reasonable under the issuer's circumstances" to ensure compliance with the FCPA's accounting provisions. *Id.*

[94]   *See* 15 U.S.C. § 78m(b)(2)(A).

[95]   *See* 15 U.S.C. § 78m(b)(7).

[96]   H. Rep. No. 94–831, at 10 (1977).

[97]   *See* § 15.21 *infra.*

[98]   *See* 15 U.S.C. § 78m(b)(2)(B).

criteria applicable to such statements, and (II) to maintain accountability for assets;

(iii) access to assets is permitted only in accordance with management's general or specific authorization; and

(iv) the recorded accountability for assets is compared with the existing assets at reasonable intervals and appropriate action is taken with respect to any differences[.][99]

In parallel with the books and records provision, the term "reasonable assurance" again means "such . . . degree of assurance as would satisfy prudent officials in the conduct of their own affairs."[100]

The Growing Field of Compliance Law. In order to ensure compliance with these internal controls requirements, basically any internationally active company now must have in place a robust "corporate compliance program." And in many large corporations, a new position of Chief Compliance Officer (CCO) is responsible for continuing compliance with the FCPA and with a whole range of similar regulatory and oversight schemes. With reference to the FCPA's internal controls requirements, therefore, CCO's job is to ensure that corporate transactions are executed and recorded properly, that only allowed payments are made, and that audits occur at "reasonable intervals."[101] Indeed, the existence of, and faithful adherence to, such a program is one of the factors the DOJ and SEC take into consideration in exercising prosecutorial discretion for potential FCPA violations.[102]

A corporate compliance program at a minimum should include the following elements: (1) a clear message from management that FCPA compliance is required and indeed is a core mission of the company; (2) a baseline assessment of the risks of prohibited payments in the various environments in which the company is active, and an adjustment of the rigor of oversight calibrated to those risks; (3) clearly defined policies and codes of conduct; (4) regularized procedures that make compliance a part of everyday

---

[99] *Id.*

[100] *See* 15 U.S.C. § 78m(b)(7).

[101] *See* 15 U.S.C. § 78m(b)(2)(B)(iv).

[102] *See* FCPA Resource Guide, *supra* note 18, at 52–53 (setting forth the DOJ's enforcement policy); 55–56 (noting that a principal consideration by the SEC in granting leniency for FCPA violations is "self-policing prior to the discovery of the misconduct, including establishing effective compliance procedures"). The SEC's general policy is set forth in its *2001 Report of Investigation Pursuant to Section 21(a) of the Securities Exchange Act of 1934 and Commission Statement on the Relationship of Cooperation to Agency Enforcement Decisions* (aka the "Seaboard Report"), *available at* https://www.sec.gov/litigation/investreport/34-44969.htm.

practice; (5) complete training of employees on FCPA compliance, along with periodic reviews; (6) periodic written certifications by key employees and foreign representatives/agents that they have been advised of and are adhering to company policies and codes of conduct; and (7) robust management review and oversight, including regular audits.[103]

With these detailed accounting and internal controls requirements of the FCPA, compliance law has become a major line of business for law firms. Most firms, large and small, now have a compliance department with a thriving business in advising internationally active enterprises on how to avoid FCPA and related problems, and how to respond if such problems arise. As Sections 15.23 through 15.27 below explain, law firms also may become involved in the indirect enforcement of the FCPA in a number of other ways, including through representing "whistleblowers" and defending corporations and individuals in prosecutions for a variety of related criminal offenses.

§ 15.18 Accounting__Liability for Accounting Violations: "Willfully" and "Knowingly"

The FCPA sets forth a formal obligation to comply with its accounting provisions: "No person shall knowingly circumvent or knowingly fail to implement a system of internal accounting controls or knowingly falsify any book, record, or account" as described above.[104] With the general use of the term "person," this obligation extends to any individual or entity that has responsibility for or control over the books of an issuer—for the Securities Exchange Act generally defines the term to include a "natural person, company, government, or political subdivision, agency, or instrumentality of a government."[105]

Willfully. As Section 15.21 below describes, a violation of this obligation subjects a responsible person to substantial criminal penalties. For a natural person, however, criminal liability attaches only for a "willful" violation.[106] Again, "willful" is not defined in the FCPA, but courts have held that the standard is the same as that for a substantive anti-bribery violation as discussed in Section 15.5 above. Thus, the Ninth Circuit declared in a case involving claimed violations of the FCPA's accounting provisions that willfully "means 'intentionally undertaking an act that one knows to be wrongful' " and that the term "does not require that the actor know specifically

---

[103] For general guidance see FCPA Resource Guide, *supra* note 18, at 56–63.

[104] 15 U.S.C. § 78m(b)(5).

[105] 15 U.S.C. § 78c(a)(9).

[106] 15 U.S.C. § 78ff(a).

that the conduct was unlawful."[107] In doing so, the court rejected an argument that "a higher scienter requirement is warranted" for the FCPA's accounting provisions.[108]

Knowingly. The predicate of a "knowing" violation does not alter this conclusion. As the Ninth Circuit observed in the same case, the FCPA provision setting forth criminal liability failing to maintain accurate books and records "means only that the defendant must knowingly commit the act of falsification" and thus it merely "protects those who accidentally record incorrect information because, for example, they are confused by accounting rules."[109] And the court expressly rejected an argument that the word "knowingly" imposes a higher scienter requirement: "On the basis of the language and structure of the statute, there is no textual reason to hold 'knowingly' . . . was intended to modify or connote a higher scienter requirement than 'willfully' " for purposes of a violation of the accounting provisions of the FCPA.[110]

§ 15.19   Enforcement of the FCPA__In General

Both the U.S. Department of Justice and the U.S. Securities and Exchange Commission have a role in enforcing the FCPA. The DOJ's principal role is the criminal enforcement of the Act, as with other federal criminal laws. The DOJ also has certain powers to enforce the FCPA through civil penalties (see § 15.20 below).

For its part, the SEC has civil enforcement authority against issuers of securities on U.S. exchanges and their agents that violate the FCPA (especially the accounting provisions). This first includes a discretionary power to institute investigations, compel testimony and production of records, and seek supporting orders from federal courts.[111] If successful in proving a violation of the FCPA, the SEC may obtain injunctive relief, civil fines, future suspensions and bans, and disgorgements of ill-gotten proceeds,[112] as well as certain monetary penalties.[113]

Statute of Limitations. Because the FCPA does not provide a specific statute of limitations for its criminal provisions, the general five-year statute of limitations applies.[114] The statute of limitations

---

[107]   United States v. Reyes, 577 F.3d 1069, 1080 (9th Cir. 2009) (*quoting* United States v. Tarallo, 380 F.3d 1174, 1188 (9th Cir. 2004)).

[108]   577 F.3d at 1080.

[109]   *Id.*

[110]   *Id.*, at 1080–1081.

[111]   *See* 15 U.S.C. § 78u(a), (b), (c).

[112]   *See* 15 U.S.C. § 78u(d).

[113]   15 U.S.C. § 78u–2.

[114]   *See* FCPA Resource Guide, *supra* note 18, at 34 (*citing* 18 U.S.C. § 3282).

for civil enforcement actions brought by the SEC also is five years.[115]

§ 15.20 Penalties__Corrupt Payment Violations

Violations of the FCPA's prohibitions on corrupt payments to influence foreign officials are subject to stiff civil and criminal penalties. Issuers, domestic concerns, or other covered entities that are not a natural person are subject to criminal penalties of up to $2,000,000 for each violation.[116] Separately, they are subject to civil penalties of up to $10,000.[117] Moreover, under the Alternative Fines Act a court may impose a fine of up to twice the ill-gotten profits from a transaction facilitated by a corrupt payment in violation of the FCPA.[118]

The criminal sanctions for individuals are even more severe. Natural persons—including officers, directors, stockholders, and agents of covered companies—who willfully[119] violate the corrupt payment provisions are subject to criminal penalties of $100,000 as well as imprisonment for up to five years (or both).[120] Separately, they are subject to civil penalties of up to $10,000.[121] And if a fine is levied against an individual for such a violation, it "may not be paid, directly or indirectly," by his employer.[122]

Again, these opportunities for enforcement of the FCPA against issuers and their officers, employees, etc. are backed up by possible injunctive relief, civil fines, bans, monetary penalties, etc. in actions brought by the SEC.[123] A recent prominent example is a civil enforcement action by the SEC against the officers of an offshore drilling company for alleged bribes paid to secure temporary permits from Nigerian customs officials.[124]

Deferred Prosecution Agreements. The U.S. government is serious about enforcing the FCPA's anti-bribery provisions. Indeed,

---

[115]   *Id.*, at 35 (*citing* 28 U.S.C. § 2462).

[116]   15 U.S.C. §§ 78dd–2(g)(1)(A), 78dd–3(e)(1)(A), 78ff(c)(1)(A).

[117]   15 U.S.C. §§ 78dd–2(g)(1)(B), 78dd–3(e)(1)(B), 78ff(c)(1)(B). For issuers that violate § 78dd–1, such civil enforcement actions are brought by the SEC. 15 U.S.C. § 78ff(c)(2)(A).

[118]   18 U.S.C. § 3571(d).

[119]   For the meaning of this term see § 15.5 *supra.*

[120]   15 U.S.C. §§ 78dd–2(g)(2), 78dd–3(e)(2), 78ff(c)(2). A separate general statute allows up to a $250,000 fine for such violations. *See* 18 U.S.C. § 3571(b)(3).

[121]   15 U.S.C. §§ 78dd–2(g)(2)(B), 78dd–3(e)(2)(B), 78ff(c)(2)(B). For officers, employees, etc. of issuers who violate § 78dd–1, such civil enforcement actions are brought by the SEC. 15 U.S.C. § 78ff(c)(2)(B).

[122]   15 U.S.C. §§ 78dd–2(g)(3), 78dd–3(e)(3), 78ff(c)(3).

[123]   *See* 15 U.S.C. §§ 78u(d), 78u–2.

[124]   SEC v. Jackson, 908 F. Supp. 2d 834 (S.D. Tex. 2012).

since 2010 the DOJ has initiated over 130 enforcement actions[125] and the SEC nearly eighty.[126] Few of the cases actually end up in court, however, especially those against large multi-national enterprises. Instead, these corporate entities prefer to accept a negotiated fine—even a very large one—rather than risk the "collateral consequences" of an FCPA conviction. These consequences include suspension or debarment from contracts with the U.S. government, exclusion from programs by multilateral development and other international banks, and revocation or suspension from important export privileges.[127] In terms of long-term effects on business opportunities and reputation, these collateral consequences can be substantially more painful than the fines contemplated by the FCPA.

Corporate defendants, therefore, have agreed to pay substantial fines in return for one of two forms of an agreement by the DOJ and SEC to suspend their enforcement actions: The first is a "deferred prosecution agreement" (DPA), under which the enforcement agencies file a charging document in court but simultaneously agree to defer prosecution. The *quid pro quo* is a payment by the charged corporate defendant of the substantial fine and a commitment to certain future compliance, monitoring, and reporting obligations.[128] The second form is a "non prosecution agreement" (NPA), which is essentially the same except that it comes before the enforcement agencies file a charging document in court.[129]

The result has been some quite spectacular agreed fines. To name just a few examples, in 2008 the German conglomerate Siemens agreed to an $800 million fine for systemic violations of the FCPA's anti-bribery provisions; in 2014, Alstom, S.A., a French power company, agreed to a $772 million fine; in 2009, KBR/Halliburton accepted a $579 million fine; and in 2010, BAE Systems, a large UK-based defense and aerospace contractor, agreed to a $400 million fine. The top ten corporate fines for violating the FCPA alone amount to over 4.6 billion dollars.[130]

---

[125]   *See* https://www.justice.gov/criminal-fraud/related-enforcement-actions.

[126]   *See* https://www.sec.gov/spotlight/fcpa/fcpa-cases.shtml.

[127]   *See* FCPA Resource Guide, *supra* note 18, at 69–71.

[128]   *See id.*, at 74–79.

[129]   *See id.*

[130]   *See* FCPA Blog, http://www.fcpablog.com/blog/2016/2/19/heres-our-new-top-ten-list-with-vimpelcom-landing-sixth.html.

§ 15.21 Penalties__Accounting Violations

The criminal and civil penalties for violating the accounting provisions of the FCPA also are substantial: Business entities that willfully violate such provisions or "willfully and knowingly" make a false or misleading statement in a filing or report are subject to a criminal penalty of up to $25 million. Individuals who commit such a violation are subject to a criminal penalty of up to $5 million and imprisonment of up to 20 years (or both).[131]

The penalty provisions of the FCPA for accounting violations nonetheless recognize a curious defense based on the so-called "No Knowledge Clause." Under this clause, "no person shall be subject to imprisonment . . . for the violation of any rule or regulation if he proves that he had no knowledge of such rule or regulation."[132] As a matter of emphasis, this provision relates only to the imposition of a sentence of imprisonment; and as an affirmative defense, "the burden to prove the defense is on the defendant."[133] The relevant lack of knowledge is not tied to the specific text of the FCPA; rather, the defense requires "proof of an ignorance of the substance of the rule, proof that the defendant did not know that [his or her] conduct was contrary to law."[134]

§ 15.22 DOJ Opinion Release Procedure

The FCPA establishes an opinion review procedure that allows certain U.S. entities to request an advance determination on whether the Department of Justice would prosecute on a stipulated set of facts.[135] In specific, it requires that the Attorney General respond to a request for guidance made by "issuers" covered by 78dd–1[136] and "domestic concerns" covered by 78dd–2[137] (both as described in Section 15.3 above).

The first step in obtaining such an opinion is for the person or company to present to the Department of Justice the details of the

---

[131]   15 U.S.C. § 78ff(a).

[132]   *Id.*, final clause.

[133]   United States v. Reyes, 577 F.3d 1069, 1081 (9th Cir. 2009).

[134]   *Id.* (*quoting* United States v. Schwartz, 464 F.2d 499, 509 n.16 (2d Cir. 1972)).

[135]   *See* 15 U.S.C. §§ 78dd–1(e), 78dd–2(f).

[136]   *See* 15 U.S.C. § 78dd–1(e) (providing with regard to "issuers" covered by § 78dd–1 that the Attorney General "shall establish a procedure to provide responses to specific inquiries by issuers concerning conformance of their conduct with . . . the preceding provisions of this section").

[137]   *See* 15 U.S.C. § 78dd–2(f) (providing with regard to "domestic concerns" covered by § 78dd–2 that the Attorney General "shall establish a procedure to provide responses to specific inquiries by domestic concerns concerning conformance of their conduct with . . . the preceding provisions of this section").

proposed transaction or conduct (most often a payment to or for the benefit of a foreign official). The DOJ must respond to such a request within 30 days stating whether the described conduct would violate the FCPA "for purposes of the Department of Justice's present enforcement policy."[138] If the DOJ responds that the described conduct in fact conforms to its present enforcement policy, the FPCA creates "a rebuttable presumption that [the] conduct . . . is in compliance" with the Act's anti-bribery provisions.[139]

This procedure has been used relatively rarely, however, with the DOJ issuing on average only three formal "FCPA Opinion Releases" per year.[140]

§ 15.23   Indirect Governmental Enforcement

The opportunities for indirect enforcement of the FCPA by the U.S. government arise from the simple fact that the prohibited conduct likely also will violate other federal criminal statutes.[141] The most prominent is the Travel Act, which as relevant here makes it a crime to use the "mail or any facility in interstate or foreign commerce" with the intent to "promote, manage, establish, carry on, or facilitate the promotion, management, establishment, or carrying on, of any unlawful activity." Criminal liability then attaches with the performance of or attempt to perform an act that promotes, manages, facilitates, etc. any such "unlawful activity."[142] Because the FCPA makes foreign bribery unlawful, and because in modern business nearly all foreign bribery schemes with any connection to the United States will use a facility of interstate commerce, a "violation of the Foreign Corrupt Practices Act . . . can be the basis for a Travel Act violation."[143]

Other options for indirect enforcement include: (a) the federal money laundering statute, which *inter alia* criminalizes the handling or transfer of funds in the United States when a person "know[s] that the property involved in a financial transaction represents the proceeds of some form of unlawful activity";[144] (b) the

---

[138]   15 U.S.C. §§ 78dd–1(e), 78dd–2(f).

[139]   *Id.*

[140]   *See* https://www.justice.gov/criminal-fraud/opinion-procedure-releases.

[141]   For a broader examination of this subject see FCPA Resource Guide, *supra* note 18, at 48–49.

[142]   *See* 18 U.S.C. § 1952.

[143]   *See, e.g.,* Worldwide Directories, S.A. De C.V. v. Yahoo! Inc., 2016 WL 1298987, at *7 (S.D.N.Y. 2016); Reich v. Lopez, 38 F. Supp. 3d 436, 446 (S.D.N.Y. 2014); Chevron Corp. v. Donziger, 974 F. Supp. 2d 362, 595–600 (S.D.N.Y. 2014), *aff'd*, 833 F.3d 74 (2d Cir. 2016).

[144]   *See* 18 U.S.C. § 1956. For an example see United States v. Esquenazi, 752 F.3d 912, 934–936 (11th Cir. 2014).

federal wire and mail fraud statutes, which *inter alia* make it a crime to transmit any information through means of interstate commerce in furtherance of a false or fraudulent scheme;[145] and (c) a variety of reporting, certification, and tax statutes.[146]

§ 15.24 No Private Right of Action Under the FCPA

A standard question with any federal statute is whether it creates an implied right of action by private parties seeking money judgments as an indirect means of enforcement. Not surprisingly, this issue has arisen as well with the FCPA based on claims by competitors that they have suffered harm from a violator's bribery of a foreign official. However, beginning with the Sixth Circuit's significant holding in *Lamb v. Phillip Morris, Inc.* in 1990[147] federal courts uniformly have held that no such private right of action exists for violations of either the FCPA's anti-bribery provisions[148] or its accounting provisions.[149]

Nonetheless, as the following Sections examine, a variety of other avenues exist for private claims indirectly based on violations of the FCPA.

§ 15.25 Indirect Private Enforcement of the FCPA__Whistleblower Claims

As noted in Section 15.21 above, in recent years compliance with the requirements and limitations of the FCPA has become a major line of business for law firms. Since 2010 this also has included a means of indirect enforcement through the "Whistleblower Bounty" provisions of the Dodd–Frank Wall Street Reform and Consumer Protection Act. Under those provisions, a person who informs the SEC of FCPA violations by a covered company may recover between 10% and 30% of collected monetary sanctions.[150] With fines and penalties by corporate offenders running into the billions of dollars (see § 15.20 above), these

---

[145]   *See* 18 U.S.C. §§ 1343, 1346.

[146]   *See generally* FCPA Resource Guide, *supra* note 18, at 49.

[147]   Lamb v. Phillip Morris, Inc., 915 F.2d 1024 (6th Cir. 1990).

[148]   *See, e.g.,* In re Key Energy Services, Inc. Securities Litigation, 166 F. Supp. 3d 822, 845 (S.D. Tex. 2016); Republic of Iraq v. ABB AG, 768 F.3d 145, 170–171 (2d Cir. 2014); Shoaga v. Maersk, Inc., 2008 WL 4615445, at *4 (N.D. Cal. 2008); Scientific Drilling Intern., Inc. v. Gyrodata Corp., 1999 WL 674511, at *3 (Fed. Cir. 1999); J.S. Service Center Corp. v. Gen. Elec. Technical Services Co., Inc., 937 F. Supp. 216 (S.D.N.Y. 1996).

[149]   *See* Earle v. Aramark Corp., 2005 WL 473675, *3 (N.D. Tex. 2005); Davis v. DCB Financial Corp., 259 F. Supp. 2d 664, 673–674 (S.D. Ohio 2003); Shields on Behalf of Sundstrand Corp. v. Erickson, 710 F. Supp. 686, 688 (N.D. Ill. 1989).

[150]   *See* 15 U.S.C. § 78u–6(b).

whistleblower suits will be an increasingly lucrative activity for law firms in the years to come.

§ 15.26 Private Enforcement__Employee Suits for Wrongful Discharge

Some courts have recognized a claim in tort by an employee who is wrongfully discharged for complying with the FCPA. The progenitor of this line is the holding of the Supreme Court of Washington in *Thompson v. St. Regis Paper Co.*[151] There, a company controller alleged that his employer discharged him for instituting accurate accounting procedures as required by the FCPA. The Court held that this stated a claim for wrongful discharge based on state public policy:

> The Foreign Corrupt Practices Act is a clear expression of public policy that bribery of foreign officials is contrary to the public interest and that specific companies . . . must institute accounting practices to ensure that this public policy is advanced. If appellant's discharge was premised upon his compliance with the accounting requirements of the Foreign Corrupt Practices Act and intended as a warning to other [employees], as appellant alleges, then his discharge was contrary to a clear mandate of public policy and, thus, tortious.[152]

A small number of other courts have recognized similar state law claims.[153] A few have refused, however, either with specific reference to the FCPA[154] or based on a general notion that violations of federal law do not form the basis of a state claim for retaliatory discharge.[155]

§ 15.27 Private Enforcement__Competitor Claims Based on RICO

Another option for private claims founded on violations of the FCPA is the Racketeer Influenced and Corrupt Organizations Act (RICO).[156] As relevant here, RICO makes it a crime for a person to

---

[151] 685 P.2d 1081 (Wash. 1984).

[152] 685 P.2d at 1090.

[153] *See, e.g.,* Kirk v. Shaw Envt'l, Inc., 2010 WL 1387887, at *6 (N.D. Ohio 2010) (applying Ohio law); D'Agostino v. Johnson & Johnson, Inc., 628 A.2d 305, 321 (N.J. 1993); Adler v. American Standard Corp., 538 F. Supp. 572, 578–579 (D. Md. 1982) (applying Maryland law), *rev'd on other grounds,* 830 F.2d 1303 (4th Cir. 1987).

[154] *See, e.g.,* Pratt v. Caterpillar Tractor Co., 500 N.E.2d 1001, 1003 (Ill. Ct. App. 1986).

[155] *See, e.g.,* McCarthy v. Tex. Instruments, Inc., 999 F. Supp. 823, 829 (E.D. Va. 1998) (applying Virginia law).

[156] 18 U.S.C. §§ 1961–1968.

use money received, directly or indirectly, "from a pattern of racketeering activity" in "any enterprise which is engaged in, or the activities of which affect, interstate or foreign commerce."[157] The Act defines "racketeering activity" to mean any indictable act under specified criminal statutes (commonly known as RICO "predicates").[158] The "pattern" requirement means at least two predicates committed within 10 years of each other,[159] but more broadly means "a series of related predicates that together demonstrate the existence or threat of continued criminal activity."[160]

RICO explicitly provides a *private* cause of action for "[a]ny person injured in his business or property by reason of a violation of" its provisions, which may include treble damages, costs, and attorney's fees.[161] The FCPA is not among the enumerated criminal statutes that may serve as a predicate for "racketeering activity" under RICO—but the federal Travel Act as well as the money laundering, mail fraud, and wire fraud statutes noted immediately above are.[162] Putting these pieces together, a violation of the FCPA's prohibitions on bribing foreign officials very often will amount to a violation of one or more of these other criminal statutes (see § 15.23 above); RICO lists a violation of these statutes as an allowed predicate for the required "pattern of racketeering activity"; thus, a pattern of violations of the FCPA's anti-bribery provisions may establish the foundation for a private cause of action under RICO. Beginning with the Third Circuit's conclusion in *Environmental Tectonics v. W.S. Kirkpatrick, Inc.* in 1988,[163] numerous federal courts expressly have so held.[164]

Nonetheless, in *RJR Nabisco, Inc. v. European Community* in 2016 the Supreme Court recognized important limitations on such a private right of action under RICO.[165] The Court first held—in

---

[157]   18 U.S.C. § 1962.

[158]   18 U.S.C. § 1961(1).

[159]   18 U.S.C. § 1961(5).

[160]   RJR Nabisco, Inc. v. European Community, ___ U.S. ___, 136 S.Ct. 2090, 2096–2097 (2016). *See also* H.J. Inc. v. Nw. Bell Tel. Co., 492 U.S. 229, 239 (1989).

[161]   18 U.S.C. § 1964(c).

[162]   18 U.S.C. § 1961(1). *See also* Reich v. Lopez, 38 F. Supp. 3d 436, 446 (S.D.N.Y. 2014) ("The FCPA, unlike the Travel Act, is not a[n] [independent] RICO predicate.") (*quoting* United States v. Young & Rubicam, Inc., 741 F. Supp. 334, 338 (D. Conn. 1990)).

[163]   847 F.2d 1052, 1067 (3rd Cir. 1988).

[164]   *See, e.g.*, Chevron Corp. v. Donziger, 974 F. Supp. 2d 362, 595–600 (S.D.N.Y. 2014), *aff'd*, 833 F.3d 74 (2d Cir. 2016); Reich v. Lopez, 38 F. Supp. 3d 436, 446 (S.D.N.Y. 2014); Dooley v. United Techs. Corp., 1992 WL 167053, at *9 (D.D.C. 1992); United States v. Young & Rubicam, 741 F. Supp. 334, 337–340 (D. Conn. 1990).

[165]   ___ U.S. ___, 136 S.Ct. 2090 (2016).

conformance with the established presumption against extraterritorial application of federal statutes[166]—that a pattern of criminal offenses may serve as a predicate for a RICO claim only if "each of those offenses violates a predicate statute that is itself extraterritorial."[167] And it gave every indication that (although not necessary for its holding) it agreed with the Second Circuit's conclusion below that the Travel Act and the federal wire and mail fraud statutes do *not* apply extraterritorially.[168] Thus, a private plaintiff must allege *domestic* conduct for each predicate violation under those statutes (subsuming the FCPA violations) to support a RICO cause of action.[169]

In addition, the Supreme Court expressly held in *RJR Nabisco* that a civil RICO plaintiff must "prove a domestic injury to business or property" and thus that RICO "does not allow recovery for foreign injuries."[170] This will severely limit the ability of foreign competitors to advance civil RICO claims premised on a pattern of violations of the FCPA's anti-bribery provisions.[171]

§ 15.28   The OECD Anti-Bribery Convention

Almost immediately upon the adoption of the FCPA in 1977, the United States began efforts to secure an international treaty to combat bribery of foreign public officials. It pursued this goal principally through the Organization for Economic Cooperation and Development (OECD). The choice was a deliberate one, for the OECD's thirty-four member states represent the most economically developed countries in the world and thus the most likely sources for "outbound" bribery of foreign public officials. The efforts of the United States bore fruit in 1997 in the form of the OECD Convention on Combating Bribery of Foreign Public Officials in International Business Transactions.[172] The United States promptly ratified this Convention and then implemented it through amendments to the FCPA in 1998.

---

[166]   *See, e.g.*, Kiobel v. Royal Dutch Petroleum Co., 569 U.S. ___, 133 S.Ct. 1659, 1663–1664 (2013); Morrison v. National Australia Bank Ltd., 561 U.S. 247, 255 (2010).

[167]   136 S.Ct. at 2101–2103.

[168]   136 S.Ct. at 2105–2106 (discussing European Community v. RJR Nabisco, Inc., 764 F.3d 129, 141 (2d Cir. 2014)).

[169]   European Community v. RJR Nabisco, Inc., 764 F.3d 129 at 141.

[170]   RJR Nabisco, Inc. v. European Community, ___ U.S. ___, 136 S.Ct. at 2111.

[171]   For an application of this point see Reich v. Lopez, 38 F. Supp. 3d 436, 451–453 (S.D.N.Y. 2014) (holding that, although a complaint alleged a sufficient domestic violation of the wire fraud statute, it failed to allege a sufficient connection with an alleged foreign bribery to form a pattern of racketeering activity).

[172]   OECD Anti-Bribery Convention, *supra* note 12.

The OECD Anti-Bribery Convention is a formal international treaty, but its substance in most respects is similar to the rules that already existed in the FCPA. In its most fundamental provision, the Convention creates an obligation for member states to criminalize under domestic law the offense of "bribery of a foreign public official."[173] The elements of this offense are quite similar to those in the FCPA:

(1) It covers an act by "any person" (including "legal persons"[174]).

(2) It requires for criminal liability that the person act "intentionally."

(3) The prohibited act is any offer, promise, or gift of "any undue pecuniary or other advantage, whether directly or through intermediaries."

(4) The prohibited recipient is "a foreign public official." The Convention defines this term quite broadly to include (a) "any person holding a legislative, administrative or judicial office of a foreign country, whether appointed or elected," (b) "any person exercising a public function for a foreign country, including for a public agency or public enterprise," and (c) "any official or agent of a public international organisation."[175]

(5) The prohibited purpose of the payment, etc. is to cause the foreign official to "act or refrain from acting in relation to the performance of official duties." This includes "any use of the public official's position, whether or not within the official's authorised competence."[176]

and

(6) The prohibited goal is to "obtain or retain business or other improper advantage in the conduct of international business."[177]

A separate provision requires the criminalization of "complicity in, including incitement, aiding and abetting, or authorization of" an act of bribery of a foreign public official, as well as related attempts or conspiracies to the extent this also is a crime regarding domestic public officials.[178]

---

[173] *Id.*, art. 1(3).

[174] *Id.*, art. 2.

[175] *Id.*, art. 1(4)(a).

[176] *Id.*, art. 1(4)(c).

[177] *Id.*, art. 1(1).

[178] *Id.*, art. 1(2).

As a matter of emphasis, the Convention requires that member states make this act of bribery of a foreign public official a *criminal* offense in domestic law. Indeed, it specifically requires that such an offense be "punishable by effective, proportionate and dissuasive criminal penalties."[179]

Again similar to the FCPA, the OECD Anti-Bribery Convention has a provision that addresses books and records. This provision obligates member states to include within their laws governing financial statements, accounting records, and auditing standards a prohibition on "off-the-book" accounts, inaccurate entries, and false documentation "for the purpose of bribing foreign public officials or of hiding such bribery."[180] The Convention then mandates that member states establish "effective, proportionate and dissuasive civil, administrative, or criminal penalties" to enforce this prohibition.[181]

Other noteworthy provisions in the Convention address consultation on issues of parallel prosecution[182] and money laundering.[183] The Convention also contains an interesting declaration that the offense of bribery of a foreign public official "shall be deemed to be included as an extraditable offence under the laws of the Parties and the extradition treaties between them."[184] This provides the legal foundation for member states to extradite persons charged with a covered offense even without a special treaty on the subject.[185]

Among the most important provisions of the OECD Convention is Article 9 on "Mutual Legal Assistance." This Article requires each member state to "provide prompt and effective legal assistance to another Party." The effect is a grant of a self-executing power to the DOJ and the SEC to exercise their statutory powers (investigations, subpoenas, etc.) to assist an investigation in a foreign country, even if no domestic FCPA investigation is pending.

---

[179] *Id.*, art. 3.

[180] *Id.*, art. 8(1) (obligating member states to "take such measures as may be necessary . . . to prohibit the establishment of off-the-books accounts, the making of off-the-books or inadequately identified transactions, the recording of non-existent expenditures, the entry of liabilities with incorrect identification of their object, as well as the use of false documents" regarding foreign bribery).

[181] *Id.*, art. 8(2).

[182] *Id.*, art. 4(3).

[183] *Id.*, art. 7.

[184] *Id.*, art. 10.

[185] *See id., Commentaries on the Convention on Combating Bribery of Foreign Public Officials in International Business Transactions*, para. 33 (November 21, 1997).

U.S. Implementation. As noted in the Introduction, the United States promptly ratified the OECD Anti-Bribery Convention (not surprisingly, as it was the main proponent) and then implemented it through amendments to the FCPA in 1998.

The most significant of these amendments expanded the Act's jurisdictional scope. First, the Convention requires member states to exercise "territorial jurisdiction," that is, to criminalize a foreign bribery if a relevant act "is committed in whole or in part in its territory."[186] This is what led to the adoption of § 78dd–3, which criminalizes any act in furtherance of foreign bribery by "any person . . . while in the territory of the United States."[187] As noted in Section 15.3 above, U.S. enforcement authorities have adopted a very expansive interpretation of this jurisdictional grant.[188]

Second, the Convention requires member states to exercise "nationality jurisdiction," that is, to establish the legal grounds for prosecuting their own nationals "for offences committed abroad."[189] This provision triggered the removal of the requirement of the use of interstate commerce for "United States persons" as described in Section 15.3 above.[190]

Other conforming amendments to the FCPA likewise were significant. The 1998 Act to implement the OECD Anti-Bribery Convention (1) expanded the scope of the FCPA to include payments made to a foreign official in order to secure "any improper advantage";[191] (2) included public international organizations within the definition of a foreign official;[192] and (3) extended criminal sanctions—not just civil penalties—to foreign nationals who participate in a bribery scheme as employees or agents of a U.S. company.[193]

Influence on the Interpretation of the FCPA. The influence of OECD Anti-Bribery Convention in U.S. law is even broader than these formal amendments. Because the Convention defines obligations of the United States under international law, and because Congress amended the FCPA in 1998 specifically to conform to those obligations, federal courts properly have recognized that the drafting history of the Convention is relevant in

---

[186]   *Id.*, art. 4(1).
[187]   *See* § 15.3, and text accompanying notes 23–24 *supra*
[188]   *See* text accompanying note 24 *supra*.
[189]   *Id.*, art. 4(2).
[190]   *See* text accompanying notes 30–33 *supra*.
[191]   *See* § 15.8 *supra*.
[192]   *See* § 15.3 *supra*.
[193]   *See id.*

interpreting the FCPA.[194] Indeed, as the Eleventh Circuit emphasized in *United States v. Esquenazi* in 2014, this even includes provisions of the FCPA that Congress did *not* amend in its implementation of the OECD Anti-Bribery Convention in 1998.[195]

Foreign Implementation. All thirty-four OECD member states have ratified the OECD Anti-Bribery Convention (as well as seven other countries), and it formally entered into force on February 15, 1999.[196] Between 1999 and early 2004, these states implemented the Convention by amending their domestic law to criminalize the "bribery of a foreign public official" as defined therein.[197]

The OECD also has a "Working Group on Bribery" that monitors implementation of the Convention by its member states.[198] The United States is an active participant.[199] In 2009, this Working Group adopted a formal document, *Recommendation of the Council for Further Combating Bribery of Foreign Public Officials in International Business Transactions*, which contains numerous explanatory notes and recommendations to assist member states in implementing and applying the Convention.[200]

The OECD Anti-Bribery Convention, however, states a floor, not a ceiling. Thus, member states remain free to impose even more exacting prohibitions and obligations. A prominent, and in part controversial, illustration of this point is the UK Bribery Act 2010. That Act differs from the FCPA in the following important respects: (a) It prohibits bribes even to *private* foreign entities; (b) it does not require a "corrupt" intent; (c) it makes it a crime to *receive* a bribe; (4) it does not have an exception for payments that facilitate routine governmental actions; and (5) it creates a strict liability offense for an organization whose employees and agents engage in bribery,

---

[194] United States v. Esquenazi, 752 F.3d 912, 924 (11th Cir. 2014); United States v. Kay, 359 F.3d 738, 754–755 (5th Cir. 2004); United States v. Aguilar, 783 F. Supp. 2d 1108, 1118 (C.D. Cal. 2011).

[195] 752 F.3d 912, 924 (11th Cir. 2014).

[196] The list of member states is available in the anti-bribery section of the OECD website, http://www.oecd.org/corruption/oecdantibriberyconvention.htm.

[197] *See* http://www.oecd.org/daf/anti-bribery/countryreportsontheimplementation oftheoecdanti-briberyconvention.htm.

[198] *See* http://www.oecd.org/corruption/anti-bribery/anti-briberyconvention/oecd workinggrouponbriberyininternationalbusinesstransactions.htm.

[199] *See* FCPA Resource Guide, *supra* note 18, at 7–8.

[200] This document is available in the anti-bribery section of the OECD website, http://www.oecd.org/daf/anti-bribery/oecdantibriberyrecommendation2009.htm.   In 2010 the Working Group supplemented these recommendations with a document on "Good Practice Guidance on Internal Controls, Ethics and Compliance." *See id.*

unless it "had in place adequate procedures designed to prevent" them from doing so.[201]

§ 15.29 Other International Efforts to Combat Corruption

A number of other treaties address the subject of anti-corruption and anti-bribery. The first, which even preceded the OECD Anti-Bribery Convention, is the Inter-American Convention Against Corruption (IACAC) adopted under the auspices of the Organization of American States in 1996.[202] Nearly every country in the Western Hemisphere has ratified this treaty, including the United States in 2000.[203]

At roughly the same time, the United Nations began work on a comprehensive treaty on the same subject. The result was a 2003 treaty, the UN Convention Against Corruption (UNCAC),[204] which entered into force in December, 2005. As of the end of 2016, 178 countries have ratified UNCAC, including the United States in 2006.[205] UNCAC is much broader in scope than the OECD Anti-Bribery Convention, for it covers domestic bribery and corruption as well as broader issues of obstruction of justice, transparency, accounting and auditing standards, and the establishment of related administrative bodies. The direct effect of UNCAC in the United States should be quite limited, however: At the time of its ratification in 2006, the United States declared that no changes in domestic law were required because "the existing body of federal and state laws will suffice to implement the obligations of the Convention."[206]

Not surprisingly, the European Union also has been active in adopting legal measures to combat corruption. Many EU member

---

[201] For analyses of this Act see Bruce W. Bean & Emma H. MacGuidwin, *Unscrewing the Inscrutable: The UK Bribery Act 2010*, 23 IND. INT'L & COMP. L. REV. 63 (2013); Margaret Ryznara & Samer Korkor, *Anti-Bribery Legislation in the United States and United Kingdom: A Comparative Analysis of Scope and Sentencing*, 76 MO. L. REV. 415 (2010); George Rosenberg, *New UK Bribery Act 2010—Draconian in Theory but Is It Enforceable in Practice?*, 5 No. 3 CONSTRUCTION L. INT'L 19 (2010).

[202] Inter-American Convention Against Corruption, March 29, 1996, S. Treaty Doc. No. 105–39, 35 I.L.M. 724, *available at* http://oas.org/juridico/english/Treaties/b-58.html.

[203] *See* http://oas.org/juridico/english/Sigs/b-58.html (listing the member states of IACAC).

[204] United Nations Convention Against Corruption, October 31, 2003, S. Treaty Doc. No. 109–6, 2349 U.N.T.S. 41, *available* at http://www.unodc.org/unodc/en/treaties/CAC/index.html.

[205] *See* http://www.unodc.org/unodc/en/treaties/CAC/signatories.html (listing the member states of UNCAC).

[206] *See* Senate Exec. Rep. 109–18, *United Nations Convention on Corruption (Treaty Doc. 109–6)*, at 6 (August 30, 2006).

states are part of the OECD and thus have ratified OECD Anti-Bribery Convention.[207] In addition, nearly all EU member states have adopted the EU Convention Against Corruption Involving Officials (1997),[208] and the Convention for the Protection of the European Communities' Financial Interests (1995), which requires EU member states to "introduce effective, proportionate and dissuasive criminal penalties to deal with fraud affecting the EU's financial interests."[209] Separately, a broader group, the Council of Europe, has adopted the Criminal Law Convention on Corruption, which has been accepted by 45 European countries.[210] A Group of States Against Corruption (GRECO) established under the auspices of the Council of Europe in 1999 monitors compliance with this Convention (and other anticorruption efforts). Although it has not ratified the Criminal Law Convention on Corruption, the United States participates in GRECO.[211]

---

[207]   See note 196 *supra*.

[208]   See Council Act of 26 May 1997, entered into force 28 September 2005, *available at* http://eur-lex.europa.eu/legal-content/EN/TXT/?uri=URISERV:l33027.

[209]   Council Act of 26 July 1995, entered into force 17 October 2002, available at http://eur-lex.europa.eu/legal-content/EN/TXT/?uri=uriserv:l33019.

[210]   Criminal Law Convention on Corruption, January. 27, 1999, 38 I.L.M. 505, *available at* http://conventions.coe.int/Treaty/en/Treaties/html/173.htm.

[211]   See FCPA Resource Guide, *supra* note 18, at 8.

Chapter 16

UNITED STATES BOYCOTT AND
ANTI-BOYCOTT LAW

Table of Sections

§ 16.1 Boycott and Antiboycott Laws

The United States engages in both boycott and antiboycott practices. In the past few decades the United States has boycotted or embargoed goods from or to such countries as Cuba, Iran, Iraq, Libya, Nicaragua, North Korea, South Africa, Rhodesia and Vietnam. The effectiveness of these boycotts in achieving political goals has been widely debated.[1] The U.S. boycotts have not all been unilateral. It has engaged in collective sanctions when many others have joined, such as the U.N. trade boycott against Iraq after the

---

[1]   *See* Gary C. Hufbauer, Jeffrey J. Schott & Kimberly Ann Elliot, ECONOMIC SANCTIONS RECONSIDERED (1990).

invasion of Kuwait,[2] against Serbia and Montenegro after the Serbian-promoted invasion of Bosnia,[3] and against Libya after killings of protesters. Less "collective" were the trade sanctions imposed on Argentina by the United States and the European Economic Community after the Argentine invasion of the Falklands/Malvinas Islands.[4]

The United States has engaged in boycotts when many have participated, such as the U.N. collective sanctions, and it has sometimes stood nearly alone among major nations in implementing boycotts, such as that directed against Cuba. Additionally, the United States has engaged in long term boycotts, notably against Cuba, and very brief boycotts, such as limits on exports to Europe which might be used in the construction of a gas pipeline from the USSR after the Soviet invasion of Poland. There is little doubt that in the future unilateral or collective boycotts will continue to be part of U.S. foreign policy.

The United States has only one significant experience with the use of the U.S. antiboycott law. That is the Arab boycott of Israel. The U.S. law was adopted exclusively because of the Arab boycott of Israel. But nowhere does the law specifically mention either Arabs or Israel. Furthermore, the law is likely to remain on the books long after the Arab boycott ends. The law is directed to prohibiting U.S. persons from participating in or supporting boycotts by foreign nations against other foreign nations friendly to the United States.

§ 16.2 Boycott Laws and International Law

International law scholars have long debated whether boycotts violate international law.[5] But boycotts have been used frequently as an instrument of international law to achieve political goals,[6] such as actions by the United Nations. A primary boycott, which involves a curtailment of trade with another nation, generally is regarded as not constituting a violation of international law. But

---

[2]   See United Nations Security Council Resolution 661 (1990).

[3]   See United Nations Security Council Resolution 757 (1992).

[4]   See Domingo E. Acevedo, *The U.S. Measures Against Argentina Resulting from the Malvinas Conflict*, 78 AM. J. INT'L L. 323 (1984).

[5]   See, e.g., Margaret P. Doxey, ECONOMIC SANCTIONS AND INTERNATIONAL ENFORCEMENT (1980); Christopher C. Joyner, *The Transnational Boycott as Economic Coercion in International Law: Policy, Place and Practice*, 17 VAND. J. TRANSNAT'L L. 205 (1984).

[6]   They may be referred to as "self-help" or unilateral measures. The Restatement (Third) of Foreign Relations Law addresses unilateral measures in § 905, as does the International Law Commission's Draft Articles on State Responsibility (Part Two), in Articles 12–14. Both assume similar approaches. Neither constitutes law; they reflect the perceptions (and sometimes goals) of their drafters.

that view may differ when the boycotted nation is little more than an economic dependent of the boycotting nation. Even when the boycott assumes secondary or tertiary characteristics, international law may not be violated. It is when the boycotting nation carries the boycott to a stage of economic warfare, such as a blockade, that it more readily conflicts with international law, especially when human rights issues arise. Further obscuring the issue is whether there must be some act by the nation boycotted which justifies the boycotting action of the other.[7]

A *blockade* of another nation may constitute a violation of international law, but some may be reluctant in labeling a blockade such a violation when it appears to be the only likely alternative to armed conflict. Few disagree as to which is the less harmful alternative, but that does not reject the idea that both may be violations of acceptable international conduct.

However elevated the argument over the norms of international law may soar to academic heights, nations will continue to use boycotts as instruments of foreign policy. The use of boycotts by the United States illustrates that it is quite an extensive, although perhaps not always effective, instrument of that policy.

§ 16.3   The Structure of United States Boycott Law

With whom the United States does *not* trade tends to be the decision of the President, although the Congress may act in special situations to deny trade benefits. Trade embargoes or other sanctions are often imposed quickly, following some act which the U.S. President finds politically unacceptable. The Department of Commerce participates in the process of enforcing trade sanctions by controls on exports to various nations. Although the Congress governs foreign commerce and specifically *exports* by means of the Export Administration Act, Congress tends to leave to presidential discretion the imposition of sanctions against specific countries. This is not always the case, however. Congress may enact specific laws targeting particular nations. An example is the Cuban Democracy Act of 1992, which placed severe limitations on trade with Cuba, including trade by U.S. controlled subsidiaries abroad.[8] When Congress does act, it usually provides that its law will be carried out with additional regulations. The Export Administration

---

[7]   A critical point is whether the boycotted state must have committed an illegal act. The majority view seems to be that the act need not be illegal; it may simply be "unfriendly."

[8]   Pub. L. No. 102–484, §§ 1706–12, 106 Stat. 2315, 2578–81 (1992).

Act has substantial regulations that are enforced largely by the Department of Commerce.

When the United States wishes to go further than to simply deny most favored nation status to a foreign nation, it may totally prohibit trade. Congressional action is likely to target a specific nation. When Congress prohibits trade, or delegates such authority to the President, there is a shift of much of the enforcement (and enactment of regulations) responsibility from the Department of Commerce to the Department of the Treasury. Part of the reason is that Treasury has an extensive framework of regulations governing the control of foreign assets.[9] The Office of Foreign Assets Control (OFAC) of Treasury has jurisdiction over a broad range of controls on transactions between U.S. persons and persons in foreign countries.[10] When those latter persons are in certain foreign countries, the controls may prohibit nearly any form of "transaction" or "transfer". A transaction or transfer may involve money or goods or services. Certain transactions or transfers may be absolutely prohibited, others may be subject to special licensing.[11]

The general regulations governing foreign assets control are followed by a series of mostly country-specific regulations.[12] These regulations vary in intensity of restrictiveness, but follow a general format including (1) the relation of the regulations to other laws and regulations, (2) what transactions are prohibited, (3) definitions, (4) interpretations, (5) licensing process, (6) reports, (7) penalties and (8) procedures. Some of the provisions are brief, others extensive. To give an idea of how these restrictions function, the experience of Cuba is outlined in the following section.

The Office of Foreign Assets Control has two forms of sanctions. One is financial sanctions and asset freezes. The second is trade and commercial embargoes. They may be used selectively or quite comprehensively. Selective sanctions may include blocking assets held in the United States, limitations on engaging in contracts, travel, transportation, or even exporting any goods or services. Selective sanctions have been used against various

---

[9]   31 C.F.R. Parts 500–585.

[10]   For a clash of OFAC and the Constitution see Looper v. Morgan, 1995 WL 499816 (S.D. Tex. 1995) (regarding the search of an attorney's briefcase upon entry to the United States in search of documents supporting violations of the Libyan sanctions).

[11]   Licensing is in 31 C.F.R. Part 500, subpart E.

[12]   OFAC's list of sanction programs in effect as of 2016, includes some or all of the Balkans, Belarus, Burma, Burundi, Central African Republic, Cote d'Ivoire, Cuba, Congo, Iran, Iraq, Lebanon, Libya, North Korea, Ukraine, Somalia, Sudan, Syria, Venezuela, Yemen, and Zimbabwe.

countries, including former "communist bloc" nations, South Africa, Iran and Angola. Comprehensive sanctions usually involve all the available options, and have been used against Cuba, Iran, Iraq, Libya, North Korea and parts of the former Yugoslavia.

The Cuban sanctions discussed immediately below represent the most severe sanctions yet adopted. They were partly used as a model for the 1996 Iran and Libya Sanctions Act, often referred to as the D'Amato Act.[13] This Act, following the Libertad Act, requires the President to impose sanctions against *foreign* companies that invest more than $20 million a year in the development of petroleum resource production in Iran, or more than $40 million in Libya. The proposed $2 billion investment in Iran by the French Total company in the late 1990s generated a conflict between France and the United States over possible sanctions, which the U.S. President did not impose although he was under pressure to do so. If sanctions had been imposed, this matter quickly would have been taken to the WTO by the European Union on behalf of France.

Although the focus of this chapter is on federal law, in the past few years a number of state and local governments have adopted boycott provisions. The provisions for the most part limit government procurement for reasons of perceived violations of human rights (a principal target has been Burma (Myanmar)), religious freedom (many countries), and the failure to deal with the return of Holocaust assets (Switzerland). These laws have created a separate (from federal sanctions) opposition among some foreign nations. The EU initiated a challenge under the WTO government procurement rules against a 1996 Massachusetts law addressed to Burma. Federal sanctions were authorized against Burma in 1997,[14] but the law did not discuss preemption. In a case against the Massachusetts law brought by the National Foreign Trade Council, the federal district court, the federal circuit court and the U.S. Supreme Court all held for the NFTC.[15] The federal ruling caused the EU to withdraw its action under the WTO dispute resolution procedures.

---

[13]   Pub.L. No. 104–172, 110 Stat. 1541 (1996).

[14]   Omnibus Consolidated Appropriations Act, Pub.L. No. 104–208, § 570, 110 Stat. 3009, 3009–166–167, on September 30, 1996.

[15]   National Foreign Trade Council v. Baker, 26 F. Supp. 2d 287 (D. Mass. 1998), *aff'd*, National Foreign Trade Council v. Natsios, 181 F.3d 38 (1st Cir.1999), *aff'd sub nom.*, Crosby v. National Foreign Trade Council, 530 U.S. 363 (2000) (holding Massachusetts' Burma law invalid under the Supremacy Clause because it threatens to frustrate federal statutory objectives).

§ 16.4 Trade Restrictions: The Case of Cuba and Normalization

The trade boycott of Cuba illustrates how the United States carries out a unilateral boycott. The Cuban boycott has endured longer than current sanctions against other nations. Furthermore, Cuba has received attention by Congress and the U.S. President of varying levels of forcefulness over the past three decades, often in direct relation to U.S. political campaigns.

The boycott of Cuba began as a response to the Cuban nationalization of all U.S. citizens' properties in 1959 and 1960,[16] and to the trade agreement concluded by Cuba with the USSR in February, 1960. The U.S. Congress amended the Sugar Act of 1948 giving the President authority to alter the Cuban sugar quota. The President used this authority during the height of the July, 1960, bitterness to nearly totally remove the extensive quotas, leaving Cuba with no access to the U.S. sugar market. In October, 1960, the President imposed an extensive embargo on shipments of goods to Cuba, except for nonsubsidized food, medicines, and medical supplies. With the cessation of diplomatic relations, the United States has continued the boycott without a break, but the intensity of the boycott has varied.

The boycott provisions were amended in 1975 to allow foreign subsidiaries of U.S. companies to trade with Cuba. These amendments followed U.S. threats to tighten controls on foreign subsidiaries that caused several foreign governments to angrily denounce the policy, and even threaten nationalization of the companies. After 1975, U.S. subsidiaries abroad developed significant trade with Cuba. This trade angered anti-Castro groups in the United States, and led to the enactment of the Cuban Democracy Act in 1992. The Cuban Assets Control Regulations were amended to reflect the Act's strict provisions. However extensive and restrictive the laws appear, the United States is one of Cuba's major trading partners.

Proponents of the Cuban Democracy Act were also urging adoption of a much harsher act, which would allow litigation by current U.S. citizens who were Cuban nationals at the time of the Castro expropriations, seeking compensation from persons currently using expropriated properties. This became the Cuban

---

[16]   The expropriations effectively commenced under the Agrarian Reform Law on June 1, 1959, but did not reach their zenith until the resolutions issued under the authority of the major nationalization law of July, 1960. *See* Michael Wallace Gordon, THE CUBAN NATIONALIZATIONS: THE DEMISE OF FOREIGN PRIVATE PROPERTY (1976).

Liberty and Democratic Solidarity (Libertad) Act (more commonly known as Helms-Burton), enacted in March, 1996,[17] only because of the emotions aroused due to the shooting down of two U.S. civilian aircraft by Cuba near Cuban territory. The Act included two very controversial sections. The first, Title III, created a right of action in U.S. courts for a U.S. national with a claim that Cuba expropriated property after January 1, 1959, against any person who is "trafficking" in such property.

Trafficking is quite broadly defined, including not only such actions as selling, buying, leasing, or transferring, but also engaging in a "commercial activity using or otherwise benefitting from confiscated property."[18] The Act authorizes the President to suspend the effectiveness of Title III actions for successive periods of six months. President Clinton issued such suspension every six months beginning in August, 1996, throughout his term, and each president elected since has continued that practice. These suspensions were the only reason the European Union deferred its request for a panel under the WTO to challenge the extraterritorial effects of the Libertad Act. The United States has stated that it would use the national security defense under the WTO, and also in response to any similar challenge brought by Canada or Mexico under the NAFTA.[19]

The second important part of the Act, Title IV, requires that the Secretary of State deny visas for entry into the United States to corporate officers, principals, shareholders and even the spouse, minor children or agents of such persons, if they are trafficking in or have confiscated property.[20] This authority has been used against officials of Canadian, Israeli, and Mexican companies.

Other nations and organizations have responded in very strong terms against the Libertad Act by adopting blocking laws and enacting resolutions.[21] Cuba enacted its own response to the Libertad Act, which, inter alia, denies any possible compensation in

---

[17]   Pub. L. No. 104–114, 110 Stat. 785 (Mar. 12, 1996).

[18]   Libertad Act § 4(13).

[19]   The use of the national security defense was strongly criticized in such a case, where there was no foreseeable security threat.

[20]   Id. at § 401.

[21]   See, e.g., Peter Glossop, Canada's Foreign Extraterritorial Measures Act and U.S. Restrictions on Trade with Cuba, 32 INT'L LAWYER 93 (1998); Jorge Vargas, Introductory Note, Mexico: Act to Protect Trade and Investment from Foreign Statutes which Contravene International Law, 36 Int'l Legal Materials 133 (1997); Douglas H. Forsythe, Introductory Note, Canada: Foreign Extraterritorial Measures Act Incorporating the Amendments Countering the U.S. Helms-Burton Act, 36 Int'l Legal Materials 111 (1997); Protecting Against the Effects of the Extraterritorial Application of Legislation Adopted by the Third Country, E.U. Council Regulation 2271/96, 1996 O.J. (L 309), reprinted in 36 Int'l Legal Materials 127 (1997).

a future settlement with the government of Cuba to anyone attempting to take advantage of the Libertad Act by using the U.S. courts under Title III.[22] Finally, the Florida legislature largely deferred to the Miami Cuban-American groups and passed a state version of Helms-Burton, essentially a "feel good" action since the federal government had pre-empted governance of trade with Cuba. Florida later passed first one law attempting to ban any Florida university researchers from traveling to Cuba using private funds, even if licensed by the federal government, and then a second, the 2008 Sellers of Travel Act, setting huge fees on federally authorized travel agencies in Florida that booked flights to Cuba. Both were quickly overturned by the federal district court. The more recent thinking from the Miami legislator who promoted those laws is to punish exiles who visit Cuba by taking away their food stamps and Medicaid.

The Cuban Assets Control Regulations, approximately four dozen pages and nearly 150 separate provisions, are the principal regulations which govern trade with Cuba.[23] The application of the Regulations is limited by the Cuban Democracy Act, which removed administrative discretion in allowing some trade with Cuba from foreign subsidiaries. Furthermore, the Regulations may not conflict with the Trading with the Enemy Act,[24] or the Foreign Assistance Act of 1961, both as amended.[25] The administration of the Regulations is delegated to the Office of Foreign Assets Control (OFAC) of the Department of the Treasury.

The Regulations prohibit certain transactions and transfers, where Cuba or a Cuban national is involved. The scope is very wide, including various transfers involving (1) currency, securities, and gold or silver coin or bullion; (2) property or indebtedness; and (3) any form where the transfer is one which attempts to evade or avoid the first two prohibitions.[26] But the Secretary of the Treasury is given authority to authorize such transfers. Imports are prohibited if (1) Cuban in origin,[27] (2) the goods have been in Cuba (including

---

[22]   Ley de Reafirmacion de la Dignidad y Soberania Cubana (Ley No. 80), Dec. 24, 1996.

[23]   31 C.F.R Part 515. OFAC publishes a useful overview of the regulations. *See* 2013 Guide to OFAC Compliance Regulations at www.OFAC-Guide.com.

[24]   The original powers of the President were in the Trading With the Enemy Act (TWEA) of 1917. The President delegated authority to Treasury in accordance with the TWEA. The International Emergency Economic Powers Act (IEEPA) was enacted in 1977 and substantially replaced the TWEA. The authority of the President continues under the IEEPA.

[25]   31 C.F.R. § 515.101.

[26]   31 C.F.R. § 515.201.

[27]   *See, e.g.,* United States v. Plummer, 221 F.3d 1298 (11th Cir. 2000).

transported through), or (3) if made from any Cuban parts.[28] There are a few exceptions to the trade restrictions. One is a limited exception allowing trade in informational materials, such as some books.[29] More recently cash sales of certain agricultural products have been allowed. The trade prohibitions conclude with a restriction that disallows (1) any vessel which has entered a Cuban port for trade purposes from entering a U.S. port for 180 days after the departure from Cuba, or (2) any vessel carrying goods or passengers to or from Cuba (or goods in which a Cuban has any interest) from entering any U.S. port with such goods or passengers on board.[30]

The Regulations were modified in 2009, to increase allowed family visits and remittances, and increase permitted telecommunications. Additionally legislation in 2009 created a new *general* license to allow travel related transactions linked to commercial marketing of agricultural commodities, medicine, or medical devices. The new U.S. administration under President Obama seemed less inclined to source U.S. foreign policy towards Cuba in Miami and a relaxation by OFAC of the zealous control demanded by a decreasing number of Cuban exiles.

The prohibitions are followed by quite extensive definitions.[31] While nearly all of the definitions create little problem, one is of considerable importance to U.S. businesses with subsidiaries. A "person subject to the jurisdiction of the United States," upon whom the Regulations impose trade restrictions, includes, "any corporation, partnership, or association, wherever organized or doing business, that is owned or controlled by persons" citizen or resident of the United States or where an entity is organized under the laws of the United States.[32] The meaning of "owned" or "controlled" is not included in the Regulations. The focus of the Cuban Democracy Act is to limit trade with Cuba from foreign subsidiaries of U.S. corporations. It has brought negative responses from the European Union (and separately from member states of the EU), Canada, Argentina, Mexico, and the U.N. General Assembly. It is one more example of the extraterritorial application

---

[28]   31 C.F.R. § 515.204.

[29]   31 C.F.R. § 515.206. But no cigars or rum. The regulations even prohibit a U.S. citizen or legal resident alien from smoking a Cuban cigar or drinking Cuban rum while in a third country. One might think that OFAC has more important things to do than produce and publish Cuban Cigar Updates.

[30]   31 C.F.R. § 515.207. These vessel restrictions were added to comply with § 1706(b) of the Cuban Democracy Act.

[31]   31 C.F.R. Subpart C.

[32]   31 C.F.R. § 515.329(d).

of U.S. laws, and one more example of foreign rejection of such application.

Until this point, the Regulations are mostly prohibitory. But the next section contains important provisions covering "licenses, authorizations, and statements of licensing policy."[33] These provisions authorize the Secretary of the Treasury to issue licenses in a wide variety of circumstances, including (1) for certain judicial proceedings to take place, (2) to determine persons to be unblocked nationals, (3) and to allow transfers by operations of law. The provisions of most importance for U.S. business interests allow some limited trade with Cuba by U.S. owned or controlled firms.[34] But it was this provision which was the principal focus of the Cuban Democracy Act, which reversed a decade old policy allowing Treasury to license foreign subsidiaries to trade with Cuba.[35] The current law prohibits the issuance of any such licenses to contracts entered into after the enactment of the Cuban Democracy Act. The governments of the foreign nations in which many U.S. subsidiaries are located, however, have enacted laws which mandate that the subsidiaries disregard the U.S. restrictions. It must be assumed that some trade continues without any attempt to obtain a license.

The subsequent subpart governs reports, and requires reports by any person engaging in any transaction subject to the Regulations.[36] Thus, a U.S. company trading through a subsidiary may twice violate the law, first by trading and second by failing to report the trade. Penalties are contained in the next provisions,[37] and are severe. Fines may reach $1 million for willful violations, with a maximum of $500,000 as civil penalties.[38] If experience with the antiboycott Regulations discussed below offers any parallel, consent decrees are likely to be the method used to respond to investigated violations. Just as the antiboycott provisions have not eliminated violations, these boycott provisions are unlikely to eliminate violations. That becomes even more clear when it is realized that with antiboycott violations there is no violation of foreign law when the violation of the U.S. law occurs. But in the case of these boycott Regulations, a U.S. firm in violation of some of the provisions may have a mitigating argument not present in the

---

[33]   31 C.F.R. Subpart E.

[34]   31 C.F.R. § 515.559.

[35]   Cuban Democracy Act § 1706(a).

[36]   31 C.F.R. § 515.601.

[37]   31 C.F.R. Subpart F.

[38]   See United States v. Brodie, 403 F.3d 123 (3d Cir. 2005); United States v. Plummer, 221 F.3d 1298 (11th Cir. 2000); United States v. Macko, 994 F.2d 1526 (11th Cir. 1993); and United States v. Ortiz de Zevallos, 748 F. Supp. 1569 (S.D. Fla. 1990), all dealing with violations of the Cuban boycott rules.

antiboycott situation—to comply with the U.S. law means violation of the law of the nation in which the U.S. subsidiary is incorporated and operating.

Normalization. In 2015, Presidents Obama and Raul Castro normalized U.S.-Cuba relations after a 54 year hiatus. The restoration of diplomatic ties and the opening of a U.S. Embassy in Havana occurred on July 20, 2015. Prisoners were swapped and the U.S. has moved to take Cuba off the list of state sponsors of terrorism. The easing of travel restrictions under 12 existing categories allows many more Americans to visit Cuba, but travel generally is still not authorized. The United States has licensed ferries and cruises to Cuba, both awaiting expanded Cuban approval. A major agreement was reached allowing extensive, regular U.S. flights to Cuba to commence in the Fall of 2016.

U.S. export restrictions on agricultural and telecommunications gear, and health and medical goods and services, will be reduced, and liberalization of U.S. banking rules are expected to permit increased family remittances, trade financing and use of U.S.-based credit cards in Cuba. Cuba has begun to expand Internet access.

No change in the U.S. boycott of Cuba has occurred, which President Castro stated was the "main issue" from Cuba's perspective. That would require an act of Congress, where opposition is significant. The first U.S. investment in Cuba, to make small tractors in the Mariel Special Development Zone, has been approved.

Some $1.9 billion ($8 billion with interest) in expropriation claims have been certified by the U.S. Foreign Claims Settlement Commission against Cuba. Cuba has raised extensive counterclaims against the United States for damages flowing from the U.S. boycott. The two governments are in negotiations over these issues.

§ 16.5 United States Reaction to the Arab Boycott of Israel: The Antiboycott Laws

Two important historic events surrounding the conflict between businesses' freedom to export and the government's political goals led to special rules governing exports. The first was the Arab nations' extensive international primary, secondary and tertiary boycott of Israel.[39] The boycott is inconsistently applied by the Arab

---

[39] A primary boycott is where one nation, for example, Oman, refuses to deal with another, for example, Israel. The boycott is secondary when the boycotting nation (Oman) refuses to deal with any third party nation, such as the United States, if that nation deals with the boycotted nation, Israel. The tertiary boycott arises when the boycotting nation (Oman) refuses to deal with the third party nation (the

nations. Where the product or project is of high priority, the Arab nations either ignore their own boycott or grant a waiver.[40]

The Arab boycott of Israel led to the adoption of U.S. laws and regulations prohibiting U.S. persons from complying with or supporting any boycott by a foreign nation against a nation friendly to the United States.[41] Nowhere in the law is there any direct reference to either Israel or any specific Arab nation, but of 376 boycott requests notified to the Office of Antiboycott Compliance in 2011, 369 involved Arab League members. The antiboycott laws owe their existence to a long and bitter struggle within Congress, and between Congress and the administration, over the creation of rules that would prohibit U.S. companies from assisting the Arab nations in their attempts to harm Israel.[42]

Prior to the enactment of federal export laws dealing with the Arab boycott of Israel, several states enacted similar laws, and the federal tax and antitrust laws were used to deter U.S. companies from compliance with boycott requests. Although the boycott of Israel by the Arab nations is the reason the federal law exists, there has been some question raised about the applicability of the law to foreign boycotts against South Africa. The Department of Commerce interpreted the law as not applicable to the (since terminated) boycotts against South Africa. The law does affect many commercial relationships between U.S. persons and Middle-Eastern governments, private individuals, and banks.

The second event leading to special rules governing exports evolved from the discovery during the Watergate investigations that many U.S. companies had made payments to foreign officials to encourage those officials to purchase the goods of the company making the payments, or extend other favors such as allowing a foreign investment. Congressional reaction was much swifter than in the case of the Arab boycott. Congress adopted amendments to the securities laws to prohibit certain payments and regulate

---

United States), if any of the elements of its products are from a fourth party nation company (e.g., The Netherlands) which trades with the boycotted nation (e.g., Israel).

[40] See Abrams v. Baylor College of Medicine, 581 F. Supp. 1570, 1576 n.3 (S.D. Tex. 1984) for an example of a waiver of the boycott regarding medical equipment from a blacklisted company.

[41] Export Administration Act of 1979, 50 U.S.C. App. § 2407; Export Administrative Regulations, 15 C.F.R. Part 760.

[42] The history of the boycott provisions is contained in Trane Co. v. Baldrige, 552 F. Supp. 1378 (W.D. Wis. 1983).

reporting of payments, in legislation called the Foreign Corrupt Practices Act.[43]

Congress instead might have further amended the Export Administration Act to prohibit such payments, but the securities laws already addressed reporting and accounting requirements and that was one method used to regulate payments abroad. The FCPA added new reporting and accounting requirements which would help identify payments abroad. Prohibiting certain payments abroad, the second part of the FCPA, could be monitored by a company's records of payments. Use of the securities laws additionally meant that the Department of Justice would be the agency to pursue violations. The antiboycott provisions were under the jurisdiction of the Department of Commerce, thought to be somewhat more lenient than Justice.[44]

§ 16.6 Export Administration Act

Enforcement of the antiboycott laws lies largely within the Department of Commerce Bureau of Industry and Security. The Export Administration Act (EAA) governs the export of goods from the United States, including the antiboycott provisions. These antiboycott provisions, and the regulations, prohibit U.S. persons from participating in boycotts by a foreign nation against third nations that are friendly toward the United States. The statutory language is very broad, not unlike the concept of the U.S. antitrust laws. The EAA structure requires the President to issue regulations that prohibit any U.S. person from engaging principally in two different areas of activity, *refusals to deal* and *furnishing information*, if such actions further or support a boycott by one foreign nation against another foreign nation that is friendly to the United States.[45]

There is a further provision that applies particularly to banks, that prohibits certain actions with regard to letters of credit which also may further or support a boycott. These prohibitions are included in six sections of the law.[46] The law subsequently states that the regulations should provide exceptions governing some six classes of activity.[47] Further mandated is reporting to the Secretary of Commerce any request to furnish information.[48] Violations of

---

[43]   Foreign Corrupt Practices Act of 1977 (as amended in 1988 and 1998), 15 U.S.C. §§ 78q(b), 78dd, 78ff(a). The FCPA is the subject of Chapter 15.

[44]   There have been attempts by businesses to shift the jurisdiction of the FCPA from the Department of Justice to the Department of Commerce.

[45]   50 U.S.C. App. § 2407(a)(1).

[46]   50 U.S.C. App. § 2407(a)(1)(A)–(F).

[47]   50 U.S.C. App. § 2407(a)(2)(A)–(F).

[48]   50 U.S.C. App. § 2407(b)(2).

these provisions are subject to the same statutes that govern other violations of the export laws.

§ 16.7   Export Administration Regulations

Supplementing the EAA are Export Administration Regulations (EAR).[49] They include very extensive examples of conduct which provide guidance in determining whether specific conduct may constitute a violation of the EAA and EAR. Many of the examples are of common occurrences where companies are in jeopardy of refusing to deal or furnishing prohibited information. Use of these examples is essential to determining both the sense of the administration in interpreting the law, and the likelihood that the conduct in question may be challenged. The examples in the regulations follow the pattern of the principal statute. Thus, the regulations begin (after a section with definitions[50]) with examples of the classes of prohibited conduct,[51] and are followed by examples of the classes of exceptions.[52] Following the regulations are a series of sixteen Supplements that include Department of Commerce interpretations of various provisions, with some suggested contractual provisions that may avoid challenges by the Department.

§ 16.8   Prohibited Actions Must Be Done Intentionally

The purpose of the antiboycott provisions is to prohibit any U.S. person "from taking or knowingly agreeing to take [certain actions] with intent to comply with, further, or support any boycott" against a country friendly to the United States.[53] It specifically exempts boycotts pursuant to U.S. law. The requirement of intent is essential, but what constitutes intent may seem marginal. In *United States v. Meyer*,[54] the defendant Meyer was held to have knowledge that a form required by Saudi Arabia to have a trademark registered in that country was not used to obtain information needed for the registration, but to further the boycott of Israel. Meyer claimed that his actions were inadvertent and not intentional, but Meyer's knowledge and intention were rather clearly illustrated by his receipt of information from the Department of State that it could not notarize the form because of

---

[49]   15 C.F.R. Part 760.

[50]   15 C.F.R. § 760.1.

[51]   15 C.F.R. § 760.2.

[52]   15 C.F.R. § 760.3.

[53]   50 U.S.C. App. § 2407(a)(1).

[54]   864 F.2d 214 (1st Cir. 1988).

the boycott, and his subsequent acquisition of a notarization through the U.S.-Arab Chamber of Commerce.[55] The *Meyer* decision involves a clear attempt to find a way past the law. *Meyer* thus is not very helpful for a case where the intent is based on less apparent criteria. But it does emphasize that *inadvertent* compliance is not a violation.

§ 16.9   Refusals to Deal

The first prohibition in the EAA is against directly refusing to do business with or in the boycotted country, or with a national or resident of that country. Also prohibited is any refusal to do business with the boycotted country by agreement with or response to requests from any other person.[56] This means a U.S. company may not refuse to do business with Israel at the request of the central boycott office of the Arab nations in Damascus. Intent to refuse to do business is not established by the absence of any business relationship with the boycotted country.

The Export Administration Regulations, which include subsections further defining the meaning of refusing to do business, expand upon this prohibition.[57] The regulations make it clear that a refusal to do business may be established by a course of conduct as well as a specific refusal, or by a use of any "blacklist" or "whitelist". They emphasize, nevertheless, that intent to comply with or support a boycott is required. The regulations also suggest what does *not* constitute a refusal to do business, such as an agreement to comply generally with the laws of the boycotting country. There does not have to be an agreement not to do business. Compliance with a request, or a unilateral decision, if for boycott reasons, will suffice. These regulations raise one especially difficult issue—the use of a list of suppliers. The regulations give a specific example, although specific examples are usually left for the "examples" section.[58] A U.S. person under contract to provide management services for a construction contract may provide a list of qualified bidders for the client if the service is customary, and if qualified persons are not excluded because they are blacklisted.

The regulations and especially the examples disclose the nearly unlimited possible configurations of fact situations that may give rise to problems. Consider only a few possible variations, from which numerous additional variations may be easily considered:

---

[55]   A strong dissent inappropriately relied on an inapplicable case to argue that the required level of intent was not met.

[56]   50 U.S.C. App. § 2407(a)(1)(A).

[57]   15 C.F.R. § 760.2(a). *See also* Supplements to Part 760.

[58]   15 C.F.R. § 760.2(a)(6).

(1)   A U.S. company is doing business in Israel, but wants to do business in Arab nations while retaining the Israel business. This creates a problem if the Arab nations have alternative sources for the goods, especially from companies in nations which do not have antiboycott laws, meaning essentially all other nations in the world.

(2)   Same as above but the company would like to terminate the business in Israel because:

(a)   it believes in or doesn't really care about the boycott. The company is in danger of challenge by the Department of Commerce. But is a business likely to state that it believes in or doesn't care about the boycott?

(b)   the Israel business is not as large as the potential Arab nations business and the company does not have the capacity to do business in both. As long as the decision is not boycott based, it is proper to drop the Israel business. But it may have to prove that its motives were business and not boycott based.

(c)   the company had planned to close the Israel business because it has been losing money. It had best be able to prove that loss.

(3)   The company trades with Arab nations and would also like to do business with Israel. It knows if it does do business with Israel it may lose the business with the Arab nations.

(4)   The same but the company is willing to drop the business with the Arab nations. It may do so without violating the boycott rules because Israel is not boycotting the Arab nations.

(5)   The company is doing business in both Israel and Arab nations. The Arabs do not know this. The company wants to drop the Israel business because it fears that the Arabs will learn of that business and terminate very profitable Arab business.

Prior to 1985–86, the focus of the Department of Commerce was on reporting violations. But in 1986 the Department, concerned about its limited resources, began to concentrate on the blacklist, religious discrimination, and refusals to deal. These are viewed by the Department as the most serious violations.

The regulations attempt to cover many variations, but obviously cannot offer an example for each possible situation.

Refusals to deal arise for reasons both directly related and totally unrelated to the boycott. When normally justified business reasons for refusing to deal begin to show a pattern of not dealing for reasons consistent with a boycott, however, the party is in some danger of a challenge from Commerce. But the law does include language of intent, which is most difficult to show from a pattern of conduct that indicates good business reasons for refusing to deal.

§ 16.10   Discriminatory Actions

The second statutorily prohibited conduct is refusing to employ or otherwise discriminating against any U.S. person on the basis of race, religion, sex, or national origin, where such conduct is intentional and in furtherance of an unlawful boycott.[59] This section addresses the Arab nations' attempts to cause harm to Jewish people wherever they may live, rather than to harm Israel as a nation. Thus, a company may not refuse to employ Jewish persons so that it may gain favor with Arab clients. In one of the few court decisions involving the antiboycott provisions, Baylor College of Medicine was found to have persistently appointed non-Jewish persons for a project with Saudi Arabia.[60]

The antidiscrimination section of the EAA includes both refusals to employ and *other discrimination*. For example, a requirement that a U.S. company not use a six-pointed star on its packaging of products to be sent to the Arab nation would be a violation because it is part of the enforcement effort of the boycott. But it is not a violation if the demand is that no symbol of Israel be included on the packaging. The former is a religious symbol generally, the latter an acceptable request which does not include reference to any person's religion.[61] This illustrates a general attempt to acknowledge that the boycotting nations are entitled to have *some* control over what comes into their nation. They are entitled to say no imports may be stamped "Products of Israel", but they may not attack the Jewish religion more broadly by requiring certification that no religious symbols appear on any packages. The United States is attempting to say by the law and regulations that the Arab nations may have a right to engage in a primary boycott

---

[59]   50 U.S.C. App. § 2407(a)(B). Even if employment discrimination is not boycott based, and thus not a violation of the EAA, it may violate other laws, such as civil rights legislation.

[60]   Abrams v. Baylor College of Medicine, 581 F. Supp. 1570 (S.D. Tex. 1984), *aff'd*, 805 F.2d 528 (5th Cir. 1986). The case also deals with the issue of the right to bring a private action. Using the *Cort v. Ash* factors test the court held that there is an implied right under the EAA.

[61]   These are examples included in 15 C.F.R. § 760.2(b), examples (viii) and (ix). *See* Supplements to Part 760.

against Israel, but they may not draw U.S. persons into supporting that boycott.

The regulations governing discriminatory actions make it clear that such actions must involve "intent to comply with, further or support an unsanctioned foreign boycott."[62] The regulations further state that the boycott provisions do not supersede or limit U.S. civil rights laws.[63]

§ 16.11   Furnishing Information Regarding Race, Religion, Sex, or National Origin

The third specific prohibition relates to the refusal to hire for reasons that would violate U.S. civil rights laws. This provision effectively means furnishing information with respect to race, religion, sex or national origin.[64] It is a brief provision is supplemented by regulations which state that it shall apply whether the information is specifically requested or offered voluntarily and whether stated in the affirmative or negative.[65] Furthermore, prohibited information includes place of birth or nationality of the parents, and information in code words or symbols that would identify a person's race, religion, sex, or national origin.[66] The regulations also reaffirm the element of intent.[67]

The examples in the regulations illustrate the difficulty of clearly defining "prohibited information". If the boycotting nation requests a U.S. company to give all employees who will work in the boycotting nation visa forms, and these visa forms request otherwise prohibited information, the company is not in violation for giving the forms to its employees or for sending the forms back to the boycotting country party. This is considered a ministerial function and not support of the boycott. But the company may not itself provide the information on race, religion, sex, or nationality of its employees, if it meets the intent requirement. The company might certify that none of its employees to be sent to the boycotting nation are women, where the laws of the boycotting country prohibit women from working. The reason for such submission has nothing to do with the boycott.

---

62   15 C.F.R. § 760.2(b)(2).

63   15 C.F.R. § 760.2(b)(3).

64   50 U.S.C. App. § 2407(a)(C).

65   15 C.F.R. § 760.2(c)(2).

66   15 C.F.R. § 760.2(c)(3).

67   15 C.F.R. § 760.2(c)(4).

§ 16.12 Furnishing Information Regarding Business Relationships: The Use of "Blacklists"

The fourth prohibition is one that is often at issue. It involves the use of blacklists. Some Arab nations maintain a blacklist of persons and companies with whom they will not do business. Arab nations often ask a prospective commercial agreement party to certify that none of the goods will include components obtained from any companies on the blacklist.

Persons are prohibited from furnishing information about an extensive list of business activities ("including a relationship by way of sale, purchase, legal, or commercial representation, shipping or other transport, insurance, investment, or supply"[68]), with an equally extensive list of business relationships ("with or in the boycotted country, with any business concern organized under the laws of the boycotted country, with any national or resident of the boycotted country, or with any other person which is known or believed to be restricted from having any business relationship with or in the boycotting country"[69]). At the end is a statement that the section does not prohibit furnishing "normal business information in a commercial context as defined by the Secretary." Thus, entities are very extensively governed with regard to the flow of information between the company and the boycotting country.

The regulations develop this already expansive section.[70] The prohibited information may not be given whether directly or indirectly requested or furnished on the initiative of the U.S. person.[71] The Secretary's definition of normal business in a commercial context is that related "to factors such as financial fitness, technical competence, or professional experience" as might be normally found in documents available to the public, such as "annual reports, disclosure statements concerning securities, catalogues, promotional brochures, and trade and business handbooks."[72] Such public information may not be supplied if in response to a boycott request.[73] But it may be supplied if it could be used by the boycotting country to further the boycott—knowledge and intent on the part of the U.S. person is the key to making the furnishing of the information unlawful. There are numerous

---

[68] 50 U.S.C. App. § 2407(a)(D).
[69] *Id.*
[70] 15 C.F.R. § 760.2(d).
[71] 15 C.F.R. § 760.2(d)(2)(ii).
[72] 15 C.F.R. § 760.2(d)(3).
[73] 15 C.F.R. § 760.2(d)(4).

examples of this prohibition, many referring to use of blacklists. For example, a person may not certify that its suppliers are not on a furnished blacklist.[74] If a company is on the blacklist, or if it wishes to know whether it is on the blacklist, it may request such information.[75] That is not furnishing information. But if it furnishes information in order to be removed, it may be in violation. If a company believes it is on the blacklist but no longer would be listed were the Arab nations to know the true facts, supplying those facts may constitute a violation.[76] The same may occur when a company believes it is mistakenly listed, and wishes to make this known to the Arab nations. Companies have removed their names, but it must be done with great care.

The most publicized blacklist case involved Baxter International Inc., a large U.S. medical supply company.[77] As a result of an informant's disclosure, Baxter was investigated and charged with violating the EAA because of the way in which it attempted to have its name removed from the Arab blacklist.[78] Commerce was prepared to charge Baxter and a senior officer with providing over 300 items of prohibited information to Syrian authorities and a Saudi Arabian firm. The company and the officer admitted civil and criminal violations and were assessed total civil penalties of $6,060,600—the highest at the time. The case would not have succeeded without the informant providing substantial documentation of the violations.

§ 16.13 Prohibition of Intentional Evasion

The EAA and the regulations each include a section that states that no U.S. person may take any action with intent to evade the law.[79] Permitted activities are not to be considered an evasion of the law. An example of an evasion is placing a person at a commercial disadvantage or imposing on that person special burdens because that person is blacklisted or otherwise restricted from business relations for boycott reasons.[80] Another evasion may be use of risk-of-loss provisions that expressly impose a financial risk on another because of the import laws of a boycotting country, unless

---

[74]   15 C.F.R. § 760.2(d) example (x).

[75]   15 C.F.R. § 760.2(d) example (xv).

[76]   A U.S. subsidiary of the French cosmetics company L'Oreal provided the parent information to assist in removal from the blacklist. Providing this information and failing to report to the Commerce department led to L'Oreal agreeing to pay $1.4 million in civil penalties. See, e.g., Los Angeles Times, August 30, 1995, at Part D.

[77]   See, e.g., The Case Against Baxter International, Business Week, Oct. 7, 1991, pg. 106.

[78]   See 5 OEL Insider 7 (Dec. 1993).

[79]   50 U.S.C. App. § 2407(a)(5); 15 C.F.R. § 760.4.

[80]   15 C.F.R. § 70.4(c).

customarily used.[81] Two final suggested evasions are the use of dummy corporations or other devices to mask prohibited activities, or diverting boycotting country orders to a foreign subsidiary.[82]

§ 16.14 Reporting Requirements

Under the title "Foreign policy controls," the EAA includes very important provisions that require the reporting of the receipt of any request for the "furnishing of information, the entering into or implementing of agreements, or the taking of any other action" outlined in the policy section[83] of the EAA.[84] The receipt of any such request must be reported to the Secretary of Commerce. Failure to report boycott associated requests is perhaps the most frequent violation of the EAA. The report must include any information the Secretary deems appropriate and must state whether the person intends to comply or has complied with the request. These reports are public records, except to the extent that certain confidential information is included that would cause a competitive disadvantage to the reporting person.

The regulations include quite extensive provisions, covering (a) the scope of reporting requirements, (b) the manner of reporting, and (c) the disclosure of information.

Scope of Reporting Requirements. Whenever a person receives a written or oral request to take any action in furtherance or support of a boycott against a friendly foreign country it must be reported. The request may be to enter into or implement an agreement. It may involve a solicitation, directive, legend, or instruction asking for information or action (or inaction). The request must be reported whether or not the action requested is prohibited, except as the regulations provide.[85] That essentially means reporting is required if the person knows or has reason to know that the purpose of the request is to enforce, implement, or otherwise support, further or secure compliance with the boycott.[86]

When a request is received by a U.S. person located outside the United States (subsidiary, branch, partnership, affiliate, office, or other controlled permanent foreign establishment), it is reportable if received in connection with a transaction in interstate or foreign

---

[81]   15 C.F.R. § 760.4(d).

[82]   15 C.F.R. § 760.4(e).

[83]   50 U.S.C. App. § 2402(5).

[84]   50 U.S.C. App. § 2407(b).

[85]   15 C.F.R. § 760.5(a)(1).

[86]   15 C.F.R. § 760.5(a)(2).

commerce.[87] A general boycott questionnaire, unrelated to any specific transaction, must be reported when that person has or anticipates a business relationship with or in the boycotting country, also in interstate or foreign commerce.

The reporting requirements apply whether the U.S. person is an exporter, bank, or other financial institution, insurer, freight forwarder, manufacturer, or other person.[88] If the information about a country's boycotting requirements is learned by means of the receipt or review of books, pamphlets, legal texts, exporter's guidebooks, and other similar publications, it is not considered a reportable request. The same is true of receipt of an unsolicited bid where there is no intention to respond.[89]

The regulations include ten specific requests that are not reportable. They were added because of the customary use of certain terms for boycott and non-boycott purposes, Congressional mandates for clear guidelines in uncertain areas, and the Department of Commerce's desire to reduce paperwork and costs. They are:[90]

(i)   request to refrain from shipping goods on a carrier flying the flag of a particular country, or that is owned, chartered, leased or operated by a particular country or its nationals or residents; or a request for certification to such effect;

(ii)   request to ship goods, or refrain from shipping goods, on a prescribed route, or a certification request of either;

(iii)   request for an affirmative statement or certification regarding the country of origin of goods;

(iv)   request for an affirmative statement or certification of supplier's or manufacturer's or service provider's name;

(v)   request to comply with laws of another country except where it requires compliance with that country's boycott laws;

(vi)   request to individual for personal information about himself or family for immigration, passport, visa, or employment requirements;

---

[87]   *Id.*, citing 15 C.F.R. §§ 760.1(c) and (d). The definition of "interstate or foreign commerce" is the subject of a Department of Commerce interpretation in Supplement No. 8 to Part 760.

[88]   15 C.F.R. § 760.5(a)(3).

[89]   15 C.F.R. § 760.5(a)(4). A definition of "unsolicited invitation to bid" is included in Supplement No. 11 to Part 769.

[90]   15 C.F.R. § 760.5(a)(5); *see also* Supplement No. 10(b) to Part 760.

(vii) request for an affirmative statement or certification stating the destination of exports or confirming or indicating the cargo will be unloaded or discharged at a particular destination;

(viii) request to supply a certificate by the owner, master, charterer, or any employee thereof, that a vessel, aircraft, truck, or other transport is eligible, permitted, nor restricted from or allowed to enter, a particular port, country or group of countries under the laws, rules, or regulations of that port, country or countries;

(ix) request for a certificate from an insurance company stating the issuing company has an agent or representative (plus name and address) in a boycotting country; or

(x) request to comply with term or condition that vendor bears the risk of loss and indemnify the purchaser if goods arc denied entry for any reason if this clause was in use by the purchaser prior to January 18, 1978.

The Department of Commerce periodically is to survey domestic concerns to determine the worldwide scope of boycott requests received by U.S. subsidiaries and controlled affiliates regarding activities outside U.S. commerce.[91] This is to cover requests that would be required to be reported but for the fact that they involve commerce outside the United States. Information collected from U.S. persons will include the number and nature of non-reportable requests received, action requested, action taken, and countries making such requests.

Manner of Reporting Requests. Every request must be reported; however, only the first need be reported when the same request is received in several forms.[92] But each different request regarding the same transaction must be reported. Each U.S. person receiving a request must report the request, but one person may designate another to make the report, such as a parent reporting on behalf of a subsidiary.[93]

Disclosure of Information. The third part of the regulations applying to reporting states that the reports shall become public records, except for "certain proprietary information."[94] The reporting party may certify that the disclosure of information

---

[91]   15 C.F.R. § 760.5(a)(7).

[92]   15 C.F.R. § 760.5(b)(1).

[93]   15 C.F.R. § 760.5(b)(2).

[94]   15 C.F.R. § 760.5(c)(1).

relating to the (1) quantity, (2) description, or (3) value of any articles, materials or supplies (including technical data and other information), may place the company at a competitive disadvantage. In such case the information will not be made public. But the reporting party must edit the public inspection copy of the accompanying documents as noted below, and the Secretary may reject the request for confidentiality for reasons either of disagreement regarding the competitive disadvantage, or of national interest in not withholding the information.[95] If such decision is made, the party must be given an opportunity to comment.

Because the report is made public, one copy must be submitted intact and the other may be edited in accordance with the above limitations. Any additional material considered confidential may also be deleted, as may be any material not required to be reported.[96] The copy is to be marked "Public Inspection Copy."

§ 16.15 Violations and Enforcement

Violations and enforcement of the antiboycott laws are subject to the same provisions as violations and enforcement of the export laws.[97] The enforcement of the antiboycott laws has generated few court decisions. Most have involved issues of constitutionality, creation of private rights of action, or the statute of limitations.[98] Several persons have had licenses suspended and fines exceeding $5 million have been levied. Most of these cases involved the receipt of requests for information from Arab countries. In instances where the companies had complied with the request, the Department of Commerce and the company usually agreed on a fine as part of a consent decree. The procedures were dealt with administratively, and the decisions are found only in some private reporters.[99] One of the largest civil penalties was imposed in a settlement with Baxter International Inc., in 1993. Baxter, a Swiss subsidiary, and an officer paid a penalty totaling $6,060,600. For all of 2011 eight companies paid penalties totaling $129,300.

---

[95] *Id.*

[96] 15 C.F.R. § 760.5(c)(2).

[97] 50 U.S.C. App. §§ 2410, 2411 and 2412. *See* Chapter 14, *supra.* Considerable information on the boycotts is at www.bis.doc.gov, including major cases.

[98] United States v. Core Laboratories, Inc., 759 F.2d 480 (5th Cir. 1985) (EAA and the statute of limitations); Abrams v. Baylor College of Medicine, 581 F. Supp. 1570 (S.D. Tex.1984), *aff'd* 805 F.2d 528 (5th Cir. 1986) (EAA and affirming private right of action); Bulk Oil (ZUG) A.G. v. Sun Co., Inc., 583 F. Supp. 1134 (S.D.N.Y. 1983), *aff'd* 742 F.2d 1431 (2d Cir. 1984) (EAA and rejecting private right of action).

[99] *See* Int'l Boycotts (Business Law Inc.); Boycott L. Bull.

The Department of Commerce began in 1986 to emphasize what it considered the most serious violations, involving the blacklist, religious discrimination and refusals to deal. The number of reported court decisions remains very small. Although in the early 1990s the number of reported Arab requests for information had diminished, cases such as Baxter illustrate that violations continue to occur.

U.S. subsidiaries that carry out boycott activities of foreign parents are within the reach of the provisions. The French L'Oreal, S.A. cosmetics company requested information from two U.S. subsidiaries, Parbel of Florida, Inc. (formerly Helena Rubenstein, Inc.) and Cosmair, Inc., about their business relationships in or with Israel. More than 100 items of information were provided, and no report of the request was made to Commerce. The two subsidiaries (and individual corporate counsel for Cosmair) agreed to fines exceeding $1.4 million in 1995.

§ 16.16   Private Right of Action

As is the case with many laws, there is no clear indication whether the EAA includes a private right of action. A federal district court in Texas, in *Abrams v. Baylor College of Medicine,*[100] addressing a claim by two Jewish medical students that Baylor University denied them opportunities when it excluded Jews from medical teams it sent to Saudi Arabia, found an implied right of action by applying the factors in the *Cort v. Ash* decision of the U.S. Supreme Court.[101] The Fifth Circuit upheld the decision. But in *Bulk Oil (ZUG) A.G. v. Sun Co.,* the Second Circuit rejected the existence of a private right of action, affirming a New York federal district court decision involving an accusation of violation of the antiboycott provisions by failing to deliver oil to Israel.[102]

---

[100]   581 F. Supp. 1570 (S.D. Tex. 1984), *aff'd* 805 F.2d 528 (5th Cir.1986).
[101]   422 U.S. 66 (1975).
[102]   583 F. Supp. 1134 (S.D.N.Y. 1983), *aff'd* 742 F.2d 1431 (2d Cir.1984).

Chapter 17

FREE TRADE AGREEMENTS
AND CUSTOMS UNIONS

Table of Sections

§ 17.1 Introduction

There is a massive movement towards free trade agreements and customs unions throughout the world, though not often of the consequence of that occurring in Europe and North America. Some of these developments are a competitive by-product of European and North American integration. Others simply reflect the desire (but not always the political will) to capture the economic gains and international negotiating strength that such economic relations can bring. This is particularly true of attempts at free trade and customs unions in the developing world. The explosion of such agreements creates systemic risks for the World Trade Organization (WTO), which reports that nearly all of its members are partners in one or more regional or bilateral trade agreements.

There is a continuum of sorts, a range of options to be considered when nations contemplate economic integration. In "free trade areas" (FTAs), tariffs, quotas, and other barriers to trade among participating states are reduced or removed while individual national trade barriers vis-à-vis third party states are retained.

"Customs unions" remove trade barriers among participating states and also create common trade barriers for all participating states as regards third-party states. "Common markets" go further than customs unions by providing for the free movement of factors of production (capital, labor, enterprise, technology) among participating states.

"Economic communities" build on common markets by introducing some harmonization of basic national policies related to the economy of the community, e.g. transport, taxation, corporate behavior and structure, monetary matters and regional growth. Finally, "economic unions" may embrace a more or less complete harmonization of national policies related to the economy of the union, e.g. company laws, commercial treaties, social welfare, currencies, and government subsidies. The difference between an economic community and an economic union relates only to the number and importance of harmonized national policies.

All such agreements are inherently discriminatory in their trade impact. As non-universalized trade preferences, they tend to simultaneously *create trade* among participating states and *divert trade* between those states and the rest of the world. Thus, while trade creation may represent an improvement in the allocation of scarce world resources, trade diversion may generate an opposite result.

With free trade agreements, diversionary trade effects are usually not distinct because of the absence of a common trade wall against outsiders. Trade diversion nonetheless occurs. "Rules of origin" in free trade area agreements keep third-party imports from seeking the lowest tariff or highest quota state and then exploiting the trade advantages within a free trade area. Under rules of origin, free trade areas are "free" only for goods substantially originating therein. This causes member state goods to be preferred over goods from other states. Rules of origin under a free trade agreement can be as trade diversionary as common external tariffs in customs unions.

§ 17.2 GATT Article 24

Article 24 of the General Agreement on Tariffs and Trade (GATT) (1947 and 1994) attempts to manage the internal trade-creating and external trade-diverting effects of FTAs, Customs Unions and similar arrangements. Proposals for free trade areas and custom unions must be submitted to a formal GATT/WTO review procedure during which "binding" recommendations are possible to bring the proposals into conformity. Such recommendations might deal with Article 24 requirements for the elimination of internal tariffs and other restrictive regulations of commerce on "substantially all" products originating in a customs union or free trade area. Or they might deal with Article 24 requirements that common external tariffs not be "on the whole higher or more restrictive" in effect than the general incidence of prior existing national tariffs. The broad purpose of Article 24, acknowledged therein, is to facilitate trade among the GATT contracting parties and not to raise trade barriers.

Most free trade and customs union agreements have passed through this review mechanism *without* substantial modification. The GATT, not economic agreements, most often has given way. For example, during GATT review of the 1957 Treaty of Rome creating what is now the European Union, many "violations" of the letter and spirit of Article 24 were cited. The derivation of the common external tariff by arithmetically averaging existing national tariffs was challenged as more restrictive of trade than previous arrangements. Such averaging on a given product fails to take account of differing national import volumes. If a product was faced originally with a lower than average national tariff and a larger than average national demand, the new average tariff is clearly more "restrictive" of imports than before. Averaging in high tariffs of countries of low demand quite plausibly created more restrictions on third-party trade. If so, the letter and spirit of Article 24 were breached.

Despite these and other arguments, the Treaty of Rome passed through GATT study and review committees without final resolution of its legal status under Article 24. Postponement of these issues became permanent. GATT attempts—through the lawyer-like conditions of Article 24 to maximize trade creation and minimize trade diversion—must be seen as generally inadequate. Treaty terms became negotiable demands that were not accepted. Decades later, the ineffectiveness of GATT/WTO supervision of free trade and customs union agreements continues. At best Article 24 exerts a marginal influence over their contents. Whether the extraordinary proliferation of preferential agreements undermines or supports WTO trade policies is hotly debated.

§ 17.3   GATS Integrated Services Agreements

Since 1995, "economic integration agreements" (EIAs) covering services are permitted under Article 5 of the General Agreement on Trade in Services (GATS). Such agreements, which can be staged, must have "substantial sectoral coverage," eliminate "substantially" all discrimination in sectors subject to multilateral commitments, and not raise the "overall" level of barriers to trade in GATS services compared to before the EIA. EIAs involving developing nations are to be accorded "flexibility." Like GATT Article 24 customs unions, there is an Article 5 duty to compensate EIA nonparticipants.

Review of GATS Article 5 notifications is undertaken, when requested by the WTO Council for Trade in Services, by the Committee on Regional Trade Agreements (CRTA). Thus, whereas CRTA examinations of GATT Article 24 agreements are required, such examinations are optional under GATS. Nevertheless, numerous Article 5 examinations have been conducted, including notably the services components of the North American Free Trade Agreement (NAFTA), the EEC Treaty (1957) and EU Enlargement (2004), Japan's FTAs with Singapore, Mexico and Malaysia, China's FTAs with Hong Kong and Macau, and various U.S. free trade agreements. None of these examinations has resulted in a final report on consistency with GATS Article 5. This pattern continues the GATT/WTO record of regulatory failure regarding economic integration agreements.

§ 17.4 The European Union

In 1957, the European Economic Community was created under the Treaty of Rome by Italy, France, West Germany, Luxembourg, Belgium and the Netherlands. Over time, this initial loose association of six nations broadened by adding additional members and strengthened through a series of treaties increasing the power of supranational institutions. In 1993, the Maastricht Treaty on European Union (TEU) was ratified by the then-10 members of the EEC, creating the European Union (EU); in 2003 the Treaty of Nice, signed by 15 member nations, amended prior treaties to restructure and strengthen European institutions; in 2007 the Reform Treaty (Treaty of Lisbon) was signed, eventually going into effect on December 1, 2009 among 27 nations. Under the latter treaty, the amended Treaty of Rome became the Treaty on the Functioning of the European Union (TFEU).[1]

With Croatia joining in 2013, the EU now has 28 member states, although in June 2016 voters in the United Kingdom approved a referendum calling for that country to leave the EU. Apart from the United Kingdom, the only major nonmember nations in Western and Central Europe are Switzerland, Norway and Iceland.

---

[1]   The official EU website is https://europa.eu/european-union/index_en. For more extensive coverage, see Ralph Folsom, PRINCIPLES OF EUROPEAN UNION LAW (4th ed. 2014).

The EU Customs Union. The free movement of goods within Europe is based upon the creation of a customs union. Under this union, the member states have eliminated customs duties among themselves.[2] They have established a common customs tariff and customs code for their trade with the rest of the world. Quantitative restrictions (quotas) on trade between member states are also prohibited, except in emergency and other limited situations.[3] The right of free movement applies to goods that originate in the Common Market and to those that have lawfully entered it and are said to be in "free circulation."[4]

The establishment of the customs union has been a major accomplishment, though not without difficulties. The member states committed themselves not only to the elimination of tariffs and quotas on internal trade, but also to the elimination of "measures of equivalent effect."[5] The elastic legal concept of measures of equivalent effect has been interpreted broadly by the European Court of Justice and the European Commission to prohibit a wide range of trade restraints, such as administrative fees charged at borders which are the equivalent of import or export tariffs.[6] Charges of equivalent effect to a tariff must be distinguished from internal taxes that are applicable to imported and domestic goods. The latter must be levied in a nondiscriminatory and non-protective manner[7], while the former are prohibited entirely,[8] There has been a considerable amount of litigation over this distinction.[9]

Nontariff trade barriers (NTBs) were the principal focus of the 1980s campaign for a fully integrated Common Market. Many legislative acts were adopted which target NTBs. When possible, a common European standard is adopted. For example, legislation on auto pollution requirements adopts this methodology. Products meeting these standards may be freely traded in the Common Market. Traditionally, this approach (called "harmonization") has required the formation of a consensus as to the appropriate level of protection.

---

[2]   Article 30, Treaty on the Functioning of the European Union (TFEU).

[3]   Articles 34–37, TFEU.

[4]   Articles 28–29, TFEU.

[5]   *See especially* Articles 30, 34 and 35, TFEU.

[6]   Rewe Zentralfinanz v. Landwirtschaftskammer Westfalen-Lippe (1973) Eur. Comm. Rep. 1039; Commission v. Italy (1969) Eur. Comm. Rep. 193. *But see* Commission v. Germany (1988) Eur. Comm. Rep. 5427.

[7]   Article 110, TFEU.

[8]   Articles 28, 30, TFEU.

[9]   *See, e.g.*, Industria Gomma, Articoli Vari v. Ente Nazionale ENCC (1975) Eur. Comm. Rep. 699.

Once adopted, harmonized standards must be followed. This approach can be deceptive, however. Some harmonization directives contain a list of options from which member states may choose when implementing those directives. In practice, this leads to differentiated national laws on the same so-called harmonized subject. Furthermore, in certain areas (notably the environment and occupational health and safety), the TFEU expressly indicates that member states may adopt laws that are more demanding. The result is, again, less than complete harmonization.

The EU Legal System. The Europeans have been creating law at dazzling though sometimes irregular speed. Without an understanding of these areas, it is almost impossible to function as a lawyer on EU matters.

The two founding treaties of the European Union, the Treaty on the Functioning of the European Union (TFEU) and the Maastricht Treaty on European Union (TEU), are the "primary" sources of regional law. They are "quasi-constitutional." The treaties have a common set of core institutions, as described below. These are the Council, the Commission, the Parliament and the Court of Justice. These institutions, supplemented by the European Council, European Central Bank and other EU bodies, and by national legislatures, courts and tribunals, have been busy generating a remarkably vast and complex body of "secondary" law.

Some law is adopted directly at the regional level, but much of it is enacted by national governments under regional "direction." Similarly, some (and the most important) of the case law is created by decisions in the European Court of Justice and its companion General Court (see below), but much development also occurs in the national courts, acting in many instances with "advisory rulings" from the Court of Justice. European secondary law also includes international obligations, sometimes undertaken through "mixed" regional and national negotiations and ratifications.

There are two main types of legislative acts, directives and regulations (see below). These acts should be distinguished from declarations, resolutions, guidelines, notices, policy statements, recommendations, opinions and individual decisions, all of which rarely involve legislative acts and are sometimes referred to as "soft law."

The Reform Treaty of 2009, in new TFEU provisions, enumerates categories and areas of exclusive, shared and supportive EU competences or powers. These enumerations determine when and to what degree the EU and/or the member states may legislate. Exclusive EU competences include the customs union, internal market competition rules, marine conservation, and the Common Commercial Policy (external trade and investment relations).[10] The Union also has exclusive competence over international agreements provided for in EU legislative acts, necessary to enable the exercise of its internal powers, or those agreements whose conclusion may affect common rules or alter their scope. In all these areas, member states may legislate only if empowered by the Union to do so, or to implement EU acts.

When the TFEU enumerates a shared competence,[11] the Union may legislate. Member states may legislate only to the extent the EU has not done so or ceased to exercise a shared competence. Shared competences include the internal market, social policy, cohesion, agriculture and fisheries, the environment, consumer protection, transport, trans-European networks, energy, the area of freedom, security and justice, and common public health safety concerns. Special more-permissive rules allow member states greater latitude in the areas of research, technology development, space, third world development and humanitarian aid.

Lastly, the Union is authorized to legislate in support of, to coordinate with, or to supplement (but not supersede) member state competence in areas designated in Article 6 of the TFEU. These include human health, industry, culture, tourism, education and training, youth, sport, civil protection and administrative cooperation. EU acts in these areas may not entail harmonization of member state laws or regulations.

EU Legislation. Article 288 of the TFEU clarifies the powers of the Council and the Commission to make regulations and issue directives. EU regulations are similar in form to administrative regulations commonly found in North America. EU directives, on the other hand, have no obvious parallel. A directive establishes regional policy. It is then left to the member states to implement the directive in whatever way is appropriate to their national legal system. This may require a new statute, a Presidential decree, an administrative act or even a constitutional amendment. Sometimes it may require no action at all. As Article 288 indicates, a directive is "binding as to the result to be achieved" but "leave[s] to the national authorities the choice of form and methods." The vast majority of the legislative acts of the 1980s single market campaign were directives. Regulations have since become more common. All directives contain time limits for national implementation. The more controversial the policy, the longer the likely allotment of time. The Reform Treaty of 2009 makes it clear member states must

---

[10]   Article 3, TFEU.

[11]   Article 4, TFEU.

adopt all measures necessary to implement legally binding Union acts.

The Commission initiates the process of legislation by drafting proposals, which the Council (comprised of ministers from the governments of the member states) has the power to adopt into law. Although the Council and Parliament may request the Commission to submit legislative proposals, neither can force the Commission to do so except through litigation before the Court of Justice. Only the Commission can draft legislative proposals. This makes the Commission the focal point of lobbying activities, a point not lost on U.S. companies with stakes in EU legislative outcomes, such as the banking, bio-tech and software directives.

The Commission's legislative proposals are always influenced by what it believes the Council and Parliament will accept. The Council, however, has the right to amend legislative proposals by unanimous vote. Parliament's role was traditionally consultative. Over time, it became and remains the source of *proposed* amendments. Note that Parliament does not have the power to enact law! This absence of legislative power is so fundamental that many observers decry a "democratic deficit" in Europe. This deficit has been partially "remedied" by conveying "co-decision" powers to Parliament. These powers amount to a Parliamentary right, in the absence of conciliation with the Council, to veto selected legislative proposals.

EU Council. The foregoing analysis of legislative process illustrates the dominant role of the Council in regional affairs. The Council, also known since 1993 as the Council of the European Union (EU Council), consists of representatives of the governments of the member states. Thus there are presently 28 Council members since the accession of Croatia in 2013. However, the people who comprise the Council change according to the topic at hand. The national ministers of foreign affairs, agriculture, economy and finance (ecofin), social affairs, environment, etc. are sent to Brussels to confer and vote on matters within their competence. Some refer to the Ecofin Council, the Environment Council, the Agriculture Council and so forth in order to differentiate the various Councils. Several different Council meetings can take place at once.

Most of the voting in the Council now takes place on a qualified majority basis. The rules that define this procedure are given in Article 238 of the TFEU. Since November 1, 2014, a qualified majority is defined as at least 55% of the members of the Council (with a minimum number of 15) who represent member states comprising 65% of the population of the Union. Any blocking minority must include at least 4 Council members. Thus a relatively simplified "double majority" voting system was undertaken in 2014.

EU Commission. The pivotal role of the European Commission in the law-making process should be evident. Apart from administrative cooperation on criminal and police matters, where a quarter of the member states can initiate EU acts, the Commission alone drafts legislative proposals. The Commission can also prosecute when proper legislative procedures are not followed. Furthermore, in certain areas, notably agricultural and competition law, the Council has delegated to the Commission the authority to issue implementing regulations and decisions that establish law. These acts detail administrative rules rather than create new or broad policies. Thus the Council establishes the "target prices" for agriculture, but the Commission issues thousands of regulations aimed at actually realizing these goals.

The Commission has also promulgated an important series of "group exemption" regulations for business competition law. These cover franchising, technology transfers, distribution and a variety of other business agreements. Lastly, the Commission is authorized by Article 106 of the TFEU to issue (on its own initiative) *directives* addressed to member states regarding public enterprises. This authority avoids the usual legislative process. The Reform Treaty of 2009 added a citizen's initiative procedure. One million EU citizens from a significant number of member states may "invite" the Commission to submit proposals in areas of regional concern.

The Commission performs a number of functions in addition to those concerning law-making. The most important of these include its prosecutorial powers against individuals and enterprises for breach of selected laws, and against member states for failure to adhere to their treaty obligations. The Commission negotiates international trade and other agreements. It also administers the EU budget and publishes a general and a series of specific annual reports (*e.g.*, on competition policy), all of which are a good way to survey regional affairs.

Unlike the ministers of the Council, Commissioners are not supposed to function as representatives of their nations. Commissioners are appointed by a qualified majority of the Council subject to Parliament's approval for five-year renewable terms. The President of the Commission is similarly appointed by the European Council and Parliament. Great pains are taken to ensure the independence of Commissioners from their home governments. Article 245 of the TFEU stipulates that Commissioners must be chosen on the basis of competence and their independence must be "beyond doubt." Any breach of this trust by Commissioners could lead to compulsory retirement or dismissal by the President of the Commission.

Court of Justice of the European Union. The EU is unique among regional economic organizations in having a powerful and active court to enforce its laws and treaties. The Court of Justice of the European Union (CJEU) rules on disputes involving EU laws and treaties. Its decisions are binding on EU institutions and the member nations' governments.[12]

The CJEU consists of three courts, the Court of Justice (informally called the European Court of Justice (ECJ)), the General Court, and the Civil Service Tribunal. The Court of Justice hears referrals from national courts regarding the proper interpretation of EU law, claims brought by the Commission against member states for failure to comply with EU obligations, claims brought by member states against EU institutions, and appeals from decisions of the General Court. The General Court hears claims by individuals and corporations (and in some cases by member states) against EU institutions. The Civil Service Tribunal hears disputes between EU institutions and their staff.

Decisions of the EU courts are binding on EU institutions, member states, and perhaps most importantly, the national courts of the member states. Over time, the EU courts have issued key decisions on a wide range of issues affecting trade and investment, including tariff policies, nontariff trade barriers, competition law and intellectual property.

The Euro. The Euro is the common currency of 19 of the 28 EU members (collectively called the "Eurozone"). It was initially adopted by 11 nations in 1999, with coins and currency introduced in 2002 and national currencies phased out and eliminated. Of the 15 EU nations in 1999, Britain, Denmark and Sweden refused to adopt the Euro, and Greece initially did not meet the fiscal qualifications (Greece joined in 2001). Since 2001, an additional 7 nations from eastern and southern Europe have adopted the Euro. In addition, a few small countries use the Euro even though they are not part of the agreements creating the monetary union, and several countries have their national currencies fixed to the Euro. Nine countries are currently members of the EU but not the Eurozone (Britain, Denmark, Sweden, Poland, Czech Republic, Hungary, Bulgaria, Romania and Croatia).

As part of the creation of the Euro, the member nations established the European Central Bank (ECB) and the European

---

[12]   *See*   https://europa.eu/european-union/about-eu/institutions-bodies/court-justice_en.

System of Central Banks (ECSB). The ECB and ECSB are governed by an executive board of six persons appointed by the member states and the governors of the national central banks. The ECB and the ECSB are independent of any other European institution and in theory free from member state influence. Their primary responsibility is to maintain price stability, specifically keeping price inflation below two percent per year. The main functions of the ECB and ECSB are: (1) defining and implementing regional monetary policy; (2) conducting foreign exchange operations; (3) holding and managing the official foreign reserves of the member states; and (4) supervising the payments systems. The ECB has the exclusive right to authorize the issue of bank notes within the Common Market and must set interest rates to principally achieve price stability.

Regrettably, the fiscal enforcement system established when the Euro was created did not work. Since 1999, many Euro states have been under threat of sanctions for failure to comply with the maximum 3 percent budget deficit rule. Yet no Eurozone member state was ever sanctioned, suggesting this system for controlling national deficits is toothless.[13] It has essentially been replaced by the 2012 Treaty on Stability, Coordination and Governance discussed below.

The global financial crisis of 2008, high debt and continuing sluggish economic performance have put intense pressure on the weaker Eurozone economies, notably Greece, Cyprus, Spain, Portugal, Ireland and Italy. Financial rescue packages ("bailouts") of debt-ridden Eurozone members have sometimes been necessary, including three successive bailouts of Greece subject to austerity conditions. In March 2012, with market pressures and threats of a Greek default or exit from the Eurozone escalating, 25 of the then-27 EU members (minus Britain and the Czech Republic) adopted a Treaty on Stability, Coordination and Governance (TSCG) intended to provide a "permanent" solution to the Euro crisis, including a permanent 900 billion Euro loan fund and ECB purchases of national government debt ("quantitative easing").

Nonetheless, Eurozone financial instability remains ongoing. Additional bailouts and ECB bond buying, significantly financed by Germany, have underwritten the Eurozone. The events of 2010–2016 have provided a stark reminder that the Euro project is not infallible nor inevitable, and that substantial differences exist among the national economies of the Eurozone members.

---

[13]   Sanctions for failure to comply with the 3 percent budget deficit rule were held unenforceable by the Court of Justice. *See* Commission v. Council (2004) Eur. Comm. Rep. I–6649 (Case C–27/04).

§ 17.5 NAFTA

The United States has entered into a growing number of major free trade agreements. The first was with Israel, enacted through the United States-Israel Free Trade Area Implementation Act of 1985.[14] The Israel-U.S. Agreement (IFTA) was fully implemented by January 1, 1995. The second was with Canada, adopted through the United States-Canada Free Trade Area Agreement Implementation Act of 1988.[15] The bilateral agreement with Canada was nothing less than path breaking: the most sophisticated free trade agreement in the world at the time. It served as the initial blueprint for the North American Free Trade Agreement (NAFTA).

Mexico in the 1980s and 1990s had been unobtrusively breaking down its trade barriers and reducing the role of government in its economy. More than half of the enterprises owned by the Mexican government were sold to private investors. Tariffs were reduced and import licensing requirements widely removed. Export promotion, not import substitution, became the highest priority. Mexico joined the GATT in 1986 and the WTO at its founding in 1995. This brought it into the mainstream of the world trading community on a wide range of fronts, including participation in nearly the full range of the GATT/WTO Uruguay Round agreements.

Presidents George H.W. Bush and Carlos Salinas, and Prime Minister Brian Mulroney, pushed hard in 1991 to open "fast track" negotiations for a free trade agreement. In 1992, NAFTA was signed by Canada, the United States and Mexico with a scheduled effective date of January 1, 1994. President Bush submitted the agreement to Congress in December 1992. President Clinton supported NAFTA generally, but initiated negotiations upon taking office for supplemental agreements on the environment and labor. This delayed consideration of the NAFTA agreement in Congress until the Fall of 1993. Ratification was considered under "fast track" procedures (see below) which essentially gave Congress 90 session days to either ratify or reject NAFTA without amendments.

After a bruising national debate that fractured both Democrats and Republicans, with each party doing its best to avoid Ross Perot's strident anti-NAFTA attacks, ratification was achieved in mid-November 1993, just weeks before NAFTA's effective date. During this same period, Canada's Conservative Party suffered a devastating defeat at the polls. This defeat was partly a response by

---

[14]   Public Law 99–47, 98 Stat. 3013, June 11, 1985.
[15]   Public Law 100–449, 102 Stat. 1851, 19 U.S.C. § 2112 Note.

the Canadian people of the earlier ratification of NAFTA under Prime Minister Mulroney.

NAFTA took effect January 1, 1994 with full implementation in nearly all areas by 2003. NAFTA was incorporated into U.S. law by the North American Free Trade Agreement Implementation Act of 1993.[16] In many ways, the title "free trade agreement" is a misnomer. In addition to free trade in goods and services, NAFTA includes intellectual property rights, foreign investment protections (see Chapter 23) and several varieties of dispute settlement.

Unlike the EU customs union, each NAFTA nation retains its own national tariffs, border controls and customs law. NAFTA trade is subject to "rules of origin" that determine which goods qualify for its duty free tariff preferences. These include goods wholly originating in the free trade area. A general waiver of the NAFTA rules of origin requirements is granted if their non-regional value consists of no more than 7 percent of the price or total cost of the goods. Goods containing non-regional materials are considered North American if those materials are sufficiently transformed so as to undergo a specific change in tariff classification. Some goods, like autos and light trucks, must also have a specified North American content. Ultimately, 62.50 percent of the value of such vehicles must be North American in origin in order to qualify for free trade under NAFTA. Every auto producer in North America, including Japanese, Korean and European firms, manufactures to meet this rule.

As this book went to press, U.S. President Donald Trump renewed his intention to renegotiate NAFTA. Mexico is particularly concerned that President Trump may, as threatened, impose high tariffs on its exports into the United States, especially on automobiles. Meanwhile, the Mexican peso dropped precipitously after the election of President Trump.

Any NAFTA nation can withdraw from the NAFTA agreement upon six months' notice.

§ 17.6 The Proliferation of Free Trade Agreements

NAFTA was a watershed event. In its wake, hundreds of free trade agreements have proliferated around the world, including for example the European Union and South Africa, Canada and Costa Rica, China and Chile, Japan and Singapore. Mexico has dozens of

---

[16] Public Law 103–182, 107 Stat. 2057. For more extensive coverage, see Ralph Folsom, NAFTA, FREE TRADE AND FOREIGN INVESTMENT IN THE AMERICAS IN A NUTSHELL (5th ed. 2014)

bilateral free trade agreements. The worldwide array of FTAs includes agreements between developed countries (such as between the United States and Australia), agreements between developed and developing countries (such as between Japan and Vietnam) and agreements between developing nations (such as between India and Sri Lanka). Leading nations have gathered together networks of free trade agreements:

(1) Japan has "Economic Partnership Agreements" (effectively free trade agreements) with Mexico, Chile, Thailand, the Philippines, Malaysia, Vietnam, Switzerland, India, Indonesia, Brunei, Singapore, Peru, Mongolia and the Association of Southeast Asian Nations (ASEAN).

(2) China has free trade agreements with its own Hong Kong and Macau Special Administrative Regions, Chile, Pakistan, Costa Rica, Peru, Singapore, New Zealand, Australia, South Korea, Iceland and ASEAN.

(3) The European Union has numerous free trade agreements, including with Algeria, Chile, Egypt, Iceland, Israel, Jordan, Lebanon, Mexico, Morocco, Norway, Serbia, South Africa, Vietnam, Tunisia and a customs union agreement with Turkey.

(4) The United States has 12 bilateral free trade agreements, with Australia, Bahrain, Chile, Colombia, Israel, Jordan, South Korea, Morocco, Oman, Panama, Peru and Singapore, plus the NAFTA agreement with Canada and Mexico and the Dominican Republic-Central America Free Trade Agreement (DR-CAFTA) with the Dominican Republic, Guatemala, Honduras, El Salvador, Nicaragua and Costa Rica.[17]

A variety of factors help explain why FTAs have become the leading edge of international trade law and policy. Difficulties encountered in the GATT/WTO Uruguay, "Seattle" and Doha Rounds of multilateral trade negotiations are certainly crucial. GATT/WTO regulatory failures regarding free trade agreements have also fueled this reality (see § 17.2).

Yet these "negatives" do not fully explain the free trade feeding frenzy. A range of attractions are also at work. For example, free trade agreements often extend to subject matters beyond WTO competence. Foreign investment law is a prime example, and many bilaterals serve as investment magnets. Government procurement,

---

[17]   *See* https://ustr.gov/trade-agreements/free-trade-agreements.

optional at the WTO level, is also often included. Competition policy and labor and environmental matters absent from the WTO are sometimes covered. In addition, free trade agreements can reach beyond the scope of existing WTO agreements. Services is one "WTO-plus" area where this is clearly true. Intellectual property rights are also being "WTO-plused" in free trade agreements.

Whether this amounts to competitive trade liberalization or competitive trade imperialism is a provocative question.

§ 17.7   U.S. Fast Track Procedures

Some recent U.S. efforts to reduce trade restrictions have been multilateral or regional efforts (*e.g.*, the WTO, NAFTA and DR-CAFTA). Others have been bilateral, such as the U.S. free trade agreements. In both situations, Congress intermittently since 1974 has given quite broad authority to the President, or the President's representative, to reduce or eliminate U.S. tariffs on a reciprocal "fast track" basis. For U.S. free trade partners, fast track generally means that once they reach a deal Congress can vote it up or down but cannot alter it, though in recent years Congress has effectively tacked on additional requirements, notably regarding labor and the environment.

Fast track originated as a compromise after Congress refused to ratify two major components of the Kennedy Round of GATT negotiations. The first such authorization lasted from 1991 to 1996, and made possible U.S. implementation of NAFTA in 1993 and the WTO package of agreements in 1995. From 1996 onward, Congress refused to grant fast track authority to President Clinton.

The Trade Act of 2002 authorized President George W. Bush to negotiate international trade agreements on a fast track basis, a procedure that requires Congress to vote within 90 legislative days up or down, without amendments, on U.S. trade agreements. In return, Congress receives substantial notice and opportunity to influence U.S. trade negotiations conducted by the U.S. Trade Representative (USTR).[18] President Bush and the USTR quickly completed and Congress approved free trade agreements with Chile and Singapore, and thereafter with Morocco, Australia, Central America/Dominican Republic (DR-CAFTA), Peru, Jordan, Oman, and Bahrain. The President's fast track authority expired in July 2007 after agreements with Colombia, Panama and South Korea had been signed. Approval of these FTAs by Congress under fast track was delayed several years into the Obama administration.

---

[18]   *See* 19 U.S.C. § 3801 *et seq.*

Congress granted fast track trade promotion authority to President Obama in the summer of 2015, lasting beyond his Presidency through June 2018. With all three NAFTA nations participating in the Trans-Pacific Partnership (TPP) agreement (discussed below), NAFTA could effectively be updated via the TPP, a prospect that now seems dim after the announcement by President Trump that he intends to withdraw from the TPP agreement.

§ 17.8 Post-NAFTA U.S. Free Trade Agreements: NAFTA Plus and Minus

U.S. free trade agreements since NAFTA have evolved substantively under a policy known as "competitive liberalization." For example, coverage of labor law has been narrowed to core International Labor Organization (ILO) principles: The rights of association, organization and collective bargaining; acceptable work conditions regarding minimum wages, hours and occupational health and safety; minimum ages for employment of children and elimination of the worst forms of child labor; and a ban on forced or compulsory labor. Coverage of labor and environmental law enforcement is folded into the trade agreement (compare NAFTA's side agreements) and all remedies are intergovernmental (compare private and NGO "remedies" in the side agreements).

Other NAFTA-plus provisions have emerged. These are most evident regarding foreign investment (discussed in Chapter 23) and intellectual property. Regarding intellectual property, NAFTA-plus has moved into the Internet age. Protection of domain names, and adherence to the World Intellectual Property Organization (WIPO) Internet treaties, are stipulated. E-commerce and free trade in digital products are embraced, copyrights extended to rights-management (encryption) and anti-circumvention (hacking) technology, protection against web music file sharing enhanced, and potential liability of Internet Service Providers detailed.

Less visibly, pharmaceutical patent owners obtain extensions of their patents to compensate for delays in the approval process, and greater control over their test data, making it harder for generic competition to emerge. They also gain "linkage," meaning local drug regulators must make sure generics are not patent-infringing before their release. In addition, adherence to the Patent Law Treaty (2000) and the Trademark Law Treaty (1994) is agreed. Anti-counterfeiting laws are tightened, particularly regarding destruction of counterfeit goods.

Other NAFTA-plus changes push further along the path of free trade in services and comprehensive customs law administration rules. Antidumping and countervailing duty laws remain applicable, but appeals from administrative determinations are taken in national courts, not binational panels. Except for limited provisions in the Chile—U.S. agreement, business visas drop completely out of U.S. free trade agreements, a NAFTA-minus development.

In sum, post-NAFTA the United States has generally used its leverage with smaller trade partners to obtain more preferential treatment and expanded protection for its goods, services, technology and investors. It has given up relatively little in return, for example a modest increase in agricultural market openings.

§ 17.9   The Trans-Pacific Partnership (TPP)

Late in 2015, the Trans-Pacific Partnership (TPP) agreement was reached among the three NAFTA nations plus Peru, Chile, Brunei, Singapore, Malaysia, Vietnam, Japan, Australia and New Zealand (but not China).[19] These Pacific Rim partners comprise roughly 40% of world trade. The TPP contains notable developments on freer agricultural and food trade, trade in automobiles and auto parts, bio-similar pharmaceuticals, protection of foreign investment, minimum wages and working hours, independent unions, technology protections, anti-corruption obligations, service sector openings, e-commerce, environmental protection and restraints on subsidies for state-owned enterprises. It contains minimal currency manipulation rules, a much debated topic. South Korea, Taiwan and Indonesia have expressed interest in joining the TPP, assuming it takes effect.

The TPP will become binding if all 12 nations ratify it within 2 years, or at least 6 nations comprising 85% of the GDP of the group (mandating U.S. and Japanese participation) do so. Ratification in the United States would be under the fast track procedures, discussed above, but President Trump's intention to withdraw from the TPP moots this possibility.

Transatlantic Trade and Investment Partnership (TTIP). The United States (under fast track) and the European Union are presently negotiating a Transatlantic Trade and Investment Partnership (TTIP) agreement that is at least as broad as the TPP outlined above. Canada already has signed a Comprehensive Economic and Trade Agreement (CETA) with the EU, although ratification has been delayed, particularly because of concerns about foreign investor-host state dispute settlement arbitrations (see Chapter 23). Britain's expected withdrawal from the EU casts

---

19   https://ustr.gov/tpp/.

further doubt on TTIP's prospects, as does the election of President Trump.

§ 17.10   Developing World Integration

Developing nations in Africa, the Caribbean, Central America, South America and Southeast Asia (among others) began adopting free trade and customs union agreements as early as the 1960s. In 1979, under what is commonly called the Enabling Clause, the GATT parties decided to permit developing nations to enter into differential and more favorable bilateral, regional or global arrangements among themselves to reduce or eliminate tariffs and nontariff barriers applicable to trade in goods. Like Article 24 of GATT, noted above, the Enabling Clause constitutes an exception to most-favored nation trade principles. It has generally been construed to authorize developing world free trade area and customs union agreements. Whether the Enabling Clause was intended to take such agreements out of Article 24 and its requirements, or be construed in conjunction therewith, is unclear. However, the creation of alternative notification and review procedures for Enabling Clause arrangements suggests Article 24 is inapplicable.

Notification to GATT of Enabling Clause arrangements is mandatory. Since 1995, the WTO Committee on Trade and Development (CTD) is the forum where such notifications are reviewed, but in practice not examined in depth. Enabling Clause arrangements should be designed to promote the trade of developing countries and not raise external trade barriers or undue trade difficulties. Consultations with individual GATT members experiencing such difficulties must be undertaken, and these consultations may be expanded to all GATT members if requested. Unlike GATT Article 24 and GATS Article 5, neither compensation to nonparticipants nor formal reporting on the consistency with the Enabling Clause of developing nation arrangements is anticipated. The ASEAN-China (2004), India-Sri Lanka (2002), and "revived" Economic Community of West African States (ECOWAS 2005) agreements illustrate notified but unexamined preferential arrangements sheltered by the Enabling Clause.

Africa. Several groups, sometimes overlapping and often poorly implemented, have been formed in Africa, a continent with little internal trade. In 1966 the central African countries of Cameroon, Central African Republic, Chad, Congo (Brazzaville) and Gabon formed the Economic and Customs Union of Central Africa (Union Douaniere et Économique de l'Afrique Centrale: UDEAC) to establish a common customs and tariff approach toward the rest of the world and to formulate a common foreign investment code.[20] In 1967 Kenya, Tanzania and Uganda created the East African Community (EAC) in an attempt to harmonize customs and tariff practices among themselves and in relation to other countries. The practical effect of that Community has frequently been negated by political strife, but of late it has enjoyed a comeback.[21] A Common Market for Eastern and Southern Africa (COMESA) wishfully embraces nineteen African states.[22]

In 1974 six French-speaking West African nations formed the West African Economic Community (known by its French initials CEAO), which expanded to become the Economic Community of West African States (ECOWAS), now encompassing 15 nations. ECOWAS was initially created by treaty in 1975 to coordinate economic development and cooperation, with a revised treaty signed in 1993.[23] Some progress on liberalized industrial trade has been made and a Cooperation, Compensation and Development Fund established. ECOWAS is also involved in peacekeeping missions in West Africa, and has established an active court, the ECOWAS Community Court of Justice. A subset of French-speaking ECOWAS countries formed the West African Economic and Monetary Union (WAEMU or UEMOA) in 1994 as a customs and monetary union, with Portuguese-speaking Guinea-Bissau joining later.[24]

In 1991, the Organization of African Unity (OAU) member states agreed to a Treaty Establishing the African Economic Community. This wide-ranging Treaty embraces 51 African nations, and includes a regional Court of Justice, although its practical prospects remain uncertain.[25] In 1995, 12 southern African countries, with post-apartheid South Africa participating for the first time, targeted free trade under the Southern African Development Community.[26]

Islamic World. Bahrain, Kuwait, Oman, Qatar, Saudi Arabia, and United Arab Emirates formed the Gulf Cooperation Council

---

[20]   This arrangement produced only limited results and was replaced in 1999 by the Central African Economic and Monetary Community (CEMAC).

[21]   The EAC now also includes Burundi, Rwanda and South Sudan. *See* http://www.eac.int/about/overview.

[22]   *See* http://www.comesa.int/comesa-members-states/.

[23]   *See* http://www.ecowas.int/.

[24]   *See* https://ustr.gov/countries-regions/africa/regional-economic-communities-rec/west-african-economic-and-monetary-union-uemoa. The UEMOA countries use the Central African Franc (CFA).

[25]   Jessica Pugliese, *Will There Be an African Economic Community?*, Brookings Institution, Jan. 9, 2014, https://www.brookings.edu/2014/01/09/will-there-be-an-african-economic-community/.

[26]   *See* http://www.sadc.int/.

(GCC) in 1981 with objectives to establish freedom of movement, a regional armaments industry, common banking and financial systems, a unified currency policy, a customs union, a common foreign aid program, and a joint, international investment company, the Gulf Investment Corporation.[27] The Council has implemented trade and investment rules concerning tariffs on regional and imported goods, government contracts, communications, transportation, real estate investment, and freedom of movement of professionals. Progress has been made on a Uniform Commercial Code and a Commission for Commercial Arbitration of the Gulf States. The GCC also has a major 1990 trade and cooperation agreement with the EU. In 2003, the non-Arab states of Iran, Pakistan, Turkey, Afghanistan and six Central Asian nations signed an Economic Cooperation Organization Trade Agreement (ECOTA).[28] In 2004, Jordan, Egypt, Tunisia and Morocco signed the Agadir free trade agreement. There is also a Greater Arab Free Trade Area, now encompassing 18 Arab nations.[29]

Latin America and Caribbean. Established in 1973, the Caribbean Community (CARICOM) now includes 15 Caribbean states.[30] The 1989 Grand Anse Declaration commits CARICOM to establishment of its own common market. Nine CARICOM members are also members of the Organisation of Eastern Caribbean States (OECS), including a 2010 agreement on economic union. Some 37 nations signed the Association of Caribbean States agreement in 1994 with long-term economic integration goals.

In 1958 Costa Rica, El Salvador, Guatemala, Honduras and Nicaragua formed the Central American Common Market (CACM), another victim of political strife, but still functioning in a limited way. Numerous countries in Latin America were members of the Latin American Free Trade Association (LAFTA) (1961) which had small success in reducing tariffs and developing the region through cooperative industrial sector programs. These programs allocated industrial production among the participating states. The Latin American Integration Association (LAIA) (1981), the eleven-member successor to LAFTA, continued arrangements for intra-community tariff concessions. They agreed to a 50 percent tariff cut on LAIA goods.

Latin America became a central focus of economic integration in the 1990s. Mexico joined NAFTA and also negotiated free trade agreements with eleven other Latin American countries, the

---

[27]   https://www.britannica.com/topic/Gulf-Cooperation-Council.

[28]   https://aric.adb.org/fta/economic-cooperation-organization-trade-agreement.

[29]   *See* http://africaecon.org/index.php/trade_agr/view_trade_agreement/7/0/_/0.

[30]   http://www.caricom.org/.

European Union and the European Free Trade Association (EFTA). Argentina, Brazil, Paraguay and Uruguay signed a treaty establishing the MERCOSUR (Southern Cone) common market in 1991, with Bolivia and Venezuela joining more recently.[31]

The Andean Community was founded by Bolivia, Chile, Colombia, Ecuador, and Peru with the Cartagena Agreement in 1969,[32] primarily to counter the economic power of Argentina, Brazil and Mexico and to reduce dependency upon foreign capital and technology. Membership has expanded and contracted over time; it currently includes the founding members except for Chile, plus Venezuela. The Community includes a regional court (the Court of Justice of the Andean Community), a free trade zone, and an agreement on a common external tariff. The Community and MERCOSUR agreed upon a free trade zone that went into effect in 2004.

§ 17.11   The Association of Southeast Asian Nations (ASEAN)

Some interesting moves toward developing world free trade and rule-making have been taken by the Association of Southeast Asian Nations (ASEAN).[33] Its problems, failures and successes are representative of developing world attempts at legal and economic integration. ASEAN has its genesis in the 1967 Bangkok Declaration,[34] with common trade rules in various states of growth, implementation and retrenchment. ASEAN has internal tariff preferences, industrial development projects, "complementation schemes," and regional joint ventures.

An important juncture in the integration process is the point in time at which member countries of a regional group accept a supranational mechanism for enforcing the regime's law irrespective of national feelings and domestic law within a member country. As discussed (§ 17.4), the 1957 Treaty of Rome provided for a supranational European Court of Justice, which decided quickly upon a mandatory enforcement stance regarding national (member state) compliance with regional law. ASEAN does not have a comparable enforcement mechanism. A vigorous administrator can also make regional law a reality. In Europe, the Commission frequently issues regulations and decisions which are binding within the territories of member states. These rules are enforced

---

[31]   http://www.mercosur.int/. Six other countries are associate members.

[32]   https://www.britannica.com/topic/Andean-Community.

[33]   http://asean.org/.

[34]   http://asean.org/the-asean-declaration-bangkok-declaration-bangkok-8-august-1967/.

through fines and penalties, and ultimately by the Court of Justice. Violations are investigated and, if necessary, prosecuted by the Commission. In contrast, the ASEAN Secretary-General once remarked that ASEAN's Secretariat was "a postman collecting and distributing letters." The surrender of national sovereignty to ASEAN institutions has been a painfully slow process. That said, NAFTA provides an alternative example of achieving free trade without significantly surrendering national sovereignty to regional institutions.

ASEAN was formed in 1967 by Indonesia, Malaysia, the Philippines, Singapore and Thailand. Brunei joined in 1984, Vietnam in 1995. Laos and Myanmar (Burma) joined in 1997, and Cambodia in 1999. Rarely have such culturally, linguistically and geographically diverse nations attempted integration. The Bangkok Declaration establishing ASEAN as a cooperative association is a broadly worded document. Later proposals were made for a formal ASEAN treaty or convention, but were rejected as unnecessary. The Bangkok Declaration sets forth numerous regional, economic, cultural and social goals, including acceleration of economic growth, trade expansion and industrial collaboration.

The Bangkok Declaration establishes several mechanisms, but little supranational legal machinery, to implement its stated goals. An annual ASEAN Meeting of Foreign Ministers is scheduled on a rotational basis among the Member States. Special meetings are held "as required." The Declaration provides for a Standing Committee composed of the Foreign Minister of the state in which the next annual Ministerial Meeting is to be held, and includes the ambassadors of other ASEAN States accredited to that state. The Declaration also provides for "Ad Hoc Committees and Permanent Committees of specialists and officials on specific subjects." Each member state is charged to set up a National Secretariat to administer ASEAN affairs within that Member State and to work with the Ministerial Meeting and the Standing Committee.

There have been relatively infrequent meetings of the ASEAN heads of government. This contrasts with the semiannual European "summits" that have kept that group moving forward along the path of integration. The third ASEAN summit was held in Manila in 1987. This summit produced an agreement for the promotion and protection of investments by ASEAN investors (national and most-favored-nation treatment rights are created), made revisions to the basic ASEAN joint venture agreement, and continued the gradual extension of regional tariff and nontariff trade preferences. Goods already covered by the ASEAN tariff scheme were given a 50 percent margin of preference. New items received a 25 percent preferential margin. The nontariff preferences generally co-opt GATT rules, *e.g.* regarding technical standards and customs valuation.

The fourth ASEAN summit in 1992 committed the parties to the creation of a free trade area within 15 years. Five years were cut from this schedule by agreement in 1994, but operational reality has eluded ASEAN free trade. In 2003, a "watershed" date for complete integration in an ASEAN Economic Community targeted 2020. In 2007, this target date was changed to 2015, a reflection of the fear that ASEAN risks being overwhelmed by the powerhouse economies of China, India and Japan. In 2016, the ASEAN common market was officially launched. Despite the fanfare, its prospects seem limited.

§ 17.12   East Asian Integration

East Asia, unlike Europe or NAFTA, has not developed a formal agreement with uniform trade, licensing and investment rules. The Asia-Pacific Economic Cooperation (APEC) group has begun to address this idea. The APEC group is comprised of 21 Asia-Pacific nations including the United States, but excluding India.[35] Late in 1994 the APEC nations targeted free trade and investment for industrial countries by 2010 and developing countries by 2020. Nine industries were selected for initial trade liberalization efforts. The uncertain Trans-Pacific Partnership (see § 17.9) includes some but not all APEC members (notably excluding China and Russia).

With the European Union and the North American Free Trade Area maturing rapidly, one provocative question is the future of Japan. It is not in the interests of any nation that Japan should feel economically isolated or threatened. To some degree, what appears to be happening is that regional integration in East Asia is growing along lines that follow Japanese investment and economic aid decisions. Japan now has "economic cooperation" agreements, the most critical of which are with ASEAN, India and Mexico, as well as the pending Trans-Pacific Partnership.

As a counterbalance to the U.S.-led APEC and TPP, China is promoting a Regional Comprehensive Economic Partnership (RCEP) with 16 nations including the 10 ASEAN nations, Australia, India, Japan, New Zealand and South Korea, but not the United States. Unlike the wide-ranging TPP, the RCEP focuses primarily upon tariff reductions on trade in goods. Early signs after President Trump announced his intention to withdraw from the TPP suggest

---

[35]   http://www.apec.org/About-Us/About-APEC/History.aspx.

China may seek to use the RCEP to integrate much of the Pacific Basin, minus the United States, with its economy.

The role of China in East Asian integration is critical. China and Japan are clearly rivals for economic leadership of the region. China is pushing for dominant influence in the East Asian economic sphere. Hong Kong's return in 1997 and Macau in 1999 moved in this direction. China is cultivating trade and investment relations with Taiwan and, to a lesser extent, Japan. China also has free trade deals that rival and/or overlap with those of Japan, notably with ASEAN, Australia and South Korea. Some commentators foresee, as a practical matter, the emergence of a powerful Southern China coastal economic zone embracing Hong Kong, Taiwan, and the Chinese provinces of Guangdong and Fujian.

Chapter 18

FRANCHISING AND TRADEMARK LICENSING

Table of Sections

§ 18.1 Franchising Abroad

Franchising constitutes a rapidly expanding form of doing business abroad. Most franchisors have established fairly standard contracts and business formulae which are utilized in their home markets, and receive counsel on the myriad of laws relevant to their domestic business operations. Approaches to developing, defining and managing franchise relationships that have worked domestically may not work abroad. For example, agreements authorizing development of multiple locations within a given territory and, possibly, subfranchising by a master franchisee are often used overseas while infrequent in the United States.

International franchising confronts the attorney with the need to research and evaluate a broad range of foreign laws which may apply in any particular jurisdiction. Such laws tend to focus on placing equity and control in the hands of local individuals and on regulating the franchise agreement to benefit the franchisees. In addition, counsel should be sensitive to the cultural impact of foreign franchising. For example, the appearance of a franchise building or trademark symbol may conflict in a foreign setting with traditional architectural forms (such as in European cities) or nationalist feelings hostile to the appearance of foreign trademarks on franchised products (such as in India or Mexico). Cultural conflicts can diminish the value of international franchises. To anticipate and solve legal and cultural problems, foreign counsel is often chosen to assist in the task of franchising abroad.

This chapter explores some of the concerns a franchisor or prospective franchisee may encounter in opting for, negotiating, drafting or enforcing an international franchise agreement. Although patents, copyrights and trademarks may all be involved in international franchising, trademark licensing is at the core of most international franchise agreements. Many rightly consider franchising to be a U.S. invention, but foreigners have rapidly been developing international franchising systems. Thus, while the primary focus in this chapter is on the problems of United States franchisors who intend to go abroad, additional coverage is given to United States law relevant to franchising.

§ 18.2 Trademark Protection

Virtually all countries offer some legal protection to trademarks, even when they do not have trademark registration systems. Trademark rights derived from the use of marks on goods in commerce have long been recognized at common law and remain so today in countries as diverse as the United States and the United Arab Emirates. The latter nation, for example, had no trademark registration law in 1986, but this did not prevent McDonald's from obtaining an injunction against a local business using its famous name and golden arches without authorization.[1] However, obtaining international trademark protection normally involves separate registration under the law of each nation. Over three million trademarks are registered around the globe each year. In the United States, trademarks are protected at common law and by state and federal registrations. Federal registration is permitted by the U.S. Trademark Office for all marks capable of distinguishing the goods on which they appear from other goods.[2] Unless the mark falls within a category of forbidden registrations (*e.g.*, those that offend socialist morality in the People's Republic of China), a mark becomes valid for a term of years following registration.

In some countries (like the U.S. prior to 1989), marks must be used on goods before registration. In others, use is not required and speculative registration of marks can occur. It is said that ESSO was obliged to purchase trademark rights from such a speculator

---

[1]   Case No. 823/85. *See* 76 Trademark Reports 356 (1986).

[2]   15 U.S.C. § 1052.

when it switched to EXXON in its search for the perfect global trademark. Since 1989, United States law has allowed applications when there is a bona fide intent to use a trademark within 12 months and, if there is good cause for the delay in actual usage, up to 24 additional months.[3] Such filings in effect reserve the mark for the applicant. The emphasis on bona fide intent and good cause represent an attempt to control any speculative use of U.S. trademark registrations.

The scope of trademark protection may differ substantially from country to country. Under U.S. federal trademark law, injunctions, damages and seizures of goods by customs officials may follow infringement. Other jurisdictions may provide similar remedies on their law books, but offer little practical enforcement. Thus, trademark registration is no guarantee against trademark piracy. A pair of blue jeans labeled "Levi Strauss made in San Francisco" may have been counterfeited in Israel or Paraguay without the knowledge or consent of Levi Strauss and in spite of its trademark registrations in those countries. Trademark counterfeiting is not just a third world problem, as any visitor to a United States "flea market" can tell. Congress created criminal offenses and private treble damages remedies for the first time in the Trademark Counterfeiting Act of 1984.

In many countries trademarks (appearing on goods) may be distinguished from "service marks" used by providers of services (e.g., the Law Store), "trade names" (business names), "collective marks" (marks used by a group or organization), and "certificate marks" (marks which certify a certain quality, origin, or other fact). Although national trademark schemes differ, it can be said generally that a valid trademark (e.g., a mark not "canceled," "renounced," "abandoned," "waived" or "generic") will be protected against infringing use. A trademark can be valid in one country (ASPIRIN brand tablets in Canada), but invalid because generic in another (BAYER brand aspirin in the United States).

Unlike patents and copyrights, trademarks may be renewed in perpetuity. A valid mark may be licensed, perhaps to a "registered user" or it may be assigned, in some cases only with the sale of the goodwill of a business. A growing example of international licensing of trademarks can be found in franchise agreements taken abroad. And national trademark law sometimes accompanies international licensing. The principal U.S. trademark law, the Lanham Act of 1946, has been construed to apply extraterritorially (much like the Sherman Antitrust Act) to foreign licensees engaging in deceptive

---

[3]　15 U.S.C. § 1051(b).

practices.[4] Foreigners who seek a registration may be required to prove a prior and valid "home registration," and a new registration in another country may not have an existence "independent" of the continuing validity of the home country registration. Foreigners are often assisted in their registration efforts by international and regional trademark treaties, discussed below.

§ 18.3   Quality Controls

Because franchising links trademarks with business attributes, there is a broad duty in the law for the franchisor to maintain quality controls over the franchisee, particularly in the business format franchise system. Any failure of the franchisor to maintain such quality controls could cause the trademark in question to be abandoned and lost to the franchisor.[5] In order to maintain adequate quality controls, the franchisor must typically police the operations of the franchisee.[6]

Broadly speaking, the duty to maintain quality controls arises because a trademark is a source symbol. The public is entitled to rely upon that source symbol in making its purchasing decisions so as to obtain consistent product quality and attributes. International franchisors operating at a distance from their franchisees must be especially concerned with quality controls. On the other hand, excessive control or the public appearance of such control may give rise to an agency relationship between the franchisor and the franchisee. Such a relationship could be used to establish franchisor liability for franchisee conduct, including international product and other tort liabilities.[7] It may be possible to minimize these risks through disclaimer or indemnification clauses in the franchise agreement.

§ 18.4   Copyright Protection in Franchising

Although franchising primarily focuses upon trademarks and trademark licensing, the use of copyrights frequently parallels such activity. For example, the designs and logos of the franchisor may be copyrighted, and certainly its instruction manual and other such written communications to franchisees should be copyrighted. These copyrights benefit in many countries from the Universal Copyright Convention (UCC) of 1952 and the Berne Convention of 1886. The

---

[4]   *See especially* Scotch Whiskey Association v. Barton Distilling Co., 489 F.2d 809 (7th Cir. 1973).

[5]   *See, e.g.,* Yamamoto & Co. v. Victor United, Inc., 219 U.S.P.Q. 968 (C.D. Cal. 1982).

[6]   *See* Dawn Donut Co. v. Hart's Food Stores, Inc., 267 F.2d 358 (2d Cir. 1959).

[7]   *See* Randall K. Hanson, *The Franchising Dilemma: Franchisor Liability for Actions of a Local Franchisee*, 19 N.C. CENTRAL L.J. 190 (1991).

United States now adheres to both of these conventions. Under the UCC, copyright holders receive national treatment, translation rights and other benefits. This convention will excuse any national registration requirement provided a notice of a claim of copyright is adequately given. However, in the United States, a reservation was made such that registration of foreign copyrights is required if the only convention under which foreigners are seeking such protection is the Universal Copyright Convention of 1952.

On the other hand, if the foreigner comes from a nation which also adheres to the Berne Convention, national treatment and a release from registration formalities is obtained. The Berne Convention permits local copyright protection independent of protection granted in the country of origin and does not require copyright notice. Prior to 1987, most United States copyright holders acquired Berne Convention benefits by simultaneously publishing their works in Canada, a member country. Since 1987, the United States has participated in the Berne Convention. This has the practical effect of eliminating registration requirements for foreign copyright holders. It also extends United States copyright relations to approximately 25 new nations.

§ 18.5   Protection of Franchise Trade Secrets

Franchise formulae often involve utilization of trade secrets. This may range from recipes and cooking techniques to customer lists, pricing formulas, market data or bookkeeping procedures. It is extremely difficult to protect such trade secrets under United States law. The first problem arises from the concept of what is a trade secret. Generally speaking, abstract ideas or business practices which do not involve an element of novelty are not considered trade secrets.[8] Even if franchise trade secrets are involved, maintaining such secrets can be difficult given the wide number of persons who may have access to the confidential information. Even though the franchisees may warrant to maintain such secrets, once released into the business public there may not be an effective way to recapture the secret or remedy the harm.[9]

The duty not to disclose trade secrets should be extended to employees of the franchisee. This can be done by permitting dissemination only on a need-to-know basis. However, it may be impossible not to permit certain employees from the knowledge of cooking procedures or recipes, for example. Once again the remedies

---

[8]   *See* Kewanee Oil Co. v. Bicron Corp., 416 U.S. 470 (1974).

[9]   *See* Smith v. Dravo Corp., 203 F.2d 369 (7th Cir. 1953).

and efforts to recapture the secret are likely to be inadequate.[10] Terminated employees and terminated franchisees are another fertile source of the loss of trade secrets. Tort remedies employing misappropriation theories may prevent the utilization or disclosure by such persons of trade secrets where there is a possibility of competition with the franchisor.[11] Damages are generally viewed as an inadequate remedy in the trade secret field because the harm of the loss of the secret is irreparable.

§ 18.6   The Franchise Agreement, U.S. Franchising

International franchising raises a host of legal issues under intellectual property, antitrust, tax, licensing and other laws. The significance of these issues is magnified by the rapid growth of international franchising. Hundreds of U.S. companies have, in total, tens of thousands of foreign franchises. Nearly 70 percent of these franchisors started in Canada, with Japan and Britain following. Some United States investors have found franchising the least risky and most popular way to enter Eastern Europe. But franchising is not just a United States export. Many foreign franchisors have entered the U.S. market.

Most franchisors have standard contracts which are used in their home markets and receive counsel on the myriad of laws relevant to their business operations. Such contracts need to be revised and adapted to international franchising without significantly altering the franchisor's successful business formula. Franchise fees and royalties must be specified, the provision of services, training, and control by the franchisor detailed, the term and area of the franchise negotiated ("master franchises" conveying rights in an entire country or region are common in international franchise agreements), accounting procedures agreed upon, business standards and advertising selected, insurance obtained, taxes and other liabilities allocated, default and dispute settlement procedures decided. At the heart of all franchise agreements lies a trademark licensing clause conveying local trademark rights of the franchisor to the franchisee in return for royalty payments.

Franchising is an important sector in the United States economy. Thousands of franchisors have created and administer franchise systems throughout the nation. U.S. franchisees number in the hundreds of thousands. These franchisees are typically independent business persons, and their local franchise outlets

---

[10]   See Shatterproof Glass Corp. v. Guardian Glass Co., 322 F.Supp. 854 (E.D. Mich. 1970) aff'd 462 F.2d 1115 (6th Cir. 1972).

[11]   See FMC Corp. v. Taiwan Tainan Giant Industrial Co., 730 F.2d 61 (2d Cir. 1984).

employ millions of people. It has been estimated that approximately one-third of all retail sales in the United States take place through franchised outlets. Just as U.S. franchisors have found franchising particularly effective for market penetration abroad, Canadian, European and Japanese companies are increasingly penetrating the U.S. market through franchising.

Franchising is a business technique that permits rapid and flexible penetration of markets, growth and capital development. In the United States, there are traditional distinctions between product franchises and business format franchises. Product franchises involve manufacturers who actually produce the goods that are distributed through franchise agreements. For example, ice cream stores, soft drink bottling companies and gasoline retailers are often the subject of product franchises. Business format franchises are more common. These do not involve the manufacture by the franchisor of the product being sold by the franchisee. More typically, the franchisor licenses intellectual property rights in conjunction with a particular "formula for success" of the business. Fast food establishments, hotels, and a variety of service franchises are examples of business format franchising.

U.S. regulation of franchise relationships occurs at both the federal and state levels of government. Such regulation can be as specific as the Federal Trade Commission Franchising Rule and state franchise disclosure duties or as amorphous as the ever present dangers of state and federal antitrust law.

§ 18.7 Regulation of International Franchising

Were franchising unaffected by regulation, the attorney's role would be limited to negotiation and drafting of the agreement. But international franchising is increasingly regulated by home and host jurisdictions, including regional groups like the European Union (EU). In third world countries, especially Latin America, technology transfer laws aimed principally at international patent and know-how licensing also regulate franchise agreements. These laws benefit franchisees and further development policies, *e.g.*, the conservation of hard currencies by control of royalty levels. In 1986, the European Court of Justice issued a major opinion on the legality of franchise agreements under EU competition law.[12] This decision indicates that Union law can depart significantly from leading United States antitrust law on market division arrangements for

---

[12]   Pronuptia de Paris GmbH v. Pronuptia de Paris Irmgard Schillgallis (1986) Eur. Comm. Rep. 353. *See* Section 18.11 *infra*.

distributors.[13] The EU first implemented a comprehensive regulation on franchise agreements in 1988.[14]

There is often a perception of being invaded culturally that follows franchising. Local laws sometimes respond to the cultural impact of foreign franchises, but this did not stop McDonald's from opening in Moscow with great success. In India and Mexico, nationalist feelings hostile to the appearance of foreign trademarks on franchised products have produced laws intended to remove such usage. For example, the Mexican Law of Inventions and Trademarks (1976) (repealed 1987) anticipated requiring use of culturally Mexican marks in addition to marks of foreign origin. Dual marks are now voluntary in Mexico and prohibited by NAFTA. Other nations require local materials (olive oil in the Mediterranean) to be substituted. This could, for example, alter the formula for success (and value) of fast food franchises. Still others (*e.g.*, Alberta, Canada) mandate extensive disclosures by franchisors in a registered prospectus before agreements may be completed. Disclosure violations can trigger a range of franchisee remedies: recision, injunctions and damages. Such laws are also found in many of the states of the United States.

Franchise advertising must conform to local law. For example, regulations in the People's Republic of China prohibit ads which "have reactionary . . . content." Antitrust and tax law are important in international franchising. Double taxation treaties, for example, will affect the level of taxation of royalties. Antitrust law will temper purchasing requirements of the franchisor, lest unlawful "tying arrangements" be undertaken. Tying arrangements involve coercion of franchisees to take supplies from the franchisor or designated sources as part of the franchise.

Such arrangements must, by definition, involve two products: the tying and tied products. They are subject to a complex and not entirely consistent body of case law under the U.S. Sherman Antitrust Act, Articles 101 and 102 of the TFEU and other laws. For example, one leading United States antitrust case treats the trademark licenses as a separate tying product and the requirement of the purchase by franchisees of non-essential cooking equipment and paper products unlawful.[15] Another case permits franchisors to require franchisees to purchase "core products" (*e.g.*, chicken)

---

[13] *Compare* Continental T.V., Inc. v. GTE Sylvania Inc., 433 U.S. 36 (1977) (location clauses not per se illegal); American Motor Inns, Inc. v. Holiday Inns, Inc., 521 F.2d 1230 (3d Cir. 1975) (allocation of franchisor/franchisee towns and territories *per se* illegal).

[14] Commission Regulation No. 4087/88, replaced by Regulation 2790/99, and replaced again by Regulation 330/10, discussed in Section 18.12 *infra*.

[15] Siegel v. Chicken Delight, Inc., 448 F.2d 43 (9th Cir. 1971).

subject to detailed specifications, or from a designated list of approved sources.[16] Sometimes the "core product" and the trademark license are treated as a single product incapable of being tied in violation of the law.[17] Still another leading case suggests that anything comprising the franchisor's "formula for success" may possibly be tied in the franchise contract.[18] This may be notably lawful if there was full pre-contract disclosure by the franchisor.

§ 18.8 The Paris Convention as Applied to Trademarks

The premium placed on priority of use of a trademark is reflected in several international trademark treaties. These include the 1883 Paris Convention for the Protection of Industrial Property, the 1957 Arrangement of Nice Concerning the International Classification of Goods and Services, and the 1973 Trademark Registration Treaty. The treaties of widest international application are the Paris Convention and the Arrangement of Nice, to which the United States is a party. The International Bureau of the World Intellectual Property Organization (WIPO) in Geneva plays a central role in the administration of arrangements contemplated by these agreements.

The Paris Convention reflects an effort to internationalize some trademark rules. In addition to extending the nondiscriminatory principal of national treatment and providing for a right of priority of six months for trademarks, the Convention mitigates the frequent national requirement that foreigners seeking trademark registration prove a pre-existing, valid and continuing home registration. This makes it easier to obtain foreign trademark registration, avoids the possibility that a lapse in registration at home will cause all foreign registrations to become invalid, and allows registration abroad of entirely different (and perhaps culturally adapted) marks. The Paris Convention right of priority eliminates the need to simultaneously file for trademark protection around the globe. Filings abroad that are undertaken within six months of the home country filing for trademark registration will take priority.

The Paris Convention has in excess of 170 member nations. Since the Convention provides that any domestic trademark

---

[16]   Kentucky Fried Chicken Corp. v. Diversified Packaging Corp., 549 F.2d 368 (5th Cir. 1977).

[17]   Krehl v. Baskin-Robbins Ice Cream Co., 664 F.2d 1348 (9th Cir. 1982) (franchisees must buy Baskin-Robbins ice cream).

[18]   Principe v. McDonald's Corp., 631 F.2d 303 (4th Cir. 1980) (franchisees required to lease land and buildings from McDonald's).

registration filing gives rise to priority in all Paris Convention countries, this means that foreign marks registered in countries that do not require use of the mark on an actual product can be obtained in the United States. In other words, foreign trademarks that are not used are entitled under the Paris Convention to U.S. trademark registration. Since 1988, the foreign applicant must state a bona fide intention to use the mark in commerce, but actual use is not required prior to registration.[19]

The Paris Convention also deals with unregistered trademarks. Article 6bis requires the member nations to refuse to register, to cancel an existing registration or to prohibit the use of a trademark which is considered by the trademark registration authorities of that country to be "well known" and owned by a person entitled to the benefits of the Paris Convention. This provision concerns what are called "famous marks" and prevents their infringement even if there has been no local registration of the mark. This is a remarkable development because it effectively creates trademark rights without registration. It has, for example, been successfully invoked in the People's Republic of China in order to protect against infringing use of Walt Disney and other well-known trademarks. In protecting such marks, China sided with the interpretation of the Paris Convention that marks that are well-known internationally deserve protection, even if not well known locally.

§ 18.9   The Nice Agreement on Trademark Classification

The Nice Agreement addresses the question of registration by "class" or "classification" of goods. In order to simplify internal administrative procedures relating to marks, many countries classify and thereby identify goods (and sometimes services) which have the same or similar attributes. An applicant seeking registration of a mark often is required to specify the class or classes to which the product mark belongs. However, not all countries have the same classification system and some lack any such system. Article 1 of the Nice Agreement adopts, for the purposes of the registration of marks, a single classification system for goods and services. This has brought order out of chaos in the field.

---

[19]   15 U.S.C. § 1126(e).

§ 18.10   International Trademark Registration Treaties

The 1973 Vienna Trademark Registration Treaty (to which the United States is a signatory) contemplates an international filing and examination scheme like that in force for patents under the Patent Cooperation Treaty of 1970.[20] This treaty has not yet been fully implemented, but holds out the promise of reduced costs and greater uniformity when obtaining international trademark protection. The 1994 Trademark Law Treaty substantially harmonized trademark registration procedures. Numerous European and Mediterranean countries are parties to the 1891 Madrid Agreement for International Registration of Marks. Since 2002, the United States has joined in the Madrid Protocol of 1989. This agreement permits international filings to obtain national trademark rights in about 90 countries and is administered by WIPO. A Common Market trademark can now be obtained in the European Union, an alternative to national trademark registrations and the "principle of territoriality" underlying IP laws.

§ 18.11   The *Pronuptia* Case

The European Union (EU) has become an active regulator of franchise agreements. Prior to *Pronuptia*,[21] the Commission had never sought to apply Article 101 of the Treaty on the Functioning of the European Union (TFEU) to franchise agreements. *Pronuptia* arose from the refusal of a franchisee to pay license fees to the franchisor. The distribution of the Pronuptia brand wedding attire in the Federal Republic of Germany was handled by shops operated by the German franchisor and by independent retailers through franchise agreements with that franchisor. The franchisee had obtained franchises for three areas (Hamburg, Oldenburg and Hannover). The franchisor granted the franchisee exclusive rights to market and advertise under the name of "Pronuptia de Paris" in these specific territories. The franchisor promised not to open any shops or provide any goods or services to another person in those territories. The franchisor also agreed to assist the franchisee with business strategies and profitability.

The franchisee agreed to assume all the risk of opening a franchise as an independent retailer. The franchisee also agreed to the following: (1) To sell Pronuptia goods only in the store specified in the contract and to decorate and design the shop according to the

---

[20]   *See* Chapter 19.

[21]   Pronuptia de Paris GmbH v. Pronuptia de Paris Irmgard Schillgallis (1986) Eur. Comm. Rep. 353.

franchisor's instructions; (2) to purchase 80 percent of wedding related attire and a proportion of evening dresses from the franchisor, and to purchase the rest of such merchandise only from sellers approved by the franchisor; (3) to pay a one-time entrance fee for exclusive rights to the specified territory and a yearly royalty fee of 10 percent of the total sales of Pronuptia and all other products; (4) to advertise only with the franchisor's approval in a method which would enhance the international reputation of the franchise; (5) to make the sale of bridal fashions the franchisee's main business purpose; (6) to consider the retail price recommendations of the franchisor; (7) to refrain from competing directly or indirectly during the contract period or for one year afterward with any Pronuptia store; and (8) to obtain the franchisor's prior approval before assigning the rights and obligations arising under the contract to a third party.

In due course, the case was referred to the European Court of Justice. The Court's judgment concentrates on the crucial issue of whether franchise agreements come within Article 101. The Court draws a preliminary distinction between "distribution" franchises such as Pronuptia as opposed to "service" and "production" franchises. The Court concludes that a franchising system as such does not interfere with competition. Consequently, clauses essential to enable franchising to function are not prohibited. Thus, the franchisor can communicate know-how or assistance and help franchisees apply its methods. The franchisor can take reasonable steps to keep its know-how or assistance from becoming available to competitors. Location clauses forbidding the franchisee during the contract, or for a reasonable time thereafter, from opening a store with a similar or identical object in an area where it might compete with another member of the franchise network were necessary for distribution franchises and therefore permissible. The obligation of the franchisee not to sell a licensed store without prior consent of the franchisor was similarly allowable.

Clauses necessary to preserve the identity and reputation of the franchise network, such as decorations and trademark usage, were upheld. The reputation and identity of the network may also justify a clause requiring the franchisee to sell only products supplied by the franchisor or by approved sources, at least if it would be too expensive to monitor the quality of the stock otherwise. Nevertheless, each franchisee must be allowed to buy from other franchisees. The requirement of uniformity may also justify advertisement approvals by the franchisor, but the franchisee must be allowed to set and advertise resale prices. The Court rejected the view that clauses tending to divide the Common Market between franchisor and franchisee or between franchisees are always necessary to protect the knowhow or the identity and the reputation of the network.

The location clause in *Pronuptia* was seen as potentially supporting exclusive territories. In combination, location clauses and exclusive territories may divide markets and so restrict competition within the network. Even if a potential franchisee would not take the risk of joining the network by making its own investment because it could not expect a profitable business due to the absence of protection from competition from other franchisees, that consideration (in the Court's view) could be taken into account only under an Article 101(3) individual exemption review by the Commission. The Commission, in fact, ultimately granted such an exemption to Pronuptia.[22]

§ 18.12   EU Regulations 4087/88, 2790/1999 and 330/10

The Commission, following the European Court of Justice decision in *Pronuptia,*[23] adopted a group exemption regulation (No. 4087/88) for franchise agreements under Article 101(3).[24] This regulation detailed permissible franchise restraints (the "white list") and impermissible obligations (the "black list"). Its terms were widely followed in drafting European franchise agreements. Any failure to adhere to the regulation could result in serious competition law (antitrust) sanctions.

Regulation 4087/88 was superseded by Regulation 2790/1999, the vertical agreements regulation. This regulation was more economic and less formalistic than Regulation 4087/88. Supply and distribution agreements of firms with less than 30 percent market shares are generally exempt; this is known as a "safe harbor." Companies whose market shares exceed 30 percent may or may not be exempt, depending upon the results of individual competition law reviews by the Commission under Article 101(3). In either case, no vertical agreements containing so-called "hard core restraints" are exempt. These restraints concern primarily resale price maintenance, territorial and customer protection leading to market allocation, and in most instances exclusive dealing covenants that last more than five years.

In 2010, a new vertical restraints Regulation 330/10 (with accompanying Guidelines) was issued. Its content is similar to that

---

[22]   Re Pronuptia, 30 O.J.Eur.Comm. 39 (L13/1987).

[23]   Pronuptia de Paris GmbH v. Pronuptia de Paris Irmgard Schillgallis (1986) Eur. Comm. Rep. 353.

[24]   O.J. 1988 L539/46.

of 1999. Restrictions on the use of the Internet by distributors with at least one "brick-and-mortar" store are treated as a hardcore restraints. For example, distributors cannot be required to reroute Internet customers outside their territories to local dealers. Nor can they be forced to pay higher prices for online sales ("dual pricing"), or be limited in the amount sales made via the Internet, although a minimum amount of offline sales can be stipulated. Generally speaking, distributors may sell anywhere in the EU in response to customer demand ("passive sales"). Restraints on "actively" soliciting sales outside designated distributor territories, including by email or banner web advertising, are permissible. *Both* supplier and distributor must have less than 30% market shares to qualify for the 2010 "safe harbor."

Chapter 19

PATENT AND KNOWHOW LICENSING

Table of Sections

§ 19.1 Protecting Patents and Knowhow

This chapter concerns the most common form of lawful international technology transfer—patent and knowhow licensing. Before any patent licensing can take place, patents must be acquired in all countries in which the owner hopes there will be persons interested in purchasing the technology. Even in countries where the owner has no such hope, patent rights may still be obtained so as to foreclose future unlicensed competitors. Licensing is a middle ground alternative to exporting from the owner's home country and direct investment in host markets. It can often produce, with relatively little cost, immediate positive cash flows. After a brief introduction to patents and knowhow, the main themes of this chapter are standard licensing contract terms and the regulation of international licensing agreements.

§ 19.2 The Nature of Patents

For the most part, patents are granted to inventors according to national law. Thus, patents represent *territorial* grants of exclusive rights. The inventor receives Canadian patents, United

States patents, Mexican patents, and so on. There are relatively few jurisdictions without some form of patent protection. However, legally protected intellectual property in one country may not be protected similarly in another country. For example, many third world nations *refuse* to grant patents on pharmaceuticals. These countries often assert that their public health needs require such a policy. Thailand has been one such country and unlicensed "generics" have been a growth industry there. Similarly, most European countries do not grant patents on medical and surgical therapeutic techniques for reasons of public policy.

Nominal patent protection in some developing nations may lack effective forms of relief—giving the appearance but not the reality of legal rights. Since international patent protection is expensive to obtain, some holders take a chance and limit their applications to those markets where they foresee demand or competition for their product. Nevertheless, U.S. nationals continue to receive tens of thousands of patents in other countries. But the reverse is also increasingly true. Residents of foreign countries now receive over 50 percent of the patents issued under United States law. In many countries, persons who deal with the issuance and protection of patents are called patent agents. In the United States, patent practice is a specialized branch of the legal profession. Obtaining international patent protection often involves retaining the services of specialists in each country.

What constitutes a "patent" and how it is protected in any country depends upon domestic law. In the United States, a patent issued by the U.S. Patent Office grants the right for 20 years to exclude everyone from making, using or selling the patented invention without the permission of the patentee.[1] The United States traditionally granted patents to the "first to invent," not (as in many other countries) the "first to file." In 2013, the U.S. switched to first to file rules. Patent infringement can result in injunctive and damages relief in the U.S. courts. "Exclusion orders" against foreign-made patent infringing goods are also available. Such orders are frequently issued by the International Trade Commission under Section 337 of the Tariff Act of 1930,[2] and are enforced by the U.S. Customs Service. A U.S. patent thus provides a short-term legal, but not necessarily economic, monopoly. For example, the exclusive legal rights conveyed by the patents held by Xerox on its photocopying machines have not given it a monopoly in the marketplace. There are many other producers of non-infringing photocopy machines with whom Xerox competes.

---

[1]   35 U.S.C. § 154.

[2]   *See* Chapter 20.

There are basically two types of patent systems in the world community, registration and examination. Some countries (*e.g.*, France) grant a patent upon "registration" accompanied by appropriate documents and fees, without making an inquiry about the patentability of the invention. The validity of such a patent grant is most difficult to gauge until a time comes to defend the patent against alleged infringement in an appropriate tribunal. In other countries, the patent grant is made following a careful "examination" of the prior art and statutory criteria on patentability or a "deferred examination" is made following public notice given to permit an "opposition." The odds are increased that the validity of such a patent will be sustained in the face of an alleged infringement. The United States and Germany have examination systems.

To obtain U.S. patents, applicants must demonstrate to the satisfaction of the Patent and Trademark Office that their inventions are novel, useful and nonobvious. Nevertheless, a significant number of U.S. patents have been subsequently held invalid in the courts and the Patent Office has frequently been criticized for a lax approach to issuance of patents. Much of this growth is centered in high-tech industries, including computer software and business methods patents, for example Amazon's "Buy Now with 1-Click" software patent. The U.S. has also been criticized for sometimes allowing patents on "traditional knowledge" (*e.g.*, Mexican Enola Beans) found primarily in the developing world.

The terms of a patent grant vary from country to country. For example, local law may provide for "confirmation," "importation," "introduction" or "revalidation" patents (which serve to extend limited protection to patents already existing in another country). "Inventor's certificates" and rewards are granted in some socialist countries where private ownership of the means of production is discouraged. The state owns the invention. This was the case in China, for example, but inventors now may obtain patents and exclusive private rights under the 1984 Patent Law.

India requires pharmaceutical patents to be "more efficacious" than existing drugs, an "anti-evergreening" requirement the Indian Supreme Court applied to deny Novartis a patent for its cancer drug Gleevac. Some countries, such as Britain, require that a patent be "worked" (commercially applied) within a designated period of time. This requirement is so important that the British mandate a "compulsory license" to local persons if a patent is deemed unworked. Many developing nations have similar provisions in their patent laws . . . the owner must use it or lose it.

§ 19.3   The Nature of Knowhow and Trade Secrets

Knowhow is commercially valuable knowledge. It may or may not be a trade secret, and may or may not be patentable. Though often technical or scientific, *e.g.*, engineering services, knowhow can also be more general in character. Marketing and management skills as well as simply business advice can constitute knowhow. If someone is willing to pay for the information, it can be sold or licensed internationally.

Legal protection for knowhow varies from country to country and is, at best, limited. Unlike patents, copyrights and trademarks, you cannot by registration obtain exclusive legal rights to knowhow. Knowledge, like the air we breathe, is a public good. Once released in the community, knowhow can generally be used by anyone and is almost impossible to retrieve. In the absence of exclusive legal rights, preserving the confidentiality of knowhow becomes an important business strategy. If everyone knows it, who will pay for it? If your competitors have access to the knowledge, your market position is at risk. It is for these reasons that only a few people on earth ever know the Coca Cola formula, which is perhaps the world's best kept knowhow.

In the United States, the Economic Espionage Act of 1996 creates *criminal* penalties for misappropriation of trade secrets for the benefit of foreign governments or anyone. For these purposes, a "trade secret" is defined as "financial, business, scientific, technical, economic or engineering information" that the owner has taken reasonable measures to keep secret and whose "independent economic value derives from being closely held." In addition to criminal fines, forfeitures and jail terms, the Act authorizes seizure of all proceeds from the theft of trade secrets as well as property used or intended for use in the misappropriation (*e.g.*, buildings and capital equipment).

Protecting knowhow is mostly a function of contract, tort and trade secrets law. Employers will surround their critical knowhow with employees bound by contract to confidentiality. But some valuable knowledge leaks from or moves with these employees, *e.g.*, when a disgruntled retired or ex-employee sells or goes public with the knowhow. The remedies at law or in equity for breach of contract are unlikely to render the employer whole. Neither is tort relief likely to be sufficient since most employees are essentially judgment proof, although they may be of more use if a competitor induced the breach of contract. Likewise, even though genuine trade secrets are protected by criminal statutes in a few jurisdictions, persuading the prosecutor to take up your business problem is not easy and criminal penalties will not recoup the trade secrets (though they may make the revelation of others less likely in the future).

Despite all of these legal hazards, even when certain knowhow is patentable, a desire to prolong the commercial exploitation of that knowledge may result in no patent registrations. The international chemicals industry, for example, is said to prefer trade secrets to public disclosure and patent rights with time limitations. Licensing or selling such knowhow around the globe is risky, but lucrative.

§ 19.4 International Patent and Knowhow Licensing

This section concerns the most common form of lawful international technology transfer-patent and knowhow licensing. Before any patent licensing can take place, patents must be acquired in all countries in which the owner hopes there will be persons interested in purchasing the technology. Even in countries where the owner has no such hope, patent rights may still be obtained so as to foreclose future unlicensed competitors. Licensing is a middle ground alternative to exporting from the owner's home country and direct investment in host markets. It can often produce, with relatively little cost, immediate positive cash flows.

International patent and knowhow licensing is the most critical form of technology transfer to third world development. From the owner's standpoint, it presents an alternative to and sometimes a first step towards foreign investment. Such licensing involves a transfer of patent rights or knowhow (commercially valuable knowledge, often falling short of a patentable invention) in return for payments, usually termed royalties. Unlike foreign investment, licensing does not have to involve a capital investment in a host jurisdiction and may be tax-advantaged. However, licensing of patents and knowhow is not without legal risks.

From the licensee's standpoint, and the perspective of its government, there is the risk that the licensed technology may be old or obsolete, not "state of the art." Goods produced under old technology will be hard to export and convey a certain "second class" status. On the other hand, older more labor intensive technologies may actually be sought (as sometimes done by the PRC) in the early stages of development. Excessive royalties may threaten the economic viability of the licensee and drain hard currencies from the country. The licensee typically is not in a sufficiently powerful position to bargain away restrictive features of standard international licenses. For all these reasons, and more, third world countries frequently regulate patent and knowhow licensing agreements. Such law is found in the Brazilian Normative Act No. 17 (1976) and the Mexican Technology Transfer Law (1982) (repealed 1991), among others. Royalty levels will be limited, certain clauses prohibited (*e.g.*, export restraints, resale price maintenance, mandatory grantbacks to the licensor of improvements), and the desirability of the technology evaluated.

Regulation of licensing is not limited to the developing world. The European Union extensively regulates patent and knowhow licensing.[3] In the United States, there is a less direct form of licensing regulation via antitrust law.[4]

The licensor also faces legal risks. The flow of royalty payments may be stopped, suspended or reduced by currency exchange regulations. The taxation of the royalties, if not governed by double taxation treaties, may be confiscatory. The licensee may abscond with the technology or facilitate "gray market" goods[5] which eventually compete for sales in markets exclusively intended for the licensor. In the end, patents expire and become part of the world domain. At that point, unless the technology is somehow tied to a protected trade secret, the licensee has effectively purchased the technology and becomes an independent competitor (though not necessarily an effective competitor if the licensor has made new technological advances).

Licensing is a kind of partnership. If the licensee succeeds, the licensor's royalties (often based on sales volumes) will increase and a continuing partnership through succeeding generations of technology may evolve. If not, the dispute settlement provisions of the agreement may be called upon as either party withdraws from the partnership. Licensing of patents and knowhow often is combined with, indeed essential to, foreign investments. A foreign subsidiary or joint venture will need technical assistance and knowhow to commence operations. When this occurs, the licensing terms are usually a part of the basic joint venture or investment agreement. Licensing may also be combined with a trade agreement, as where the licensor ships necessary supplies to the licensee, joint venturer, or subsidiary. Such supply agreements have sometimes been used to overcome royalty limitations through a form of "transfer pricing," the practice of marking up or down the

---

[3]   *See* Section 19.8.

[4]   *See generally* Antitrust Guidelines for the Licensing for Intellectual Property issued by the U.S. Dept. of Justice and the Federal Trade Commission, April 6, 1995. BNA-ATRR, Vol. 68, No. 1708 (April 13, 1995), Special Supplement. These Guidelines are primarily domestic in orientation, but also apply to international licensing.

[5]   *See* Chapter 20.

price of goods so as to allocate revenues to preferred parties and jurisdictions (*e.g.*, tax havens).

§ 19.5   International Acquisition of Patents

The principal treaties regarding patents are the 1970 Patent Cooperation Treaty and the 1883 Paris Convention for the Protection of Industrial Property, frequently revised and amended. To some extent, the Paris Convention also deals with trademarks, servicemarks, trade names, industrial designs, and unfair competition. Other recent treaties dealing with patents are the European Patent Convention (designed to permit offices at Munich and The Hague to issue patents of all countries party to the treaty), the European Community Patent Convention (designed to create a single patent valid throughout the EU) and the 1994 Eurasian Patent Convention (which does the same for Russia and the Central Asian states).

Paris Convention. The Paris Convention,[6] to which over 170 countries including the U.S. are parties, remains the basic international agreement dealing with treatment of foreigners under national patent laws. It is administered by the International Bureau of the World Intellectual Property Organization (WIPO) at Geneva. The "right of national treatment" (Article 2) prohibits discrimination against foreign holders of local patents and trademarks. Thus, for example, an American granted a Canadian patent must receive the same legal rights and remedies accorded Canadian nationals. Furthermore, important "rights of priority" are granted to patent holders provided they file in foreign jurisdictions within twelve months of their home country patent applications. But such rights conceivably may not overcome prior filings in "first to file" jurisdiction.

Patent applications in foreign jurisdictions are not dependent upon success in the home country: Patentability criteria vary from country to country. Nevertheless, the Paris Convention obviates the need to file simultaneously in every country where intellectual property protection is sought. If an inventor elects not to obtain patent protection in other countries, anyone may make, use or sell the invention in that territory. The Paris Convention does not attempt to reduce the need for individual patent applications in all jurisdictions where patent protection is sought. Nor does it alter the various domestic criteria on patentability.

---

[6]   21 U.S.T. 1583, T.I.A.S. No. 6295, 828 U.N.T.S. 305 (Stockholm revision).

Patent Cooperation Treaty. The Patent Cooperation Treaty (PCT),[7] to which about 140 countries including the U.S. are parties, is designed to achieve greater uniformity and less cost in the international patent filing process, and in the examination of prior art. Instead of filing patent applications individually in each nation, filings under the PCT are done in selected countries. The national patent offices of Japan, Sweden, Russia and the United States have been designated International Searching Authorities (ISA), as have the European Patent Offices at Munich and The Hague. The international application, together with the international search report, is communicated by an ISA to each national patent office where protection is sought. Nothing in this Treaty limits the freedom of each nation to establish substantive conditions of patentability and determine infringement remedies.

However, the Patent Cooperation Treaty also provides that the applicant may arrange for an international preliminary examination in order to formulate a nonbinding opinion on whether the claimed invention is novel, involves an inventive step (non-obvious) and is industrially applicable. In a country without sophisticated search facilities, the report of the international preliminary examination may largely determine whether a patent will be granted. For this reason alone, the Patent Cooperation Treaty may generate considerable uniformity in world patent law. In 1986 the United States ratified the PCT provisions on preliminary examination reports, thereby supporting such uniformity. China, Japan and South Korea now account for the largest number of PCT applications, with Germany and the United States declining in utilization.

§ 19.6 Intellectual Property Rights as European Trade Barriers

A truly remarkable body of case law has developed around the authority granted national governments in Article 36 of the Treaty on the Functioning of the European Union to protect industrial or commercial property by restraining imports and exports. These cases run the full gamut from protection of trademarks and copyrights to protection of patents and knowhow. There is a close link between this body of case law and that developed under Article 101 concerning restraints on competition.

Trade restraints involving intellectual property arise out of the fact that such rights are nationally granted. Owners of intellectual property rights within the Union are free under most traditional

---

[7]   28 U.S.T. 7645, T.I.A.S. No. 8733.

law to block the unauthorized importation of goods into national markets. There is a strong tendency for national infringement lawsuits to serve as vehicles for the division of the Common Market. Common Market IP regimes provide an alternative to, but do not replace, national intellectual property rights. In 1993, for example, the Council reached agreement on a Common Market trademark regime. And the Council adopted Directive 89/104, which seeks to harmonize member state laws governing trademarks. In the copyright field, several directives have harmonized European law, perhaps most importantly mandating copyrights for computer software.

Exhaustion Doctrine. The European Court of Justice has addressed the problems under Article 36 and generally resolved against the exercise of national intellectual property rights in ways which inhibit free internal trade. In many of these decisions, the Court acknowledges the existence of the right to block trade in infringing goods, but holds that the *exercise* of that right is subordinate to the TFEU. The Court has also fashioned a doctrine which treats national intellectual property rights as having been *exhausted* once the goods to which they apply are freely sold on the market. One of the few exceptions to this doctrine is broadcast performing rights which the Court treats as incapable of exhaustion.[8] Records and CDs embodying such rights are, however, subject to the exhaustion doctrine once released into the market.[9] Such goods often end up in the hands of third parties who then ship them into another member state.

The practical effect of many of the rulings of the Court of Justice is to remove the ability of the owners of the relevant intellectual property rights to successfully pursue infringement actions in national courts. When intellectual property rights share a common origin and have been placed on goods by consent, as when a licensor authorizes their use in other countries, then infringement actions to protect against trade in the goods to which the rights apply are usually denied. It is only when intellectual property rights do not share a common origin or the requisite consent is absent that they stand a chance of being upheld so as to stop trade in infringing products.[10] Compulsory licensing of patents, for example, does not involve consensual marketing of products. Patent rights may therefore be used to block trade in goods produced under

---

[8]   *See* Coditel v. Ciné Vog Films SA (1980) Eur. Comm. Rep. 881; (1982) Eur. Comm. Rep. 3381.

[9]   Musik-Vertrieb membran Gmbh v. GEMA (1981) Eur. Comm. Rep. 147.

[10]   *See* CNL-Sucal v. HAG (1990) Eur. Comm. Rep. 3711 (Case C–10/89) (wartime expropriation of trademark removes common origin).

such a license.[11] But careful repackaging and resale of goods subject to a common trademark may occur against the objections of the owner of the mark.[12]

Centrafarm Case. An excellent example of the application of the judicial doctrine developed by the Court of Justice in the intellectual property field under Article 36 can be found in the *Centrafarm* case.[13] The United States pharmaceutical company, Sterling Drug, owned the British and Dutch patents and trademarks relating to "Negram." Subsidiaries of Sterling Drug in Britain and Holland had been respectively assigned the British and Dutch trademark rights to Negram. Owing in part to price controls in the UK, a substantial difference in cost for Negram emerged as between the two countries. Centrafarm was an independent Dutch importer of Negram from the UK and Germany. Sterling Drug and its subsidiaries brought infringement actions in the Dutch courts under their national patent and trademark rights seeking an injunction against Centrafarm's importation of Negram into The Netherlands.

The Court of Justice held that the intellectual property rights of Sterling Drug and its subsidiaries could not be exercised in a way which blocked trade in "parallel goods." In the Court's view, the exception established in Article 36 for the protection of industrial and commercial property covers only those rights that were specifically intended to be conveyed by the grant of national patents and trademarks. Blocking trade in parallel goods after they have been put on the market with the consent of a common owner, thus exhausting the rights in question, was not intended to be part of the package of benefits conveyed. If Sterling Drug succeeded, an arbitrary discrimination or disguised restriction on Union trade would be achieved in breach of the language which qualifies Article 36. Thus the European Court of Justice ruled in favor of the free movement of goods within the Common Market even when that negates clearly existing national legal remedies.

Only in the unusual situation where the intellectual property rights in question have been acquired by independent proprietors under different national laws may such rights inhibit internal

---

[11]   Pharmon BV v. Hoechst AG (1985), Eur. Comm. Rep. 2281.

[12]   Hoffman-LaRoche & Co. AG v. Centrafarm Vertriebsgesellschaft Pharmazeutischer Erzeugnisse mbH (1978) Eur. Comm. Rep. 1132; Pfizer, Inc. v. Eurim-Pharm GmbH (1981) Eur. Comm. Rep. 2913.

[13]   Centrafarm BV and Adriaan de Peipjper v. Sterling Drug Inc. (1974) Eur. Comm. Rep. 1147.

trade.[14] While the goal of creation of the Common Market can override national intellectual property rights when internal trade is concerned, these rights apply fully to the importation of goods from outside the European Union.[15] North American exporters of goods allegedly subject to rights owned by Europeans may therefore find entry into the EU challenged by infringement actions in national courts. This is notably true regarding trade in gray market goods.[16] Levi Strauss successfully cited *Silhouette* to keep low-price (made in the USA) Levi's out of the EU.

§ 19.7 European Patents

The 1973 European Patent Convention (EPC)[17] established the European Patent Offices (EPO) in Munich and The Hague. It allows applicants to simultaneously apply for national patent rights in any of the contracting countries. These include all of the EU nations save Spain, plus a number of other European states. The applicant must meet the requirements for patentability established by the EPC. Challenges to patentability decisions by the EPO may be made within 9 months after granting of the patent. Thereafter, challenges must be made in national courts subject to national patent laws. Thus, the EPC basically presents a one-stop opportunity to obtain a basket of national patents in Europe. It does not foreclose the option of individual national patent applications.

A European Union Unitary Patent Convention finally came into force in 2014. The Convention originally provided that it had to be ratified by all members before becoming effective. It was agreed in 1985 that if unanimous ratification was not achieved by December 31, 1991, a lesser number of required ratifications would suffice. The Convention was therefore expected to come into force before the end of 1992, but realization of this goal remained elusive until 2012 when 25 of the EU member states agreed to move forward on "enhanced cooperation" to create a "unitary" patent. The abstainers were Italy and Spain, miffed because their languages are not used, only French, English and German.

---

[14]   *See* Terrapin (Overseas) Ltd. v. Terranova Industrie CA Kapferer & Co. (1976) Eur. Comm. Rep. 1039; CNL-Sucal v. HAG (1990) Eur. Comm. Rep. 3711 (Case C–10/89).

[15]   *See* E.M.I. Records Ltd. v. CBS United Kingdom Ltd. (1976) Eur. Comm. Rep. 811 and Silhouette International v. Hartlauer, No. C–355/96 (July 16, 1998) (gray market goods).

[16]   *See* Chapter 20 and Silhouette International v. Hartlauer (1998) Eur. Comm. Rep. I–4799 (Case C–355/96); Zino Davidoff SA v. A + G Imports Ltd. (2001) Eur. Comm. Rep. I–8691 (Cases C–414/99 to 416/99).

[17]   13 Int'l Legal Mats. 268 (1974).

The Unitary Patent regime allows applications for a Common Market patent valid in 25 contracting states. Applications will be handled by the EPO in Munich. A Unitary Patent may be granted, revoked or transferred. Licenses for part of the Union will be possible. The Unitary Patent will be an alternative to (but not a replacement for) national or EPO patent rights. Its signatories are required to harmonize national patent laws to conform to Unitary Patent rules on infringement, litigation procedures, exhaustion of rights and other issues.

A new Unified Patent Court primarily based in Paris will become the final arbiter on patent disputes, though references to the European Court of Justice on questions of interpretation of Unitary Patent regulations and the EU directive in biotech inventions are mandatory. By 2021, patent disputes concerning nationally issued or EPO patents will also be exclusively resolved by the Unified Patent Court. A special Court of Appeals for patent matters will be created in Luxembourg.

§ 19.8 European Patent and Knowhow Licensing

In its 1982 *Maize Seed* judgment, the European Court of Justice addressed patent license restrictions under the Community's competition rules.[18] The Commission waited for this judgment before publishing the 1984 group exemption under Article 101(3) TFEU for patent licensing agreements. In this case, a research institute financed by the French government (INRA) bred varieties of basic seeds. In 1960, INRA assigned to Kurt Eisele plant breeder's rights for maize seed in the Federal Republic of Germany. Eisele agreed to apply for registration of these rights in accordance with German law. In 1965, a formal agreement was executed by the parties. This agreement consisted of five relevant clauses.

Clause 1 gave Eisele the exclusive rights to "organize" sales of six identified varieties of maize seed propagated from basic seeds provided by INRA. This enabled Eisele to exercise control over distribution outlets. Eisele undertook not to deal in maize varieties other than those provided by INRA. Clause 2 required Eisele to place no restriction on the supply of seed to technically suitable distributors except for rationing in conditions of shortage. The prices charged to the distributors by Eisele were fixed in consultation with INRA, according to a specified formula. Clause 3 obligated Eisele to import from France for sale in Germany at least two-thirds of that territory's requirements for the registered varieties. This restricted Eisele's own production and sale to only one-third of the German market. Clause 4 concerned the protection

---

[18]   Nungesser v. Commission (1982) Eur. Comm. Rep. 2015.

by Eisele of INRA's proprietary rights, including its trademark, from infringement and granted Eisele the power to take any action to that end. Clause 5 contained a promise by INRA that no experts to Germany of the relevant varieties would take place otherwise than through the agency of Eisele. This meant that INRA would ensure that its French marketing organization would prevent the relevant varieties from being exported to Germany to parallel importers.

In September 1972, it became apparent that dealers in France were selling the licensed varieties of maize seed directly to German traders who were marketing the products in breach of the breeder's rights claimed by Eisele. This resulted in an action by Eisele in the German courts against one of the traders. The parties reached a court approved settlement under which the French trader promised to refrain from offering for sale without permission any variety of maize seed within the rights held by Eisele, and to pay a fine. In February 1974, another breach took place, this time advertising in the German press by a French dealer. In response to threats of legal proceedings, this dealer lodged a complaint with the Commission alleging breach of the Treaty of Rome competition rules.

The Commission considered both the agreement and the settlement to violate Article 101(1) because they granted an exclusive license and provided absolute territorial protection. The Court of Justice reversed the Commission with respect to exclusivity, but upheld the Commission with respect to absolute territorial protection. The Court drew a distinction between "open" licenses which do not necessarily fall under Article 101(1), and "closed" licenses which do so.

Open license agreements are those which do not involve third parties. In *Maize Seed,* the obligation upon INRA or those deriving rights through INRA to refrain from producing or selling the relevant seeds in Germany was treated as an open license term. The Court held such clauses necessary to the dissemination of new technology inasmuch as potential licensees might otherwise be deterred from accepting the risk of cultivating and marketing new products. The Court defined closed licenses as those involving third parties. Thus, the obligation upon INRA or those deriving rights through INRA to prevent third parties from exporting the seeds into Germany without authorization, Eisele's concurrent use of his exclusive contractual rights, and his breeder's rights, to prevent all imports into Germany or exports to other member states were invalid under Article 101(1).

The Commission of the European Community adopted in 1984 a patent licensing group exemption regulation under Article

101(3).[19] It acknowledged that patent licensing improves the production of goods and promotes technical progress by allowing licensees to operate with the latest technology. The Commission also believes that patent licensing increases both the number of production facilities and the quantity and quality of goods in the Common Market. Commission Regulation 2349/84 covered patent licensing agreements and licensing agreements for both patents and knowhow. Commission Regulation 556/89 covered pure knowhow licensing agreements, also exempting them under the terms of Article 101(3). Knowhow was broadly conceived in this regulation. Nonpatented technical information (*e.g.,* descriptions of manufacturing processes, recipes, formulae, designs or drawings) was the focus of Regulation 556/89.

§ 19.9   European Transfer of Technology Regulation

In 1996 the Commission enacted Regulation 240/96 on the application of Article 101(3) TFEU to transfer technology agreements. The intention of this Regulation was to combine the existing patent and knowhow block exemptions into a single regulation covering technology transfer agreements, and to simplify and harmonize the rules for patent and knowhow licensing. It was also intended to encourage dissemination of technological knowledge and promote the manufacture of more technologically advanced goods.

Transfer of Technology Regulations 772/2004, 316/2014. The detailed regulation of technology transfer agreement clauses contained in Regulation 240/96 was replaced by Regulation 772/2004 and subsequently Regulation 316/2014. The latter Regulation and its accompanying Guidelines apply to patent, know-how, production trademark and some software copyright licensing agreements.

The new Regulations distinguish agreements between those of "competing" and "noncompeting" parties, the latter being treated less strictly than the former. Parties are deemed "competing" if they compete (without infringing each other's IP rights) in either the relevant technology or product market, determined in each instance by what buyers regard as substitutes. If the competing parties have a *combined* market share of 20 percent or less, their licensing agreements are covered by group exemption under Regulation 316/2014. Noncompeting parties, on the other hand, benefit from the group exemption so long as their *individual* market shares do

---

[19]   Commission Regulation 2349/84.

not exceed 30%. Agreements initially covered by Regulation 316/2014 that subsequently exceed the "safe harbor" thresholds noted above lose their exemption subject to a two-year grace period. Outside these exemptions, a "rule of reason" approach applies.

Inclusion of certain "hardcore restraints" causes license agreement to lose their group exemption. For competing parties, such restraints include price fixing, output limitations on both parties, limits on the licensee's ability to exploit its own technology, and allocation of markets or competitors (subject to exceptions). Specifically, restraints on active and passive selling by the licensee in a territory reserved for the licensor are allowed, as are active (but not passive) selling restraints by licensees in territories of other licensees. Licensing agreements between noncompeting parties may not contain the "hardcore" restraint of price fixing. Active selling restrictions on licensees can be utilized, along with passive selling restraints in territories reserved to the licensor or in most cases another licensee. For these purposes, the competitive status of the parties is decided at the outset of the agreement.

Other license terms deemed "excluded restrictions" also cause a loss of exemption. Such clauses include: (1) mandatory grant-backs or assignments of severable improvements by licensees, excepting nonexclusive license-backs; (2) no-challenges by the licensee of the licensor's intellectual property rights; and (3) for noncompeting parties, restraints on the licensee's ability to exploit its own technology or either party's ability to carry out research and development (unless indispensable to prevent disclosure of the licensed Know-how). The 2014 Guidelines clarify that IP settlement agreements (*e.g.*, "pay-for-delay" or "reverse payment" agreements) may not impose more restrictive settlement terms than would have been accepted solely on the basis of the strength and validity of the licensor's technology. The Guidelines further detail the permissible limits of technology pooling and essential patent product standards.

In all cases, exemption under Regulation 316/2014 may be withdrawn where in any particular case an agreement has effects that are incompatible with Article 101(3) TFEU. Regulation 316/2014 provided a one year time limit that ended May 1, 2015, to conform existing technology transfer agreements to its rules.

§ 19.10 Technology Transfers

The process of transferring technology involves an agreement which outlines the relationship between the transferor and the transferee. The extent to which the agreement is detailed may depend upon the character of the transferee.

Subsidiary or Affiliate as Transferee. Even when the technology is transferred to a wholly owned subsidiary in a foreign nation, there is almost always some agreement, at the very least for tax purposes. The corporate structure using a parent and subsidiary (the latter being an entity incorporated under the laws of the foreign host nation) demands that the separate nature of the two entities be maintained. If not, the parent may be held responsible for the debts of the subsidiary under veil piercing theory. Consequently, the transfer of technology from a parent to a subsidiary should be at arms length and represented by a written agreement.[20] But if the parent is convinced that there is little likelihood that the subsidiary's management will adversely affect the value of the technology, or produce poor quality goods using the technology, there are likely to be fewer provisions in the agreement than where the transferee is an independent entity, unrelated to the transferor.

Independent Transferee. When the agreement is to transfer technology to an entity which is not part of the transferor's corporate structure, such as a subsidiary or affiliate, there will be a sense that more detail ought to appear in the technology agreement. For example, disputes will not be settled "within" the company, as they may when the transfer of technology is to a subsidiary, but by judicial or arbitral tribunals. A transfer within a corporate structure is usually easily worked out, but a transfer to an independent transferee may involve considerable negotiation of many details.

§ 19.11   Regulations in the Country of the Transferee

When there are no transfer of technology rules in the country of the transferee, the technology transfer agreement is the conclusion of the bargaining of the two parties, the transferor and the transferee. The agreement will not be public; it will not be registered. But when the transfer of technology is to some nations, especially developing nations and nonmarket economy nations, there may be a third party, i.e., the government, involved both in the determination and regulation of what may and may not be included in the technology transfer agreement, and in approving the agreement. During the 1970s a number of developing nations enacted transfer of technology laws.[21] The laws were adopted both

---

[20]   If it is not an arms' length transaction, there may be accusations that transfer pricing is involved.

[21]   For example, Mexico adopted a transfer of technology law in 1972. It was amended in 1982 but remained restrictive. In 1991 it was replaced by a law which

as part of the general attempt to control foreign investment and technology transfers, but also to preserve scarce hard currency at a time of severe balance of payment problems. The developing nations viewed technology transfers as an area of investment where there were serious abuses, and believed that their laws would adequately address these issues.[22] The principal abuses were thought to include the following:

(1)   Transfer of obsolete technology;

(2)   Excessive price paid for the technology;

(3)   Limitations on use of new developments by the transferee by grantback provisions;

(4)   Little research performed by the transferee;

(5)   Too much intervention by the transferor in transferee activities;

(6)   Limitations on where the transferee may market the product;

(7)   Requirements that components be purchased from the transferor which are available locally or could be obtained from other foreign sources more cheaply;

(8)   Inadequate training of transferee's personnel to do jobs performed by personnel of the transferor;

(9)   Transfer of technology which has adequate domestic substitutes and is therefore not needed;

(10) Too long a duration of the agreement; and

(11) Application of foreign law and use of foreign tribunals for dispute resolution.

These do not establish an exclusive list. Some nations had different reasons for wishing to more closely govern technology transfers. But these reasons provide an outline of what areas transfer of technology laws in the 1970s attempted to govern.

The result of these restrictive laws was the transfer of less technology, and of technology less valuable to the parent. It was often older technology over which the company was willing to relinquish some control. The bureaucracies established to register and approve or disapprove the agreements were often staffed with

---

removed the focus on restrictions and replaced this focus with more investment encouraging and protecting provisions.

[22]   *See* Robert J. Radway, *Antitrust, Technology Transfers and Joint Ventures in Latin American Development*, 15 LAWYER AM. 47 (1983).

persons who knew little about technology, less about international business, but who possessed all of the inefficiency and incompetence of many developing nation government agencies. The laws did not bring in more technology, but less. The consequence was that they did not serve the purpose of helping the balance of payments. Furthermore, the nations which adopted strict rules regulating the transfer of technology often did not have laws which protected intellectual property.

In the 1980s, these restrictive laws were dismantled in many countries, whether by formal repeal or replacement by more transfer encouraging and intellectual property protecting laws, or by a relaxed interpretation of the laws and a general automatic approval of what the transferor and transferee agreed upon. In the 1990s transferring technology increased.[23] Ironically, some technology agreements which were used in the 1960s before the enactment of the strict laws, and which became unusable after such enactments, are now once again be used in the developing world but regulated in the European Union (above).

§ 19.12 Technology Agreements as Part of a Foreign Direct Investment

Any foreign direct investment which includes the transfer of some technology may include the transfer in an agreement which also includes the direct investment, quite possibly in a joint venture contract. Whether there is such an agreement will depend on the laws of the host nation. Sometimes foreign direct investment requires nothing more than entering the host nation with a branch operation or establishing a local wholly owned subsidiary. The articles of incorporation of the subsidiary will not include anything relating to the transfer of technology to the subsidiary. There will be a separate transfer of technology agreement.

But in many nations which restrict foreign investment, there may be an agreement which expresses the total relationship, including the transfer of technology.[24] Investment in nations which mandate joint ventures are the most likely situations where the investment agreement will also include the technology transfer

---

[23] But it has only increased when the nations not only dismantled their restrictive transfer of technology laws but also adopted laws protecting intellectual property, including knowhow.

[24] For example, the few foreign investments established in Cuba must comply with the broad and often vague provisions of the out-of-date 1982 joint venture law. That law notes the need for foreign technology and that a formal agreement with the government for an investment must also outline the nature of any technology transfers. Little technology is being transferred because there is little protection to technology under Cuban law.

provisions. There is nothing wrong with combining transfer of technology provisions in a larger scope agreement, but the agreement ought to be just as detailed regarding technology provisions as it would standing alone as a separate agreement.

Where technology is transferred within the context of a joint venture or other form of investment agreement, the agreement ought to be clear as to the access of the host nation joint venture partner to any sensitive technology. Particularly where there is knowhow transferred, the foreign investor may wish to control the local party's access to the technology.[25] India demanded in the 1970s that the Coca-Cola company alter its structure from a wholly foreign owned investment to a joint venture. While the Indian government did not expressly state that the foreign parent would have to share the secret formula, the government did say that such sharing would be the natural consequence of the partnership sense of the joint venture. Coca-Cola would not disclose the technology, and withdrew from India, not to return until the 1990s, when India had relaxed its previously strict foreign investment rules.

---

[25] While the local party may be one trusted by the foreign investor, unless there are restrictions on the transfer of ownership interests, that party may change and bring into the ownership and management persons less trusted.

Chapter 20

COUNTERFEIT, INFRINGING AND GRAY MARKET IMPORTS— UNITED STATES SECTION 337 PROCEEDINGS

Table of Sections

---

§ 20.1 Trade in Counterfeit Goods

The predominant vehicle for controlling technology transfers across national borders is the "license" or "franchise" contract. See Chapters 18 and 19. The holder of a patent, copyright or trademark in one country first acquires the legally protected right to the same in another country. This is a time consuming and expensive process.

Theft of intellectual property and use of counterfeit goods are rapidly increasing in developing and developed countries. Such theft is not limited to consumer goods (Pierre Cardin clothing, Rolex watches). Industrial products and parts (*e.g.*, automotive brake pads) are now being counterfeited. Some countries see illegal technology transfers as part of their strategy for economic development. They encourage piracy or choose not to oppose it. Since unlicensed producers pay no royalties, they often have lower production costs than the original source. This practice fuels the fires of intellectual property piracy. Unlicensed low-cost reproduction of entire copyrighted books (may it not happen to this book) is said to be rampant in such diverse areas as Nigeria, Saudi Arabia, and South Korea. Apple computers have been inexpensively counterfeited in Hong Kong. General Motors estimates that about 40 percent of its auto parts are counterfeited in the Middle East. Recordings are duplicated almost everywhere without license or fee. The Internet fuels film and TV piracy . . . try a Google search. And the list goes on.

Among the industrialized countries, efforts occur to acquire (even by way of stealing) "leading edge" technology. One example in the 1980s involved attempted theft of IBM computer technology by Japanese companies ultimately caught by the F.B.I. In the United States, the Office of Export Administration uses the export license procedure to control strategic technological "diversions." But falsification of licensing documents by prominent Norwegian and Japanese companies allowed the Soviets to obtain the technology for making vastly quieter submarine propellers. In the ensuing scandal, "anti-Toshiba" trade sanctions were adopted in the United States. Leading Japanese executives resigned, which is considered the highest form of apology in Japanese business circles.

In 2009, U.S. officials seized about $260 million in counterfeit goods. Chinese gangs accounted for the bulk of these goods, which were most often footwear, consumer electronics, luxury goods and pharmaceuticals. U.S. military and civilian procurement agencies have begun actively targeting counterfeit suppliers. In 2012, the European Union seized over $1.3 billion in counterfeit goods, roughly two-thirds of which came from China. Cigarettes comprised the biggest counterfeit seizures.

§ 20.2 Counterfeit Goods, U.S. Remedies

Legal protection against intellectual property theft and counterfeit goods is not very effective. The four principal U.S. remedies are: (1) seizure of goods by Customs; (2) infringement actions in federal courts; (3) criminal prosecutions or treble damages actions under the Trademark Counterfeiting Act of 1984; and (4) Section 337 proceedings. Each of these is discussed below.

The Anticounterfeiting Consumer Protection Act of 1996, Public Law 104–153 (110 Stat. 1386), made a number of statutory changes intended to combat counterfeiting. Trafficking in counterfeit goods is now an offense under the RICO Act (Racketeer Influenced and Corrupt Organizations Act). Importers must disclose the identity of any trademark on imported merchandise, ex parte seizures by law enforcement officers of counterfeit goods and vehicles used to transport them are widely authorized, damages and civil penalties that can be recovered from counterfeiters and importers were increased, and the Customs Service's authority to return counterfeit merchandise to its source (and potential re-entry into commerce) has been repealed. Customs must now destroy all counterfeit merchandise that it seizes unless the trademark owner otherwise consents and the goods are not a health or safety threat.

In the United States, the Copyright Felony Act of 1992 criminalized all copyright infringements. The No Electronic Theft Act of 1997 (NET) removed the need to prove financial gain as element of copyright infringement law, thus ensuring coverage of copying done with intent to harm copyright owners or copying simply for personal use. The Digital Millennium Copyright Act of 1998 (DMCA) brought the United States into compliance with WIPO treaties and created two new copyright offenses; one for circumventing technological measures used by copyright owners to protect their works ("hacking") and a second for tampering with copyright management information (encryption). The DMCA also made it clear that "webmasters" digitally broadcasting music on the internet must pay performance royalties. Criminal and civil sanctions apply.[1]

§ 20.3 U.S. Customs Service Seizures

United States trademark and copyright holders may register with the Customs Service and seek to block the importation of pirated items made abroad. Such exclusions are authorized in the Tariff Act of 1930 and the Copyright Act of 1976.[2] The thrust of these provisions is that unauthorized imports bearing U.S. registered trademarks or copyrights may be seized by the Customs Service. Trade names that have been used for at least six months can also be recorded with the Customs Service. Such recordation

---

[1]   See, e.g., Universal City Studios, Inc. v. Reimerdes, 111 F. Supp. 2d 294 (S.D.N.Y. 2000) (injunction against anti-encryption software).

[2]   See 19 U.S.C. § 1526(a) (trademarks) and 17 U.S.C. § 602(b) (copyrights). See also 19 C.F.R. § 133, Parts A, D.

permits those names to receive the same relief accorded registered trademark and copyright holders when imports that counterfeit or simulate those trade names are found.[3] Since these trademark, copyright and trade name remedies are only available to United States citizens, distributors of foreign goods must ordinarily be assigned United States trademark rights held by foreigners. Such assignments would permit the distributor to seek a new registration from the Patent and Trademark Office so as to be able to invoke these trade remedies.

The importation of semiconductor chip products or equipment that contains a semiconductor chip design or "mask work" registered with the U.S. Copyright Office is prohibited.[4] As with trademarks, copyrights and trade names, the owner of such a mask work may register it with the U.S. Customs Service or the U.S. International Trade Commission so as to invoke trade remedies which will preclude infringing products and equipment from entering into the United States. The Customs Service also administers a high-tech copyright protection program specially targeted at pirated computer programs.[5] Generally, the Customs Service will seize infringing programs if there is proof of access by the infringer and a "substantial similarity" between the imports and the registered program.[6]

There are some differences in Customs Service seizure proceedings depending upon whether the product seized is alleged to be a trademark counterfeit or a copyright counterfeit. The Customs Service rules indicate that in administrative hearings the burden is on the importer to demonstrate why allegedly counterfeit trademarked goods should be released, whereas the burden is on the copyright owner to prove that copyrighted goods are being pirated. These burdens are different because of the greater difficulties in proving copyright infringements. The Second Circuit has ruled that the Customs Service must employ the "average purchaser test" in determining whether imports are counterfeits subject to seizure and forfeiture.[7] In this case, the Service had used experts to determine differences in the trademark such that it was deemed not a counterfeit (merely infringing) and therefore admissible if the confusing mark was obliterated. The consumer test

---

3   *See* 19 C.F.R. § 133, Parts B, C.

4   *See* 17 U.S.C. § 601(a).

5   *See* 19 C.F.R. § 133.31 *et seq.*

6   *See* Webster and Pryor, *Customs Administration of the High-tech Copyright Protection Program*, 73 J. PAT. & TRADEMARK OFF. SOCIETY 538 (1991).

7   Montres Rolex, S.A. v. Snyder, 718 F.2d 524 (2d Cir. 1983).

mandated by the Second Circuit should give greater protection from counterfeits.

Attorneys invoking the Customs Service process frequently sense the inadequacy of relief against counterfeit goods. The first problem is simply knowing when counterfeit goods are likely to enter the United States market. The Customs Service has enormous duties and can only pay limited attention to the possibility that certain goods are pirated. This is understandable. How is the Customs Service officer to know that the goods are pirated? Can the Customs Service do anything more than look at the invoice in a cursory way? Pirates often take great pains to imitate the logo and trademarks they are copying. This makes such piracy non-obvious.

Copyright piracy of sound recordings is even more difficult to ascertain. It cannot reasonably be expected of the Customs Service that they will play records and tapes in order to determine that they are counterfeit goods. To make customs relief effective it is necessary for private interests to notify the Customs Service that a suspected shipment of counterfeit goods is about to or has arrived in the United States. Companies are increasingly hiring private detectives in order to assist with this task. Private detectives might also be used to try to locate pirated copies and counterfeiting operations inside the United States.

A second frustration with Customs Service relief concerns narrow Customs Service interpretations, such as in the *ROMless Computers* case.[8] In that decision, the Customs Service refused to seize ROMless computers alleged to be in violation of Apple Computer Company copyrights. The practical effect of this decision was to permit ROMless computers to enter the U.S. market, and thereafter be altered in rather simple fashion so as to become effective competitors and arguably infringers of copyrights held by the Apple Computer Company. By removing the ROM (Read Only Memory operating system computer program) unit from the computers, the importers eliminated the only copyrighted element in the computer and thereby nullified attempts at blocking importation of these goods:

> Assuming without deciding that the making of the "ROMless" computers constitutes a contributory infringement against the copyright holder's copyrights, the importation of such merchandise is not prohibited by 17 U.S.C. 602(b). While the phrase "an infringement of copyright" arguably includes contributory copyright infringement, preventing the importation of "ROMless"

---

8   *See* 9 BNA U.S. Import Wkly 1062 (May 30, 1984).

computers would be inconsistent with other language in the statute. The objects against which the provisions of 17 U.S.C. 602(b) are directed are copies or phonorecords of a work that have been acquired outside the United States.

With regard to the very computer programs in issue, the statutory copyright requirement of fixation has been held to be satisfied through the embodiment of these programs in ROM devices. . . . Furthermore, computer programs contained in ROMs can be perceived, reproduced, or otherwise communicated therefrom with the aid of other computer equipment. Accordingly, the provisions of 17 U.S.C. 602(b) are operative against ROMs (or diskettes, tapes, or other devices for fixed storage of software) that contain unlawful reproductions of copyrighted computer software, for these items are copies within the meaning of that section. . . . Therefore, inasmuch as "ROMless" computers do not include such copies upon arrival in the United States, they may enter the country without violation of 17 U.S.C. 602(b).

§ 20.4   U.S. Section 337 Proceedings (Intellectual Property)

This section focuses on the application of Section 337 of the Tariff Act of 1930 to imports that infringe U.S. intellectual property rights. A later section in this chapter focuses upon non-intellectual property rights' cases, and there are two additional sections discussing Section 337 procedures and remedies generally.

Patent piracy is most often challenged in proceedings against unfair import practices under Section 337 of the Tariff Act of 1930.[9] Section 337 proceedings traditionally have involved some relatively complicated statutory provisions. Prior to 1988, the basic prohibition was against: (1) unfair methods of competition and unfair acts in the importation of goods (2) the effect or tendency of which is to destroy or substantially injure (3) an industry efficiently and economically operated in the U.S. Such importation was also prohibited when it prevented the establishment of an industry, or restrained or monopolized trade and commerce in the U.S. Section 337 proceedings are *in rem* which explains why they are preferable to a series of *in personam* actions for infringement in the federal courts.

The Omnibus Trade and Competitiveness Act of 1988 revised Section 337. The requirement that the U.S. industry be efficiently

---

[9]   19 U.S.C. § 1337.

and economically operated was dropped. Proof of injury to a domestic industry is *not* required in intellectual property infringement cases. The importation of articles infringing U.S. patents, copyrights, trademarks or semiconductor chip mask works[10] is specifically prohibited provided a U.S. industry relating to such articles exists or is in the process of being established. Such an industry exists if there is significant plant and equipment investment, significant employment of labor or capital, or substantial investment in exploitation of the intellectual property rights (including research and development or licensing). This test has origins in prior ITC case law.[11] There is also prior case law on the question of whether an American industry is "in the process of being established."[12]

Determination of violations and the recommendation of remedies to the President under Section 337 are the exclusive province of the International Trade Commission (ITC). Most of the case law under Section 337 concerns the infringement of patents. Trademark, copyright and mask work infringements may also be pursued under Section 337.[13] In copyright cases, the petitioner must prove ownership of the copyright and the fact of copying.[14] While not quite a per se rule, it is nearly axiomatic that any infringement of United States patent rights amounts to an unfair import practice for purposes of Section 337.[15] Both product and process patents are entitled to protection under Section 337. But in a major decision affecting biotechnology firms, the Federal Circuit Court of Appeals

---

[10]   The Semiconductor Chip Protection Act of 1984 (17 U.S.C. §§ 901–914) provides a national system for the registration of original mask works. Only a mask work that was first commercially exploited in the United States, or which was owned by a national or domiciliary of the United States or a national, domiciliary, or sovereign authority of a foreign nation that is a party to a treaty affording protection to mask works to which the United States is also a party or a stateless person at the time of its first commercial exploitation outside the United States, is entitled to registration. The owner of a registered mask work has exclusive rights to reproduce the work by optical, electronic, or any other means and to import or distribute a semiconductor chip product in which the mask work is embodied. The violation of any of these exclusive rights would amount to infringement. However, the owner of a particular semiconductor chip product made by the owner of the mask work, or by any person authorized by the owner of the mask work, may import, distribute, or otherwise dispose of or use, but not reproduce, that particular semiconductor chip product without the authority of the owner of the mask work. Reverse engineering of the mask work is permitted for the purpose of teaching, analysis or evaluation or for the purpose of making another original mask work.

[11]   *See* Airtight Cast-Iron Stoves, 3 ITRD 1158, U.S.I.T.C. Pub. No. 1126 (1980).

[12]   *See* Caulking Guns, 6 ITRD 1432, U.S.I.T.C. Pub. No. 1507 (1984).

[13]   19 U.S.C. § 1337(a).

[14]   *See* Coin-Operated Audio-Visual Games and Components, 1981 WL 50518, U.S.I.T.C. Pub. No. 1160 (June 1981).

[15]   *See* Synthetic Star Sapphires, § 316, No. 13 (Sept. 1954), *aff'd sub nom.* In re Von Clemm, 229 F.2d 441 (C.C.P.A. 1955).

refused relief when the U.S. patent owner had no claim either to the final product or the process used to create it even though the foreign party had to use the patented product to create the product being imported into the United States.[16] Had the same activity been undertaken in the U.S., an infringement would most probably have been found. Section 337 can be used to obtain exclusionary orders based upon misappropriation abroad of trade secrets of U.S. companies. Such complaints are governed by federal common law (not state law).[17]

All legal and equitable defenses (but not counterclaims) may be presented, including attacks upon the validity or enforceability of the patent.[18] A patent license term requiring all "litigation" to take place in California barred pursuit of Section 337 relief.[19] The ITC's refusal to entertain a Section 337 proceeding because the complainant's patent was unenforceable due to prior inequitable conduct was upheld by the Federal Circuit Court of Appeals.[20] This decision illustrates the power of the ITC, as a practical matter, to rule on patent validity. International Trade Commission decisions on patent validity, and Federal Circuit Court of Appeals opinions on appeal from the ITC, can be treated as preclusive fact findings under collateral estoppel principles in ordinary federal court proceedings.[21] Res judicata effect is ordinarily denied given the fundamental differences between ITC administrative and federal judicial proceedings concerning patent validity.[22]

Patent-based Section 337 proceedings are multiplying. ITC decisions take about 12 to 15 months, versus three to five years for federal court lawsuits. General exclusion orders are typically sought. Hearings are held before one of four administrative law judges specializing in patent law, with final decisions taken by the ITC. Infringing products are excluded from importation during the appeals process. About one-fourth of all 337 proceedings find infringements. In 2007, in a major decision, the ITC excluded the importation of cell phones containing Qualcomm microchips found to infringe Broadcom parents. In 2012, Samsung succeeded before

---

[16]   Amgen, Inc. v. U.S. Int'l Trade Commission, 902 F.2d 1532 (Fed. Cir. 1990).

[17]   See TianRui Group Co. Ltd. v. U.S. Int'l Trade Commission, 661 F.3d 1322 (Fed. Cir. 2011) (misappropriation in China from licensees of wheel production trade secrets of U.S. manufacturer).

[18]   19 U.S.C. § 1337(c).

[19]   Texas Instruments Inc. v. Tessera, Inc., 231 F.3d 1325 (Fed. Cir. 2000).

[20]   LaBounty Manufacturing, Inc. v. U.S. Int'l Trade Commission, 958 F.2d 1066 (Fed. Cir. 1992).

[21]   In re Convertible Rowing Exerciser Patent Litigation, 814 F. Supp. 1197 (D. Del. 1993).

[22]   Id.

the ITC in alleging patent infringement by imported Apple cellphones, but the President denied a general exclusion order because the patents in question were part of an industry standard and thus he determined it was against the public interest to exclude the imports on the basis of such patent infringement. This was the first denial of ITC-recommended Section 337 relief since President Reagan. Apple's subsequent attempt to bar Samsung cellphones on patent infringement grounds were upheld by the ITC. Absent involvement of industry standards, no Presidential veto was forthcoming.

An increasing number of foreign owners of U.S. patents are invoking 337 procedures. About half of all such complaints are settled, often using cross-licensing among the parties. Section 337 proceedings can result in general exclusion orders permitting seizure of patent counterfeits at any U.S. point of entry. Apple Computer, for example, was able to get such an order against computers sold under the label "Orange" that contained infringing programs and color display circuits.[23] However, as previously noted, the Customs Service finds it extremely difficult when inspecting invoices and occasionally opening boxes to ascertain which goods are counterfeit or infringing. Many counterfeits do look like "the real thing." For most seizure remedies to work, the holder must notify the Customs Service of an incoming shipment of patent offending goods. Such advance notice is hard to obtain.

Section 337 exclusion orders can be used against gray market imports. In one decision, the Federal Circuit Court of Appeals upheld the ITC's order against used Kubota-brand tractors.[24] This decision relies heavily on the existence of material differences between the gray market tractors and those distributed by authorized Kubota dealers in the U.S. These differences included parts and the absence of English-language labels and instructions.

A 1989 decision by a General Agreement on Tariffs and Trade (GATT) panel ruled that Section 337 violates the national treatment provisions of Article III:4 of the GATT. The panel was persuaded that imported goods are treated less favorably (i.e., more severely) under Section 337 in terms of patent infringement remedies than domestic goods which are remedied in the federal courts. The panel's decision was ultimately adopted by the GATT Council and the U.S. indicated that it would consider ways to reach compliance after the TRIPs accord was finalized. The Uruguay Round

---

[23]   In re Certain Personal Computers and Components Thereof, 6 ITRD 1140, 1984 Copr.L.Dec. p 25651, U.S.I.T.C. Pub. No. 1504.

[24]   Gamut Trading Co. v. U.S. Int'l Trade Commission, 200 F.3d 775 (Fed. Cir. 1999).

Agreements Act of 1994 did not alter the substance of Section 337 law. It did make procedural changes (such as allowance of counterclaims in Section 337 proceedings) intended to address the issue of an imbalance in patent infringement remedies. The federal district courts must stay infringement proceedings at the request of the respondent to Section 337 actions.

§ 20.5 Infringement Actions

Another alternative available to counsel attempting to assist U.S. firms combating foreign counterfeiting of their products is infringement relief, including temporary restraining orders, injunctions, damages and an award of the defendant's profits. The major problem with infringement relief is the inability of United States trademark, patent and copyright owners to get effective jurisdiction over and relief from foreign counterfeiters. Infringement and contributory infringement actions can be used more effectively against the importers, distributors or retailers of counterfeit goods. But relief against one such party may merely shift counterfeit sales to another who must then be brought to court, and then another, and another, etc. While such proceedings can result in *ex parte* seizure orders of counterfeit goods already in the United States, they do not represent a long term solution to production of counterfeit goods in foreign jurisdictions.

Most injunctive and damages relief remains illusory, but it can sometimes be useful. For example, it has been held that counterfeit goods seized *ex parte* under the Lanham Trademark Act can be destroyed upon court order.[25] Civil remedies are *not* limited to simply removing the offending trademark.[26]

Infringement and treble damages actions may be commenced in United States courts against importers and distributors of counterfeit goods, but service of process and jurisdictional barriers often preclude effective relief against foreign pirates. Even if such relief is obtained, counterfeiters and the sellers of counterfeit goods have proven adept at the "shell game," moving across the road or to another country to resume operations. Moreover, the mobility and economic incentives of counterfeiters have rendered the criminal sanctions of the Trademark Counterfeiting Act of 1984 (below) largely a Pyrrhic victory. Ex parte seizure orders are also available under the 1984 Act and the Lanham Trademark Act when counterfeit goods can be located in the United States. Goods so seized can be destroyed upon court order.

---

[25]   Fendi S.a.s. Di Paola Fendi E Sorelle v. Cosmetic World, Ltd., 642 F. Supp. 1143 (S.D.N.Y. 1986).

[26]   *Id.*

§ 20.6 Criminal Prosecutions

Many states have enacted criminal statutes to combat increased counterfeiting of goods and services in the United States. After much debate, Congress enacted the Trademark Counterfeiting Act of 1984.[27] Criminal penalties are established for anyone who "intentionally traffics or attempts to traffic in goods or services and knowingly uses a counterfeit mark on or in connection with such goods or services." Treble damages or profits (whichever is greater) and attorney fees may be recovered in civil actions unless there are "extenuating circumstances." Ex parte seizure orders for counterfeit goods may be issued by the federal courts. Parallel imports of genuine or "gray market goods" (goods legitimately produced overseas but imported into the United States via unauthorized distribution channels, infra) and "overruns" (goods produced without authorization by a licensee) are expressly *excluded* from the Act's coverage. The real problem with criminal sanctions as a remedy for counterfeiting is to persuade public prosecutors to take these crimes seriously and to allocate law enforcement resources to them.

§ 20.7 International Solutions

International solutions to the problem of intellectual property piracy have been no less elusive. A draft "Anti-Counterfeiting Code" received close scrutiny in the Uruguay Round of negotiations. Although the TRIPs accord incorporates some coverage of counterfeiting, it is not the encompassing anti-counterfeiting code that the developed world sought. The TRIPs agreement does mandate border measures to block the release of counterfeit goods into domestic circulation. It also requires criminal penalties for willful trademark counterfeiting or copyright piracy undertaken on a commercial scale. However, the TRIPs agreement does not reject the practice of re-exportation of counterfeit merchandise. Re-exportation has the practical effect of pushing the problem on some other jurisdiction and does not represent a final solution from the point of view of the infringed party.

France and Italy have made it illegal to knowingly purchase counterfeit goods. For example, if a student buys a "Louis Vuitton" bag for $15 in a Paris or Florence flea market, he or she may be arrested, fined and imprisoned. France has gone a step further. A new agency monitors Internet piracy. French offenders are subject to a "three strikes" rule: Two warnings are issued before Net accesses can be terminated and fines imposed by court order. South

---

[27] 18 U.S.C. § 2320 *et seq.*

Korea and Taiwan also employ warnings and penalties against illegal downloading.

Various United States statutes authorize the President to withhold trade benefits from or apply trade sanctions to nations inadequately protecting the intellectual property rights of U.S. citizens. This is true of the Caribbean Basin Economic Recovery Act of 1983,[28] the Generalized System of Preferences Renewal Act of 1984,[29] the Trade and Tariff Act of 1984 (amending Section 301 of the 1974 Trade Act), and Title IV of the 1974 Trade Act as it applies to most-favored-nation tariffs.[30] Slowly this carrot and stick approach has borne fruit. Under these pressures for example, Singapore drafted a new copyright law, Korea new patent and copyright laws, and Taiwan a new copyright, patent, fair trade and an amended trademark law. Brazil introduced legislation intended to allow copyrights on computer programs. Though these changes have been made, there is some doubt as to the rigor with which the new laws will be enforced when local jobs and national revenues are lost.

§ 20.8 Gray Market Goods

One of the most controversial areas of customs law concerns "gray market goods," goods produced abroad with authorization and payment but which are imported into unauthorized markets. Trade in gray market goods has dramatically increased in recent years, in part because fluctuating currency exchange rates create opportunities to import and sell such goods at a discount from local price levels. Licensors and their distributors suddenly find themselves competing in their home or other "reserved" markets with products made abroad by their own licensees. Or, in the reverse, startled licensees find their licensor's products intruding on their local market shares. In either case, third party importers and exporters are often the immediate source of the gray market goods, and they have little respect for who agreed to what in the licensing agreement. When pressed, such third parties will undoubtedly argue that any attempt through licensing at allocating markets or customers is an antitrust or competition law violation.

In times of floating exchange rates, importers have found that by shopping around the world for gray market goods they can undercut local prices with "parallel imports." This explains in large part the dramatic growth in trade in gray market goods in recent years. Gray market goods have become an important source of price

---

28   See Chapter 10.
29   See Chapter 10.
30   See Chapter 10.

competition in the United States marketplace, particularly in years when the U.S. dollar is strong. Some retail firms, like K-Mart, are major traders of gray market goods.

A decline of the dollar against the Japanese Yen or the Euro would decrease the flow of gray market *imports* from those sources, but perhaps increase the flow of gray market *exports* from the United States to those countries. For example, assume a Cadillac sells in the United States for $30,000 and a Mercedes sells in Germany for 30,000 Euros. At an exchange rate of .75 dollars to the Euro, the dollar is very strong. The Mercedes sells in Germany for $22,500; the Cadillac sells in the United States for 40,000 Euros. This encourages importing cars bought in Germany to the United States. The cars are converted to U.S. specifications for $2,000 and sold for $24,500 by nonauthorized companies, often independent Mercedes repair shops. Then the dollar drops in value to 1.50 dollars to the Euro. Now you must pay $45,000 in Germany to buy a Mercedes, but need only 20,000 Euros to buy a Cadillac. This encourages exporting cars bought in the United States to Germany.

In most cases, the manufacturer is not unhappy at selling the product, whether it is sold in the regular market or gray market. But the manufacturer may do better when its product is sold through the regular distributor. First, this lessens the need to face angry authorized distributors as in the above Mercedes situation. Furthermore, when the dollar is strong there is a very substantial price differential. This profit is effectively divided between the manufacturer and the U.S. distributor.

§ 20.9 Gray Market Goods__The U.S. Customs Service Position

In the early part of the 20th century, gray market litigation provoked a Supreme Court decision blocking French cosmetics from entering the United States.[31] A United States firm was assigned the U.S. trademark rights for French cosmetics as part of the sale of the United States business interests of the French producer. The assignee successfully obtained infringement relief in federal district court against Katzel, an importer of the French product benefiting from exchange rate fluctuations. On appeal, the Second Circuit vacated this relief in a holding which followed a line of cases allowing "genuine goods" to enter the U.S. market in competition with established sources. The Supreme Court ultimately reversed the Second Circuit emphasizing the trademark ownership (not

---

[31]   A. Bourjois & Co. v. Katzel, 260 U.S. 689 (1923).

license) and independent public good will of the assignee as reasons for its reversal.

Genuine Goods Exclusion Act. Congress, before the Supreme Court reversal, passed the Genuine Goods Exclusion Act, now appearing as Section 526 of the Tariff Act of 1930.[32] This Act bars *unauthorized importation* of goods bearing trademarks of U.S. citizens. Registration of such marks with the Customs Service can result in the seizure of unauthorized imports. Persons dealing in such imports may be enjoined, required to export the goods, destroy them or obliterate the offending mark, as well as pay damages.

The Act has had a checkered history in the courts and Customs Service. The Customs Service view (influenced by antitrust policy) was that genuine (gray market) goods may be excluded only when the foreign and U.S. trademark rights are not under common ownership or control, or those rights have been used without authorization. The practical effect of this position was to admit most gray market goods into the U.S., thereby providing substantial price competition, but uncertain coverage under manufacturers' warranty, service and rebate programs. Some firms, like K-Mart, excel at gray market importing and may provide independent warranty and repair service contracts. Since 1986, New York and California require disclosure that manufacturers' programs may not apply to sellers of gray market goods.

An attempt in 1985 by Duracell to exclude gray market batteries alternatively under Section 337 of the Tariff Act of 1930 as an unfair import practice was upheld by the U.S. International Trade Commission, but denied relief by President Reagan in deference to the Customs Service position.[33] Despite that position, injunctive relief under trademark or copyright law is sometimes available against gray market importers and distributors.[34] Injunctive relief, however, applies only to the parties and does not prohibit gray market imports or sales by others. This remedy is thus useful, but normally insufficient.

A split in the federal Courts of Appeal as to the legitimacy in light of the Genuine Goods Exclusion Act of the Customs Service position on gray market imports resulted in a U.S. Supreme Court

---

[32]   19 U.S.C. § 1526.

[33]   *See* Duracell, Inc. v. U.S. Int'l Trade Commission, 778 F.2d 1578 (Fed. Cir. 1985). Compare Bourdeau Bros. Inc. v. U.S. Int'l Trade Commission, 444 F.3d 1317 (Fed. Cir. 2006) (goods produced in U.S., exported to Europe, importation can be blocked if materially different from goods sold in USA).

[34]   *See especially* CBS, Inc. v. Scorpio Music Distributors, Inc., 569 F. Supp. 47 (E.D. Pa. 1983), *aff'd* 738 F.2d 424 (3d Cir. 1984) (copyright infringement relief granted); NEC Electronics, Inc. v. CAL Circuit Abco, Inc., 810 F.2d 1506 (9th Cir. 1987) (trademark infringement relief denied).

ruling.[35] In an extremely technical, not very policy-oriented decision, the Supreme Court arrived at a compromise. The Customs Service can continue to permit entry of genuine goods when there is common ownership or control of the trademarks. The Service must seize such goods only when they were authorized (licensed), but the marks are not subject to common ownership or control. For these purposes, "common ownership or control" is defined as a 50 percent shareholding or the effective control of policy and operations.

Gray market goods originating from such "affiliated companies" will still be allowed to enter the United States.[36] However, a Fifth Circuit decision indicates that close and profitable business ties between a foreign trademark owner and the foreign owner of U.S. trademark rights do not amount to "common control." Rolex was thus able to obtain a Customs Service forfeiture ruling against gray market imports of its watches by Wal-Mart. The court applied a strict common ownership test to Section 526.[37] The Tenth Circuit affirmed summary judgment in favor of an Oklahoma company owning U.S. trademark rights to "Vittoria" for bicycle tires. The rights were transferred by an Italian company, the maker of the tires. The "common control" exception to gray market trademark protection did not apply because there was at most "a close business relationship" between the two companies.[38]

Many believe that the bulk of U.S. imports of gray market goods have continued under the Supreme Court's *K Mart* ruling. However, this perspective is somewhat undermined by treatment of gray market imports under other statutory regimes.

§ 20.10 Gray Market Goods__Trademark and Copyright Remedies

Section 42 of the Lanham Trademark Act prohibits the importation of goods that copy or simulate a registered U.S. trademark.[39] In *K Mart,* the U.S. Supreme Court specifically declined to review the legality of barring gray market goods under this provision. Some courts have denied relief under Section 42 against gray market imports. These cases stress the absence of consumer confusion when genuine goods are involved.[40] Other

---

   35   K Mart Corp. v. Cartier, Inc., 486 U.S. 281 (1988).

   36   *See* 19 C.F.R. §§ 133.21(c), 133.2(d).

   37   United States v. Eighty-Three Rolex Watches, 992 F.2d 508 (5th Cir. 1993).

   38   Vittoria North America, LLC v. Euro-Asia Imports, Inc., 278 F.3d 1076 (10th Cir. 2001).

   39   15 U.S.C. § 1120.

   40   *See, e.g.,* Monte Carlo Shirt v. Daewoo International (America) Corp., 707 F.2d 1054 (9th Cir. 1983); Bell & Howell: Mamiya Co. v. Masel Supply Co. Corp., 719 F.2d 42 (2d Cir. 1983).

courts have reached conclusions that in the absence of adequate disclosure Section 42 is actionable against gray market goods that materially differ in physical content from those sold in the United States.[41] However, when there are material differences, labeling suffices to avoid Section 42.[42]

A Second Circuit decision relying upon Section 32 of the Lanham Act also supports blocking imports of materially different gray market goods.[43] In this case, Cabbage Patch dolls produced in Spain under license came with birth certificates, adoption papers and instructions in Spanish, but were otherwise the same product. The U.S. manufacturer refused to register these dolls, leading to numerous complaints by parents and children. These complaints supported the court's injunction against importation of the dolls from Spain under Section 32. Section 32 provides trademark owners with remedies against persons who, without consent by the owner, use a "reproduction, counterfeit, copy or colorable imitation" of a mark so as to cause confusion, mistake or deception.[44] However, a Ninth Circuit decision relying of Sections 32 and 43(a) (country of origin markings) of the Lanham Act leads to the opposite conclusion, finding no support for the argument that gray market imports can be remedied under those provisions.[45]

Sections 103 and 602 of the Copyright Act provide that importing goods into the U.S. without the consent of copyright owners is an infringement.[46] But Section 109 limits the distribution rights of copyright owners under what is known as the "first sale doctrine."[47] This doctrine limits the owner's control over copies to their first sale or transfer. Two Third Circuit decisions split on the use of copyright law against gray market imports in spite of the first sale doctrine.[48] In *Sebastian,* the Third Circuit held that a U.S. manufacturer who sells goods with copyrighted labels to foreign distributors is barred by the first sale doctrine from obtaining

---

[41]   *See* Lever Bros. Co. v. United States, 877 F.2d 101 (D.C. Cir. 1989); Ferrero U.S.A., Inc. v. Ozak Trading, Inc., 753 F. Supp. 1240 (D.N.J. 1991), *aff'd* 935 F.2d 1281 (3d Cir. 1991); Société Des Produits Nestle, S.A. v. Casa Helvetia, Inc., 982 F.2d 633 (1st Cir. 1992); Lever Bros. Co. v. United States, 981 F.2d 1330 (D.C. Cir. 1993).

[42]   *See* 19 C.F.R. § 133.23.

[43]   Original Appalachian Artworks v. Granada Electronics, Inc., 816 F.2d 68 (2d Cir. 1987). *Accord* Société Des Produits Nestle, S.A. v. Casa Helvetia, Inc., 982 F.2d 633 (1st Cir. 1992).

[44]   15 U.S.C. § 1114.

[45]   NEC Electronics v. CAL Circuit Abco, Inc., 810 F.2d 1506 (9th Cir. 1987)

[46]   17 U.S.C. § 106.

[47]   17 U.S.C. § 109.

[48]   Columbia Broadcasting System v. Scorpio Music Distributors, 569 F. Supp. 47 (E.D. Pa. 1983), *aff'd* 738 F.2d 424 (3d Cir. 1984) (relief granted); Sebastian Int'l, Inc. v. Consumer Contacts (PTY), Ltd., 847 F.2d 1093 (3d Cir. 1988) (relief denied).

import infringement relief. In *Scorpio,* where the goods were manufactured abroad under license by the U.S. copyright holder, such relief was granted. The Supreme Court subsequently held that the first sale doctrine bars injunctive relief under the Copyright Act[49] against goods previously exported from the United States. Reversing the Ninth Circuit, the Supreme Court has also barred injunctive relief under the Copyright Act even if the goods are foreign made.[50]

§ 20.11 Gray Market Goods in Other Jurisdictions

An excellent review of the treatment of gray market goods in other jurisdictions is presented in a somewhat dated article by Takamatsu.[51] This review may be of particular interest to U.S. *exporters* of gray market goods. For the most part, his 1982 review indicates that other jurisdictions permitted gray market goods to enter. This was true of the *Parker Pen* cases under Japanese law,[52] the *Maja* case under German law[53] and the *Agfa-Gevaert* case in Austria,[54] all of which are reviewed by Takamatsu. Canadian Supreme Court law strongly supports free trade in gray market goods.[55]

The legal analysis contained in these opinions has been very influential in European Union licensing law.[56] EU law basically posits that once goods subject to intellectual property rights of common origin have been sold on the market with authorization, the holders can no longer block importation of those goods ("parallel imports") through the use of national property rights. Such use is not thought to have been intended as part of the original grant of rights and is said to have been "exhausted" upon sale. An extensive

---

[49]   Quality King Distributors, Inc. v. L'anza Research International, Inc., 523 U.S. 135 (1998).

[50]   *See* Kirtsaeng v. John Wiley & Sons, 133 S.Ct. 1351 (2013) (*reversing* Parfums Givenchy, Inc. v. Drug Emporium, 38 F.3d 477 (9th Cir. 1994)) and Costco Wholesale Corp. v. Omega SA, 562 U.S. 40 (2010) (*affirming by a tie vote,* 541 F 3d 982 (9th Cir. 2008)).

[51]   Kaoru Takamatsu, *Parallel Importation of Trademarked Goods: A Comparative Analysis,* 57 WASH. L. REV. 433 (1982).

[52]   NMC Co. v. Schulyro Trading Co., Feb. 20, 1970 (Osaka Dist. Ct., 234 Hanrei Taimuzu 57), reprinted in English at 16 JAPANESE ANNUAL OF INT'L LAW 113 (1972) affirmed by Osaka High Court. *See* Nestle Nihon K.K. v. Sanhi Shoten (unreported Tokyo Dist. Ct. May 29, 1965) summarized in T. Doi, DIGEST OF JAPANESE COURT DECISIONS IN TRADEMARKS AND UNFAIR COMPETITION CASES (1971).

[53]   Fed. Sup. Ct. (W.Ger.), Jan. 22, 1964, 41 Bundesgerichtshof 84 summarized in 54 Trademark Rep. 452 (1964).

[54]   Agfa-Gevaert GmbH v. Schark, Sup. Ct. (Aus.), Nov. 30, 1970.

[55]   Consumers Distributing Co., Ltd. v. Seiko Time Canada Ltd., 1 Sup. Ct. 583 (1984). *But see* Mattel Canada Inc. v. GTS Acquisitions, 27 C.P.R. (3d) 358 (1989) (preliminary injunction against identical gray market goods).

[56]   *See* Chapter 19.

body of law permits parallel imports (even of qualitatively different goods) as part of the promotion of the Common Market and rejects attempts to divide the market territorially along the lines of national property rights. Product labeling as to source and contents is thought sufficient notice to consumers that qualitatively different goods are involved.

In a major decision, the European Court of Justice has ruled that trademark rights can be used to block gray market imports into the Common Market. These rights are not exhausted once the goods are voluntarily put into the stream of international commerce. An Austrian maker of high-quality sunglasses was therefore entitled to bar imports from Bulgaria.[57] In *Zino Davidoff, SA*, and *Levi Strauss* the European Court of Justice affirmed the right of trademark owners to block gray market sales of their goods sold at prices below those they utilize in the EU. No "implied consent" to gray market imports was found via the sale of goods outside the EU.[58]

§ 20.12 Section 337 Proceedings___Complaint and Response

Section 337 complaints may be filed by domestic producers with the International Trade Commission in Washington, D.C., provided the complainants have not agreed by contract to litigate all disputes elsewhere.[59] The complainant must be a representative of the industry. The complaint itself must contain a statement of the facts alleged to constitute unfair import methods or acts. The complaint must also specify instances when unlawful importations occurred, the names and addresses of respondents, and if they exist, a description of any related court proceeding. The complaint must describe the domestic industry that is affected by the import practices and the petitioner's interest in that industry. If the case involves intellectual property rights, detailed information regarding the patent, copyright, trademark or mask work must be provided. Lastly, the complaint must indicate what relief is sought.[60] Section 337 complainants are subject to the "duty of candor" recognized in *Convertible Rowing Exercisers*.[61] This duty is violated by (1) a

---

[57] Silhouette International v. Hartlauer, 1998 WL 1043033 (July 16, 1998).

[58] Cases C–414–99, 415/99 and 416/99, 2001 WL 1347061 (Levi jeans sold by supermarket in Britain) (Nov. 20, 2001).

[59] *See* Texas Instruments Inc. v. Tessera, Inc., 231 F.3d 1325 (Fed. Cir. 2000) (agreement that all litigation must take place in California precludes Section 337 complaint).

[60] C.F.R. § 210.20 (1990).

[61] Inv. No. 337–TA–212, U.S.I.T.C. Pub. No. 2111 (1988).

failure to disclose material information or a submission of false material information and (2) an intent to mislead.

Once a complaint is filed, or the Commission decides to start a Section 337 proceeding on its own initiative, an investigation is normally commenced. The Commission takes the position that it is not obliged to commence an investigation after the filing of a private complaint. Its Office of Unfair Imports (OUI) takes 30 days to examine the sufficiency of the complaint. This Office is an independent party in Section 337 proceedings charged with representing the public interest. Pre-filing review of draft complaints by the OUI is possible, and counsel for the respondents may also seek to have the OUI recommend against proceeding with a Section 337 complaint. Although it is a rare event, the Commission occasionally has declined to pursue a Section 337 investigation. If this happens, the complaint is dismissed.[62]

The Commission has maintained its discretionary authority to review Section 337 complaints despite statutory language which would appear to be mandatory.[63] Thus, it has dismissed complaints where there is insufficient data to support the allegations, or the allegations themselves are insufficient to prove a Section 337 violation.[64] The complainant may of course amend and refile its complaint. Furthermore, a rejection of Section 337 complaints by the Commission can be appealed to the Federal Circuit Court of Appeals.[65] The Commission serves the complaint on foreign parties, thus avoiding the delay of international service of process. Parties who fail to appear can default, and have exclusion orders automatically entered against them.

The respondents in Section 337 proceedings are given an opportunity to submit written briefs regarding the complaint. Such briefs should respond to each allegation in the complaint and set forth any defenses. Section 337 complaint and response requirements are reproduced in Section 20.27 of this chapter. Failure to provide a response to the complaint can result in a determination that the facts alleged in the complaint are deemed admitted.[66] For example, if the complaint is based upon patent infringement, the respondent would typically allege non-infringement by suggesting that the product is not covered by the

---

[62]   See 19 C.F.R. § 210.12.

[63]   See 19 U.S.C. § 1337(b)(1).

[64]   See Certain Fruit Preserves in Containers Having Lids With Gingham Cloth Design, Docket 1056 (May 21, 1984); Certain Architectural Panels, Docket 1122 (November 30, 1984).

[65]   See Syntex Agribusiness, Inc. v. U.S. Int'l Trade Commission, 617 F.2d 290 (C.C.P.A. 1980) and 659 F.2d 1038 (C.C.P.A. 1981).

[66]   19 C.F.R. § 210.21.

patent and/or the invalidity of the patent. An unusual aspect of Section 337 proceedings is the appointment of an investigative attorney by the ITC to represent the public interest. This attorney is a party to the investigation and may participate in discovery and hearings to the full extent of the complainant and respondent.[67]

§ 20.13   Section 337___Temporary Relief

If the Commission decides, in the process of its investigation, that there is reason to believe that a violation of Section 337 has occurred, it may order the goods to be excluded from entry into the United States or permit entry only under a bond as a temporary remedy.[68] Such remedies require proof not only of the reasons to believe in the violation, but also of an immediate and substantial injury to the domestic industry in the absence of a temporary remedy.[69] The statute now requires that the Commission consider the public interest in making temporary remedial decisions in connection with Section 337.

Thus, the Commission ends up balancing the probability of the complainant's success on the merits, the prospect for immediate and substantial harm to the domestic industry if no relief is granted, the harm to the respondent if such relief is granted, and the effect that temporary remedies would have on the public interest.[70] If the Commission is concerned that the complainant may possibly have filed a frivolous claim or that the harm to the respondent is particularly large, it can require the complainant to post a bond in order to get temporary relief. Decisions about temporary relief are made by the administrative law judge in the case, although they may be modified or vacated by the Commission upon review.[71]

§ 20.14   Section 337___Administrative Process

Section 337 investigations normally last one year but may be extended to eighteen months in complicated cases. This relatively short period has been described as "due process with dispatch." Section 337 investigations are the only investigations conducted by the International Trade Commission that are governed by the Administrative Procedure Act. Thus, the investigation will follow the established procedures for discovery under the Federal Rules of Civil Procedure, pre-hearing conferences, an initial determination of the issues by an administrative judge, and final review by the

---

[67]   19 C.F.R. § 210.4.

[68]   19 U.S.C. § 1337(e).

[69]   *See* Certain Apparatus, 12 ITRD 1841, U.S.I.T.C. Pub. No. 1132 (April 1981).

[70]   19 U.S.C. § 1337(e).

[71]   19 C.F.R. § 210.24(17).

Commission.[72] One problem is the frequent need for extraterritorial discovery in Section 337 cases. Another issue is sanctions for abuse of discovery,[73] although findings of default can be made. Section 337 discovery responses are typically due in 10 days, much more rapidly than in civil litigation. Although the Commission is authorized to promulgate rules allowing costs and attorneys' fees as sanctions, it has not yet done so.

In contrast, the Commission has aggressively enforced its protective orders against disclosure of confidential and business information of a proprietary character.[74] At any point during its investigation, the Commission may decide to settle the proceedings by consent order or by agreement of the parties. This happens reasonably often, especially when the parties to an intellectual property case agree to a licensing arrangement. In either case, the Commission will review the motion to terminate or a proposed consent order from the standpoint of the public interest in the proceeding. An arbitration agreement between parties who are contesting a Section 337 proceeding is no grounds for terminating the ITC investigation.[75]

When the International Trade Commission reviews the advisory decision of the administrative law judge in Section 337 proceedings, it need not undertake a review of that entire determination. It is sufficient for purposes of appeal that the Commission decides the case on the basis of a single dispositive issue. For example, in patent infringement litigation, if the Commission decides that there was no infringement, it need not render decisions concerning any other issues in the Section 337 proceeding.[76] Thus it was only this issue that could be appealed to the Federal Circuit Court of Appeals. Put another way, the only issues that can be appealed are those upon which the Commission has decided, and this is true even in cases concerning temporary relief under Section 337.[77]

§ 20.15 Section 337__Sanctions

If the Commission ultimately decides that an unfair import method or act has been committed, it is authorized to issue a cease

---

[72]   See 19 C.F.R. §§ 2210.1–2210.71.

[73]   See Certain Concealed Cabinet Hinges and Mounting Plates, 12 ITRD 1841 (Jan. 8, 1990).

[74]   See Certain Electrically Resistive Monocomponent Toner, 10 ITRD 1672 (1988).

[75]   Farrel Corp. v. U.S. Int'l Trade Comm'n, 949 F.2d 1147 (Fed. Cir. 1991).

[76]   Beloit Corp. v. Valmet Oy, 742 F.2d 1421 (Fed. Cir. 1984).

[77]   See Warner Bros., Inc. v. U.S. Int'l Trade Commission, 787 F.2d 562 (Fed. Cir. 1986).

and desist order or an exclusion order barring the goods from entering the United States. Any violation of those orders is punishable by civil penalties up to $100,000 per day or twice the value of the merchandise in question. Final ITC determinations under Section 337 are appealed directly to the Federal Circuit Court of Appeals.

The Federal Circuit Court of Appeals has ruled that the ITC may impose civil penalties for violation of consent orders (as well as cease and desist orders) that terminate patent infringement investigations under Section 337.[78]

§ 20.16 Section 337__Settlements

As the Section 337 investigation proceeds, the complainant may move for a summary determination by the ITC. This is analogous to summary judgment under the Federal Rules of Civil Procedure.[79] If the complaint concerns patent infringement, one solution is for the parties to enter into a licensing agreement. However, the parties must give the Commission a copy of their complete agreement. The Commission's investigative attorney then comments on the settlement and the administrative law judge makes an initial decision as to whether to terminate the investigation on the basis of the settlement. This determination is sent to the Commission for final approval.[80] The purpose of these procedures is to insure that the public interest is preserved as part of the patent infringement dispute settlement.

In non-patent cases, the typical route for settlement is by consent order. To do this, a joint motion is filed by all of the complainants, the Commission's investigative attorney, and one or more of the respondents.[81] This typically occurs before the commencement of the hearing before the administrative law judge. Consent settlements of this type must contain admissions of all jurisdictional facts, waivers of rights to seek judicial review or other means of challenging the consent order, and an agreement that the enforcement, modification and revocation of the order will be undertaken pursuant to ITC rules. The consent order typically is not deemed to constitute an admission of a violation of Section 337 and usually states that it is undertaken solely for settlement purposes.[82] There is a ten-day notice period which allows any

---

[78] San Huan New Materials High Tech, Inc. v. U.S. Int'l Trade Commission, 161 F.3d 1347 (Fed. Cir. 1998).

[79] 19 C.F.R. § 210.50.

[80] 19 C.F.R. § 210.51.

[81] 19 C.F.R. § 211.20.

[82] 19 C.F.R. § 211.22.

interested party to comment on the proposed termination of a Section 337 proceeding on the basis of a consent order.[83]

§ 20.17   Section 337__ITC Public Interest Review

The International Trade Commission is not required to impose a Section 337 remedy if it finds a violation. Its remedial powers are discretionary. In deciding whether to accept proposed consent orders or to impose any remedy, the Commission is required to consider all of the public comments that have been received, the effect upon the public health and welfare of the United States, the effect upon competitive conditions in the U.S. economy, the effect on production of like or directly competitive articles in the United States, and its effect upon U.S. consumers.[84] The Commission has rarely invoked the public interest exception to Section 337 relief. When it has, the domestic industry typically was unable to supply critically needed items[85] or the public's strong interest in the research overrode patent rights.[86]

§ 20.18   Section 337__ITC General Exclusion of IP Infringing Imports and Cease and Desist Orders

The International Trade Commission may issue three different kinds of remedies under Section 337. The first is an exclusion order of a limited or general nature, and this type of relief predominates in intellectual property cases. The second is a cease and desist order, and this type of relief is often issued if there are significant inventories of the offending product already imported into the United States. The effect of such a cease and desist order is to prevent further distribution within the country. The Commission is expressly authorized to issue exclusion orders and cease and desist orders together.[87] In either case, the Commission may authorize entry of the goods under bond pending the President's final determination in the proceeding. The amount of the bond varies from case to case, but is generally intended to offset the competitive advantages that are perceived to exist. Such bonds have ranged upwards to 600 percent of the value of the imports.[88] Many Section 337 bonds have been determined by measuring the difference

---

[83]   19 C.F.R. § 211.20.

[84]   19 U.S.C. § 1337(d), (e), (f).

[85]   *See* Automatic Crankpin Grinders, 2 ITRD 5121, U.S.I.T.C. Pub. No. 1022 (1979) (engine parts needed to meet fuel efficiency standards); Certain Fluidized Supporting Apparatus, 7 ITRD 1089 (1984).

[86]   Certain Inclined-Field Acceleration Tubes, 2 ITRD 5572 (1980).

[87]   19 U.S.C. § 1337(f).

[88]   *See* Certain Cube Puzzles, *supra*.

between the complainant's prices in the U.S. and the customs value of the imports. Forfeiture orders are relatively uncommon and typically follow notice by the Secretary of the Treasury that forfeiture would result from further importation of goods that offend Section 337.

Plaintiffs usually wish to obtain general exclusion orders in intellectual property cases. Such orders will keep out all infringing products. The problem with this approach is that it may unfairly bar the importation of goods that resemble but do not infringe the patented product. This is a generally undesirable result that the Commission will try to avoid.[89] Consequently, the Commission requires those seeking general exclusion orders to prove a widespread pattern of unauthorized use of the patented invention and reasonable inferences that foreign manufacturers other than the respondents may attempt to enter the United States market with infringing goods.[90]

A widespread pattern of unauthorized use can be demonstrated by the importation of the infringing goods by numerous companies, by pending foreign infringement suits based upon foreign patents which correspond to the United States patent at issue, or by other evidence which demonstrates a history of unauthorized foreign use of the invention.[91] In providing evidence that it is reasonable to infer that other foreign manufacturers may attempt to enter the U.S. market, plaintiffs may offer proof of the established demand for the product, the existence of a distribution system in the United States for its marketing, the cost to foreigners of manufacturing or creating a facility capable of manufacturing the goods, the ease and number of foreign manufacturers who could retool so as to produce the offending article, and the cost of such retooling.[92] As these criteria suggest, obtaining a general exclusion order is not always easy, and certainly not automatic.

§ 20.19 Section 337__Presidential Veto

Any order issued by the International Trade Commission under Section 337 goes into effect immediately. However, the President may veto that order for public policy reasons.[93] Vetoes by the President of Commission orders in Section 337 proceedings are rare

---

[89]   *See* Certain Cloisonne Jewelry, 8 ITRD 2028, U.S.I.T.C. Pub. No. 1822 (March 1986).

[90]   *See* Certain Airless Spray Pumps and Components Thereof, 3 ITRD 2041, U.S.I.T.C. Pub. No. 1199 (1981).

[91]   *Id.*

[92]   *Id.*

[93]   19 U.S.C. § 1337(j).

and not generally reviewable by the courts.[94] The President has sixty days within which to make a decision concerning ITC orders under Section 337. If the President does not take action within this period, then the order becomes final.[95] Final ITC orders under Section 337 remain in effect until the Commission decides that there is no longer reason to continue the order.[96] Any violation of an outstanding ITC order under Section 337 can incur a civil penalty of up to $10,000 per day or twice the domestic value of the goods sold, whichever is greater.[97]

§ 20.20 Section 337__ITC Opinion Letters

The ITC follows the practice of issuing informal or formal opinion letters in connection with Section 337 matters. Requests for informal opinions from the ITC staff should be addressed to the Assistant General Counsel of the Commission. Formal opinions actually issued by the Commission itself may be obtained if the staff opinion letter is adverse or a formal opinion is just simply necessary. Requests for such opinions are filed with the Secretary of the Commission.[98]

---

[94]   Duracell, Inc. v. U.S. Int'l Trade Commission, 778 F.2d 1578 (Fed. Cir. 1985).

[95]   *Id.*

[96]   19 U.S.C. § 1337(k).

[97]   19 U.S.C. § 1337(j).

[98]   19 C.F.R. § 211.54.

Chapter 21

INTRODUCTION TO FOREIGN DIRECT INVESTMENT

Table of Sections

§ 21.1 Why Invest Abroad?

Foreign direct investment (FDI) may be defined as sending capital and establishing business operations abroad in hopes of earning a profit. It often occurs after less extensive contact with the foreign country in the form of selling goods or transferring technology to have goods produced under license in a foreign nation. Individuals and multinationals have many reasons to invest abroad. It may be part of an initial overall plan to produce goods or provide services worldwide. It may be a strategy for expansion after the home market is saturated. It may be done to take advantage of lower production costs, as a result of cheaper labor, less regulation or lower taxes. A further step, increasingly undertaken by companies in the United States and the European Union, is to move the corporate headquarters or place of incorporation to another country where the organizational and regulatory laws are more favorable.

A foreign investment may be less than fully voluntary in some instances. Avoiding high tariffs may be a factor in deciding whether to invest. An investment might be considered when a licensee abroad is creating problems and the investor believes it can make a better product or provide a better service on its own. Poor-quality products or services produced by licensees is often the reason for assuming control of production abroad.

Enterprises which undertake foreign investment are referred to by several names, including multinational corporations (MNCs) or multinational enterprises (MNEs), or transnational corporations (TNCs) or transnational enterprises (TNEs). Foreign investment is a major part of the business of many companies, particularly those chartered in developed nations. Especially since the 1980s, multinational enterprises have moved toward global production and division of labor.

§ 21.2 The Law Governing Foreign Investment

There is no single comprehensive source for the law of foreign investment. Rather, governance of multinational enterprises and their operations may be divided into three spheres: governance by the home nation (that is, the country where the investor is based); governance by the host nation (that is, the country where the investment is made); and governance by international organizations and international law. As described below, home countries generally impose relatively few restrictions on foreign investment, and international governance remains infrequent and contested. As a result, foreign investment is most broadly regulated by the country in which it is located.

Governance by Home Nations. Under international law, countries are generally entitled to regulate the extraterritorial activities of their citizens (including corporations and other business entities created under their laws).[1] However, in practice extraterritorial activities are often not regulated, or regulated only to a limited extent.

Extraterritorial regulation may arise in two ways. First, laws may be enacted to deal with domestic issues but worded broadly so that they could also apply to activities elsewhere. As discussed below, in the United States there is a presumption against extraterritorial application of U.S. law.[2] However, some important regulatory regimes, most notably antitrust, have been applied

---

[1]   Restatement (Third) of Foreign Relations Law of the United States, § 402 (1987). "Extraterritorial" refers to activities not within a nation's territory.

[2]   RJR Nabisco, Inc. v. European Community, 136 S.Ct. 2090 (2016); Morrison v. National Australia Bank Ltd., 561 U.S. 247 (2010). *See* Chapter 26, § 26.8.

extraterritorially to conduct with effects in the United States.[3] Second, laws may address specific foreign policy issues with the express understanding that they apply to foreign conduct. Examples include the Foreign Corrupt Practices Act (FCPA), export licensing regulations and antiboycott laws.[4] There are other laws that affect multinationals' actions abroad, such as tax laws that may encourage investment in friendly nations, customs provisions allowing assembly abroad of U.S.-made parts with duties applied only to the value added abroad when the products re-enter the United States, and the generalized system of preferences (GSP) that is intended to assist development. In general, however, home nations tend to enact laws that are in the best interests of the home nation, not to protect the interests of the host nations or their citizens.[5]

Governance by Host Nations. Because the activities and operations of foreign investment take place principally in the host nation, it is not surprising that they are principally governed by host-country law. In part, this is simply because the investment is subject to the general laws of the place where it is located, as are all other persons and entities, domestic or foreign, located there. In addition, however, most countries (especially in the developing world) have laws that apply specifically to foreign investment. These laws may be favorable, to the extent countries want to encourage foreign investment as a means of economic development, or they may be unfavorable, reflecting fears that foreign investment can be a threat to national sovereignty or to the well-being of local people and businesses.

Host nation laws enacted in the 1960s and 1970s to govern foreign investment tended to be very restrictive. Some of their characteristics are discussed below.[6] Mandatory joint ventures and other restrictions on foreign ownership and management were key elements.[7] But foreign investors in developing nations with restrictive laws often were able to avoid joint ventures and related limitations. An "operational code" or unwritten law existed that allowed much-needed foreign investment to avoid the harsh rules of the host nation that were generally believed to be mandatory.[8]

---

[3]   *See, e.g.*, Hartford Fire Ins. Co. v. California, 509 U.S. 764 (1993) (antitrust); Steele v. Bulova Watch Co., 344 U.S. 280 (1952) (trademarks).

[4]   *See* Chapters 14, 15 and 16.

[5]   A partial exception in U.S. law is the Alien Tort Statute, which may provide some remedy against human rights abuses. *See* § 21.12 below.

[6]   *See* §§ 21.3–21.5 below.

[7]   *See, e.g.*, Wolfgang G. Friedmann & J.P. Beguin, JOINT INTERNATIONAL BUSINESS VENTURES IN DEVELOPING COUNTRIES (1971).

[8]   *See* § 21.6 below.

Beginning in the late 1980s and continuing to the present, the restrictive laws began to be dismantled. By the early 1990s the earlier laws had often been replaced by laws encouraging foreign investment. The changes were both internally induced after the financial crises of the early 1980s, when foreign debts could not be paid by many nations, and externally induced in order to participate in the World Trade Organization (WTO) and in regional pacts such as the North American Free Trade Agreement (NAFTA).[9] In addition, the fall of the Soviet Union and the opening of many formerly nonmarket economies to the international economy resulted in more destinations for investment and further contributed to a global embrace of market economics. Thus the nationalizations of the 1960s and 1970s gave way to privatizations in the 1980s and 1990s; investment restrictions gave way to investment incentives, as nations that had rejected foreign investment now welcomed it, and involuntary joint ventures gave way to voluntary joint ventures or wholly foreign-owned investment. Today, many host nations (and states or provinces within nations) often strongly promote foreign investment and offer diverse incentives to foreign investors.[10]

But even though this liberalization has provided investors with significant opportunities in many foreign nations, obstacles to foreign investment remain, and old ones may be exhumed as governments change.[11] Subsequent sections focus on some of the typical regulations that investors may confront in attempting to establish, operate and withdraw from enterprises in foreign countries.

Governance by International Organizations and International Law. International organizations have accomplished little in regulating international investment. One obvious possible source of regulation is the United Nations, whose various committees[12] have considered the issues arising from multinational corporations and sought to develop various guidelines for conduct. But the United Nations and its subsidiary organizations have had little success in developing an effective, widely accepted regulatory scheme for multinationals. This should not be surprising because the United

---

[9]   *See* Chapter 17.

[10]   *See, e.g.*, Ajay Sharma, *A Comparative Analysis of the Chinese and Indian FDI Regimes*, 15 CHI.-KENT J. INT'L & COMP. L. 35 (2015); Rodrigo Polanco Lazo, *Legal Framework of Foreign Investment in Chile*, 18 L. & BUS. REV. AM. 203 (2013).

[11]   Recent years have seen sharp turns away from foreign investment in some countries formerly open to it, such as Venezuela.

[12]   *E.g.*, the U.N. Conference on Trade and Development (UNCTAD), the U.N. Commission on International Trade Law (UNCITRAL), and the U.N. Economic and Social Council (ECOSOC).

Nations is a large organization with diverse cultural, economic, and political norms. However laudable have been the efforts to develop a code of conduct for multinationals, the record to date has not been impressive.

Another source of international guidelines is the Organisation for Economic Cooperation and Development (OECD). The OECD is composed of the principal developed nations plus a number of higher-income developing countries. The OECD recommends only a modest form of "governance" through model laws that can be enacted into national laws, as well as model bilateral treaties such as tax treaties and guidelines for the conduct of multinational enterprises. The OECD also sponsors multilateral treaties such as the Convention on Combating Bribery of Foreign Officials in International Business Transactions (see Chapter 15) and the unsuccessful Multilateral Agreement on Investment (see Chapter 23).

Treaties play an important though limited role in governing international investment. As discussed below in Chapter 23, Bilateral Investment Treaties (BITs) attempt to provide some protection for foreign investors and investments. Similar protections are often incorporated into free trade agreements (FTAs) such as NAFTA. The WTO also has an Agreement on Trade-Related Investment Measures (TRIMs), which provides some protection. These agreements do not, however, typically govern the activities of the investor.

Finally, customary international law[13] may play a role in foreign investment in two senses. First, as discussed in Chapter 24, customary international law provides some protection for investments against expropriation and related interference by the host government, although the extent of that protection is debated. Second, international law may provide some basic rules regarding protection of human rights and the environment that investments must respect, although again the scope of these rules is much debated (see Section 21.12 below). In both cases, even if there is theoretical agreement on standards, enforcement may be difficult.

§ 21.3   Host Country Restrictions on Foreign Investment___Restrictions on Entry

Some nations make *entry* very difficult by mandatory review of proposed investments, requirements of joint ventures or exemptions gained only after long negotiation and concessions, restrictions on

---

[13]   Customary international law is unwritten law that "results from a general and consistent practice of states followed by them from a sense of legal obligation." Restatement (Third) of Foreign Relations Law of the United States, § 102(2) (1987).

acquisitions, and numerous levels of permission required from various ministries and agencies. For example, Mexico, until the late 1980s, had all of these restrictions. But by 1994 it had repealed nearly all of them, a necessary change for Mexico to participate in NAFTA. As discussed above, in general the trend has been toward much greater openness to foreign investment, although that varies from country to country, and even relatively open countries may have significant restrictions in some areas.

Prohibitions on Ownership in Certain Sectors. Almost every nation prohibits foreign investment in certain sectors of its economy. Both developed and developing nations limit investment where national security is threatened. (See Chapter 22.) But developing nations often have much wider prohibitions based on the belief that certain sectors of the economy should be owned by the state rather than operated privately for profit. Foreign investment is most often prohibited in the exploitation of the nation's most important natural resources. Mexico, for example, until recently prohibited nearly all foreign investment in the petroleum industry.[14] Other areas often restricted in various nations relate to the nation's infrastructure, such as transportation, communications and electricity, or industrial sectors such as petrochemical production. U.S. investors in particular may be surprised by the extent to which other nations restrict all private ownership in certain sectors and industries.[15]

Reservation of Investment to Domestic Private Investors. There may also be industries where private rather than national ownership is permitted, but the private owners must be host-nation nationals. The reasons may be no greater than protectionism and the power of lobbying efforts of domestic industry which does not wish to compete with foreign-owned investment, although it may also reflect strategic decisions about the control of key sectors of the economy.

For example, Canada's early foreign investment regulations discouraged foreign investment in railroads by limiting ownership of Canadian railroads receiving government aid to British subjects. Canada also restricted investment in natural resources, limiting oil

---

[14] *See* Tim R. Samples, *A New Era for Energy in Mexico? The 2013–14 Energy Reform*, 50 TEX. INT'L L.J. 603 (2016); Kyle Doherty, *From "The Oil Is Ours!" to Liberalization: Resource Nationalism and the Mexican Energy Reform*, 53 HOUS. L. REV. 245 (2015).

[15] As in Mexico, these restrictions may appear in a nation's constitution. If a foreign investment law is inconsistent with the nation's constitution, but is not questioned by the current government, problems may arise for the foreign investor if a later government is not inclined to view the investment law as liberally as the prior government. There may be no process of judicial review to test legislation against the constitution.

and gas leases, mining, and exploration assistance grants to Canadian companies, or foreign companies having at least 50 percent Canadian ownership or being listed on the Canadian stock exchange. Similarly, India reserved some industries to its public sector in its Industrial Policy Resolution of 1948, and in the 1970s India took such a strong position about limiting foreign investment that it attempted to force foreign-owned corporations in India to reduce ownership to less than 50 percent. IBM and Coca-Cola withdrew. Like many nations, India has substantially relaxed its restrictions in the modern era.[16]

In the modern era, if a nation admits private ownership in a specific industry, it may have difficulty reserving that industry for its own nationals; in general, the WTO requires that nations offer the same investment opportunities to foreigners that they offer to their own nationals, under the concept of national treatment.[17]

Foreign Investment Allowed but Limited. Foreign private ownership, even if allowed, may be limited to joint ventures, and possibly to only minority interests. In some joint venture laws, it appears at first that all areas are open to foreign investment, because the law does not reserve any spheres of activity for the state or its nationals. But if investments must be approved by a government agency exercising broad discretion, investment may in practice be refused if it is not structured as a joint venture.

The equity percentages allowed to be owned by foreign investors have varied with the type of industry and the host nation's goal in applying the restriction. Sometimes a regime may be flexible to allow the amount to depend on what the investment is perceived to offer the nation, such as needed technology. Sometimes the restrictions may be driven by an economic/social philosophy that majority foreign ownership is inherently threatening to sovereignty. The former concerns may be overcome by the foreign investor through negotiation; the latter often may not.

When nations adopt mandatory joint venture rules, they may limit foreign ownership to a minority share, usually 49 percent. The reason is stated to be a preference to keep a majority of the ownership and control in the hands of nationals. If the nation decides to allow majority control to be owned by foreign investors, it often takes the additional step of allowing the investment to be wholly foreign owned. Equity percentage limitations often do not remain static over time nor are they always enforced consistently.

---

[16]   Gucharan Das, INDIA UNBOUND: FROM INDEPENDENCE TO THE GLOBAL INFORMATION AGE (2000); Note, *Foreign Investment in India*, 26 COLUM. J. TRANSNAT'L L. 609 (1988).

[17]   *See* Chapter 23, § 23.5.

An unwritten code usually allows selective, needed investment to
enter with total foreign ownership. The host nation often will waive
restrictive equity limitations. Several reasons are commonly found
in exception provisions in written investment laws, or in the
unwritten policy of the government (the "operational code"). They
include the following:

(1) *Technology.* Some companies with advanced
technology have been able to avoid joint venture mandates
and retain total ownership. What form of technology will
gain such a waiver is likely to vary from one nation to
another. Where there is a transfer of technology law, it is
likely to state several reasons for registering a technology
agreement which discloses the nation's interests. They
include technology that assists import substitution, the
most up-to-date technology, technology in high priority
areas such as computers, technology intended to enhance
job opportunities, and technology viewed as reasonable in
cost.

(2) *Plant Location.* The willingness to locate a production
facility away from already saturated areas, such as the
most populated cities, will increase chances of gaining a
waiver. Some countries specify areas that the nation feels
are already sufficiently industrialized; others specify areas
that they have designated for industrial development, or
simply mention "less developed" areas.

(3) *Education.* The willingness to establish training
centers in the host nation, especially centers that will
teach jobs to function with new technology, is a method of
gaining a waiver.

(4) *Research and Development.* A major criticism by
many nations is that multinationals only export their
technology while undertaking all the research to develop
that technology in their home nation. Being willing to
undertake some research and development in a host
nation may gain a waiver of maximum equity
participation requirements.

(5) *Balancing Imports with Exports.* Because of chronic
shortages of hard currencies, many host nations grant
waivers of investment restrictions where the investment
will require little demand on the host nation's scarce hard
currency reserves. Thus, exporting part of the production
to earn sufficient hard currency to pay for imports and
cover profit and royalty payments may be decisive. The

host nation's appreciation will increase as the export earnings continue to exceed the import demand.[18]

(6) *Sourcing Capital from Abroad.* In addition to shortages of foreign currency, some nations have shortages of domestic currency to lend to companies. They often wish to reserve that lending capacity for locally owned business. Thus, commencing an investment with capital from outside the host nation is another possible key to gaining a waiver.

Not only developing nations have experimented with limitations on foreign ownership of domestic business. During the 1970s, Canada enacted a restrictive investment law, although the provisions were never as restrictive as the foreign investment laws of major developing nations such as India, Mexico, and Nigeria. Canada's Foreign Investment Review Act of 1973 had complex rules governing foreign investment, especially acquisitions. There was a Foreign Investment Review Agency with powers not greatly different than the powers of the Mexican Foreign Investment Commission. But this restrictive Canadian law was replaced in 1985 with a more investment-encouraging law—the Investment Canada Act. Parts of that Act have remained in place and were integrated into the framework of investment rules under the Canada-United States Free Trade Agreement and subsequently NAFTA.

Reasons for Accepting Equity Restrictions. Foreign investors generally prefer to have total ownership of their foreign investments. Why would a foreign investor agree to limit participation to a minority interest?

An investment in place at the time of enactment of a government demand to either convert to a joint venture or withdraw from the nation may be less costly to continue as a joint venture with a minority position than to withdraw. A local partner may be an asset if market penetration is difficult or political contacts are critical. But it is unlikely that the parent company will increase its investment or transfer the latest technology to the joint venture enterprise. The foreign entity will thus become quite unlike other wholly owned foreign investments of the multinational. It will remain relatively static while other foreign wholly owned company investments receive any needed additional capital and the latest technology.

---

[18]   *See* Vivienne Bath, *Foreign Investment, the National Interest and National Security—Foreign Direct Investment in Australia and China,* 34 SYDNEY L. REV. 5 (2012).

If the market in the host nation has good long term prospects, and the restrictive joint venture laws are viewed as being transitory and likely to be modified in the future, it may be appropriate to accept a joint venture and invest. In Mexico in the 1970s, the willingness of Japanese investors to enter joint ventures with minority participation placed pressure on U.S. firms to accept the same limits on ownership, and even to offer better deals because of the growing Mexican desire to lessen reliance on U.S. investment. But new investment was never as extensive as it would have been without the restrictive laws of the 1970s, illustrated by the rapid increase in new foreign investment since those laws were repealed in the 1990s as Mexico entered the WTO and NAFTA.

If the host nation offers attractive investment incentives, accepting limitations on equity and management participation may be a fair trade, especially if the incentives are available immediately and the joint venture rules are likely to fade in time.

Limitations on Acquisitions. A common method to invest abroad, especially for investments in developed nations, is to acquire a locally owned company in the foreign nation. These acquisitions may encounter additional barriers for a variety of reasons, including antitrust concerns, national security and replacement of a locally owned business by a foreign owned business. Limitations on acquisitions are discussed further in Chapter 22.

§ 21.4 Host Country Restrictions on Foreign Investment___Restrictions During Operations

Some nations allow entry with comparative ease. Once established, however, the operation of the enterprise may be subject to various restrictions that divert time and resources from the main purpose of the investment. Government oversight may be extensive, with frequent visits from different officials to the degree that it becomes more harassment than regulation. These may be part of the nation's general regulatory environment, or they may be (officially or unofficially) directed particularly to foreign investments. For example, restrictions are often imposed on repatriating capital or sending profits or royalties abroad, or receiving hard currency to pay for needed imports.

Limitations on Management. A limitation on the permitted foreign equity may not mean an inability to control the investment. Host nation majority owners may elect foreign management. Some host nation laws, however, stipulate that the percentage of foreign management may be no greater than the permitted equity participation.[19] But even this limitation may be unimportant if the local board is dominated by host nation nationals who are profit-motivated entrepreneurs whose interests are far more aligned with the foreign parent than with host nation government officials who believe that local management should be committed to pursuing the nation's social goals.

Performance Requirements. Performance requirements are typically directed only to foreign investment and take a variety of forms. They may mandate that manufactured products contain a certain minimum percentage of local content, thus protecting many smaller local suppliers. Other requirements may address the use of local labor. Labor requirements may cover both employing local persons and establishing facilities for training new employees, including management level positions. The performance requirements may also mandate that a certain percentage of the production be exported, often in order to balance import needs against exports to avoid drawing on scarce foreign exchange.[20] Finally, there may be mandates regarding the level of technology used in the production, often requiring that the technology be as current as technology of the company used in the home nation. Transfer of technology requirements may also include mandated licenses to locals, or stipulations as to what technologies the investor may introduce. The elimination of performance requirements has been a focus of multinational negotiations, especially in the WTO TRIMs Agreement and in BITs and FTAs, which have diminished use of such restrictions.[21]

§ 21.5 Host Country Restrictions on Foreign Investment__Restrictions on Withdrawal

The withdrawal of foreign investment may be subject to restrictions. These restrictions may affect the ability to repatriate capital, the liability of the foreign parent or other subsidiaries in the country for debts of the withdrawing entity, and the removal of physical assets from the country. Potential investors should

---

[19] Mexico's 1973 Investment Law stated: "The participation of foreign investment in the administration of the business enterprise may not exceed its participation in the capital." Law to Promote Mexican Investment and to Regulate Foreign Investment, art. 5 (1973). The provision does not appear in Mexico's current investment law.

[20] Mexico's 1989 investment regulations required that a company established under the regulations (which exempted the company from joint venture mandates) maintain "during the first three years of its operations, a position of equilibrium in its balance of foreign currency." Regulations of the Law to Promote Mexican Investment and to Regulate Foreign Investment, Diario Oficial, art. 5, IV, 16 May 1989.

[21] *See* Chapter 23.

evaluate the restrictiveness at each level in determining whether or not to invest. Termination of an investment by bankruptcy may introduce the foreign investor to different theories of bankruptcy, including liability of the parent for debts of the foreign subsidiary. Although transnational bankruptcy is a complex subject beyond the scope of this book, at minimum foreign investors should not assume that the effects of failure of a foreign investment can be limited to a single country.[22]

§ 21.6   The Unwritten Law: Operational Codes[23]

If one is asked how multinationals are governed, the common response is to concentrate exclusively on those written laws of host nations that directly or indirectly regulate foreign direct investment. This "Public Code" is typically written law, in contrast to the what might be called Aspirational Declarations—policy statements of national or international institutions[24] which are written but are not law—and the "Operational Code," which as discussed below is often not written but is an essential element of the actual restraints faced by foreign investment. A nation's Public Code includes constitutional provisions affecting foreign direct investment (such as labor and social security rules), statutes, published administrative regulations and widely distributed regulations or decisions of foreign investment agencies.

A nation's Public Code governing foreign direct investment serves as the basis—the mental framework—of regulation of foreign direct investment for that developing nation. But even in those nations that have an extensive Public Code, multinational advisors should not rely on that written law as constituting the total

---

[22]   *See* Paul J. Keenan, *Chapter 15: A New Chapter to Meet the Growing Need to Regulate Cross-Border Insolvencies*, 15 J. BANKR. L. & PRAC. 2 Art. 4 (2006); Jonathan L. Howell, *International Insolvency Law*, 42 INT'L LAW. 113 (2008). UNCITRAL has drafted a Model Law on Cross-Border Insolvency, which has been adopted in approximately 20 countries (including Mexico). *See* United Nations Commission on International Trade Law, UNCITRAL Model Law on Cross-Border Insolvency: The Judicial Perspective (2013), http://www.uncitral.org/uncitral/uncitral_texts/insolvency/2011Judicial_Perspective.html.

[23]   This material is extracted from Michael Wallace Gordon, *Of Aspirations and Operations: The Governance of Multinational Enterprises by Third World Nations*, 16 INTER-AMERICAN L. REV. 301 (1984).

[24]   For example, statements of U.N. bodies regarding foreign investment typically are not law but may reflect the way U.N. members wish foreign investment might be governed. Aspirational Declarations have particular importance not because they constitute international law but because they disclose current sentiments and the direction of possible future law. They create a norm of expected conduct, a moral code promoted by nations as proper and reasonable conduct for multinationals. But they are more than a moral code. They may be a precursor of customary international law or they may become part of the written or unwritten laws of specific host nations governing foreign investment.

framework of investment regulation. Awareness of the Operational Code is necessary, as is awareness of any impact that the nation's participation in the formulation of Aspirational Declarations would have on the functioning of both the Operational and Public Codes.

The Operational Code is the pivotal concept for multinational enterprises to understand. It is important largely because it is not written, or, where written, is not publicly disclosed. Indeed, by definition it may not be publicly disclosed. When elements of the Operational Code become so well-known to the investing community and are no longer considered secret, these elements tend to assume the status of the Public Code, yet remain unwritten. There is consequently a small part of the Public Code which is not formally written. But it is likely to become part of the written Public Code in its next revision. Nevertheless, the government may continue to deny its existence, even in the face of overwhelming public acknowledgment of its existence.

The definition of the Operational Code suggests that it excludes formal unwritten regulations and decisions, but it may also include formal written regulations and decisions that are not publicly available or discoverable. In contrast to formally non-disclosed pronouncements, there are regulations issued by various ministries which have not been kept secret. Although technically part of the Public Code, they exist in such large numbers and are so difficult to locate that they must be considered part of the Operational Code. Brazilian lawyers deal with such rules in the form of what are known as "drawer" regulations. These are regulations that have been issued by various ministries that, even though not labeled secret, have not been publicly disseminated. They are kept in a ministry official's drawer, removed on one occasion when considering a proposed foreign investment, and left in the drawer on another. Even when a drawer regulation is noted by the official it may be applied with an inconsistency permitted by the lack of public disclosure.

The Operational Code is always somewhat at variance with the Public Code, but it must not deviate from the Public Code so extensively that it generates uncertainty that reduces foreign investor confidence in the regulatory structure. The Operational Code directly conflicts with the Public Code when, although positive law provisions of the Public Code do not contain exceptions, the law is waived according to the Operational Code. Any such waiver would be an Operational Code provision directly contrary to written law, which would constitute a serious source of misunderstanding for potential foreign investors. This would be a far more serious problem than where a sizable variance exists between the Codes only in an indirect form. A direct conflict with the Public Code may lead to litigation against a host country over the Operational Code.

An indirect variance exists when positive statements of the Public Code are conditioned by exception provisions, but the government so routinely grants exceptions that the positive law effectively becomes a nullity. It is a potential source of conflict because unknowing foreign investors may believe the Public Code to be routinely applied. If the variance between the Operational Code and Public Code becomes extreme, it is in the best interest of a nation to enact a new investment law. The new law should add to the Public Code those elements of the Operational Code the government wishes to acknowledge as now being appropriately part of the Public Code, and those which it believes create unacceptable conflicts by remaining within the Operational Code. The government will still not acknowledge Operational Code provisions it does not want admitted to the public. For example, Operational Code requirements mandating payments to government officials to expedite services, to grant exceptions, or even to refuse to enforce the Public Code, are not appropriate subjects to publicly acknowledge, and thus remain perpetually hidden in the Operational Code.

It is as important for a host nation government to be aware of the divergence of its Operational Code from the Public Code as it is for multinationals to be aware of that divergence and the progressively changing content of the Operational Code. A company failing to appreciate these movements is not in a secure position to predict future movements if it is ignorant of the existence of the Operational Code and the degree to which it varies from the Public Code. The Operational Code may have different rules applicable to multinationals with different levels of power to demand a lenient Operational Code. If a dominant multinational enterprise in that nation is able to influence the Operational Code, it may function according to a lenient Operational Code but defend its actions on the basis of the more restrictive Public Code. There may be a benefit to the nation because it limits the single, dominant multinational to benefitting from the lenient Operational Code and enforces the more restrictive Public Code for other new investments. The Operational Code thus reflects the nation's need to be flexible so as to obtain investment, particularly in crucial areas. The Operational Code under which a technology company functions in many nations, where it has a monopoly position and where such technology is of critical need to development, is in stark contrast to the Operational Code applicable to a multinational entering an industry saturated by domestic-owned enterprises.

The Operational Code occupies an important position in a host nation's governance of foreign direct investment because it allows the government to treat different multinational enterprises in specific ways thought to be best for the nation. It may even treat different nations' multinational enterprises differently, hidden from obligations of most-favored nation (MFN) treatment. An investor with leverage may be able to enter without accepting a joint venture with majority host nation equity, but other enterprises, even those manufacturing similar products, may be required to comply with a Public Code mandating the joint ventures. More important than permitting unequal treatment, however, is that a potentially unpopular, flexible, Operational Code is hidden from public criticism. Nationalistic pressures may have caused the enactment of a restrictive Public Code for foreign investment that is unrealistic and certain to discourage all investment. By use of a liberal Operational Code, however, the government is able to function pragmatically while public opinion remains nationalist. Conversely, a restrictive Operational Code may continue to reflect nationalistic impulses despite a liberal Public Code imposed by treaty obligations.

The most successful multinational enterprises are those that are aware of the various sources of law affecting foreign investment. This awareness, however, should not be misinterpreted as constituting control by the multinational enterprise. A multinational that appears to have a foreign investment with attributes that differ from provisions of the Public Code may simply understand the Operational Code better than others. The Operational Code cloaks much activity of foreign direct investment. It may lead to increased criticism from the public sector, particularly the press and academia, that may identify practices of multinationals which appear to the public to be at variance with the Public Code. The multinationals, however, have not necessarily violated the law; they have rather followed the Operational Code completely in accordance with the practices of the host nation government.

§ 21.7 Structuring the Foreign Investment

Foreign investment is often done through a subsidiary (a company owned, in whole or part, by the investing company). Sometimes this is a legal requirement, as in countries that require local operations to be conducted by companies incorporated in that country or partially owned by nationals of that country. Often it is a strategic decision. Investors may be allowed to structure their foreign operations as a branch of their larger business, without any legal separation. However, for tax and liability purposes, they will generally prefer to operate through a separate subsidiary, or sometimes through multiple tiers of subsidiaries. Where this structure is adopted, counsel must assure that legal formalities are followed; otherwise the parent and subsidiary might be deemed "alter egos" and treated as a single company, thus losing the benefits of corporate separateness.

The investment subsidiary (sometimes called the "operating company") may be incorporated in the home country, the host country or in a third country, depending on particular circumstances. Often this choice is driven by legal and tax considerations, although it may also reflect strategic choices. Some countries may require or highly prefer a locally incorporated subsidiary, even where the ultimate ownership is foreign. As discussed below, there may be advantages in locating a subsidiary in a low-tax jurisdiction.

Foreign investment may be structured as a joint venture, meaning that ownership is shared between two or more independent foreign investors, or between foreign investors and local investors. As discussed above, sometimes the latter arrangement is required by local law. A joint venture is not typically a distinct corporate form; rather, it usually involves creating a subsidiary to own the investment, with ownership of the subsidiary divided among the joint venturers.[25]

§ 21.8 Financing the Foreign Investment

Some foreign investment is financed using the parent corporation's retained earnings or using traditional borrowing sources for investments in the home country. The foreign investment opens new possible sources, including lending institutions in the foreign host nation and international banks specializing in such projects. Additional possible sources exist, such as government institutions that seek to encourage foreign investment. An example is the U.S. Overseas Private Investment Corporation (OPIC), which in addition to acting as an insurer (see Chapter 25) also provides funds for foreign investment projects.

Project Financing. "Project financing" is a specialized form of financing that is typically used for large industrial, infrastructure and resource extraction projects. Even quite substantial enterprises may not have the ability or desire to take on the debt burdens (often, many billions of dollars) these projects require. Also, agreements with existing lenders may disallow additional

---

[25] A joint venture could be a partnership rather than a corporation, but because of tax and liability issues this is not common.

borrowing if it would exceed defined levels or ratios (such as assets to debts).

The innovation of project financing is that the project itself represents the source for repayment of the project debt.[26] The enterprise that initiates the project (the "sponsor") will create the legal structures for the project, secure the financing, and otherwise arrange the myriad related contracts—but lenders and other creditors must look only to the revenues and assets of the *project* for payment. The sponsor will establish a separate legal entity (a "special purpose vehicle") as a wholly or partially owned subsidiary to construct, own, and operate the project. The separate legal entity, and not the sponsor, will then serve as the borrower for project loans.

This arrangement contains two significant elements. First, the project debt is "off balance sheet" for and "nonrecourse" to the sponsor. That is, the project sponsor does not include the debt on its own books and has no direct legal obligation to repay the debt if the project fails. Second, and closely related, the viability of the project financing—the ability to attract lenders and other investors—will depend on the merits of the project and not on the credit of the sponsor. This means that the sponsor will need to convince the project finance lenders that the project will generate sufficient revenue to repay the loans, with interest, and satisfy any priority claims of other investors. Thus, secure and sufficient revenue from the project represents the foundation of project financing. The project also will need to provide collateral to protect the lenders upon default, and the lenders will need to be assured that they will have secure, first-priority access to that collateral under applicable legal rules.

International Financial Institutions. The principal international financial institutions are the International Monetary Fund (IMF)[27] and the International Bank for Reconstruction and Development (called the World Bank).[28] Both institutions arose from the 1944 Bretton Woods conference, which laid the foundations for the post-

---

[26]   *See* John D. Finnerty, PROJECT FINANCING: ASSET BASED FINANCIAL ENGINEERING (3rd ed. 2013); E.R. Yescombe, PRINCIPLES OF PROJECT FINANCE (2d ed. 2013).

[27]   http://www.imf.org/external/about.htm.

[28]   Technically, the World Bank now consists of two entities, the International Bank for Reconstruction and Development (IBRD) and the International Development Association (IDA), which focuses on the poorest nations. These two and three other entities—the International Finance Corporation (IFC), the Multilateral Investment Guarantee Agency (MIGA), and the International Centre for the Settlement of Investment Disputes (ICSID), make up the World Bank Group. *See* http://www.worldbank.org/en/about.

World War II international financial order. Over 180 countries are now members of the IMF and the World Bank.

The World Bank was designed to facilitate loans by capital surplus countries such as the United States to countries needing foreign investment for economic redevelopment after World War II. Today its principal goal is to assist economic growth in developing countries. The World Bank makes direct loans to governments. and also provides funds to private infrastructure projects through its International Finance Corporation (IFC).[29] The World Bank's Multilateral Investment Guarantee Agency (MIGA) offers investment insurance to private projects (see Chapter 25).

The IMF's goals are to facilitate the expansion and balanced growth of international trade, to assist in the elimination of foreign exchange restrictions which hamper the growth of international trade, and to shorten the duration and lessen the disequilibrium in the international balances of payments of members.[30] The mitigation of wide currency fluctuations is achieved through a complex lending system which permits a country to borrow money from other Fund members or from the Fund (by way of Special Drawing Rights or SDRs) for the purpose of stabilizing the relationship of its currency to other world currencies.

The IMF's activities focus on loans to governments rather than support of particular foreign investments.[31] However, IMF activities can have enormous significance for foreign investment. In the modern era, IMF loans have normally been "conditioned" upon adoption of specific economic reforms by debtor states, especially in Asia and Latin America, and commercial and national banks often conform their loans to IMF conditions. This has led to the perception that the IMF is the world's sheriff, setting the terms for refinancing national debts and protecting the interests of commercial bank creditors. These IMF conditions can have dramatic political and social repercussions in debtor nations, often stoking resentment and criticism as infringements on sovereignty.

The IMF plays a critical role in global financial crises such as the one that began in 2008, providing loans to countries it considers sound but facing liquidity problems. The IMF has also been heavily involved in the bailouts of weaker economies in the European Union such as Greece that have faced mounting pressures as a result of their membership in the Euro (see Chapter 17, § 17.4).

---

[29]   *See* http://www.ifc.org/wps/wcm/connect/corp_ext_content/ifc_external_corporate_site/home.

[30]   *See* http://www.imf.org/external/np/exr/facts/glance.htm.

[31]   *See* http://www.imf.org/external/np/exr/facts/howlend.htm.

§ 21.9   Currency Issues

When a business invests in a foreign nation with a different currency, many issues arise. They may generally be grouped into two categories. The first is valuation. Currencies change value relative to each other—sometimes gradually, sometimes abruptly. If the investment's revenues and expenses are in a foreign country, they may be denominated in the foreign currency; if the currency gains or loses value relative to the investor's home country currency, the investor may find that in terms of the home country currency the expenses are much greater, or the revenues much less, than expected.

Currencies are typically either fixed rate currencies or floating rate currencies. A floating rate currency changes its value continuously based on market conditions—that is, how much people are willing to pay in one currency to obtain a unit of the other currency. The currencies of most major developed nations, including the U.S. dollar, the U.K. pound, the Euro and the Japanese yen, are floating rate currencies (as are the currencies of a number of developing nations). A fixed rate currency has its value tied to another currency by government decree. For example, the government might declare that one unit of its currency is worth one U.S. dollar. Some nations have intermediate approaches such as a "managed float" in which the government frequently changes the fixed rate to approximate market rates or where the government participates in currency markets to try to achieve a desired rate.

One might suppose that a fixed rate is more attractive to foreign investors, but that is not necessarily so. For one thing, fixed rates are hard to maintain because they will get out of alignment with the market rate (that is, what the rate would be if it were allowed to be determined by the market). Thus the government will come under pressure to change the fixed rate, which it may do dramatically and without warning. It is important to remember that fixed rates are fixed only until the government changes them, which it can do at any time. In addition, to maintain a fixed rate, the government may engage in various types of currency controls to manage problems created by a fixed rate that is out of alignment with the market rate. As discussed below, currency controls are a serious threat to the viability of foreign investment.

A related aspect of currency valuation is the idea of "hard" and "soft" currencies. A hard currency is one that tends to hold its value relative to other currencies, while a soft currency is one that tends to lose value over time. The currencies of most major developed countries, most of the time, have been hard currencies. Though they change in value relative to one another over time, they (usually) do not experience dramatic declines. But that has not always been true; external events, difficult economic situations and misguided government policies have caused abrupt collapses in even supposedly "hard" currencies.[32] Many developing nations have soft currencies, generally meaning a fairly gradual but sustained loss in value over time—due to high inflation, economic conditions and government policy—with the risk of more rapid loss. Foreign investors obviously prefer hard currencies and see substantial risk in soft currencies: keeping money in a foreign soft currency may result in substantial loss of value relative to the home currency.

The second major area of currency risk for foreign investors is currency exchange controls and related regulations of currency exchange and repatriation. Host government regulations may prevent the foreign currency from being be readily converted into dollars or other hard foreign currency.

Exchange controls may arise from political motivations—for example, to keep foreign investors from taking "excess" profits out of the country rather than reinvesting them. Commonly, they arise from fixed exchange rates that do not align with market rates and thus result in shortages of hard foreign currency in developing nations; in such a circumstance the government will not want the foreign investor to exchange local currency for scarce foreign currency it plans to take out to the country.

Exchange controls take a great variety of forms. They may involve specific limitations on the amount of currency that can be converted or removed from the country. They may involve limits on the categories of funds that can be removed—for example, repatriation of profits might be limited while funds to acquire technology to bring into the country might be allowed. Sometimes a regulatory agency such as the central bank must approve transfers, often with considerable discretion whether to approve or not approve. Some controls are imposed on a temporary basis in response to financial emergencies, while others may be a permanent part of the nation's economic policy.

These issues create significant planning problems for foreign investors. How should revenues and expenses to be incurred in foreign currency be valued? How much local currency should be retained for business needs? The investor must learn about hedging—buying contracts that assure later currency conversion at a determined rate. Planning for currency issues can be expensive, but not planning for currency risk can be disastrous.

---

[32] For example, the U.K. pound fell sharply in June 2016 after the United Kingdom voted to leave the European Union.

§ 21.10   Taxation of Foreign Investment

Even though a nation may have a liberal foreign investment law, unless there is a reasonably clear expression of the form of taxation facing the investment, investment will be slow to enter. Some nations offer tax incentives to foreign investment, such as tax holidays that defer tax for a certain number of years, or rebates when profits are reinvested rather than repatriated. The tax benefits are often linked to investment in high priority areas, such as those that generate foreign exchange for the host country. Tax benefits may extend beyond a tax on profits to taxation of royalties, taxes on imports and exports, sales and consumption taxes, and taxes on personal income of foreign nationals.

One problem for foreign investors is the dynamics of taxation in foreign nations. Tax burdens change frequently and incentives received one year may be far less valuable or available in another. A possible solution is to incorporate tax benefits into an investment contract with the foreign government. However, there may be substantial doubts whether such contracts are enforceable.

Foreign investors will also be concerned about the tax they pay in their home countries. Many developed nations, including the United States, have concluded tax treaties with nations in which their multinationals invest to avoid double taxation. How each of these treaties operates is of great importance to foreign investors. In addition, typically the United States does not tax foreign investment income earned by subsidiaries until it is repatriated (that is, brought back to the United States). As a result, corporate investors may seek to avoid, or at least defer, U.S. taxes on foreign investment income by holding the income abroad, often in "tax havens" such as the Cayman Islands or Bermuda. (These are countries with relatively stable political systems but little or no corporate taxation). Thus, foreign investments may be structured with an intermediate subsidiary in a low-tax jurisdiction. Not surprisingly, taxation issues have enormous impact on the structure and operation of foreign investment.[33]

§ 21.11   Transfer Pricing

Transfer pricing refers to the exchange of goods, services and technologies between related entities such as a parent and a subsidiary.[34] For example, suppose a U.S. parent company supplies

---

[33]   Taxation of cross-border transactions is extremely complex and beyond the scope of this book. For a useful simplified treatment, see Richard Doernberg, INTERNATIONAL TAXATION IN A NUTSHELL (10th ed. 2015).

[34]   See OECD Transfer Pricing Guidelines for Multinational Enterprises and Tax Administrations (2010), http://www.oecd.org/publications/oecd-transfer-pricing-

parts and technology to its manufacturing subsidiary in China. How is the value of the parts and technology to be determined for purposes of calculating profits and losses of the parent and the subsidiary? In a transaction between unrelated entities (an "arm's length transaction"), the price would be negotiated. But if the parent owns and controls the subsidiary, it can set any price it wants. A high price for the parts and technology will increase profits at the parent level and reduce profits of the subsidiary; a low price will make the subsidiary appear more profitable and the parent less profitable.

There are several reasons a company might wish to manipulate the price of transfers between itself and its subsidiaries. If a U.S. investment in another nation faces laws that restrict repatriating profits to the parent, but allow payments for technology, perhaps the parent will simply raise the price it charges the foreign subsidiary for technology and thus operate without showing any profits abroad that if they existed would be frozen in the non-transferrable foreign currency. In addition, transfer pricing can be used to shift profits to jurisdictions with lower taxes. For example, if the U.S. parent's subsidiary is located in a country with lower taxes than the United States, the parent might want to show more profits in the subsidiary (and less in the parent) by charging a low price for transferred goods, services and technology. Finally, transfer pricing may be used to divert profits away from joint venture partners. For example, a U.S. parent with a majority owned subsidiary might charge a high price for technology transfers to its subsidiary; the joint venture partners would lose dividends because the subsidiary's profits (in which they would share) would be transformed into technology payments (in which they would not share).

Because transfer pricing can lead to various abuses, including manipulation of tax laws and unfair treatment of minority shareholders, it is closely regulated (at least in theory) in most jurisdictions. In addition to national laws, bilateral tax treaties often address, among other things, transfer pricing.[35] In general, the regulating authority will require the related companies to price their transfers as if they were arm's-length transactions (that is, market-based transactions between unrelated parties).[36] This is an easy rule

---

guidelines-for-multinational-enterprises-and-tax-administrations-20769717.htm; Note, *Regulation of Transfer Pricing in Multinational Corporations: An International Perspective*, 10 NYU J. INT'L L. & POLITICS 67 (1977).

[35]   *See* OECD Model Tax Convention on Income and on Capital, Art. 9 (2015), http://www.oecd.org/tax/treaties/model-tax-convention-on-income-and-on-capital-2015-full-version-9789264239081-en.htm.

[36]   *See, e.g.*, 28 U.S.C. § 482 (regulating transfer pricing for U.S. tax purposes); OECD Transfer Pricing Profiles, http://www.oecd.org/ctp/transfer-pricing/transfer

to state, and it may be an easy rule to apply if the items transferred are generic goods for which a price can readily be found on the open market. However, when the transferred items are unique—such as proprietary technology or services of particular individuals—the "arm's length" price may be difficult to identify. In addition, it may not be obvious that companies are using inappropriate pricing unless they are closely scrutinized by knowledgeable regulators, which may be especially difficult for developing nations.

§ 21.12   Human Rights and Environmental Litigation Involving Foreign Investment

Foreign investment, like any business operation, involves risks of ordinary litigation regarding contracts, employment, etc. A further risk to consider is the extent to which the investment or the parent company might be held liable for human rights violations or environmental damage in private tort litigation.

Litigation in U.S. Courts: The Alien Tort Statute. The U.S. Alien Tort Statute (ATS) provides that U.S. federal courts have jurisdiction over suits by aliens for torts that violate international law.[37] In the modern era, this statute has been used to bring international human rights claims against foreign government officials for conduct that occurred outside the United States.[38] Prior to 2013, this statute was also widely used by foreign plaintiffs to sue multinational corporations for complicity in human rights violations by the governments of developing nations in which they operated.[39] For example, in *Kiobel v. Royal Dutch Petroleum Co.*,[40] Nigerian plaintiffs sued Royal Dutch, a British-Dutch company, for aiding and abetting the Nigerian government's violations of their international human rights. Similar suits against both U.S. and non-U.S. companies have been brought for alleged complicity in the abusive

---

pricingcountryprofiles.htm (providing country profiles on transfer pricing legislation and practices for OECD member countries and observers).

[37]   28 U.S.C. § 1350.

[38]   *E.g.,* Filártiga v. Peña-Irala, 630 F.2d 876 (2d Cir. 1980) (suit by Paraguayan citizens against Paraguayan official for torture and murder that occurred in Paraguay); Kadic v. Karadžić, 70 F.3d 232 (2d Cir. 1995) (suit by Bosnian Muslims against Bosnian Serb commander for genocide during Bosnian civil war).

[39]   *See, e.g.,* Doe v. Unocal, 395 F.3d 932 (9th Cir. 2002) (alleging human rights violations by the defendant corporation for complicity with the government in using forced labor in the construction of an oil pipeline). None of these cases resulted in a judgment against a corporate defendant, but some (including *Unocal*) were settled. The chronology of corporate liability under the ATS is recounted in Presbyterian Church of Sudan v. Talisman Energy, Inc., 244 F. Supp. 2d 289, 308 (S.D.N.Y. 2003). *See also* Courtney Shaw, *Uncertain Justice: Liability of Multinationals Under the Alien Tort Claims Act,* 54 STAN. L. REV. 1359 (2002).

[40]   133 S.Ct. 1659 (2013).

conduct of governments in, among others, Burma (Myanmar), Indonesia, South Africa, Sudan, Colombia and Argentina.

In 2013, the U.S. Supreme Court held in *Kiobel* that the presumption against extraterritoriality (see Chapter 26) barred application of the ATS to claims that did not "touch and concern" the United States. It accordingly directed dismissal of the claim in *Kiobel*,[41] and after *Kiobel* numerous ATS claims against multinational corporations have similarly been dismissed.

It is unclear which, if any, ATS claims remain viable after *Kiobel*. If the defendant is a U.S. corporation (instead of a non-U.S. corporation as in *Kiobel*), and especially if some of the corporation's decisionmaking regarding the alleged harmful acts took place in the United States, it is possible that the presumption against extraterritoriality would be overcome (or would not apply).[42] However, post-*Kiobel* courts have generally not been hospitable to ATS claims.[43]

Even if the ATS applies, there is a question of what level of involvement in the government's harmful conduct is required for liability. As a threshold matter, there must be a violation of international law. Not all harms, even grievous ones, violate international law. For example, environmental harms, at least if occurring in only one country, may not be sufficient to come within the statute.[44] How expansive an interpretation should be given the ATS's "violation of the law of nations" language is yet undetermined. Certainly torture and extra-judicial killing are such violations. In *Sosa v. Alvarez-Machain*,[45] a case that did not involve a corporate defendant, the Supreme Court urged judicial caution in finding international law violations under the ATS.

In addition, in most corporate ATS cases the primary wrongdoer is the foreign government and the allegation is that the multinational

---

[41]   *Id.*

[42]   *See, e.g.*, Licci v. Lebanese Canadian Bank, 834 F.3d 201 (2d Cir. 2016) (allowing claim against foreign bank that provided banking services through an account in New York); al Shimari v. CACI Premier Technology, Inc., 758 F.3d 516 (4th Cir. 2014) (allowing claim against U.S. corporation for torture at Abu Ghraib prison in Iraq); Mastafa v. Chevron Corp, 770 F.3d 170 (2d Cir. 2014) (finding some claims based on injuries in Iraq had enough connection to the United States to survive *Kiobel* but dismissing on other grounds).

[43]   *E.g.*, Doe v. Drummond Corp., 782 F.3d 576 (11th Cir. 2015) (dismissing claims by Colombian victims in Colombian civil war); Cardona v. Chiquita Brands Int'l, Inc., 760 F.3d 1185 (11th Cir. 2014) (same); Balintulo v. Daimler AG, 727 F.3d 174 (2d Cir. 2013) (dismissing suit by South African plaintiffs for injuries under South African apartheid regime).

[44]   *See* Beanal v. Freeport-McMoran Inc., 197 F.3d 161 (5th Cir. 1999) (claimed harms were not violations of international law and so not cognizable under the ATS).

[45]   542 U.S. 692 (2004).

corporation assisted the violation.[46] In *Presbyterian Church of Sudan v. Talisman Energy, Inc.,*[47] the court of appeals held that for ATS liability the defendant corporation must have intended that the government's wrongful conduct occur. However, other courts have allowed ATS claims if the corporation knew (or should have known) of the violations and acted in ways that facilitated them, even absent intent that they occur.[48]

Although the threat of ATS litigation has diminished after *Kiobel*,[49] U.S. companies need to carefully assess investments in countries with abusive governments. Various codes of conduct, developed by industry groups and international organizations, suggest ways that corporations can ethically conduct business in countries with such governments. Many multinational corporations develop internal codes of conduct and hire compliance officers and consultants to assist in monitoring the ATS and related risks.

Litigation in U.S. Courts: Other Sources of Law. In addition to the ATS, suits might be brought in U.S. courts under other U.S. laws, state law or foreign law. Application of U.S. federal law would have to overcome the presumption against extraterritoriality,[50] but that might be possible for some statutes.[51] In the case of a U.S. defendant, a state in which the defendant is incorporated or headquartered might apply its law to foreign activity, including for such traditional actions as wrongful death, false imprisonment, assault, intentional

---

[46]   A few international law violations can be committed by a private corporation alone, including genocide and slavery, but most require some government involvement.

[47]   582 F.3d 244 (2d Cir. 2009).

[48]   *See, e.g.,* Aziz v. Alcolac, Inc., 658 F.3d 388 (4th Cir. 2011) (following *Talisman*); Doe v. ExxonMobil Corp., 654 F.3d 11 (D.C. Cir. 2011) (rejecting *Talisman* and allowing claim if corporation knew or should have known of violations).

[49]   There is also a question whether the ATS applies to corporations at all. The Second Circuit in *Kiobel* held that it does not, 621 F.3d 111 (2d Cir. 2010), but the Supreme Court did not adopt that reasoning. Other courts have rejected it. *E.g.,* Flomo v. Firestone National Rubber Co., 643 F.3d 1014 (7th Cir. 2011). *But see* In re Arab Bank PLC Alien Tort Statute Litigation, 808 F.3d 144 (2d Cir. 2015) (reaffirming the Second Circuit rule after *Kiobel* while questioning its basis).

[50]   *See* RJR Nabisco, Inc. v. European Community, 136 S.Ct. 2090 (2016) (assessing extraterritoriality of Racketeer Influenced and Corrupt Organizations (RICO) Act). The presumption is discussed below, Chapter 26, § 26.8.

[51]   A federal statute, the Torture Victim Protection Act (TVPA), 28 U.S.C. § 1350 Note, allows claims for some extraterritorial human rights violations, but it applies only to individual defendants. *See* Mohamad v. Palestinian Authority, 132 S.Ct. 1702 (2012). However, claims might be brought against individual corporate officers. *See, e.g.,* Doe v. Drummond Corp., 782 F.3d 576 (11th Cir. 2015) (generally allowing such claims but dismissing for lack of proof in the particular case); In re Chiquita Brands International, Inc. Alien Tort Statute and Shareholder Derivative Litigation 2016 WL 3247913 (S.D. Fla. 2016) (finding plaintiffs stated claim under TVPA against corporate officers and directors).

infliction of emotional distress and negligence. And in general, courts in the United States will apply foreign law in appropriate circumstances. There may, however, be substantial procedural barriers to these approaches.[52]

Litigation in Foreign Courts. Foreign investors have always faced possible litigation in the host nation. Jurisdiction in the host nation is rarely a problem because the company is clearly present and doing business. But a foreign-owned subsidiary in the host nation may have few assets in that nation. While those may be sufficient to satisfy judgments dealing with such common issues as a job-related injury to an employee or a contract breach, they are insufficient when multi-plaintiff actions are brought for alleged large-scale injuries such as environmental damage or labor abuses. In such actions the defendants may include both the foreign parent and the host nation subsidiary, leading to jurisdictional issues if the suit is brought in the host nation.

Historically multinational investors faced relatively little risk of private suits for human rights and environmental claims in the host-country courts of developing nations. The host-country legal systems typically did not embrace mass tort claims or substantial damage awards. However, this seems to be changing. In a well-known recent case, Ecuadorian plaintiffs sued Chevron Corp., a U.S. corporation, in Ecuador, claiming environmental torts by a company Chevron had acquired.[53] The Ecuadorian courts delivered a very large judgment against Chevron, which the company has resisted paying on grounds that it was obtained by fraud.[54] Other host-country courts, particularly in Latin America, have also begun to award substantial damages against foreign corporations in environmental and human rights cases.[55]

---

[52]   *See* Chapter 26; *see also* Christopher A. Whytock, Donald Earl Childress III & Michael D. Ramsey, *After Kiobel—International Human Rights Litigation in State Courts and Under State Law*, 3 UC IRVINE L. REV. 1 (2013); Donald Earl Childress III, *The Alien Tort Statute, Federalism, and the Next Wave of Transnational Litigation*, 100 GEO. L.J. 709 (2012).

[53]   The plaintiffs initially brought the case in the United States, but the defense successfully argued, perhaps unwisely, that it should proceed in Ecuador instead. *See* Aguinda v. Texaco, Inc., 303 F.3d 470 (2d Cir. 2002).

[54]   *See* Chevron Corp. v. Naranjo, 667 F.3d 232 (2d Cir. 2012); Chevron Corp. v. Donziger, 2016 WL 4173988 (2d. Cir. 2016).

[55]   *See, e.g.,* Osorio v. Dole Food Co., 665 F.Supp.2d 1307 (S.D. Fla. 2009), *aff'd,* Osorio v. Dow Chemical Co., 635 F.3d 1277 (11th Cir. 2011). As these cases reflect, and as discussed in Chapter 26, these judgments often have been difficult to enforce.

Chapter 22

CROSS-BORDER MERGERS AND ACQUISITIONS

Table of Sections

§ 22.1 Introduction

For investors wishing to establish business operations in a foreign country, there are two basic options. The first is to build up a new business (a "greenfields" investment); the second is to acquire or merge with an existing business. Where a cross-border merger or acquisition is selected, there may be additional legal barriers to consider. Even nations that are generally open to foreign investment may restrict mergers and acquisitions, in particular for national security, economic and antitrust reasons. This chapter considers those and similar limitations, as well as privatization, a special form of acquisition that involves purchase of a previously government-owned business.

§ 22.2 National Security and National Economic Considerations

Nations commonly restrict mergers and acquisitions in areas that affect national security, even if they do not formally restrict national-security-related sectors to local or government ownership. Restriction of foreign acquisitions is often done through an administrative review process. For example, as discussed below, the United States may require foreign investment acquisitions in areas affecting national security to be reviewed by an administrative board called the Committee on Foreign Investment in the United

States (CFIUS).[1] Canada has an approval process under the Investment Canada Act (1985), as amended (ICA),[2] which governs foreign investment in Canada—especially acquisitions. Treaties protecting foreign investment (see Chapter 23) often have exceptions for national security review; for example, review of acquisitions under the ICA are generally exempt from the dispute settlement provisions of the North American Free Trade Agreement (NAFTA).[3]

Nations vary considerably in the scope of their review of acquisitions. As discussed below, the U.S. review process centers only on national security, which is generally understood principally to encompass military and related technology sectors. Canada, in contrast, has a broader review, asking whether new investment will "significantly benefit" Canada, including the effects on economic activity, participation by Canadians, productivity, efficiency, innovation, technological development, competition, culture, and role in world markets.[4] However, most new foreign investment in Canada is not reviewed,[5] review being generally limited to acquisitions[6] above a minimum threshold value.[7]

Apart from national security, nations may oppose acquisitions by foreign investors if the acquisition targets large employers or famous companies strongly associated with the nation's national identity (sometimes called "national champions" or "national

---

[1]   See below, §§ 22.3, 22.4.

[2]   R.S. 1985, ch. 28 (1st Suppl.), *as amended,* and Investment Canada Regulations SOR/85–611, *as amended* by SOR/89–69.

[3]   *See* NAFTA ch. 11, Annex 1138.2. Similarly, NAFTA specifically allows Mexico to retain review by the Mexican National Commission on Foreign Investment, with such review of acquisitions not subject to the Chapter 11 or Chapter 20 dispute resolution panels and procedures. The United States reserved no process of review of acquisitions in NAFTA, but there is no exception for NAFTA countries in the U.S. foreign investment review statute.

[4]   Investment Canada Act of 1985, art. 20. *See* Simone Collins, *Recent Decisions under the Investment Canada Act: Is Canada Changing Its Stance on Foreign Direct Investment?,* 32 NW. J. INT'L L. & BUS. 141 (2011); Michel Gélinas, Jeffrey Brown & Tania Djerrahian, *A Primer on Canadian Foreign Investment Rules Including Recent Developments*, 2016-Apr. BUS. L. TODAY 1; Gil Lan, *Foreign Direct Investment in the United States and Canada: Fractured Neoliberalism and the Regulatory Imperative*, 47 VAND. J. TRANSNAT'L L. 1261 (2014).

[5]   Canada has reserved the right to review investment in certain stipulated cultural industries. *See* ICA arts. 14.1(9), 15. This right is retained in NAFTA.

[6]   The earlier Canadian Foreign Investment Review Act did provide for a review of new investment, with complex provisions regarding investor eligibility and control. Under the Investment Canada Act, new investment is generally subject only to notification procedures. Part III, Arts. 11–13.

[7]   By 2008 the threshold for investments from World Trade Organization (WTO) countries had been increased to Can$295 million. For non-WTO countries and certain industries, such as culture, transportation, and financial services, there is a low Can$5million threshold.

treasures"). For example, Britain reacted strongly against foreign acquisition of the iconic Cadbury candy manufacturer, as did France against the rumored foreign acquisition of Danone, a famous producer of yogurt and bottled water.[8] Nations may not want to see these companies fall under foreign control for abstract reasons of national pride, or they may have specific fears that the new foreign owners will dismantle or move operations, resulting in job losses and other economic injury. Acquisitions by potentially hostile nations may also raise security concerns even if they are not in defense-related industries. For example, in recent years Chinese companies have aggressively sought foreign acquisition and have often encountered resistance.[9]

§ 22.3 U.S. Regulation of Foreign Investment— Background

Although the United States is relatively open to foreign investment, it is subject to recurrent concerns over foreign investment's national security implications. U.S. foreign investment law has been gradually tightened to provide for review and rejection of foreign investment that threatens national security, although in practice relatively few investments have actually been blocked.

The President initially created the Committee on Foreign Investment in the United States (CFIUS) in the 1970s, when there was concern over widespread Arab buyouts of U.S. businesses. CFIUS was designed as an interagency, interdepartmental group to investigate inward foreign investment and recommend policy. CFIUS at this point had no real screening or review power and was used infrequently; for example, President Carter's administration investigated only one transaction. During the 1980s, the concern turned more toward large inflows of Japanese foreign investment. The administration began to intervene in these inflows more frequently, especially when they constituted planned acquisitions of U.S. companies. The policy of open versus controlled investment seemed most confused when the Japanese electronics conglomerate Fujitsu sought to acquire an 80 percent share in Fairchild Semiconductor. Fairchild had openly solicited the bid. Even though the French company Schlumberger already owned Fairchild, the

---

[8]   Following speculation that Danone might be acquired by the U.S. company PepsiCo Inc., France developed rules to protect French companies from hostile foreign companies, known as the Danone law. *See* David Rothnie, *US Companies May Bid for Danone Division*, Financial News, June 28, 2007, http://www. efinancialnews.com/story/2007-06-28/us-companies-may-bid-for-danone-division.

[9]   For example, Australia has blocked the purchase by a Chinese company of land amounting to around one percent of Australia's total land area. Claire Zillman, *Australia Is Blocking China from Buying 1% of Its Land Mass*, Fortune, Apr. 29, 2016.

Commerce, Defense, and Justice Departments joined to oppose the proposed acquisition. The Department of Justice was concerned with antitrust implications,[10] while the Departments of Commerce and Defense appeared to object primarily in order to force Japanese markets to open more. Because of the extensive concern, Fujitsu withdrew its proposed acquisition, even though CFIUS at the time lacked the power to block the sale.

In 1988, frustrated by the generally weak response to foreign acquisitions, Congress enacted the Exon-Florio amendment to the Defense Production Act of 1950. Exon-Florio gave the President power to investigate and suspend or prohibit transactions leading to control of U.S. firms by foreign persons, based on national security concerns. While Exon-Florio included a list of factors to be considered in the evaluation of a transaction's national security implications, there nevertheless remained concern about its broad language. CFIUS interpreted national security on a case-by-case basis, leaving investors somewhat baffled about the criteria used to evaluate transactions. Although interference with acquisitions remained relatively rare, there were a few prominent cases, including China National Aero Technology Import and Export Corp. (CATIC) attempting to buy MAMCO Manufacturing Inc., a U.S. company that manufactured parts for Boeing aircraft, and Thomson-CSF, a conglomerate majority owned by the French government, attempting to buy the missile division of LTV Corp.[11] The former transaction was blocked by the President after CFIUS review; the buyer withdrew from the latter transaction when it seemed likely CFIUS would recommend that the President block it.[12]

After several prominent proposed acquisitions in the 2000s (including a bid by the China National Offshore Oil Corporation (CNOOC) for Unocal, Inc. and Dubai Ports' bid to take over operation of several U.S. ports), in 2007 Congress enacted the Foreign Investment and National Security Act (FINSA),[13] further amending the Defense Production Act. FINSA substantially revised and updated Exon-Florio, and remains the basic framework for reviewing foreign acquisitions that implicate national security.

---

[10]   *See Division Is Probing Effects of Merger of California, Japanese Computer Firms*, 51 Antitrust & Trade Reg. Rep. (BNA) No. 1282, 803 (Nov. 27, 1986).

[11]   *See Foreign Investment: Thomson-CSF Bid for LTV "Watershed Event," Leading to New Controls, ABA Seminar Told*, 9 Int'l Trade Rep. (BNA) 1781 (Oct. 14, 1992). Following the LTV episode, Congress enacted further amendments expanding CFIUS's review authority and obligations.

[12]   For concern about national security implications of foreign investment during this period, *see* Martin Tolchin & Susan J. Tolchin, SELLING OUR SECURITY: THE EROSION OF AMERICA'S ASSETS (1992).

[13]   Pub. L. 110–49, 121 Stat. 246, 50 U.S.C. App. § 2170.

FINSA was principally intended to amend Exon-Florio to reform the process by which CFIUS undertakes national security reviews of proposed foreign acquisitions of U.S. businesses, with special scrutiny of acquisitions by foreign state-owned corporations. FINSA made other important changes, including identifying critical infrastructure that is to be reviewed, codifying modifications to CFIUS, emphasizing the importance of national security, and expanding the number of risk factors taken into consideration in CFIUS reviews.

§ 22.4 U.S. Regulation of Foreign Investment Under FINSA

As prescribed by FINSA, national security review potentially covers "any merger, acquisition, or takeover . . . by or with any foreign person which could result in foreign control of any [entity] engaged in interstate commerce in the United States."[14] FINSA continues presidential authority through CFIUS to investigate effects on national security from covered transactions. It sets forth eleven statutory factors to be considered.[15] If national security is threatened, the President may prohibit the acquisition. The law additionally limits the sale of defense-related U.S. companies to entities controlled by foreign governments.[16] FINSA has caused a significant increase in the proposed transactions subject to review.

Most investigations are at the discretion of CFIUS after receipt of written notification as prescribed by the regulations, although review must occur if the purchasing foreigner is controlled by or acting on behalf of a foreign government.[17] CFIUS has 30 days after notification to decide whether to investigate, and 45 days after that to investigate and make a recommendation to the President. The President then has 15 days to either suspend or prohibit the acquisition, merger, or takeover, or seek divestiture for an already completed transaction.[18] The President may direct the Attorney

---

[14]   50 U.S.C. App. § 2170(a)(3).

[15]   50 U.S.C. App. § 2170(f).

[16]   50 U.S.C. App § 2170a.

[17]   *See* 50 U.S.C. App. § 2170(b). This was part of the 1992 amendments resulting from the Thomson/LTV case discussed above.

[18]   Notice may be submitted and CFIUS review commenced at any time while the transaction is pending or after it is completed, subject to a three-year limitation after the transaction is completed, unless the CFIUS chairman, consulting with other members, requests an investigation. To avoid the possibility of having a completed transaction questioned, companies sometimes submit a voluntary notice to commence review before completing the transaction. Any transaction that has been the subject of CFIUS review or investigation is not subject to later presidential action. Thus, even when there seems to be little apparent impact on national security, a review request might be useful.

General to seek appropriate relief in U.S. district court to enforce the decision.

The President must make two findings to block a transaction. First, there must be "credible evidence" that the foreign interest would exercise "control" which might threaten "national security." Second, other provisions of law, aside from the International Emergency Economic Powers Act, must provide inadequate authority to safeguard national security. These findings are not subject to judicial review under the statute.

Any information filed with CFIUS is largely confidential, although some releases of information may be made to authorized members of Congress. Critics have charged that CFIUS has abused the confidentiality provisions in some cases, and also has left important players out of the investigation process until after CFIUS has made its decisions. The confidentiality provision has made official reports of cases impossible but has protected both the interests of foreign investors and national security. The manner in which CFIUS and the President have applied the law, and the criticism generated from such application, have focused on the proper meaning of three terms—"mergers, acquisitions, and takeovers," "control," and "national security."

A recent prominent dispute under FINSA involved two Chinese investors who sought to develop wind energy projects near a U.S. military reservation. Acting through Ralls Corp., a U.S. company that they controlled, the investors purchased four U.S. companies with property, assets and approvals necessary for the projects. Ralls notified CFIUS of the acquisition and submitted various documents; after review, CFIUS found a threat to national security. On CFIUS's recommendation the President issued an order blocking the project and requiring Ralls to divest itself of all interests in the acquired companies.[19] Ralls successfully challenged the order in U.S. court on the ground that the review process had not been fair under the U.S. Constitution's due process clause because Ralls had not been given adequate opportunity to review and rebut the evidence on which CFIUS relied.[20] It is not clear, however, how much protection this decision will ultimately provide foreign investors because it relates only to CFIUS's procedures; as noted, the President's ultimate decision is shielded from judicial review.[21]

---

[19]   Ralls Corp. v. Committee on Foreign Investment in the United States, 758 F.3d 296 (D.C. Cir. 2014).

[20]   *Id.*

[21]   Ralls subsequently reached a settlement with the United States and sold its investment. *See* Stephen Dockery, *Chinese Company Will Sell Wind Farm Assets in*

Another recent dispute arose from CFIUS's 2013 approval of the acquisition of Smithfield Foods Inc. by a Chinese company, Shuanghui International Holdings. Some members of Congress argued that CFIUS should have blocked the acquisition because it posed risks to the national food supply.[22] In general, critics of CFIUS argue that it should take a broader view of national security, or perhaps that its review should be expanded beyond national security to include something like the "best interests" test applied in Canada.

§ 22.5 Antitrust Issues in Mergers and Acquisitions

When a company acquires or merges with an enterprise in the same line of business, or with a supplier or retailer of its products, the transaction may raise antitrust issues because it reduces competition. Most developed countries and many developing countries have some form of supervision of mergers and acquisitions for antitrust purposes, although the extent of regulation and enforcement varies widely.[23] Two of the more aggressive regimes, discussed below, are the United States and the EU.

It is important to note that U.S. and EU antitrust laws, as well as those of some other jurisdictions, are applied extraterritorially where the conduct at issue has effects in the regulating jurisdiction, even if the conduct itself occurs outside the jurisdiction. In the case of mergers and acquisitions, this means that the combination of two companies located in the same jurisdiction may nonetheless also be regulated by another jurisdiction in which those companies do business. For example, the merger of two U.S. companies, both doing business in the EU as well as the United States, might be subject to regulation by both U.S. authorities and EU authorities— and those authorities might have different views about whether the combination represents a threat to competition.

A typical regime of mergers and acquisitions regulation subjects the proposed transaction to advance regulatory review for its effect on competition. There may be a threshold transaction value that triggers review, or the regulatory authorities may have broad discretion whether to investigate and possibly block the

---

CFIUS Settlement, Wall St. J., Nov. 4, 2015, http://blogs.wsj.com/riskandcompliance/2015/11/04/chinese-company-will-sell-wind-farm-assets-in-cfius-settlement/.

[22]   *See* William Mauldin & Brent Kendall, *Appeals Court Faults Government Order Prohibiting Ralls Corp. Wind Farm Deal*, Wall St. J., July 15, 2014, http://www.wsj.com/articles/appeals-court-faults-government-order-prohibiting-ralls-corp-wind-farm-deal-1405439077.

[23]   *See generally* Einer Elhauge & Damien Geradin, GLOBAL ANTITRUST LAW AND ECONOMICS (2007).

transaction. Mergers and acquisitions, even within industries, are usually not categorically prohibited; rather the regulatory authorities are tasked with determining whether the transaction has too great a potential effect on competition (with the specific standard being stated in different ways in different jurisdictions). If the regulatory authorities find the transaction to be anti-competitive, they typically have power to block the transaction. The authorities and the acquiring company may also reach a settlement whereby the acquiring company agrees to certain conditions and restrictions in return for approval. Regulatory decisions may be subject to judicial review, under varying standards of deference.

§ 22.6 Mergers and Acquisitions Under U.S. Antitrust Law

U.S. federal merger and acquisition law rests principally on the Clayton Antitrust Act of 1914, as amended.[24] Since 1975, this includes "premerger notification" requirements (sometimes known as "Hart-Scott-Rodino" notifications) stipulating that parties to large mergers and acquisitions must give the Department of Justice and the Federal Trade Commission advance notice of their intentions.[25] This advance notice allows the government antitrust authorities to review proposed mergers and acquisitions for their potential to violate Section 7 of the Clayton Act[26] and the desirability of challenging them in court. Of all the mergers that take place in the United States annually, including those involving takeovers by foreign firms, probably less than 1 percent are required to be notified to the federal antitrust authorities.

A second statute, the Federal Trade Commission Act (FTC Act), enacted in 1913, established the Federal Trade Commission (FTC) as an independent agency with broad regulatory and enforcement powers.[27] Section 5 of the FTC Act prohibits "unfair methods of competition." As interpreted by the U.S. Supreme Court, Section 5 covers all of the types of activities prohibited by the Sherman and Clayton Acts as well as anticompetitive methods that are not clearly prohibited by those statutes but which the FTC determines to be unfair. Thus the FTC Act is said to fill in the gaps of federal antitrust law.

---

[24]   Pub. L. 63–212, 38 Stat. 730, codified at 15 U.S.C. §§ 12–27, 29 U.S.C. §§ 52–53; see generally Dale Oesterle, MERGERS AND ACQUISITIONS IN A NUTSHELL (2d ed. 2008).

[25]   15 U.S.C. § 18a.

[26]   15 U.S.C. § 18 (prohibiting acquisitions where "the effect of such acquisition may be substantially to lessen competition, or to tend to create a monopoly").

[27]   15 U.S.C. §§ 41–58, as amended.

Over the years, the FTC has had a sporadic record in accomplishing its mission. It is composed of five persons nominated by the President and confirmed by the Senate, no more than three of whom can be from the same political party. Despite the political nature of the appointment process, the FTC is supposed to exercise its statutory authority to act against unfair methods of competition without influence from the President or Congress. However, Presidents (through appointments) and Congress (through the budgetary process) have increasingly involved themselves in FTC policy and enforcement decisions.

The FTC is authorized to issue cease and desist orders against parties found to violate Section 5 of the FTC Act. Additional remedies can follow, including civil penalties and restitution, if there is noncompliance with such orders. The FTC can also enforce the prohibitions found in the Clayton Act. In the modern era, the FTC's primary merger-related activity is evaluating transactions under the premerger notification rules of Section 7 of the Clayton Act. It is hard to see that the Commission's efforts have lent much precision to the field of antitrust law. It has instead become a variable agency often swinging from periods of inaction to dramatic enforcement proceedings along with the tides of United States politics and the prevailing winds of antitrust.

Private challenges to mergers and acquisitions, including cross-border transactions involving foreign companies, can also be brought under the Clayton Act. A notable example involved the hostile takeover of British Consolidated Gold Fields by Minorco (a Luxembourg company controlled by the two leading South African gold producers). Gold Fields sought to block the takeover on antitrust grounds in the United States, Britain, South Africa, Australia and the EU. These efforts failed everywhere except in a private action in the United States, where a U.S. federal district court judge enjoined the takeover.[28]

U.S. states also have antitrust laws that may restrict mergers and acquisitions. Some mergers approved by the federal authorities have been subsequently challenged by a state attorney general.[29] The states have, in general, become quite active in the mergers area and have adopted their own set of Horizontal Merger Guidelines through the National Association of Attorneys General (NAAG).[30]

---

[28]   Consolidated Gold Fields v. Anglo American Corp., 698 F.Supp. 487 (S.D.N.Y.1988), *affirmed* 871 F.2d 252 (2d Cir. 1989).

[29]   *See* California v. American Stores Co., 495 U.S. 271 (1990).

[30]   http://www.naag.org/assets/files/pdf/at-hmerger_guidelines.pdf.

§ 22.7   Mergers and Acquisitions Under EU Competition Law

Original Articles 81 and 82 of the EC Treaty, renumbered by the Lisbon Treaty of 2009 as Articles 101 and 102 of the Treaty on the Functioning of the European Union (TFEU), provide the foundation for EU regulation of mergers and acquisitions. Article 101 prohibits agreements and practices "which have as their object or effect the prevention, restriction or distortion of competition within the common market." Article 102 includes the important language prohibiting "abuse . . . of a dominant position." These two prohibitions, and regulations developed under them, are generally referred to as "competition law," and are approximate counterparts to U.S. antitrust law under the Sherman, Clayton and FTC Acts.[31]

Although Articles 101 and 102 do not expressly regulate mergers, the European Commission[32] in the *Continental Can* case asserted authority to regulate mergers that might be harmful to consumers, and the European Court of Justice agreed.[33] The Commission concluded that Continental Can abused its dominant positions in the manufacture of meat and fish tins and metal caps in Germany by announcing an 80 percent control bid for the only Dutch meat and fish tin company. The Commission reasoned that Continental Can would strengthen its dominant German market position through this Dutch acquisition to the detriment of consumers, and that this amounted to an abuse. The Commission emphasized that potential competition between companies located within Europe would be eliminated. On appeal to the European Court of Justice, Continental Can argued that the Commission was acting beyond its powers in attempting to control mergers under Article 102.[34] The Court, agreeing with the Commission, went beyond the language of Articles 101 and 102 and interpreted them in light of basic EU tasks and activities. The Court reasoned teleologically that both Articles were intended to assist in the maintenance of nondistorted competition. If businesses could freely merge and eliminate competition, a "breach in the whole system of competition law that could jeopardize the proper functioning of the common market" would be opened.

There may therefore be abusive behavior if an enterprise in a dominant position strengthens that position so that

---

[31]   *See* Ralph H. Folsom, PRINCIPLES OF EUROPEAN UNION LAW (3d ed. 2011).

[32]   The European Commission is the executive body of the EU. *See* Chapter 17, § 17.4.

[33]   (1972) Common Mkt. L. Rep. D11.

[34]   (1973) Eur. Comm. Rep. 215.

the degree of control achieved substantially obstructs competition, i.e. so that the only enterprises left in the market are those which are dependent on the dominant enterprise with regard to their market behavior.[35]

One problem with relying on Article 102 for control of mergers and acquisitions was the absence of any pre-merger notification system. Once a merger is completed, it is always difficult to persuade a court or tribunal that dissolution is desirable or even possible. The key to effective merger regulation, as the United States has learned under its Hart-Scott-Rodino pre-merger notification rules,[36] is advance warning and sufficient time to block anticompetitive mergers before they are implemented.

Eventually the EU Council of Ministers adopted Regulation 4064/89 on the Control of Concentrations Between Undertakings ("Mergers Regulation"). This regulation, effective in 1990, was expanded in scope by amendment in 1997 (Regulation 1310/97) and significantly revised in 2004.[37] It gives the Commission the exclusive power to oppose large-scale mergers and acquisitions of competitive consequence to the Common Market.

Applicability and Advance Notice. For EU regulatory purposes, a "concentration" includes almost any means by which control over another firm is acquired.[38] This could be by a merger agreement, stock or asset purchases, contractual relationships or other actions. "Control" can be achieved by minority shareholders, such as when they exercise decisive influence over strategic planning and investment decisions.[39] Cooperative joint ventures between independent competitors may also be subject to the Mergers Regulation.[40]

The review process established by the Mergers Regulation commences when a concentration must be notified to the Commission. Meeting in advance of notification with members of the Commission on an informal basis in order to ascertain whether the "concentration" has a regional dimension and is compatible with the Common Market has become widely accepted. Such meetings provide an opportunity to seek waivers from the various requests for information contained in the applicable form.

---

[35]   *Id.*

[36]   15 U.S.C. § 18A.

[37]   Council Regulation (EC) No 139/2004 of 20 January 2004 on the control of concentrations between undertakings, Official Journal L 24, 29.01.2004, p. 1–22.

[38]   Mergers Regulation, Article 3.

[39]   *See* Conagra/IDEA, 1991 O.J. C175/18; EIF/BC/CEPSA, 1991 O.J. C172/8; Usinor/ASD 1991 O.J. C193/34.

[40]   Mergers Regulation, Article 3(4).

The Commission must be notified of concentrations above a specified value prior to their implementation.[41] The Commission can fine any company for failing to notify it as required.[42] The duty to notify is triggered only when the concentration involves enterprises with a combined worldwide and/or regional sales turnover of a specified value.[43] As a general rule, concentrations meeting these criteria cannot be put into effect and fall exclusively within the Commission's domain. The objective is to create a one-stop regulatory system. However, certain exceptions apply that allow national authorities to challenge some mergers. For example, this may occur under national law when two-thirds of the activities of each of the companies involved take place in the same member state.[44] Member states can also oppose mergers by appealing Commission decisions when their public security is at stake, to preserve plurality in media ownership, when financial institutions are involved or other legitimate interests are at risk.[45] If the threshold criteria of the Mergers Regulation are not met, member states can ask the Commission to investigate mergers that create or strengthen a dominant position in that state.[46] Similarly, if the merger only affects a particular market sector or region in one member state, that state may request referral of the merger to it.

Once a concentration is notified to the Commission, the Commission has one month to decide to investigate the merger. If a formal investigation is commenced, the Commission ordinarily then has four months to challenge or approve the merger.[47] During these months, in most cases, the concentration cannot be put into effect. The Commission evaluates mergers in terms of their "compatibility" with the Common Market. Since 2004, the applicable test is a prohibition against mergers that "significantly impede effective competition" by creating or strengthening dominant positions.[48] Thus the test focuses on effects not dominance. The Guidelines on Horizontal Mergers issued by the Commission in 2004 elaborate upon this approach.

During a mergers investigation, the Commission can obtain information and records from the parties, and request member states to help with the investigation. Fines and penalties back up

---

[41]   *Id.*, Article 4.

[42]   *Id.*, Article 14(1).

[43]   *Id.*, Article 2.

[44]   *Id.*, Article 1(2).

[45]   *Id.*, Article 21(3).

[46]   *Id.*, Article 22.

[47]   *Id.*, Article 10.

[48]   *Id.*, Article 2.

the Commission's powers to obtain records and information from the parties.[49] If the concentration has already taken effect, the Commission can issue a "hold-separate" order.[50] This requires the corporations or assets acquired to be separated and not, operationally speaking, merged. Approval of the merger may involve modifications of its terms or promises by the parties aimed at diminishing its anticompetitive potential. If the Commission ultimately decides to oppose the merger in a timely manner, it can order termination of the merger by whatever means are appropriate to restore conditions of effective competition (including divestiture, fines or penalties). Such decisions can be appealed to the EU's General Court under "fast track" procedures intended to promote judicial review within a year. As a practical matter, most merger proposals do not last that long. Hence, a negative Commission decision usually kills a merger.[51]

The Commission may be found liable in damages for intervening unlawfully against mergers, notably when making manifest procedural errors. Commission decisions to clear joint ventures or mergers can, in rare cases, be annulled.

Cross-Border Implications. EU competition law, including regulation of mergers and acquisitions, looks at the effect within the Common Market, not at the location of the companies involved. (This is similar to the extraterritorial application of U.S. antitrust law). Thus cross-border mergers, or even mergers of companies located outside the EU, are subject to EU regulation and disapproval, as several classic cases illustrate.

The first merger actually blocked by the Commission on competition law grounds was the attempted acquisition of a Canadian aircraft manufacturer (DeHaviland, owned by Boeing) by two European companies, Aerospatiale SNI of France and Alenia e Selenia Spa of Italy.[52] Prior to this rejection in late 1991, the Commission had approved over 50 mergers, obtaining modifications in a few instances. In the DeHaviland case, the Commission took the position that the merger would have created an unassailable dominant position in the world and the European market for turbo prop or commuter aircraft. If completed, the merged entity would have had 50 percent of the world market and 67 percent of the European market for such aircraft. In contrast, the Commission approved (subject to certain sell-off requirements) the acquisition of

---

[49]   *Id.*, Articles 11–15.

[50]   *Id.*, Articles 7 and 10.

[51]   *See* Gencor Ltd. v. EC Commission, 1999 CEC 395. *See also* France v. EC Commission, 1998 Eur. Comm. Rep. I–1375.

[52]   1991 O.J. L334/42.

Perrier by Nestlé.[53] Prior to the merger, Nestlé, Perrier and BSN controlled about 82 percent of the French bottled water market. Afterwards, Nestlé and BSN each had about 41 percent of the market. The sell-off requirements were thought sufficient by the Commission to maintain effective competition. The case also presents interesting arguments that the Commission, in granting approval, disregarded fundamental workers' social rights. This issue was unsuccessfully taken up on appeal by Perrier's trade union representative.

In 1997, the European Commission dramatically demonstrated its extraterritorial jurisdiction over the proposed merger of Boeing Co. and McDonnell Douglas Co., two leading U.S. aircraft manufacturers. The merger had already been cleared by the U.S. Federal Trade Commission.[54] The European Commission, however, asserted jurisdiction based on the companies' sales in the EU and threatened to block to transaction. Ultimately Boeing made important concessions, including abandonment of exclusive supply contracts with three U.S. airlines and licensing of technology derived from McDonnell Douglas' military programs at reasonable royalty rates, to receive the European Commission's approval.[55]

The Commission blocked the merger of MC Worldcom and Sprint, two U.S. companies, in 2001, as did the U.S. Department of Justice. Both authorities were worried about the merger's adverse effects on Internet access. For the Commission, this was the first block of a merger taking place outside the EU between two firms established outside the EU. Much more controversy arose when in 2001 the Commission blocked the merger of General Electric and Honeywell, also both U.S. companies, after the merger had been approved by U.S. authorities. The Commission was particularly concerned about the potential for bundling engines with avionics and non-avionics to the disadvantage of rivals. This reasoning was rejected on appeal by the European Court of Justice, but the merger was never completed. The United States and the EU, in the wake of the GE/Honeywell case, have agreed to follow a set of "Best Practices" on coordinated timing, evidence gathering, communication and consistency of remedies.

---

[53]   O.J. L356/1 (Dec. 5. 1992).

[54]   Matter of Boeing Company/McDonnell Douglas Corporation, U.S. Federal Trade Commission, Statement, July 1, 1997.

[55]   Commission of the European Union Decision, 30 July 1997 (Case No. IV/M.877—Boeing/McDonnell Douglas)(97/816/EC).

§ 22.8 Privatization

Privatization refers to the sale of formerly state-owned enterprises to private investors. Although such sales are not necessarily made to foreign investors, foreign capital is often necessary to make the sale realistic. Privatization received substantial impetus in the 1990s after the collapse of the Soviet Union and the transition of many formerly nonmarket economies, especially in eastern and central Europe, to market-based systems. During this time, other developing countries sought to reduce the role of the state in the economy, often at the behest of the International Monetary Fund (IMF) in connection with IMF loans to heavily indebted countries. Although the pace of privatization has declined somewhat in the 21st century, it remains an important aspect of foreign investment in countries seeking to raise hard currency revenue, reduce the budgetary impact of inefficient money-losing state firms, or reduce the government's role in the economy.[56]

Many transitional and developing nation governments are theoretically committed to the idea of a market economy, but it is often difficult to gain public acceptance of the idea when populist remnants endure, and even assume control. While privatization has important economic consequences for the nation, it is always the result of political decisions, and thus can be a fundamentally politicized process. There are many obstacles to privatization, which if not corrected or surmounted tend to return the plan to mythology. These include:

Absence of an Adequate Legal and Physical Infrastructure. Developing nations usually have in place a legal infrastructure with market economy characteristics, but there are often inadequate structures to help raise capital, such as a viable stock market and securities regulation law. Also, few developing nations have effective rules governing monopolies and restrictive trade practices. They may lack effective company laws, commercial codes, laws governing property transfers, and bankruptcy or insolvency laws. There also may be inadequate or unreliable judicial systems. Even when the laws and institutions are created there may be an absence of the educated human resources required to function effectively. The result may be no enforcement or a very harsh and arbitrary enforcement.

---

[56] For example, the recent EU/IMF bailout of Greece set goals for privatization of Greek state-owned companies. *See* Simon Nixon, *New Test for Greece's Alexis Tsipras: Privatization,* Wall St. J., July 19, 2015; Nekaria Stamouli, *Greece Expected to Miss 2016 Privatization Target,* Wall St. J., Dec. 8, 2015.

Another infrastructure often lacking in developing nations is the infrastructure of airports, roads, ports, waterways, telecommunications, water treatment, and power plants, all needed to allow business to function and grow. Often these are state-owned and operated inefficiently and without adequate capital. They are areas where privatization is often most needed to diminish such a serious obstacle to encouraging foreign investment. In recent years there has been a major emphasis in some developing nations, especially in Latin America, in developing this infrastructure with foreign private assistance.

Government Approval Process. Because the essence of privatization is the sale of state-owned properties, the government is obviously involved. Often, the state creates a privatization commission to carry out the process. But where a specific case becomes a public issue, there may be pressure on the central administration to influence decisions of the special commission. Privatization can become a volatile issue, especially when the workers feel threatened by the process and seek public support for stopping the process.

Government approval creates opportunities for requests for bribes. Many developing nations' governments have institutionalized corruption. The privatization process creates new opportunities and new forms of corruption. Management (i.e., government employees) of the state-owned enterprises may oppose the privatization unless they are paid off, or hired, by the purchasers. Many government employees see the proceeds of the sale as a one-time windfall, which they have an opportunity to share in personally. It is difficult to participate in privatization in many countries without confronting demands for payments that will likely create issues under the U.S. Foreign Corrupt Practices Act.[57]

Participation of Workers in the Approval Process. Workers often view privatization as a threat to their jobs. They have good reason. Usually the state enterprise has more employees than are needed to perform the business function. Privatization means a reduction of the workforce in most cases. As a consequence, workers are sometimes given some voice in the sale of an enterprise. But they are rarely given the final say, since they are likely to vote against the sale to preserve their jobs. They may receive rights to participate in the equity of the new privately owned enterprise.

Rights of Nationals to Preferences. While employees may participate in the approval process, all nationals may have

---

[57]   *See* Chapter 15.

preference rights to purchase shares in the entity being sold. The reason is to allow nationals to share in the sale of assets. When governments set aside so much of the enterprise to be privatized for possible purchase by nationals or employees, they may issue coupons or vouchers to the nationals or employees. The vouchers may be used for any privatization, or for a specific industry being privatized. A danger is allowing too much of the enterprise to be acquired by nationals at a nominal price paid for the coupons or vouchers. The purchaser of the majority interest may not be willing to subsidize the acquisition of shares by nationals.

Method of Valuation. There is probably no more difficult aspect of privatization than establishing a value for an enterprise to be privatized. The book value of a state-owned company is not likely to be any more reflective of the value than in the case of a privately owned business in the United States.

Where it is difficult to determine a fair value, the government may wish to have an auction. Foreign investors may not wish to engage in a bidding process, and the auction process clearly drives away some prospective buyers. Most purchasers wish to be the only negotiating company, so as to avoid the expense of competitive bidding.

Valuation difficulty is not limited to developing nation privatizations. There have been experiences in developed nations that have privatized state-owned companies at either too high prices (bringing no interest), or too low prices (bringing many buyers and the creation of a second market after the sale at a considerably higher price).

Treatment of Foreign Investment. The privatization process in developing nations typically assumes the participation of foreign investment. There is usually thought to be insufficient capital in the private sector to purchase the enterprises. However, some enterprises which are to be privatized may be limited to private ownership by host nation nationals. Or there may be limitations on the foreign share acquired, bringing into the privatization mandatory joint ventures. Sometimes there are attempts to first sell the business to nationals, with a subsequent opening of the remaining shares to foreign investment. This is not likely to attract many foreign investors when it means acquisition of a minority share. The reality is that the capital needed to privatize is usually mostly located abroad, and sooner or later the nation must adapt the privatization plan to include foreign investors. If there are limits on foreign investment, the largest industries will go unsold.

Miscellaneous. Privatization contains many unknowns for both the government and potential foreign investors. The government views the process as relieving it of a financial burden and acquiring a substantial payoff. The foreign investor often views the process as a means of entering the nation and obtaining a good investment at a favorable price. Neither the nation nor the foreign investor may be fully satisfied, and they may discover that the time and expense necessary to complete the privatization is far in excess of what was expected.

Additional problems that face foreign investors acquiring an enterprise through privatization include the possibility that there may be demands that the company continue to produce the same products, or export so much production. The company must know what the demands will be that will interfere with its making choices.

Privatization has been especially successful in formerly nonmarket economies with small to medium businesses. But in developing nations, there are usually few state-owned small to medium sized business. Selling the largest businesses in any form of economy has more complex problems than selling smaller businesses. The workforce is likely to be more vocal and more powerful in the largest businesses. Valuation is usually more difficult, and there are fewer buyers who can afford such businesses. In many cases, the largest business have been acquired by consortia, often comprising investors from several foreign nations.

Chapter 23

TREATIES AND AGREEMENTS PROTECTING FOREIGN INVESTMENT

Table of Sections

§ 23.1 Bilateral Investment Treaties (BITs)

For U.S. investors, the United States' Treaties of Friendship, Navigation and Commence (FCN Treaties) and similar bilateral agreements such as Treaties of Amity and Economic Relations provided some of the earliest treaty-based investment protections. These agreements, many of which were signed in the mid-twentieth century or earlier, covered a range of topics and often included basic commitments against expropriation and other interference with foreign investment absent compensation.[1]

Beginning in the 1980s, the United States undertook a new program of treatymaking specifically aimed at investment protection. These Bilateral Investment Treaties (BITs) were designed to replace and extend the protections offered by FCN Treaties and other similar agreements, particularly with regard to

---

[1]   For litigation involving the expropriation provisions of these treaties, see McKesson Corp. v. Islamic Republic of Iran, 539 F.3d 485 (D.C. Cir. 2008) (U.S.-Iran Treaty of Amity, Economic Relations and Consular Rights); Kalamazoo Spice Extraction Co. v. Provisional Military Government of Socialist Ethiopia, 729 F.2d 422 (6th Cir. 1984) (U.S.-Ethiopia Treaty of Amity and Economic Relations).

dispute resolution.[2] The United States currently has BITs with approximately 40 nations.[3] While many are with small developing countries,[4] the United States has also signed BITs with more important investment destinations such as Argentina, Turkey and a number of eastern European countries.[5] However, many of the most important countries for U.S. investment are not parties to U.S. BITs.

The U.S. BITs tend to have very similar language, although they have evolved somewhat over time and may vary according to the particular needs of the other nation. The United States has a model BIT,[6] which it seeks to use as a template in negotiating new treaties, but variations are permitted. Thus, while BITs can be described generally, specific reference must be made to each treaty to confirm the details of its operation.

Most BITs address both investment protection and investor access to each other's markets. They provide rules which each country must follow with respect to investors and investments from the other party.[7] Investor access provisions address both express barriers to foreign investment, such as prohibitions on foreign ownership, and investment regulations that operate as implicit barriers, such as requirements to hire as managers only nationals of the host government.[8] Under the typical BIT, explicit freedom to hire home-country nationals exists in a narrow range of management provisions, helping roll back the traditional requirement of local management. But investment screening mechanisms and key sectors often remain exempt from BIT protections, typically listed in an Annex to the BIT. While elimination of investment screening and performance requirements

---

[2]   *See* K. Scott Gudgeon, *United States Bilateral Investment Treaties,* 4 INT'L TAX & BUS. LAW. 105 (1986); Pamela Gann, *The United States Bilateral Investment Treaty Program,* 21 STANFORD J. INT'L L. 373 (1985).

[3]   *See* http://www.state.gov/e/eb/ifd/bit/117402.htm (listing U.S. BITs).

[4]   For an early example, see the 1989 U.S.-Cameroon treaty, http://2001-2009. state.gov/documents/organization/43543.pdf.

[5]   *E.g.,* http://2001-2009.state.gov/documents/organization/43475.pdf (investment treaty with Argentina); http://www.state.gov/documents/organization/210528.pdf (investment treaty with Poland); http://2001-2009.state.gov/documents/organization/ 43615.pdf (investment treaty with Turkey). An investment treaty with Russia was signed but not ratified. The most recent U.S. BIT is the 2012 treaty with Rwanda, see http://www.state.gov/documents/organization/101735.pdf.

[6]   http://www.state.gov/documents/organization/188371.pdf.

[7]   An investor's nationality under the BITs is often not well-defined. *See id.,* art. 1 (definition of "investor of a Party"). For example, there may be dispute whether a subsidiary incorporated in the United States whose parent is incorporated in another country should be treated as a U.S. investor.

[8]   *Id.,* art. 9. *Compare* Sumitomo Shoji America v. Avagliano, 457 U.S. 176 (1982) (FCN Treaty did not prohibit restrictions on hiring home-country management).

has been an object of the BIT program, these provisions of the model BIT have been weakened in many treaties currently in force.[9]

The BITs do not prohibit nations from enacting investment laws, but they provide that any such laws should not interfere with any rights in the treaty. The free access aspect of some BITs may not be perceived as a right. Thus investment laws might be enacted that limit access to certain areas, but would not create a right of the other party to challenge the law under the BIT.

The BITs also contain important protections for an investment once it is established. Typically (though not always) these are reflected in four principal categories: (a) national treatment; (b) most favored nation treatment; (c) protection against expropriation; and (d) minimum standard of treatment. National treatment means that the foreign investment will not be treated any worse than investments owned by nationals of the host nation.[10] It is thus effectively an anti-discrimination rule. Although it is sometimes difficult to apply, as it may be difficult to agree on what constitutes equivalent treatment, this is an important correction to the common practice of treating local businesses more favorably. Most-favored-nation treatment means that the investor will not be treated less favorably than foreign investors from other nations (that is, there will be no discrimination among foreign investors).[11] This sort of discrimination is less common, but the provision protects against retaliation or other unfavorable treatment based on the host nation's dislike of a particular foreign country.

Expropriation refers to the host government's seizure of or other interference with the investment (see Chapter 24). The United States seeks to include in its BITs its preferred "prompt, adequate and effective" concept (if not always the language) of compensation subsequent to expropriation.[12] Many nations that have recently agreed to this language previously disputed its appropriateness during the nationalistic North-South dialogue years of the 1960s and 1970s. But as developing nations began to promote rather than restrict investment, they began to accept the idea that expropriated investment had to be compensated reasonably soon after the taking ("prompt"), with compensation

---

[9]   *See* K. Scott Gudgeon, *United States Bilateral Investment Treaties,* 4 INT'L TAX & BUS. LAW. 105, 126–27 (1986) (observing that BITs with Egypt, Haiti, and Zaire (Congo) have the weakest language ["shall seek to endeavor/avoid" trade related performance requirements], while BITs with Senegal and Panama include qualifications, such as exemption for Panama's investment incentive program).

[10]   *See* U.S. Model BIT, Art. 3, http://www.state.gov/documents/organization/188371.pdf.

[11]   *See id.,* art. 4.

[12]   *See id.,* art. 6.

based on a fair valuation ("adequate") and paid in a realistic form ("effective"). For example, the Argentina-United States BIT uses language referring to the "fair market value . . . immediately before the expropriatory action."[13] Recent BITs contain language further explaining and limiting the definition of expropriation, especially as applied to indirect (regulatory) expropriation.[14]

The provision for a "minimum standard of treatment"[15] of the investment is the most difficult to apply. As most BITs specifically explain, this is intended to refer to the standard for "fair and equitable treatment and full protection and security" as established under customary international law.[16] This provision typically goes on to provide that "(a) 'fair and equitable treatment' includes the obligation not to deny justice in criminal, civil, or administrative adjudicatory proceedings in accordance with the principle of due process embodied in the principal legal systems of the world; and (b) 'full protection and security' requires each Party to provide the level of police protection required under customary international law."[17] However, as explained in more detail in Chapter 24, customary international standards for treatment of an investment are sharply disputed. As a result, investors may often be able to claim they have been treated unfairly under this standard, but establishing that claim will be much more difficult.

Other common protections include requirements for free transfer of funds[18] and prohibitions on performance requirements.[19]

---

[13] Argentina-United States BIT, art. IV(1), http://2001-2009.state.gov/ documents/organization/43475.pdf. For further discussion of compensation standards following expropriations, see Chapter 24, § 24.7.

[14] *See* U.S. Model BIT, Annex B, § 1 (explaining that the treaty "is intended to reflect customary international law concerning the obligation of States with respect to expropriation"), https://ustr.gov/sites/default/files/uploads/agreements/bit/asset_ upload_file748_9005.pdf; *id.*, Annex B, § 2 (explaining that "[a]n action or a series of actions by a Party cannot constitute an expropriation unless it interferes with a tangible or intangible property right or property interest in an investment"); *id.*, Annex B, § 4(b) (providing that "[e]xcept in rare circumstances, non-discriminatory regulatory actions by a Party that are designed and applied to protect legitimate public welfare objectives, such as public health, safety, and the environment, do not constitute indirect expropriations.") *See also, e.g.*, Treaty Between the United States of America and the Oriental Republic of Uruguay Concerning the Encouragement and Reciprocal Protection of Investment, Nov. 1, 2006 (adopting these provisions), https://ustr.gov/sites/default/files/uploads/agreements/bit/asset_upload_file748_9005. pdf. Under the latter provision, the potential for succeeding with regulatory takings claims against the host government appears reduced.

[15] *See* U.S. Model BIT, art. 5, http://www.state.gov/documents/organization/ 188371.pdf.

[16] *Id. See also id.,* Annex A (stating that customary international law "results from a general and consistent practice of States they follow from a sense of legal obligation").

[17] *Id.,* art. 5, § 2.

[18] *Id.,* art. 7.

Especially in more recent BITs, there may be special provisions on environmental and labor law relating to investments.[20]

The BITs' most significant innovation has been in the area of dispute resolution. Most BITs contain provisions that allow an investor, in the event of a dispute with the host government, to submit the dispute to arbitration.[21] The host government is required to accept arbitration and to satisfy any arbitration awards against it. Thus BITs provide more options to investors to seek remedies against host governments that interfere with investments. In Latin America, for example, such provisions override traditional "Calvo Clause" rules limiting foreign investors to host country remedies. Indeed, BIT arbitration remedies have encouraged "treaty shopping" through strategic or mailbox investments in countries that provide access to such remedies.[22] Philip Morris, for example, restructured a Hong Kong investment in order to challenge foreseeable (but not yet enacted) Australian cigarette packaging regulations via the Hong Kong-Australia BIT remedies.[23] Romanian and other companies are reported to be using Dutch mailbox companies as the vehicle for investments in their own home countries in order to avoid local law and assertedly corrupt local courts. Naturally such firms are not keen on exclusive EU investment treaty jurisdiction, which will in time presumably eliminate this treaty shopping option. (For more on BIT arbitrations, see Chapter 28).

Most BITs include provisions for consultations when differences arise in the interpretation of the treaty,[24] and they may also require prior exhaustion of local remedies before resort to arbitration.[25]

---

[19]   *Id.*, art. 8.

[20]   *Id.*, arts. 12–13.

[21]   *Id.*, art. 24.

[22]   Julien Chaisse, *The Treaty Shopping Practice: Corporate Structuring and Restructuring to Gain Access to Investment Treaties and Arbitration,* 11 HASTINGS BUS. L.J. 225 (2015).

[23]   The arbitrators found that Philip Morris had engaged in an "abuse of rights" and rejected all of its claims. *See* Kavaljit Singh, *ISDS Arbitration Upholds Australia's Plain Packaging Laws,* EAST ASIA FORUM, Jan. 15, 2016, http://www.eastasiaforum.org/2016/01/15/isds-arbitration-upholds-australias-plain-packaging-laws/.

[24]   *See* U.S. Model BIT, art. 23, http://www.state.gov/documents/organization/188371.pdf.

[25]   *See* BG Group, PLC v. Republic of Argentina, 134 S.Ct. 1198 (2014) (discussing exhaustion requirement in U.K.-Argentina BIT). The U.S. Model BIT does not have this requirement.

European Union countries have also pursued BITs, with some 1,200 bilateral investment agreements between member states and non-EU countries. The EU brought foreign investment under exclusive EU competence in the Lisbon Treaty, which became effective in 2009. In late 2012 the EU adopted a new regulation on bilateral investment agreements. It affects both existing agreements, which the EU will attempt to replace over time, and new EU-wide agreements, including existing agreements (ratification pending) with Canada and Vietnam.

BITs are an important contribution of the developed home nation to their multinationals investing abroad. They establish some ground rules for investment on a bilateral treaty basis that should not be unilaterally altered by the host nation to impose restrictions on the investments that are inconsistent with the BIT. Certainly, revolutionary governments have ignored similar agreements in the past and may in the future. But the BITs do provide some investment security, at least as long as the host governments remain relatively stable, and receptive to foreign investment.

BITs have significance beyond the particular countries involved in at least two important respects. First, after an initial slow start, there has been a surge in arbitration cases brought under U.S. and non-U.S. BITs asking arbitrators to apply protections against discrimination, expropriation, and unfair treatment. Since these concepts are also part of the customary international law of foreign investment, the arbitrators' decisions transcend the immediate dispute and have contributed to the expansion and definition of this part of international law. Second, as discussed below, the BITs' investment protections have also been incorporated into regional and bilateral free trade agreements, beginning with the North American Free Trade Agreement (NAFTA).

§ 23.2 The Convention on the Settlement of Investment Disputes Between States and Nationals of Other States (ICSID Convention)

More than 140 nations including the United States are parties to the 1966 Convention on the Settlement of Investment Disputes Between States and Nationals of Other States (the ICSID Convention).[26] The Convention provided for the creation of the International Centre for the Settlement of Investment Disputes

---

[26] *See* https://icsid.worldbank.org/apps/ICSIDWEB/icsiddocs/Pages/ICSID-Convention.aspx. The Convention is implemented in the United States by 22 U.S.C. §§ 1650–1650a.

(ICSID) as part of the World Bank.[27] The Convention and Centre provide a forum for arbitration of investment disputes, offering an institutional framework for the proceedings. Jurisdiction under the Convention extends to "any legal dispute arising directly out of an investment, between a Contracting State or . . . any subdivision . . . and a national of another Contracting State." The parties must consent in writing to the submission of the dispute to the Centre. Once given, the consent may not be unilaterally withdrawn.[28]

ICSID arbitration is only for disputes involving nations that are both parties ("Contracting States") to the ICSID Convention. Concern regarding the jurisdictional limitations led to the creation of the ICSID Additional Facility, which may be used for conciliations and arbitrations for special disputes in which only one party is (or is a national of) an ICSID member.[29] It was not created to deal with ordinary investment disputes but with disputes between parties with long-term special economic relationships involving substantial resource commitments. The Additional Facility may be used only with the approval of the ICSID Secretary General.

Most BITs allow (but do not require) investors to select ICSID arbitration in the event of an investment dispute if the host nation is an ICSID member.[30] As discussed below, the investment protections of most free trade agreements also incorporate ICSID arbitration, and it can also be selected in private contracts between an investor and the host government.

§ 23.3 The Investment Protections of the North American Free Trade Agreement (NAFTA)

As discussed in Chapter 17, the North American Free Trade Agreement (NAFTA) is a major regional free trade agreement among the United States, Canada and Mexico, which went into effect in 1994. As is typical in free trade agreements, it primarily addresses cross-border trade in goods and services. In addition, however, NAFTA contains a set of provisions protecting foreign

---

[27] The Centre publishes a useful journal, the ICSID Review—Foreign Investment Law Journal, http://icsidreview.oxfordjournals.org/. *See, e.g.,* Alexander A. Ekpombang, *The Legal Framework of Foreign Investment in Rwanda,* 26 ICSID REV. 123 (2011); Otto Sandrock, *Right of Foreign Investors to Access German Markets,* 25 ICSID REV. 268 (2010).

[28] ICSID arbitration is discussed in more detail in Chapter 28.

[29] The Additional Facility has its own arbitration rules.

[30] *See* U.S. Model BIT, art. 24(3), http://www.state.gov/documents/organization/188371.pdf.

investment similar to those of the BITs.[31] Investment, for these purposes, is broadly defined to cover virtually all forms of ownership and activity, including real estate, stocks, bonds, contracts and technologies.

NAFTA's investment protections are relevant not just to its three member nations. A subsidiary of a non-NAFTA corporation, if incorporated and having substantial business operations in a NAFTA country, will be treated as a NAFTA investor. For example, an Asian or European subsidiary incorporated with substantial business operations in Canada will be treated as a Canadian investor for purposes of NAFTA.

The NAFTA investment provisions, in Chapter 11 of the Agreement, are divided into two major sections. Section A covers investment rules, and Section B covers the settlement of investment disputes. Chapter 11 applies to all investments, as defined in Article 1139, with exemptions for financial services contained in Annex III, and where special social services (police, public health, etc.) are performed. But if a provision of Chapter 11 conflicts with a provision in another chapter, the latter prevails.

Like the BITs, Section A of NAFTA Chapter 11 requires each party to provide specific treatment to investors of each other party, including *national treatment* (requiring treatment of investors of another party "no less favorable than that it accords" to the party's own investors); *most-favored-nation treatment* (requiring that a party accord investors of another party treatment no less favorable than it accords to investors of any other party or non-party); and a *minimum standard of treatment* (incorporating a rule of "international law, including fair and equitable treatment and full protection and security").[32]

One ongoing concern of foreign investors has been *performance requirements,* local mandates that a certain percentage of the goods or services be exported, or be of domestic content, or meet a balance between import needs and exports, or link local sales to the volume of exports, or contain certain technology transferred from abroad, or mandate meeting certain exclusive sales targets. Each of these is disallowed by NAFTA, with certain exceptions. Perhaps the second most disliked domestic restrictions on foreign investment are

---

[31]   *See generally* Gloria L. Sandrino, *The NAFTA Investment Chapter and Foreign Direct Investment in Mexico: A Third World Perspective,* 27 VAND. J. TRANSNAT'L L. 259 (1994); Stephen Zamora, *NAFTA and the Harmonization of Domestic Legal Systems: The Side Effects of Free Trade,* 12 ARIZ. J. INT'L & COMP. L. 401 (1995).

[32]   In a subsequent official interpretation, the NAFTA parties clarified that this standard does not require treatment beyond what is required by customary international law. *See* http://www.state.gov/documents/organization/38790.pdf.

mandated levels of local equity (the *involuntary joint venture*). A prohibition against a minimum level of domestic equity is included in the national treatment provision. There is also a prohibition against requirements that a minimum number of local persons being appointed to senior management. But there may be a local requirement that a majority of the board of directors (or a board committee) be nationals or residents, as long as the investor is not therefore impaired in controlling the investment. A fourth investor concern is free transferability of profits, royalty payments, etc., both during operation and upon liquidation of the investment. NAFTA provides a general right to convert and transfer local currency at prevailing market rates for earnings, sale proceeds, loan repayments and other investment transactions, with exceptions for good faith and nondiscriminatory restraints upon monetary transfers arising out of bankruptcy, insolvency, securities dealings, crimes, satisfaction of judgments and currency reporting duties.

The above areas of concern deal mostly with the ability to commence and operate an investment free from certain restrictions. There is another time in the life of a business that has perhaps long been the most significant risk for foreign investors: when the business is nationalized or expropriated. NAFTA includes an eight-part article outlining rules for both takings and compensation. Direct and indirect expropriations of investments of NAFTA investors are precluded except for public purposes and if done on a nondiscriminatory basis following due process of law. A right of compensation without delay at fair market value plus interest is recognized. The words "prompt, adequate, and effective" are not used, although that has long been the standard the U.S. government has argued to be the mandate of international law. That standard was specifically rejected by Mexico subsequent to the nationalization of its petroleum industry in 1938. The language of NAFTA addresses each of these areas, however. Compensation shall be "equivalent to the fair market value of the expropriated investment immediately before the expropriation took place . . . ," The adequacy issue is covered by NAFTA's requirement of "fair market value," and the effectiveness by the requirement of payment in a "G7 currency," or by implication one convertible to such currency. The expropriation article has been the subject of considerable debate, especially when it is used to challenge actions that are not traditional nationalizations but are more common regulatory standards that impede the effective operation of an investment.[33]

---

[33] *See, e.g.,* Anthony DePalma, *Mexico is Ordered to Pay a U.S. Company $16.7 Million,* N.Y. Times, Aug. 31, 2000, at C4 (state government's enforcement of environmental laws amounted to an expropriation); Timothy Pritchard, *Law Suits*

The NAFTA investment rules do not apply to Mexican constitutionally-reserved sectors (*e.g.*, energy, railroads and boundary and coastal real estate) nor Canada's cultural industries. Maritime, airline, broadcasting, fishing, nuclear, basic telecommunications, and government-sponsored technology consortia are exempt from the NAFTA investment rules. The NAFTA countries have agreed not to lower environmental standards to attract investment and to permit (as Mexico requires) environmental impact statements for foreign investments.

Section B of NAFTA Chapter 11 governs the settlement of investment disputes between a party and an investor of another party.[34] In the event of a dispute, a NAFTA investor may seek monetary (but not punitive) damages through binding arbitration under the ICSID Convention (if both nations are parties),[35] the ICSID Additional Facility Rules (if only one nation is a party to the Convention), or the arbitration rules of the U.N. Commission on International Trade Law (UNCITRAL). An arbitration tribunal for investment disputes will be established by the Secretary-General of ICSID if the parties are unable to select a panel by choosing one arbitrator each and having those arbitrators choose a third. However, there are no time limits for the arbitration and either side may appeal the award to the courts. Alternatively, the investor may pursue judicial remedies in courts of the host state.

There have been numerous investor-state claims proceedings under NAFTA's Chapter 11, Section B.[36] Relatively few have been successful for the investor. For example, a U.S.-based company successfully sued Mexico after state and local authorities in Mexico refused to issue environmental permits for its hazardous waste processing facility.[37] Another U.S.-based waste processing company successfully sued Canada after Canada effectively prohibited the export of hazardous waste from Canada.[38] In a case that stirred

---

are Prompting Calls for Changes to Clause in NAFTA, N.Y. Times, June 19, 1999, at C2 (Canadian corporation claiming California environmental law violated Ch. 11); William Glaberson, *NAFTA Invoked to Challenge Court Award*, N.Y. Times, Jan. 28, 1999, at C6 (Canadian company claiming Mississippi jury award violated Ch. 11).

[34]   *See* Donald S. Macdonald, *Chapter 11 of NAFTA: What Are the Implications for Sovereignty?*, 24 CAN.-U.S. L.J. 281 (1998).

[35]   The United States has been a party to the ICSID Convention since 1966; Canada joined in 2013. Mexico is not an ICSID member.

[36]   *See* William L. Owen, *Investment Arbitration under NAFTA Chapter 11: A Threat to Sovereignty of Member States?*, 39 CAN.-U.S. L.J. 55 (2015); Ralph H. Folsom, NAFTA, FREE TRADE AND FOREIGN INVESTMENT IN THE AMERICAS IN A NUTSHELL, ch. 6 (2014).

[37]   Metalclad Corp. v. United Mexican States, ICSID Case No. ARB (AF)/97/1, ¶ 107 (2001).

[38]   S.D. Myers, Inc. v. Canada, 40 I.L.M. 1408 (2001) (decision of Nov. 12, 2000).

considerable controversy, a Canadian funeral home operator challenged an adverse Mississippi court judgment on the ground that there had been unfair discrimination against it in the court proceedings.[39] Another controversial case, in which the parties reached a settlement, involved a Canadian province's seizure of property and equipment of a U.S. investor.[40] However, a number of claims relating to regulatory actions have been rejected.[41]

As discussed in Chapter 17, the newly elected administration of President Trump in the United States may substantially renegotiate NAFTA, or perhaps withdraw from it altogether, although the objections are principally centered on NAFTA's trade provisions, not its investment provisions.

§ 23.4 Investment Protections in Other Free Trade Agreements

Following the example of NAFTA, the United States commonly included investment protections in subsequent free trade agreements (FTAs). These include both bilateral free trade agreements, such as the United States has with, for example, South Korea, Chile and Colombia, and the regional free trade agreement among the United States, the Dominican Republic and five Central American countries (DR-CAFTA).[42] The pending Trans Pacific

---

[39] Loewen Group, Inc. v. United States, ICSID Case No. ARB(AF)/98/3 (June 26, 2003), http://www.italaw.com/cases/632. The arbitral tribunal allowed a challenge to court proceedings as a general matter, but rejected the particular claim on a technicality.

[40] See AbitibiBowater Inc. v. Canada, Notice of Intent to Submit a Claim to Arbitration (23 April 2009); Canada—Department of Foreign Affairs and International Trade, Foreign Affairs and International Trade, Canada Issues Statement on AbitibiBowater Settlement, DFAIT Press Release 2010 No. 268 (Aug. 24, 2010), http://www.italaw.com/cases/39.

[41] E.g., Waste Management, Inc. v. United Mexican States, ICSID Case No. ARB(AF)/00/3, Award of April 30, 2004, http://www.italaw.com/cases/1158 (rejecting U.S. investor's claim relating to breach of agreement to provide waste disposal services in Acapulco, Mexico); Glamis Gold, Ltd. v. United States of America, Award of June 8, 2009, http://www.state.gov/documents/organization/125798.pdf (rejecting Canadian investor's claim for U.S. regulations of mining operation); Methanex Corp. v. United States, NAFTA/UNCITRAL (Aug. 3, 2005), http://www.state.gov/documents/organization/51052.pdf (rejecting Canadian investor's claim arising from California's environmental regulation of the gasoline additive MBTE). For a list of all investment claims filed under NAFTA, see U.S. Department of State, NAFTA Investor-State Arbitrations, http://www.state.gov/documents/organization/38790.pdf.

[42] See, e.g., DR-CAFTA Free Trade Agreement, ch. 10, https://ustr.gov/sites/default/files/uploads/agreements/cafta/asset_upload_file328_4718.pdf; U.S.-Korea Free Trade Agreement, ch. 11, https://ustr.gov/trade-agreements/free-trade-agreements/korus-fta/final-text. Australia refused to accept investor-state arbitrations under the U.S-Australia free trade agreement. For further discussion of free trade agreements and a complete list of U.S. FTAs, see Chapter 17, § 17.6.

Partnership (TPP)[43] also contains investment protections, as does a proposed agreement, called the Transatlantic Trade and Investment Partnership (TTIP), being negotiated between the EU and the United States. The FTAs typically track the BITs both in the nature of the protections provided and in the method of dispute resolution.[44] Non-U.S. free trade agreements, such as the FTAs between South Korea and Canada and between South Korea and Australia, also commonly have investment protections, usually in language parallel to the U.S. agreements.[45]

§ 23.5   The WTO Agreement on Trade Related-Investment Measures (TRIMs)

The GATT Uruguay Round, which led to the establishment of the World Trade Organization (WTO),[46] included some investment rules. Prior to this Round, the General Agreement on Tariffs and Trade (GATT) had not directly governed foreign investment.[47] The new rules were thus a somewhat significant development. But as must be expected with any large organization with members possessing divergent views, the WTO investment provisions are not as comprehensive as those in the much smaller NAFTA or in bilateral agreements.

The WTO investment rules are included in the Agreement on Trade-Related Investment Measures (called TRIMs), one of the

---

[43]   *See* Chapter 17, § 17.9. The TPP makes several material reforms in the investment protection area, mostly limiting available protections. For example, financial stability regulation falls outside indirect expropriation claims, tobacco regulation may not be challenged, mere frustration of profit expectations is insufficient to pursue investor-state arbitrations, the burden of proof falls on investor claimants, no shell companies may be used to access investor-state arbitral remedies, and state-owned enterprises along with authorized government agents are made subject to the agreement's dispute settlement regime. In addition, the TPP agreement mandates public access to hearings and documents, allows amicus briefs, facilitates expedited dismissals of frivolous claims, and generally protects existing intellectual property license royalties and durations from alteration. As indicated in Chapter 17, the TPP appears unlikely to be ratified due to the opposition of the new administration in the United States.

[44]   *See* § 23.1 above. Among other things, recent FTAs typically contain the restrictive definitions of "fair and equitable treatment" and expropriation found in recent BITs.

[45]   *See* Canada-Korea Free Trade Agreement, ch. 8 (2015), http://www. international.gc.ca/trade-agreements-accords-commerciaux/agr-acc/korea-coree/toc-tdm.aspx?lang=eng; Korea-Australia Free Trade Agreement, art. 11 (2014), http://dfat.gov.au/trade/agreements/kafta/official-documents/Pages/default.aspx.

[46]   *See* Chapter 9.

[47]   Foreign investment was originally to have been governed by a proposed World Trade Organization discussed at the Bretton Woods conference near the end of World War II. The U.S. Senate was hostile to the idea and the ensuing GATT did not regulate foreign investment. *See* Chapter 9.

many agreements constituting the WTO.[48] The Agreement sets forth a national treatment principle. TRIMs which are considered inconsistent with WTO obligations are listed in an annex, and include such performance requirements as minimum domestic content, imports limited or linked to exports, and restrictions on access to foreign exchange to limit imports for use in the investment. Developing countries are allowed to "deviate temporarily" from the national treatment concept, diminishing the effectiveness of the WTO investment provisions and discouraging investment in nations which have a history of imposing investment restrictions—and thus making such agreements as NAFTA all the more useful and likely to spread.

The essence of the WTO TRIMs Agreement is to establish the same principle of national treatment for investments as has been in effect for trade. TRIMs are incorporated in the overall structure of the WTO, alongside trade measures, rather than being treated as a distinct area. The WTO's investment protections are narrower than those included in bilateral investment treaties and free trade agreements. In addition (and perhaps more importantly) the WTO TRIMs Agreement's dispute resolution process is the same as the dispute resolution for other WTO Agreements: it involves only state-to-state dispute resolution with state-to-state retaliation as the only remedy.[49] Thus, much of the international law of foreign investment has developed and likely will continue to develop under BITs and FTAs rather than within the WTO. That said, about a dozen WTO complaints have successfully challenged local content performance requirements for auto production by foreign investors. The United States and the European Union, for example, overcame Indonesian performance requirements of this sort via WTO proceedings.

§ 23.6 The Multilateral Agreement on Investment (MAI)

In the 1990s a large number of nations aggressively pursued a worldwide agreement on foreign investment, to be called the Multilateral Agreement on Investment (MAI), through the Organisation for Economic Cooperation and Development (OECD). However, irreconcilable disputes between developed and developing nations, and even among developed nations, led to the collapse of

---

[48]   https://www.wto.org/english/docs_e/legal_e/18-trims.pdf.

[49]   *See* Chapter 9. For a list of WTO disputes involving the TRIMs Agreement, see https://www.wto.org/english/tratop_e/dispu_e/dispu_agreements_index_e.htm?id= A25#.

the negotiations in 1998.[50] Although there are periodic suggestions that the idea be revived, there seems no immediate prospect that it will be. This failure illustrates the wide differences remaining among nations on the subject of foreign investment, despite the general relaxation of earlier antagonistic rhetoric and the general embrace, at least in principle, of foreign investment's positive attributes.

---

[50]   *See* OECD, Multilateral Agreement on Investment: Documentation from the Negotiations, http://www.oecd.org/daf/mai/intro.htm.

Chapter 24

EXPROPRIATION OF AN INVESTMENT

Table of Sections

§ 24.1 Introduction

When a foreign investment is made, assets are in effect placed within the power of the host government. This creates the substantial risk that the host government will simply seize the investment. Such seizures are variously called nationalization, confiscation or expropriation. They may come as part of a wider social movement such as a revolutionary change of government; they might come in retaliation for acts of the investor's home government or of the investor itself; or they might be part of an economic restructuring of a particular industry or region. There are both good and bad reasons that an investment might be seized. From the investor's perspective, however, the question is how the risk can be mitigated. This chapter considers the extent to which legal protections and remedies may exist.

While most attention focuses on direct expropriation—when part or all of the investment is taken by the host nation government—governments may also take actions that essentially amount to expropriation because they make continuation of the investment impossible, such as excessively high tax rates, forced

779

joint ventures, excessive government control, mandatory use of domestic inputs, and mandatory export levels. It is debated whether these actions, sometimes called indirect expropriation or (if they occur in stages) creeping expropriation, should be analyzed in parallel with "true" expropriation. There may often be a difficult line between indirect expropriation and legitimate regulation in the public interest.

The risk of expropriation cannot be fully avoided, and insurance should be considered, especially the insurance provided by the U.S. Overseas Private Investment Corporation (OPIC) (for U.S. investors) or the World Bank's Multilateral Investment Guarantee Agency (MIGA).[1] A significant development has been the increasing use of bilateral investment treaties (BITs) and Free Trade Agreements (FTAs) that include requirements of prompt, adequate, and effective compensation (or equivalent language) in the event of expropriation, and that require arbitration of investment disputes between the investor and the host government.[2]

§ 24.2 What Law Applies and What Is That Law?

A threshold question is what law applies to the legality of the expropriation and (most importantly for the investor) the requirement of compensation. There has been continuing debate about both the choice of law issue with respect to expropriation law and, assuming international law applies or is to be considered, what that law requires. For example, the Mexican expropriation of foreign petroleum interests in 1938 commenced a dialogue between Mexico and the United States regarding the applicable law.[3] Mexico insisted that Mexican domestic law applied, which required compensation. The United States insisted that international law applied, which also required compensation. The United States argued that compensation had to be made in accordance with an alleged "prompt, adequate, and effective" international law standard, while the Mexican government had a different view of compensation. The U.S. government position has continued to be that the standard is "prompt, adequate, and effective," even though this view receives inconsistent support abroad and even within the United States by many jurists. The U.S. business community, nevertheless, tends to support the U.S. government position.

---

[1]   *See* Chapter 25.

[2]   *See* Chapter 23.

[3]   The views expressed in letters exchanged by the governments are included in 3 Green H. Hackworth, DIGEST OF INTERNATIONAL LAW 655–65 (1942).

BITs and FTAs with investor protection provisions attempt to resolve this dispute by providing agreement on common principles such as rules governing what compensation is required, when it must be paid, and in what form. However, these agreements may necessarily be somewhat vague on some issues, so areas of disagreement remain.

§ 24.3 Applying the Domestic Law of the Taking Nation

While there is agreement among developed nations that international law applies to takings of foreign property, that has been challenged in two ways. First, the U.N. Charter of Economic Rights and Duties of States affirms the right of nations to expropriate property and declares that compensation issues are to be settled by the "domestic law of the nationalization State," unless otherwise agreed.[4] Second, when a nation expropriates foreign property, it tends to find greater comfort in arguing the applicability of its own law, which is usually less demanding in requiring compensation than whatever standard the international community has endorsed. Thus, expropriating countries may insist that the only applicable law is their own law, unless they have agreed to international protections by treaty (as in a BIT). Obviously a country's receptiveness to the international law of expropriation is a consideration in investing, as is the degree of protection offered by its domestic law. However, both of these may change abruptly after the investment is made if there is a change in government or a change in governmental attitudes.

§ 24.4 Applying International Law

Even if the parties agree that international law is applicable, it may be difficult to determine what international law requires. There is no global lawmaker, nor is there a comprehensive worldwide treaty governing investment.[5] In the absence of a bilateral or regional treaty or similar agreement, international investment law is determined by custom. "Customary international law results from a general and consistent practice of states followed

---

4   Dec. 12, 1974, U.N.G.A. Res. 3281 (XXIX), 29 U.N. GAOR, Supp. (No. 31) 50, U.N. Doc. A/9631 (1975), reprinted in 14 Int'l Legal Mat. 251 (1975). This Charter, which does not constitute international law, was passed over objections to this provision by 16 nations, mostly the largest industrialized nations, including the United States. The Charter illustrates the diversity of opinion regarding expropriation arising with the achievement of independence by many former colonies of the industrialized nations.

5   Such an agreement, called the Multilateral Agreement on Investment (MAI), was pursued in the 1990s but ultimately abandoned. See Chapter 23, § 23.6.

by them from a sense of legal obligation."[6] Particularly in the area of expropriation and compensation, determining the content of this customary law has proved challenging. The U.S. Supreme Court observed:

> There are few if any issues in international law today on which opinion seems to be so divided as the limitations on a state's power to expropriate the property of aliens. . . . The disagreement as to relevant international law standards reflects an even more basic divergence between the national interests of capital importing and capital exporting nations, and between the social ideologies of those countries that favor state control of a considerable portion of the means of production and those that adhere to a free enterprise system.[7]

For example, as discussed below, it may be especially difficult to determine the "customary" standard for compensation after an expropriation. It may be "prompt, adequate and effective" compensation, as the United States argues, or "just" compensation, as the Restatement of Foreign Relations Law suggests, or "appropriate" compensation, as U.N. Resolution 1803 proposed in 1962, and which seems to have been adopted by tribunals and courts more than any other standard. Nonetheless, in the modern era, most countries that accept a customary international law standard for expropriation agree that it contains three basic rules: the expropriation must be (a) for a public purpose; (b) non-discriminatory; and (c) accompanied by at least some form of compensation[8] (although the extent of compensation required remains contested).

§ 24.5 Public Purpose Under International Law

A sovereign nation has full and permanent sovereignty over its natural resources and economic activities.[9] That sovereignty gives the nation the right to take privately owned property, whether that property is owned by the country's nationals or foreigners. These are long-held concepts that exist on both an international and domestic level. Most national (and state or provincial) constitutions

---

6 Restatement (Third) of Foreign Relations Law of the United States, § 102(2) (1987).

7 Banco Nacional de Cuba v. Sabbatino, 376 U.S. 398 (1964). For more on the *Sabbatino* case, see Chapter 27.

8 *See* Restatement (Third) of Foreign Relations Law of the United States, § 712(1) (1987).

9 U.N. Resolution on Permanent Sovereignty Over Natural Resources, Dec. 14, 1962, U.N.G.A. Res. 1803 (XVII), 17 U.N. GAOR, Supp. (No. 17) 15, U.N.Doc. A/5217 (1963), reprinted in 2 Int'l Legal Mat. 223 (1963).

express this right. But the theory of taking does not allow the taking for any reason or upon any whim of the prevailing government. There must be a public purpose. There are two problems with the public purpose requirement, however: its definition, and determining who is to measure public purpose.

There has never been a clear definition of public purpose. It is often expressed in such broad words as "improvement of the social welfare or economic betterment of the nation." Does this mean such specific goals as improved infrastructure, better medical care, lower rates for basic services such as electricity, more adequate housing, or a lower infant-mortality rate? Or does it mean something more general, such as a shift to a different fundamental economic theory, by increasing or making exclusive the state ownership of the means of production and distribution?[10] The practical definition may be what the taking nation says it is, but at least there seems to be agreement that some legitimate public purpose is a necessary component of a lawful expropriation, and the taking nation must offer some rational public purpose for the taking.

Defining public purpose does not end the problem. When one state has taken the property of nationals of another, what court should sit in judgment of the public purpose issue, both to define it and to determine whether it has been met? A court in the taking nation is not likely to invalidate the taking for lack of public purpose justifications.[11] A venue for establishing these rules might be the International Court of Justice, but that court has not proven to be an effective body to develop an international law of expropriation due to a lack of cases. Such development is thus left to national courts and various tribunals. These have tended to shy away from addressing the public purpose issue.[12] That has been because of both the conceptual difficulty of the issue and the fact that foreign investors whose properties have been expropriated usually are not interested in restitution of their property as long as the taking government is in office. The foreign investors are interested in receiving compensation. Consequently, while the public purpose element of expropriation is present and should be considered, there are other elements of expropriation more likely to be the subject of investor concern.

---

[10]   Public purpose, with respect to the Cuban expropriations, is explored in Michael Wallace Gordon, THE CUBAN NATIONALIZATIONS: THE DEMISE OF FOREIGN PRIVATE PROPERTY (1976).

[11]   See Kelo v. City of New London, 545 U.S. 469 (2005) (rejecting challenge to a taking's public purpose under U.S. constitutional law).

[12]   See Martin Domke, Foreign Nationalizations, 55 AM. J. INT'L L. 585 (1961).

§ 24.6   Retaliation and Discrimination Under International Law

An expropriation may also be unlawful if it is in retaliation for acts of the government of the investor, or if it discriminates against a particular person or particular nationalities.[13] The 1960 Cuban expropriations were examples of both. The first expropriations were exclusively of U.S. property (i.e., discrimination), and were in response to the United States eliminating the Cuban sugar quota (i.e., retaliation).

The taking of property of only one nation's nationals is not necessarily discriminatory. A country may decide to nationalize one sector, such as mining. That sector might be owned exclusively by nationals of one foreign nation. It could be difficult in such case to decide whether the taking was based on the desire to have the state own all mining interests, because that was believed more sound economically or preferable for national security reasons, or was based on an intention to discriminate against one nation and take its property, whether it consisted of mining properties or hotels or anything else.

§ 24.7   The Requirement of Compensation

However important it may be to understand the issues of public purpose, retaliation and discrimination, the real issue is likely to be the payment of compensation. If a foreign investor is compensated satisfactorily, there may be little concern with the technical lawfulness or unlawfulness of the taking under international law. Conversely, a ruling that the expropriation was unlawful is an empty victory if there is no satisfactory compensation.

The U.S. government's repeatedly stated position is that compensation is required under international law and must be prompt, adequate, and effective.[14] The first view, that international law requires compensation, is generally shared by jurists within the United States and abroad. But the second view, the prompt, adequate, and effective standard, is the subject of vigorous debate and is rejected by many U.S. and foreign jurists.

The first international court case that discussed expropriation is the 1928 *Chorzów Factory* decision of the Permanent Court of

---

[13]   *See* Helmerich & Payne Intern. Drilling Co. v. Bolivarian Republic of Venezuela, 784 F.3d 804 (D.C. Cir. 2015) (finding expropriation to be discriminatory).

[14]   *See* Oscar Schachter, *Editorial Comment, Compensation for Expropriation*, 78 AM. J. INT'L L. 121 (1984).

International Justice (PCIJ).[15] That case referred only to a duty of "payment of fair compensation." That seems less stringent than the "prompt, adequate, and effective" standard alleged to be the prevailing international law by U.S. Secretary of State Hull in 1938 in his notes to the Mexican government.[16] There has been little further guidance from the PCIJ or its successor, the International Court of Justice (ICJ). The narrow focus in the latter's *Barcelona Traction* decision[17] added very little, if anything, to the international law of expropriation compensation.

The ICJ subsequently decided a dispute involving an Italian government intervention which allegedly caused a U.S. company to file for bankruptcy.[18] The decision turned on the interpretation of the Treaty of Friendship, Commerce, and Navigation between the United States and Italy, specifically issues regarding interference with the U.S. company's right to "control and manage" its operation in Italy. The measure of damages became an issue, and was not dealt with clearly, partly because of the uncertainty of the company's ability to function during the period of intervention and the appropriateness of damages after filing bankruptcy. But the ruling was that Italy had not violated international law in its requisition or intervention. Furthermore, since the damages were conditioned upon liability, there was no final decision as to their measure.

Debate over the proper level of compensation continues without a consensus. But some standards have developed that might be applied by a court or tribunal. The alternatives seem to use elastic words or terms, but when further defined, there may be less difference than is at first thought to exist.

---

[15]   Factory at Chorzów (Germany v. Poland), P.C.I.J., Ser. A, No. 17 (1928). The earlier 1922 Norwegian Shipowners' Claims arbitration referred to "just compensation" as determined by the "fair actual value at the time and place." Norwegian Shipowners' Claims (Norway v. United States), 1922 1 U.N. Rep. Int'l Arb. Awards 307.

[16]   3 Green H. Hackworth, DIGEST OF INTERNATIONAL LAW 655 (1942).

[17]   Barcelona Traction, Light & Power Co. (Second phase) (Belgium v. Spain), 1970 ICJ Rep. 3. The case is discussed in Herbert W. Briggs, *Barcelona Traction: The Jus Standi of Belgium*, 65 AM. J. INT'L L. 327 (1971); F.A. Mann, *The Protection of Shareholders' Interests in the Light of the Barcelona Traction Case*, 67 AM. J. INT'L L. 259 (1973). It held only that Belgium lacked standing to espouse claims of its nationals who were owners of an expropriated investment because the investment company was incorporated elsewhere.

[18]   Elettronica Sicula S.p.A. (ELSI), Judgment (United States v. Italy), 1989 ICJ Rep. 15. The case is discussed in Ignaz Seidl-Hohenveldern, *ELSI and Badger: The Two Raytheon Cases*, 26 RIVISTA DE DIRITTO INTERNAZIONALE PRIVATO E PROCESSUALE 261 (1990); F.A. Mann, *Foreign Investment in the International Court of Justice: The ELSI Case*, 86 AM. J. INT'L L. 92 (1992).

Prompt, Adequate and Effective Compensation. The "prompt, adequate and effective" standard is likely to be applied by (1) U.S. courts or tribunals applying a U.S norm of compensation theory or searching for an international standard, or (2) U.S. courts or tribunals applying an agreement between the parties or nations that calls for the application of the prompt, adequate, and effective standard, such as a BIT. There is no assurance, however, that a U.S. court or tribunal searching for "the" international law will arrive at a prompt, adequate, and effective standard. The 1981 *Banco Nacional v. Chase Manhattan Bank* decision suggested that the consensus of nations was to apply an "appropriate" standard and quoted one highly regarded U.S. author who rejected the prompt, adequate, and effective standard as a norm of international law.[19]

Because of the very limited number of judicial decisions discussing the compensation issue, arbitration decisions are often useful to compare with cases. In the *LIAMCO* arbitration, the arbitrator suggested that the prompt, adequate, and effective standard was not the only standard and concluded that under general principles of law only "equitable" compensation was required.[20] But the arbitrator included in the award a substantial amount for lost profits, a conclusion suggesting adoption of a *full* compensation standard.

Appropriate Compensation. The "appropriate" compensation norm is the standard in U.N. Resolution 1803 of 1962, which in the view of many jurists[21] remains the most likely norm to be applied. It was suggested as the standard in the *Banco Nacional* decision noted above and in at least two important international arbitrations, the *TOPCO* and *AMINOIL* cases.[22]

Fair Compensation. The "fair" compensation standard was used in the much-discussed but little followed *Chorzów Factory* PCIJ decision, noted above. However, fair compensation has not generally been accepted as the proper standard, and has not become an accepted norm of international law. That is at least partly due to

---

[19] Banco Nacional de Cuba v. Chase Manhattan Bank, 658 F.2d 875 (2d Cir. 1981), quoting Professor Wolfgang G. Friedmann.

[20] Libyan American Oil Co. (LIAMCO) v. Libyan Arab Republic, 20 Int'l Legal Mat. 1 (1981).

[21] *See, e.g.,* Richard B. Lillich, *The Valuation of Nationalized Property in International Law: Toward a Consensus or More "Rich Chaos"?,* in Richard B. Lillich (ed. & contrib.), 3 THE VALUATION OF NATIONALIZED PROPERTY IN INTERNATIONAL LAW 183 (1975).

[22] Texaco Overseas Petroleum Co. (TOPCO) v. Government of the Libyan Arab Republic, 17 Int'l Legal Mat. 1, 3, 29 (1978); Arbitration between Kuwait and the American Independent Oil Co. (AMINOIL), 21 Int'l Legal Mat. 976 (1982).

the broad sense of what "fair" might include. A legal norm deserves greater definition.

Just Compensation. The Restatement (Third) of the Foreign Relations Law of the United States adopted "just" in place of "appropriate,"[23] largely to avoid a possible inclusion of deductions demanded by the host nation under an "appropriate" standard. Several expropriating nations had calculated compensation by taking the company's value of the property and deducting what were called "excess profits" or "improper pricing" of resources to arrive at a conclusion that either no compensation was due or that the company actually owed the expropriating nation. But it is hard to envision a taking nation agreeing that while such deductions could be allowed under an "appropriate" standard, they could not be allowed under a "just" standard.

Mandatory Questions Under Any Standard. Whatever standard is chosen, three questions must be asked. First, *how much* is to be paid? Second, in *what form* is it to be paid? And third, *when* must it be paid? If the answers to these questions are the full value of the property, in convertible currency, and immediately or very soon, then the standard being applied seems to approximate the "prompt, adequate, and effective" standard favored by the United States. The Iran-United States Claims Tribunal (discussed below) never formally applied a "prompt, adequate, and effective" standard.[24] But claims approved by the tribunal have been paid *promptly* from the funds established for the purpose, they have been paid in dollars (that surely constitutes *effective* payment), and the methods of valuation used seem to satisfy any reasonable *adequacy* standard.[25]

If the consensus is an "appropriate" standard, tribunals that have gained the respect of the majority of the international community, including the main industrialized nations, seem to be applying a standard that is "fair, just, and appropriate" as well as "prompt, adequate, and effective." For now, and perhaps until or unless the investment restrictiveness of the 1970s returns, the

---

[23]   Restatement (Third) of Foreign Relations Law of the United States, § 712(1) & comment d (1987).

[24]   The Tribunal has used a "just" standard, which is stated in the U.S.-Iran Treaty of Amity, Economic Relations and Consular Rights, Aug. 15, 1955, 8 UST 899, ITAS No. 3853, 284 UNTS 93 ("prompt payment of just compensation"). But the treaty goes on to state that it must be paid in "an effectively realizable form" and must be for the "full equivalent of the property taken," thus becoming nearly a prompt, adequate, and effective standard. *See* David Caron, *The Nature of the Iran-United States Claims Tribunal and the Evolving Structure of International Dispute Resolution,* 84 AM. J. INT'L L. 104 (1990).

[25]   The Iran-United States Tribunal is unusual, however, because of the initial agreement to deposit considerable funds in dollars to meet approved claims.

demand for a norm allowing only partial compensation has little backing.[26]

§ 24.8 Restitution as a Substitute for Compensation

The expropriated foreign investor may prefer to have the property returned rather than receive compensation. Among other things, that avoids difficult questions of the adequacy of compensation. It is not likely to be favored where a revolution has installed an investment-hostile government, as in Cuba, but it may be appropriate where a counter-revolution has soon restored an investment-welcoming government. There is some precedent for restitution. In the *TOPCO* arbitration, following expropriations of Texas Overseas Petroleum Corporation and California Asiatic Oil Company by Libya, the sole arbitrator, Professor Dupuy (Secretary General of the Hague Academy of International Law), noted that the *Chorzów Factory* decision suggested that *restitutio in integrum* remains international law, and ordered Libya to resume performance of the agreement.[27] But in the *BP Arbitration* the arbitrator, Swedish Judge Lagergren, stated that the *Chorzów Factory* rule of *restitutio in integrum* was meant only to be used to calculate compensation, suggesting adherence to a full compensation theory.[28]

§ 24.9 Exhaustion of Local Remedies

Seeking compensation from the expropriating government's courts or administrative agencies is not only appropriate, but may be a precondition for initiating a claim elsewhere.[29] It is reasonable to first seek compensation from the one who has committed the wrong. Some BIT treaties have an exhaustion of local remedies provision, and some courts hearing claims against foreign sovereigns have imposed such a requirement.[30] Whether international law requires exhaustion remains debated.

---

[26] *See* Patrick M. Norton, *A Law of the Future or a Law of the Past? Modern Tribunals and the International Law of Expropriation*, 85 AM. J. INT'L L. 474 (1991).

[27] Texaco Overseas Petroleum Co. (TOPCO) v. Government of the Libyan Arab Republic, 17 Int'l Legal Mat. 1, 32 (1978).

[28] British Petroleum Exploration Co. v. Libyan Arab Republic, 53 ILR 297 (1973).

[29] Restatement (Third) of Foreign Relations Law of the United States, § 713 comment f (1987).

[30] *See* Abelesz v. Republic of Hungary, 692 F.3d 661 (7th Cir. 2012) (requiring exhaustion in Hungary before suit in United States); Fischer v. Magyar Államvasutak Zrt., 777 F.3d 847 (7th Cir. 2015) (same); BG Group, PLC v. Republic of Argentina, 134 S.Ct. 1198 (2014) (discussing exhaustion requirement in U.K.-Argentina BIT).

Exhaustion makes sense when the expropriation is not part of a total change in economic theory following a revolution that includes the expropriation of all private property. The taking nation may be prepared to compensate takings in a selective nationalization, such as a taking of all telecommunications or air transportation enterprises. But when a nationalization occurs of the dimensions of those in the former Soviet Union, China, Eastern Europe, and Cuba, there is little reason either for the expropriated property owner to attempt to exhaust local remedies or for that party to be forced to do so before the presentation of insurance claims. Nevertheless, it is probably appropriate for the expropriated party to make some attempt against the taking government, if nothing more than a formal written protest of the taking and a demand for compensation.

A problem arises when the taking nation expresses a willingness to hear takings claims but the circumstances and unfolding facts seem clearly to suggest that the willingness to discuss compensation is illusory.[31] The expropriated property owner may need to establish that local remedies are inadequate before seeking remedies at home or in third party nations or international tribunals.[32] Adequate proof justifying the futility of pursuing local remedies may take time to accumulate. The proof should illustrate deficiencies with the court or tribunal system of the taking nation, the method of valuation, the ability of the country to pay settled claims, and the appropriateness of the form of any payment the taking nation can afford. The experience with taking nations where the taking is part of a major economic, political, and social revolution indicates that local remedies are likely to be unsatisfactory to the expropriated property owners, who will have to seek assistance outside the taking nation.

§ 24.10 Assistance of the Home Government and the "Calvo Clause"

Expropriated U.S. investors usually report the expropriation to the U.S. Department of State. Diplomatic pressure may be essential to success in dealing with the taking nation. The U.S. executive branch has frequently intervened diplomatically after foreign nationalizations of U.S. property. Diplomatic intervention may be helpful and may lead to government sanctions against the taking nation, but it may also be resented by the taking nation. For a time,

---

[31]   Cuba offered compensation in the form of bonds that deserved the term "junk bonds" long before Wall Street popularized that term decades later.

[32]   *See* BG Group, PLC v. Republic of Argentina, 134 S.Ct. 1198 (2014) (discussing claim that exhaustion would be futile).

capital-importing countries, especially in Latin America, attempted to counter this move by imposing a so-called "Calvo Clause" or something comparable.[33]

The Calvo Clause reflects a theory, sometimes expressed in an agreement signed by the foreign investor, that a foreign investor is entitled to treatment no different than that given domestic investors, and recourse to diplomatic channels may result in forfeiture of the property. A Calvo Clause was included in Article 3 of the restrictive 1973 Mexican Investment Law, but there were no instances of property forfeiture in Mexico (or in other nations which have either adopted the Calvo Clause concept formally in investment legislation or made it a part of investment rhetoric). The concept of the Calvo Clause improperly frustrates the right of a nation to diplomatic intervention to protect property of its citizens. If a government does intervene, it may not be clear whether it does so at the request of the expropriated foreign investor or on its own initiative. If the latter, it is unfair to conclude that the property is therefore forfeited because of an act of the investor. While the idea that foreign investors ought to be entitled to no better treatment than nationals may seem sensible, the real world does give foreign investors alternatives not available to nationals. One is diplomatic negotiations. When the Calvo Clause goes beyond being a statement of exhaustion of local remedies to being an exclusionary rule precluding any other subsequent remedies, it loses much of its respect and viability.

With the general political climate in developing nations growing more favorable to foreign investment, interest in Calvo clauses has broadly declined. The concept was not included in the 1993 Mexican Investment Law, which is more investor friendly than the 1973 law. The NAFTA foreign investment provisions eliminated the Calvo Clause as a threat to a Canadian or U.S. investors, a major concession by Mexico.

§ 24.11 Lump-Sum Agreements and Claims Commissions

Where there has been an extensive nationalization of foreign property, such as by the Soviet Union, China, and Eastern European nations, a common resolution has been lump-sum settlements under the terms of a later bilateral agreement. Lump-sum settlements are questionable as a part of the jurisprudence of

---

[33]   Donald R. Shea, THE CALVO CLAUSE (1955). The clause draws its name from the Argentinian jurist Carlos Calvo.

the customary international law of compensation.[34] Typically they are made for amounts far below the amount of losses claimed. Any agreed-upon lump sum is subsequently divided among claimants who may have filed claims years earlier, soon after the expropriations occurred, or who may be entitled to file claims with a commission once the settlement is reached.[35]

Lump-sum settlements are typically distributed to claimants by a claims settlement commission established either by the settlement agreement or by national law. These commissions may be either mixed commissions, composed of members from both nations, or national commissions, with only members from the claiming country. In the latter case, the host nation pays a fixed sum and leaves it entirely to the home country to decide how payment is distributed.

Lump-sum settlements have a long history in U.S. practice. A mixed commission to settle claims was created following the U.S. revolutionary war.[36] But it was not effective and was followed by a national commission to determine claims after a lump-sum settlement agreement was concluded in 1803. Over the next century the United States established national commissions to distribute funds received in settlements with Great Britain, Brazil, China, Denmark, France, Mexico, Peru, the Two Sicilies, and Spain. Between World Wars I and II both national and mixed claims commissions were used, but the national commission prevailed.

The U.S. Foreign Claims Settlement Commission (FCSC) was established in 1954 as a separate entity when the earlier International Claims Commission was abolished. Its function is essentially judicial, and the benefit of its existence (as opposed to using the district courts, for example) is its ability to acquire expertise in the narrow area of adjudication of foreign claims. Evidence of valuation of property lost abroad is difficult to obtain, and the form of evidence demanded in the courts is rarely available. In 1980, after a number of years of relative inactivity, the FCSC was transformed into a separate and independent agency within the

---

[34] Dictum in *Barcelona Traction* suggests that lump-sum settlements are not sources of law for compensation. Barcelona Traction, Light & Power Co., Ltd. (Belgium v. Spain), 1970 I.C.J. 3, 40. *See also* Brice Clagett, *Just Compensation in International Law: The Issues Before the Iran-United States Claims Tribunal*, in 4 THE VALUATION OF NATIONALIZED PROPERTY IN INTERNATIONAL LAW 31 (Richard B. Lillich ed. 1987). Other scholars dispute this narrow view of international law sources.

[35] *See generally* Richard B. Lillich, INTERNATIONAL CLAIMS: THEIR ADJUDICATION BY NATIONAL COMMISSIONS (1962).

[36] The Jay Treaty of 1794 established the first claims commission for the new United States.

Department of Justice. Any sums obtained by the United States are distributed according to the statute.

Special funds have been created in the Treasury for specific claims relating to claims and agreements with Yugoslavia and the People's Republic of China. Each real or expected settlement with an expropriating nation must necessarily be kept separate from another; thus the statutes have titles covering special procedures for various specific takings. These include claims against (1) Bulgaria, Hungary, Romania, Italy, and the Soviet Union; (2) Czechoslovakia, Cuba and China; (3) the German Democratic Republic; and (4) Vietnam. Each is related to takings following significant disturbances, principally war and revolution. The statutes illustrate a pattern of procedural provisions which will likely be adopted for any future losses by U.S. citizens abroad where the takings are of all the property of U.S. citizens.[37]

The Iran-United States Claims Tribunal is a striking example of a mixed claims commission. It was created in 1981 as part of the settlement of the 1979–1980 Iran-United States dispute arising from the hostage-taking at the U.S. embassy in Tehran. The tribunal was funded by frozen Iranian assets in the United States. Approximately 1,000 claims were filed for amounts of $250,000 or more, and 2,800 were filed for smaller claims. Most claims have been satisfied but a few large and complex claims remain.

The Tribunal has tended to interpret its obligation to provide full compensation to mean something closer to going concern value than book value.[38] Arguing for acceptance of a claim under a going concern value does not assure that one will receive that higher amount, but it may mean a claim accepted for an amount higher relative to other U.S. claimants, and thus ultimate receipt of a

---

[37]   The 1964 Cuban Claims Act provided for claims arising from the Cuban nationalizations to be filed between 1965 and 1967, extended later to 1972. At the end claims allowed amounted to U.S. $1.76 billion. *See* Michael Wallace Gordon, *The Cuban Claims Act: Progress in the Development of a Viable Valuation Process in the FCSC*, 13 SANTA CLARA LAWYER 625 (1973). The valuation method ranged from strict reliance on book value to a usually much higher going concern value. The statute governing the FCSC authorizes the use of several methods of valuation. *See* 22 U.S.C. § 1623(a)(2)(B). The valuation is to use "applicable principles of international law, justice, and equity." *Id. See* 22 U.S.C. § 1623(k). However, no lump sum settlement with Cuba has been achieved nor seems likely to be achieved.

[38]   The experience with Iran differs markedly from the case of Cuba. Iran agreed to the payment of claims only because it had very substantial sums on deposit in the United States, which were blocked. Iran agreed to the claims process as a means to gain access to those funds. But Cuba had no such large sums in foreign banks. Sums that remain frozen in U.S. banks will probably be part of a future settlement agreement, with additional sums to be paid from renewed trade with the United States, possibly with restoration of some sugar quota.

higher amount in the pro rata apportioning of any agreed settlement.

Some claimants might prefer bringing their own suits against a foreign government if they can locate property owned by that foreign government in the United States. That has not proven very successful in most cases, however. When a nation undertakes a massive expropriation of the property of a foreign nation it usually removes as much property as possible from that nation. The inability of Iran to do so motivated Iran to agree to the Iran-United States Claims Tribunal. Cuba successfully transferred large sums out of the United States before remaining assets were frozen by Congress. Thus, there may be little sense in seeking a judgment in a U.S. court if there is no property to attach and it is evident that the hostile taking nation will reject any attempt to enforce the judgment. Furthermore, the United States may make filing claims before a claims commission the only available procedure. Many investors who were in the process of suing Iran at the time of the resolution of the hostage dispute and the establishment of the claims tribunal were angered that the agreement included removal of their claims from U.S. courts to the Tribunal.[39] Requiring all U.S. claimants to use this same process may benefit relations between the nations, but may not satisfy some claimants who were able to attach specific property of the foreign government and who believe they might receive a greater share of their claim by separate litigation.

§ 24.12   Private Remedies Through Litigation and Arbitration

Private litigation outside the taking nation may be attempted by frustrated expropriated investors, perhaps more successfully when the expropriations have not been massive takings as discussed above, but more selective takings of only certain property. Thus, some thought should be given to these individual suits against foreign governments for expropriations. The difficulty is finding a court or other dispute settlement body able to hear the claim and provide a remedy.

Suit in International Courts. There is no international court generally available to hear investment disputes. The International Court of Justice (ICJ) is a possible venue, and as discussed it has heard occasional claims regarding expropriations. However, it is limited in at least two important respects. First, only nations can be

---

[39]   *See* Dames & Moore v. Regan, 453 U.S. 654 (1981) (upholding order that all claims against Iran must be filed exclusively with the Tribunal against challenge by party with pending litigation in U.S. court).

parties to a claim at the ICJ. Nations can "espouse" the claims of their nationals, including expropriation claims, but the private party must persuade its government to bring a claim on its behalf. Second, ICJ jurisdiction is based on consent. That is, both parties (including the nation against which the claim is brought) must agree to ICJ jurisdiction, either in advance through a treaty, or ad hoc by a submission agreement. Relatively few nations have been willing to accept ICJ jurisdiction.

Suit in Home Country Courts. An investor may bring a claim against a foreign government in its home courts. However, there are substantial barriers to this approach. As discussed in Chapter 27, in the United States foreign sovereign immunity and the act of state doctrine make suits for foreign expropriations difficult, although not impossible. Moreover, even if such suits are successful, the resulting judgment may be difficult to enforce, either because the losing nation has removed its assets from the jurisdiction or its assets are protected by immunity (see Chapter 27, § 27.9).

Investor-State Arbitration. The most common forum for settlement of modern expropriation disputes is through arbitration. Like ICJ jurisdiction, arbitration depends on consent of the taking nation. However, nations anxious to attract foreign investment have increasingly been willing to sign treaties (BITs and FTAs) with mandatory arbitration provisions for investment disputes. A growing number of arbitration panels have been convened to hear investment disputes under these agreements. (Nations may also agree to arbitration in private contracts with investors). Investor-state arbitration is discussed further in Chapter 28.

Chapter 25

OPIC AND MIGA INVESTMENT INSURANCE

Table of Sections

§ 25.1 Introduction

As discussed in prior chapters, foreign investment faces substantial threats of interference from the host country's government. These risks are especially problematic because judicial remedies against an interfering government may be greatly limited (see Chapters 26–27). One potential solution allowing the investor to mitigate these risks is insurance.

Many private insurers are reluctant to insure against risks related to foreign governments (called "political risks"). Unlike ordinary risks such as fire and floods, political risk is difficult to assess and thus is difficult to price under conventional insurance industry approaches. As a result, political risk insurance may be available only through public entities such as the U.S. government's Overseas Private Investment Corporation (OPIC) or the World Bank's Multilateral Investment Guarantee Agency (MIGA). These agencies reflect a public commitment to encourage foreign investment. They also may be more effective insurers than private companies because host governments may be more reluctant to interfere with investments backed by the U.S. government or the World Bank.

Like private insurers, OPIC and MIGA charge substantial premiums for their insurance. Thus obtaining political risk insurance will add to the cost of the investment, and investors must consider whether it is worth the price. In many cases, lenders such as banks that are financing an investment will require the investor to obtain political risk insurance.

§ 25.2   The Overseas Private Investment Corporation (OPIC)___Role and Structure

The Overseas Private Investment Corporation (OPIC) was established by statute in 1969 with a mandate to "mobilize and facilitate the participation of United States private capital and skills in the economic and social development of less developed countries and areas, thereby complementing the development assistance objectives of the United States."[1] In selecting projects to insure, OPIC is guided by the expected economic and social development impact of a project and its compatibility with other U.S. projects, with preferential consideration given to investment projects in countries having low per-capita income and investments in high-income countries generally excluded from coverage.[2] The President may designate other countries as beneficiaries under separate authority.[3] OPIC insurance may be denied to projects in countries that do not extend internationally recognized workers' rights to workers in that country, but the President may waive this prohibition on national economic interest grounds.[4]

OPIC insures U.S. investment abroad against political risks including inconvertibility of local currency, expropriation, and losses due to war, revolution, insurrection, or civil strife (as discussed further in § 25.4 below).[5] In the event of a loss, the investor's claims will be paid by OPIC, with OPIC then being subrogated to the investor's claims against the host government. OPIC often becomes involved in negotiations when a dispute arises over an insured investment.[6] The U.S. government has far more leverage in negotiations than single investors.

---

[1]   22 U.S.C. § 2191. OPIC's website is https://www.opic.gov/.

[2]   22 U.S.C. § 2191.

[3]   19 U.S.C. § 2702.

[4]   22 U.S.C. § 2191a.

[5]   22 U.S.C. § 2194.

[6]   *See* https://www.opic.gov/what-we-offer/political-risk-insurance/examples-of-advocacy (giving examples).

In general, OPIC will cover up to $250 million per project, for up to 20 years. OPIC's obligations are backed by the full faith and credit of the U.S. government.[7]

OPIC has broad power to engage in insurance activities including to insure, reinsure,[8] cooperate in insuring,[9] enter into pooling or risk-sharing agreements, and hold ownership in investment insurance entities.[10] In addition to insuring investment risks, OPIC has some financing authority.[11] It provides loans to projects that are sponsored by or significantly involve U.S. small businesses. OPIC may also guarantee loans, regardless of the size of the company. It is also directed to take actions to promote the expansion of private risk insurance.[12] OPIC provides insurance worldwide but only for projects in nations with bilateral agreements with OPIC.

OPIC operates with a fifteen member board of directors that includes eight members appointed by the President, with the advice and consent of the Senate, from outside the government.[13] At least two of the eight must be experienced in small business, and one each in organized labor and cooperatives. Other members of the board include the Administrator of the U.S. Agency for International Development, the U.S. Trade Representative or the Deputy, the President of OPIC, and four members who are senior officials of such entities as the Department of Labor. The OPIC President and Chief Executive Officer is appointed by the President, with the advice and consent of the Senate, taking into account private business experience.[14] This composition causes OPIC to be referred to as a "quasi private/quasi public" organization.

§ 25.3 OPIC__Investor Eligibility

OPIC is a U.S. program for U.S. business. Eligibility is limited to U.S. citizens, U.S. corporations, partnerships, or other

---

[7]   https://www.opic.gov/what-we-offer/political-risk-insurance/benefits-of-working-with-opic. For a critical assessment, see Bryan Riley & Brett D. Schaefer, *Time to Privatize OPIC* (Heritage Foundation 2014), http://www.heritage.org/research/reports/2014/05/time-to-privatize-opic.

[8]   22 U.S.C. § 2194(f).

[9]   22 U.S.C. § 2194(a)(2).

[10]   22 U.S.C. § 2194(f).

[11]   22 U.S.C. § 2194(c). *See* https://www.opic.gov/what-we-offer/financial-products. OPIC also sponsors private equity funds that invest in emerging markets. *See* https://www.opic.gov/what-we-offer/investment-funds.

[12]   22 U.S.C. § 2194b.

[13]   22 U.S.C. § 2193(b).

[14]   22 U.S.C. § 2193(c).

associations "substantially beneficially owned" by U.S. citizens.[15] "Substantial beneficial ownership" ordinarily means that more than 50 percent of each class of issued and outstanding stock must be directly or beneficially owned by U.S. citizens. Foreign corporations, partnerships and other associations are also eligible if they are 95 percent owned by U.S. citizens.[16] If it appears from all the circumstances that foreign creditors can exercise effective control over an otherwise eligible corporation, no insurance will be written.

§ 25.4 OPIC___Insurance Programs

The three principal investment risks insured by OPIC are (1) inconvertibility of currency, (2) expropriation or confiscation of property, and (3) property loss caused by war, revolution, insurrection, or civil strife. A fourth class has been added, called "business interruption" due to any of the principal three risks.[17]

Inconvertibility. Inconvertibility specifically refers to "inability to convert into United States dollars other currencies, or credits in such currencies, received as earnings or profits from the approved project, as repayment or return of the investment therein, in whole or in part, or as compensation for the sale or disposition of all or any part thereof."[18] Before insurance against inconvertibility of currency is approved, the investor must obtain assurance from the host country that investor earnings will be convertible into dollars and that repatriation of capital is permitted. If the currency thereafter becomes inconvertible by an act of the host government, OPIC will accept the foreign currency, or a draft for the amount, and will provide the investor with U.S. dollars.

Expropriation and Other Forms of Unlawful Government Interference. Expropriation is broadly defined and "includes, but is not limited to, any abrogation, repudiation, or impairment by a foreign government . . . of its own contract with an investor with respect to a project, where such abrogation, repudiation, or impairment is not caused by the investor's own fault or misconduct, and materially adversely affects the continued operation of the project."[19] OPIC contracts have followed a more specific and

---

[15]   22 U.S.C. § 2198(c). *See* https://www.opic.gov/doing-business-us/applicant-screener (providing eligibility details). Some other capital-exporting nations have similar programs available to their nationals.

[16]   22 U.S.C. § 2198(c).

[17]   22 U.S.C. § 2194(a).

[18]   *Id. See* https://www.opic.gov/what-we-offer/political-risk-insurance/types-of-coverage/currency-inconvertability.

[19]   22 U.S.C. § 2198(b). OPIC also offers insurance against "arbitral award default" (meaning the government fails to satisfy a valid arbitration award). *See* https://www.opic.gov/what-we-offer/political-risk-insurance/types-of-coverage/expropriation.

enumerative approach, because the law does not further define what actions constitute expropriation. OPIC's standard insurance contract contains a lengthy description of what is considered expropriatory action sufficient to require OPIC payment. That definition may help an investor in drafting a contract with the foreign host government, because that government will have to deal with OPIC once OPIC has paid the investor's claim.

The OPIC-insured investor must exhaust local remedies before OPIC is obligated to pay any claim. All reasonable action must be taken by the investor, including pursuing administrative and judicial claims, to prevent or contest the challenged action by the host government. Upon payment of the claim, OPIC is subrogated to all rights to the investor's claim against the host government. Because the United States (OPIC) must deal with the foreign government, OPIC will not write any insurance for projects in a foreign country until that country agrees to accept OPIC insurance and thus to negotiate with OPIC after claims have been paid.[20]

Political Violence. The third form of coverage, political violence, is not defined by the statute, but is understood by OPIC to include property loss due to (1) declared or undeclared war, (2) hostile actions by national or international forces, (3) revolution, insurrection, and civil strife, and (4) terrorism and sabotage.[21]

Business Interruption. Business interruption insurance is available for losses due to business interruption caused by any of the three foregoing risks. Business interruption is not further defined in the statute.[22]

The OPIC statute provides:

Before issuing insurance for the first time for loss due to business interruption, and in each subsequent instance in which a significant expansion is proposed in the type of risk to be insured under the definition of "civil strife" or "business interruption", the Corporation shall . . . submit to [Senate and House Committees] . . . a report with respect to such insurance, including a thorough analysis of the risks to be covered, anticipated losses, and proposed rates and reserves and, in the case of insurance for loss due to business interruption, an explanation of the

---

[20]   *See* https://www.opic.gov/content/bilateral-agreements (listing countries with such agreements).

[21]   https://www.opic.gov/what-we-offer/political-risk-insurance/types-of-coverage/political-violence.

[22]   See   https://www.opic.gov/what-we-offer/political-risk-insurance/types-of-coverage/political-violence (offering coverage for "[i]ncome losses resulting from damage to assets of the foreign enterprise caused by political violence/terrorism.").

underwriting basis upon which the insurance is to be offered.[23]

§ 25.5   OPIC___Eligible Investments

The applicable statute authorizes OPIC to carry out its functions "utilizing broad criteria."[24] OPIC must consider investment eligibility in accordance with extensive guidelines that require OPIC to conduct operations on a self-sustaining basis. It must consider the economic and financial soundness of the project; use private credit and investment institutions along with OPIC's guarantee authority; broaden private participation and revolve its funds through selling its direct investments to private investors; apply principles of risk management; give preferential consideration to projects involving small business (at least 30 percent of all projects); consider less-developed nation receptiveness to private enterprise; foster private initiative and competition and discourage monopolistic practices; further balance of payment objectives of the United States; support projects with positive trade benefits to the United States; advise and assist agencies of the United States and other public and private organizations interested in projects in less-developed nations; avoid projects which diminish employment in the United States; refuse projects which do not have positive trade benefits to the United States; and refuse projects which pose an unreasonable or major environmental, health, or safety hazard, or result in significant degradation of national parks and similar protected areas. OPIC must also operate consistently with the goals of U.S. law relating to protection of the environment and endangered species in less developed nations. Additionally, it must limit operations to nations which provide or are in the process of providing internationally recognized rights for workers. That includes the right of association, the right to organize and bargain collectively, prohibition of forced or compulsory labor, minimum age for employment, and acceptable conditions of work. This requirement is often observed more on paper than in practice in many of the countries listed as acceptable for OPIC assistance. Finally, OPIC must consider the host nation's observance of and respect for human rights.[25]

OPIC is categorically prohibited from supporting activities that may have an irremediable impact on the environment, an adverse impact on the U.S. economy or employment, or an adverse impact

---

[23]   22 U.S.C. § 2194(a)(4).

[24]   22 U.S.C. § 2191.

[25]   *Id.*

on public health and safety.[26] OPIC is also precluded from competing with private insurance, and so can insure a project only where no private insurance is available.[27]

OPIC participates only in new investments (loans or insurance) because its role is to encourage new investment, not to facilitate existing investment. OPIC will not provide insurance where an investment has already been established, or generally where an irrevocable commitment to invest has been made.[28] Each proposed investment is evaluated by OPIC to consider, in addition to the above eligibility requirements, the extent to which the U.S. participant has long-term management arrangements with the new enterprise, the extent of private participation and whether the project is likely to assist further development of the host nation's private sector. Loans or the contribution of goods or services to foreign governments will not be insured unless they are part of a construction contract. OPIC will not insure the credit or solvency of the foreign government. OPIC insures or provides a guarantee only for projects in countries that have signed an agreement with the United States for OPIC programs, which currently includes over 150 developing nations.[29]

§ 25.6 OPIC__Claims and Dispute Settlement

Claims presented to OPIC by insured investors are "settled, and disputes arising as a result thereof may be arbitrated with the consent of the parties, on such terms and conditions as [OPIC] may determine."[30] OPIC insurance contracts provide that "[a]ny controversy or claim arising out of or relating to this contract shall be determined by arbitration in Washington D.C. according to then prevailing International Arbitration Rules of the American Arbitration Association."[31] The arbitration process is important:

---

[26]   https://www.opic.gov/doing-business-us/applicant-screener/insurance-eligibility-checklist. For a detailed list of prohibited projects, see https://www.opic.gov/doing-business-us/applicant-screener/insurance-eligibility-checklist#1.

[27]   *Id.*

[28]   https://www.opic.gov/doing-business-us/applicant-screener/insurance-eligibility-checklist.

[29]   *See* https://www.opic.gov/content/bilateral-agreements (listing countries with such agreements). *See also, e.g.,* Agreement on Incentives for Investments, U.S.-Chile, Sept. 22, 1983, available at https://www.opic.gov/sites/default/files/docs/latin-america/BL_Chile-09-22-1983.pdf (example of OPIC bilateral agreement). From time to time, OPIC may suspend new insurance issuance in particular countries due to lack of cooperation from their governments.

[30]   22 U.S.C. § 2197(i).

[31]   *See* Big Sky Juice, LLC v. Overseas Private Investment Corp., ICDR case no. 50 195 T 00233 12 (International Centre for Dispute Resolution, 2014) (quoting OPIC arbitration clause).

OPIC has challenged a number of claims presented to it by insured investors.[32]

From its inception to 2016, OPIC has paid over 300 insurance claims totaling over $1 billion.[33] OPIC has denied thirty claims, fourteen of which were submitted to arbitration by the investors.[34]

OPIC must deny loss claims if the investor, a controlling shareholder, or any agent of the investor has engaged in any act which resulted in a conviction under the Foreign Corrupt Practices Act (FCPA) and such act was the "preponderant" cause of the loss.[35] There have been few convictions under the FCPA, however, since most charges lead at most to a consent decree involving a fine.

§ 25.7   The Multilateral Investment Guarantee Agency (MIGA)

In 1988, an international convention established the Multilateral Investment Guarantee Agency (MIGA) as part of the World Bank.[36] This agency is designed to encourage increased investment in developing nations by offering investment insurance and advisory services.[37] Over 180 countries are members.[38] Voting power is equally divided between the industrial and developing nation groups. Shares are proportional to member nations' shares of World Bank capital. Unlike OPIC, MIGA is not also a lending agency, but its parent organization—the World Bank—serves principally as a lender.

Creating MIGA within the World Bank structure offers benefits a separate international organization would lack. MIGA has access to World Bank data on nations' economic and social status. This gives considerable credibility to MIGA and encourages broad participation. MIGA complements national programs such as OPIC (and similar programs in other countries) by offering an alternative for investors from that country. A U.S. company, for example, may prefer dealing with OPIC because of greater

---

[32]   *See* https://www.opic.gov/what-we-offer/political-risk-insurance/arbitral-awards (listing OPIC arbitrations).

[33]   https://www.opic.gov/what-we-offer/political-risk-insurance/benefits-of-working-with-opic.

[34]   https://www.opic.gov/what-we-offer/political-risk-insurance/claims-and-arbitral-awards. For a list of claims outcomes, *see* https://www.opic.gov/what-we-offer/political-risk-insurance/claims-determinations.

[35]   22 U.S.C. § 2197(l).

[36]   Convention Establishing the Multilateral Investment Guarantee Agency, https://www.miga.org/Documents/MIGA%20Convention%20February%202016.pdf.

[37]   *See* https://www.miga.org/who-we-are/overview. MIGA also has a newsletter, available at https://www.miga.org/Lists/Newsletter/CustDisp.aspx?ID=4.

[38]   https://www.miga.org/who-we-are/member-countries/.

confidence of claims being paid, of maintaining information confidentiality, and benefiting from legal processes established in bilateral investment treaties. But U.S. companies may find that MIGA insurance is available where OPIC is not, or that MIGA provides better terms for some kinds of projects. Numerous U.S. companies have obtained MIGA insurance, either instead of OPIC insurance or in conjunction with it. Since its inception, MIGA has issued over $28 billion in insurance for projects throughout the world.[39]

Banks have found MIGA attractive because bank regulators in some countries have exempted commercial banks from special requirements for provisioning against loss where loans or investments are insured by MIGA. Furthermore, investors from nations without adequate national insurance programs have welcomed MIGA's creation. MIGA is not intended to replace national programs but to extend the availability of investment insurance to many areas where it was not previously available, which in turn is expected to assist economic development in those areas.

Unlike national programs such as OPIC, MIGA has the leverage of a large group of nations behind it when it presses a claim. MIGA's intention is to avoid political interference and consider the process solely as creating legal issues.

§ 25.8   MIGA__Insurance Programs

Risks covered by MIGA include risks of currency transfer; expropriation; war, terrorism, and civil disturbance; breach of contract; and failure to honor sovereign financial obligations, all actions by the host government. Only developing nations are eligible locations for insured investments.

Currency Transfer. This insurance is similar to that offered by OPIC. It covers losses incurred when an investor is unable to convert host nation currency into foreign currency and transfer that currency abroad.[40] Host nation currency may be obtained from profits, principal, interest, royalties, capital, etc. The insurance covers refusals and excessive delays where the host government has failed to act, where there have been adverse changes in exchange control laws or regulations, or where conditions in the host nation that govern currency transfer have deteriorated.

---

[39]   https://www.miga.org/who-we-are/overview.

[40]   *See* https://www.miga.org/Pages/Investment%20Guarantees/Overview/Types OfCoverage.aspx#toc1.

Currency devaluations are not covered. Devaluations often cause substantial losses, but in MIGA's view these are commercial losses attributed to changes that are to some extent predictable and are not carried out by host nations to harm investment. Indeed, currency devaluations are usually extreme measures to address changing demand for the nation's currency.

Expropriation. This insurance covers partial or total loss from acts that reduce ownership of, control over, or rights to the insured investment. It includes "creeping" expropriation, where a series of acts has the same effect as an outright taking.[41] It does not cover nondiscriminatory actions of the host government exercising its regulatory authority.

Valuation for compensation is net book value; that may mean inadequate compensation where book value reflects historic costs. Loans and loan guarantees are compensated to the extent of the outstanding principal and interest. When compensation is paid, the insured investor assigns its rights in the investment to MIGA, which then may take action against the expropriating government.

War, Terrorism, and Civil Disturbance. This category includes losses for damage, disappearance, or destruction to tangible assets by politically motivated acts of war or civil disturbance, such as revolution, insurrection, *coups d'etat*, sabotage, and terrorism. Compensation is for the book value or replacement cost of assets lost, and for the repair of damaged assets. Business interruption insurance is also available for these risks.[42]

Breach of Contract. This insurance covers losses caused by the host government's breach or repudiation of a contract. When there is an alleged breach or repudiation, the foreign investor must invoke an arbitration clause in the contract and obtain an award for damages. If that award is not paid by the host government, MIGA provides compensation.[43]

Failure to Honor Sovereign Financial Obligations. More recently added, this insurance is for losses from the failure of a government to make payments when due where there is an unconditional (not subject to defenses) obligation or guarantee related to an eligible investment. The investor does not need to obtain an arbitral award.[44]

---

[41]   *Id.*

[42]   *Id.*

[43]   *Id.*

[44]   *Id.*

§ 25.9   MIGA___Eligible Investments

MIGA insurance may cover new equity investments (and in some cases existing investments), shareholder loans or guaranties, and non-shareholder loans. Coverage may also include technical assistance and management contracts, asset securitization, capital market bond issues, leasing, services, and franchise and licensing agreements. MIGA will insure acquisitions under privatization programs.

Two MIGA member countries must be involved. First, investors must be from a member country, and generally only foreign investors qualify: An investor seeking MIGA insurance must be a national of a member country other than the country in which the investment is to be made. The test of nationality for corporations is incorporation and principal place of business in a member nation, or being majority owned by nationals of a member nation. Commercially operated state-owned corporations are eligible, as are non-profit organizations if they operate on a commercial basis. With special MIGA approval, domestic investors may receive coverage for projects where they bring assets back to their nation from abroad. This provision is intended to promote the return of capital transferred to safe havens during times of political or economic uncertainty.

Second, the investment must be located in a developing nation that is a MIGA member and approves the insurance. When MIGA was first created, there were proposals to limit insurance to developing nations that adopted standards for protecting foreign investment, but the final Convention did not include any such limits or standards. Host nation standards for protecting foreign investment may nevertheless be a factor in writing insurance.[45] Investment projects must be financially and economically viable and meet MIGA's social and environmental performance standards.[46]

§ 25.10   MIGA___Scope of Coverage

MIGA covers investments for a standard term of fifteen years, which may be increased to twenty years if MIGA determines that the longer term is justified by the nature of the project. If the insurance is for a loan, the term follows the duration of the loan agreement. Once the insurance is written, MIGA cannot terminate

---

[45]   On eligibility, see generally https://www.miga.org/investment-guarantees/overview/eligibility/.

[46]   *See* https://www.miga.org/Pages/Projects/Environmental%20and%20Social%20Sustainability/Performance-Standards.aspx.

the coverage except for default by the investor. The insured investor may cancel the insurance on any anniversary date after the third.

MIGA can insure up to $250 million per project. Premiums are based on a risk assessment, which includes consideration of the political and economic conditions in the host nation, as well as an assessment of the project's viability. They average about one percent of the insured amount per year, but vary depending on the industry and type of coverage.[47] MIGA can insure equity investments to ninety percent of the initial contribution, plus 180 percent to cover earnings. Contracts such as for technical assistance are covered to ninety percent of the value of the payments due under the agreement. Loans and loan guarantees are also insured to ninety percent of the principal and interest that will accrue over the term of the loan. These figures are maximum available guarantees. The *current* amount is that in force for the given year. The difference between the maximum and current amount is referred to as the *standby* amount of guarantee, and constitutes a reserve coverage that the investor may place in effect each year to cover changes in the value or amount of investment at risk.

§ 25.11 MIGA___Claims

MIGA seeks to resolve potential investment disputes through negotiation before claims are submitted. It requires investors to provide early notification of emerging disputes and uses the substantial leverage of the World Bank to prevent investment losses. MIGA reports that "[t]o date, MIGA has been able to resolve disputes that would have led to claims in all but two cases, and both of those claims were paid. MIGA also has paid six claims resulting from damage related to war and civil disturbance."[48]

If an investor brings a claim, MIGA will review the claim and, if it is valid, pay the insured amount. The MIGA Convention then allows MIGA to seek reimbursement from the host government.[49] In the event of a dispute between MIGA and an investor over a claim, arbitration will be provided under the terms of the insurance contract, pursuant to arbitration rules developed by MIGA.[50]

---

[47]   https://www.miga.org/investment-guarantees/overview/terms-and-conditions/.

[48]   https://www.miga.org/Documents/Dispute_Resolution_and_Claims.pdf.

[49]   https://www.miga.org/investment-guarantees/dispute-resolution/.

[50]   *See* Multilateral Investment Guarantee Agency, Rules for Arbitration of Disputes under Contracts of Guarantee (1990), https://www.miga.org/Documents/Master-Rules-of-Arbitration.pdf.

Chapter 26

INTERNATIONAL BUSINESS LITIGATION

Table of Sections

---

§ 26.1 Introduction

Even though parties may hope and expect that no disputes will arise in their business ventures, considering methods of dispute resolution is an essential part of business planning. This Chapter provides an overview of the procedures of international business litigation, with particular attention to steps parties may take in advance, such as choice of law clauses and choice of forum clauses, to mitigate the uncertainties of such litigation. Chapter 28 below explores arbitration and other methods of alternative dispute resolution that the parties might select in place of litigation.

Many of the topics covered in this chapter, such as personal jurisdiction, service of process, and *forum non conveniens,* should be familiar to any law student who has completed a course in U.S. domestic Civil Procedure. But disputes between parties from different U.S. states are fundamentally different from ones between parties from different nations. In some cases, while the doctrines are similar, the stakes are greatly raised. It is one thing if lack of personal jurisdiction requires suit to be brought in a different state; it is quite another if lack of personal jurisdiction requires suit to be brought on a different continent. Other doctrines may be new, or applied in new ways: discovery abroad is fundamentally different from discovery within the United States, as is the enforcement of judgments from other jurisdictions.

§ 26.2 Personal Jurisdiction

Personal jurisdiction refers to a court's ability to hear claims against a particular defendant. It is a common issue in U.S. domestic litigation because it is typically determined on a state-by-state basis (that is, for a suit in California, for example, the question is whether personal jurisdiction exists in California, even if the defendant is a U.S. party from another state). In international litigation in the United States, however, disputes over personal jurisdiction are of much greater consequence to the parties; lack of personal jurisdiction may result in the case having to be brought, not in another state with similar laws, customs and procedures, but in a different country with entirely different law, customs and procedures.

Personal jurisdiction requirements arise from the due process clauses of the U.S. Constitution. Courts may be further limited by state statutes and state constitutional limitations, but many states have "long-arm" statutes that extend jurisdiction to the federal constitutional limits. Generally federal courts use the rules for personal jurisdiction of the state in which they sit, although for cases involving federal law special federal rules apply.[1]

The classic test for personal jurisdiction, enunciated in domestic cases, is that the defendant must have "minimum contacts" with the jurisdiction.[2] If the minimum contacts test is satisfied, the court next considers reasonableness—whether exercising jurisdiction comports with "notions of fair play and substantial justice."[3]

General and Specific Jurisdiction. Personal jurisdiction may be either general or specific. Under specific jurisdiction, the court may only adjudicate claims related to the defendant's contacts with the forum, while general jurisdiction envisions adjudication of any claims against the defendant because of the aggregate of the defendant's contacts with the forum.[4]

General jurisdiction exists at a person's place of residence (for a corporation, at its headquarters and its place of incorporation). In addition, general jurisdiction may arise when the defendant's

---

[1]   *See* Federal Rules of Civil Procedure, Rules 4(k)(1), 4(k)(2).

[2]   International Shoe Co. v. Washington, 326 U.S. 310 (1945).

[3]   *Id.*

[4]   *See* Tuazon v. R.J. Reynolds Tobacco Co., 433 F.3d 1163 (9th Cir. 2006).

activities constitute "continuous and systematic general business contacts" with the forum.[5] In recent years, the Supreme Court has apparently scaled back the reach of "continuous and systematic contacts" jurisdiction.[6] General jurisdiction based on continuous and systematic contacts (other than residence or corporate location) is generally not recognized in Europe or elsewhere, and so may cause difficulties in enforcing U.S. judgments abroad (see Section 26.11 below).

Specific jurisdiction, in contrast, can arise from as little as a single contact with the forum (but as noted allows only suits arising out of such contacts). In general, it requires a showing that the defendant "purposefully availed" itself of the jurisdiction of the forum by taking some action within or directed to the territory of the forum.[7] It is not clear whether specific jurisdiction requires an additional consideration of reasonableness once sufficient contacts are established.[8]

Jurisdiction Arising from Sales of Products. In *World-wide Volkswagen Corp. v. Woodson,*[9] the Supreme Court held that specific jurisdiction could be established where a defendant "purposefully directed" its activities toward the forum state by the sale of moveable goods which placed them into the "stream of commerce." The defendant would have to have anticipated being subjected to the forum state's courts, and there should be some link between the injuries and the defendant's activities in the state. The Court listed several factors, emphasizing the number, nature, and quality of contacts, as well as the source and connection of the action with the contacts.

In *Asahi Metal Indus. Co., Ltd. v. Superior Court*, the Court applied this result to an international transaction.[10] A motorcycle tire failed and the driver and passenger were injured and killed, respectively. The valve stem was allegedly the defective part of the tire, and had been made by Asahi, a company in Japan. It was purchased by the Taiwanese tire manufacturer. The tire manufacturer was sued in California state court and cross-

---

[5]   Helicopteros Nacionales de Colombia, S.A. v. Hall, 466 U.S. 408, 416 (1984); Perkins v. Benguet Consol. Mining Co., 342 U.S. 437 (1952).

[6]   Goodyear Dunlop Tires Operations, S.A. v. Brown, 131 S.Ct. 2846 (2011); Daimler AG v. Bauman, 134 S.Ct. 746 (2014).

[7]   *E.g.*, GT Securities, Inc. v. Klastech GmbH, 2014 WL 2928013 (N.D. Cal. 2014) (applying specific jurisdiction analysis to tort and contract claims).

[8]   *See* Benton v. Cameco Corp., 375 F.3d 1070 (10th Cir. 2004) (in contract case, finding minimum contacts but nonetheless finding exercise of jurisdiction unreasonable).

[9]   444 U.S. 286 (1980).

[10]   480 U.S. 102 (1987).

complained against Asahi. The California Supreme Court upheld jurisdiction over Asahi, but the U.S. Supreme Court reversed. The Court was unanimous in ruling that jurisdiction was improper, but the reasoning was not unanimous. There was general agreement that the *International Shoe* decision applied and that there must be both minimum contacts and constitutional due process. But there was disagreement regarding the standard to determine minimum contacts. Four justices found the "stream of commerce" theory insufficient, because the product was brought into the forum by the consumer. Some action by the defendant was needed to satisfy a substantial connection theory. The defendant would have to take some action "purposefully directed toward the state."[11] Four other justices preferred the stream of commerce theory without additional conduct. The split of opinion regarding minimum contacts has not helped subsequent cases; federal circuits and state courts have also split on which side they favored.[12] In a subsequent similar case involving an injury in New Jersey from a machine manufactured in England, the Court again failed to assemble a clear majority position.[13]

Asahi suggests consideration of the burden on the defendant of litigating in the forum state, the interests of the foreign state, the interests of the plaintiff in obtaining relief, the interests of the interstate judicial system in efficient resolution of cases, and the shared interests of the states in furthering substantive social policies.[14] The Court in *Asahi* was concerned with the burden placed on the Asahi company in defending the action in a foreign (U.S.) forum. It additionally noted that "great care and reserve should be exercised when extending our notions of personal jurisdiction in the international field."[15]

Affiliate and Agency Jurisdiction. When the defendant is the parent or affiliate of a corporation located in or doing business in the United States, a court may attribute the jurisdictional contacts of the subsidiary to the parent or affiliate. Most obviously, if the two entities are "alter egos"—that is, not really separate corporations

---

[11]   480 U.S. at 112 (emphasis in original).

[12]   *See, e.g.*, Gould v. P.T. Krakatau Steel, 957 F.2d 573 (8th Cir. 1992) (sale of Indonesian company's product to New York corporation with subsequent sending of product to Arkansas does not meet test); Mason v. F. LLI Luigi & Franco Dal Maschio Fu G.B. s.n.c, 832 F.2d 383 (7th Cir. 1987) (sale of Italian goods to Maryland with subsequent sending of product to Illinois meets test); Microsoft Corp. v. Very Competitive Computer Products Corp., 671 F.Supp. 1250 (N.D. Cal. 1987) (sale of Taiwanese product to California through another Taiwanese company meets test).

[13]   J. McIntyre Machinery, Ltd. v. Nicastro, 131 S.Ct. 2780 (2011).

[14]   *See also* Burger King Corp. v. Rudzewicz, 471 U.S. 462 (1985).

[15]   480 U.S. at 114.

for liability purposes—such attribution seems appropriate.[16] But some courts have gone further to extend jurisdiction to the parent in what is often a poorly analyzed piercing of the corporate veil. Veil piercing usually involves linking the two enterprises, but in jurisdiction cases, the analysis often appears less demanding, using agency concepts more freely.[17] This looser approach may result in finding personal jurisdiction over foreign corporations much more easily.

Jurisdictional Analysis in Foreign Courts. Jurisdiction in other nations, in particular civil law based nations, usually is not divided into personal and subject matter jurisdiction as in the United States, but is treated as a single topic of the court's authority to hear the case. This authority is typically described by code or statute (as in the EU). The EU regulations generally provide that suit may be brought at a person's residence or a corporation's place of incorporation or principal place of business (similar to U.S. general jurisdiction), or at the place a tort occurred or a contract was signed or to be performed (similar to U.S. specific jurisdiction). Unlike in the United States, in the EU once jurisdiction is established the court is typically obligated to hear the case; as discussed in the sections below, U.S. courts have various ways to dismiss a case even when jurisdiction is established.

§ 26.3 Subject Matter Jurisdiction

In the United States, subject matter jurisdiction typically refers to the ability of a federal court to hear a case. State courts are courts of general jurisdiction, subject to some provisions for exclusive jurisdiction in federal court for particular topics. Federal courts, in contract, are courts of limited jurisdiction; a source of jurisdiction must be identified in federal law and in Article III of the U.S. Constitution.

For international business litigation, the most common sources of federal jurisdiction are that the claim arises under federal law ("arising under" jurisdiction)[18] or that the claim involves parties from different states or nations ("diversity" jurisdiction).[19] For

---

[16]   *See* Ranza v. Nike, Inc., 793 F.3d 1059 (9th Cir. 2015) (contacts not attributed to parent in absence of alter ego relationship); Singh v. Daimler AG, 902 F. Supp. 2d 974 (E.D. Mich. 2012) (same).

[17]   *E.g.*, Bauman v. DaimlerChrysler Corp., 644 F.3d 909 (9th Cir. 2011), *rev'd* Daimler AG v. Bauman, 134 S.Ct. 746 (2014); Wiwa v. Royal Dutch Petroleum Co., 226 F.3d 88 (2d Cir. 2009). After the Supreme Court's decision in *Bauman*, the Ninth Circuit adopted a more restrictive view. Ranza v. Nike, Inc., 793 F.3d 1059 (9th Cir. 2015) (finding that *Bauman* rejected the circuit's earlier approach).

[18]   28 U.S.C. § 1331.

[19]   28 U.S.C. § 1332. In addition, the amount in controversy must exceed $75,000.

diversity jurisdiction, there must be "complete" diversity (no plaintiffs can be from the same state as any defendant). In addition, diversity jurisdiction does not exist for suits between non-U.S. parties; at least one party must be a U.S. citizen or entity.

In general, if federal jurisdiction does not exist the case may be heard in state court, except in unusual circumstances (such as foreign sovereign immunity, see Chapter 27 below) where subject matter jurisdiction does not exist in any U.S. court. Unlike personal jurisdiction, lack of subject matter may not be waived, and may be raised by the parties or *sua sponte* by the court at any stage of the litigation.

§ 26.4   Service of Process

Service of process involves providing official notice of the suit to the defendant. It will be ineffective, and may be grounds for dismissing the suit or overturning a judgment, if it is not made in conformance with the law of the forum. In the United States, service for suits in federal court is governed by Rule 4 of the Federal Rules of Civil Procedure, while state courts use the applicable state law. Rule 4 has specific provisions relating to service on defendants located abroad.[20]

For foreign defendants, plaintiffs must also consider the service rules in the country where the defendant's assets are located. Defective service is one ground for refusing to enforce a foreign judgment (see Section 26.11 below). This is particularly problematic because many foreign countries have different and stricter ideas about what constitutes adequate service. U.S. plaintiffs suing foreign defendants too often attempt to use shortcuts that prove to be the plaintiff's downfall. For example, the U.S. plaintiff may not adequately provide translations of the papers required abroad for a recognized claim. The U.S. concept of "tag" jurisdiction allows service in person, perhaps by serving the foreign party in a New York City airport while awaiting the final leg on a flight to Europe from Brazil. The advantages perceived to be gained by the U.S. party in tracking down the defendant during a layover in the airport may not seem so clever when a later judgment is rejected when an attempt is made to enforce it abroad.

Service of process abroad is facilitated by two conventions. The larger in scope is the Hague Convention on the Service Abroad of Judicial and Extrajudicial Documents (called the Hague Service

---

[20]   Federal Rules of Civil Procedure, Rule 4(f), 4(h)(2).

Convention).[21] The second is the Inter-American Convention on Letters Rogatory.[22] Rule 4(f) of the Federal Rules of Civil Procedure provides for the service of process abroad, requiring use of the treaties if they are applicable. If service is not available under the treaties, the Rule provides for alternative means of service. Use of the treaty process should result in service acceptable to the foreign country, but use of the alternative means may not. When using alternative means, consideration must be given to the rules in the country where service is to be made. Ineffective service will make enforcement of a judgment very unlikely in the foreign nation.

Service under the Hague Convention is available in approximately seventy participating countries, including the United States and most major commercial nations. Some participating countries have made special reservations which affect the method of service. The Convention is the exclusive method of service for foreign defendants located in member countries; it states that the Convention "shall apply in all cases, in civil or commercial matters, where there is occasion to transmit a judicial or extrajudicial document for service abroad."[23] Service is made through a designated "central authority" in the foreign nation, which subsequently transmits the documents to the proper location.

Article 10 of the Convention arguably allows service by mail directly on the defendant (an approach that is common in the United States for domestic suits). Some Convention members have made reservations or declarations prohibiting service by mail within their nation. In the United States, courts are divided as to whether and when Article 10 and Federal Rule 4(f) allow mail service abroad.[24] Mail service is thus a form that should be used very carefully.

Although the Hague Service Convention is usually exclusive for service abroad in a member nation, it does not apply if service can be made on a foreign defendant in the United States. In *Volkswagenwerk Aktiengesellshaft v. Schlunk*,[25] service made on

---

[21]   Hague Convention on the Service Abroad of Judicial and Extrajudicial Documents in Civil or Commercial Matters, Nov. 15, 1965, 20 U.S.T. 362, https://assets.hcch.net/docs/f4520725-8cbd-4c71-b402-5aae1994d14c.pdf.

[22]   Inter-American Convention on Letters Rogatory, *done* Jan 30, 1975, *entered into force for the United States*, Aug. 27, 1988, S. Treaty Doc. 98–27, 98th Cong., 2d Sess. (1984); Additional Protocol to the Inter-American Convention on Letters Rogatory, *done* May 8, 1979, *entered into force for the United States,* Aug. 27, 1988, S. Treaty Doc. 98–27, 98th Cong., 2d Sess (1984).

[23]   Hague Service Convention, Art. 1.

[24]   *See, e.g.*, Brockmeyer v. May, 383 F.3d 798 (9th Cir. 2004); Ackermann v. Levine, 788 F.2d 830 (2d Cir. 1986); Bankston v. Toyota Motor Corp., 889 F.2d 172 (8th Cir. 1989).

[25]   486 U.S. 694 (1988).

Volkswagen of America, a subsidiary located in the United States. was held proper under local law to reach Volkswagenwerk, the German parent corporation. The Supreme Court concluded that the Convention was not applicable to service effected within the United States, even if the party served was located abroad.

The Inter-American Convention and its Additional Protocol have been ratified by most Latin American nations and the United States. The Convention is limited to letters rogatory, essentially requests from one country through its courts to another country through its courts to assist the administration of justice. Its purpose is similar but less encompassing than the Hague Service Convention. If both are applicable, the Inter-American Convention applies. But the Inter-American Convention is not exclusive, as is the Hague Service Convention. A party thus might use state methods of service that if transmitted to an Inter-American Convention nation would be effective, but that if transmitted to a Hague Service Convention nation not a party to the Inter-American Convention would fail because the Hague Service Convention would be applicable and exclusive.

Service which does not comply with an applicable convention will likely cause any judgment to be rejected if there is an attempt to enforce it abroad. The German government made it very clear in the *Schlunk* case that unless service was made under the Convention, German courts would not enforce a judgment.[26]

Where there is no applicable treaty, U.S. law allows various approaches to service abroad. Service may be effected through a letter rogatory, which is a diplomatic request to the foreign nation. Where this appears futile, courts may approve novel methods of service, including service by email or social media.[27]

§ 26.5 Choice of Forum

In international business litigation, there will often be several sets of courts with jurisdiction to hear the parties' dispute. If the parties have not made a prior agreement as to forum, initially the choice falls to the plaintiff, who decides where to file. (Of course, the defendant may seek to move the litigation elsewhere, using the various strategies discussed elsewhere in this chapter). A plaintiff needs to think carefully about the choice of forum, because the

---

[26]   Brief for Volkswagenwerk AG at 16, Volkswagenwerk Aktiengesellschaft v. Schlunk, 486 U.S. 694 (1988).

[27]   *See* Rio Properties, Inc. v. Rio International Interlink, 284 F.3d 1007 (9th Cir. 2002) (service by email); FTC v. Pecon Software, Ltd., 2013 WL 5288897 (S.D.N.Y. 2013) (service by email and Facebook); Lexmark Int'l Inc. v. Ink Technologies Printer Supplies, LLC, 291 F.R.D. 172 (S.D. Ohio 2013) (service by email).

choice of forum may affect other aspects of the litigation—including the applicable procedural and substantive law, the methods of discovery that will be permitted, and the ability to enforce any resulting judgment against the defendant's assets.

To avoid the uncertainties of forum selection, many international business contracts contain a forum selection clause, by which the parties agree to submit any disputes relating to the contract to a particular court system. (An alternative, discussed in Chapter 28 below, is to select arbitration instead of litigation). Forum selection clauses are usually exclusive[28]—that is, the dispute may only be resolved in the chosen forum—and are often accompanied by choice of law clauses (see Section 26.8 below). In agreeing to a forum selection clause, parties must understand that they are picking much more than just the location. Choosing a nation with a civil law tradition legal system, for example, introduces a very different form of litigation, where there will be a process of gathering evidence by the assigned judge until the case is ready for a decision. There is no jury trial as known in common law systems. For parties in civil law nations, the idea of a jury trial may be as much of a concern as the absence of one to a party from a common law system.

Selecting a forum may be useful for contract disputes, but it is often not possible for torts. However, some torts are covered by choice of law agreements where the parties also have a contractual relationship, as in the purchase of tickets for a vacation, shares of stock, or an automobile.

Historically courts were reluctant to enforce forum selection clauses. However, today most jurisdictions accept the parties' forum selection, subject to limited defenses. In the United States, the decisive case was *M/S Bremen v. Zapata Off-Shore Co.*, in which the Supreme Court (reversing the lower court) enforced a forum selection clause between a U.S. party and a German party that chose the courts of the United Kingdom.[29] A subsequent case, *Carnival Cruise Lines, Inc. v. Shute*,[30] enforced a forum selection clause contained in small print on the back of a pre-printed cruise ticket. The Supreme Court rejected arguments that the forum selection provision was never negotiated and that it would be an unreasonable burden on the plaintiff to bring suit in the chosen

---

[28]   Parties must be sure to draft the clause to be exclusive if that is what is intended. *See* Albemarle Corp. v. AstraZeneca UK Ltd., 2009 WL 902348 (D. S.Car. 2009) (finding ambiguous clause to be permissive rather than exclusive).

[29]   407 U.S. 1 (1972).

[30]   499 U.S. 585 (1991).

forum (Florida). The Court found it reasonable for Carnival to want to consolidate cases brought against it in its home state of Florida.

Forum selection clauses are subject to standard contract defenses such as fraud and duress, and they may also be found unreasonable if they choose a forum that seems designed to prevent litigation rather than to serve the interests of the parties.[31] Typically such challenges will arise when one party files suit in a forum other than the one selected, and the other party seeks dismissal on the basis of the clause.[32]

Forum selection clauses are usually held to waive objections to personal jurisdiction in the chosen forum. However, a choice of forum agreement does not establish subject matter jurisdiction. A choice of forum clause choosing the court in which litigation is brought may be grounds to reject a defendant's motion to dismiss for *forum non conveniens* (see Section 26.6 below).[33]

There is some doubt whether and to what extent the concept of mandatory law limits forum selection. Mandatory law means law that may not be derogated from. An example is the Carriage of Goods at Sea Act (COGSA). If COGSA is the governing law, can it be ousted by an agreement that chooses another nation's courts? The Supreme Court, in *Vimar Seguros y Reaseguros, S.A. v. M/V Sky Reefer*,[34] held that that there was no mandatory law exception to the parties' ability to choose arbitration, assuming that the arbitrators would apply the U.S. law. It is not clear how this ruling affects forum selection clauses that choose foreign courts, which might or might not apply U.S. law.

EU law generally enforces forum selection clauses, subject to limited defenses.[35] A proposed treaty, the Hague Convention on Choice of Courts Agreements, is intended to enforce private party agreements choosing a forum and includes rules for recognizing and enforcing decisions of the forum so selected.[36] However, to date, it has been adopted by only one country (Mexico), although the EU

---

[31]   Liles v. Ginn-La West End, Ltd., 631 F.3d 1242 (11th Cir. 2001) (describing grounds for non-enforcement); *see* Petersen v. Boeing Co., 715 F.3d 276 (9th Cir. 2013) (clause selecting Saudi Arabian courts not enforced); Sun Trust Bank v. Sun Int'l Hotels, Ltd., 184 F. Supp. 2d 1246 (S.D. Fla. 2001) (forum selection clause not enforced where plaintiff, a hotel guest, had no ability to reject it).

[32]   A district court's refusal to dismiss on the basis of a forum selection clause is generally not subject to interlocutory appeal. *See* Lauro Lines S.R.L. v. Chasser, 490 U.S. 495 (1989).

[33]   AAR Int'l, Inc. v. Nimelias Enterprises, S.A., 250 F.3d 510 (7th Cir. 2001).

[34]   515 U.S. 528 (1995).

[35]   *See* EU Regulation No. 1215/2012 on Jurisdiction and the Recognition and Enforcement of Judgments in Civil and Commercial Matters (Recast), Art. 25.

[36]   http://www.hcch.net/index_en.php?act=conventions.text&cid=98.

and the United States have both signed it and are considering ratification.

§ 26.6   *Forum Non Conveniens*

Forum non conveniens is a common law doctrine that allows a court to dismiss a case it believes is better brought in another forum. Many nations do not recognize the doctrine, although some reach a similar conclusion under other names.[37] The U.S. doctrine has origins in *Gulf Oil Corp. v. Gilbert*,[38] a case involving two U.S. forum choices but with immense impact on the use of the theory in international litigation when the alternate forums are two different countries. In *Gilbert*, the Supreme Court allowed courts to decline to exercise jurisdiction where public and private factors favored another forum. This theory was adopted in two important international cases. First, in *Piper Aircraft Co. v. Reyno*,[39] the Supreme Court approved a *forum non conveniens* motion to dismiss a suit in the United States in favor of suit in Scotland; the plaintiffs represented Scottish decedents in a crash of a U.S.-made aircraft flown by a Scottish pilot that crashed in Scotland. Scottish law was clearly less favorable to the plaintiffs, but the Court significantly discounted this consideration, emphasizing the difficulty of bringing witnesses and evidence to the United States and Scotland's closer connection to the event. Second, in *In re Union Carbide Corp. Gas Plant Disaster*,[40] the court dismissed a case on behalf of numerous Indian nationals injured in an explosion at a Union Carbide subsidiary's plant in Bhopal, India. The court conditioned dismissal on Union Carbide's agreement to submit to jurisdiction in India, a condition that has become common in *forum non conveniens* dismissals.

The *forum non conveniens* test has evolved to include several considerations. There must be an available and adequate alternative forum. The plaintiff's choice is then weighed against private and public interests in the location of the litigation.[41]

---

[37]   *See, e.g.*, Republic of Bolivia v. Philip Morris Companies, 39 F.Supp.2d 1008 (S.D. Tex. 1999). There appear to be some Scottish origins to the *forum non conveniens* doctrine. *See generally* Paxton Blair, *The Doctrine of Forum Non Conveniens in Anglo-American Law*, 29 COLUM. L. REV. 1 (1929).

[38]   330 U.S. 501 (1947).

[39]   454 U.S. 235 (1981).

[40]   809 F.2d 195 (2d Cir. 1987).

[41]   In an analysis similar to *forum non conveniens*, courts may also dismiss cases in favor of foreign forums on the basis of international comity. *See, e.g.*, Mujica v. AirScan, Inc., 771 F.3d 580 (9th Cir. 2014) (dismissing claims by Colombian citizens against U.S. corporations for injuries suffered in Colombian civil war).

Available and Adequate Alternative Forum. Forum non conveniens entails the conclusion that there is a *better* forum. Therefore, a threshold question is whether the supposed alternate forum is in fact adequate and available. The law applied in any alternate forum will likely be different from that where the suit was filed. That is not sufficient in itself to find the alternative forum inadequate. Only if the plaintiff has no reasonable possibility of recovery will the forum be held inadequate on this ground.[42]

Many nations have suspect legal systems that only by stretching the definition provide due process. But U.S. courts are hesitant to reject a *forum non conveniens* motion when the plaintiff's opposition is based on the objection that the foreign forum is inefficient, corrupt, and/or has a judiciary subject to intimidation. Only a few cases in U.S. courts have rejected *forum non conveniens* motions for these reasons,[43] even though every lawyer engaged in international litigation can list nations where they do not believe fairness is part of the procedure or a principal goal of the judges.

Private and Public Interest Factors. U.S. courts start with a presumption favoring the plaintiff's initial choice of forum, at least if the plaintiff is a U.S. citizen or resident.[44] They then consider private and public interest factors. Private factors include location of the witnesses, ability to depose persons, access to sources of proof such as important records, ability to implead possible third-party defendants, need to translate documents, language of the chosen forum, and other matters going to the general convenience of the parties. Public interest factors involve matters of public policy and the relative interests that the two jurisdictions have in the dispute.[45]

Forum non conveniens is generally not available in civil law countries (including the EU). In the view of many civil law jurists, it

---

[42]   *See* Loya v. Starwood Hotels & Resorts Worldwide, Inc., 583 F.3d 656 (9th Cir. 2009) (finding Mexico an adequate alternative forum despite much lower damages and lack of contingency fees).

[43]   *See* DiFederico v. Marriott Int'l, Inc., 714 F.3d 796 (4th Cir. 2013) (finding Pakistan not an adequate alternative for resolving terrorism-related claims).

[44]   *E.g.,* Guidi v. Inter-Continental Hotels, Corp., 224 F.3d 142 (2d Cir. 2000). Non-U.S. plaintiffs must show convincing reasons for their choice. Often the choice is made to obtain punitive damages and representation on a contingent fee basis; neither is sufficient justification for retaining the suit in the forum chosen by the plaintiff.

[45]   For example, in *Reyno,* private interests included the difficulty of bringing witnesses and evidence to the United States and the difficulty of impleading third-party defendants; public interests included Scotland's interest in resolving disputes over accidents in its territory.

interferes with the idea that jurisdiction should not be declined if it is present.[46]

Forum non conveniens motions are brought by defendants as part of litigation strategy. An important aspect of *forum non conveniens* is that the court is not forcing the case upon the foreign courts. Whether the plaintiff re-files in the foreign forum is the plaintiff's choice. The truth is usually that the U.S. forum was chosen because of the availability of legal representation on a contingent fee basis and the possibility of receiving a very large award because of punitive damages. Few courts outside the United States offer such large returns on such small investments. If the *forum non conveniens* motion is successful, the defendant hopes that the case will end because the plaintiffs no longer have visions of large punitive damage awards and may otherwise find it impractical or not worthwhile to pursue the claim. The defendants in both the *Piper* and *Bhopal* cases were obviously pleased with the outcome. The *Piper* case never went to trial in Scotland. The *Bhopal* case resulted in a settlement far less than what might have been a jury's award in the United States, and there is doubt that the settlement funds ever reached the injured plaintiffs. Courts have thus increasingly asked about the nature of the proceeding in the foreign forum, especially about the nature of the process.

One concern for defendants and their attorneys in obtaining a successful *forum non conveniens* ruling is that control over the case may be diminished or lost. If the case is moved abroad, the attorneys likely will not be able to appear before the foreign court, and foreign counsel must be hired. The U.S. defendant will have to learn about the foreign law and legal system. In addition, defendants should not assume that if the case is moved from the United States, that will be an end of it. Foreign courts, even in developing nations, are increasingly able to undertake sophisticated litigation and may render very large judgments, perhaps without the procedural protections for defendants that the United States has.[47] The better choice for a defendant may be to keep the matter in U.S. court but seek application of foreign law, which may be more favorable to the defense. It is a difficult choice for lawyers because the law of *forum non conveniens* seems sufficiently elastic that it is

---

[46]   *See* Owusu v. Jackson, C–281/02 [ECJ 2005] (rejecting British court's use of *forum non conveniens*).

[47]   For example, in *Aguinda v. Texaco, Inc.*, 303 F.3d 470 (2d Cir. 2002), the defendant successfully moved for *forum non conveniens* dismissal on the ground that the case should be litigated in Ecuador. The plaintiffs then refiled in Ecuador and won a very large judgment. The defendant resisted enforcement of the Ecuadorian judgment on the ground that it was obtained by fraud. *See* Chevron Corp. v. Naranjo, 667 F.3d 232 (2d Cir. 2012).

hard to predict the outcome, and it is additionally hard to predict possible outcomes in the foreign court.

§ 26.7 Parallel Proceedings

International litigation may result in a situation where a plaintiff initiates suit in one nation and the defendant in the first suit then sues the plaintiff in a different nation's courts. This situation is called parallel proceedings—that is, two suits, involving substantially the same parties and issues, are going forward in two different jurisdictions.

When parallel proceedings arise, a party may seek to stay or dismiss the action in which it is the defendant so the other suit may proceed to judgment. This motion is called *lis alibi pendens*, or just *lis pendens*. Generally courts say that they will grant such a motion only in extraordinary circumstances.[48] There is no presumption against parallel proceedings; rather the presumption is that parallel suits may both go forward, with the one reaching judgment first then being potentially conclusive on the other, assuming it is recognized and enforced in the second jurisdiction (see Section 26.11 below). In practice, however, courts will sometimes grant *lis alibi pendens* motions on what may not seem to be exceptional facts.[49]

Another approach is for a party to ask the court in which it is the plaintiff to block the other suit (in which it is the defendant). For example, when Laker Airways initiated litigation in the United States against several U.S. and foreign airlines, including two from the United Kingdom,[50] the British airlines sued in an English court to enjoin Laker from pursuing the suit in the United States because the litigation had only one proper forum—England. This is called an "antisuit injunction." In *Laker*, the U.S. court rejected the injunction granted by the English court, and a serious conflict was avoided only after the House of Lords overturned the injunction, although preserving the concept.

Although the U.S. court in *Laker* rejected the English antisuit injunction, the concept is accepted in U.S. courts. Some federal circuits have granted antisuit injunctions, generally applying a multi-part test which considers such issues as whether the foreign litigation would frustrate a policy of the U.S. forum, be vexatious or

---

[48]   *E.g.*, Royal and Sun Alliance Ins. Co. of Canada v. Century Int'l Arms, Inc., 466 F.3d 88 (2d Cir. 2006); Ingersoll Milling Mach. Co. v. Granger, 833 F.2d 680 (7th Cir. 1987).

[49]   *E.g.*, Finova Capital Corp. v. Ryan Helicopters U.S.A., Inc., 180 F.3d 896 (7th Cir. 1999); Posner v. Essex Ins. Co., Ltd., 178 F.3d 1209 (11th Cir. 1999).

[50]   Laker Airways, Ltd. v. Sabena, Belgian World Airlines, 731 F.2d 909 (D.C. Cir. 1984).

oppressive, threaten the court's jurisdiction, or prejudice other considerations.[51] *Laker*, however, had a narrower view, recognizing antisuit injunctions only to protect the jurisdiction of the court or prevent the litigant from evading public policies of the forum. Since *Laker*, courts have applied different standards.[52]

Antisuit injunctions, like *lis alibi pendens* stays or dismissals, are unusual because courts often allow parallel proceedings to continue in two jurisdictions. A judgment of a U.S. court may be considered *res judicata* in the foreign court, while the foreign judgment might be considered res judicata in the U.S. court. (This depends on issues involving recognition and enforcement of foreign judgments, discussed in Section 26.11 below). Thus, the party that receives the first judgment may have the advantage, encouraging a race to judgment. But, however undesirable it is to encourage such races, U.S. courts have not acted just to stop them.

In the EU, the general rule is that the first case to be filed is the one that should proceed, while the other is stayed or dismissed.[53] While this not an express rule in the United States, it is a consideration—perhaps a dominant consideration—in deciding when to issue stays and injunctions.

§ 26.8   Choice of Law and Extraterritorial Law

Where a transaction involves more than one jurisdiction—whether by the location of the parties, the relevant actions, or the relevant effects—more than one set of laws may potentially be applicable. Because national laws vary substantially, deciding what law governs may effectively decide the case.

Extraterritorial Law. In general, an activity is governed by the law where it takes place. However, nations sometimes also extend their laws to "extraterritorial" activities—that is, those that take place beyond the nation's borders. This happens most commonly when nations seek to regulate the conduct of their citizens abroad or to regulate activities abroad that have effects in their territory.

---

[51]   In re Unterweser Reederei, GmbH, 428 F.2d 888 (5th Cir. 1970), *affirmed en banc*, 446 F.2d 907 (5th Cir. 1971); Seattle Totems Hockey Club, Inc. v. National Hockey League, 652 F.2d 852 (9th Cir. 1981).

[52]   For decisions subsequent to *Laker*, see Quaak v. Klynveld Peat Marwick Goerdeler Bedrijfsrevisoren, 361 F.3d 11 (1st Cir. 2004) (upholding injunction); Kaepa, Inc. v. Achilles Corp, 76 F.3d 624 (5th Cir. 1996) (upholding injunction); China Trade & Dev. Corp. Ltd. v. M.V. Choong Yong, 837 F.2d 33 (2d Cir. 1987) (reversing injunction); Gau Shan Co. v. Bankers Trust Co., 956 F.2d 1349 (6th Cir. 1992 (reversing injunction).

[53]   EU Regulation No. 1215/2012 on Jurisdiction and the Recognition and Enforcement of Judgments in Civil and Commercial Matters (Recast), Art. 29(1).

With respect to U.S. federal law, a U.S. court will apply a law to extraterritorial conduct if it finds Congress intended the law to so apply (possibly subject to very minimal due process limitations). In recent years the Supreme Court has invoked a presumption against extraterritoriality, meaning that courts should not apply a law to extraterritorial conduct unless the law clearly states its extraterritorial scope.[54]

If a U.S. law specifically contemplates extraterritorial application, it will overcome the presumption against extraterritoriality. For example, two laws that are specifically and intentionally directed to cross-border conduct are the antiboycott provisions of the Export Administration Act and the Foreign Corrupt Practices Act. The former provisions were enacted to address the Arab boycott of Israel; the latter addresses what are referred to as "corrupt" payments made by U.S. persons and businesses to foreign officials. These two laws by their language were intended to apply to extraterritorial conduct and they have been so applied for decades.

Some laws that are less specific about their extraterritorial scope are also applied extraterritorially. Most notably, the U.S. antitrust laws were held to apply abroad prior to the modern articulation of the presumption against extraterritoriality,[55] and they continue to be so applied.[56]

The conflicts that have arisen over extraterritorial application of U.S. law—especially antitrust law—are numerous. The debate has led to the adoption by many nations of laws that attempt to nullify or minimize the impact of U.S. laws affecting the foreign nation's sovereignty. That includes the adoption of such laws as the U.K.'s Protection of Trading Interests Act of 1980, the theory of which has been copied in many nations in what are called "blocking statutes." It includes such areas as discovery abroad, taking evidence abroad, and enforcing judgments abroad, especially when U.S. courts award damages that are for the most part unheard of outside the United States. Some nations, including the U.K., have gone further, allowing a "clawback" of certain damages. However, it

---

[54]   RJR Nabisco, Inc. v. European Community, 136 S.Ct. 2090 (2016); Kiobel v. Royal Dutch Petroleum Co., 133 S.Ct. 1659 (2013); Morrison v. National Australia Bank Ltd., 561 U.S. 247 (2010); E.E.O.C. v. Arabian American Oil Co., 499 U.S. 244 (1991).

[55]   United States v. Aluminum Co. of America, 148 F.2d 416 (2d Cir. 1945); Continental Ore Co. v. Union Carbide & Carbon Corp. 370 U.S. 690 (1962).

[56]   See Hartford Fire Insurance Co. v. California, 509 U.S. 764 (1993) (applying U.S. antitrust law to conduct occurring in the U.K.). But see F. Hoffmann-La Roche Ltd. v. Empagran S.A., 542 U.S. 155 (2004) (limiting extraterritorial reach of antitrust law to conduct affecting the United States).

is important to note that many nations other than the United States—notably including the European Union—apply some laws extraterritorially.[57]

Choice of Law. Courts in the United States apply a somewhat different approach when they are choosing between the law of two states, or between the law of a U.S. state and a foreign nation. Called "choice of law" or "conflicts of law," this approach involves the court deciding which law has the closest relationship to the transaction or events forming the basis of the suit.

Choice of law rules are a matter of state law in the U.S. system. Unfortunately, they vary widely from state to state, and in most states are a matter of common law rather than statute. The approaches may be loosely grouped as "First Restatement" rules, derived from the initial Restatement of Conflict of Laws, and "Second Restatement" rules, derived from the Restatement (Second) of Conflict of Laws.[58]

Some laws and treaties applicable to international transactions have their own choice of law provisions. For example, as discussed in Chapter 2 above, the U.N. Convention on International Sale of Goods (CISG) generally provides that it applies to sales of goods between parties located in two different nations that are members of the Convention.

Unfortunately, many cases are filed in U.S. courts with a complaint drafted without any thought that foreign law might be applicable. The complaint may include several counts that may correctly refer to U.S. law but have no relevance if foreign law applies. For example, most civil law nations do not provide causes of action based on civil conspiracy or unjust enrichment. Additionally, most foreign legal systems do not grant punitive damages. Sometimes the plaintiff will attempt to equate a foreign concept with a U.S. concept. Thus, when a plaintiff has asked for punitive damages, and the law of Mexico is to apply, Mexico's "moral damage" law may be misconstrued to be the same as punitive damages.

There is a relationship between choice of law and *forum non conveniens* (see Section 26.6 above). When a court considers a motion to dismiss for *forum non conveniens*, the court may believe a

---

[57]   *See* Ralph Folsom, PRACTITIONER TREATISE ON INTERNATIONAL BUSINESS TRANSACTIONS (2012), Chapter 20 (EU Business Competition Law).

[58]   *See* Restatement of Conflicts of Law (1934) (generally attempting to provide precise rules for choosing applicable law); Restatement (Second) of Conflicts of Law § 188 (1971) (generally providing that court should choose law that has the "most significant relationship to the transaction").

foreign forum is more appropriate because the law of that foreign nation is the proper choice of law.

Choice of Law Clauses. Parties to commercial contracts are allowed in most jurisdictions to choose the applicable law in their contract. Choice of law clauses (often used in conjunction with choice-of-forum clauses, see Section 26.5 above), are very common in international transactions. They may apply not only to contractual disputes but sometimes also to designate the applicable law (and forum) for torts arising between parties with a contractual relationship, such as contracts selling vacations, cruises, etc. These clauses are often enforced.[59]

The parties should be fully aware of the substance of each possibly applicable law before stipulating the chosen law. For example, a U.S. party selling goods to a German party might discover that the German law favors the seller in such a transaction. The U.S. party in such case would want to specify that German law applies, and might even gain concessions from the German party on other issues if the German party prefers German law not because it has been researched but because it seems more familiar to the German party.

Courts usually respect a choice of law provision, especially in a commercial contract where the choice is between the laws of the parties' nations. Enforcement of the clause is less likely where the choice has no relevance to the contract, such as if German and U.S. parties chose the law of Mongolia.[60] A court is likely to reject such choice, perhaps because the chosen law has no linkage to the case, but also because the court may feel uncomfortable in applying the law of a nation without a highly developed contract law that may be difficult to prove. Enforcement of a choice of law clause may also be denied on ordinary contract principles such as fraud or duress, as well as on grounds of public policy.[61]

One important issue with choice of law clauses involves mandatory law—that is, laws of a jurisdiction that necessarily apply to parties' conduct. Parties cannot defeat the application of

---

[59]   *E.g.*, Cooper v. Meridian Yachts, Ltd., 575 F.3d 1151 (11th Cir. 2009).

[60]   *See* Restatement (Second) of Conflict of Laws, § 187(2)(a) (allowing choice of law clause to be disregarded if "the chosen [jurisdiction] has no substantial relationship to the parties or the transaction and there is no other reasonable basis for the parties' choice").

[61]   *See id.*, § 187(2)(b) (allowing court to disregard choice of law clause if "application of the law of the chosen [jurisdiction] would be contrary to a fundamental policy of a [jurisdiction] which has a materially greater interest" in the transaction). *See also* Johnson v. Ventra Group, Inc., 191 F.3d 732 (6th Cir. 1991) (rejecting claim that clause violated public policy).

mandatory law through a choice of law clause, but it may often be difficult to tell what laws are mandatory.[62]

§ 26.9 Proving Foreign Law

If parties in litigation intend to rely on foreign law, they will have to prove the content of that law. Typically procedural rules of the forum will direct how this occurs. For example, in U.S. federal court, Rule 44.1 of the Federal Rules of Civil Procedure provides:

> A party who intends to raise an issue concerning the law of a foreign country shall give notice in his pleadings or other reasonable written notice. The court, in determining foreign law, may consider any relevant material or source, including testimony, whether or not submitted by a party or admissible under the federal Rules of Evidence. The court's determination shall be treated as a ruling on a question of law.[63]

Proving foreign law in U.S. court likely will include various forms of written and oral testimony. Often affidavits of experts are submitted,[64] with the experts appearing at trial to support and respond to questions about their opinions. Usually when foreign law must be proved, experts will be practitioners or academics from the foreign country. But unless they have received some legal education in the United States, those persons may not be effective in explaining a very different legal system to a U.S. judge. In such case U.S. comparative law experts may be helpful in explaining to the judge the differences between the laws of the two nations.[65]

If the opposing lawyers do not recognize that the case involves the application of foreign law and proceed on the assumption that U.S. law applies, the ability to use foreign law may be waived.[66] Alternatively, the court may ask them to present opinions on the foreign law. A court may conduct its own research, which also may

---

[62]   *See* Richards v. Lloyd's of London, 135 F.3d 1289 (9th Cir. 1988) (en banc) (upholding choice of law clause even though it avoided application of U.S. securities laws); Mitsubishi Motors Corp. v. Soler Chrysler-Plymouth, Inc., 473 U.S. 614 (1985) (indicating that antitrust laws are mandatory law).

[63]   Federal Rules of Civil Procedure, Rule 44.1.

[64]   *See* Bing v. Halstead, 495 F. Supp. 517 (S.D.N.Y. 1980) (affidavits resulting in granting summary judgment).

[65]   *See generally* Peter Hay, *The Use and Determination of Foreign Law in Civil Litigation in the United States*, 62 AM. J. COMP. L. 213 (2014).

[66]   *See* In re Magnetic Audiotape Antitrust Litigation, 334 F.3d 204 (2d Cir. 2003); Laminoirs-Trefileries-Cableries de Lens, S.A. v. Southwire Co., 484 F. Supp. 1063, 1067 (N.D. Ga. 1980).

be helpful when the experts are divided on the meaning of the foreign law (as is usually the case).[67]

Proof of foreign law often requires obtaining translations. Some foreign laws are available in English, especially constitutions and important codes such as civil and commercial codes. If there is a published version of the foreign statute, it is likely to have been translated objectively and thus will be accepted by the court. Where the parties have to translate foreign statutes or cases, they may do so with a choice of words favoring their case. The court may have to choose between two versions. Translations of foreign cases are not often undertaken, sometimes because of their length and thus expense, and sometimes because they are written very abstractly and are difficult to understand by a U.S. judge who lacks experience with foreign materials. When translations do exist, they may be very helpful because a U.S. judge may not wish to interpret a foreign statute in a manner that is not clear from the language unless the foreign court has already given a similar or consistent interpretation.[68] If the parties do not submit adequate proof of foreign law, the court may choose to apply the substantive law of the forum.[69]

§ 26.10 Depositions and Document Discovery Abroad

For a trial in the United States, gathering evidence is far easier when both the defendant and the evidence are in the United States. But when the evidence is located abroad, obtaining evidence may become very difficult.

The rules for obtaining evidence are the rules of procedure of the forum, including any applicable international conventions or treaties such as the Hague Evidence Convention (discussed below). In U.S. federal court, the applicable rules are the Federal Rules of Civil Procedure, Rules 26–37, which generally allow courts to order broad discovery. One difficulty with discovery abroad, however, is that the U.S. court may not have jurisdiction over the target of the discovery. If the target is a party to the litigation, presumably the

---

[67]   *See* Bodum USA Inc. v. La Cafetière, Inc., 621 F.3d 624 (7th Cir. 2010) (debating whether judges should rely principally on experts or principally on their own research into foreign law).

[68]   *See* Federal Rules of Civil Procedure, Rule 44(a)(2) (governing proof of official foreign records).

[69]   *See* Naghiu v. Inter-Continental Hotels Group, Inc., 165 F.R.D. 413 (D. Del. 1996).

court will have jurisdiction, but if not, discovery may depend on the cooperation of the foreign country.[70]

This raises two difficulties. The first is that the methods of obtaining discovery may be different in other countries. For example, it may be that deposition evidence can only be collected by a court, not by private lawyers. Indeed, some practices of obtaining evidence permitted in the United States constitute *criminal* conduct in foreign nations.

Second, the foreign country may have different ideas about what evidence should be available for discovery. If U.S. notions of proper evidence paralleled those in foreign nations there would be far less trouble. The problem in gathering evidence abroad is not that foreign nations prevent other nations from obtaining evidence in their territory; it is that the U.S. concept of evidence extends beyond nearly all other nations' rules regarding what may be obtained. In most civil law tradition nations, judges with substantial discretion closely regulate gathering evidence. Attorneys are for the most part not left on their own to collect what they think would be useful, with occasional forays into court for new orders of production, as in the United States.

Civil law nation judges determine who may be witnesses. The judges ask questions they originate or those referred to them by the lawyers which they have approved. Requests for documents must be specific, disallowing requests, for example, for any documents that might have affected the design and manufacture of a product involved in an injury. If we sometimes think of U.S. process as condoning "fishing expeditions" for evidence, other nations are likely to interpret the U.S. method of fishing as using drift nets miles long that catch everything that the net surrounds. Other nations have effectively banned our nets.

As litigation unfolds in the United States, the search for evidence begins at an early stage, well before the trial. Much that the lawyers are seeking will help in the further development of the case. There may have been very little, if any, evidence present when a complaint was filed. Much of what *is* subsequently obtained will never be used. This pretrial discovery is neither fully understood nor accepted by many civil law tradition nations.

Obtaining evidence abroad comes in two general areas, deposing witnesses and obtaining physical evidence, principally written documents. If depositions are permitted by the foreign

---

[70]   If the target is a U.S. citizen or resident, however, a U.S. court may subpoena the target to appear in the United States and produce specified documents. 28 U.S.C. § 1783(a).

nation, they are sometimes taken before a person commissioned by the U.S. court.[71] U.S. consular officers are ordinarily used as the designated commissioners to take the testimony, but a foreign official or private person may be appointed. In some countries the testimony may only be taken under rules of the country that disallow the use of a commissioner appointed by the U.S. court. The foreign rules may even prohibit taking any testimony by deposition. In such case the U.S. court may be able to issue a letter of request to a court in the foreign nation asking that it issue an order to take the testimony.[72] The letter may be accepted under notions of comity, but it may not be accepted if the scope of the evidence sought or the method of seeking it is incompatible with the foreign nation's practices and assumptions.

Discovery Under the Hague Convention. To manage the problems of transnational discovery, many countries, including the United States, are parties to the Hague Evidence Convention.[73] This Convention provides for three principal methods of obtaining evidence abroad. The first is use of a letter of request to the "Central Authority" in the foreign nation.[74] That authority sends the request to the appropriate court. The second is by means of a request to take evidence before a diplomatic or consular officer in the foreign country. Third, a request may be made to have a commissioner appointed to take evidence.

The common dislike for U.S.-style pretrial evidence collection is apparent in the Convention, which allows a Convention party to make a declaration that disallows requests seeking "pretrial discovery of documents."[75] Most parties to the Convention (other than the United States) have made such a declaration, undermining the usefulness of the Convention to U.S litigants. As a result, U.S. litigants generally prefer to use the Federal Rules (or similar state law procedures) rather than the Convention, if the U.S. court has jurisdiction over the target of the discovery.

In *Société Nationale Industrielle Aerospatiale v. U.S. District Court,*[76] the U.S. Supreme Court held that the Convention is not the

---

[71]   Fed.R.Civ.P. 28(b)(4).

[72]   Some nations require the letters of request to be submitted through diplomatic channels rather than court-to-court.

[73]   Hague Convention on the Taking of Evidence Abroad in Civil or Commercial Matters, Mar. 18, 1970.

[74]   *See* Pronova BioPharma Norge A.S. v. Teva Pharmaceuticals USA Inc., 708 F. Supp. 2d 450 (D. Del. 2010); In re Urethane Antitrust Litigation, 267 F.R.D. 361 (D. Kan. 2010).

[75]   *Id.*, Art. 23.

[76]   482 U.S. 522 (1987). For subsequent application, see, *e.g.*, In re Automotive Refinishing Paint Antitrust Litigation, 358 F.3d 288 (3d Cir. 2004) (allowing discovery under Federal Rules for evidence located abroad); Costa v. Kerzner Int'l

exclusive method to seek discovery abroad; indeed the Court did not even require that the Convention be used first, with subsequent resort to the rules of the forum. Thus for discovery targeted at parties or their affiliates, or at persons over whom the U.S. court otherwise has jurisdiction, parties will typically seek to use the Federal Rules rather than the Convention.

Discovery that Conflicts with Foreign Law. When a court in the United States approves discovery of evidence abroad, the laws of the foreign nation may block disclosure of the requested evidence. This might result from national security laws, privacy laws, or even laws specifically designed to block U.S. discovery (called "blocking statutes").[77] In general, U.S. law allows courts to order discovery prohibited by foreign law, often placing the discovery target in an uncomfortable situation of having to violate either the U.S. court order or the foreign law.[78] However, U.S. courts are encouraged to take hardship to the parties and the legitimate interests of the foreign nation into account in crafting their orders.[79]

§ 26.11 Recognition and Enforcement of Foreign Judgments

A party may obtain a court judgment in international business litigation but find that the losing party's assets are located in a different jurisdiction. If the losing party refuses to satisfy the judgment voluntarily, the winning party will have to ask the courts of the second jurisdiction to enforce the judgment. That process is far from automatic, and varies considerably from country to country.

Enforcing Foreign Judgments in the United States. Judgments in one state of the United States must be recognized and enforced in other U.S. states under the "full faith and credit" clause of the U.S. Constitution.[80] This doctrine does not apply to foreign judgments. No rule exists in the United States prohibiting enforcement of foreign judgments, but no federal rule requires it either.[81]

Resorts, Inc., 277 F.R.D. 468 (S.D. Fla. 2011) (same, as to evidence held by defendants' affiliates).

[77]   *E.g.*, the U.K.'s Protection of Trading Interests Act of 1980.

[78]   *See* In re Air Cargo Shipping Services Antitrust Litigation, 2010 WL 2976220 (E.D.N.Y. 2010); Strauss v. Credit Lyonnais, S.A., 242 F.R.D. 199 (E.D.N.Y. 2007); Richmark Corp. v. Timber Falling Consultants, 959 F.2d 1468 (9th Cir. 1992).

[79]   *See* Restatement (Third) of Foreign Relations Law of the United States, § 442 (1987); Reinsurance Co. of America, Inc. v. Administratia Asigurarilor de Stat, 902 F.2d 1275 (7th Cir. 1990) (refusing to order discovery in violation of Romanian law).

[80]   U.S. Const. art. IV, § 1.

[81]   Negotiations have been pursued at The Hague for an international convention on jurisdiction and the enforcement of foreign judgments but have not

Enforcement is currently a matter for each state to decide, as matter of state law. Federal courts in diversity actions must follow the law of the state in which they sit.

Hilton v. Guyot, an influential early decision by the U.S. Supreme Court,[82] adopted a rule based on comity. *Hilton,* in considering whether to enforce a French judgment in the United States, assessed whether there had been an opportunity for a fair trial before a court of competent jurisdiction and whether the system of justice was impartial. Although it found the French judgment adequate on these grounds, the court nonetheless refused to enforce it because it found that French courts would not enforce a U.S. judgment, and thus there was no reciprocity. This decision did not establish a federal rule effective in the states, although the evolving state law has drawn heavily from the *Hilton* decision.

Beginning in 1962, many states adopted the Uniform Foreign Money-Judgments Recognition Act (UFMJRA). As of 2016, about 30 states have adopted a form of the uniform law, including its updated version, the 2005 Uniform Foreign-Country Money Judgments Recognition Act (UFCMJRA). Under the Uniform Acts, a foreign money judgment will be recognized and enforced unless a listed exception applies. Specifically, a court must not recognize or enforce a judgment if (1) the foreign judicial system does not provide impartial tribunals or procedures compatible with due process; or (2) the foreign court did not have personal or subject matter jurisdiction.[83] In addition, a court need not recognize or enforce a foreign judgment for a number of other reasons, including that the defendant lacked adequate notice; that the judgment was obtained by fraud; that the judgment or the cause of action is repugnant to the public policy of the enforcing state; or that the judgment was rendered in circumstances that raise substantial doubt about the integrity of the foreign court.[84]

States that have not adopted the Uniform Acts generally recognize and enforce judgments after applying tests similar to the approach in *Hilton.*[85] Notably, the Uniform Acts do not require reciprocity, although some states have added that requirement, and states that have not adopted the Uniform Acts differ on whether to include reciprocity as a requirement for enforcement.

---

produced a final document. If that is accomplished, there is no certainty that it will be adopted in the United States.

[82]   159 U.S. 113 (1895).

[83]   UFCMJRA § 4(b).

[84]   *Id.,* § 4(c) (also setting out additional exceptions).

[85]   *See, e.g.,* Koster v. Automark Ind., Inc., 640 F.2d 77 (7th Cir. 1981).

Courts applying either the Uniform Acts or non-uniform state law commonly enforce foreign judgments after considering the factors described above.[86] However, courts have sometimes refused recognition and enforcement, especially with regard to judgments from nations with corrupt or poorly developed judicial systems.[87] For example, several judgments in Nicaraguan courts against U.S. corporations for alleged injuries to Nicaraguan workers resulted in awards of many millions of dollars. The decisions were riddled with inequities and failure to include the most fundamental due process, and have been rejected by U.S. courts.[88] Occasionally, even judgments of developed-nation courts may be refused enforcement if they reflect fundamental differences in public policy.[89]

Enforcing U.S. Judgments in Foreign Nations. Foreign judgments are recognized and enforced in many nations, but only under often strict rules that allow careful scrutiny of many aspects of the original judgment. Some nations refuse to enforce foreign judgments (or refuse to do so absent a bilateral treaty), thus requiring re-litigation. Although a number of developed nations have enforcement practices similar to the United States, enforcement of some U.S. judgments may still be difficult because those nations may have different standards of personal jurisdiction, service of process and discovery, as well as differences on remedies such as punitive damages.[90]

Currency Issues in Enforcement. A related issue is what the enforcing state should do when the original judgment is in a foreign currency. Judgments are usually given in the currency of the forum,

---

[86]   *E.g.,* DeJoria v. Mahgreb Petroleum Exploration, S.A., 804 F.3d 373 (5th Cir. 2015) (reversing district court's refusal to enforce Moroccan judgment); Society of Lloyd's v. Turner, 303 F.3d 325 (5th Cir. 2002) (enforcing U.K. judgment); Society of Lloyd's v. Ashenden, 233 F.3d 473 (7th Cir. 2000) (same); Southwest Livestock and Trucking Co., Inc. v. Ramon, 169 F.3d 317 (5th Cir. 1999) (recognizing Mexican judgment).

[87]   *E.g.,* Bridgeway Corp. v. Citibank, 45 F.Supp.2d 276 (S.D.N.Y. 1999) (refusing to enforce judgment from Liberia); Bank Melli Iran v. Pahlavi, 58 F.3d 1406 (9th Cir. 1995) (refusing to enforce Iranian judgment).

[88]   *See* Osorio v. Dole Food Co. 665 F. Supp. 2d 1307 (S.D. Fla. 2009), *aff'd* 635 F.3d 1277 (11th Cir. 2011). In 2016, the Second Circuit upheld a lower court order under the federal Racketeer Influenced and Corrupt Organizations (RICO) statute and state law that effectively prohibited enforcement of an Ecuadorian judgment found to be procured by fraud. Chevron Corp. v. Donziger, 2016 WL 4173988 (2d Cir. 2016).

[89]   *E.g.,* Telnikoff v. Matusevitch, 347 Md. 561 (1997) (refusing to enforce U.K. libel judgment).

[90]   *See* Samuel Baumgartner, *Understanding the Obstacles to the Recognition and Enforcement of U.S. Judgments Abroad,* 45 N.Y.U. J. INT'L L. & POL. 965 (2013).

and in some cases this is a mandatory rule.[91] The principal issue for courts has been establishing the time of conversion of the currency of the judgment to the currency of the enforcing forum.[92] Some jurisdictions use the time of the act establishing the cause of action, others use the date of the judgment and others use the date of payment.[93] The Uniform Foreign Money Claims Act has adopted the date of payment.[94] The Restatement (Third) of Foreign Relations Law suggests use of the date which would best "serve the ends of justice in the circumstances."[95]

---

[91]   Judgments in U.S. courts may be in foreign currencies. *See, e.g.*, In re Oil Spill by the Amoco Cadiz Off the Coast of France on March 16, 1978, 954 F.2d 1279, 1328 (7th Cir. 1992).

[92]   *See* Jennifer Freeman, *Judgments in Foreign Currency—A Little Known Change in New York Law*, 23 INT'L LAW. 73 (1989) (noting adoption of a date-of-judgment rule).

[93]   *See* Manches & Co. v. Gilbey, 419 Mass. 414 (1995).

[94]   About twenty states have adopted this uniform law. *See* http://uniformlaws. org/LegislativeFactSheet.aspx?title=Foreign%20Money%20Claims%20Act.

[95]   Restatement (Third) of the Foreign Relations Law of the United States § 823 (1987).

Chapter 27

LITIGATION INVOLVING FOREIGN SOVEREIGNS

Table of Sections

§ 27.1 Foreign Sovereign Immunity and the Act of State Doctrine

In addition to the challenges of ordinary transnational business litigation, as described in Chapter 26, litigation involving foreign governments or their instrumentalities presents special difficulties. Two legal doctrines make such litigation complex. The first is foreign sovereign immunity—the rule that foreign sovereigns and their instrumentalities have immunity from suit in U.S. (and other nations') courts, subject to various exceptions. The second is the act of state doctrine, which holds that acts of a foreign government done in its own territory cannot be questioned by U.S. courts (again subject to various exceptions). In the United States, foreign sovereign immunity is mainly governed by a federal statute, the Foreign Sovereign Immunities Act (FSIA),[1] while the act of state doctrine is a common law rule developed by court decisions.

---

[1]   28 U.S.C. §§ 1330, 1602–1611.

§ 27.2 History and Rationale of Foreign Sovereign Immunity

Foreign sovereign immunity arises in part from the international law principle of equality of nations (thus, no nation may be the judge of another), and in part from a practical necessity for courts not to interfere with diplomatic relations among nations. As a rule of international law, it is present in most developed legal systems, although it is implemented in different ways and to different extents.[2]

The roots of foreign sovereign immunity law in the United States go back to *The Schooner Exchange v. McFaddon*.[3] Chief Justice Marshall stated in this Supreme Court decision that U.S. courts lacked jurisdiction over an armed ship of a foreign state (France) located in a U.S. port. When engaged in official acts *(jure imperii)* the sovereign (whether ancient prince or modern state),

> [b]eing in no respect amenable to another; and being bound by obligations of the highest character not to degrade the dignity of his nation, by placing himself or its sovereign rights within the jurisdiction of another, can be supposed to enter a foreign territory only under an express license, or in the confidence that the [absolute] immunities belonging to his independent sovereign station, though not expressly stipulated, are reserved by implication, and will be extended to him.[4]

In subsequent cases, foreign sovereign immunity was found to be absolute, regardless of the nature of the activity.[5] The doctrine of sovereign immunity might have caused little difficulty had sovereigns engaged only in "sovereign" acts. But modern nations engage in many private transactions *(jure gestionis)*. Many nations became private traders, engaging in the operation of transportation, telegraph and telephone services, radio and television communications, and the production of goods (extraction of natural resources, tobacco and matches, etc.). Commercial transactions gave rise to disputes and brought into the courts of one nation the public trading entities of another. Eventually, the doctrine of absolute immunity gave way to a "restrictive" theory that denied immunity

---

2   For example, in Britain it is implemented by the State Immunity Act 1978 and in some European countries through the European Convention on State Immunity.

3   11 U.S. 116 (1812).

4   *Id.* at 137.

5   *See* Berizzi Brothers Co. v. The Pesaro, 271 U.S. 562 (1926).

when (among other situations) the sovereign acted in the market place.

National courts were initially slow to alter the absolute immunity doctrine. Rather surprisingly, in civil law tradition nations in Europe the evolution from absolute immunity to restrictive immunity occurred in case law. As early as 1857 in Belgium, in *Etat du Pérou v. Krelinger,*[6] courts began to accept the restrictive theory. An Italian decision in 1882, *Morellet C. Governo Danese,*[7] continued the movement, as did Austrian and German courts in the 20th century.

In the mid-twentieth century, U.S. courts shifted to a view that immunity decisions should rest largely with the U.S. executive branch. The U.S. Department of State regularly requested immunity when friendly nations were sued in U.S. courts. But in 1952, the State Department sent what became known as the "Tate Letter" to the Department of Justice, announcing that its policy would be "to follow the restrictive theory of sovereign immunity in the consideration of requests of foreign governments for a grant of sovereign immunity."[8] The letter stated:

> It is realized that a shift in policy by the executive cannot control the courts but it is felt that the courts are less likely to allow a plea of sovereign immunity where the executive has declined to do so. There have been indications that at least some Justices of the Supreme Court feel that in this matter courts should follow the branch of the Government charged with responsibility for the conduct of foreign relations.

Although the Tate Letter announced an acceptance of the restrictive theory of sovereign immunity, it offered no guidelines or criteria to distinguish a nation's public acts from its private acts. Until the passage of the Foreign Sovereign Immunities Act twenty-four years later, the application of the restrictive theory proved troublesome. The courts generally complied with "suggestions" of immunity from the Department of State, and foreign sovereigns were sometimes successful in urging the Department to support immunity for the kind of private acts the restrictive theory was intended to address.

In 1976, Congress enacted the Foreign Sovereign Immunities Act (FSIA) to relieve the government of diplomatic pressures relating to immunity, "thereby eliminating the role of the State

---

[6]   P.B. 1857–II–348.

[7]   (1882) Guir. It. 1883–I–25.

[8]   24 Dept. State Bull. 984 (1952).

Department in such questions and bringing the United States into conformity with the immunity practice of virtually every other country."[9] The FSIA additionally illustrated to litigants that sovereign immunity decisions would be made on legal rather than political grounds. In adopting the restrictive theory, the FSIA established legal standards applicable to claims of immunity made by foreign sovereigns, whether the litigation was in a state or federal court in the United States. The FSIA also guaranteed foreign states the right to remove civil actions from state court to federal court, thus allying fears of "local" treatment and contemplating the development of a fairly uniform body of law in the federal courts.

A further goal of the FSIA was to provide a procedure for serving process and obtaining personal jurisdiction, thus avoiding the past practices of plaintiffs seizing property of foreign states to force an appearance. And finally, the FSIA allows execution upon commercial assets of foreign states, although the requirements for execution are stricter than those for jurisdiction to adjudicate.

§ 27.3   Basic Structure of the FSIA

The FSIA is federal law. Its approach is that a foreign state is immune from the subject matter jurisdiction of U.S. courts unless an exception set forth in the statute applies.[10] Subject matter jurisdiction is conferred to permit a nonjury civil action against a foreign state not entitled to immunity.[11] According to the Supreme Court, the FSIA is the sole basis for obtaining jurisdiction over a foreign state.[12] If the court has subject matter jurisdiction, and if proper service of process is made,[13] the statute also provides for personal jurisdiction over the foreign state.[14] The Supreme Court even found that the FSIA provides federal jurisdiction over suits between foreign sovereigns and non-U.S. plaintiffs,[15] even though

---

[9]   Martropico Compania Naviera S.A. v. Perusahaan Pertambangan Minyak Dan Gas Bumi Negara (Pertamina), 428 F. Supp. 1035, 1037 (S.D.N.Y. 1977).

[10]   28 U.S.C. §§ 1694, 1605. See Saudi Arabia v. Nelson, 507 U.S. 349 (1993).

[11]   28 U.S.C. § 1330(a).

[12]   Argentine Republic v. Amerada Hess Shipping Corp., 488 U.S. 428 (1989).

[13]   The FSIA, 28 U.S.C. § 1608, has special mandatory provisions for serving process on foreign sovereigns and their instrumentalities.

[14]   28 U.S.C. § 1330(b). It is unclear whether a foreign sovereign defendant could mount a constitutional due process challenge to personal jurisdiction. See Price v. Socialist People's Libyan Arab Jamahiriya, 294 F.3d 82 (D.C. Cir. 2002) (foreign state not protected by due process clause); Frontera Resources Azerbaijan Co. v. State Oil Co. of the Azerbaijan Republic, 582 F.3d 393 (2d Cir. 2009) (foreign state-owned corporation may be protected by due process clause).

[15]   Verlinden B.V. v. Central Bank of Nigeria, 461 U.S. 480 (1983).

typically suits between non-U.S. parties are not within federal jurisdiction unless there is a federal claim involved.

As discussed below, the FSIA provides separate immunities for foreign sovereign property against attachment and execution in satisfaction of a judgment. Thus, even if there is jurisdiction to hear a case against a foreign sovereign, there might not be any ability to enforce a resulting judgment.

§ 27.4   What Entities Are Covered by the FSIA?

A critical threshold inquiry is whether a defendant entity is covered by the FSIA's definition of "foreign state." If so, it can only be sued under an FSIA exception to immunity, and it is protected by other FSIA provisions such as special rules on service of process and enforcement of judgments. If it is not covered by the FSIA, immunity may still exist as a matter of common law (but as to business entities this is unlikely).

Under the statute's definitions section, a "foreign state" includes "a political subdivision of a foreign state or an agency or instrumentality of a foreign state."[16] An "agency or instrumentality of a foreign state" is any entity:

(1) which is a separate legal person, corporate or otherwise, and

(2) which is an organ of a foreign state or political subdivision thereof, or a majority of whose shares or other ownership interest is owned by a foreign state or political subdivision thereof, and

(3) which is neither a citizen of a State of the United States [as defined in the Act], . . . nor created under the laws of any third country.[17]

Critically for international business transactions, this definition includes many corporations that may appear to be ordinary commercial entities, if their stock is majority-owned by a foreign government. In *Dole Food Co. v. Patrickson*,[18] the Supreme Court held that the definition of "foreign state" did not extend to second-tier (and beyond) subsidiaries. Thus a corporation owned by a corporation owned by a foreign state is not an agency or instrumentality of the foreign state, and so is not covered by the FSIA.[19] The Court also held in *Patrickson* that the categorization of

---

[16]   28 U.S.C. § 1603(a).

[17]   28 U.S.C. § 1603(b).

[18]   538 U.S. 468 (2003).

[19]   In unusual circumstances, a subsidiary might be an "organ" of the foreign state and thus included in the definition of foreign state, see 28 U.S.C. § 1603(b)(2),

the defendant as a foreign state depends on ownership at the time suit is filed. Thus a business entity that was not a "foreign state" at the time a transaction is negotiated may become one later (and vice-versa).

The distinction between a foreign state and its agencies or instrumentalities is important: a foreign state is not liable for the acts of its agencies or instrumentalities in the absence of piercing the corporate veil. There is a presumption that the foreign state is separate from its instrumentalities, which may only be overcome by showing that (1) the corporate entity was so controlled that there was a principal/agent relationship, or (2) allowing the distinction would work fraud or injustice.[20]

Some entities may present particular challenges in characterizing them. The Vatican has been held to be a foreign state.[21] The Palestinian Liberation Organization (PLO) has been denied such status.[22] Courts have denied "foreign state" status to the Organization of Petroleum Exporting Countries (OPEC)[23] and granted it to the British West Indies Central Labour Organization.[24] In 2010, overturning a line of lower court decisions,[25] the Supreme Court held that the FSIA does not apply to government officials.[26]

If a person or entity associated with a foreign sovereign is not covered by the FSIA, immunity may still exist as a matter of common law or another statute or treaty. For example, foreign heads of state and other government officials may have common law immunity.[27] International organizations such as the United Nations may have immunity as a result of particular treaties.

It is also important to remember that if an entity is covered by the FSIA, that does not mean it necessarily has immunity; it only means that a statutory exception to immunity must be found.

---

even if not directly owned by the foreign state. *See* Calif. Dep't of Water Resources v. Powerex Corp., 533 F.3d 1087 (9th Cir. 2008).

[20]   First Nat'l City Bank v. Banco Para El Comercio Exterior de Cuba (Bancec), 462 U.S. 611 (1983).

[21]   English v. Thorne, 676 F.Supp. 761 (S.D. Miss. 1987).

[22]   National Petrochemical Co. of Iran v. M/T Stolt Sheaf, 860 F.2d 551 (2d Cir. 1988).

[23]   International Ass'n of Machinists and Aerospace Workers v. OPEC, 477 F.Supp. 553, 560 (C.D. Cal. 1979), *aff'd*, 649 F.2d 1354 (9th Cir. 1981).

[24]   Rios v. Marshall, 530 F.Supp. 351 (S.D.N.Y. 1981).

[25]   *E.g.*, Chuidian v. Philippine National Bank, 912 F.2d 1095 (9th Cir. 1990).

[26]   Samantar v. Yousuf, 130 S.Ct. 2278 (2010).

[27]   Yousuf v. Samantar, 699 F.3d 763 (4th Cir. 2012).

§ 27.5 Exceptions to Foreign Sovereign Immunity__Waiver

A foreign state is not immune in any case "in which [it] has waived its immunity either explicitly or by implication, notwithstanding any withdrawal of the waiver . . . except in accordance with the terms of waiver."[28]

Explicit waivers are found in treaties and in private contracts. For example, some treaties of Friendship, Commerce, and Navigation (FCN) waive immunity with respect to commercial and other activities. Waivers in private contracts with foreign states, such as bond indentures relating to sovereign debt obligations, have commonly been enforced.[29] The language used in the waiver is important—a commonly used provision in FCN treaties that immunity shall not be claimed from "suit, execution or judgment, or other liability" is not an explicit waiver from prejudgment attachment.[30]

Implied waivers are not easily established. A foreign state does not waive its immunity by entering into a contract. The contract may give rise to a commercial activity exception (see Section 27.6 below), but a waiver must be intentional and knowing.[31] Similarly, failure to defend against a claim is not a waiver, although regular participation in litigation might constitute one.[32]

§ 27.6 Exceptions to Foreign Sovereign Immunity__Commercial Activity

The FSIA's commercial activity exception[33] is probably the most important to international business. It reflects the core of the "restrictive" theory of foreign sovereign immunity—that the sovereign should not be immune when it acts like a private party in the marketplace. However, the commercial activity exception has proved difficult to apply and is the source of an enormous amount of litigation under the FSIA.

---

[28]   28 U.S.C. § 1605(a)(1).

[29]   *E.g.*, Capital Ventures International v. Republic of Argentina, 552 F.3d 289 (2d Cir. 2009); *but see* World Wide Minerals, Ltd. v. Republic of Kazakhstan, 296 F.3d 1154 (D.C. Cir. 2002) (express waivers narrowly construed).

[30]   Libra Bank Ltd. v. Banco Nacional de Costa Rica, S.A., 676 F.2d 47 (2d Cir. 1982).

[31]   Transamerican Steamship Corp. v. Somali Democratic Republic, 767 F.2d 998 (D.C. Cir. 1985).

[32]   *See* Siderman de Blake v. Republic of Argentina, 965 F.2d 699 (9th Cir. 1992).

[33]   28 U.S.C. § 1605(a)(2).

The FSIA defines "commercial activity," somewhat unhelpfully, as:

> either a regular course of commercial conduct or a particular commercial transaction or act. The commercial character of an activity shall be determined by reference to the nature of the course of conduct or particular transaction or act, rather than by reference to its purpose.[34]

In 1992, resolving considerable disagreement in the lower courts, the U.S. Supreme Court addressed the definition of commercial activity and came down strongly against any interpretation based on the *purpose* of the activity.[35] The Court said the issue is whether the actions that the foreign state "performs (whatever the motive behind them) are the type of actions by which a private party engages in 'trade and traffic or commerce.' " The Court held that issuing sovereign bonds is a commercial activity, even though the proceeds from the bonds would be used for governmental purposes. Thus, if the activity is one which normally could be engaged in by a private party, it is commercial and a foreign state is not immune, but if the activity is one in which only a state can engage, it is noncommercial under the FSIA.[36] The focus is not on whether the defendant generally engages in commercial activities, but on the particular conduct giving rise to the action.[37]

In most cases, expropriations will be considered non-commercial sovereign acts. The general view is that a "nationalization is the quintessentially sovereign act, never viewed as having a commercial character."[38] Thus suits based on expropriation generally cannot proceed under the commercial activity exception. The exception contained in § 1605(a)(3), discussed in the next section below—rights taken in violation of international law—may apply to some nationalizations, depending on the relation of the property located in the United States to the property nationalized.

---

[34]   28 U.S.C. § 1603(d).

[35]   Republic of Argentina v. Weltover, Inc., 504 U.S. 607 (1992).

[36]   *See* Saudi Arabia v. Nelson, 507 U.S. 349 (1992) (wrongful detention of plaintiff by Saudi police not commercial activity even if done in cooperation with plaintiff's employer); Guevara v. Republic of Peru, 468 F.3d 1289 (11th Cir. 2006) (offering a reward for information is a commercial activity).

[37]   Brazosport Towing Co., Inc. v. 3,838 Tons of Sorghum Laden on Board, 607 F. Supp. 11 (S.D. Tex. 1984).

[38]   Carey v. National Oil Co., 453 F. Supp. 1097 (S.D.N.Y. 1978).

Even where a commercial activity is found, it must also bear some relationship to the United States. The FSIA recognizes exceptions for commercial activity in three circumstances:

A foreign state shall not be immune from the jurisdiction of courts of the United States or of the States in any case . . . in which the action is based [1] upon a commercial activity carried on in the United States by the foreign state; or [2] upon an act performed in the United States in connection with a commercial activity of the foreign state elsewhere; or [3] upon an act outside the territory of the United States in connection with a commercial activity of the foreign state elsewhere and that act causes a direct effect in the United States.[39]

The first of these—an "action based upon a commercial activity carried on in the United States by the foreign state"—is the easiest to apply, although there may be questions about how much commercial activity was done in the United States and what link there is between the claim and the U.S.-based commercial activity.[40]

The second category deals with an "act performed in the United States in connection with a commercial activity of the foreign state performed elsewhere." It is the least used of the three categories, and it is somewhat hard to imagine what sort of claims would fit within it.

The third category, an "act outside . . . the United States in connection with a commercial activity of the foreign state and that act causes a direct effect in the United States," has been the most difficult to define. Since most foreign sovereign acts occur outside the United States, the "direct effect" language is often the focus of attention. The Supreme Court found a direct effect where the foreign government had an obligation to pay money in New York and failed to pay. In the Court's view, an effect is direct if it "follows 'as an immediate consequence of the defendant's . . . activity.' "[41]

---

[39] 28 U.S.C. § 1605(a)(2).

[40] *See* OBB Personenverkehr AG v. Sachs, 136 S.Ct. 390 (2015) (claim for railway injury in Austria was not "based on" a commercial activity carried on in United States even though ticket was purchased in United States).

[41] Republic of Argentina v. Weltover, Inc., 504 U.S. 607 (1992), citing Texas Trading & Milling Corp. v. Federal Republic of Nigeria, 647 F.2d 300, 311 (2d Cir. 1981).

§ 27.7   Exceptions to Foreign Sovereign Immunity—Violations of International Law

Claims for rights in property taken in violation of international law are an exception to sovereign immunity in two circumstances. The first is if:

> that property or any property exchanged for such property is present in the United States in connection with a commercial activity carried on in the United States by the foreign state . . . [42]

This section may be used to respond to noncompensated expropriations of property, but its "property tracing" feature severely limits its use.

The FSIA also provides an exception for claims to expropriated property where:

> that property or any property exchanged for such property is owned or operated by an agency or instrumentality of the foreign state and that agency or instrumentality is engaged in a commercial activity in the United States.[43]

This exception may be somewhat more useful because it does not require the property to be brought into the United States, but it depends on the foreign state structuring its property holding in a way that leaves it open to suit.[44] As a result, claims for expropriation are often difficult to bring in U.S. courts due to foreign sovereign immunity.

§ 27.8   Other FSIA Exceptions

The FSIA contains a number of additional exceptions to immunity. Many of them are not generally helpful to international business transactions (such as the exception for torts committed in the United States),[45] or are helpful only in particular circumstances (such as the exceptions for counterclaims, for certain maritime claims, and for terrorism).[46] Suits involving rights to real property located in the United States are an exception, as are suits to enforce arbitration agreements and arbitral awards (see Chapter 28).[47]

---

[42]   28 U.S.C. § 1605(a)(3).

[43]   *Id.*

[44]   *See* Agudas Chasidei Chabad of U.S. v. Russian Federation, 528 F.3d 934 (D.C. Cir. 2008); Cassirer v. Kingdom of Spain, 616 F.3d 1019 (9th Cir. 2010) (en banc).

[45]   28 U.S.C. § 1605(a)(5).

[46]   28 U.S. C. §§ 1605(b), 1605A, 1607.

[47]   28 U.S.C. §§ 1605(a)(4), 1605(a)(6).

§ 27.9   Immunity Against Execution

Even if an exception to immunity can be found and a judgment can be obtained against a foreign sovereign, that may not be sufficient to provide a remedy. The FSIA contains a separate immunity for foreign sovereign property against "attachment arrest or execution," subject to certain exceptions.[48] Property of the sovereign itself is only subject to attachment and execution if it is used for commercial purposes.[49] That is true even if the sovereign has waived its immunity: waiver is not effective for non-commercial property. Agencies and instrumentalities, however, can waive immunity for non-commercial property if they are engaged in commercial activity.[50] The execution immunities do not preclude other orders a court might issue relating to enforcement of judgments.[51]

§ 27.10   The Act of State Doctrine

In addition to sovereign immunity, the act of state doctrine is a further barrier to claims involving foreign sovereigns. The doctrine's basic rule is that U.S. courts may not question the validity of the act of a foreign sovereign done in its territory. Although related, the two rules are distinct, and one may apply even if the other is defeated.[52]

Unlike foreign sovereign immunity, which is jurisdictional, the act of state "operates as an issue preclusion device."[53] It does not deprive a court of jurisdiction; if it applies, the court may proceed to issue a judgment, but in doing so it must assume the foreign sovereign act is valid. The act of state doctrine in the United States is for the most part not governed by statute but rather by case law that is sometimes confusing and difficult to apply. Like the FSIA, the doctrine has various exceptions, but they are less well established. That case law includes debate regarding its application to violations of international law such as expropriations;[54] whether the doctrine applies to bar a counterclaim; whether it applies to an

---

[48]   28 U.S.C. §§ 1609–1611.

[49]   28 U.S.C. § 1610(a).

[50]   28 U.S.C. § 1610(b).

[51]   Republic of Argentina v. NML Capital, Ltd., 134 S.Ct. 2250 (2014) (court may order discovery of sovereign assets); NML Capital, Ltd. v. Republic of Argentina, 727 F.3d 230 (2d Cir. 2013) (court may enjoin sovereign payments to third parties).

[52]   *E.g.*, World Wide Minerals, Ltd. v. Republic of Kazakhstan, 296 F.3d 1154 (D.C. Cir. 2002) (act of state doctrine precluded claims for which foreign sovereign immunity had been waived).

[53]   National American Corp. v. Federal Republic of Nigeria, 448 F. Supp. 622, 640 (S.D.N.Y. 1978), *aff'd*, 597 F.2d 314 (2d Cir. 1979).

[54]   Banco Nacional de Cuba v. Sabbatino, 376 U.S. 398 (1964).

act in violation of a treaty; uncertainty over the situs of an act of state; and whether it applies to motives rather than acts of foreign state officials. Of most concern to those engaged in international business transactions is the debate regarding the existence of waiver and commercial activity exceptions to the doctrine.

§ 27.11   History of the Act of State Doctrine

The doctrine has been traced to the 1674 English case *Blad v. Bamfield.*[55] The initial important U.S. decision is *Underhill v. Hernandez.*[56] There the Supreme Court stated:

> Every sovereign state is bound to respect the independence of every other state, and the courts of one country will not sit in judgment on the acts of the government of another, done within its own territory. Redress of grievances by reason of such acts must be obtained through the means open to be availed of by sovereign powers as between themselves.[57]

The *Underhill* litigation arose from claimed damages suffered by the plaintiff (Underhill) at the hands of a Venezuelan revolutionary army commander (Hernández) during an alleged false arrest in Venezuela. The Court held that the commander's actions could not be questioned in U.S. court. Several subsequent cases reaffirmed the doctrine in the context of the seizure of property.[58]

Banco Nacional de Cuba v. Sabbatino began the contemporary history of the act of state doctrine and its applicability to expropriations.[59] The case involved rights to property (sugar) affected by the Cuban nationalization of property in 1960. After the sugar was sold, the proceeds were paid to the former owners, and the Cuban government (through Banco Nacional) sued to obtain the money. The former owners, represented by Sabbatino, defended on the ground that the nationalization was invalid because it violated international law. The court refused to consider the defense, stating:

> [T]he Judicial Branch will not examine the validity of a taking of property within its own territory by a foreign sovereign government, extant and recognized by this country at the time of suit, in the absence of a treaty or

---

[55]   36 All Eng. Rep. 992, applied in Buttes Gas and Oil Co. v. Hammer (No. 3), [1981] 3 All E.R. 616.

[56]   168 U.S. 250 (1897).

[57]   *Id.* at 252.

[58]   Oetjen v. Central Leather Co., 246 U.S. 297 (1918); Ricaud v. American Metal Co., 246 U.S. 304 (1918).

[59]   376 U.S. 398 (1964).

other unambiguous agreement regarding controlling legal principles, even if the complaint alleges that the taking violates customary international law.[60]

Accordingly, the Court gave judgment for Banco Nacional.

The *Sabbatino* decision affected the contours of the act of state doctrine in several key respects. First, although it did not find the doctrine constitutionally compelled, it said the doctrine had "constitutional underpinnings" in the separation of powers— notably, the executive's control over foreign relations. Thus the doctrine was not so much about the rights of the foreign sovereign, but rather about the best way to conduct U.S. diplomacy. Second, it found that the doctrine was a matter of federal common law, and so binding on state courts as well. Third, it implied that there might be exceptions to the rule, such as for "a treaty or other unambiguous agreement" in the quoted language above.

The Supreme Court decision was not well received by Congress, and its specific outcome was reversed by statute (see § 27.14 below). However, it remains the foundation of the modern act of state doctrine.

§ 27.12   Elements of the Act of State Doctrine

The act of state doctrine is best understood as a general rule subject to a series of exceptions. There are three basic elements of the general rule:

(1)   An act of a foreign state;

(2)   committed in its territory; and

(3)   a claim or defense that questions the validity of that act.

As to the first element, not all acts of governmental actors or entities rise to the level of acts of state. In *Alfred Dunhill of London, Inc. v. Republic of Cuba*,[61] the Supreme Court found that the refusal of government employees running a Cuban state-owned business to reimburse overpayments was not an act of the Cuban state, and so was not protected by the doctrine.[62]

The second element is straightforward, although it may present difficulties in particular cases. Determining that the situs of the activity is not in the foreign state may cause judicial rejection of

---

[60]   *Id.* at 428.

[61]   425 U.S. 682 (1976).

[62]   *See also* McKesson Corp v. Islamic Republic of Iran, 672 F.3d 1066 (D.C. Cir. 2012) (acts of government agents on company's board of directors not protected by act of state doctrine).

the doctrine. This has proven important to the international debt issue. If nonpayment is held to have occurred at the office of the lending bank in the United States, the doctrine may be rejected as a defense.[63]

The third element is the hardest to understand, and it was read narrowly in the 1990 Supreme Court case *W.S. Kirkpatrick & Co. v. Environmental Tectonics Corp., Int'l.*[64] In *Kirkpatrick,* Environmental Tectonics alleged that the reason it had lost a contract with Nigeria was that Kirkpatrick had bribed Nigerian government officials. Environmental Tectonics sought damages against Kirkpatrick, and Kirkpatrick raised the act of state doctrine in defense, pointing out that proof of the bribe might require the court to consider an act of the foreign state. The court of appeals declined to apply the act of state doctrine because the Department of State said that such inquiry would not cause embarrassment to U.S. foreign relations. But the Supreme Court rejected that reasoning, instead refusing to apply the doctrine because the plaintiff's claim did not involve an inquiry into the lawfulness of an act of the foreign government; it merely required the consideration of the motivations of foreign officials. The case might cause embarrassment to the foreign state or to U.S. foreign relations, but that was insufficient to invoke the doctrine.

Although it may not always be easy to apply the *Kirkpatrick* ruling, the core aspects of the doctrine are not affected by it. In *Sabbatino,* for example, it is clear that the defense sought to invalidate the nationalization act of the Cuban government, which clearly implicates the act of state doctrine even after *Kirkpatrick.*

As *Kirkpatrick* indicates (and as several early cases held),[65] the act of state doctrine can be applied even in cases involving only private parties. If one party relies on the foreign sovereign act to justify its own conduct, and the other party challenges that justification, the act of state doctrine is implicated even if the foreign sovereign is not part of the suit.

§ 27.13   Act of State and the Separation of Powers

As explained in *Sabbatino,* the act of state doctrine rests upon considerations of international comity and separation of powers between the executive and judicial branches of the government. It is

---

[63]   Allied Bank Int'l v. Banco Crédito Agrícola de Cartago, 757 F.2d 516 (2d Cir. 1985).

[64]   493 U.S. 400 (1990).

[65]   Oetjen v. Central Leather Co., 246 U.S. 297 (1918); Ricaud v. American Metal Co., 246 U.S. 304 (1918).

intended to avoid embarrassment in the conduct of the nation's foreign relations.

The doctrine's foundation in separation of powers raises the question whether it can be waived by the executive branch. In *Bernstein v. N.V. Nederlandsche-Amerikaansche Stoomvaart-Maatschappij,*[66] the court of appeals was inclined to apply the act of state doctrine, but the Department of State urged the court to refrain and to proceed with an examination of the legal issues. The court concluded:

> [I]n the prior appeal in this case . . . because of the lack of a definitive expression of Executive Policy, we felt constrained to follow . . . [the act of state doctrine] . . . Following our decision, however, the State Department issued . . . [a policy statement intended] . . . to relieve American courts from any [such] restraint upon the exercise of their jurisdiction [in this case]. . . . In view of this supervening expression of Executive Policy, we amend our mandate . . . [67]

However, in a subsequent case, a fractured Supreme Court appeared to reject this "*Bernstein* exception," at least to the extent that the State Department's position should not be conclusive on the courts.[68] A later dissenting opinion explained:

> [S]ix members of the Court in *First National* . . . disapproved finally the so-called *Bernstein* exception to the act of state doctrine, thus minimizing the significance of any letter from the Department of State . . . [T]he task of defining the role of the Judiciary is for this Court, not the Executive Branch.[69]

Constitutional effect aside, a *Bernstein* letter from the Department of State to a court may be quite persuasive in providing the court a reason to avoid application of the act of state doctrine. Lack of such a letter may not result in a reverse conclusion; in 1982, the Department advised that "courts should not infer from the silence of the Department of State that adjudication in . . . (a pending) case would be harmful to the foreign policy of the United States."[70]

---

[66]   210 F.2d 375 (2d Cir. 1954).

[67]   *Id.* at 375–376.

[68]   First National City Bank v. Banco Nacional de Cuba, 406 U.S. 759 (1972). The lead opinion for the Court declared that it was adopting the *Bernstein* exception, but it gained only three votes. The other concurring and dissenting opinions rejected the exception.

[69]   Alfred Dunhill of London, Inc. v. Republic of Cuba, 425 U.S. 682 (1976).

[70]   *See* 22 Int'l Legal Mat. 207 (1983).

The *Kirkpatrick* decision (see § 27.12 above) supports the view that it is the function of the judiciary rather than the executive to define the role of the judiciary in addressing acts of foreign states. The Supreme Court in *Kirkpatrick* did not reject any role for the executive, but clearly rejected conclusive reliance on letters from the State Department.

§ 27.14   Exceptions to the Act of State Doctrine

As in the case of sovereign immunity, there are exceptions to the act of state doctrine. Unlike sovereign immunity, however, the exceptions are not clearly stated in a statute, and in many cases it is unclear whether they are valid exceptions.

Treaty Exception. As noted, *Sabbatino* expressly contemplated that the act of state doctrine might not apply where there was "a treaty or other unambiguous agreement regarding controlling legal principles." In *Kalamazoo Spice Extraction Co. v. The Provisional Government of Socialist Ethiopia,*[71] the court of appeals endorsed this suggestion, finding that a provision in an bilateral treaty requiring compensation for expropriation was sufficient to defeat the act of state doctrine. One might also argue that an *unambiguous* rule of customary international law should be sufficient to defeat the doctrine[72] (the problem in *Sabbatino* being that the international law rule was disputed).

Waiver. A foreign sovereign might expressly waive its right to raise the act of state defense, for example in a contract with a private party. Like a treaty, a private contract might represent an "agreement regarding controlling legal principles" as suggested in *Sabbatino*. But it is not clear whether the sovereign could retract the waiver. If the waiver is revocable, it would seem that the doctrine actually cannot be waived. Moreover, because the act of state doctrine addresses the relationship between two branches of the U.S. government, it is not clear that it is waivable by the foreign government. A clear and unambiguous statement by a foreign state that it does not object to judicial scrutiny of a state act may influence a court, but other factors may also be considered.[73] Waiver of foreign sovereign immunity does not in itself waive application of the act of state doctrine.[74]

---

[71]   729 F.2d 422 (6th Cir. 1984).

[72]   *See* Doe v. Unocal Corp., 395 F.3d 932 (9th Cir. 2002).

[73]   Compania de Gas de Nuevo Laredo, S.A. v. Entex, Inc., 686 F.2d 322 (5th Cir. 1982).

[74]   *See* World Wide Minerals, Ltd. v. Republic of Kazakhstan, 296 F.3d 1154 (D.C. Cir. 2002).

A further question is whether the imposition of a counterclaim by a foreign sovereign defendant constitutes a waiver. A majority of the Court in the *First National* decision suggested no, but it was not part of the opinion. As *Sabbatino* made clear, if the sovereign brings an action in a U.S. court, it may invoke the act of state doctrine to defeat a defense to its claim; presumably this also applies to a counterclaim.

Governments No Longer in Existence. Multiple cases have held that acts by governments that no longer exist are not protected by the act of state doctrine.[75] However, this exception does not apply where the successor government has adopted the acts of the prior government.[76]

Commercial Activity. Uncertainty also clouds the existence of a commercial activity exception to the act of state doctrine. The Supreme Court plurality in the *Dunhill* case argued:

> [T]he concept of an act of state should not be extended to include the repudiation of a purely commercial obligation owed by a foreign sovereign or by one of its commercial instrumentalities. . . . In their commercial capacities, foreign governments do not exercise powers peculiar to sovereigns. . . . Subjecting them in connection with such acts to the same rules of law that apply to private citizens is unlikely to touch very sharply on "national nerves."[77]

However, only four justices joined that part of the opinion, and four other justices wrote:

> [I]t does not follow that there should be a commercial act exception to the act of state doctrine. . . .
>
> The carving out of broad exceptions to the doctrine is fundamentally at odds with the careful case-by-case approach adopted in *Sabbatino*.[78]

The ambiguity of the Court has led to different views in lower federal courts. One court stated:

> [C]onsideration of the commercial nature of a given act is compelled if the doctrine is to be applied correctly. In this connection, attention is owed not to the purpose of the act but to its nature. The goal of the inquiry is to determine if

---

[75]   *E.g.*, Bigio v. Coca-Cola Co., 239 F.3d 440 (2d Cir. 2001); Republic of Philippines v. Marcos, 806 F.2d 344 (2d Cir. 1986).

[76]   Konowaluff v. Metropolitan Museum of Art, 702 F.3d 140 (2d Cir. 2012) (act of state doctrine protects acts of former Soviet Union).

[77]   Dunhill, 425 U.S. at 695.

[78]   *Id.* at 725.

denial of the act of state defense in the case under consideration will thwart the policy concerns in which the doctrine is rooted.[79]

But another court observed:

> While purely commercial activity may not rise to the level of an act of state, certain seemingly commercial activities will trigger act of state considerations. . . . When the state *qua* state acts in the public interest, its sovereignty is asserted. The Courts must proceed cautiously to avoid an affront to that sovereignty. . . . [W]e find that the act of state doctrine remains available when such caution is appropriate regardless of any commercial component of the activity involved.[80]

Expropriation. As noted, after the *Sabbatino* decision Congress enacted a provision—called the Second Hickenlooper Amendment, for its sponsor—to overturn it. The Amendment states:

> [N]o court in the United States shall decline on the ground of the federal act of state doctrine to make a determination on the merits giving effect to the principles of international law in a case in which a claim of title or other right to property is asserted by any party including a foreign state . . . based upon . . . a confiscation or other taking . . . by an act of that state in violation of the principles of international law, including the principles of compensation. . . .[81]

This Amendment led to a reversal of *Sabbatino*'s outcome on remand.[82] But subsequent courts have not applied it enthusiastically. For example, a number of courts have limited it to situations precisely tracking *Sabbatino*, where the property at issue is present in the United States.[83] Thus it is not clear that the Amendment is generally helpful to expropriation claims.

---

[79] Sage Int'l, Ltd. v. Cadillac Gage Co., 534 F. Supp. 896, 905 (E.D. Mich. 1981).

[80] International Ass'n of Machinists and Aerospace Workers v. OPEC, 649 F.2d 1354, 1360 (9th Cir. 1981); *see also* Honduras Aircraft Registry, Ltd. v. Government of Honduras, 129 F.3d 543 (11th Cir. 1997) (rejecting commercial exception).

[81] 22 U.S.C. § 2370(e)(2).

[82] Banco Nacional de Cuba v. Farr, 243 F.Supp. 957 (S.D.N.Y. 1965), *aff'd*, 383 F.2d 166 (2d Cir. 1967).

[83] *E.g.*, Compania de Gas de Nuevo Laredo, S.A. v. Entex, Inc., 686 F.2d 322 (5th Cir. 1982); Restatement (Third) of Foreign Relations Law of the United States § 444, comment (e) (1987).

Chapter 28

INTERNATIONAL COMMERCIAL ARBITRATION

Table of Sections

§ 28.1   Introduction to Alternative Dispute Resolution

Parties concerned about the uncertainties, costs and delays of international business litigation may seek some form of alternative dispute resolution (ADR). Most legal systems allow parties by contract to select ADR prior to or instead of litigation.

Some versions of ADR are designed to encourage voluntary resolution of differences. These include contractual requirements that the parties engage in good faith negotiation, conciliation or mediation prior to filing suit. Mediation, a popular choice, involves a neutral third party (the mediator) who encourages the parties to resolve their dispute but has little power to compel a resolution. Conciliation is a similar approach.[1] Another strategy is referral to

---

[1]   *See* Michael McIlwrath, Elpidio Villarreal & Amy Crafts, *Finishing Before You Start: International Mediation,* in INTERNATIONAL LITIGATION STRATEGIES AND PRACTICE 41 (Barton Legum ed. 2006).

an expert, in which the parties present their case to a neutral third party having expertise in the field, who gives a nonbinding assessment of the dispute. When parties agree to such procedures by contract, courts typically require them to be undertaken before litigation can proceed. However, if no voluntary resolution is achieved through these measures, litigation may follow.

Parties may want to remove their dispute from courts altogether and substitute a different decisionmaker. Usually, this involves selecting arbitration, in which the parties arrange for a panel of neutral persons (or sometimes a single person) to hear the dispute and issue a binding decision. Although historically courts resisted enforcing arbitration agreements and arbitration awards, in the modern era such enforcement has become common and routine, supported by international treaties and national laws. In the United States, for example, commercial arbitration is governed by the Federal Arbitration Act (FAA),[2] which broadly promotes the use of arbitration. Applying the FAA, U.S. courts have become very supportive of arbitration, and arbitration clauses in international business contracts will usually be enforced. The U.S. Supreme Court has strongly embraced arbitration, to the extent of becoming very hostile to state laws that appear to limit it.[3]

In addition to arbitration, there are even less formal alternate dispute resolution mechanisms. The mini-trial, for example, comes in a variety of packages, each with a different impact on resolution of the dispute. It can be nonbinding if used with a "neutral advisor," it can be semi-binding if its results are admissible in later judicial proceedings, or it can be binding before a court appointed master. Arbitration may also be combined with other forms of ADR through the use of "step clauses," which might for example require the parties first to try mediation and then proceed to arbitration if the dispute still cannot be resolved.

ADR procedures are common in domestic business relationships as well, and in the United States much of the caselaw relating to enforcement of arbitration agreements and awards arises from domestic disputes. However, as discussed below, international commercial arbitration has its own set of laws arising from international treaties, most notably the U.N. Convention on the Recognition and Enforcement of Foreign Arbitral Awards (called the New York Convention),[4] which encourages enforcement of

---

[2]   9 U.S.C. § 1 *et seq.*

[3]   *E.g.*, AT&T Mobility LLC v. Concepcion, 563 U.S. 333 (2011).

[4]   U.N. Convention on Recognition and Enforcement of Foreign Arbitral Awards (1958), 21 U.S.T. 2517, 330 U.N.T.S. 38.

arbitration clauses and arbitration awards. Most major commercial nations are parties to the Convention, including the United States.

§ 28.2 Why Arbitrate?

Uncertainty about where a dispute may be heard, about procedural and substantive rules to be applied, about the degree of publicity to be given the proceedings and the judgment, about the time needed to resolve a dispute, and about the enforcement of court judgments all combine to make arbitration a preferred mechanism for solving international commercial disputes. Thus the growth of international commercial arbitration is in part a retreat from the vicissitudes and uncertainties of international business litigation.[5] More positively, international commercial arbitration offers predictability, neutrality, and the potential for specialized expertise. It also allows the parties to select and shape the procedures and costs of dispute resolution. In addition, one of the most attractive attributes of international commercial arbitration is the enforceability in national courts of arbitral awards under the New York Convention and related national laws. As discussed above,[6] there is no comparable international convention for the enforcement of court judgments.

Arbitration has potential disadvantages. Its procedures are often informal and not laden with legal rights. To quote Judge Learned Hand:

> Arbitration may or may not be a desirable substitute for trials in courts; as to that the parties must decide in each instance. But when they have adopted it, they must be content with its informalities; they may not hedge it about with those procedural limitations which it is precisely its purpose to avoid. They must content themselves with looser approximations to the enforcement of their rights than those that the law accords them, when they resort to its machinery.[7]

Although arbitration is sometimes assumed to be cheaper and faster than litigation, that is not necessarily true, and both costs and delays appear to be increasing. Another potential concern is the general lack of pre-trial provisional remedies.[8] In addition, arbitrators may focus on splitting the differences between the parties rather than fully vindicating legal rights which in court

---

[5]   *See* Chapter 26.

[6]   Chapter 26, § 26.11.

[7]   American Almond Products Co. v. Consolidated Pecan Sales Co., 144 F.2d 448, 451 (2d Cir. 1944).

[8]   *See* Borden, Inc. v. Meiji Milk Products Co., 919 F.2d 822 (2d Cir. 1990).

might result in "winner takes all" judgments. But one-sided results could permanently disrupt otherwise longstanding and mutually beneficial business relationships, so "splitting the baby" through arbitration may really be the optimal outcome.

Clearly international commercial arbitration has its pros and cons, and it may be more appropriate for some transactions than others.[9] Whatever the right conclusion, the use of arbitral dispute resolution is increasingly common. One distinguished set of authors believes that this trend is not surprising. Here is their analysis of why:

> Trade and investment across state lines is on the rise, and parties from different jurisdictions who engage in such activity frequently seek the comparative neutrality of a non-state tribunal to resolve their differences. Parties to a transaction from different states may be reluctant to submit to the jurisdiction of the courts of the other. This reluctance may arise from lack of enthusiasm about operating in another language, or according to the procedures and, insofar as it infiltrates procedure, the substantive law of another state. In some circumstances, one party may fear that the courts of the other may have a preference for their own nationals, may share a dislike of a particular foreign nationality or may, in cases involving very large amounts of money, lean toward finding in favor of their national because of the consequences for their national economy and political system. Where one of the parties is a state or state agency, a non-state party may prefer arbitration to submitting a dispute to the courts of the other contracting party. Arbitration may thus serve to "equalize" the non-state entity by transferring the dispute to a setting which may be designed to minimize or ignore the sovereign character of one of the parties rather more than would a national court.

> Arbitration may also be utilized because the various national laws which might be relevant have not developed enough to treat problems raised in a pioneer industry. Thus issues regarding intellectual property rights in computer software of companies from different states may be submitted to arbitration as a way of resolving a dispute by shaping new law on the matter. In some circumstances potential litigants may also seek out arbitration because it

---

9   *See* Michael McIlwrath & John Savage, INTERNATIONAL ARBITRATION AND MEDIATION: A PRACTICAL GUIDE 97–101 (2010) (discussing factors in choosing between arbitration and litigation).

is touted as more rapid, private and cheaper than domestic adjudication, though many of these characteristics of international commercial arbitration may be relative and sometimes overstated.

International commercial arbitration is also on the increase because many national court systems not only help international arbitration but appear anxious to externalize a larger amount of the disputes that are formally within their jurisdiction. The willingness of national courts to compel parties who have made prior commitments to engage in private arbitration and then to enforce the awards that ensue, subject only to limited judicial review, increases the likelihood that parties will resort to that mode of dispute resolution.[10]

Other distinguished authors are more critical of international commercial arbitration, suggesting its benefits may have been over-sold:

> The [parties] hope that arbitration will prove speedy, cheap, informal and confidential. Such hopes are sometimes disappointed. A determined and evasive opponent can introduce a variety of delays into the process, by going to court to contest the validity of the contract clause calling for arbitration, by challenging arbitrators as biased, and by resisting enforcement of the award. States pay for judges, but the costs of arbitrators and those who administer the process must be borne by the parties. The leading arbitrators generally receive more in compensation for their services than judges get by way of salaries, and there have been complaints about the fees charged by major arbitration centers. In any case, expensive counsel must spend time away from home, usually in expensive hotels located in cities where the cost of living may be even higher than New York. Nor should one assume that arbitration will always be confidential. Generally, such confidentiality requires the agreement of both of the parties, and may be lost at the enforcement stage if resort must be had to a national court.[11]

---

[10]   W. Michael Reisman, W. Laurence Craig, William W. Park & Jan Paulsson, INTERNATIONAL COMMERCIAL ARBITRATION (2d ed. 2015).

[11]   Detlev F. Vagts, William S. Dodge, Harold Hongju Koh & Hannah L. Buxbaum, TRANSNATIONAL BUSINESS PROBLEMS (5th ed. 2014).

§ 28.3   Ad Hoc and Institutional Arbitration

There are two basic types of international commercial arbitrations: ad hoc and institutional. Ad hoc arbitrations involve selection by the parties of the arbitrators and rules governing the arbitration. The classic formula involves each side choosing one arbitrator who together agree upon a third arbitrator. Typically the parties provide by contract a set of procedural rules (such as the UNCITRAL Arbitration Rules discussed below), or the ad hoc panel may select its own procedural rules. Ad hoc arbitration can be agreed upon in advance or, quite literally, selected ad hoc as disputes arise.

Institutional arbitration involves selection of a specific arbitration center, sometimes called a "court of arbitration," typically accompanied by its own rules and personnel. Institutional arbitration is in a sense pre-packaged, and the parties need only "plug in" to the arbitration system of their choice. There are numerous competing centers of arbitration, discussed in more detail below.

Ad hoc arbitration presupposes a certain amount of goodwill and flexibility between the parties. It can be speedy and less costly than institutional arbitration. The latter, on the other hand, offers easy incorporation into an international business agreement, supervisory services, experienced arbitrators and a fixed fee schedule. The institutional environment is professional, a quality that sometimes can get lost in ad hoc arbitrations. Awards from well-established arbitration centers (including default awards) are more likely to be favorably recognized in the courts if enforcement is contested. Many institutional arbitration centers now also offer "fast track" or "mini" services.

§ 28.4   Choosing Arbitration Rules: UNCITRAL Rules and Alternatives

Private parties' agreements to arbitrate are typically reflected in an arbitration clause in the contract establishing their business relationship. (In some cases parties agree to arbitrate after a dispute has arisen, but this is not common). Parties and their attorneys must take care to draft a clause that anticipates uncertainties that may arise in the arbitration.

Parties choosing ad hoc arbitration may draft their own set of procedures for the arbitration, but this is not advised because of the difficulty and complexity in identifying and agreeing upon all of contingencies for which rules will be needed. Instead, parties usually specify only a few basic rules, such as the number of arbitrators, the method of selection, the place and language of the arbitration and perhaps a timeline for submission. The parties then typically choose a set of default arbitration rules published by an international organization or private entity.[12]

UNCITRAL Rules. The UNCITRAL Rules refer to the Model International Commercial Arbitration Rules issued in 1976 by the U.N. Commission on International Trade Law (UNCITRAL), as revised periodically (most recently in 2013).[13] The UNCITRAL Rules are intended to be acceptable in all legal systems and in all parts of the world. Developing countries favor the Rules because of the care with which they were drafted and because UNCITRAL was one forum for formulating arbitration rules in which their concerns would be heard. Additionally, the UNCITRAL Rules are not identified with any national or international arbitration organization, a factor supporting their use as "neutral" arbitration rules.

Among other things, the UNCITRAL Rules provide that an "appointing authority" shall be chosen by the parties or, if they fail to agree upon that point, shall be chosen by the Secretary-General of the Permanent Court of Arbitration at the Hague. The UNCITRAL Rules also cover notice requirements, representation of the parties, challenges of arbitrators, evidence, hearings, the place of arbitration, language, statements of claims and defenses, pleas to the arbitrator's jurisdiction, provisional remedies, experts, default, rule waivers, the form and effect of the award, applicable law, settlement, interpretation of the award, and costs. In 2012, UNCITRAL issued its "Recommendations to assist arbitral institutions and other interested bodies with regard to arbitration under the UNCITRAL Arbitration Rules as revised in 2010."[14]

UNCITRAL also promulgated the 1985 Model Law on International Commercial Arbitration (amended in 2006),[15] the 1996 Notes on Organizing Arbitral Proceedings, and the 2002 Model Law on International Commercial Conciliation. The 1985 Model Law has been enacted in approximately fifty countries (and the 2006

---

[12]   *See, e.g.,* International Centre for Dispute Resolution (ICDR), Guide to Drafting International Dispute Resolution Clauses, https://www.adr.org/cs/idcplg?Idc Service=GET_FILE&dDocName=ADRSTG_002539&RevisionSelectionMethod=Lates tReleased.

[13]   http://www.uncitral.org/pdf/english/texts/arbitration/arb-rules-2013/ UNCITRAL-Arbitration-Rules-2013-e.pdf.

[14]   http://www.uncitral.org/pdf/english/texts/arbitration/arb-recommendation-2012/13-80327-Recommendations-Arbitral-Institutions-e.pdf.

[15]   http://www.uncitral.org/pdf/english/texts/arbitration/ml-arb/07-86998_Ebook. pdf (2006 revision); http://www.uncitral.org/pdf/english/texts/arbitration/ml-arb/06-54671_Ebook.pdf (original 1985 text).

amendment in a half-dozen), as well as in a number of U.S. states. In Model Law jurisdictions, an arbitral award may be set aside by local courts on grounds that virtually track those specified as permissible for denials of recognition and enforcement of awards under the New York Convention (discussed below). Under the UNCITRAL Model Law, submission to arbitration may be *ad hoc* for a particular dispute but is accomplished most often in advance of the dispute by a general submission clause within a contract. Under Article 8 of the Model Law, an agreement to arbitrate is specifically enforceable.

In addition to many private commercial disputes, the UNCITRAL Rules are used in some investor-state arbitrations (see below, § 28.11). The Iran-U.S. Claims Tribunal, discussed in Chapter 24, has used the UNCITRAL Rules in dealing with claims arising out of the confrontation between the two countries in 1979–80. Trade agreements such as the North American Free Trade Agreement (NAFTA) typically allow the use of UNCITRAL Rules in investment disputes.

Other Sources of Arbitration Rules. In addition to UNCITRAL, various private institutions have published sets of arbitration rules that parties may select. If the parties choose institutional arbitration (see below), they will necessarily choose the rules of the arbitral institution selected.

§ 28.5 Institutional Arbitration: International Chamber of Commerce, London Court of International Arbitration, and Others

There are many institutional arbitration centers from which parties may choose. Some are long-established with heavy workloads, while others are more recent and may be struggling for business.

One leading arbitration center is the Court of Arbitration of the International Chamber of Commerce (ICC) at Paris.[16] The ICC Rules are modern, most recently updated in 2012, and often used in international arbitration. Over 11,000 arbitrations have been administered by the ICC.[17]

The ICC International Court of Arbitration is not a court in the judicial meaning of that label; its primary role is to administer arbitrations. The Court does not itself resolve disputes, but instead facilitates independent arbitral tribunals appointed under the ICC

---

[16] http://www.iccwbo.org/products-and-services/arbitration-and-adr/arbitration.

[17] *See* http://www.iccwbo.org/products-and-services/arbitration-and-adr/arbitration/; W. Laurence Craig, William W. Park and Jan Paulsson, INTERNATIONAL CHAMBER OF COMMERCE ARBITRATION (4th ed. 2017).

Rules. A major goal of the Court is to see that arbitral awards are enforceable in national courts.

The London Court of International Arbitration (LCIA), with roots to 1883, is another leading global forum for dispute resolution using arbitration.[18] It also is active in mediation. The London Court has its own rules and procedures.

The ICC Court of Arbitration in Paris recommends use of the following model clause for the adoption of its rules:

> All disputes arising in connection with the present contract shall be finally settled under the Rules of Arbitration of the International Chamber of Commerce by one or more arbitrators appointed in accordance with the said Rules.[19]

Parties who wish to refer any dispute to the LCIA may use the following model clause:

> Any dispute arising out of or in connection with this contract, including any question regarding its existence, validity or termination, shall be referred to and finally resolved by arbitration under the LCIA Rules, which Rules are deemed to be incorporated by reference into this clause. The number of arbitrators shall be [one/three]. The seat, or legal place, of arbitration shall be [City and/or Country]. The language to be used in the arbitral proceedings shall be [ ]. The governing law of the contract shall be the substantive law of [ ].[20]

Another common choice for U.S. parties is the International Centre for Dispute Resolution (ICDR), which is associated with the American Arbitration Association (AAA).[21] There are countless other arbitration institutions throughout the world.

§ 28.6   Treaties and Laws Affecting International Arbitration

The principal international treaty affecting international commercial arbitration is the U.N. Convention on Recognition and Enforcement of Foreign Arbitral Awards (the New York

---

[18]   *See* http://www.lcia.org/.

[19]   http://www.iccwbo.org/products-and-services/arbitration-and-adr/arbitration/standard-icc-arbitration-clauses/.

[20]   http://www.lcia.org/Dispute_Resolution_Services/LCIA_Recommended_Clauses.aspx.

[21]   *See* https://www.icdr.org/.

Convention).[22] The Convention applies to both the enforcement of arbitration agreements (§ 28.7 below) and the enforcement of arbitration awards (§ 28.8–§ 28.10 below). In general, the Convention directs that both arbitration agreements and arbitration awards shall be enforced by national courts in nations that are parties to the Convention, subject to very limited exceptions.

The 1975 Inter-American Convention on International Commercial Arbitration,[23] to which the United States and most major Latin American countries are parties, has provisions that substantially track the New York Convention.

As discussed in § 28.12 below, the ICSID Convention provides for arbitration of certain investor-state disputes. Also as discussed below, Bilateral Investment Treaties (BITs), Free Trade Agreements (FTAs) and other bilateral or regional agreements often call for mandatory arbitration of investor-state disputes.

Most developed legal systems have laws governing the enforcement of arbitration agreements and awards. In the United States, the principal statute is the Federal Arbitration Act (FAA),[24] first enacted in 1925 and revised to provide for implementation of the New York Convention[25] and the Inter-American Convention.[26] The FAA is discussed further in § 28.10 below. As noted in Section 28.4 above, UNCITRAL has drafted a Model Law on arbitration that has been adopted in many nations and some U.S. states.

§ 28.7 Enforcing Arbitration Agreements

Even if parties agree to arbitration in advance, once a dispute arises one party may decide it prefers litigation (or it might refuse to participate in any dispute resolution). As a result, the usefulness of arbitration clauses depends on courts' willingness to enforce them. Where one party resists arbitration and files suit instead, the other party will seek to stay or dismiss the litigation and compel arbitration.

The New York Convention and the laws of most major legal systems (including the United States) commit courts to recognize

---

[22]   21 U.S.T. 2517, 330 U.N.T.S. 38. *See* http://www.newyorkconvention.org/ (overview); http://www.newyorkconvention.org/11165/web/files/original/1/5/15432.pdf (text).

[23]   http://www.oas.org/juridico/english/treaties/b-35.html. A subsequent treaty, the 1979 Inter-American Convention on Extraterritorial Validity of Foreign Judgments and Arbitral Awards, http://www.oas.org/juridico/english/treaties/b-41.html, applies to arbitral awards not covered by the 1975 convention.

[24]   9 U.S.C. § 1 *et seq.*

[25]   9 U.S.C. §§ 201–208.

[26]   9 U.S.C. §§ 301–307.

and enforce arbitration clauses and separate arbitration agreements for the resolution of international commercial disputes.[27] Under the Convention, there must be an "agreement in writing," which "shall include an arbitral clause in a contract or an arbitration agreement, signed by the parties or contained in an exchange of letters or telegrams."[28] Where the court finds such an arbitral clause or agreement, it "*shall* . . . refer the parties to arbitration, unless it finds that the said agreement is null and void, inoperative, or incapable of being performed" (emphasis added).[29]

Whether a valid agreement to arbitrate exists depends on the specifics of the arbitration clause, not the entire business agreement. The arbitration clause is severable, and issues of validity (such as fraud in the inducement of the arbitration clause and unconscionability) are directed to it.[30] Many courts will stretch the limits of the Convention to uphold an arbitration clause.[31] When there is a battle of forms, the same judicial bias towards arbitration is often found.[32] But, in most cases, the disputes must "arise under" the business transaction to be arbitrable,[33] and legal claims falling outside the transaction remain in court.[34]

Questions of validity and other issues concerning the appropriateness of arbitration are often submitted to the arbitral panel. The U.S. Supreme Court has repeatedly affirmed that arbitrators have jurisdiction to decide their own jurisdiction (competence).[35] For example, the Court held that a claim that a contract containing an arbitration provision is void for illegality should be decided by arbitration rather than by a court.[36] Similarly, the Court held (in the context of investor-state arbitration) that the question whether the investor was excused from a contractual

---

[27]   New York Convention, Art. II(1); FAA, 9 U.S.C. § 2.

[28]   New York Convention, Art. II(1), II(2).

[29]   *Id.*, Article II(3).

[30]   Prima Paint Corp. v. Flood & Conklin Mfg. Co., 388 U.S. 395 (1967). *See* Republic of Nicaragua v. Standard Fruit Co., 937 F.2d 469 (9th Cir. 1991); Hunt v. Up North Plastics, Inc., 980 F. Supp. 1046 (D. Minn. 1997).

[31]   *See* Sphere Drake Insurance PLC v. Marine Towing, Inc., 16 F.3d 666 (5th Cir. 1994) (absence of signature to standard insurance policy contract no barrier to arbitration).

[32]   *See* I.T.A.D. Associates, Inc. v. Podar Bros., 636 F.2d 75 (4th Cir. 1981).

[33]   *See* Mediterranean Enterprises, Inc. v. Ssangyong Corp., 708 F.2d 1458 (9th Cir. 1983).

[34]   *Id. See* Coors Brewing Co. v. Molson Breweries, 51 F.3d 1511 (10th Cir. 1995).

[35]   *See, e.g.,* Howsam v. Dean Witter Reynolds, Inc., 537 U.S. 79 (2002); Pacificare Health Systems, Inc. v. Book, 538 U.S. 401 (2003).

[36]   Buckeye Check Cashing, Inc. v. Cardegna, 546 U.S. 440 (2006).

requirement to exhaust local remedies before pursuing arbitration should be decided by the arbitral panel.[37]

The Supreme Court also indicated that the question whether the parties agreed to submit a dispute to arbitration may be decided by the arbitrators if the parties manifested a clear willingness to submit that question to arbitration. However, silence or ambiguity should favor judicial resolution of the issue.[38] Arbitration clauses that adopt the UNCITRAL Rules meet this requirement because Article 21 conveys jurisdictional issues to the tribunal.

Procedures for Enforcement. Disputes over arbitration agreements often arise when a party that has agreed to arbitration in a contract nonetheless files suit in court. The other party will then typically respond with a motion to dismiss or stay the litigation and a motion to compel arbitration, based on the arbitration agreement.[39] As noted, under the New York Convention and the FAA, the court should grant the motion absent unusual circumstances.[40] If no such motion is made, and a court judgment is rendered (even by default), the right to arbitrate may be waived.[41] Delays in triggering arbitration or invocation of litigation rights may constitute a waiver of arbitration rights.[42]

Occasionally, when a party files suit in a dispute governed by an arbitration agreement, the other party may seek to enjoin the litigation in a different court. For example, if one party files suit in France, the other party might seek an injunction from a U.S. court ordering the plaintiff in the French suit to discontinue the proceedings. This is a version of the anti-suit injunction discussed in Chapter 26. Such suits may not be successful because the U.S. court will presume that the French court would not proceed if arbitration is warranted. However, if the foreign court allows the litigation to proceed, an injunction may be issued.[43]

---

[37]   BG Group, PLC v. Republic of Argentina, 134 S.Ct. 1198 (2014).

[38]   First Options of Chicago, Inc. v. Kaplan, 514 U.S. 938 (1995).

[39]   Prokopeva v. Carnival Corp., 2008 WL 4276975 (S.D. Tex. 2008); Apple & Eve, LLC v. Yantai North Andre Juice Co. Ltd., 499 F. Supp. 2d 245 (E.D.N.Y. 2007). *See* 9 U.S.C. § 206.

[40]   *See, e.g.,* Freudensprung v. Offshore Tech. Servs., Inc., 379 F.3d 327 (5th Cir. 2004); Lim v. Offshore Specialty Fabricators, Inc., 404 F.3d 898 (5th Cir. 2005); Francisco v. Stolt Achievement MT, 293 F.3d 270 (5th Cir. 2002); Motorola Credit Corp. v. Uzan, 388 F.3d 39 (2d Cir. 2004).

[41]   *See* Menorah Insurance Co. v. INX Reinsurance Corp., 72 F.3d 218 (1st Cir. 1995).

[42]   *See* O.J. Distributing, Inc. v. Hornell Brewing Co., 340 F.3d 345 (6th Cir. 2003); Colón v. R. K. Grace & Co., 358 F.3d 1 (1st Cir. 2003); Apple & Eve, LLC v. Yantai North Andre Juice Co., Ltd., 610 F. Supp. 2d 226 (E.D.N.Y. 2009).

[43]   *E.g.,* Karaha Bodas Co. L.L.C. v. Perusahaan Pertambangan Minyak Dan Gas Bumi Negara, 500 F.3d 111 (2d Cir. 2007) (enjoining suit in the Cayman

Most arbitration rules allow the arbitration to proceed even if one party refuses to participate. The non-participating party may go to court to seek an injunction against the arbitration. This is not likely to succeed under the New York Convention, since there are few grounds to resist an agreement to arbitrate. However, some country's courts—especially countries that are not party to the New York Convention—may be willing to issue injunctions because they disfavor arbitration, or perhaps to favor a local business or public entity. A party proceeding to arbitration despite an injunction not to do so incurs various risks, including that the award will not be enforced (especially in the jurisdiction issuing the injunction).

Grounds for Non-Enforcement. Arbitration agreements may be resisted under standard contract defenses such as fraud, duress or incapacity (although these are unusual). As noted, Article II(2) of the New York Convention requires members to recognize written arbitration agreements *signed* by the parties "or contained in an exchange of letters or telegrams."[44] In most jurisdictions exchanges of fax, email, and the like embracing arbitration will also be recognized. However, arbitration clauses in unsigned purchase orders do not amount to a written agreement to arbitrate.[45] Another possible objection is that the agreement is too vague or unspecific to be performed—for example, it does not specify the place of arbitration or the rules to be used.[46] Courts tend to be reluctant to refuse to enforce agreements on this ground, often implying reasonable terms when there are none specified.[47] However, parties can and should avoid this problem through careful drafting of the arbitration agreement. The closure or misdescription of an arbitration center designated in the agreement (*e.g.*, the New York Chamber of Commerce) is no barrier to arbitration. A substitute arbitrator can be appointed by the court if the parties cannot agree.[48]

Islands); Paramedics Electromedicina Comercial, Ltda. v. GE Medical Systems Information Technologies, Inc., 369 F.3d 645 (2d Cir. 2004) (enjoining litigation in Brazil).

[44]   *See* Norcast, S.À.R.L. v. Castle Harlan, Inc., 2014 WL 43492 (S.D.N.Y. 2014) (denying motion where party did not sign agreement); AGP Indus. SA (Peru) v. JPS Elastromerics Corp., 511 F. Supp. 2d 212 (D. Mass. 2007) (same).

[45]   Kahn Lucas Lancaster, Inc. v. Lark Int'l Ltd., 186 F.3d 210 (2d Cir. 1999).

[46]   *E.g.*, Jain v. de Mere, 51 F.3d 686 (7th Cir. 1995) (agreement void where no arbitration site was selected).

[47]   *See, e.g.*, Apple & Eve, LLC v. Yantai North Andre Juice Co. Ltd., 499 F. Supp. 2d 245 (E.D.N.Y. 2007) (contract failed to specify arbitration center to handle the dispute).

[48]   *See* Astra Footwear Industry v. Harwyn International, Inc., 442 F. Supp. 907 (S.D.N.Y. 1978).

Another defense to compelled arbitration is that the dispute is not covered by the arbitration clause. Poorly drafted arbitration clauses may allow a party to claim a dispute is not covered even if the other party intended otherwise, so again care should be taken at the drafting stage and clauses should be drafted broadly (assuming that is the intent).

Arbitrability. A further defense to compelled arbitration is that by law certain types of claims must be decided in court (that is, they are non-arbitrable). This is likely to arise for claims arising under "mandatory law," *i.e.* public law that private parties cannot avoid by contract.

In the United States, initially some lower courts held that mandatory laws could not be the subject matter of arbitration because of the public interest indicated by the legislative intent underlying the enactment of mandatory law and the public policy favoring judicial enforcement of such law. However, the Supreme Court rejected that doctrine in *Scherk v. Alberto-Culver Co.,*[49] holding that securities law issues arising out of an international contract were subject to arbitration under the FAA despite the public interest in protecting U.S. securities markets. In *Mitsubishi Motors Corp. v. Soler Chrysler-Plymouth, Inc.*[50], the Court held that antitrust claims arising out of an international transaction were arbitrable, despite the public interest in a competitive national economy and legislative pronouncements favoring enforcement by private parties. In *Vimar Seguros y Reaseguros, S.A. v. M/V Sky Reefer,*[51] the Court rejected claims that the foreign arbitrators would not apply the U.S. Carriage of Goods by Sea Act (COGSA) on the ground that the United States could "review" the arbitral award at the award-enforcement stage. (That power may, however, be very narrow under the New York Convention, as discussed below).

§ 28.8   Enforcing and Challenging Arbitral Awards

Once an arbitral panel issues its decision (called an "award"), the losing party may refuse to honor it. Since a panel has no enforcement power, the winning party may have to turn to national courts. Similarly, the losing party may ask national courts overturn the result of the arbitration.

---

[49]   417 U.S. 506 (1974).

[50]   473 U.S. 614 (1985). Lower courts have held after *Mitsubishi* that private antitrust claims are arbitrable. *E.g.,* Seacoast Motors of Salisbury, Inc. v. DaimlerChrysler Motors Corp., 271 F.3d 6 (1st Cir. 2001).

[51]   515 U.S. 528 (1995).

This litigation may occur at the place where the arbitration took place (called the "seat"). National law of that jurisdiction will govern the circumstances under which a court will confirm or invalidate the arbitration award. Most arbitration-friendly jurisdictions have national law (such as the U.S. FAA) that limit courts' ability to invalidate arbitration awards to narrow circumstances.

Either party may bring an action in the courts of the arbitration seat. The winning party may seek to have the award "confirmed" so that it can be enforced against the losers' assets. The losing party may seek to have the award set aside ("invalidated" or "annulled") as permitted under local law.

Often, however, the losing party will not have assets located in the jurisdiction of the arbitration seat. (The location of the arbitration is often chosen for its neutrality and its friendliness to arbitration rather than its connection to the parties). Thus, the winning party may need to seek enforcement of the award in a different jurisdiction—for example, an award by the ICC Court of Arbitration in Paris might need to be enforced against the assets of the losing party located in the United States. As discussed in Chapter 26, enforcing foreign court judgments is often a difficult enterprise. The treaties and laws relating to arbitration, particularly the New York Convention and implementing national laws such as the FAA, make enforcement of foreign arbitral awards somewhat easier.

Courts in countries other than the arbitral seat cannot invalidate arbitration awards, but they can refuse to recognize and enforce them. Thus a claim regarding a foreign arbitral award is typically brought by the winning party seeking enforcement against the losing party's assets, and the losing party will defend by asking the court not to enforce the award. An award need not be confirmed in the seat prior to being enforced elsewhere (although, as discussed below, if it is annulled at the seat enforcement abroad is likely to be very difficult).

§ 28.9 Enforcing Arbitral Awards Under the New York Convention

In approximately 150 countries, the enforcement of foreign arbitral awards is facilitated by the New York Convention.[52] The Convention commits the courts in each Contracting State to recognize and enforce (under local procedural rules) arbitral awards

---

[52] 21 U.S.T. 2518, T.I.A.S. No. 6997, 330 U.N.T.S. 38, implemented in the United States by 9 U.S.C. §§ 201–208.

made by arbitral panels in any other "Contracting State" (that is, a country that is a member of the Convention).[53] Thus whether the Convention applies generally turns on where the award was or will be made, not the citizenship of the parties.[54]

The Convention also sets forth limited grounds under which courts may refuse recognition and enforcement. These include:

(1)   incapacity or invalidity of the agreement containing the arbitration clause "under the law applicable to" a party to the agreement,

(2)   lack of proper notice of the arbitration proceedings, the appointment of the arbitrator or other reasons denying an adequate opportunity to present a defense,

(3)   failure of the arbitral award to restrict itself to the terms of the submission to arbitration, or decision of matters not within the scope of that submission,

(4)   composition of the arbitral tribunal not according to the arbitration agreement or applicable law, and

(5)   the arbitral award is not yet binding on the parties under applicable law or has been set aside or suspended by a court in the place it was made.[55]

In addition, recognition or enforcement may be refused if it would be contrary to the public policy of the country in which enforcement is sought or if the subject matter of the dispute cannot be settled by arbitration under the law of that country.[56]

§ 28.10   Enforcing Arbitration Awards Under U.S. Law

As a party to the New York Convention, the United States applies the Convention to enforce foreign arbitral awards. Chapter 2 of the FAA was added to provide for implementation of the Convention. "[T]he principal purpose underlying American ... implementation ... was to encourage the recognition and enforcement of commercial arbitration agreements in international contracts and to unify the standards by which agreements to

---

[53]   Article I(1) of the Convention states that it applies to arbitral awards made in any foreign nation. However, Article I(3) allows a member nation to declare that it will only apply the Convention to awards made in another member nation, and most member nations (including the United States) have made such a declaration.

[54]   *But see* 9 U.S.C. § 202 (award between two U.S. citizens may not be covered by Convention).

[55]   New York Convention, Article V(1).

[56]   *Id.*, Article V(2).

arbitrate are observed and arbitral awards are enforced in the signatory countries."[57]

In the United States an award rendered in another Convention member state is considered to be governed by the Convention (and thus by Chapter 2 of the FAA) if it is "commercial." However, an award arising out of a relationship "which is entirely between citizens of the United States shall be deemed not to fall under the Convention unless that relationship involves property located abroad, envisages performance or enforcement abroad, or has some other reasonable relation with one or more foreign states."[58]

Under Chapter 2 of the FAA, the grounds for refusing to recognize and enforce an award track those in the New York Convention (see § 28.9 above). In general, U.S. courts have applied those grounds narrowly and resisted calls to imply additional ones.[59] For example, courts in the United States have taken the position that the "public policy limitation on the New York Convention is to be construed narrowly [and] to be applied only where enforcement would violate the forum state's most basic notions of morality and justice."[60] The U.S. Supreme Court has held that arbitrators are subject to "requirements of impartiality" and must "disclose to the parties any dealings that might create an impression of possible bias."[61] But most U.S. courts hesitate to intrude or vacate an arbitration award on disclosure grounds.[62]

The New York Convention and the FAA allow (but do not require) courts to refuse enforcement where foreign arbitral awards are annulled at their seat. In general, U.S. courts have refused enforcement of annulled awards,[63] except in exceptional circumstances.[64] A U.S. court refused to honor the annulment of an

---

[57]   Scherk v. Alberto-Culver Co., 417 U.S. 506, 520 n.15 (1974).

[58]   9 U.S.C. § 202. An award between two foreign parties, even though rendered in the United States, may be covered by the Convention. Bergesen v. Joseph Muller Corp., 548 F. Supp. 650 (S.D.N.Y. 1982).

[59]   Parsons & Whittemore Overseas Co., Inc. v. Societe Generale De L'Industrie Du Papier (RAKTA), 508 F.2d 969 (2d Cir. 1974).

[60]   Fotochrome, Inc. v. Copal Co., Ltd., 517 F.2d 512 (2d Cir. 1975).

[61]   Commonwealth Coatings Corp. v. Continental Casualty Co., 393 U.S. 145 (1968).

[62]   See Andros Compania Maritima v. Marc Rich & Co., 579 F.2d 691 (2d Cir. 1978).

[63]   TermoRio S.A. E.S.P. v. Electranta S.P., 487 F.3d 928 (D.C. Cir. 2007)); Baker Marine (Nig.) Ltd. v. Chevron (Nig.) Ltd., 191 F.3d 194 (2d Cir. 1999); Thai-Lao Lignite (Thailand) Co., Ltd. v. Government of the Lao People's Democratic Republic, 997 F. Supp. 2d 214 (S.D.N.Y. 2014); Spier v. Calzaturificio Tecnica, S.p.A., 71 F. Supp. 2d 279 (S.D.N.Y. 1999).

[64]   See TermoRio S.A. E.S.P. v. Electranta S.P., 487 F.3d 928 (D.C. Cir. 2007) (suggesting court may enforce an annulled award if the judgment annulling the award "violated . . . basic notions of justice to which we subscribe").

arbitral award by an Egyptian court because the parties had agreed not to appeal the award,[65] and another U.S. court enforced an award that had been annulled at the seat (Mexico) because it found the annulment proceedings violated basic notions of justice.[66]

For domestic arbitrations, U.S. courts have historically implied an additional ground of "manifest disregard of the law" to bar enforcement of an arbitral award.[67] It is not clear whether this approach remains valid after the Supreme Court's decision in *Hall Street Associates LLC v. Mattel*,[68] which indicated that the grounds for nonenforcement in the FAA cannot be varied. Even if "manifest disregard" survives in domestic cases,[69] it is doubtful whether this implied ground also applies to awards covered by the Convention. Article V of the Convention does not recognize manifest disregard of the law as a basis for denial of enforcement, and a number of courts have held that for cases covered by the Convention the expressly listed grounds are exclusive.[70] However, as noted, the U.S. Supreme Court in *Mitsubishi* and related cases seemed to assume that U.S. courts would be able to review arbitrators' application of U.S. mandatory law, at least to some extent, at the enforcement stage.[71] In addition, some courts have held that review for "manifest disregard of the law" is available where the action is to invalidate an award made in the United States, as opposed to an action to confirm a foreign award, even if it is covered by the Convention.[72]

---

[65]   Chromalloy Aeroservices v. Arab Republic of Egypt, 939 F.Supp. 907 (D.D.C. 1996).

[66]   Corporación Mexicana de Mantenimiento Integral, S. de R.L. de C.V. v. PEMEX-Exploración y Producción, 962 F.Supp.2d 642 (S.D.N.Y. 2013); *aff'd* 2016 WL 4087215 (2d Cir. 2016).

[67]   *E.g.*, Fahnestock & Co. v. Waltman, 935 F.2d 512 (2d. Cir. 1991).

[68]   552 U.S. 576 (2008) (holding that parties to an arbitration agreement could not add additional grounds for nonenforcement of the award).

[69]   *See* STMicroelectronics, N.V. v. Credit Suisse Securities (USA) LLC, 648 F.3d 68 (2d Cir. 2011) (noting the issue). Lower courts have reached various conclusions. *See, e.g.*, Robert Lewis Rosen Assoc., Ltd. v. Webb, 566 F.Supp.2d 228 (S.D.N.Y. 2008); F. Hoffman-LaRoche Ltd. v. Qiagen Gaithersburg, Inc., 2010 WL 3184228 (S.D.N.Y. 2010); Ramos-Santiago v. United Parcel Service, 524 F.3d 120 (1st Cir. 2009); Comedy Club, Inc. v. Improv West Associates, 553 F.3d 1277 (9th Cir. 2009); Citigroup Global Mkt., Inc. v. Bacon, 562 F.3d 349 (5th Cir. 2009).

[70]   *E.g.*, M & C Corp. v. Erwin Behr GmbH & Co., KG, 87 F.3d 844 (6th Cir. 1996); Int'l Standard Elec. Corp. v. Bridas Sociedad Anónima Petrolera, Industrial y Comerical, 745 F.Supp. 172 (S.D.N.Y. 1990).

[71]   *See above,* § 28.7.

[72]   Yusuf Ahmed Alghanim & Sons v. Toys 'R' Us, Inc., 126 F.3d 15 (2d Cir. 1997); Westerbeke Corp. v. Daihatsu Motor Co., Ltd., 304 F.3d 200 (2d Cir. 2000); Duferco International Steel Trading v. T. Klaveness Shipping, 333 F.3d 383 (2d Cir. 2003); Hardy v. Walsh Manning Securities, LLC, 341 F.3d 126 (2d Cir. 2003); *but see* Industrial Risk Insurers v. M.A.N. Gutehoffnungshutte GmbH, 141 F.3d 1434 (11th Cir. 1998).

Another issue concerning the New York Convention is whether to adjourn U.S. enforcement proceedings if parallel proceedings to vacate the award have been commenced in the country of arbitration. Despite the risks of forum shopping and delay, the Second Circuit indicated that adjournment can be appropriate, depending upon the circumstances.[73] The Second Circuit has also denied use of 28 U.S.C. § 1782 to obtain compulsory non-party discovery in private commercial arbitrations. The issue was whether the I.C.C. in Paris constitutes a "tribunal" within the scope of that statute.[74] The Second Circuit has also held that the doctrine of *forum non conveniens* applies in arbitral award confirmation proceedings under the New York Convention.[75]

Cases in the United States have pointed out that parties cannot refer a dispute to a court while an arbitration is in progress,[76] or block enforcement of an award in the United States in reliance upon the fact that the award, although binding in the country where rendered, is being challenged in court there.[77] Interim orders of arbitrators, such as records disclosures, may be enforceable "awards" under the Convention.[78]

Under the Supreme Court's decision in *Hall Street* (discussed above), parties may not expand the scope of judicial review of arbitration awards.[79] Attempts at narrowing statutory standards of review are also likely to be rejected.[80]

§ 28.11   Investor-State Arbitration

Investor-State arbitration (also called investor-state dispute settlement or ISDS) refers to arbitration of a dispute between a private party and a foreign government. (There are also "state-state" arbitrations, involving disputes between two governments, but these do not usually involve business matters). As discussed in Chapter 23, investor-state arbitration is often the result of treaties, such as Bilateral Investment Treaties (BITs) and free trade

---

[73]   Europcar Italia, S.p.A. v. Maiellano Tours, Inc., 156 F.3d 310 (2d Cir. 1998).

[74]   National Broadcasting Co. v. Bear Stearns & Co., 165 F.3d 184 (2d Cir. 1999).

[75]   In re Monegasque de Reassurances S.A.M. v. Nak Naftogaz of Ukraine, 311 F.3d 488 (2d Cir. 2002).

[76]   Siderius, Inc. v. Compania de Acero del Pacifico, S.A., 453 F. Supp. 22 (S.D.N.Y. 1978).

[77]   Fertilizer Corp. of India v. IDI Management, Inc., 517 F. Supp. 948 (S.D. Ohio 1981).

[78]   *See* Publicis Communication v. True North Communications, Inc. 206 F.3d 725 (7th Cir. 2000).

[79]   Hall Street Associates, LLC v. Mattel, Inc., 552 U.S. 576 (2008).

[80]   *E.g.*, Hoeft v. MVL Group, Inc., 343 F.3d 57 (2d Cir. 2003).

agreements (FTAs) that require the host nation to guarantee certain protections to foreign investment and to submit to mandatory arbitration in the event of a dispute with a private investor from another country that is party to the treaty.[81] Private parties and foreign governments may also provide for investor-state arbitration by contract.

Most treaties providing for investor-state arbitration allow the investor to pursue arbitration under either the ICSID Rules (discussed below) or the UNCITRAL Rules (see § 28.4 above). Many arbitrations have been conducted in recent years in accordance with BIT or FTA provisions, with some resulting in substantial awards in favor of investors.

§ 28.12   The International Center for the Settlement of Investment Disputes (ICSID)

The 1966 Convention on the Settlement of Investment Disputes Between States and Nationals of Other States, to which over 100 countries including the United States are parties, provided for the establishment of an International Center for the Settlement of Investment Disputes (ICSID) as a non-financial organ of the World Bank (the International Bank for Reconstruction and Development). ICSID is designed to serve as a forum for both conciliation and arbitration of disputes between private investors and host governments. It provides an institutional framework within which arbitrators, selected by the disputing parties from an ICSID Panel of Arbitrators or from elsewhere, conduct arbitration in accordance with ICSID Rules of Procedure for Arbitration Proceedings. Arbitrations are held in Washington D.C. unless agreed otherwise.[82]

Under the Convention, ICSID's jurisdiction extends only "to any legal dispute arising directly out of an investment, between a Contracting State or . . . any subdivision . . . and a national of another Contracting State, which the parties to the dispute consent in writing to submit to the Centre." No party may withdraw its consent unilaterally.[83]

If one party questions jurisdiction, the issue may be decided by the arbitration tribunal.[84] A party may seek annulment of any award by an appeal to an ad hoc committee of persons drawn by the Administrative Council of ICSID from the Panel of Arbitrators

---

[81]   *See* BG Group, PLC v. Republic of Argentina, 134 S.Ct. 1198 (2014).

[82]   *See* Lucy Reed, Jan Paulsson & Nigel Blackaby, GUIDE TO ICSID ARBITRATION (2004).

[83]   ICSID Convention, Art. 25.

[84]   ICSID Rule 41.

under the Convention.[85] Annulment is available only if the Tribunal was not properly constituted, exceeded its powers, seriously departed from a fundamental procedural rule, failed to state the reasons for its award, or included a member who practiced corruption.

The Convention's jurisdictional limitations prompted the ICSID Administrative Counsel to establish an Additional Facility to conduct conciliations and arbitrations for disputes which do not arise directly out of an investment and for investment disputes in which one party is not a Contracting State to the Convention or not a national of a Contracting State. The Additional Facility is intended for use by parties having long-term relationships of special economic importance to the State party to the dispute and which involve the commitment of substantial resources on the part of either party. The Facility is not designed for disputes which fall within the 1966 Convention or which are "ordinary commercial transaction" disputes. ICSID's Secretary General must give advance approval of an agreement contemplating use of the Additional Facility. Because the Additional Facility operates outside the scope of the 1966 Convention, the Facility has its own arbitration rules and its awards can be reviewed by national courts. Numerous NAFTA investor-state arbitrations have operated under the Additional Facility.

The ICSID Convention is implemented in the United States by statute.[86] An arbitral money award rendered pursuant to the Convention is entitled to the same full faith and credit in the United States as a final judgment of a court of general jurisdiction in a state of the United States and thus is effectively not reviewable by U.S. courts.

The ICSID process has become somewhat controversial in recent years. In particular it has been charged with bias in favor of investors, lack of transparency and conflicts of interest.[87] Several nations (including Venezuela, Ecuador and Bolivia) have withdrawn from the ICSID Convention, and some countries (including Brazil and South Africa) generally decline to agree to ISDS in any form.[88]

---

[85]   ICSID Convention, Art. 52.

[86]   22 U.S.C. § 1650 and § 1650a.

[87]   See Martin Khor, The Emerging Crisis of Investment Treaties, GLOBAL POLICY FORUM, Nov. 21, 2012; Leon E. Trakman, The ICSID Under Siege, 45 CORNELL INT'L L.J. 603 (2012); European Federation for Investment Law and Arbitration, A Response to the Criticism against ISDS (2015), http://efila.org/wp-content/uploads/2015/05/EFILA_in_response_to_the-criticism_of_ISDS_final_draft.pdf.

[88]   See Diana Marie Wick, The Counter-Productivity of ICSID Denunciation and Proposals for Change, 11 J. INT'L BUS. & L. 239 (2012).

However, many BITs and FTAs with investor-state arbitration provisions continue to be concluded among nations.

§ 28.13   Enforcing Arbitration Awards Against Foreign Sovereigns

Like private parties, governments and their instrumentalities may refuse to satisfy adverse arbitral awards. Unlike private parties, non-paying sovereign entities may present additional enforcement complexities due to sovereign immunity and related issues.[89]

In the United States, foreign sovereign immunity is governed by a statute, the Foreign Sovereign Immunities Act (FSIA),[90] as discussed in Chapter 27. The FSIA specifically denies immunity to foreign sovereign entities for actions to enforce arbitration agreements and to recognize and enforce arbitral awards.[91] However, that does not resolve all enforcement issues, because the FSIA separately grants immunity against execution on sovereign property.[92] Thus, facing a recalcitrant sovereign, a party seeking to enforce an arbitral award cannot seize sovereign property in satisfaction unless an exception exists. The FSIA recognizes execution exceptions to enforce arbitration awards against foreign sovereign property only for commercial property.[93] For foreign sovereign instrumentalities engaged in commercial activity in the United States, enforcement is also allowed against noncommercial property (subject to exceptions) if the instrumentality has waived its enforcement immunity.[94]

---

[89]   *See* Chapter 27.

[90]   28 U.S.C. § 1602 *et seq.*

[91]   28 U.S.C. § 1605(a)(6) (as to arbitrations in the United States or governed by international treaties, among others).

[92]   *Id.*, § 1609.

[93]   *Id.*, § 1610(a)(6), subject to exceptions in § 1611.

[94]   *Id.*, § 1610(b)(1), subject to exceptions in § 1611.

Table of Cases

Index

References are to Sections